APL

An Interactive Approach

An Interactive Approach

Third Edition

Leonard Gilman
International Business Machines Corporation

Allen J. Rose
Allen Rose Associates

JOHN WILEY & SONS, Inc.   **New York · Chichester · Brisbane · Toronto · Singapore**

Library of Congress Cataloging in Publication Data

Gilman, Leonard, 1930-
  APL : an interactive approach.

  Includes index.
  1. **APL** (Computer program language) I. Rose,
Allen J. II. Title. III. Title: A.P.L.

QA76.73.A27G54   1983   001.64'24   83-14716

Printed in the United States of America

10 9 8 7 6

Concept HDS is registered trademark of Human Designed Systems, Inc.
Spinwriter is reg. tm. of Nippon Electric Corp.
Sharp APL is reg. service mark of I. P. Sharp Associates, Ltd.
APL★PLUS is reg. service mark of STSC, Inc.
TRS80 is reg. tm. of Tandy Corp.
PacMan is reg. tm. of Atari, Inc.

Foreword

APL is both a programming language and a system that supports the writing, editing, using, saving and sharing of programs. It is appropriate to think of them as one since all use of APL involves both in an integrated way.

The two are interactive and mediated from terminals so that personal involvement is continual and natural and—for computer systems—relatively effortless. As this book so admirably illustrates, one can 'sneak up' on the mastery of APL starting from an almost negligible investment in language and system techniques. At the other extreme, once one has mastered APL one has accomplished something of permanent value and benefit: programs of great value and interest can be written by one person that in other languages would require a team!

The power of the APL language comes from its direct manipulation of aggregates of data in the form of arrays. Everyone recognizes that computers excel where aggregates are manipulated, where the descriptive details of a function do not grow with the size of the aggregates being manipulated, and where one description suffices to cover a large population of aggregates. Most other languages require their programs to penetrate these structures, manipulate the components individually even in order to achieve a uniform effort. It is not surprising that APL programs are significantly shorter and more lucid than programs in most other languages. In programming, clarity is not a consequence of discursiveness or low information density in the program text.

Because of its power in aggregate and component manipulation, APL has many more primitive functions than other languages. Rather than adding to complexity, this multiplicity actually simplifies. When a typical processing need arises, APL has a primitive function that naturally performs it. Learning the properties and uses of these primitives adds but a little to the labor of APL mastery. Shortly after encountering a function one sees how it 'falls:in' with others already understood and soon it begins to participate in program constructions in a natural way.

Programmers are surprised and pleased to discover that all APL primitive functions get used and that none are arcane and of questionable utility. Even more, one soon acquires skill in combining these functions artfully into phrases commonly called 'idioms', that are frequently used and that extend every programmer's arsenal of programming constructions. No other language supports such a rich development of idioms, or even permits one to think idiomatically.

It is often said of APL that it provides too much choice for programmers—there are too many ways to perform desired functions, and among a group of APL programmers the same task will often lead them to create quite different programs. Consequently, reading APL programs is not trivial. Considering that APL text is often one-third to one-fifth the size of equivalent text in another language, APL programs turn out to be as understandable as those in other languages. The very richness of the set of APL functions that makes its mastery so challenging makes the learning of other languages much easier once APL is learned.

APL has its own operating system and thus use of APL is much the same (but alas not identical) on all computers, from the smallest and cheapest to the largest and most expensive. Unlike BASIC, for which each computer has its own idiosyncratic version, APL is a paragon of constancy between machines.

The workspace in which the user's APL traffic is organized is a natural, simple and friendly environment in which to compute. Its permanence is set by the individual user and can comfortably be thought of as an immense personal blackboard. Indeed, each user has a large number of such blackboards identified by chosen names and between which the user can flit and transfer data and function. Best of all, a workspace can be frozen, suspended in time, saved and resumed in the future as though no time had passed. A collection of workspaces forms a library and the user has access to both public and private libraries to which he has been granted access.

More idiosyncratic than the workspace, APL supports large files—but differently on most machines. A recent development in APL is heterogeneous nested arrays. Their value is unquestioned, but the permanence of their definition and form within the APL language is still under study. Like all living languages APL changes, but more slowly and carefully than most others. Unlike most other languages APL affects the way one thinks about programming: familiarity with BASIC or PASCAL does not automatically translate over to expertise in APL.

This is not a book on programming or even programming in APL. Instead it is a carefully organized journey through the APL language and system. The journey is amazingly smooth and painless. The book reads very well. One does not have to be a computer specialist to understand the material. The exercises are by and large elementary, though a few difficult problems are scattered throughout. No book on APL can present a complete specification of the APL language and system and still be readable. However, this book, in conjunction with an APL system, provides the basic spectrum of insights into APL behavior:

(a) Read the material on issue X.

(b) Do a sample of the exercises.

(c) Execute some obvious instances of X at the terminal.

(d) Pose questions about X of the form 'What if... .' Execute them at the terminal. Between the results obtained and a re-reading of the text one will soon say, 'Ah, that is why this happened and I now understand issue X.'

By the time one has read the book, the details of APL behavior will have become so engraved in one's skull that one will think naturally at the programming level but perform at the primitive function level. One will have become an APL programmer.

Alan J. Perlis
New Haven, Conn.
August 1983

Preface

Today's APL systems are substantially more powerful than the APL described in the first edition of 'Interactive Approach' in 1970. During that time APL has evolved from a language with 'funny looking symbols' used as a novel calculator of small scientific problems into a full-featured general purpose programming system.

The community of APL users has grown also—over 250,000 copies of the previous editions of this work have been circulated worldwide. Well-attended international APL conferences are regularly sponsored by major computing societies.

The interests of APL users are as varied as people themselves, and we are still surprised and impressed by the breadth and sophistication of applications of APL that we see. We believe the next few years will yield an even more rapid rate of growth for APL, largely due to its availability on low cost, individual processors such as the IBM Personal Computer.

It has not been easy for us to keep current with all the changes in APL and its uses. We wanted to retain in this edition the informality and readability that our readers told us were in the previous editions, and yet include the important language extensions and their application. All this for an audience that ranges from high school to MBA candidates, and includes casual do-it-yourselfers, educators and professional programmers.

This edition emphasizes practical information-processing applications somewhat more than scientific examples. Engineering and mathematical material is included, but we indicate what may be skipped without loss of continuity. Our guide is the rule 'what you don't know shouldn't hurt you.'

At the suggestion of nearly everyone, we take up elementary function definition (programming) quite early—most readers will be able to write simple programs in their first session on the computer. Advanced topics such as report formatting, generalized arrays, files, and interacting with the operating system are deferred and can be read in any sequence, or skipped entirely. All of the programs and examples displayed in the book can be entered from the keyboard, or may be purchased in machine readable form for popular systems. See inside the back cover for details.

Like the previous editions, this book has been designed and tested for use in formal courses as well as for self study. In either case we recommend that Chapters 1 through 16 be read in sequence, and that the reader have access to an APL system to try things out (after all, the subtitle is *An Interactive Approach*). It isn't necessary to memorize the details in these chapters because the index (prepared by an APL program, of course) is thorough enough that the book serves as a reference manual as well as a text.

We hope you enjoy this book as much as we have enjoyed writing it for you. It is the interaction with our readers that helps us keep a pulse on APL usage. We encourage you to correspond with either or both of us.

Many people have contributed to this book indirectly through their efforts on the previous editions, where they are cited. For this edition, we are grateful for the good work of Ms. Jillian Wade, an author in her own right and an accomplished APL programmer and instructor. She entered, edited, criticized, and verified much of the text and provided ideas which were significant improvements over our own. We thank Mr. Alan Graham for his guidance and the problem set for the chapter on nested arrays, as well as for many other suggestions that have been incorporated into this edition.

Leonard Gilman
19 Horseshoe Road
Mt. Kisco, NY 10549

Allen J. Rose
Box 58, Kinue Road
Captain Cook, Hawaii 96704

September, 1983

CONTENTS

APL

An Interactive Approach

Chapter 1: Getting started

Imagine having a mindless assistant at your beck and call who will readily and accurately carry out your every instruction. However, he requires that you be extremely precise in your instructions: that you neither leave out any detail nor give him conflicting instructions. Your communication with this faithful person would become very precise. In contrast, natural languages are filled with inherent ambiguities. For example, a telegram reading 'STRIKE AT MINE. COME AT ONCE' means one thing to a mining engineer, and quite another thing to a shop steward from the miners' union. Hence, you and he might develop and adopt some artificial language which is (1) well suited to the type of instructions being communicated; (2) easily learned and remembered by you and your assistant; (3) not prone to ambiguities; (4) extendable to cope with future unanticipated needs; and (5) terse, so that no time is wasted in idle conversation.

Assuming that the tasks put to this assistant are mostly record keeping and arithmetic in nature, it is likely that the language would readily lend itself to expressing instructions. If this faithful assistant does nothing other than what you direct, and if you direct him to do only work that you would have done otherwise, isn't he being used as a *tool*? A special type of tool to be sure—one that we *communicate* with rather than just push, pull or turn.

Now no one wants to be thought of as a tool. And no one has to, at least as far as record keeping and calculations are concerned. Computers do that type of work better, cheaper, faster and more accurately than any human. But like our faithful assistant (and unlike other tools), we communicate with a computer to get it to work.

A *programming language* is the means through which we tell the computer what to do and it tells us what it has done. It would be desirable to use a language well suited to the tasks to be done. *Natural* languages such as English, French or German are simply too ambiguous and too verbose for the task.

As a result of the development of time-sharing, in which regular telephone lines are used to connect inexpensive remote typewriters and display screens equipped for teleprocessing ('terminals') to a single central computer, and the more recent availability of low cost personal computers, a number of specialized languages have appeared with features adapted to this environment. Among them is APL, the name being an acronym for *A Programming Language*, which is the title of a book by Dr. K. E. Iverson (New York, John Wiley, 1962) defining a notation for mathematics which has evolved to the APL that is presented in this book.

Not only is APL similar in many respects to algebraic notation, but it also contains many useful functions not expressible concisely with conventional symbols. It has been proven to be very efficient for describing algorithms (problem-solving procedures). And because of the ease with which complicated problems can be expressed in APL, it has been very useful where fast answers are needed for one-time problems (so-called 'quick-and-dirty' solutions) or to model applications, particularly where the application itself is expected to undergo frequent change.

The text will therefore concentrate on the use of APL for problem-solving on a computer. This detailed exposition will begin soon, but first we will give a brief introduction to the operation of the computer or terminal and the establishment of the telephone connection. In this introduction, little consideration will be given to the characteristics and operation of any of the other parts of the APL system, since the user of a time-sharing system is removed from the immediate vicinity of the computer and usually need not worry about anything other than his terminal and his problem needing solution. The user of a personal computer should consult his owner's manual for instructions specific to his computer.

What the APL system does

The following is an example of a user interacting with an APL computer. First, he can enter arithmetic problems and the computer will display the answers:

        2+2
4

```
      3÷4
0.75

      3.1×5
15.5
```

As the examples show, APL can be used much like a hand calculator. Instructions and data are entered by the user through the keyboard beginning six spaces to the right of the margin, and shown in boldface in this book. After each line is entered, the RETURN key is pressed to signal the computer that the entry is complete. The computer's response begins on the next line, at the left margin.

We can assign (store) a string of numbers to a variable called X, and ask the computer to execute the instruction shown, $+/X$ (read as 'sum over X'), with a response of 17.1:

```
      X←3  4  1.1  3  6
      +/X
17.1
```

The variable X can be used repeatedly as, for example,

```
      2+X
5  6  3.1  5  8
```

And we have the ability to call on programs previously stored in the computer. Here is one that carries out statistical calculations on data that we enter. The following examples were obtained from a terminal with access to programs that probably aren't available to the reader at this point. Hence, attempts to duplicate these results may not be successful.

```
      STATISTICS
ENTER DATA
□:
      4  3  4.4  5  1  6.2
6 OBSERVATIONS ENTERED
AVERAGE IS 3.933333333
RANGE IS 5.2
STANDARD DEVIATION IS 1.787363048

□:
      8  9  7.8  6.4
4 OBSERVATIONS ENTERED
AVERAGE IS 7.8
RANGE IS 2.6
STANDARD DEVIATION IS 1.070825227
□:
      STOP
```

As the instructions indicated, we terminated execution by typing $STOP$.

The hardware

Let's take a brief look at the terminal and telephone and associated equipment. It will be assumed in the remainder of this book that the communications terminal you will be using is equipped with the APL character set and capable of corresponding with an APL computer system.

APL KEYBOARD

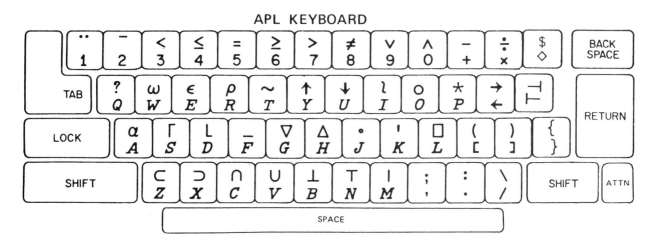

The space bar is at the bottom of the keyboard and the alphabetic and numeric characters are in the conventional typewriter positions. But you will find some of the other symbols unfamiliar, and some of the familiar symbols may not be located where you might expect them. There may also be minor differences in the number and arrangement of the keys, depending on the terminal manufacturer.

The SHIFT key is used in the usual manner for upper shift characters, and the RETURN key (or EXECUTE or ENTER on some terminals) on the right is used to tell the system that you are finished with whatever you are entering, and are now ready for the terminal to respond.

Somewhere on the terminal is an ON-OFF switch, which is the main power control. Also located on the terminal may be a switch marked LOCAL-REMOTE or ONLINE-OFFLINE. When the switch is in the LOCAL or OFFLINE position the terminal can be used as an ordinary electric typewriter. The REMOTE or ONLINE position is the correct one for APL.

Besides the typewriter-like terminals, another type features a video display instead of a printer. An example of this type is the IBM 3278 display terminal, with this keyboard

IBM 3270 APL Data Analysis Feature Keyboard

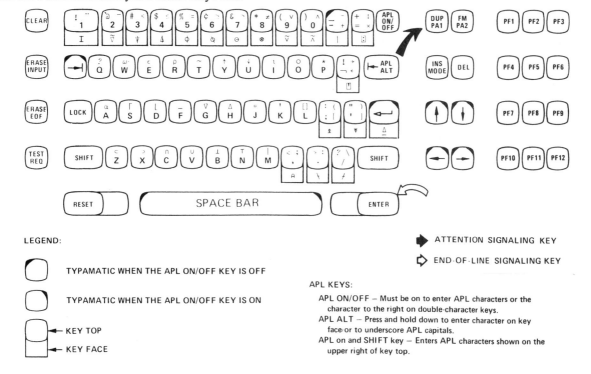

LEGEND:

ATTENTION SIGNALING KEY

END-OF-LINE SIGNALING KEY

TYPAMATIC WHEN THE APL ON/OFF KEY IS OFF

TYPAMATIC WHEN THE APL ON/OFF KEY IS ON

← KEY TOP

← KEY FACE

APL KEYS:

APL ON/OFF — Must be on to enter APL characters or the character to the right on double-character keys.

APL ALT — Press and hold down to enter character on key face or to underscore APL capitals.

APL on and SHIFT key — Enters APL characters shown on the upper right of key top.

There are three shifts on this keyboard. The regular APL characters on the tops of the keys are obtained in the same manner as on other terminals, that is, by using the shift keys. The compound characters on the front of some keys and all the underscored alphabetic characters are produced by holding down the APL ALT key along with the desired character.

These display terminals are usually 'hardwired' to a computer. Turning on the power is all you need to establish the connection. They are capable of producing all the characters shown, both EBCDIC and text. To sign on APL, press the ENTER and APL ON/OFF keys, and follow the instructions below for entering your personal ID.

The keyboard of the IBM Personal Computer equipped with STSC's APL*PLUS software is similar to that of the IBM 3278. The APL*PLUS PC System has two principal modes of operation: it can be used as a stand-alone APL system in the usual sense, and it can also be used as a dial-up or hardwired terminal connected to a time-shared computer. In fact, it can even operate in both modes simultaneously (see page 241), but for now you can switch it from stand-alone to time-sharing or back by pressing both the ALT and F8 keys.

Turn on your terminal or computer and set the LOCAL-REMOTE switch (if there is one) to LOCAL. Practice entering your sign-on identification in the form *)usernumber:password*. The sign-on for user 1500 with the password *DGIL* would be entered as

)1500:DGIL

The use of the password is optional, but strongly recommended for security reasons. If a password is not used, the sign-on command is simply of the form *)usernumber*.

Should you forget to hold down the shift key, you will get] instead of). That is an incorrect entry and you would not be able to sign on. Repeat the above exercise. When you are finished practicing, set the LOCAL-REMOTE switch to REMOTE and leave the power switch on.

If you are using a stand-alone APL system such as for the IBM Personal Computer, you are both the user and the computer manager. As a user, you only need to know how to use APL as presented in this book. However, because it is a personal system, there isn't any central staff (other than yourself) to run backups, install system upgrades, etc. Hence, if you value the continuity of your data and programs, follow the vendor's system management advice.

Those of you using a time-sharing system will need to know the telephone access number, how to set the switches on your terminal and dataset, modem or accoustic coupler, and the particular sequence of network control codes to get you properly connected. There are so many variants possible that we can't begin to help you here. Moreover, most of the system and equipment manuals are difficult for the novice to decipher. Your best bet is to ask someone on the staff of your vendor or information center to help you get connected. After the first few tries things will work smoothly, and by experimentation you may even be able to understand the manuals.

Some APL systems will conceal the sign-on by overprinting random characters (on print terminals) or blanking it out (on display terminals). These features may be automatically invoked at sign-on or triggered by a command like a simple right parenthesis or *)BLOT*. They are intended to protect your user number from unauthorized use, and should be used if available.

A typical sign-on with the terminal response looks like this:

)1500:DGIL
OPR: SYSTEM AVAILABLE TO 10 PM TONIGHT
057) 9.44.03 10/25/82 LGILMAN

    WELCOME TO APL

057) tells which port (telephone line) connects you to the computer, and it is followed by the time in hours, minutes, and seconds, the date and the user's name. The next line identifies the system. Sometimes there may also be a message from the computer operations center with news for all users.

Having signed on, we are ready to do some simple calculations:

    3+5
8
    2+2
4

There may well be variations in the above sign-on procedure in different APL systems and with different terminals. For example, when using an ASCII terminal at 30 characters per second on many commercial time-sharing systems, you must enter ○ (shift *O*) before the right parenthesis. You should consult your computer center for specific sign-on instructions and hints. For stand-alone small computers that can also be used as terminals, consult the manufacturer's reference manual for more detailed sign-on instructions. Likewise, VS APL running under various environments requires a sign-on sequence that may differ from one installation to another.

Sign-off

At this point let's assume you have successfully signed onto an APL system and are ready to try it out. However, before we get into how you use it, we want to mention how you sign off. Don't actually sign off now, if you want to try out APL.

Here is the sign-off procedure: enter) *OFF*, press RETURN and wait for the computer's response. After that, turn the power switch off. If you are using an acoustic coupler, turn it off and hang up the telephone.

```
)OFF
057  10.04.15 10/25/82  LGI
CONNECTED 0.20.12 TO DATE   4.19.26
CPU TIME  0.00.01 TO DATE   0.01.03
```

Sign-on and sign-off are APL *system commands*. They tell the computer to do something for you. There are many such commands, like)*ERASE*,)*CLEAR*,)*LOAD*,)*COPY* that will be introduced as needed.

All times shown are in hours, minutes and seconds. The cumulative connect time for this user in this billing period is 4 hours, 19 minutes and 26 seconds. The cumulative computer usage time is 1 minute and 3 seconds.

Different APL systems may use accounting displays other than the one shown here. In any case it is wise to make sure you understand how you're being charged or budgeted. Contact your sales representative if you are using a commercial system, or the computer center management otherwise.

To change the password, or include one for the first time, the sign-off command is modified to be)*OFF* : new password, while to remove the password enter)*OFF* :. Some systems may also have a special command for this,)*PASSWORD* old password : new password. Passwords may be any combination of letters and numbers, only the first eight of which are recognized by APL. To ensure security and privacy they should be randomly chosen and not be too short. Your computer center management may have further instructions for their proper use.

From now on we assume you are seated at an active terminal or have ready access to one. Many of the chapters will have instructions to get you into a special workspace, which is a block of internal storage (called 'memory'), and in which there are programs and exercises for your use. More about this later.

In the early chapters try to get as much finger practice as you can. Remember that the slowest part of the APL system is you, the user. You are limited by the speed with which you can enter information at the keyboard. If you are a typist, learn to touch-type your APL rather than use the 'two-finger' method.

Elementary arithmetic operations

We'll begin with the simple arithmetic operations, + × − ÷, the symbols for which are in the upper right portion of the keyboard. The decimal point is in the lower right part of the keyboard. All the symbols are used in the conventional manner.

In many places in this book, when there are a few short examples in sequence, we will place them across rather than down the page, to save space.

Addition

```
        3+4                    .5+.6                      1.45+5.99
7                       1.1                    7.44
```

You've just barely started, but already there is one error you are free to make. Suppose you enter

```
    3+
```

You ask '3+ what?' It isn't a meaningful statement because you haven't indicated a second value for the plus symbol to operate on. The computer responds by displaying

```
SYNTAX ERROR
    3+
      ^
```

This error message tells you that the statement has been improperly formulated in APL, i.e., is 'ungrammatical' in the sense that we are using perfectly good symbols, but using them incorrectly. The caret (∧) marks where the error was detected. The exact form of the error display, including the position and number of carets, may vary slightly with different versions of APL.

Multiplication

```
        5.1×7.9                    3×6
40.29                       18
```

The symbol for multiplication is ×. It must always be explicitly used in APL. In conventional notation expressions like A(B) or even AB mean multiply A by B; however, in APL it must be written $A \times B$.

Subtraction

```
        5−2                     2−5
3                        ¯3
```

Notice the overbar (¯) in the last response. The symbol means 'negative.' In a way it is a description, like the decimal point, attached to the number that follows it. It is *not* an indication of an operation to be performed. For that, the subtraction sign (−) is used.

Let's try some more examples using the negative sign (upper shift 2):

```
        3+¯2                    ¯2+3                    −2+3
1                       1                   ¯5
```

If you think there's something peculiar about the last example, where a subtraction sign was used in place of the negative sign, relax; the distinction will be made in Chapter 7.

Division

```
        3÷5                    5÷3
0.6                     1.666666667
```

By now you have probably noticed in your own practice with the arithmetic operations that at most ten significant figures will be displayed in the response. Most APL systems carry out calculations to approximately sixteen figures and round off to ten figures in the display. Trailing zeros are not displayed. In Chapter 17 a command will be introduced that will allow the number of places displayed to vary from 1 to 16.

So far so good. But how about

```
      5÷0
DOMAIN ERROR
      5÷0
      ∧
```

Here we see a different type of error. The operation is a valid one, but we tried to divide by 0, which is not in the *domain* of possible divisors. This seems reasonable enough, until you try 0÷0: you get a 1. The version of APL used here follows the rule that any real number divided by itself is 1.

Corrections and comments

Now suppose we have to enter numbers that are a little harder to type than what we have been using thus far, and (heaven forbid) we made a mistake. Specifically, suppose we entered 2×3.14169 and really meant 2×3.14159, but haven't yet pressed the RETURN key.

The error can easily be corrected. On print terminals, strike the BACKSPACE key (gently, because it may be a 'repeating' key on some terminals) to move the cursor, or position indicator, over to where the error begins. Then press the LINEFEED key. The cursor will move down. This signifies that everything above and to the right has been wiped out from the memory of the system and won't be seen by the computer:

```
      10+3.14159
      2
13.142
```

In the following examples we want 23×506 but actually enter 3×506. All we need do is to backspace just before the 3 and type 2 as shown, provided, of course, that RETURN hasn't yet been pressed:

```
      23×506
11638
      3×506
1518
```

```
      3×506
      2
11638
```

The fact that the 2 is shown on another line is immaterial, since the system doesn't know that we moved the roller and paper manually for illustrative purposes here. We can also glean from this example that the order in which characters are entered at the keyboard is immaterial. What you see on the paper or screen is what you get with APL.

You have undoubtedly concluded by this time that the way to get rid of a whole line is to backspace all the way to the left margin and press ATTN:

```
      1234567×12345678
∨
```

On most APL systems using ASCII terminals, BREAK will get rid of the line without having to backspace. If you are using a display terminal like the IBM 3278, corrections are made by entering new characters in place of the old after moving the cursor to the appropriate position. Furthermore, you may use the DELETE and INSERT keys to change the entry, or the ERASE INPUT key to erase the characters in the input area of the screen, or the CLEAR key to clear the entire screen.

The combination of upper shift *C* (∩) and the small circle (upper shift *J*, ○) overstruck means that a comment follows. Comments may contain any APL symbols and call for no response from the system.

```
      ⍝ THIS IS HOW TO MAKE A COMMENT
```

This doesn't mean that all combinations of overstruck characters are possible in APL. The times and divide signs have been overstruck in the example below, with a resulting *ENTRY ERROR (CHARACTER ERROR* on some systems). Allowable overstrikes will be taken up as needed in succeeding chapters.

```
      34∗73
ENTRY ERROR
      34▨      (The display is moved forward one line here for illustrative purposes.)
        ×73
2482
```

Note that the original input is reproduced only up to the first illegal character, here indicated by the ▨, where the cursor comes to rest. At the same time the keyboard is unlocked and ready to accept the correct characters for processing and display, as though you had entered the entire line at once.

Occasionally the computer will report an error even when you haven't made one. At other times there may be misprints not traceable to mechanical or electrical problems in the terminal itself. This happens when there is a faulty telephone connection. If errors are reported frequently, hang up the phone and dial in again. At times transmission difficulties may result in a *RESEND* message. When this happens, the input line is lost and must be reentered.

An introduction to vectors

Imagine a store which, following a disastrous fire, is left with just three items for sale, A, B, C. Here is the sales record of the number of items sold over a two-week period:

```
           |   A       B       C
  ---------+--------------------------
  WEEK  1  |   9       7       8
  WEEK  2  |   3       4       5
```

Before the store goes out of business, what are the total sales for each item? The obvious answer is to add the weekly totals for each item separately as

```
      9+3                 7+4                 8+5
12                  11                  13
```

In APL there is a much more compact way to do this:

```
      9 7 8+3 4 5
12 11 13
```

This leads us into a unique and time-saving feature of APL: its ability to process arrays of numbers. In the previous example the array was one-dimensional, with the elements all arranged in a single string, called a *vector*. We'll see later that APL can handle multidimensional arrays as well.

Let's now change the problem:

```
           |   A       B       C
  ---------+--------------------------
  WEEK  1  |   9       7       8
  WEEK  2  |   5       5       5
```

Treating this as a problem involving vectors, we enter

```
      9 7 8+5 5 5
14 12 13
```

To save still more entry time, where all the elements of one of the vectors are identical, just enter that value once, and APL will extend it automatically to match the other vector in length:

```
      9 7 8+5
14 12 13
```

Now for some do's and don'ts. First, suppose we run all the numbers together:

```
      978+555
1533
```

The absence of space between the digits causes the system to interpret the series as a single number. Again, what you see is what you get. Does this mean that the numbers or the operation symbol must be separated by any fixed number of blanks? The following example makes clear that one blank is sufficient as a separator, but extra blanks don't hurt:

```
      9    7 8+    5
14 12 13
```

What if the two vectors don't have the same number of elements?

```
      9 7 8 + 5 3
LENGTH ERROR
      9 7 8 + 5 3
            ∧
```

We get an error message because the computer doesn't know which number goes with which. The only exception to this is where all the elements are identical, in which case only one of them need be entered, as in the example 9 7 8 + 5 above.

Some people have felt that in a problem like 9 7 8 + 5 3, APL should supply a trailing zero. However, other people feel it should supply the zero on the left side (0 5 3 versus 5 3 0). In general, where there's no unambiguous best way to do it, APL simply doesn't take short cuts.

This *parallel processing* of vectors, to give it a name, works equally well with other arithmetic operations:

```
      1 2 3 4×2
2 4 6 8
```

If, for example, a cookie recipe required 6, 4 and 2 cups respectively of three ingredients, and we wished to make only one-third of a batch, then the required amounts are

```
      6 4 2÷3
2 1.333333333 0.6666666667
```

Again, suppose that the above three ingredients cost respectively 1, 5 and 7 cents per cup. What is the total cost for each ingredient?

```
      6 4 2×.01 .05 .07
0.06 0.2 0.14
```

As we shall see soon, there are many operations that can be used with vectors. We will also be able to invent functions that behave just like our ordinary arithmetic operations in that they can be used with vectors.

PROBLEMS

1. DRILL. (Some of the drill problems in this chapter and others may result in error messages.)

```
6  8  2  4+3  9  1  1        5  4  3×6              1  2  8÷1  2  0
1  0  9  8-4  2  2  3        10÷10  5  2  1         ¯2  0  .81+15  6  ¯5
3-¯1  ¯56.7  0  ¯.19        3  4×1  2  3            2¯¯3
```

2. Additional finger exercises. (What happens if you leave out the comment symbol?)

```
ⁿNOW IS THE TIME FOR ALL GOOD MEN TO COME TO THE AID
ⁿIF AT FIRST YOU DON'T SUCCEED, TRY AGAIN
ⁿHOW NOW BROWN COW
ⁿPRACTICE MAKES PERFECT
ⁿTHE SLOWEST PART OF THE APL SYSTEM IS USUALLY THE USER
```

3. At a basketball game a ticket seller sold 155 adult tickets at $1.25 each, 89 student tickets at .50 each, and accepted 45 courtesy passes at .25 each. Write an APL expression which gives the income from each class of tickets.

4. A taxi fleet owner recorded mileages of 1263, 1997 and 3028 for his three cars. Operating expenses for each car during the same period were $59.50, 79.88 and 83.00, respectively. What was his cost per mile for each car?

5. An inept salesperson sells four radios for $47, $18, $68 and $10 but forgets to collect the 5% sales tax. How much was lost on each radio?

6. A car dealer illegally resets the odometers of some used cars on his lot. If the odometers read 45201, 64677, 52468 and 68893 miles *after* setting each one back 15000 miles, what is the true mileage for each car?

7. Four hundred responses to a survey were received. For the five questions on the survey there were 356, 205, 189, 322 and 257 'yes' answers. What fraction of the respondents gave positive answers to each question?

8. (For terminals with a backspace key.) Type 3 − 2. Backspace and overstrike the subtract sign with a plus sign (without using ATTN or LINEFEED). Then press RETURN and explain the result.

Chapter 2: Useful tools

All of our work so far has been done in hand calculator or *immediate execution* mode. This has the disadvantage that once we enter the numbers and the operation symbol to be used and then press RETURN, execution proceeds and we get an answer (unless we tried something illegal). But the work is lost. It is no longer available to us for any future calculation, except on some display terminals where we can 'page' or 'scroll' back.

You will now be introduced to the data storage feature of APL. This will permit reusing data without having to reenter it. Then, as an extension of the concept of a vector, two-dimensional arrays will be examined in the latter part of the chapter.

Assignment

Any good calculator has the ability to store constant factors so that they can be used over and over again without having to be reentered each time. For instance, suppose we are given a series of problems all involving the constant 0.75:

```
     2×.75            4+.75                .75×.75
1.5                4.75              0.5625
```

As it stands, .75 has to be typed each time. What we'd like is some way to save this number and have it available for reuse. It may seem trivial at this point because our repeated factor, .75, doesn't take many keystrokes, but what if the expression you had to repeat had a large number of digits in it?

In APL, the term *assignment* is used to describe the placing of the results of an expression in storage. It works this way:

```
     A←.75
```

The expression above is read as '*A* is assigned the value .75'. From this point on, unless the contents of our *workspace* (the place in the computer where our work is being done) are destroyed or a different value is assigned to *A*, entering *A* will be equivalent to entering .75. Since *A* is a name to which we are free to assign any value we want, even though we chose a specific one here, it and other names used in a similar manner are called *variables*.

Here are some calculations you can do with *A*:

```
     2×A              4+A                  A×A
1.5                4.75              0.5625
```

Flushed with success, you ought to be ready to try your hand at another assignment:

```
     B←1 2 3 4 5              2×B
                        2 4 6 8 10
```

A, like death and taxes, is still with us. So try

```
     A+B                           B×B
1.75 2.75 3.75 4.75 5.75       1 4 9 16 25
```

If we keep this up, sooner or later we will run out of letters of the alphabet. What then? The next logical step is to use multiple letter names:

```
     PI←3.14159              PI×PI
                        9.869587728
```

The name in the example above wasn't chosen haphazardly. Subject to restrictions on length and usable characters (to be discussed later in this chapter), you have a wide choice of possible names for objects in APL. We suggest as a general rule that names be chosen for their mnemonic utility. This simplifies identification and enhances consistency, making it easier for you and others to follow what has been done.

You may have noticed above that when an assignment is made, the terminal doesn't display its result. This is reasonable enough, since all we are asking when we make an assignment is for something to be placed in storage. And if we don't tell it where to go, it goes on the paper, like a well-trained house pet.

A is still in storage. Here it is again:

        A
`0.75`

What happens if we mistakenly or otherwise use *A* for a second assignment? For instance,

        A←2+B

If we display *A* now, we get

        A   *2+B*
`3  4  5  6  7        3  4  5  6  7`

The new values of *A* replace the old, which are lost. Moral of the story: if you want to save the values stored in a variable name, don't override the assignment. Use a different name instead.

There are several ways to extend the number of possibilities for variable names. Underlining (upper shift *F*) is one way:

        A̲←3.2   *A̲+5*   *A̲*
                   `8.2`   `3.2`

A̲ is clearly different from *A*, which still has its last assigned value. In effect this gives us 52 letters to choose from, alone or in multiple character names like

        DATA←5 2 7 8

Most major APL systems allow up to 77 characters in a variable name, but it doesn't pay to make it too long. Remember, *you* are the one who will have to enter it. Numbers can also be included in any position except the first, as shown by

        X3Y2←20   *3XY2←20*
                          SYNTAX ERROR
                              `3 XY2←20`
                                `∧`

but special symbols for operations, spaces and punctuation marks may not be used in a name. Exceptions: the symbols ∆ (upper shift *H*) and ∆̲ are treated as alphabetic characters, and some systems allow the characters _ and ‾ (shift *F* and shift 2) to be used in names, but not in the first position. Incidentally, APL did put the value 2̄0 (see above) in storage under the name *XY*2:

        XY2
`20`

You can make multiple assignments in the same statement. In certain cases this is a handy timesaver. Here is an example:

        A←2+B←3 1 5   *A*   *B*
                             `3  1  5`   `5  3  7`

However, don't use multiple assignments unless there is a clear and obvious relation among the variables; it can cause more confusion than it's worth.

Now let's try

        A+W
VALUE ERROR
        A+W
          `∧`

It should be obvious what's wrong. The computer didn't recognize the variable name W because there hasn't been any value assigned to that name. A is still a valid variable, but not W:

```
        A                       W
5  3  7                 VALUE ERROR
                            W
                            ∧
```

This raises another question: how can you find out what variable names you already have in storage? The command $)VARS$ (for 'variables') produces an alphabetized listing of the variables in storage:

```
      )VARS
A        B        DATA    PI       X        XY2      X3Y2      A
```

A partial listing of the variable names beginning with a given letter or letters, say PE, to the end of the alphabet can be obtained with:

```
      )VARS PE
PI       X        XY2      X3Y2      A
```

and in APL2 $)VARS$ PE ST lists alphabetically all variables from PE through ST.

Underlined letters such as $\underline{A}$ come after all nonunderlined letters, so far as their display order is concerned. For a long listing, if you don't want to continue the display, press ATTN (BREAK on an ASCII terminal, or CLEAR on the IBM 3278) to stop it. This technique can be used to interrupt execution of any expression currently being processed.

Expressions starting with a right parenthesis are known as *system commands*. You have already used two of them, sign-on and sign-off, and $)VARS$ is another. More will be introduced as the need arises.

Getting back to our $VALUE$ $ERROR$, if we give W a value and then call for $A+W$, we no longer get an error message,

```
      W←0.1                 A                    A+W
                      5  3  7            5.1  3.1  7.1
```

and not only is execution successful, but W is added to the list of variables in storage:

```
      )VARS
A        B        DATA    PI       W        X        XY2      X3Y2      A
```

Now W behaves just like the other variables and can be reassigned:

```
      W                     W←2×W                   W
0.1                                             0.2
```

Suppose that you want to get rid of one or more variables while still actively working in APL. Entering

```
      A←
```

buys you nothing since the response of the system is

```
SYNTAX ERROR
      A←
        ∧
```

and entering $A←0$ also gets you nowhere, since the only thing that happens is that the value 0 is assigned to A.

Another system command, $)ERASE$, is useful here. This command is followed by the name(s) of the variables to be erased. Its execution elicits no response from the system other than the cursor moving over 6 spaces:

```
      )ERASE A B DATA
      )VARS
PI       W        X        XY2      X3Y2      A
```

An introduction to matrices

While useful in and of itself, the concept of a vector, introduced at the end of the first chapter, is far too limited in the real world. We would certainly stand accused of myopic vision if, like the strange inhabitants of Flatland, we didn't recognize the need for arrays which are multidimensional.

The sales record table on page 8

```
        |    A        B        C
--------+---------------------------
WEEK  1 |    9        7        8
WEEK  2 |    3        4        5
```

is an obvious case in point. For tabulating data or correlating information which purports to relate two quantities or more, an array of two dimensions, called a *matrix*, is necessary.

We could continue this discussion and come up into a general n-dimensional array, but our finite minds are likely to boggle at the conception of any array beyond three dimensions. Also, since the great majority of users of arrays don't normally require more than two dimensions, we'll stick with two dimensions until much later in the text, after a firm foundation has been laid.

Now for the goodies. Before using matrices we have to know how to create them. Unlike vectors, which can be created in APL by simply typing the elements in a single line, matrices require two more pieces of information: how many rows and how many columns. Incidentally, the words *dimension* and *axis* are frequently used to refer to a direction along which an array extends in space. Loosely speaking, they are somewhat interchangeable with the word *dimension* as we used it previously. Put another way, we need to state how big the array will be in each direction, that is, how many rows and columns. More specifically, the example matrix

```
1   2   3   4
5   6   7   8
9  10  11  12
```

has 3 rows and 4 columns, i.e., its *shape* is 3 4. The first dimension, which gives the number of *rows*, is of length 3, which corresponds to the size of one column, while the second dimension, of length 4, gives the number of *columns*, and corresponds to the size of one row.

If you're still with us, let's now take a look at how we can build these matrices. The symbol ρ (upper shift *R*) is employed for array construction. In use, the numbers on the left specify the shape of the resulting matrix, and consist of two integers detailing the number of rows and columns, in that order. The numbers on the right are the elements to be included in the array, with these elements ordered by rows. Here are some examples:

```
      2 3ρ4 7 8 2 4 6
   4  7  8
   2  4  6
```

```
      A←4 2ρ7 8 4              B←3 4ρ1 2 3 4 5 6 7 8 9 10 11 12 13 14
      A                        B
   7  8                      1   2   3   4
   4  7                      5   6   7   8
   8  4                      9  10  11  12
   7  8
```

Two pertinent comments need to be made at this point. First, if there aren't enough elements to make up the array, APL goes back to the beginning of the 'storage pile' on the right and starts over as in *A* above. Second, if there are too many elements, only those needed are used and the rest ignored, as in *B*.

The symbol ρ used in this manner is called *reshape*. It takes what is on the right, which could be a single number, vector, matrix, three-dimensional or higher array, and reshapes it according to the numbers on the left. The following example is illustrative:

```
      2 3ρB                  10ρB
   1  2  3              1 2 3 4 5 6 7 8 9 10
   4  5  6
```

The shape of the result is dependent on the number and magnitude of the elements on the left:

```
        8ρ3 0 1                           3 2ρ100                      2 3 4ρ7 8 2 2 3
3 0 1 3 0 1 3 0                        100 100              7 8 2 2
                                       100 100              3 7 8 2
                                       100 100              2 3 7 8

                                                            2 2 3 7
                                                            8 2 2 3
                                                            7 8 2 2
```

If there is one element on the left, the result is a vector; two elements form a matrix; three elements form a three-dimensional array, etc. Don't be alarmed by the last example, which is three-dimensional, consisting of 2 planes (or pages) each of which contains 3 rows and 4 columns. It is included at this point only for illustrative purposes.

How large an array can be defined? Every APL system limits the numbers of elements an array can have. The limit is based on such factors as the size of the workspace, the amount of other data already stored in the workspace, and certain characteristics of the data itself (an integer usually takes less space than a mixed fraction, for example). We'll cover this matter in more detail later. But for now, if you get the message *WS FULL* you'll know that you have tried to deal with more data than your system allows.

Operations with matrices

Now that you know how to build and store matrices, there are many things you can do to manipulate their elements. We begin by defining two matrices M and N:

```
M←4 3ρ1 2 0 1 3 2 3 4 2 3 3 0
N←4 3ρ2 3 7 8 1 4 2 5 0 0 7 6

        M                    N
1 2 0              2 3 7
1 3 2              8 1 4
3 4 2              2 5 0
3 3 0              0 7 6
```

As an extension of our earlier work with vectors in the last chapter, we can add 2 to each element of M, or divide each element by 3:

```
     2+M                    M÷3
3 4 2              0.3333333333    0.6666666667    0
3 5 4              0.3333333333    1               0.6666666667
5 6 4              1               1.333333333     0.6666666667
5 5 2              1               1               0
```

We can multiply two matrices together element-by-element, or subtract one matrix from another:

```
      M×N                    M−N
 2   6   0          ¯1  ¯1  ¯7
 8   3   8          ¯7   2  ¯2
 6  20   0           1  ¯1   2
 0  21   0           3  ¯4  ¯6
```

PROBLEMS

1. Assign the vector 3 4 5 6 7 to the name *A* and make *B* equal to two times *A*.

2. Which of the following are valid variable names in APL?

   SPACEMAN   *B+ALPHA*   *SIXTY-FOUR*
   X SQUARED   *Δ3X*   *4BY5*

3. Construct **A** matrix *M* with 5 rows and 3 columns, consisting entirely of the number 7, and **B** matrix *Q* of the same size as *M*, each of whose rows contains 4 9 11.

4. Convert the matrix *M* from problem 3 into a matrix *N* of all 1's in at least two different ways.

5. A store sells 3 items, A, B, C. Over a one-week period, the amounts sold are respectively 8, 15, 7. The following week's sales record is 12, 4, 0. Put this data in a matrix *S*, each of whose rows represents a week's sales. The prices of A, B, C the first week are respectively \$3.10, 2.00, 4.17, but because of rapid inflation, these prices increase to 3.50, 2.75, 4.35 in the second week. Put this data in a matrix *P* and use it to construct a table of total sales revenue by item over the two-week period.

6. The base pay for shipping clerks in a warehouse is \$4.50 per hour, with time-and-a-half after 40 hours. If in a certain week the 5 clerks working put in 40, 55, 46, 40 and 40 hours respectively, compute their gross pay for the week. (What if someone worked less than 40 hours? We'll see how to handle that problem in the next chapter.)

7. The year of birth of each member of a family is stored in a vector *BIRTH*. Compute for each member of the family **A** age, **B** year of retirement (at age 65), **C** number of years left until retirement. Assume the present year is *YR*.

8. Using the data from problem 7, Chapter 1, what fraction of the respondents gave 'no' answers to each question?

9. A company charges a flat fee *PH* for postage and handling on all orders, plus the applicable sales tax. If the day's sales are stored in the vector *SALES* and the tax rates in the vector *TAX* (one element for each element in *SALES*), what is the total cost to each customer?

Chapter 3: Additional operations and tools

In the previous chapters we dealt with individual numbers, which we will now call *scalars*; strands of numbers, for which the term *vectors* was used; and two-dimensional arrays, which we called *matrices*. Left partly unanswered at that time was the question of what combinations of these are allowed in APL, as well as what the shape of the result might be. Let's now direct our attention to the question by formulating a few simple rules and giving appropriate names for the concepts to be considered.

Primitive scalar dyadic functions

There are seven rules that govern the ways in which vectors, scalars and matrices can be combined. In what follows, the letter f stands for any of the arithmetic operations that we have already introduced. Later in this section we'll further classify and categorize these operations to make it easier for you to relate them to others that are yet to come.

rule	result		arguments
1	SCALAR	←	SCALAR f SCALAR
2	VECTOR	←	SCALAR f VECTOR
3	VECTOR	←	VECTOR f SCALAR
4	VECTOR	←	VECTOR f VECTOR
5	MATRIX	←	SCALAR f MATRIX
6	MATRIX	←	MATRIX f SCALAR
7	MATRIX	←	MATRIX f MATRIX

The terms under 'result' tell us the shape of the result when the function is performed on various combinations of argument shapes.

In some newer versions of APL, these rules have been extended so that, for example, it is now possible to add a vector to each column of a matrix. The vector, of course, would still have to match the length of the column. This extension is discussed in more detail on page 211.

This is as good a place as any to introduce a little additional terminology. Why? you ask. Naming something doesn't tell us any more about it and it might even mislead us by making it easy for us to talk glibly of things we may not know much about. But mathematicians especially, being the perverse creatures that they are, insist on more formal names for the tools and concepts they work with. And having a name for something does have the advantage of letting the namer identify without ambiguity (we hope!) that which is under discussion.

First, if F stands for an operation to be performed, the things it is to operate on will be called *arguments*. In support of our previous comment we quote here (out of context) Samuel Johnson: 'I have found you an argument, but I am not obliged to find you an understanding.'

Thus, in the expression 5×6, the left argument is 5, and the right argument is 6. Both arguments can be scalars (rule 1),

```
      3+5
8
```

or one can be a vector, either on the right or the left (rules 2 and 3), or both arguments can be vectors (rule 4).

```
      2+3 5 7                5 6 8×3                3 6 8÷2 1 4
5 7 9                  15 18 24               1.5 6 2
```

The only stipulation is that both arguments be the same length. As an obvious corollary, the lengths of the resulting vectors in the above two examples are the same as those of the vector arguments.

By substituting the words *size* or *shape* for *length* in the last two sentences, the same reasoning can be shown to hold for various combinations of matrices and scalars (rules 5, 6, 7). In fact, an inspection of the seven rules and the examples will convince you that they can all be boiled down into a single rule for operations on n-dimensional arrays (n=0,1,2, with 0 being associated with scalars), provided that appropriate size restrictions in the arguments are observed. Can you state this rule?

The operators that we have been working with are more properly called *functions*, because a result is obtained as a consequence of the function operating on its argument(s). (One of the dictionary meanings of 'function' is 'performance' or 'execution.')

Furthermore, the word *dyadic* is associated with these functions, since they require *two* arguments (at least as we have been using them thus far). They are also called *primitive* because they are immediately available on the APL keyboard. And finally (at long last!), they are referred to as *scalar* because functions of this type are defined first for scalars and then extended element by element to vectors, matrices and other arrays. In summary, the operations + − × ÷ are called *primitive scalar dyadic functions*.

Operation tables for the arithmetic functions

For each of the functions thus far introduced, we can construct an *operation table*, with the left argument down the vertical column on the left and the right argument across the top. To save space, only the integers 1 2 3 4 will be used as arguments:

```
+| 1 2 3 4      -| 1    2    3   4      ×| 1  2   3   4      ÷| 1   2    3    4
-+--------      -+-----------------      -+----------------      -+---------------
1| 2 3 4 5      1| 0   ⁻1   ⁻2  ⁻3      1| 1  2   3   4      1| 1  1÷2  1÷3  1÷4
2| 3 4 5 6      2| 1    0   ⁻1  ⁻2      2| 2  4   6   8      2| 2   1   2÷3  2÷4
3| 4 5 6 7      3| 2    1    0  ⁻1      3| 3  6   9  12      3| 3  3÷2   1   3÷4
4| 5 6 7 8      4| 3    2    1   0      4| 4  8  12  16      4| 4   2   4÷3   1
```

Since it is a downright nuisance to construct these operation tables by hand, let's use this opportunity to introduce a new APL feature which behaves somewhat differently from the simple arithmetic functions used so far, but which, nevertheless, will be a great timesaver for us in the future.

We'll begin by introducing a problem that involves a large number of multiplications. It asks that we compute the taxes to be paid for items costing varying amounts and taxed at different rates:

```
   TAX     |    TAX RATES
  TABLE    |  .01   .02   .05
---------+------------------
         1 |  .01   .02   .05
  COST   2 |  .02   .04   .10
  OF     3 |  .03   .06   .15
  ITEM   4 |  .04   .08   .20
         5 |  .05   .10   .25
```

The result desired is the matrix which is obtained by getting all possible products of costs and rates. You can see that if the cost and tax rate vectors had large numbers of noninteger elements, this procedure could involve a lot of work.

Outer product

APL has an *operator*[1] which may be applied to arrays in precisely the way needed to fill in the table above. It is called the *outer product* or *outer result*. To illustrate it, let the left argument be the vector of costs *A* and the right argument the tax rates *B*:

    A←1 2 3 4 5   B←.01×1 2 5

---

[1] Formally speaking, an APL operator is something which works on a function to change in some systematic way the result that would normally be obtained from that function.

The outer product is

```
    A∘.×B
0.01          0.02          0.05
0.02          0.04          0.1
0.03          0.06          0.15
0.04          0.08          0.2
0.05          0.1           0.25
```

which is read 'A jot dot times B.' The little circle, called *jot*, is the upper shift J. Clearly, the outer product in this case gives all possible multiplications of the left and right arguments, i.e., a modified 'times' table.

Any primitive scalar dyadic function can be used after the period in place of ×, as for instance,

```
    A∘.+B
1.01          1.02          1.05
2.01          2.02          2.05
3.01          3.02          3.05
4.01          4.02          4.05
5.01          5.02          5.05
```

Notice that the shape of the result is the catenation (chaining together) of the shapes of the two arguments. In this case it is a matrix with five rows and three columns.

The outer product lets us do a wide variety of things. For example, here we produce an addition table and a subtraction table:

```
    A∘.+A                        A∘.−A
2   3   4   5   6        0  ‾1  ‾2  ‾3  ‾4
3   4   5   6   7        1   0  ‾1  ‾2  ‾3
4   5   6   7   8        2   1   0  ‾1  ‾2
5   6   7   8   9        3   2   1   0  ‾1
6   7   8   9  10        4   3   2   1   0
```

The other operation tables can be obtained in the same way. We'll have more to say about outer product in Chapter 21.

In the meantime, to continue our story, here is an operation table for which no function is specified. Can you guess what it is?

```
    |  1   2   3    4
 ---+-------------
  1 |  1   1   1    1
  2 |  2   4   8   16
  3 |  3   9  27   81
  4 |  4  16  64  256
```

Power function

You should be able to see that the previous table represents raising to powers. The left argument values are raised to the powers indicated by the right argument. This power function exhibits the characteristics we would expect from a primitive scalar dyadic function. All we need is a symbol for it. This brings up an interesting aspect (or failing, if you prefer) of conventional mathematical notation, and one which will become even more apparent as we go along.

Notice how we write the four arithmetic functions:

$$2 + 3$$
$$2 - 3$$
$$2 \times 3$$
$$2 \div 3$$

And then we come along and write for the power function

$$2^3$$

The operation to be performed is specified not by a symbol but by position, which is not only inconsistent but potentially dangerous since it is very easy sometimes to miss the elevated position of the power in writing or reading.

In APL the symbol * (upper shift *P*) is used to represent raising to a power, as in

```
      2*3
8
```

Like the other primitive scalar dyadic functions, it extends to vectors and matrices as well:

```
      2 4 3*2
4 16 9
      A←2 3ρ1 2 3 4 5 6

      A                      A*3
 1 2 3                   1    8   27
 4 5 6                  64  125  216
```

In algebra, roots are shown to be the same as fractional powers, e.g., finding the square root of a number is the same as raising it to the one-half power. So instead of writing $\sqrt{2}$ to mean the square root of 2, in APL this is

```
      2*.5                  9 64*.5
1.414213562              3 8
```

The power function is the key to compound interest calculations. If you were to start a savings account with a $500 deposit (principal) and your banker offers you 6% interest for a year's use of the money, you would have $530 at the end of the first year. Now if that sum were saved for another year at the 6% rate, you would then have $561.80 (530+.06×530). The general formula to compute the future value F of P dollars saved for N years with an annual interest rate of R in conventional notation is

$$F = P \times (1+R)^n$$

Thus, the future value of $500 over 8 years at .06 annual interest rate is

```
      RN←1.06*8                   500×RN
                             796.9240373
```

Or, you can watch your money grow each year by doing

```
      RN←1.06*1 2 3 4 5 6 7 8
      500×RN
530 561.8 595.508 631.23848 669.1127888 709.2595561 751.8151295 796.9240373
```

On the other hand, if the same annual interest rate, 6%, were offered by another bank, but here the compounding were done quarterly, the future worth of $500 over 8 years would be

$$500 \times \left(1 + \frac{.06}{4}\right)^{4 \times 8}$$

yielding

```
      RN←1.015*32                 500×RN
                             805.1621601
```

Negative powers, which are the equivalent of the reciprocal of the number raised to the corresponding positive power, are also available to the APL user, as in the following:

```
      2*¯2
0.25
```

And now that we have the power function at our disposal, it can be used to generate very large numbers, as, for instance,

```
      100*8
1E16
```

which raises the question of whether there is any largest number in APL. You may want to experiment on the terminal to determine what, if any, it is.

Scaled or exponential notation

In the last example you saw a new notation, which some of you may recognize as being similar to what is used in other higher level programming languages and many 'scientific' hand calculators. It is intended to avoid writing a monster like 10,000,000,000,000,000. The E may be interpreted as 'times ten to the ... power.'

This notation is equally convenient for very small numbers,

```
      .01*9
1E‾18
```

and can be employed in many different ways to express the same number, say, 530:

```
530        =        53×10
5.3E2               5.3×100
.0053E5             .0053×100000
530E0               530×1
5300E‾1             5300×.1
```

APL not only produces results in scaled notation, but lets you enter data this way also:

```
      1+33              1+3.3E1              1+.33E2              1+330E‾1
34                 34                   34                   34
```

Users have considerable freedom in formatting their inputs, although the common practice of using commas to separate groups of digits isn't allowed because the comma itself is an APL function, to be discussed later. The results generated by the APL system are somewhat more restricted. Problems 1 and 2 at the end of the chapter will give you some clues as to these limitations.

The rest of this chapter and the next will introduce more primitive dyadic functions. Some of these will be employed frequently by most APL users; others, like logarithms and combinations, will be of value to a more specialized fraternity, nonmembers of which should feel free to study them with no more than passing interest, or for that matter, ignore them completely.

Logarithms

The logarithm function is an inverse of the power function. The logarithm of a number N to the base B is that power to which B must be raised to equal N. In APL this is written $B \circledast N$, the symbol being that for power ($*$) overstruck with the large circle (upper shift O).

Thus, since it is true that $10*3$ is 1000, then the base-10 log (to use the usual abbreviation) of 1000 is written as $10 \circledast 1000$. Of course, this function also works with vector and matrix arguments:

```
      10⊛1000                     2 2 10⊛4 8 1000
3                            2 3 3

      X←2 3ρ1 2 3 4 5
      X                               2⊛X
1 2 3                       0             1             1.584962501
4 5 1                       2             2.321928095   0
```

Notice that the base is the left argument and the number whose log is being found is the right argument.

Logarithms, like powers, are often used in financial calculations involving compound interest. For example, to find how many years it would take for your savings to double at 5, 6, 7, 8, 9 or 10 percent annual compound interest,

```
      RATES←.01×5 6 7 8 9 10
      RATES←1+RATES
      RATES
1.05 1.06 1.07 1.08 1.09 1.1
      RATES⊛2
14.20669908 11.89566105 10.24476835 9.006468342 8.043231727 7.272540897
```

We admit that powers and logarithms are a bit tougher to grasp than our old friends $+ - \times \div$. But they are so useful in helping to solve money-related problems that we felt you should be exposed to them early in this book. To give you a breather, we're now going to end this chapter with two uncomplicated but very useful new functions.

Maximum and minimum

Try the following exercises, exploring the working of the symbol ⌈ (upper shift *S*):

  3⌈5   **5⌈3**   **5⌈5**

5 ˋ   5   5

Lest you be tempted to think that ⌈ always generates a 5, look at

  3⌈1

3

If you experiment with this function for a while, you will see that it selects the larger of the left and right arguments and is appropriately named the *maximum* function. Its operation table looks like this:

```
      1 2 3 4 5∘.⌈1 2 3 4 5
1  2  3  4  5
2  2  3  4  5
3  3  3  4  5
4  4  4  4  5
5  5  5  5  5
```

Since there's a maximum function, you would expect a companion *minimum* function. It is found on the upper shift *D* key, and it selects the smaller of the two arguments:

  3⌊5   **5⌊3**   **¯5⌊3**   **¯5⌊¯3**

3   3   ¯5   ¯5

    B←2 3ρ3 4 0 1 7 9
    C←2 3ρ1 2 3 4 5 6

    B   *C*   *B⌊C*

3 4 0   1 2 3 1 2 0
1 7 9   4 5 6 1 5 6

```
      1 2 3 4 5∘.⌊1 2 3 4 5
1  1  1  1  1
1  2  2  2  2
1  2  3  3  3
1  2  3  4  4
1  2  3  4  5
```

'Smaller' and 'larger' are relative terms, and, indeed, the mathematician defines them according to position on the real number line:

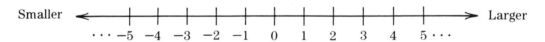

Smaller ⟵ ··· −5 −4 −3 −2 −1   0   1   2   3   4   5 ··· ⟶ Larger

Thus, the smaller of two numbers is that one which is farther to the left, and the larger one, farther to the right. That's why ¯5 is a smaller value than ¯3 or 3.

Let's consider a couple of simple problems. There are three students who got grades of 90, 80 and 55 in an exam, and on a retest received 70, 80 and 75, respectively. Their kind-hearted instructor wishes to record for each student only the larger of the two grades received. How can he do it? The right answers are 90 for the first student, 80 for the second, and 75 for the third. In APL this is obtained by

  90 80 55⌈70 80 75

90 80 75

A second problem: we have purchased an odd lot of lumber consisting of four boards of lengths 5, 8.1, 10 and 7.9 feet. Unfortunately, our truck can carry boards no longer than 8 feet without running afoul of the law. Boards longer than 8 feet have to be trimmed to 8 feet. The 'trimming' is done in APL by

```
      8⌊5 8.1 10 7.9
5  8  8  7.9
```

and the second and third boards are the ones which get cut down. These are two trivial examples, but here are some with great practicality.

The 1983 rules for U. S. Social Security withholding state that the employee pays 6.70% of the lesser of his annual salary or \$35,700. The equivalent expression in APL is $BASE \leftarrow SALARY \lfloor 35700$ followed by $WHOLD \leftarrow .0670 \times BASE$.

Remember problem 10 of Chapter 2? It awarded time-and-a-half for all hours worked over 40. When we left it, we still didn't have a way to calculate wages if someone worked less than 40 hours. That can now be fixed by following $OT \leftarrow HOURS - 40$ with $OT \leftarrow 0 \lceil OT$. This changes any 'negative' overtime to zero overtime.

Of all the primitive scalar dyadic functions learned so far ($+ \ - \ \times \ \div \ \star \ \circledast \ \lceil \ \lfloor$), maximum and minimum are different from all the others in one significant respect: no knowledge of an operation table is needed to use them—only the ability to distinguish larger and smaller. They are inherently simpler than even addition and subtraction. In fact, very young children can conceptualize $\lceil$ and $\lfloor$ before they can + and −.

User-defined functions

Up to now you've worked only with some of the primitive APL functions available directly to you on the keyboard. If you wanted to solve the same problem several times with different arguments, your knowledge of APL thus far would dictate that the instructions would have to be repeated for each set of arguments.

In common with other higher level programming languages, APL offers users the ability to define their own functions (within limits) using names instead of symbols. We will give you a bare-bones look at this feature, with a fuller treatment to start in Chapter 8. There will be a minimum of explanations at this time, since we are reserving our detailed commentary for later.

Let's use as an example the compound interest problem on page 20. Assume our principal is \$1. If we had a special function, call it ▨, available to us on the keyboard to do the calculation, then we could write $FV \leftarrow R▨Y$, where FV is the future value of \$1 at $R\%$ for Y years. The symbol ▨ would have to have been so defined by the implementors of the APL system that whenever it was encountered, it would add 1 to .01 times the left argument and raise that number to the power represented by the right argument.

Needless to say, no such symbol exists since the APL system is a general one, not specifically designed for financial analysis. The primitive functions that are provided, however, can be combined to do just about anything.

Enough said. To define a function to compute future value, enter the following:

$$\nabla Z \leftarrow L \ \ FV \ \ R \qquad \text{(RETURN)}$$

∇ (called *del*) is the symbol that tells APL you are about to define a function. The $Z \leftarrow$ (any variable name will do) will make your function behave like a primitive. L and R are arbitrary variable names for the arguments, and FV is the name chosen for the function. The system responds with a [1], ▨ indicating where the cursor is, waiting for some instruction(s) on line 1.

```
[1]    ▨
```

Enter

```
[1]    L←.01×L
```

followed by a return to indicate you are through with the line. The system responds with [2] and the remaining instruction is now entered:

```
[2]    Z←(1+L)*R    (RETURN)
[3]    ▨
```

To tell the system that you are finished defining this function, enter a second ∇. The cursor comes to rest in its usual position, outside the function:

```
[3]     ∇
       Ａ
```

Now we can use *FV* to compute future values:

```
     FUT1←10 FV 8
     FUT1
2.14358881
     500×FUT1              ⍝ FUTURE VALUE OF $500
1071.794405
     10 FV 1 2 3 4 5 6 ⍝ FUTURE VALUE OF $1 FOR EACH YEAR UP TO 6
1.1 1.21 1.331 1.4641 1.61051 1.771561
```

To define and use even simple functions you need to know a little more than what we've said so far. First, the arguments are subject to the same rules as the primitives (page 17). Second, the result, like the primitives, may be stored in a variable. Third, multiple line instructions are executed sequentially. And last, that line of the function that produces the final result (here, line 2) must begin in the same way as the *header* (top line with all the names), in this case, Z←, for the result to be storable.

What happens if you make a mistake? APL provides excellent editing capability (Chapter 10), but only a few simple commands will be introduced now.

To display the list of defined functions, enter)*FNS*, while the command ∇*FUNCTIONNAME*[□]∇ displays the function itself:

```
      )FNS
FV
      ∇FV[□]∇
    ∇ Z←L FV R
[1]   L←0.01×L
[2]   Z←(1+L)*R
    ∇
```

A function may be erased with)*ERASE*, or a line replaced by the command ∇*FUNCTIONNAME* [*LINENUMBER*] *new instructions* ∇. For example, if we wanted to change the instruction on line 2 of *FV* to (1+L)×R (that's wrong, of course, but who cares?), we would enter ∇*FV*[2]Z←(1+L)×R∇. To get rid of a line, enter ∇*FUNCTIONNAME*[△*linenumber*]∇.

Some systems offer other ways to define functions. In particular, a method called *direct definition* is gaining popularity among academic users. If that's your calling, you may want to take a peek at **page 298**.

PROBLEMS

1. DRILL

```
¯2*.5                    1 10⊕1                 10⊕0
3*4 3 2 1 0 ¯5           2*.5 .333 .25 .2       1 9 ¯5 ¯2⌊0 6 4 3
21.268E1+4.56E¯2         1*0 1 10 100 1000      ¯8*.3333333333333
5 0 ¯22 15⌈3 7 ¯10.8 2   8.3E0×7.9E¯3 56        ¯7.11E4÷9.45E¯3
2 3 4 5⊕2                ¯2⊕25                  346×2E3.7
```

2. Key in 1*E*0, 1*E*1, etc. to 1*E*11. Do likewise for 1*E*¯1 through 1*E*¯6. Note where the break point is in APL for the display on large and small numbers in *E*-notation.

3. Given a cube each of whose edges have length *L*. Write the APL steps needed to find its surface area. Execute for *L*←3 7 15 2.7.

4. Assign *A*←1 2 3 4 and *D*←3×*A*. Execute *A*∘.×*D* and *D*∘.*A*.

5. Use the outer product to generate a table of squares and square roots of the integers 1 through 5.

6. Express the number of seconds in the year (365 days) in scaled notation.

7. A journeyman snail finishing his apprenticeship is now allowed by the union to travel at a snail's pace (12 ft. per day). Express this in miles per hour.

8. Execute ‾8*.5. Why the error message?

9. An astronomical unit (AU) is approximately 93,000,000 miles, the distance from Earth to Sun. Using scaled notation, find the distance in AU's of an object that is 1,500,000,000 miles away.

10. Store A sells 4 kinds of vegetable for 15, 20, 32 and 29 cents a pound. At store B the prices are 18, 20, 10 and 49 cents a pound, respectively. The policy of a third store, C, is to meet the competition's prices. Write an APL expression to determine store C's selling prices for the 4 items.

11. The pH of a solution is a measure of its acidity or basicity, and is defined as the logarithm (base 10) of the reciprocal of the hydrogen ion concentration in moles/liter of solution. Use APL to express the pH of a solution whose concentration is C.

12. You are given two matrices of prices, A and B. Define a new matrix C such that each element of C is the smaller of the corresponding elements of A and B.

13. **A** What is the future value of $1000 in ten and one half years if it earns 8% annual interest, compounded monthly? **B** Is this better than a 7.9% annual interest compounded daily? Use 360 as the number of days in a year.

14. Fold a piece of paper. It's now twice as thick as it was before. If the paper is .01 cm thick, how many times do you have to fold it to make it at least a kilometer thick?

15. A certain bacterium is known to grow 15% in a day. How long does it take for it to be 1000 times its starting size?

16. As I was going to St. Ives, I met a man with 7 wives. Each wife had 7 sacks. Each sack held 7 cats. How many cats? How many sacks? How many wives? How many were going to St. Ives?

17. Using the outer product, show the future value of $1 compounded annually at 0, 2, 4, 6, 8 and 10 percent for 1 through 10 years.

18. If inflation reduces the purchasing power of saved cash by 10% per year compounded, how long will it take for a dollar saved today to be worth only one fourth as much in real purchasing power?

Chapter 4: More primitive dyadic functions

This chapter introduces the remaining primitive dyadic functions, which will complete the set begun with $+ - \times \div \star \circledast \lceil \lfloor$. While we will be discussing 13 new ones, it really won't be very difficult; after we struggle through the first two individually, the remaining ones fall into two simple categories that are easy to learn and remember.

Combinations

A relatively simple combinatorial problem in mathematics is to find the number of ways one can group 2 things out of a population of 4. Let's solve the problem by brute force, with 4 objects, A, B, C, D. The possible combinations are AB AC AD BC BD and CD. We'll assume the order isn't significant, so that CA and AC, for example, will be considered to be the same. Thus, there are 6 ways of grouping 2 things out of a population of 4.

In combinatorial theory it is shown that the formula (in conventional notation)

$$\frac{m!}{n!(m-n)!}$$

gives the number of ways of grouping m objects n at a time. For the case above, this would be (in conventional notation)

$$\frac{4!}{2!(4-2)!}$$

or 6. To remind those of you whose math is rusty, m! means $m \times (m-1) \times (m-2) \times ... \times 1$, so that 4! is the same as $4 \times 3 \times 2 \times 1$.

As you might hope, the process is somewhat easier in APL. It is done with the same symbol !, called *binomial* or *combinations*. The symbol is formed by striking the period, BACKSPACE and the quote symbol (upper shift *K*) so that the two characters line up. Of course, if your keyboard has the ! symbol, use it directly.

```
      2!4
6
```

When formed by overstriking, the symbols ' and . *must* be lined up. If they aren't, different things (none of them good) happen, depending on which APL system you use. Some will admonish you with *SYNTAX ERROR* or *OPEN QUOTE*, others will both admonish you and supply a second quote, and yet others will act dead regardless of what you do, until you figure out that you have to enter another quote. More about the use of quotes in Chapter 13.

The primitive scalar dyadic function ! can take both vector and matrix arguments:

```
      0 1 2 3 4!4
1 4 6 4 1

      X←2 3ρ0 1 2 3 4 5
      2!X
 0   0   1
 3   6  10
```

Its operation table looks like this:

```
         0  1  2  3  4 ∘.!0  1  2  3  4
1  1  1  1  1
0  1  2  3  4
0  0  1  3  6
0  0  0  1  4
0  0  0  0  1
```

That portion of the table consisting of the nonzero integers can be removed to form what in mathematics is called Pascal's triangle,

```
                1
             1     1
          1     2     1
       1     3     3     1
    1     4     6     4     1
```

which, if you're interested, is a way to calculate and display the coefficients generated in the expansion of an expression of the form $(A+B)^n$ by the Binomial Theorem.

Finally, to complete the picture, our arguments don't have to be integers:

```
      2.1!5.6
13.48487115
```

For the benefit of the more mathematically sophisticated, this is related to the complete beta-function of probability theory. Don't panic. It won't be mentioned again!

Residue

The next primitive scalar dyadic function to learn is called *residue*. We can illustrate it with a trivial example. Assume that we are at the zoo with only 8 peanuts and 3 children who are to share the wealth evenly. We aren't able to cut up a single peanut. How many do we have left?

The simple-minded way to do this would be to start with 8 and take away 3, leaving 5. Then take 3 more away, with 2 remaining, too few to distribute to the children. In formal language, the 3-residue of 8 is 2. This isn't, of course, the only way to solve the problem. We could also divide 8 by 3, see that it goes in twice and get a remainder of 2.

The symbol for residue is |, which is the upper shift *M* . In APL, the 3-residue of 8 is entered as 3 | 8.

Our peanut problem can be enlarged by considering the distribution of varying amounts of peanuts to the 3 children:

```
      3|0  1  2  3  4  5  6  7  8
0  1  2  0  1  2  0  1  2
```

Here is another problem in which 5 peanuts are distributed among 1, 2 and 3 children:

```
      1  2  3|5
0  1  2
```

The residue function is a handy one for generating all kinds of useful results. For instance, asking for the 1-residue of a number is a convenient way to get the fractional part of the number:

```
      1|2.5 31.23
0.5  0.23
```

Now what about the residues of negative numbers, say 3 | ⁻4? Previously we saw that a recurring pattern was generated by

```
      3|0  1  2  3  4  5  6  7  8
0  1  2  0  1  2  0  1  2
```

So when we try

```
        3|¯4 ¯3 ¯2 ¯1 0 1 2 3 4 5 6 7 8
2 0 1 2 0 1 2 0 1 2 0 1 2
```

we expect, and get, a continuation of the recurring pattern. If you think about it a bit, you will see another way to obtain the residue of a negative number. For our example above, add 3 to ¯4 to get ¯1. Then add 3 again to get 2. In general, the rule is to keep adding until the result is zero or positive.

Suppose the left argument is negative. Then the result is also negative, or 0 if the right argument is a multiple of the left argument:

```
       ¯8 3 ¯3 ¯2|¯4
¯4 2 ¯1 0
```

Applications requiring negative left arguments are few and far between. However, if you insist on pursuing this, try a few examples. Observe that the residue always lies between 0 and the value of the left argument. More formally, the result of $L|R$ is R if L is zero; otherwise it equals $R-(N \times L)$ for some integer N.

There is one residue class of particular interest in the computing industry, the 2-residues of the integers:

```
       2|0 1 2 3 4 5
0 1 0 1 0 1
```

Here we have a continuing pattern with 0 and 1 as its only elements. If we so choose, we can let 0 represent the state of a circuit with the switch open (no current) and 1 with the switch closed. Data that has values of 0 or 1 only is often called *bit* data. We'll have more to say about this soon.

Relational functions

In APL there are six *relational* functions, < ≤ = ≥ > ≠, which are found on the keyboard as the upper shift 3 through 8. They have the usual mathematical meanings, *less than, not greater than, equal, not less than, greater than* and *not equal*, respectively. The reason they are called *relational* is that they inquire about the truth or falsity of the relationship between two quantities.

For example, consider the statement A<B. It is really a question asked of the computer: 'Is A less than B?' It calls for a response of 'yes' or 'no', because either A is less than B or it isn't. Let's try this on the terminal:

```
     3<5              5<3              3<3
1                 0                0
```

Clearly, a 1 response means the statement is true, and 0 false. Indeed, the only two values you ever get from any of the relational functions are 0 and 1.

```
     3<1 2 3 4 5              A←2 3ρ1 2 3 4 5 6
0 0 0 1 1                     2<A
                         0 0 1
                         1 1 1
```

We can now use this function to help us in a selection problem. Suppose as store owners we have a number of accounts, with $3, $¯2, $0, $2 and $¯3 as balances, and we want to flag or mark those accounts which are overdrawn (represented by negative values). The *less than* function will solve our problem.

```
     3 ¯2 0 2 ¯3<0
0 1 0 0 1
```

Does < have all the qualities of a primitive scalar dyadic function? Here is its operation table:

```
     1 2 3 4∘.<1 2 3 4
0 1 1 1
0 0 1 1
0 0 0 1
0 0 0 0
```

By this time you ought to be able to convince yourself that *less than* meets our criteria for a primitive scalar dyadic function, as do indeed the rest of the relationals. We won't go through them all, but let's explore just one more, =. Entering

```
      3 ¯2 0 2 ¯3=0
0  0  1  0  0
```

generates a listing of those accounts from the previous example whose balance is 0. You should be able to see many other possibilities. For instance, to get vectors of all 1's or all 0's, try

```
      0 1 2 3=0 1 2 3                0 1 2 3=3 2 1 0
1  1  1  1                       0  0  0  0
```

Logical functions

Not all the juice has yet been squeezed out of the subset 0 1 of the real numbers. Here is a function ∧ (upper shift 0), called *and*, whose entire operation table is

```
      0 1∘.∧0 1
0  0
0  1
```

The result is 1 if and only if both arguments are 1, otherwise it is 0.

You have probably noticed that only 0 and 1 were used as arguments for *and*. Notice what happens when we try

```
      2∧0
DOMAIN ERROR
      2∧0
      ∧
```

Just as zero is not in the domain for division, all values other than 0 and 1 are not in the domain for ∧; and attempts to use them result in *DOMAIN ERROR*s.

For those who have some background in mathematical logic, the analogy between 0 and 1 and the true-false entries in the truth table for *and* will be apparent. In any event, this function provides yet another means of generating 0's and 1's, and will be useful in writing programs later on. The *and* function is an example of a class of functions called *logical* or *Boolean*.

Some of you will no doubt immediately see uses for this function. Others may be encountering it for the first time. For those of you in the latter category we offer the following example.

You have two vectors containing respectively the prices and amounts in inventory of each item sold. You want to generate a vector of 0's and 1's showing which items have to be reordered (less than 5 in inventory) and which at the same time sell for $50 or more. The following function will do the job:

```
      ∇RESULT←PRICE REORD INVENTORY
[1]   PRICES50←PRICE≥50
[2]   INVENTORY5←INVENTORY<5
[3]   RESULT←PRICES50∧INVENTORY5
[4]   ∇
```

Another logical function is ∨ (upper shift 9), called *or*. The result is 1 if either or both of the arguments are 1:

```
      0 1∘.∨0 1
0  1
1  1
```

Referring to the inventory example above, suppose now you want to identify those items the orders for which exceed the number in inventory or for which there are less than 5 in stock.

```
      ∇RESULT←ORDERS IDENT INVENTORY
[1]   ORDERS←ORDERS>INVENTORY
[2]   RESULT←ORDERS∨INVENTORY
[3]   ∇
```

There are yet two more functions in this class, ⍲ and ⍱, (*nand* and *nor*). You may have guessed already that *nand* stands for 'not and' and *nor* for 'not or.' The overstruck character ~ (upper shift T) implies negation. Below are their operation tables:

```
        0  1∘.⍲0  1                    0  1∘.⍱0  1
  1  1                          1  0
  1  0                          0  0
```

You can see that everywhere 0 appears in the table for ∧, a 1 appears for ⍲, and vice versa. The same holds for ∨ and ⍱.

Logical functions are used in programming to test a set of conditions (true and false usually being represented by 1 and 0 respectively), and then to take actions based on the outcome of the tests. Logical functions are also widely used to represent or simulate switching circuits.

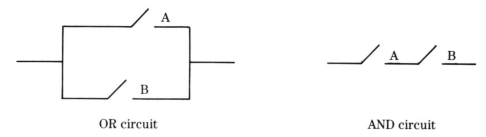

OR circuit   AND circuit

In the left figure electricity flows if either switch A or switch B is on, while in the right figure electricity flows only if both A and B are on. Read '0' for off and '1' for on, and the figures correspond to the *or* and *and* tables respectively. Keep in mind that it is a short step to go from simple electrical circuits like these to the fundamentals of digital computer design.

There are 16 possible logical connectives, although we have taken up only 4 of them. To illustrate how others can be generated, let's assume we need a function that gives us an *exclusive or*, with operation table

```
    |  0  1
  --+-----
  0 |  0  1
  1 |  1  0
```

the result being 0 if and only if both arguments are 0 or both are 1. Can we produce this table in APL?

The answer is yes. It is that part of the operation table for ≠ where both arguments are 0 or 1. A similar approach yields many of the other logical connectives.

```
        0  1  2  3∘.≠0  1  2  3
        1  1
        1  1
  1  1  0  1
  1  1  1  0
```

Summary

We have now introduced and illustrated almost all of the primitive scalar dyadic functions. Before going on, here is a brief recapitulation:

$A+B$	sum of A and B	$A<B$	
$A-B$	B subtracted from A	$A\le B$	Relationals all yield
$A\times B$	product of A and B	$A=B$	1 if true
$A\div B$	A divided by B	$A\ge B$	0 if false
$A\star B$	A raised to the power B	$A>B$	
$A\circledast B$	base-A logarithm of B	$A\ne B$	
$A\lceil B$	larger of A and B	$A\vee B$	logical or of A and B
$A\lfloor B$	smaller of A and B	$A\wedge B$	logical and of A and B
$A\mid B$	A residue of B	$A\,⍱\,B$	logical nor of A and B
$A!B$	combinations of B items taken A at a time	$A\,⍲\,B$	logical nand of A and B

Any of these functions can be used to replace the character f in the rules (**page 17**) for combining scalars, vectors and matrices.

PROBLEMS

1. DRILL

```
1  9  8│3  4  6                              1│3.4  ¯2.2  .019
0  1  2  3  4!3  4  5  6  7                   0│1  2  3
3│¯3  ¯1  0  1  2  3                          ¯2  4  ¯5│8  13  3.78
0  0  1  1∨0  1  0  1                         2  3  0<5  ¯1  4
1  0  1  0∧1  0  0  1                         3  1  2≠1  2  3
2  4  7  ¯2>6  ¯1  0  4                       0  1  2  3=0  1  3  2
4  ¯5  ¯1  ¯6.8≥4  1  ¯1  2                   0  0  1  1⍱0  1  0  1
8  7  6  5  4  3  2  1≤1  2  3  4  5  6  7  8  1  0  1  0⍲1  0  0  1
```

2. How can the functions = and | be used in APL to identify the factors of an integer N?

3. *A* is a vector of accounts, with the negative values representing those overdrawn. Use one or more of the relational functions to flag those accounts *not* overdrawn.

4. Write an APL expression to return a 1 if either condition A is true or condition B is false.

5. Execute 0 1∘.=0 1. Contrast this with the operation table on **page 30**. What name would be appropriate to assign to this logical connective?

6. You happen to have in storage a vector *S* of four positive elements. Use *S* to generate each of the following in at least five different ways: **A** a vector *Z* of four zeros, and **B** a vector *Y* of four ones.

7. Write APL statements which will produce a logical vector *C* with 1's corresponding to the even numbers in a vector *A*←¯6 7 2 4 ¯21.

8. Obtain as many of the remaining logical connectives as you can from the functions introduced so far.

9. Execute the following outer products for *A*←0 1:   *A*∘.×*A*   *A*∘.⌊*A*   *A*∘.⌈*A*   *A*∘.*A   *A*∘.|*A*   *A*∘.!*A*. What logical or relational function is each equivalent to?

10. How can the residue function be used to tell whether one number A is exactly divisible by another number B?

11. Write an APL expression to tell what clock time it is, given the number of elapsed hours H since midnight.

12. How many quadrilaterals can be formed by joining groups of 4 points in a collection of 30 points in a plane.

13. If 1 | *N* produces the fractional part of *N*, how can the residue function be used to get the integral part of the number?

14. Write an expression to get the fractional part of a negative number.

15. A student's answers (0 for no, 1 for yes) to a survey are stored in a vector *RESP*1. Six months later the student again takes the same survey. His latest answers are stored in *RESP*2. Show how to identify the questions **A** to which the responses both times were 'yes' and **B** which were answered differently in the two surveys.

16. (For lovers of FORTRAN or BASIC.) In other programming languages you may run across statements like I=I+1, where I is a counter for some iterative procedure. There is, of course, no finite real number that equals itself when 1 is added to it. This statement is to be interpreted as 'increment I by 1 and *store* the result in I'. What is its APL equivalent?

Chapter 5: Algorithms, reduction and scanning

We now introduce the concept of an *algorithm*, which is nothing but a series of steps that together comprise a prescription for defining a function or solving a problem. Two examples will be given. The first, taken from plane geometry, will involve no new APL functions and will be used solely as an illustration of an algorithm. The second example, although very useful in its own right, quite frankly, is an excuse to introduce one of the most widely used APL operations, *reduction*, which allows us to compute among the elements of a single vector or matrix. Finally, *scan*, which can be thought of as a powerful extension of reduction, will be introduced.

Algorithms

Here is the example referred to above, which everyone should recognize as the butt of numerous jokes and misspellings of its name. The problem is to calculate the hypotenuse of a right triangle, given the sides as shown:

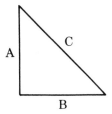

A convenient and time-honored rule for finding C is the Pythagorean Theorem. It states that to get C we have to square A, add it to the square of B, and then find the square root of this sum.

Here is how this sequence of steps can be executed in APL:

```
      A←3
      B←4
      A2←A*2
      A2
9

      B2←B*2
      S←A2+B2
      S
25

      C←S*.5
      C
5
```

Of course, if we didn't want to save the result by storing it in C, we could have eliminated its assignment and displayed the result directly by entering $S*.5$.

Now think about this: we had to assign A and B initially in the sequence; otherwise, when we called for the values of $A2$, $B2$ and S along the way as checks on our work, we would have gotten *VALUE ERROR*s, or perhaps some previously assigned value. We'll see later, when we learn how to store instructions (programming), that this assignment of values for the variables need not be done beforehand.

Let's assign new values to A and B, this time solving two triangles simultaneously:

```
        A←1  3
        B←1  4
        C
5
```

What happened? Why did we get the same value for C even though A and B changed? We answer this question by asking another: when we assign a quantity like $A2+B2$ to some variable S, what is it that is stored? Not the *instruction* $A2+B2$, but the result of executing that instruction with the numbers stored in $A2$ and $B2$. Thus, assignment can't ordinarily be used to store instructions; only *values* can be stored this way.

```
     A2←A*2                    B2←B*2                      S←A2+B2
     A2                        B2                          S*.5
1  9                   1  16                       1.414213562  5
```

However, instructions *can* be stored in a user-defined function:

```
        ∇C←A HYP B
[1]     A2←A*2                        1 3 HYP 1 4
[2]     B2←B*2                1.414213562  5
[3]     S←A2+B2
[4]     C←S*.5
[5]     ∇
```

A set of instructions like the above, that collectively represents a prescription for solving a particular problem, is called an *algorithm*. Defined functions in APL, therefore, are a mechanism for saving and calling algorithms.

Finally, we can check on the variables in storage in the usual manner,

```
        )VARS
A         A2        B         B2        C         M         N         PI
RATES     RN        S         W         X         XY2       X3Y2      A
```

and the new variables specified in our right triangle algorithm are now included. Of course, your listing may differ from this if you happen to have defined additional variables in the current terminal session. However, it should contain at least these names.

Reduction

You saw how working with vectors and matrices allowed us to do *parallel processing* of data, with a resulting saving in time and number of keystrokes required. We now extend this concept to show how meaningful operations can be effectively performed on the elements of a single vector or matrix. Continuing with the analogy with electrical circuits, we may call such work *series processing*.

Let's begin with a common business calculation, an invoice extension. Assume that several different items have been purchased. We'll use Q and C to represent the quantities and the costs, respectively.

```
     Q←6  2  3  1  0              C←2  4  3  5  10
```

To get the vector of total costs, we execute

```
     X←Q×C                    X
                        12  8  9  5  0
```

But now, to obtain the grand total, we have to add up all the elements of this vector. In conventional notation, the mathematician indicates the sum of the elements of a vector by writing

$$\sum_{i=1}^{n} x_i$$

$\sum$ means 'sum' while i is a running variable from 1 to n, identifying the individual elements of the vector. The total number of elements is n, 5 in the invoice extension problem we are working on. If this seems potentially like a lot of work, don't be too concerned. In what follows we will show how to carry out the summation in APL with minimal effort.

Getting back to the problem at hand, our objective is to sum across the elements of a vector. We do this in APL with $+/X$. This is read as 'plus reducing X,' or 'the plus reduction of X.' The symbol $/$ (lower right corner of the keyboard) is called *reduce*, because it reduces the vector to a single element:

```
    +/X
34
```

How this operator works is worth discussing in more detail. The APL system inserts the function symbol which appears to the left of the $/$ between each pair of elements of the vector, and groups them so that the order of execution is $12+(8+(9+(5+0)))$.

The reason for the grouping is that each function operates on everything to the right of it. If you think about what this means, you will see that this is equivalent to operating on the rightmost pair of elements first, taking that answer together with the next element to the left, and so on. Following this through step by step, we obtain

```
12+(8+(9+(5+0)))
12+(8+(9+  5  ))
12+(8+  14     )
12+  22
    34
```

You may be inclined to argue that we are making a big to-do about nothing, since with addition it doesn't really matter whether we work from right to left or left to right. We'll see later, however, that arbitrary order of execution (called *commutativity*) is not general. For the time being, just remember that in APL reduction proceeds from right to left.

Times reduction

Now consider still another problem. A rectangular box has the dimensions 2 by 3 by 4 centimeters. What is its volume? To answer the question we obviously want

```
    2×3×4
24
```

If we assign the vector of the dimensions to Z, then $×/Z$ should give us our answer:

```
    Z←2 3 4
    ×/Z
24
```

In this case, $×$ is planted between each neighboring pair of elements, and the internal calculation is carried out in this sequence:

```
2×(3×4)
2×  12
   24
```

Since raising to integer powers is the same as repeated multiplication, then a clumsy alternative to $1.06*4$ (future value of a dollar compounded annually for 4 years at a constant rate of 6%) is $×/1.06\ 1.06\ 1.06\ 1.06$. That's not very exciting itself, but it does lead to methods for dealing with varying interest rates. For example, the future value of a dollar compounded for 4 years with annual interest rates of 5%, 7%, 6% and 5.5% for each of the years in turn is simply $×/1.05\ 1.07\ 1.06\ 1.055$.

Reduction on matrices

A matrix has two dimensions to be concerned about, and that makes reducing matrices a little harder than reducing vectors. Suppose we have sales information by weeks showing the numbers sold of each of five items, as in the table below:

```
         |      ITEMS
   SALES|  1   2   3   4   5
   -----+-----------------
W    1 | 15  18   9   2   7
E    2 |  4  15   1   8   6
E    3 |  0   4   0   8   3
K    4 | 12  10  13   7   9
```

It is reasonable to ask what the sales record is by item for the month (i.e., over the 4-week period). This involves a summation along the columns, or, put another way, across the *first* dimension of the matrix.

To show this operation in APL, we first put the matrix in storage:

```
      S←4 5⍴15 18 9 2 7 4 15 1 8 6 0 4 0 8 3 12 10 13 7 9
      S
15 18  9  2  7
 4 15  1  8  6
 0  4  0  8  3
12 10 13  7  9
```

The desired summation is obtained by

```
      +⌿S
31 47 23 25 25
```

⌿ is the symbol for reduction overstruck with the subtract sign. It is used for summing the elements in each *column* of a matrix. The result is a vector with as many elements as there are *columns* in the matrix.

If in the above example we wanted gross sales records by weeks, we would obtain it by entering

```
      +/S
51 34 15 51
```

This sums the elements in each *row* of the matrix, that is, across the *last* dimension. The result is a vector with as many elements as there are *rows* in the matrix.

In summary, +⌿ causes a reduction across the *first dimension* of any array, and +/ reduces across the *last dimension* of any array. A vector has only one dimension, so that +⌿ and +/ will have the same effect.

The word 'reduce' was selected because it does indeed reduce the number of dimensions. A matrix reduces to a vector, and a vector reduces to a scalar.

Algorithms for averaging and counting

We can now profitably talk about an algorithm to get the average of the elements of a vector such as

```
      X←2 4 3 3 2.5 2
```

To get an average we need two things: the sum of all the elements in the vector we are averaging, and the number of elements. The first is easy: +/X is 16.5. We could then get the average by dividing this sum by the number of elements obtained by manually counting them. One way to 'count' the number of elements using APL is

```
      X=X
1 1 1 1 1 1
```

The result of all 1's is no surprise, since each element of X is equal to itself. As you can see, this generates a vector consisting of as many 1's as there are elements in X. But where does that lead us? Now all we have to do is add up those 1's to find the number of elements:

```
      M←X=X              N←+/M                    N
                             6
```

We can now complete the calculation of the average of 2 4 3 3 2.5 2:

```
      T←+/X            T                  T÷N
                 16.5               2.75
```

The expression +/X=X is a rather awkward way to obtain a count of the number of elements in a vector. As a reward for your patience, we'll now introduce the *shape* function, ⍴. Its job is to return the size of the array to its right.[1]

---

[1]Since ⍴ in this context has only a single argument (as opposed to A⊕B, which has a left and right argument), it is called a *monadic* (rather than dyadic) function. More about this in Chapter 7.

Our algorithm for averaging can now be more succinctly expressed as

```
    T←+/X              N←ρX              T÷N
                                 2.75
```

or even more usefully as a defined monadic function:

```
        ∇ T←AVERAGE X
[1]     T←+/X ⋀ NOTE USE OF T FOR STORING INTERMEDIATE RESULT.
[2]     T←T÷ρX
[3]     ∇
        AVERAGE X
2.75
```

When you apply *shape* to a matrix, the result isn't simply a count of elements, but rather is a vector holding the numbers of rows and the number of columns.

```
      A←2 3ρ1 4 5 6 8 9              B←1 2 3∘.⌈1 2 3 4
      A                             B
  1 4 5                          1 2 3 4
  6 8 9                          2 2 3 4
      ρA                         3 3 3 4
  2 3                                ρB
                                  3 4
```

Maximum, minimum and logical reduction

Plus reduction and minus reduction are very common in APL. But reduction isn't limited to just + and ×. Any primitive scalar dyadic function can be used. Here is an illustration using the maximum function. Remember Z, the vector of dimensions of the rectangular box we introduced earlier?

```
      Z
2 3 4
```

Suppose we wanted to get the longest dimension in Z, i.e., pick out the maximum value. Then by analogy, just as we had

```
        2+(3+4)  is2+7  or  9
        2×(3×4)  is  2×12  or  24
```

for +/Z and ×/Z, respectively,

```
        2⌈(3⌈4)  is  2⌈4  or  4
```

represents ⌈/Z, and returns the largest value in Z.

On the terminal, try

```
    ⌈/Z                 ⌊/Z
4                     2
```

The last example, minimum reduction, is carried out like this:

```
        2⌊(3⌊4)  is  2⌊3  or  2
```

Note that the symbol before the reduction operator is again placed between each pair of neighboring elements, and the groupings are the same as before.

Yet another simple application involves the logical functions in an accounts identification problem. Let X be a vector of balances:

```
    X←3 4 2 ¯2 1
```

Our job is to see if any of the balances are overdrawn (negative). The first step is to assign a vector of the same length as X, containing a 1 in each place where X is less than 0. Then use *or* reduction:

$LZ \leftarrow X < 0$	LZ	$\lor/LZ$
	0 0 0 1 0	1

(Remember that *or* returns a 1 if either or both arguments are 1.) Our answer can be interpreted as follows: if 1, then at least one account is negative; if 0, then no accounts are negative.

Let's reset X and repeat the problem to illustrate the other possibility:

$X \leftarrow 3\ 6\ 1\ 0\ 3$	$LZ \leftarrow X < 0$	$\lor/LZ$
		0

Can you tell what the significance of the answers might be if we had used $\land/LZ$ in the algorithm instead of $\lor/LZ$?

Minus reduction

This use of reduction is only for those of a mathematical persuasion. All others should skip this section.

```
      -/3 2 1 4
_2
```

Because of the right-to-left sequence of execution of APL, $-/3\ 2\ 1\ 4$ is equivalent to $3-2+1-4$ in conventional notation—in other words, it produces the *alternating sum*. You can view it as $3-(2-(1-4))$.

Here is a somewhat messy example, an expression to calculate π:

$$\pi = 4 \times \left(\frac{1}{1} - \frac{1}{3} + \frac{1}{5} - \frac{1}{7} + \frac{1}{9} - \cdots + \cdots \right)$$

Let's translate this into APL. Our first step is to get the vector of denominators, stopping after 10 terms. Next, we take their reciprocals, find the alternating sum and multiply it by 4.

Practically speaking, this isn't a very good way to get π because the series converges so slowly that a very large number of terms is needed to obtain an accurate value. However, it's dandy for illustrative purposes. First, we generate the vector $1\ 3\ 5\ \ldots\ 19$ from the vector $1\ 2\ 3\ \ldots\ 10$:

```
      N←1 2 3 4 5 6 7 8 9 10
      N←2×N
      N
2 4 6 8 10 12 14 16 18 20
      N←N-1
      N
1 3 5 7 9 11 13 15 17 19
```

The reassignment of N and $2 \times N$ and $N-1$ destroys the previously assigned values of N, as discussed on page 12.

The reciprocals can be obtained by assigning

```
      R←1÷N
      R
1 0.3333333333 0.2 0.1428571429 0.1111111111 0.09090909091 0.07692307692
    0.06666666667 0.05882352941 0.05263157895
```

and the alternating sum by

```
      T←-/R
```

Our answer for π (at last!) is

```
      4×T
3.041839619
```

which is about 0.1 off because we used too few terms for such a slowly converging series. However, after all this work, you will be pleased to hear that APL provides a primitive function for π, that it is alive and well, and is discussed in Chapter 7.

A defined function to compute π with this algorithm would look like this:

```
      ∇Z←PICALC N
[1]   Z←2×N
[2]   Z←Z-1
[3]   Z←1÷Z
[4]   Z←-/Z
[5]   Z←4×Z
[6]   ∇
      PICALC 1 2 3 4 5 6 7 8 9 10
3.041839619
```

If $-/$ is the alternating sum, then $÷/$ is the alternating product, which you can verify for yourself on the terminal.

Scanning

There are many instances when you may want to operate on the elements of an array one at a time and cumulatively with some primitive dyadic function, i.e., do a series of 'partial reductions' as you 'scan' the array. The simple example which follows illustrates the use of APL's scan operator.

Suppose you opened a bank account. You deposit $100 the first week, and in weeks two, three and four you write checks for $25, $50 and $33 respectively. In the fifth week you deposit $80, and then withdraw $40 and $10 during the following two weeks. If you store the data in a vector M, using negative values to represent outgoing funds,

```
      M←100 ¯25 ¯50 ¯33 80 ¯40 ¯10
```

then the balance at the close of the seventh week is $+/M$ or $22. More interesting yet is keeping track of the balance on hand each week. Using reduction, you could find this by executing

```
      +/100
100
      +/100 ¯25
75
      +/100 ¯25 ¯50
25
      +/100 ¯25 ¯50 ¯33 ⍝ WHAT IS THE SIGNIFICANCE OF A NEGATIVE RESULT?
¯8
      +/100 ¯25 ¯50 ¯33 80
72
      +/100 ¯25 ¯50 ¯33 80 ¯40
32
      +/100 ¯25 ¯50 ¯33 80 ¯40 ¯10
22
```

The plus-scan, which uses the symbol \, found on the same key as /, does it all at once:

```
      +\100 ¯25 ¯50 ¯33 80 ¯40 ¯10
100 75 25 ¯8 72 32 22
```

The shape of the result is the same as the shape of the argument. The last element is what would have been obtained had you performed a reduction instead of a scan.

Using the matrix S entered earlier in this chapter, you can scan across the second dimension or across the first dimension:

```
        S                    +\S                     +⌿S
15 18  9  2  7        15 33 42 44 51         15 18  9  2  7
 4 15  1  8  6         4 19 20 28 34         19 33 10 10 13
 0  4  0  8  3         0  4  4 12 15         19 37 10 18 16
12 10 13  7  9        12 22 35 42 51         31 47 23 25 25
```

In the examples above, the last column or row is the same as what would have been obtained by reduction along the same dimension.

Any of the primitive dyadic functions can be used with scan, just as with reduction. Here is our π-finding algorithm using scan instead of reduction. You can see how the accuracy of the result improves as the number of terms increases:

```
      R←1÷1 3 5 7 9 11 13 15 17 19
      T←-\R
      4×T
4 2.666666667 3.466666667 2.895238095 3.33968254 2.976046176 3.283738484
        3.017071817 3.252365935 3.041839619
```

Logical scans

Scans of arrays that consist only of zeros and ones are particularly interesting. $\wedge\setminus$ applied to a logical vector LV results in a vector of ones up to the first zero of LV and zeros thereafter. It is often used to count the number of elements until some condition changes, such as a space character following a word. A common expression in APL is $+/\wedge\setminus LV$, which returns a count of the number of leading ones in LV.

Other useful logical scans are $\vee\setminus LV$, which returns zeros up to the first one in LV, and $<\setminus LV$, which returns a vector of all zeros except for a one in the position corresponding to the first one in LV. $\neq\setminus LV$ can be used for parity indication. The result is one if the sum of the number of ones encountered so far is odd, and zero if even. An equivalent expression is $2\,|\,+\setminus LV$.

PROBLEMS

1. DRILL

```
+/3 7 ¯10 15 22          -/2 4 6 8 10          ×/2 4 6 8 10
÷/3 5 2                  */3 2 1               ∧/1 0 1 1
∧/1 1 1                  ∨/0 1 0 1             ∨/0 0 0
=/3 2 2                  >/1 ¯2 ¯4             ⌊/¯2 4 0 ¯8
⌈/1 ¯14.7 22 6           ×\3 2 7 9             ⌈\4 12 7 14
```

2. State in words what tests are represented by ∧/, ∨/ and =/.

3. For $AV \leftarrow 3\ 6\ 8\ 2\ 4$, evaluate $+/3 \times AV$.

4. Write a one-line APL expression to assign Q as the vector 1 7 ¯2 ¯3 and find the largest element in Q.

5. Set up an algorithm in APL to calculate the area of a triangle by Hero's formula, Area $= \sqrt{S(S-A)(S-B)(S-C)}$. A, B and C are the lengths of the sides of the triangle, and S is the semiperimeter. In your algorithm use L as the vector of sides of the triangle.

6. Write an APL expression to give the slope of the line passing through the points with coordinates (X_1, Y_1) and (X_2, Y_2). By definition, the slope of a straight line is the difference in the values of the vertical coordinates of two points on the line divided by the difference in the values of the corresponding horizontal coordinates.

7. Each row of a matrix S represents sales by weeks of some item over a two-month period. Create a new matrix SR which gives a running tally of cumulative sales over this time period.

8. Explain the action of each of the following on a logical vector LV: ∧\LV, <\LV, ∨\LV.

9. You are given a vector of sales transactions $SALES$, with taxes not included. Write expressions to determine **A** the number of transactions, **B** the highest and lowest sales, **C** the total sales, **D** the amount due on each transaction including a 4% sales tax, **E** the average sale.

10. Incredible Charlie, a used car dealer sold 6, 2, 1, 8, 4 and 3 cars during successive days of a sale-a-thon. **A** How many did he sell altogether? **B** If 15 customers traded in their cars, and 4 of those were immediately wholesaled to another dealer, by how much did the inventory of cars in stock change? **C** What is the average profit per sale if total profit is $6300? **D** How much was paid out in sales commissions if they average $75 per car sold?

11. Execute $T \leftarrow 10 \rho 1$ and then $+\backslash T$. The result is not surprising; however, would you have thought to use scan to generate a sequence like this?

Chapter 6: Order of execution

In the last chapter we saw that in reduction the effective order of execution was from right to left, since each functional symbol operated on everything to the right of it. It was as a result of this rule that $-/$ gave us the alternating sum. Does this order of execution concept apply to all functions of APL? You should make up some examples to convince yourself at this point that it does.

One good illustration is the problem on page 37 that calculates a value for π. There we used a large number of steps to get the result; but a much neater and more elegant way to write the algorithm is

```
        ∇Z←PI1 N
[1]     Z←4×-/1÷ ¯1+2×N
[2]     ∇
        PI1 1 2 3 4 5 6 7 8 9 10
3.041839619
```

Here, working from right to left, first the computer produces the sequence 2 4 6 ... by multiplying 1 2 3 ... by 2. Then ¯1 is added, which gives us the odd numbers 1 3 5 ... These are divided into 1, yielding the reciprocals. After $-/$ makes an alternating sum out of the reciprocals, the result is multiplied by 4 to give π.

The same approach can be taken with our old friend the invoice extension problem (page 33). In this case the total cost of the products Q with individual costs C can be written as $+/Q×C$. Numerically it can be expressed as

```
        +/6 2 3 1 0×2 4 3 5 10
34
```

Changing the order of execution

Don't be tempted by these examples into thinking that all problems can be solved this neatly. A case in point is the calculation of the hypotenuse. See what happens as we foolishly enter the following sequence:

```
        A←3
        B←4
        A*2+B*2*.5
22041.01477
```

Why this result? Working from right to left, $2*.5$ is 1.414223562, and 4 is raised to the 1.41413562 power, giving 7.102993301. Then 2 is added, giving 9.102993301. Lastly, 3 is raised to that power, giving the (undesired) result 22041.01477.

The correct way to carry out the hypotenuse algorithm on one line follows. You should study the sequence in which things are calculated in it:

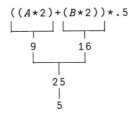

This is a good place to make three observations: (1) pairs of parentheses are used in APL in exactly the same way as in conventional mathematical notation, that is, the normal order of execution is interrupted and expressions within parentheses are evaluated separately; (2) aside from the above use of parentheses, there is no hierarchy of functions specifying the order of execution in APL; and (3) a single right parenthesis is used in APL to denote system commands, as contrasted to their use in calculations, where a pair is required.

Having said this much, we now hedge a bit to point out that APL2 treats order of execution in a slightly different way; although there still is no hierarchy of functions, nor of operators, operators take precedence over functions.

Getting back to the hypotenuse example, *A* and *B* are squared, then added, and finally this sum is raised to the .5 power. Let's executed this for specific values of *A* and *B*:

```
     A←3
     B←4
     ((A*2)+(B*2)).5
SYNTAX ERROR
     ((A*2)+(B*2)) 0.5
              ^
```

The omission of the symbol * before the .5 was deliberate. We needed an excuse once again to call a subtle point to your attention. In conventional notation you were able to get away with expressions like A(B+C) because tradition allowed it. But in APL there is no such assumption. If some function *f* is meant, then *f* must be explicitly used. It certainly helps to keep the language concise and free of ambiguities.

Reentering the line correctly produces the hypotenuse:

```
     ((A*2)+(B*2))*.5
5
```

As you can see in the following example, which omits the parentheses around *B* * 2, parentheses aren't always needed. (Why not in this example?)

```
     ∇C←A HYP1 B
[1]  C←((A*2)+B*2)*.5
[2]  ∇
     3 HYP1 4
5
```

Now one more rehash of an old problem, the calculation of averages. We saw that it was necessary to get the sum of the elements of the vector *X* and divide this by the number of elements in *X*:

```
     ∇Z←AVERAGE1 X
[1]  Z←(+/X)÷ρX
[2]  ∇
```

From right to left, ρX yields the number of elements of *X*, which in turn is divided into the sum of the three elements of *X*.

Parentheses aren't needed around the expression $+/X$ on the extreme left, but for a reason different from what you might expect. This can be shown by looking at $+/1\ 2\ 3÷3$, which is arithmetically equivalent to $(1÷3)+(2÷3)+(3÷3)$, or 2. This is exactly the same as $(1+2+3)÷3$. It doesn't make one bit of difference if we divide the elements of the vector by 3 before summing or after, since, of course, the divisor (here 3) is the same for all elements. However, it does make a difference *computationally* because it is a matter of three divisions and three additions in one case as compared to one division and three additions in the other.

A natural extension of this algorithm can be used to get row and column averages for a matrix. For example, let the matrix *M* be the number of units sold for 4 products (across) during 3 weeks (down):

```
     M←3 4ρ6 7 9 10 4 0 4 8 3 1 9 7
     M
6  7  9 10
4  0  4  8
3  1  9  7
```

The average number of units sold per week over the 4 products is

```
     (+/M)÷4
8 4 5
```

and the average number of units of each product sold per week over the three weeks is

```
     (+⌿M)÷3
4.333333333 2.666666667 7.333333333 8.333333333
```

Can you write a one-line expression to get the grand average of all the elements of the array? And while you're at it, can you think of a way to get the APL system to generate the number of elements in the rows and columns?

The elegant simplicity of APL's right-to-left sequence of execution means that we don't have to remember arbitrary rules of precedence as found in conventional notations. This is particularly advantageous because APL has many more primitive functions. Having to pay attention to arbitrary rules of precedence would just make life harder.

However, we predict that you will have trouble breaking away from one part of conventional notation: what does 3×2+4 mean to you? If you said 10, you're still doing your multiplications before your additions, as in conventional notation. In APL, 3×2+4 is 18, because in the strict right-to-left sequence, 2+4 is 6, and then 3×6 is 18. If you are uncomfortable with this departure with tradition, we suggest that you use parentheses liberally to give your statements clarity. For example, if you really wanted to calculate (3×2) +4, then enter it that way. Note, however, that the experienced APL'er would probably express it as 4+3×2, because that takes less time to enter on the terminal.

As you begin to exercise your skills building expressions with many functions, don't hesitate to over-parenthesize. When you are more at home in your understanding of the APL language, you can experiment with omitting nonessential parentheses.

A polynomial illustration

An elegant demonstration of the order of execution rule and the power and versatility of APL can be seen in the following example showing how polynomials can be written and evaluated. Consider the typical algebraic polynomial expression $3-2X+9X^2+4\times X^3$ (conventional notation) which we want to evaluate for X, say 10. How can this be represented in APL?

We'll start with the most obvious, a direct transliteration from the conventional notation:

```
      X←10
      3+(¯2×X)+(9×X*2)+4×X*3
4883
```

A little better version, which eliminates the parentheses, is

```
      3+X×¯2+X×9+X×4
4883
```

Observe the sequence of steps APL takes to obtain the result.

$$3 \ + \ 10 \ \times \ ^-2 \ + \ 10 \ \times \ 9 \ + \ 10 \ \times \ 4$$

$$\longleftarrow 40 \longrightarrow$$
$$\longleftarrow 49 \longrightarrow$$
$$\longleftarrow 490 \longrightarrow$$
$$\longleftarrow 488 \longrightarrow$$
$$\longleftarrow 4880 \longrightarrow$$
$$\longleftarrow 4883 \longrightarrow$$

But you can't really appreciate the economy of the APL notation until you have taken advantage of its ability to handle arrays. Here is the *pièce de résistance* of our polynomial example:

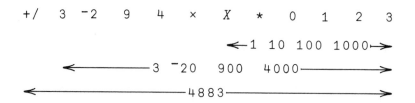

Lines and statements

Now that you can express complete formulas on one line, you may be tempted to pack as much on a single line as possible. An exercise of this sort has its good and bad points. First the good news: it has the effect of forcing you to review all the APL you know while looking for the proper combination of symbols and order that solves the problem. And now the bad news: lines of APL so written are frequently difficult for others to read and understand. To show that you really do have sympathy for others, as well as to enhance the concepts involved, you should arrange your lines so that each one represents a distinct part of the algorithm and can stand more or less on its own feet.

Every APL author has his or her own stable of favorite horror stories in this connection. One of ours is the following, which happens to be a one-line representation of the calculation of the correlation coefficient from statistics. If you're not mathematically inclined, don't worry. This isn't designed to scare you out of several days' growth, but rather to cause you to swear off such activity in the future. Here it is:

$$R \leftarrow (+/X \times Y) \div ((+/(X \leftarrow X - (+/X) \div \rho X) * 2) \times +/(Y \leftarrow Y - (+/Y) \div \rho Y) * 2) * .5$$

In the above line, aside from the fact that it's almost impossible to read, there is the latent risk that in some future APL implementation it might not work at all and indeed is pornographic! Pornography is as elusive and hard to define in APL as it is in the courts. Most experienced APL users will agree that they know it when they see it, but refuse to be pinned down to a definition.

A better arrangement for the correlation algorithm is

```
X←X-(+/X)÷ρX
Y←Y-(+/Y)÷ρY
R←(+/X*2)×+/Y*2
R←(+/X×Y)÷R*.5
```

On some APL systems, the economy of the one-liner can be achieved by employing the diamond ◊. It lets you put related statements on the same line, without sacrificing brevity or clarity. Each statement is separated by diamonds; and the system executes the first statement on the left, then the next, and so on until the last (rightmost) statement on the line is executed. The usual order of execution rules apply within each statement. Here is one way to write the above algorithm with the diamond:

```
X←X-(+/X)÷ρX  ◊  Y←Y-(+/Y)÷ρY
R←(+/X*2)×+/Y*2  ◊  R←(+/X×Y)÷R*.5
```

The two lines above could have been pushed into one long one with another diamond, but that might look too formidable. In the final analysis, how much you put on one line is a matter of personal taste, but you should avoid constructing long lines (without the diamond) which might be hard for others to follow.

Another feature of many newer systems is that a comment can be placed on any line. The rule is that all characters to the right of the ⍝ symbol are ignored by the computer:

```
X←X-(+/X)÷ρX  ◊  Y←Y-(+/Y)÷ρY  ⍝ CENTER X AND Y
R←(+/X*2)×+/Y*2  ⍝ CALCULATE DIVISOR - SQUARED
R←(+/X×Y)÷R*.5  ⍝ FINAL RESULT R IS CORRELATION
```

PROBLEMS

1. DRILL

```
4*3⌈3*4                    5*3×5                      76÷+/2+3×1 2 3 4
(4*3)⌈3*4                  1÷2+⁻5 6 0 8 ⁻6            6÷2-4*3
```

2. Which of the following six expressions have the same value?

```
(B*2)-4×A×C                B*2-4×A×C                  B×B-(4×A)×C
((B*2)-4×(A×C))            (B×B)-(4×A)×C              (A×⁻4×C)+B*2
```

3. Construct APL expressions for each of the following: **A** three-fourths plus five-sixths minus seven-eighths; **B** the quotient of the two differences, nine-sevenths minus eight-tenths, and one-third minus two-fifths.

4. The geometric mean of a set of N positive numbers X is the Nth root of their product. Write an APL expression to calculate this for $X←1$ 7 4 2.5 51 19.

5. What is wrong with the expression $A+B=B+A$ to show that the operation of addition is commutative, i.e., the order of the arguments is immaterial?

6. The Gregorian calendar provides that all years from 1582 to about 20,000 that are divisible by 4 are leap years, with the adjustment that of the centesimal years (1600, 1700, etc.) only those divisible by 400 are leap years, and of the millenial years those divisible by 4000 are not. Write a one-line APL expression to determine whether a given year Y is a leap year.

7. Why is this APL expression, $(X*2)-(2×X×Y)+Y*2$, wrong for X²−2XY+Y² (conventional notation)? Correct it.

8. Rewrite the polynomial APL expression $(⁻3×X*4)+(2×X*2)-8$ without parentheses. Do *not* use reduction.

9. Write an APL expression to compute the root-mean-square of the elements of a vector. (This is the square root of the average of the squares.)

10. What is a possible interpretation of the following?

```
PROPOSE←RING∧WEATHER∧(JILL<JACK)∧JACK<AGELIMIT
```

11. Rewrite as a single expression the future value algorithm (page 20) to calculate the interest on P dollars at R percent compounded annually for T years. How would you change the expression to provide for compounding quarterly?

12. You are required to assign 5 to C if A is greater than B; otherwise, C is assigned the value 4. Similarly, if A is greater than B, and D is less than E, then C is 10. Otherwise, C is 8.

13. Without executing it on the terminal, what is $2+2$ $2+2$?

14. You are an industrial spy working for a bank, and have managed to steal a vector from a rival bank. The APL vector V contains all their accounts. Find: **A** how many accounts they have; **B** the average value of the accounts; **C** how many accounts are in the red; **D** how many are exactly zero; **E** the values of the largest and smallest accounts; **F** the percentage of accounts above $100; **G** the number of accounts between $100 and $200 inclusive; **H** how many of the nonnegative accounts are exact multiples of $100.

15. Construct an APL expression that will yield a value A if A is greater than B, otherwise zero.

16. The Sharp-as-a-Tack Company offers to sell one square inch of Klondike land for $0.25. Compute the gross income per acre (an acre is 160 square rods and one rod is 16.5 feet).

17. A resort hotel charges $235 per person double occupancy for seven days, six nights (Modified American Plan). Extra nights are $39 per person. Children under 12 are half-price. With a service charge of $3.20 per person per day and $4 daily tax on the M.A.P. rate, what is the cost for a family of 5 (2 under 12) staying 10 days, 9 nights?

18. Carry out the following instructions and explain the results.

$A \leftarrow 15.8$	$A \leftarrow 15.8$
$B \leftarrow (A \leftarrow 4) \times A$	$B \leftarrow (A \leftarrow 4) \times 0 \lceil A$
B	B
16	63.2

19. The matrix $FUND$ (shape 3 by 10) records the shares a broker sold of each of 10 stocks during the first three trading hours of the day. If the vector $COMM$ contains the per share brokerage fee for each of the stocks, find the total commission earned during the three hours.

20. A customer paid for three kinds of dried fruit at a health food store: $5 for apricots at $2.75/pound, $4.50 for banana chips at $1.80/pound and $7.25 for papayas at $3/pound. What was the largest quantity purchased?

21. Write an expression to determine whether a given matrix A consists of all 0's and 1's.

22. A store has a vector of the current year's transactions called $BILLS$. There is a parallel vector in the same order called $DATE$, which contains the Julian dates of the transactions (days are numbered consecutively from 1 to 365). Write an instruction to update $BILLS$ by adding 1.5% to those bills over 30 days. The current Julian date is the variable $TODAY$.

23. You own three cars:

car	year	price	cumulative gas cost	cumulative miles driven
Chevy	1975	$5200	$9660	98,730
Ford	1981	$8100	$8556	84,000
Lincoln	1980	$8450	$3080	28,000

    If gas prices averaged $1.35/gallon for the Chevy, $1.30 for the Ford, and $1.47 for the Lincoln during the entire period of ownership, and the sales tax on each was 4% of the prices shown, calculate: **A** gallons of gas used for each car and all three; **B** tax paid for each car and all three; **C** average number of miles per year for each car; **D** average miles per gallon for each car; **E** average gas cost per year for each car; **F** average gas cost per mile for each car and for all three; **G** total gas cost; **H** total number of miles; **I** average number of miles per year driven.

24. Compute the net pay for each of a group of workers if R is the hourly rate, H the number of hours worked and S, $I1$ and $I2$ are the current percentage deductions for social security, Federal and State income taxes.

25. An office equipment salesperson sold 2, 4, 0, 1 and 3 typewriters (stored in the vector $SALES$) during a five-day period. **A** Was the sales quota for the week (6) made? **B** If there is a commission of $50 on each unit sold, how much was earned in commissions each day? **C** For 5 of the typewriters trade-ins were taken at an average value of $75 each. If the units sold for $600 each, what is the net revenue to the company after payment of commission?

26. A store creates its own special assortment of mixed nuts from cashews (30% by weight), pecans (10%), almonds (10%), walnuts (10%), Brazil nuts (5%) and peanuts (35%). A batch of 10 pounds is to be made up. However, the person doing the mixing is crazy about pecans and eats half as much as goes into the mixture. If the nuts cost wholesale $2, $2, $1.50, $1.25, $1.80 and $.40 a pound respectively, and the store has to make a profit of $1 per pound sold, what should be the minimum selling price?

27. Telegrams (remember them?) between two cities are $2.50 for the first 15 words or fewer and $.10 per additional word. Write an expression to give the cost of any telegram based on the number of words.

28. You are given the following vectors for a group of employees: M (marital status, 0 for single and 1 for married), S (sex, 0 for male and 1 for female), A (age in years), L (amount of group life insurance carried). Write an expression to pick out those employees who are at the same time married, male, younger than 55, and carry more than $50,000 of life insurance.

Chapter 7: Monadic and circular functions

Primitive scalar monadic functions

Just as on page 18 we introduced the term *dyadic* to describe functions which require two arguments, so we will use the term *monadic* where only a single argument is needed. Let's now take a look at how some monadic functions are represented in conventional mathematical notation:

$$-x \quad \text{arithmetic negation}$$
$$x! \quad \text{factorial}$$
$$|x| \quad \text{.absolute value}$$
$$x^{-1} \text{ or } 1/x \quad \text{reciprocal}$$
$$e^x \quad \text{exponential}$$
$$\ln x \quad \text{natural logarithm}$$
$$\sqrt{x} \quad \text{square root (dyadic)}$$
$$\bar{x} \quad \text{logical negation}$$

Whatever other merits this mishmash has, consistency certainly isn't one of them; for the symbol which is the functional indicator may appear on the left, the right, both sides, on top, or be in a special position, or be represented by an alphabetical name!

These same functions are represented in APL as follows:

$$-X \quad \text{arithmetic negation}$$
$$!X \quad \text{factorial}$$
$$|X \quad \text{absolute value}$$
$$\div X \quad \text{reciprocal}$$
$$\star X \quad \text{exponential}$$
$$\circledast X \quad \text{natural logarithm}$$
$$X\star.5 \quad \text{square root (dyadic)}$$
$$\sim X \quad \text{logical negation}$$

Notice that for all the monadic functions in this list, the symbol comes before the argument. Many of the symbols are also used for dyadic functions, but the meanings may not always be closely related.

Let's explore some of them on the terminal. For any of them, you can use scalars, vectors and matrices as arguments. The more mathematical of these functions, such as factorial, exponential, logarithm and the circular functions (to be discussed later in this chapter) may be omitted from your study without loss of continuity if you won't be using them in your later work.

Arithmetic negation

This function, also called *negative* and additive inverse, simply negates the argument that follows it:

```
      -3 4 ¯1 0 ¯8                      -2 3ρ1 2 0 ¯3 ¯5 ¯8
¯3 ¯4 1 0 8                        ¯1 ¯2  0
      --2 1 0 ¯1 ¯2                  3  5  8
2 1 0 ¯1 ¯2
```

Don't confuse the negative sign (¯) with arithmetic negation (−). As pointed out on page 6, the negative sign should really be thought of as punctuation, not an operation to be performed; hence, the error message in the following:

```
      A←3 ¯1 0                           ¯A              ¯A
                           ¯3 1 0               SYNTAX_ERROR
                                                     ¯A
                                                     ∧
```

Factorial

An expression like `!X` (for X an integer) means the product $1 \times 2 \times 3 \times \ldots (X-1) \times X$. For example,

```
     !4                      !1 2 3 4                      !2 2ρ1 5 2 4
24                      1 2 6 24                      1 120
                                                     2  24
```

If you got a *SYNTAX ERROR*, it was probably due to your failure to line up `'` and `.` as discussed on page 26.

For those with a considerable background in mathematics, the factorial can be defined by the use of the gamma function, given by the following integral

$$\Gamma(n+1) = \int_0^\infty x^n \, e^{-x} \, dx$$

which is equivalent to n! with n not restricted to integer values (negative integers are out of the domain, however).

```
     !2.5 0 ¯2.5
3.32335097 1 2.363271801
```

For those with minimal math background, forget it.

Magnitude

The *magnitude* (absolute value) function is defined as X if $X \geq 0$, or $-X$ if $X < 0$. In plain English, take the magnitude of the number and ignore any negative sign that may be present. Here are some examples:

```
      |3 5 ¯2 7 ¯3                       |2 3ρ3 ¯1 0 1 ¯5 ¯6
3 5 2 7 3                          3 1 0
                                   1 5 6
```

Reciprocal

In APL the division symbol, `÷`, used monadically, is the multiplicative inverse, or reciprocal. Taking the reciprocal of a number is the same as dividing one by that number. As expected, `÷0` is a *DOMAIN ERROR*.

```
     ÷1 2 3 4 5                            1÷1 2 3 4 5
1 0.5 0.3333333333 0.25 0.2        1 0.5 0.3333333333 0.25 0.2

     ÷÷1 2 3 4 5                            ÷2 2ρ1 ¯2.5 4 5
1 2 3 4 5                          1              ¯0.4
                                   0.25            0.2
```

Exponential, natural logarithm and roots

The expression `*X` is equivalent to raising e, the base of the system of natural logarithms, which has the value 2.71828..., to the X power. This means that `*X` is the same as `e*X`. In this example, the second element of the argument results in the value of e itself:

```
     *2.5 1
12.18249396 2.718281828
```

Natural logarithms are obtained by the monadic `⍟`. `⍟X` yields the same result as the dyadic logarithm using e, 2.17828... as the left argument. Since the base e is frequently used in mathematics, conventional notation for it is 'ln' or 'log$_e$'. Logarithms were originally invented as an aid in doing calculations involving products, quotients, powers and roots. With the advent of modern calculators and computers they are rarely used for this purpose. What's more important, however, is that they do occur frequently in the solutions of equations representing many physical problems. This is generally the case where the changes involved in the phenomena to be analyzed are exponential in nature, such as unrestrained population growth or monetary calculations for compound interest.

Here is a sample:

```
      ⍟1 10 100 1000
0 2.302585093 4.605170186 6.907755279
```

Logarithms and exponentials are inverse functions, that is, each undoes the effect of the other as the example below shows:

```
      ⍟*1 2 3
1 2 3
```

Furthermore, the dyadic logarithm function $B⍟N$ (page 21) can be defined as $(⍟N)÷⍟B$.

No special symbol is provided for the square root (or any other root) in APL. To take the Nth root of X, use $X*÷N$. Recall that in algebra, roots are shown to be equivalent to fractional powers (see **page 20**).

Logical negation

Like the dyadic logical functions ∧ ∨ ⍲ ⍱, logical negation, also called *not* and using the symbol ~, can have only 0 or 1 as an argument. As you have probably guessed, ~1 is 0 and ~0 is 1.

```
      ~1 0 1 1              ~2 2⍴1 0 1 1                  ~3
0 1 0 0               0 1                    DOMAIN ERROR
      ~~1 0 1          0 0                         ~3
1 0 1                                              ∧
```

The last two examples show that ~ is its own inverse, and works only for 0's and 1's.

Ceiling and floor

There are a few more monadic functions in APL that don't have corresponding symbols in conventional notation, yet are important to know. The first of these is *ceiling*. It uses the symbol ⌈, and is defined as the smallest integer not smaller than the argument. Practically speaking, taking the ceiling of a number 'rounds up' the number.

```
      ⌈3.14 3.9 4 4.1
4 4 4 5
```

Its usefulness becomes apparent when you have to change a decimal fraction to the next higher integer. For example, the U. S. Postal Service charges 20 cents for the first ounce of first class mail and 17 cents for each additional ounce (at this writing). Any fractional ounces are counted as a full ounce. If X is the actual weight of a letter, then .03+.17×⌈X is the cost in dollars.

Floor (⌊) is a mirror image of ceiling. It results in the largest integer not larger than the argument ('rounding down').

```
      ⌊3.14 3.9 4 4.1              ⌊2 3⍴2.999 3.542 7.931 6 1.08 4
3 3 4 4                         2 3 7
                                6 1 4
```

What about the ceiling and floor of a negative number? Let's try two examples:

```
      ⌈¯4.1              ⌊¯4.1
¯4                      ¯5
```

If this puzzles you, it can be cleared up by reference to the number line (page 22). Rounding ¯4.1 up gives the next larger integer, ¯4, while rounding down gives the next smaller integer, ¯5.

Finally, before going on to an illustrative problem, if we assign *X* as

```
X←1.1 4.2 ¯3.9 0 3
```

then by executing

```
      ⌊X                        ⌈X
1 4 ¯4 0 3               2 5 ¯3 0 3
     -⌈-X                       -⌊-X
1 4 ¯4 0 3               2 5 ¯3 0 3
```

we can see that our APL system is richer by two identities, no simple equivalent of which exists in conventional notation. Other identities will be introduced from time to time in the text.

Now back to earth. Here is a practical problem which uses the floor and ceiling functions. It involves rounding off bills with fractional pennies (so-called half-cent adjustment). For purposes of illustration let's assign a vector *X* as

```
X←3 3.1 3.49 3.5 3.51 3.9 4
```

To make the half-cent adjust work properly, we round up if the fractional part is 0.5 or more, and round down if it is less than 0.5. So for the above values we want the result to be 3 3 3 4 4 4 4.

Looking at the floor of *X*, we get

```
  ⌊X
3 3 3 3 3 3 4
```

This isn't exactly what we want. What about the ceiling?

```
  ⌈X
3 4 4 4 4 4 4
```

which isn't right either.

Suppose we add 0.5 to each element of *X* and then try the floor again:

```
  X+.5
3.5 3.6 3.99 4 4.01 4.4 4.5
  ⌊X+.5
3 3 3 4 4 4 4
```

Success! And the result suggests that a half-cent adjustment that rounds down (that is, makes 3.5 come out to 3 instead of 4) is done this way:

```
  ⌈X-.5
3 3 3 3 4 4 4
```

Roll

Let's try the monadic function *roll*, whose symbol is *?* (upper shift Q):

```
   ?6 6                ?6 6                    ?3 4⍴6
1 5                 3 4                   2 1 5 5
                                          6 3 4 5
                                          1 1 4 5
```

What kind of oddball function can this be that doesn't return the same result each time? We seem to be getting numbers at random from it. Indeed, if you play around with it some more, you will see that *? X* returns a random integer chosen from the integers 1 to *X* inclusive.

This means that *?*6 6 simulates the roll of a pair of dice, while

```
  ?2
```

is a simulation of a coin toss, with 1 standing for heads, say, and 2 for tails.

Where you put the symbol makes an important difference:

```
      ?3 4ρ6                    3 4ρ?6
3 1 3 5                  6 6 6 6
4 6 6 4                  6 6 6 6
1 4 3 5                  6 6 6 6
```

The example on the right generates only one random value and then repeats that value twelve times, as contrasted to the left example, which first made a matrix of 6's and then randomized the values.

When we try to execute the roll function with a noninteger, or with zero or a negative number, a *DOMAIN ERROR* results. The domain of the roll function consists of positive integers only.

Each time you sign on the terminal you will get the same sequence of random numbers if the same arguments are used. When you check out algorithms (called *debugging*), it is often desirable for testing purposes to use the same set of numbers so that valid comparisons can be made of successive runs. In Chapter 28 we'll show how to change the starting value for the built-in APL algorithm that generates random numbers.

Direction

Occasionally you may need to know whether a value is positive, negative or zero. The function $\times X$, called *direction*, does this for us. It returns as results 1, ¯1, or 0. Don't confuse it with $\times/X$:

```
      ×2 2ρ¯1 4 0 ¯8            ×1 ¯3 0            ×/1 ¯3 0
 ¯1  ¯1                  1 ¯1 0                  0
  0  ¯1
```

Pi times

The function $\circ X$ is equivalent to πX. It uses the large circle $\circ$ (upper shift *O*):

```
      ○¯1 0 1 2 3
¯3.141592654 0 3.141592654 6.283185307 9.424777961
```

Note that $\circ 1$ is π itself.

A short lesson on probability

The discussion which follows exercises some of the monadic functions introduced in this chapter. It may be of interest to the mathematically inclined or to those who visit Las Vegas or Monte Carlo. If you are of neither persuasion, we won't be disappointed if you skip this section and the next (trigonometry and related functions) and go directly to the drill on page 52.

A fallen member of Gamblers Anonymous with a flair for numbers comes up with the following formula for the probability of having exactly one match in a random matching of two equivalent decks of 52 distinct cards:

$$\text{P1} = \frac{1}{0!} - \frac{1}{1!} + \frac{1}{2!} - \frac{1}{3!} + \cdots - \cdots + \frac{1}{52!}$$

He notes that this can be readily modified for 2, 3, ...m matches.

APL notation makes easy work of this formula. First, we develop the vector of denominators, stopping after 10 terms:

```
      D←!0 1 2 3 4 5 6 7 8 9
```

The reciprocals can be obtained by assigning

```
     R←÷D
     R
1  1  0.5  0.1666666667  0.04166666667  0.008333333333  0.001388888889  0.0001984126984
        2.48015873E¯5  2.755731922E¯6
```

and the alternating sum is given by

```
     P1←-/R
     P1
0.3678791887
```

Putting all of this together we have

```
     ∇P1←MATCH N                    MATCH 0 1 2 3 4 5 6 7 8 9
[1]    P1←-/÷!N                     0.3678791887
[2]    ∇
```

The series converges rapidly because of the factorials in the denominators. And, as our backsliding gambler soon found out, the probability P_m of m matches is approximately $e^{-1}/m!$, or $PM←(\star ¯1)÷!M$.

Circular, hyperbolic and pythagorean functions

For those of you who have an interest, be it perverse or legitimate, in the circular, hyperbolic and pythagorean functions, they are available as primitive scalar dyadics. As with π, the function symbol is the large circle.

Strictly speaking, these functions, being dyadic, don't belong in this chapter. Most users of APL will never need them. However, for those of you with a scientific bent, they are mentioned here.

0○X	(1-X*2)*.5	¯1○X	arcsin X
1○X	sine X	¯2○X	arccos X
2○X	cosine X	¯3○X	arctan X
3○X	tangent X	¯4○X	(¯1+X*2)*.5
4○X	(1+X*2)*.5	¯5○X	arcsinh X
5○X	hyperbolic sine of X (sinh X)	¯6○X	arccosh X
6○X	hyperbolic cosine of X (cosh X)	¯7○X	arctanh X
7○X	hyperbolic tangent of X (tanh X)		

The rules for conformability of the arguments are the same as for the standard scalar dyadic functions; that is, the shapes of the arguments must match, or either can be a scalar. The left argument cannot be any values other than those shown above, and is used to select which of the functions is to be performed. For the trigonometric functions, the right argument is taken to be radians (multiply degrees by ○÷180). The inverse (arc) functions return only the principal value of the angle.

Here is a simple example testing the oft-heard rumor that $\sin^2\theta + \cos^2\theta = 1$ (at least for an angle of 45 degrees):

```
     THETA←45×○÷180
     +/(1 2○THETA)*2
1
```

Finally, besides their direct use in problems, readers familiar with the calculus will appreciate the value of having a complete set of circular functions. See any handbook containing tables of derivatives and indefinite integrals.

A drill exercise

On most APL systems there is a drill exercise in the various functions that have been described so far (it's located in common library 1 of the system on which this text is based). This is a stored program, much like STATISTICS in the first chapter. The details of how such programs are written and stored will be covered in later chapters.

Follow this sequence carefully on your terminal. You should also check to see what other exercises, if any, are available on your system. The more practice you get at this early stage, the better you will understand how the individual functions of APL can be used in programming.

First execute the following command:

```
)LOAD 1 AIDRILL
SAVED   14.15.05 07/06/79
```

A message comes back stating when the workspace *AIDRILL* (a block of storage containing the drill programs) was last saved. The *)LOAD* command, about which more will be said later, puts an exact image of the workspace *AIDRILL* in a place where you can use it directly.

You are about to go through an exercise in which you and the APL system will exchange roles. It will ask you to do problems and you will be required to enter the answers. To start off, enter *EASYDRILL* and put a *Y* under each function for which you want practice, as shown in the copy below. Be sure to type *Y* for the exercises in vectors because vectors are so important in APL. Also reply *Y* to the question about reduction. None of the problems require answers which are not integers, and the problems are relatively easy computationally. We suggest, however, that the first time through, you select only the easier functions.

```
EASYDRILL
TYPE Y UNDER EACH FUNCTION FOR WHICH YOU WANT EXERCISE
SCALAR DYADIC FUNCTIONS
+-×÷*⌈⌊<≤=≥>≠!|∧∨⊕↑↓
YY          YY   YY
SCALAR MONADIC FUNCTIONS
YY  YY

TYPE Y IF EXERCISE IN VECTORS IS DESIRED, N OTHERWISE
Y

TYPE Y IF EXERCISE IN REDUCTION IS DESIRED, N OTHERWISE
Y
```

Here are some sample problems generated by the program. These will be different each time you use the program, and different for each user as well.

```
                  ¯1  9  ¯9  5  >  ¯8  ¯10  4  8
□:     1  1  0  0
                  -8  ¯6  ¯4  ¯3  0
□:     ¯8  6  4  3  0
```

If the problem is correctly answered, you get another problem as your reward. Let's enter a wrong answer for the next one:

```
               ⊕/  2  2
□:       0  1
TRY AGAIN
□:       1
```

You get three tries altogether, after which you are given the correct answer, and, to add insult to injury, you get another problem of the same general kind:

```
               ∨/  0  0  1  1
□:       1
               ⌊  ¯2.333333333  ¯2  1.666666667  ¯2.666666667  ¯3

□:     3  4  5  6
TRY AGAIN

□:     4  2  10  4
TRY AGAIN

□:     3  1  9  7
ANSWER IS   ¯3  ¯2  1  ¯3  ¯3
               ⌊ ¯1

□:       ¯1
               ×  ¯7  ¯4
□:       ¯1  ¯1
```

Entering $PLEASE$ gives you the answer and another problem of the same kind, while $CHANGE$ gives you the answer and moves you on to another problem involving a different function. To get out of the drill, enter $STOP$, after which you will receive a record of your performance, only part of which is shown here. $STOPSHORT$ exits you from the program but doesn't display your record, in case you're too embarrassed to look at it.

```
              ⌊ 1.333333333  ‾0.6666666667
□:    PLEASE
ANSWER IS   1  ‾1
              ⌊ 0.5 1.75

□:    STOP

YOUR RECORD IS
FUNCTION          FIRST TRY   SECOND TRY   THIRD TRY   FAILED
     +
     ‾
     >                1
     ≢
     ∨                1
     ⍟                                        1
     ×                1
     ‾
     ⌈                                                    1
     ⌊                2
```

PROBLEMS

1. DRILL

```
⌊‾2.7|‾15              |3.1 0 ‾5.6 ‾8          ?10 10 10 10
*3 4.7 ‾1.5           !3 5 7 4               ⍟14.1 86 .108
⌈‾1.8 0 ‾21 5.6       ⌊5.5 6.8 ‾9.1 ‾.12     ×‾5.6 0 42
?3 4 5                ?‾1.2 ‾6.7 .52 19.5    ~0 1 1 0
÷3.5 ‾10 ‾.287        4×⌈5.8×‾31.046         1○○1 2
○1÷180                4○1 2 3                ‾1 ‾2○1 10.5
```

2. Using the residue function, write one-line definitions in APL of $\lfloor X$ and $\lceil X$.

3. If $A \leftarrow 3$ and $B \leftarrow 3\ 2\ 1\ ‾6$, evaluate

```
*2+A1←(‾1+A*3)÷2
~(2≤A)∧∨/3=B
C≠⌊C←((A*2)+(A+1)*2)*.5
```

4. Write an algorithm to test an integer N for the following: if the final digit is deleted, the original number is divisible by the new one.

5. January 1 fell on Thursday (the fifth day of the week) in 1970. Determine the day of the week on which January 1 falls in any given year Y. For simplicity, assume any year divisible by 4 is a leap year.

6. Given a vector V which is made up of one-and two-digit integers. **A** Write an expression that will yield a logical vector whose 1's correspond in position to the one-digit members of V; **B** do the same for the two-digit members of V.

7. Let $M \leftarrow 84.6129999993$. Display M. Compare $1E5 \times M$ with $\lfloor 1E5 \times M$. (See *comparison tolerance* on page 295 for an explanation.)

8. Construct an APL expression that will determine whether or not the first N significant figures of two whole numbers X and Y are identical.

9. **A** You are given D dollars with which to make purchases of books at B dollars each. How many books can be purchased? **B** How many books can be bought if it is required that the D dollars be used up and supplemented, if necessary?

10. **A** Write a general expression to round any number N to D positions to the right of the decimal point. **B** How does your answer change if the rounding is to take place to the Dth position to the *left* of the decimal point?

11. Write an APL expression that rounds numbers down if the decimal part is less than .5, and up if greater than .5. For numbers ending in .5, your expression should round to the nearest *even* integer.

12. For $A \leftarrow 0\ 1\ 0\ 1$, $B \leftarrow 1\ 0\ 0\ 1$ and $C \leftarrow 1\ 1\ 0\ 0$ evaluate **A** $(\sim A) \vee \sim B$; **B** $A \vee C \wedge B$; **C** $(A \wedge \sim B) \wedge A \vee C$; **D** $(\sim B) \vee A \vee \sim C$

13. Show in APL that the following identity holds: $\cos 2x = \cos^2 x - \sin^2 x$

14. Use reduction to express the identity $\sin^2 x + \cos^2 x = 1$

15. Write an APL expression to construct a $4\ 4$ matrix made up of random integers in the range 1 to 100.

16. A certain number N may be either positive or negative. Write a one-line APL expression to compute its square root if it is positive or its square if it is negative.

17. Write APL expressions for each of the following. Use S for 'Sam's a ham', J for 'Joe is so-so' and T for 'Teddy is ready.' **A** Sam's a ham and Teddy is not ready; **B** Joe is not so-so or Teddy is ready; **C** Teddy is ready and Sam's a ham or Joe is so-so.

18. For the arbitrary vectors $V1 \leftarrow 0\ 1\ 1\ 1\ 0\ 1$ and $V2 \leftarrow 1\ 1\ 0\ 1\ 0\ 1$ show that $\sim(V1 \wedge V2)$ is equivalent to $(\sim V1) \vee \sim V2$ and $\sim(V1 \vee V2)$ is equivalent to $(\sim V1) \wedge \sim V2$.

19. A teacher gives the following grades in an exam: 40 55 75 92 98 60 71 74 59 67 ($GRADES$). On a retest the same pupils scored 67 79 81 90 95 62 68 75 54 80 ($NEWGRADES$). The teacher (a rare and generous soul!) decides to record only the new grades or 20% more than the old grades, whichever is greater. What grades (whole numbers, no grades higher than 100) are actually recorded?

20. An insurance company sells three types of homeowners' policies with optional deductible amounts of $100, $250 and $500 respectively. The total number of policies of each type sold by one of their agencies is 608, 1277 and 942. If the agency's experience is that in a given year 2%, 3.5% and 5% of the three types of policies suffered losses in excess of the deductible, how much money beyond the premiums was paid out by the owners themselves?

21. The Board of Directors of a company decides to split the stock by issuing one additional share for each four now held. Fractional shares are to be redeemed in cash at the rate of $16.50 a share. If stockholder holdings are stored in the vector $SHARES$, how many additional shares are to be issued to each stockholder? How much does each receive in cash for fractional shares?

22. Convert a vector $DATES$ written as YYMMDD to the format MMDDYY.

23. Write an expression to extract out of a vector of numbers the digits in a specified position. Assume the positions are specified as...2 1 0 ‾1 ‾2... for ...hundreds, tens, units, tenths, hundredths,...

24. A school district buys pencils for its elementary school population of 3412 pupils and 175 teachers, administrators and others. Each individual is expected to use 11 pencils a year on the average. If pencils are sold only in boxes of one gross (144), and it is desired to have 20 extra boxes for stock, how many gross should be purchased?

25. The rounding algorithm $\lfloor X + .5$ on page 50 gives inconsistent results with negative numbers ending in $.5$. Rewrite it to take care of this exception.

Chapter 8: Function definition

In Chapter 3 we introduced the concept of a user defined function to supplement the primitive functions available on the keyboard. In this and the next few chapters we will review and considerably extend that concept, which allows you to develop (or borrow from other users with similar interests) and store functions of your choice on the APL system. This is equivalent to giving you the ability to tailor the generalized APL system to suit your own requirements. You can't use symbols like the hypothetical ⍟ in Chapter 3 (at least not in most commercially available APL systems), but, as you have already seen, you are able to use multiple character names with potential for mnemonic meanings, such as *HYP* for computing the length of the hypotenuse of a right triangle from the lengths of its legs. With this facility, solutions like (12 *HYP* 5)+4 *HYP* 3 become available.

The Defined Function HYP

The function *HYP* has already been developed and stored by the authors, and you may 'borrow' it by entering

```
    )COPY 1 CLASS HYP
SAVED  14.45.33 02/20/83
```

Don't worry at this point about the details of the above entry and response (unless you got a message like *WORKSPACE NOT FOUND* or *OBJECT NOT FOUND*, in which case check with your system librarian); we'll cover that later. The workspace 1 *CLASS*, incidentally, contains many illustrations and examples that will be of use throughout this book.

Experiment with *HYP* by entering

```
    3 HYP 4              (12 HYP 5)-4 HYP 3            1 3 12 HYP 1 4 5
5                       8                        1.414213562 5 13
```

The last example shows that *HYP* works with vector arguments as well as scalars. In fact, the defined function *HYP* has the same requirements on the shapes of its arguments as the primitive scalar dyadic functions + or × or ⌈.

So far, we've looked only at the external behavior of the function *HYP*. Before we can design our own functions we will have to be able to understand how *HYP* and similar functions are constructed.

Displaying a defined function

You have already seen the command which displays functions like *HYP* stored in the APL system. It is ∇*HYP*[⎕]∇, which you should carefully enter on your keyboard at this point. *Do not* press RETURN until your entry looks exactly like the one below. If you make a mistake, correct it before you press RETURN, not after, using the correction procedure introduced on page 7.

```
    ∇HYP[⎕]∇
```

The symbol ∇ is the upper shift *G* and the box ⎕ (called a *quad*) is the upper shift *L*. We won't explain the rationale behind the particular combination of symbols now, but you will see in Chapter 10 how this command relates to others that will be needed to define, display and edit functions.

Here is the system's response:

```
    ∇C←A HYP B
[1]    C←((A*2)+B*2)*0.5
    ∇
```

The first line, beginning with ∇, is called the *header* of the function. *HYP* is the name of the function; it has two arguments, *A* and *B*, with a *result* *C* (i.e., the answer). Notice that the arguments are separated from the function name by spaces. Can you imagine what would happen if the spaces were omitted?

Line 1 gives the familiar algorithm for calculating the hypotenuse. As has been pointed out, the ∇s send signals to the system that function definition is about to begin or end.

HYP can be used like a primitive scalar dyadic function, though an error results if we try to execute *HYP*/3 4, *HYP*\ι10 or *A∘.HYP B* in many APL implementations.

Interface diagrams

To help you understand the role of defined functions like *HYP*, here is a pictorial representation, called an *interface diagram*, of the entry and execution of *HYP*. Think of the outer box as holding the entire APL system:

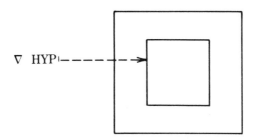

The first ∇ 'opens the door' to an appropriate place in storage (inner box) for the instructions comprising the function *HYP*. Entering the final ∇ in effect 'closes the door,' and the system reverts to execution mode.

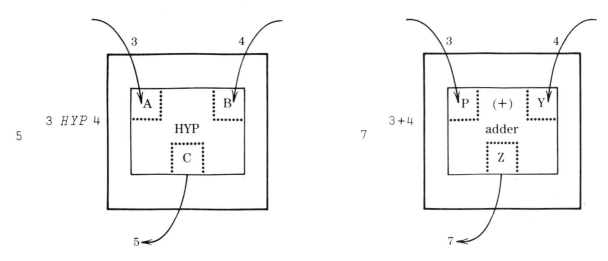

After opening, the paths leading to the dotted boxes *A* and *B* (left diagram), and the path leading from the dotted box *C* are set up automatically as part of the instructions incorporated in *HYP* to allow for receipt of data (*A* and *B*) and for temporary storage of the answer *C* before release to the outside. These latent paths are transformed into operational ones when the function is executed. Dotted boxes *A*, *B* and *C* have a similar ephemeral existence, coming into play only during function execution. In this example, the process shown is really not much different from that involved in a simple addition problem, summing 3 and 4 to give 7 (right diagram).

    3 *HYP* 4
5

In the diagram of the adder the temporary boxes have been given arbitrary names *P*, *Y* and *Z*. The two pictures are conceptually identical, except that in the second case the box representing the adder is a primitive part of APL, courtesy of the designers and implementors of the APL system. You may wonder what purpose the dotted storage boxes serve. More about this in Chapter 9.

Composing and entering functions

Now get some practice entering functions yourself. First enter,

)*CLEAR*
CLEAR WS

which is a system command that clears out your active workspace (where you are doing your APL work) and replaces it with a fresh blank workspace, just like the one you received when you signed on.

Suppose we try to execute *HYP* now:

        3 *HYP* 4
SYNTAX ERROR
        3 *HYP* 4
            ∧

Are you surprised that we got an error message? You shouldn't be. After all, our new workspace isn't supposed to have anything in it, and this leaves the way open for us to insert the function *HYP* ourselves. Start by entering

        ∇*C←A HYP B*
[1]   *C←((A*2)+B*2)*.5*
[2]   ∇

The initial ∇, as pointed out previously, tells the system you want to enter a function and 'opens the door' to a place in storage. More formally, after you enter the opening ∇, you are said to be in *function definition mode*, as opposed to *execution mode*. The rules for making up function names in APL, by the way, are the same as those for variable names (see page 12).

The rules for entering a function in APL2 are similar, but the system response is slightly different. After the header is entered it is returned as line zero ([0]), and subsequent lines are not numbered by the system until after the function is closed out.

This completes entry of the function *HYP*, and it can now be executed:

        3 *HYP* 4
5

If at this point you don't get 5 as your result, enter)*CLEAR* and repeat the previous steps.

We haven't squeezed all the juice out of *HYP* yet. Just as we can enter

        2+3×4
14

so we can ask the system for

        2+3 *HYP* 4
7

What makes this possible is the fact that the calculation involved in *HYP* produced a result which was stored away *temporarily* under the name *C* and hence was available for further calculations. Such a function is said to *return an explicit result*.

Using an interface diagram for this example, we can see that the existence of the temporary storage box C makes the result of 3 HYP 4 available to the adder, which adds it to 2, to yield the final result 7.

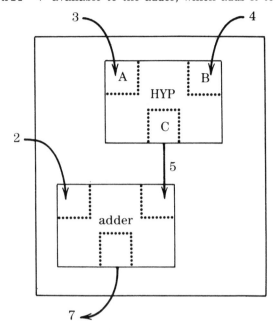

In the next chapter we'll explore the uses and consequences of writing headers *without* results, equivalent in our diagram above to leaving out the box C.

A defined monadic function

As a concession to those of you with backgrounds in other programming languages we'll now define a function to simulate $A*.5$, that is, a square root. It's unnecessary, but who cares? It makes an interesting simple illustration. If we had such a function, say $SQRT$, then line 1 of HYP could be   [1] $C \leftarrow SQRT$ $(A*2)+B*2$ instead of   [1] $C \leftarrow ((A*2)+B*2)*.5$.

Now define such a function by entering the header

    ∇$R \leftarrow SQRT$ X
[1]

Don't forget the space between $SQRT$ and X. Only the one argument X is needed here (the numbers we are calculating the square root of). It is placed to the *right* of the function name. The system responds, as before, with [1]. Incidentally, this suggests that a good way to tell whether you are in function definition or execution mode is to see if you get a number in brackets when RETURN is pressed. Just remember that if you do get it, anything you enter from that point on until the closing ∇ becomes part of the function you are defining.

If you were to press RETURN again, you would once more get [1], indicating that the system is still waiting for line 1.

Now enter the algorithm and close out the function. A couple of examples show that $SQRT$ seems to work acceptably.

[1] $R \leftarrow X*.5$ $SQRT$ 1 2 4
[2]   ∇   1 1.414213562 2

Earlier we had suggested that $SQRT$ could be used to simplify the function HYP. Having just defined $SQRT$, let's now write another HYP function in which $SQRT$ can be embedded. Starting off as before, enter the function header and wait for the response:

    ∇$R \leftarrow A$ HYP B
$DEFN$ $ERROR$
      ∇$R \leftarrow A$ HYP B
           ∧

But this time it appears that something is wrong. Apparently reentering the function with the same name and in the same workspace doesn't wipe out the old function. There is no analogy between the behavior of a function header and an assignment of values to a variable, the old values of which are lost when a new assignment is made.

You may argue that this replacement feature could be a very handy thing to have around for function headers, but if you think about it you will see that it can have some very grave consequences too. Suppose, for example, you had a big complicated function that was really valuable in your work, and you inadvertently used the same function name for something else. All your hard work, unless you kept a record of it somewhere else, would then be gone. So the APL system deliberately makes it hard for you to destroy defined functions.

This leaves you with two alternatives for redefining HYP. You can get rid of HYP by an appropriate system command (to be taken up later) or, better yet, use a different name for your new function, say, HY. Here is the function HY, which works just as well as HYP did:

```
      ∇C←A HY B
[1]   C←SQRT (A*2)+B*2
[2]   ∇
```

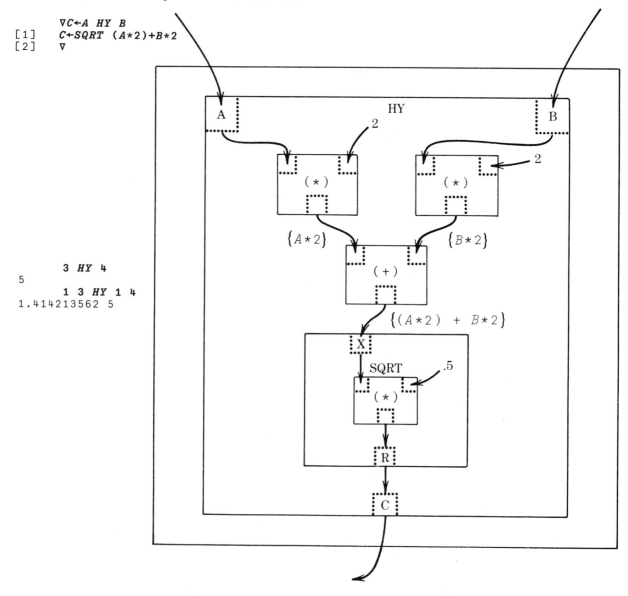

```
      3 HY 4
5
      1 3 HY 1 4
1.414213562 5
```

The interface diagram shows $SQRT$ embedded within HY, along with the square and adder (not detailed). The arrow leading to the box X in $SQRT$ carries the result of the operation on A and B of the square and adder functions.

Documenting functions

Most of the APL expressions and functions that we have seen so far are so simple that they are self-explanatory to an experienced user. However, suppose a function to calculate cosines was called C instead of $COSDEM$. How long might it take you to discover what it really does? You'd be wise to include comment statements in your functions to avoid the frustrating experience of not being able to figure out what you did a month or two later (and as a way of showing mercy to others who may be working with your functions).

With this in mind, here is a documented function that uses a MacLaurin series to calculate the cosine of an angle. You needn't know anything about cosines or MacLaurin series to appreciate the importance of some of the comments:

```
      ∇T←COSDEM X
[1]    ⍝ COSINE EXAMPLE.  ARGUMENT IS IN DEGREES.  DEMONSTRATES CONVERGENCE
[2]    ⍝ GILMAN AND ROSE, 1980
[3]    T←0 2 4 6 8 10 12 14 16
[4]    ⍝ T ABOVE IS USED AS A TEMPORARY VARIABLE.
[5]    T←-\((○X÷180)*T)÷!T
[6]    ⍝ FOR PRODUCTION WORK OR COMPARISON, USE 2○○X÷180
[7]    ∇
```

On older APL systems a separate line must be used for comments, but on most modern systems a comment can be put on the same line as instructions. The rule is that everything to the right of a ⍝ is taken as commentary.

Unfortunately, most casual APL users (as opposed to professionals) seem to develop all kinds of afflictions when it comes to documenting. They suddenly become blind, deaf and dumb. The typical arguments (no pun) given as to their failure to document include the following gems:

Who needs it?

It's obvious

APL is self-documenting

No one else will ever use my functions.

Hogwash! People with those attitudes act as though they're going to be around in the same job forever, which is absurd. They refuse to leave an understandable legacy to their successors. Moreover, if they haven't used some of their own (nontrivial) code for some time and then need to modify it, the odds are great that they'll have as much difficulty picking through their *own* undocumented functions as someone else's!

This whole topic deserves much more attention than we can give it here. Many information systems managers require formal documentation of functions, groups of related functions comprising major production applications, and workspaces. Whether you are a casual user or full-time programmer, some record of what you did and how it works is useful.

System commands to list and delete functions

Our workspace, which was originally empty, now has four functions. We can find out what functions are in our workspace with the system command $)FNS$, introduced in Chapter 3,

```
      )FNS
COSDEM  HY      HYP     SQRT
```

which works in exactly the same way as $)VARS$ did earlier; that is, it provides us with an alphabetized listing of the functions available in the active workspace. As was the case for the command $)VARS$, if the listing is long and we are interested only in whether a particular name, say, HYP is included, we can ask for

```
      )FNS HY
HY      HYP     SQRT
```

and we get that part of the listing from the letter sequence HY on. The display can be interrupted at any time by pressing ATTN or its equivalent on your terminal.

We can watch the behavior of the system as we add and delete functions. For example, let's include the following simple monadic function designed to give the square of a number:

```
      ∇R←SQ U
[1]   R←U×U∇
```

Two observations should be made at this point. First, the rule could have been stated in either of two ways: $U \times U$ or $U*2$. Second, waiting until the next line number is returned by the system is really unnecessary. Since the function is finished at the end of line 1, it's perfectly proper to close it out there, as was done in this case.

SQ seems to be in working order,

```
      SQ 4
16
```

and in fact SQ and $SQRT$ are inverse functions, with one undoing the effects of the other:

```
      SQRT SQ 4
4
```

Displaying the list of functions now available, we see SQ has been added to the list:

```
      )FNS
COSDEM  HY      HYP     SQ      SQRT
```

To delete functions that are no longer needed in the workspace, use the system command $ERASE$ introduced earlier:

```
      )ERASE HYP
```

A new display of functions shows that HYP is gone:

```
      )FNS
HY      SQ      SQRT
```

The $ERASE$ command can be used to delete several functions and variables at the same time. Just separate the names you want deleted. If you try to erase nonexistent objects, APL will let you know which ones weren't there.

Of course, to get rid of all the functions and variables at once, use

```
      )CLEAR
CLEAR WS
```

Now the commands $)FNS$ and $)VARS$ will elicit 'empty' responses. The cursor just moves over six spaces.

Some observations on function definition

Now that you have been introduced to function definition, called 'programming' in other languages, some guidelines on the subject are in order. Let's look first at what is involved: formulating the problem, developing the algorithm, translating the algorithm into APL instructions, testing and debugging the resulting functions, and documenting.

The user's imagination and creativity are called on to a far greater extent in the first two of these activities than in the others, which are generally more mechanical. Half the battle is formulating the problem well. And victory can be almost guaranteed if, building on this foundation, intelligent algorithms can be developed. Many of the errors that must be identified and removed in debugging arise because the user rushed into an APL translation of a half-baked algorithm. While it is true that APL instructions can be changed easily in defined functions (see Chapter 9), and error messages are usually a clue as to what is wrong, nonetheless, in APL as in medicine, an ounce of prevention is worth a pound of cure. Our advice to you, therefore, is to spend more time thinking through the problem and how you plan to solve it. If you do this, you will spend considerably less time correcting mistakes after the fact.

Moreover, if the developed function will be used by you again in the future, or will be used by others, it should be documented. For simple applications comments within the function will suffice, but for extensive work, formal users' manuals and maintenance aids should be written.

Those of you who are following the discussion of direct definition are reminded to see page 298.

PROBLEMS

We haven't explained how to correct typographical errors in defined functions (Chapter 10), so for now you'll have to be very careful entering these exercises. If you do make mistakes, $)CLEAR$ and reenter. Most of the exercises don't depend on any other, so you can usually $)CLEAR$ before each exercise. On some systems you can't even $)CLEAR$ while in function definition, so you may have to enter a ∇ (to close function definition) before you can $)CLEAR$.

1. Define a function EQ which evaluates the expression $(X-2) \times X - 3$ for various integer values of X and identifies the solutions to the equation $0 = (X-2) \times X - 3$.

2. Define a function BB which generates the batting averages of players by dividing the number of hits obtained by the number of times at bat for each player.

3. Define a function $HERO$ to calculate the area of a triangle by Hero's formula. (See problem 5, Chapter 5.)

4. The ABC Manufacturing Company reimburses its employees 100% of the first $200 spent per semester for college work in an approved program, and 50% of the next $300. No reimbursement is made for expenses above $500 per semester. Write a function called $REFUND$ that will calculate the refund due each employee in the program.

5. A well-known formula (Ohm's Law) in electrical work gives the combined resistance RT of several resistances R1, R2, etc., wired in parallel as follows (conventional notation):

$$\frac{1}{RT} = \frac{1}{R_1} + \frac{1}{R_2} + \cdots$$

Define a function PR that will calculate RT for a vector M of resistances in parallel.

6. To find the standard deviation of a set of numbers, the following steps are necessary: (1) compute the mean; (2) find the difference of each number from the mean; (3) square these differences; (4) take the square root of the average of step 3. Write a function SD to compute the standard deviation of some data X. Assume you already have a monadic function AVG (which computes averages) in storage.

7. In relativity theory the mass of a body depends on its velocity V relative to the observer. Specifically, in conventional notation $m = m_0 \div \sqrt{1 - v^2/c^2}$ where m_0 is the mass of the object at rest and c is the velocity of light (3E8 meters/sec.). Write a defined function REL to compute the mass of a body moving at speed V and with a rest mass MR.

8. Define functions called $PLUS$, $MINUS$, $TIMES$, $DIVIDEDBY$ to give mathematical meaning to these words, e.g., 3 $PLUS$ 4 returns 7, etc.

9. (For the more sophisticated) Rewrite HYP using one or more of the circular functions introduced in Chapter 7.

10. Write a function that does what $\div$ does, except that any number divided by zero results in a zero, rather than an error.

11. A well known rule of thumb in personal finance states that the number of years required to double money on deposit is roughly equal to 72 divided by the annual interest rate in percent. Write a function to estimate the doubling time for various rates of interest.

12. A company wants to maximize its profit (who doesn't?) on a new line of widgets. The cost accountants estimate that the overhead of the assembly line making the widgets is $50,000 regardless of the number sold. The first 5000 are calculated to cost $20 each, and all those in excess of 5000 cost $25 each. **A** Define a function $EXPENSE$ to calculate the total cost based on the number produced. **B** A survey shows the probable sales expected for a range of possible prices. Use the function $EXPENSES$ along with the revenue estimates from the survey to obtain the potential profit at each price.

Chapter 9: The syntax of functions

The last chapter showed how to enlarge the set of functions that is a primitive part of APL with functions of your own choosing or need. We observed that no matter how many primitive functions APL has, you are likely to need some that the implementors didn't anticipate. And even if there were many more primitive functions, the keyboard would have to be so large to incorporate them that it would be physically impractical. Actually, the ability to define functions (that is, to program) is what separates general purpose computer systems from fixed-application devices such as calculators, automated bank tellers and airline reservation systems.

Analogous to the primitive functions, we've seen two forms of defined functions: the dyadics *HYP* and *HY*, and the monadics *SQRT* and *SQ*. There are four more variants to learn about, helpful illustrations of which are stored in the workspace 1 *CLASS*, which was accessed in the last chapter. Let's reload this workspace and find out what is in it by executing the following sequence of commands. The system responses are included after each command:

```
        )LOAD 1 CLASS
SAVED   14.45.33 02/20/83

        )FNS
ADD       AGAIN     AREA      AUTO      AVG       AVG1      AVG2      AVG3
AVG4      AVG5      AVG6      CHANGE    CHARMAT   CLR       CMP       CMPN
CMPX      CMPY      COMPINT   COMPOSE   COS       CP        C2GT99    DEC
DENUMCODE           DESCRIBE            DICE      DUPLICATES          ENT
EVAL      F         FACT      FACTORIALS          FIND      FINDROW   FIX
FUNEDIT   GAME      GEO2      GEO3      GETFN     GO        GRAPH     HEXA      HY
HYP       INPUT     INT       INVOICERUN          LASTVISIT           MEAN
NAMESONLY           NEWPATIENT          NEWVISIT            NUMCODE   OBSERVE   ON
PEREL     RECT      REP       REPF      REPL      REPLENISH           RETIE
RIGHTJUST           ROWNAMES            RUN       SALES     SD        SELECT
SELECT    SETUP     SHOWME    SIGN      SLAM      SORT      SPELL
SPLINECALC          SPLINEEVAL          SPRED     SQ        SQRT      STAT      STATEMENT
STATISTICS          SUB       SUBST     SUM       SUSPENDED           TOSS
TOTVISITS           TRANSP    VIG       WSSHOW    DSLOPE    ESLOPE    XSLOPE
```

Your listing may not be identical to this one, since changes are made from time to time in the common library workspaces. Be that as it may, most of the functions in this list will be illustrated and explained as we go through the remaining chapters. The ones we will be interested in now are *HYP*, *SIGN*, *DICE*, *RECT*, *STAT* and *GAME*.

Remember that to display the contents of a function, enter ∇name[□]∇, after which the system displays the function header followed by all the steps which comprise the function, including even the opening and closing dels. Here is our old friend *HYP*:

```
      ∇ HYP[□]∇
    ∇  C←A HYP B
[1]    C←((A*2)+B*2)*0.5
    ∇
```

This display command will be useful as we examine in the rest of this chapter some additional ways of constructing defined functions.

Function Headers

There are six types of APL function headers. Each has its own particular uses, as will be seen from the illustrative examples to be displayed. These six forms are summarized in the table below.

	Dyadic	Monadic	Niladic
Returns Explicit Result	$\nabla E \leftarrow A\ HYP\ B$	$\nabla R \leftarrow SIGN\ X$	$\nabla R \leftarrow DICE$
No Explicit Result	$\nabla L\ RECT\ H$	$\nabla STAT\ X$	$\nabla GAME$

Don't worry for the moment about what all this means; all in good time.

The formal term for the number of explicit arguments that a function takes is *valence*. It also refers to the number of operands (the functions or arrays on which an operator acts to produce a derived function) associated with an operator. Some APL systems return a *VALENCE ERROR* instead of some other error message whenever you try to execute a monadic function (with no dyadic definition) with left and right arguments, or a primitive dyadic function (with no monadic definition) with a right argument only.

Functions with explicit results

To start off, display the function $SIGN$:

```
    ∇SIGN[□]∇
  ∇ R←SIGN X
[1]   R←(X>0)-X<0
  ∇
```

It takes a single argument which, if negative, returns ¯1, if positive, 1 and if zero, it returns 0. In fact, it duplicates the monadic direction function introduced earlier. Executing this for various arguments, we get

```
    SIGN ¯5.2            SIGN 0              SIGN 3 ¯2 0
¯1                           0            1 ¯1 0
```

You can see how $SIGN$ works by tracing through it with a few examples. If X is negative, $X<0$ would be 1 and $X>0$ would be 0. So $0-1$ gives ¯1. Similarly, for X positive, $X<0$ is 1, with $1-0$ resulting in 1. And for $X=0$, $X<0$ is 0 and $X>0$ is also 0, so that $0-0$ gives 0.

Here is an interface diagram for $SIGN$:

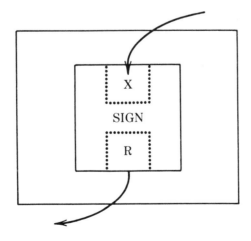

Now enter *DICE* a few times and then display it.

```
        DICE
9

        DICE
4

        DICE
4

        ∇DICE[☐]∇
      ∇ R←DICE
[1]     R←+/? 6 6
      ∇
```

DICE simulates the sum of a random roll of two dice. The header has no arguments. It is a *niladic* function, to coin a word. The function really doesn't need any arguments. It selects the numbers for the roll itself, using the random number generator. As shown by the interface diagram, there is no external input path because the data required comes from within the APL system itself (dotted arrow):

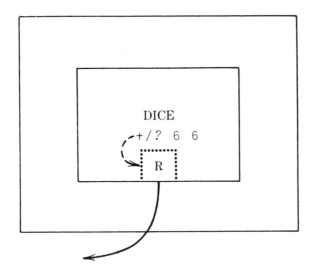

Functions without explicit results

We have just seen examples of function headers that take no arguments (*DICE*), one (*SIGN*), or two (*HYP*). They all returned *explicit results*, that is, a result that could be used for subsequent computation. Now let's look at one that doesn't give explicit results, but merely displays them, the function *RECT*:

```
        ∇RECT[☐]∇                    3 RECT 4
      ∇ L RECT H                   14
[1]     2×L+H                       5
[2]     L HYP H                    12
[3]     L×H
      ∇
```

The first thing that should hit your eye is that there is no arrow in the header. Line 1 gives the perimeter of a rectangle of length *L* and height *H*; line 2 is the length of the diagonal, using the previously defined *HYP*; line 3 is the area of the rectangle. Notice also that there is no assignment arrow on any line. This means that the results of each line aren't stored anywhere but will be displayed.

This function displays information, but that information can't be easily used for further work. Watch what happens when we try to use its 'result' for further computation:

```
        5+3 RECT 4
14
5
12
VALUE ERROR
        5+3 RECT 4
             ∧
```

Here the results of the three lines of the function again are displayed, but we can't add 5 to them because the numbers weren't stored anywhere, as contrasted to

> **5+3 *HYP* 4**
>
> 10

A comparison of their interface diagrams highlights their differences:

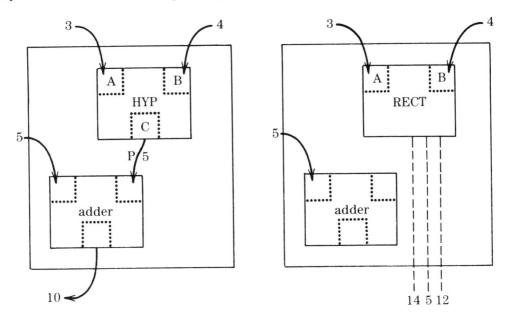

In the diagram for *RECT* one of the input paths has no values to feed into the adder, since the output from *RECT* was 'deposited' on the paper or display screen but not retained anywhere else. By contrast, the output from *HYP* was stored temporarily in *C* to permit its movement to the adder.

The two headers ∇*C*←*A HYP B* and ∇*A RECT B* differ in that an assignment (←) is made in *HYP* and not in *RECT*, and in the body of *RECT* there are no assignments of results to any variables. We'll have more to say about the significance of the variables used in the header and in the function itself later in this chapter.

Now consider the monadic function *STAT*:

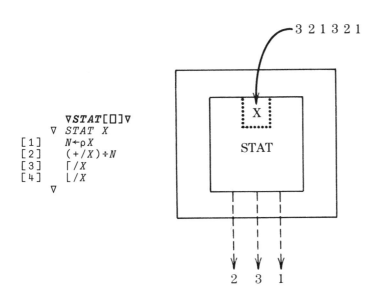

```
      ∇STAT[▯]∇
    ∇ STAT X
[1]    N←ρX
[2]    (+/X)÷N
[3]    ⌈/X
[4]    ⌊/X
    ∇
```

Again the header has no explicit result, and the display will be three lines. The first two compute the average of the elements of X and could easily have been combined into one line. N is just a convenient handle for transferring the results of line 1 (which is the number of elements) to line 2. Line 2 displays the average, and lines 3 and 4 display the largest and smallest elements of X. Executing $STAT$ we get

        $STAT$ **3 2 1 3 2 1**
2
3
1

Since no explicit results are returned, it doesn't make any sense to try to work further with them. If we do try it, we get an error message as before:

        2×$STAT$ 8 1 4 10
5.75
10
1
$VALUE$ $ERROR$
        2×$STAT$ 8 1 4 10
             ∧

To complete the table on page **65**, display the function $GAME$:

        ∇$GAME$[□]∇
    ∇ $GAME$
[1] $MINE←DICE$
[2] $YOURS←DICE$
[3]   ×$MINE-YOURS$
    ∇

After executing the function a few times,

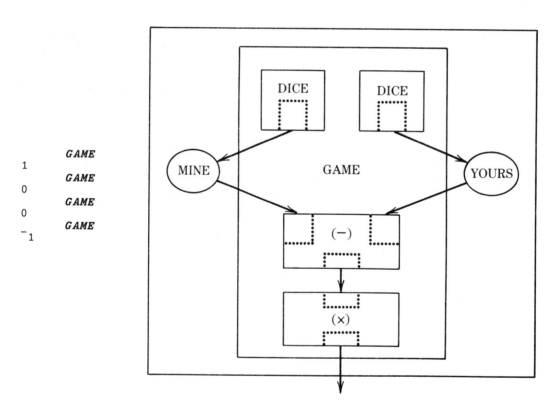

```
          GAME
1
          GAME
0
          GAME
0
          GAME
 ¯1
```

you should be able to see that this function simply generates one of the three random integers ¯1, 0, 1. It needs no arguments because the random numbers come from the niladic function $DICE$.

The interface diagram for *GAME* shows the results of *DICE* being ultimately deposited in permanent (as opposed to temporary) storage boxes in the APL system.

Another function like *GAME* that you have already encountered is *EASYDRILL* in the workspace 1 *AIDRILL*. This also required no arguments and returned no explicit results. It displayed the answers and accepted inputs, but you couldn't do any computations with them. Functions of this type are commonly called *main programs*.

Some of these programs can be quite large. In most systems the only limit is the space available, but VS APL has a limit of 2047 lines in a single function. Of course, common sense should tell you not to make your programs too long because they will be hard to read and maintain. A good rule of thumb to follow is to keep the length to a page or less.

Different types of variables

The variables that we have encountered so far all appeared to have similar behavior. Now we will see that this isn't quite true, and that APL has a feature that provides protection against variables being accidentally respecified as a result of function execution. Another aspect of this feature lets the same variable name be used repeatedly in different functions without the possibility of confusion.

In the workspace 1 *CLASS*, which you should now load,

```
)LOAD 1 CLASS
SAVED   14.45.33 02/20/83
```

there are five functions, *AVG*1, *AVG*2, *AVG*3, *AVG*4, *AVG*5, which are quite similar and which are all intended to calculate averages. We will use the small but significant differences among them to study the different kinds of variables that can exist in APL.

Dummy variables

Display *AVG*1. The header shows it to be a monadic function that returns an explicit result. The first line gives the number of elements in *X* and stores that value in *N*, while the second line divides the sum of the elements by *N* and stores it temporarily in *R* when the function is executed.

```
      ∇AVG1[□]∇
    ∇  R←AVG1 X
[1]    N←ρX
[2]    R←(+/X)÷N
    ∇
```

Let's give *X* and *N* values and then execute *AVG*1 with an arbitrary argument. What will happen to *X* and *N*?

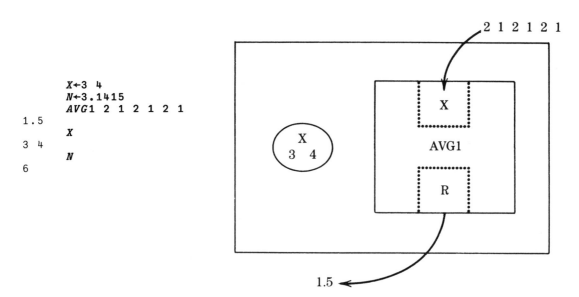

```
        X←3  4
        N←3.1415
        AVG1 2 1 2 1 2 1
1.5
        X
3  4
        N
6
```

Is something wrong here? We put in 3.1415 for N and got back 6. On the other hand, X was set at 3 4 and apparently wasn't affected, although we used the vector 2 1 2 1 2 1 for the argument X in the header of $AVG1$. According to what was presented in an earlier chapter, the latest value of X is supposed to supersede a previous value. So why didn't we get 2 1 2 1 2 1 when we called for X?

For a clue look at the function header. One of its arguments is named X. Apparently this isn't the same variable as the X we set before (3 4), even though the symbols are the same. When we executed this function for 2 1 2 1 2 1, *for the time being* X inside the function must have had the value 2 1 2 1 2 1. The X outside (3 4) wasn't affected, since we were able to retrieve it afterwards unaltered. Are there then really two X's?

This can be clarified by reference to an interface diagram for $AVG1$. The X in the header is a *temporary* storage box for the argument (dotted box). It is filled in this case by the vector 2 1 2 1 2 1, while the variable X previously assigned the value 3 4 is sitting elsewhere in storage (oval). The X within $AVG1$ is a different X from the X in the oval.

If, however, we failed to specify another argument for $AVG1$, and instead executed $AVG1$ X, the data flow would look as in this interface diagram.

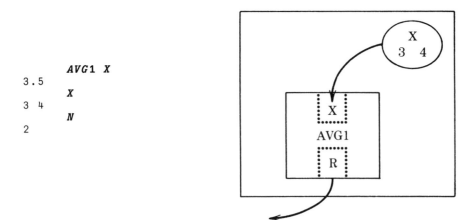

```
        AVG1 X
3.5
        X
3  4
        N
2
```

It's as though the system looked around for an X in storage to use as an argument and found 3 4. This situation is exactly the same as though we had called for $AVG1$ A for some A in storage. What may be confusing is the use of the same name at two different levels here.

The variables used as the argument and result of the header are in a very real sense 'dummy' variables. This means that they have values assigned to them only *inside* the function itself. We can find out what these values are only when we ourselves are 'inside' the function, that is, when execution is suspended part way through because we interrupted it or because of an error.

To illustrate the point further, define this function and then execute it with arguments 3 and 4:

```
      ∇Z←A FN G                    3 FN 4
[1]   Z←A+G∇                  7
```

If after execution we ask for A, G and Z, we get *VALUE ERROR*s instead, because A, G and Z simply don't exist once the function *FN* is completed.

```
        A                     G                     Z
VALUE ERROR           VALUE ERROR           VALUE ERROR
        A                     G                     Z
        ∧                     ∧                     ∧
```

Interface diagrams of the situations during and after execution show this graphically:

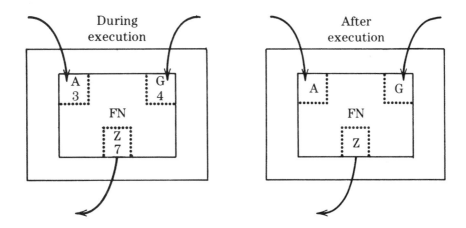

Since the A and G boxes are empty after execution, the *VALUE ERROR* messages received above should be understandable. However, now let's assign A and G and then display them after execution of *FN*:

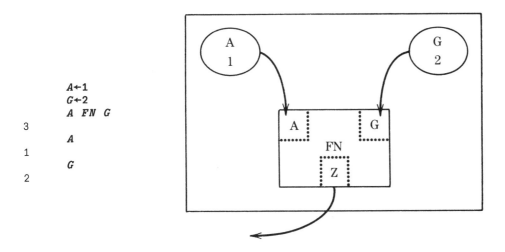

```
      A←1
      G←2
      A FN G
3
      A
1
      G
2
```

The values of A and G stored outside the function (ovals) weren't affected by the execution, even though copies of their constants were fed into the A and G dotted boxes.

It may be dawning on you by this time that it doesn't make any difference what names we use for the arguments of a function. They serve only to indicate that two arguments are called for and to indicate which is which. In a sense, they act like the zeros in the number .00032. All the zeros do is fill up space, but you need them to read the number correctly. This is why the arguments associated with the function name are sometimes called *dummy variables* and have values only within the function, acquired during execution and disappearing when execution is complete. They are special cases of a general class of variables called *local variables*. More about this later.

As the interface diagrams suggest, we can make similar points about results in the headers. They also are dummy variables, and may acquire values during execution. And in the case of the arguments, once execution is finished, the value is lost. That's why Z produced a *VALUE ERROR* in the previous example.

Global variables

There is still a little more juice to be squeezed out of the original function $AVG1$. We have answered the question of why calling for X returned the value 3 4. But what about N?

In contrast to X, N does not appear in the header, but only in the body of the function. Lacking any instructions from us to the contrary, it ought to behave the same way all of our variables had been behaving before we learned about function definition. That is to say, whenever the system encounters an instruction reassigning a variable whose value has been previously set, it changes that value accordingly. In our case, N was originally set at 3.1415, but during execution it was reset to 6 as a result of the instructions in line 1 of $AVG1$. Interface diagrams would show N as follows:

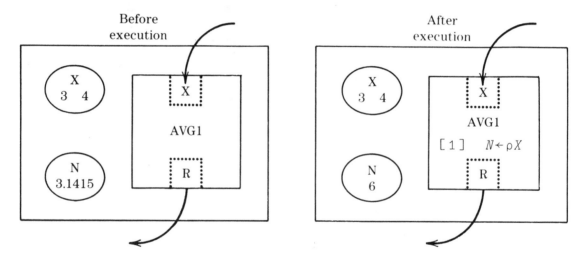

When the variable N is given a value during execution, that new value replaces any existing value of N outside $AVG1$; or if N didn't exist, N is created for the first time (again outside $AVG1$). The key word here is *outside*, with variables like N, appearing in the executable lines of a function (but not in the header), ending up outside the function once a value has been assigned to them. In this sense they behave exactly like the variables you worked with in Chapter 2, and are called *global variables*.

The next section will describe how these variables can be protected from surprise replacement by having the names appear in the header of the function.

Local variables

Let's look at another way in which variables can be used in function definition. For this, display $AVG2$:

```
        ∇AVG2[□]∇
    ∇ R←AVG2 X;N
[1]    N←ρX
[2]    R←(+/X)÷N
    ∇
```

Something new has been added to the header: a variable N, preceded by a semicolon. When a variable is used in the header in this fashion, it is a *local variable*, whose value can be set and used only within the function itself. It behaves like the dummy variables we discussed previously.

To restore the values of the variables to what they were before we first executed $AVG1$ for comparison purposes, reset N:

```
    N←3.1415
    X
3 4
```

Using the same argument as before, let's execute $AVG2$ and then display X and N:

```
    AVG2 2 1 2 1 2 1         X               N
1.5                      3 4            3.1415
```

As you expected, X hasn't changed. This time N still holds the original value set when we made it a global variable. The instructions for N on line 1 now refer to a *local* N within the function itself, it being only an accident of choice that we used the same name for both a local and a global variable.

In the following interface diagrams for $AVG2$ we see an example of how local variables such as N, in a very real sense *shield* or protect previously defined names.

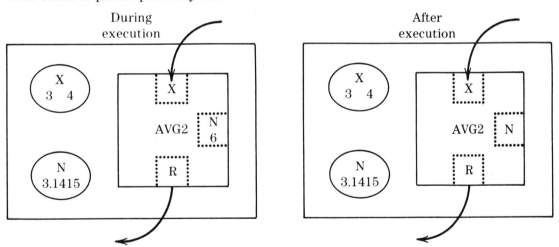

It should now be clear that the APL system keeps the record straight for variables used in these different ways. This is fortunate for us because we may have used the same variable name previously for something entirely different and probably want to preserve it. To prevent accidental reassigning of the variable, it is wise to make it local by putting it in the header preceded by a semicolon. If more than one variable is to be localized, they can be strung out, separated from each other and the rest of the header by semicolons.

$AVG3$ is another example of the use of a local variable. It has a local variable P and is a niladic function returning an explicit result:

```
        ∇AVG3[□]∇            AVG3
    ∇ R←AVG3;P            3.5
[1]    P←ρX
[2]    R←(+/X)÷P             X
    ∇                    3 4
```

You ought to be able to figure out for yourself why the result 3.5 was returned. (Hint: is X a local, global or dummy variable?) In any event, $AVG3$ is a poorly designed function because it depends on the existence of the global variable X for its successful execution. Such dependencies should be employed only when there are no reasonable alternatives, and they should always be documented.

Now reassign X and execute $AVG3$ again. Clearly, the X being averaged is from the most recent global assignment:

```
      X←2  1  2  1  2  1
      AVG3
1.5
```

Things get more complicated when you define functions that in turn execute other functions (subroutines). Local variables in the outermost function still shield globals of the same name from the inner functions as well. And if there is local name duplication in the subroutine, the value associated with it is that in the particular subroutine being executed at the moment.

The following example will either clarify the confusion above, or cause you to swear off duplication of names in subroutines altogether.

```
      ∇R←A OPN B;D              ∇Z←OPN1 A              D←5
[1]   D←A+B              [1]    A                      3 OPN 4
[2]   R←OPN1 D ∇        [2]    D                  7
                        [3]    Z←A*2 ∇             7
                                                  49
```

Global variables as counters

$AVG4$ adds a new twist:

```
      ∇AVG4[□]∇
    ∇ R←AVG4 X
[1]   R←(+/X)÷ρX
[2]   COUNT←COUNT+1
    ∇
```

This function is intended to illustrate a practical reason to change the value of a global variable inside a function. It is designed so that each time it is used a counter (called $COUNT$) increases by one. A record can thus be kept of the total number of times the function is executed.

Here is an attempted execution of $AVG4$:

```
      AVG4 2 1 2 1 2 1
VALUE ERROR
AVG4[2] COUNT←COUNT+1
        ∧
```

Why do we get an error message? If you think about it, you will see that we goofed by failing to assign an initial value for $COUNT$. So naturally the system didn't know where to start counting, and was unable to execute line 2. This is confirmed by asking for the value of $COUNT$:

```
      COUNT
VALUE ERROR
      COUNT
      ∧
```

Setting $COUNT$ to 0 and reexecuting $AVG4$ twice, we get

```
      COUNT←0
      AVG4 2 1 2 1 2 1              AVG4 5 4 3 2 1
1.5                          3
      COUNT                        COUNT
1                            2
```

$COUNT$ now behaves as we had intended. It is a global variable because it doesn't appear in the header.

In *AVG*5 below, *COUNT* is a local variable:

```
    ∇AVG5[□]∇                          AVG5 2 3 2 3
  ∇ R←AVG5 X;COUNT                  VALUE ERROR
[1]   R←(+/X)÷ρX                    AVG5[2] COUNT←COUNT+1
[2]   COUNT←COUNT+1                         ∧
  ∇
```

What's wrong? *COUNT* was set earlier to 0, so why the error message? True, *COUNT* was set, but as a global variable. Its value can't be used in *AVG*5 because we said in the header that *COUNT* was local. There's no way this function can work, because the local *COUNT* shields the global *COUNT*.

Suppose we put a line before line 1 which sets *COUNT* to 0. Then each time we executed it, the local variable *COUNT* would be reset to 0. It would never get beyond 1. Furthermore, because it would be local, all trace of it would be lost once we exited the function.

Up to this point in the chapter we have managed to bungle the execution of two functions, *AVG*4 and *AVG*5. Such partial executions, called *suspensions*, stay with us until we sign off or remove them. They take up valuable space and may cause other unanticipated things to happen. For the time being, clear up each such suspension by typing →, followed by *RETURN*. More about this phenomenon in Chapter 16.

There is a limitation on the use of local variables. It isn't possible to use a subfunction by the same name as a local variable. For example, if *COUNT* were also a function, we couldn't ask for it to be executed in *AVG*5 and still retain *COUNT* as a local variable.

By this time you should be getting an appreciation of the usefulness of local variables, as well as an awareness (we hope) of some of their pitfalls. It is not only variables that can be localized; functions can be made local to functions. This advanced concept is treated in Chapter 24.

Before leaving the topic this is a good place to point out that most people have difficulty remembering more than a half dozen things at a time. This physiological limitation suggests that you would do well to restrict the number of different variables you use in your programs. They not only take up space in the workspace, but also make your programs harder to read and maintain. If you use the same names over again in another part of your program, make sure it is in a place where no confusion is likely to arise when the statements are reviewed later, and use comments liberally to document your techniques.

PROBLEMS

Define the functions as required in problems 1 to 6:

1. Dyadic, explicit result: to calculate the FICA (social security tax) at the rate of P percent on gross yearly income IN up to an annual maximum of MAX.

2. Dyadic, no explicit result: to store in the variable T the square of the difference of its two scalar arguments.

3. Monadic, explicit result: to generate a limited set of prime numbers, using Fermat's formula 2^{2^n} (conventional notation).

4. Niladic, no explicit result: to see if either of two previously defined variables A and B divides the other evenly. The answer should be 1 if they divide evenly, or 0 otherwise.

5. Monadic, no explicit result: accepts a vector argument V and makes these changes to global variables:**A** adds to NV the number of numbers in V; **B** adds to SV the sum of the elements in V; **C** adds to $SVSQ$ the sum of the squares of the elements in V. Don't $)CLEAR$ yet; problem 6 uses these variables.

6. Niladic, explicit result: uses NV, SV and $SVSQ$ of problem 5 to compute the sample standard deviation, using the formula $((SVSQ-(SV*2)\div NV)\div {}^-1+NV)*.5$.

7. What is wrong with the following function headers (A and B are arguments)?
   A SQ A $\nabla Z \leftarrow B$ HYP ∇A $1FIB$ B ∇A HYP B C ∇A HYP $B;B;C$

8. Enter the function HYP (page 56) and use it to evaluate each of the following:
   $(3$ HYP $4)$ HYP 3 HYP 1 $4+3$ HYP $4-3$ $(4+3)$ HYP $4-3$

9. $)LOAD$ 1 $CLASS$ and then define a dyadic function D which returns an explicit result that is the larger of its two arguments. Explain the system's behavior.

10. Define a dyadic function $ROUND$ that returns an explicit result which is the right argument rounded off to the number of decimal places indicated in the left argument. Example:
    2 $ROUND$ 123.456 1.33333 3.5 gives 123.46 1.33 3.5

11. $)LOAD$ 1 $CLASS$. Enter $CLR \leftarrow 52$ 78 90 and account for the result.

12. $)LOAD$ 1 $CLASS$ and enter this function :

    ```
         ∇F
    [1]  Z←(A*2)+B*2
    [2]  Z←Z*.5∇
    ```

    After assigning arbitrary values for A and B, execute $T \leftarrow F+7$ and $T \leftarrow Z+7$. Explain your results.

13. $)CLEAR$ and define these three functions:

    ```
         ∇PERIM1              ∇R←B PERIM2 C           ∇R←PERIM3 C
    [1]  R←2×B+C∇        [1]  R←2×B+C∇           [1]  R←2×B+C∇
    ```

    Now make these assignments $R \leftarrow 3$ $B \leftarrow 2$ $C \leftarrow 5$ $M \leftarrow 7$ $S \leftarrow 1$.
    A Execute $PERIM1$. Observe the changes to the variables.
    B Reset the variables R, B, C, M and S to their original values and execute $S \leftarrow M$ $PERIM2$ R. Again observe the changes to the variables.
    C Reset the variables again and execute $S \leftarrow PERIM3$ R. Observe the changes to the variables. Can you explain every change?

14. Write a function $MARGIN$, which returns an explicit result, to solve the following problem. Experience shows that sales S of a toy depend on the price, P, as $40000-5000 \times P$. The total cost C of production is $C \leftarrow 35000+2 \times S$. For each price \$1, \$2, \$3, \$4, \$5, \$6 and \$7, what is the profit margin?

15. Write a function $COST$ to figure the total cost of a shopping trip by adding the cost of nontaxable items to that of the taxable items (on which 5% sales tax must be calculated).

Chapter 10: Function editing

The two previous chapters explained how to enter and use different types of functions, but didn't show how to change a function which had an error in it. Since we can't do much without the capability for such change, this chapter will be concerned with ways of editing functions after they have been written and entered.

To speed things up, we'll use the prepared function $STAT$ in the workspace 1 $CLASS$:

```
      )LOAD 1 CLASS
SAVED  14.45.33 02/20/83

      ∇STAT[□]∇
    ∇ STAT X
[1]    N←ρX
[2]    (+/X)÷N
[3]    ⌈/X
[4]    ⌊/X
    ∇
```

It isn't possible to enter it or redefine it because we already have a copy of it in our workspace. Suppose we didn't know that it was already in and tried to reenter it:

```
      ∇STAT X
DEFN ERROR
      ∇STAT X
            ∧
```

As was discussed earlier on **page 59** the error message shows that the system has built-in protection against accidental replacement of a function. However, we can make changes to functions that have already been defined, as we shall see. Given our all too-human propensity to make mistakes or to change our minds, this APL feature is an obvious necessity.

Adding a line

The four lines of the function $STAT$ as presently written give information on the average and largest and smallest elements of a vector argument X. Suppose we want to add a fifth line which will give the range (difference between the largest and smallest element).

How is this done? The first step is to open up the function by entering a single ∇ and the function name, followed by RETURN as usual:

```
      ∇STAT
[5]
```

Notice that the system replies with [5]. In general the next available line number will be returned. It's as though we had just entered the first four lines and are ready to continue our writing on the fifth line. (This is a way, if somewhat sneaky, to find out how many lines are in the function.) Now enter

```
[5]    (⌈/X)-⌊/X
[6]    ∇
```

and we see that the system replies with a [6], waiting for the next line of input. Since we don't want to add anything further, a closing ∇ has been entered as a signal that we want to get back into execution mode.

Execution with a vector 2 9 1 gives us four lines of output, the fourth line being range as we had intended, and a display of the function now shows that line 5 has indeed been added:

```
        STAT 2 9 1                              ∇STAT[□]∇
4                                        ∇  STAT X
9                                  [1]      N←ρX
1                                  [2]      (+/X)÷N
8                                  [3]      ⌈/X
                                   [4]      ⌊/X
                                   [5]      (⌈/X)−⌊/X
                                      ∇
```

Replacing a line with another line

Also in the workspace 1 *CLASS* is a function called *AVG* which computes the average of the elements of an argument *X*. We are going to change line 2 of *STAT* to *AVG*, but first we'll check out *AVG* to see if it works:

```
    AVG 1 2 3
2
```

To replace line 2, we need to open up the function as before by entering

```
    ∇STAT
```

The system's response is [6], which we override with [2]:

```
[6]    [2]
```

After pressing RETURN, the system replies with a [2] and we can now enter *AVG X*:

```
[2]    AVG X
```

Having accepted the change to line 2, the system displays [3], anticipating that's the next line you want to change. Since we aren't going to make any more changes right now, ∇ is used to close out the function:

```
[3]    ∇
```

It should be emphasized that in making this change, only line 2 was changed. All the other lines of the function were *not* affected.

Here is an execution of *STAT* and a display of the revised function:

```
        STAT 2 9 1                              ∇STAT[□]∇
4                                        ∇  STAT X
9                                  [1]      N←ρX
1                                  [2]      AVG X
8                                  [3]      ⌈/X
                                   [4]      ⌊/X
                                   [5]      (⌈/X)−⌊/X
                                      ∇
```

The change has been made and the rest of the function is unaltered.

Changing the header

You can change the header itself in exactly the same way as any other line by using [0] as the line number:

```
        ∇STAT                           ∇STAT[□]∇
[6]    [0]                        DEFN ERROR
[0]    NEWNAME X                        ∇STAT
[1]    ∇                                   ∧
```

Since *STAT* as been renamed *NEWNAME*, we get an error message when we attempt to display *STAT*, because it no longer exists. Naturally, any changes in the header must be consistent with what is in the body of the function itself, unless of course the corresponding changes are made in the body of the function also.

You can display *NEWNAME* now if you wish, but after you do, change the name of the function back to *STAT* because there are more function editing commands yet to learn, and it will be easier if we get back on track.

```
        ∇NEWNAME
[6]     [0]
[0]     STAT X
[1]     ∇
```

Inserting a line between two other lines

Suppose we want to insert between lines 1 and 2 a statement whose purpose is to display the original values of *X*. This is done by first opening the function as usual, and then entering some number in brackets that is between 1 and 2, say [1.1]:

```
        ∇STAT
[6]     [1.1]
```

Any number will do as long as it is between the numbers of the two lines bracketing the location of the insertion. The system returns [1.1] and we can then enter *X*, which when encountered during execution will cause the values of *X* to be displayed.

```
[1.1]   X
[1.2]
```

The next line number provided by the system is 'one greater' in its last significant digit to provide for still other entries between lines 1 and 2. Let's ask first for a display of what we have so far while we're still in function definition mode, and then close it out:

```
[1.2]   [□]∇
        ∇ STAT X
[1]     N←ρX
[1.1]   X
[2]     AVG X
[3]     ⌈/X
[4]     ⌊/X
[5]     (⌈/X)-⌊/X
        ∇
```

Your cursor should have moved over six spaces after this. If it did, you are in execution mode. However, if a number in [ ] was returned, then enter ∇, followed by RETURN.

Of course, a line numbered 1.1 is somewhat awkward, to say the least. Fortunately, after the function is closed out the lines are automatically renumbered, as seen in the following display:

```
        ∇STAT[□]
        ∇ STAT X
[1]     N←ρX
[2]     X
[3]     AVG X
[4]     ⌈/X
[5]     ⌊/X
[6]     (⌈/X)-⌊/X
        ∇
[7]
```

The lines of the function have been renumbered. But since [7] was returned, we are still in function definition mode. Pressing RETURN gives [7] again, and since there is to be no more entry at this time, we close out the function to get back to execution mode.

```
[7]     ∇
```

Doing several things at once

It is possible to put several of the editing instructions on a single line. For our example we'll take line 3, *AVG X*, change it back to what it was originally, and then return to execution mode. To do this, enter the following:

∇*STAT*[3](+/*X*)÷*N*∇

The [3] moves control to line 3, what follows it becomes the new line 3, and the second ∇ closes it out after the change. We can now check this by displaying the function in the usual manner:

```
        ∇STAT[□]∇
      ∇ STAT X
[1]     N←ρX
[2]     X
[3]     (+/X)÷ρX
[4]     ⌈/X
[5]     ⌊/X
[6]     (⌈/X)-⌊/X
      ∇
```

But observe the following entry, which inserts a comment after line 5:

∇*STAT*[5.1] ⍝ *NEXT LINE DISPLAYS RANGE* ∇
[5.2]

Why is function definition still open? The reason is that even though a closing ∇ was entered, it came after a comment symbol ⍝, and hence was taken as part of the comment itself. Entering a ∇ on the *next* line now closes the function and renumbers the comment as line 6.

[5.2] ∇

Deleting a line

How do we remove a line completely? For example, suppose we want to get rid of line 4. As usual, we first open up the function and direct control to line 4:

∇*STAT*[4]

The computer responds with [4], indicating it is ready to work on line 4. What you do next depends on the particular APL system you are using. On many older versions of APL, the only way you can delete a line is to press ATTN followed by RETURN. For most modern systems, [∆4] deletes line 4, but on APL*PLUS Systems it is [~4].

[4]   [∆4]

Next, [8] is displayed, it being the next available line at the end of the function. We now ask for a display of the function, but without closing it out:

```
[8]    [□]
      ∇ STAT X
[1]     N←ρX
[2]     X
[3]     (+/X)÷N
[5]     ⌊/X
[6]   ⍝ NEXT LINE DISPLAYS THE RANGE∇
[7]     (⌈/X)-⌊/X
      ∇
[8]
```

Notice that line 4 has been deleted and the display continues with [8]. Let's remove line 6 (incidentally, some systems let you remove many lines at once, e.g., [∆4 6 7]) and close the function:

[8]   [∆6]∇

Since the function is closed, the lines are now renumbered:

```
      ∇STAT[□]∇
    ∇ STAT X
[1]    N←ρX
[2]    X
[3]    (+/X)÷N
[4]    L/X
[5]    (⌈/X)-L/X
    ∇
```

Just remember that if the number of ∇'s *you* (and not the system) have entered is even, you are in execution mode; if odd, you are in function definition mode. An exception is ∇'s following a comment; they are regarded as part of the comment itself.

Erasing the entire function

Occasionally, while making extensive changes, you might get so messed up that you want to start over. You can get rid of the entire function using the system command)*ERASE* followed by the name of the function you no longer want. Don't do it now, because we need *STAT* for some more examples. The response to a successful erasure is simply that the cursor moves over six spaces. As you would expect, attempts to display an erased function result in an error message.

Locking functions

You can lock a function by closing it with the ⍢ character (formed by overstriking ∇ and ~) instead of ∇. On some systems you can use ⍢ for either starting or ending functions to be locked. Once a function is locked, it can't be edited or displayed, although it can be executed and erased. Make sure you keep an unlocked reference version as a base for future work. Locking is useful for protecting proprietary algorithms or things like classroom exercises which a teacher might not want students to see, or to prevent others from tampering with the programs. APL2 has a more general way to lock functions using the dyadic system function □*FX*, described in Chapter 24.

Displaying only part of a function

Thus far we have asked for the entire function to be displayed. What if the function is a long one and we are interested only in a single line, say, 4? The display command for this is very similar to what we have used previously:

```
      ∇STAT[4□]∇
[4]    L/X
```

If there had been no second ∇, line 4 would have been displayed and then the system would ask us what we wanted to do to it by returning [4] again,

```
      ∇STAT[4□]
[4]    L/X
[4]
```

and now we can close out the function by entering ∇:

```
[4]    ∇
```

By now you should be getting the idea that the □ (quad) is used in APL to display things. Fancifully speaking, you can think of it here as a window to see what's going on inside the function. The rules are that [□] displays everything, [n□] displays the particular line, and [□m] displays all lines beginning with the one specified to the end of the function.

```
      ∇STAT[□3]
[3]    (+/X)÷N
[4]    L/X
[5]    (⌈/X)-L/X
    ∇
[6]
```

After listing lines 3, 4 and 5, the system offers the next available line number, 6, to let us continue adding lines. What's a user to do if the function has, say, fifty lines and he wants to display only lines 3, 4 and 5? The way to display only these lines is to enter [☐3] and let it run until you've seen what you need to see. Just press ATTN or BREAK to stop the display. However, unless the original display command was closed with a ∇, you will be in function definition mode after interrupting. Plan your next step accordingly.

Detailed editing of part of a line

Getting into more specific and limited changes, let's start over again with a fresh copy of 1 *CLASS*.

```
)LOAD 1 CLASS
SAVED  14.45.33 02/20/83
```

As we've already said, this wipes out what was in the active workspace and replaces it with an exact image of the workspace being loaded.

Now display *STAT*, but without the closing ∇:

```
        ∇STAT[☐]
    ∇ STAT X
[1]   N←ρX
[2]   (+/X)÷N
[3]   ⌈/X
[4]   ⌊/X
    ∇
[5]
```

It is again in its original form, and the system is waiting for us to enter line 5.

Up to now we have replaced entire lines. But suppose a line is very long and complicated, and our change is to involve only a few characters. For example, say we'd like to change the variable *N* to *COUNT* in lines 1 and 2 of *STAT*. Obviously, in this case we could type both lines over since they are quite short. However, it will be more instructive to use the detailed editing capabilities of APL to make the changes.

We're still in function definition mode, since pressing RETURN gets

```
[5]
```

To direct the cursor to the specific characters that need revising, what we enter has the following format:

[line number ☐ estimate of what display position the first change occurs at]

In this case we'll deliberately make the cursor space over twenty positions (from the left margin) and then backspace manually to the *N* just to show that our estimate doesn't have to be accurate:

```
[5]    [1☐20]
```

The system will respond by displaying [1] and then positioning the cursor twenty spaces over on the next line:

```
[1]   N←ρX
                ⍺
```

We wish to strike out the letter *N*. For this, the slash (/, same symbol as reduction) is used. *COUNT* has five characters for which space needs to be provided. To be sure we get enough space we enter 8 after the slash as shown, once we have manually backspaced the cursor to the *N*. This inserts eight spaces just prior to the character (here ←) above the number entered:

```
[1]   N←ρX
      /8
```

After pressing RETURN, the system responds as follows, with the cursor finally resting at the position where ⍺ is shown.

```
[1]     ⍺          ←ρX
```

We can now enter $COUNT$ in the space provided:

```
[1]    COUNT    ←ρX
```

Having made this change we are asked if we want to do anything with line 2. Before doing anything else, display line 1:

```
[2]    [1□]
[1]    COUNT←ρX
[1]
```

N is gone, $COUNT$ has been inserted, and the extra blanks have been deleted.

Now directing control to the eighth position on line 2, we use the same procedure to insert $COUNT$ at the end of the line. Eight positions are too few in this case, so we'll have to use the space bar to move the cursor over some more after it comes to rest in the eighth position:

```
[1]    [2□8]
[2]    (+/X)÷N
              /
[2]    (+/X)÷COUNT
[3]    ∇
```

Since the insertion is to be made at the end of the line, no provision for extra space is necessary. Displaying the entire revised function, we see that the changes have been made:

```
       ∇STAT[□]∇
[1]    COUNT←ρX
[2]    (+/X)÷COUNT
[3]    ⌈/X
[4]    ⌊/X
    ∇
```

Here are more things you can do with detailed editing. First, the command [n□0] displays line n and moves the cursor to the end of the line to allow for additions on the right as shown,

```
       ∇STAT[2□0]
[2]    (+/X)÷COUNT▨
```

and we can now extend the line:

```
[2]    (+/X)÷COUNTER∇
```

Local variables are conveniently added to the header of a function by using [0□0] to position the cursor at the right end of the header line.

Second, if more than nine spaces have to be inserted at any one place in a line, the letters of the alphabet may be used, each letter being assigned a numerical value equal to five times its index position in the alphabet. Here is an example:

```
       ∇STAT[1□12]
[1]    COUNT←ρX
              B
[1]    COUNT▨                ←ρX
```

The letter B causes 10 spaces to be inserted, and the cursor comes to rest at the position marked by the ▨ above. Now it's as though *you* had entered the line as shown above, and you can make whatever additions you choose. In the example below, the letters ER are entered in that space and followed by ∇ at the end of the line:

```
[1]    COUNTER        ←ρX∇
```

You can apply detailed editing to the line number itself. The effect is to generate a new line with the new number. The old line still remains. If you make other changes, those changes are carried to the new line, but the original line is unchanged.

The APL*PLUS and Sharp Systems make use of the comma, period and semicolon to give added flexibility to detailed line editing. When a comma is entered, all characters following it are placed directly in the line to be changed, and then the line is redisplayed. The cursor comes to rest at the first created blank position, or at the end of the line if there were no blank positions created. For example:

```
        ∇STAT[1□7]
[1]     COUNTER←ρX
        ///////,N
[1]     N←ρX▨
```

Pressing RETURN now directs control to the next line. Alternatively, if you have more than one change to make on the same line, use the semicolon instead of the comma. It works the same way, except that the line is again displayed, with the cursor coming to rest just after the last character you inserted. If you have only one change to make to the line, use the period instead of the comma or semicolon. In this case the change is inserted as usual, but control goes immediately to the next line.

```
[2]     [2□10]
[2]     (+/X)÷COUNTER
                ///////.N
[3]     ∇
```

Editing the last line entered in calculator mode

On the APL*PLUS and Sharp Systems, you can apply detailed editing to the last line you entered in calculator mode. You inform the system you wish to make changes to the last line entered by the system command)EDIT followed by the position number. That is,)EDIT 12 is similar to [n□12]. The line is redisplayed, and you can now use any of the characters / , ; . as well as digits and letters to delete, insert or position changes to the line. When the editing is complete, the line is again executed for you, or at least attempted, if you make a mistake like the one that follows here:

```
        X←2 3 7 4 2
        +/X
4.5
        )EDIT 7
        +/X
        /..5×(⌈
SYNTAX ERROR
        0.5×(⌈/X
              ∧
        )EDIT
        0.5×(⌈/X)+⌊/X
```

In the last example,)EDIT without a number following it is equivalent to [n□0]—the cursor moved to the end of the line to allow for additions to the right.

)EDIT works on the last executable line only. It ignores intervening system commands entirely. It also ignores all lines entered in function definition. However, there is one very interesting and useful quirk in its behavior. It can be used to capture the last executed line and include it in a function. This can be a real blessing when developing subsequent lines of a function by experimenting with each line in execution mode. Suppose you had just developed an algorithm for midrange, .5×(⌈/X)+⌊/X, in execution mode and now wanted to include it as the last line in STAT:

```
        ∇STAT
[5]     )EDIT
[5]     0.5×(⌈/X)+⌊/X∇
```

Because)EDIT is such a popular feature, it has been made even easier to use. The entry)20 is just as good as)EDIT 20, and) is equivalent to)EDIT or)EDIT 0.

Other ways to edit functions and lines

Besides the editing facilities that are provided as an inherent part of APL systems, many terminals provide features that can be employed to edit lines and functions. On the IBM 3278 display terminal, for instance, the cursor may be moved under any line previously displayed, even on a prior page, or belonging to some other function. After RETURN is pressed, the line, complete with its line number, appears in the input area of the screen. The INSERT and DELETE keys may then be used with the cursor to perform very detailed and sophisticated editing. However, no matter what value you give m in the command [n□m], the cursor comes to rest at the end of the line. In other words, it is always equivalent to [n□0].

There are additional variants on the standard APL editing commands which are available in APL2. These make life a little easier for the user who may have access to them.

commands	[Δ]	all lines (be careful!)
to delete	[ΔS]	all lines in vector S
	[ΔL1−L2]	all lines from $L1$ through $L2$
	[Δ−L2]	all lines from the beginning through $L2$
	[ΔL1−]	all lines from $L1$ to the end
commands	[□S]	all lines in S
to display	[□L1−L2]	all lines from $L1$ through $L2$
	[□−L2]	all lines from the beginning through $L2$
	[□L1−]	all lines from $L1$ to the end

Should you goof in deleting lines, the action can be rescinded with [→] or →, which restores the function.

Full screen editors

Many APL systems which support display terminals also offer more advanced editing capabilities than those included in the traditional APL editor described in this chapter. These full-screen editors differ from system to system in how they are invoked and in the specific commands and features available to the user.

But they all have these common characteristics: (1) changes can be made in place anywhere on the screen; (2) there are commands to do global finds of names, etc. within the function and change them; and (3) users always see the current version of the function displayed (although line renumbering still doesn't take place until after the function is closed and redisplayed). If you have a display terminal on a system which offers this capability, use it. The ease with which changes can be made will more than compensate for having to learn the commands specific to the editor.

Much later in the book we will discuss other powerful ways to modify functions, which provide an adjunct or alternative to the ones of this chapter. There are even ways to convert a function to a character variable, change the character variable under program control, and then reconvert it to a function.

Summary of editing features

The editing facilities covered in this chapter will 'soak in' as you write more involved functions. You should refer to this chapter frequently until editing becomes second nature for you. For that reason, we provide the following synopsis of the major features:

∇*FN*	open *FN*, ready for entry of first new line.
[3]	ready for entry or reentry of line 3.
[3.1]	ready for entry of a line to follow line 3.
[3□]	display line 3, ready for reentry of line 3.
[□]	display entire *FN*, ready for entry of first new line.
[□3]	display line 3 and all following ready for entry of first new line.
[Δ3]	(or [~3]) delete line 3, ready for entry of first new line.
[3□0]	display line 3, ready to add onto end of line 3.
[3□10]	display line 3, cursor at position 10 ready for insertions.
/	delete character above.
digit	insert specified number of spaces.
letter	insert 5 spaces for *A*, 10 for *B*, etc.
.	insert following text, ready for next line (Sharp and APL*PLUS Systems).
,	insert following text, ready at end of same line (Sharp and APL*PLUS Systems).
;	insert following text, cursor positioned at end of inserted text (Sharp and APL*PLUS Systems).
∇	close function definition.
⍫	close function definition and lock function.
)*ERASE FN*	erase function entirely.
)*EDIT* 10	display last line executed, ready to insert at position 10 (Sharp and APL*PLUS Systems).
)10	display last line executed, ready to insert at position 10 (Sharp and APL*PLUS Systems).
)*EDIT*	display last line executed, ready at end of line (Sharp and APL*PLUS Systems).
)	display last line executed, ready at end of line. (Sharp and APL*PLUS Systems).

PROBLEMS

)*LOAD* 1 *CLASS* and enter the following sample program to calculate the standard deviation of a set of numbers (see problem 6, Chapter 8):

```
      ∇ STD N
[1]     R←AVG N
[2]     R←R-N
[3]     R←AVG R*2
[4]     ANS←R*0.5 ∇
```

1. Display the function and direct control to line 5.

2. Use detailed editing to change *ANS* on line 4 to *R*.

3. Edit the header to return an explicit result *R*.

4. Eliminate line 2.

5. Display the function and remain in function definition mode.

6. Change line 3 to *R←AVG(R-N)*2*.

7. Display lines 3 and 4.

8. Close out the function.

9. Use a single entry to open up the function again and reinsert the original contents of line 2.

10. Change line 3 back to its original form with detailed editing.

11. Insert just prior to line 1 a command that will display the number of elements in *N*. Then close out the function.

12. Delete the function from the active workspace.

13. Without reloading the workspace or copying the function you just erased, try to display it now.

Chapter 11: Workspaces

In the previous chapters, all variables that you assigned and functions that you defined were lost whenever you signed off. The only recoverable work was in 1 *CLASS* and 1 *AIDRILL*. And the only reason you could still access them was that when you loaded one of these workspaces into your own active workspace, you were actually taking an exact *image* of the original, not the original itself. Although you lost the image whenever you signed off, you could always obtain another image later.

We need to know how to preserve what we do for posterity. In this chapter we'll go through a series of exercises designed to show how you can manipulate workspaces. To ensure continuity while learning the features covered in this chapter, you should repeat the entire sequence of commands exactly as they are given in this chapter. Diagrams of the workspace contents are included at appropriate points to help you.

Workspace contents

Start off by entering

```
)CLEAR
CLEAR WS
```

As we pointed out earlier, this is one of a family of system commands, like the sign-on and sign-off. It has the effect of wiping out all the work done in the active workspace and replacing it with a clean workspace, such as is normally obtained at the sign-on. Remember that the active workspace is the one that you have currently available to you, in which all your work is now being done.

In VS APL the)*CLEAR* command may be followed by a number, e.g.,)*CLEAR* 256000, to set up a clear workspace whose size in *bytes* (a byte is a space needed for one character) is the number entered.

To show that this workspace is now empty as a result of the)*CLEAR* command, we can use the commands

```
)FNS
)VARS
```

ACTIVE WS

```
CLEAR WS
- - - - - -
```

to see that there isn't anything in the active workspace.

Since the purpose of this chapter is to show you how to save functions and variables for future use, we'll need some example functions. For this, let's enter the function *HYP*:

```
      ∇R←A HYP B
[1]   R←((A*2)+B*2)*.5∇
```

ACTIVE WS

```
CLEAR WS
- - - - - -

HYP
```

Let's now set a couple of variables and observe that they appear in the $)VARS$ listing:

```
PI←3.14159
V←1  2  3  4  5
```

ACTIVE WS

```
┌─────────────┐
│ CLEAR  WS   │
│─ ─ ─ ─ ─ ─  │
│ HYP      PI │
│          V  │
│             │
└─────────────┘
```

and the command

```
        )VARS
PI       V
```

For a second function, enter

```
        ∇TOSS
[1]     ?2∇
```

and then obtain a new listing of functions to confirm that $TOSS$ has indeed been stored.

```
        )FNS
HYP       TOSS
```

ACTIVE WS

```
┌─────────────┐
│ CLEAR  WS   │
│─ ─ ─ ─ ─ ─  │
│ HYP      PI │
│ TOSS     V  │
│             │
└─────────────┘
```

Saving and recovering a workspace

We could continue entering functions and variables, but for purposes of illustration let's pretend that we're through with our work at this point and want to preserve these functions and variables for use later.

The system command $)SAVE$ does this. It puts an image of the active workspace into a more permanent storage facility, called your *private library*. When a workspace is saved, you give it a name so that it can be retrieved later. Many systems limit the name to eight or fewer characters. There is no relation between this name and the names of variables and functions inside the workspace, although you should always try to select names with some mnemonic content.

We'll use the name $FIRST$ for the work previously entered:

```
        )SAVE FIRST
14.12.04 02/26/83
```

We get a message back giving the time and date. This means that $)SAVE$ was successful and an image of the workspace is now stored with the name $FIRST$ in your private library.

There is a command which lists the names of all the saved workspaces in your library. This command is $)LIB$ or $)WSLIB$, depending on the particular system.

```
        )LIB
FIRST
```

ACTIVE WS

```
┌─────────────┐
│ FIRST       │
│─ ─ ─ ─ ─ ─  │
│ HYP      PI │
│ TOSS     V  │
│             │
└─────────────┘
```

PRIVATE LIBRARY

```
┌─────────────┬──────┐
│ FIRST       │      │
│─ ─ ─ ─ ─ ─  │─ ─ ─ │
│ HYP      PI │      │
│ TOSS     V  │      │
│             │      │
```

Only one workspace is listed because that's all we have saved so far.)*FNS* shows that *HYP* and *TOSS* are still around:

```
        )FNS
HYP     TOSS
```

Remember that we saved an *image* of the active workspace. Let's now get a fresh workspace:

```
        )CLEAR
CLEAR WS
```

ACTIVE WS	PRIVATE LIBRARY
CLEAR WS	*FIRST*
	HYP *PI* *TOSS* *V*

Imagine that it's now the following day and we are ready to do some work with *HYP* and *TOSS*. They were lost from the active workspace when we cleared, but there is an exact image stored in our library in the workspace named *FIRST*. To recover this image, execute the command

```
        )LOAD FIRST
SAVED  14.12.04 02/26/83
```

The response tells when it was last saved. In VS APL, the)*LOAD* command can be followed by a number specifying a desired size of the active workspace. For example,)*LOAD FIRST* 200000 changes the size of the active workspace to 200000 bytes. Or, if the size of the saved workspace forces a change of size for the active workspace, you'll get a *WS SIZE IS...* message.

Our functions and variables are available to us once again:

```
        )FNS
HYP     TOSS
        )VARS
PI      V
```

ACTIVE WS	PRIVATE LIBRARY
FIRST	*FIRST*
HYP *PI* *TOSS* *V*	*HYP* *PI* *TOSS* *V*

Let's check on *V* to see whether it's still what it's supposed to be:

```
        V
1 2 3 4 5
```

Most people have more than one project cooking at any one time, and usually save a separate workspace for each project. How is this done? To illustrate the procedure,

```
        )CLEAR
CLEAR WS
```

ACTIVE WS	PRIVATE LIBRARY
CLEAR WS	*FIRST*
	HYP *PI* *TOSS* *V*

and define the function $SQRT$:

```
    ∇R←SQRT X
[1]   R←X*.5∇
```

ACTIVE WS		PRIVATE LIBRARY	
CLEAR WS		FIRST	
SQRT		HYP PI TOSS V	

Now save an image of the active workspace (which contains only the function $SQRT$) with the name $SECOND$:

```
    )SAVE SECOND
 14.12.21 02/26/83
```

Before going on, let's be sure we understand that all we have immediate access to at this point is the active workspace with only the function $SQRT$ in it. An image of this workspace, with the name $SECOND$, is also in your private library.

```
    )FNS
SQRT
    )LIB
FIRST
SECOND
```

ACTIVE WS		PRIVATE LIBRARY		
SECOND		FIRST	SECOND	
SQRT		HYP PI TOSS V	SQRT	

If we want to use any of the functions or variables in the workspace named $FIRST$ now, we must load it. Then we see that HYP and $TOSS$ are back in the active workspace:

```
    )LOAD FIRST
SAVED  14.12.04 02/26/83
    )FNS
HYP     TOSS
```

ACTIVE WS		PRIVATE LIBRARY		
FIRST		FIRST	SECOND	
HYP PI TOSS V		HYP PI TOSS V	SQRT	

Now we'll load $SECOND$ and look at its contents. We don't need to clear between loadings because the act of loading replaces the contents of the active workspace with the material in the workspace being loaded.

```
    )LOAD SECOND
SAVED  14.12.21 02/26/83
    )FNS
SQRT
```

ACTIVE WS		PRIVATE LIBRARY		
SECOND		FIRST	SECOND	
SQRT		HYP PI TOSS V	SQRT	

The examples above show that we can access the contents of only one workspace at a time, specifically, the one whose image is in the active workspace.

Let's save yet another workspace with the name $THIRD$. This time, just to be different, load 1 $CLASS$, and get a list of the functions:

```
      )LOAD 1 CLASS
SAVED  14.45.33 02/20/83

      )FNS
ADD       AGAIN    AREA     AUTO     AVG      AVG1      AVG2     AVG3     AVG4     AVG5
AVG6      CHANGE   CHARMAT  CLR      CMP      CMPN      CMPX     CMPY     COMPINT  COMPOSE
COS       CP       C2GT99   DEC      DENUMCODE          DESCRIBE          DICE
DUPLICATES         ENT      EVAL     F        FACT         (list interrupted.)
```

ACTIVE WS	PRIVATE LIBRARY		
1 *CLASS*	*FIRST*	*SECOND*	
ADD AUTO *AGAIN AVG* *AREA* · · ·	*HYP PI* *TOSS V*	*SQRT*	

The contents (or more precisely, an *image* of the contents) of 1 *CLASS* will now be saved as *THIRD*:

```
      )SAVE THIRD
14.12.35 02/26/83
```

Our listing of saved workspaces has grown:

```
      )LIB
FIRST
SECOND
THIRD
```

ACTIVE WS	PRIVATE LIBRARY		
1 *CLASS*	*FIRST*	*SECOND*	*THIRD*
ADD AUTO *AGAIN AVG* *AREA* · · ·	*HYP PI* *TOSS V*	*SQRT*	*ADD AUTO* *AGAIN AVG* *AREA* · · ·

The *LIB* command produces an alphabetized list. Furthermore, just as with *FNS* and *VARS*, a partial listing can be obtained:

```
      )LIB SE
SECOND
THIRD
```

APL2 allows a variant of this command:)*LIB PE ST* lists all workspaces whose names begin with *PE* through *ST*.

Let's clear again, define a couple of variables, and save them in *FOURTH*:

```
      )CLEAR
CLEAR WS
      X←4 6 8 10
      Y←2 5 8

      )SAVE FOURTH
NOT SAVED, USER STORAGE FULL
```

We are told, in effect, that we have only three workspaces allotted to us and they are used up, so we're out of luck.

Some versions of APL have a)*QUOTA* command. In APLSV, the first number in the reply is the number of workspaces allowed and the fourth number is the number of workspaces actually used. (The other parts of the reply will be explained later.) In VS APL, the amount of library space is based on the number of bytes actually stored rather than the number of workspaces. The first line of the reply tells the total number of bytes permitted in your private library and the number of bytes already used.

Dropping a saved workspace

If X and Y were really some big functions or tables of data and we wanted desperately to save them, then our question is: which of the three workspaces in our library can we afford to sacrifice? Again, look at the list:

```
      )LIB
FIRST
SECOND
THIRD
```

Assuming we don't need $THIRD$, let's try to save X and Y, which are still in the active workspace, in $THIRD$:

```
      )SAVE THIRD
NOT SAVED, THIS WS IS CLEAR WS
```

We are prevented from saving it in $THIRD$ because we already stored a workspace named $THIRD$. Again APL keeps you from inadvertently destroying a saved workspace by replacing it with another workspace with the same name.

As we'll soon see, there is a way to include X and Y in $THIRD$ without destroying what is already there. But for now, suppose we really wanted to get rid of $THIRD$. The command

```
      )DROP THIRD
14.12.47 02/26/83
```

does this, the response giving the time and day when the workspace was dropped. $THIRD$ is now gone, as shown by

```
      )LIB
FIRST
SECOND
```

ACTIVE WS	PRIVATE LIBRARY		
CLEAR WS	FIRST	SECOND	
X	HYP PI		
Y	TOSS V	SQRT	

We have no functions in the active workspace, but it still contains the two variables X and Y:

```
      )FNS
      )VARS
X       Y
```

This isn't a surprise, since we haven't done anything to the active workspace yet. Now that there is room available, let's save these variables in a workspace called $XYDATA$.

```
      )SAVE XYDATA
14.12.48 02/26/83
      )LIB
FIRST
SECOND
XYDATA
```

ACTIVE WS	PRIVATE LIBRARY		
XYDATA	FIRST	SECOND	XYDATA
X	HYP PI		X
Y	TOSS V	SQRT	Y

Altering a saved workspace

What if we wanted to merge the variables X and Y into $FIRST$? Here is what happens when we try this:

```
      )SAVE FIRST
NOT SAVED, THIS WS IS XYDATA
```

What this means is that the contents of our active workspace have already been saved with the name *XYDATA* and therefore can't be saved also with the name *FIRST*. To save the material in the active workspace into *FIRST*, we would have to drop *FIRST* and then save the active workspace with the name *FIRST*. Later we'll see how the *COPY* command can be used to merge two workspaces.

Another way to change the status of a saved workspace is illustrated by the following sequence:

```
      )LOAD FIRST
SAVED  14.12.04 02/26/83
```

ACTIVE WS		
FIRST		
HYP	*PI*	
TOSS	*V*	

PRIVATE LIBRARY		
FIRST	*SECOND*	*XYDATA*
HYP *PI*		*X*
TOSS *V*	*SQRT*	*Y*

Let's now define the function *SIGN*:

```
      ∇R←SIGN X
[1]   R←(X>0)-X<0∇
      )FNS
HYP      SIGN     TOSS
```

ACTIVE WS		
FIRST		
HYP	*PI*	
SIGN	*V*	
TOSS		

PRIVATE LIBRARY		
FIRST	*SECOND*	*XYDATA*
HYP *PI*		*X*
TOSS *V*	*SQRT*	*Y*

Here is what happens when we try to save this active workspace into *SECOND*:

```
      )SAVE SECOND
NOT SAVED, THIS WS IS FIRST
```

We are again prevented from doing so because the active workspace contains an image of *FIRST*, not *SECOND*. However, we can save into *FIRST*. Since the active workspace has the name *FIRST* already associated with it, when we now save, it isn't necessary to repeat the name *FIRST* (though it wouldn't hurt matters any to use it):

```
      )SAVE
14.13.00 02/26/83 FIRST
```

ACTIVE WS		
FIRST		
HYP	*PI*	
SIGN	*V*	
TOSS		

PRIVATE LIBRARY		
FIRST	*SECOND*	*XYDATA*
HYP *PI*		*X*
SIGN *V*	*SQRT*	*Y*
TOSS		

The response is the time of the saving and the name of the saved workspace.

FIRST is now updated. This can be shown by clearing and reloading. Notice that the time and day reported by the *LOAD* are those associated with the most recent *SAVE*.

```
      )CLEAR
CLEAR WS
      )FNS
      )LOAD FIRST
SAVED  14.13.00 02/26/83
      )FNS
HYP      SIGN     TOSS
```

The CONTINUE workspace

On time sharing systems each user has provision for a special workspace named *CONTINUE*. Should you lose your telephone connection with the APL system before signing off, everything in your active workspace would be available automatically to you when you sign back on. This is because the system places an image of your active workspace into a workspace named *CONTINUE*, and reloads it at the next sign-on, as indicated by the response *SAVED...* following the system identification message.

CONTINUE is really an extra workspace that isn't part of the regular user allotment, and it can be used for emergencies if the other workspaces aren't available. However, you have to be very careful with it. Usually, whenever there is a failure in the system or the telephone lines, the contents of *CONTINUE* are replaced by whatever is in the active workspace. So if you must, you can save work into *CONTINUE*, since it is always available to you. But it isn't a wise move for long-term storage because of the danger posed by the possible involuntary replacement of its contents.

Following our example, let's define a vector *X* in the active workspace:

X←2 3 7 4 2

ACTIVE WS		PRIVATE LIBRARY		
FIRST		*FIRST*	*SECOND*	*XYDATA*
HYP *PI*		*HYP* *PI*		*X*
SIGN *V*		*SIGN* *V*	*SQRT*	*Y*
TOSS *X*		*TOSS*		

If you were to lose your connection with the computer at this point, an image of your active workspace would be automatically placed in *CONTINUE*. And of course your active workspace doesn't exist when you're not signed on. The next time you sign on, rather than starting with a clear workspace, the *CONTINUE* workspace is automatically loaded for you.

ACTIVE WS		PRIVATE LIBRARY				
CONTINUE		*FIRST*	*SECOND*	*XYDATA*		*CONTINUE*
HYP *PI*		*HYP* *PI*		*X*		*HYP* *PI*
SIGN *V*		*SIGN* *V*	*SQRT*	*Y*		*SIGN* *V*
TOSS *X*		*TOSS*				*TOSS* *X*

You can simulate losing your telephone connection with the *)CONTINUE* command. It places an image of your active workspace in *CONTINUE*, then signs you off the system and severs the phone connection as does *)OFF*. *)CONTINUE HOLD* and *)OFF HOLD* are similar except that they keep the phone line active briefly so someone else can sign on without having to redial.

Locked workspaces

Workspaces which contain material of a sensitive or private nature can be protected with passwords in a manner similar to the user sign-on. A password, whose use is strictly optional, may be included, changed or dropped when saving the workspace. Once included, it must be be used to load it:

```
      )LOAD FIRST
SAVED  14.13.00 02/26/83
      )SAVE FIRST:GW33
  14.13.10 02/26/83
      )LOAD FIRST
WS LOCKED
      )LOAD FIRST:GW33
SAVED  14.13.10 02/26/83
```

A password is removed by resaving the workspace using the colon only, as follows:

)SAVE FIRST:
14.13.11 02/26/83

In VS APL the password is ignored for your own workspaces.

Using other people's libraries

You know how to use the *LIB* command to get a listing of the saved workspaces in your private library. Someone else may have saved workspaces in his private library with the same names as yours, but there is never any confusion, since each user's workspaces are associated with his own user identification (same as sign-on).

In APLSV, Sharp and APL*PLUS Systems you can load an image of someone else's workspaces into your active workspace like this:

)LOAD 78974 INTERACT
SAVED 12.30.59 05/09/80

ACTIVE WS	PRIVATE LIBRARY 78974
78974 *INTERACT* ----------- (*FNS*) (*VARS*)	78974 *INTERACT* ----------- (*FNS*) (*VARS*)

Here we are loading the workspace named *INTERACT* that is stored in user 78974's private library. Since for reasons of privacy you can't execute *)LIB* on anyone else's library, user 78974 would have had to tell you which workspace names he is using for you to load them.

Such easy promiscuity isn't possible in VS APL. Instead, VS APL has a feature called a *project library* for groups of users who need to freely share workspaces. For authorized users, loading and copying material from their project library takes place in the same way as common libraries (see below).

VS APL workspaces can be moved between people who are not in the same project, but it is a cumbersome procedure. You should consult your system administrator for assistance should you need to do this.

Common libraries

The libraries with numbers between 1 and 999 are intended to hold workspaces of general or common interest, and are called *common libraries*. The contents of any of these can be displayed using the *LIB* command followed by the library number. As discussed on page 91, a partial listing beginning, say, at *AI* can be obtained by:

)LIB 1 AI
AIDRILL
CLASS
FILEAID
FILEPRINT
FILES
FORMAT
NEWS
TYPEDRILL
WSFNS

ACTIVE WS	COMMON LIBRARY 1			
78974 *INTERACT* ----------- (*FNS*) (*VARS*)	*APLCOURSE* *DESCRIBE* *EASYDRILL* *TEACH*	*CLASS* *ADD AUTO* *AGAIN AVG* *AREA ...*	*NEWS* (*FNS*) (*VARS*)	*TYPEDRILL* (*FNS*) (*VARS*)

The list you get will probably differ from what is shown here because common libraries aren't static; they are different on each APL system, and they change from time to time. Notice that *CLASS* and *AIDRILL*, which have been used before, are in the list. Ordinarily, individual APL users cannot save material into a common library or drop any workspaces from it. If you were to try to save an image of your active workspace into someone else's private library or into a common library such as 1 *CLASS*, you would not be permitted to because yours wasn't the user number that saved it the first time:

```
     )SAVE 1 CLASS                           )SAVE 78974 LITTER
NOT SAVED, THIS WS IS 78974 INTERACT    IMPROPER LIBRARY REFERENCE
```

In some systems certain libraries have been designated as 'load only' for security reasons. Attempts to save, rename or copy workspaces in such a library won't be successful.

Library 1 is a general interest library on most APL systems. Other common libraries may or may not be present on a given system. The library listings may seem meaningless to you, but there are practical ways to find out what is in a strange workspace. As an example, enter

```
     )LOAD 1 CLASS
SAVED  14.45.33 02/20/83
```

The load commands are slightly different for one's own workspaces as compared to those in the common libraries or other private libraries: you must include the library number. Its use is optional for your own library.

Having loaded the workspace 1 *CLASS*, the first thing to do is to get a list of the functions and variables:

```
     )FNS
ADD        AGAIN    AREA     AUTO     AVG     AVG1     AVG2     AVG3    AVG4      AVG5
AVG6       CHANGE   CHARMAT  CLR      CMP     CMPN     CMPX     CMPY    COMPINT   COMPOSE
COS        CP       C2GT99   DEC      DENUMCODE         DESCRIBE         DICE
DUPLICATES          ENT      EVAL     F       FACT     FACTORIALS        FIND      FINDROW
FIX        FUNEDIT  GAME     GEO2     GEO3    GETFN    GO       GRAPH   HEXA      HY
HYP        INPUT    INT      INVOICERUN       LASTVISIT         MEAN    NAMESONLY
NEWPATIENT          NEWVISIT          NUMCODE OBSERVE ON        PEREL   RECT      REP
REPF       REPL     REPLENISH         RETIE   RIGHTJUST         ROWNAMES          RUN
SALES      SD       SELECT   SELECT   SETUP   SHOWME   SIGN     SLAM    SORT      SPELL
SPLINECALC          SPLINEEVAL        SPRED   SQ       SQRT     STAT    STATEMENT
STATISTICS          SUB      SUBST    SUM     SUSPENDED         TOSS    TOTVISITS
TRANSP     VIG      WSSHOW   DSLOPE   ESLOPE  XSLOPE

     )VARS
A          ADBASE   B        CARDS    CIRCUIT D        FURN     M       MILEAGE NUMDATA
P          PREVIOUSTIME      PRODREV  QUOTE   SPL      TAB0     TAB1    TAB2     TAB3
VECT       X        Y        WSID     ACH
```

Look for names that are suggestive of instructions, like *HOW* or *DESCRIBE*. Executing a few of them will usually give you the information you need, since most professional APL system librarians and managers use these conventions.

```
     DESCRIBE
THE FUNCTIONS IN THIS WORKSPACE ARE USED AS EXAMPLES IN THE TEXT,
APL - AN INTERACTIVE APPROACH (THIRD EDITION),
BY LEONARD GILMAN AND ALLEN J. ROSE (WILEY, 1983).

CONTENTS OF THIS WORKSPACE ARE COPYRIGHT 1983 BY GILMAN AND ROSE.
```

Even if there is no description of the contents of a workspace, you can often gain some information by displaying functions with interesting names. In particular, looking at the header will tell you how many arguments a function has and whether it returns an explicit result.

Some workspaces require so much description that complete documentation in the workspace would take up too much space and take a lot of time to display. For many of these, separate instruction manuals may be available or the documentation may be stored in another workspace.

Workspace descriptions are very important. You'll realize just how important the first time you have to use someone's workspace which is not adequately described. Furthermore, you should always prepare descriptions for your own workspaces. It makes it much less painful to use the functions after they and you have lain fallow for a while.

The workspace identification command

After an hours-long session at the keyboard, with your fingers worn down to the bone, you can't be blamed for having forgotten the name of the workspace you started with. The command)*WSID* (for *workspace identification*) command will tell you:

```
    )WSID
IS 1 CLASS
```

ACTIVE WS	PRIVATE LIBRARY			
1 CLASS	FIRST	SECOND	XYDATA	CONTINUE
ADD AUTO	HYP PI		X	HYP PI
AGAIN AVG	SIGN V	SQRT	Y	SIGN V
AREA ...	TOSS			TOSS X

It gives the name (and library number, if not your own) of the last workspace you loaded or saved. In other words, when you save an image of the active workspace, the workspace identification of the active workspace becomes the name of the saved workspace. Of course, if you just signed on and haven't yet loaded or saved a workspace,)*WSID* replies with *CLEAR WS*.

The)*WSID* command can also be used to change the workspace identification of the active workspace:

```
    )WSID XYDATA
WAS 1 CLASS
```

ACTIVE WS	PRIVATE LIBRARY			
XYDATA	FIRST	SECOND	XYDATA	CONTINUE
ADD AUTO	HYP PI		X	HYP PI
AGAIN AVG	SIGN V	SQRT	Y	SIGN V
AREA ...	TOSS			TOSS X

At this point, you have tricked the active workspace into thinking it came from *XYDATA*. If you now issue a *SAVE*, it will put an image into saved workspace *XYDATA*:

```
    )SAVE
14.13.36 02/26/83 XYDATA
```

ACTIVE WS	PRIVATE LIBRARY			
XYDATA	FIRST	SECOND	XYDATA	CONTINUE
ADD AUTO	HYP PI		ADD AUTO	HYP PI
AGAIN AVG	SIGN V	SQRT	AGAIN AVG	SIGN V
AREA ...	TOSS		AREA ...	TOSS X

Without)*WSID*, the shortest way you could have moved the contents of the active workspace to workspace *XYDATA* would have been)*DROP XYDATA* followed by)*SAVE XYDATA*.

Copying a workspace

The command)*COPY* provides the very important ability to gather selected functions and variables from saved workspaces into the active workspace without having to reenter them at the keyboard. Unlike the)*LOAD* command,)*COPY* doesn't replace the contents of the active workspace. It merges the copied variables and functions with those already there.

The following sequence puts the function *SIGN* (from workspace *FIRST*) in workspace *SECOND*:

)LOAD SECOND
SAVED 14.12.21 02/26/83

ACTIVE WS	PRIVATE LIBRARY			
SECOND	*FIRST*	*SECOND*	*XYDATA*	*CONTINUE*
SQRT	*HYP PI* *SIGN V* *TOSS*	*SQRT*	*ADD AUTO* *AGAIN AVG* *AREA ...*	*HYP PI* *SIGN V* *TOSS X*

)COPY FIRST SIGN
SAVED 14.13.11 02/26/83

ACTIVE WS	PRIVATE LIBRARY			
SECOND	*FIRST*	*SECOND*	*XYDATA*	*CONTINUE*
SIGN *SQRT*	*HYP PI* *SIGN V* *TOSS*	*SQRT*	*ADD AUTO* *AGAIN AVG* *AREA ...*	*HYP PI* *SIGN V* *TOSS X*

While the active workspace now contains the function *SIGN*, the saved workspace *SECOND* doesn't until it is saved again:

)SAVE
14.13.46 02/26/83 *SECOND*

ACTIVE WS	PRIVATE LIBRARY			
SECOND	*FIRST*	*SECOND*	*XYDATA*	*CONTINUE*
SIGN *SQRT*	*HYP PI* *SIGN V* *TOSS*	*SIGN* *SQRT*	*ADD AUTO* *AGAIN AVG* *AREA ...*	*HYP PI* *SIGN V* *TOSS X*

Here are some variants of the *)COPY* command, shown by examples:

)COPY 1 CLASS AVG1   **)COPY 78974 INTERACT FREQ**
SAVED 14.45.33 02/20/83   *SAVED* 17.20.57 08/28/82

For security reasons, you can't copy from a *CONTINUE* workspace belonging to someone else. When copying from someone else's workspace or a common library workspace, the number (and password, if present) must be included. Several functions and variables may be copied at once. Just separate them with spaces. A *)COPY* command without a list of objects copies *all* functions and variables in. It is useful when you want to merge the contents of two workspaces, but shouldn't be used as an alternative to loading a workspace. A *COPY* uses much more computer resources than a *LOAD* does (like emptying a bag of sugar one spoonful at a time, instead of dumping it all at once).

Protected copying

If you copy a function or variable from some saved workspace, and there already is an object with the same name in the active workspace, then the new object replaces the old one in the active workspace *without warning*. If that's what you intended to do, fine. But with the ability to copy all objects without giving a specific list of which ones to copy, it's almost too easy to clobber something you wanted to keep.

To avoid this problem, use the *)PCOPY* command. It works exactly like *)COPY*, except that if there is an ambiguity (same name in the active workspace and the copied workspace), the object is *NOT COPIED*, preserving the original object in the active workspace.

Groups

Users who often have to copy a collection of objects from a heavily used workspace, their own or in a common library, will be pleased to hear that APL provides a facility to make such copying less burdensome.

This feature lets the owner of the workspace *group* a collection of global objects. Users of that workspace can then copy (or erase from their own version of the workspace) the entire group as though it were a single object.

For example, let's group in workspace $SECOND$ the various functions (copied from 1 $CLASS$) that attempt to calculate averages:

```
        )COPY 1 CLASS AVG1 AVG2 AVG3 AVG4 AVG5 AVG6
SAVED   14.45.33 02/20/83
        )GROUP AVGFNS AVG1 AVG2 AVG3 AVG4 AVG5 AVG6
        )SAVE SECOND
    14.14.06 02/26/83
        )CLEAR
CLEAR WS
        )COPY SECOND AVGFNS
SAVED   14.14.06 02/26/83
        )FNS
AVG1    AVG2     AVG3     AVG4     AVG5     AVG6
```

The assigned name of the group immediately follows the group command. It obeys the same rules for naming functions and variables, but cannot be the same as that of any other global object in the workspace. In other words, you use the same rules for naming variables, functions and groups, but any chosen name can be used only for one object at a time.

To display the groups in a workspace use the command $)GRPS$, or $)GRPS$ MA to get a partial listing starting at, say, MA. The command $)GRP$ $AVGFNS$ displays the members of the group $AVGFNS$.

The group $AVGFNS$ can be enlarged to incorporate new variables and functions:

```
        DATA←ι0
        )GROUP AVGFNS AVGFNS DATA
        )GRP AVGFNS
AVG1    AVG2     AVG3     AVG4     AVG5     AVG6     DATA
```

It may be *dispersed* (i.e., broken up, but with its members not erased) by entering

```
        )GROUP AVGFNS
        )GRPS
        )FNS
AVG1    AVG2     AVG3     AVG4     AVG5     AVG6
```

All the objects in a group may be erased at one time by executing $)ERASE$ on the group name, which is handy when you want to make room in the workspace, or frustrating if you had intended only to disperse the group.

Finally, groups can be made up of other groups. However, in copying, the constituent objects of the copied group aren't copied over—just the group name is.

Groups are convenient for a lot of activities, but they are not as well thought out as most other parts of APL systems, and their behavior may differ widely on different APL systems. For these reason, we suggest you not make heavy use of groups, but rather use the storage management techniques covered later in this book.

As if in recognition of this fact, APL2 doesn't support the group commands. Instead, it provides two facilities called *indirect copy* and *indirect erase*, which use the conventional $COPY$ and $ERASE$ commands with character matrices each of whose rows contains the name of an object to be copied or erased. The matrix must be enclosed in parentheses in the name list following the command.

```
        )CLEAR
CLEAR WS
        )COPY SECOND AVG1 AVG2 AVG3 AVG4 AVG5 AVG6
SAVED   14.14.06 02/26/83 (GMT-5)
```

```
      ANAMES←7 6ρ'AVG1  AVG2  AVG3  AVG4  AVG5  AVG6  ANAMES'
      )SAVE APL2DEMO
 14.20.55  2/28/83 (GMT-5)
      )ERASE (ANAMES)
      )FNS
      )COPY APL2DEMO (ANAMES)
·SAVED  14.20.55 02/28/83 (GMT-5)
      )FNS
AVG1    AVG2    AVG3    AVG4    AVG5    AVG6
      )VARS
ANAMES
      )ERASE (ANAMES)
      )FNS
      )VARS
```

The name of the matrix itself can be included as one of its own rows, so that it can be erased at the same time.

System functions that match system commands

On most APL systems, system commands cannot be included inside a function, but in many cases *system functions* are provided which achieve the desired effect. For example, to copy the variable $TAB3$ from 1 $CLASS$ on the APL*PLUS System, use $\square COPY$ '1 $CLASS$ $TAB3$' and to erase $TAB3$ from the active workspace use $\square EX$ '$TAB3$'. Most of the system functions return explicit results (sometimes coded) that are equivalent to the corresponding replies or error messages from the system commands. Those that most directly match the system commands treated in this chapter are in the table below. We'll deal with system functions in depth later; for now just be aware that they exist.

A summary of the effects of system commands on workspaces

To avoid unpleasant surprises such as having used)$DROP$ where you meant)$ERASE$, learn how each system command affects your stored and active workspaces. The equivalent system functions listed below aren't all available in every APL system.

SYSTEM COMMAND	CHANGES ACTIVE WS NAME	CHANGES ACTIVE WS CONTENTS	CHANGES LIBRARY CONTENTS	INFORMATION ONLY	EQUIVALENT SYSTEM FUNCTION
CLEAR	X	X			
CONTINUE	X		X		
COPY		X			$\square COPY$ 'WS OBJ'
DROP			X		
ERASE		X			$\square EX$ 'OBJ'
FNS				X	$\square NL$ 3
GROUP		X			
GRP				X	
GRPS				X	
LIB				X	$\square LIB$
LOAD	X	X			$\square LOAD$
OFF	X	X			
OFF HOLD	X	X			
PCOPY		X			$\square PCOPY$ 'WS OBJ'
SAVE			X		
SAVE NAME	X		X		
VARS				X	$\square NL$ 2
WSID				X	$\square WSID$
WSID NAME	X				
WSLIB				X	$\square WSLIB$

Some thoughts about workspace storage

We can't end this chapter without a few words about the limitations imposed on the APL user who insists on storing information only in workspaces. It should be apparent by this time that workspaces are somewhat constrained in what they can hold (although less so in VS APL than in other versions). As you become more knowledgeable you will learn other ways to 'stretch' the workspace by using space-saving algorithms, the APL equivalent of cars that get more miles to a tank of gasoline. But all they can accomplish for you is to let you go a bit farther with what you have.

This doesn't help you when you have a database which may be, say, ten times as large as the workspace you want to put it in. Something more is needed. This something is the notion of *files*, which are collections of information stored in a place other than the workspace. To manipulate such data in APL it has to be brought into the active workspace in appropriate sized chunks, although some systems have facilities for doing certain tasks in a non-APL environment like CMS. More about files later in the book.

PROBLEMS

1. Carry out the following instructions and APL system commands in the order given.

    Define a few arbitrary functions and variables. Then enter

)SAVE WORK1
)CLEAR
    and repeat these instructions several times until your workspace quota is used up. Use workspaces named WORK2, WORK3, etc.

)LIB

    How many workspaces can you save in your APL system?

)DROP WORK1
)LIB
)LOAD WORK3
)FNS
)VARS

    Define additional functions and variables.

)SAVE WORK2

    Why wasn't the material saved?

)WSID WORK2
)SAVE
)CLEAR
)LOAD WORK2
)FNS
)VARS

    Has WORK2 been superseded?

    Delete several functions and variables from WORK2.

)ERASE FN1 FN2 V1 V2 ...
)SAVE
)LIB
)FNS
)VARS

2. Follow the instructions given and carry out the indicated system commands:

>   )*LIB* 1
>   )*LOAD* 1 *ADVANCEDEX*

(If your system does not have workspace 1 *ADVANCEDEX*, load any other workspace from common library 1.)

>   )*FNS*
>   )*VARS*

If there is a function or variable named *DESCRIBE* or *HOW*, execute it.

>   )*WSID*

Define a function *RECT* which gives only the area of a rectangle of length L by W. Display it after executing.

>   )*COPY* 1 *CLASS RECT*

Was your own defined function *RECT* unchanged?

>   )*ERASE RECT*

Redefine *RECT* as above to give only the area of a rectangle.

>   )*PCOPY* 1 *CLASS RECT*

Does this command behave the same as)*COPY*?

>   )*SAVE JONES*

If the workspace was not saved, drop one of those in your library and then save it. Then change the name of your active workspace to *SMITH*.

>   )*WSID SMITH*
>   )*SAVE*
>   )*CLEAR*
>   )*LOAD* 1 *ADVANCEDEX* (or whichever *LIB* 1 workspace you used before)
>   )*SAVE* 1 *ADVANCEDEX*

Why couldn't *ADVANCEDEX* be saved?

>   )*CONTINUE HOLD*

Now sign on again.

>   )*LIB*
>   )*FNS*
>   )*VARS*

3. You have saved your work in a workspace called *GOOD* and have just developed a function *OK* in your active workspace. Write out a sequence of commands which will get *OK* into *GOOD* without carrying with it any unwanted 'trash' which may be in the active workspace.

4. Compose a group A consisting of the variables *TAB*0, *TAB*1, *TAB*2, *TAB*3 and a group B consisting of functions *AVG*1, *AVG*2, *AVG*3, *AVG*4, *AVG*5 of workspace 1 *CLASS*. Enlarge group A by including the variable *PI*. List the groups, list the members of group A, and then disperse group A.

Chapter 12: Mixed functions

Thus far we have worked mainly with primitive scalar dyadic and monadic functions. One of their characteristics is that the shape of the result is the same as the shape of the argument. For example, if the arguments are vectors, so is the result. If the arguments are scalars, then the result is a scalar. In this and subsequent chapters, functions will be introduced for which the result has the *data type* (i.e., character or numeric) of the right argument, but the contents and shape depend on the arguments in some way. These are appropriately called *mixed* functions. Both dyadic and monadic ρ, introduced in Chapter 2, are examples of mixed functions.

Interval

Regular sequences of numbers like 1980 1981 1982 1983 or .05 .06 .07 .08 .09 .10 are frequently used in business. You may already have discovered that you could generate the sequence 1 2 3 4 5 by expressions like +\5ρ1 and probably wondered why it takes so much effort to get such a simple result.

Rest assured that the developers of APL knew you would often need this type of result, and they provided a monadic mixed function to do it for you. It is called the *interval function* or *interval generator* or *count*, and it employs the ι symbol (shift *I*, also referred to as *iota*).

We can see what it does by entering a few examples,

```
      ι5                  ι6                    ι10                          ι2
1 2 3 4 5          1 2 3 4 5 6       1 2 3 4 5 6 7 8 9 10           1 2
```

but suppose we want the sequence 1980 1981 1982 1983. It's pretty easy. Just cook up the sequence 1 2 3 4 and add 1979 to it:

```
      1979+ι4
1980 1981 1982 1983
```

Similarly, to get the sequence .05 .06 .07 .08 .09 .10 enter

```
      .04+.01×ι6
0.05 0.06 0.07 0.08 0.09 0.1
```

Not quite so intuitive, but it surely works. Very often a need for a sequence will be expressed in terms of 'I want numbers starting at .05 up to .1 in steps of .01'. The function *STEP* does this for us:

```
      ∇Z←L STEP R;POINTS;RANGE
[1]   ⍝L IS START,END; R IS INCREMENT
[2]   ⍝NO ERROR CHECKING   AJ ROSE SEPT 1982
[3]   RANGE←--/L ⍝ HIGH-LOW
[4]   POINTS←⌊RANGE÷R ⍝ INCLUDE BOTH ENDS
[5]   Z←0,(×POINTS)×ι|POINTS ⍝ INCLUDE BOTH END POINTS
[6]   Z←R×Z ⍝ SCALE RESULT
[7]   Z←(1ρL)+Z ⍝ DISPLACEMENT
[8]   ⍝ ON ONE LINE: Z←(1ρL)+R×0,ι⌊(--/L)÷R
[9]   ∇
```

```
      .05 .1 STEP .01
0.05 0.06 0.07 0.08 0.09 0.1
```

```
      1980 1983 STEP 1
1980 1981 1982 1983
```

The ability to deal with sequences makes it easier to explore functions with operation tables—you don't have to do the counting.

	(ι5)∘.≤ι5				(1.075 1.15 *STEP* .025)∘.*10 12 *STEP* 1		
1	1	1	1	1	2.061031562	2.215608929	2.381779599
0	1	1	1	1	2.59374246	2.853116706	3.138428377
0	0	1	1	1	3.247321025	3.653236154	4.109890673
0	0	0	1	1	4.045557736	4.652391396	5.350250105
0	0	0	0	1			

You may recognize the second result above as compound interest at 7.5%, 10%, 12.5% and 15% over 10, 11 and 12 periods.

The remainder of this section is for those readers who are of a mathematical bent. We'll meet the rest of you at the next section.

Remember the card matching algorithm (page 51),

$$P1 = \frac{1}{0!} - \frac{1}{1!} + \frac{1}{2!} - \frac{1}{3!} + \cdots - \cdots + \frac{1}{52!}$$

With interval we can simplify our execution of the function *MATCH*:

```
    ∇P1←MATCH N                MATCH 5                  MATCH 20
[1]    P1←-/÷!ιN ∇           0.6333333333            0.6321205588
                               MATCH 10                 MATCH 52
                            0.6321205357            0.6321205588
```

Its evaluation for a varying number of terms indicates that this probability estimate converges very rapidly as the number of terms increases.

Index set

This APL2 function is a close cousin of the interval function. Its symbol is the *squad* (skinny quad), R▯, formed by overstriking the left and right brackets. Applied monadically to a scalar or vector of nonnegative integers, it produces all permutations of the intervals of the argument:

```
      R▯4                    R▯2 3
 1  2  3  4                    1  1
                              1  2
                              1  3

      R▯1 2                    2  1
 1  1                         2  2
 1  2                         2  3
```

Empty vectors and vectors of length one

These concepts, which are not intuitively apparent to most of us, are important to master. We have previously covered certain topics which we suggested most students might want to skip; however, *everyone* needs to understand empty vectors and vectors of length one.

Look at the following examples:

```
    ι3              ι2             ι1              ι0
 1  2  3         1  2             1
```

ιN obviously generates a *vector* of N elements, starting with 1. That doesn't bother you as long as N is 2 or greater, but what about ι1? Is it a vector with one element, or is it the same as the scalar 1?

        1
1

They look the same, but they are not the same. The expression 1 (or 1-0, or ×72, etc.) results in a scalar. The result of ι 1 is a vector, even though it is only a single element. In mathematics there is a term which is associated with the distinction—*rank*, which we introduced earlier and about which we will have more to say shortly.

We have seen the results of ι5, ι4, ι3, ι2 and ι1. Now we're ready to examine ι0. This is a vector of *no* elements. The system in its response is trying to display a vector of length 0, but there just aren't any elements to display! The important thing to remember is that ι*N* always returns a vector, and the length of that vector is *N*.

Of what use is a vector of length 0? A good question. One might ask, 'What use is an empty warehouse?' The empty warehouse is a place in which goods can be stored. An empty vector (you should pardon the comparison) is somewhat analogous. Think about this: if you needed to generate vectors of varying length and you were looking for a starting place to store elements as they were accumulated, what better place to start with than a vector of no elements, an empty 'warehouse,' the vector ι0? Although you won't really appreciate its many uses until you begin to get more deeply involved in function definition in APL, some examples of empty vectors will be introduced in this and subsequent chapters to help motivate you.

Shape

In Chapter 5 the shape function ρ was introduced and used to give information about the sizes of vectors, matrices and other arrays. It was stated that ρ could be applied to *any* array. Let's explore this by using some samples that are in 1 *CLASS*. Bring copies of these arrays, called *TAB*0, *TAB*1, *TAB*2 and *TAB*3 into your active workspace with the *COPY* command:

```
)COPY 1 CLASS TAB0 TAB1 TAB2 TAB3
SAVED   14.45.33 02/20/83
```

Display *TAB*0:

        ***TAB*0**   ρ*TAB*0
4.1

It's just the scalar number 4.1 and has *no* dimensions. Hence, ρ*TAB*0 results in a vector with *no* elements. Unlike vectors and matrices, scalars don't 'extend out' in any direction. In this sense scalars are like idealized geometric points, which are also considered to be dimensionless.

Let's now investigate *TAB*1:

        ***TAB*1**   ρ*TAB*1
1.414213562 1.732050808 2 2.236067977   4

*TAB*1 is obviously a vector of four elements. ρ*TAB*1 confirms that *TAB*1 has only one dimension, with four elements along that dimension.

Now display *TAB*2:

```
    TAB2              ρTAB2
 3   1   7      4  3
 7  10   4
 6   9   1
 1   6   7
```

Here we have a two-dimensional array (matrix), with four elements along one dimension (number of rows) and three elements along the other (number of columns).

Finally, display $TAB3$:

```
        TAB3                    ρTAB3
 111  112  113          2  4  3
 121  122  123
 131  132  133
 141  142  143

 211  212  213
 221  222  223
 231  232  233
 241  242  243
```

This may look peculiar, but remember that we are restricted to two-dimensional paper to depict a three-dimensional array. The result of $\rho TAB3$ indicates that we do indeed have a three-dimensional array, two elements deep (number of planes), four elements down (number of rows), and three elements across (number of columns).

If you are wondering how $TAB3$ was constructed, here's how it was done. Try both the following algorithms which use the outer product twice:

```
    100 200∘.+10 20 30 40 ∘.+ι3              (100×ι2)∘.+(10×ι4)∘.+ι3
 111  112  113                           111  112  113
 121  122  123                           121  122  123
 131  132  133                           131  132  133
 141  142  143                           141  142  143

 211  212  213                           211  212  213
 221  222  223                           221  222  223
 231  232  233                           231  232  233
 241  242  243                           241  242  243
```

Rank

Rank was mentioned as a way to talk about the number of dimensions of an array. Let's see how this is handled in APL. First consider

```
    ρρTAB0
0
```

An unexpected response? Not really, when you think about it. Let's see if we can construct a plausible explanation. First, we'll line up the responses from $\rho TAB0$, $\rho TAB1$, $\rho TAB2$ and $\rho TAB3$:

```
        ρTAB3                    ρρTAB3
 2  4  3                      3

        ρTAB2                    ρρTAB2
 4  3                         2

        ρTAB1                    ρρTAB1
 4                            1

        ρTAB0                    ρρTAB0
                  0
```

What do you see? The shape of an array of N dimensions is itself a vector of N elements. So $\rho TAB0$ must really be a vector with no elements (same as $\iota 0$), and $\rho\rho TAB0$ is equivalent to $\rho \iota 0$.

Thus, $\rho \rho$ of any array gives the number of dimensions of the array. We have already attached the name *rank* to this concept. A scalar has rank 0; a vector, rank 1; and a matrix, rank 2. Arrays of rank 3 and higher don't have generally accepted names.

At last we are ready to tell the difference between 1 and $\iota 1$. This distinction was left unanswered when it was introduced on **page 104**. They have different shapes and different ranks:

```
        1                    ρ1                  ρρ1
 1                                    0
        ι1                   ρι1                 ρρι1
 1                     1                    1
```

In spite of the identical appearance of the results of 1 and ι 1 on the screen or paper, 1 and ι 1 are viewed as different in the APL system. Your failure to observe the difference can lead to the downfall and subsequent painful debugging of otherwise well-constructed programs.

Catenate

You have probably sensed a need to have a way to stuff more elements into a vector. This would certainly be desirable if the vector represented, say, the individual charges run up over a period of time by a customer in a department store. Our only recourse thus far has been to reassign the vector by reentering it with both old and new values—an unsatisfactory method.

APL does have a function which allows us to enlarge an array. To illustrate how it can be done, let's design a simplistic calculator capable of summing a list of numbers. Here is its description:

key	purpose or action
CLR	clears accumulator
ENT	allows entry of values and prints number of values accumulated since last entry
SUM	prints sum of accumulated numbers

A simulation of this calculator is provided in 1 *CLASS*. Let's use it first and then see how it's constructed.

```
      )LOAD 1 CLASS
SAVED  14.45.33 02/20/83
```

First, we clear the 'memory':

```
      CLR
```

Next, enter *ENT* followed by some data as shown:

```
      ENT 5 3 1
3
```

The system responds with a 3, indicating that three values have been entered. Make another entry:

```
      ENT 5 6
5
```

Entering *SUM* gives the sum of the values accumulated:

```
      SUM
20
```

We can continue to enter values and get the sum:

```
      ENT 2
6
      SUM
22
```

Now clear the memory again and make a new entry:

```
      CLR
      SUM
0
      ENT 1 2 3
3
      SUM
6
```

What do the functions look like that comprise this simple calculator?

```
      ∇CLR[□]∇              ∇ENT[□]∇               ∇SUM[□]∇
    ∇ CLR                 ∇ ENT X                ∇ SUM
[1]   VECT←ι0        [1]    ρVECT←VECT,X     [1]    +/VECT
    ∇                     ∇                      ∇
```

CLR is niladic and doesn't return an explicit result. Reasonable enough, since its purpose is only to set the accumulator *VECT* to ⍳0 each time it is executed. *VECT* is a global variable. It is initialized as an empty vector, a good place to start.

ENT takes the elements in its argument *X* and joins them onto the end of *VECT*. This result is stored in *VECT* and the number of elements resulting is displayed. In effect, we update *VECT* and display information about its elements at the same time. A new dyadic function is introduced in *ENT*. It is called *catenate*, the symbol for which is the comma. Its job is to join or chain together its two arguments.

All the third function *SUM* does is calculate and display the sum of the values that have been accumulated in *VECT*.

The catenate function has some noteworthy characteristics. For example, if we make the assignments

        J←⍳3   *K←9 8 7 6*

and catenate *J* and *K*, putting the result in *Y*, then there are seven elements in *Y*:

        Y←J,K   *Y*   ρ*Y*
                          1 2 3 9 8 7 6   7

Two vectors can be catenated. What about a scalar? Can it be catenated to a vector? Consider

        J,6
1 2 3 6

For the purpose of catenation, scalars are regarded as vectors of length 1. Therefore, catenation of two scalars makes a vector:

        X←3,5   *X*   ρ*X*
                          3 5   2

Catenating ⍳0 to a vector gives the same vector, as we would expect:

        J,⍳0   (⍳0),*J*
1 2 3   1 2 3

What about catenating a vector of length 0 to a scalar?

        R←6   *T←R,⍳0*
        R   *T*
6   6
        ρ*R*   ρ*T*
                                 1
        ρρ*R*   ρρ*T*
0   1

T is a vector of one element, while *R* is a scalar. Anytime you catenate vectors or scalars in any combination, the result is always a vector.

When applied to matrices, catenation allows us to increase the number of rows or columns. This extension of the function is often needed to merge data from several sources, or to tack on a row or column of totals to some table. It will be discussed in Chapter 19.

Ravel

If we're not careful, the distinction between vectors and scalars can cause difficulties. Sometimes it's advantageous to have a vector of length one instead of a scalar. As an example consider *AVG* in 1 *CLASS*, which you should still have in your active workspace. When used on a vector argument, it works as expected, but see what it does with a scalar argument:

        AVG 2 3 4   *AVG* 4
3

Something must be wrong. Check to see what ρAVG 4 is:

```
      ρAVG 4
0
```

This means that AVG 4 must result in a vector of length 0. Why should this be? Let's display the function:

```
      ∇AVG[□]∇
    ∇ R←AVG X
[1]   R←(+/X)÷ρX
    ∇
```

Working from right to left on line 1, if X is a scalar, then ρX is an empty vector. But the algorithm calls for dividing $+/X$ (a scalar) by ρX (in this case a vector of length 0). Dividing a scalar by a vector gives a result which has the same shape as the vector argument. Need we say more?

Interesting though all this may be, it doesn't solve our problem. Our function, to be consistent, should return a result of 4 in this case. We have to make the argument X a vector if it isn't one already. The monadic function *ravel* is used for this. It uses the same symbol, the comma, as the dyadic function catenate. Let's insert a comma between ρ and X in AVG:

```
      ∇AVG[1□16]
[1]   R←(+/X)÷ρX
      1
[1]   R←(+/X)÷ρ,X∇
```

Now executing AVG 4, we get the desired result:

```
      AVG 4

      4
4
```

Ravel has some interesting uses. $TAB2$ is a good example. Notice that the last dimension is raveled first, and that there are as many elements in the result as in the original array:

```
      TAB2                 ρTAB2                 ,TAB2
   3   1   7            4 3                 3 1 7 7 10 4 6 9 1 1 6 7
   7  10   4
   6   9   1            ×/ρTAB2               ρ,TAB2
   1   6   7         12                   12
```

Raveling proceeds similarly on a three-dimensional array like $TAB3$. The last dimension is again raveled first. No matter what the rank of the array with which we start, ravel converts the array to a vector.

```
      TAB3
 111 112 113
 121 122 123
 131 132 133
 141 142 143

 211 212 213
 221 222 223
 231 232 233
 241 242 243
      ,TAB3
 111 112 113 121 122 123 131 132 133 141 142 143 211 212 213 221 222 223 231 232
     233 241 242 243
```

In APL2 ravel has been extended to allow raveling along an existing axis, or the creation of a new one:

```
      R←2 3ρι6                      ,[1 2]R
      R                      1 2 3 4 5 6
1 2 3                              ,[2 3]2 3 4ρι24
4 5 6                        1   2   3   4   5   6   7   8   9 10 11 12
      ,[1]R                  13 14 15 16 17 18 19 20 21 22 23 24
1 4                                ,[ι0]5 6
2 5                          5
3 6                          6
```

```
        ,[1.5]1 2                    ,[2.2]2 2ρι4
1                            1
2                            2
        ,[.2]1 2
1  2                         3
                             4
```

The result, for A a scalar or vector of integer axes (only continuous and increasing order allowed) combines those axes and has rank $1 + (\rho \rho R) - \rho , A$ where R is the argument and A the axis specifiers. For fractional axis specifiers the result has in the appropriate position in its shape a new axis and has rank $1 + \rho \rho R$. (See page 183 for a discussion of axis specifiers.)

Similar extensions to catenate are found in other APL systems, and are described in Chapter 19.

Reshape

This function was introduced in Chapter 2. By way of review, assign

```
    U←4  3  5  7  8  9
```

Suppose we want to build a two-dimensional table with the first row 4   3   5 and the second row 7 8 9. The reshape function rearranges the elements in the right argument to have the shape of the left argument:

```
      2  3ρU
4  3  5
7  8  9
```

Here is an example where the left argument contains a single element:

```
      3ρU
4  3  5
```

The number of elements in the left argument gives the rank of the resulting array. Here are some more examples:

```
      5ρ3              5ρ0 1            1 5ρ0 1              5 1ρ0 1
3  3  3  3  3      0  1  0  1  0      0  1  0  1  0              0
                                                               1
                                                               0
                                                               1
                                                               0
```

So far our right arguments have been vectors or scalars. What happens when the right argument of ρ is a matrix?

```
      A←2  3ρ2 3 4 5 6 7          5ρA              3 4ρA
      A                      2  3  4  5  6      2  3  4  5
2  3  4                                         6  7  2  3
5  6  7                                         4  5  6  7
```

From this we can conclude that whatever the shape of the right argument for ρ, for reshaping purposes it is in effect , A. This is perfectly reasonable, since raveling an array of rank 2 or more before reshaping is just what most people would do if they had to do it by hand.

Finally, what if the right argument contains no elements, i.e., is an empty vector?

```
      3ρι0
LENGTH ERROR
      3ρι0
        ∧
```

There are no elements on the right with which to carry out the desired reshaping, so the instruction can't be executed. But now try these two examples:

```
      0ρι0                    (ι0)ρι0
                       LENGTH ERROR
                             (ι0)ρι0
                               ∧
```

Can you explain the results?

PROBLEMS

1. DRILL Assign $A \leftarrow 0$ 8 ‾3 4 6 10, $M \leftarrow 2$ 4$\rho \iota 8$ and $V \leftarrow$ 3 3$\rho \iota 9$ and execute

ρA	ρM	$\bar{} 7 \times \iota 1$	$\div \iota 5$
$\rho \rho A$	$(\bar{} 2)$ 1 2	$\iota \lceil /A$	$\iota 28 \div 3 + 1$
$\rho \rho \rho A$	$\iota 10$	$\bar{} 2$, 1 2	$\rho \rho V$
$A \lceil 0.8 \times \iota 6$	$(\iota 5) + 3$	$+/ \iota 15$	V, M

2. What is the difference in meaning of the two expressions $\rho A = 6$ and $6 = \rho A$?

3. Load 1 *CLASS* and execute each of the following:

   $\times / \rho TAB 0$ $\qquad$ $\times / \rho TAB 1$ $\qquad$ $\times / \rho TAB 2$ $\qquad$ $\times / \rho TAB 3$

   What information is gained from these instructions?

4. For the vector A (problem 1) execute $\iota \rho A$ and $\rho \iota \rho A$. What meaning can be assigned to each of these expressions?

5. Write one-line monadic functions returning an explicit result to give: **A** the sum of the square roots of the first N positive integers; **B** the square root of the sum of the first N positive integers; **C** the geometric mean of the first N positive integers (the Nth root of the product of the N numbers)

6. Construct each of the following sequences using ι:

1 3 5 7 9 11 13 15	‾250 ‾150 ‾50 50 150 250
‾7 ‾2 3 8 13	5 4 3 2 1
0 0.3 0.6 0.9 1.2 1.5	1 0 1 0 1 0

7. Enter $\iota 3 \star \iota 3$. Account for the error message.

8. Fill in the blanks in the following expressions to generate 50 1's:

   _____50 $\qquad$ 50_____ $\qquad$ _____50_____50

9. Rewrite each of the following statements without parentheses:

   $\bar{} 1 + (-/(\iota 5)) \times 2$ $\qquad$ $+/(\iota 5) - 1$ $\qquad$ $+/((\iota 5) + 1) = 5$ $\qquad$ $+/0 = (\iota 5) = 6$

10. Write functions that would approximate each of the following series to N terms:

    A $$1 - \frac{1}{2} + \frac{1}{3} - \frac{1}{4} + \cdots$$

    B $$\frac{1}{0!} + \frac{x^1}{1!} + \frac{x^2}{2!} + \cdots$$

11. Write an APL expression that yields 1 if the array A is a scalar, 0 otherwise.

12. What is the difference between $\rho A, \rho B$ and $(\rho A), \rho B$ for two vectors A and B?

13. Assume you have defined a dyadic function E. How could you tell the difference between it and, say, $6E8$ in scaled notation?

14. Make the scalar S a vector without using the ravel function.

15. Construct a table of sines of angles from 0 to $O \div 2$ radians in steps of $O \div 20$ radians.

16. Show how to find the sum of the alternate elements in ιN, beginning with the second.

17. How do you set up an 'empty' matrix with 5 columns?

18. Express each of the following numbers in APL and determine which is the smallest:

$$\frac{321,400}{\sqrt{27.8}} - \frac{17}{.00065} \qquad \log_5 \frac{1}{\sqrt[4]{.0000068}} \qquad \sqrt[9]{(32,200)^2}$$

19. Find the sum of the first 30 terms in the series $\quad 1 - \dfrac{1}{2} + \dfrac{1}{4} - \dfrac{1}{6} + \dfrac{1}{8} - \cdots + \cdots$

20. Create an $N \times N$ matrix with an arbitrary vector of elements V along the major diagonal and 0's elsewhere.

21. Use the outer product to form the $4 \quad 4$ matrix

```
1 1 1 1
2 2 2 2
3 3 3 3
4 4 4 4
```

22. You owe a kind-hearted loan shark $10,000 and are required to pay as interest 1/2 of this sum the first year. Because of the lender's generosity, the second year you pay only 1/2 of the first year's repayment, and during the third year, only 1/2 of the second year's payment, etc. in perpetuity. There being no discount for prepayment, how much would you have to repay to wipe out the debt?

23. Write expressions to generate logical vectors of length L and **A** R leading ones **B** R trailing ones.

Chapter 13: Character data

All of the functions, problems and solutions you've learned so far have been fundamentally quantitative or numerical in nature. However, computers are used as much for nonnumerical work as for numerical work. Just consider all the applications of word processing, information retrieval, electronic mail, language translation and 'talkative' computer games that abound. And don't forget that most quantitative applications (such as business reports) combine text and data to provide meaningful headings and descriptions for those who receive the reports.

Simple titles for results

In workspace 1 *CLASS* the function *RECT* calculates and displays the length of the perimeter, the length of the diagonal and the area of a rectangle. Load 1 *CLASS*, try *RECT* for a rectangle with sides 3 and 4, and then display the function:

```
      )LOAD 1 CLASS                    ∇RECT[□]∇
SAVED  14.45.33 02/20/83           ∇ L RECT H
      3 RECT 4                  [1]    2×L+H
14                              [2]    L HYP H
5                               [3]    L×H
12                                 ∇
```

The three lines of output are the perimeter, diagonal and area (in that order) of the rectangle whose sides are 3 and 4. But we had to look inside the function to see what each of the answers represented. Even if you had used comments, they wouldn't help identify the results when you execute the function.

Now try the function *GEO2*, which is similar to *RECT*:2

```
      3 GEO2 4                        ∇GEO2[□]∇
PERIMETER IS:                      ∇ L GEO2 H;X
14                              [1]    X←' IS:'
AREA IS:                        [2]    'PERIMETER',X
12                              [3]    2×L+H
DIAGONAL IS:                    [4]    'AREA',X
5                               [5]    L×H
                                [6]    'DIAGONAL',X
                                [7]    L HYP H
                                   ∇
```

Line 1 looks like nothing we've done so far. It introduces a new use for the quote symbol, to enclose characters. As a matter of fact, not only are there obvious alphabetic characters *I* and *S* but also a colon used as a punctuation mark, and even a blank space at the beginning.

APL interprets each of these, including the blanks, as a separate character. But it does more than that. Since in line 2 catenation is used betweeen the set of characters on the left and those on the right (stored in *X*), there is a strong suggestion that such characters are elements of an array, in this case of rank 1. It's a fancy way of calling what is between the quotes a vector. However, since we could conceivably have a table (or matrix) of characters, the rank will depend, as with numerical information, on the shape. *X* here is a vector of length 4.

Continuing down the function, lines 4 and 5 respectively catenate the words '*AREA*' and '*DIAGONAL*' to *X*, which consists of the characters ' *IS:*'.

You don't have to be in function definition mode to use characters literally. For instance:

```
A←'HELLO '
```

Again, notice the space after the `'O'`. Counting the space, it's a vector of length 6:

```
     ρA
6
```

We can do some pretty cute things with character data. If we assign

```
     B←'HOW ARE YOU'
```

then catenation forms the message

```
     A,B
HELLO HOW ARE YOU
```

Now back to more serious business. Suppose we had a family of rectangles we wanted information about:

```
     1 3 5 GEO2 1 4 12
PERIMETER IS:
4 14 34
AREA IS:
1 12 60
DIAGONAL IS:
1.414213562 5 13
```

Our answers are OK, but the grammar is a little peculiar. It would be nice to have identification that matches the output grammatically. Specifically, the labels should be followed by `'ARE'` or `'IS'`, depending on the number of elements in the arguments. Let's now explore the function `GEO3`:

```
        ∇GEO3[□]∇
     ∇ L GEO3 H;X;FLAG
[1]    FLAG←((ρ,L)>1)∨(ρ,H)>1
[2]    X←((4×~FLAG)ρ' IS:'),(6×FLAG)ρ'S ARE:'
[3]    'PERIMETER',X
[4]    2×L+H
[5]    'AREA',X
[6]    L×H
[7]    'DIAGONAL',X
[8]    L HYP H
     ∇
```

```
     1 3 5 GEO3 1 4 12
PERIMETERS ARE:
4 14 34
AREAS ARE:
1 12 60
DIAGONALS ARE:
1.414213562 5 13
     3 GEO3 4
PERIMETER IS:
14
AREA IS:
12
DIAGONAL IS:
5
```

`GEO3` does exactly what we want it to, and changes the alphabetic information to fit the conditions of the problem. The first thing to note is the presence of the two local variables `X` and `FLAG`. On line 1, if there is more than one element in either `L` or `H`, then the variable `FLAG` is set to 1; otherwise it is 0. If the result of line 1 is 1 (i.e., we ask for information about more than one rectangle), `6×FLAG` is 6 and `6ρ'S ARE:'` is simply the characters `'S ARE:'`. At the same time `~FLAG` would be 0 and `4×0` is 0, so `0ρ' IS:'` results in an empty vector. Thus, no characters are displayed. When catenated, the effect is just `'S ARE:'`. You should be able to figure out for yourself what happens in this line if `FLAG` is 0. Line 2 tells the system to pick up `'IS:'` or `'S ARE:'`, depending on the length of the arguments. The rest of the function is like `GEO2`. Finally, some food for thought before leaving this function: why must the arguments `L` and `H` in line 1 be raveled?

Mixed output

You may have wondered why in both `GEO2` and `GEO3` the numeric and alphabetic information was placed on separate lines when a more natural format would call for them to be on the same line, as, for example, `'PERIMETERS ARE: 4 14'`.

Unless you are using an APL system that allows mixed arrays (page 257), attempts to catenate characters and numeric values run into trouble:

```
     M1←'GIVE '              M2←' DOLLARS'              COST←15
     M1,COST,M2
DOMAIN ERROR
     M1,COST,M2
     ∧
```

While character data and numeric data can't be catenated directly, numeric data can be converted to character data using the monadic *format* function ⊤, formed by overstriking ⊤ and ○ (upshift *N* and *J*). What you get is a character vector or character scalar that when displayed looks exactly like the original numeric value.

```
      ⍕COST              ρ⍕COST
15                    2
```

Using ⍕ we can now make more natural looking displays:

```
      M1,(⍕COST),M2
GIVE 15 DOLLARS
```

Practice makes perfect, so you should now go back and modify *GEO*2 and *GEO*3 to give more attractive displays.

The format function has many other uses than the simple conversion to characters shown here. Chapter 17 will discuss these in more detail.

Assigning character variables

Character data must begin and end with quotes. It's important that when character data is entered, *both* quotes are present. Otherwise you have an open quote, the results of which are system dependent, as described on page 26.

Occasionally you may need to use a word with an apostrophe in it. Since this is the same character as the quote, how can it be handled? For example, look at the following attempted assignment:

```
      'ISN'T'
SYNTAX ERROR
      'ISN'T'
         ∧
```

That didn't help at all. Use double quotes to get the apostrophe in:

```
      W←'ISN''T'
      W
ISN'T
```

A handy rule to remember when using quotes is that there must be an even number on any line (but comments don't count). Some early APL systems won't give an error message for unmatched quotes, but rather appear to gobble up whatever you enter like some voracious video game monster. The only way to stop it is to enter a matching quote.

Character variables can contain any of the printable characters, including the overstruck ones, that can be entered at the keyboard. Besides these, you can also use certain special effects characters such as *new line*, *linefeed* and *backspace*. They are described on page 238.

Functions that work with characters

What about all the functions we've studied so far? Do they work with characters? Let's try some and see:

```
      A←'X'              A+B              A<B
      B←'Y'         DOMAIN ERROR     DOMAIN ERROR
                        A+B              A<B
                        ∧                ∧
```

These functions make no sense operating on characters because characters aren't orderable. That is, 5.3 is greater than 2.45, but who can say whether the character '*F*' is greater or lesser than the character '*∗*'? Indeed, most of the primitive functions behave similarly. But consider

```
      A=B              A≠B
0                    1
```

Here we are asking the system to compare each element of the left argument A with the corresponding element of B. There is only one element on each side, and they don't match, so we get the responses shown.

A more sophisticated application of = is shown in the following example, which asks how many occurrences of the letter `'E'` there are in a vector:

```
    D←'ENGINEER'               'E'=D                    +/'E'=D
                      1 0 0 0 0 1 1 0              3
```

Another function which works with a character argument is the dyadic ρ, which isn't surprising since all it does is reshape the argument:

```
    ALF←'ABCDEFGHIJKLMNOPQRSTUVWXYZ'
    4 6ρALF
ABCDEF
GHIJKL
MNOPQR
STUVWX
```

We can create all kinds of interesting character arrays this way. Here is another example in which words that will comprise the rows are of varying lengths:

```
    FURN←4 6ρ'DESKS CHAIRSTABLESFILES '
    FURN
DESKS
CHAIRS
TABLES
FILES
```

In such cases you should be extra careful to 'pad' each prospective row with the right number of blanks to ensure a proper display. Otherwise the consequences can be ludicrous:

```
    4 6ρ'DESKSCHAIRSTABLESFILES'
DESKSC
HAIRST
ABLESF
ILESDE
```

You will find the function $ROWNAMES$ in workspace 1 $CLASS$ convenient for making character matrices without having to count the number of characters between words. $ROWNAMES$ makes use of a few APL features to be described later. But because it is so handy for building matrices of names or titles, we are introducing it here. However, don't bother to try to understand why it works. Just use it.

```
    )COPY 1 CLASS ROWNAMES
SAVED  14.45.33 02/20/83

    ∇ROWNAMES[□]∇
    ∇ Z←S ROWNAMES T;A;B;R
[1]    T←,T ◇ B←T=1↑T
[2]    A←(+/B)↑⍒B ◇ A←(1↓A,□IO+ρT)-1+A ◇ R←⌈/A
[3]    Z←((ρA),R)ρ(,A∘.≥(~□IO)+⍳R)\(~B)/T ◇ R←ρZ
[4]    S←2↑(2× 3 2 ⊥(ρ,S),0=¯1↑S)↓((¯2↑0,S),R,-R)[2 3 2 3 2 1 2 5 0 1 0 5 +□IO]
[5]    →BY×Rv.≠S
[6]  BY:Z←(S× 1 ¯1 ⌈×S)↑Z ◇ →OUT×0>¯1↑S
[7]  OUT:Z←(1-(Z=' ')⍳1)⌽Z
    ∇
```

```
    FURNV←'/DESKS/CHAIRS/TABLES/FILES'              FURN2
    FURN2←(⍳0)ROWNAMES FURNV                  DESKS
    ρFURN2                                    CHAIRS
4 6                                           TABLES
                                              FILES
```

The right argument of $ROWNAMES$ is a character vector. Its first character is arbitrary (we used the `'/'`) and serves as a *delimiter* (separator). The resulting matrix has as many rows as there are delimiters. The left argument can be a variety of things. If it is an empty vector, as above, the result contains as many columns as the longest character sequence between delimiters. If it is a scalar positive integer, then the number of columns is chopped (or extended with blanks). If the left argument is a scalar zero, each column is as long as the longest character sequence between delimiter characters, but each row is *right-justified*:

```
        4 ROWNAMES FURNV                    0 ROWNAMES FURNV
DESK                                    DESKS
CHAI                                    CHAIRS
TABL                                    TABLES
FILE                                    FILES
```

If the left argument is a negative number, then that sets the number of columns, with each row again right-justified. Finally, if the left argument is a two-element vector, the first element sets the number of rows (positive from the top or negative from the bottom), while the second element controls the configuration of the columns, as in the scalar left arguments described above:

```
      ¯9 ROWNAMES FURNV                    ¯3 5 ROWNAMES FURNV
    DESKS                               CHAIR
   CHAIRS                               TABLE
   TABLES                               FILES
    FILES
```

Characters that look like numbers

Up to this point we have used only letters, punctuation marks and space as characters. Any keyboard character, including overstruck ones, can be employed in this manner. This can lead to some mystifying situations with numbers:

```
    T←'10'            (or T←⍕10)

    T
10
```

But *T* doesn't have the value of 10:

```
    T=10
0  0
```

Neither element of *T* matches the '10' on the right! If this is puzzling to you, remember that *T* is a *vector* of two elements, '1' and '0', neither of which is equal to the numeric value 10.

On page 115 we saw how the format function ⍕ was used to convert a numeric value to its character representation. That function can be used to test whether a variable contains character information or numeric information. The trick is based on the fact that ⍕ applied to numeric values converts it to characters.

The following commented function is the test. It covers all cases except where the argument is empty; that's treated on page 131.

```
      ∇R←TYPE VAR
[1]     VAR←1⍴VAR ⍝ DEALS ONLY WITH FIRST ELEMENT--FAILS IF VAR IS EMPTY
[2]     R←(9×∧/VAR=⍕VAR)⍴'CHARACTER' ⍝ IF CHARACTER, OTHERWISE R IS EMPTY.
[3]     R←R,(7×∨/VAR≠⍕VAR)⍴'NUMERIC' ⍝ IF NUMERIC--HENCE R IS EITHER
[4]     ⍝THE VECTOR 'CHARACTER' OR THE VECTOR 'NUMERIC'
[5]     ∇
```

Just as ⍕ is used to convert numeric data to its character representation, ⍎ (upshift B with upshift J), called *execute*, can be used to convert character vectors to their numeric representation.

```
    V←'10 72.4 93'        VN←⍎V              VNV←⍕VN
    V                     VN                 VNV
10 72.4 93           10 72.4 93          10 72.4 93
    ⍴V                    ⍴VN                 ⍴VNV
10                   3                   10
    TYPE V               TYPE VN             TYPE VNV
CHARACTER            NUMERIC             CHARACTER
```

For users of APL*PLUS and APL2 there is a primitive function *type*, monadic ∊, that gives the same information as the defined function *TYPE*. It returns a zero for numeric values and a blank for character values:

```
       εV                              εVN
                          0  0  0
       ρεV                              ε2  4ρι8
10                          0  0  0  0
       +/' '=εV                    0  0  0  0
10
```

Executing character strings

The execute function does much more than just converting character representations into numbers. Execute treats its character vector argument as though you had entered it in calculator mode. For example, $A \leftarrow 'B \leftarrow 2+3' \diamond \underline{\Delta} A$ is equivalent to your having entered $B \leftarrow 2+3$ at the keyboard. This means you can assign character variables which will subsequently be executed.

Both execute and direct definition (see page 298) give you a vast increase in programming flexibility and power because you can reassign the character variables on which they are based, under program control. This leads to application systems that can appear intelligent (in the sense of programs that write or edit other programs), a topic we address in Chapter 24.

Ranking

Earlier in this chapter we said that character data is unorderable. Yet there are many times when it is necessary to impose an artificial ordering on character data. Dictionaries and telephone books would be impossible if words or names weren't listed in some order.

To see how this can be done, let's first assign a vector consisting of the letters of the alphabet in their normal sequence:

```
       X←'ABCDEFGHIJKLMNOPQRSTUVWXYZ'
```

Now try

```
       Xι'CAFE'
3  1  6  5
```

The dyadic use of ι (called *ranking* or *index of*) can be used to convert a character vector such as $'CAFE'$ above to a numeric vector holding the index position of each character in the left argument. In other words, $'C'$ is the *third* element of X, $'A'$ is the *first*, $'F'$ is the *sixth* and $'E'$ the *fifth*.

The following function uses *index of* to convert a character vector or scalar to a single number, which can then be ordered:

```
       ∇S←ORDER CONVERT CHVEC;WEIGHTS;INDEX              X CONVERT 'CAFE'
[1]    CHVEC←, CHVEC                             3010605
[2]    WEIGHTS←100*(ρCHVEC)-ιρCHVEC                      X CONVERT 'CHAD'
[3]    INDEX←ORDERιCHVEC                         3080104
[4]    S←+/INDEX×WEIGHTS∇                                X CONVERT 'CASH'
                                                 3011908
```

This method has some flaws, however. It won't work reliably for vectors of more than 8 characters because the computer can store only about 16 decimal digits in a scalar (that value will vary from system to system). To see the failure, compare X $CONVERT$ $'ABCDEFGHIJKLMN'$ with X $CONVERT$ $'ABCDEFGHIJKLMZ'$.

A second flaw is apparent in the following examples:

```
       X CONVERT 'DAME'                    X CONVERT 'DAY'
4011305                               40125
```

We would expect $'DAY'$ to appear in the dictionary after $'DAME'$; this method doesn't work unless the compared words are the same length. This can be dealt with by making all words the same length inside the function, and by augmenting to include a blank as its first element (since $'DAM'$ should come before $'DAME'$). A new function to do this has a built-in ranking vector, and makes all arguments eight characters long:

```
        ∇S←CONV2 CHVEC;WEIGHTS;INDEX
[1]     CHVEC←8ρCHVEC,'        '
[2]     WEIGHTS←100*8-ι8
[3]     INDEX←' ABCDEFGHIJKLMNOPQRSTUVWXYZ'ιCHVEC
[4]     S←+/INDEX×WEIGHTS ∇

        CONV2 'DAME'                    CONV2 'DAY'
5.02140601E14                   5.02260101E14
```

Here are a few more details to know about dyadic ι. Its left argument must be a vector, but its right argument can be arrays of any shape whatever. The shape of the result is always the same as that of the right argument.

```
    M←2 3ρ'CATDOG'              XιM                ρXιM
                             3  1 20           2 3
                             4 15  7
```

What happens if the right argument contains a character which isn't present in the left argument, or if the same character appears more than once in the right argument?

```
        Xι'BABBAGE, CHAS.'
2 1 2 2 1 7 5 27 27 3 8 1 19 27
```

The example shows you that all characters that aren't found (such as the comma, space and period) result in a value that is one larger than the length of the left argument. Generally, the left argument should contain all characters you expect to encounter in the right argument. Any repeated characters in the right argument return the same value: that of the *first match* in the left argument. This is true even if the left argument has duplicate occurrences.

```
        'BABBAGE, CHAS.'ι'BABBAGE, CHAS.'
1 2 1 1 2 6 7 8 9 10 11 2 13 14
```

Note that the repeated letters aren't used up. This feature can be used to test whether a vector has duplicate characters or not:

```
        TD←'BABBAGE'                TU←'COMPUTER'
        TDιTD                      TUιTU
1 2 1 1 2 6 7                 1 2 3 4 5 6 7 8
        (TDιTD)=ιρTD              (TUιTU)=ιρTU
1 1 0 0 0 1 1                 1 1 1 1 1 1 1 1
        ∧/(TDιTD)=ιρTD            ∧/(TUιTU)=ιρTU
0                             1
```

Ranking works with numeric arrays in exactly the same way that it does with characters.

Membership

Suppose you want to know which characters in some vector are also present in some other vector 'CHSET'. One way to do it is this:

```
        CHSET←' ABCDEFGHIJKLMNOPQRSTUVWXYZ0123456789'
        (1+ρCHSET)≠CHSETι'ALL FOUND'
1 1 1 1 1 1 1 1 1
        (1+ρCHSET)≠CHSETι'SOME NOT FOUND'
1 1 1 1 1 0 0 0 1 1 1 1 1 1
```

A more direct way to check for membership is to use the *membership* function, ∈, found on the E key:

```
        'ALL FOUND'∈CHSET                 ∧/'ALL FOUND'∈CHSET
1 1 1 1 1 1 1 1 1                1                         1
        'SOME NOT FOUND'∈CHSET            ∧/'SOME NOT FOUND'∈CHSET
1 1 1 1 1 0 0 0 1 1 1 1 1 1                                0
```

For membership, the shape of the result is always the same as that of the left argument. Both arguments may be arrays of any rank whatever:

```
      (3 4ρι12)ε2 2ρ4 15 2 ¯3                    (2 2ρ4 15 2 ¯3)ε3 4ρι12
 0 1 0 1                                     1 0
 0 0 0 0                                     1 0
 0 0 0 0
```

A few more points about character data

Look at this sequence of entries:

```
    ρ'ABC'                 ρ'AB'                ρ'A'              ρ''
3                      2                    1                0
```

A single character in quotes in APL is a scalar, while any other number of characters in quotes is a vector. Of course, to make a single character a vector, just ravel it.

```
    ρ,'A'
1
```

Don't make the common mistake of putting the comma inside the quotes. Why?

And finally, `' '` is an empty vector, just as `ι0` is an empty vector. There is actually a difference between `' '` and `ι0`, but don't worry about that now.

PROBLEMS

1. DRILL: Assign $X \leftarrow 'MISSISSIPPI'$ and $Y \leftarrow 'RIVER'$

   ```
   'ABCDE'='BBXDO'         1 2<'MP'           ρρAL←3 3ρ'ABCDEFGHI'
   ρV←'3172'               YεX                X='S'
   (ρV)ρV                  +/X='S'            +/'P'=X
   3172=V                  +/X≠'S'            +/(X,' ',Y)≠'S'
   X,Y                     X,' ',Y            ∨/X='R'
   ```

2. Determine what D is from the following record of executions:

   ```
            D
           ρD
   15
           5×D
   DOMAIN ERROR
           5×D
           ∧
         ' '=D
   1 1 1 1 1 1 1 1 1 1 1 1 1 1 1 1
   ```

3. Define a function F which takes a single argument A and displays its shape, rank and number of elements with appropriate descriptive messages. Assume rank $A \geq 1$.

4. Show how to display 1-and 2-digit positive integers I so that 1-digit integers are indented one space and the 2-digit integers begin at the left margin.

5. Copy the functions HYP and $GEO3$ in 1 $CLASS$. Open up the function and direct control to line $[0.5]$. Use the comment symbol ⍝ on this line and the next to write a message describing what the function does. Then close out the function, display it and execute it. Do comments introduced in this manner affect execution?

6. The matrix $GR3$ contains the grade records (A, B, C, D and F) of 25 students in a class, with the first row listing the number of A's received by each student, the second row the number of B's, etc. Each course represented in the matrix is three credits. A similar matrix $GR2$ records grades for two-credit courses, and $GR1$ for one-credit courses. Write a program to calculate the grade point average for each student and for the class. (The grade point average is computed by multiplying 4 times the number of A credits, 3 times the number of B credits, etc., adding them up and dividing by the total number of credits earned.)

7. How many consonants are in the vector $CHAR \leftarrow 'WHY AM I DOING THIS PROBLEM?'$?

Chapter 14: Selecting data from an array

Most of the time we find ourselves in possession of far more data (from business records, surveys, experiments, observations of natural phenomena, government statistics, etc.) than we need for the job to be done. So the problem of how to pull out the 'good stuff' from the mass of extraneous information is an important one for most APL users. In fact, data selection is one of the most common activities in APL, and for that matter, in any computer language. This chapter will describe five mixed functions that will assist you in the data selection process.

Indexing

Of all the selection functions *bracket indexing* is the most general. Let's define a character vector X:

        X←'ABCDEFGHIJK'

We can select from X the characters forming the word CAFE by

        X[3 1 6 5]
    CAFE

The expression in square brackets (not parentheses) is usually read as 'X sub 3 1 6 5' (for *subscripting*).

Any valid APL expression that results in integers can be used for indexing. For instance, execute

        X[2 5ρ3 1 8 9 4 2 10 6 7 5]   X[4ρ3]
    CAHID   CCCC
    BJFGE

The result has the shape of the expression in the brackets. But the following produces a new kind of error:

        X[12]
    INDEX ERROR
        X[12]
        ∧

To avoid an error message the expression in brackets must refer only to left argument indices that exist. In the last example, because X has just 11 characters there is no way to get the twelfth one.

Not only does bracket indexing have a different form from the other functions, it is also unique in being the only function that can appear on the left side of the assignment arrow (except in APL2; see Chapter 25). For example, suppose we want to change the character 'D' in X above to the character '$?$':

        X   X[4]←'?'   X
    ABCDEFGHIJK   ABC?EFGHIJK

The replacement has taken place.

More generally, elements can be rearranged by indexing:

        X   X[5 6]←X[6 5]   X
    ABC?EFGHIJK   ABC?FEGHIJK

If no indices are entered, every element of the vector is changed to the specified value:

        X   X[]←'T'   X
    ABC?FEGHIJK   TTTTTTTTTTT

You can index numeric as well as character arrays. Say we are given the heights (in inches) of five students:

```
L←51 63 60 62 59 62
```

If the third student's height had been entered incorrectly, and should have been 61 instead of 60 inches, the change can be made easily by

```
L[3]←61
L
51 63 61 62 59 62
```

Indexing matrices

To illustrate bracket indexing on a two-dimensional array, let's define a matrix which contains a company's revenue (in thousands of dollars) over a four-month period for three products:

```
            |        M O N T H
            |    1     2     3     4
      ------+---------------------------
PRODUCTS  A |   11    23    80   100
          B |   18    19    99   122
          C |   16    14   128   112
```

The sales data is stored in a matrix called *PRODREV* in 1 *CLASS*.

```
)COPY 1 CLASS PRODREV              PRODREV
SAVED  14.45.33 02/20/83        11   23   80  100
                                18   19   99  122
                                16   14  128  112
```

To specify any element of this array requires two numbers, one to tell the row and the other the column in which the element is located. Suppose we want the element in the second row and fourth column. The expression

```
     PRODREV[2 4]
RANK ERROR
     PRODREV[2 4]
     ∧
```

doesn't work because the two elements of the expression in the brackets refer to two different dimensions of the array *PRODREV*. We get a *RANK ERROR* message because we have failed to take into account that *PRODREV* is of rank 2, not rank 1. What is needed here is a separator for the row number and column number. The semicolon is used for this purpose.

```
     PRODREV[2;4]
122
```

More than one element can be specified at a time, like the sales of products A and C in the second month or that of product C in months 1 and 2:

```
     PRODREV[1 3;2]              PRODREV[3;1 2]
23 14                         16 14
```

There is a shorthand way of specifying *all* the elements along a particular dimension. Curiously enough, it's done by not entering *any* indices of the dimension in question. This is an extension to two dimensions of a previous example, $X[]←'T'$. If we wanted to see the sales for product C for all the months stored, we could enter either of the following:

```
     PRODREV[3;1 2 3 4]            PRODREV[3;]
16 14 128 112                  16 14 128 112
```

Similarly, we can get the revenue for all products for the fourth month with

```
     PRODREV[;4]
100 122 112
```

This implies that to get all of *PRODREV* we could use

```
      PRODREV[;]
11   23   80  100
18   19   99  122
16   14  128  112
```

which is perhaps a bit silly, but at least consistent.

As with vectors, you can change values in a matrix by using bracket indexing to the left of the assignment arrow. For example, to change the sales figures for month 1, products C and D, enter

```
PRODREV[1;3 4]←90 105                    PRODREV
                                   11   23   90  105
                                   18   19   99  122
                                   16   14  128  112
```

Unless the right argument is a single element, its shape must match the shape of the part of the array being indexed on the left.

Now for some miscellaneous but useful observations about bracket indexing. When indexing a matrix, there must be one semicolon to separate the row and column indices. But since vectors are one-dimensional, no semicolon is needed. Scalars are dimensionless and cannot be indexed at all.

The shape of the result in bracket indexing is the same as the shape you would get by taking outer products among the indices. This may not seem significant to you, but it does explain the following:

```
      X←2 3ρι6
      X[1 2;3]
3  6

      ρX[1 2;3]                      ρ1 2∘.+3
2                            2

      X[1 2;,3]
   3
   6

      ρX[1 2;,3]                     ρ1 2∘.+,3
2  1                         2  1
```

Previously you saw that APL permitted multiple assignments. If you are using this feature extensively, you should observe and remember this example, whose result varies on different APL systems:

```
      X←5ρ0              Z←X[2 3 4]←1              X                    Z
                                            0  1  1  1  0           1
```

We close this section on indexing by posing a question. Given the array *FURN* (page 116), how do you select the scattered elements '*F*', '*I*', '*R*' and '*E*'? If you have been thinking about how bracket indexing works, you will already be aware that it is the nature of the beast to couple in all possible combinations the indices specified for each dimension. You can't use this form of indexing directly to index scattered points in an array unless they all lie along a single row or column. Here is how you would pick out the vector '*FIRE SALE*' from the matrix *FURN*. We readily agree that it's a lot of work. If you have access to APL2, Chapter 25 describes functions that select scattered elements from arrays of any rank.

```
      FURN
DESKS
CHAIRS
TABLES
FILES
      FURN[4;1 2],FURN[2 3;5],FURN[1;6],FURN[1 2;3],FURN[3;4 5]
FIRE SALE
```

Replication and Compression

Replicate is a function whose left argument elements specify how many copies of corresponding right argument elements are to be selected. It uses the same symbol, /, as does reduction, but there's no confusion because reduction always has a function (such as + or ×) to its left while replicate has a vector of nonnegative integers. For vector right arguments the shape of the result of replicate is the sum of the left argument.

```
      2 3 0 1 3/10 20 30 40 50
10 10 20 20 20 40 50 50 50
```

Replicate is a relatively new function in the world of APL. Some older systems don't have it, and for them we provide the following simulation:

```
      )COPY 1 CLASS REP REPF REPL
SAVED   14.45.33 02/20/83
```

```
      ∇REPF[□]∇                              ∇REPL[□]∇
    ∇ Z←L REPF R;AXIS                      ∇ Z←L REPL R;AXIS
[1]   ⍝ SIMULATION OF L/[1]R         [1]   ⍝ SIMULATION OF L/[ρρR]R
[2]   ⍝ JILL WADE   SEPT. 82         [2]   ⍝ JILL WADE   SEPT. 82
[3]   ⍝ AXIS IS GLOBAL TO REP        [3]   ⍝ AXIS IS GLOBAL TO REP
[4]   AXIS←1 ◇ Z←L REP R             [4]   AXIS←1⌈ρρR ◇ Z←L REP R
    ∇                                    ∇
```

The function *REP* which is used by *REPF* and *REPL* does contain some features not yet covered in the text—don't worry, we'll get to them soon.

```
      ∇REP[□]∇
    ∇ Z←L REP R;IX;RHO;RT;TRANS
[1]   ⍝ SIMULATES Z←L/[AXIS] R   USED BY REPF AND REPL (JILL WADE SEPT 82)
[2]   ⍝ CREATE A MATRIX WHOSE LAST DIMENSION CONTAINS THE REQUIRED
[3]   ⍝ DATA, INDEX WHAT'S NEEDED, THEN REARRANGE SHAPE OF RESULT
[4]   R←1/R ◇ L←((ρR)[AXIS]ρ1)/L ⍝ DEAL WITH SCALAR ARGUMENTS
[5]   IX←(,L∘.≥⍳⌈/L)/,(⍳ρL)∘.×(⌈/L)ρ1 ⍝  INDICES IN REQUIRED DIMENSION
[6]   TRANS←((AXIS≠⍳ρρR)/⍳ρρR),AXIS ◇ RT←(⍋TRANS)⍉R
[7]   RHO←ρRT ◇ RT←((×/¯1↓RHO),¯1↑RHO)ρRT ⍝  RESHAPE TRANSPOSED ARRAY
[8]   Z←TRANS⍉((¯1↓RHO),ρIX)ρRT[;IX⌊¯1↑ρRT] ⍝ ADJUST FOR SCALAR RIGHT ARGUMENT
    ∇
```

When the left argument of replicate consists of only 0's and 1's, it is usually called *compression*. Compression is on virtually all APL systems, and it is a very popular function because it has so many uses.

In Chapter 4 we examined a group of relational functions which resulted in logical arrays (1's and 0's only) when applied to data. These logical arrays can be used as 'sieves' with holes where the 1's are, and barriers for the 0's to strain out unwanted data.

The vector *L* represents the heights of a group of students. We could find the heights of the second and third students by indexing, but we could as well use compression:

```
      L
51 63 61 62 59 62
      L[2 3]
63 61
      0 1 1 0 0 0/L
63 61
```

This can be read as 'the 0 1 1 0 0 0 compression of L.' Where there is a 0 in the left argument, the corresponding element on the right isn't picked up. The only elements returned are in those positions where there is a 1 to match it on the left. This means that for vector arguments the lengths must be the same.

To illustrate a practical use of compression, here is a bank account problem. For *A*, a vector of accounts with the negative values representing overdrawn accounts, the instruction $A < 0$ produces a vector with 1's in the positions of the offenders and 0's elsewhere. This is made to order for compression,

```
      A←3 ¯4 5 0 ¯6            A<0              (A<0)/A
                           0 1 0 0 1          ¯4 ¯6
```

and we have extracted from *A* only the overdrawn accounts.

We can go a little further with compression. For instance, the instruction

```
      (A<0)/⍳ρA
```

tells us that accounts 2 and 5 are the guilty parties and should be flagellated, dunned or whatever, depending on the circumstances.

Both arguments normally must have the same length, unless the left argument is a scalar. If all or none of the elements are desired, use a single 1 or 0:

```
     A←'ABCDEF'                    1/A              0/A                2/A
                               ABCDEF                             AABBCCDDEEFF
```

Otherwise, if the lengths don't agree, an error message results:

```
     1  0  1 0/A
LENGTH ERROR
     1 0 1 0 /A
          ∧
```

In `1 CLASS` the function `CMP` uses compression to compare two scalar arguments for size and returns a character vector stating whether the left argument is less than, equal to or greater than the right argument. Use the `COPY` command to get it into your active workspace, try it out on a few examples and display it.

```
     )COPY 1 CLASS CMP
SAVED  14.45.33 02/20/83
     3 CMP 5                  5 CMP 3               5 CMP 5
LESS                     GREATER                EQUAL

     ∇CMP[□]∇
   ∇ A CMP B
[1]   ((A>B)/'GREATER'),((A=B)/'EQUAL'),(A<B)/'LESS'
   ∇
```

It doesn't return an explicit result, since we wouldn't be apt to have any further use for the result. Notice the practical use for catenation with characters, not unlike line 2 of the function `GEO3` on page 114. Starting from the right, we pick up either all of the character vector `'LESS'` or none of it, depending on whether A is less than B. The vectors `'EQUAL'` and `'GREATER'` are treated similarly and catenated. Since only one of the three conditions can possibly hold at any one time, we are actually catenating two empty vectors and one nonempty character vector to get the right display. The fact that the left argument of compression is a logical vector makes it an ideal candidate for selecting on the basis of a true-false condition, as `CMP` shows.

There are several other ways of doing what `CMP` does, but most of them require features that we haven't introduced yet. They'll be discussed in Chapter 22. One method that we can explore now, however, employs indexing rather than compression:

```
     (3 7ρ'LESS    EQUAL   GREATER')[2+×A-B;]
```

It is further evidence that the old adage 'There's more than one way to skin a cat' holds for most problems in APL, and reflects the richness of the language.

Replication and compression on two-dimensional arrays

When using replication or compression with two-dimensional arrays, you have to keep one additional piece of information in mind: the left argument must have as many elements as the number of elements in the dimension across which replication or compression occurs. The symbol / works along the second dimension of a matrix, and ⌿ along the first dimension. Here are examples in which the third month (column 3) in `PRODREV` is elided, and `'CHAIRS'` is repeated three times but `'DESKS'` and `'FILES'` are elided in `FURN`:

```
     )COPY 1 CLASS PRODREV FURN
SAVED  14.45.33 02/20/83

     PRODREV                    1 1 0 1/PRODREV
  11  23  80 100            11  23 100
  18  19  99 122            18  19 122
  16  14 128 112            16  14 112
```

```
        FURN                    0 3 2 0⌿FURN
DESKS                   CHAIRS
CHAIRS                  CHAIRS
TABLES                  CHAIRS
FILES                   TABLES
                        TABLES
```

Formally, the conditions for replication or compression of matrices are as follows:

If $Z \leftarrow L/R$, then
1. L must be a vector or a scalar consisting of nonnegative integers
2. ρL must be $(\rho R)[1]$ for ⌿, or $(\rho R)[2]$ for /
3. $\rho\rho Z$ is $\rho\rho R$

Unlike indexing, replication and compression can't reorder data. Although their selection capability is limited to a single dimension, they can pick out elements, rows, columns or planes that aren't adjacent, but only in the order in which they occur. So to select products A and C for months 2 and 3 in *PRODREV* (represented by *PRODREV* [1 3;2 3]) we would have to compress twice:

```
     1 0 1⌿0 1 1 0/PRODREV
 23   80
 14  128
```

The replicate function on APL2 also permits the use of negative integers in the left argument. Wherever they occur, as many copies of the fill element (zero for numeric arrays, blank for characters) as the magnitude of the (negative) integer are inserted into the result. This allow you to compress, replicate and expand in one step:

```
     0 1 2 ‾2 1 1 0 ‾2/0 5 10 15 20 25
 5 10 10 0 0 15 20 0 0
```

Selecting data with membership

Membership, because it produces a logical array based on the presence or absence of elements, is frequently used as the left argument for compression. Like the relational and logical functions, it acts like a sieve to separate wanted from unwanted elements in an array. The following example removes vowels from a sentence:

```
     PHRASE←'THE QUICK BROWN FOX JUMPED OVER THE LAZY PROGRAMMER'
     (~PHRASE∊'AEIOU')/PHRASE
TH QCK BRWN FX JMPD VR TH LZY PRGRMMR
```

Most systems don't have a primitive function that says 'not a member of.' To get results like 'those elements of L that aren't members of R,' use membership with logical negation.

```
     L←1 5 50 17 13
     R←13 45 17 5 50 19

     (L∊R)/L                    (~L∊R)/L
 5 50 17 13                 1
```

However, APL2 does have a dyadic function *without*, ~, whose action is equivalent to the expression $(~L\in R)/L$. Its syntax is L~R. R may be any array, while L is a scalar or vector. The result is the vector of elements in L which aren't in R.

```
     'HELP'~'L'          3 1 5 6 7~1 3 7          3 1 5 6 7~2 3ρ⍳6
HEP                   5 6                      2 4
```

The idiom L~L~R gives the *intersection* (i.e., the common items) of L and R:

```
     3 1 5 6 7~3 1 5 6 7~1 3 7
 3 1 7
```

Expansion

Just as compression gives us a way to get a subset of an array, so there is also in APL a function called *expansion*, which allows us to insert additional elements. The symbol for expansion is \, the backward pointing slash, on the same key as the compression symbol.

```
      1 0 1 0 0 1 1 1 1 1\'ABCDEFG'                    1 0 0 1 0 1\3 2 3
A B  CDEFG                                          3 0 0 2 0 3
```

These examples show that where 0 appears in the left argument, a blank (for characters) or 0 (for numeric array) is inserted in the result, which otherwise is identical to the right argument. Notice also that the number of 1's in the left argument must be the same as the dimension of the right argument, i.e., we have to pick up *all* of the right argument.

The following example shows that when a scalar right argument is used, it is repeated to match the number of 1's in the left argument, with the shape of the result the same as the shape of the left argument:

```
      1 0 0 1 0 1\323
323 0 0 323 0 323
```

With two-dimensional arrays the treatment is similar to that for compression.

```
      PRODREV                          1 1 1 0 1 0\PRODREV
  11  23  80 100            11  23  80   0 100   0
  18  19  99 122            18  19  99   0 122   0
  16  14 128 112            16  14 128   0 112   0
```

We made room for two new columns by inserting zeros in the positions shown. To place `'LAMPS'` between `'DESKS '` and `'TABLES'` in `'FURN'`, use this sequence:

```
      FURN
DESKS
CHAIRS
TABLES
FILES
```

```
      MOREFURN←1 0 1 1 1\FURN              MOREFURN[2;]←'LAMPS '

      MOREFURN                              MOREFURN
DESKS                                 DESKS
                                      LAMPS
CHAIRS                                CHAIRS
TABLES                               TABLES
FILES                                FILES
```

Here is a summary of the conditions governing the use of the expansion function on matrices:

If $Z \leftarrow L \backslash R$, then
1. L must be a vector consisting of all 1's and 0's.
2. $(+/L)$ must be $(\rho R)[1]$ for $\nmid$ or $(\rho R)[2]$ for $\backslash$.
3. (ρZ) is $(\rho L),(\rho R)[2]$ for $\nmid$ and $(\rho R)[1],\rho L$ for $\backslash$.

Although it may seem a bit far-fetched, in a way, expansion is a selection function since it allows us to 'select' everything and make room for extra elements needed in the array.

Take and drop

Besides compression and indexing, there are two other versatile function which select portions of an array. Their behavior and syntax are best explained with a few well-chosen examples. First, let's examine the *take* function ↑, (upper shift Y), with vector and scalar right arguments:

```
      V←8 5 3 9 ¯1 ¯4
      1↑V                              ¯1↑V
8                                   ¯4
      2↑V                              ¯2↑V
8 5                                 ¯1 ¯4
      8↑V                              ¯8↑V
8 5 3 9 ¯1 ¯4 0 0             0 0 8 5 3 9 ¯1 ¯4
      2 3↑5                            ¯2 ¯3↑'X'
5 0 0                               X
0 0 0
```

If L is the left argument and is positive, ↑ selects the first L elements from the right argument. If L is negative, the last $\mid L$ elements are taken. When L is greater than ρR the result is R with sufficient 0's (or blanks for character data) on the right or left to make a vector of length L. L must be an integer or a vector of integers. With a vector left argument and a scalar right argument, ↑ returns an array whose shape is the left argument and whose elements consist of zeros (or blank characters), except for the element in the upper left corner.

Here is how ↑ can be applied to $PRODREV$. In each case the elements of the left argument refer to what is to be taken across each dimension:

```
      PRODREV              2  3↑PRODREV              2  ‾3↑PRODREV
 11   23   80  100      11 23 80                23   80  100
 18   19   99  122      18 19 99                19   99  122
 16   14  128  112           ‾2  3↑PRODREV           ‾2  ‾3↑PRODREV
                        18   19   99             19   99  122
                        16   14  128             14  128  112
```

Drop, ↓, (upper shift U) behaves in much the same way, except that if A is the left argument, A elements are dropped instead of taken. As with ↑, A must be a scalar integer or a vector of integers.

```
        0↓V                   2↓V            8↓V              ‾2↓V
 8  5  3  9  ‾1  ‾4      3  9  ‾1  ‾4               8  5  3  9
```

Again, here are some illustrations with $PRODREV$.

```
      2  1↓PRODREV          ‾1  2↓PRODREV            2  ‾1↓PRODREV
 14  128  112            80 100               16   14  128
                         99 122                    ‾2  3↓PRODREV
                                             100
```

Generally speaking, for $Z \leftarrow L \downarrow R$, ρZ is $(\rho R) - \mid L$. This means that the result always has the same rank as the right argument. In the example $\;\;‾2\;\;3 \downarrow PRODREV\;\;$ above, the result is a matrix (one row and column), *not* a scalar. Similarly, the result of $\;\;‾2\;\;1 \downarrow PRODREV\;\;$ is also a matrix (one row, three columns) even though it looks like a vector.

Take and drop allow only solid blocks of data to be selected, with no capability to reorder or replicate. Where large blocks of data are needed, ↑ and ↓ are much faster than bracket indexing on most APL systems.

As you saw above in the examples using $PRODREV$, ↑ and ↓ are handy for picking out corners of an array, and appropriate combinations of them can be used to select a solid block located away from a corner. For example, here are some ways to 'take the edges' off a matrix:

```
    MAT←4  6ρι24
    MAT                     ‾1  ‾1↓1  1↓MAT            2  4↑1  1↓MAT
 1   2   3   4   5   6     8   9 10 11              8   9 10 11
 7   8   9  10  11  12    14  15 16 17             14  15 16 17
13  14  15  16  17  18
19  20  21  22  23  24
```

In APL2 take and drop have been extended to allow for selection along specified axes. The extended form and its equivalent in other APL systems are shown side-by-side:

```
    1↑[1]MAT                  1  6↑MAT
 1 2 3 4 5 6              1 2 3 4 5 6

    2↑[2]MAT                  4  2↑MAT
 1   2                    1   2
 7   8                    7   8
13  14                   13  14
19  20                   19  20

    2↓[1]MAT                  2  0↓MAT
13  14  15  16  17  18    13  14  15  16  17  18
19  20  21  22  23  24    19  20  21  22  23  24
```

Reshape

This function was introduced in Chapter 2 and has been used right along in the text. Reshape isn't commonly thought of as a selection function. However, when you're interested in the front of an array, it's a handy way of picking out elements. For example,

```
      6ρPRODREV
11 23 80 100 18 19
```

picks out the first 6 elements, while

```
      3 3ρPRODREV
 11  23  80
100  18  19
 99 122  16
```

selects the first 9 and reshapes them—not too useful in this example but handy in building *identity matrices* used in matrix algebra. These are simply square matrices with 1's on the major diagonal and 0's elsewhere:

```
      4 4ρ1, 4ρ0
1 0 0 0
0 1 0 0
0 0 1 0
0 0 0 1
```

You may wonder what happens when the left argument of ρ is an empty vector. Let's explore this with the matrix *PRODREV*:

```
      (⍳0)ρPRODREV                    ''ρPRODREV
11                                11
```

The shape of the result is a scalar, the first element of the right argument. You should be able to figure out for yourself why it has to be a scalar.

We can enlarge any array with reshape as well as shrink it, provided we don't mind replicating data from the front end:

```
      4 7ρPRODREV
 11  23  80 100  18  19  99
122  16  14 128 112  11  23
 80 100  18  19  99 122  16
 14 128 112  11  23  80 100
```

In a way reshape is like APL food. Too much and you have a 'fat' array; too little and your array may end up looking like a dieter's delight.

More APL2 functions

Many APL'ers have wished for a primitive function that locates where in an array another array is. Although you would have to define a function for it in most APL systems, APL2 provides a *find* function, ⍷ (ε overstruck with underbar) that does just that.

It's as easy to use as membership—no restrictions on the sizes, shapes and ranks of the arguments. The result is a logical array of the same shape as that of the left argument *L* (the array being searched), with a 1 in every position of *L* where the pattern (the right argument *R*) begins. Find may be used with an axis specifier to indicate a direction other than the normal last axis.

```
      L←'ABRACADABRA'              L⍷'AB'          L⍷[1]'AB'
      L⍷'AB'                     1 0 0 0 0       0 0 0 1 0
1 0 0 0 0 0 0 1 0 0 0           0 0 1 0 0       0 0 1 0 0
      1 2 3 4 1 2 3 4⍷1 2       0 1 0 0 0       0 0 0 0 1
1 0 0 0 1 0 0 0                 0 0 0 1 0       0 0 0 1 0
      L←5 5ρL                    0 0 1 0 0       0 0 0 0 0
```

```
        L                                  L∈2 2ρ'ABAD'           L∈2 1ρ'AB'
   ABRAC                              1  0  0  0  0           0  0  0  1  0
   ADABR                              0  0  0  0  0           0  0  1  0  0
   AABRA                              0  1  0  0  0           0  0  0  0  1
   CADAB                              0  0  0  0  0           0  0  0  1  0
   RAABR                              0  0  0  0  0           0  0  0  0  0
```

A companion function is *find index*, ⍳. Its result is a matrix of integers containing the indices of the starting positions of the pattern. Again the arguments, like find, have no restrictions on them:

```
     L⍳'AB'          L⍳2 1ρ'AB'          L⍳[1]'AB'          L⍳2 2ρ'ABAD'
 1  1            1  4                 1  4                 1  1
 2  3            2  3                 2  3                 3  2
 3  2            3  5                 3  5
 4  4            4  4                 4  4
 5  3
```

Another selection function available in APL2 is *unique*, ∩. As its name suggests, when applied to any array R the result is a logical array of the same shape, with 1's marking the first occurrence of the items of R in row major order:

```
        ∩R←3 2 3 4 2 1 0 1                    ∩2 4ρ1 2 1 3 2 4 3 6
 1  1  0  1  0  1  1  0                  1  1  0  1
        (∩R)/R                           0  1  0  1
 3  2  4  1  0
```

One or more axes may be specified in testing for uniqueness:

```
        R←5 5ρ'HE    SELLSWHAT HE    SELLS'
        R                                      ∩[1]R
 HE                                        1  1  1  0  0
 SELLS
 WHAT
 HE
 SELLS
```

Putting the functions to work

Our parting gifts to you before leaving this chapter are two useful defined functions for working with character data. It is well worth your time to understand how these functions work, and why.

The first, *SQUEEZE*, is a monadic functions that removes contiguous blank characters in a vector of text. It works by comparing each element to its immediate neighbor. If both are blank, then the second of the pair is compressed out. Notice also the treatment of leading and trailing blank elements.

```
        ∇Z←SQUEEZE X
[1]     ⍝REDUCES CONSEC. BLANKS
[2]     Z←((X≠' ')∨(1↓X≠' '),1)/X∇

        SQUEEZE ' HOW      NOW BROWN    COW      '
 HOW NOW BROWN COW

        SQUEEZE 'BEES    KNEES'
 BEES KNEES
```

Does it work on *all* vectors? Will it work on empty vectors?

The next function converts a vector of text into a matrix with no more than one word per row. It is a simpler version of *ROWNAMES* (page 116).

```
      )COPY 1 CLASS CHARMAT
SAVED  14.45.33 02/20/83

      CHARMAT ' HOW     NOW BROWN COW'
HOW


NOW
BROWN
COW

      CHARMAT SQUEEZE ' HOW     NOW BROWN COW'
HOW
NOW
BROWN
COW

      ∇CHARMAT[□]∇
    ∇ Z←CHARMAT V;A
[1]   V←V,' ' ◇ A←Vε' ,' ◇ V←(~A)/V ⍝ V HAS COMMA, SPACES REMOVED
[2]   A←A/ιρA ⍝ A IS LOCATIONS OF COMMAS, SPACES
[3]   A←A-1+0,¯1↓A ◇ A←(A≠0)/A ⍝ A IS LENGTHS OF RESULTANT ROWS.
[4]   A←A∘.≥ι⌈/0,A ⍝ A IS LOGICAL MATRIX FOR EXPANSION.
[5]   Z←(ρA)ρ(,A)\V ⍝ RAVEL A TO EXPAND, THEN RESHAPE RESULT.
    ∇
```

Our last function is a classical idiom for determining whether a variable is character or numeric. It depends on the fact that ↑ (and \) fills in with blanks for character data and 0's for numeric data. Note that even when an APL array is empty, its type (character or numeric) is still preserved.

```
      ∇Z←DATATYPE R
[1]   Z←' '=1↑0ρR ⍝ 1 FOR CHARACTER, 0 FOR NUMERIC
[2]   ∇
```

Summary

Before leaving the subject of data selection, let's summarize the selection capabilities of traditional APL:

function	syntax	description
indexing	$A[B]$	picks out isolated elements, rows, columns, etc. in known positions
replication, compression	B/A	selects repeated items (or none at all) along some dimension
expansion	$B\backslash A$	inserts zeros or blanks along some dimension
take, drop	$B{\uparrow}A$ and $B{\downarrow}A$	selects a chunk of an array by specifying its boundaries
reshape	$B\rho A$	selects data from the front of an array, recycling if needed
membership	$B\epsilon A$	tests for presence of elements in an array.

There is still one more selection function, the transpose, $A\lozenge B$, which can be used to select elements lying on a diagonal plane. This advanced function will be discussed in Chapter 19.

PROBLEMS

1. DRILL. Assign

```
A←0 ¯5 ¯8 6.2 15 ¯2 25
B←1 0 0 1 0 1 1
C←'ABCDEFGHIJKLMNOPQRSTUVWXYZ ?'
M←3 4ρι12
```

(2<ι5)/ι5	M[2;3 1]	1 0 1≠M
B/A	1 1 0 1\'TWO'	A[1]+A[2 3 4]×A[7]
A[ρA],B[¯2+ρB]	A[8]	1 0 0 1 1 1\M
A[3 6]←2E5 4E¯4	Aι⌈/A	B\2 3 4 5
'ABD'∈C	2 10 15∈M	0 2↓M
4↑A	¯3↓C	1 3↑M
2 3ρM	3 3ρ1,3ρ0	10ρ100

2. Assign $D←¯2.1$ 4 1.9 0 ¯1 ¯4 ¯1.4 .7 2.5 2. Select those elements which are **A** less than .5 **B** positive **C** equal in magnitude to 4 **D** negative and greater than ¯1 **E** equal to 2 **F** less than 1 and greater than or equal to ¯2.

3. Define a monadic function to insert the character ∘ between each pair of adjacent elements in vector V.

4. For any arbitrary vector V write a function $INCR$ to compute increments between adjacent elements.

5. For mathematicians only: obtain the approximate area under the curve $Y = 3X^2$ between X_1 and X_2 by breaking it up into rectangles of width I in that interval. Hint: first define F to compute $3 \times X \star 2$.

6. Write a program $WITHIN$ to select from a vector W those elements which lie within an interval R on either side of the average of W.

7. Write an APL expression to select those elements in a vector which are integers.

8. Define a function IN to tell what percent of the elements in a vector A lie within the interval B $\pm$C.

9. Construct an expression that selects the largest element in a three-element vector V and displays a 1 if it exceeds the sum of the remaining two elements, 0 otherwise.

10. Show how to select the elements with even indices in a vector Y.

11. You are given a vector X whose elements are all different and arranged in ascending order. Write a program to insert a given scalar S into the appropriate place in the sequence so that the result is still in ascending order. Be sure that your function is able to handle the case where S is identical to some element in X.

12. Define functions to remove from a vector V all duplicate elements.

13. Write a program $SELECT$ which takes two arguments and prints that element in the left argument X whose position corresponds to the position of the largest element in the right argument Y.

14. Why is $V[¯1+ιρV]$ not executable?

15. Write an APL expression which returns the index of the largest element in a vector W.

16. V is a vector of bank account balances. Write expressions to get: **A** negative balances; **B** total of all the negative balances; **C** account number(s) (consecutive, beginning with 1) of the positive balances; **D** account number(s) with the largest balance; **E** sum of the balances in accounts 1, 5 and 6. Ditto for 2, 4 and 8.

17. Write an APL expression to calculate the sum of the first eight elements of a vector Q (or all of them if the number of elements is less than eight).

18. You are given a matrix M whose shape is 4 5. Use drop to pick out the section of M represented by $M[2 3; 2 3 4]$

19. Construct APL expressions to insert for $V \leftarrow \iota N$ a zero **A** between each two adjacent elements of V; **B** before each even element of V; **C** after each odd element of V.

20. Write a function whose explicit result is all the factors of a given integer N (i.e., the integers which divide evenly into N).

21. Define a monadic function which takes a character argument and selects the longest word in it. Hint: look for the longest set of consecutive nonblank characters.

22. Define a function $COMFACT$ to display a list of common factors, if any, of two integers A and B.

23. Write an expression to eliminate from a vector V elements with specified indices I.

24. What is the difference between $M[1;2]$ and $M[,1;,2]$?

25. Write an APL expression to delete the letter A from a character vector W.

26. Show how to pick out the elements of a vector X which are **A** divisible by 2 and/or 3, and **B** divisible by neither 2 nor 3.

27. A vector A contains the ages of all the employees of the Zee Manufacturing Company. Define an APL function that will yield the two ages which are closest to one another.

28. For an arbitrary matrix, $M \leftarrow 5 \ 5 \rho \iota 25$, show how to obtain **A** the first three rows of M; **B** the four elements in the upper left corner; **C** the last two columns of M; **D** the four corner elements.

29. Redo problem 23, Chapter 6, assuming that all the data is stored in a 3 5 matrix $INFO$. The fifth column is the average cost per gallon of gas.

30. The auditors of a progressive company find that the total cost of sampling information for accounting purposes can be described by the expression $(.08 \times N) + 10.24 \div N \star .5$ where N is the number of items to be sampled, $\$.08$ the unit cost of sampling an item and $\$10.24$ the cost of a unit error in estimation. How many items should be sampled to minimize the total cost? Assume $N \leq 50$.

31. Write a function $CENTER$ to center the title T above the body of a report R.

32. Use expansion to double-space a character matrix M.

33. A vector V is broken up into fields marked by a delimiter character W. Write a function $FWIDTH$ to return the widths of these fields.

34. A survey is conducted in which interviewers are asked 10 questions to which they must respond 'yes' or 'no.' Find the percentages of positive responses to each question if the answers are stored in a logical matrix ANS, with one row for each person interviewed.

35. You are given a vector of stored messages $V \leftarrow 'GOOD \ DAYHI \ YOURSELFHELLO \ AND \ WELCOMEGO \ AWAY \ I''M \ BUSY'$. Define a function HI to return a random message from V.

36. **A** Construct a matrix whose shape is always random and not greater than 8, made up of elements which are random positive integers not greater than 150. **B** Modify your result to make the upper bound for the elements itself a random number less than 300.

37. Use the membership function to identify and select the one-digit integer elements of a vector V.

38. Write an APL expression to determine if two sets of numbers, $S1$ and $S2$, have identical elements, except possibly for order.

39. You are given a vector of characters $S \leftarrow 'WE \ ARE \ ALL \ GOOD \ MEN'$. Write an APL expression to determine how many occurrences of the letters $'ABCDEFGHIJKL'$ are in S.

40. Let C be a vector of characters. Construct an expression which replaces every $'X'$ in C with a $'Y'$.

41. For a vector of eight elements, construct two expressions for selecting the last three elements. Use the compression function in one and the take function in the other.

42. Write an APL expression to select N random elements from a matrix M.

43. Show how to add a scalar N to each element in the even columns of a matrix M.

44. You are given five vectors $V1$ through $V5$ of invoices from fifteen customers. The first represents bills under 30 days old, the second 30 through 59 days old, the third 60 through 89 days, etc. All entries with a given index are associated with the same customer. Write a program that will **A** construct a matrix of these invoices with each vector $V1$ through $V5$ occupying a single row; **B** print the total amount of receivables in each category and separately for each customer, with an appropriate message; **C** print the grand total of all receivables with an identifying message; and **D** identify which customers are deadbeats (have invoices outstanding more than 59 days).

45. Using *only* the take ($\uparrow$) function, select from the character vector $V \leftarrow {}' INDUBITABLY'$ the characters ${}'DUB'$. Ditto for drop($\downarrow$).

46. As production and sales manager for one of your company's products, you must decide how much to produce and what to charge for it. Your compensation is a salary plus 2% of the total receipts from the sale of the product. The company will not sell the product for less than $7.00. At the same time, if the price goes above $7.50 then the company's facilities are liable to be picketed by local consumer groups. The demand function for this product is $Q = 600\text{-}3.7P^2$, where Q is the quantity sold and P the price charged. What price should you charge and how much should you produce to maximize your personal income? Assume you produced only enough to cover sales, and can vary the price only in increments of one cent.

47. Write an APL expression to compare two sets of 50 random integers each (generated without duplication from $\iota 100$) and select those integers common to both.

48. Given $V1 \leftarrow 2\ 3\ 4\ 5\ 6\ 9\ 15$ and $V2 \leftarrow 4\ 9\ 15\ 6\ 20\ 25\ 40$, write APL expressions to find **A** those elements in both $V1$ and $V2$; **B** those elements in either $V1$ or $V2$; **C** those elements of $V1$ not in $V2$.

49. Write an expression to delete a specified row R from a matrix M, storing the result in $M1$.

50. Write an expression to take from a vector V all the elements after the first occurrence of a specified element, S. That is, if $V \leftarrow 3\ 1\ 2\ 7\ 2\ 1\ 1\ 2\ 6$ and $S \leftarrow 2$, the result should be $7\ 2\ 1\ 1\ 2\ 6$.

51. Why does $MAT[I;] \iota VECTOR$ give a $RANK\ ERROR$ for some row I?

52. The $4\ 3$ matrices $PRICES$ and $ORDERS$ contain information about four sizes (S,M,L,XL) and three styles (A,B,C) of shirts from a manufacturer. When the prices on style B are decreased by 10% to meet competition, the orders received increase by 15% for all sizes in that style. How does total revenue from all styles now compare with the original?

53. Again with $PRICES$ and $ORDERS$, **A** identify those sizes and styles that sold less than 10,000 and were also high priced (more than $20); **B** how many combinations fall in this category?; **C** how much revenue is attributable to them?

Chapter 15: Transformations and rearrangements

One of the earliest commercial uses of computers was rearranging data, particularly alphabetic information (commonly referred to as *sorting*). Those of you who are jigsaw puzzle buffs or who have had to produce an index for a book such as this will appreciate the desirability of having a systematic way to go about the job.

And who is there among us who hasn't at one time or another wondered why the grated cheese in certain supermarkets is to be found over the frozen foods, rather than being nestled among the boxes of pasta and tomato sauce, where you might expect it? Then there's the frustration we have all felt when a house number in an unfamiliar neighborhood isn't where it's 'supposed to be.' The need for order when searching clearly permeates most everyday activities.

This chapter is concerned with rearranging data in arrays. The topic isn't really new because some of the functions covered already, like bracket indexing and reshape, can be used to rearrange data as well as to select data.

Two very common rearrangements are reversing or rotating the elements in an array. For example, if you wished to reverse the elements of a vector V you could use the expression $V[1+(\rho V)-\iota\rho V]$. And the expression $V[1+(\rho V)|^-1+\iota\rho V]$ will rotate the elements N positions to the left. Reversal and rotation requirements occur frequently enough that APL provides functions specifically designed for the jobs.

Reverse

To *reverse* the elements in a vector, use the symbol ϕ (O overstruck with |). As with all selection and rearrangement functions, reverse can be applied to character data as well as numeric data:.

```
     ϕ10 10 20 12         ϕι3        ϕ'ABCDEF'        ϕ'POTS'
12 20 10 10               3 2 1      FEDCBA           STOP
```

When applied to matrices, ϕ reverses the order of the columns (last dimension). To reverse the order of the rows (first dimension), use $\ominus$ (O and −) instead. The example matrix $DATA$ here was chosen so that you can easily see how the elements are moved:

```
    DATA←(10×ι5)∘.+ι4
```

```
    DATA              ϕDATA                 ⊖DATA
11 12 13 14        14 13 12 11        51 52 53 54
21 22 23 24        24 23 22 21        41 42 43 44
31 32 33 34        34 33 32 31        31 32 33 34
41 42 43 44        44 43 42 41        21 22 23 24
51 52 53 54        54 53 52 51        11 12 13 14
```

To reverse both columns and rows, use either of

```
    ϕ⊖DATA               ⊖ϕDATA
54 53 52 51        54 53 52 51
44 43 42 41        44 43 42 41
34 33 32 31        34 33 32 31
24 23 22 21        24 23 22 21
14 13 12 11        14 13 12 11
```

Reverse is a very easy function to remember. The shape of the result is always the same as the shape of the argument, as for the primitive scalar monadic functions. The elements themselves are unchanged, but they appear in element reverse order for vectors or reverse row ($\ominus$) or column (ϕ) order for matrices.

Rotate

The same symbols φ and ⊖, when used dyadically, mean *rotation*. For vectors, the left argument is the number of positions to rotate, while the right argument is the array to be rotated:

```
      2φ10 10 20 12                    2φ⍳3                  1φ'ABCDEF'
20 12 10 10                      3 1 2                 BCDEFA
      0φ10 10 20 12                   ‾1φ⍳3                ‾5φ'ABCDEF'
10 10 20 12                      3 1 2                 BCDEFA
```

There are always as many elements in the result as in the right argument. The shape of the result is the same as the right argument. The elements are just pushed left for positive left arguments or right for negative left arguments.

What happens if you rotate more positions than there were in the vector originally?

```
      103φ'ABCDEFGHIJ'                 ‾30φ1 2 3
DEFGHIJABC                       1 2 3
```

This little function, which can be regarded as a *formal description*, tells what really happens:

```
     ∇ R← N ROTATE V
[1]    ⍝FORMAL DESCRIPTION OF ROTATION.  NOTE USE OF RESIDUE
[2]    N←(ρV)|N ◇ R←NφV ∇
```

Matrices can be rotated as well. If the left argument is a single number, then all rows or columns are rotated the same amount:

```
        DATA                     1φDATA                   ‾2⊖DATA
11 12 13 14               12 13 14 11              41 42 43 44
21 22 23 24               22 23 24 21              51 52 53 54
31 32 33 34               32 33 34 31              11 12 13 14
41 42 43 44               42 43 44 41              21 22 23 24
51 52 53 54               52 53 54 51              31 32 33 34
```

Each row or column can be rotated an independent amount. For those cases, the left argument must be a vector containing one element for each row or column of the right argument. That is, for φ, ρLEFT must be ‾1↑ρRIGHT and for ⊖, ρLEFT must be 1↑ρRIGHT:

```
      1 2 0 ‾1 5φDATA               3 2 1 0⊖DATA
12 13 14 11                    41 32 23 14
23 24 21 22                    51 42 33 24
31 32 33 34                    11 52 43 34
44 41 42 43                    21 12 53 44
52 53 54 51                    31 22 13 54
```

Applications of rotation

Here are some applications of rotation drawn from text processing, finance and mathematics. If you're not interested in any of these topics, you can skip to the next section.

Given a matrix of words, we want to *right justify* each row; that is, slide each word to the right so that the right margin lines up.

```
      )COPY 1 CLASS FURN RIGHTJUST
SAVED  14.45.33 02/20/83

      ∇RIGHTJUST[▯]∇
     ∇ R←RIGHTJUST M;BLANKS;TRAILBLANKS
[1]    ⍝RIGHT JUSTIFY CHARACTER MATRIX.  AJR/LG AUG 1980.
[2]    BLANKS←M=' ' ◇ TRAILBLANKS←∧\φBLANKS ◇ R←(-+/TRAILBLANKS)φM
     ∇
```

```
      FURN                    RIGHTJUST FURN
DESKS                         DESKS
CHAIRS                        CHAIRS
TABLES                        TABLES
FILES                          FILES
```

For our second application let's multiply two polynomials. The longhand method is shown here:

$$x^3 + 3x^2 + 5x - 6$$
$$2x^2 - 4x + 7$$
$$\overline{}$$
$$2x^5 + 6x^4 + 10x^3 - 12x^2$$
$$-\ 4x^4 - 12x^3 - 20x^2 + 24x$$
$$+\ 7x^3 + 21x^2 + 35x - 42$$
$$\overline{2x^5 + 2x^4 +\ \ 5x^3 - 11x^2 + 59x - 42}$$

In APL it can be worked this way:

```
P1←1 3 5 ¯6
P2←2 ¯4 7
PROD←P1∘.×P2
AUGMENT←((ρP1),¯1+(ρP1)+ρP2)↑PROD
SHIFTED←(1-ιρP1)⌽AUGMENT
```

```
       PROD                    AUGMENT                      SHIFTED
   2  ¯4    7           2  ¯4    7   0   0   0       2  ¯4   ¯7   0   0   0
   6 ¯12   21           6 ¯12   21   0   0   0       0   6 ¯12 ¯21   0   0
 ¯10 ¯20   35         ¯10 ¯20 ¯35   0   0   0       0   0  10 ¯20  35  ¯0
 ¯12  24  ¯42         ¯12  24 ¯42   0   0   0       0   0   0 ¯12  24 ¯42
    +⌿SHIFTED
 2  2 5 ¯11 59 ¯42
```

The interesting part of the method is augmenting the outer product result matrix with enough columns of zeros to permit lining up each row of coefficients properly.

An important financial planning use of rotation is in calculating leading or lagging cash flows. For example, a planner knows that 50% of his customers pay in the month they are billed, 30% pay in the first following month, 10% pay in the second following month, and 5% in the third following month. The rest of the customers are deadbeats who never pay. If the expected monthly billings are as shown in the vector *BILLINGS*, what is the cash stream?

```
BILLINGS←1000 1020 1350 1200 900 950 990 1030 1000 800 800 900
LAGPAY←.5 .3 .1 .05

      ∇CASHSTREAM←B FLOW L;T
[1]    T←B∘.×L
[2]    T←(+\ρT)↑T ⍝ ENLARGE TO PREVENT WRAP-AROUND
[3]    T←(1-ι1↑ρT)⌽T ⍝ LAG EACH ROW ONE MORE MONTH
[4]    CASHSTREAM← ¯1↓+⌿T∇

      BILLINGS FLOW LAGPAY
500 810 1081 1157 996 932.5 930 952 955.5 852.5 791.5 820 390 130 45
```

Transpose

Transposition is the interchanging of elements along two or more dimensions. The *transpose* function ⍉ has both monadic and dyadic forms. This chapter will consider only monadic transpose, leaving dyadic transpose (powerful, but difficult for many people to master) for a later chapter.

Monadic transpose applied to a matrix simply turns the matrix on its side:

```
      DATA                    ⍉DATA
  11 12 13 14            11 21 31 41 51
  21 22 23 24            12 22 32 42 52
  31 32 33 34            13 23 33 43 53
  41 42 43 44            14 24 34 44 54
  51 52 53 54                ρ⍉DATA
      ρDATA            4  5
  5  4
```

In other words, any element that could be reached by $DATA[I;J]$ can be reached as $(\lozenge DATA)[J;I]$ and $\rho DATA$ is the same as $\phi \rho \lozenge DATA$. It doesn't make any sense to transpose vectors or scalars; in both cases the results are the same as the arguments.

Transposition is almost indispensable for some tasks. Suppose you wanted to produce a compound interest table for 5%, 7.5% and 10% interest for 1, 2, 3 and 4 years, but with the interest rates running across the page and the periods running down:

```
     ⍉(1+0.05 0.075 0.1)∘.*⍳4
1.05               1.075          1.1
1.1025             1.155625       1.21
1.157625           1.242296875    1.331
1.21550625         1.335469141    1.4641
```

You would be hard pressed to think of any way to get this result *without* transpose. You certainly can't do it with $(\iota 4)\circ.*1+0.05\ 0.075\ 0.1$ because * isn't commutative.

A transformation mnemonic

By this time you have probably noticed that the appearance of the symbols ϕ, $\ominus$ and $\lozenge$ is related to the kind of transformation which results when they are applied to certain arrays.

```
       DATA              φDATA                ⊖DATA                  ⍉DATA
  11 12 13 14        14 13|12 11         51 52 53 54          11 21 31 41 51
  21 22 23 24        24 23|22 21         41 42 43 44          12 22 32 42 52
  31 32 33 34        34 33|32 31         31 32 33 34          13 23 33 43 53
  41 42 43 44        44 43|42 41         21 22 23 24          14 24 34 44 54
  51 52 53 54        54 53|52 51         11 12 13 14
```

In each case the slant of the line in ϕ $\lozenge$ and $\ominus$ represents the axis (shown as a dotted line) about which the transformation occurred.

Arranging data in ascending and descending order

A director of a musical comedy has the following dancers available for the chorus line:

```
     )COPY 1 CLASS ROWNAMES
SAVED   14.45.33 02/20/83

     NAMES←(⍳0) ROWNAMES '/JUDY/MINDY/JEFF/JILL/DAVID/ANNETTE/LISA'
     EMPNO←⍳7

     HEIGHT←63 65 69 62 69 64 64

     RECORDS←(⍒⍉2 7⍴EMPNO,HEIGHT),' ',NAMES

     RECORDS
 1 63 JUDY
 2 65 MINDY
 3 69 JEFF
 4 62 JILL
 5 69 DAVID
 6 64 ANNETTE
 7 64 LISA
```

He wants to line them up so that the shortest dancer is at the left and the tallest is at the right. If he were to do this manually, he might designate an area as the place to line up, and then ask the shortest person in the set of dancers to report there. He would repeat the procedure until no dancers were left in the original place.

With APL he can move them all at once:

```
     ORDER←⍋HEIGHT
     ORDER
4  1  6  7  2  3  5
```

```
        NAMES[ORDER;]                        RECORDS[ORDER;]
JILL                                  4 62 JILL
JUDY                                  1 63 JUDY
ANNETTE                               6 64 ANNETTE
LISA                                  7 64 LISA
MINDY                                 2 65 MINDY
JEFF                                  3 69 JEFF
DAVID                                 5 69 DAVID
```

The new symbol above, ⍋, *grade up*, formed by overstriking the Δ and the |, is the key to this type of ordered rearrangement. When applied to a vector of numbers it gives the indices of the lowest, next lowest, and so on to the highest value in the original vector. Thus, the result always has the same shape as the argument.

The result is frequently used to index some related array to reorder it, as we did with *NAMES* above. We could have applied it to *HEIGHT* as well, producing them in ascending order:

```
        HEIGHT[⍋HEIGHT]
62 63 64 64 65 69 69
```

If there are two or more identical values in the original vector, the first from the left is taken as the lowest. Look at the last two elements of *ORDER*. The first 69 encountered was the third element of *HEIGHT*, and the next 69 was in the fifth element. And if all the elements of the vector were identical, then ⍋*VECTOR* would be the same as ⍳ρ*VECTOR*.

Sometimes you need to arrange data in descending order. An obvious approach is to reverse the results of ⍋:

```
        HEIGHT
63 65 69 62 69 64 64
```

```
        ⍋HEIGHT                         ⌽⍋HEIGHT
4 1 6 7 2 3 5                       5 3 2 7 6 1 4
```

```
        HEIGHT[⌽⍋HEIGHT]                ⌽HEIGHT[⍋HEIGHT]
69 69 65 64 64 63 62                69 69 65 64 64 63 62
```

```
        NAMES           NAMES[⌽⍋HEIGHT;]               ⊖NAMES[⍋HEIGHT;]
JUDY                DAVID                          DAVID
MINDY               JEFF                           JEFF
JEFF                MINDY                          MINDY
JILL                LISA                           LISA
DAVID               ANNETTE                        ANNETTE
ANNETTE             JUDY                           JUDY
LISA                JILL                           JILL
```

But a specific function, ⍒, *grade down*, does it directly:

```
        ⍒HEIGHT              HEIGHT[⍒HEIGHT]                NAMES[⍒HEIGHT;]
3 5 2 6 7 1 4           69 69 65 64 64 63 62           JEFF
                                                       DAVID
                                                       MINDY
                                                       ANNETTE
                                                       LISA
                                                       JUDY
                                                       JILL
```

Observe that while this gives an equally good arrangement for the chorus line, it is not identical to ⊖*NAMES*[⍋*HEIGHT*;] or *NAMES*[⌽⍋*HEIGHT*;]. This is because both ⍋ and ⍒ start their search for smallest or largest from the left end of the vector:

```
        ⍋HEIGHT                         ⍒HEIGHT
4 1 6 7 2 3 5                       3 5 2 6 7 1 4
        ⌽⍒HEIGHT                        ⌽⍋HEIGHT
4 1 7 6 2 5 3                       5 3 2 7 6 1 4
```

You can sometime take advantage of this subtle difference. For instance, a test for unique elements is ∧/(⍋*VECTOR*)=⌽⍒*VECTOR*, although ∧/(*VECTOR*⍳*VECTOR*)=⍳ρ*VECTOR* may be easier to understand.

Grading matrices up and down

In most APL systems, grade up and grade down work only on vectors. If that's the case on your system, read the rest of this section and the next on alphabetic sorting. If you are using APL2, skip to page 142, advanced grade features. While the result of $\triangle$ or $\triangledown$ can be used to rearrange a matrix, as we did with *NAMES*, sometimes a matrix has to be rearranged taking into account more than one column.

For example, each row of the following table represents the date of hiring of a group of employees:

month	day	year
5	12	1970
6	3	1969
5	12	1965
3	30	1965
6	3	1969
1	12	1970

There are several ways to do the reordering, but they all depend on one principle: rearrange on the least significant column first (days), and do the most significant column last (years).

The first approach simply converts each three-part date into a single number:

```
H←6 3ρ5 12 70 6 3 69 5 12 65 3 30 65 6 3 69 1 12 70
H[;3]←H[;3]+1900
H
5   12 1970
6    3 1969
5   12 1965
3   30 1965
6    3 1969
1   12 1970
```

Each row of the data matrix *H* is now converted to a single element in a new vector in which years have the greatest weight, months have an intermediate weight, and days have the least weight:

```
SQUASHED←+/H×(ρH)ρ100 1 10000
SQUASHED
19700512  19690603  19650512  19650330  19690603  19700112

   ↑SQUASHED
4 3 2 5 6 1

   H[↑SQUASHED;]
3   30 1965
5   12 1965
6    3 1969
6    3 1969
1   12 1970
5   12 1970
```

Well, it worked. We took advantage of the fact that no value in the 'days' column would exceed 99 and that the months also would not exceed 99. All in all, we took up around 8 decimal digits for each value in *SQUASHED*. But if we had had many data columns to include in the 'squashed' ordering, this method wouldn't work because most APL systems can't handle more than around 16 decimal digits in one element.

A more general approach is to reorder the array once for each column that contributes to the ordering:

```
HD←H[↑H[;2];]            HMD←HD[↑HD[;1];]          HYMD←HMD[↑HMD[;3];]
HD                       HMD                       HYMD
6    3 1969              1   12 1970               3   30 1965
6    3 1969              3   30 1965               5   12 1965
5   12 1970              5   12 1970               6    3 1969
5   12 1965              5   12 1965               6    3 1969
1   12 1970              6    3 1969               1   12 1970
3   30 1965              6    3 1969               5   12 1970
```

This approach also worked, and it was not limited by the number of columns involved in the ordering. But we moved a *lot* of data around to get it done. All the elements of what was *H* were moved three times. A better method is to move only the elements of the grade vector for each column, and rearrange the original matrix only after all the grading is complete, as in the following sequence:

```
      GD←⍋H[;2]                              H[GYMD;]
      GMD←GD[⍋H[GD;1]]                  3    30 1965
      GYMD←GMD[⍋H[GMD;3]]              5    12 1965
                                        6     3 1969
                                        6     3 1969
                                        1    12 1970
                                        5    12 1970
```

With only three columns to arrange, a hard-coded solution in a defined function doesn't appear unreasonable here:3

```
      ∇R←GRADE3 M
[1]   ⍝REARRANGES 3-COLUMN NUMERIC MATRIX.  GILMAN, OCT 1980
[2]   R←⍋M[;2]
[3]   R←R[⍋M[R;1]]
[4]   R←R[⍋M[R;3]] ∇
```

We feel compelled to cite an instance where an APL one-line solution for this problem achieved conciseness, but destroyed readability. Here is the controversial one-liner:

```
      ∇R←ONELINEGRADE M
[1]   R←R[⍋M[R←R[⍋M[R←R[⍋M[;3]];2]];]]∇
```

Alas, it works, but not in all APL implementations

Alphabetic sorting

Rearranging the rows of character matrices in alphabetic order is not different from working with numeric matrices, once you get past the first step: changing the characters to their index positions in some character set, called a *collating sequence*.

```
      NAMES                    ' ABCDEFGHIJKLMNOPQRSTUVWXYZ,.'⍳NAMES
JUDY               11 22   5 26  1  1  1
MINDY              14 10 15   5 26  1  1
JEFF               11  6  7  7  1  1  1
JILL               11 10 13 13  1  1  1
DAVID               5  2 23 10  5  1  1
ANNETTE             2 15 15  6 21 21  6
LISA               13 10 20  2  1  1  1
```

Again the rearranging begins in the least significant column. But because there are many columns to do, it's wise to write a little function to make entry easier.

```
      ∇R←C UP V
[1]   ⍝USES GLOBAL MATRIX ND.  V IS LESS SIGNIFICANT GRADE VECTOR.
[2]   ⍝C IS COLUMN OF ND TO BE GRADED.  R IS NEW GRADE VECTOR.
[3]   R←V[⍋ND[V;C]]∇
      ND←' ABCDEFGHIJKLMNOPQRSTUVWXYZ,.'⍳NAMES

      NAMES[1 UP 2 UP 3 UP 4 UP 5 UP 6 UP 7 UP ⍳1↑⍴NAMES;]
ANNETTE
DAVID
JEFF
JILL
JUDY
LISA
MINDY
```

Why the ⍳1↑⍴NAMES? That's the original grade vector, meaning that NAMES[⍳1↑⍴NAMES;] is identical to NAMES itself. Also, see how we have taken advantage of APL's right-to-left execution sequence.

You must be thinking that there's got to be a better way to alphabetize than using 1 UP 2 UP 3 UP... etc., and there is, but it comes in a later chapter.

Advanced grade features

In APL2, ⍋ and ⍒ have been enhanced to accept arrays of rank greater than one:

```
      TAB2                    ⍋TAB2
  3   1   7            4  1  3  2
  7  10   4
  6   9   1
  1   6   7
```

The shape of the result is the same as the first dimension of the argument and places the subarrays of the argument (defined along the first dimension) in ascending order.

The most interesting part of the extension is with character arrays,

```
    NAMES               ⍋NAMES              NAMES[⍋NAMES;]
JUDY             6  5  3  4  1  7  2      ANNETTE
MINDY                                     DAVID
JEFF                                      JEFF
JILL                                      JILL
DAVID                                     JUDY
ANNETTE                                   LISA
LISA                                      MINDY
```

using the default sort sequence ' _AAaBB_b ... 0 1 2 3 4 5 6 7 8 9 '. If, as frequently happens, we have a list which is a combination of alphabetic and numeric characters (for example, a parts list), then ⍋ will neatly sort the alphabetic prefixes and numeric suffixes:

```
      INV←6 4ρ'CX20AC10AM2 AB8 AB3 CD14'

      INV                 INV[⍋INV;]
CX20                    AB3
AC10                    AB8
AM2                     AC10
AB8                     AM2
AB3                     CD14
CD14                    CX20
```

Any desired sort sequence can be used with a dyadic version of grade. For instance, let $S←'\square*LX0'$ and $M←5$ $3ρ'***XXXZZZ\llcorner\llcorner\llcorner\square\square\square'$:

```
      S⍋M                 M[S⍋M;]
  5  1  4  2  3         □□□
                        ***
                        ⌊⌊⌊
                        XXX
                        ZZZ
```

As with dyadic ⍳, characters not present in the sort sequence are relegated to the end of the list.

Exotic uses of grade

Grade up and grade down are easy enough to work with for their obvious applications in rearranging vectors or matrices for display. However, don't think that's all they are good for. They are profoundly versatile, and professional APL'ers continue to discover interesting uses for them. This section mentions a few of the more surprising ones. Some of the points are admittedly of academic or recreational interest only. You can skip this entire topic if you wish, without loss of continuity.

⍋ and ⍒ can be used instead of monadic ⍳:

```
      ⍳5                   ⍋5ρ0                 ⍒5ρ0
 1 2 3 4 5           1 2 3 4 5            1 2 3 4 5
```

The more curious among you may wonder whether ⍋⍋VECTOR has any special meaning. Let's explore it with

```
      Z←40 80 50 10 40                ⍋Z                  ⍋⍋Z
                               4  1  5  3  2         2  5  4  1  3
```

What you get is the cardinal ordering of each of the elements of the original vector. ⍋⍋*Z* tells you that *Z*'s first element is the second largest, its second element is the largest, its third element is the fourth largest, and so on.

⍋⍋ can be used to *merge* or *collate* two or more arrays much as you would collate pages of paper from several stacks into one. For example, the two matrices *ITEMS* and *SUMMARIES* can be merged in whatever pattern is required:

ITEMS	*SUMMARIES*	*LINES*
REVENUES	*GROSS MARGINS	REVENUES
COST OF GOODS	*TOTAL EXPENSES	COST OF GOODS
SELLING EXPENSE	*NET BEFORE TAX	*GROSS MARGINS
GEN AND ADMIN	*NET AFTER TAX	SELLING EXPENSE
TAXES		GEN AND ADMIN
		*TOTAL EXPENSES
		*NET BEFORE TAX
		TAXES
		*NET AFTER TAX

```
    TEMP←((ρITEMS)+1 0×ρSUMMARIES)ρ(,ITEMS),,SUMMARIES
    LINES←TEMP[⍋⍋1 1 2 1 1 2 2 1 2;]
```

Observe that the result of ⍋*VECTOR* is always some permutation of the numbers ⍳ρ*VECTOR*. *Permutation vectors* have interesting mathematical properties when used with functions ⍋, ⍒, monadic ⌽, dyadic ⍳ and indexing. We'll state a few of the identities here as brain teasers. All of these examples assume that *P* is a vector consisting of the numbers ⍳*N*, but scrambled in an arbitrary manner.

⍒*P*	⌽⍋*P*		*P*	⍋⍋*P*	⍒⍒⍒⍒*P*
⍒⍋*P*	⌽*P*		⍋*P*	⍋⍋⍋*P*	⍋⍒⍋*P*
P[*P*]	(⍋*P*)⍳*P*		*P*[⍋*P*]	(⍋*P*)[*P*]	⍳ρ*P* *P*⍳*P*

Another practical use of ⍋ and ⍋⍋ is in the following linear interpolation algorithm. Given a set of actuarial data like the following,

PRESENT AGE	1	5	10	20	30	50	65	70
ADDITONAL LIFE EXPECTANCY	75	74	66	54	40	23	9	7

calculate the expectancies for a group of people aged 5, 20, 24, 61 and 12. The first two are easy and can use dyadic ⍳ directly,

```
    AGE←1 5 10 20 30 50 65 70             EXP[AGE⍳24 61 12]
    EXP←75 74 66 54 40 23 9 7         INDEX ERROR
    EXP[AGE⍳5 20]                         EXP[AGE⍳ 24 61 12]
74 54                                             ∧
```

but those that don't match exactly will require us to estimate between values. One of the simpler methods for doing this is linear interpolation. For example, age 24 is four-tenths the distance between 20 and 30, and the corresponding life expectancies are 54 and 40:

```
    54+((24-20)÷30-20)×40-54
48.4
```

The question is, how to find that 24 is between the 20 and the 30; and the answer is a clever use of grade up:

```
    ⍋⍋AGE,24
1 2 3 4 6 7 8 9 5
```

The last element represents the relative ranking of 24 among the elements of the vector *AGE*. From here it's all downhill (pun intended):

```
    POS←¯1↑⍋⍋AGE,24
    EXP[POS-1]+((24-AGE[POS-1])÷-/EXP[POS-1 0])×-/EXP[POS-1]
69.42857143
```

This will interpolate only one value at a time. But one of the major beauties of APL is its ability to work with arrays of data. The following function interpolates entire arrays, and even extrapolates if the values are outside the range of numbers.

```
    )COPY 1 CLASS INT
SAVED  14.45.33 02/20/83
```

```
      (⍉ 2 8⍴AGE,EXP) INT 5 20 61 24 12
74 54 12.73333333 48.4 63.6

      ∇INT[⎕]∇
    ∇ R←X INT D;DI;Y;RQ;P
[1]   ⍝LEFT ARG IS 2 COL MATRIX. COL 1 IS INDEPENDENT VARIABLE
[2]   ⍝COL 2 IS RESULT VARIABLE.
[3]   ⍝RIGHT ARG IS VALUES [SCALED TO COL 1] TO BE INTERPOLATED
[4]   ⍝     OR EXTRAPOLATED INTO COL2.  AJROSE 26 AUG 79.
[5]   RQ←⍴D ◇ DI←⍋D←,D ◇ D←D[DI] ◇ Y←X[;2] ◇ X←X[;1]
[6]   P←¯1+2⌈(((⍴X)↓⍋⍋X,D)-¯1+⍳⍴D)⌊⍴X
[7]   R←(Y[P]+((D-X[P])÷-/X[P∘.+ 1 0])×-/Y[P∘.+ 1 0])[RQ⍴⍋DI]
    ∇
```

Match

Occasionally there is a need to determine whether two arrays are identical, that is, their contents, shape and rank are the same. APL2 and APL*PLUS both provide a dyadic function *match*, ≡ (= overstruck with _) to do the checking. It returns a scalar 1 if the arguments are identical, 0 otherwise. Note its behavior on these look-alikes:

```
      '' ≡ ⍳0
0

      1 ≡ ,1
0

      (2 3⍴⍳6) ≡ 2 3⍴⍳6
1

      '23' ≡ 23
0
```

Deranged data

All of this chapter has focused on transforming or rearranging data into some orderly pattern. Now we're going to introduce a function that deliberately scrambles data.

Suppose, for example, that the dancers' union protests having the chorus line in ascending order, and demands that each person be given an even chance of being in any position. A way to do it fairly would be to write each dancer's identification number on a slip of paper, put it in an urn, and have an honest person, blindfolded, sequentially draw slips from the urn and announce the lineup. The function *deal*, ?, does exactly that.

Ordering for the dancers could be any of these:

```
      7?7                      7?7
4 2 5 3 7 6 1          3 1 2 7 4 6 5

      ARB←7?7               ARB
                       3 1 6 2 7 5 4
      NAMES                NAMES[ARB;]
JUDY                   JEFF
MINDY                  JUDY
JEFF                   ANNETTE
JILL                   MINDY
DAVID                  LISA
ANNETTE                DAVID
LISA                   JILL
```

We've already used the symbol ? in a monadic sense to mean *roll*. Roll, you may recall, selects each value with possible replacement. Thus, ?7⍴7 may or may not have values repeated in it, while 7?7 is guaranteed not to have any repeats.

Suppose you needed only 5 dancers. Then

```
      5?7                    5?7                   5?7
3  2  1  7  4          1 2 6 5 3           3  1  4  7  6
```

is a way to select 5 items from a population of 7, again without repeats. Both arguments must be single integers, and the left argument must not be larger than the right. The result is a vector whose length is the same as the value of the left argument.

To help you keep deal and roll straight, associate their names with games of chance. Deal implies random selection of a subset (or complete set) of unique objects like a deck of cards (4 13ρ52?52 is a perfect way to simulate a bridge round). Roll implies random selection with the possibility of repeated values, as in a roll of dice (?2ρ6), the readout of a one-armed bandit (?3ρ10), or even a coin toss (?2). Of course, 1?N and ?N both select one number from ιN, although their ranks may differ.

Both roll and deal are random selections from an underlying uniform frequency distribution, each value of which has an equal chance of being selected. Suppose you wanted to build a game of chance, such as Russian roulette (a six-position revolver with only one live bullet). Here the probability of living is 5/6 and the probability of dying is 1/6 on any given spin and trigger pull.

This function would do it:

```
        ∇RISKY
[1]     [1] ((2 4ρ'LIVEDEAD')[1 1 1 1 1 2;])[1?6]∇
```

The program *TEACH* in the next section employs a similar technique, assuring that all exercises have a chance of being selected, but weighting the probability of choice toward those on which the student has done poorly.

Another drill

In Chapter 7 the tutorial exercise *EASYDRILL* was introduced to give you practice in the functions discussed up to that point. You're ready now for some tougher problems. In workspace 1 *AIDRILL* there is a drill called *TEACH*. Load the workspace and type *TEACH*. Indicate which functions you want practice in. Be brave and try exercises with vectors of length 1 and 0. Here is a short sample session with *TEACH*:

```
      )LOAD 1 AIDRILL
SAVED  14.15.05 07/06/79

      TEACH
ARE YOU ALREADY FAMILIAR WITH THE INSTRUCTIONS? (TYPE
Y FOR YES AND N FOR NO.
NO

THIS IS AN EXERCISE IN SIMPLE APL EXPRESSIONS.  YOU WILL FIRST
HAVE THE OPPORTUNITY TO SELECT THE FEATURES YOU WISH TO BE
DRILLED IN.  THE EXERCISE THEN BEGINS.  FOR EACH PROBLEM YOU MUST
ENTER THE PROPER RESULT.  ANSWERS WILL CONSIST OF SCALAR INTEGERS
IF EXERCISES WITH VECTORS ARE NOT DESIRED; OTHERWISE ANSWERS WILL
CONSIST OF SCALARS OR VECTORS.  A VECTOR OF LENGTH ZERO REQUIRES
THE RESPONSE ι0, A VECTOR OF LENGTH ONE REQUIRES THE RESPONSE ,X
WHERE X IS THE VALUE OF THE ELEMENT.  YOU HAVE THREE TRIES FOR
EACH PROBLEM.  TYPE STOP AT ANY TIME TO TERMINATE THE EXERCISE
AND PRODUCE A RECORDING OF YOUR PERFORMANCE.  TYPING STOPSHORT
WILL TERMINATE THE EXERCISE BUT WILL NOT PRODUCE A RECORD OF
PERFORMANCE.  TYPING PLEASE FOR ANY PROBLEM WILL LET YOU PEEK AT
THE ANSWERS.  TYPE Y UNDER EACH FUNCTION FOR WHICH YOU WANT
EXERCISE:

SCALAR DYADIC FUNCTIONS
+-×÷*⌈⌊<≤=≥>≠!|∧∨⊛⍀⍦
     YY       YY

SCALAR MONADIC FUNCTIONS
+-×÷⌈⌊!|~
   Y  Y

TYPE Y IF EXERCISES ARE TO USE VECTORS, N OTHERWISE
Y
```

TYPE Y IF REDUCTION EXERCISES ARE DESIRED, N OTHERWISE
Y

TYPE Y IF VECTORS OF LENGTH ZERO OR ONE ARE DESIRED,
N OTHERWISE
Y

MIXED DYADIC FUNCTIONS
ρι,∈⊥⊤/↑↓\φ
YYY

MIXED MONADIC FUNCTIONS
ιρ,φ
YY

```
                        !,0
□:
        1
TRY AGAIN
□:
          ,1

                        !ι0
□:
        ι0

                        ρ0
□:
        ι0

                        ÷ 1 ¯1 0.1111111111
□:
        1 ¯1 9

                        ⌈/ ¯8 ¯10 4
□:
        4

                        ι5
□:
        STOPSHORT
```

PROBLEMS

1. DRILL.   Assign $A \leftarrow 3 \ 2 \ 0 \ ^-1 \ 5 \ ^-8$, $N \leftarrow 4 \ 3\rho 9 \ 7 \ 1 \ 2 \ 3 \ 5 \ 6 \ 9 \ 15 \ 22 \ 1$ and
   $M \leftarrow 3 \ 4 \rho \iota 12$.

$3\phi A$	$\phi 0, \iota 3$	$A[\Psi 0 \ 1 \ 0 \ 1 \ 0 \ 1]$
$2\phi A[\iota 4]$	$2\phi\phi\iota 7$	$2\phi 1\Theta M$
$\spadesuit\Psi A$	$\phi\Theta N$	$(\phi\iota 6)\iota M$
$2\uparrow ^-3\phi A$	$A[\spadesuit\spadesuit A]$	$(\iota 6)=\spadesuit A[\spadesuit A]$
$^-2 \ 1 \ 3\phi M$	$M[\spadesuit M[1;];]$	$\Diamond N$

2. Use APL to rearrange the character vector $S \leftarrow$ '*THE QUICK BROWN FOX JUMPS OVER THE LAZY DOG*' so that the letters (including duplicates and blanks) are in alphabetical order.

3. Construct this matrix using the monadic transpose:

   ```
   0 3 2 1
   1 0 3 2
   2 1 0 3
   ```

4. For an arbitrary numerical vector V which has been sorted in ascending order, show how to insert another vector $V1$ so as to preserve the ordering.

5. For a given numeric vector V of length N, write an APL expression that tests whether V is some permutation of the vector ιN (i.e., every element of V is in ιN and vice versa).

6. Write a program to find the median of a set of numbers. The median is defined as the scalar in the middle of the list after it has been sorted. When the number of elements is even, average the two middle elements.

7. Define a function to delete all leading, trailing and redundant occurrences of some element S in a vector V.

8. If the lengths of the sides of a box are stored in the 3-element vector $LENGTHS$, write expressions to compute **A** the volume of the box, and **B** its surface area (assuming it is closed on all sides).

9. Define a function $STRAIGHTLINE$ to compute a straight line depreciation schedule. The function should take a 3-element vector as its argument indicating the initial value of the asset, its life in years and its salvage value, in that order. It should return a vector showing the depreciated value of the asset at the end of each year. For example, $STRAIGHTLINE$ 1000 4 200 should result in 1000 800 600 400 200.

10. Write an expression to move all elements greater than 10 in a vector V to the front of the vector.

11. (A toughie!) A magic square of order n is one made up of the integers 1 through n. The sums over each row, column and diagonal are the same. One way to construct the squares of odd order is to start with a matrix of the right size, made up of the successive integers ordered rowwise. Then set up a vector of n successive integers with 0 in the middle to rotate the matrix successively over the last and first dimensions. Define a monadic function MS to do this.

12. You are given a 13-card bridge hand whose face values are the top row of a character matrix $HAND$ and the corresponding suit the bottom row (T=10):

   ```
            HAND
   JA9T36QTQ48K7
   DHCHSCHSCHDHD
   ```

   Write instructions to sort the hand **A** by suit, **B** by value and **C** by value within suit.

13. Write a function to separately sort each row of a numeric matrix M.

14. Construct a function LOC that locates all occurrences of a word or phrase W in a character vector V.

15. The vector G contains the grade point averages of all the seniors in a certain college. Find the two highest grades.

16. Show how to use ∧\ and ⌽ to **A** left-justify a matrix M, and **B** right-justify it.

17. Use the results of problem 16 to rotate a function that centers each line in a matrix whose lines before padding are of different lengths.

18. The vector S lists the amounts of individual holdings of shares of stock in the Squeaky Wheel Company. Show how to find the smallest number of individuals who together control 50% of the shares.

19. You are given a vector V of scholastic grades. Write an expression to drop off the lowest four and find the average of the rest.

20. Using *only* four characters, construct an expression that returns 1 if the first element in a given vector V is the largest, and 0 otherwise.

21. Write an APL expression that returns the index of the rightmost nonzero element in a vector V, that is, we get 5 for $V \gets 3\ 2\ 0\ 0\ 8\ 0\ 0$.

22. $NAMES$ is a character matrix containing the names of golf players in a tournament. The numeric vector $SCORES$ contains their scores in the same order as $NAMES$. Print $NAMES$ and $SCORES$ together and rank them high to low score.

23. Generate the indices of the last occurrences of elements $V1$ in vector $V2$.

24. Use ranking to delete the **A** leading and **B** trailing occurrences of some scalar S from a vector V.

25. Define a function $TRIANGLE$ to construct an n-row triangle out of the character ' ○ '.

26. Construct a function $SUBST$ that makes a simple letter substitution for a message M which uses only the 26 letters of the alphabet (no blanks).

27. (For cryptography buffs). Design a function VIG to simulate the Vigenère code, which adds a 'key' to the indices resulting from $ALF \iota MESSAGE$.

28. Write a program to decode the message resulting from execution of the function $SUBST$ (problem 26).

29. Execute the following instructions and explain what they do:

$$B \gets \phi A \gets \iota 25 \qquad \square 3\ 25 \rho A, B, A \times B$$

Chapter 16: Branching

One of the more prominent features of most programming languages is the concept of program flow and control, commonly referred to as *branching*. If you are familiar with other languages, you may be wondering why this notion, which involves selection of only some of the steps of a function or causes repeated execution under specified conditions, hasn't yet been presented in this text. The reason is that APL solves many problems in a more straightforward way, without branching.

The branch instruction

A branch instruction is usually called for whenever an algorithm requires a choice to be made as to what the next step should be, based in the results of some previous step. It is nothing more than an instruction to alter the regular sequence of steps.

We can demonstrate how this can be done by using a function called *SORT* in 1 *CLASS*. The problem that *SORT* is designed to handle is a very simple one: rearrange the elements of a vector in ascending order. Actually, there isn't any need to write a function to do this, since grade up can be used with indexing to accomplish the same thing very concisely (see page 140). The function, however, is a classic example of controlling the sequencing of the steps in a program.

Let's talk ourselves through the algorithm needed to solve the problem. The first and most obvious step is to start with a clean sheet of paper. Don't laugh. Try doing a large sorting problem by hand without it (or its equivalent). And as we'll see when we 'translate' the steps required into their APL equivalents, this part of the algorithm really does have an APL analogue.

The sensible next step is to pick out the smallest value in the vector. Right? Yes, but... suppose this value occurred many times (say, 100) in the vector. Then we would be inefficiently searching the vector 100 times for the same value. Wouldn't it make more sense to pick up all occurrences of that value in a single pass? Having done that, we write the smallest value 100 times on our paper and cross them off the original vector, go back and pick out the smallest value from what's left and repeat the process until all the numbers are used up.

It isn't any great challenge to devise a function to go through the repetitive steps, but it would need a safeguard built into it. We know when to stop, but a function would have to be explicitly instructed; otherwise it would continue to cycle through the sequence of steps indefinitely. This means that our algorithm needs a step which says in effect: 'look each time through to see if any numbers are left in the vector. If there are any, go on; if not, stop.'

Now we are ready to explore the function *SORT*.

```
      )LOAD 1 CLASS                    ∇SORT[□]∇
SAVED  14.45.33 02/20/83               ∇ R←SORT X
      SORT 2 3 7 4 4 2           [1]     ⍝BRANCHING EXAMPLE NO. 1.
2 2 3 4 4 7                      [2]     R←⍳0
                                 [3]     TEST:→(DONE,MORE)[1+×⍴X]
                                 [4]     MORE:R←R,(X=⌊/X)/X
                                 [5]     X←(X≠⌊/X)/X
                                 [6]     →TEST
                                 [7]     DONE:⍝SORT IS COMPLETED.
                                         ∇
```

It is a monadic function and expects a numeric vector argument X. The result is to be the numbers in X arranged in ascending order (same as $X[\spadesuit X]$). Line 2 defines R as an empty vector (remember the clean sheet of paper?).

Line 3 is the branch instruction. If X were empty (i.e., nothing to sort), then $\times \rho X$ is 0 and $(DONE, MORE)[1 + \times \rho X]$ would select $DONE$, whose value is 7. The arrow $\rightarrow$, *branch*, then directs the computer to move immediately to line 7, bypassing all the others. In other words, a sorted empty list is still an empty list.

On the other hand, if X were not empty, then $\times \rho X$ is 1 and $(DONE, MORE)[1 + \times \rho X]$ is $MORE$, whose value is 4. The arrow then directs the computer to line 4, where all copies of the smallest value in X are catenated to R, the equivalent of writing them on the clean sheet of paper. On line 5, all copies of the smallest value in X are compressed out of X.

Line 6 gives the computer no choice whatsoever. It is an instruction to go directly to the line on which $TEST$: appears. The above sequence of instructions is repeated until there are no numbers left to sort.

Labels

In the $SORT$ function above, $TEST$, $MORE$ and $DONE$ are *labels*. Labels follow the same naming rules as variables, functions and groups. A label is set off from the rest of the line by a colon. Although they are local to the function, they don't appear in the header. Labels can be used like scalar variables or constants, except that you can't assign new values to them; their values are the line numbers on which they appear. If the line number changes (by editing the function), so does the value of the label.

Infinite loops

It takes no great talent to write functions that will run forever. For example, if line 5 of $SORT$ had been omitted, X would never become empty. The result R would grow wildly until the inevitable $WS\ FULL$ stopped execution. What do you think would happen if line 3, which is a checkpoint, were left out?

Errors in the calculation of which line to branch to next are also common. And it can be hard to ferret out these errors, particularly in functions with many branches.

For these reasons, we make an obvious recommendation: don't use branches unless you have to. If you don't have iterative branching (also called *looping*), you can't have an infinitely running program. But there are still many algorithms that either can't be executed without branching, or which are easier to develop using branches; so you're not going to be able to avoid branching forever. Fortunately, APL provides features which help you to figure out what's happening inside functions with branches. The next two sections treat the most fundamental of these.

Tracing the sequence of execution

Suppose you just wrote your first function using branches, and it doesn't work. What do you do? Let's assume you don't have an APL expert handy, so you have to find the problem and fix it yourself. First, get a new listing of the function and review it for obvious errors. Ask yourself if the APL expressions on each line do what they are supposed to do, especially in the branch instructions themselves.

But it is likely that you won't catch many subtle errors this way. You really need a way to watch each line as it is executed, and see if it is delivering what you expected at that point.

APL comes to the rescue! The *trace* system function does exactly that. To trace each execution of every line in $SORT$, enter

```
      (ι7) □TRACE 'SORT'
      SORT 30 70 40 40
SORT[1]
SORT[2]
SORT[3]→4
SORT[4]30
SORT[5]70  40  40
SORT[6]→3
SORT[3]→4
SORT[4]30  40  40
```

```
SORT[5]70
SORT[6]→3
SORT[3]→4
SORT[4]30 40 40 70
SORT[5]
SORT[6]→3
SORT[3]→7
SORT[7]30 40 40 70
```

(On older systems, use $T\Delta SORT \leftarrow \iota 7$ instead.) As you can see, the result of each line and branch is shown. If you have avoided using long, complicated expressions it will be easier to trace because more intermediate results will be displayed.

Rather than tracing all the lines of a function, you can select only those lines that are central to the analysis. This avoids voluminous displays that don't add to the understanding.

```
      3 4 □TRACE 'SORT'
      SORT 30 70 40 40
SORT[3]→4
SORT[4]30
SORT[3]→4
SORT[4]30 40 40
SORT[3]→4
SORT[4]30 40 40 70
SORT[3]→7
30 40 40 70
```

The trace stays set until you change it or remove it. You can view the current trace setting by the monadic use of □TRACE, and you can remove all tracing by using an empty left argument:

```
      □TRACE                              (ι0) □TRACE 'SORT'
3 4                                       SORT 30 70 40 40
                         30 40 40 70
```

Stopping the sequence of execution

Sometimes tracing isn't enough; and you'd like to halt execution dead in its tracks so you can poke around. It is very unlikely that you can stop a running function at the right place using BREAK—APL moves too swiftly for that. One simplistic approach is to deliberately cause an error where you want to stop. For example, if line 6 of *SORT* were →*TEST*÷0 instead of →*TEST*, you'd have a *DOMAIN ERROR* every time you got to line 6.

But there is a cleaner way to do it. You can set *stops* before whichever lines you wish in a manner similar to the trace:

```
      6 □STOP 'SORT' ⍝FOR OLDER SYSTEMS, USE S∆SORT←6
      SORT 2 3 7 4 4 2
SORT[6]
```

Now you can view any of the variables that have acquired values prior to (but not including) line 6. At this point you are free to change the variables or enter other commands as though they were already lines of the function. And most important, you can resume execution by issuing a branch instruction:

```
      →6
SORT[6]
```

The function stopped again before line 6. Let's look at *R* and *X*:

```
      R                  X                    →3
2 2 3              7 7 4                  SORT[6]
```

When we resumed execution (→3), we bypassed line 6. No harm was caused in this particular function, but in general it's not a wise procedure.

This time, after viewing *R* and *X* and having concluded that the function is running properly, we remove the stop. The function runs uninterrupted to completion.

```
      R                          (ι0) □STOP 'SORT'
2 2 3 4 4                         →6
      X                     2 2 3 4 4 7
7
```

Suspended functions

When a function is interrupted by encountering a stop (or by an error, or by your having pressed BREAK), it is called *suspended*. As you saw in the last section, you can explore, or even do unrelated calculations while suspended.

It is easy to forget that your function is suspended, because most of APL's features are still available to you. Most novices will stubbornly start another execution of the function while suspended. This is a bad practice. Without going into detail now, two of the horrors that result are that some of your global variables may be shielded, and your workspace becomes littered with a stack of partly executed functions and their associated variables. This littering reduces the space available to you for other work, and increases your storage charges on commercial systems.

Hence, always remove a suspension as soon as you have fixed whatever caused it. The usual fix is a branch to the proper line to continue running, but there are other alternatives, to be discussed soon.

You can produce a list of the suspensions with the system command $)SI$ (for *state indicator*). Let's now define a trivial function $FAILURE$ to generate suspensions:

```
        ∇FAILURE
[1]     5÷0
[2]     5 □STOP 'SORT'
[3]     SORT 2 3 7 4 2
[4]     (2+3 ∇
```

There are three potential suspensions above: line 1 will cause a $DOMAIN\ ERROR$; line 2 will cause $SORT$ to suspend at its line 5; and line 4 is an obvious $SYNTAX\ ERROR$.

Here goes $FAILURE$:

```
        FAILURE                          )SI
DOMAIN ERROR                      FAILURE[1]*
FAILURE[1] 5÷0
          ^
```

It is hung as expected on line 1. Now push on to line 2:

```
       →2                                )SI
SORT[5]                           SORT[5]*
                                  FAILURE[3]
```

Note that the stack of litter has grown. Not only is $SORT$ suspended, but $FAILURE$, which initiated $SORT$ on line 3, is also on the stack. Manually execute $FAILURE$ again:

```
        FAILURE                          )SI
DOMAIN ERROR                      FAILURE[1]*
FAILURE[1] 5÷0                    SORT[5]*
          ^                       FAILURE[3]
```

What a mess! But look carefully at the $)SI$ report. The most recent suspension appears at the top, the oldest at the bottom. Did you observe the *'s following the top two entries? They indicate that these are true suspensions; on the other hand, $FAILURE[3]$ (without a *) indicates that it is *pendent*, not having been suspended itself, but rather waiting for $SORT$, which it invoked, to finish.

As promised, there are several ways to reduce the $)SI$ stack. Saving the workspace, clearing, and copying the entire workspace will remove all the stack. Copying removes all stops and traces as well.

```
       )SAVE CONTINUE                      )COPY CONTINUE FAILURE SORT
21.29.25 12/09/82                 SAVED   21.29.25  12/09/82
       )CLEAR                              )SI
CLEAR WS
```

Many APL systems support the system command)*RESET*, which removes all the clutter:

```
    )LOAD CONTINUE                                    )RESET
SAVED  21.29.25 12/09/82                              )SI
    )SI
FAILURE[1]*
SORT[5]*
FAILURE[3]
```

Occasionally, when an error halts execution in a lengthy run, you may want to 'back out' part way to preserve some of the work. A branch to zero (→0) will remove the immediate suspension:

```
    )LOAD CONTINUE                                    )SI
SAVED  21.29.25 12/09/82                        SORT[5]*
    )SI                                         FAILURE[3]
FAILURE[1]*                                            →0
SORT[5]*
FAILURE[3]                                      2 2
    →0                                          SYNTAX ERROR
                                                FAILURE[4] (2+3
                                                           ∧
                                                     )SI
                                                FAILURE[4]*
```

It hung again, but this time because of the missing parenthesis on line 4 of *FAILURE*. When backing out, it is wise to set stops in the pendent function which invoked the suspended one. This gives you a chance to look around and maybe patch up some errors, so you may resume your execution.

The arrow used by itself is called a *naked branch*. It removes the current suspension and any pendencies that invoked it. After using it, the stack still has earlier suspensions in it. In other words, each time you use → alone, you 'peel' one layer from the suspension stack.

```
    →
    )SI
```

In our case, since there was only one suspension in the stack, entry of → restored the stack to its normal, empty state.

Two variants of the)*SI* system command are available in some APL systems. They give more detail about the suspensions.)*SINL* (or)*SIV* on older systems) reports suspensions like)*SI* and lists the local variables for each suspended or pendent function.)*SIS* (in APL2) lists the statements being executed at the time of suspension, with an indication (as in the typical error message) of the point where the suspension happened and the statements being executed at the time.

Some APL systems treat locked functions as though they were primitives. Unlike old soldiers, locked functions do die when execution is interrupted. To avoid compromising security they are never suspended or pendent. Three kinds of error message are possible: *DOMAIN ERROR* if there was an actual error, *WS FULL* (or something similar) if a system limitation halted execution, or *INTERRUPT*. See page 300 if you need more detail.

The line counter system function

Some of the same information reported by)*SI* is available in a feature called the *line counter system function*, □*LC*. It results in a vector whose first element is the most current line number that is suspended or being executed, whose second element is the most immediate previous line, etc. Compare the following displays:

```
    )LOAD CONTINUE              )SI                □LC
SAVED  21.29.25 12/09/82   FAILURE[1]*          1  5  3
                           SORT[5]*
                           FAILURE[3]
```

Its most important use is to resume execution at the point of interruption by the instruction →□*LC*. In the case above, this would result in the function *FAILURE* restarting at line 1.

$\Box LC$ is also used to direct control to some line that is a fixed number of lines distant from the present one. For example, here's a stupid way to sum a vector, somewhat reminiscent of more primitive programming languages:

```
[N]     S←0
[N+1]   I←0
[N+2]   I←I+1
[N+3]   →(2×I>ρVECTOR)+1+□LC[1]
[N+4]   S←S+VECTOR[I]
[N+5]   →□LC[1]-2
[N+6]   ...
```

No matter where these statements are in a program (so long as they are adjacent), line [N+5] causes a branch back two lines. And line [N+3] causes a branch ahead one line, provided that all the elements in VECTOR haven't been added yet, or ahead 3 lines, if they have all been added. Caution: if you use this method instead of the using labels, you must be sure to make appropriate adjustments if you insert or delete lines.

Another simple use of the line counter is using $\rho \Box LC$ to test how deep you are in the suspension stack. It's shorter, albeit less informative, than)SI.

Absolute branches

It is technically possible to branch to an absolute line number instead of to a label or relative to $\Box LC$. For example, SORT could have been written as

```
      ∇R←BADSTYLESORT X
[1]   ⍝USES ABSOLUTE BRANCHES; SHOWN ONLY AS COUNTEREXAMPLE
[2]   R←⍳0
[3]   →(7  4)[1+ρX]
[4]   R←R,(X=⌊/X)/X
[5]   X←(X≠⌊/X)/X
[6]   →3
[7]   ⍝SORT IS COMPLETED
[8]   ∇
```

However, this style is not recommended because it requires too much maintenance for even simple changes. For example, in BADSTYLESORT, if a new line were inserted between lines 1 and 2, all the line numbers would have to be changed. About the only absolute branch in lieu of a label that is condoned is →0, which means 'leave the program immediately.' And even here it is recommended that the function have only one exit point, preferably the last line.

Conditional branching

A branch expression consists of right arrow followed by an APL expression (naked branch is a special case). The expression must result in scalar or vector integer values. Decimals, characters and arrays of rank greater than 1 cause an error. If it is a vector, only the first element is used for the branch. If the value (including labels) matches a line in the function, then that line is executed next. If the value doesn't match (for example, →100 in a function with 20 lines, or →0 in any function), then execution is ended and control returns to the pendent function which used it, or to calculator mode if the stack is empty.

An important, special case is a branch to an empty vector (→⍳0). Then *no branch* happens, since there is no first element in the vector. Control flows to the next statement as though the branch expression wasn't there at all.

This gives rise to the most popular use of branching—one which causes a branch if some logical condition is met. For example, here is a more efficient version of SORT:

```
      ∇R←SORT X
[1]   ⍝BRANCHING EXAMPLE NO. 3
[2]   R←⍳0
[3]   LOOP:→(0=ρX)/DONE
[4]   R←R,(X=⌊/X)/X
[5]   X←(X≠⌊/X)/X
[6]   →LOOP
[7]   DONE:⍝SORT IS COMPLETED.
[8]   ∇
```

An even shorter version would omit line 7 entirely, and change line 3 to $LOOP:→(0=\rho X)/0$.

Examples of branch expressions

There are many ways to compute the branch target in APL—any expression that returns an integer scalar or vector with integer first element would do. In the list of popular forms that follows, $L1, L2, L3$ are labels, X and Y are numeric scalars to be compared, I is an iteration counter, and N is the relative distance between the line being executed and the target line.

1) Branch unconditionally to a fixed point in the function:
$$\rightarrow 5$$
$$\rightarrow LABEL$$

2) Branch unconditionally out of the function:
$$\rightarrow 0 \quad \text{(or any nonexistent line number)}$$

3) Branch to one of the two possible lines:
$$\rightarrow (L1, L2)[1 + X \geq Y]$$
$$\rightarrow ((X \geq Y), \sim X \geq Y)/L1, L2$$
$$\rightarrow (1 \ 0 \neq X \geq Y)/L1, L2$$

4) Branch to one of several lines:
$$\rightarrow (L1, L2, L3)[2 + \times X - Y]$$
$$\rightarrow ((X > Y), (X < Y), X = Y)/L1, L2, L3$$
$$\rightarrow I \phi L1, L2, L3, \ldots$$
$$\rightarrow I + \Box LC$$

5) Branch to a given line or drop through to the next line:
$$\rightarrow (X \geq Y)/L1$$
$$\rightarrow (X \geq Y) \rho L1$$
$$\rightarrow (\times X - Y) \uparrow L1, L2$$
$$\rightarrow L1 \lceil \iota X \geq Y$$
$$\rightarrow (L2, L3, L1)[I] \times \iota X \geq Y$$
$$\rightarrow ((X > Y), (X < Y))/L1, L2$$

6) Branch to a line a fixed distance from the current line:
$$\rightarrow N + \Box LC$$

7) Branch out of the program or to a specific line:
$$\rightarrow ((X \geq Y), X < Y)/L1, 0$$
$$\rightarrow L1 \times X \geq Y$$

8) Branch to a given line or the line following it:
$$\rightarrow L1 + X \geq Y$$

Rules for branching

As you can see below, the rules for branching in defined functions are very simple, yet using these rules most popular forms of structured programming can be emulated.

$$\rightarrow \text{(any APL expression)}$$
is

INVALID   if the expression results in other than an integer or a vector whose first element (the only one which can cause a branch) is an integer or a valid label.

VALID   if the expression results in
(a)   an empty vector, which causes a branch to the next statement ($\rightarrow \iota 0$ for example).
(b)   an integer outside the range of statement numbers of the function, which causes an exit from the function (such as $\rightarrow 0$, but don't confuse with $\rightarrow \iota 0$).
(c)   an integer inside the range of statement numbers of the function, which causes a branch to that line number.
(d)   a label, which causes a branch to that line of the function on which the label is to be found.

Structured branching and control

In the 1970's much was written about *structured programming*. Some of its advocates have charged APL with being devoid of structure. No doubt the allegation comes from the fact that APL has only one form of program control, the branch expression. Virtually anything goes in that expression, as we saw in the last section. There are situations where too much variety can blemish the appearances of functions. The careful user should consider limiting his choice of branching techniques to the following forms.

Normal program flow should be downward, rather than jumping around. Error or warning messages should appear immediately after the test. For APL*PLUS and Sharp Systems, the message can even appear on the same line as the test, by using diamonds.

```
→(VALUE>0)/L3
'NEGATIVE VALUE ENCOUNTERED FOR SQUARE ROOT'
'CHANGING TO POSITIVE AND PROCEEDING'
VALUE←|VALUE
L3:R←VALUE*.5
```

The notion of branching if some logical condition exists is so prevalent that it's wise to employ a function whose name is descriptive:

```
      ∇R←BRANCH IF CONDITION              →L3 IF VALUE ≥0
[1]   R←CONDITION/BRANCH ∇                L3:R←VALUE*.5
```

Iteration, particularly when based on some arithmetic progression, such as 'do some sequence of lines for *J* having values of 10, 12, 14, 16, 18 and 20,' should follow a pattern like this:

```
J←10
LOOPJ:→(J>20)/PASTJ
(whatever is to be done based on J)
J←J+2
→LOOPJ
PASTJ:
(whatever should follow)
```

Many users prefer to increment on the same line as the test. While it does use embedded assignment, it's worthwhile in this case.

```
J←8 ⍝ NOTE STARTING VALUE
LOOPJ:→(20<J←J+2)/PASTJ
(whatever is to be done based on J)
→LOOPJ
PASTJ:
(whatever is to follow the loop)
```

Because this type of iteration is so common, we have a gift for you: a set of functions that will let you write the above sequence as

```
J←DO 8 20 2
(whatever is to be based on J)
→NEXT J
```

We now present the functions *DO*, *NEXT*, *SETDO* and *OUT*. Although they use no new primitives, the techniques employed are tricky, to say the least. Understanding how they work is not a prerequisite for using them.

```
      ∇R←DO X;N
[1]   ⍝X IS 3 ELEMENT VECTOR: START, END, INCREMENT
[2]   ⍝DC IS A GLOBAL VARIABLE THAT CONTROLS IT ALL.
[3]   ⍝LAST TWO ELEMENTS ARE BOOLEAN INDICATORS.
[4]   →(∧/ 0 1 = ‾2↑DC)/POST ⍝ OTHERWISE THIS IS A NEW DO STMT.
[5]   N←⌊(X[2]-X[1])÷X[3]+X[3]=0 ⍝N IS NUMBER OF ITERATIONS TO DO.
[6]   →((N>0)∧X[3]≠0)/OK
[7]   'LINE ',(⍕⎕LC[2]),' INFINITE LOOP: ',⍕X
[8]   DC← 1 1 ⍝RESET DC IN HOPELESS SITUATION.
[9]   → ⍝ AND BLAST OUT OF )SI STACK.
[10]  OK:DC←0,(N+1),X[1 3],⎕LC[2],DC ⍝ SET UP FOR THIS LEVEL.
[11]  POST:R←DC[3]+DC[1]×DC[4] ⍝RETURN VALUE FOR THIS ITERATION.
[12]  DC[1]←1+DC[1] ⍝COUNT THIS ITERATION.
[13]  DC[⍴DC]←0 ⍝ 0 MEANS JUST EXECUTED DO.  SEE NEXT[4].
[14]  ∇
```

```
         ∇ R←NEXT X
[1]      ⍝X IS IGNORED, BUT RECOMMENDED. USE NAME OF ITEᴦATION VARIABLE.
[2]      R←(DC[1]≠DC[2])/DC[5] ⍝BRANCH TO DO OR BEYOND.
[3]      DC[¯1+ρDC]←DC[1]=DC[2] ⍝1 MEANS COMPLETED ITERATION.
[4]      DC[ρDC]←1 ⍝1 MEANS JUST EXECUTED NEXT.  SEE DO[13].
[5]      →PEEL×DC[1]=DC[2]
[6]      PEEL:DC←5↓DC ∇

         ∇ R←TD OUT CONDITION
[1]      ⍝SPECIAL FUNCTION FOR PREMATURE ESCAPE FROM LOOP.
[2]      ⍝TD[1] IS TARGET LINE, TD[2] IS NUMBER OF LEVELS OUT.
[3]      R←CONDITION/TD[1]
[4]      →REALLYOUT×CONDITION
[5]      REALLYOUT:DC←(5×TD[2])↓DC ⍝CHOP 5 ELEMENTS OFF FOR EACH LEVEL.
[6]      ∇

         ∇ SETDO
[1]      ⍝EXECUTE THIS TO INITIALIZE AND AFTER ANY ABORTED RUN.
[2]      DC← 1 1 ⍝ INITIAL SETTING FOR DO CONTROL.
[3]      ∇
```

Here is an example of the use of looping functions to perform a matrix multiplication (the hard way—APL has a built-in function we'll see later):

```
         ∇ C←A MATMULT B;I;J;K;T               A←2 3ρ⍳6
[1]      SETDO                                 A
[2]      →((¯1↑ρA)=1↑ρB)/OK                 1 2 3
[3]      'ERROR - DIMENSIONS DO NOT MATCH'    4 5 6
[4]      S∆MATMULT←⎕LC+1
[5]      OK:C←((1↑ρA),¯1↑ρB)ρ0                B←100×3 4ρ⍳12
[6]      I←DO 1,(1↑ρA),1                       B
[7]      J←DO 1,(¯1↑ρB),1                100  200  300  400
[8]      T←0                            500  600  700  800
[9]      K←DO 1,(¯1↑ρA),1               900 1000 1100 1200
[10]     T←T+A[I;K]×B[K;J]
[11]     →NEXT K                              A MATMULT B
[12]     C[I;J]←T                       3800  4400  5000  5600
[13]     →NEXT J                        8300  9800 11300 12800
[14]     →NEXT I ∇
```

Some thoughts on branching

Branching in APL is a powerful programming tool about which much sense (and nonsense) has been written. There is one school of thought that says 'avoid branching wherever possible.' Two reasons are usually given by adherents of this school: (1) each time around there is a costly translation of source code into internal code, and (2) branching complicates the normal flow of a program, and therefore makes it harder to debug and maintain.

A second school proclaims the virtues of 'intelligent' loops which can run rings around (sorry about that) complicated one-liners.

As usual, neither side has a monopoly on wisdom. The truth lies somewhere in between. While it's true that some loop programs are virtually indecipherable, that is probably the fault of the coder, not APL. You will find many occasions where branching just can't be avoided or where the nonbranch solution, while ingenious, is unnatural. So branch if you must, but do so with style.

If the previous section on structured programming touched a responsive chord, you are well prepared. If not, here are a few simple guidelines with illustrations to help you avoid pitfalls in branching.

1. Avoid branching around a branch. Instead of

```
    →(A=B)/L1
    →L2
```

use

```
    →(A≠B)/L2
L1:
```

2. Put the test for a condition at the beginning of a loop (*leading decision*) rather than at the end (*trailing decision*). This tends to eliminate unnecessary looping. The function $SORT$ at the beginning of this chapter employs a leading decision. It branches immediately to the end if the argument X has no elements.

3. Replace branches with array operations. The function below uses looping to summarize by quarter the sales for each item (row) in a matrix, each of whose 12 columns contains the sales for a particular month:

```
        ∇R←SUMQ M;I
[1]     R←((1↑ρM),4)ρ0
[2]     I←1
[3]     →(5=I)/0
[4]     L:R[I;]←+/M[;(3×I-1)+ι3]
[5]     I←I+1
[6]     →L ∇
```

This problem is one of those that can be solved without branching:

```
        ∇R←BETTERSUMQ M                        ∇R←BESTSUMQ M
[1]     R←(+\M)[;3×ι4]              [1]     R←+/((1↑ρM),4 3)ρM ∇
[2]     R[;2 3 4]←R[;2 3 4]-R[;1 2 3] ∇
```

$BESTSUMQ$ reshapes the sales matrix to a three-dimensional array (see Chapter 19) each of whose planes represents a single item. Within any plane each row contains a quarter's sales data. The reduction is carried out over the rows. The lesson learned here is that thinking the problem through again may lead to a different solution which takes advantage of APL's lesser used, but no less powerful features, or suggests the use of a higher dimensional array than was initially contemplated.

4. Always branch to a label, not a line number. We've said it before (**page 154**), but it bears repeating here.

5. Do as much as possible a) before you enter a loop, and b) with each iteration, testing and incrementing counters no more than is absolutely necessary. This last guideline is proposed to get you 'thinking lean,' to reduce the overhead involved in looping.

6. Avoid 'gluing.' Even the best APL'ers do it, but that doesn't make it right:

```
        →LABEL,0ρ□←'THIS IS A MESSAGE TO THE USER'
```

Here two completely unrelated concepts, the message and the branch, are placed in a single executable line. Just as in writing there should be but one idea in a sentence, so having one concept (or at least only closely related concepts) makes an APL line more readable. Besides, in some cases gluing another instruction might change the rank of an array and lead to an error. These problems can be avoided by using separate lines for the unrelated pieces, or the diamond as a separator if your system supports it.

Even when the ideas are closely related, problems can arise when execution is interrupted. For instance, in the last section an example was given which incremented a counter on the same line as the test:

```
        LOOPJ:→(20<J←J+2)/PASTJ
```

If the function is interrupted past the point where J is incremented but *before the line is completed*, when execution is resumed the entire line will be reexecuted with an incorrect value for J. Hence branch lines, like all the others, should be written to be *restartable* in case of interruption.

There is another technique that avoids branching altogether by the use of *execute*. This concept will be discussed in Chapter 24.

The foregoing discussion has touched on only one aspect of style in writing APL programs, although an important one. Programming style is a whole subject in itself, and one about which reasonable people can differ. Indeed, whole books have been written just on the related subject of structured programming.

Our intent is to be expository, and not dogmatic, since no one can dictate by fiat what 'good' style is. Whatever it is, it certainly changes with time, like fashions in clothes, and depends on the features available on the system being used.

'Good' can probably be best translated as 'readable,' which isn't necessarily synonymous with efficiency of execution and effective use of storage. Those of you who have to modify or maintain someone else's code will appreciate our emphasis on readability. But don't be too quick to point a finger at others. We assure you that your own code is just as likely to be unreadable after you haven't looked at it for six months.

Recursion

This section is entirely optional. Recursion is rarely used in practical business programming. But it is an intriguing topic for most neophyte computer scientists, so we include it for your entertainment.

The classic example of recursion is that of the factorial. An alternate way to describe how to calculate the factorial of N is to multiply N by the factorial of $N-1$. But that would require being able to calculate the factorial of $N-2$ and so on. That is a recursive definition. To make sense out of it, there must be some special ending value or else the dependencies go on forever. In the case of factorials, the special ending value is the factorial of zero, defined to be 1. Once you have that, you can work your way out and ultimately produce the factorial of N. Now, here is what we just said, but written in APL:

```
      )COPY 1 CLASS FACT COMB
SAVED   14.45.33 02/20/83

      ∇FACT[□]∇
    ∇ R←FACT N;NM1
[1]    →(N≠|⌊N)/0
[2]    →(N=0)/L6
[3]    NM1←N-1
[4]    R←N×FACT NM1
[5]    →0
[6]  L6:R←1
    ∇
```

As you can see, the function $FACT$ calls upon itself. And as you can also see, if it didn't have (or can't get to) an ending value of 0, you would be in deep trouble. You might want to set $□TRACE$ or $□STOP$ on this function and explore it with *small* positive integer arguments.

Recursive techniques are used in sophisticated computer programs for artificial intelligence research, compilers and interpreters. An example is wading through sets of nested parentheses in APL statements to get to the innermost level, and then working the way out with the solution.

One of the more useful examples of recursion is the following function $COMB$ that enumerates all combinations of N things taken from a population of P. This function is particularly interesting because it calls upon itself twice (line 2) at each level of the recursion.

```
      ∇COMB[□]∇                                    3 COMB 4
    ∇ R←M COMB N                          1 2 3
[1]   →(M=1,N)/L,R  ⍝RECURSIVE    AJROSE 1976    1 2 4
[2]   R←1+(0,(M-1) COMB N-1),[1] M COMB N-1      1 3 4
[3]   →0                                         2 3 4
[4]  L:R←(⍳N)∘.×⍳1
[5]   →0                                         5 COMB 5
[6]  R:R←(⍳1)∘.×⍳N                     1 2 3 4 5
    ∇
```

PROBLEMS

1. Tell what each of the following does:

   A $\rightarrow((5<W),5>W)/\ 3\ 2$ **F** $\rightarrow {}^-1\uparrow\phi\ 3\ 4\ 7\ 9$

   B $\rightarrow 3\times\iota A=8$ **G** $\rightarrow 8\times\iota 0\neq J\leftarrow J-1$

   C $\rightarrow END\times Y>,R\leftarrow\ 1\ 1\ \rho 1$ **H** $\rightarrow 4\times(|X)\geq I\leftarrow I+1$

   D $\rightarrow(\vee/,B\epsilon C)/7$ **I** $\rightarrow AGAIN\lceil\iota N=2\times 1\rho R\leftarrow\ 2\ 4\ \rho\ 5\ 7\ 1\ 8$

   E $\rightarrow\ 5\ 0[1+A>C]$

2. Let T be a vector of 'trash' characters, some of which may occur in the character vector V. Define an APL function that will eliminate the trash from V.

3. Write a version of the function CMP (page 125) that uses branching.

4. Use branching to find the median of a set of numbers. (see problem 6, Chapter 15 for more information about the median.)

5. Define a dyadic function $DUPL$ that will locate all occurrences of some scalar N in a vector V and print an appropriate message if the desired scalar is not present.

6. Design an APL function so that it ignores all nonscalar input and takes the square root of any scalar argument. Assume all input is positive.

7. Take the opening two sentences of this chapter, eliminating all punctuation, underlining and blanks, and define a function to arrange the characters in alphabetic order.

8. Write an APL program to find the *mode* (most frequently occurring number) of a set of data.

9. The Fibonacci series is of the form 1 1 2 3 5 8 13 ..., where each term after the first two is the sum of the preceding two terms. Define a function which prints N terms of the series.

10. Define a function which will produce a histogram of a vector A of nonnegative integers, i.e., the height of the histogram for $A[1]$ is $A[1]$, the height for $A[5]$ is $A[5]$, etc. Show how the histogram can be 'cleaned up' by replacing the 0's with blanks and the 1's with $*$'s.

11. Use branching to construct a function which prints an annual compound interest table. Design your function to produce three columns, the first to be the year, the second the value of the principal at the beginning of the year, and the third the interest accumulated during the year. Include appropriate column headings and round off each figure to the nearest cent.

12. Estimate the odds that 3 or more cards of any one suit will appear in a 5-card poker hand from a well-shuffled deck.

13. ACK is a function constructed for the purpose of proving that nonprimitive recursive functions do exist, and is named after its creator (see Communications of the ACM, page 114, Vol. 8, No.2, February 1965.) Use *small* integers for I and J. Follow the execution of ACK with the trace and stop controls:

```
        ∇R←I ACK J
[1]     →(0=I,J)/4 3
[2]     R←(I-1) ACK I ACK J-1 ◇ →0
[3]     R←(I-1) ACK 1 ◇ →0
[4]     R←J+1∇
```

14. Write a program $EQUAL$ that compares any two APL arrays and returns a 1 if they are identical, 0 otherwise.

15. Define a dyadic function $PRINT$ to print a message (argument) if a given condition (other argument) is met.

16. Define a program $DELE$ to delete a given name from a matrix of names or print an appropriate message if the name isn't in the matrix.

17. Use branching to solve the matrix grade problem cited on **page 140** in the last chapter.

18. Define a function $FINDROW$ that locates those lines in a literal matrix that match a given name.

19. Write a function $CARDSORT$ that uses the cardsort technique (from the days of mechanical punched card sorters) to sort one column of a literal matrix at a time, working backwards from right to left.

20. Redo problem 9 and define a dyadic recursive function $FIB1$ whose right argument A specifies the first two terms of·the series, with the left argument N the number of terms desired.

Chapter 17: Report formatting

This chapter covers what you need to know to produce a neat report for someone else. You have probably observed by now that you haven't been able to exercise much control over the way APL prints numeric results on the terminal. If this limit on your options for producing attractive reports doesn't bother you, skim over this chapter lightly. If on the other hand you have developed some concern (or consternation) over this, then you will find the features described here very helpful.

Thus far it would appear that APL decides how displayed numbers will be formed, how they will be spaced, and how many significant digits will be shown. However, while you can always get the answers out in a readable form, they may not necessarily be in the proper shape to hand to your boss, who may have a preference for reports with such features as column and row headings, and data with a fixed number of decimal positions, each neatly lined up. Be tolerant. The boss needs good formatting because as he gets older his eyes start to go. More seriously, if the data that you submit to him is easy for him to read, the quicker he can make his business decisions. And besides, you owe it to yourself to finish up any important programming assignment by producing the final results in an attractive format.

The treatment in this chapter is intended to be only an introduction, covering some elementary ideas to get you started. Many APL systems include prepared formatting packages to make life easier for you. The more elaborate format packages generally have user guides to assist both the novices and the pros. Consult your computer center management for further information.

The monadic format function

In Chapter 13 we introduced ⍕ as a device to convert numeric values to their character representation. While we used it only for scalars there, it can take any array as its argument, and the result is a character array whose appearance when displayed is identical to the original argument. In this example we have a table of compound interest (on one dollar) for interest ranges of 4, 8 and 12 percent, for years 1 through 4:

```
      TABLE←((1+.04×⍳3)∘.*⍳4)-1
      TABLE
0.04        0.0816        0.124864      0.16985856
0.08        0.1664        0.259712      0.36048896
0.12        0.2544        0.404928      0.57351936
```

Now suppose we didn't want to see all those digits, three digits being sufficiently accurate for our purpose. If we use a rounding algorithm such as

```
      .001×⌊.5+TABLE×1000
0.04        0.082         0.125         0.17
0.08        0.166         0.26          0.36
0.12        0.254         0.405         0.574
```

the numbers are still spread out more than is desired. Some of the blank columns could be eliminated by storing a character representation of *TABLE* as *CTABLE* and then compressing out some of the blank columns:

```
      CTABLE←⍕TABLE
      ⍴CTABLE
3 64
      CTABLE
0.04        0.0816        0.124864      0.16985856
0.08        0.1664        0.259712      0.36048896
0.12        0.2544        0.404928      0.57351936
```

While *TABLE* had only four columns of numbers, *CTABLE* has 64 columns of characters. In general, monadic ⍕ preserves all the dimensions of the array argument except for the last dimension.

```
      (64ρ16↑7ρ1)/CTABLE
0.04    0.081   0.124   0.169
0.08    0.166   0.259   0.360
0.12    0.254   0.404   0.573
```

Printing precision

In the above example, we did eliminate the trailing digits, but the numbers are truncated (chopped off) rather than rounded. We could combine the rounding algorithm with compression to fix it, but it seems a lot of work for something that can be stated as simply as 'I want three digits of printing precision.' APL to the rescue! The *printing precision* system variable, $\Box PP$, is a special feature (actually, there are many system variables and system functions in APL, but we'll hold back on a general discussion so we don't clutter up the presentation of the present topic) that lets you control the maximum number of digits that are displayed for a numeric array, or the number of significant digits that are provided in the result of ⍕ for each column of its argument.

The default value of $\Box PP$ on most APL systems is 10. That's why we never showed a result with more than 10 significant digits. But you can change it on most systems to any integer value between 1 and 16:

```
      □PP
10
      ÷7
0.1428571429
```

```
      □PP←1
      ÷7
0.1
```

```
      □PP←16
      ÷7
0.1428571428571428
      □PP←10
```

Monadic ⍕ uses the present $\Box PP$ setting in determining the width of the result. The rules for spacing with monadic ⍕ (and APL raw output as well) differ from system to system, and are subject to change. And while the above formatting was a little easier to do, it's still not an ideal result. No more than three significant digits are shown, and the result is properly rounded in the last digit, but the display still looks ragged. For these reasons feel free to use monadic ⍕ and $\Box PP$ for casual displays, but avoid them in applications where the result must be aligned with other displays, such as headings and titles. Read on, the next section contains one answer.

The dyadic formatting function

The dyadic use of ⍕ extends the control you have over printed results. Its right argument is the data to be formatted, and its left argument holds the format instructions, which are the total number of characters in the result and the number of decimal positions to be shown. The following example forms each column of $TABLE$ into a *field* six characters wide, with three decimal places:

```
      6 3⍕TABLE
 .040   .082   .125   .170
 .080   .166   .260   .360
 .120   .254   .405   .574
```

The left argument 6 3 was (conceptually) repeated for each column of $TABLE$. On the other hand, if you enter

```
      (8ρ8 3 7 4)⍕TABLE
 .040   .0816    .125   .1699
 .080   .1664    .260   .3605
 .120   .2544    .405   .5735
```

```
      ρ(8ρ8 3 7 4)⍕TABLE
3 30
```

you get a pattern of alternating field specifications. ⍕ applies each *pair* of numbers in the left argument to a column of the right argument. The format function returns an explicit result which is a character representation (in this case a matrix) of the right argument.

The shape of the result is the same as the shape of the right argument, except that the last dimension of the result is the sum of the field widths. Thus, if the right argument is a (numeric) vector, the result is a (character) vector. Of course, if the right argument is a scalar, you'll still get a vector as a result. If you want a complete table with numeric row and column headings, the following program will do it:

```
      ∇RATES COMPINT TIMES
[1]   (4ρ' '),6 0⍕TIMES
[2]   (4 2,(2×ρTIMES)ρ6 3)⍕RATES,((1+RATES)∘.*TIMES)-1 ∇
      (.04×⍳3) COMPINT ⍳5
              1      2      3      4      5
      .04   .040   .082   .125   .170   .217
      .08   .080   .166   .260   .360   .469
      .12   .120   .254   .405   .574   .762
```

If the number of decimal positions is given as zero, as in line one of *COMPINT*, then the decimal point itself is suppressed. The result is rounded, not truncated.

If the second number of the pair is negative, then the corresponding field will be printed in scaled notation. Most commercial reports don't employ scaled notation, so unless you are making reports involving very large or very small numbers, skip the rest of this paragraph. If in spite of this warning you're still here, the first number in the pair still dictates the field width, but the second number controls the minimum number of significant digits of *mantissa* (the number before the *E*) that will be produced. The magnitude of this number must be at least six smaller than the field width to allow for a negative sign and the characters of the exponent itself, as for example

```
      10 ¯4 20 ¯3 10 ¯4⍕12345 .000001234567 ¯1
1.23450E4            1.235E¯6 ¯1.00000E0
```

To recap, we have seen that the shape of the left argument must be a vector with either two elements (implied replication) or with one pair of elements for each column in the right argument. The first element of the pair gives the field width, and the second gives the number of digits after the decimal point (or the number of significant digits for scaled notation). If the second element of the pair is zero, the result appears as an integer, with no decimal point at all.

Special cases of dyadic format

If the first element of the pair is zero, the width is then taken to be whatever is required to represent the value, allowing for one blank space in front. Fractional values (i.e., have no integer parts) are formed without a zero before their decimal points. Look at this example:

```
      0 5 0 0 0 4 0 4⍕101.49  101.49 .1234 ¯.1234
101.49000 101 .1234 ¯.1234
```

If you format a matrix using zero (automatic) width specification, the resulting width is whatever is needed to cause each column of the result to line up properly and yet not run together, as shown by

```
      X←2 2ρ¯79.68 ¯.91 .5 1234567
      0 3 0 0⍕X
¯79.680           ¯1
   .500    1234567
```

When using implied replication and automatic widths (that is, formatting several columns of the right argument using a left argument pair of elements the first of which is zero), the width is based on the number of characters required to represent the largest value in the right argument, rather than dealing with it column by column. Observe the difference in these two examples:

```
      0 2 0 2⍕X
¯79.68            ¯.91
   .50    1234567.00

      0 2⍕X
¯79.68            ¯.91
   .50    1234567.00
```

As a special case, the left argument can be a single element. If it is a positive value, the result has automatic width, with the number of decimal positions taken from the left argument:

```
      Y←20 .012345 ¯7.2
      5⍕Y
20.00000   .01235 ¯7.20000
```

If the left argument is a single zero, the result will be formed with automatic width and no decimal positions. When the left argument is a negative integer, the result is formed in scaled notation:

```
         0⍕Y                        ¯3⍕Y
20    0  ¯7                2.0000E1   1.235E¯2  ¯7.2000E0
```

Lest you have any doubts, a character array as an argument is a *DOMAIN ERROR*, and left arguments that aren't scalars or vectors give *RANK ERROR*s. A vector left argument must be the proper length (2 or $2 \times ^{-}1 \uparrow \rho ARRAY$) to avoid a *LENGTH ERROR*. And, not unexpectedly, if the field width specified is too small to accommodate the display without overlap, a *DOMAIN ERROR* results.

A method for producing complete reports

Most commercial reports consist of at least some title lines, column headings and line names, as well as the data in the body of the report. As we pointed out earlier, this pattern is so common that most commercial APL systems provide report writing programs to make it easy for the user (who may not even know how to program in APL!) to produce decent-looking reports. We can't assume you have access to such facilities on your system, but we'll provide you with a method which will help you produce the reports you need.

The fundamental idea here is to use a character matrix whose dimensions are large enough to hold all the information that must be in the report—in other words, think of a page of paper if you are using a printing terminal, or one full screen if you are using a display terminal, many of which are 24 vertical lines by 80 characters across.

The illustration which follows produces an expense report for a traveling salesperson addicted to three-martini lunches and living high on the hog. As you study it, make sure you understand how each of the parts of the report goes into the character matrix *PAGE*. A display of the completed report is at the end of this section.

```
        ∇DATA PLACE INDS;ROWIND;COLIND
[1]     ⍝PLACES CHAR MATRIX DATA IN GLOBAL CHAR MATRIX PAGE
[2]     ⍝   STARTING AT POSITIONS GIVEN BY INDS.   A.J.ROSE   DEC 18 1980
[3]     DATA←(¯2↑ 1 1 ,⍴DATA)⍴DATA ⍝MAKE VECTORS, SCALARS INTO 1-ROW MATRIX
[4]     ROWIND←INDS[1]+¯1+⍳(⍴DATA)[1]
[5]     →(∧/ROWIND≤(⍴PAGE)[1])/L1 ◇ 'ROW INDEX TOO LARGE' ◇ →0
[6]     L1:COLIND←INDS[2]+¯1+⍳(⍴DATA)[2]
[7]     →(∧/COLIND≤(⍴PAGE)[2])/L2 ◇ 'COLUMN INDEX TOO LARGE' ◇ →0
[8]     L2:PAGE[ROWIND;COLIND]←DATA∇

        )COPY 1 CLASS ROWNAMES
SAVED   14.45.33 02/20/83

        PAGE← 24 80 ⍴' '
        LODGING← 45.7 60.42 55.2 0 50.19
        TRAVEL← 94.65 0 42.8 23.34 76
        FOOD← 40.25 51.4 66.5 42.34 35.9
        MISC← 37.9 32.2 28.75 0 35.45
        EXPENSES←⍉ 4 5 ⍴LODGING,TRAVEL,FOOD,MISC
        'GAIL PATTERSON' PLACE 1 1
        'EXPENSE REPORT FOR WEEK OF 12/3/82' PLACE 2 1
        (,¯8 ROWNAMES ' LODGING TRAVEL FOOD MISC. TOTAL') PLACE 4 11
        (40⍴' ------- ') PLACE 5 11
        (10 ROWNAMES ' MONDAY TUESDAY WEDNESDAY THURSDAY FRIDAY  TOTAL') PLACE 6 1
        (8 2 ⍕EXPENSES) PLACE 6 11
        (8 2 ⍕ 5 1 ⍴+/EXPENSES) PLACE 6 43
        (40⍴' ------- ')PLACE 11 11
        (8 2 ⍕(+⌿EXPENSES),+/+⌿EXPENSES) PLACE 12 11

        PAGE
GAIL PATTERSON
EXPENSE REPORT FOR WEEK OF 12/3/82
```

	LODGING	TRAVEL	FOOD	MISC.	TOTAL
	-------	------	-----	------	------
MONDAY	45.70	94.65	40.25	37.90	218.50
TUESDAY	60.42	.00	51.40	32.20	144.02
WEDNESDAY	55.20	42.80	66.50	28.75	193.25
THURSDAY	.00	23.34	42.34	.00	65.68
FRIDAY	50.19	76.00	35.90	35.45	197.54
	-------	------	-----	------	------
TOTAL	211.51	236.79	236.39	134.30	818.99

Dressing up displayed values

Most business people like to see their numbers decorated more than just aligning decimal points. Three of the most common requests are currency symbols such as ' $ ' in front of the values, commas in every third position of the integer parts, and negative values placed in parentheses instead of using the APL ' ‾ ' symbol. Virtually all commercial APL systems provide this sort of thing (see the next chapter); but for those of you who don't have such access, we provide the following functions. Besides, understanding how these functions work will help improve your own APL skills.

The function *FLOAT* takes a single character as its left argument and a character matrix or vector (the result of a ⍕) and places the symbol just before each leading nonblank character. It's the user's responsibility to make sure the matrix has enough blank spaces to get the result looking right.

```
      ∇R←SYMBOL FLOAT MATRIX;SHAPE
[1]   SHAPE←ρMATRIX
[2]   R←,MATRIX
[3]   R[((R=' ')∧1⌽R≠' ')/⍳ρR]←SYMBOL
[4]   R←SHAPEρR∇
```

```
      DATA←4 2ρ1 2.75 .5 12345.678 ‾12 ‾.03 0 999
```

```
    10 2⍕DATA                   ' $ ' FLOAT 10 2⍕DATA
    1.00        2.75            $1.00        $2.75
     .50    12345.68            $.50    $12345.68
 ‾12.00        ‾.03          $‾12.00       $‾.03
     .00      999.00            $.00      $999.00
```

Placing a comma between every third digit in the integer parts is a tougher job. The function *COMMAS* is one way to do it. If you're looking for a challenge, rewrite *COMMAS* so that it can handle more than one field across, with varying field widths. You may want to employ loops to do it.

```
      ∇R←DEC COMMAS N;B;D;S;T;U
[1]   N←(‾2↑1 1,ρN)ρN ⍝ SHAPE INTO MATRIX
[2]   R←DEC ⍕((×/ρN),1)ρN ⍝ FORMAT
[3]   T←ρR
[4]   D←R[1;]⍳'.' ⍝ FIND DECIMAL PT (IF ANY)
[5]   B←⌽(⌊4×(D-1)÷3)ρ1 1 1 0 ⍝ SET UP EXPANSION
[6]   B←B,(1+(1↑ρR)-D)ρ1 ⍝ REST OF EXPANSION
[7]   R←B\R ⍝ EXPAND RESULT AND
[8]   R[;(~B)/⍳1↑ρR]←',' ⍝ PUT COMMAS IN
[9]   U←ρR
[10]  R←,R
[11]  B←R∈','
[12]  S←B/⍳ρB ⍝ REMOVE COMMAS AS IN ,123 OR ,‾12
[13]  S←((R[(ρR)⌊1+S]∈' ')∨R[1⌈‾1+S]∈' ‾ ')/S
[14]  R[S]←' '
[15]  R←(1 ‾1×T)↑UρR
[16]  R←((1↑ρN),T[2]×1↑ρN)ρR∇
```

```
    15 2 COMMAS 6 1 ρ0 1 123 1234 123456 1234567.89
              .00
             1.00
           123.00
         1,234.00
       123,456.00
    1,234,567.89
```

Our final task for this section is to develop a function to place parentheses around negative numbers. Placing the left parenthesis in front of the negative values is easy enough—simply replace the ‾ by a (. However, to line up the positive values with the negative values, it is necessary to shift every character left one position, and then insert the) only in those fields that start with (, as shown in the following function:

```
      ∇Z←DEC PARENS N;L;R;S;T
[1]     T←ρN
[2]     N←1⌽DEC⍕((×/ρN),1)ρN ⍝ RESHAPE AND FORMAT
[3]     S←' '=N ⍝ IDENTIFY POSN OF LEFT PAREN
[4]     S[;¯1↑ρS]←2×+/S ⍝ IDENTIFY POSN OF RIGHT PAREN
[5]     S←,S
[6]     L←(S=1)/⍳ρS ⍝ LOCATIONS OF LEFT PARENS
[7]     R←(S=2)/⍳ρS ⍝ LOCATIONS OF RIGHT PARENS
[8]     N←,N
[9]     N[L]←'('
[10]    N[R]←')'
[11]    Z←((1↑T),(ρN)÷1↑T)ρN⍝
```

```
      12 2 PARENS ¯5  0 ¯.00003 ¯55559.98 123.4
      (5.00)
         .00
         .00
   (55559.98)
      123.40
```

Picture format

Some versions of APL, including IBM's APL2, offer an enhanced format feature called *picture format*, and a *format control* system variable, ⎕FC, used with ⍕.

⎕FC is a 6-element character vector whose default value is '.,*0_J', with the following definitions:

⎕FC element	default	use in picture format
1	.	decimal point
2	,	comma
3	*	fill to replace blank
4	0	fill to indicate overflow
5	_	fill to display blank
6	J	complex number formatting (to be discussed in Chapter 28)

The picture format is a character vector used as the left argument of ⍕. As its name suggests, it specifies the pattern to be applied to the right argument. Digits are control characters. Their positions show where digits will appear in the result. All other characters (called *decorators*) are displayed in the result. The dot and comma are used as a decimal point and comma in the usual sense.

Each control character has a specific meaning:

0 pad result with zeros up to this position
1 float decorator if negative
2 float decorator if nonnegative
3 float decorator
4 do not float nearest decorator
5 display digit
6 end field at right of noncontrol character
7 exponential E at right of noncontrol character
8 fill with ⎕FC[3] when blank
9 if nonzero, pad result with zeros to this position
. decimal point
, comma

Here are some examples:

```
      ' 5555.5'⍕6 0 45.26 350          ⍝ WHEN ONLY 5'S ARE USED, LEADING AND
  6              45.3   350                TRAILING ZEROS ARE SUPPRESSED

      ' 5.5 55.5 5555.55'⍕7.5 62.78 100.452
7.5 62.8   100.45

      ' 005 5.550'⍕32.56 4.1           ⍝ 0 PADS A FIELD WITH ZEROS
033 4.100

      '05/05/05'⍕20382                 ⍝ USE OF EMBEDDED DECORATORS
02/03/82

      ' ‾51.550'⍕‾6 0 6 ‾12.24         ⍝ 1 FLOATS DECORATOR AGAINST NEGATIVE NUMBERS
 -6.000      .000    6.000 -12.240

      '(51.550)'⍕‾6 0 6 ‾12.24
(6.000)    .000    6.000 (12.240)

      ' +52.552'⍕‾6 0 6 ‾12.24         ⍝ 2 FLOATS DECORATOR AGAINST POSITIVE NUMBERS
  6                +6        12.24

      ' $53.552'⍕‾6 0 6 12.24          ⍝ 3 FLOATS DECORATOR AGAINST ALL NUMBERS
 $6               $6        $12.24

      ' $51.45*'⍕‾6 0 6 ‾12.24         ⍝ 4 BLOCKS EFFECT OF 1,2 OR 3
 $6      *       *   6    * $12.24*

      '06/06/06'⍕2 3 82                ⍝ 6 ENDS A FIELD
02/03/82

      '1.700E0'⍕342.789                ⍝ 7 INDICATES EXPONENTIAL E
3.428E2

      '1.700*00'⍕342.789               ⍝ * REPLACES E
3.428*02

      ⎕FC[3]←'?'
      ' 8855.5'⍕6 0 6 12.24            ⍝ 8 REPLACES BLANK POSITIONS WITH ⎕FC[3]
???6    ????    ???6    ??12.2

      ' 55.59'⍕6 0 6 12.24             ⍝ 9 PADS ONLY NONZERO FIELDS WITH ZEROS
 6.00           6.00 12.24

      ' 55,555'⍕32879                  ⍝ USE OF COMMA IN PICTURE FORMAT
32,879

      ⎕FC[4]←'*'                       ⍝ ⎕FC[4] FILLS IN FOR OVERFLOWING FIELD
      2 0 4 1 4 2⍕2 3⍴4 7 32 2 1 .4
4 7.0****
2 1.0 .40
      ' 555'⍕36824
***

      ⎕FC[4]←'0'
      ' 555'⍕36824                     ⍝ ⎕FC[4] DEFAULT VALUE (0) CAUSES ERROR
DOMAIN ERROR
      ' 555'⍕36824
           ∧
      ⎕FC[5]←'A'
      ' $AA35555.5'⍕43287              ⍝ ⎕FC[5] IN PICTURE FORMAT PRODUCES BLANKS
 $   43287
```

Is the report still useful?

We can't resist one last tip, based on our own extensive and sometimes unhappy experience with business reports generated by others. It is that periodic reports, once begun, seem to take on a life of their own, and continue to be produced even when no one needs them. Circumstances do change. The initial recipients die or move on. Their successors wonder why they keep getting those weighty and impressive reports, but are reluctant to take their names off the distribution list or to question their value.

If you are the producer of such a long-lived 'standard' report, you might after a while unilaterally and without fanfare terminate it, and wait for a reaction. The odds are high that few of the recipients will even notice the loss. And you will have done your employer a service by reducing his overhead.

PROBLEMS

1. Format the array $TABLE$ (page 161) according to each of the following specifications: **A** field width 10, 4 decimal places; **B** field width 10, E-notation, 3 mantissa places; **C** automatic width, 3 decimal places; **D** columns 1 and 3 having 3 decimal places and field width 8, columns 2,4,5 having 5 decimal places and width 10.

2. Use ⍕ to display a logical matrix more compactly.

3. Define a dyadic function SAL to print a table of salaries showing the amount earned per week, month and year for a specified range and given increments of weekly salaries.

4. Design a report for a bank to identify currently overdrawn accounts, those with more than $100, and the weekly high and low balances for all accounts for the month. Assume you have two tables, $NAMES$ for customer names and $ACTIVITY$ for the weekly activity during the month (deposits −withdrawals). Each column in $ACTIVITY$ represents the net activity by customer for a particular week. Negative values mean withdrawals exceeded deposits. The first week's activity includes the opening balance.

5. Write a function which uses ⍕ to distinguish between literal and numeric arguments.

6. DAT is a numeric table whose columns contain respectively part numbers, quantity in inventory, quantity on order (by customer), unit cost and standard reorder quantity. Produce a report with appropriate column headings and a set of stars to flag those items for which the number in stock is less than the standard reorder quantity.

7. Insurance coverage in a dental plan pays 60% of all costs over $15 for each visit. Write a function to display the bill, amount paid by insurance and net cost to the policy holder for a given visit.

8. Format a date which is in numeric form, e.g., 121582 becomes 12/15/82.

9. Write a function $FORM$ to replace with blanks all zero elements in a matrix M.

10. Define a function $COLHEAD$ to spread the rows of a matrix of column headings across the top of a report. The left argument should have two elements, the first being the number of positions from the left margin at which printing begins, the second the column width.

Chapter 18: Comprehensive report formatting

Given dyadic ⍕ and a lot of enthusiasm, the accomplished APL programmer can produce formatted number displays with infinite variety and utility. However, it is time-consuming to develop functions like $FLOAT$, $COMMAS$ and $PARENS$ (Chapter 17). Besides, functions like those seem to use up more computer resources than you may feel appropriate; after all, they do apparently obvious, simple things to the display. Even worse is that unless you invest a vast amount of time in design and analysis, they won't work well together. Suppose you needed floating currency symbols, commas and negative numbers in parentheses all in the same formatted value?

Most commercial APL systems offer powerful solutions to this dilemma. In this and the following sections we'll discuss the dyadic system function $\Box FMT$. The version we will discuss is that of Sharp APL and the APL*PLUS System, but variants are found on other systems as well.

The left argument is always a character vector with its own set of rules about how the data, which is the right argument, will be formatted and decorated. Regardless of the shape of the right argument, the result is always a character matrix. The left argument is called the *format string* and the right argument the *data list*. Going over the examples used in Chapter 17, we first format the variable $TABLE$ so that each field is six characters wide, with three digits after the decimal point:

```
      TABLE←((1+.04×⍳3)∘.*⍳4)-1
      'F6.3' □FMT (TABLE)
0.040 0.082 0.125 0.170
0.080 0.166 0.260 0.360
0.120 0.254 0.405 0.574
```

Parentheses aren't really needed around the right argument. However, since you'll need the parentheses later to format two or more data items at the same time, you might as well form the habit now. One difference from ⍕ is that for all numbers between ¯1 and 1, leading zeros are produced in the result.

Let's now examine the format string. The character F indicates that the result is to be produced in *fixed point*; in other words, a decimal point will be present. The 6 indicates the fields are to be six characters wide, and the 3 calls for three positions after the decimal point.

In the above example, it is implied that the *format phrase* $F6.3$ is repeated once for every column in the data list. To produce fields of varying width, use format strings composed of several format phrases, with each phrase set off by a comma:

```
      'F8.3,F7.4,F8.3,F7.4,F8.3' □FMT (TABLE)
0.040 0.0816   0.125 0.1699
0.080 0.1664   0.260 0.3605
0.120 0.2544   0.405 0.5735
```

For that matter, since $\Box FMT$ will cycle through a list of format phrases and start again at the front (much like the dyadic ⍴) 'F8.3,F7.4' could have been used above as well.

Integer formatting is done using the letter I instead of F, followed by the desired field width. If the value to be formatted by an I-code is not an integer, it is rounded to the nearest integer. Look carefully at the next example, because we're sneaking in yet another new feature:

```
      'I4,2F10.5,I4' □FMT ((⍳4)∘.*1 .5,(÷3),2 3)
   1   1.00000   1.00000   1    1
   2   1.41421   1.25992   4    8
   3   1.73205   1.44225   9   27
   4   2.00000   1.58740  16   64
```

The above table of numbers, square roots, cube roots, squares and cubes has two main formats. The $I4$ produced fields one, four and five, and the $F10.5$ produced fields two and three. The new feature we introduced

169

was the explicit *replication factor*, namely, the 2 that comes before the $F10.5$. Its meaning is straightforward: you could just as well replace the phrase $2F10.5$ by the two phrases $F10.5,F10.5$.

Replication factors can apply to several format phrases by using parentheses. For example, $2(I4,2F10.3)$ is the same as $I4$, $F10.3$, $F10.3$, $I4$, $F10.3$, $F10.3$ and $I4$, $2(F6.2,2(I3,I2),I5),F10.6$ is the same as $I4$, $F6.2$, $I3$, $I2$, $I3$, $I2$, $I5$, $F6.2$, $I3$, $I2$, $I3$, $I2$, $I5$, $F10.6$.

You can express results in scaled notation by using a format phrase of the form $E14.8$. The 14 stands for the field width, and the 8 stands for the number of significant digits in the mantissa that will be represented. The number of significant digits requested must always be at least six less than the width to allow for the letter E, the decimal point, possible negative signs in the mantissa and exponent, and the two-digit exponent itself. To give you the flavor of the E-format code, try some variants of this example:

```
      'I4,E10.3,E20.12' ⎕FMT (2 ¯5 10 ∘.* 1 ¯4 15)
   2  6.25E¯2    3.27680000000E4
  ¯5  1.60E¯3   ¯3.05175781250E10
  10  1.00E¯4    1.00000000000E15
```

So far every illustration we have used as the right argument to $⎕FMT$ has been a matrix. When the data list contains a vector, it is treated as though it were a one-column matrix, as in

```
      'I1' ⎕FMT (!ι4)
1
2
6
*
```

which produces a character matrix with four rows and one column. This is particularly handy because a very common use of $⎕FMT$ is to list several data items side-by-side. Note that stars are produced whenever the value is too big for the field width.

Here is an example which displays the first five integers, their factorials, reciprocals, exponentials and natural logarithms:

```
      '2I4,F15.7,2E14.6' ⎕FMT (ι5;!ι5;÷ι5;*ι5;⍟ι5)
1   1    1.0000000    2.71828E0    0.00000E0
2   2    0.5000000    7.38906E0    6.93147E¯1
3   6    0.3333333    2.00855E1    1.09861E0
4  24    0.2500000    5.45982E1    1.38629E0
5 120    0.2000000    1.48413E2    1.60944E0
```

Since semicolons are used to separate items in the data list, parentheses aren't needed for any of the expressions.

Suppose you really wanted the example $'I4'$ $⎕FMT$ $(!ι6)$ to produce a one-line result. You could do it either by making the data items into a one-row matrix or by raveling the result:

```
      'I4' ⎕FMT (1 6⍴!ι6)           ,'I4' ⎕FMT (!ι6)
1    2   6  24 120 720       1    2   6  24 120 720
```

The shape of the first result is a matrix with one row and 24 columns, and the shape of the second result is a character vector with 24 elements. Can you explain the difference?

Working with alphabetic data

Most business reporting has character information (such as names of items or people) shown next to whatever numbers apply to them. For example, with this data

```
      NAMES←4 6⍴'NUTS  SCREWSBOLTS NAILS '
      COSTS←.05 .03 .20 .01
      QUANT←150 200 4 1000
```

a quite readable report (or invoice) can be obtained:

```
        '6A1,F10.2,I8,F10.2'  □FMT (NAMES;COSTS;QUANT;(COSTS×QUANT),+/COSTS×QUANT)
NUTS         0.05       150      7.50
SCREWS       0.03       200      6.00
BOLTS        0.20         4      0.80
NAILS        0.01      1000     10.00
                                24.30
```

The main point here is the format phrase $6A1$. The A-code is used to format character data items. Its width specification is usually 1, and its repetition factor is usually the number of columns in the character matrix you are formatting. But width factors other than 1 can be useful, as shown here:

```
        '6A2'  □FMT (NAMES)
N  U  T  S
S  C  R  E  W  S
B  O  L  T  S
N  A  I  L  S
```

Each character position in the variable $NAMES$ produced two positions in the result. In a sense, this is a very limited way to perform an expansion on the second dimension of a character matrix. However, it is introduced here because reports can sometimes be made more attractive by spreading out the text a bit.

It is easy to get messed up when using the A-code if you forget that each column of a character array is a separate entity. We will emphasize that point by this example:

```
        '2A1,A4'  □FMT (NAMES)
|NU|   T |S  |     |
|SC|   R |EW|  S|
|BO|   L |TS|   |
|NA|   I |LS|    |
     2A1    A4   2A1   A4
```

Dotted lines have been drawn to emphasize the result produced by each part of the format string.

The picture code

The picture code helps you produce specialized decorative effects. Embellishments such as placing slashes between the day, month and year in a date, separating the parts of a Social Security number, or 'dressing up' a telephone number are easily accomplished. To use it, the letter G is followed by a *picture pattern*. The pattern starts with the character ⊂ and ends with ⊃, and the result field width is the number of characters between ⊂ and ⊃. The characters between determine how the result appears: a character 9 says 'put a digit here,' and the character Z says 'if this position would have been a leading or trailing zero, put a blank here, otherwise use the appropriate digit character.' Any other character that appears in the picture pattern is literally placed in the result in that position.

```
        X←72.71 0 ‾12 .026
```

```
        'G⊂ZZZ9⊃'  □FMT (X)                    'G⊂ZZZZ⊃'  □FMT (X)
  73                                      73
   0
 ‾12                                     ‾12
   0
```

```
        'G⊂9999⊃'  □FMT (X)                    'G⊂$Z9.99⊃'  □FMT (X)
0073                                     $  0.73
0000                                     $  0.00
****                                     $ ‾0.12
0000                                     $  0.00
```

Only the integer part of the values are taken, as for an I-code. In the top right example, those values that would have printed as all zeros have disappeared (replaced by blanks). You may be surprised by the stars in the lower left example. The reason they appear is that the G-code demanded that every position be a digit, and there wasn't room for the negative sign here.

Even though a period was used in the bottom right example, it didn't scale the data. The period has no special meaning in a picture code. You have two options for properly placing the decimal point: you can multiply the data by the appropriate power of 10 before $□FMT$ works on it; or you can use the scaling code, K:

```
      'G⊂$ZZ9.99⊃' ⎕FMT (100×X)                    'K2G⊂$ZZ9.99⊃' ⎕FMT (X)
$ 72.71                                        $ 72.71
$  0.00                                        $  0.00
$⁻12.00                                        $⁻12.00
$  0.03                                        $  0.03
```

The K-code is preferred, because it uses fewer computer resources. The number following K is the power of 10 (either positive or negative) by which the data is to be multiplied. You may find it easier to think of it as the number of positions that the decimal point is being shifted over. The K-code can be used with F, I and E as well, although its use there is rather infrequent.

Here are some examples of typical uses of the G-code. Pay special attention to the first example; it shows a common error. Characters taken from the picture pattern are placed in the result field only if they would be surrounded by digits in the result field. This may be frustrating when dealing with decimal points, but quite handy when placing commas. See how the value .87 is treated in the next examples:

```
      'K2G⊂$ZZZ,ZZZ.99 REFUND⊃' ⎕FMT (1063.24 .87 150)
$   1,063.24 REFUND
$         87 REFUND
$     150.00 REFUND

      'K2G⊂$ZZZ,ZZ9.99 REFUND⊃' ⎕FMT (1063.24 .87 150)
$   1,063.24 REFUND
$       0.87 REFUND
$     150.00 REFUND

      'G⊂PHONE (999) 999-9999⊃' ⎕FMT (9143475565 5198373216)
PHONE (914) 347-5565
PHONE (519) 837-3216
```

Qualifiers

If you are warming up to the idea that APL can do commercial formatting, you will be convinced after learning about *qualifiers* and *decorations*, which are much like the control characters used in APL2 (Chapter 17). They are used with format codes F, I and G to tailor the report further to specific needs. All qualifiers and decorations come after the repetition factor, if there is one, and before the format codes. Here is an example using two qualifiers:

```
      'BCF13.2' ⎕FMT (10 ⁻4 0 1234567.9 ⁻.004 ⁻1000)
    10.00
   ⁻4.00


 1,234,567.90

    ⁻1,000.00
```

The B-qualifier says 'if the number would have been represented as a zero, make the field all blanks.' Notice that since we're showing only two decimal positions, the result is rounded to the nearest whole number, and hence the value ⁻.004 is rounded to zero and subsequently blanked. The C-qualifier simply inserts commas separating the digits of the integer parts in groups of three.

The Z-qualifier is used to insert leading zeros (instead of leading blanks) in a field. It would ordinarily be used when preparing output destined for punched card transfer to another (non-APL) computer as shown:

```
      'ZI9,⍫/⍫' ⎕FMT (3 4⍴⍳12)
000000001/000000002/000000003/000000004/
000000005/000000006/000000007/000000008/
000000009/000000010/000000011/000000012/
```

In the following illustration, the L-qualifier is used to *left-justify* the represented values within the field:

```
      ∇FACTORIALS
[1]   28⍴14↑' N  !N'
[2]   'I2,X2,LI10,I2,X2,LI19' ⎕FMT (⍳10;!⍳10;10+⍳10;!10+⍳10) ∇
```

```
          FACTORIALS
   N   !N            N   !N
   1   1            11   39916800
   2   2            12   479001600
   3   6            13   6227020800
   4   24           14   87178291200
   5   120          15   1307674368000
   6   720          16   20922789888000
   7   5040         17   355687428096000
   8   40320        18   6402373705728000
   9   362880       19   1216451004088320__
  10   3628800      20   2432902008176640___
```

Note the dashes at the lower right of the display. They appear because the internal value stored in APL is accurate only to approximately 16 decimal places, and the positions shown as dashes indicate that there is no accuracy in those positions.

We've already seen the K-qualifier applied to the G-code, so we'll just remind you that it can also be used with F-, I-and E-codes.

Decorations

The codes $MNOPQR$, each followed by a string of text enclosed between ⊂ and ⊃, are used to inject that text into the field according to these rules:

> M⊂text⊃   places text to left of negative result
> N⊂text⊃   places text to right of negative result
> O⊂text⊃   substitutes this text in place of zero result
> P⊂text⊃   places text to left of nonnegative result
> Q⊂text⊃   places text to right of nonnegative result
> R⊂text⊃   fills in 'unclaimed' spaces with text.

Since some people still aren't accustomed to the way negative numbers are shown in APL, you can use the M-decoration to replace the APL overbar by the dash:

```
     'M⊂-⊃P⊂$$⊃F10.2'  []FMT (¯79.32 10000 0 ¯123.45)
      -79.32
  $$10000.00
      $$0.00
     -123.45
```

Besides using the M-decoration to get the minus sign in the above example, P was used to place two dollar signs before each nonnegative value. This is called a 'floating currency symbol' because it is placed adjacent to the first visible digit.

It is often desirable to substitute some indication like $NONE$ or N/A for those fields that would print only zeros, such as the third row in the above example. Use the O-decorator for that:

```
      'O⊂NONE⊃P⊂$$⊃F10.2'  []FMT (¯79.32 10000 0 ¯123.45)
    _ ¯79.32
  $$10000.00
      _ NONE
     ¯123.45
```

If the O-decorator is not present, zero fields are decorated with P-text and Q-text. If the O-code is used, however, it takes precedence over P and Q.

Business reports often indicate losses or decreases by placing any negative values in parentheses, rather than prefixing them with a negative sign. This can be done with the following combination of codes:

```
     'M⊂(⊃N⊂)⊃Q⊂ ⊃CI10'  []FMT (¯79 1000 0 ¯123.45)
      (79)
    1,000
        0
      (123)
```

Do you know why the Q⊂ ⊃ decoration is used in this example?

The next illustration shows a typical 'check protection' application in which the field is protected against someone tampering with the printed value. The *R*-text fills in all 'unclaimed' positions, except that if an *O*-code is also present, it dominates:

```
      'O⊂NIL⊃P⊂$⊃CR⊂*⊕⊃F14.2' ⎕FMT (7932.56 .002 312.5)
★⊕★⊕★$7,932.56
★⊕★⊕★⊕★⊕★NIL
★⊕★⊕★⊕★$312.50
```

Stars in the result

Decorations and qualifiers consume additional character positions, and the field width must be sufficient to hold them all. If you try to put more characters in a field than will fit, the field will be entirely filled with the ★ character, but no other indication of error is given. This is so that in an involved commercial format, you can see which field caused the problem and revise your format string.

The most frequent cause of ★'s appearing is the attempt to format character data with an *F*-, *I*-, *E*-or *G*-code, or trying to format numeric data with the *A*-code. This often happens when you haven't counted the number of columns carefully in a character matrix, so that there is a mismatch between the format phrases and the columns of the data items in the right argument. For example, if you used the format

```
      '5A1,F10.2,I5,F10.2' ⎕FMT (NAMES;COSTS;QUANT;COSTS×QUANT)
NUTS ★★★★★★★★★    0     150.00★
SCREW★★★★★★★★★    0     200.00★
BOLTS★★★★★★★★★    0       4.00★
NAILS★★★★★★★★★    0    1000.00★
```

you get the stars in the second field because the matrix *NAMES* has six columns instead of five. The remaining data items are displaced one field to the right, with the consequences shown.

Filler and positioning codes

So far we've covered the *F*-, *I*-, *E*-and *G*-codes for formatting numeric values, and the *A*-code for formatting character values. The remaining formatting codes don't associate with any data in the right argument, but rather are used to supply filler spaces or text between fields. The *X*-code supplies blanks:

```
      'I4,X3,6A1' ⎕FMT (ι4;NAMES)
   1    NUTS
   2    SCREWS
   3    BOLTS
   4    NAILS
```

Can you think of an alternate way to produce this display without using the *X*-code?

Fields of constant character information can be sandwiched between data fields in the result by placing the text between ⊂ and ⊃:

```
      '⊂PRODUCT⊃,I2,⊂ IS ⊃,6A1' ⎕FMT (ι4;NAMES)
PRODUCT 1 IS NUTS
PRODUCT 2 IS SCREWS
PRODUCT 3 IS BOLTS
PRODUCT 4 IS NAILS
```

The last of the codes is the *T*-code (for horizontal tabbing). It is used to specify in which visible column of the result the next characters will be placed. For example,

```
      'I3,T20,I1' ⎕FMT (ι3;2×ι3)
   1               2
   2               4
   3               6
```

starts the second field in column 20 of the result. *T* and *X* are quite similar. The major difference is that *X*-positioning is relative to the present position, while *T*-positioning is relative to the left margin. Both *T*-and *X*-

codes may be used to position to the left (backwards). For instance, assume you are presently at display position 50. The phrase $T40$ will cause the characters that were in position 40 and beyond to be replaced by any following formatted characters. X^-10 moves backward 10 positions from wherever it presently is.

The T-code, when used without a number following it, repositions the cursor to the right to the first 'unused' position. You'd use it in a very complicated formatting job in which backspacing is needed.

Substitution of standard symbols

The previous discussion introduced some characters with special meanings in $\Box FMT$ left arguments and results. Here is a summary of them:

character	code	meaning
9	G	digit selector
Z	G	zero-suppress digit selector
∗	F G I	overflow indicator
.	F	decimal point
,	C	comma insert
_	F G I	nonsignificant digit marker
$\bar{0}$	Z	fill character
(blank)	G	lead zero fill character

For special effects, any of the above can be replaced by a different character through use of the S-qualifier. The first character in each pair is the standard symbol, and the second is the substitute. In this expression commas are replaced by dashes and the star by a question mark:

```
     'S⊂,-*?⊃CI10' ⎕FMT (1234567 123456789)
 1-234-567
 ?????????
```

The characters Z and 9 are reserved in their use in the picture code. If you ever had to use them literally (for example, to include the word $'FRAZZLE'$ or $'MODEL\ Z9'$ in a picture), you'd be in trouble without the S-qualifier. It works this way: if you put $S⊂9⊛ZZ⊃$ in front of the G, then for that picture, $⊛$ now means 'put a digit here' and Z has the meaning that Z used to have, so that 9 and Z are released from their regular duties, as shown below:

```
     'S⊂9⊛ZZ⊃G⊂ZZZ⊛ UNITS OF PRODUCT Z9⊃' ⎕FMT (73)
 73 UNITS OF PRODUCT Z9
```

The characters used to enclose text, $⊂$ and $⊃$, can also be substituted by other characters if you need to use $⊂$ and $⊃$ within the text itself. Other pairs that are valid are <text>, ⎕text⎕ and ⎕text⎕. Thus, $G⎕999Z⎕$ is the same as $G⊂999Z⊃$.

Symbol substitution is a convenient way to match the European number formatting convention, in which commas and periods are interchanged from the North American style:

```
     'S⊂.,,.⊃CF14.2' ⎕FMT (123479.32 10000000 123.456)
     123.479,32
 10.000.000,00
         123,46
```

Ragged data

$\Box FMT$ really doesn't care whether all of the data items have the same number of rows; it simply fills in any 'ragged edges' with blank fields. Note how we can produce the whole report, including a total line at the bottom:

```
        QC←COSTS×QUANT ◊ NAMT←5 6ρ(,NAMES),'TOTAL '
        '6A1,F10.2,I5,F10.2' ⎕FMT (NAMT;COSTS;QUANT;QC,+/QC)
 NUTS        0.05   150      7.50
 SCREWS      0.03   200      6.00
 BOLTS       0.20     4      0.80
 NAILS       0.01  1000     10.00
 TOTAL                      24.30
```

This implies that $\Box FMT$ can be used to join character matrices together, even if they aren't the same size.

Chapter 19: More on higher dimensional arrays

Most APL users feel quite comfortable with scalars, vectors and matrices. Which is why, except for a few illustrations earlier in the text, that's all we have used so far. But when it comes to three-(and higher-) dimensional arrays, the story is quite different. The comfort vanishes, to be replaced by queasiness and a lingering suspicion that there's something fishy about how APL manipulates such arrays.

Perhaps this is due to our inability to visualize them satisfactorily on a two-dimensional screen or paper. Or maybe our brains can't operate readily on more than two dimensions at a time. Be that as it may, this chapter will attempt to give you a warm feeling for three-dimensional arrays and how they can be used more effectively than a collection of matrices containing the same data.

As for arrays of rank greater than three (some APL implementations can deal with up to 63 dimensions), we concede that a certain measure of dedication and ingenuity is required, though the rewards are often commensurate with the effort. Also to be described in this chapter will be an extension of catenate and a new function, *laminate*, which allows us to construct arrays of rank greater than those of the arguments.

There are many examples of potential three-dimensional arrays which suggest themselves, more often than not as a set of separate two-dimensional arrays. For instance, an accounting system may be set up with 4 expense categories for each of 7 departments to keep track of expenditures by month. We could store each month's data in a separate 4 by 7 matrix. But it then becomes awkward to generate reports on selected departments and categories over a span of many months. However, if we structure the data as a single three-dimensional array, each of whose planes (or pages, if you prefer) contains all the data for a single month, we can slice up the data in many ways to answer any request the auditors may make.

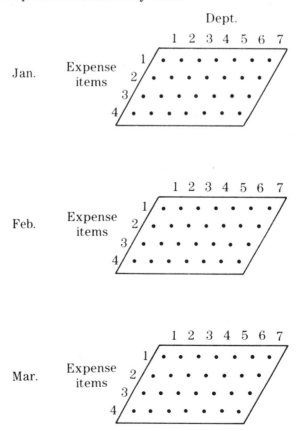

Three-dimensional arrays

We'll use as our primary example a couple of three-dimensional databases which will consist of 2 planes, one for each of two months. Each plane has 4 rows (for different sizes) and 3 columns (for different styles). The data elements are orders and wholesale prices:

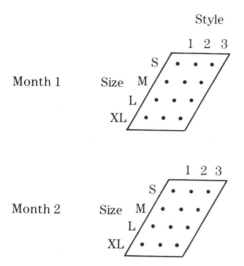

```
ORD←2 4 3ρ50 88 32 34 62 20 10 21 5 3 4 2 15 30 10 20 50 20 5 12 2 1 2
PRICE←20 22 19 20 22 9 20 22 19 22 24 21
PRICE←2 4 3ρPRICE,36 40 34 36 40 34 36 40 34 38 42 36
```

```
      ORD                PRICE
50  88  32           20  22  19
34  62  20           20  22   9
10  21   5           20  22  19
 3   4   2           22  24  21

15  30  10           36  40  34
20  50  20           36  40  34
 5  12   2           36  40  34
 1   2   1           38  42  36
```

Observe how *ORD* and *PRICE* were built by reshaping a vector of data. The left argument of dyadic ρ dictates that the result is of shape 2 by 4 by 3, just as in the expression $T←5\ 8ρι40$ the result will be a matrix of shape 5 by 8.

All of the standard scalar functions work on three-dimensional arrays in the same way they work on arrays of lesser rank. For example, to get the total revenue for each month-size-style (with prices increasing uniformly by 15%), enter

```
   ORD×1.15×PRICE
1150          2226.4           699.2
 782          1568.6           207
 230           531.3           109.25
  75.9         110.4            48.3

 621          1380             391
 828          2300             782
 207           552              78.2
  43.7          96.6            41.4
```

The new revenues can be rounded to the nearest hundred with

```
        100×⌊.5+(ORD×1.15×PRICE)÷100
1200 2200  700
 800 1600  200
 200  500  100
 100  100    0

 600 1400  400
 800 2300  800
 200  600  100
   0  100    0
```

The rules for primitive scalar dyadic and monadic functions stated earlier can be boiled down to

any-dimensional array ← any-dimensional array f any-dimensional array
any-dimensional array ← g any-dimensional array

with f standing for any primitive scalar dyadic function and g standing for any primitive scalar monadic function. The arrays must have identical dimension and rank (or one can be a single element).

Indexing multidimensional arrays

To index an item or items of a multidimensional array, you must provide an index for each of the dimensions of the array. A quick check is whether you have used exactly one fewer semicolon than the rank of the array. Thus, to get the scalar value corresponding to the second month, fourth size, third style of ORD, use

```
    ORD[2;4;3]
1
```

or to get the matrix that is all of the second month's data,

```
    ORD[2;;]
15 30 10
20 50 20
 5 12  2
 1  2  1
```

Operations along a single dimension

In Chapter 5 we saw how reduction could be used along the rows or columns of a matrix with / and ⌿ respectively. But what symbols do we use when there are more than two dimensions? APL has a feature called the *axis* operator. It has the syntax [I], where I is a scalar or one-element vector representing the index of the axis or dimension along which the associated function is to be applied. What this means is that +/[1]M is the same as +⌿M and +/[ρρM]M is the same as +/M (that is, reduce over the last dimension). The need for the brackets when dealing with three-dimensional objects should be obvious: there should be a way to reduce over any dimension. For instance, in the example used previously, here are some ways to get summaries:

```
      +/[1]ORD      ⍝ BY SIZE AND STYLE FOR ALL MONTHS (COULD BE +⌿ORD)
 65 118  42
 54 112  40
 15  33   7
  4   6   3
      +/[3]ORD      ⍝ BY SIZE FOR ALL STYLES FOR EACH MONTH (COULD BE +/ORD)
170 116  36  9
 55  90  19  4
      +/[2]ORD      ⍝ BY STYLE FOR ALL SIZES FOR EACH MONTH (ONLY WAY
 97 175  59          TO DO THIS ONE)
 41  94  33
```

As you can see from the three examples above, $f/[K]ARRAY$ results in an array whose shape is the same as $\rho ARRAY$, except that the K-th dimension or axis disappears. Hence the term *reduction*—the result is reduced in rank. More formally, $\rho f/[K]ARRAY$ is $(K \neq \rho ARRAY)/\rho ARRAY$.

The dyadic function *MEAN* takes a given dimension of an array and divides the sum across that dimension by the number of elements comprising that sum. Its left argument is the dimension of the array across which we are averaging:

```
      )COPY 1 CLASS MEAN               ∇MEAN[□]∇
SAVED  17.28.02 06/12/81          ∇ R←K MEAN X
                                 [1]   R←(+/[K] X)÷(ρX)[K]
                                  ∇
```

Let's try it on *ORD*:

```
      1 MEAN ORD      ⍝AVERAGE ORDERS FOR ALL MONTHS BY SIZE AND STYLE
32.5            59              21
27              56              20
 7.5            16.5             3.5
 2               3               1.5

      2 MEAN ORD      ⍝AVERAGE ORDERS FOR EACH STYLE FOR EACH MONTH
24.25           43.75           14.75
10.25           23.5             8.25

      3 MEAN ORD      ⍝AVERAGE ORDERS FOR EACH SIZE FOR EACH MONTH
56.66666667     38.66666667     12              3
18.33333333     30               6.333333333    1.333333333
```

The overall average is

```
      1 MEAN 2 MEAN 3 MEAN ORD      ⍝AVERAGE ORDER FOR ANY MONTH, SIZE AND STYLE
20.79166667
```

Can you think of why 3 *MEAN* 2 *MEAN* 1 *MEAN ORD* won't work?

The same dimension selection scheme outlined above for reduction applies to other operators and functions as well. Here are a few representative examples using *TAB*3:

```
      )COPY 1 CLASS TAB3
SAVED  14.45.33 02/20/83

      TAB3                    +\[3]TAB3
111 112 113             111 223 336
121 122 123             121 243 366
131 132 133             131 263 396
141 142 143             141 283 426

211 212 213             211 423 636
221 222 223             221 443 666
231 232 233             231 463 696
241 242 243             241 483 726

      +\[1]TAB3               1⌽[3]TAB3 ⍝OR 1⌽TAB3
111 112 113             112 113 111
121 122 123             122 123 121
131 132 133             132 133 131
141 142 143             142 143 141

322 324 326             212 213 211
342 344 346             222 223 221
362 364 366             232 233 231
382 384 386             242 243 241

      +\[2]TAB3               (2 3ρ1 2 3 2 0 1)⌽[2]TAB3
111 112 113             121 132 143
232 234 236             131 142 113
363 366 369             141 112 123
504 508 512             111 122 133

211 212 213             231 212 223
432 434 436             241 222 233
663 666 669             211 232 243
904 908 912             221 242 213
```

The last illustration needs careful examination to see what is happening. Note that the left argument is itself a matrix:

```
      2 3ρ1 2 3 2 0 1
1 2 3
2 0 1
```

To see what is happening, look at the value in row 2, column 3. It is 1 and therefore rotates $TAB3[2;;3]$ one position. Can you describe the result of $(4 3ρ\iota12)\ominus TAB3$?

Here are some more examples:

```
      1 0/[1]TAB3 ∩OR 1 0≠TAB3          1 1 1 0 1\[2]TAB3
111 112 113                       111 112 113
121 122 123                       121 122 123
131 132 133                       131 132 133
141 142 143                         0   0   0
      1 2 ‾2↑TAB3                  141 142 143
112 113
122 123                           211 212 213
      R←2 4ρTAB3                   221 222 223
      R∈TAB3                       231 232 233
1 1 1 1                              0   0   0
1 1 1 1                            241 242 243

      TAB3∈R                            1 ‾1 2↓TAB3
1 1 1                             213
1 1 1                             223
1 1 0                             233
0 0 0

0 0 0
0 0 0
0 0 0
0 0 0
```

Note that $+\backslash[2]TAB3[;4;]$ is the same as $+/[2]TAB3$. Can you generalize this?

Catenation

Our earlier discussion of catenation (Chapter 12) was limited to combinations of vectors and scalars, with the result always a vector. Now that we have the axis operator [n] as an APL 'signpost' to mark the dimension over which we want to use a function, we can extend catenation to arrays of all shapes.

This is easier to see than to talk about in the abstract. The character arrays P, Q, R, S and T will be used here for illustration. But first, a couple of brief rules. Two arrays whose shapes are *conformable* (i.e., the 'right size') can be joined along an existing dimension. If no dimension is specified, the catenation is along the last dimension:

```
      P←2 2 7ρ'P'              Q←4 7ρ'Q'                R←2 7ρ'R'
      P                        Q                        R
PPPPPPP                  QQQQQQQ                  RRRRRRR
PPPPPPP                  QQQQQQQ                  RRRRRRR
                         QQQQQQQ                        S←7ρ'S'
PPPPPPP                  QQQQQQQ                        S
PPPPPPP                                           SSSSSSS
                                                       T←4ρ'T'
                                                       T
                                                 TTTT

      Q,[1]R                   Q,[1]S                   Q,T  ∩OR  Q,[2]T
QQQQQQQ                  QQQQQQQ                  QQQQQQQT
QQQQQQQ                  QQQQQQQ                  QQQQQQQT
QQQQQQQ                  QQQQQQQ                  QQQQQQQT
QQQQQQQ                  QQQQQQQ                  QQQQQQQT
RRRRRRR                  SSSSSSS                        ρQ,T
RRRRRRR                        ρQ,[1]S            4 8
      ρQ,[1]R            5 7
6 7
```

A scalar argument is extended for purposes of catenation:

```
      W←'W'
      Q,W ∧OR Q,[2]W              Q,[1]W                       W,[2]P
QQQQQQQW                    QQQQQQQ                     WWWWWWW
QQQQQQQW                    QQQQQQQ                     PPPPPPP
QQQQQQQW                    QQQQQQQ                     PPPPPPP
QQQQQQQW                    QQQQQQQ
     ρQ,W                   WWWWWWW                     WWWWWWW
4 8                              ρQ,[1]W                PPPPPPP
                           5 7                          PPPPPPP
                                                             ρW,[2]P
                                                       2 3 7
```

Remember the function *PLACE* in Chapter 17? We used it to create a report with row and column headings by placing the pieces in the desired row and column positions in a predefined character matrix or page. Here is an alternative approach, which emphasizes catenation. First, let the expenses be stored in the matrix *EXP*:

```
      EXP←45.7 94.65 40.25 37.90 60.42 0 51.40 32.2 55.2 42.8 66.5 28.75
      EXP←5 4ρEXP, 0 23.34 42.34 0 50.19 76 35.9 35.45
```

Now we append the row totals:

```
      EXP1←EXP,+/EXP ◊ EXP1
45.7         94.65        40.25         37.9        218.5
60.42        0            51.4          32.2        144.02
55.2         42.8         66.5          28.75       193.25
 0           23.34        42.34          0           65.68
50.19        76           35.9          35.45       197.54
```

To include the column totals and the grand total, enter

```
      EXP2←EXP1,[1]+/EXP1 ◊ EXP2
45.7         94.65        40.25         37.9        218.5
60.42        0            51.4          32.2        144.02
55.2         42.8         66.5          28.75       193.25
 0           23.34        42.34          0           65.68
50.19        76           35.9          35.45       197.54
211.51       236.79       236.39        134.3       818.99
```

The numeric matrix is then converted to characters by

```
      EXP3←11 2▼EXP2 ◊ EXP3
  45.70       94.65        40.25        37.90       218.50
  60.42         .00        51.40        32.20       144.02
  55.20       42.80        66.50        28.75       193.25
    .00       23.34        42.34          .00        65.68
  50.19       76.00        35.90        35.45       197.54
 211.51      236.79       236.39       134.30       818.99
```

The row headings are formatted next. We could assign them as

```
      ROWS←7 9ρ'         MONDAY    TUESDAY  WEDNESDAYTHURSDAY FRIDAY    TOTAL      '
```

(why the spaces before *MONDAY*?), but if you are doing a lot of this it would be handy to have a utility like the following:

```
      )COPY 1 CLASS ON
SAVED   14.45.33 02/20/83

      ∇ON[□]∇
    ∇ Z←A ON B;PAD
[1]    A←(¯2↑ 1 1 ,ρA)ρA ∧ FORCE A TO BE A MATRIX
[2]    B←(¯2↑ 1 1 ,ρB)ρB ∧ FORCE B TO BE A MATRIX
[3]    PAD←(¯1↑ρA)⌈¯1↑ρB ∧ PICK LARGER DIMENSION FOR PAD
[4]    Z←(((1↑ρA),PAD)↑A),[1]((1↑ρB),PAD)↑B
    ∇

      ROWS←'' ON 'MONDAY' ON 'TUESDAY' ON 'WEDNESDAY'
      ROWS←ROWS ON 'THURSDAY' ON 'FRIDAY' ON 'TOTAL'
```

Next we form a vector of the column headings, keeping in mind that $ROWS$ is 9 positions wide and each of the columns in $EXP3$ was formatted as a field of width 11:

```
HDGS←5 11↑'LODGING' ON 'TRAVEL' ON 'FOOD' ON 'MISC' ON 'TOTAL'
HDGS←,(-+/∧\⌽HDGS=' ')⌽HDGS ⍝ RIGHT ADJUSTS
```

To complete the body of the report the pieces are catenated:

```
RPT←ROWS, HDGS,[1]EXP3 ⍝ OR ROWS, HDGS ON EXP3
RPT
              LODGING      TRAVEL        FOOD        MISC       TOTAL
MONDAY          45.70       94.65       40.25       37.90      218.50
TUESDAY         60.42         .00       51.40       32.20      144.02
WEDNESDAY       55.20       42.80       66.50       28.75      193.25
THURSDAY          .00       23.34       42.34         .00       65.68
FRIDAY          50.19       76.00       35.90       35.45      197.54
TOTAL          211.51      236.79      236.39      134.30      818.99
```

Suppose we belatedly discover that the amount for food on Tuesday is incorrect. It should be \$54.50 instead of \$51.40. $EXP3$ is a character array on which we can't do calculations. So unless we want to go to the bother of figuring out the exact positions in $EXP3$ to change, it's back to the original numeric array EXP or intermediate steps $EXP1$ or $EXP2$. Do you now see the wisdom in saving it separate from the augmented and formatted version?

The final step is to put the title on. First, let's add some space on top of RPT,

```
RPT←' ' ON RPT
```

and then execute the utility function $CENTER$, since titles on reports are generally centered:

```
        ∇Z←T CENTER R
[1]      Z←(¯1↑⍴R)-⍴T
[2]      Z←((⌈.5×Z)⍴' '),T
[3]      Z←Z ON ' ' ON R∇

        'JILLIAN AUSTEN' CENTER 'EXPENSE REPORT FOR WEEK OF 12/3/80' CENTER RPT
                              JILLIAN AUSTEN

               EXPENSE REPORT FOR WEEK OF 12/3/80

              LODGING      TRAVEL        FOOD        MISC       TOTAL
MONDAY          45.70       94.65       40.25       37.90      218.50
TUESDAY         60.42         .00       51.40       32.20      144.02
WEDNESDAY       55.20       42.80       66.50       28.75      193.25
THURSDAY          .00       23.34       42.34         .00       65.68
FRIDAY          50.19       76.00       35.90       35.45      197.54
TOTAL          211.51      236.79      236.39      134.30      818.99
```

If you had guessed wrong on the spacing in $HDGS$, it's no big deal to go back and reassign it, particularly if you are working on a display terminal with good editing capabilities. It would be much nicer if we had still another utility that would take a matrix of column headings and spread it over the columns of data, no matter how they might be spaced. This capability, as well as other cosmetic features needed for professional formatting, is generally included in the formatting packages found in most APL systems.

Lamination

By now you have probably tried on at least one occasion to make a matrix out of two vectors of the same length, using catenate:

```
V←⍳5                        V,[1]V                       V,[2]V
V,V                   1 2 3 4 5 1 2 3 4 5          INDEX ERROR
1 2 3 4 5 1 2 3 4 5                                    V,[2] V
                                                          ∧
```

Catenate can be used only to produce a result of the same *rank*, but enlarged *shape*. (The sole exception is when both arguments are scalars; in this case they are treated as vectors of length one.)

What we were trying unsuccessfully to do with V above was to make a matrix (rank 2) out of two vectors (rank 1). This means joining the vectors along a new, not yet existing dimension. If you think about the vectors as layers of data, the technique of forming a matrix out of them is akin to the building up of a sheet of plywood, that is, the data is *laminated*.

The *laminate* function, which shares the use of the comma with catenation, does this. Don't be intimidated by the fractional axis specifiers in the following examples; they're not as haphazardly chosen as they seem to be (ρQ is 4 7, ρR is 2 7 and W is a scalar):

```
        Q,[.5]W                 Q,[1.4]W                 R,[2.9]W
QQQQQQQ                  QQQQQQQ                  RW
QQQQQQQ                  WWWWWWW                  RW
QQQQQQQ                                           RW
QQQQQQQ                  QQQQQQQ                  RW
                         WWWWWWW                  RW
WWWWWWW                                           RW
WWWWWWW                  QQQQQQQ                  RW
WWWWWWW                  WWWWWWW
WWWWWWW                                           RW
        ρQ,[.5]W         QQQQQQQ                  RW
2  4  7                  WWWWWWW                  RW
                                 ρQ,[1.4]W        RW
                         QQQQQQQ                  RW
                         WWWWWWW                  RW
                         4  2  7                  RW
                                                  RW
                                                  RW
                                                       ρR,[2.9]W
                                                  2  7  2
```

```
        L←3 4ρ'ABCDEFGHIJKL'            L,[1.1]R          L,[2.75]R  L,[.5]R
        R←3 4ρ'1234567890KR'    ABCD              A1                  ABCD
                                1234              B2                  EFGH
                                                  C3                  IJKL
                                EFGH              D4
                                5678                                  1234
                                                  E5                  5678
                                IJKL              F6                  90KR
                                90KR              G7
                                                  H8

                                                  I9
                                                  J0
                                                  KK
                                                  LR
```

Here is a way to think about laminating arrays. Suppose you wish to laminate two matrices of shape 3 by 4. The result will have *three* dimensions, and the shape will be 3 4 2, 3 2 4 or 2 3 4. The only question is where the 2 will go. Much like inserting a line in a function, to squeeze the 2 between the existing dimensions, use a value between 1 and 2; in the first position use a number between 0 and 1. As in catenation, scalars are extended to match the array being laminated. The catenation of two scalars to form a two-element vector is really an example of lamination.

Laminate is commonly used to build up a three-dimensional array from already existing matrices. As an example, let's use the two separate planes of ORD (here we obtain them by indexing):

```
        )COPY 1 CLASS TAB3
SAVED   14.45.33 02/20/83

        TB1←TAB3[1;;]            TB2←TAB3[2;;]
        TB1                      TB2
111 112 113              211 212 213
121 122 123              221 222 223
131 132 133              231 232 233
141 142 143              241 242 243
```

These two arrays can be combined in several ways:

```
        TB1,[.4]TB2              TB1,[1.3]TB2              TB1,[2.5]TB2
111 112 113                  111 112 113              111 211
121 122 123                  211 212 213              112 212
131 132 133                                           113 213
141 142 143                  121 122 123
                             221 222 223              121 221
211 212 213                                           122 222
221 222 223                  131 132 133              123 223
231 232 233                  231 232 233
241 242 243                                           131 231
        ρTB1,[4]TB2          141 142 143              132 232
2  4  3                      241 242 243              133 233
                                     ρTB1,[1.3]TB2
                             4  2  3                  141 241
                                                      142 242
                                                      143 243
                                                              ρTB1,[2.5]TB2
                                                      4  3  2
```

These laminations produced three-dimensional arrays, while the following catenations give us only larger matrices, as we pointed out earlier:

```
        TB1,[1]TB2                   TB1,[2]TB2
111 112 113                  111 112 113 211 212 213
121 122 123                  121 122 123 221 222 223
131 132 133                  131 132 133 231 232 233
141 142 143                  141 142 143 241 242 243
211 212 213
221 222 223
231 232 233
241 242 243
```

Dyadic transpose

ORD, you will recall, is a three-dimensional array with two planes (one for each of two months), four rows (sizes) and three columns (styles). In the last section, we used laminate to reconstitute the display with differing points of view, as it were. A more general method of interchanging among planes, rows and columns employs the dyadic transpose function, ⍉. First, let's rearrange the data so that the planes are style and the columns are months. In other words, if the original data was in month, size, style order, we now want style, size, month.

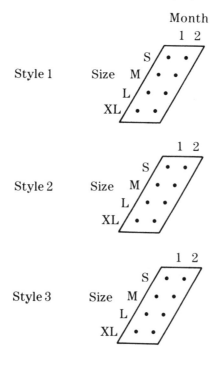

What was the third dimension becomes the first, the second remains as the second, and the new third dimension is what was the first. The result is identical to that obtained from the monadic transpose, ⍉ORD:

3 2 1⍉ORD		**⍉ORD**		**ρORD**	
50	15	50	15	2 4 3	
34	20	34	20	**ρ⍉ORD**	
10	5	10	5	3 4 2	
3	1	3	1	**ρ3 2 1⍉ORD**	
				3 4 2	
88	30	88	30		
62	50	62	50		
21	12	21	12		
4	2	4	2		
32	10	32	10		
20	20	20	20		
5	2	5	2		
2	1	2	1		

Another transpose makes the styles the rows and the sizes the columns, leaving the planes as months:

```
      1 3 2⍉ORD
50 34 10   3
88 62 21   4
32 20  5   2

15 20  5   1
30 50 12   2
10 20  2   1
      ρ1 3 2⍉ORD
2 3 4
```

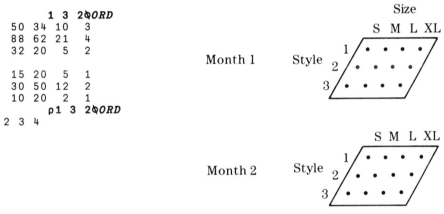

Month 1 Style

Size
S M L XL

Month 2 Style

In this case the first dimension is unchanged, but what was the third dimension becomes the second, and what was the second becomes the third.

Note how dyadic transpose allows alteration of the axes in the last two and next four examples:

```
    2 1 3⍉ORD          2 3 1⍉ORD          3 1 2⍉ORD          1 2 3⍉ORD
50 88 32          50 34 10   3       50 15             50 88 32
15 30 10          15 20  5   1       88 30             34 62 20
                                     32 10             10 21  5
34 62 20          88 62 21   4                          3  4  2
20 50 20          30 50 12   2       34 20
                                     62 50             15 30 10
10 21  5          32 20  5   2       20 20             20 50 20
 5 12  2          10 20  2   1                          5 12  2
                        ρ2 3 1⍉ORD   10  5             1  2  1
 3  4  2          3 2 4              21 12                   ρ1 2 3⍉ORD
 1  2  1                             5  2             2 4 3
      ρ2 1 3⍉ORD                      3  1
4 2 3                                 4  2
                                      2  1
                                          ρ3 1 2⍉ORD
                                    4 3 2
```

You should now be able to determine for yourself how different left arguments rearrange the month, style and size data. By the way, the 1 2 3⍉ isn't very useful since the result is the same as the right argument, but we included it for completeness. There are 6 (!3) different transpositions of three-dimensional objects into three-dimensional objects.

For transposition, the left argument meets the requirement that each element of the normal axis order (1,2,3,...) is replaced by the axis number it is to end up as in the result. In the example   3   1   2⍉ORD, month (axis 1 originally) is now the third axis, while size (axis 2) is now planes (first axis), and style (original third axis) is now rows (second axis).

Confused? We're not through yet. The following section looks at ways to take diagonal slices of an array with the dyadic transpose. In the authors' experience, this is one of the most difficult features of APL. For that reason the section is optional and left to those readers who are looking for a challenge.

Using dyadic transpose to get a diagonal slice

The sales analyst for the company whose database is the array *ORD*, a true APL buff, decides to examine the data in still other ways. Comparison of each line with the other lines of the plane from which it was taken shows that in the second month, the best seller was actually a size larger than the best selling size in the first month! The analyst concludes that the advertising campaign was aimed at the fashion setters, who tend to be smaller, and awareness of the product only gradually filtered through to those for whom the blouses the company makes would be less flattering.

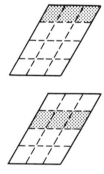

All the relevant data can be extracted with

```
      1  1  2⍉ORD
50  88  32
20  50  20
```

Here the desired plane and row indices are the same.

The transposition

```
      2  2  1⍉ORD
50  20
88  50
32  20
```

gives the same information, but the result is the (monadic) transpose of the previous result, as can be seen if we remove duplicate elements from the left argument.

A second slice is the 2 1 1 (or 1 2 2) transpose, which consists of all elements whose row and column indices are the same:

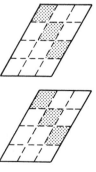

```
      2  1  1⍉ORD              1  2  2⍉ORD
50  15                   50  62   5
62  50                   15  50   2
 5   2
```

This extracts for each month the sales for style A small size, style B medium size and style C large size.

The final slices are

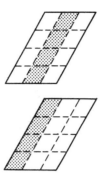

```
        1  2  1⍉ORD              2  1  2⍉ORD
  50  34  10   3            50  30
  30  50  12   2            34  50
                            10  12
                             3   2
```

which gets those elements whose first and third indices are identical. The result is the sales for style A the first month and style B the second month.

What about left arguments like

```
        1  3  3⍉ORD
DOMAIN ERROR
      1  3  3  ⍉ORD
            ∧
```

All positive integers up to the largest one present in the left argument must be included to avoid the error message. In the example, 2 was missing.

The most commonly used diagonal slice is that of a matrix (usually a square one), and fortunately it's an easy one to remember—the 1 1⍉.

```
   M←3 3⍴⍳9               M              1  1  ⍉M
                      1  2  3          1  5  9
                      4  5  6
                      7  8  9
```

As in the above matrix example, in a three-dimensional array the 1 1 1 ⍉ selects those elements all of whose indices are the same.

Although the dyadic transpose is one of the most powerful APL functions, its action on arrays of rank greater than 2 isn't always easy to see. For that reason, the function is not among the more popular with many APL users. And that's a pity, because it is so useful. You can do quite well experimenting at the terminal to find the proper transpose. If you do experiment, avoid arrays with the same dimension—it's much clearer to deal with an array of shape 2 by 4 by 3 than one of shape 3 by 3 by 3.

Using the relationships below will help you become a dyadic transpose expert, if that's your goal in life. The rules apply only when the elements of the left argument are all different; in other words, the rules don't apply for diagonal slices.

```
        ρ right argument is (ρ result)[left argument]
        left argument is (ρ,result) ⍳ρ right argument
        ρ result is (ρ right argument)[left argument ⍳ ⍳ρ left argument]
```

An application of dyadic transpose

Here is an application which uses dyadic transpose to reformat a character matrix (each row representing a word) into several columns of words, so that the order is preserved by reading down the first column, then the second, etc. The function is *SPRED* and the sample matrix is *SPL*:

```
      )COPY 1 CLASS SPRED SPL                        SPL
SAVED  14.45.33 02/20/83                           ZERO
      ∇SPRED[□]∇                                    ONE
    ∇ R←F SPRED X                                   TWO
[1]    R←⌈(ρX)[1]÷F ⍝CALCULATE AND PAD EXTRA        THREE
[2]    X←((R×F),1↓ρX)↑X ⍝BLANKS IF F IS NOT A       FOUR
[3]    X← 2 1 3 ⍉(F,R,1↓ρX)ρX ⍝FACTOR OF 1↑ρX       FIVE
[4]    R←(×/ 2 2 ρ1,ρX)ρX ⍝GILMAN AND ROSE, 1976    SIX
    ∇                                               SEVEN
      ρSPL                                          EIGHT
10 5                                                NINE
```

To produce a two-field spread and a three-field spread, try

```
      2 SPRED SPL,' '                3 SPRED SPL,' '
ZERO   FIVE                    ZERO   FOUR   EIGHT
ONE    SIX                     ONE    FIVE   NINE
TWO    SEVEN                   TWO    SIX
THREE  EIGHT                   THREE  SEVEN
FOUR   NINE                          ρ3 SPRED SPL,' '
      ρ2 SPRED SPL,' '          4 18
5 12
```

Do you know why a column of blanks was catenated to *SPL* in these examples?

Indexing scattered points

As we pointed out in Chapter 14, it isn't possible to pick out scattered elements of arrays of rank greater than one with primitive bracket indexing without getting more than we need. However, the previous sections showed how dyadic transpose can select various slices of an array. You may have a sneaking suspicion that if indexing is used to select parts of an array that include the desired points, maybe the dyadic transpose can then pull out the right slice.

Let's put this to the test on the array *CARDS* in 1 *CLASS*:

```
      )COPY 1 CLASS CARDS
SAVED  14.45.33 02/20/83

      CARDS
SPADE
CLUB
HEART
DIAMOND
```

The following set of separate indices will produce the characters *SUITS*,

```
      CARDS[1;1],CARDS[2;3],CARDS[4;2],CARDS[3;5],CARDS[1;1]
SUITS
```

but if the indices are merged, the result looks like some long-dead ancestor of the English language:

```
      AA←CARDS[1 2 4 3 1;1 3 2 5 1]
      AA
SAPES
CUL C
DAIOD
HAETH
SAPES
```

Each index is coupled with *all* the other indices along the remaining dimension.

If you're looking for *SUITS* in this mess, you probably noticed that the correct combinations of indices are those along the major diagonal of *AA*. But we already know how to get these points:

```
      1 1◊AA
SUITS
```

It isn't too difficult a generalization to extend this to three dimensions. Say the elements 112 142 143 221 are wanted from *TAB*3:

```
    TAB3                  1 1 1◊TAB3[1 1 1 2;1 4 4 2;2 2 3 1]
111 112 113            112 142 143 221
121 122 123
131 132 133
141 142 143

211 212 213
221 222 223
231 232 233
241 242 243
```

By taking other slices of a three-dimensional array, you can index scattered rows or columns.

The use of dyadic transpose for scatter-indexing may be summarized as follows, where *P*,*R*,*C* are the vectors of plane, row and column indices:

select scattered	from a matrix	from a rank-3 array
points	1 1◊M[R;C]	1 1 1◊T[P;R;C]
columns	M[;C]	2 1 2◊T[P;;C]
rows	M[R;]	1 1 2◊T[P;R;]
planes	M	T[P;;]

Those users who have access to APL2 or APL*PLUS will find that scatter-indexing can be done more easily with the index or choose functions (page 264).

PROBLEMS

1. Drill. Assign $U \leftarrow 2 \ 3 \ 4\rho\iota24$, $C \leftarrow 2 \ 4 \ 3\rho$'*ABCDEFGHI*'

```
⌈/⌈/⌈/U          +/+U[;2;3]         ◊C             ⊖C
⌈/,U             ‾1 1 2↓C          1 0 1 0/[2]C    3 1 2◊C
×/U              (2 4ρι3) ⌽C       0 2 2↓U         1 2 2◊U
+/[2]U           +/U[;1;3]
```

2. Make the first row first plane of *U* equal to the third row second plane of *U*.

3. Starting with a matrix $M \leftarrow 3 \ 4\rho\iota4$, produce another matrix *R* whose shape is 3 3 4 and made up of the columns of *M*. Use only indexing.

4. Write a one-line function to produce a table of three columns listing the integers 1 through *N*, their factorials and their reciprocals.

5. The XYZ advertising agency currently has 10 accounts. Each of these accounts represents an amount of money which is budgeted to be spent over a 12-month period in the following categories: 1) radio, 2) TV, 3) newspapers, 4) magazines, 5) direct mail. Assume the financial data is stored in an array *BUDGET* whose first dimension is time (in months), whose second dimension consists of the cost categories above, and whose third dimension is the accounts themselves. Write APL expressions to answer each of the following:
   A Find the total yearly cost for accounts 4 and 10.
   B How much was spent for the year for newspaper advertising in account 6?
   C What is the total yearly cost by account?
   D Which account spent the least money on TV during any month? In which month did this occur?
   E How much was spent each month in accounts 1 and 3 for magazine and direct mail advertising?
   F Construct a matrix of total monthly costs/account. Include appropriate row and column headings.
   G Enlarge the array *BUDGET* to include extra planes after the 6th and 12th months that will contain cumulative semiannual or annual costs/account/budget category.

6. You are given a long character vector V. Use laminate to follow each character with a semicolon.

7. A magazine subscription service sells 25 different magazines in 16 cities. The 12 by 25 by 16 array $MAGSALES$ contains a record of the number of subscriptions sold by month, magazine and city. Construct a function that will print in matrix form the name of the leading magazine each month. Assume the names of the magazines are stored in a matrix $MAGNAMES$, with the names of the months in the matrix CAL. Ignore the possibility of a tie for total sales per month to simplify the algorithm.

8. Write a program to underline nonblanks in a character vector V.

9. The 5 4 4 array SP contains selling price information on a company's primary product. Each plane represents data for one year (1978-82) for each of four models A, B, C, D (rows) in each of four sizes S, M, L, XL (columns). A similar array $SALES$ has the number of units sold each year for each model and size. Find the
   A gross volume for 1979
   B sales by size for 1980 and 1981
   C increase in sales volume by model from 1978 to 1982
   D revenue for models A and C (medium size) in 1978 and 1979
   E total revenue for 1982.
   F create a new table for 1983 prices (20% higher than 1982) and append it to SP.

10. Using the same three-dimensional database as in problem 9,
    A By what percent did sales in 1980 for mediums (all models) exceed those for extra large?
    B How many units (by model) were sold during 1981 and 1982 of those models whose sales exceeded 50,000 for all sizes sold?

11. During the year a hardware store bought each quarter a certain amount of nails, tacks and screws. The pounds of each bought per quarter are stored in the 3 by 4 table HWR. Print a report with an appropriate title and row and column headings and totals showing the year's purchases.

12. Write a function to number a given list of names.

13. Define a function $TABLE$ which formats a numeric table M as a character table with no decimal places if all the elements are integers, otherwise 2. The table should be bordered by '_' and '¯', and the columns separated and bordered by '|'.

14. Write functions $WITH$ and $ABOVE$ to do the following: $WITH$ is to append and pad out row headings (stored in $SIDE$); $ABOVE$ is used to append column headings (stored in TOP). The expression $SIDE\ WITH\ TOP\ ABOVE\ DATA$ should then return a report which includes row and column headings.

15. Define a function $BESIDE$ to join two matrices of different shapes horizontally.

16. Decorate (i.e. outline) a literal matrix M with a character A.

17. For a 5 by 5 matrix $SALES$, use ⍉ to construct a new matrix $SALES1$ with column headings 10 through 14 and row headings $STORE1$ through $STORE5$.

18. Use the dyadic transpose to add a vector V to each row of a vector M.

19. Write an expression to obtain the diagonal that runs from the upper right to the lower left of a matrix.

Chapter 20: Generalized inner product and matrix inverse

In Chapter 2 the concept of an operator was introduced as something which can be applied to a function to obtain a different function; i.e., like the action of an adverb on a verb in grammar, operators modify a function. The operators common to most versions of APL are the outer product $\circ.f$, reduction $f/$, scan $f\backslash$, the axis operator $f[n]$, and the *inner product* $f.g$. It is this last very useful operator which will be introduced in this chapter.

We illustrate the inner product with a common problem. A company employs three sales persons who are engaged in selling four products A,B,C,D. Their sales volumes are shown in the matrix $VOLS$. $COSTS$ contains the price for each product and the shipping charges per unit.

Costs

Product	Unit price	Unit ship cost
A	4	0.05
B	2	0.06
C	1	.03
D	1	.02

Salesperson	A	B	C	D
1	2	3	0	1
2	0	2	1	4
3	1	1	2	1

Volumes

```
VOLS←3 4ρ2 3 0 1 0 2 1 4 1 1 2 1
COSTS←4 2ρ4 .05 2 .06 1 .03 1 .02
```

The total revenue generated by salesperson 1 can be calculated as either of

```
      +/2 3 0 1 × 4 2 1 1                    +/VOLS[1;]×COSTS[;1]
15                              15
```

and in the same way we can generate the total shipping costs for salesperson 3:

```
      +/1 1 2 1 × .05 .06 .03 .02            +/VOLS[3;]×COSTS[;2]
0.19                                 0.19
```

In fact, *all* the revenue and shipping costs associated with the three salespersons can be obtained by executing

```
      +/VOLS[1;]×COSTS[;1]                    +/VOLS[1;]×COSTS[;2]
15                                     0.3
      +/VOLS[2;]×COSTS[;1]                    +/VOLS[2;]×COSTS[;2]
9                                     0.23
      +/VOLS[3;]×COSTS[;1]                    +/VOLS[3;]×COSTS[;2]
9                                     0.19
```

or, more compactly, with

```
      +/[2]1 2 2 3 ⍉VOLS∘.×COSTS
  15              0.3
   9              0.23
   9              0.19
```

Inner product

The inner product concisely states and executes this complete set of instructions:

```
      VOLS+.×COSTS
15              0.3
 9              0.23
 9              0.19
```

This particular operator, $+.\times$, corresponds to *matrix multiplication* in mathematics. With matrix arguments it separately multiplies each row of the left argument by each column of the right argument and then carries out plus-reduction on the results. The inner dimensions must agree. That is, the number of columns in the left argument must match the number of rows in the right argument. Hence, the name *inner product*.

We're not through with this problem yet. Let's try

```
      VOLS⌈.×COSTS
8               0.18
4               0.12
4               0.06
```

By the same reasoning as before this represents the greatest revenue and shipping charge per item produced by each salesperson.

In present implementations of APL there are 441 distinct inner products possible, although most users tend to stay with $+.\times$, $\wedge.=$, $\vee.\neq$, $\wedge.\neq$, $\lfloor.+$ and $\lceil.+$. There appears to be plenty of room for those of you who are adventurous enough to explore new uses for the remaining 435. Who knows? You may become famous!

The inner product is *not* the same as $A\circ.+B$ or $A\circ.\times B$ and it can't even be compared with $A\times B$ since the latter operation works only when the two arrays are the same size, and the multiplication is carried out between corresponding elements only. The inner product, $Af.gB$, operates on any pair of arrays, provided that the last dimension of the left argument is the same as the first dimension of the right argument. Except for scalar arguments, the dimensions of the result in each case are $(^-1\downarrow\rho A),1\downarrow\rho B$. Here are more examples involving scalars, vectors and multidimensional arrays:

```
      10+.×3 2 8                       (2 3 4⍴⍳24)+.-4 2⍴⍳8
130                              ¯6  ¯10
      1 2 3 4+.*0 1 2 3           10    6
76                               26   22
      2 1 6+.×3 2⍴⍳6
35 44                            42   38
      (3 4⍴⍳12)+.=⍳4              58   54
4 0 0                            74   70
```

Numerical applications of the inner product

One interesting application involves a pipeline network between cities on a map. The diagram below shows not only the intercity pipeline lengths in miles between A, B, C and D, but also the directions in which they are measured:

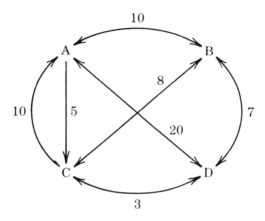

```
FM↓ TO→| CITY A   CITY B   CITY C   CITY D
-------|----------------------------------
CITY A |    -        10        5        20
CITY B |   10         -        8         7
CITY C |   10         8        -         3
CITY D |   20         7        3         -
```

Notice that the distances are not necessarily the same in both directions between any two cities. This is to allow for the most general case where there may be competing pipelines between two cities along different rights of way. The same information is provided in 1 *CLASS* as the variable *MILEAGE*. Believe it or not, a table of the longest pipeline distances from any city to any other city passing through some intermediate city is given by *MILEAGE⌈.+MILEAGE*:

```
     )LOAD 1 CLASS
SAVED  14.45.33 02/20/83
```

```
        MILEAGE                  MILEAGE⌈.+MILEAGE
   0  10   5  20              40  27  23  20
  10   0   8   7              27  20  15  30
  10   8   0   3              23  20  16  30
  20   7   3   0              20  30  25  40
```

The longest distance from A to B is 27 miles (A→D→B), from B to C 15 miles (B→A→C), etc.

Why does this work? Let's arrange the matrices for the inner product in the same form used for the the last section:

0	10	5	20
10	0	8	7
10	8	0	3
20	7	3	0

$\lceil . +$

0	10	5	20
10	0	8	7
10	8	0	3
20	7	3	0

[1;1]	[1;2]	[1;3]	[1;4]
[2;1]	[2;2]	[2;3]	[2;4]
[3;1]	[3;2]	[3;3]	[3;4]
[4;1]	[4;2]	[4;3]	[4;4]

The longest distance from B to C is represented by the contents of box [2;3]. This is formed by operating on the second row of the left argument and the third column of the right argument. It requires adding 10 and 5, and taking the greater of that sum and the sum of 0 and 8, which is 15, then taking the greater of 15 and the sum of 8 and 0, which is still 15, and finally taking the greater of 15 and the sum of 7 and 3.

There are many other interesting and useful variants of the inner product, only a few of which will be considered here. For instance, the shortest two-leg pipeline distance is $MILEAGE\lfloor.+MILEAGE$. The shortest distance from A to C is 5 miles, which is A→A→C or A→C→C. We are allowed this possibility because the distance from each city to itself is zero (the entries on the major diagonal of $MILEAGE$):

```
        MILEAGE                    MILEAGE⌊.+MILEAGE
    0  10   5  20                   0  10   5   8
   10   0   8   7                  10   0   8   7
   10   8   0   3                  10   8   0   3
   20   7   3   0                  13   7   3   0
```

One way to prevent such a sneaky result is to put arbitrarily large numbers along the major diagonal of a new array Q (to avoid destroying or rewriting $MILEAGE$). Then $Q\lfloor.+Q$ is the matrix of shortest two-leg distances, given that the intermediate city is different from the start or end. The shortest such distance from A to C is 18 miles (A→B→C). Application of this operation a second time ($Q\lfloor.+Q\lfloor.+Q$) gives the shortest three-leg distances:

```
      Q←MILEAGE+1000×(ι4)∘.=ι4
          Q                         Q⌊.+Q                    Q⌊.+Q⌊.+Q
 1000    10     5    20        15  13  18   8           23  15  11  20
   10  1000     8     7        18  14  10  11           20  18  14  13
   10     8  1000     3        18  10   6  15           16  14  18   9
   20     7     3  1000        13  11  15   6           21  13   9  18
```

We can continue this process ad nauseam, but there is a prepared function $AGAIN$ in 1 $CLASS$ that will do it for us. It is niladic and simply reassigns a global T as $T\lfloor.+Q$. If we set T equal to Q initially, the first time we execute $AGAIN$ we will get the shortest two-leg distances, the next time the shortest three-leg distances, and so on:

```
      ∇AGAIN[□]∇              T←Q  ◇  AGAIN            AGAIN                  AGAIN
    ∇  AGAIN              15  13  18   8        23  15  11  20        21  19  23  14
[1]    T←T⌊.+Q           18  14  10  11        20  18  14  13        24  20  16  17
[2]    T                 18  10   6  15        16  14  18   9        24  16  12  21
    ∇                    13  11  15   6        21  13   9  18        19  17  21  12
```

Circuit analysis applications

Imagine a circuit with six functional units connected as follows:

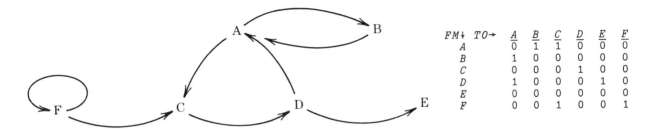

FM↓ TO→	A	B	C	D	E	F
A	0	1	1	0	0	0
B	1	0	0	0	0	0
C	0	0	0	1	0	0
D	1	0	0	0	1	0
E	0	0	0	0	0	0
F	0	0	1	0	0	1

A, B, C, D, E and F are some kind of functional units which can be either energized or not. The circuit works this way: if C is energized, after a certain increment of time D is energized, and after another increment of time E and A are energized; if A is energized, after an increment of time C and B are energized, etc. F is the oddball unit here. Once it is energized it stays on permanently, but unless we start with F on there is no way to turn it on. E is a terminus. It doesn't turn anything on. All this information is summarized in the matrix *CIRCUIT*, with 1 standing for the existence of a connection from the unit named on the left to the one whose name is on the top:

```
      CIRCUIT
0 1 1 0 0 0
1 0 0 0 0 0
0 0 0 1 0 0
1 0 0 0 1 0
0 0 0 0 0 0
0 0 1 0 0 1
```

We can assign a vector *ST* with six elements (one for each unit in the circuit) in which a 1 signifies that that unit is energized initially. For example, if only A is on, we assign *ST* as

```
      ST←1 0 0 0 0 0
```

What units are on after one increment of time? From the matrix *CIRCUIT* it appears that B and C will be turned on and all the others, including A, will be off. The result should be 0 1 1 0 0 0, which can be achieved by

```
      STv.∧CIRCUIT
0 1 1 0 0 0
```

(Why is ∨.∧ used?) and after another increment of time,

```
      0 1 1 0 0 0v.∧CIRCUIT
1 0 0 1 0 0
```

A is energized during alternate cycles because of the loop between A and B.

To step this through several increments of time use the function *RUN* in 1 *CLASS*:

```
      ∇RUN[□]∇
    ∇ NETWORK RUN STATUS;COUNT
[1]    COUNT←0
[2] LOOP:COUNT
[3]    STATUS
[4]    STATUS←STATUSv.∧NETWORK
[5]    COUNT←COUNT+1
[6]    →LOOP
    ∇
```

The left argument is *NETWORK*, the matrix which describes the circuit connections. The right argument *STATUS* represents the initial conditions. *COUNT* is a local variable which is set to 0 on line 1 and displayed on line 2. Line 3 prints the current status of the circuit elements. *STATUS* is updated on the next line and the counter upped on line 5. The final line causes a branch to line 2.

Does this program look a bit peculiar to you? It should. There is no safeguard in it to turn it off once it starts, and it will run forever! The proper thing to do would be to put a line in it that will cause execution to cease once *COUNT* reaches a certain value. Since there is no such check, we'll let it go and manually interrupt execution when we've seen enough.

Start by turning on only A:

```
      ST←1 0 0 0 0 0

      CIRCUIT RUN ST
0
1 0 0 0 0 0

1
0 1 1 0 0 0

2
1 0 0 1 0 0

3
1 1 1 0 1 0

4
1 1 1 1 0 0

5
1 1 1 1 1 0

6
1 1 1 1 1 0

7
1 1 1 1 1 0
RUN[3]
      )SI
RUN[3]  *
      COUNT
10
```

Execution has been manually interrupted, as discussed above, and we are suspended on line 3. F will never turn on no matter how many runs we make, while *COUNT* is up to 10, the display having lagged behind execution. Ordinarily we can't get a value for *COUNT* because it is a local variable. But remember that we are still in the function as a result of the suspension. Don't forget to remove the suspension by → or)RESET.

Character applications

One of the most frequent applications of inner product is finding which row of a character matrix matches a given character vector, commonly called *table lookup*. For example, if *DATA* is a matrix with each row holding the name of a product,

```
      DATA←'TACO' ON 'BURRITO' ON 'ENCHALADA' ON 'TOSTADA' ON 'TUMS'
```

then a function like this

```
      ∇HITS←MATRIX FIND VECTOR
[1]     HITS←MATRIX∧.=(1↓ρMATRIX)↑VECTOR∇
```

returns a bit vector with a 1 corresponding to which rows of the matrix match the vector.

```
      DATA FIND 'TOSTADA'
0 0 0 1 0
```

By this time some of you may be thinking how nice it would be if the example above could be modified to handle a matrix right argument, i.e., to simulate ranking. Let's see how a function can be built to do this.

Remember that ranking locates the first match of right argument elements in the left argument:

```
        A←3 4 ρ1 4 3 28 10 50 60 15 4 9 13              B←3 10 15 3 8
        A                                               B⍳A
  1   4   3 28                                      6 6 1 6
 10  50  60 15                                      2 6 6 3
  4   9  13  1                                      6 6 6 6
```

The 6's represent those elements in A not found in B. The right argument can be of any shape, but the left argument must be a vector.

A useful extension of this idea is locating the indices of rows in the left argument which are the first occurrences of matches to rows of the right argument. If we had such a function, MDI, for the arrays

```
        FURN1←5 6ρ'DESKS CHAIRSTABLESFILES CHAIRS'
        LOOKUP←4 6ρ'CHAIRSLAMPS PHONESTABLES'

        FURN1              LOOKUP
DESKS               CHAIRS
CHAIRS              LAMPS
TABLES              PHONES
FILES               TABLES
CHAIRS                    ρLOOKUP
      ρFURN1               4 6
5 6
```

then FURN1 MDI LOOKUP should return 2 6 6 3.

How do we go about building MDI? Two ideas suggest themselves here. The inner product ∧.= will be useful for getting matches of the rows. Locating the *first* match is trickier. In Problem 8, Chapter 5, we showed that ∧\ on a logical vector returns 1's until the first 0 is encountered, with all 0's thereafter. These two techniques are the basis for MDI.

We can't execute FURN1∧.=LOOKUP (why not?), but the expression A1←FURN1∧.=⍉LOOKUP works quite nicely. The 'highest' 1 in each column marks the spot. To turn that into a recognizable index, we'll first define A2←∧⍀~A1 and then add 1 to A2's column sums:

```
        A1←FURN1∧.=⍉LOOKUP            A2←∧⍀~A1            A3←1++⌿A2
        A1                            A2                  A3
0 0 0 0                         1 1 1 1              2 6 6 3
1 0 0 0                         0 1 1 1
0 0 0 1                         0 1 1 0
0 0 0 0                         0 1 1 0
1 0 0 0                         0 1 1 0
```

The function MDI, assembled from these steps, is shown below, along with another version, MDI1, which works no matter what the rank of LOOKUP.

```
        ∇Z←MATRIX MDI LOOKUP              ∇Z←MATRIX MDI1 LOOKUP
[1]     Z←1++⌿∧⍀MATRIX∧.=⍉LOOKUP∇    [1]  Z←1++/∧\LOOKUP∨.≠⍉MATRIX∇
```

The inner product ∨.≠ returns a result which is the logical complement of that from ∧.=. In all cases, of course, the shapes of the two arrays must be acceptable for use with the inner product.

The rest of this chapter is optional. It covers, at least superficially, many uses of APL in matrix algebra, curve-fitting and splines. If you are a member of that class of users for whom the above topics are esoterica, skip to the next chapter. But if your curiosity has gotten the better of you, or you have a genuine need to know, read on.

Linear equations

There are many uses for APL in the branch of mathematics known as *matrix algebra*. Since this text is a teaching introduction to the language, only a few of these will be considered, the first being the solution of a set of exactly determined simultaneous linear equations.

For those who have forgotten their high school algebra, simultaneous linear equations are of this form in conventional notation,

$$aX + bY + cZ = r$$
$$dX + eY + fZ = s$$
$$gX + hY + iZ = t$$

the problem being to find values of the variables X, Y, Z that satisfy all the equations. a, b, c,..., i and r, s, t are numerical constants.

Suppose that in three successive weeks we bought quantities of items A, B and C, spending the amounts listed:

	TOTAL	A	B	C
WEEK 1	$1.10	4	6	0
WEEK 2	$0.59	3	2	2
WEEK 3	$0.78	1	3	4

What are the unit costs of the various items? The answer happens to be $.05 for A, $.15 for B and $.07 for C. Let's work back from the answer to see how we can solve similar problems. From our previous work with the inner product, we ought to be able to get the vector of total costs from the number-of-items matrix and the unit-costs vector (try this for yourself). We'll call the total-costs vector D, the matrix of the number of each item purchased X, and the unit-costs vector B. Our trouble is that in a real problem we would know X and D but not B.

Before proceeding, here is a quick review of some elementary rules about matrices. M, N, P and R are matrices of the appropriate size and $+.\times$ is ordinary matrix multiplication. You can demonstrate all of these rules on any APL system:

(1)   If M equals N, then $R+.\times M$ equals $R+.\times N$
(2) $(M+.\times(N+.\times P))$ equals $(M+.\times N)+.\times P$
(3)   If M has an inverse, MI, then $MI+.\times M$ equals I, where I is the identity matrix
(4) $(M+.\times I)$ equals $(I+.\times M)$ equals M

The third fact introduces two new concepts, the *identity matrix* and the *matrix inverse*. The identity matrix is simply a square matrix with ones on the major diagonal and zeros elsewhere. An identity matrix of size N can be formed by $(\iota N)\circ.=\iota N$ or $(N,N)\rho 1,N\rho 0$. It is called the identity matrix because when any matrix is multiplied (in the $+.\times$ sense) by it, the result is unchanged.

The matrix inverse concept is similar to other types of inverses we have encountered. For example, adding the additive inverse to a number results in 0, the identity element for addition, while multiplying a number by its multiplicative inverse results in 1:

```
   R←ι5
 0=R+-R                    1=R×÷R
1 1 1 1 1                 1 1 1 1 1
```

$-R$ here is the additive inverse and $\div R$ the multiplicative inverse. So the inverse of a matrix M is a matrix which, when it multiplies M (matrix multiplication, not element-by-element), yields the identity matrix.

If $M+.\times MIR$ results in I, then MIR is said to be a *right inverse*. If $MIL+.\times M$ results in I, MIL is a *left inverse*. If the same matrix is both a left and a right inverse of M, then M must be square (why?), and we refer to *the inverse* of M. From this point on, MI will stand for *the inverse* of M.

Now getting back to our problem, with the dimensions underneath as shown, we had

$$\begin{array}{cccc} D & \leftarrow & X & +.\times & B \\ (3) & & (3\ 3) & & (3) \end{array}$$

and we want to find B. The following sequence of algebraic substitutions does it for us. The rules are the ones stated above.

$$\begin{array}{lll} XI+.\times D & \text{is } XI+.\times(X+.\times B) & \text{rule 1} \\ & \text{or } (XI+.\times X)+.\times B & \text{rule 2} \\ & \text{or } I+.\times B & \text{rule 3} \\ & \text{or } B & \text{rule 4} \end{array}$$

The last line is our conclusion, that $B \leftarrow XI+.\times D$.

To find the inverse of a matrix, APL provides a primitive monadic function ⊞, formed by overstriking the quad and divide symbols, and usually called *quad-divide, domino* or *matrix divide*. Let's use it to solve the unit costs problem at the beginning of this section.

```
         X                        ⊞X
   4  6  0          ¯0.03846153846    0.4615384615   ¯0.2307692308
   3  2  2           0.1923076923   ¯0.3076923077    0.1538461538
   1  3  4          ¯0.1346153846    0.1153846154    0.1923076923
         D                      (⊞X)+.×D
   1.1  0.59  0.78       0.05  0.15  0.07
```

If the right argument X is a scalar, then ⊞X is equivalent to ÷X, while for X a vector, ⊞X returns a vector result which is a multiple of X.

Use of the inner product in the solution of simultaneous equations can be eliminated by the dyadic matrix divide, $R \leftarrow D⊞X$, instead of (⊞X)+.×D. The right argument is the matrix of coefficients, and the left argument the vector of constants:

```
     D⊞X
0.05  0.15  0.07
```

More generally, for ⊞M to yield a result, the matrix must be invertible, i.e., have at least as many rows as columns. Its determinant must not be zero, otherwise a *DOMAIN ERROR* results. If M is nonsquare, the result is a left inverse,

```
     M←4 2ρ2 1 1 3 4 5 6 7
     ⊞M
 ¯0.3377926421   ¯0.3913043478    0.003344481605    0.1170568562
 ¯0.2575250836    0.347826087     0.05685618729    ¯0.01003344482
```

while if the matrix is square, the result is the inverse of the matrix:

```
     P←3 3ρ3 4 5 6 7 8 9 10 2
     ⊞P
 ¯2.444444444     1.555555556    ¯0.1111111111
  2.222222222    ¯1.444444444     0.2222222222
 ¯0.1111111111    0.2222222222   ¯0.1111111111
```

In the first case, ρ⊞M equals ρ⍉M. The use of the dyadic ⊞ as in $R \leftarrow B⊞A$, requires that ρρA be 2, with ρρB either 1 or 2. The first dimension of A must be equal to or greater than the second dimension of A, and must equal the first dimension of B. A right argument which is nonsquare (first dimension greater than second dimension) indicates a system of equations with more equations than unknowns, and the solution is a *least-squares* solution (next section). It is also possible for both A and B to be vectors. In this case the result is a scalar. Similarly, if A and B are both scalars, $A⊞B$ is equivalent to $A÷B$.

APL2 offers more advanced matrix algebra features. ⎕IR (implicit result) holds the rank (matrix algebra definition, largest submatrix with an inverse) of the right argument of the last execution of ⊞. ⊟, polynomial zeros, is a monadic function whose argument is the coefficients of the powers (decreasing to the right) of the polynomial. The result is a vector containing the roots of the polynomial. ⍉ (eigen) is a monadic function whose argument must be a square matrix of real numbers and whose result is a matrix with one more row than the argument. The first row is the *eigenvalues* of the argument, and the remaining rows are the right *eigenvectors*.

Least square fits, trend lines and curve fitting

If you wish to fit a straight line of the form $Y = a + bX$ through two points, such as (1.5,2) and (3.5,3), you can use the dyadic ⊞ as shown:

```
     2 3⊞2 2ρ1 1.5 1 3.5
1.25  0.5
```

1.25 is the value of the Y-intercept, and 0.5 is the value for b, the slope. Any predicted Y-value along the line can be found by the defined function *EVAL*:

```
        ∇EVAL[□]∇
      ∇ Y←EVAL X
[1]     Y←(X∘.* 0 1)+.× 1.25 0.5
      ∇

        EVAL 0 .5 1 1.5 2 2.5 3
   1.25 1.5 1.75 2 2.25 2.5 2.75
```

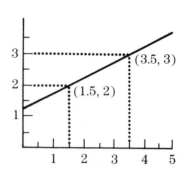

Now suppose a business analyst has spent effort, time and funds obtaining the following data, and wishes to find the linear (straight line) relation between X and Y:

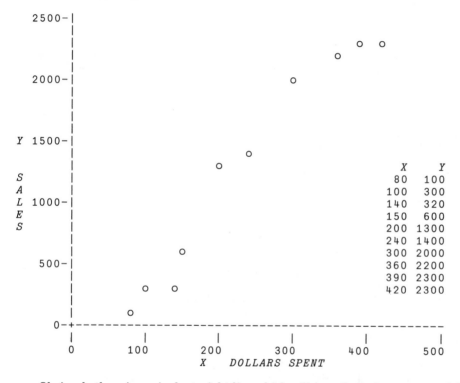

X	Y
80	100
100	300
140	320
150	600
200	1300
240	1400
300	2000
360	2200
390	2300
420	2300

Obviously there is no single straight line which will pass through every one of the points. We are left with the problem of choosing the one particular straight line which is 'best' in some sense.

One approach in wide use is to fit a line such that the sum of the squared vertical distances from the line to each point is the smallest possible value—the *least squares* fit. The problem, therefore, is to find the coefficients a and b such that $+/(((b,a)+.×X∘.*0\ 1)-Y)*2$ is the smallest possible value. The expression $Y⌹X∘.*0\ 1$ does it, and is called a *linear least squares* solution. There is no other set of coefficients you can pick which will get a smaller sum-of-squares of differences, given that you decide a straight line is the correct *model*.

The following figures use a typical graphics workspace as found on commercial time sharing systems or available for purchase. It is one of a family of graphics workspaces for specific models of printing terminals, in this case an Anderson-Jacobsen Model 832 or 833 terminal).

```
    X←80 100 140 150 200 240 300 360 390 420
    Y←100 300 320 600 1300 1400 2000 2200 2300 2300
    PX←(⌊/X)+0,(⍳100)×.01×(⌈/X)-⌊/X
    OT←PX,[1.5](PX∘.*0 1)+.×Y⌹X∘.*0 1
```

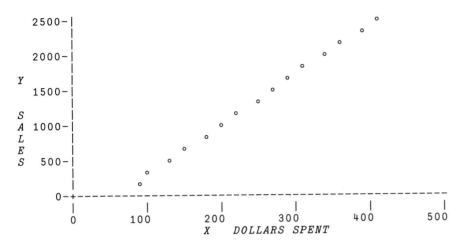

Alternatively, you might want to fit a simple curved line through the points. There are an infinite number of curved lines you could pick, but a typical first choice is to fit a quadratic of the form $Y = a + bX + cX^2$. a, b and c are the three elements of the result of

```
R←Y⌹X∘.*0 1 2
R
```
¯996.8729766 13.2153557 ¯0.01230306278

There is no other set of three values which will give a smaller result to the expression `+/((R+.×X∘.*0 1 2)-Y)*2`.

```
OT←PX,[1.5](PX∘.*0 1 2)+.×Y⌹X∘.*0 1 2
```

Statisticians concern themselves with selecting the proper model (should it be $A + B \times X$, or $A + (B \times X) + C \times X * 2$, or something else?) and then making formal tests of statistical significance. Usually these tests involve comparison of the size of the coefficients to the sum of the squares of the differences. You should *not*, however, conclude that the models used above exhaust the ingenuity of statisticians and mathematicians.

Splines

Since the computer has made their calculation manageable, a great deal of research effort has gone into models called *splines*. A spline is a mathematical analogue of a draftsman's curve-fitting instrument. Splines have a solid mathematical basis, and they also have the desirable property of fitting curves to a set of points in an esthetic fashion. Their greatest application is for graphing data for which the underlying model is unknown (or even nonexistent !).

It is far beyond the scope of this book to treat splines in any detail. We will present working programs for evaluating natural cubic splines, with no comment on the programming style or algorithms.

```
        ∇SPLINECALC[□]∇
    ∇   C←X SPLINECALC Y;N
[1]     N←4×¯2+ρY←0,Y
[2]     C← 1 0 0 0 0 0 1 1 1 1 0 0 0 0 1 2 3 0 ¯1 0 0 0 2 6 0 0 ¯2
[3]     C←(N- 2 0)ρ(4+4×N)ρ(5,N)↑ 4 7 ρC
[4]     C←(C,[1] N↑ 0 0 2),[1](-N)↑ 2 6
[5]     C←X,((ρX),4)ρY[,1⌈(1↓ιρX)∘.+ 0 1 ,2ρ-N]⊞C
    ∇

        ∇SPLINEEVAL[□]∇
    ∇   R←X SPLINEEVAL C;J
[1]     J←1⌈+/X∘.>R←C[;1]
[2]     R←+/C[J;1+ι4]×((X-R[J])÷((1↓R)-¯1↓R)[J])∘.*¯1+ι4
    ∇

        OT←PX,[1.5] PX SPLINEEVAL X SPLINECALC Y
```

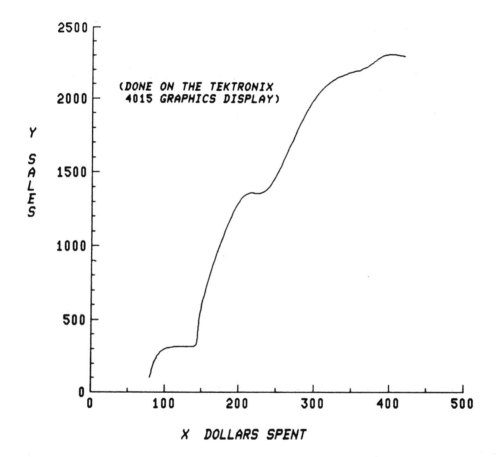

Notice that the spline technique ingeniously fits the curve through each of the points, without any jagged edges.

The few examples shown barely begin to cover the wide range of possible applications of the inner product. Many of the problems appearing in the previous chapters can be redone more compactly with the inner product. Exercises for the reader are deferred to the end of Chapter 21, which covers the outer product.

Chapter 21: Generalized outer product

This chapter is somewhat anticlimactic in that there are no surprises or new APL features in it. The outer product, you will recall, was introduced way back in Chapter 3 as a shortcut to generate operation tables for the primitive scalar dyadic functions, and has been used in most of the succeeding chapters. Here we will review the syntax of the outer product and emphasize it with suitable examples other than just the vectors and scalars used heretofore.

The arguments of the outer product can be arrays of any rank. And the *rank* of the result in all cases is the *sum of the ranks* of the arguments, while the *shape* of the result is the *catenation of the shapes* of the arguments. Below are some examples:

```
      3 6 ∘.⌈ 5 8 7 ¯1 ⍝ALL POSSIBLE COMBINATIONS OF ELEMENTS OF THE TWO VECTORS
5 8 7 3
6 8 7 6

      'HELLO'∘.='GOODBYE' ⍝OCCURRENCES OF LEFT ARG ELEMENTS IN RIGHT ARG
0 0 0 0 0 0 0
0 0 0 0 0 0 1
0 0 0 0 0 0 0
0 0 0 0 0 0 0
0 1 1 0 0 0 0
      SOLD←2 3⍴3 8 5 10 6 20 ⍝ SALES OF PRODUCT OVER 2 WEEKS BY 3 SALESPEOPLE
      COST←2 2⍴11 15 30 20 ⍝ POSSIBLE TEST PRICES FOR THE PRODUCT
      COST∘.×SOLD ⍝ RESULT HAS 4 DIMENSIONS
 33  88  55
110  66 220

 45 120  75
150  90 300


 90 240 150
300 180 600

 60 160 100
200 120 400
```

Some of the patterns in the result are interesting. Here again is the identity matrix (see page 198) of order 4 and its logical complement:

```
      (⍳4)∘.=⍳4               (⍳4)∘.≠⍳4
1 0 0 0                  0 1 1 1
0 1 0 0                  1 0 1 1
0 0 1 0                  1 1 0 1
0 0 0 1                  1 1 1 0
```

The other relational functions also yield interesting patterns of 1's and 0's, which when 'overlaid' by multiplication on a matrix of the same size, will sieve out unwanted elements by replacing them with 0 while leaving alone the others:

```
      (⍳5)∘.≤⍳5         M←5 5⍴⍳25            M×(⍳5)∘.≤⍳5
1 1 1 1 1                             1  2  3  4  5
0 1 1 1 1                             0  7  8  9 10
0 0 1 1 1                             0  0 13 14 15
0 0 0 1 1                             0  0  0 19 20
0 0 0 0 1                             0  0  0  0 25
```

Some uses for the outer product have already been explored in the text and exercises. Others will be found in the problems at the end of this chapter. Until then, for those of you in whom the gambling instinct runs strong and unrestrained, consider the following 'practical' problem: you wish to use the facilities of APL to simulate 20 rolls of a single die. Identify those successive rolls which between them result in a 7.

We must first generate the 20 rolls by

```
      R←?20ρ6
      R
1 5 3 4 2 1 5 5 6 3 4 5 1 1 4 5 1 3 1 3
```

The corresponding vector of the 'neighbors' of these rolls is easily obtained by $1\phi R$ and the sums by $^-1\downarrow R+1\phi R$. Why is $^-1$ used?

```
      1φR
5 3 4 2 1 5 5 6 3 4 5 1 1 4 5 1 3 1 3 1
      ¯1↓R+1φR
6 8 7 6 3 6 10 11 9 7 9 6 2 5 9 6 4 4 4
```

Those successive rolls adding up to 7 can be identified by

```
      HIT←(7=¯1↓R+1φR)/ι¯1+ρR
      HIT
3 10
```

while the rolls represented by HIT are $HIT\circ.+0\ 1$ and the actual values of R selected can be displayed with $R[HIT\circ.+0\ 1]$:

```
      HIT∘.+0 1              R[HIT∘.+0 1]
   3  4                    3 4
  10 11                    3 4
```

As a corollary to the last problem, consider the following question: how many 4's are there in R? Clearly this is $+/R=4$. But suppose we modify the question slightly and ask how many times each of the integers 1 through 6 occurs in R. We could repeat the above expression for each integer. But the outer product lets us do it all at once:

```
      +/R∘.=ι6
6 1 4 3 5 1
```

If you are still in a gambling mood you might try your luck by defining a function to simulate the action of a slot machine, the so-called 'one-armed bandit,' to see how many times you get, say, three 'lemons' or three 'cherries.' You may find the outer product useful here, or, as is frequently the case given the richness of the APL language, come up with a completely new and innovative approach.

String searching

Our next example is a function $STRINGSEARCH$ designed to locate all occurrences of a given phrase W in some character vector T of text, sometimes called a *string*. There are several ways in which the problem can be approached. The one to be shown here makes use of the fact that an outer product with vector arguments results in a matrix, each of whose rows corresponds to the execution of the given function between each element of the left argument and the entire right argument. (Compare with $R\circ.=ι6$ in the last example.)

With the function $=$, this will result in a logical matrix, each row of which checks for the presence of one character of the phrase W in the text T. To illustrate, assign

```
      W←'IN'                 T←'IT DOES NOT RAIN IN SPAIN'          AA←W∘.=T
      AA
1 0 0 0 0 0 0 0 0 0 0 0 0 1 0 0 1 0 0 0 0 0 1 0
0 0 0 0 0 0 0 0 1 0 0 0 0 0 1 0 0 1 0 0 0 0 0 1
```

The interesting thing about this array is the location of the 1's in the rows, corresponding to the occurrences of I and N in T. Note the shift of the 1 corresponding to the location of N in the second row, compared with the location of I in the first row (except the letter N in the word NOT).

One way to distinguish between occurrences of IN and those of isolated I's and N's is to shift the second row one element to the left, which produces columns of all 1's, corresponding to the locations of IN:

```
      BB←(¯1+⍳⍴W)⌽AA
      BB
1 0 0 0 0 0 0 0 0 0 0 0 0 0 0 1 0 0 1 0 0 0 0 0 1 0
0 0 0 0 0 0 0 1 0 0 0 0 0 0 0 1 0 0 1 0 0 0 0 0 1 0
```

Next, to identify these columns, ∧-reduce across the first dimension:

```
      CC←∧⌿BB
      CC
0 0 0 0 0 0 0 0 0 0 0 0 0 0 0 1 0 0 1 0 0 0 0 0 1 0
```

This result can now be used to pinpoint in T the indices representing the locations of the first elements of occurrences of IN in W:

```
      CC/⍳⍴T
15  18  24
```

Finally, the complete defined function looks like this:

```
      ∇R←T STRINGSEARCH W
[1]     R←(∧⌿(¯1+⍳⍴W)⌽W∘.=T)/⍳⍴T ∇
```

What would change if we wanted to locate all occurrences of the *word* IN instead of just the successive *characters* I and N?

$STRINGSEARCH$ isn't very efficient in its use of space or time if T is very large. If we really wanted to produce, say, a concordance of a text, first, the text itself isn't likely to fit into the available workspace and would therefore have to be stored on a file (Chapter 27), to be brought in one piece at a time. Second, the individual words would be pre-indexed, and the search would then be confined to identifying words with the same indices as the ones desired.

Text processing is such an important application that some systems provide special system functions for doing it efficiently. On many systems $T \ \square SS \ W$ is equivalent to $∧⌿(¯1+⍳⍴W)⌽W∘.=T$, but runs much faster.

Our next illustration also has to do with text searches. The problem is to replace all occurrences of a single character in a character vector with a specified string. This is a simpler version of the customary replacement of a given string by another string, wherever it occurs in the text.

We first define a character vector:

```
      VEC←'HOT POT'
```

The character $'T'$ is to be replaced by the string $'CUS'$.

Let's build a function $REPSTRING$ to do this. First, we catenate the string to each element of VEC:

```
      AA←,VEC,((⍴VEC),⍴'CUS')⍴'CUS'
      AA
HCUSOCUSTCUS CUSPCUSOCUSTCUS
↑   ↑   ↑↑↑↑   ↑   ↑   ↑↑↑
```

The arrows show the characters to be selected. Next, we use the outer product to define a sieve of 1's and 0's to do the selection and then compress to get the desired result:

```
      BB←,(VEC='T')∘.=0,(⍴'CUS')⍴1          BB/AA
                                        HOCUS POCUS
```

The function $REPSTRING$ which incorporates this algorithm is show below:

```
      ∇R←V REPSTRING C;STR;TEMP1;TEMP2          VEC REPSTRING 'T','CUS'
[1]     STR←1↓C                              HOCUS POCUS
[2]     TEMP1←,V,((⍴V),⍴STR)⍴STR
[3]     TEMP2←,(V=1↑C)∘.=0,STR=STR
[4]     R←TEMP2/TEMP1 ∇
```

This sneaky solution is an ingenious but slower alternative to looping, a more natural approach for most people:

```
       ∇R←V REPSTRING1 C;STR;TEMP1;TEMP2
[1]    R←'' ⍝ TO HOLD RESULT
[2]    STR←1↓C  ⍝ REPLACEMENT STRING
[3]    C←1↑C ⍝ CHARACTER TO BE REPLACED
[4]    TEMP1←(C=V)/⍳⍴V ⍝ ALL OCCURRENCES OF C IN V
[5]    TEMP1←⁻1+TEMP1-0,⁻1↓TEMP1 ⍝ CHARACTERS BETWEEN ADJACENT C'S
[6]    L:→END IF 0≥⍴TEMP1 ⍝ EXIT IF NO MORE REPLACEMENTS
[7]    TEMP2←1↑TEMP1 ⍝ CHARACTERS TO NEXT C
[8]    R←R,(TEMP2↑V),STR ⍝ MAKE THIS REPLACEMENT IN R
[9]    TEMP1←1↓TEMP1 ⍝ REMOVE THIS OCCURRENCE
[10]   V←(1+TEMP2)↓V  ⍝ STRIP THE CHARACTERS OFF V
[11]   →L⍝ TO REPEAT PROCESS
[12]   END:R←R,V ⍝ IF NO CHARACTERS REMAIN IN V
[13]   ∇
```

Removing duplicate rows from a matrix

Frequently it happens that we have a table which contains duplicate rows, for example, a mailing list, to be cleaned up. The key to the problem is to find a way to identify the duplicate rows.

We'll use the matrix $NAMS$ to illustrate the technique:

```
       NAMS←5 3ρ'ANNJOEJOEMAYANN'              AA←NAMS∧.=⍉NAMS
       NAMS                                     AA
ANN                                             1 0 0 0 1
JOE                                             0 1 1 0 0
JOE                                             0 1 1 0 0
MAY                                             0 0 0 1 0
ANN                                             1 0 0 0 1
```

AA indicates that rows 1 and 5 of $NAMS$ are duplicates, as are rows 2 and 3. What we need is a vector whose elements are 1 1 0 1 0. This can be gotten by $BB←(\iota 1↑\rho NAMS)\circ.>\iota 1↑\rho NAMS$ which produces a lower triangle of 1's, and combining it with the array AA:

```
       BB←(⍳1↑ρNAMS)∘.>⍳1↑ρNAMS              CC←AA∧BB
       BB                                     CC
 0 0 0 0 0                                    0 0 0 0 0
 1 0 0 0 0                                    0 0 0 0 0
 1 1 0 0 0                                    0 1 0 0 0
 1 1 1 0 0                                    0 0 0 0 0
 1 1 1 1 0                                    1 0 0 0 0
```

Notice that there are now 1's only in the duplicate rows. The rest is easy:

```
       (~∨/CC)⌿NAMS
ANN
JOE
MAY
```

Here is the complete algorithm:

```
       ∇R←DUPELIM X;T                           DUPELIM NAMS
[1]    T←X∧.=⍉X                              ANN
[2]    R←(~∨/((⍳1↑ρT)∘.>⍳1↑ρT)∧T)⌿X          JOE
[3]    ⍝ OR  R←(∧/T≠(⍳1↑ρT)∘.>⍳1↑ρT)⌿X ∇      MAY
```

Graphing

This topic has to do with the use of the outer product to build up a simple-minded but instructive graphing function. To begin with, define

```
      X←¯5+ι9                          Y←φX
      X                                Yι
¯4 ¯3 ¯2 ¯1 0 1 2 3 4            4 3 2 1 0 ¯1 ¯2 ¯3 ¯4
```

Because the middle elements in both X and Y are 0's, their outer product will produce 0's along the 'axes' of the matrix:

```
      M←Y∘.×X
```

The next step is to replace the 0's with some character, say, +, and everything else with blanks. One way to do this is to use the matrix M to index a suitable character vector:

```
      ' +'[1+0=M]
      +
      +
      +
      +
+++++++++
      +
      +
      +
      +
```

Since the horizontal axis looks somewhat out of scale (one horizontal character space isn't as wide as one vertical character space), we adjust our 'graph' as follows:

```
      (18ρ1 0)\' +'[1+0=M]
      +
      +
      +
      +
+ + + + + + + + +
      +
      +
      +
      +
```

Suppose now we wish to plot on this set of axes a number of points (X,Y), where $Y←X+1$. Our axes are made up of characters, so that the points themselves would have to be represented as characters to include them. It is more interesting, however, to go back to our original outer product, which is numeric, and superimpose the desired set of points FP on it before converting to characters:

```
      FP←Y∘.=X+1
      FP
0 0 0 0 0 0 0 1 0
0 0 0 0 0 0 1 0 0
0 0 0 0 0 1 0 0 0
0 0 0 0 1 0 0 0 0
0 0 0 1 0 0 0 0 0
0 0 1 0 0 0 0 0 0
0 1 0 0 0 0 0 0 0
1 0 0 0 0 0 0 0 0
0 0 0 0 0 0 0 0 0
```

FP produces a matrix of 1's where the points are. We next add the matrices FP and $1+2×0=M$. You should be able to see why multiplication by 2 is necessary if you execute the next step but with and without the multiplication by 2:

```
        FP+1+2×0=M                        FP+1+0=M
   1  1  1  3  1  1  2  1          1  1  1  2  1  1  2  1
   1  1  1  3  1  2  1  1          1  1  1  2  1  2  1  1
   1  1  1  3  2  1  1  1          1  1  1  2  2  1  1  1
   1  1  1  4  1  1  1  1          1  1  1  3  1  1  1  1
   3  3  4  3  3  3  3  3          2  2  3  2  2  2  2  2
   1  2  1  3  1  1  1  1          1  2  1  2  1  1  1  1
   2  1  1  3  1  1  1  1          2  1  1  2  1  1  1  1
   1  1  1  3  1  1  1  1          1  1  1  2  1  1  1  1
```

Finally, our expanded plot is

```
        (18ρ1 0)\' o+o'[FP+1+2×0=M]
           +           o
           +        o
           +     o
                 o
   +  +  +  o  +  +  +  +  +
        o     +
      o       +
    o         +
              +
```

Now that we have built up the algorithm for the plot routine, we can incorporate it into a defined function, *GRAPH*, and try it out after setting *FP* and *X*:

```
        ∇Z←GRAPH
[1]     Z←((2×ρX)ρ1 0)\' o+o'[FP+1+2×0=(φX)∘.×X] ∇
        X← ¯5+ι9
        FP←(φX)∘.=X+1

        GRAPH
           +           o
           +        o
           +     o
                 o
   +  +  +  o  +  +  +  +  +
        o     +
      o       +
    o         +
              +
```

Plotting functions can get quite complicated when it is necessary to include such amenities as labeling of the axes, provision for changing the scale of the plot, and rounding off the computed values for the coordinates, since the terminal can't type characters between lines and spaces. Most APL systems provide prepared plotting routines in the common libraries. Some of these, however, may be specific packages designed to work only on graphics terminals like those manufactured by Tektronix or Hewlett-Packard Corporations. The plotting facilities available may differ somewhat from system to system, so carefully read the instructions in *DESCRIBE* or *HOWPLOT* or whatever your system provides. Problem 11 will give you some practice in simple plotting, using a widely distributed APL workspace.

Operators

This section is optional. Its purpose is twofold: to discuss in more detail the nature of the class of APL features called 'operators,' and second, to describe APL2 enhancements in this area.

One reason for this emphasis on operators is that, as the present and preceding chapters show, a single operator, because it can act on many different functions, becomes a powerful tool in the hands of a knowledgeable user. Just inner products alone added 441 possible derived functions to your APL vocabulary.

Quantity, of course, doesn't automatically make for quality. But the operator concept has been generalized to enrich the APL dictionary in the same way that the ability to convert old words or coin new ones has greatly broadened the scope and versatility of the English language.

Let's now look at the operator itself. As we mentioned earlier in the text, an operator takes a function (sometimes with another function or an array) and converts it into something different, called a *derived function*.

Those functions or arrays that the operator acts upon are formally called *operands*. They are analogous to the arguments of functions.

The left operand of an operator must be a function, while the right operand may be either a function or an array. Reduce is an example of a monadic operator, while inner and outer products are dyadic. For, say, +/, + is the left operand of the reduce operator /, while for ∘.× and +.×, ∘ and + are left operands, with × the right operand.

We mentioned in Chapter 6 that there is a sort of hierarchy in APL after all. It's limited to operators taking precedence over functions. Operators are said to have 'long scope' on the left, which means that the left operand is the longest function expression on the left. If the operator is dyadic, it has 'short scope' on the right, that is, its right operand is the single function or array on the right. Functions, by way of contrast, have long scope on the right.

You'll appreciate what all this means by following this APL2 example:

```
      A←2 3ρι6              B←3 4ρι12                A+.×.⌈B
      A                     B                   45 120 122 384
1 2 3                 1   2   3   4          180 240 308 384
4 5 6                 5   6   7   8
                      9  10  11  12
```

It isn't as weird as it looks. The rows of *A* combine, using ⌈, with the columns of *B* in the usual manner of the inner product to give

```
1   2   3   4
5   6   7   8
9  10  11  12

4   4   4   4
5   6   7   8
9  10  11  12
```

and then +.×/ is carried out on each column of this intermediate result. But what kind of oddball expression is +.×/ ?

Three comments are in order here. First, the reason that the expression +.×.⌈ was grouped as (+.×).⌈ is that operators have long left scope and short right scope. Second, the sensible (and correct) way to look at +.×/ is to put × between every pair of elements in each column and perform +/ on the result. The first column in the first plane, for example, becomes +/1×5×9, or 45. And last, the plus reduction bought us nothing since it was carried out on a scalar. The original extended inner product would have made more sense on higher-dimensional arguments.

Reduce and scan have been extended in APL2 to allow the use of any dyadic function, including defined functions, that produces a result. This can lead to some interesting possibilities. In what follows, the new expression on the left side is equivalent to the traditional expression on the right:

```
      ρ/2 3                        2ρ3
3 3                         3 3


      ρ/2 2ρ2 1 3 2              2 3ρ1 2
1 2 1                       1 2 1
2 1 2                       2 1 2
```

If this last example seems incomprehensible to you, look at it this way:

$$\begin{pmatrix} 2 \\ 3 \end{pmatrix} \rho \begin{pmatrix} 1 \\ 2 \end{pmatrix}$$

ρ is applied to the subarrays along the last dimension, giving 2 3ρ1 2.

```
      ,/2 3ρ2 1 3 2 4 5               2 2,1 4,3 5
2 2 1 4 3 5                   2 2 1 4 3 5
```

```
        HYP/12 3 4                              12 HYP 3 HYP 4
13                                      13

        +.,≠2 3ρ⍳6                              +/⍳6
21                                      21

        °.+≠2 3ρ⍳6                              1 2 3 °.+4 5 6
5 6 7                                   5 6 7
6 7 8                                   6 7 8
7 8 9                                   7 8 9
```

You can get partial reductions across an array in APL2. This *n-wise reduction* has the syntax $Z \leftarrow L\ F/R$, where F is any dyadic function producing a result and L is any integer. It works like this:

```
        5+/1 2 3 4 5                            0+/1 2 3 4 5
15                                      0 0 0 0 0

        4+/1 2 3 4 5                            2+≠3 3ρ⍳9
10 14                                   5  7  9
        3+/1 2 3 4 5                    11 13 15
6 9 12                                          3,/5 6 7 8 9
        2+/1 2 3 4 5                    5 6 7 6 7 8 7 8 9
3 5 7 9                                         ¯2-/1 5 8 14 50
        1+/1 2 3 4 5                    4 3 6 36
1 2 3 4 5
```

A negative value for L reverses the subarrays before applying the function.

If your system supports this extension, don't confuse these two similar appearing expressions:

```
        2+/1 2 3 4 5                            2++/1 2 3 4 5
3 5 7 9                                 17
```

Inner and outer products have also been generalized to allow any primitive or defined function that produces a result:

```
        A←2 3ρ1 0 1 1 1 0              A,./C                  2 4 6⌊.⍳B
        B←3 3ρ1 2 2 4 5 6 7 8 9  1  9                  2 1 1
        C←3 4ρ⍳12                2 10
        A                        3 11                  2 3°.HYP 3 4
1 0 1                            4 12           3.605551275 4.472135955
1 1 0                                           4.242640687 5
        B                        1  5
1 2 2                            2  6                   2 3+.HYP 3 4
4 5 6                            3  7           8.605551275
7 8 9                            4  8
        C
1  2  3  4                       ρA,./C
5  6  7  8                2 4 2
9 10 11 12
```

You might be surprised at the shape of the result of outer product, and we suggest you draw a table like the one on the right to see that it works out the same as any other outer product:

```
        ρ1 2 3 °., 10 20 30 40
3 4 2
        1 2 3 °., 10 20 30 40
  1 10
  1 20
  1 30
  1 40

  2 10
  2 20                    , |    10        20        30        40
  2 30            --- +---------------------------------------
  2 40             1 | (1,10)   (1,20)   (1,30)   (1,40)
                   2 | (2,10)   (2,20)   (2,30)   (2,40)
  3 10             3 | (3,10)   (3,20)   (3,30)   (3,40)
  3 20
  3 30
  3 40
```

We didn't tell you the whole story earlier when we said that the shape of the result was the catenation of the shapes of the two arguments. APL2 uses a definition common to all IBM versions of APL, in which for $Z \leftarrow L \circ .fR, \rho Z$ is $(\rho L),(\rho R),\rho S1fS2$, where $S1$ and $S2$ are scalars. Since $\rho S1fS2$ is empty for scalar functions, the difference never showed up before.

There are two more primitive operators available in APL2. *Each* ($\ddot{}$) applies a function to each element in an array. Since its usefulness is more apparent with nested arrays, discussion is deferred to Chapter 25. Another operator is *bracket axis*. It specifies the subarrays to which a function is to be applied *and* the axes along which to assemble the result.

Here we have to digress to describe a somewhat similar operator which is available in most APL systems, but which is restricted to a few functions that transform an array or select from it. We refer here to *axis specification*, which you have already seen with reduction, scan and the mixed functions replicate, expand, rotate, catenate and laminate. APL2 permits it to be used also with ravel, take and drop, unique, find and find index. These extensions have been described where the functions are introduced in the text. Those specific to nested arrays are described in Chapter 25.

That's only part of the story. APL2 extends axis specification to all primitive scalar monadic and dyadic functions. Now you can do what you wanted to do at the beginning of the text: add a vector to a matrix.

```
      1 2 3 +[2]2 3ρι6                    (2 3ρι6) +[1 2] 2 3ρ5+ι6
2 4 6                              7  9 11
5 7 9                             13 15 17

      5 6+[1]2 3ρι6                        (2 3ρι6) +[2 1] 2 3ρ5+ι6
 6  7  8                           7  9 11
10 11 12                          13 15 17
```

Let's get back to *bracket axis*. Two forms are recognized:

```
Z←  F[AZ;AR] R
Z←L F[AZ;AL;AR] R
```

The names in the brackets refer to axes associated with the right and left arguments (AR and AL) and the result (AZ). If no values are specified for AR or AL, all axes are taken. If there is no value given to AZ, the last axes of Z are taken.

Although there appear to be similarities between this operator and axis specification (which has no semicolons), the way in which the latter works is function dependent, while bracket axis, like other operators, acts on functions in a consistent way, independent of the specific functions. It can be used with any function that produces a result.

Bracket axis works with defined functions as well as primitive functions. If AR or AL is empty ($\iota 0$), the monadic F is applied to each subarray (i.e., is like $F\ddot{}$).

```
      A←2 3ρι6              ,[;1]A                   ,[1;]A
      A                   1  4               1 2 3 4 5 6
1 2 3                    2  5                     ,[1;ι0]A
4 5 6                    3  6               1 2 3
      ,[;ι0]A                                4 5 6
1                          ,[;2]A                  ,[1;1]A
2                       1 2 3                1 2 3
3                       4 5 6                4 5 6
                             ,[;1 2]A              ,[1;2]A
4                       1 2 3 4 5 6          1 4
5                                            2 5
6                                            3 6

      A1←2 3ρ1 0 2 ¯7 ¯8 0
      ×[;1]A1
 1 ¯1
 0 ¯1
 1  0

      A2←3 4ρ5 2 0 4 ¯5 6 15 1 8 3 11 ¯5
      A2                                          ⍋[;1]A2
 ¯5  2  0  4                               2 1 3
 ¯5  6 15 ¯1                               1 3 2
  8  3 11 ¯5                               1 3 2
                                           3 2 1
```

So far we haven't shown you anything which couldn't be obtained in other ways without too much fuss. But here's a perhaps unanticipated goody which falls out of all this: you can convert a character matrix directly into a number matrix (in other APL systems ♠ works only on scalars and vectors).

```
      CHAR←▼A                        NUM←♠[;2]CHAR
      CHAR                           NUM
1  2  3                           1  2  3
4  5  6                           4  5  6
      ρCHAR                          ρNUM
2  5                              2  3
```

With dyadic functions, if *AR* or *AL* is empty, the other subarrays will be replicated like a scalar:

```
      10 20 30 40,[;ι0;ι0]ι4              10 20 30 40,[;1;ι0]ι4
10  1                          10 20 30 40   1
20  2                          10 20 30 40   2
30  3                          10 20 30 40   3
40  4                          10 20 30 40   4

      10 20 30 40,[;ι0;1]ι4               10 20 30 40 [;1;1]ι4
10   1  2  3  4                10 20 30 40   1   2   3   4
20   1  2  3  4                      10 20 30 40 [1;ι0;ι0]ι4
30   1  2  3  4                10 20 30 40
40   1  2  3  4                    1   2   3   4

      10 20 30 40[1;ι0;1]ι4              10 20 30 40[1;1;ι0]ι0
10 20 30 40                   10 10 10 10
 1  1  1  1                   20 20 20 20
 2  2  2  2                   30 30 30 30
 3  3  3  3                   40 40 40 40
 4  4  4  4                       1   2   3   4
```

Defined operators

Just as the concept of a defined function allowed us to assemble various combinations of primitive functions and operators for repeated use with different arguments, so the idea of a *defined operator*, available in APL2, lets you invent your own operators, to be used with different operands. Defined operators are handy when you need to apply several different functions in the same way to data in a manner not already covered by the existing operators.

There are eight allowable header forms, depending on the number of arguments and operands and whether an explicit result is to be returned:

	return result	no result
2 arguments, 2 operands	$Z←L \ (F \ OP \ G)R$	$L \ (F \ OP \ G) \ R$
2 arguments, 1 operand	$Z←L \ (F \ OP) \ R$	$L \ (F \ OP) \ R$
1 argument, 2 operands	$Z←(F \ OP \ G) \ R$	$(F \ OP \ G) \ R$
1 argument, 1 operand	$Z←(F \ OP) \ R$	$(F \ OP) \ R$

F and *G* are operands, *L* and *R* are arguments, and *OP* is the name of the defined operator.

Operators are defined in the same way as functions, subject, of course, to the header format restrictions above. Here is a universal operator that tries to be all things to all users:

```
      ∇Z←L (F ALLPURP) R
[1]   Z←R F L
[2]   ∇

      R←5 12
      L←.5
      L *ALLPURP +/R*2      ⍝ FINDS HYPOTENUSE OF RT TRIANGLE WITH LEGS R
13

      R←'ABCDEFGHIJKLMNOP'
      L←'HELP'
      L ιALLPURP R      ⍝ SIMULATES RANKING
8 5 12 16
```

Another problem: suppose you had to do different outer products on square matrices of the same size and wanted to limit the arithmetic to the elements on or above the main diagonal. The following defined operator will do it:

```
     ∇Z←L (F OUTP) R;K;M
[1]  K←ι1↑ρL
[2]  M←K∘.≤K
[3]  Z←(M×L)∘.F M×R
[4]  ∇
```

Thus, the outer products could be easily executed on L and R by expressions of the form L $+OUTP$ R, L $×OUTP$ R, L $⌈OUTP$ R, etc.

To complete the picture and help you keep track of defined operators in your workspace, a system command $)OPS$ is provided that works like $)FNS$ and $)VARS$.

PROBLEMS

1. DRILL. Assign $A←ι4$, $B←2$ $3ρ'ABCDEF'$, $C←'ABD'$, $D←3$ $1ρι3$, $E←3$ 4 5, $F←4$ $3ρι10$, $G←3$ $4ρφι7$

$C∘.=B$	$A∘.+3×D$	$~(A∘.=A)∘.∧1$ 0 0 1
$D∘.×A$	$D∘.÷A$	$⍉D∘.*A$
1 3 $9∘.>D$	$B∘.≠C$	$A∘.⌈¯1$ 3 2 4
$E+.=E$	$E∧.>G$	$F×.=E$
$F×.-G$	$E∨.≠F$	$G|.-F$
$F∨.<G$	$3+.×F$	$(⍉G)⌈.+E$

2. What is the shape of the result when the outer product is used to add the elements of a vector of length 4 to the elements of a 2 2 matrix?

3. Define a function $DIST$ that computes the rounded off (nearest integer) distances between any two cities whose X and Y coordinates are given in a matrix L. Assume $ρL$ is N, 2 and the cities are all located north and east of the origin of the coordinate system.

4. Write an APL expression to find the number of occurrences of each of the letters $ABCDEFG$ in the word $CABBAGE$.

5. Construct expressions which will give the sum and carry digits for addition of two numbers in any number system B (for B less than 10). Write a function to generate an additional table of a set of integers INT in the base B.

6. For mathematicians only: write a program to multiply two polynomials together. Assume their coefficient vectors $C1$ and $C2$ are arranged in descending order of powers of X.

7. Use the function $GRAPH$ (page 208) for each of the following:
   A $Y←|X←¯5+ι9$
   B $Y←¯5+X*2$
   C $Y≤X+1$
   D $(Y≤X+1)∧Y≥3-|X$
   E $Y≤3|X$

8. Execute the following instructions in order and explain the resulting display.

   ```
   X←¯13+ι20
   Y←φX
   R←(0=(¯3×Y)∘.+(2×X)-2)∨0=(2×Y)∘.+X-8
   R
   ```

9. Modify $GRAPH$ (page 208) to scale down all the data X by a factor S.

10. Write an expression to show the growth of various amounts of principal accumulating interest compounded at different rates and for different numbers of years.

11. After loading the workspace with plotting routines in your APL system, execute each of the following. (As pointed out at the end of the chapter, the syntax, name of the function, and auxiliary features may be different, so be sure to call for *DESCRIBE* or *HOWPLOT* or *HOWFORMAT*, or whatever instructions are available in your system.)

A $X \leftarrow \iota 20$
          $Y \leftarrow X \star 2$
          $Z \leftarrow 2 \times X \star 2$
          20 60 *PLOT X VS Y*
          20 60 *PLOT* (*Y AND Z*) *VS X*

B $X \leftarrow 1, 50 \times \iota 7$
          $Y \leftarrow \div X$
          20 60 *PLOT Y VS X*
          20 30 *PLOT Y*[$1 + \iota 7$] *VS X*[$1 + \iota 7$]

12. To evaluate the strength of a bridge hand (13 cards dealt from a standard deck), a point count is used. This assigns 4 points for each Ace, 3 for each King, 2 for each Queen and 1 for each Jack. Out of a possible 40 points in the deck, a particular hand can have up to 37 high card points (HCP), with the average being 10. Define a function to simulate the dealing of a large number of bridge hands and use a histogram (problem 10, Chapter 16, or in the *PLOT* workspaces if available) to determine the shape of the HCP distribution.

13. Modify the function *STRINGSEARCH* (page 205) so that it uses $\uparrow$ to point to occurrences of W in T.

14. **A** For two vectors A and B of the same length, and the matrices M and U ($U \leftarrow (\iota N) \circ . \leq \iota N$) give a meaning to each of the following:

    A $A \wedge . = B$ $M \wedge . = B$ $A + . \neq B$ $(M = 0) \wedge . \geq U$ $A \times . \star B$
    B For a logical square matrix N, what is the significance of $R \leftarrow N \vee . \wedge N$?
    C For the matrices C and D, what is the meaning of $C + . = D$ and $C \lceil . \lfloor D$?

15. (Again for the math buffs.) Write a program to evaluate at various points X a polynomial with coefficients C. Assume the terms of the polynomial are arranged in ascending order of powers of X. Use the inner product.

16. The Parochial Computing Systems Corporation reimburses its employees for travel on company business at the rate of 20 cents per mile for the first 100 miles, 15 cents per mile for the next 50 miles and 10 cents per mile for all mileage in excess of 150. Define a monadic function which uses the inner product to compute mileage allowances for employees.

17. Redo using the inner product
    A problem 6, Chapter 6
    B problem 4, Chapter 8
    C problem 5, Chapter 16

18. The Shallow Water Pump Company manufactures four different sump pumps. Each model requires different numbers of five basic parts:

part type		1	2	3	4	5
	1	1	2	0	5	2
pump	2	0	3	0	1	5
model	3	1	1	4	2	2
	4	1	2	4	5	5

The Company anticipates orders for 300 of model 1, 500 of model 2, 200 of model 3 and 1000 of model 4. Assuming no margin for bad parts, how many of each part should be ordered from the vendors? These parts cost respectively $32.00, $9.75, $3.20, $.78, $7.20. What is the cost of all the parts needed? What is the cost of each pump model?

19. The Shocking Appliance Company has a distribution system which consists of 2 warehouses, 8 distribution centers and 100 stores. Highway distances between the warehouses and distribution centers are stored in the 2 by 8 matrix WD, while the distances between the centers and stores are in the 8 by 100 matrix DS. Find the shortest distance between each warehouse and store, given that merchandise must pass through a distribution center on its way to the store.

20. A solution in search of a problem: for a given vector A what does $A < . \geq 1 \phi A$ do?

21. The table below shows how many kilograms of each fruit were purchased at what cost in four trips made to the supermarket.

item	kilograms/trip				cost/kilogram
apples	5	2	6	8	$.89
oranges	2	4	3	1	.50
pears	5	6	2	5	.95
grapes	2	2	4	3	1.70
bananas	5	6	2	7	.55

Assume that the item names are stored in the matrix $FRUIT$, the purchased amounts in $QUANT$ and the cost per kilogram in the vector $VCOST$. Find the

A cost of each trip
B total weight purchased each trip
C total weight of each fruit purchased
D total cost of each fruit
E total cost of the four trips
F largest amount paid for a single fruit in each trip
G average cost/kilogram of all fruit purchased.
H amount spent on grapes ('grapes' may not necessarily be the fourth rows of $FRUIT$ and $QUANT$)

22. Another puzzler: what is the significance of the inner product $(M,0)<.-\lozenge M,0$ for M an integer matrix?

23. Use the inner product to locate the index of the first occurrence of a vector in a table.

24. Find the inverse of the identity matrix.

25. Use ⊞ to solve the following set of equations:

$$
\begin{aligned}
2x + y + 3z &= 10 \\
4x + 3y - z &= 13 \quad \text{(conventional notation)} \\
2x + y - 4z &= 3
\end{aligned}
$$

26. In algebra it is shown that for the system of equations

$$
\begin{aligned}
ax + by &= c \quad \text{(conventional notation)} \\
dx + ey &= f
\end{aligned}
$$

the application of Cramer's rule gives as solutions

$$
\begin{aligned}
x &= (ce - bf) \div (ae - bd) \quad \text{(conventional notation)} \\
y &= (af - cd) \div (ae - bd)
\end{aligned}
$$

Write an APL program to solve by Cramer's rule a given set of two linear equations and print the message $NO\ UNIQUE\ SOLUTION$ if ae - bd = 0. Then define a function $SOLVE$ which uses ⊞ to solve the equations.

27. Nearly every calculus book ever printed has a problem similar to the following: A farmer has 300 feet of fencing material which he wants to use to enclose as large a rectangular area as possible. One side of the property to be enclosed is a relatively straight stretch of river, and needs no fencing. How should the fence be put in? (To solve this problem, set up an expression for the area, apply the $SLOPE$ function to it, and see where the slope is 0. This corresponds to a maximum point on the graph of area vs the variable representing the length of one side.)

28. Sales forecasters for the Sticky Wicket Company predict the following sales for the next 7 years (in millions of dollars):

year	sales
1985	38
1986	52
1987	64
1988	82
1989	98
1990	128
1991	156

Assuming a linear model, find the equation which best fits this data.

29. (For matrix algebra buffs). A factory makes three finished products, P1, P2, P3. Four subassemblies A1, A2, A3, A4 are involved, along with two detail parts D1, D2. The table below shows how many of each (row) part are used directly in each (column) part:

	P1	P2	P3	A1	A2	A3	A4	D1	D2
P1	0	0	0	0	0	0	0	0	0
P2	0	0	0	0	0	0	0	0	0
P3	0	0	0	0	0	0	0	0	0
A1	1	2	0	0	0	0	0	0	0
A2	0	1	1	0	0	0	0	0	0
A3	0	0	2	1	1	0	0	0	0
A4	0	0	0	1	2	2	0	0	0
D1	3	2	0	0	0	0	1	0	0
D2	0	0	0	0	0	1	3	0	0

What are the total parts required? Hint: if the above matrix is designated as U and the requirements matrix as R, then the following matrix equation (conventional notation) is true: R=UR+I (I is the identity matrix).

30. Tests conducted by the U.S. Environmental Protection Agency yielded the following data on fuel economy of light duty vehicles:

weight class	fuel consumption, gal/100 mi.
2000	4.14
2200	4.67
2500	5.35
2750	5.61
3000	6.77
3500	7.39
4000	9.29
4500	10.45
5000	10.95
5500	12.16

Find the linear least-squares fit of fuel consumption to weight.

Chapter 22: The representation and storage of data

It is impossible to think of a number in the abstract without associating it with some concrete representation. Take the number 3, for instance. Can you think of the concept of 'threeness' without imagining three objects or visualizing the character 3 in some system of notation, be it Roman numerals, scaled notation, base-2 notation or whatever?

No matter how many different ways of depicting the number 3 we may come up with, they all stand for the same thing—the abstract notion of *threeness*. Yet most of the time we have no difficulty recognizing the number if it is embedded in a context which conditions our thinking along the right lines:

0.03E2

003

3.0000

EXACTLY***$3*DOLLARS*AND*00*CENTS

III

00011

The last line above might be eleven in decimal notation, but because of the other more familiar ways of expressing three that preceded it, we would quite likely accept it as being the value 3 in its binary representation.

What it all boils down to is this: just as a rose by any other name is still a rose and smells just as sweet, so there are many ways to express the same number; and their value to us depends on what we are most used to, and what form is most useful to us.

Thus far in all our APL work we have been using ordinary decimal notation. But many other systems are in common use. Mixed systems like clock time and number systems to the bases 2, 8 and 16 are examples. In this chapter we will examine how APL makes it possible for us to switch conveniently from one number system to another. For this, two powerful functions, *decode* and *encode*, will be introduced.

Decode

Suppose we are in a room whose length is 3 yards, 0 feet and 1 inch. This is an example of the English system of measurement at its worst! How can we express the length in a single unit of measure, say inches? If we were to do it by hand, we would probably set up something like the following:

3 yds
×(12×3)
———
108   +

0 ft
×12
———
0   +

1 in
×1
———
1   =   109 in

APL has a dyadic function that makes this conversion for us. It is called the *base* or *decode* function, and its symbol is the upper shift B, $\bot$. The right argument is the array to be converted, while the left argument is a vector whose elements are the increments needed to make the conversion from one unit to the next, like from yards to feet. Since each of the elements on the left can be thought of as acting somewhat like the base of a number system (sometimes called a *radix*), the left argument is usually referred to as the *radix vector*.

In a *mixed number system* like the one involving our length measurements of the room, the syntax of $\bot$ requires that the number of elements in both arguments be the same. There is one exception to this, namely, that either argument may be a scalar or vector of length 1, a case which will be considered shortly. For our particular problem, we'll use 1760 (the number of yards per mile) as the multiplying factor for the next increment even though it won't be used specifically in the conversion:

      1760 3 12⊥3 0 1
109

As a matter of fact, any number will do in that position, as long as there is something there:

    0 3 12⊥3 0 1　　　　　　　　　　　**3 1⊥3 0 1**
109　　　　　　　　　　　　　　　　　*LENGTH ERROR*
　　　　　　　　　　　　　　　　　　　　3 1 ⊥ 3 0 1
　　　　　　　　　　　　　　　　　　　　　　　∧

Here is another example, the conversion to seconds of 2 minutes and 10 seconds:

     60 60⊥2 10　　　　　　　　　**0 60⊥2 10**
130　　　　　　　　　　　　　130

We can formally express the action of the radix vector on the right argument by letting $W[J]$ be the weighting factor that tells us what the increments should be from one unit to the next in our reduction. In our example of the room size, if A is the radix vector and B is the right argument, then $W[3]$ is 1, $W[2]$ is $A[3] \times W[3]$ or 12, $W[1]$ is $A[2] \times W[2]$ or 3×12. This is equivalent to $+/36\ 12\ 1 \times 3\ 0\ 1$, or $+/W \times B$.

Clock time and English length measurements are examples of mixed number systems. The decode function works equally well for decimal or other uniform base number systems. For instance, suppose the following is a picture of the odometer reading (in miles) of a car:

This can be regarded as a scalar 3521 or a vector 3 5 2 1. If it is a vector, we can convert it to the scalar number 3521 by executing

    10 10 10 10⊥3 5 2 1　　　　　　**0 10 10 10⊥3 5 2 1**
3521　　　　　　　　　　　　　　　3521

The decode function can be applied to number systems other than decimal. Here is a binary counter:

1	0	1	1	0

This can be converted to a decimal number by

    2 2 2 2 2⊥1 0 0 1 1
19

But if the counter were to be interpreted as readings on an odometer, our result will be different:

    10 10 10 10 10⊥1 0 0 1 1
10011

Obviously, we need to know what the representation is to tell what a particular number stands for.

As we have already seen with many primitive functions, APL extends a scalar argument to match the length of the other argument:

    10⊥3 5 2 1　　　　　　　**2⊥1 0 0 1 1**　　　　　　**10 10 10 10⊥5**
3521　　　　　　　　　19　　　　　　　　　5555

To help you understand how the decode function works, we diagram the last three problems side-by-side:

	room length	odometer	binary counter
radix vector R	1760 3 12	10 10 10 10	2 2 2 2 2
weighting vector $W \leftarrow \phi 1 , \times \backslash 1 \downarrow R$	36 12 1	1000 100 10 1	16 8 4 2 1
vector to be decoded B	3 0 1	3 5 2 1	1 0 1 1 0
result $+ / W \times B$	109	3521	22

The weighting matrices are obtained by cumulative multiplication, so that the Kth element is the product of the elements 1 to K-1 of the radix vector beyond the first K. For mixed radix systems such as English length measure, you have to use that much detail to describe it, but for uniform radix systems such as the odometer or binary counter examples, the weighting vectors are simply the radix raised to the powers ...3 2 1 0.

Decoding matrices

Although decode acts on any multidimensional array, we'll introduce here only a few simple examples with matrices. The array $SAMPLE$ will be used for illustration:

    $SAMPLE \leftarrow 4 \ 4 \rho 10 \ 15 \ 8 \ 14 \ 13 \ 1 \ 18 \ 25 \ 10 \ 15 \ 1 \ 14 \ 2 \ 15 \ 2 \ 27$

Let's assume we want to get the 100 decode of the rows. Since decode acts along the first dimension, we'll have to transpose the sample:

    $DCD \leftarrow 100 \perp \lozenge SAMPLE$
    DCD
10150814 13011825 10150114 2150227

We must confess that the matrix $SAMPLE$ isn't completely arbitrary, but was derived from

    $ASAMPLE \leftarrow 4 \ 4 \ \rho 'JOHNMARYJOANBOB \ '$

so that $SAMPLE$ is equivalent to $' \ ABCDEFGHIJKLMNOPQRSTUVWXYZ' \iota ASAMPLE$. Although it may not be obvious, $\spadesuit DCD$ applied to the rows of $SAMPLE$ yields the same results as the defined function $GRADE3$ (page 141), which was used to sort the columns in a numeric matrix beginning at the right, and $ASAMPLE[\spadesuit DCD ;]$ is really an alphabetic sort!

    $\spadesuit DCD$ $ASAMPLE[\spadesuit DCD;]$
4 3 1 2 BOB
               JOAN
               JOHN
               MARY

All of this is incorporated in a program $ALFSORT1$ (B is the radix for decoding):

```
      ∇Z←B ALFSORT1 M;ALF
[1]   ALF←' ABCDEFGHIJKLMNOPQRSTUVWXYZ0123456789'
[2]   Z←M[♠,B⊥⍉ALFιM;]∇
```

This method avoids a looping solution which might seem more natural to those of you who were brought up on card sorters and the like. But we must warn you that it has several disadvantages. First, with large tables there are apt to be $WSFULL$ problems. Second, there is a limitation to the ability of the function to discriminate among long, nearly identical rows because the large numbers which result can't be represented in APL as distinct numbers. For example, if $B \leftarrow 38$, then rows whose first 10 or more columns are the same won't be differentiated. And third, if there are too many columns you may get a $DOMAIN \ ERROR$ because of the very large values resulting from the decoding. An algorithm to determine how many columns can be handled by one decimal number is $\lfloor 56 \div 2 \circledast \rho ALF$, 56 being the number of usable bits in a decimal (floating point) number. B should also be at least 1 greater than ρALF.

$ALFSORT2$ completes the picture, when one field is required to be in sequence within another:

```
        ∇Z←BFLDS ALFSORT2 M;ALF;B
[1]     ALF←' ABCDEFGHIJKLMNOPQRSTUVWXYZ0123456789'
[2]     B←1↑BFLDS
[3]     BFLDS←1↓BFLDS
[4]     Z←M[♠B⊥⍉ALF⍳M[;BFLDS];]∇
```

In this function, $BFLDS$ contains the radix as its first element. The remaining elements in $BFLDS$ are the selected column indices used to key the sort (leftmost values are the most major fields).

$ALFSORT1$ and $ALFSORT2$ will handle most ordinary sorting problems. However, if the sort sequence is very long and you run into the limitations mentioned earlier, you might try sorting in two passes, first the minor, then the major fields. There are many variations employed in sorting, particularly where upper and lower case alphabets are involved. Programs to handle these and other cases are found in utility workspaces in nearly every APL system. If you are using an APL system that has enhanced primitive grade capability (Chapter 15), then the use of sorting routines like the above is unnecessary.

Like the dyadic transpose (Chapter 19), decode can be employed to select or identify scattered elements in a matrix. Let's get a sample matrix to work on:

```
      )COPY 1 CLASS TAB2               TAB2
SAVED  14.45.33 02/20/83          3   1   7
                                  7  10   4
                                  6   9   1
                                  1   6   7
```

Suppose you wanted to select from $TAB2$ a vector consisting of $TAB2[1;3]$, $TAB2[4;2]$, $TAB2[3;2]$, $TAB2[1;1]$. If you place all the desired indices in a matrix and apply $⊥$ to that array,

```
      PICK←4 2⍴1 3 4 2 3 2 1 1           1+(⍴TAB2)⊥⍉PICK-1
      PICK                              3  11  8  1
   1  3
   4  2
   3  2
   1  1
```

what you get are the positions you want if $TAB2$ were raveled (check it!). This gives rise to a general method for selecting arbitrary elements from an array:

```
      ∇R←DATA SELCT INDICES
[1]   ⍝INDICES IS A MATRIX WITH AS MANY ROWS AS DATA HAS RANK.
[2]   R←(,DATA)[1+(⍴DATA)⊥⍉INDICES-1] ∇
      TAB2 SELCT PICK
7  6  9  3
```

The diagram below clarifies how the raveled positions (RP) are related to the original positions (OP). In each case, $RP←1+(⍴DATA)⊥^-1+OP$.

value	OP	RP	value	OP	RP	value	OP	RP
3	1 1	1	1	1 2	2	7	1 3	3
7	2 1	4	10	2 2	5	4	2 3	6
6	3 1	7	9	3 2	8	1	3 3	9
1	4 1	10	6	4 2	11	7	4 3	12

Here's an offbeat but useful application of $⊥$. Suppose you have an 'irregular' matrix of characters M (the irregularity is really illusory since the apparently ragged edges are padded with blanks that don't show):

```
      M←5 6ρ' ANN      EVA JILL              JANICE'
      M
ANN
   EVA
JILL

JANICE
```

The problem is to right-justify the matrix (see also the defined function *ROWNAMES*, page 116). We first identify the location of the blanks with $M=$ ' '. This logical matrix, used as the left argument of the decode function with 1 as the right argument, results in a vector whose elements are related to the number of blanks to the right of the first nonblank character in each line of M (why?):

```
      Q←(M=' ')⊥1             Q
                      3 2 3 6 1
```

Subtracting Q from 1 should tell us how much to shift each line to the right (any value will do for the fourth row):

```
      QS←1-Q              QS              QSϕM
                 ‾2 ‾1 ‾2 ‾5 0          ANN
                                        EVA
                                       JILL

                                      JANICE
```

Putting all this in one expression, the completed algorithm is (1-(M=' ')⊥1)ϕM. Another way to do the same thing, not using ⊥, is (-+/∧\ϕM=' ')ϕM (page 136).

Encode

Like so many of the other functions we've encountered in APL, there is a function that 'undoes' the work of the decode function, that is, converts from a value to some predetermined representation. Appropriately, it is called *representation* or *encode*, and its symbol is T (upper shift *N*). Thus, if we execute

```
      2 2 2 2⊥0 1 0 1
5
```

then the function T brings back our initial argument:

```
      2 2 2 2T5
0 1 0 1
```

Here are our room length and odometer problems in reverse:

```
      1760 3 12T109               10 10 10 10T3521
3 0 1                          3 5 2 1
```

The latter example describes how 3521 would appear on a 4-digit odometer. How would 43521 appear on the same odometer?

```
      10 10 10 10T43521
3 5 2 1
```

We can draw an analogy here. It's like an odometer which reads only up to 9999 and then starts over from 0 again. In fact, in this case the right argument has been reduced by $10*4$:

```
      (10*4)|43521
3521
```

What happens when we're not sure how many elements are needed in the radix vector, yet we don't want to lose anything, as was unfortunately the case in the example above? Using zero as the first element of the left argument puts everything remaining in the first element of the result, as shown below:

```
      0 10 10 10T43521             0 60T130
43 5 2 1                       2 10
```

The encode function also operates on matrices. This feature doesn't have many uses, and will not be reviewed here. Both encode and decode yield some rather interesting results when used with negative numbers and nonintegers. Explore these on your own, because we're hard put to think of practical examples for them.

Hexadecimal to decimal conversion

An obvious application is the conversion of decimally represented information to another numbering system. Since the bases 2, 8 and 16 have been used extensively for computers, our first illustration builds an algorithm to convert from the decimal to the *hexadecimal* (base-16) system.

In our ordinary decimal (base-10) system, we require ten distinct symbols 0123456789, and in the base-16 system, 16 symbols are needed. Values larger than 9 in the base-10 system are represented by adding positions on the left (provided, of course, we are talking about whole numbers and not fractions). For example, 10 is a two-position number, 9 being the largest number that can be represented by a single symbol.

In the hexadecimal system the symbols are 0123456789ABCDEF. If you were to ask why the letters ABCDEF, the most appropriate response would be, why not? We need symbols for each of the values 10 through 15. New symbols could be invented or old ones used differently (like upside down or with a bar across them), but it really doesn't matter as long as they are distinct from one another and are used consistently.

A decimal system number such as 6325 can be represented in so-called expanded notation as $6 \times 10^3 + 3 \times 10^2 + 2 \times 10^1 + 5 \times 10^0$. We can represent a hexadecimal number in exactly the same way, except that powers of 16 instead of powers of 10 are involved. Here is the expansion of the hexadecimal number 1AF2, which is equivalent to 6898 in decimal form: $1 \times 16^3 + 10 \times 16^2 + 15 \times 16^1 + 2 \times 16^0$.

In 1 *CLASS* there is a dyadic function *HEXA* which makes the conversion for us. The left argument is the number of positions we want to see represented; the right argument is the value to be converted:

```
        )COPY 1 CLASS HEXA
SAVED   14.45.33 02/20/83
        ∇HEXA[□]∇
    ∇ R←N HEXA X
[1]     R←'0123456789ABCDEF'[1+(Nρ16)TX]
    ∇
```

```
      3 HEXA 254
0FE

      2 HEXA 254
FE

      1 HEXA 254
E
```

$Nρ16$ generates a vector of N elements, each of which is 16. If, for example, N is 3 and X is 254, $(Nρ16)TX$ is $(3ρ16)T254$ or 0 15 14. In expanded notation this is the same as $0 \times 16^2 + 15 \times 16^1 + 14 \times 16^0$.

Looking through the vector of characters 0123456789*ABCDEF*, we see that the 0 is in the first position, 1 in the second position, etc. It is necessary to add 1 to $(3ρ16)T254$ to pick up the subscripts for the proper characters:

```
      1+(3ρ16)T254
1 16 15
```

Now let's execute *HEXA* for, say, the number 257, for which at least three hexadecimal positions are needed: $1 \times 16^2 + 0 \times 16^1 + 1 \times 16^0$.

```
      4 HEXA 257
0101
```
```
      2 HEXA 257
01
```

We get a false result if we don't specify sufficient positions. Incidentally, 0101 is a vector of characters. Do you see why?

```
      ρ4 HEXA 257
4
```

What about the reverse operation, converting from hexadecimal to decimal representation? The function *DEC* in 1 *CLASS* does this. It is monadic and requires a character argument:

```
        )COPY 1 CLASS DEC
SAVED   14.45.33 02/20/83
        ∇DEC[□]∇
    ∇ R←DEC H
[1]     R←16⊥¯1+'0123456789ABCDEF'ιH
    ∇
```

```
      DEC '0FE'
254

      DEC 'FE'
254

      DEC 'E'
E
```

H represents the vector of characters in hexadecimal notation. The ranking picks up the positions of the corresponding characters in the left argument. Trying this out with *0FE*, we get

        '0123456789ABCDEF'ι'0FE'
1 16 15

which is one position too high to use as the right argument of ⊥. Hence ‾1 is added before the decode function is applied:

        16⊥0 15 14
254

DEC doesn't need a left argument because the decode function automatically extends the scalar 16 to match the shape of the right argument.

If we were to try *DEC* with undefined characters, say, *WER*, we still get a result,

        DEC 'WER'
4336

but it is meaningless. To find out why, remember what ranking does for an element in the right argument not found on the left. It will produce here the vector 17 15 17; and after adding ‾1 to each element we have

        16⊥16 14 16
4336

Now try

        DEC 5 HEXA 321   **DEC 2 HEXA 321**
321   65

and we see that *DEC* and *HEXA* are inverse functions, provided that sufficient positions have been allowed.

Numeric encrypting

In some of the problems at the end of Chapter 15 we experimented with cryptographic techniques by converting readable messages into 'scrambled' characters. Using ⊤ and ⊥ we can now code several characters into a single number. The function *NUMCODE* (from 1 *CLASS*) breaks up a character vector *M* into groups of four characters each, and codes each group into a single numerical value. *B* is a scalar which must be at least one greater than ρ*ALF*. The key to this function is line 4, which takes the four-row character matrix into which *M* has been transformed (lines 2 and 3), converts it into indices (*ALF*ι*M*) and then changes each column into a unique number in base *B*. As you will learn in the next section, there is an upper limit on the value of *B* which depends on the way in which numbers are represented in the computer. Decrypting can be done using *DENUMCODE*, provided that one knows the base *B*:

```
    ∇NUMCODE[□]∇                    ∇DENUMCODE[□]∇
  ∇ Z←B NUMCODE M                 ∇ Z←B DENUMCODE MESSAGE
[1]   M←(4×⌈0.25×ρM)↑M       [1]    MESSAGE←(4ρB)⊤MESSAGE
[2]   M←(4,0.25×ρM)ρM        [2]    Z←,ALF[MESSAGE]
[3]   Z←B⊥ALFιM                 ∇
  ∇
```

        ALF←' ABCDEFGHIJKLMNOPQRSTUVWXYZ'

        M←'REBELS ADVANCING ON ALL FRONTS'

        MESSAGE←30 NUMCODE M

        MESSAGE
517537 183199 83266 175545 354681 549410 40891 61231

        30 DENUMCODE MESSAGE
REBELS ADVANCING ON ALL FRONTS

How data is stored in APL

In the IBM based versions of APL (VS APL, STSC, Sharp, APL2) discussed in this book, a number can have 16 decimal digits without loss of precision. More specifically, the mantissa is represented as 56 binary elements, and $10 \otimes 2 \star 56$ is 16.8+, which suggests that each 16-bit machine 'word' can pack eight 2-digit numbers. Before showing how decode can be used to do the packing, let's examine the way in which APL stores information.

Ultimately, every numeric or character element that you use in APL is represented inside the computer as a sequence of binary (0 or 1) values or *bits*. Each character is represented internally as 8 bits, called a *byte*. This implies that APL has a maximum of 256 ($2 \star 8$) different characters. Your terminal can represent about 150 of them. These are the display characters, including the overstruck ones such as $\lozenge \ominus \boxed{\square} \neq \underline{A} \underline{Z} \cap$.

Integers in the range ⁻2147483648 to 2147483647 are usually stored in 32 adjacent bits, called a *word*. Here is what the number 5 looks like internally:

$$00000000000000000000000000000101$$

Negative numbers are denoted with a 1 in the leftmost position, and the number itself is stored as $(32\rho 2)\top VALUE$, called 2's *complement* form. Some examples follow:

⁻2147483648	10000000000000000000000000000000
⁻2147483647	10000000000000000000000000000001
⁻2147483646	10000000000000000000000000000010
⁻2	11111111111111111111111111111110
⁻1	11111111111111111111111111111111
0	00000000000000000000000000000000
1	00000000000000000000000000000001
2	00000000000000000000000000000010
2147483646	01111111111111111111111111111110
2147483647	01111111111111111111111111111111

Nonintegers, as well as integers smaller than ⁻2147483648 or larger than 2147483647, take 64 bits for internal storage, called *double-word floating point*. But the value isn't represented in a straightforward manner like 2's complement. Rather, it is stored as follows:

bit 1	Sign of mantissa (1 if negative, 0 if positive or 0)
bits 2 to 8	Value of exponent, in hexadecimal. Decode as $16 \star (2 \bot STORAGE[1+\iota 7])-64$
bits 9 to 64	Value of mantissa, as a binary fraction. Decode as $(2 \bot STORAGE[8+\iota 56])\div 2 \star 56$ or $.5 \bot 0, STORAGE[65-\iota 56]$

The value is assembled by the computer with this algorithm:

$$\underset{\text{(sign)}}{(1-2\times STORAGE[1])} \times \underset{\text{(mantissa)}}{(.5\bot 0, STORAGE[65-\iota 56])} \times \underset{\text{(exponent)}}{(16 \star ⁻64+2\bot STORAGE[1+\iota 7])}$$

Positive and negative values within the approximate range $10 \star ⁻75$ and $10 \star 75$ can be accommodated.

When the values you use in APL are only 0 or 1, each is stored as a single *bit*. This is an extremely compact way to store information, and in part explains why APL is so well suited for analysis of binary choice data—market research studies, for example. You can pack 32 times as much of this kind of information into a workspace as you could if you were using integers, or 64 times as much as when using floating point.

Conversion from one storage type to another

An important factor to consider is that if one element of an array requires integer (32 bits) or floating point (64 bits) internal representation, then *every* element in the array is stored in the same manner. Thus, we have:

0 1 1 0 1 1 0 0	takes 8 bits, or 1 byte
0 1 1 0 2 1 0 0	takes 256 bits, or 32 bytes
.5	takes 512 bits, or 64 bytes
'01101106'	takes 64 bits, or 8 bytes.

Although on most older APL systems characters and numeric values can't be mixed in the same array, APL2, Sharp and APL*PLUS Systems have relaxed the restriction (see page 257).

APL tries to pick the most compact internal representation for your data, but in the interests of practicality, certain types of checking are not done by the computer. For example, when you multiply two integers, the result is integer (32 bits) if it fits; otherwise the result is made floating (64 bits). However, if you multiply .2 by 10, the result is stored as floating, even though it would be expressible as an integer. Likewise, $5-4$ results in integer (32 bits) storage, rather than taking only one bit.

You can usually force APL to store data the way you wish by using $X \leftarrow \lfloor X$ or $X \leftarrow \lceil X$ to convert from floating to integer. The only time it won't work is when the integer part is too large to fit into a 32-bit word. Use $X \leftarrow 2 \times .5 \times X$ to convert bits or integers to floating point representation. To convert integer or floating to bit storage, use $X \leftarrow \sim \sim X$ or $X \leftarrow X = 1$. $\sim \sim X$ gives $DOMAIN\ ERROR$ if any of the values to be converted are neither 0 nor 1, while $X = 1$ will produce 0 for any value not equal to 1.

These conversions may differ from system to system. If these matters are important to you, you'll have to ask someone who knows the particulars of your system, or do lots of experimentation.

Finally, here is a function which will internally represent any numeric array in the most compact manner:

```
      ∇R←INTREP N;S;NULL
[1]   S←ρN
[2]   NULL←(×/S)ρ0
[3]   NULL[]←N
[4]   R←SρNULL∇
```

All of the above discussion was specific to APL on IBM 370-based hardware. Things may be entirely different on other computers. For example, on STSC's TRS80 model III and IBM PC versions, integers are 16 bits long and there is no bit type storage at all! Binary data is stored as integer instead, taking 16 bits for storing each bit. On those systems, floating point data still uses 64 bits per number, but the mantissa and exponent arrangement differs. You can get a hint of that by trying $\lfloor / \iota 0$.

Measuring the amount of storage

The amount of storage available in your active workspace can be measured by the $\square WA$ (for *working area*) system variable. Its result is a scalar holding the number of bytes available to you. When you define a variable, you will find that $\square WA$ decreases roughly by the number of bytes actually taken by the data. It isn't usually exact because of storage taken by the name and the dimension information, as well as other scraps of internal information that the APL system stores or erases, almost as though it has a mind of its own.

```
      ☐WA              Q←10000ρ'CLUTTER '              ☐WA
149544                                              139524
```

If you explore $\square WA$, make sure your tests use enough data to get accurate readings. Also, in some systems vectors of the form $D + M \times \iota N$ aren't stored as N-element vectors, but rather as only three elements holding D, M and N. Some systems are clever enough to save only one copy of data from a sequence like $B \leftarrow 99\ 6\rho 'BOTTLE'$ followed by $C \leftarrow B$.

$\square WA$ can be employed in programs which use an alternative algorithm (usually involving looping) to solve a problem when there isn't enough space to do the job directly. The value of $\square WA$ in a clear workspace varies from system to system, usually between 24000 and 256000, as decided by the system management.

Data compaction

To illustrate how decode can be used to pack data in a form requiring less internal storage, we first define

```
      NUMBERS←100-ι8
      NUMBERS
99 98 97 96 95 94 93 92

      ☐WA
139468

      PACKED←100⊥NUMBERS

      PACKED
9.998979696E15
```

```
      □PP←16

      PACKED
9998979695949392

      )ERASE NUMBERS
      □WA
139480
```

As you might expect, to unpack the numbers use ⊤:

```
      (8ρ100)⊤PACKED
99 98 97 96 95 94 93 92
```

We can easily demonstrate the inability to pack accurately more than eight 2-digit numbers:

```
      NUMBERS←100-ι9                    PACKED←100⊥NUMBERS
      NUMBERS                           (9ρ100)⊤PACKED
99 98 97 96 95 94 93 92 91        99 98 97 96 95 94 93 92 80
```

Generally speaking, packing like this isn't recommended because it tends to obscure what's going on. Moreover, how much you can pack is very implementation dependent. You will very likely have to redo all compaction work if you change systems. Because APL does a pretty good job conserving storage, it isn't necessary for you to resort to techniques like this unless there's a desperate need to conserve space.

In-place storage

During execution APL usually needs space for both the argument and the result at the same time. This is why you may encounter *WS FULL* when trying to catenate a row to a very large array in a workspace whose □*WA* indicates lots of space available.

Most APL implementations are sophisticated enough to sense when the result will fit into the space occupied by an argument and use the same space for it. For example, in the instruction *R←+\ι1000* the result is in-place storage, with *R* replacing the temporary values ι1000. However, for *R←+\R*, the scan argument isn't temporary, and there is no in-place storage.

Some other functions for which there is in-place storage are rotate, reshape, bracket indexing and addition. The first two will make copies if room exists, and use in-place storage only to avoid *WS FULL*'s.

Some instructions produce a result that is the same as the argument. These cause no data movement in the workspace and take up no extra storage (e.g., *A[ ]*). And finally, there are a few instructions which appear to defy logic by requiring much less space to execute than you might expect. One such example is the common expression *V/ιρV*, which needs space only for the result. Another is →□*LC*, which takes only 40 bytes no matter how big □*LC* itself is.

These space-saving features are highly implementation dependent and may even change from release to release.

Hints for saving storage

As applications grow and become more sophisticated, storage requirements tend to grow also. Sooner or later you reach a point where something has to go to make room for currently needed functions and data, unless your computer center upgrades its machines to provide bigger workspaces. With VS APL you may be able to stave off the inevitable for a while because of the large workspace size, but even here there are steps you can take to save space. Some are obvious and have already been discussed; others will be taken up in later chapters.

Localize variables. If you must use global variables don't enter them into a function as arguments, to avoid doubling the space required.

Expunge unneeded information.

Load or copy only what you need.

Store large amounts of data and functions on files.

Segregate data by data type where practicable, e.g., don't mix one column of floating point with 10 columns of integers.

Pack data if feasible into characters or use ⊥ to store more than one value in a single element. Scale decimal data by a power of 10 to convert it to integers.

Avoid APL operations that require an array argument to coexist temporarily with the result.

Store large character matrices with many trailing blanks in raveled form with the blanks removed. Use a table of pointers to record start and stop positions for each item in the vector.

Eliminate unnecessary suspensions.

Production programming

Having said all this, we now make some observations about the *production* environment (tested and debugged programs to be used generally by others), contrasted with that of the do-it-yourselfer. In the latter case no one really cares if your specifications are nonexistent, the code is inefficient and is giving the computer a headache, or the program itself is likely to fail if it encounters an unusual situation (sometimes called an edge condition) such as empty vectors or negative inputs.

But when programming for production, this laissez-faire attitude leads to disaster. Programs whose code is obscure, whose design is illogical and whose resistance to modification would make a diamond seem soft by comparison, are the bane of support groups who try to maintain them. There are two choices: change either APL or the programmers' work habits and style. Since the former occurs only slowly, and then with much disagreement on how to change it, the only reasonable alternative is to change the way programmers write APL.

This is where standards come in. Reasonable people can (and do) differ about them. In a way it's like asking how much government regulation is necessary to protect people from themselves and others without stifling individual initiative. It is not the authors' intent to prescribe a set of guidelines, which probably wouldn't help those of you whose anarchical bent is beyond redemption, but to sensitize you to the fact that the production environment is, and must be, more restrictive than the personal environment.

Application to computer design

This optional section is intended for those of you who are curious about the design of computers. APL has been widely used to design and simulate digital devices. Here is an example of how the addition operation of a typical 16-bit microcomputer can be simulated. The addition operation adds the 16 bits of its argument $WORD$ to the accumulator $\underline{A}$, itself a 16-bit register, and sets the carry flag $\underline{C}$ (a 1-bit register) to 1 if the result would have 'overflowed' into a seventeenth binary position.

```
      ∇ADD16 WORD;TEMP
[1]   TEMP←(17ρ2)⊤(2⊥A)+2⊥WORD
[2]   A←1↓TEMP
[3]   C←1↑TEMP∇
```

This use of APL as a *formal definition* of a digital system or subsystem is a viable alternative to the lengthy (and often ambiguous or incomplete) written specifications that are normally used for this purpose. With APL, the formal definition is a program that can be tested, validated and run.

Check protection

Our last illustration is the function CP, which fills in the space before a number with stars up to a preset position. Its use for check protection should be evident. CP, which is in 1 $CLASS$, is dyadic. The left argument is the number of characters in the result (field width), and the right argument is the amount of the check. The function is superfluous for those APL systems with picture format, $\square FMT$, or their equivalent (Chapters 17 and 18).

```
      )COPY 1 CLASS CP                                5 CP 301
SAVED  14.45.33 02/20/83                          **301
      ∇CP[▯]∇                                         5 CP 12345
   ∇ R←N CP X;P                                   12345
[1]    R←'0123456789'[1+(Nρ10)⊤X]                    5 CP 0031
[2]    P←¯1+(R≠'0')ι1                             **301
[3]    R←(Pρ'*'),P↓R ∇
```

Line 1 makes a vector of characters out of X, the argument, and adds enough 0's in front to make ρR equal to N. Line 2 sets P as one less than the index of the first nonzero character, while line 3 puts into R, P copies of $*$ followed by all but the first P elements of R.

PROBLEMS

1. DRILL

    ```
    (3ρ40)⊥8 7 2           2⊥5 1 9 6            1 4 7⊥3 5ρι15
    1 ¯4.1 .8⊥1 2 3        7 8 9⊥7 8 9          3⊤5217
    3 3⊤5217               3 3 3⊤5217           (5ρ3)⊤5217
    (4ρ8)⊥¯14              1 4 6⊤345            2 4 5⊤78
    ```

2. Write APL expressions to **A** convert 2 gallons, 8 quarts and 1 pint to pints; **B** find the number of ounces in 3 tons, 568 pounds and 13 ounces.

3. Find the

    A base-8 value of 2 1 7 7
    B base-2 value of   1 0 1 1 0 1
    C base-3 representation of 8933
    D base-5 representation of 4791

4. Write expressions that will show that ⊥ and ⊤ are inverses of each other (not, however, for all arguments).

5. Define a function to remove commas from a character vector consisting of digits and commas, and convert the result to a numerical vector.

6. Write an APL expression which determines whether or not, for a given three-digit number N, N is equal to the sum of the cubes of its digits.

7. For $M←$'1234583', what are the differences between each of the following expressions?

    A $M←¯1+$'0123456789'$ιM$
    B $M←10⊥¯1+$'0123456789'$ιM$
    C $M←10⊥0 1 2 3 4 5 6 7 8 9[$'0123456789'$ιM]$

8. It is a fact that a number N is divisible by 11 if the alternating sum of its digits is divisible by 11. Construct an expression that uses the encode function with this condition to test for divisibility by 11.

9. Write an APL function to illustrate the following well-known arithmetic 'trick': given any 3-digit number N whose first and last digits are different, reverse the digits and subtract the smaller number from the larger. Reverse the digits in the answer and add this value to the original difference. The sum will always be 1089.

Problems 10-14 are designed to show you a little of the often unappreciated power of the decode and encode functions.

10. Describe the action of each of the following (N a scalar and V a vector): **A** 1⊥V **B** 0⊥V **C** ¯1⊥φV **D** 0 1⊤N

11. Use ⊥ to write a dyadic function $EVAL$ to evaluate at the point X a polynomial with coefficients C (descending powers of X). Compare with page 43.

12. Define a function $ENCODE$ to simulate ⊤ and provide the necessary number of positions in the left argument.

13. How can you use decode on the room measurement example (page 217) to get the answer in feet or yards?

14. Show how to delete **A** leading and **B** trailing occurrences of some element S from a vector V.

15. Array C contains the costs for various items of clothes purchased by Abigail Adams for Polly Jefferson and her maid in 1787. (First column is pounds, second column shillings and the third is pence.) The total submitted to Thomas Jefferson was 10 pounds, 15 shillings, 8 pence. Jefferson changed this to 11 pounds, 16 shillings and 2 pence. Which sum is correct? (Pound=20 shillings; shilling=12 pence.)

```
C←0 5 6 3 10 0 0 15 0 1 10 0 0 6 6 0 5 0 0 7 6 0 13 0
C←C,0 2 4 0 5 10 0 13 6 0 3 0 0 5 6 0 1 6 1 5 6 0 7 4
C←20 3ρC,0 6 0 0 2 0 0 4 6 0 6 8
```

16. Define a function $DIAG$ that takes as its right argument a matrix M whose elements are positive integers, and forms a decimal number out of the diagonal elements.

17. A challenge for those of you who are so in love with APL they can't fall asleep at night without saying to themselves 'Let me count the ways ...' Find at least 9 different ways to compute the average of a vector of numbers.

18. Execute `1000 100 10 1 +.×3 5 2 1` (the odometer problem). What does the result tell you about the relationship between inner product and decode?

Chapter 23: Input and output

Observe the following dialogue with a computer, using a program which simulates a psychiatrist (derived from the program *Eliza*, J.Weisenbaum, *Communications of the ACM*, Volume 9, Number 1, January 1966).

WOULD YOU PREFER TO TALK TO A DOCTOR (CLIENT-CENTERED PSYCHOTHERAPIST),
OR A FREAK (LONG-HAIRED STUDENT TYPE)?
TYPE 'DOCTOR' FOR THE DOCTOR, OR 'FREAK' FOR THE STUDENT.
☐: **DOCTOR**

YOU MAY END THE CONVERSATION ANYTIME BY TYPING THE SINGLE WORD 'BYE'

HOW DO YOU DO. PLEASE STATE YOUR PROBLEM
☐: **I AM TRYING TO LEARN ABOUT INPUT AND OUTPUT.**
DO YOU BELIEVE IT IS NORMAL TO BE TRYING TO LEARN ABOUT INPUT AND OUTPUT
☐: **IN THE CONTEXT OF AN APL COURSE IT IS NORMAL.**
WHAT DOES THAT SUGGEST TO YOU
☐: **THAT I MAY HAVE TO LEARN EVEN MORE**
YOU SAY THAT YOU MAY HAVE TO LEARN EVEN MORE
☐: **YES, I NEED TO GAIN AN UNDERSTANDING OF IT.**
I SEE
☐: **WHAT DO YOU SEE?**
WHAT ANSWER WOULD PLEASE YOU MOST
☐: **I DON'T KNOW. YOU ARE NOT VERY HELPFUL.**
DO YOU WISH TO BE ABLE TO KNOW
☐: **WHAT SORT OF QUESTION IS THAT?**
THAT'S A FREAKY QUESTION
☐: **THIS CONVERSATION IS GETTING SILLY.**
I'M NOT SURE I UNDERSTAND YOU FULLY
☐: **I SAID, I DON'T THINK YOU KNOW WHAT YOU'RE DOING.**
DO YOU SAY YOU SAID FOR SOME SPECIAL REASON
☐: **WHAT?**
ARE SUCH QUESTIONS MUCH ON YOUR MIND
☐: **NOT UNTIL I STARTED TALKING TO YOU.**
YOU SEEM TO NEED TO STARTED TALKING TO ME
☐: **THAT'S SILLY.**
PLEASE GO ON
☐: **I DON'T WANT TO GO ON; I WANT TO STUDY MORE.**
WHY DO YOU WANT TO GO ON
☐: **I DON'T WANT TO GO ON.**
WHAT DOES WANTING TO GO ON HAVE TO DO WITH THIS DISCUSSION
☐: **THAT'S WHAT I'D LIKE TO KNOW.**
HAVE YOU ASKED SUCH QUESTIONS BEFORE
☐: **GOOD HEAVENS.**
WHAT DOES THAT SUGGEST TO YOU
☐: **HELP!**

PLEASE GO ON
☐: **HOW DO I GET OUT OF HERE?**
HAVE YOU ASKED SUCH QUESTIONS BEFORE
☐: **BYE**

I EXPECT TO TALK TO YOU AGAIN SOON

The function appears to converse or interact with the user. While running, it prompts the user for an entry on the keyboard, comes up with an appropriate answer (well, most of the time) and decides what the next prompt is. This is different from all of the programs and functions you have written so far; all your functions communicated with the user only through arguments or global variables, and as a consequence the user had to know *something* about APL to use them. With the facility to 'converse' with the computer, users need to know only how to type an appropriate response. Depending on the level of sophistication that the program employs to deal with a user's entry, it can appear almost human in its reply. In particular, if the program lets the user know what his choices are, treats him gently when he errs, and can deal with minor typing errors, the program can rightly be termed *user friendly*.

Accepting character data

The most important APL feature to accept input from the user is the *quote-quad*, ⍞. When it is encountered in an APL statement, the computer accepts whatever characters the user types at the keyboard, until he enters RETURN. The characters that have been entered are then available for assignment to a variable as a character vector or for other purposes.

Here is an APL function that you might employ to deal with yes-or-no choices in a user-friendly application. Its argument is used as a prompt. The explicit result is a 1 for a *YES* reply or 0 for *NO*.

```
        ∇Z←YESORNO PROMPT;TRIES;ANS
[1]     ⍝ RETURNS 1 FOR YES, 0 FOR NO.
[2]     ⍝ AFTER 3 UNSUCCESSFUL TRIES, WARNS USER AND EXITS.
[3]     ⍝ A.J. ROSE SEPT 1982
[4]     TRIES←0
[5]     AGAIN2:PROMPT
[6]     AGAIN1:ANS←,⍞
[7]     Z←((2 3ρ'YESNO ')∧.=3↑ANS)/1 0
[8]     →(1=ρZ)/0
[9]     TRIES←TRIES+1 ◊ 'PLEASE ANSWER YES OR NO'
[10]    →(AGAIN1,AGAIN2,DEFAULT)[TRIES]
[11]    DEFAULT:'WARNING - BECAUSE I CANNOT UNDERSTAND YOUR REPLY,'
[12]    'YOUR INTENTIONS WILL BE INTERPRETED AS ''NO'''∇
```

```
        YESORNO 'DO YOU UNDERSTAND WHAT THIS FUNCTION DOES?'
MAYBE
PLEASE ANSWER YES OR NO
???
PLEASE ANSWER YES OR NO
DO YOU UNDERSTAND WHAT THIS FUNCTION DOES?
PERHAPS
PLEASE ANSWER YES OR NO
WARNING - BECAUSE I CANNOT UNDERSTAND YOUR REPLY,
YOUR INTENTIONS WILL BE INTERPRETED AS 'NO'
0
```

The input is accepted on line 6. The effect of ⍞ is to halt execution at that point until you press the RETURN key. Whatever characters you typed on the line prior to RETURN will be in the variable *ANS* as a character vector. (Some older APL systems treat a single character of ⍞ input as a scalar. For them, you should ravel so that you are always dealing with a vector.)

You can use your APL system as a word processor or electronic typewriter to help you edit text. The following program both accepts text and lets you edit what you've entered.

```
        )COPY 1 CLASS CHANGE COMPOSE
SAVED   14.45.33 02/20/83

        ∇CHANGE[⎕]∇
     ∇  Z←CHANGE TEXT;CMD;W;C
[1]     Z←W←0 ◊ →(1=ρρTEXT)/L2 ◊ 'NOT A VECTOR' ◊ →0 ⍝ DEMO TEXT
   EDITOR. AJR 10/1/82
[2]     L2:CMD←'' ◊ →(0=ρTEXT)/INS ◊ →(' '=1↑0ρTEXT)/EDIT ◊ 'NOT CHARACTER' ◊ →0
[3]     EDIT:(50↑W↓TEXT), 7 0 ▼W+1 ◊ CMD←,⍞ ◊ →(0=ρCMD)/HELP
[4]     Z←+/∧\' '=CMD ◊ C←1↑Z↓CMD ◊ CMD←(1+Z)↓CMD
[5]     →(C='H0123456789FBL/\EI')/HELP,(10ρDIG),FWD,BACK,LOC,SL,SL,END,INS
[6]     'UNKNOWN COMMAND' ◊ →EDIT
[7]     HELP:'NNN          MOVE WINDOW TO NNN'
[8]     'FNNN  BNNN   MOVE FORWARD OR BACK NNN CHARACTERS'
[9]     'F     B      MOVE FORWARD OR BACK 50 CHARACTERS'
[10]    'LPHRASE      MOVE TO NEXT PHRASE'
[11]    '//NEW \\NEW  REPLACE WHAT''S OVER // OR \\ BY NEW'
[12]    'E           END THE PROGRAM'
```

```
[13]    'H               HELP MESSAGES'
[14]    'INEW            INSERT NEW AT THIS POINT, SWITCH TO ENTRY MODE'
[15]    'SPACES          SWITCHES FROM ENTRY MODE TO EDIT MODE'
[16]    →EDIT
[17]  DIG:W←0⌈(⁻50+ρTEXT)⌊⍋C,(∧\CMD∈'0123456789')/CMD ◇ →EDIT
[18]  FWD:W←0⌈(⁻50+ρTEXT)⌊W+Z+⁻1↑⍋'50 ',(∧\CMD∈'0123456789')/CMD ◇ →EDIT
[19]  BACK:W←0⌈(⁻50+ρTEXT)⌊W+Z-⁻1↑⍋'50 ',(∧\CMD∈'0123456789')/CMD ◇ →EDIT
[20]  LOC:W←W+Z ◇ CMD←∧≠/(⁻1+⍳ρCMD)ΦCMD∘.=W↓TEXT ◇ →(∨/CMD)/HIT
      ◇ 'NOT FOUND' ◇ →EDIT
[21]  HIT:W←⁻1+W+CMD⍳1 ◇ →EDIT
[22]  SL:W←W+Z ◇ Z←+/∧\C=CMD ◇ TEXT←(W↑TEXT),(Z↓CMD),(W+Z+1)↓TEXT ◇ →EDIT
[23]  INS:W←W+Z ◇ Z←(W↑TEXT),CMD,(' '≠⁻1↑CMD)/' ' ◇ TEXT←W↓TEXT
[24]  INMORE:CMD←,⍞ ◇ →(' 'v.≠CMD)/INM2 ◇ TEXT←Z,TEXT ◇ →EDIT
[25]  INM2:Z←Z,CMD,(' '≠⁻1↑CMD)/' ' ◇ →INMORE
[26]  END:Z←TEXT
      ∇
```

The argument is a character vector, $TEXT$. If $TEXT$ is not empty, $CHANGE$ assumes you want to edit $TEXT$; line 3 then assigns to CMD those characters which you enter on the keyboard. In particular, if you enter only RETURN, then CMD is an empty vector and execution moves to line 7 where user instructions are displayed. Entry of valid commands (see lines 7 to 15) causes the appropriate action to be performed, after which execution moves to line 3 again.

$CHANGE$ starts out in entry mode if the argument was empty. In this mode, new characters are repeatedly accepted in line 24 and catenated to Z. If the entered line doesn't end with a space character, one is supplied so that words don't run together. Entry of a totally blank line causes a switch to edit mode as in the previous paragraph. You can switch from edit mode to entry mode with the I command. Whatever follows I becomes part of the newly entered text.

```
        NT←CHANGE ''
BECAUSE THE ARGUMENT WAS EMPTY, WE START IN
ENTRY MODE AND STAY THERE UNTIL AN ENTIR
ELY BLANK LINE IS INPUT.

BECAUSE THE ARGUMENT WAS EMPTY, WE START IN ENTRY         1
LENTIRELY
NOT FOUND
BECAUSE THE ARGUMENT WAS EMPTY, WE START IN ENTRY         1
LENTIR
ENTIR ELY BLANK LINE IS INPUT.                          80
/////////COMPLETELY
COMPLETELY BLANK LINE IS INPUT.                         80
B20
STAY THERE UNTIL AN COMPLETELY BLANK LINE IS INPUT      60
                          /
 COMPLETELY BLANK LINE IS INPUT.                        78
                            IHERE WE SWITCH
BACK TO ENTRY MODE.

HERE WE SWITCH BACK TO ENTRY MODE.                      111
                        /AND BACK AGAIN TO EDIT MODE.
AND BACK AGAIN TO EDIT MODE.                            144
B10
CH BACK TO ENTRY MODEAND BACK AGAIN TO EDIT MODE.       123
                    / A
 AND BACK AGAIN TO EDIT MODE.                           144
0
BECAUSE THE ARGUMENT WAS EMPTY, WE START IN ENTRY         1
F
MODE AND STAY THERE UNTIL A COMPLETELY BLANK LINE       51
STOP
UNKNOWN COMMAND
MODE AND STAY THERE UNTIL A COMPLETELY BLANK LINE       51
END
        20↑NT
BECAUSE THE ARGUMENT
```

Although it doesn't contribute to our discussion of ⍞, $CHANGE$ needs a companion function, $COMPOSE$, to produce final copy. The right argument is a vector of $CHANGE$d text, and the left argument is whatever maximum line width you want.

```
        ∇COMPOSE[□]∇                        40 COMPOSE NT
      ∇ N COMPOSE TEXT;P              BECAUSE THE ARGUMENT WAS EMPTY, WE START
 [1]    LOOP:→(N≤ρTEXT)/MORE ◇ TEXT ◇ →0   IN ENTRY MODE AND STAY THERE UNTIL A
 [2]    MORE:P←(TEXT=' ')/ιρTEXT      COMPLETELY BLANK LINE IS INPUT. HERE WE
 [3]    P←¯1↑N,(P≤N+1)/P             SWITCH BACK TO ENTRY MODE AND BACK AGAIN
 [4]    P↑TEXT ◇ TEXT←P↓TEXT ◇ →LOOP  TO EDIT MODE.
      ∇
```

Escaping from quote-quad

The following program has a fatal flaw. It swallows up whatever you enter at the keyboard like an APL equivalent of the video game PacMan:

```
        ∇TEXT←GOTCHA
 [1]    TEXT←''
 [2]    MORE:'GIMME SOME WORDS'
 [3]    TEXT←TEXT,⍞
 [4]    →MORE∇
```

No matter what you type (including character errors) the program continues to gobble up your input (until you ultimately reach *WS FULL*). You can't even sign off because *')OFF'* would just be catenated to *TEXT*! But there is an emergency escape from situations like this—entering the sequence *O* backspace *U* backspace *T* RETURN will rescue you, as will use of the CLEAR or PA2 keys or their equivalent on terminals that don't have a backspace. The exact form of rescue may differ, though on most systems you will be suspended. Check *)SI* to be safe.

Needless to say, programs that don't include a graceful way to escape a ⍞ loop shouldn't be written. Plan for some sequence of characters which when entered will provide an escape from the loop. Typical escapes are entry of a blank line, or only the RETURN key, or some word like *END*, *STOP*, *QUIT* or *HELP*. It's very important for the program to tell the user what his choices are and how to escape. Programs that don't are user-hostile, and they are largely responsible for the feeling of alienation that many people have for computers and computer programmers.

Prompts and replies on the same line

Most of the techniques described here differ significantly in their details from one system to another. You will need to try these ideas and experiment on your own to discover the idiosyncrasies of your system.

Just as in the expression *REPLY←,⍞* you move characters from the keyboard into the variable *REPLY*, in the expression *⍞←PROMPT* characters are being moved from the variable *PROMPT* to the terminal's printer or screen. Using this form of display, no new line signal is sent to the printer or screen. That means that if you follow *⍞←PROMPT* with an expression like *REPLY←,⍞*, then the prompt and reply are on the same line. In a very real sense ⍞ is a window between APL and the outside, sharing information between the two environments.

The following example shows how this feature, called *bare output* works in APLSV and VS APL:

```
      ∇ Z←BAREOUTPUT R                  REPLY←BAREOUTPUT 'ENTER YOUR NAME: '
 [1]    ⍞←R                     ENTER YOUR NAME: FLOYD
 [2]    Z←,⍞ ∇                          REPLY
                                                  FLOYD
                                 ρREPLY
                          22
```

REPLY has 22 elements because in these versions of APL the input is prefixed with as many space characters as there are characters in the prompt.

Removal of the blanks is easy. We'll change line 2 and reexecute to show that the result now has only the characters that were entered:

```
     ∇BAREOUTPUT[2]Z←(ρR)↓,⍞ ∇
     ρBAREOUTPUT 'ENTER YOUR NAME: '
ENTER YOUR NAME: FLOYD
5
```

On some other systems, the reply holds an image of the prompt instead of the blanks above. On still other systems only the characters that were typed in are retained. But APL2 lets you decide for yourself how to treat replies on the same line as the ⍞ prompt. Whatever value you set in the *prompt replacement* system variable is what goes into the reply. Its default value is ⎕PR←' ', which matches the behavior of APLSV and VS APL by supplying leading blanks. Here are some other values:

```
    ⎕PR←'∘'                                ⎕PR←''
    BAREOUTPUT 'TEST'                      BAREOUTPUT 'TEST'
TESTENTRY                              TESTENTRY
∘∘∘∘ENTRY                              ENTRY
```

Setting ⎕PR to an empty character vector, '', eliminates the leading blanks.

Evaluated input

One application of ⍞ input occurs so frequently that it has been given a separate symbol, the ⎕ (quad). When control in a line of APL reaches a ⎕, the prompt ⎕: is displayed. Whatever you enter on the keyboard is accepted as though you were in calculation mode, rather than accepting the characters literally as with ⍞. Informally, this is what ⎕ does in terms of ⍞:

```
       ∇R←QUADINPUT
[1]    ⍝ INFORMAL SIMULATION OF ⎕ FOR INPUT. DOES NOT HANDLE
[2]    ⍝ EDGE CONDITIONS SUCH AS ∇ FN DEF, )SYS COMMANDS, BLANK LINES
[3]    ⍞←'⎕:',⎕TCNL,6ρ' ' ◊ R←⍎⍞ ∇
```

The symbol ⍎ on line 3 was mentioned on page 117 and is called *execute*; it treats character vectors as though they were entered in calculation mode. (In other words, Z←⍎'2+3' or ⍎'Z←2+3' is equivalent to Z←2+3. More in Chapter 24). ⎕TCNL (page 238) makes the next display start on a new line.

Any valid APL expression can be entered through ⎕. Recall that the drill *TEACH* in workspace 1 *AIDRILL* accepts the student's replies through ⎕. Here is a much simpler computer drill—one to exercise a child's skills in elementary subtraction:

```
       SUB                                ∇ SUB;HELP;STOP;P1;P2
ENTER STOP TO STOP                 [1]     HELP←∘∘1 ◊ STOP←∘∘∘1
14-10                              [2]     'ENTER STOP TO STOP, HELP FOR HELP'
⎕:                                 [3]   L3:P1←?20
                                   [4]     P2←¯1+?P1+1
       4                           [5]     (⍕P1),'-',⍕P2
THATS RIGHT                        [6]   L6:→((1↑,⎕)=(P1-P2),HELP,STOP)/OK,HELP,0
19-7                               [7]     (⍕P2),' + ___ = ',(⍕P1),⎕TCNL,'TRY AGAIN'
⎕:                                 [8]     →L6
                                   [9]   OK:'THATS RIGHT'
       11                          [10]    →L3
7 + ___ = 19                       [11]  HELP:(P1ρ'∘'),' TAKE AWAY',⎕TCNL,P2ρ'∘'
TRY AGAIN                          [12]    →L6 ∇
⎕:

       HELP
∘∘∘∘∘∘∘∘∘∘∘∘∘∘∘∘∘∘∘ TAKE AWAY
∘∘∘∘∘∘∘
⎕:

       12
THATS RIGHT
11-9
⎕:

       STOP
```

Line 1 assigns values to *HELP* and *STOP* that are unlikely to be matched by a student's entry at the keyboard. On line 3 a random integer from 1 to 20 is stored in *P1*. *P2* is then assigned a random integer from 0 to *P*. This guarantees that *P2* will never be greater than *P1*, so that no problems requiring negative answers will be generated. Line 5 displays the problem. Line 6 accepts input, tests the correctness of the answer and branches. If *HELP* was entered, the branch is to line 11, where a hint is offered to the student. Entering *STOP* causes execution to cease.

If an incorrect answer is entered, line 7 rephrases the problem. If the problem is answered correctly this time we go to line 9 and then to line 3 for a new problem to solve.

In this exercise, *HELP* and *STOP* are local variables with unlikely (but arbitrary) values. This technique is a simple way to give programs a touch of user-friendliness, although for serious applications ⍞ should be used instead. Even in *SUB*, a student could cheat on the answer by replying with $P1-P2$; he would be right every time!

As with ⍞, it is possible to write loops including ⎕ which don't have planned escapes. Emergency escape from ⎕ input differs from one system to another. Try → or)RESET or BREAK or O backspace U backspace T. One or more of these will likely work.

Other uses and limitations of the quad

Don't get the impression from the previous section that ⎕ must be used only within defined functions. When entering voluminous data, ⎕ is very handy for coping with entries that would overrun the right margin. Suppose within some function there are lines like

```
[9]    'ENTER DATA'
[10]   'SUM IS ',⍕+/⎕
```

If the number of values being added is large, ⎕ can be used in the manner shown below:

```
ENTER DATA
⎕:
      5 9 14 6 3 12 15,⎕
⎕:
      6 2 3,(10ρ21),8,7,⎕
⎕:
      3 2 1
SUM IS 306
```

It works because ⎕ admits any APL expression, including ⎕ itself. A line of numeric input that ends with ,⎕ has the meaning 'to be continued.'

Here are some limitations of ⎕ input. You can't use it for function definition; it is intended only for APL statements which return an explicit result. System commands entered as ⎕ input are executed, but the response to the command isn't considered as input. If you reply to ⎕ with just a RETURN or spaces and RETURN, it acts as though you haven't entered anything and comes back with another ⎕: prompt. If your reply to ⎕ is a line with multiple statements, the rightmost statement must return an explicit result, or a *VALUE ERROR* is produced. *GAME* in this example does not have an explicit result:

```
        Z←⎕                          STMT1              ∇GAME[⎕]∇
⎕:                          5                        ∇ GAME
        STMT1←2+3 ◊ GAME             Z               [1]    MINE←DICE
1                           VALUE ERROR              [2]    YOURS←DICE
VALUE ERROR                          Z               [3]    ×MINE-YOURS
        Z←⎕                          ∧                        ∇
        ∧
```

⎕ can also be used on the left side of the assignment arrow. A statement like ⎕←2 3ρι6 has the same effect as simply 2 3ρ6; but to both display and store the values *STORE*←⎕←2 3ρι6 or ⎕←*STORE*←2 3ρι6 replaces the two statements *STORE*←2 3ρι6 ◊ *STORE*. Some APL experts always use ⎕← instead of implicit output because they feel the explicit reference makes the programs more readable.

If you are lost in some horribly complicated APL line trying to figure out what went wrong, it may be helpful to temporarily embed ⎕← at critical points to detail the sequence of events, as we demonstrate on our old friend *HYP*. ⎕← used in this way serves as a trace within the line.

```
        ∇HYP[⎕]∇                           ∇HYP[1⎕10]
      ∇ C←A HYP B               [1]     C←((A*2)+B*2)*0.5
[1]     C←((A*2)+B*2)*0.5               22    2
      ∇                         [1]     C←(⎕←(⎕←A*2)+⎕←B*2)*0.5
                                [2]   ∇
        3 HYP 4                        →1
5                               16 144 10000
        3 5 HYP 4 12 100        9 25
LENGTH ERROR                    LENGTH ERROR
HYP[1] C←((A*2)+B*2)*0.5        HYP[1] C←(⎕←(⎕←A*2)+⎕←B*2)*0.5
       ∧                               ∧
```

Conversions of character input to numeric values

Many large commercial applications have need to accept voluminous numeric data from the terminal. Often the people assigned to entering the data are not experienced in the use of computers. To err is human; to forgive is user-friendly. So it is important that your programs handle input errors gently. For that reason, most applications use ▯ input instead of ▯, with the input being checked in the program for errors before being converted to numeric values.

The usual means of doing the conversion is with the execute function, ♠ (see Chapter 24). However, input validation must be done first or else the program may suspend with errors from invalid data. In both Sharp and APL*PLUS Systems, monadic system functions $\Box FI$ and $\Box VI$ are provided to do this efficiently. $\Box FI$ takes as its argument a character vector (or scalar) and converts it to a vector of numbers, using a subset of the rules for ▯ input. If there is anything in the argument that can't be converted, a zero is placed in that position of the result.

```
      □FI '10    25.4 9'                    □FI '10 23SKIDOO 9 ¯.25'
10 25.4 9                            10  0  9 ¯0.25
```

To distinguish between true zeros and those arising from bad data, the system function $\Box VI$ may be used. It accepts the same arguments as $\Box FI$, but returns a vector with 1's in the positions where the result is valid, and 0's where it isn't.

```
      □VI '10    25.4 9'                    □VI '10 23SKIDOO 9 ¯.25'
1  1  1                            1  0  1  1
```

$\Box FI$ and $\Box VI$ are both usually employed in a sequence like this:

```
      INPUT←,▯
      →(0ε□VI INPUT)/ERRORANALYSIS
      DATA←□FI INPUT
```

Friendly design

The last section described facilities for checking and cleaning up entries and thereby protecting naive users from the consequences of their limited experience. It is a fact that input and output considerations consume a vast amount of the time and energy of computer people. Perhaps more than any other single factor, properly designed input and output is what lets non-computer people use computers. Imagine the chaos that would result if an automatic bank teller machine didn't have built-in error checking to exclude unacceptable input!

When someone begins using an application, he benefits by explicit prompts and unabbreviated replies, all of which tend to reinforce learning the application. As he gains experience, the prompts can become more terse, and abbreviated replies are sufficient. This holds true for most applications. $YESORNO$ at the beginning of this chapter is a trite example of generic prompting functions.

Most commercial APL systems feature libraries of prompting and input functions that can be embedded in your applications. If you have access to such functions, you should use them rather than write your own, because they save development time and tend to make for more consistent use of prompts and input conventions across diverse applications.

We've only hinted at some of the ways to deal with naive users so far. Those of you who will be designing applications for others to run should always take the user's viewpoint, skill and experience level to heart. Test your work on people who are representative of the ultimate audience. Don't rely on your own judgment; the fact that you've arrived here in this book says you are no longer a novice, and prompts that suit you may be too cryptic for a truly naive user.

Direct communication with the operator and other users

Most time-shared APL systems provide ways to send messages to other users via shared files or shared variables. The messages are kept in a common file until the intended recipient decides to read his 'mail.' However, there is occasional need to contact another user immediately, and system commands are provided for this purpose. The system command $)PORTS$ gives a listing of *port numbers* (remember your first sign-on in Chapter 1?) and the three-letter codes for the users presently signed on. This command, as well as the message commands described below, is usually not supported on personal computer systems when used as a stand-alone, since there is no one else to send messages to.

```
     )PORTS
OPR OPE      036 LGI      226 ADF
003 AJR      064 JIL
035 LMB      079 KEI
```

In the interests of privacy, the $)PORTS$ command is usually restricted on commercial APL systems. But if you know the three-letter code, say, JIL, for the person you want to reach, you can enter

```
     )PORT JIL
064 JIL
```

You can communicate with that person by the $)MSG$ or $)MSGN$ commands. The command consists of $)MSG$ or $)MSGN$ followed by the port number and your one-line message.

```
     )MSG 64 THIS IS AL. DID YOU FIX THE PLANNING PROGRAM?
```

The message will not be sent while the other user is typing, and your keyboard is locked during that time. As soon as he enters a RETURN, the message will appear on his terminal,

```
003:R THIS IS AL. DID YOU FIX THE PLANNING PROGRAM?
```

and you will get the message $SENT$ on your terminal. If you used $)MSGN$ instead of $)MSG$ (i.e., no reply expected, as evidenced by the absence of R in the message received), your terminal unlocks as soon as the message $SENT$ appears on your terminal. In either case, a lock can be broken at any time by BREAK, but $MESSAGE$ $LOST$ appears on your terminal if you do so prematurely.

A message can be sent to the computer operator with the command $)OPR$ or $)OPRN$, followed by your message. With $)OPR$, your terminal remains locked, while it becomes available for use immediately after the $SENT$ message is you used $)OPRN$.

```
     )OPR A.J. ROSE HERE; MAY I PLEASE HAVE 2 MORE WORKSPACES?
SENT
OPR: DONE ... /BETSY
     )OPRN THANKS
SENT
```

Good manners are even more important in the use of APL's message commands than in voice telephone communication. Do not send messages capriciously, as you may disturb some important report being prepared by the other user. Remember also that a one-line printed message cannot carry your voice inflections, so be very explicit when you request something or when you reply to a request for information.

To avoid the intrusion of a message while you are working at the terminal, use $\Box MSGR$ $'OFF'$. Then no one (except the operator to advise you of an emergency) can send you a message. The would-be sender is informed (by seeing $INCOMMUNICADO$) that you're not willing to take messages. When you're ready to receive them again, use $\Box MSGR$ $'ON'$.

You can use $\Box KEYB$ $'LOCK'$ to place your terminal in a permanently locked state, so that messages can be received even if you've stepped away from the terminal. To use the terminal, just press BREAK before each line of input. To restore the keyboard to its normal state use $\Box KEYB$ $'OPEN'$.

$\Box KEYB$ and $\Box MSGR$, along with $\Box HT$ and $\Box PW$ (to be introduced later in this chapter), are session-related system variables. That means that their values don't get reset when you $)LOAD$ a new workspace, but rather they stay until sign-off or until you deliberately reset them.

Special characters

Most terminals have features such as backspace, linefeed, new line, and bells (or even whistles) that you may wish to exercise. Inside APL, these features are represented as characters; for example, if you had a character vector containing `'OVERBAR'`, three backspace characters, and three overbars (`'¯'`), then on most terminals it would display as $OVER\overline{BAR}$.

The rub is there's no direct way to enter the backspace character from the keyboard. But there are ways to get it. The system variable □*AV* (atomic vector) contains the entire character set, including overstruck characters like ⍉, ⍐ and ≠, as well as terminal control characters such as the backspace.

The definition of □*AV* is completely dependent on the particular implementation of APL being used. Hence, you should avoid expressions with □*AV* within functions which may be transferred to a different version of APL.

All is not lost, however, since some systems provide the more useful special characters in an alternate form:

Character	Sharp, SV	□AV position VS	APL2	APL*PLUS	special terminal character APL2	APL*PLUS
linefeed	160	170	38	202	□TC[3]	□TCLF
backspace	165	38	23	201	□TC[1]	□TCBS
new line	157	74	22	203	□TC[2]	□TCNL
idle	1	1	1	205		□TCNUL
audible tone				204		□TCBEL

For other characters consult your local information center, system manager or system manual.

Some of the 256 elements of □*AV* may produce weird results on your terminal; some are associated with characters not reproducible with your particular display or keyboard printer; and some may vary from country to country. There are even combinations of characters which have a particular significance on specific terminals. For instance, a user of the Tektronix 4015 graphics terminal on APLSV may blank the screen by entering □*AV*[47 92 47 91] or trigger the Tektronix 2631 hard copy unit with □*AV*[47 92 47 87]. On other terminals these instructions would simply appear as ωFωE and ωFωA respectively, or as pure gibberish.

Sophisticated APL programmers occasionally employ □*AV* to save space when storing data which is known to have 256 or fewer different possible values. For example, imagine dealing with survey data in which multiple choice replies were 1 2 3 4 5 6. Storing each value as an integer would consume 32 bits (on IBM 370 or equivalent systems; varies on other systems). If you were to convert each value to character, as in $CODED\leftarrow$□*AV*[*INTEGERS*], there would be a four-fold saving in space because each character consumes only 8 bits (see page 224). You can reconstitute the original values by □*AV* ⍳ *CODED* whenever you need them. Caution: if you use this technique, do not attempt to display the coded values on your terminal. It may produce unpredictable results and might even cause physical damage!

Getting the most out of your terminal

APL can be run on a wide variety of terminals. For much of what you do with APL you don't have to worry about the type of terminal you are using; however, you can take advantage of the special features of your terminal if you want to.

If your terminal is equipped with horizontal tabs, you can speed up significantly the printing of reports with a lot of 'white space' between the columns of information. Some screen display terminals come with built-in tab stops, usually 6 apart. To use them simply inform the APL system you are using tabs with □*HT*←6×⍳20 for a terminal with 120 characters per line, or □*HT*←6×⍳13 for one with 80 characters.

Printing terminals usually require that you set their physical or electronic tab stops. Page 240 gives an example of setting tabs. Once they are set, use the □*HT* system variable to inform the APL system where you have set the tabs. Some systems require that tabs be evenly spaced (i.e. some multiple of ⍳*N*) but IBM APL systems are more permissive, allowing any integer values up to the width of the printer. You then proceed without any further consideration of tabs. Whenever it takes less time for APL to tab over to the next printed position (rather than spacing over), it will do so automatically. □*HT* by itself gives you the present tab settings.

For input, entry of the TAB key is treated exactly like the equivalent number of spaces. A novel application of this involves using ⍞ input to build the rows of a character matrix. If the tabs are set to the column dimension of the result matrix, then tabbing to the next typed word ensures that the result matrix will have text left-justified on each row.

Here is an example with tabs set at 10, 20, 30 etc. The symbol ⍈ denotes where the TAB key was pressed:

```
      □HT←6×⍳20                                ρT
      ∇R←INPUT                          3  10
[1]   R←,⍞ ◇ R←(⌈(ρR)÷10),10)ρR ∇              T
      T←INPUT                          PICKLES
PICKLES⍈ONIONS⍈KETCHUP⍈                ONIONS
                                       KETCHUP
```

Not all terminals can print the same number of characters on a line. For example, many desktop printing terminals provide 130 or more characters per line, but screen display devices often provide only 40, 64 or 80. Professional business reports should be designed to fit on the narrowest terminal likely to be used for the application, to ensure that nothing is lost by trying to display lines too long to fit. Most APL systems assume a display width of 60 to 130 characters. Longer displays are continued on following lines. You can usually tell when a display has been continued because all lines after the first are indented six spaces.

If your application requires it, and if your terminal has the physical capability, you can vary the print or display width from 30 to about 250 characters. The way to do it is with the □PW (print width) system variable.

```
      □PW
130
      □PW←60
      90ρ'1234567890'
1234567890123456789012345678901234567890123456789012345678901234567890
      1234567890123456789012345678901234567890

      ÷⍳10
1 0.5 0.3333333333 0.25 0.2 0.1666666667 0.1428571429
      0.125 0.1111111111 0.1

      □PW←50
      90ρ'1234567890'
1234567890123456789012345678901234567890123456789012345678901234567890
      1234567890123456789012345678901234567890
```

As you can see, character displays are broken at exactly the specified width, but numeric displays are broken earlier to avoid splitting a value in the middle. The □PW system variable is handy when you have to make emergency use of a terminal that is narrower than your usual one, or when your application requires wide lines and you have access to a terminal with suitable width.

The print width setting is ignored for entry of data from the terminal. Even if the print width is set to 50, you are free to enter characters up to the right margin. Similarly, direct messages from the operator or other users ignore the print width.

Many screens don't need the built-in delays and idles required by electromechanical typewriter-style terminals, and on some systems the □TERM system function can be used. □TERM 'NOIDLES' removes all delays; □TERM 'IDLES' restores them.

To permit the use of new overstruck symbols on display terminals such as the IBM 3278, which doesn't have a backspace character, APL2 includes the system command)PBS followed by a nonblank character of your choice. If, for example, you entered)PBS ←, then to simulate the equal underbar ≡, you enter =←_ or _←=. Only legitimate new overstruck characters can be represented in APL2 (at this writing) in this way (⍒ ⍳ ⍷ ≡ ⍇ ⍈ ⍤).

For applications that might be run at a variety of terminals, such as electronic mail applications for traveling executives, the program can even determine the terminal type (□TT, but interpretation varies from system to system) and set □PW, □HT and □TERM to suit.

If a given application will be run so frequently as to dominate the use of the terminal, you should consider acquiring the right terminal for that job. This means shopping carefully and evaluating the features. You can get a good start by reading 'A Consumers' Guide to Choosing an APL Terminal', by Carl M. Cheney and Scott N. McAuley, pages 356-367 of *APL In Practice* (Wiley, 1980).

Arbitrary output and input

The rest of this chapter discusses features and details useful for tailored input and output applications, including intersystem communication and making the terminal do tricks. You may safely skip it without loss of continuity.

APL*PLUS and Sharp APL Systems provide the system functions, $\Box ARBOUT$ and $\Box ARBIN$ which, while a little trickier to use than $\Box AV$, give you total control and flexibility in moving information between the computer, the terminal and the outside world.

$\Box ARBOUT$ is a monadic system function which does not have an explicit result. Rather, it sends unadorned byte sequences to the terminal without any delays, idles, linefeeds or other padding that is normally transmitted when producing character results on the terminal. It is inadvisable to rely on the $\Box HT$ settings when using $\Box ARBOUT$ because the terminal needs certain delays and padding to physically move the printing mechanism to the right position. Ironically, the tab stops themselves are usually set by a $\Box ARBOUT$ sequence. For instance, to set tabs on a NEC Spinwriter to correspond to $\Box HT \leftarrow 10 \times \iota 10$, use the sequence $\Box ARBOUT$ 27 55, 120ρ(10ρ32),27 49.

To switch the display of a Human Design Systems Concept 400 terminal from white-on-black to black-on-white (i.e., reverse video image), the terminal must first be placed in 'programmer mode' by $\Box ARBOUT$ 27 85, and then $\Box ARBOUT$ 27 68 will produce the reverse image (found by reading the HDS manual):

```
      ⎕ARBOUT 27 85 27 68
'THIS IS BLACK ON WHITE'
```

Now all following displays show as black on white. You can switch back to white-on-black by $\Box ARBOUT$ 27 100, and disable programmer mode with $\Box ARBOUT$ 27 117.

But suppose you want to switch to and from reverse image in the middle of a line. To do that, use $\Box ARBOUT$ for the entire line, including the characters that you would normally print directly. The phrase *WATCH IT SWITCH* is coded into the argument here:

```
      ⎕ARBOUT 119 97 116 99 104 32 27 100 105 116,⎕
⎕:
      27 68 32 115 119 105 116 99 104 13
WATCH IT SWITCH
```

The numbers in $\Box ARBOUT$'s argument correspond to ASCII (American Standard Code for Information Interchange) codes and can be found in their published tables. Because APL overstruck characters like ⍵ aren't in the table, they are formed with sequences such as 79 8 63 or 63 8 79.

Just as you can send any arbitrary byte pattern from the computer to the terminal, you can also send arbitrary patterns from the terminal or other input device to the computer. $\Box ARBIN$ is a function (monadic or dyadic depending on the system) that accepts signals from an outside source (typically the keyboard but could be an analog sensor, voice input, bar code reader, or whatever) and translates those signals to $\Box ARBOUT$-compatible values. $\Box ARBIN$'s right argument is a prompt, and it works much like $\Box ARBOUT$. To suppress the prompt just use $\iota 0$.

On the APL*PLUS VM System, $\Box ARBIN$ is monadic, as shown by the following:

```
      ARB←⎕ARBIN 101 110 116 101 114 62 ⍝  ⎕ARBIN VALUES FOR 'ENTER:'
ENTER:THIS IS O̅V̅E̅R̅
      ARB
244 232 233 243 160 233 243 160 239 246 229 242 136 136 136 13
6 192 192 192 192 141
      ⎕ARBOUT ARB
THIS IS O̅V̅E̅R̅
```

Every keystroke is taken verbatim, which means that there are three elements for APL overstruck characters such as ⍝. $\Box ARBIN$'s result may differ from the expected value in the ASCII table by 128, depending on how the parity switch on the terminal was set. It's always safe to resolve that by $ARB \leftarrow 128 | ARB$.

Intersystem communication and distributed computing

On STSC's APL*PLUS systems for small computers, $\square ARBIN$ is a dyadic function. The right argument, which may be character, is the prompt, and the left argument is an integer vector specifying how, where and when the signals will be sent.

element no.	possible values	meaning
1 outbound	0	No outport used
	1	Send to first serial (ASCII) port
	2	Send to second serial port
	3	Send to parallel port (usually a printer)
	4 - 15	Other ports or peripheral devices
2 inbound	0	No response is expected
	1	Response comes from first serial port
	2 - 15	Response comes from designated port
3 translation	$^{-}1$	Untranslated numeric codes are transmitted and received
	0 - 2	Various ASCII translations (0 is normal for APL)
	3	IBM and Epson parallel printer graphics mode
4 protocol	0 - 3	3 is normal for many time sharing computers
5 wait	positive integer	If no response in this number of seconds, continue execution of program (called a dead-man timer)
	0	No response expected; no wait (similar to use of $\square ARBOUT$)
	negative integer	Infinite wait
6 char limit	positive integer	Maximum number of characters accepted in response
	0	Default value (check for your computer)
7 terminators	list of values, 0 to 255	$\square ARBIN$ stops accepting data when any transmission code in the list is encountered (the list can be empty)

What this all means is that $\square ARBIN$ will send information to, and accept information from, the ports designated in elements 1 and 2. It will stop accepting signals when the time limit has been reached, or the maximum number of characters has been received, or a terminating code was entered or the BREAK key was pressed.

$\square INKEY$ is a special niladic system function for working with the display screen to do full-screen management. It accepts a single keystroke, which may occur anywhere on the screen. As soon as you have entered one keystroke, the program resumes (without waiting for you to press RETURN). In this manner you can manage the screen on a character by character basis.

If you use a line like $REP \leftarrow 1\ 1\ 0\ 1\ 20\ 250\ 7\ 10\ 13\ \square ARBIN\ 'PROMPT'$, it means you are sending $PROMPT$ to serial port 1, and you expect a reply to come from there as well. Input continues to be accepted until 20 seconds have elapsed since the last character was entered, or 250 characters have been received, or a RETURN, LINEFEED or BACKSPACE has been entered. The result will be characters.

You can tell which one of the termination rules stopped the transmission by looking at the last element of the result (caution, system dependent):

last value in result	what caused termination	relevant elements
One of the termination codes	Termination code encountered	7 and beyond
129 or $\square AV[129+\square IO]$	Time limit exceeded	5
130 or $\square AV[130+\square IO]$	Character count exceeded	6
131 or $\square AV[131+\square IO]$	BREAK was pressed	not applicable

The most important thing about $\square ARBIN$ is that with it you can use a low-cost personal computer such as the TRS80 Model III or the IBM Personal Computer as an intelligent node of a distributed computing network. A typical configuration might consist of several IBM PCs attached via modems to a time-sharing APL system running in a VM environment on an IBM 3081 or other large-scale computer.

The function *ET* (for executed transmission) lets the remote user phone his home base and transfer data between the time-sharing computer and the personal computer. *ET* is a rather primitive function, but it does demonstrate distributed computing capabilities. Assume the time-sharing computer's active workspace is 1 *CLASS*. The dialogue below is on the remote personal computer:

```
        )CLEAR
CLEAR WS

        ∇Z←ET R
[1]     ⍝ EXECUTES R ON TIME+SHARING COMPUTER
[2]     ⍝ RESULT TRANSMITTED TO REMOTE PERSONAL COMPUTER
[3]     Z←1 1 0 1 ¯1 32000 7 ⎕ARBIN R,⎕TCNL ⍝ STOP ON ⎕TCBEL
[4]     ⍝ TO TIME+SHARING COMPUTER, APPEARS AS KEYBOARD USER
[5]     Z←2↓¯9↑Z ⍝ CHOP OFF TRANSMISSION EMBELLISHMENTS - MAY VARY ON OTHER SYSTEMS
[6]     Z←(Z≠⎕TCLF)/Z ⍝ MAY VARY ON OTHER SYSTEMS
[7]     ∇
        ET ')LOAD 1 CLASS'
SAVED  21.53.11 02/19/83

        LV←ET ')WSID'

        LV
IS 1 CLASS

        ⎕←X←ET 'TAB1'
1.414213562 1.732050808 2 2.236067977

        ⍴X ⍝ X IS CHARACTERS
37
        X←⍎X ⍝ CONVERT TO NUMERIC
```

The transactions above moved an image of *TAB*1 on the time-sharing computer into *X* on the personal computer. Data and programs can also be moved from the personal computer to the time-sharing computer:

```
        X←X+3
        ET 'NEWX←',⍕X
        ET 'NEWX'
4.414213562 4.732050808 5 5.236067977

        NEWX
VALUE ERROR
        NEWX
        ∧
```

We generated that last *VALUE ERROR* on purpose to demonstrate that *NEWX* is in the time-sharing computer, not the personal computer.

Elaborations of this general idea of intercommunicating computers make possible such sophisticated activities as a small personal computer programmed to dial a larger one to access a database, or to hand off some computing task that's too intensive for a small machine.

PROBLEMS

1. Define a function that will give multiplication drill with integers $?N$ for some argument N in the header. Have your function print a message TRY $AGAIN$ for wrong answers. Use $STOP$ as a variable for escape from the function.

2. Modify your answer to the above problem so that three tries are allowed, after which the correct answer is printed and another problem is posed.

3. Add a further refinement to the multiplication drill so that when $HELP$ is typed, the answer to the problem is given as $X[1]$ rows of $X[2]$ stars each, with an appropriate message and a repetition of the problem. X is the vector of random integers generated in the problem.

4. Still another refinement: keep track of the number of right answers and display the percent right when finished.

5. Since quote-quad input doesn't prompt with ⍞, show how to force literal input and display ⍞ at the same time.

6. Replace the message TRY $AGAIN$ on line 6 of $SPELL$ (in 1 $CLASS$) with a statement that reveals the answer.

7. Define a function $ENTER$ that will take the literal spelling of numbers, like those in SPL (in 1 $CLASS$), and put them in successive rows of a 20-column matrix. Exit from the function will be effected by entering an empty vector.

8. Define a dyadic function $LIST$ that lets you input and list a specified number of names of specified length.

9. Write a monadic function $LOOKUP$ whose right argument is a list L of names in matrix form, and which asks you to input a name to be looked up by the function, identifies its row location(s), or prints an appropriate message.

10. Define a function $BALANCE$ to prompt for an opening balance and a vector of transactions (positive for deposits and negative for withdrawals) and produce a report showing the opening and closing balances, total deposits and total withdrawals.

11. Write a function whose syntax is $Z \leftarrow MAT$ INS N to prompt for a vector to be inserted after row N in a literal array MAT.

12. Define a function $MONTHLYINPUT$ to ask for 12 months of data and a control total. If the control total equals the sum of the first 12 numbers, the program should return these 12 numbers as a result. Any error should cause an appropriate error message to be printed and prompt for the numbers again.

Chapter 24: Advanced programming features and techniques for controlling exceptions

With the rapid spread of microcomputers and the phenomenal growth of end-user application packages designed for them, there has developed great interest in the concept of user friendly programs. This chapter will concentrate on those features of APL that will, when properly used, dissuade users from heading for the nearest bar to drown their frustrations.

Consider the following compound interest program, which was written to be used by a friend who doesn't like computers:

```
        ∇SAVINGS;PIN;P;I;R;CF
[1]     TOP:'ENTER PRINCIPAL, INTEREST RATE AND NUMBER OF PERIODS'
[2]     PIN←□
[3]     P←PIN[1] ◊ I←PIN[2] ◊ N←PIN[3]
[4]     CF←P×(1+I)*⍳N
[5]     'BALANCE EACH PERIOD ',8 2⍕CF ∇
        SAVINGS
ENTER PRINCIPAL, INTEREST RATE AND NUMBER OF PERIODS

□:
        1000 .08 4.5
DOMAIN ERROR
SAVINGS[4]  CF←P×(I-1)*⍳N
                   ∧
```

A person who started out with a dislike for computers would not be won over by the display above. While professionals understand the meaning and intent of the diagnostic message *DOMAIN ERROR*, its tone is unfriendly to the naive user.

We would like to insulate unwitting users from such messages. There are two traditional means of keeping the user out of trouble: the first is to admonish the user to follow the instructions precisely (e.g., put in a positive integer only, or else suffer embarrassment or frustration). The second is for the application developer to anticipate every possible thing that can go wrong (ha!) and include steps to deal with these potential errors, or events, or exceptions. The first approach is inhumane to the user; the second is inhumane to the developer. If one had to choose between the two, the recommended choice would be to put the burden on the developer to do it right.

Error trapping

Some modern APL systems provide a third option, to 'trap' the unfriendly message just before it is displayed, replace it by something less offensive, and even fix or bypass the problem and keep running. The underlying philosophy is that an error is an exception to the normal running of the program. The default behavior of APL when an exception happens is to display the cause of the exception and halt execution.

On APL*PLUS Systems, □*ELX* (for exception *latent* expression) is used to change what the system does when an exception (i.e, an error like *DOMAIN ERROR*) happens. You assign □*ELX* as a character vector holding whatever APL statement you would like executed should an error occur.

For example, if you wanted the *SAVINGS* program to print 'I CANNOT UNDERSTAND YOUR REQUEST, PLEASE TRY AGAIN' and branch to line 1, set

```
□ELX←'MESSAGE◊→TOP'
MESSAGE←'I CANNOT UNDERSTAND YOUR REQUEST, PLEASE TRY AGAIN'
```

```
        SAVINGS
ENTER PRINCIPAL, INTEREST RATE AND NUMBER OF PERIODS
□:
        1000 .08 4.5
I CANNOT UNDERSTAND YOUR REQUEST, PLEASE TRY AGAIN

ENTER PRINCIPAL, INTEREST RATE AND NUMBER OF PERIODS
□:
        1000 .08 5
BALANCE EACH PERIOD   1080.00 1166.40 1259.71 1360.49 1469.33
```

Now, when an error happens, regardless of what error it is, whatever is in $\Box ELX$ gets executed rather than the normal system behavior of displaying the diagnostic message and halting. You can even take different actions depending on the type of error, since $\Box DM$ (next section) holds the text of the diagnostic message. $\Box ELX$'s default value is '$\Box DM$'; that is, display the error message (and halt execution).

A similar facility is found on APL2. There the dyadic system function $\Box EA$ (for execute alternate) is used. Its right argument is the APL expression you wish to compute; and its left argument is what to do if there is an exception in the right argument.

```
        ∇SAVINGS[4] '→ERCODE' □EA 'CF←P×(1+I)*ιN'
[5]     →0 ⍝ NORMAL EXIT
[6]     ERCODE:'I CANNOT UNDERSTAND YOUR REQUEST, PLEASE TRY AGAIN'
[7]     →TOP ∇
```

Analyzing the diagnostic message

For both versions above, the same treatment was given without regard to the type of the exception or where it happened. Most professional applications benefit by more detailed analysis of the nature of the exception; depending on what happened it might be possible to make changes and move on. For example, you might decide that a noninteger N could be rounded up, but other exceptions, such as character data, should result in a halt.

Both APL*PLUS and APL2 capture the most recent diagnostic message, albeit somewhat differently. On the APL*PLUS System, the system variable $\Box DM$ is a character vector holding the last diagnostic message encountered ($\Box DM$ is an empty vector if no exceptions have happened). On APL2, the same information is in the system variable $\Box EM$ (for event message), but as a character matrix. $\Box EM$ starts out as 3 0ρ' '.

```
        ρ□DM ⍝ APL*PLUS SYSTEMS            ρ□EM ⍝ APL2 SYSTEM
63                                    3 25
        □DM                               □EM
DOMAIN ERROR                          DOMAIN ERROR
SAVINGS[4]   CF←P×(1+I)*ιN            SAVINGS[4]   CF←P×(1+I)*ιN
                   ^                                    ^
```

The first row of $\Box EM$ contains the error message, the second the offending statement, and in the third carets point to where the error occurred and the extent of the execution prior to the error. There may be further information in following rows.

```
        ⍙'1 2+3 4 5'
LENGTH ERROR
        1 2+3 4 5
        ^   ^
        ⍙'1 2+3 4 5'
        ρ□EM
5 18
```

APL2 provides additional information about the most recent event or exception with $\Box ET$, for event type. Its value starts as 0 0, and is reset by each error. At this writing, there are 32 codes:

0 0	No error	3 1	*VALUE*, name with no value
0 1	Unclassified (monadic *□ES*)	3 2	*VALUE*, no result for function
1 1	*INTERRUPT* (attn)		
1 2	*SYSTEM ERROR*	4 1	Implicit *□PP ERROR*
1 3	*WS FULL*	4 2	Implicit *□IO ERROR*
1 4	*SYSTEM LIMIT*, symbol table	4 3	Implicit *□CT ERROR*
1 5	*SYSTEM LIMIT*, shares	4 4	Implicit *□FC ERROR*
1 6	*SYSTEM LIMIT*, interface quota	4 5	Implicit *□RL ERROR*
1 7	*SYSTEM LIMIT*, interface capacity	4 6	Implicit *□MD ERROR*
1 8	*SYSTEM LIMIT*, array rank	4 7	Implicit *□PR ERROR*
1 9	*SYSTEM LIMIT*, array size		
1 10	*SYSTEM LIMIT*, array depth	5 1	*VALENCE ERROR*
1 11	*SYSTEM LIMIT*, prompt length	5 2	*RANK ERROR*
		5 3	*LENGTH ERROR*
2 1	*SYNTAX*, no array (3÷)	5 4	*DOMAIN ERROR*
2 2	*SYNTAX*, ill-formed line [( ]	5 5	*INDEX ERROR*
2 3	*SYNTAX*, name class 13←*A*	5 6	*AXIS ERROR*
2 4	*SYNTAX*, context (*X←Y*)←0		

Controlling interruptions

APL*PLUS Systems treat differently those exceptions caused by errors and those caused by the user pressing BREAK or ATTN. *□ALX*, for *attention latent expression*, works like *□ELX*, but traps only BREAKs. You would use it to prevent a program from halting in a critical section, such as an update of a database. For instance, place the statements *GLOBSW←0 ◊ □ELX←'→RESUME'*   prior to the critical section, with this program to handle the interruption:

```
      ∇Z←RESUME;□ALX
[1]   □ALX←'→□LC' ◊ GLOBSW←1 ⍝ LOCAL □ALX TO PREVENT SECOND INTERRUPTION HERE
[2]   'I AM WORKING ON A CRITICAL PART OF YOUR JOB'
[3]   'AND WILL HALT WHEN I GET TO A SAFE PLACE'
[4]   Z←1↓(0≠□LC)/□LC ∇
```

At the end of the critical section, reset *□ALX* to turn off its current action (if it was not localized), and test *GLOBSW* to see if an interrupt had been deferred.

Interruptions in APL2 are handled with *□EA* and the detection of the code 1 1 in *□ET*. There is also a dyadic *□FX* (*fix*) that can make a function uninterruptable. The left argument is a four-element vector consisting of ones and zeros signifying whether certain properties are active or not:

element	effect
1	function cannot be displayed or edited
2	function cannot be suspended
3	weak interrupts (attn or break) are ignored
4	most errors are changed to *DOMAIN ERROR*

A left argument value of 0 0 0 0 is equivalent to a normal unlocked function, and a value of 1 1 1 1 is equivalent to using ∇ to lock the function. In particular, setting element three to 1 prevents interruptions in the function.

□FX's right argument requirements will be covered later in this chapter, but for now you can impose the effects you want using sequences like 0 1 1 0 *□FX □CR 'FNNAME'*, where *FNNAME* is the name of the unlocked function that you want to make uninterruptable.

Simulating events

Sometimes when testing a new application system, you may need to simulate an error or event even though one hasn't happened. Or you may want the application to signal an exception to the function which called the currently executing function. The unmodified hypotenuse program below will display a diagnostic message and halt if its arguments disagree in shape or rank, or if either is character:

```
      )LOAD 1 CLASS
SAVED   14.45.33 02/20/83

      1 2 3 HYP 'ABC'
DOMAIN ERROR
HYP[1]  C←((A*2)+B*2)*0.5
               ^
      )RESET
```

Suppose we don't want to leave the function suspended, but prefer instead to compose a friendlier message and pass it to the calling environment. ⎕ERROR is an APL*PLUS monadic system function whose character argument is the message to be carried back to the calling environment; it will be displayed as though it were the diagnostic message.

```
      ∇HYP[0] C←A HYP B;⎕ELX
[1]   [.1]⎕ELX←'⎕ERROR ''PLEASE REENTER WITH A DIFFERENT '',(∧\⎕DM≠'' '')/⎕DM'∇
      3 5 HYP 4 12
5 13
      1 2 3 HYP 4 12
PLEASE REENTER WITH A DIFFERENT LENGTH
      1 2 3 HYP 4 12
               ^
      ⎕DM
PLEASE REENTER WITH A DIFFERENT LENGTH
      1 2 3 HYP 4 12
               ^
```

In the above example, ⎕ERROR doesn't actually get invoked unless an exception occurs which wakes up ⎕ELX. If ⎕ERROR's argument is empty, then ⎕ERROR does not become effective. This feature can be used to conveniently control conditional use of the facility.

In APL2, the event simulation system function is ⎕ES. In its dyadic form, the left argument is the character vector message to be carried back to the calling environment. The right argument is usually a two-element integer vector which sets ⎕ET.

Here is HYP in APL2 form:

```
      ∇C←A HYP2 B
[1]   'ALT' ⎕EA 'C←((A*2)+B*2)*.5'∇
      ∇ALT;ERTEXT
[1]   ERTEXT←(∧\(⎕EM[1;]≠' ')/⎕EM[1;] ⍝ UP TO FIRST SPACE
[2]   ('PLEASE REENTER WITH A DIFFERENT ',ERTEXT) ⎕ES ⎕ET ∇
```

As with ⎕ERROR, if ⎕ES's right argument is an empty vector, then ⎕ES does not become effective, permitting conditional control.

⎕ES also has a monadic form whose argument may be a character vector or scalar or a zero or two-element integer vector. Non-empty character vectors are displayed and an error condition generated in the statement executing the function containing ⎕ES. ⎕ET is set to 0 1 (unclassified). If the argument of ⎕ES is a two-element integer vector, it goes into ⎕ET and an event simulation generated in the statement executing the function containing ⎕ES, along with an error message if the argument is a legitimate error code for ⎕ET. Finally, if the argument is 0 0, the workspace is cleared unless the error is trapped with ⎕EA.

Controlling the environment

Normally, when a user signs onto an APL system, the terminal keyboard becomes 'open' to the user's taking control of the session. There are situations, however, where it is undesirable for the user to have such power. An automated banking application, for instance, would be chaotic if a customer were to gain control: he might break the bank!

We have already seen some control mechanisms in ⎕EA, ⎕ELX and ⎕ALX. Once a program starts running, control can be maintained with these. Still to be considered are ways to start a session under complete control, and how to keep control when a function completes.

The latent expression and variants of workspace loading

The system variable $\Box LX$ causes a workspace to 'come out running' in the sense that when it is loaded, a designated APL expression begins executing immediately:

```
      )CLEAR
CLEAR WS
      )COPY 1 CLASS SPELL SPL GO
SAVED  14.45.33 02/20/83

      ∇GO[□]∇
    ∇ GO
[1]   'TIME FOR YOUR SPELLING EXERCISE!'
[2]   □RL←⌈1000×□TS[6]
[3]   SPELL
    ∇

      □LX←'GO'
      )SAVE SPELIT
 14.43.44 02/26/83
```

The *latent expression* can be any APL expression held in a character vector. It is executed when the workspace is loaded, as seen from the following display:

```
      )LOAD SPELIT
SAVED  14.43.44 02/26/83

TIME FOR YOUR SPELLING EXERCISE!
5
FIVE
THATS RIGHT

8
EIGHT
THATS RIGHT
2
STOP
```

Besides making the use of application and tutorial workspaces convenient for non-APLers, the latent expression provides a valuable assist to restarting critical applications after a communications line failure. Since $\Box LX$ can be reassigned any number of times, you can store anticipatory resumption instructions in it. Particularly in shared file or shared variable applications (Chapters 27 and 28), you will probably need different resumption actions depending on whether a sequence of file updating statements was completed or not.

When a user signs on again after a line failure, his $CONTINUE$ workspace is loaded for him, and the latent expression executes. It may reactivate relevant files, and it should branch into the interrupted program at whatever line is appropriate (within noncritical sequences), or it should force a complete restart if there is no way to resume at the interruption.

On the APL*PLUS System, $\Box LX$ can be used in conjunction with $\Box LOAD$, $\Box QLOAD$ and $\Box XLOAD$ to develop application systems that encompass many workspaces, loading the next one automatically. Each initiates loading of a designated workspace. The argument is the name (and number and lock, if necessary) of the workspace to be loaded. An example is $\Box LOAD$ '1 $CLASS$'. $\Box LOAD$ and $\Box QLOAD$ operate identically, except that $\Box LOAD$ prints the $SAVED$ message while $\Box QLOAD$ does not.

Usually, the succeeding workspaces are saved with a latent expression set by the author of the application system. Just prior to executing $\Box LOAD$, all pertinent intermediate data is placed on a file. Then $\Box LOAD$ brings in the next workspace, and the latent expression brings in the data that was placed on the file and executes the main function of that workspace. Using these techniques, very large applications are tackled conveniently and economically.

$\Box XLOAD$ and its companion system command $)XLOAD$ cause the workspace to be loaded without the latent expression being activated. This is so that the application developer has a way to maintain the programs in an unencumbered manner. Only the owner of a workspace can load it with $\Box XLOAD$ or $)XLOAD$; other users are prohibited for security considerations.

Keeping control when the program stops

When a function stops running because of an untrapped exception or interruption, or a simulated event, or a □STOP, or even a normal finish, control is usually turned over to the user. But in some applications (or for some users) this may not be desirable; you may want the user to be prohibited from free-form use of the system, constraining him to the use of specific applications only. A global declaration of □EA or □ELX or □ALX (perhaps in □LX itself) will trap the exceptions. What remains to be discussed is what to do with the session if it can't be resumed or if the application has completed normally.

On APL2 you can force a *CLEAR WS* by using an expression like ('*CLEARING THE WORKSPACE*' □ES 0 0) as the left argument to □EA. That is, a □ES right argument of 0 0 is a special signal to clear the active workspace. This prevents users from poking around in the functions.

APL*PLUS systems clear the active workspace with the expression □SA '*CLEAR*'. □SA (for stop action) operates in a latent manner; that is, you can set it early in the program but it doesn't become effective until the function is about to halt. Of course, if you had set □ELX or □ALX they would dominate. □SA is the ultimate tool to use where □ELX or □ALX haven't been set, or where they themselves fail, or when the function completes normally.

Besides □SA '*CLEAR*' you can use □SA '*EXIT*' to have the same effect as → (i.e., clearing the □SI to the most recent suspension), or □SA '*OFF*' to sign off the system, or □SA '' to reset its original, default condition of no stop action.

Automatic program generation and modification

Since the earliest days of the stored program computer there has been speculation (mostly in jest, but some serious) about when computers would become self-perpetuating. We will not join this discussion here, except to note that one technological requirement for that to happen would be the ability of a computer to write computer programs by itself.

No, your APL system can't write or modify programs without your active participation. But it can reduce the amount of work you do by taking over virtually all aspects of the job except thinking. As such, your APL computer is considerably more than the mindless assistant we described in the opening pages of this book.

The rest of this chapter considers programs that help write programs and modify programs. The need for this ability is apparent: suppose you had written a 30-line function making frequent use of a local variable P and you now wish to change every occurrence of it to T. Or you may want to include in a function you are developing large chunks of other, existing functions. Making those changes manually is tedious work.

To modify a program, we will first convert it to a character variable because it is easy to make changes to character variables in APL. For example, to change all occurrences of the letter P in the vector VEC to T, use $VEC[(VEC='P')/\iota\rho VEC]\leftarrow'T'$. Then after the desired changes are made, the character variable is reconverted to a defined function.

The system function □CR (for canonical representation) produces a character matrix in which each row is a line of the function.

```
      )LOAD 1 CLASS
SAVED  14.45.33 02/20/83


      ∇SUB[□]∇
   ∇ SUB;HELP;STOP;P1;P2;BR
[1]   HELP←oo1 ◊ STOP←ooo1
[2]   L2:P1←?20 ◊ P2←¯1+?P1+1
[3]   (⍕P1),'-',⍕P2
[4]   L4:BR←(1↑,□)=(P1-P2),HELP,STOP
[5]   →BR/OK,HELP,0
[6]   (⍕P2),' +  ___  = ',(⍕P1)
[7]   'TRY AGAIN' ◊ →L4
[8]   OK:'THATS RIGHT' ◊ →L2
[9]   HELP:(P1ρ'o'),' TAKE AWAY'
[10]  P2ρ'o' ◊ →L4
    ∇
```

```
      XSUB←□CR 'SUB'
      ρXSUB
11 30
      XSUB
SUB;HELP;STOP;P1;P2;BR
HELP←oo1 ◊ STOP←ooo1
L2:P1←?20 ◊ P2←¯1+?P1+1
(⍕P1),'-',⍕P2
L4:BR←(1↑,□)=(P1-P2),HELP,STOP
→BR/OK,HELP,0
(⍕P2),' +  ___  = ',(⍕P1)
'TRY AGAIN' ◊ →L4
OK:'THATS RIGHT' ◊ →L2
HELP:(P1ρ'o'),' TAKE AWAY'
P2ρ'o' ◊ →L4
```

The name of the function to be worked on must be supplied as a character vector argument. There doesn't have to be any relation between the name of the function being converted and the name of the result, but you may find it convenient to choose related names.

The function header line becomes the first row of the result. Line numbers themselves, as well as the starting and closing ∇s, are stripped off. Each line of the function is left-justified, and the column dimension is determined by the number of characters in the longest line.

When you have a canonical representation of a function, you can apply all the character-manipulating tricks of APL to do function editing and searching for patterns. You could, for example, find the row and column positions of each occurrence of the letter P with this sequence:

```
     1+(ρXSUB)⊤¯1+('P'=,XSUB)/⍳ρ,XSUB
  1   1   1   1   2   2   3   3   3   4   4   5   5   5   6   7   7  10  10  11
  8  13  15  18   4  15   4  13  20   3  12  15  18  25  30  11   3  21   4   7   1
```

Let's change the message *TAKE AWAY* to *SUBTRACT* (note that line 9 of the function is row 10 of its character representation):

```
     XSUB[10;]←(1↓ρXSUB)↑'HELP:(P1ρ''∘''),'' SUBTRACT'''
```

We haven't changed the function *SUB* yet. All we've done is change the variable *XSUB*. A canonical representation is converted to a function by the monadic system function □*FX*, for *fix*:

```
     □FX XSUB
SUB
```

If the canonical representation is proper, □*FX* returns a character vector consisting of the name of the function. That the function has been replaced becomes obvious by displaying part of it in the normal manner:

```
     ∇SUB[□8]∇
[8]   OK:'THATS RIGHT' ◇ →L2
[9]   HELP:(P1ρ'∘'),' SUBTRACT'
[10]  P2ρ'∘' ◇ →L4
     ∇
```

The canonical representation being converted to a function must be properly formed. If the argument is numeric, you get *DOMAIN ERROR*. If it isn't a matrix, you get *RANK ERROR*. You can fix suspended or pendent functions, but no change takes place in the definition until execution is completed. It's best to clear the state indicator before making changes to functions.

Other errors, such as improperly formed headers, blank rows, unmatched quotes and characters which cannot be entered in normal function definition mode (like backspace) get you an explicit numeric result indicating the first row of the function that is causing the problem. To help catch these kinds of errors, people frequently use tools like this one to 'cover' □*FX*:

```
     ∇FIX[□]∇
   ∇ FIX X;Z
[1]   →(' '=1↑0ρZ←□FX X)/0
[2]   'CANNOT CONVERT ';X;' ERROR AT ';Z
   ∇
```

Besides □*CR*, APL*PLUS Systems offer □*VR*, for *vector representation*. Like □*CR*, it is monadic, and its argument is a character vector holding the name of a function. The result of □*VR* is a character vector, which when displayed looks exactly as though you had displayed the function in the normal manner. Both the starting and trailing ∇'s are in the vector. Also present are the line numbers in brackets, and a new line character at the end of each line. □*VR*'s result usually requires less space than that of □*CR* because there is no 'padding' to fill out short lines. Which one to use in a given application depends on space considerations and whether what you want to do is easier with the function in vector form or matrix form. Generally speaking, use □*CR* if you are displaying or changing entire lines; use □*VR* if the changes tend to be less structured. Doing things like changing all occurrences of *P*1 to *FIRSTNUM* is much easier with □*VR* than with □*CR*.

Here is a very useful function employing □*VR* to search and modify functions. It employs *CHANGE* (page 231) to do the actual modification of the character vector *TEXT*:

```
     □VR 'FUNEDIT'
   ∇ R←FUNEDIT X;TEXT;REPLY
[1]   ⍝PROTOTYPE MODEL OF APL*PLUS WS 11 FNED FNED
[2]   ⍝ORIGINAL BY J. M. SPENCER AND C. E. YATES
```

```
[3]    START:TEXT←□VR X ◇ →(' '=1↑0ρTEXT)/REWORK ◇ 'CANNOT EDIT ',X ◇ →0
[4]    REWORK:TEXT[(TEXT=□TCNL)/ιρTEXT]←'田' ◇ 'USE 田 TO STAND FOR CARRIER RETURN'
[5]    TEXT←CHANGE TEXT ∩ LET USER EDIT AS HE WISHES.
[6]    TEXT[(TEXT='田')/ιρTEXT]←□TCNL ∩REPLACE CARRIER RETURNS
[7]    R←□DEF TEXT ∩ ATTEMPT TO RECONSTITUTE FUNCTION
[8]    →(' '=1↑0ρR)/0 ∩ IF CHARACTER RESULT IT WAS SUCCESSFUL.
[9]    →(E1,E2,E3,E4,E5,E6,E7)[1↑R] ∩EXPLAIN ERRORS
[10]   E1:'WS FULL: NOT ENOUGH ROOM FOR THE FUNCTION DEFINITION.' ◇ →EX
[11]   E2:'DEFN ERROR: MALFORMED HEADER; FN NAME IN USE; MISSING OR EXTRA ∇ OR ⍒;'
[12]    'MISSING A LINE NUMBER [N]; OR NONCONSECUTIVE LINE NUMBERS' ◇ →EX
[13]   E3:'CHAR ERROR: CONTAINS CHARACTER SUCH AS □TCNL OR □TCBS' ◇ →EX
[14]   E4:'SYMBOL TABLE FULL: CREATING THE FUNCTION WOULD REQUIRE MORE'
[15]    'SYMBOL TABLE ENTRIES THAN ARE AVAILABLE' ◇ →EX
[16]   E5:'UNMATCHED QUOTES: THERE IS AN ODD NUMBER OF QUOTES' ◇ →EX
[17]   E6:'*** UNUSED □VR ERROR CODE.  ERROR IN CHANGE PROGRAM'
[18]    'ABANDONING EFFORT.  CONTACT A. J. ROSE.' ◇ →0
[19]   E7:'EMPTY LINE: NO TEXT BETWEEN TWO CARRIAGE RETURNS' ◇ →EX
[20]   EX:'ERROR OCCURRED AROUND POSITION ',⍒R[2]
[21]   PROMPT:□←'REWORK, START OVER, QUIT? ' ◇ REPLY←1↑□
[22]    →(REWORK,START,0,PROMPT)['RSQ'ιREPLY]
       ∇
```

Rather than using $□FX$, line 7 of $FUNEDIT$ uses $□DEF$ (*define*), a somewhat more powerful cousin of $□FX$ on the APL*PLUS System. It can accept matrices and properly formed character vectors as its argument. A vector must be similar to the result of $□VR$. New line characters not contained within quotes are used to mark the lines of the function. The characters up to the first new line character make up the function header. Headers must begin with a ∇ or ⍒ (if ⍒, then the function is created as a locked function). As in the result of $□VR$, the lines of the argument must be numbered consecutively beginning with 1, and must be contained within brackets. A trailing ∇ or ⍒ is required, and it may appear on or after the last numbered line.

If $□DEF$ can't convert its argument to a function, its result is a two-element numeric vector. The first element is the error code (see lines 10-19 of $FUNEDIT$). The second element is the location of the error—the character position for a vector argument, or the row number for a matrix argument.

Local functions

The example here creates, executes and discards a local function:

```
      ∇XSLOPE[□]∇

  ∇ Z←X∆X XSLOPE F;X;∆X;F;SINK
[1]   ∩ CALCULATES SLOPE OF CURVE F AT POINT X.
[2]   X←1↓X∆X ◇ ∆X←X∆X[1]
[3]   SINK←□FX F
[4]   Z←((F X)-F X-∆X)÷∆X
  ∇
      (.0001,ι5) XSLOPE 2 13ρ'Y←F X          Y←(3×X*2)+5×X'
10.9997 16.9997 22.9997 28.9997 34.9997
```

Line 3 of the function is the important one here. The character matrix right argument of $XSLOPE$, F, was made into the function F. The explicit result of $□FX$ is stored in $SINK$ simply to avoid its being implicitly displayed. Another way to suppress it is 0 $0ρ□FX$ F.

Then line 3 was executed, and we got the expected result. However, were we to display $)FNS$ after the execution, we find that the function F isn't there. That's because it was declared to be a *local function* by the presence of F in the header. And like any local variable, when the function $XSLOPE$ finishes executing, F disappears and the space it had taken is freed up.

The slope example we used here is a trivial one, because ⌹ does it more directly. But remember that ⌹ can handle only one line at a time, and it is clumsy with branching, while $□FX$ has no such restrictions.

An important use of local functions is storing functions in their character array representation as components of an APL file, and bringing into the workspace only those needed for the particular job at the time they are needed.

Local functions follow the same conventions as local variables. You can have a global and a local function with the same name. The display of a function using $□CR$ or $□VR$ displays the local version.

Erasing objects under program control

Functions, variables and group can be erased with the $)ERASE$ system command, but like all system commands this requires manual intervention. The monadic system function $\Box EX$ (for *expunge*) is provided to erase functions and variables under program control.

To erase a function named $STAT$ from the workspace, use $\Box EX$ $'STAT'$. You can erase several things at once by making the argument a character matrix with each row an object to be erased. On APL*PLUS Systems the argument can also be a character vector in which spaces separate names to be erased.

$\Box EX$ always returns a vector of 1's and 0's whose length matches the number of names in the argument. 1 means that the object either didn't exist in the first place or that it was successfully erased. 0 means that the object either could not be erased ($\Box EX$ won't let you erase a label or group, or (except in APL2) a function that is currently in the state indicator). And it won't work if the name you supplied was an impossible one, such as $23SKIDOO$. $\Box EX$ operates on the most local version of the object, while $)ERASE$ operates only on global objects.

Locking functions

$\Box DEF$ produces a locked function if the argument is in vector form and $\nabla\!\!\!\sim$ is used instead of the starting or ending ∇. However, there is no way to contain locking instructions in the matrix form. For this reason the $\Box LOCK$ system function is provided on the APL*PLUS System. Its argument is a character vector or matrix holding the names of the functions to be locked. The result is an empty matrix (its shape is 0 0) if all the names were in fact functions; otherwise it is a character matrix holding the names that could not be locked. APL2 provides dyadic $\Box FX$ for locking functions. The right argument is the canonical representation of the function to be locked, and the left argument is a four element binary vector (see page 300). If the first element is a 1, the function will be locked.

Name list and name classification

We have just seen how functions can be created, modified and erased using $\Box CR$, $\Box FX$, $\Box VR$, $\Box DEF$, $\Box LOCK$ and $\Box EX$. They wield substantial power over their weaker brothers, the system commands and ∇ editing of Chapter 10, particularly because they can be executed under program control. To complement these facilities, some inquiry functions are also provided. The first is $\Box NL$, for *name list*. The argument of $\Box NL$ is the class of the object you are inquiring about. Its result is a character matrix holding names of objects satisfying the inquiry.

$\Box NL$ can be either monadic or dyadic. If monadic, the right argument is a scalar or vector of coded values (1 for labels, 2 for variables and 3 for functions) of the classes of objects you are trying to list. For example, to find all function and variable names in the workspace, use $R\leftarrow\Box NL$ 2 3. The most local definition of the object is used.

When $\Box NL$ is used in dyadic form, the left argument is a character vector or scalar. Only objects whose names start with a character in the left argument are returned. Thus, to get a list of all labels starting with P or Q or R, use $LIST\leftarrow'PQR$ $'\Box NL$ 1.

The monadic system function $\Box NC$ is closely related to $\Box NL$. The argument is a character matrix of names (APL*PLUS Systems also allow a character vector), and the result is a numeric vector telling how each of the names is used. The most local use of the names is given.

result	interpretation
0	The name is not in use at this level of the state indicator, and hence can be used to define a function, label, variable or group.
1	The name is in use as a label.
2	The name is in use as a variable.
3	The name is in use as a function.
4	The name is not available for use (i.e., it is a group, and the state indicator is empty and the name is not shielded, or the name is not properly formed).

In APL2, $\Box NL$ and $\Box NC$ have been extended. $\Box NL$ accepts 4 as an argument to list defined operators (page 212), and $\Box NC$ returns $^{-}1$ for an invalid name. The return code of 4 for $\Box NC$ means the name is in use as a defined operator. There is also a related system command $)NMS$. An example of its use is $)NMS$ PE ST, which lists the names of all global variables, defined functions and defined operators from PE through ST (optional), along with an integer designating the name class.

Functions on files

Here is the key part of a system for using functions stored on files (see Chapters 26 and 27) as a means of conserving workspace. The general idea is to pull in functions only when they are needed, and to erase functions when required to make room for new ones. Component one of the file is a directory holding the names of the functions that are on file.

```
      ∇GETFN[☐]∇
    ∇ Z←NAME GETFN FILENO;IF;ROWMATCH;DIR;SINK;STK;CANERASE;HOWMANY;LOCVEC;SIZES
[1]   ⍝BRINGS FN NAME IN FROM FILE FILENO [IF IT CAN]   AJROSE NOV 82
[2]   ⍝FIRST COMPONENT OF FILE IS DIRECTORY MATRIX;
[3]   ⍝   FIRST ROW IS '***DIRECTORY'
[4]   ⍝   OTHER ROWS HOLD FN NAMES; ROW INDEX IS COMPONENT NO.
[5]   ⍝RESULT CODES:   1 IF SUCCESSFUL, NAME ASSEMBLED
[6]   ⍝   2 NAME ALREADY IN WS       3 ERROR, NAME NOT ON FILE
[7]   ⍝   4 ERROR, NOT ENOUGH WS    5 ERROR IN FILED FUNCTION
[8]   SINK←☐DEF 2 8 ρ'Z←B IF C  Z←C/B ' ⍝ IF IS A LOCAL FN
[9]   SINK←'∇Z←L ROWMATCH R',☐TCNL ⍝ROWMATCH IS A LOCAL FN
[10]  SINK←☐DEF SINK,'[1]Z←1+(¯1↑ρL)⌈¯1↑ρR◇Z←(((¯1↑ρL),Z)↑L)∧.
=(Z,1↓⌽ρR)↑⍉R∇',☐TCNL
[11]  NAME←(NAME≠' ')/NAME ◇ Z←2 ◇ →0 IF∨/(☐NL 3) ROWMATCH NAME ⍝IF ALREADY IN WS
[12]  DIR←☐FREAD FILENO,1 ◇ LOCVEC←DIR ROWMATCH NAME
[13]  →(∨/LOCVEC)/L1 ◇ Z←3 ◇ →0 ⍝ IF NAME NOT IN FILE
[14]  L1:STK←☐SI ⍝BUT MUST REMOVE ALL BUT THE FN NAMES FROM IT
[15]  STK←(ρSTK)ρ(,∧\STK≠'[')\(,∧\STK≠'[')/,STK
[16]  →L3 IF WA>5000
[17]  ⍝THIS IS THE TRICKY PART.   TRY TO ERASE FNS TO MAKE SOME ROOM.
[18]  ⍝ERASE LARGEST FNS THAT ARE IN WS, ON FILE, BUT NOT IN STK.
[19]  CANERASE←(∨/(☐NL 3) ROWMATCH DIR)≠☐NL 3
[20]  CANERASE←(~∨/CANERASE ROWMATCH STK)≠CANERASE
[21]  SIZES←☐SIZE CANERASE
[22]  HOWMANY←1++/(+\SIZES[♥SIZES])<5000-☐WA ⍝ERASE AT LEAST 5000 BYTES
[23]  →L2 IF HOWMANY≤ρSIZES ◇ Z←4 ◇ →0
[24]  L2:SINK←☐EX CANERASE[HOWMANY↑♥SIZES;]
[25]  L3:SINK←☐DEF ☐FREAD FILENO,(DIR ROWMATCH NAME)⍳1
[26]   Z← 1 5[1+0=1↑0ρSINK] ⍝ IF NUMERIC RESULT, IT WAS UNSUCCESSFUL
    ∇
```

Here is a narrative of what happens. If the function is already in the workspace, exit (line 11). Otherwise, check if the function is in the file: if it isn't, exit (lines 12 and 13). If there was no exit, clean up the execution stack (lines 14 and 15) for later use. If there aren't 5000 bytes of storage available (line 16), try to make space by erasing the largest functions which are reconstitutable and not in the execution stack (lines 19 through 22). If there is not enough space after that attempt, exit (line 23). Finally, erase the old function (line 24) and bring the new function from the file (line 25), and exit with result code (line 26).

This function was written to be an expository prototype rather than a comprehensive production program. In particular, *GETFN* can't deal with functions whose names conflict with local variables. This problem is usually circumvented in production systems by using very unlikely (and unmnemonic) names for the locals such as Δ1, Δ2, Δ3, etc.

Two local functions are embedded in *GETFN. IF* (line 8) is kept in ☐CR form, while *ROWMATCH* (lines 9 and 10) is kept in ☐VR form. There was no particular reason for the choice of forms in this example except to demonstrate both forms to the reader.

GETFN employs ☐SIZE on line 21 to help determine which functions should be erased, the idea being to erase a few large ones rather than a lot of little ones. ☐SIZE finds the amount of space used by objects in the workspace. The right argument is either a character vector with the names separated by blanks, or a character matrix with one name per row. The result is a numeric vector, one element per name holding the number of bytes used. Unused names result in a zero, while for groups the value is the sum of the space taken up by the individual objects, plus some overhead for the group name itself.

Execute

This monadic function, whose symbol is ⍕, is a partial alternative to $\Box FX$ or $\Box DEF$ in that it allows the direct evaluation of character vectors. Indeed, its argument is a character vector (or scalar), and the result (explicit or not) is what would have happened if you had entered the characters in calculator mode. Compare these examples:

```
      A←ι5                    ⍕'A←ι5'                  A←⍕'ι5'
      R←A+2                   ⍕'R←A+2'                 R←⍕'A+2'
      R                       R                        ⍕'R'
3 4 5 6 7              3 4 5 6 7               3 4 5 6 7
```

When used within a function, statements like [5] $X←⍕'3+Y'$ or [8] $→⍕'LOOP'$ are equivalent to [5] $X←3+Y$ or [8] $→LOOP$.

You can overcome APL's limit of two arguments per function by passing a character matrix holding the names, all in one argument. Here, for example, is a function that displays whatever information (such as shape, datatype, size, etc.) is requested about named objects in the workspace:

```
      ∇SHOWME[□]∇
    ∇ LIST SHOWME ACTION;OBJ
[1]    ⍕(2≠ρρLIST)/'LIST←(ι0) ROWNAMES LIST' ∩CONDITIONAL EXECUTION.
[2]  LOOP:→(0=1↑ρLIST)/0 ◊ OBJ←LIST[1;] ◊ LIST← 1 0 ↓LIST
[3]    OBJ ◊ OBJ←⍕OBJ ◊ ⍕ACTION ◊ →LOOP
    ∇
```

```
      ' TAB0 TAB1 TAB2 TAB3' SHOWME '''RANK='',(⍕ρρOBJ),''   SHAPE='',⍕ρOBJ'
TAB0
RANK=0   SHAPE=
TAB1
RANK=1   SHAPE=4
TAB2
RANK=2   SHAPE=4 3
TAB3
RANK=3   SHAPE=2 4 3
```

Execute is frequently used as an alternative to simple conditional branching as it was on line 1 of $SHOWME$. Now for another example, in which if the variable DC doesn't exist, it is created as the vector 1 1, but if DC already exists, nothing is done: $⍕(0=\Box NC\ 'DC')/'DC←1\ 1'$. Can you see how inclusion of this expression in the function DO (page 156) eliminates the need for $SETDO$ for initialization?

Execute is useful for numerical approximations to the functions of calculus because the *form* of an expression (rather than the *value*) can be used as an argument. The mathematical representation of the slope of a function f(X),

$$\frac{F(x + \Delta x) - F(x)}{\Delta x}$$

can be evaluated with the following function. Note that the left argument of $\underline{E}SLOPE$ passes the formula to the function, avoiding having to hard-code the formula in $\underline{E}SLOPE$.

```
      ∇ESLOPE[□]∇
    ∇ Z←FX ESLOPE XΔX;FX;FXΔX;ΔX
[1]  ∩RIGHT ARG IS 2-ELE VECTOR X AND ΔX    AJROSE NOV 82
[2]  ∩LEFT ARG IS FORMULA IN TERMS OF X.
[3]    X←XΔX[1] ◊ ΔX←XΔX[2]
[4]    FX←⍕FX ∩EVALUATE AT X
[5]    X←X-ΔX
[6]    FXΔX←⍕FX ∩EVALUATE AT X-ΔX
[7]    Z←(FX-FXΔX)÷ΔX
    ∇
```

```
      '(3×X*2)+5×X' ESLOPE 4 .001
28.997
      '(3×X*2)+5×X' ESLOPE 4 .00001
28.99997
```

This function can be adapted to handle more than one X and ΔX with this change,

```
∇ESLOPE[3] X←XΔX[1;;] ◊ ΔX←XΔX[2;;]∇
```

which expects the right argument to be a three-dimensional array whose first plane is X values and whose second plane is ΔX values.

The function $SLAM$ can be used to format sets of X's and ΔX's together:

```
∇SLAM[□]∇
  ∇ XΔX←X SLAM ΔX
[1]  ⍝USED IN CONJUNCTION WITH SLOPE FUNCTIONS. AJR NOV 82
[2]  X←,X ◊ ΔX←,ΔX ⍝ MAKE ARGUMENTS VECTORS.
[3]  XΔX←(⍉((ρΔX),ρX)ρX),[0.5]((ρX),ρΔX)ρΔX
  ∇
```

```
      4 5 6 SLAM .01 .001 .0001 .00001
4.000000000E0    4.000000000E0    4.000000000E0    4.000000000E0
5.000000000E0    5.000000000E0    5.000000000E0    5.000000000E0
6.000000000E0    6.000000000E0    6.000000000E0    6.000000000E0

1.000000000E¯2   1.000000000E¯3   1.000000000E¯4   1.000000000E¯5
1.000000000E¯2   1.000000000E¯3   1.000000000E¯4   1.000000000E¯5
1.000000000E¯2   1.000000000E¯3   1.000000000E¯4   1.000000000E¯5

      '(3×X*2)+5×X' ESLOPE 4 5 6 SLAM .01 .001 .0001 .00001
      28.97          28.997          28.9997          28.99997
      34.97          34.997          34.9997          34.99997
      40.97          40.997          40.9997          40.99997
```

Which method of automatic program generation to use (canonical or vector representation, or execute, or direct definition) depends on three factors: what is supported on your system, your personal taste, and which technique most closely fits the job at hand. If you are anticipating moving an application from one system to another, $\Box CR$ and ⍎ tend to be consistent on most systems. $\Box VR$ differs from system to system in its fussiness (presence of new lines, starting and ending ∇'s, etc.).

PROBLEMS

1. Write a function $ARITH$ with argument $DATA$ to branch (using execute) to ADD, SUB or BAL if the first element of a vector $DATA$ is 15, 25 or 35 respectively. Otherwise, the branch is to ERR.

2. Show how execute can be used to **A** generate a new name for some data DAT, and **B** change a standard variable name NAM to $NAM1$, $NAM2$ etc. for various data D.

3. Write a function $DECOM$ to decomment any function, using $\Box CR$.

4. Rewrite the recursive function $FACT$ (page 159) using $\pmb{\triangle}$.

5. Generalize problem 2B to select the Ith column of an array M of unknown rank (but either 2 or 3).

6. If you have the diamond $\Diamond$ available on your system, show how to recursively execute (although inefficiently) an instruction *outside* function definition mode.

7. Write a function that will erase all functions in the workspace except those in the argument M.

8. What does $A \leftarrow \pmb{\triangle} (\, \overline{\pmb{\triangle}} A\,) , \, ' \quad ' , \Box$ do if executed within a function?

9. Define functions to edit a matrix as though it were a function.

10. Write a calling function $REPORT$ which prompts a user for the name of a report and then executes a program of the same name as the report he has chosen.

11. Define a function $OMIT$ to prompt for a matrix name and the rows to be omitted from it.

12. After loading $1 \; CLASS$, define a function $DRILL$ which allows the user to choose between the exercises SUB, ADD and $SPELL$, and automatically initiates execution once a choice has been made.

13. Use execute to define a function with header $A \; CHECK \; B$ that prints $TRUE$ or $FALSE$ for $A > B$.

14. Edit the canonical representation of CMP in $1 \; CLASS$ to change $GREATER$ to $MORE$.

15. Make HYP local to the function $RECT$ in $1 \; CLASS$.

16. Construct a function $DISP$ to display automatically the canonical representations of functions beginning with specified letters.

17. Write APL instructions that force an absolute branch ($\rightarrow$) whenever there are more than six entries in the state indicator.

18. Define a function $LIST$ to display all the functions in a given workspace. (Hint: use $\Box NL$ to get the names, and convert them to character representation.)

19. Construct a dyadic function $OPROD$ to produce operation tables, given that the left argument is an APL operator and the right argument R is a two-element vector of positive integers such that the table is made up of combinations of $\iota 1 \uparrow R$ and $\iota 1 \downarrow R$.

Chapter 25: Nested arrays

Some APL systems now allow you to build *nested arrays* made up of other arrays of different shape, rank and type (i.e., mixed character and numeric). This added power doesn't come for free, however. You will have to learn new concepts about data, and quite a few new functions as well.

But it will be well worth it. For example, defined functions will now accept multiple explicit arguments and yield multiple explicit results. Numeric and character data may now be directly combined in a single variable for convenient formatting and storage. Mixed data in files is easier to read and write. The need for looping is significantly reduced. In building arrays there is no need to count characters to insure proper padding, and because padding isn't needed, storage is conserved. These are just a few of the many uses of nested arrays that illustrate, more than anything you have seen so far, the power of APL.

Mixed arrays

You learned in Chapter 13 that character and numeric data could not normally be mixed in an array. On several occasions we have discussed methods for converting from numeric to character or vice versa to compensate for the inability to handle mixed data types. You still can't mix types in most APL systems, but some newer versions have removed the restriction. For example, in APL2 and newer APL*PLUS Systems the following works:

```
      V←'T',4 12,'PEOPLE'                      M←2 7ρι14
      V                                        M[1;1+ι6]←'2BV~2B'
T 4 12 PEOPLE                                  M
      ρV                                 1  2  B  V  ~  2  B
9                                        8  9 10 11 12 13 14
      Vει20                                    Mε□AV
0 1 1 0 0 0 0 0 0                         0  0  1  1  1  1  1  1
      Vε□AV                                    0  0  0  0  0  0  0
1 0 0 1 1 1 1 1 1
```

As you can see, each position in an array can now be either character or numeric, and both types can be in the same array.

The *type* function, ε, a new member of the family of primitive scalar monadic functions, indicates which items are numeric (returns a 0) or character (returns a blank):

```
      εV                                       εM
0 0                                      0
      ρεV                                0 0 0 0 0 0 0
9                                              0≠εM
      0≠εV                               0 1 1 1 1 1 1
1 0 0 1 1 1 1 1 1                         0 0 0 0 0 0 0
      ' '=εV
1 0 0 1 1 1 1 1 1
```

You may recall that for uniform arrays (all character or all numeric), the fill element for expand and take was zero for numbers and blank for characters. For mixed arrays, the fill element is determined by the type of the first item. If the first item is numeric, the fill element is zero, while for a character first item the fill element is the blank. The fill element of an empty array is determined by the type of the most recent first item:

```
      V                         M                            ‾3 8 ↑M
T 4 12 PEOPLE             1  2  B  V  ~  2  B           0 0  0  0  0  0  0 0
      (18ρ 0 1)\V         8  9 10 11 12 13 14           1 2  B  V  ~  2  B 0
T 4   12  P E O P L E                                   8 9 10 11 12 13 14 0
```

257

All APL functions work on mixed arrays. In particular, those for selecting or rearranging require no change in thinking at all. You still can't do arithmetic on the character items, but it's very easy to compress them out. For example, you can sum all the numeric items in a vector V by $+/(0=\epsilon V)/V$.

Vector notation and nested arrays

In traditional APL, numeric vectors are implied whenever two numeric values are separated only by spaces. Thus, $V2\leftarrow 4\ 12$ is a two-element uniform numeric vector. Similarly, character vectors are implied when two or more characters are surrounded by single quotes. For example, $V3\leftarrow$ '$PEOPLE$' is a six-element uniform character vector, while $S1\leftarrow$ 'T' is a character scalar.

Nested array systems extend the concept of vector notation by allowing *variables* separated only by spaces to be regarded as the *items* of a vector. The expression $V2\ \ V3$ is a two-element nested vector (sometimes called a *strand*), while $V2,V3$ is an eight-element simple mixed vector.

One benefit of this extension is easier expression of commonly used idioms. Just as you would write $5\ \ 3\rho\iota15$ rather than $(5,3)\rho\iota15$ in traditional APL, you can now write $A\ \ B\ \rho\iota15$ instead of $(A,B)\rho\iota15$ (assuming A is 5 and B is 3). Seasoned APL'ers reading this section may cry heresy; however, the evidence is strong that new APL users, unbiased by habit, readily take to this notational freedom.

To encourage you to read on, see if you can figure out these examples:

```
      ρ'T', 4 12 ,'PEOPLE'
9

      ρ'T' 4 12 'PEOPLE'
4

      S1←'T' ◊ V2← 4 12 ◊ V3←'PEOPLE'
      ρS1,V2,V3
9

      ρS1 V2 V3
3
```

The expression $S1\ \ V2\ \ V3$ above—three variables with no functions between them—yielded a three-item vector. Let's capture the result to examine it more closely:

```
      NA←S1 V2 V3           NA                      ⌽NA
      ρNA              T  4 12  PEOPLE         PEOPLE  4 12  T
3
      NA[1]                NA[2]                   NA[3]
T                    4 12                    PEOPLE
      ρρNA[1]              ρρNA[2]                 ρρNA[3]
0                    0                       0
```

The display of the result gives some clue about what's going on. Notice the extra spaces in some of the results. They indicate that the items between extra spaces are enclosed by an incredible shrinking process so that it is stored in a single array position as though it were a scalar. To make the point even more dramatic, in the APL*PLUS System NA would have been displayed as $T\ \ (4\ \ 12)\ \ (PEOPLE)$, the parentheses showing exactly where the nesting has occurred. From all appearances, it seems that the number vector $4\ \ 12$ and the character vector '$PEOPLE$' have been enclosed so that each vector is now stored in a single array position as though it were a scalar.

The enclose function

That's exactly what happened. Each item of the result has become a nested scalar. The enclosures in our example happened as an implicit effect of vector notation, but there are also explicit ways to enclose arrays to make them nested scalars. The *enclose* function is the monadic use of the symbol $\subset$:

```
      S3←⊂'PEOPLE' ∧ OR S3←NA[3]
      ρS3

      ρρS3
0
      S3
PEOPLE
```

Because $S3$ is a scalar, its contents can be stored in a single position of any array:

```
       M                                      M[2;3]
 1  2   B  ∨   ~    2   B           10
 8  9  10 11  12  13  14                      M[2;4]
       M[2;4]←S3                       PEOPLE
       M                                      M[2; 3 4]
 1  2   B  ∨         ~    2   B       10  PEOPLE
 8  9  10   PEOPLE   12  13  14
       ρM
2 7
```

Simple scalars (contrasted to nested scalars) cannot be enclosed; for them the application of ⊂ is ignored. All other arrays can be enclosed. The result of ⊂ is always a scalar, either simple (the do-nothing case) or nested. See how the vector , 'V' can be nested while the scalar 'S' cannot:

```
        'S'                        ,'V'
S                          V
        ⊂'S'                       ⊂,'V'
S                          V
        ⊂⊂⊂'S'                     ⊂⊂⊂,'V'
S                                V
```

Actually, there are two major schools of thought about nested arrays, and the difference centers on whether a simple scalar can be enclosed or not. The systems described in this book are termed *floating*, and do not enclose simple scalars. Those systems that do allow scalars to be enclosed are called *grounded*. For elementary uses such as described in this book either system will do, and the differences won't be dramatic. However, for advanced use and commercial applications the distinction becomes important.

The depth function

The *depth* function, monadic ≡ (= overstruck with _), indicates the maximum nesting of an array. It always returns a scalar result. When applied to a simple scalar the result is 0, and for other simple arrays the depth function returns 1.

```
      ≡5                    ≡⍳10                  ≡ 2 3 4 9 ρ'FOO'
0                       1                      1
```

Nested arrays are another story. For them the result is the maximum nesting expressed as a positive scalar integer one more than the number of nest levels:

```
      U←2ρ⊂⊂⊂4 1ρ'NEST'        U[2]←⊂U[2]              U[2]←25
      U                        U                       U
   N        N               N        N              N     25
   E        E               E        E              E
   S        S               S        S              S
   T        T               T        T              T
      ≡U                       ≡U                      ≡U
4                       5                      4
```

APL*PLUS Systems determine depth somewhat differently. There, ≡A is always 0 for any simple array; for nested arrays the result is positive if the nesting is uniform, and negative otherwise. The results for the examples in this section would be 0, 0, 0, 3, ¯4, 3.

Simple scalars, such as the most recent $U[2]$, don't figure into the determination of nesting depth or uniformity, just as scalars don't affect the shape of the result of primitive scalar dyadic functions like + −
× and ÷ (remember them?).

Enclose with axis

APL2 features an interesting extension to enclose which can change simple arrays to nested arrays or increase the nesting depth. It works like this:

```
      ⊂[1]3 2ρι6              ⊂[2]3 2ρι6
 1 3 5   2 4 6          1 2   3 4   5 6
      ρ⊂[1]3 2ρι6             ρ⊂[2]3 2ρι6
2                      3
```

```
      ARG←2 3 5ρ'HOW   NOW   BROWNCOW   SO    QUIET'
HOW
NOW
BROWN                    ⊂[1 3]ARG                      ⊂[2 3]ARG
                     HOW      NOW     BROWN         HOW      COW
COW                  COW      SO      QUIET         NOW      SO
SO                                                  BROWN    QUIET
QUIET                    ρ⊂[1 3]ARG                     ρ⊂[2 3]ARG
                3                              2
```

If $Z←⊂[K]ARG$, except when K is empty and ARG is simple, $ρρZ$ is $(ρρARG)-ρ,K$, and each item in the result has rank $ρ,K$. The shape of the result is $(∼(ιρρARG)∈K)/ρARG$. Alert readers will note some similarities between this use of enclose and the function $SPRED$ (Chapter 19), which used dyadic transpose to restructure arrays for display.

APL*PLUS provides a function similar to enclose with axis, *split*, the monadic ↓. If no axis is specified, it encloses along the last axis; otherwise it encloses on the axis given.

```
      ↓ARG                   ↓[1]↓[3]ARG                 ↓[2]↓[3]ARG
HOW    NOW    BROWN      HOW    NOW    BROWN         HOW    LOW
COW    SO     QUIET      COW    SO     QUIET         NOW    SO
                                                     BROWN  QUIET
      ρ↓ARG                   ρ↓[1]↓[3]ARG                ρ↓[2]↓[3]ARG
2 3                     3                           2
```

The first function

You have already seen that when a nested item is selected from a nested array, it is obtained as a nested scalar. In other words, it still 'wears' its enclosure implicitly:

```
      NA
 T  4 12    PEOPLE
      X←NA[3]
      X
PEOPLE
      ρρX
0
```

The *first* function (also called *disclose*), monadic ⊃, removes one level of enclosure from an item:

```
      ⊃X                     ρ⊃X                 ρρX
PEOPLE                      6                   1
```

When first is applied to an array with more than one item, the result is the first item and all the others are ignored:

```
      NA
 T  4 12    PEOPLE
      ⊃NA                     ⊃⊃NA                    ⊃⊃⊂NA
T                        T                       T
      ⊃φNA                    ⊃⊃φNA                   ⊃⊃⊃φNA
PEOPLE                   P                       P
      ⊃NA[2]                  ⊃⊃NA[2]                 ⊃⊃⊃NA[2]
4 12                     4                       4
```

If the item is not nested (in other words, it is already a simple scalar), then first just delivers that scalar as its result.

Disclose with axis

This function has the syntax $Z⊃[K]ARG$, where all the nonscalar items in ARG must have rank $ρ,K$. K itself is a simple scalar or integer vector (except that if ARG consists of scalar items only, K must be empty). The depth of the result Z is less than that of ARG (except when ARG is simple and K is empty). For the case where the items of ARG have different shapes, they are padded on the right with their fill elements to conform to the shape of the biggest item. One other point: unlike its use in other axis sensitive functions, $[K]$ refers to the axes of the result rather than the axes of the argument.

```
      Z←⊃[1](3 2 4)(10 8 16)              Z←(3 2ρ'ABCDEF')(3 2ρ'UVWXYZ')
           Z                                    Z
 3  10                                    AB   UV
 2   8                                    CD   WX
 4  16                                    EF   YZ

           ρZ                                  Z←⊃[2 3]Z
 3  2                                          Z
      Z←⊃[2](3 2 4)(10 8 16)              AB
      Z                                   CD
  3   2  4                                EF
 10   8 16
      ρZ                                  UV
 2  3                                     WX
      Z←⊃[1]'ABC' 'DEFG'                  YZ
      Z                                        ρZ
 AD                                      2 3 2
 BE                                            Z←⊃[2](2 3)(4 5 6)
 CF                                            Z
  G                                      2 3 0
                                         4 5 6
```

The APL*PLUS System uses the function *mix*, monadic ↑, to replace a level of nesting by a new axis. It uses the same fractional index notation as laminate; however, while in laminate the new axis has only two levels, mix produces as many levels as there were nested objects in the argument. If there is no index specified for mix, the new axis becomes the last axis of the result:

```
      ↑[0.5]'ABCD' 'EFGH' 'IJKL'
 AEI
 BFJ
 CGK
 DHL
```

```
      ↑[1.5]'ABCD' 'EFGH' 'IJKL'                    ↑'ABCD' 'EFGH' 'IJKL'
 ABCD                                          ABCD
 EFGH                                          EFGH
 IJKL                                          IJKL
```

The items being disclosed by mix must be of identical shape; otherwise $RANK$ or $LENGTH$ $ERROR$s result:

```
      ↑(1 2 3)(4 5)(6 7 8)
 LENGTH ERROR
      ↑(1 2 3)(4 5)(6 7 8)
      ∧
```

Split and mix (or enclose and disclose with axis) can rearrange arrays to achieve transpose-like effects. For $X←3$ $4ρι12$, all the following expressions get the same result. Can you think of any others?

```
      ↑[0.5]↓X          ↑⊂[1]X          ⊃[1]⊂[2]X          ⊃[2]⊂[1]X
```

Pick

The dyadic form of disclose is called *pick*. When applied to a nested vector right argument, it selects the item named on the left, with a layer of enclosure removed. Each item of the left argument picks through a progressively deeper layer of the nest. Picking a nonexisting item causes an error:

```
      NA
  T  ·4  12    PEOPLE
        1⊃NA                2 1 ⊃NA                3 1 ⊃NA
  T                    4                      P
        2⊃NA                2 2 ⊃NA                3 2 ⊃NA
  4  12                12                     E
        3⊃NA                2 3 ⊃NA                3 3 ⊃NA

  PEOPLE               INDEX ERROR            O
                         2 3 ⊃NA                     3 1 1 ⊃NA
                            ^                LENGTH ERROR
                                                    3 1 1 ⊃NA
                                                       ^
```

The results of using pick on vectors are simpler than the arguments, as the above examples show. Successive applications of pick show this clearly:

```
      V←'APL' 2 (5ρ'ABC' 'XYZ')
      V
  APL 2   ABC XYZ ABC XYZ ABC
      ρV
  3
      3 4 2⊃V
  Y
```

```
      A←3⊃V                   B←4⊃A              C←2⊃B
      A                       B                  C
  ABC XYZ ABC XYZ ABC         XYZ         Y

      ρA                      ρB                 ρC
  5                       3
      ρρA                     ρρB                ρρC
  1                       1               0
```

When the right argument is more complicated than a vector, the items of the left argument must be nested vectors, indicating the axes of the right argument to be picked:

```
      M                                   (⊂ 1 1)⊃M              (⊂ 2 4)⊃M
  1 2  B  v         ~  2  B          1                     PEOPLE
  8 9 10  PEOPLE   12 13 14                                    5⊃(⊂2 4)⊃M
                                         (⊂ 1 3)⊃M          L
                                     B
```

Pick can do many of the same things that traditional bracket indexing can. In general, the disclosed item in the *I*;*J*th position of a matrix can be selected by ⊃*ARRAY*[*I*;*J*] or (⊂*I* *J*)⊃*ARRAY*. But there are differences between pick and indexing: pick is restricted to getting single items, while indexing can get various slices or planes of items. That is, pick has no direct analogue for *ARRAY*[*I*;]. Another obvious difference is that while indexing selects *elements*, pick selects *items*.

Pick is very powerful in its ability to reach into an array of any shape whatsoever and draw out desired data. However, like some other powerful functions, it requires a lot of learning to use it for complicated cases.

By the way, did you notice anything odd about the statement *V*←'APL' 2 (5ρ'ABC' 'XYZ')? It ends with a right parenthesis, and that is indeed never required—for traditional APL. But the convenience of strand notation costs you here. The *DOMAIN ERROR* below comes from trying to use the strand 'APL' 2 5 as the left argument to reshape.

```
      'APL' 2 5ρ'ABC' 'XYZ'
  DOMAIN ERROR
      'APL' 2 5ρ'ABC' 'XYZ'
         ^        ^
```

Assigning to vectors of variables

A bonus feature of the nested arrays facility is the ability to disperse the items of a vector into a group of variables. For example, the three items of the nested vector *NA* can be stored in three variables with a statement like this:

```
      ITA ITB ITC←NA
      ITA                        ITB                        ITC
T                            4 12              PEOPLE
```

The item to the right of the assignment must be a scalar or vector (higher dimensional arrays won't work and will result in *RANK ERROR*), and there must be exactly as many variable names on the left as there are items on the right (*LENGTH ERROR* otherwise). As with pick and disclose, one layer of enclosure is removed by vector notation assignment. A handy consequence of all this is that you can now exchange the contents of two variables. Try doing *ITA ITB←ITB ITA* in one step in traditional APL!

Vector notation can be used to remove the limitation of two arguments in defined functions. Here is a function to replace a substring in text. Focus your attention on the argument and line 2. The rest of the function is a mundane looping solution.

```
      ∇Z←REPLACE R;TEXT;OLD;NEW;LOC
[1]   ⍝ R IS A 3-ELEMENT NESTED VECTOR
[2]   TEXT OLD NEW←R
[3]   Z←''
[4]   LLP:LOC←(∧/(¯1+⍳⍴OLD)⊖TEXT∘.=OLD)⍳1
[5]   ⍝ABOVE FINDS LOCATION OF FIRST OCCURRENCE OF OLD IN TEXT.
[6]   →(LOC=1+⍴TEXT)/DONE
[7]   Z←Z,((LOC-1)↑TEXT),NEW
[8]   TEXT←(¯1+LOC+⍴OLD)↓TEXT
[9]   →LP
[10]  DONE:Z←Z,TEXT ∇

      REPLACE 'VECTOR ← VECTOR + VECTOR' 'VECTOR' 'MATRIX'
MATRIX ← MATRIX + MATRIX
```

Selective assignment

In traditional APL you could assign an entire variable (*Z←* ...) or parts of a variable using bracket indexing (*Z[* ... *]←* ...). In APL2 this idea of assigning parts has been broadened. Most of the selection and ordering functions now work on the left of the assignment arrow. For example, (1 1⍉*MATRIX*)←0 sets the diagonal of a matrix to zero. To change the last element of a vector to twice what it was, execute (¯1↑*VECTOR*)←2×¯1↑*VECTOR*.

Selective assignment considers the expression on the left as an array of locations, or positions that can be indexed, for the variable being assigned. It works with those functions that select or rearrange elements without changing their values.

Unite

In APL2 there is a handy function, *unite*, monadic ∪, which does just what it says. On simple arrays it is equivalent to ,*ARG*:

```
      ARG←∪(3 5 6) (2 3⍴⍳6) (⍳0)
      ARG
3 5 6 1 2 3 4 5 6
      ⍴ARG
9
```

One consequence of this is that we can easily partition a vector. Try doing the following example in traditional APL:

```
      V←'NORTH/SOUTH/EAST/WEST'
      V[(V='/')/⍳⍴V]←⊂''' '''
      V
 NORTH ' ' SOUTH ' ' EAST ' ' WEST
```

```
      NV←'''',(∪V),''''
      NV
'NORTH' 'SOUTH' 'EAST' 'WEST'

      NV←⍕NV
      NV
 NORTH  SOUTH  EAST  WEST
      ρNV
4
```

Scatter-indexing

Besides its traditional uses to obtain single items or vectors or planes of items, indexing has been extended in some APL*PLUS Systems to allow working with scattered items. This form of indexing is called *choose*:

```
      X← 2 3 ρ'BAFDEC'
      X
BAF
DEC

      X[1;2],X[1;1],X[2;3]
ABC
      X[(1 2)(1 1)(2 3)]
ABC
```

The rule is that each item of the (nested) array in the brackets must call for a valid position of the left argument. The same idea can be used to assign into indexed positions. To swap $X[1;2]$ with $X[2;3]$ you can use $X[(1 2)(2 3)]←X[(2 3)(1 2)]$. You can use either traditional bracket indexing with semicolons or the new choose form, but you can't use them together in the same selection.

Index

APL2 extends indexing through the dyadic function *index*, ⌷. Its left argument L is a simple integer array whose values are in the range 1 to the axis length to be indexed in the right argument R. Each column of L is associated with an axis of R, and each element in L determines the element to be selected along the associated axis of R. This means, for example, that $2\ 1\ 3\ ⌷\ R$ is the same as $R[2;1;3]$. The real benefit comes when L itself is multidimensional, with each row of L then indexing R independently. The function then scatter indexes.

```
      3⌷10×⍳4                              (10×⍳4)[3]
30                                    30
      R←3 5ρ'DRINKWATEROFTEN'
      2 3⌷R                                R[2;3]

T                                     T
      (3 2ρ⍳4)⌷R                           R[1;2],R[3;4],R[1;2]
RER                                   RER
```

Conformability requires that $ρρR$ be the same as $^-1↑1,ρL$.

An extension of index is *index with axis*. It works the same way as index except that the left argument contains indices only for the axes selected. For the other axes all the indices are used, like bracket indexing when axes are omitted. Unselected axes are placed last in the result.

```
      2⌷[1]R                               R[2;]
WATER                                 WATER
      3⌷[2]R                               R[;3]

ITT                                   ITT
      (2 1ρ2 3)⌷[1]R                       R[2 3;]
WATER                                 WATER
OFTEN                                 OFTEN
      (2 1ρ2 3)⌷[2]R                       R[;2 3]
RAF                                   RAF
ITT                                   ITT
```

Match

To check that two arrays are exactly identical, use dyadic *match* (= overstruck with _). This function returns a scalar 1 if the two arguments are identical in shape, rank, nesting and contents, and returns scalar 0 if there are any differences at all.

```
        (×/ι0)≡5-4                    (,1)≡⊂1                        (ι0)≡''
1                                                    0
        1≡,1                          (,1)≡⊂,1                       (⊂ι0)≡⊂''
0                                                    0
        1≡⊂1                          (⊂1)≡⊂,1                       (ι0)≡0↑ι5
1                                                    1
        1≡⊂,1                         (⊂,1)≡⊂,,1                     ''≡0ρ'ABC'
0                                                    1              1
```

The each operator

This powerful operator, *each*, ¨, greatly reduces the need to use looping or complicated loopless APL idioms. The formal definition is deceptively simple: the each operator applies a function to its arguments item by item. The best way to understand each's potential is to write some examples to show how they would be done both with and without each:

```
        'ABC',¨'EFG'                         ('A','E')('B','F')('C','G')
  AE  BF  CG                           AE  BF  CG

        1 2 3 ρ¨10                            (1ρ10)(2ρ10)(3ρ10)
  10    10 10   10 10 10            10    10 10   10 10 10

        ×/¨ι¨ι3
  1 2 6

        ×/¨(1)(1 2)(1 2 3)                   (×/1)(×/ 1 2)(×/ 1 2 3)
  1 2 6                               1 2 6
```

The arguments of each follow the rules for scalar dyadic functions; that is, both arguments must have the same shape, unless one of them is a single element.

How traditional APL operators work on nested arrays

When working with the operators outer product, reduction, scan and inner product in the next few pages, think about the rules for defining the shape of the result. Even though the arguments can now be nested arrays, in each case the rules for determining the shape of the result haven't changed:

```
Z←L ∘.f R      (ρZ) is (ρL),ρR   (catenation of all the axes)
Z←f/[K]R       (ρZ) is (K=ιρρR)/ιρR   (all axes except the one reduced over)
Z←f\[K]R       (ρZ) is ρR   (all axes preserved)
Z←L f.g R      (ρZ) is (¯1↓ρL),1↓ρR   (catenation of all axes except the inner two)
```

The rules above look simple enough; however, it may take some examples to convince you they really work on nested arrays. First, we explore outer product:

```
      A←(1 2 3)(4 5)
      B← 10 20 30
      A∘.+B
  11 12 13   21 22 23   31 32 33
  14 15      24 25      34 35
```

To see what's happening, set up an operation table and start filling it in.

```
      +    |     10          20          30
  ---------+-----------------------------------
      1 2 3 |   11 12 13    21 22 23    31 32 33
      4 5   |    14 15       24 25       34 35
```

You may be surprised to find that $A \circ .+A$ won't work. That's because it would require a table like

```
    +   |    1 2 3              4 5
--------+----------------------------------
  1 2 3 |    2 4 6        LENGTH ERROR
    4 5 | LENGTH ERROR        8 10
```

In other words, even though the shapes of the arrays are conformable for outer product, the individual items must be conformable for addition, and 1 2 3 + 4 5 won't work.

When you apply the each operator to outer product, you get entirely different results; an outer product is performed on each pair of items:

```
      A∘.+¨A
 2  3  4    8  9
 3  4  5    9 10
 4  5  6
```

Think of this as $(1 \ 2 \ 3 \ \circ.+ \ 1 \ 2 \ 3) \ (4 \ 5 \ \circ.+ \ 4 \ 5)$ and you'll see how the result is developed. However, $A \circ .+¨B$ won't work because A's first item, $(1 \ 2 \ 3)$, would be added with B's first item, 10, and A's second item, $(4 \ 5)$, would be added with B's second item, 20; but there would be no match for the third item of B.

You know that reduction over simple arrays is equivalent to writing the function between adjacent items; that is, $+/1 \ 2 \ 3$ is the same as $1+2+3$. The same holds true with nested arrays, as you can see by writing out the steps:

```
      +/(10 20 30) 4 (5 6 7)
 19 30 41
      (⊂ 10 20 30)+4+⊂5 6 7
 19 30 41

      ρρ+/(10 20 30) 4 (5 6 7) ⍝NOTE THE RESULT IS A NESTED SCALAR
 0
      ⊂(10+4+5)(20+4+6)(30+4+7)
 19 30 41
```

Moreover, the shape of the result still follows the familiar rules for reduction of simple arrays: all axes are preserved except the one being reduced.

```
      ρTAB3
 2 4 3
      T3X←⊂[3] TAB3
      T3X
 111 112 113   121 122 123   131 132 133   141 142 143
 211 212 213   221 222 223   231 232 233   241 242 243

      ρT3X
 2 4

      ⌈/[1] T3X
 211 212 213   221 222 223   231 232 233   241 242 243
      ρ⌈/[1] T3X
 4
```

Suppose you want to obtain a result consisting of the sum of the elements of each item? That's literally how you do it:

```
      +/¨(1 2 3) 4 (5 6 7) ⍝ READ AS SUM OVER EACH
 6 4 18
      (+/ 1 2 3)(+/4)(+/ 5 6 7)
 6 4 18
```

Since scan is the repeated application of reduction, it follows that it will work where reduction works:

```
      +\(10 20 30) 4 (5 6 7)
 10 20 30  14 24 34  19 30 41
      +\¨(10 20 30) 4 (5 6 7)
 10 30 60  4  5 11 18
```

Incidentally, because of mixed arrays, some *DOMAIN ERROR*s associated with scan no longer appear; =*'AAAA'* produces the mixed vector *A* 1 0 0 rather than *DOMAIN ERROR*.

Inner products calculated with nested arrays are also possible, but in practice are rarely used. Since inner product includes repeated application of reduction, all the conformability rules for reduction apply here as well. Inner product will result in a *LENGTH ERROR* unless each of the items of both arguments are the same shape or are scalars.

You must be ready now to leap on your terminal to try out all this new power that nested arrays brings to you. But hold on—one of the bigger surprises is just about to be disclosed (no pun) to you. Here it is: all of the traditional operators, reduction, scan, inner and outer products, now work with dyadic mixed functions as well as the dyadic scalar functions. We already saw in Chapter 21 that catenation could be used with the outer product. It wasn't mentioned at that time, but the result of 1 2 3∘.,10 20 30 40 is nested.

Practical applications? You bet. For example, here's how to read the first three records of a file (next chapter) tied to 20 on an APL*PLUS System:

```
        DATA←□FREAD¨20∘.,⍳3        or        DATA←□FREAD 20,¨⍳3
        ⍴DATA
3
        DATA
 100 103   200 201 202   300 301 302 303 304 305
```

How traditional APL functions work on nested arrays

Many of the APL functions take on additional capabilities in the world of nested arrays. We have already encountered the shape function, monadic ⍴, in this chapter. It gives the shape of the array at the outermost level:

```
        A←(2 3 ⍴'HOWNOW') 'BROWN' 'COW'
        A
 HOW   BROWN   COW
 NOW
        ⍴A
3
```

To see the shapes of items at the next level of nesting, use the each operator with shape (think of 'the *shape* of *each* item'). To get the ranks at the next level, apply the 'shape of each' twice:

```
        ⍴¨A
 2 3   5   3
        ⍴¨⍴¨A
 2   1   1
```

To see how these work, look at the process in detail:

```
        ⍴¨⍴¨A
 2   1   1

        ⍴¨⍴¨(2 3 ⍴'HOWNOW') 'BROWN' 'COW'
 2   1   1

        ⍴¨(⍴ 2 3 ⍴'HOWNOW')(⍴'BROWN')(⍴'COW')
 2   1   1

        ⍴¨(2 3)(,5)(,3)
 2   1   1

        (⍴ 2 3)(⍴,5)(⍴,3)
 2   1   1

        (,2)(,1)(,1)
 2   1   1
```

The items of the result are enclosed because they are one-item vectors. To remove the enclosure, use ⊃¨⍴¨⍴¨A or ,↑⍴¨⍴¨A.

Here is how you would calculate the averages of the nested vector *DATA* gathered in the last section:

```
      (+/¨DATA)÷ρ¨DATA
101.5   201  302.5
```

Those mixed functions that select or rearrange generally work on the items of nested arrays as they do on simple arrays. This includes reverse, rotate, compress (replicate), expand, index, transpose, take, drop, reshape, ravel, catenate and laminate, as well as the new ones, enclose, disclose, split and mix. For all the dyadic ones except catenate and laminate, the left argument must be simple (that is, not nested).

All the functions above work at the outer level only. For instance, reverse changes the order of the three items in *A*, but not the order of the characters enclosed in those items:

```
        ΦA                              Φ¨ΦA
COW     BROWN   HOW             WOC     NWORB   WOH
                NOW                             WON

        Φ¨A                             ΦΦ¨A
WOH     NWORB   WOC             WOC     NWORB   WOH
WON                                             WON

        Φ¨Φ¨A                           Φ¨¨¨A
HOW     BROWN   COW             HOW     BROWN   COW
NOW                             NOW
```

Φ¨¨¨ reaches into the second level of the nest, which consists of scalars. That's why the last example above has no effect.

Here are some more examples for you to ponder:

```
        2↑A                             ,¨A
HOW     BROWN                   HOWNOW   BROWN    COW
NOW                             2↑¨,¨A
        2↑¨A                    HO   BR   CO
LENGTH ERROR                    (ι3)↑¨,¨A
        2↑¨A                    H    BR   COW
        ∧
```

Index of (dyadic ι) and membership also work on the outer level of nested arrays. Their results are simple and the shape of the result is still the same as the shape of the right argument for ranking or the left argument for membership. Technically, the implied = comparison is replaced by ≡.

```
        AιA                 'NOW' 'COW' ιA              Aε 'NOW' 'COW'
1  2  3                   3  3  2                      0  0  1
```

The rest of the mixed functions, monadic ⊞ ⍋ ⍒ ⍉ and dyadic ⊞ ⊤ ⊥ ⌽ \ ⍋ ⍒ work only on non-nested arrays. Thus, ⍋(20 10 5 10) (20 30 10) won't work, but you can grade each of the items:

```
      ⍋¨(20 10 5 10)(20 30 10)
3 2 4 1   3 1 2
```

Rearranging the contents of the items according to their grades (the equivalent of X[⍋X] for a non-nested vector) is somewhat harder to do. Bracket indexing can't be used with each, so pick has to be used. Note that the items have to be enclosed one more level (by ⊂¨X) to make it work.

```
      X←(20 10 5 10) (20 30 10)
      (⍋¨X)⊃¨¨¨⊂¨X
(5 10 10 20) (10 20 30)
```

All the primitive scalar functions, dyadic + − × ÷ * ⊛ ⌈ ⌊ | ! ○ < ≤ = ≥ > ≠ ∨ ∧ ⍲ ⍱ and monadic + − × ÷ * ⊛ ⌈ ⌊ | ! ○ ~ ? ε work on the data at the bottom of the nest, as opposed to the mixed functions, which work on the items at the outermost level of the nested array:

```
        A                     'O'=A                      ('O'=A)+2×'W'=A
HOW     BROWN   COW     0 1 0   0 0 1 0 0   0 1 0    0 1 2   0 0 1 2 0   0 1 2
NOW                     0 1 0                         0 1 2
```

As with simple arrays, scalars and one-element arrays are conformable for the dyadic functions. Remember that the functions associate with each pair of items and you'll understand why these work: $(1 \quad 2 \quad 3) \quad 4 \quad +$ $(, 5) (20 \quad 30)$ is the same as $(1 \quad 2 \quad 3 + , 5) \quad (4 + 20 \quad 30)$. It's as though the each operator were applied an arbitrary number of times.

Since the primitive scalar functions already work on the data at the bottom of the nest (the formal term is *pervasive*), each does not have any effect on them. For that reason, $(1 \quad 2 \quad 3) \quad 4 + \overset{\cdots}{} (, 5) (20 \quad 30)$ is the same as $(1 \quad 2 \quad 3) \quad 4 \quad + \quad (, 5) (20 \quad 30)$.

When and where to use nested arrays

Some people feel that the concept of nested arrays and the associated extensions to traditional APL is as significant an advance as APL was over other programming languages. In terms of the new power and freedom of expression that is no doubt true, but there is a dark side to the story also.

Others feel that APL has been made more confusing by all these new features—for example, no longer can arrays be regarded as just plain rectangular. Moreover, at this writing there are differences among the various commercial implementations which can affect the portability of applications.

We suggest that you do explore nested arrays, but that you adopt a limited approach to its use. Begin by avoiding the use of nesting for data that has permanence (i.e., is filed or stored in the workspace between sessions). On the other hand, do employ nested arrays and the new functions in local algorithms if they make programming easier for you. As with the rest of APL, shorter is probably clearer, but make sure you use comments liberally. And be prepared to revise your work if you must change APL systems. When you gain experience and confidence in nested arrays it is then appropriate to use them for saved data. Ultimately, nested arrays gives you the power to represent data realistically and naturally, without artifices like padding.

Our own experience in adapting to nested arrays was that it was harder for us than for our students. This we attribute to our own habits formed by sixteen years of traditional APL use. Newcomers to the APL scene accept nested arrays as useful, powerful, and not particularly difficult to learn.

If you are beginning to see how nested arrays can be put to practical use, you'll appreciate the applications illustrated in some of the problems. We especially recommend that you work through problems 9 (report formatting), 13 (branching), 14 (side-by-side display), 15 (text processing) and 16 (vectors of different lengths).

PROBLEMS

1. On each expression indicate if the array produced is simple or nested.

```
3  4  5            3 (4 'A')          'ABC'  'XYZ'
(,3)(,4)(,5)       ((3)(4)(5))        'ABC','XYZ'
(3)(4)(5)          (,3),(,4),(,5)     'A' 'B' 'C'
3  4  'A'          3  4  'AB'         'A' ('B' 'C')
```

2. Given the variables $A \leftarrow 2 \quad 3 \rho \iota 6$ $B \leftarrow 99$ $C \leftarrow 'APL'$, show the depth, shape, rank and display of the array produced by each expression.

```
⊃A                 (⊂A),(⊂B),(⊂C)     2  3ρC  C
⊂A                 ⊃⊃A                2  3ρ⊂C
⊂⊂A                3  4ρA  B  C       B  B  B
⊂⊃A                2  3ρC             ⊂A  B  C
```

3. Using the variables defined above and $D \leftarrow A \ B \ C$, show the depth, shape and display of the array produced by each expression.

D	$(\supset D[1]),D[2]$	$\supset^{..}D$
$D[1]$	B	$,^{..}D$
$\supset D[1]$	$\subset B$	$\rho^{..}D$
$\supset \supset D[1]$	$\subset \subset B$	$\rho^{..}\rho^{..}D$
$D[2]$	$\supset B$	$\supset \rho^{..}\rho^{..}D$
$\supset D[2]$	$\supset \supset B$	$+/^{-}1 \downarrow D$
$D[1],D[2]$	$C,^{..}B$	$(\subset A),^{..}C$
$D[1 \ 2]$	$A,^{..}B$	

4. Describe what these expressions do: $1 \ge = A$ and $\square CR^{..}\subset[2]\square NL \ 3$

5. Write an expression to change a vector of character vectors that contains no blanks into a simple vector with one blank between each of the original vectors. For example, $'APL' \ 'IS' \ 'FUN'$ would be changed to $'APL \ IS \ FUN'$.

6. Write an expression to change a simple vector that may contain blanks into a vector of vectors that are split at the blanks. Do not include the blanks in the result. For example, $'APL \ IS \ FUN'$ would be changed to $'APL' \ 'IS' \ 'FUN'$.

7. Write an expression that will enclose an array only if the array is simple.

8. Write an expression to attach row numbers onto the left edge of any matrix.

9. Given the variables

        COLS←'JANUARY' 'FEBRUARY' 'MARCH'
        ROWS←'SHOES' 'TIES' 'WORK BOOTS' 'SHIRTS'
        DATA←2 3ρ100 523 0 95 0 192 3 12 18 38 0 0
    Write an expression to produce the following display:

	JANUARY	FEBRUARY	MARCH
SHOES	100	523	0
TIES	95	0	192
WORK BOOTS	3	12	18
SHIRTS	38	0	0

    The expression should work regardless of the number of items or their length as long as $\rho ROWS$ is $1 \uparrow \rho DATA$ and $\rho COLS$ is $^{-}1 \uparrow \rho DATA$.

10. Write a monadic function named $SHAPES$ that takes as its argument any array and returns a nested vector of the shapes of all the simple arrays that it contains. For example, $SHAPES \ 'APL' \ (45 \ ((3 \ 4 \ \rho \iota 6) \ (\iota 0)))$ results in $(,3) \ (\iota 0) \ (3 \ 4) \ (,0)$

11. The following function is very similar to monadic format. How does it differ and why?

        ∇ Z←FORMAT A
    [1]   Z←0 1↓0 ¯1↓⍕⊂((-2⌈ρρA)↑1 1,ρA)ρA ∇

12. If $X \leftarrow P1 \supset V$, $Y \leftarrow P2 \supset V$ and $Z \leftarrow P3 \supset V$, express $P1 \ P2 \ P3 \supset^{..} \subset V$ in terms of X , Y and Z .

13. Use pick with execute to branch to $L1$ if $X > Y$, $L2$ otherwise.

14. For $A \leftarrow 3 \ 4\rho \iota 12$ and $B \leftarrow 4 \ 2\rho 10 \times \iota 8$, display A , B and $A + . \times B$ side by side.

15. Show how to **A** get a count of the number of occurrences of each word in a text string $TEXT \leftarrow 'THIS \ IS \ AN \ EXAMPLE \ OF \ WORD \ PROCESSING \ IN \ THIS \ CHAPTER'$; **B** check for the presence of the phrase $'AN \ EXAMPLE'$; **C** produce a listing of those words in $TEXT$ not in the word list $REFERENCE$.

16. You are a businessman with only three accounts, each of which consists of debits for goods purchased and credits for returned goods. The data is stored in a nested vector $ACCOUNTS$, with two vectors (debits, credits) for each account: $ACCOUNTS \leftarrow ((100 \ 350) \ (10)) \ ((5000 \ 290 \ 450 \ 600) \ (\iota 0)) \ ((150) \ (\iota 0))$. **A** Find the total credits and debits by account; **B** Find the net sales for each account.

Chapter 26: Introduction to Data Files

Almost all commercial data processing applications and a good many scientific applications involve more data than can be jammed into a workspace. Even though sophisticated coding and packing techniques may be employed, sooner or later the workspace will fill up. Also, there is a class of applications, such as airline reservation systems, in which several users must be able to read or update values almost simultaneously. For example, imagine that your terminal is one of many serving as a reservation station, and you and the other reservation agents are all trying to sell whatever seats are still unclaimed. There would have to be a variable to serve as an inventory record to keep count of how many seats remain. It would be decreased whenever any agent reserves a seat or increased when a seat is cancelled.

Both of these classes of applications can be handled through careful and tedious use of the system commands $)COPY$ and $)SAVE$, but at best they would be prone to error. Furthermore, in the case of a reservation system, you would have the problem of deciding whose saved workspace holds the most recent updating of the inventory. There are good odds that you would never resolve the situation of two agents attempting to decrement the inventory at the same time.

Large database applications and shared database applications are both properly handled using a *file system*. There are many different file systems, but the two major types are those based on IBM's *shared variables* concept (next chapter) and those based on the *component file* concept (here). The examples used in this chapter are based on STSC's APL, but Sharp's is almost identical, the major difference being the names used. For example, STSC uses $\Box FCREATE$ and $\Box FREAD$ to create a file and to read from it, while Sharp uses $\Box CREATE$ and $\Box READ$.

A *file* is a place to put data so that it is available to the programs in your active workspace, but doesn't take any space away from the active workspace. You don't have to be concerned with where the data is actually put; it is enough to say that it is stored in the same type of equipment that holds the workspaces of your library.

Like workspaces, files have names, and data can be stored in them. In fact, the data items stored in a file can have the same variety of structures that variables have. However, unlike workspaces, instead of referring to a data item by name, you refer to it by a number, that number being the position of that data item in the file. Each data item in a file is called a *component* (instead of a variable) and the file itself consists of a sequence of these components. You could have a file with, say, three thousand components, and each component could be a character matrix of shape 100 by 90. This would amount to nearly three million bytes if you had to stuff it into a workspace all at once, which would be impossible in most APL systems and grossly inefficient in the rest. When using files you have to contend with only one component at a time in your workspace.

File creation

Now that we have the generalities out of the way, let's approach learning file use by considering an example of a simplistic customer information system containing both identifying and geographic data.

Imagine that you are responsible for keeping business related data on some 5000 customers. When a new customer is added to the list, 25 items of information, including size, address, type of business, etc., are recorded. Some customers may have multiple locations, which may change from time to time as, say, branch offices, warehouses or factories are opened or closed. We will assume that no company in our customer set has more than 100 locations.

A reasonable structure for holding this data (if it could fit in the workspace) would be a three-dimensional array of customers by location and by associated data category (25 items). There would be lots of wasted space because the second dimension, locations, would either have to be as long as the number of locations associated with the most dispersed customer or limited to some fixed amount, say, 100, as suggested above.

In the file we're going to create, the component numbering will correspond to the first dimension of this hypothetical three-dimensional array, and each component will consist of a given customer's data. Each component will be a matrix whose row dimension is the number of locations recorded, with 25 columns for the 25 pieces of associated data.

Let's name the file we will create `'CUSTOMERS'`:

> `'CUSTOMERS' ⎕FCREATE 98`

The dyadic function `⎕FCREATE` is used to create the file. Its left argument is the name of the file. The naming rules are similar to those of workspaces: names must consist of letters and numbers, and can be up to eleven characters in length. Note that the name is in quotes, which is different from the way workspaces are referenced in system commands.

The right argument is called the *file tie number*. It is a unique number for referencing the file when it is in active use. A number is used rather than the file name so that if you have two or more files active (tied) at the same time, you can 'index' from file to file much as you index an array in the workspace. The number you choose doesn't really matter much except that it must be a positive integer, and there must be a different number for each file in active use at any one time. You can find out which files are tied at any time by the niladic function `⎕FNAMES`:

> `⎕FNAMES`
> `78975 CUSTOMERS`

The result is a 22-column character matrix. Columns 1 through 10 hold the user numbers of the owners of the files, column 11 is blank and columns 12 through 22 hold the names of the files. Our particular matrix has only one row, but if you had six files active, the matrix would have six rows. The order of the file names in the matrix corresponds to the chronological order in which they were tied.

A listing of file tie numbers in use can be obtained by the niladic function `⎕FNUMS`:

> `⎕FNUMS`
> `98`

The result is a vector holding the file tie numbers in the same sequence as the names in `⎕FNAMES`. Thus, if you already have some files tied, to find a unique file number for activation of another file, execute

> `1+⌈/0,⎕FNUMS`
> `99`

In the expression above, the 0 is necessary to cover the case where no files are currently activated. Without it, the result would be `⌈/⍳0`, which is `¯7.237005577E75`. Of course, 1 added to that is not a positive number.

Whenever you sign off or lose your telephone connection, your files are automatically deactivated or *untied*. They are *not* automatically reactivated when you sign back on, even if `CONTINUE` is reloaded. You have to reactivate them with the `⎕FTIE` function:

> `'CUSTOMERS' ⎕FTIE 76`

The syntax is similar to `⎕FCREATE`, except that this function is used to tie files that had been created previously. Actually, `⎕FCREATE` both *creates* and *ties* a file, while `⎕FTIE` only *activates* a file. Note that in this session, we tied `'CUSTOMERS'` to the number 76 instead of the number 98. There is no permanent connection between a file name and a file tie number. A file can be tied to whatever number you choose in any session.

To untie a file in midsession, use the monadic function `⎕FUNTIE`. Its argument is the vector of tie numbers of the files that you want to deactivate. `⎕FUNTIE ⎕FNUMS[ρ⎕FNUMS]` would untie the file that was tied most recently in this session.

`⎕FSIZE` is a 'shape of' operation applied to a file. It is monadic, and takes an active file tie number as its argument. The result is a four-element vector holding (1) the lowest numbered component in the file, (2) the number of the next available component in the file, (3) the amount of space that you are presently using in the file and (4) the total space available in the file.

```
      ⎕FSIZE 79              ⎕FSIZE 76
FILE  TIE ERROR         1  1 128 100000
      ⎕FSIZE 79
      ∧
```

We got an error because there is no file tied with 79. But 76 is an active tie number for the `'CUSTOMERS'` file.

The lowest component in our file is 1, but the next available component is also 1. This tells you that the file is empty, which is certainly what we'd expect for a file that we had never put anything into. The third element is the amount of storage currently used by the file. Depending on which system you are using, it may be zero for a new file, or it may be a small amount of overhead storage that even an empty file needs. The last element is 100000, the nominal amount of space available for storage in this file. Both the third and fourth elements are expressed in bytes and their values may differ from system to system.

Our file certainly doesn't have the capacity to hold all the data we intend for it. There are two ways to provide this space. If we had created the file as `'CUSTOMERS 52000000'` `⎕FCREATE` 98, then it would have had the required capacity (computed from 4 bytes per integer to be stored, times 5000 customers, times 100 rows, times 25 columns), plus 4 percent overhead. Alternatively, we could have used the dyadic function `⎕FRESIZE`, whose right argument is the file tie number, and whose left argument is the amount of space to be reserved for the file:

```
      52000000 ⎕FRESIZE 76              ⎕FSIZE 76
                                   1 1 128 52000000
```

Updating a file

Let's now store some data in the file. We'll use the following variables as data for two customers:

```
      C1←2 25ρι50
      C2←(ι4)∘.×φι25
```

We are simulating customer 1 with two locations and customer 2 with four locations. In particular, *C1[1;1]* is 1 and *C2[1;1]* is 25. Let's put customer 1 on the file, using the dyadic function *⎕FAPPEND*:

```
      C1 ⎕FAPPEND 76
      ⎕FSIZE 76
1 2 384 52000000
```

⎕FAPPEND puts the value of its left argument as a new component at the end of the file designated in the right argument. The lowest component is still number 1, but the next available component is now number 2. (Incidentally, some file systems would return the component number being appended as an explicit result.) Continuing, we add customer 2:

```
      C2 ⎕FAPPEND 76
      ⎕FSIZE 76
1 3 840 52000000
```

The amount of space used (third element of the result of *⎕FSIZE*) increases as you store more data. Although it may appear to increase erratically, it is that the file system reclaims space where possible, and occasionally uses extra chunks of space to manage its internal directories.

Now we're going to do what looks like a foolhardy act:

```
      )CLEAR
CLEAR WS
```

Before you began using files, doing that operation would have meant permanent loss of the data (unless, of course, you had)*SAVE*d an image of the workspace). However, our customer data is stored safely in a file and isn't affected by clearing the workspace.

We now have to learn how to read information from files, using *⎕FREAD*:

```
      C1←⎕FREAD 76 1              C2←⎕FREAD 76 2
      ρC1                         ρC2
2 25                         4 25

      C1[1;1]                     C2[1;1]
1                          25
      ρC2
VALUE ERROR
      ρC2
      ^
```

The ⎕*FREAD* function brings into the active workspace an image of what's in the file component that you ask for. Note that, as in Chapter 11, we used the term *image*. The file is no more changed by reading it than a variable in the workspace is changed by using it as part of an expression. Also, while we frequently read the values back into the same variables that they came from, it is not a requirement. For example, we could have entered *C2*←⎕*FREAD* 76 1 and *C1*←⎕*FREAD* 76 2, which would interchange the data for customers 1 and 2 in the workspace (but *not* in the file).

You may have observed that the file tie numbers are preserved even if the workspace is cleared. File tie numbers are changed only by the functions ⎕*FCREATE*, ⎕*FTIE*, ⎕*FUNTIE*, ⎕*FSTIE* or ⎕*FERASE* (the last two will be explained subsequently), or by signing off.

Here is a simple function to find the total number of locations of all customers (that is, the total number of rows in the file):

```
        ∇R←TOTCUST N;I
[1]     ⍝N IS THE FILE NUMBER
[2]     R←0 ◊ I←(¯1+⎕FSIZE N)[1]
[3]     LOOP:I←I+1 ◊ →(I=(⎕FSIZE N)[2])/0 ◊ R←R+1↑ρ⎕FREAD N,I ◊ →LOOP ∇
        TOTCUST 76
6
```

By this time you should be catching on to the use of files. More file operations will be introduced later in the chapter, along with example functions to utilize our customer database. There are two operations that are obvious necessities: (1) establishing a new customer in the file by methods a bit more friendly than what was done above; and (2) adding a new location to any individual customer's data already in the file. The first is handled by the defined function *NEWCUST*:

```
        ∇NEWCUST N
[1]     ⍝N IS THE FILE NUMBER
[2]     ⍝ APPENDS AN EMPTY MATRIX FOR NEW CUSTOMER
[3]     ⍝ AND PRINTS THE CUSTOMER NUMBER ASSIGNED.
[4]     (0 25ρ0) ⎕FAPPEND N
[5]     'THIS IS CUSTOMER ',⍕(⎕FSIZE N)[2]-1 ∇
```

CUSTDATA records the data gathered on a customer:

```
        ∇C CUSTDATA N;DATA
[1]     ⍝C IS CUSTOMER NUMBER, N IS TIE NUMBER
[2]     →((C≥(⎕FSIZE N)[1])∧C<(⎕FSIZE N)[2])/OK
[3]     'NO SUCH CUSTOMER NUMBER' ◊ →0
[4]     OK:'ENTER 25 VALUES' ◊ →(25=ρDATA←,⎕)/UPDATE
[5]     'INVALID INPUT' ◊ →0
[6]     UPDATE:DATA←(⎕FREAD N,C),[1]DATA ◊ DATA ⎕FREPLACE N,C ∇
```

You probably spotted the new file function ⎕*FREPLACE* on line 6. It replaces the *C*-th file component with new data from the workspace. In our case it's the catenation of the existing component with another row, *DATA*, on the bottom. There doesn't need to be any relation between what is being replaced and what you're replacing it with, although in the above case there happened to be. The requirement that only the first 100 locations are to be kept in the file can be satisfied simply by changing the second statement on line 6 to read (100 25↑*DATA*) ⎕*FREPLACE N,P*.

Getting data from a file

Having written functions to enter a new customer and his associated data, we now turn to programs for getting selected data from the file. *Information retrieval* is the computer industry's term for this procedure. Much effort is spent by computer professionals to develop and improve both file design (how the data is laid out in the files) and functions to access the database. In general, it requires more time to take one value from each of several components than it does to take several values out of one component. And if your database includes vast amounts of data, you really need to study how the information is to be used before you choose the layout of your file. As you have already seen, the nature of APL is such that even if you first happen to choose the wrong layout for your file, it's no big deal to revise it. However, the limited scope of this text doesn't permit our going into all the fine points of file design.

Complete data on each customer can be obtained by reading his component. Here is a function for obtaining a matrix of data from one or more customers' latest locations added to the database:

```
      ∇R←V LASTLOC N
[1]   AV IS CUSTOMER NUMBER; N IS TIE NUMBER
[2]   R←0 25ρ0
[3]   LOOP:→(0=ρV)/0 ◇ R←R,[1]¯1 25↑□FREAD N,1↑V ◇ V←1↓V ◇ →LOOP ∇
```

The following function returns a vector of customer numbers with at least one location having more than 99 employees (item number 2, i.e., the second column):

```
      ∇R←C2GT99 N
[1]   R←ι0 ◇ I←(□FSIZE N)[1]
[2]   LOOP:→(I=(□FSIZE N)[2])/0
[3]   R←R,(∨/(□FREAD N,I)[;2]>99)/I
[4]   I←I+1 ◇ →LOOP ∇
```

The approach in $C2GT99$ can be generalized to produce a function which returns customer numbers all of which satisfy some relation on some column; for example, all customers who have ordered product 100 (the 25th column), or all customers whose state code is less than 7 (the New England states) in column 12:

```
      ∇R←REL SELECT NCV;N;C;V;COMP;T
[1]   ANCV IS 3-ELE VECTOR - TIE NUMBER, COLUMN, VALUE
[2]   A REL IS RELATION SYMBOL (<≤=≥> OR ≠) AS A CHARACTER SCALAR
[3]   N←NCV[1] ◇ C←NCV[2] ◇ V←NCV[3]
[4]   R←ι0 ◇ I←(□FSIZE N)[1]
[5]   REL←(LT,LE,EQ,GE,GT,NE)['<≤=≥>≠'ιREL]
[6]   LOOP:→(I=(□FSIZE N)[2])/0 ◇ COMP←(□FREAD N,I)[;C] ◇ →REL
[7]   LT:T←∨/V<COMP ◇ →XX
[8]   LE:T←∨/V≤COMP ◇ →XX
[9]   EQ:T←∨/V=COMP ◇ →XX
[10]  GE:T←∨/V≥COMP ◇ →XX
[11]  GT:T←∨/V>COMP ◇ →XX
[12]  NE:T←∨/V≠COMP ◇ →XX
[13]  XX:R←R,T/I ◇ I←I+1 ◇ →LOOP ∇

      '=' SELECT 76 25 100
2

      '<' SELECT 76 12 7
1 2
```

More file functions

Some additional useful file functions will now be discussed briefly. First, the $□FLIB$ function is used to list the file names in a *library* of files. $□FLIB$, with your user number as an argument, produces an explicit result: a character matrix with 22 columns and as many rows as you have different file names. Columns 1 through 10 hold your user number; column 11 is blank; and columns 12 through 22 hold the file name.

To illustrate the next function, $□FDROP$, consider a file application involving order entry and invoicing. As each order is received, the pertinent information is appended as a new component on a file. Each order shipped causes an invoice to be produced, and the order information for that order is no longer needed. Most of the time, but not always, orders will be shipped in the order of receipt. It makes sense to let the component number be the order/invoice number, since there will be a different component for each one.

The only fly in the ointment is how to dispose of all the components holding order information that has already been invoiced. For that, we use $□FDROP$. It is monadic, and its argument is the file number and the number of sequential components you want to drop from the front end (positive number) or back end (negative number) of the file.

For example, if some file tied to the number 20 presently has 153 components (that is, $□FSIZE$ 20 results in 1 154 40028 100000), then dropping 15 components from the front end ($□FDROP$ 20 15) leaves 139 components. Then $□FSIZE$ 20 would now yield 16 154 35630 100000. Note that component numbering now starts with 16. If you now drop the last nine components, ($□FDROP$ 20 ¯9), the result of $□FSIZE$ 20 would be 16 145 34918 100000.

An application in which components are appended to the file and other components are later dropped from the front end, is called FIFO (first-in, first-out), while an application which appends and drops from the back end is called LIFO (last-in, first-out).

Our order/invoice application is a member of the FIFO category. Here is a possible program to process an invoice, the argument *N* being the invoice number (component number) to be processed:

```
        ∇INVOICERUN N;ORD;FN
[1]     'ORDERS' ⎕FTIE FN←1+⌈/0,⎕FNUMS
[2]     →(1=+/N<2↑⎕FSIZE FN)/OK1
[3]     'THIS NUMBER NOT IN FILE' ◊ ⎕FUNTIE FN ◊ →0
[4]     OK1:ORD←⎕FREAD FN,N ◊ →(0≠ρORD)/OK2
[5]     'THIS NUMBER ALREADY PROCESSED' ◊ ⎕FUNTIE FN ◊ →0
[6]     OK2: PRINTINVOICE ⍝ INVOICE PRINTING PROGRAM NOT SHOWN HERE
[7]     (⍳0) ⎕FREPLACE FN,N ⍝ REPLACE WITH EMPTY AFTER PROCESSING
[8]     DROPLOOP:→(=/2↑⎕FSIZE FN)/DONE ⍝ DONE IF FILE IS EMPTY
[9]     →(0≠ρ ⎕FREAD FN,1↑⎕FSIZE FN)/DONE
[10]    ⍝ STOP WHEN FIRST COMPONENT NOT EMPTY
[11]    ⎕FDROP FN,1 ◊ →DROPLOOP
[12]    DONE:⎕FUNTIE FN ∇
```

We have departed from a pure FIFO scheme in using an empty vector to signal that an invoice has been processed. After processing, any empty components on the front end of the file are dropped.

When a file is no longer needed, it can be removed by the ⎕FERASE function. Once ⎕FERASE has been applied to a file, that file name no longer exists and any storage used by the file is available for reuse. The file to be erased must be tied. ⎕FERASE is a dyadic function whose left argument is the file name and whose right argument is the file tie number. It may seem redundant that both the name and tie number are required, but this is done to protect you from erasing the wrong file by accident.

```
    'CUSTOMERS' ⎕FERASE 76
```

File access

Our discussion so far has assumed that you are the only person to access and update your files. This is satisfactory for many applications, but what do you do if the file in question contains, say, airline flight reservations which may be updated by any of thousands of ticket or travel agents across the country? We need a mechanism that permits sharing data among multiple users. To make a file shareable, its owner must overtly arrange for others to share it. For reasons of data security, when a file is first created, it is personal (i.e., not available to anyone other than the owner).

When a file owner decides to share his file, he must determine the type of *access permission* he wants to give others. For example, a bank systems manager may own (and hence control) a file of customer transactions. He might also want to allow the bank tellers to append new transactions on the file, but prevent their reading any of the already filed material. He might also want the bank president to be able to read any transaction, but (because the president has clumsy fingers) might not be willing to let him replace or append any components. And the people in the accounting department may have read, replace and append access, but are not allowed to drop or erase any transactions.

In the APL*PLUS and Sharp file systems, all these access rules are determined and recorded in an *access matrix*. Each file has associated with it an access matrix with three columns: the first contains the user numbers of those who have been given access permission of some sort; the second is the sum of *access codes* granted to each individual; and the third is an *access passnumber*, which provides a level of security to be discussed later in this chapter. For the time being the third column will be kept at zero, which means no access passnumber is required.

Here are the codes used to grant accesses to a file:

1 allows ⎕FREAD	128 allows ⎕FRENAME
2 allows ⎕FTIE	512 allows ⎕FRDCI
4 allows ⎕FERASE	1024 allows ⎕FRESIZE
8 allows ⎕FAPPEND	2048 allows ⎕FHOLD
16 allows ⎕FREPLACE	4096 allows ⎕FRDAC
32 allows ⎕FDROP	8192 allows ⎕FSTAC

A file's access matrix is brought into the workspace by an expression of the form $AM←⎕FRDAC \; FN$, where *FN* is the file number. As mentioned earlier, *AM* will always have 3 columns. For a file which has no accesses set, ρAM is 0 3.

Say you wanted user 7 8 9 7 5 to be permitted to read components on a file which you own, and user 1 7 2 9 to be able to append and replace components on your file. You would construct a matrix like this:

```
      AM←2  3ρ78975  1  0  1729  24  0
      AM
78975      1       0
 1729     24       0
      AM ⎕FSTAC 20
```

The ⎕FSTAC function is used to change the accesses for a file. Its left argument will be the access matrix of file 20 in this example. User 7 8 9 7 5 has read access to the file because of the 1 in column two, and user 1 7 2 9 has append and replace access because of the 2 4 (i.e., 8 for append plus 16 for replace) in $AM[2;2]$.

Given that someone has granted you access to his file, how do you actually do it? You can list the file names to which another user (say 4 1 7 6 3 8 2) has given you some kind of access by using ⎕FLIB:

```
      ⎕FLIB 4176382
4176382 BONDS
4176382 STOCKS
```

Now that you know what files you have access to, you can tie them with ⎕FSTIE:

```
      '4176382 STOCKS' ⎕FSTIE 909
```

The left argument is the owner's user number and file name. ⎕FSTIE works much like the function ⎕FTIE introduced earlier. Once ⎕FSTIE has been executed, you can perform any of the file functions for which access permission has been granted.

Any number of users may tie the same file at the same time using ⎕FSTIE (called a *shared tie*), but only one person may tie a file using ⎕FTIE (*exclusive tie*). Normally, when using someone else's files, you 'share-tie' them. In fact, most shared applications don't permit ⎕FTIE (as controlled by the access matrix) except for emergency maintenance. ⎕FSTIE permission comes along with giving permission to do any of ⎕FREAD, ⎕FSIZE, ⎕FAPPEND, ⎕FREPLACE, ⎕FDROP, ⎕FHOLD, ⎕FRDAC, ⎕FSTAC, ⎕FRDCI, ⎕FRENAME and ⎕FRESIZE, while the function ⎕FERASE requires that the file be exclusively tied.

Here is another example of the use of shared files. Imagine that there is a class of students in a course in computer technology and that the instructor tells them to 'mail' their semester project reports as character vectors appended to a file he created, called *PROJECT*. The students' user numbers are 1001, 1002, 1003, ... ,1020. Since the instructor doesn't want them to read each other's work, the access permissions are set at 8, i.e., append only:

```
      'PROJECT' ⎕FCREATE 90
      ((1000+ι20),20 2ρ8 0) ⎕FSTAC 90
      ⎕FUNTIE 90
```

Each student can either share-tie and append his result, or he can append more than one component. Now there's always one wise-guy in a class of students who figures he can write whatever sort of graffiti he chooses into his instructor's file. But he won't go undetected. The function ⎕FRDCI (for *read component information*) is designed to let you know who did what to your file. Its syntax is like ⎕FREAD. The argument is a two-element vector consisting of the file number and component number.

The result is always a three-element vector. The first element is the number of bytes the component would use up if it were read into the workspace. This gives you the opportunity to bypass reading a large component in a crowded workspace. The second element is the user number of the person who last appended or replaced this particular component. A user who appends or replaces a component cannot suppress this information. The third element is the *timestamp*: when the component was appended or last replaced. This can be very useful when trying to analyze past actions performed on a file. The time is computed in milliseconds since midnight, January 1, 1900.

In workspace 0 or 1 *FILEAID* on APL*PLUS systems, you will find the monadic function *TIMEN*. Use the third element of ⎕FRDCI's result as its right argument. It will convert the argument into a more readable form, a six-element vector consisting of the year, month, day, hour, minute and seconds.

Real-time systems

The □*FHOLD* function is employed in sophisticated real-time systems where it is important that changes to the database be synchronized among several sharers. For example, suppose you had a shared file in which one component is a character matrix of names and another component is a vector of associated numbers (one number per row of the character matrix), and you did the following update:

```
NAMES←□FREAD 1 1 ◇ VEC←□FREAD 1 2
NAMES[K;]←20↑◙ ◇ VEC[K]←□
NAMES □FREPLACE 1 1 ◇ VEC □FREPLACE 1 2
```

There is a risk that some other user might execute

```
NAMES←□FREAD 1 1 ◇ VEC←□FREAD 1 2
```

and get the data that existed on the file for the time between when you entered *NAMES* □*FREPLACE* 1 1 and *VEC* □*FREPLACE* 1 2. If that were to happen, he'd have the new name but the old value.

To prevent this, the □*FHOLD* function is used. It is monadic, its argument consisting of the tie numbers of those shared files for which you want *temporary exclusive access*. The general idea is to bar you and the other sharers from doing anything with the file, if any of the sharers has already begun a critical updating sequence.

Thus, your update section should look like

```
NEWNAME←,◙ ◇ NEWVALUE←□
□FHOLD 1 ◇ NAMES←□FREAD 1 1 ◇ VEC←□FREAD 1 2
NAMES[K;]←20↑NEWNAME ◇ VEC[K]←NEWVALUE
NAMES □FREPLACE 1 1 ◇ VEC □FREPLACE 1 2
□FHOLD ι0
```

and the other user's retrieval section should be

```
□FHOLD 1 ◇ NAMES←□FREAD 1 1 ◇ VEC←□FREAD 1 2 ◇ □FHOLD ι0
```

What actually happens when you execute □*FHOLD* is that a request for temporary exclusive use of the files is entered. If no one presently has the files in temporary exclusive use, you get them. If someone has an active □*FHOLD*, execution of your function is suspended until his □*FHOLD* is broken (and all users who had executed □*FHOLD* prior to your request have been satisfied). Then it's your turn. To avoid hard feelings among disgruntled users, extensive updating should be done at times when the use of the file by others is likely to be minimal.

You might think that an uncooperative sharer could hog the file by executing a □*FHOLD* and not breaking it; however, □*FHOLD* is broken by any of these actions:

1. An interruption at the keyboard
2. Executing another □*FHOLD*
3. Any return to execution mode
4. Untying the file
5. Signing off or being bounced

□*FHOLD* ι0 in the above example relinquishes your hold so that others don't have to wait unnecessarily to use the file. The conversational input *NEWNAME*←,◙ ◇ *NEWVALUE*←□ was moved outside the domain of □*FHOLD* for a similar reason. Other users might waste a lot of time waiting for you to input at the keyboard while hogging the file, although in some applications this might be a perfectly valid technique.

Transferring ownership and renaming files

The □*FRENAME* function, as its name suggests, lets you rename a file. The left argument is the new name, and the right argument is the tie number. If you rename a file belonging to someone else (he would have to have given you access permission to do so), you now own it. Of course, □*FRENAME* can also be used to change the name of one of your own files.

Access passnumbers and secure applications

Even though you can control what types of file accesses a person can make through the access codes in the second column of a file access matrix, this is usually not enough. For example, you might have a file in which a certain user is permitted to read only the fifth component of a file, or one in which you won't permit him to append a component with more than, say, 500 elements.

Access passnumbers, the third column of the access matrix, are used to gain this level of security control. It works this way: if the access passnumber for a user is *not* 0, then to use the file, that person must supply the identical value in his file functions. Suppose user 666666 has been granted access to the file '78974 *STREAK*' by this row in the access matrix: 666666 25 6948520. This means that user 666666 has permission to share-tie, read, append and replace, but he must use expressions like this:

```
'78974 STREAK' ⎕FSTIE 1 6948520
X←⎕FREAD 1 10 6948520
```

The access passnumber, when required, is the last element of the right argument of the file functions. The only exception is for ⎕FHOLD. For it, use a 2-row matrix. The first row is the tie numbers of the files to be held, and the second row is the corresponding access passnumbers:

```
⎕FHOLD 2 1⍴1 6948520
```

It doesn't make such sense to go through all the bother of setting up a passnumber and then telling the user what that number is, so locked functions are employed. In secure applications, the designer or owner of the file usually supplies his correspondents with locked functions to do the file accessing. For instance, the following simple program allows other users to access only the even-numbered components of the file:

```
    ∇ Z←READ N
[1]   Z←⎕FREAD N[1],(N[2]×0=2|N[2]),6948520 ∇
```

Since the function is locked, there is no way the user can disclose the passnumber. Any attempts to read odd-numbered components will result in a *FILE INDEX ERROR*.

Summary of file functions

Here is a table showing all the file functions. *Z←* means that there is an explicit result. *tn*, *cn* and *pn* mean respectively file tie number, component number and access passnumber. The passnumber is required only if there is a nonzero value in column three of the access matrix. The access codes (column 2 of the access matrix) are shown for your convenience.

	function		code
arg	⎕FAPPEND	tn,pn	8
arg	⎕FCREATE	tn	none
	⎕FDROP	tn,arg,pn	32
arg	⎕FERASE	tn,pn	4
	⎕FHOLD	tn,tn,...	2048
Z ←	⎕FLIB	arg	none
Z ←	⎕FNAMES		none
Z ←	⎕FNUMS		none
Z ←	⎕FRDAC	tn,pn	4096
Z ←	⎕FRDCI	tn,cn,pn	512
Z ←	⎕FREAD	tn,cn,pn	1
arg	⎕FRENAME	tn,pn	128
arg	⎕FREPLACE	tn,cn,pn	16
arg	⎕FRESIZE	tn,pn	1024
Z ←	⎕FSIZE	tn,pn	any
arg	⎕FSTAC	tn,pn	8192
arg	⎕FSTIE	tn,pn	any
arg	⎕FTIE	tn,pn	2
	⎕FUNTIE	tn,tn,...	none

Chapter 27: Shared variables and communicating with other systems

IBM's shared variables concept is a general means of communication between your own APL programs and those of others, both APL and non-APL. The latter may even include the operating system under which APL and other (non-APL) services are running. A shared variable is, therefore, a window between your program and other environments to which your computer allows access.

What shared variables is all about

Chapter 23 introduced a feature that permits sharing a variable (though without specifically labelling the process as such)—the ☐ used for APL input and output. There, the ☐ is shared between you at your terminal and APL. We will now define a set of system functions that will generalize this simple sharing concept to include many other environments.

Just as you and your active workspace comprise a team to share the work of solving a problem, teams can be formed among two APL users and their active workspaces. Teams can also consist of an APL active workspace and the parent system that lives in the inner depths of the computer, and which controls all APL activities. They can further come into being between the parent APL system and alien languages or systems running on the same computer, such as FORTRAN, COBOL, Assembler language and their associated storage mechanisms.

For example, on most APL systems you can print voluminous reports on the high-speed printer attached to the computer, instead of at your terminal. This involves you, your terminal, your active workspace, the parent APL system, the system that runs the printer, the printer itself and the person at the computer center who puts the proper paper on the printer and delivers the printed results to you.

In practice, most APL users overlook most of these distinctions as unnecessary philosophy. But the ability to model shared processes is a characteristic of APL that is worth knowing. In this chapter we'll consider the formal sharing between a variety of commonly encountered environments.

Any APL variable in your active workspace, global or local, can be shared with any other consenting user. Both you and he can give the variable a new value. Then, when one of you uses the variable, it will have the most recent value that was given by either. A variable can be shared with the dyadic $\square SVO$ (shared variable offer) system function. For example, the expression $78974 \ \square SVO \ 'X'$ is an offer to share your variable X with user 78974.

User 78974 must make a similar offer to share his variable X with you. If your user number is 3677758, then he executes $3677758 \ \square SVO \ 'X'$. $\square SVO$ returns an explicit result, called the *degree of coupling*. The result is 1 when the first user has made an offer, and 2 when the second user makes a matching offer. A result of 2 indicates that the sharing arrangement has been consummated. A result of 0 means no offer has been made.

It isn't necessary that the two consenting users use the same name to refer to the shared variable. For example, users 78974 and 3677758 might agree that 3677758's variable $MZ3$ and 78974's variable SX are to be the same thing. Then, after 3677758 executes $MZ3 \leftarrow 'HELLO'$, 78974 would find that his SX is the character vector $'HELLO'$. Any of the following three independent sequences would have the same effect:

```
        USER 3677758                          USER 78974

   ------------------------------------------------------------------
           78974 □SVO 'MZ3'                      3677758 □SVO 'SX MZ3'
   1                                      2
   ------------------------------------------------------------------
           78974 □SVO 'MZ3 SX'                   3677758 □SVO 'SX'
   1                                      2
   ------------------------------------------------------------------
           78974 □SVO 'MZ3 COMM'                 3677758 □SVO 'SX COMM'
   1                                      2
   ------------------------------------------------------------------
```

The second name mentioned in the right argument is called a *surrogate name*. It serves as a common link to establish the sharing. This is most evident in the third sequence, where both users offer the new name $COMM$ as the surrogate. Surrogate names may not be more than 15 characters long.

You can make several offers to share at the same time. The right argument is then a matrix of names (one row per name, and if there is to be a surrogate it must be separated from the name by a blank). The left argument is a vector of coupling users, one for each variable of the right argument that is to be shared polygamously. The combination of a scalar left argument and matrix right argument offers to share all the variables with that user. For example,

```
      78974 □SVO 3 3ρ'MZ3MZ4MZ5'
1 2 2
```

offers to share variables $MZ3$, $MZ4$ and $MZ5$, but user 78974 has already offered variables $MZ4$ and $MZ5$.

You can find out what variables are presently being offered for sharing with the $□SVQ$ (shared variable query) monadic system function. It has two modes of operation. If the argument is an empty vector, the result is a vector holding the user numbers of all people offering to share something with you. And if the argument is one of those numbers, the result is a character matrix holding the names of the variables that user is offering to you. This matrix holds only the names that are *offered* for sharing, and not those which are presently being shared.

To determine whether a variable has been offered for sharing, is shared or hasn't been offered, use the monadic $□SVO$ system function. Its argument is a character vector (or matrix) holding the names of the variables you are inquiring about. The result is a scalar (or vector) holding the degree of coupling: 0 if the variable has not been offered, 1 if it has been offered, and 2 if it is presently being shared with someone. For those cases where the degree of coupling is 1 or 2 the dyadic $□SVO$ may also be used for inquiry, since a repeated offer under those conditions does not change the status of the original offer.

There are several possible error conditions that may occur. Attempts to exceed the quota of shared variables assigned by the system management result in $INTERFACE$ $QUOTA$ $EXHAUSTED$ messages. Unavailability of the shared variable facility itself causes the report NO $SHARES$.

A variable need not have been assigned to share it. Or it is possible that both users have assigned a value to it prior to sharing. Here is how potential conflicts are resolved: if neither sharer has assigned a value, an attempt to use the variable results in the normal $VALUE$ $ERROR$. If only one user has assigned it, that value is taken. If both have assigned values prior to sharing, then the value taken is the one set by the first person to make the offer to share.

For the lonely hearts among our readers, an offer to share a variable with user number 0 means you're willing to share it with any user who happens to be signed on at that time. Such unbounded generosity, however, can be reciprocated only with a counter-offer that specifically identifies the user making the original general offer.

After a variable is shared, it can be used much like any other variable. For example, you can set the (shared) variable $MZ3$ by $MZ3 \leftarrow 56$. You or anyone else among the sharers can now 'read' it in the usual way:

```
      MZ3
56
```

Since any sharer can read or reassign it at any time independently of other sharers, the process is completely unconstrained. If $MZ3$ represented a sharer's bank balance, such anarchy would lead to chaos if there were no rules governing who is allowed to do what under various conditions.

This *access protocol* is defined by the dyadic system function □*SVC* (shared *variable* control). Its right argument is a vector (or matrix) of the names of the variables whose access protocol is to be changed. The left argument is a four-element vector (or matrix with four columns) whose values can be only 0 or 1 as specified below:

If the first element is 1	Your sharer must read or assign a value to the shared variable before you can reassign it.
If the second element is 1	Your sharer cannot reassign the shared variable until you either read or assign a value to it.
If the third element is 1	You cannot read the shared variable a second time unless your sharer has reassigned it.
If the fourth element is 1	Your sharer cannot read the shared variable a second time unless you have reassigned it.

It would appear that you can control your sharer's every move. That's not exactly the case, however, since he can make similar restrictions apply to your use of the shared variable. In fact, the resulting access protocol is determined by the logical OR (∨) of both your access requests. Hence, the effect is always to become more restrictive. In one sense this is good, because there is no way that an uncooperative user can negate restrictions you have set. As a byproduct, dyadic □*SVC* returns an explicit result which is the new setting of the access protocol combining your specifications with those of the sharer. It is the same shape as the left argument.

Monadic □*SVC*, whose argument is a character vector (or matrix) holding names of shared variables, returns the present access protocol as seen by the user, but doesn't change any of the control settings.

In actual operation, when one of the sharers is inhibited from proceeding and awaits some interlocking action on the part of the other sharer, his execution is held up until the action is performed. As soon as the conditions are satisfied, his execution continues. Interrupting may disturb the sharing aspects of a particular system.

An existing sharing arrangement can be retracted by the monadic system function □*SVR* (shared *variable* retraction). The argument is a character vector (or matrix) holding the names of the variables you wish to stop sharing. The explicit result is the degree of coupling that the variables had prior to being withdrawn. Thus, you can annul an offer to share even before a prospective sharer has consummated the sharing arrangement.

A variable also ceases to be shared if you sign off, are disconnected because of a telephone failure, load or clear a workspace, or if the shared variable was local to some function which has completed execution, or if you erase the variable.

Once a variable has been offered for sharing, its access protocol does not have to be respecified. That is to say, after a nullification and subsequent offer to share again, the access protocol is whatever it was the last time it was set with □*SVC*. However, it's a good idea to verify the degree of coupling from time to time if the other sharer is believed to be unstable.

A variable can be shared with only one other person at any time. Polygamous sharing of information can be done by having one of the people serve as a steward, or 'communication center.' By sharing at least one variable with each of the other people, the communication center can mediate and route information among any of the people with whom he shares a variable.

System dependence

The shared variable commands described so far are fairly consistent across most APL systems offering them. Once we begin to use them to communicate with non-APL environments all sorts of system dependencies arise, which makes for problems in transporting APL data or programs from one system to another. Common sense suggests that to minimize the difficulty of making the required changes under these circumstances, the communication instructions should be isolated and well documented in a small number of subroutines. This has the obvious benefit of making the instructions to be changed not only more accessible but also more understandable.

Those non-APL programs that use the shared variable concept to interface with APL are called *auxiliary processors* (AP's). They provide access to many different non-APL environments. The rest of this chapter discusses some AP's found in various IBM systems, in particular *Time Shared Input/Output AP* (TSIO), which lets you use the data management facilities of the OS/VS and MVS operating systems and AP 100, 110, 111 and 123, found in CMS, a system operating in the virtual machine environment VM/370. They allow you to read and write files, execute VM and CMS commands, and access various peripheral devices. These AP's are also associated with other systems, such as TSO and CICS. (The authors regret having to deal with the computerese acronyms that pepper this section. We debated omitting the material entirely, but deferred because the facility provides the only way in many cases to use APL for important information handling tasks.)

TSIO file processing

This section will describe the access functions in the IBM supplied workspaces *APLFILES* and *TSIO* as part of APLSV. These workspaces let you use both TSIO and shared variables to set up, store and access files outside your workspaces.

```
    )LOAD 1 APLFILES
SAVED   8.27.13 02/20/83
```

A file is created by using the dyadic function *CREATE*. The right argument, a character vector, is the name to be associated with the file. The left argument is a three-element vector. Element one contains the maximum number of components (APL arrays) that you can store in the file. Element two is the size (in characters) of the chunks[1]. A component may use several chunks, but a chunk cannot be used by two components. Therefore, use of many small chunks for a component results in a greater amount of retrieval time, while large chunks mean a lot of wasted storage in your file. The third element consists of the total number of chunks allowed.

For casual use of *CREATE*, you need not worry about all these details. If the third element is not given, 1.1 times the value of element one is supplied automatically. If the second element is not given, a chunk size of 550 is assumed. And if the first element is not supplied (that is, the left argument is $\iota 0$), then a file with a capacity for 100 components is created:

```
    (ιO) CREATE 'SMALLFILE'
```

Here a file named *SMALLFILE* has been created with 100 components and a total of 110 chunks of 550 characters each.

Once a file has been created, it can be activated with the *USE* function:

```
    USE 'SMALLFILE'
```

If you are using someone else's files, his user number must precede the file name and be separated by a blank, for example, *USE* '1234 DATA'. Use of that file by someone else doesn't preclude your reading it. *Caution*: the *USE* function sets three global variables, the first of which begins with the letters *CTL* and is followed by your file name. The second begins with the letters *DAT* and the last begins with *FD*. Avoid using these variables directly, as they are a critical part of the operation of the file processor.

Data is put on the file by using the function *SET*, aided by the function *AT*, in an expression of the form (*FILENAME AT COMPONENTNO*) *SET DATA*. As an example, let's put the character vector '3000 WESTCHESTER AVENUE' into the fifth component of the file *SMALLFILE*:

```
    ('SMALLFILE' AT 5) SET '3000 WESTCHESTER AVENUE'
```

The fifth component can be set without having set components one through four. However, you can't set any components beyond 100 with this particular file since only 100 were implied when the file was created.

Data is read from the file with the *GET* and *AT* functions. If you attempt to *GET* a component which has not been set, a *FILE INDEX ERROR* results.

```
    R←GET 'SMALLFILE' AT 5
    R
3000 WESTCHESTER AVENUE
```

The function *EXIST* can be used before *GET* to determine which components already have values. The result is ‾1 for components out of range, 0 for those components in the range but having no value, and 1 for those that do have values:

```
    EXIST 'SMALLFILE' AT 3 4 5 6 100 101 102
0 0 1 0 0 ‾1 ‾1
```

---

[1] *Chunk* is the authors' term to refer to any physical or logical borders in storage such as tracks, sectors, extents, granules, etc., which impose some restriction on the smooth and contiguous storage of data in space set aside for you.

For files shared among users, you can tell who last set a particular component and its timestamp with the *GETL* function. *GETL FILENAME AT COMPONENTNO* returns the number of the user who has set the component, and when it was set.

A component can be removed with the *ERASE* command, which frees up the storage:

        ERASE 'SMALLFILE' AT 5
        EXIST 'SMALLFILE' AT 5
0

When there is only one file for an application, or when you reference the same file again, you can omit the *AT* and its right argument with *SET*, *GET*, *ERASE* and *EXIST*. These functions all use the global variable *FILEID*, which holds the name of the file last used as an argument to *USE* or *AT*.

Finally, when access to a file is no longer required, use the *RELEASE* function. *RELEASE* returns an explicit result 1 if the file was in use at the time of release, or 0 if it wasn't. *RELEASE* doesn't destroy the file, but simply retires it from active use. *USE* must be executed to regain access to a file after it has been released:

        RELEASE 'SMALLFILE'
1

DELETE is used when a file is to be destroyed. It makes the file permanently unavailable, removes the file name and frees the previously occupied storage space for reuse:

        DELETE 'SMALLFILE'

Other TSIO functions

Besides the TSIO functions in *APLFILES*, there are cover functions distributed with *APLSV* that provide an interface to the TSIO processor and incorporate the commands needed to share variables. There are two which are particularly useful, *TRY* and *CHK*.

TRY offers a share to the TSIO processor, uses surrogate names, checks for acceptable completion codes and sets up an interlock and file access. Here is an example:[1]

        'A' TRY 'SW DSN=DS1'

CHK enables you to check the return codes (it is used by *TRY*):

        B CHK C

B is a vector of return codes for which a message will *not* print. *C* is the shared variable. *CHK*'s result is a vector of length *B* with a 1 corresponding to the return code found and 0 elsewhere. If *B* is an empty vector, all error messages will be printed.

There are three global variables used in *TRY* and *CHK*. They are set by the application:

Q	error conditions (1-31)
QLE	error messages corresponding to *Q*
PID	processor ID (most often 370)

If TSIO returns a code not in *Q*, the error message will be printed.

Although many of the error messages are self-explanatory (e.g., 12 *DATA SET NOT FOUND*), you may have to refer for help to the table of TSIO messages in the IBM publication SH 20-9087, APL Shared Variable Users Guide.

The rest of the discussion of TSIO will be concerned with the *direct* use of TSIO, as opposed to the cover functions like *USE*, *GET*, *ERASE* etc., that we have just described.

---

[1]With apologies to our readers, the standard terminology used in this and many subsequent commands in the rest of this chapter now begins to stray a little from 'looking like APL.' SW, to be explained later, stands for 'sequential write,' and DSN for 'dataset name.' A is the surrogate name of the control variable.

You may already have heard other programmers use words like *blocks* and *records* and wondered what they meant. To help you, we include a brief glossary of commonly used terms relating to how files are organized in many systems.

Terminology

dataset	The name given to a file in the operating system
block	A chunk of a dataset moved between the internal memory of the computer and the external device (tape, disk, etc.,) on which the dataset is stored.
record	A subunit of a block which contains the information you would normally access when you read or write to a dataset. It is sometimes called a *logical record*.
blocked (unblocked) data	Datasets whose blocks contain more than one data record are said to be blocked; otherwise they are unblocked.
fixed (variable) length	Applies to both blocks and records.
self-describing records	Begins with an indication of how long it is.
record format (RECFM)	A description of how blocks and records of a dataset are organized.
sequential access	Reading (SR) or writing (SW) records in a dataset in sequential order.
indexed access	Reading (IR) or writing (IW) records in a dataset by selecting the desired indices (records are indexed sequentially beginning with 0).

Our discussion of files hinted that the internal architecture of a block may differ significantly from one file to another, not just in the length of the records or the number of records in the block, but also in the kind of information in the record and in how it is encoded. The record format describes the organization of the block.

There are six different record formats provided in TSIO:

RECFM	Fixed length blocks
F	One fixed length record
FBS	The same number (>1) of fixed length records, each sent as a matrix
U	One variable length record
FB	Some number of fixed length records, each sent as a vector
V	One self-describing variable length record
VB	Some number of self-describing variable length records

The information itself may be stored in many different ways: in floating point, integer, character, APL or APL-EBCDIC representation. As you might expect, only the APL representation carries with it the shape and type of data. The others use only vectors.

Communicating with TSIO

In the description of the cover function *USE* (page 283), we pointed out that the file processor used several global variables. These variables are key to letting TSIO know that you want to work with a file.

The first of these is a *control variable* whose name must start with CTL, followed by a dataset name. It serves two masters, letting you give commands to TSIO and letting TSIO in turn tell you how you made out with your commands. Where there may be multiple simultaneous accesses, TSIO uses this variable to keep things straight.

The second is a *data variable* whose name must start with DAT, followed by a dataset name. For each data variable there is an associated control variable, the association being denoted by the use of the same dataset name (or surrogate name) with both variables. For example, if the dataset is DS1, the variables would be $CTLDS1$ and $DATDS1$. Of course, more than one control variable (or associated control/data variables) may be shared simultaneously for concurrent access to the dataset.

We haven't yet said how you identify the TSIO processor when you make your offer to share. On many (but not all) systems it is labeled '370'. Your sharing instruction would therefore be

```
370 ⎕SVO 'CTL'
```

1

Creating a dataset

A dataset may be built up only by writing records to it sequentially. If it has been sequentially written with RECFM=F, it may be indexed read or rewritten later.

To create a new dataset CTL must be set with several commands, SW for sequential writing, DSN=[name of dataset], DISP(for disposition)=NEW, RECFM=F (for indexed access, otherwise the default is RECFM=V), and BLKSIZE=[number of records per block]. Here is an example:

```
CTL←'SW DSN=DS1,DISP=NEW,RECFM=F,BLKSIZE=750'
CTL
```
0   (indicates successful execution)

Missing from the above is the space to be allocated and the data representation (default is CODE=A, for APL).

Now you are ready to write records to the data set. Once again the control variable is the key:

```
CTL←'RECORD1'
CTL←2 3ρφι6
CTL←10 20 30
CTL←'MARY HAD A LITTLE LAMB'
CTL←ι0
CTL
```
0

The data set is closed by assigning an empty vector to CTL.

Finally, to reopen an existing dataset, say, DS1, for sequential writing, set

```
CTL←'SW DSN=DS1'
```

Since DISP=OLD is the default value and the block size and record format are already known to TSIO, the dataset is ready for you to sequentially write records.

Now you have a problem. The above command erases the existing records and starts writing again with the first record. Most of the time, however, you merely want to write additional records to an existing dataset. For this use the command

```
CTL←'SW DSN=DS1, DISP=MOD'
```

To change the name of a dataset use the $RENAME$ command

```
CTL←'RENAME DSN=FRANKS, NEWNAME=HOTDOGS'
```

and to get rid of a dataset use $DELETE$:

```
CTL←'DELETE DSN=HOTDOGS'
```

Reading a dataset

As you might expect, you can sequentially read DS1 by the following commands:

```
CTL←'SR DSN=DS1'        (opens DS1)

CTL
```
0
```
CTL
```
RECORD1
```
CTL
```
3 2 1
6 5 4
```
ρ□←CTL
```
10 20 30

3
```
CTL
```
MARY HAD A LITTLE LAMB

   ρ*Z←CTL*   (end of dataset)

0

   CTL

0

If the empty vector had actually been entered as data, the response code to *CTL* would have been 14.

Indexed reading and writing

  Thus far we have described how to sequentially read or write to a dataset starting at the first record. Many applications require access only to particular records in a dataset. TSIO provides this capability by associating sequential indices with the records. The numbering begins with 0, not 1. To index read or write a record two variables are needed—*CTL* to indicate whether we want to read or write, and *DAT* to send the data. As with *CTL*, *DAT* first has to be offered for sharing:

   370 □*SVO* '*DAT*'

1

The following sequence of commands allows you to read the dataset:

   CTL←'*IR DSN=DS1*'   (open DS1 for indexed read)

   CTL

0

   *CTL←*0 2   (read [0 indicates read] third record)

   CTL

0

   DAT   (third record)

   *CTL←*0 0   (read first record)

   DAT

*RECORD*1   (first record)

   CTL←''   (close DS1)

   CTL

0

  To read and write the commands are modified slightly:

   CTL←'*IRW DSN=DS1*'   (open DS1 for indexed read/write)

   *CTL←*0 2   (read third record)

   DAT   (third record)

10 20 30

   DAT←'*WHITE PLAINS, N.Y.*'

   *CTL←*1 2   (write [1 indicates write] over third record with *DAT*)

   *CTL←*0 2   (read third record)

   DAT

WHITE PLAINS, N.Y.   (third record)

Sharing TSIO datasets

  An owner may designate his dataset for sharing by DISP=SHR. Others may obtain access to it by also indicating DISP=SHR. Now the fun begins. If two users want to read the dataset at the same time, there is no problem since the contents of the dataset are static. But if writing is involved, there may be synchronization problems as to who does what when.

Much depends on what is being written. If the two users write independent records, they are home free. Even if they write the same record there is no difficulty, provided that what they write doesn't depend on what was previously in the record. TSIO acts as a scheduler, allowing one user to write and then the other.

The troublesome case arises where one user reads, say, record 20 and then decides, on the basis of what is in record 20, to add 5 to it. In the interval between his reading and writing of record 20, a second user reads record 20 and decides to add 10 to it. By the time he gets around to writing it, the first user has already rewritten record 20, so the change that the second user wants to make is based on an old reading of the record.

TSIO again comes to the rescue, with provisions for exclusive as well as shared holds on records, parts of datasets, functions on the datasets, or even things not connected with datasets at all, such as printers. All the things that a hold can be associated with are collectively designated as *facilities*, each of which is represented by a number.

A hold is exercised by setting

$$CTL \leftarrow C, F$$

F is the integer associated with the facility in question. C designates the type of hold desired. It has values 2,3,4 or 5 with the following meanings:

C	request for
2	Exclusive hold. Allow only if there is no current hold on *F*. The response code indicates whether the hold was successful. Continue execution.
3	Exclusive hold, but delay execution until all existing requests for holds on *F* have been fulfilled and the holds released.
4	Shared hold. Allow only if there are no existing requests for exclusive holds.
5	Shared hold, but delay execution as in C=3.

A second hold request on a facility releases an existing hold, as will retraction of the shared variable or its disappearance. Setting F=0 will also release a hold without requesting another. More than one hold can be requested by using multiple control variables.

Protection of datasets

TSIO automatically identifies every dataset you create by your account number. Explicitly adding your account number at the time of creation is allowable, but superfluous, much like loading or copying from one of your own workspaces:

    CTL←'SW DSN=123456 DS1, DISP=NEW, BLKSIZE=700'

But when you execute with a *negative* account number,

    CTL←'SW DSN=¯123456 DS1, DISP=NEW, BLKSIZE=700'

DS1 becomes a *reserved* dataset. Only you can access it, unless another APL user sets CTL with an *indirect command*, IC:

    CTL←'IC DSN=¯123456 CDS(10)'

¯123456 *CDS* is called a *command dataset*. Put simply, it is a 'laundry list' of commands each of which has associated with it a list of the users authorized to use that command. The example above refers to the 10th command stored in the dataset ¯123456 *CDS*:

    SW DSN=DS1, DISP=NEW, BLKSIZE=700

If you are not on the list, access is denied. The dataset owner, of course, is free to access his reserved datasets at any time. To make it easy for administrators of collections of datasets designed to be accessed by large numbers of authorized users, many APL systems have utility functions which create and update command datasets.

There are other ways to control the setting up of files and use of specific devices. System administrators can allow users to allocate a certain amount of space on a storage device on their own to create new datasets, for example, 100 tracks on a disk. A dataset requiring more than 100 tracks would have to be specifically authorized by the system administrator. A user may be permitted to read other users' nonreserved datasets provided he knows their names. And some users (for example, systems programmers) may have special authorization for additional commands and reserved dataset access.

APL/TSIO datasets are really OS/VS datasets. They may be read directly, bypassing APL security, unless the system administrator has taken steps to prevent or control this access.

Finally, users authorized to allocate specific devices may perform physical I/O through TSIO. They can, for example, read a tape by including in the SR command the appropriate parameters like DENSITY, LABEL, UNIT, VOLUME.

VS APL file processing

In the VM environment programs run on *virtual machines*. This means each user has the perception that all the computer's resources are at his disposal, and are for him only. Since all the users are therefore virtual machine users, direct sharing of variables with others isn't possible. However, auxiliary processors enable users or APL functions to share variables in this environment.

Although there are many AP's in VS APL, our discussion in this chapter will address only those which are useful in working with files and in display screen management. At this time (1983) not all AP's are available or work in the same way in all host environments.

Cover functions

Just as a set of cover functions was provided in the workspace *APLFILES* to assist the TSIO user, so a series of environment dependent and file AP workspaces have been made available in VS APL. Those of you who have read the section on TSIO files will find the names of many of the cover functions similar to their TSIO counterparts. It is expected that more cover functions will be available in time to help the APL user. Readers wishing to explore the literature of the AP's in more detail should consult the references at the end of the chapter. Before reviewing these cover functions, here is an example using AP 110.

AP 110

Let's look at how a CMS file can be read or written using AP 110. Suppose, for example, we want to access the CMS file CUSTOMERS with fixed length records and character translation to the VS APL character set. The command

        DATA←'CUSTOMERS (FIX 192'

initializes the variable *DATA* with the name of the file to be accessed and the options to be used.

The next step is to offer the variable *DATA* for sharing with the AP:

        110 □SVO 'DATA'
2

AP110 then checks the initial value of the variable and assigns a return code. Each subsequent reference to the variable returns a record from the file:

        DATA
SMITH PUBLISHING COMPANY, NEW YORK, NY
        DATA
JONES AND KILPATRICK, INC., MOLINE, ILLINOIS

A new record is added to the file with

        DATA←40↑🖬
MURPHY AND GREENBERG CO., ST. LOUIS, MO

and the file is closed by expunging the variable:

□EX 'DATA'

Here is a set of utility functions to do this. We must warn you that these utilities may not exist on all VS APL systems; or if they do exist, they may have different names, syntax, restrictions or defaults from those listed here.

action	syntax	comment
file open	*FILEN OPEN R*	Opens the file *FILEN*, which may be new. *FILEN* is a character vector. *R* contains all the (optional) information needed to open the file: file type, mode, fixed length records, access control and conversion options. If missing there are default options.
file write	*Z←DAT PUT FILEN* or *DAT PUTFILE FILEN*	Puts the data in *DAT* sequentially into the file. *DAT* is a character vector in *PUT* and a character matrix in *PUTFILE*.
file read	*Z←GET FILEN* or *Z←GETFILE FILEN*	Gets the next sequential record in the file. The argument of *GETFILE* may contain, besides the file name, file type, mode and conversion option.
file close	*Z←CLOSE FILEN* *Z←CLOSEALL*	Closes the file and expunges the associated shared variables. *CLOSEALL* expunges all outstanding shared variables.

For the TSO environment there are similar functions available, along with a function *Z←FILEN RECID RECNO* which is used with *GET* and *PUT* to directly access a particular record, e.g., *GET CUSTOMER RECID 30* will read record number 30 in the file *CUSTOMER*.

The CICS environment uses AP 132 to access what are called *transient data files*, which allow data to be exchanged with other CICS transactions. The files can be thought of as first in, first out queues where reading destroys a record at one end while writing appends it at the other.

file activated	*USE FILEN*	
file write	*QWRITE DAT*	A character scalar or vector is written at the back end of the current queue.
file read	*Z←QREAD*	Reads record at front end of queue and removes it from queue.
file close	*CLOSE*	Closes file and expunges shared variables.

Reading and writing APL variables

AP 121 reads and writes APL variables in their internal form. Objects are stored as they appear in the workspace. Here are the key functions:

file create	*L ACREATE FILEN*	Creates an APL file. *L* is a character vector beginning with *'S'* for a sequential file, otherwise a direct file is assumed. A numeric ending for *L* is the file size in bytes (default size if absent).
file activated	*USE FILEN*	Makes the referenced file available for reading or writing.
file write	*AWRITE DAT*	Writes *DAT* to the file. An empty vector closes it.
file read	*Z←AREAD*	Reads the next record (sequential) sequentially.
file read	*Z←AGET RECNO*	Reads the specified (direct) record number.
file update	*RECNO ASET DAT*	Replaces record *RECNO* with *DAT*.
file close	*CLOSE*	Closes currently open file and expunges associated shared variables.
file delete	*DROP FILEN*	Deletes the file.

Two monadic functions are provided to store large variables. *STORE VAR* (*VAR* is a character vector or scalar holding the name of the variable) creates an APL sequential file with the same name as in *VAR*, writes the variable as a single record, then expunges *VAR* from the workspace. *RETRIEVE VAR* opens the file and recreates *VAR* in the workspace.

For those users who have to access VSAM files, a similar set of utilities is provided. These are described in detail in the IBM manual 'A Guide to the VS APL Workspace Library,' Document Number GG22-9263.

Designing and using full-screen panels

Most computer systems these days provide facilities for full-screen panel design to take advantage of the capabilities available on newer display terminals. The miracles of modern electronics make it possible to access and use the entire screen, so that users aren't limited by the unidirectional start-stop movements of the keyboard printers that were popular when APL was in its infancy. VS APL provides AP 126 to assist in both designing and using the panels in APL programs.

In common with the other AP's, a set of cover functions has been developed to assist users in designing their own panels. Although the details may differ from system to system, the tasks which any good full-screen manager has to perform are the same. They include:

1. starting and stopping the use of AP 126
2. managing the pages themselves (creating, deleting, accessing, storing)
3. formatting text fields (defining new fields, reformatting existing fields, defining field attributes (e.g., color, highlighting, symbol sets, use of light pen, etc.)
4. managing screen I/O, including getting the output from 3 above to the screen so that it can be used
5. writing and reading text and attributes
6. getting screens to a printer
7. error handling
8. translating characters

A comprehensive set of cover functions that manage these tasks is in the distributed workspace *FSM*, which uses the IBM GDDM Program Product. To make things easier there is a companion workspace *FSDESIGN* which is a step-by-step do-it-yourself program, called *DESIGN*, that allows the user to query the process at each stage for a complete description of what is happening. The PF keys of the IBM 3278 terminal are employed in *DESIGN* not only to get help, stop execution or go back to the master design-control panel, but also to manipulate the viewing area of the screen as the panel is being laid out. Users will find the last two references particularly helpful here.

References (IBM Documents)

APLSV Shared Variables User's Guide, SH20-9087

VS APL for CMS, Terminal User's Guide, SH20-9067

VS APL for TSO, Terminal User's Guide, SH20-9180

VS APL for CICS, Terminal User's Guide, SH20-9167

Presentation Graphics Feature User's Guide, SC33-0102

Graphical Data Display Manager User's Guide, SC33-0101

A Guide to the VS APL Workspace Library, GG22-9263.

Chapter 28: Et cetera

This chapter consists of topics that didn't fit conveniently elsewhere. Some of it is very implementation specific. Nonetheless, these topics are important for advanced APL usage.

Working with time

Most APL systems have a clock that is accessed for a wide range of uses. In the case of a personal computer the user sets the clock when he turns on the computer; on larger systems the clock is set by the operations staff. The accuracy of the clock is no better than the accuracy of its initial setting, and it is possible that the clock may run slightly slow, particularly on small computers, if the system is heavily used.

The first manifestation of the clock that a user sees is typically in his sign-on banner, which will report the time and date.

When a workspace is saved a *timestamp* is supplied by the system; that timestamp is displayed when the workspace is loaded or copied. It can be invaluable to a developer trying to figure out which workspace is the most recent version.

On APL*PLUS Systems, the system variable $\Box WSTS$ is a scalar containing the time the active workspace was last saved. It is stored in millionths of a second from midnight January 1, 1900. In workspace 1 *FILEAID* the monadic functions *TIMEN* (for a result compatible with $\Box TS$, below) and *TIME* (for a character vector result) are often used to convert this representation to year, month, day, hour, minute and second.

Similarly, when a file component is stored (via $\Box FAPPEND$ or $\Box FREPLACE$), a timestamp is stored with it. That timestamp can be retrieved by accessing the third element of $\Box FRDCI$'s result. It is in the same format as $\Box WSTS$.

The principal means of obtaining the current time on most APL systems is via the niladic system variable $\Box TS$, for time stamp. Its result is a vector whose elements are year, month, day, hour, minute, seconds and milliseconds. For example,

```
      □TS
1983 3 10 21 54 7 867
```

means that the date and time is March 10, 1983, at 21:54 (9:54 p.m.) and 7.867 seconds.

On APL2 you can find the time when a function was last fixed by 2 $\Box AT$ R where R is a character vector holding the name of the function. The result is in the same format as $\Box TS$. The full use of $\Box AT$ is covered on page 300.

The system clock on most time-sharing APL systems is set according to the time zone in which the system is located. On APL2 systems, however, the time stamp is Greenwich Mean Time (GMT) but you can change it to your local time by setting the system variable $\Box TZ$, for time zone. You would use $\Box TZ \leftarrow {}^{-}8$ for Pacific Standard Time, or $\Box TZ \leftarrow 1$ for European Standard Time. The permissible values are integers between ${}^{-}11$ and 13 inclusive.

Most systems make *account* information available to the user with the $\Box AI$ system variable. $\Box AI$ is quite system dependent, but a representative one produces a 4-element integer vector consisting of your user number, the amount of computer time used in the session, the amount of connect time since you signed on, and the typing time (that part of the elapsed time when it was your turn to type, as opposed to the time APL was typing or when the keyboard was locked). The last three elements are in milliseconds. To convert them to more comprehensible numbers (like hours, minutes, seconds and milliseconds) use a sequence such as

```
      X←□AI
      X
78975 1517 3809817 3113100
      ⍝0 60 60 1000⊤1↓X
1517 3809817 3113100
      0   0   1 517      1.517 seconds of CPU time
      1   3  29 817      1 hour, 3 minutes and 29.817 seconds of connect time
      0  51  53 100      51 minutes and 53.1 seconds of open keyboard time.
```

$\Box AI$ in some systems may measure other usage, such as the number of characters transmitted, or the number of disk accesses or file resource units. Check your system reference manual for details.

Timing algorithms and applications

You can get an overall measure of how much time an application takes by the difference in $\Box TS$ before and after running the application. On time-sharing systems the elapsed time an application takes depends also on how much resources the other users are taking, and elapsed times can vary widely. To smooth out these irregularities you should measure the application at different times and days, and average the results. You should run small applications in a loop several times so that your numbers are large enough to go beyond the granularity of the system clock. Also, do the same tests (including the loop, but with a placebo application instead) to account for the overhead of the test method itself. Besides measuring $\Box TS$, which is an approximation of elapsed time, consider some of the other resources reported in $\Box AI$.

The following program is a reasonably complete and precise tool for measuring the resources consumed. Its right argument is the character string representation of the statement to be timed, and the left argument is the number of repeated executions you want. The resources consumed are returned in the same format as $\Box AI$.

```
      ∇ ΔAI←N TIMER EXPR;FN;HEADER;WIDTH;TIMER
[1]   ⍝ TAKES TIMINGS FOR N ITERATIONS OF EXPR   BRIAN BECKER 3/83
[2]   ⍝ ASSUME EXPR RETURNS AN EXPLICIT RESULT; DISCARD IT IN SINK.
[3]   EXPR←'SINK←',EXPR ⍝ BEGIN TO BUILD LOCAL FUNCTION.
[4]   EXPR←(N,ρEXPR)ρEXPR ⍝ REPEATS THE EXPRESSION N TIMES
[5]   HEADER←'TIMER;SINK' ◇ WIDTH← ⌈/(ρHEADER),ρEXPR
[6]   FN←□FX (WIDTH↑HEADER),[1](N,WIDTH)↑EXPR ⍝ CREATE THE FUNCTION
[7]   ΔAI←□AI ◇ TIMER ◇ ΔAI←□AI-ΔAI ⍝ PRETIME, RUN, TAKE DIFFERENCE
      ∇
```

Delaying execution

$\Box DL$ causes a *delay* for a fixed period of time. Its argument is the number of seconds of delay that is desired. The result is the number of seconds that actually transpired, because you may be delayed slightly longer than called for if the system is used heavily, or less if you interrupted by BREAK. When $\Box DL$ is executed, your terminal keyboard stays locked, as when computing, but no computer time is used.

Asynchronous devices

Time is an important consideration when dealing with independent processors or devices. If your APL system communicates with devices such as microcomputers, printers, voice simulators or remote sensors, they must be synchronized, or chaos results. Often the application requires delaying the APL processing until a signal is received from the device. Much of this signalling happens automatically, as with buffered printers. For other devices or other applications you may have to specify the communication protocol.

One of the important considerations is what to do if the device doesn't respond when it should, similar to your own behavior when the system simply doesn't respond to your entries. $\Box ARBIN$ (page 240), with its timeout feature, can be a lifesaver for this situation.

Imagine a time-shared computer that is programmed to routinely call several remote microcomputers and transfer the previous day's business transactions. The process needs to take alternate action if the telephone line was busy (try later), or if there was no answer (message the communications manager). During a successful connection there is the possibility of garbled transmission, indeterminate delays or unrecoverable communications failure. Detection and recovery, or at least alternate actions, are possible for all of these, and need to be developed if the application is to run without human intervention.

Detached and deferred tasks

The exact details of these facilities differ significantly from system to system. We will give only an introduction here. If you need these features for your application, consult your system reference manual.

Some time-sharing systems have facilities for initiating sessions without having a terminal attached. The *detached task* can communicate with regular users (here called *attached tasks*) via shared files or shared variables. Applications of this technology parallel supervisory or stewardship activities among humans. A major use of detached tasks is to serve as a 'security officer' to a shared database. The detached task intercepts the user's interactive request for data, and limits the flow to only that information to which the user is authorized.

A simple but useful application of detached tasks is to eliminate the use of a connected terminal for those jobs that aren't inherently interactive. You sign on the system from a regular terminal and create a detached task through the $\square SIGNON$ (for APL*PLUS) or $\square RUN$ (for Sharp APL) system function. Its argument consists of items like the name of the workspace to load (which usually has a latent expression set), the files that are to be used for input and output (in lieu of terminal keyboard and display), usage limits (to prevent runaways such as infinite loops), and what to do if there are untrappable errors.

When a detached task is running, the owner (that is, the user who initiated the task) can monitor it with the $\square TASKS$ or $\square RUNS$ system variable. The result is a matrix of task numbers and usage figures for all tasks currently running, including the current attached task. The result of $\square TASKS$ is roughly equivalent to $\square AI$, but for all tasks. A detached task can be terminated by the attached task or an initiating detached task using the $\square BOUNCE$ system function.

There is also a way to cause a detached task to 'wake up' much as you would set an alarm clock to wake you in the morning. The activation instructions can be very specific, and contingent on other tasks having completed, or a certain time having arrived, or certain data being available, or on a regular schedule such as every Friday night at 10 p.m. The specification is usually done by prompted programs supplied with the system. Detached tasks initiated in this manner are called *deferred tasks*. They are the ultimate mechanism for automating applications because once they are set up, no human need attend to them. This eliminates both the unnecessary human effort and errors. Where the deferred tasks are done at times other than normal working hours, they help to even out system workloads and thus make better use of the computing facilities.

Changing the index origin

APL normally operates in index origin 1. This means that the first element of a vector is obtained by $VECTOR[1]$. But there are branches of mathematics where by convention the first element of a vector is called the zero-th. To make APL more closely represent this convention, you can change the index origin to 0 by $\square IO \leftarrow 0$. Then the first element of a vector is obtained by $VECTOR[0]$. Affected are the monadic and dyadic forms of ι, $?$, $\spadesuit$ and Ψ, all forms of indexing and axis designation, and the left argument of ϕ.

```
      □IO←0                X←2 6ρ'CHAIRSTABLES'          0 0 ⌽X
      ι5                   X[0;0 1 5]                CA
0 1 2 3 4            CHS                                 X,[0] 'DESKS '
      'ABCD'ι'CAXB'             +/[0]X='E'          CHAIRS
2 0 4 1              0 0 0 0 1 0                     TABLES
      ?1                       +/[1]X='E'            DESKS
0                   0 1                                   'CAT',[¯.5]'DOG'
      3?3                                            CAT
0 1 2                                                DOG
```

These are the only things affected. In particular, the lines of functions still start at [1], file component numbers are always referenced in origin 1, and the shape of objects (ρ) is unchanged. The current origin can be determined by $\square IO$ and it can be reset with $\square IO \leftarrow 1$:

```
      □IO                  □IO←1                    □IO
0                                          1
```

$\Box IO$ can be localized in defined functions, but you must give it a value before it is used by any of the affected primitive functions, or an *IMPLICIT ERROR* will result. Only 0 and 1 are acceptable values for $\Box IO$.

You may well ask what advantages there may be to work in either origin. To most do-it-yourselfers, 1 seems more 'natural.' But there are applications which seem made for 0-origin. For instance, algorithms like *HEXA* and *DEC* (Chapter 22) no longer need to add or subtract to adjust the indices. Boolean numbers are directly usable as indices, as in the branch instruction $\rightarrow(L1,L2)[X \geq Y]$.

In most APL systems, storage is saved by working in origin 0 if the results are in bit rather than integer form:

```
M←0  2  5  6  10  16  20  15  8  9  7  2
□IO←0                          □IO←1
SPACE←□WA                      SPACE←□WA
DATA0←M∘.≥1+⍳⌈/M               DATA1←1+M∘.≥⍳⌈/M
SPACE-□WA                      SPACE-□WA
116                      1008

      ' □'[DATA0]                    ' □'[DATA1]
```

```
□□                             □□
□□□□□                          □□□□□
□□□□□□                         □□□□□□
□□□□□□□□□□                     □□□□□□□□□□
□□□□□□□□□□□□□□□□                □□□□□□□□□□□□□□□□
□□□□□□□□□□□□□□□□□□□□            □□□□□□□□□□□□□□□□□□□□
□□□□□□□□□□□□□□□□                □□□□□□□□□□□□□□□□
□□□□□□□□                       □□□□□□□□
□□□□□□□□□                       □□□□□□□□□
□□□□□□□□                       □□□□□□□□
□□                             □□
```

Many programmers localize $\Box IO$ in every main function, setting it at the start and thereby passing it on to each function called by it (unless it is localized again). But the best solution is to write origin-independent APL instructions whenever possible, as for example:

```
V[⍳4]              instead of    V[1 2 3 4]
→(X>Y)↑LABEL                     →LABEL  ×⍳X>Y
M,[□IO]V                         M,[1]V
V[1 7-~□IO]                      V[1 7]
```

Random link

When *roll* and *deal* were explained, we commented that you get the same sequence of random numbers each time you sign on. More accurately, there is a *random link*, $\Box RL$, associated with each workspace. Each time you use *?*, a random number is generated based on the present value of $\Box RL$, and $\Box RL$ itself changes, ready for the next execution of *?*. Actually, the numbers provided aren't really random; they cycle (on the IBM 370-based APLs) every 2147483646 numbers, but that's more than sufficient for practical purposes.

The value of $\Box RL$ in a clear workspace is 16807 ($7 * 5$). It can be manually reset by assigning $\Box RL$ any value from 1 to 2147483646. The current random link can be captured by $X \leftarrow \Box RL$. $\Box RL$ can be localized, and must be assigned before any use of roll or deal.

There are two main reasons for changing the random link. You might want to reset it to some known previous value if you were rerunning some *simulation* or game to check its computations, or you might want to set it to an arbitrary random starting point, as happens in the exercise programs *EASYDRILL* (page 53) and *TEACH* (page 145). This is usually done by basing $\Box RL$ on $\Box TS$ or $\Box AI$. One of the more novel expressions is $\Box RL \leftarrow +/\Box AI$.

Comparison tolerance

On page 224 we mentioned that only about 16 decimal positions are kept in floating point internal representation. Thus, a rational number like $1\,1/3$ is accurate to approximately 1.333333333333333, which is slightly different from an exact value of $1\,1/3$. If you ponder this for a while, you'll accept the fact that it would take an infinite number of bits (as opposed to the 56 used for representation of the mantissa in floating point) to represent that number exactly.

If you must deal with rational numbers with exact precision, consider representing each value as a numerator and denominator pair of integer elements in an array, and developing a set of APL functions to perform rational arithmetic.

If $1 \ ^1/_3$ is represented in floating point storage as 1.333333333333333 then $3 \times 1 + \div 3$ should be 3.999999999999999. Why is it, then, that $4 = 3 \times 1 + \div 3$? They aren't *exactly* equal! The reason is that APL uses a little 'common sense' when comparing two numeric values. If values differ by no more than one part in 10000000000000, APL considers them equal. This feature is called the comparison *tolerance* (or *fuzz*, if you prefer), and is used by APL in the functions $< \ \le \ = \ \ge \ > \ \ne \ \iota \ \epsilon \ \lceil \ \lfloor \ \cap \ \top \ \underline{\epsilon} \ I$ and $|$.

You can change the comparison tolerance with the system variable $\Box CT$. It can take any value between 0 and just under 1:

```
      X←□CT                    □CT←0
      X                        4=3×1+÷3
1.419697693E¯14          0
      4=3×1+÷3                 □CT←X
1
```

$\Box CT$ can be localized in defined functions, but it must be assigned before any of the primitives that use it are executed, or an *IMPLICIT ERROR* results.

In APL2 there is a similar, but unrelated system variable $\Box MD$, for matrix divide tolerance, which may be set to any scalar nonnegative number. It acts for matrix divide and matrix inverse in the same way that $\Box CT$ does for functions which do comparisons. For singular right arguments, or those with more columns with rows, $\Box MD$ is a fuzz on the algebraic determination of the rank of R.

Horizontal tabs

For those APL users who work at typewriter terminals and some nonintelligent displays, the *horizontal tabs* system variable, $\Box HT$, is a scalar or vector containing tab settings. The cursor will move over to these tab settings on execution for faster output. Physical tab settings on the terminal must agree with those in $\Box HT$. $\Box HT$ is reset to $\iota 0$ when the current session is ended.

Terminal type

For those users who wish to create special effects that may be available only on certain terminals, there is a system variable $\Box TT$, for *terminal type*, which may be incorporated in a defined function to identify the terminal being used. There are five possible return codes (on VS APL—yours may differ): 0 for indeterminate; 1 for correspondence; 2 for PTTC-BCD; 3 for 1050; 4 for 3270 with APL; 5 for 3270 without APL.

User load

This system variable, $\Box UL$, returns the number of users on the system. In the early days of APL usage this was the main indicator of how saturated the system was. For versions of APL running on virtual machines or personal computers $\Box UL$ returns 1, which isn't particularly useful.

The symbol table

On most APL systems, there is a limit to how many different symbols (variables, functions, labels and groups) you can have in a workspace. That limit is quite liberal for most purposes. But as you might expect, sooner or later you may exceed the limit and get a *SYMBOL TABLE FULL* message (*SYSTEM LIMIT* on APL2).

You can view the current symbol table status by the system command $)SYMBOLS$:

```
      )LOAD 1 CLASS                    )CLEAR
SAVED  23.54.04 12/10/82       CLEAR WS
      )SYMBOLS                         )SYMBOLS
IS 512; 201 IN USE             IS 512; 0 IN USE
```

A symbol is used whenever you mention a new variable, function, label or group. However, if a name is used over again (such as $L1$ used as a label in one function, as a local variable in another, and as a group in the workspace) it doesn't increase the symbol count.

On the other hand, erasing variables or functions doesn't decrease the symbol count. Indeed, the symbol count is increased even by innocently mistyping a variable name:

```
      XY                              )SYMBOLS
VALUE ERROR                    IS 512; 1 IN USE
      XY
      ∧
```

and it can increase substantially by forgetting to use quotes, as in this entry:

```
      XY←THIS IS AN ERROR            )SYMBOLS
VALUE ERROR                    IS 512; 5 IN USE
      XY←THIS IS AN ERROR
                   ∧
```

If you use a workspace for extensive development and maintenance, eventually you will name more symbols than are allowed, as we have done maliciously here:

```
      ∇SYMBFULL                       SYMBFULL
[1]   I←1                       SYMBOL TABLE FULL
[2]   LP:♠'A',(⍕I),'←99'        SYMBFULL[2]  LP:♠'A',(⍕I),'←99'
[3]   I←I+1                                     ∧
[4]   →LP ∇                            )SYMBOLS
                               IS 512; 512 IN USE
```

When this happens, you should erase whatever variables, groups and functions you don't need and use the following sequence (assuming the original workspace was named $OLDWS$):

```
      )SAVE CONTINUE
      )CLEAR
      )COPY CONTINUE
      )WSID OLDWS
      )SAVE
```

This 'purifies' the workspace so that expired symbols are not retained. It is advisable to do this to a developing workspace every few weeks. On some systems, $)RESET$ performs a similar cleanup of the symbol table.

Lest you feel that our example $SYMBFULL$ is contrived, recall that any application using automatic program generation ($\Box FX$, $\Box DEF$, ♠, direct definition and latent expressions) can create new symbols. Similarly, applications that let the user roam in an executable environment (as opposed to keeping him tethered with ⍞) are vulnerable to $SYMBOL\ TABLE\ FULL$s.

You can change the number of symbols, if you genuinely need more than the default, by an entry like $)SYMBOLS\ 1000$. This works only in a clear workspace, so you would still use the sequence above, resetting $)SYMBOLS$ just before the $)COPY$. Increasing the symbol capacity decreases the available workspace (as measured by $\Box WA$) by as much as eight bytes per symbol, so plan accordingly. You can also specify fewer symbols, which gives you more $\Box WA$.

Some systems also offer a system variable, $\Box SYMB$. You can't use it to change the number of symbols, but you can use it in applications to see if the symbol table is getting full. Its result is a two-element vector holding the capacity and the number in use.

Direct definition

Direct definition is a form of expressing executable algorithms that most closely parallels the formal use of functions in mathematics. For this reason it is a popular APL feature in academic circles. For example, a mathematical definition of the conversion from Fahrenheit to Celsius is C(F)=(F-32)×(5÷9). Here is the same formula expressed and evaluated in defined function form and direct definition form on the Sharp APL System:

```
      )LOAD 1 DIRECTDEF
SAVED  10.59.31 09/25/80

      ∇C←FROMFAHREN F                    DEFINE
[1]    C←(F-32)×5÷9 ∇            DDFROMFAHREN:(ω-32)×5÷9

      FROMFAHREN 0 32 98.6 212          DDFROMFAHREN 0 32 98.6 212
¯17.77777778 0 37 100             ¯17.77777778 0 37 100
```

At this writing, direct definition has not stabilized in the APL language. APL2 doesn't have it at all. It is generally available on the Sharp APL System, but only as a simulation (workspace 1 *DIRECTDEF*) rather than as part of the APL system itself. On STSC's APL it has been implemented only on the 'experimental' system presently (August, 1983). Moreover, the syntax of direct definition used on each system is different.

But in spite of these drawbacks, direct definition has its advocates and its place in APL, particularly in expository work involving straightforward mathematics. It might be just right for you. However, if you came here from Chapter 3, you probably should go back there now, as the following paragraphs use features covered after Chapter 3.

On both systems the general idea is to provide a facility which lets you express your algorithms in an unencumbered way. For monadic functions on Sharp APL that idea carries well (the argument is always represented by ω):

```
      DEFINE                    DEFINE
SQRT:ω*.5                    SQ:ω×ω
      SQRT 1 2 4                    SQ 4
1 1.414213562 2              16
      SQ SQRT 1   4
1 2 4
```

On the STSC system, algorithms are stored as character vectors, and the operator ∇ is used to execute them:

```
      SQRT←'ω*.5'                    SQ←'ω×ω'
      (∘∇ SQRT) 1 2 4              (∘∇ SQ) 4
1 1.414213562 2              16
      (∘∇ SQ)(∘∇ SQRT) 1 2 4
1 2 4
```

The ∘ is used as a place holder to tell whether the function is being used as though it were monadic (∘∇ *NAME*) or dyadic (*NAME* ∇∘). Both Sharp and STSC use α to represent the left argument. The following examples compare the systems:

	traditional	*Sharp*	STSC
	∇Z←SUM W	DEFINE	
[1]	Z←+/W ∇	SUM:+/ω	SUM←'+/ω'
	∇Z←AVG W	DEFINE	
[1]	Z←(SUM W)÷ρW ∇	AVG:(SUM ω)÷ρω	AVG←'((∘∇SUM)ω÷ρω'
	AVG 2 3 7 4 2	AVG 2 3 7 4 2	(∘∇ AVG) 2 3 7 4 2
3.6		3.6	3.6
	∇Z←CEN W	DEFINE	
[1]	Z←W-AVG W ∇	CEN:ω-AVG ω	CEN←'ω-(∘∇ AVG)ω'

```
        ∇Z←SSQ W                      DEFINE                        SSQ←'(∘∇ SUM)
[1]     Z←SUM (CEN W)*2 ∇         SSQ:SUM (CEN ω)*2                    ((∘∇ CEN)ω)*2'


        ∇Z←VAR W                      DEFINE                        VAR←'((∘∇ SSQ)ω)
[1]     Z←(SSQ W)÷ρW ∇            VAR:(SSQ ω)÷ρω                        ÷ρω'


        ∇Z←SD W                       DEFINE                        SD←'((∘∇ VAR)ω)*.5'
[1]     Z←(VAR W)*.5 ∇            SD:(VAR ω)÷ρω                   (∘∇ SD) 2 3 7 4 2
        SD 2 3 7 4 2                  SD 2 3 7 4 2              1.854723699
1.854723699                    1.854723699
```

The final two examples are dyadic. In traditional APL they appear as

```
        ∇Z←A SXY W
[1]     Z←SUM (CEN A)×CEN W ∇

        ∇Z←A COR W
[1]     Z←(A SXY W)÷((SSQ A)×SSQ W)*.5 ∇i

        2 3 7 4 2 COR 2 4 7 3 2
0.9418604651
```

and they follow closely in Sharp APL:

```
        DEFINE
SXY:SUM (CEN α)×CEN ω

        DEFINE
COR:(α SXY ω)÷((SSQ α)×SSQ ω)*.5

        2 3 7 4 2 COR 2 4 7 3 2
0.9418604651
```

But the form is quite different in APL*PLUS:

```
        SXY←'(∘∇ SUM)((∘∇ CEN)α)×(∘∇ CEN)ω'
        COR←'(α(SXY ∇∘)ω)÷(((∘∇ SSQ)α)×(∘∇ SSQ)ω)*.5
        2 3 7 4 2 COR 2 4 7 3 2
0.9418604651
```

As you can see, direct definition starts out simple, but tends toward long one-liners as the work gets more complicated. Although we won't cover it here, both systems allow more than one line, and they even have ways to branch or conditionally execute. The authors' feelings are that while direct definition is useful for very simple functions, the majority of users will continue to prefer and use regular function definition for most of their work.

More APL2 system functions and variables

The rest of this chapter explains still more advanced features of APL2. If you are new to APL, you can ignore them for now. Indeed, although these features are very powerful, you may not need them for years—the original APL was implemented in 1966, and none of these features existed until around 1982. That tells you that a lot of people somehow got by without them!

Attributes

This is a handy dyadic system function, represented by $\square AT$, which tells you in detail about the attributes of various objects in the workspace. The right argument is a character matrix of names, as for $\square NC$, while the left argument is 1, 2 or 3. Here is a table of results for each left argument value:

description	value	result position	meaning
valences	1	1	returns explicit result (0,1)
		2	function valence (0,1,2)
		3	defined operator valence (0,1,2)
fix time	2	1 through 7	$\square TS$ at fix time
execution properties	3	1	nondisplayable (0,1)
		2	nonsuspendable (0,1)
		3	weak interrupts ignored (0,1)
		4	nonresource errors converted to $DOMAIN\ ERRORs$ (0,1)

For variables, fix times and execution properties are all meaningless and zeros are returned. The execution properties may be independently set by use of the dyadic $\square FX$. The result is a numeric matrix with one row for each object whose attributes are being inquired after, and 3, 7 or 4 columns, depending on the value of the left argument.

```
      )LOAD 1 CLASS
SAVED  14.45.33 02/20/83

      □FX 'Z←(F REDUCE) R',[1]14↑'Z←F/R'
REDUCE

      1 □AT 3 7ρNAMES←'RECT    REDUCE MILEAGE'
0 2 0
1 1 1
1 0 0

      2 □AT NAMES
1982 10  7  9 22 35 685
1983  1  6 11 44 51 220
   0  0  0  0  0  0   0

      0 1 1 1 □FX 'L FN R',[1]6↑'L×R'
FN

      3 □AT 'FN'
0 1 1 1
```

Transfer forms

The dyadic system function $\square TF$ transforms an array or function into a character vector consisting of a data type code (F, N or C for a function, simple numeric array or simple character array), followed by the name of the object and a blank, the rank and shape of the array and a blank, and a raveled version of the array. Defined functions are represented in their raveled canonical form.

```
      ARRAY←3 3ρι9
      Z←1 □TF 'ARRAY'
      Z
NARRAY 2 3 3 1 2 3 4 5 6 7 8 9
      Z←1 □TF 'HYP'
FHYP 2 2 16 C←A HYP B          C←((A*2)+B*2)*.5
```

There is an extended transfer form which has 2 as its left argument instead of 1 and displays the name and value of a variable or a (displayable) defined function or operator:

```
      2 ⎕TF 'ARRAY'
ARRAY←3 3ρι9
      2 ⎕TF 'HYP'
⎕FX 'C←A HYP B' 'C←((A*2)+B*2)*.5'
```

The result for a defined function or operator is a vector of vectors of the canonical form, beginning with ⎕FX, if no execution properties have been set. Otherwise, the same display is prefixed by the execution properties:

```
      2 ⎕TF 'FN'
0 1 1 1 ⎕FX 'L FN R' 'L×R'
```

This transfer form is equivalent to the monadic ⎕TF R.

The value of the transfer form is that it puts objects in a workspace in a standard form which allows for easy movement to another system which may be running a different version of APL. Once transferred, the character vectors containing the transfer forms can be executed to reconstitute the objects.

To assist users in the transfer, APL2 has two helpful system commands.)OUT filename creates a transfer file containing the transfer forms of objects in the active workspace. It may be followed by an optional list of specific objects (including system variables) to be transferred. At the receiving end)IN filename reads the file and defines the objects in the active workspace.

Left argument and right argument

These variables, ⎕L and ⎕R, are shared with the system. They are the array values of the referenced arguments of a function which has been interrupted by an error (except *SYNTAX ERROR* and *VALUE ERROR*). After the suspension is removed, they disappear.

```
      3 5 HYP 4 12 20                      ⎕R
LENGTH ERROR                          16 144 400
HYP[1]    C←((A*2)+B*2)*.5                 ⎕L
          ^        ^                   9 25
```

Execution can proceed if we reassign ⎕L or ⎕R:

```
      ⎕R←16 144
      →ι0
5 13
```

National language translation

A simple character vector is used as an argument to ⎕NLT. It determines the language to be used for reporting errors and what language (besides English) will be accepted for system commands. The only recognized values at this time are

'DANSK'	Danish	'FRANCAIS'	French
'DEUTSCH'	German	'NORSK'	Norwegian
'ENGLISH'	English	'SUOMI'	Finnish
'ESPANOL'	Spanish	'SVENSKA'	Swedish

Anything other than the above sets ⎕NLT to English. This variable can be set only for a session, but is not affected by clearing and loading.

System labels

APL2 provides two *system labels*, $\square FL$ (fill) and $\square ID$ (identity), which are used in defined functions and defined operators. The fill label $\square FL$ is activated when the each, bracket axis, outer product and inner product operators are applied to certain empty arrays. It produces an empty result and avoids the *DOMAIN ERROR*s which would otherwise be produced. There is an elaborate set of conditions governing the use of this label and $\square ID$ which interested users can reference in the IBM APL2 Language Manual SB21-3015.

Here is an example of how $\square FL$ is used in a defined function with outer product:

```
       ∇Z←L POWER R                    ρ1 2 ∘.POWER 0ρ0
[1]    Z←L*R                    0 0
[2]    →0                              1 2 ∘.POWER 3 4
[3]    □FL:Z←L*R+2 ∇
                               1   1
                               8  16
```

The identity label $\square ID$ works similarly. It is activated when a dyadic defined function is applied to an empty array through the reduce operator or inner product whose intermediate result is empty along the last axis. In the following example the identity element is 3:

```
       ∇Z←L ADD R                      ADD/1ρ2
[1]    Z←L+R                    2
[2]    →0                              ADD/0ρ2
[3]    □ID:Z←((L≠ιρρR)/ρR)ρ3 ∇B
                               3        ADD/2 0ρ2
       ADD/2 5                          3 3
7
```

Complex arithmetic

APL2 treats all numbers as members of the complex number field. All arithmetic operations are defined on complex numbers, so that the real numbers with which we have been working thus far are only a subset of what is possible.

Here is how complex numbers may be represented:

APL2	conventional notation
2J3	2+3i
0J1	i
3.4E2J⁻2E⁻3	340−.002i
2R.5	2(cos.5 + i sin .5) in radians
2D50	2(cos 50 + i sin 50) in degrees

Our assumption is that if you are reading these words now, you don't need Gilman and Rose's handy guide to what complex numbers are all about. We'll just briefly describe the actions of those primitive APL2 functions that may not be obvious when used with complex numbers. In what follows, to save space R and I refer to the real and imaginary parts of a complex number RJI, with Z the result of some primitive function. Functions not shown can be expected to follow the same rules with both real and complex numbers.

	L and ⌈	rounds R and I
	+	negates the imaginary part
monadic	×	Z has magnitude 1 with same phase as RJI
functions	|	Z is $((R*2)+I*2)*.5$
	−	negates R and I
	÷	takes reciprocal of R and I
	8○	Z is $-(\,{}^-1-RJI*2)*.5$
	⁻8○	Z is $(\,{}^-1-RJI*2)*.5$
	9○	returns R
	⁻9○	returns RJI
	11○	returns I
	⁻11○	Z is $0J1 × RJI$

$$\begin{array}{l} \text{-}120 \quad Z \text{ is phase } R \\ \text{-}120 \quad Z \text{ is } \texttt{*0J1} \times RJI \end{array}$$

`⁻40,⁻80,80`   holds only for complex numbers in first quadrant

`L,⌈,<,≤,>,≥` RJI must be within system fuzz of a real number to avoid *DOMAIN ERROR*

`*`   for multiple roots, Z is the root with the least nonnegative angle in the complex plane.

Fortunately or unfortunately, depending on your point of view, operations in APL2 which result in complex numbers, even from real input (e.g., `⁻1*.5`) will return a complex result instead of the usual *DOMAIN ERROR* found on most systems. If this bothers you, you will have to bypass it with appropriate program instructions, since there is no way to 'turn it off' at the keyboard.

PROBLEMS

1. Use $□AI$ **A** to pass through only those users whose sign-ons are in the vector $NUMBERS$, and **B** to quit a function if the elapsed time is greater than, say, 100 seconds.

2. Write an expression to create a dollar sign character if your system doesn't have one.

3. A company records billing dates and order numbers of its bills rendered in a numeric matrix $BILLS$ in the form

   ```
   12345    10     5    1982
   14872    11    13    1982
   15112     1    30    1983
   ```

   the first column being the order numbers. Use $□TS$ to determine which bills are overdue (same date of month following above billing date).

4. Write an expression to convert a vector V of positive integers into a logical matrix with one row for each integer I in the vector and I leading 1's.

5. Define a function $DISTRDS$ to do distributive rounding to some decimal position DEC, i.e., make sure that the sum of the rounded values equals the rounded sum of the unrounded values.

6. Just to test your alertness: what happened to the space in the following sequence?

   ```
          □WA
   125840
          SMASH
          □WA
   132
          )FNS
   SMASH
   ```

7. Devise a scrambling scheme which keys the account number to the random link to encrypt any array.

8. How do you decrypt the results of problem 7?

9. Using $□TS$, construct a niladic function $TIME$ that will result in the current time expressed as, for example, `4:47:22` *PM EASTERN*. Truncate to seconds.

10. Define an APL function that will generate today's date as $MM/DD/YEAR$.

11. Define a niladic function that will, when executed, display a message for only those whose user numbers have been incorporated in the function.

12. Assign $A←9.222222222222222$ and $B←9.222222222222227$ and execute $A=B$, $A∈B$ and $A-B$. Repeat after setting $□CT←0$. Account for the responses.

13. Why is the expression $A[\iota N]$ independent of the index origin?

14. Execute $\iota 0$ and $\iota 1$ after setting $\Box IO \leftarrow 0$. Are they vectors? Of what size?

15. Define a function to identify whether it is morning, afternoon or evening and print an appropriate message.

16. Use $\Box DL$ to write a function that executes $DICE$ (page 58) N times, with a built-in delay of D seconds between repetitions.

17. Modify the multiplication drill function of problem 1, Chapter 23 to include a statement which gives the time required to get the correct solution.

18. Use $\Box LX$ to automatically display one message for authorized users 1500 and 1600, and another for all others when the workspace is loaded. Assume the messages are lines of a two-row matrix M.

19. Write a program to execute an APL statement and report how much time and space are used.

Answers to problems

Some of the problems will have more than one solution given. This will generally occur when there is more than one sound approach to the solution. The proposed solutions, because they are keyed to the operations presented up to that point in the text, will not always be the most concise or elegant possible, with the drill problems occasionally returning error messages. For this reason, an occasional solution will have forward references to simplify the task of defining the expressions needed to solve the problem.

Answers for Chapter 1

```
1.            6  8  2  4+3  9  1  1
       9  17  3  5
             1  0  9  8  -  4  2  2  3
      ‾3  ‾2  7  5
             3-‾1  ‾56.7  0  ‾.19
      4  59.7  3  3.19
             5  4  3×6
      30  24  18
            10÷10  5  2  1
      1  2  5  10
             3  4  ×1  2  3
      LENGTH ERROR
             3  4  ×  1  2  3
                   ^
             1  2  8÷1  2  0
      DOMAIN ERROR
             1  2  8  ÷  1  2  0
                       ^
            ‾2  0  .81+15  6  ‾5
      13  6  ‾4.19
             2‾‾3
      SYNTAX ERROR
             2  ‾  ‾  3
                 ^
```
Reminder: the negative sign is a mark of punctuation, not a function.

```
3.           155  89  45×1.25  .50  .25
      193.75  44.5  11.25
4.           59.50  79.88  83.00÷1263  1997  3028
      0.04711005542  0.04  0.02741083223
5.           .05×47  18  68  10
      2.35  0.9  3.4  0.5
6.           45201  64677  52468  68893  +  15000
      46701  66177  53968  70393
7.           356  205  189  322  257÷400
      0.89  0.5125  0.4725  0.805  0.6425
```
8. The answer is the same as 3+2, or 5. −overstruck with + still looks like +. This exercise emphasizes again that in APL what you see is what you get.

Answers for Chapter 2

1.
```
        A←3 4 5 6 7
        B←2×A
```
2. *SPACEMAN* and Δ3X are valid. The others are invalid because they contain special characters (blank, +, −) or begin with a digit.

3.
```
        M←5 3ρ7
   Q←5 3ρ4 9 11
```
4.
```
        N←M÷7
        N←M−6
        N←8−M
```
5.
```
        S←2 3ρ8 15 7 12 4 0
        P←2 3ρ3.10 2.00 4.17 3.50 2.75 4.35
        TOTSALES←S×P
```
6.
```
        HRS←40 55 46 40 40
        OT←HRS−40
        OTPAY←OT×1.5×4.5
        REGPAY←40×4.5
        GROSSPAY←REGPAY+OTPAY
```
   After you learn how APL handles multiple instructions in a single line (Chapter 6), you'll be able to write the answer as $GROSSPAY←(4.5×40)+4.5×1.5×HRS−40$.

7. A
```
        AGE←YR−BIRTH
```
    B
```
        RET←BIRTH+65
```
    C
```
        REMYRS←RET−YR
```
8.
```
        YES←356 205 189 322 257
        NO←400−YES
        FRNO←NO÷400
```
9.
```
        ST←SALES×TAX
        CHARGES←SALES+ST+PH
```

Answers for Chapter 3

1.
```
         ¯2*.5
DOMAIN ERROR
         ¯2*0.5
           ∧
         3*4 2 1 0
81 27 9 3 1
         21.268E1+4.56E¯2
212.7256
         ¯5 0 ¯22 15⌈3 7 ¯10.8 2
5 7 ¯10.8 15
         2 3 4 5⍟2
1 0.6309297536 0.5 0.4306765581
         1 10⍟1
1 0
         2*.5 .333 .25
1.414213562 1.25962998 1.189207115
         1*0 1 10 100 1000
1 1 1 1 1
         8.3E0×7.9E¯3 56
0.06557 464.8
         ¯2⍟25
DOMAIN ERROR
         ¯2⍟25
           ∧
         10⍟0
DOMAIN ERROR
         10⍟0
          ∧
```
Both arguments must be greater than 0. If the left argument is 1, the right argument must be 1 also.
```
         ¯1 9 ¯5 ¯2⌊0 6 4 3
0 6 ¯5 ¯2
```

```
      ¯8*.33333333333
DOMAIN_ERROR
      ¯8*0.33333333333
          ∧
```

Why the *DOMAIN ERROR* in this example and the first above? Try adding a few more 3's on the right and reexecuting.

```
      ¯7.11E4÷9.45E¯3
¯7523809.524
      346×2E3.7
SYNTAX ERROR
      346×2000 . 7
              ∧
```

2.
```
          1E0
1
          1E1
10
          1E6
1000000
          1E9
1000000000
          1E10
1E10
          1E¯1
0.1
          1E¯2
0.01
          1E¯4
0.0001
          1E¯5
1E¯5
          1E¯6
1E¯6
```

3.
```
      L←3 7 15 2.7
      F←L*2
      AREA←6×F
      AREA
54 294 1350 43.74
```

4.
```
      A←1 2 3 4
      D←3×A
      A∘.×D
  3   6   9 12
  6  12  18 24
  9  18  27 36
 12  24  36 48
      D∘.*A
      3       9      27      81
      6      36     216    1296
      9      81     729    6561
     12     144    1728   20736
```

5.
```
      1 2 3 4 5∘.*2 .5
      1              1
      4              1.414213562
      9              1.732050808
     16              2
     25              2.236067977
```

6. There are 86400 seconds in a day.
```
      86400×365
31536000 (which is 3.1536E7 seconds per year)
```

7.
```
      5280×24
126720
      12÷126720
9.46969697E¯5 (miles per hour)
```

8. The *DOMAIN ERROR* results because there is no real number that gives ¯8 when squared. APL2 gives an answer in the complex domain.

9.
```
      1.5E9÷9.3E7
16.12903226
```

10.   `15 20 32 29⌊18 20 10 49`
   `15 20 10 49`

11.   `10⍟1÷C`

This is a bit ahead of the game in that we haven't said anything yet about order of execution, where multiple operations occur in a single expression. See Chapter 6 for more details. You can, of course, always write this as two steps, $D \leftarrow 1 \div C$, followed by $10 \circledast D$.

12.   `C←A⌊B`

13. **A**   `RATE←.08÷12`
         `RN←(1+RATE)*126`
         `1000×RN`

   B   `RATE1←.079÷360`
         `RN1←(1+RATE1)*3780`
         `1000×RN1`

14.   A kilometer is equivalent to 1000 meters or 1000×100 (100000) cm. Each fold doubles the thickness. The problem (in conventional notation) can be stated as $.01 \times 2^x = 100000$. Take the log of both sides and solve for X: `X←(10⍟100000÷.01)÷10⍟2` which is a little more than 23 folds.

15.   `1.15⍟1E3`

   (The problem is simplified by using 1.15 as the base for taking logarithms. With APL there's no need to use base 10.)

16.   `MEN←7*0`
         `WIVES←7*1`
         `SACKS←7*2`
         `CATS←7*3`

   or, more compactly, `7*0 1 2 3` for the number of men, wives, sacks and cats respectively.

17.   `GROWTH←1.00 1.02 1.04 1.06 1.08 1.10`
         `FUTVAL←GROWTH∘.*1 2 3 4 5 6 7 8 9 10`

18.   `.9⍟.25`
   (see comment at end of problem 15.)

Answers for Chapter 4

1.   `1 9 8|3 4 6`
      `0 4 6`
             `0 1 2 3 4!3 4 5 6 7`
      `1 4 10 20 35`
             `3|¯3 ¯1 0 1 2 3`
      `0 1 0 1 2 0`
             `0 0 1 1∨0 1 0 1`
      `0 1 1 1`
             `1 0 1 0∧1 0 0 1`
      `1 0 0 0`
             `2 4 7 ¯2>6 ¯1 0 4`
      `0 1 1 0`
             `4 ¯5 ¯1 ¯6.8≥4 1 ¯1 2`
      `1 0 1 0`
             `8 7 6 5 4 3 2 1≤1 2 3 4 5 6 7 8`
      `0 0 0 0 1 1 1 1`
             `1|3.4 ¯2.2 .019`
      `0.4 0.8 0.019`
             `0|1 2 3`
      `1 2 3`
             `¯2 4 ¯5|8 13 3.78`
      `0 1 ¯1.22`
             `2 3 0<5 ¯1 4`
      `1 0 1`
             `3 1 2≠1 2 3`
      `1 1 1`
             `0 1 2 3=0 1 3 2`
      `1 1 0 0`
             `0 0 1 1⍱0 1 0 1`
      `1 0 0 0`
             `1 0 1 0⍲1 0 0 1`
      `0 1 1 1`

2.   The factors of an integer N are those integers which divide N. Hence, set $0 = 1\ 2\ 3\ \ldots\ N\,|\,N$.

3. $A \geq 0$ or $0 \leq A$ yields a logical vector with 1's in those positions corresponding to the accounts not overdrawn.

4.   Let $C \leftarrow 0 = B$. Then $A \vee C$ works if either or both conditions hold, while $A \neq C$ works when only one of the conditions holds, but not both. Later, when the logical negation function ($\sim$) is introduced, $A \vee \sim B$ will also be a possible solution.

5.   EXCLUSIVE NOR or NEXCLUSIVE OR.

6.   **A** $Z \leftarrow S \times 0$ $Z \leftarrow S - S$ $Z \leftarrow S \neq S$ $Z \leftarrow S\,|\,S$ $Z \leftarrow S > S$ $Z \leftarrow 0 \star S$ $Z \leftarrow 0 \lfloor S$

     B $W \leftarrow S \star 0$ $W \leftarrow S = S$ $W \leftarrow S \leq S$ $W \leftarrow S \div S$ $W \leftarrow S \circledast S$ $W \leftarrow 0\,!\,S$ $W \leftarrow S\,!\,S$

7. $B \leftarrow 2\,|\,A$
         $C \leftarrow 0 = B$

8. $0\ 1 \circ . = 0\ 1$
          $0\ 1 \circ . > 0\ 1$
          $0\ 1 \circ . < 0\ 1$
          $0\ 1 \circ . \geq 0\ 1$
          $0\ 1 \circ . \leq 0\ 1$

9. $\times$ and $\lfloor$ are equivalent to $\wedge$, $\lceil$ to $\vee$, $\star$ to $\geq$, $|$ to $<$ and $!$ to $\leq$.

10.   If the result of $B\,|\,A$ is zero, then A is divisible by B.

11.   Hours: $H - 1\,|\,H$; minutes: $60\,|\,H \times 60$. This last solution should be tried for typical values of H. You will see that H is multiplied by 60 first, and then $60\,|\,H$ is obtained.

12. $4\,!\,30$

13. $N - 1\,|\,N$ (this works only for nonnegative values of N)

14. $1\,|\ ^{-}1 \times N$ or $1 - 1\,|\,N$

15.   **A** $RESP1 \wedge RESP2$
     B $RESP1 \neq RESP2$

16. $I \leftarrow I + 1$. The left arrow is used in APL to store information, while =, like the other relationals, simply reports on the equality of the two arguments. In arithmetic the expression X=2 asserts that X is *assigned* the value 2, and is equivalent to $X \leftarrow 2$ in APL. Unfortunately, = in arithmetic is another concept that may assert equivalency, as in $1/_2 = 2/_4$. This ambiguity is absent in the APL notation.

Answers for Chapter 5

1. $+/3\ 7\ ^{-}10\ 15\ 22$
    37
        $\div/3\ 5\ 2$
    1.2
        $\wedge/1\ 1\ 1$
    1
        $=/3\ 2\ 2$
    0
        $\lceil/1\ ^{-}14.7\ 22\ 6$
    22
        $-/2\ 4\ 6\ 8\ 10$
    6
        $\star/3\ 2\ 1$
    9
        $\vee/0\ 1\ 0\ 1$
    1
        $>/1\ ^{-}2\ ^{-}4$
    0
        $\times\backslash3\ 2\ 7\ 9$
  $3\ 6\ 42\ 378$
        $\times/2\ 4\ 6\ 8\ 10$
  3840
        $\wedge/1\ 0\ 1\ 1$
    0
        $\vee/0\ 0\ 0$
    0
        $\lfloor/\ ^{-}2\ 4\ 0\ ^{-}8$
   $^{-}8$
        $\lceil\backslash4\ 12\ 7\ 14$
  $4\ 12\ 12\ 14$

2.   ∧/ returns a 1 if and only if all the elements are 1, 0 otherwise.

ᴠ/ returns a 0 if and only if all the elements are 0, 1 otherwise.

=/ (applied to a logical vector) returns 0 if there is an odd number of 0's, 1 otherwise.

3. $+/3×AV$

6 9 (which is the same as $3×+/AV$)

4. $⌈/Q←1\ 7\ ^-2\ ^-3$

5. $S←.5×+/L$

$A2←S-L$

$Q←×/A2$

$R←S×Q$

$AREA←R*.5$

After the rules of execution order are introduced in Chapter 6, this can be done more compactly as

$S←.5×+/L$

$AREA←(S×ׂ/S-L)*.5$

6.   Since the X-coordinate of a point is customarily written first, it is not enough to take $÷/Q-P$ since this results in the difference in the X-coordinates divided by the difference in the Y-coordinates, which is the reciprocal of the slope, according to the definition given. Hence, $A←÷/Q-P$ and $SLOPE←1÷A$, or more compactly, $SLOPE←1÷÷/Q-P$ (see note to problem 5).

7. $SR←+\S$

8. $∧\LV$ makes every element a 0 after the first 0.

$<\LV$ makes every element a 0 after the first 1.

$ᴠ\LV$ makes every element a 1 after the first 1.

9. **A** $TRANS←ρSALES$

B $⌈/SALES$ and $⌊/SALES$

C $TOTSALES←+/SALES$

D $1.04×SALES$

E $AVGSALE←TOTSALES÷TRANS$

10. $V←6\ 2\ 1\ 8\ 4\ 3$

A $TOT←+/V$

B $TOT-11$

C $6300÷TOT$

D $TOT×75$

11. $T←10ρ1$

$+\T$

1 2 3 4 5 6 7 8 9 10

When the interval function is introduced (Chapter 12), you will have a much faster way to generate this sequence.

Answers for Chapter 6

1. $4*3⌈3*4$

5.846006549E48

$(4*3)⌈3*4$

81

$5*3×5$

3.051757813E10

$1÷2+^-5\ 6\ 0\ 8\ ^-6$

$^-$0.3333333333 0.125 0.5 0.1 $^-$0.25

$76÷+/2+3×1\ 2\ 3\ 4$

2

$6÷2-4*3$

$^-$0.09677419355

2.   The first, second and fourth expressions are equivalent.

3. **A** $(3÷4)+(5÷6)-7÷8$ or better, $+/3\ 5\ ^-7÷4\ 6\ 8$

B $(-/9\ 8÷7\ 10)÷-/1\ 2÷3\ 5$

4. $(×/X)*1÷ρX$

6.386118449

5. B will be compared with $B+A$ for equality, with A added to that result. The expression works only when A is 0. More generally, parentheses are needed around $A+B$.

6.   Brute force solution: $(0≠4000|Y)∧(0=4|Y)∧(0=400|Y)=0=100|Y$

Better solution:

$2|+/0=4\ 100\ 400\ 4000|Y$

Still better solution: $-/0=4\ 100\ 400\ 4000|Y$

7. The minus sign in front of the middle term acts on everything to the right of it. The correct version
    is $(X*2)+(\bar{}2\times X\times Y)+Y*2$ or $(X*2)+(Y*2)-2\times X\times Y$

8. $\bar{}8+X\times X\times 2+\bar{}3\times X*2$

9. $((+/X*2)\div\rho X)*.5$

10. Jack proposes if 1) he has the ring, 2) the weather is favorable, 3) Jill is younger than Jack and 4)
    Jack isn't over the age limit for Jill's beaux.

11. Annual: $P\times(1+.01\times R)*T$
    Quarterly: $P\times(1+.01\times R\div4)*T\times4$

12. $C\leftarrow5\times(A>B)+4\times A<B$
    $C\leftarrow8+2\times(A>B)\wedge D<E$

13. `2+2 2+2`
    `6 6`
    Shame on you if you said the answer was `4 4`.

14. A ρV
    B $+/V\div\rho V$
    C $+/V<0$
    D $+/V=0$
    E $\lceil/V$
    F $100\times(+/V>100)\div\rho V$
    G $+/(V\leq200)\wedge V\geq100$
    H $+/0=100|V\times V>0$

15. $A\times A>B$

16. $.25\times16.5\times16.5\times160\times144$ or $\times/.25\ 16.5\ 16.5\ 160\ 144$
    `1568160`

17. $(7.2\times9\times5)+4\times235+39\times3$
    `1732`

18. The results of these instructions are dependent on your implementation of APL. You cannot tell
    when the system evaluates an expression in parentheses. Hence, you should avoid writing
    commands like those shown in this problem.

19. $+/COMM\times+\div FUND$

20. $\lceil/5\ 4.5\ 7.25\div2.75\ 1.8\ 3$

21. $\wedge/\wedge/A=A=1$

22. $BILLS\leftarrow BILLS\times1+0.015\times30<TODAY-DATE$

23. $YR\leftarrow75\ 81\ 80$
    $PRICE\leftarrow5200\ 8100\ 9500$
    $GAS\leftarrow9660\ 8556\ 3080$
    $MILES\leftarrow98730\ 84000\ 28000$
    $COST\leftarrow1.35\ 1.30\ 1.47$

    A $GALLONS\leftarrow GAS\div COST$ and $TGAL\leftarrow+/GALLONS$
    B $TAX\leftarrow.04\times PRICE$ and $TTAX\leftarrow+/TAX$
    C $AVMIL\leftarrow MILES\div80-YR$
    D $MPG\leftarrow MILES\div GALLONS$
    E $GASYR\leftarrow GAS\div80-YR$
    F $GASPM\leftarrow GAS\div MILES$ and $TGASPM\leftarrow(+/GAS)\div+/MILES$
    Why is this different from $(+/GASPM)\div3$?

    G $+/GAS$
    H $+/MILES$
    I $(+/MILES)\div+/80-YR$

24. $GROSSPAY\leftarrow R\times H$
    $NETPAY\leftarrow GROSSPAY-GROSSPAY\times.01\times S+I1+I2$

25. A $6\leq+/SALES$
    `1` (quota exceeded or made)
    B $50\times SALES$
    `100 200 0 50 150` (weekly earnings)
    C $((\bar{}50+600)\times+/SALES)-5\times75$
    `4575` (net revenue)

26. $WT\leftarrow10\times.3\ .15\ .1\ .1\ .05\ .35$
    $COST\leftarrow2\ 2\ 1.50\ 1.25\ 1.80\ .40$
    $SPRICE\leftarrow1+.1\times+/WT\times COST$

27. $2.50+.10\times0\lceil WORDS-15$

28. $(M=1)\wedge(S=0)\wedge(A<55)\wedge L>50000$ or $M\wedge(S=0)\wedge(A<55)\wedge L>50000$

Answers for Chapter 7

1.
```
      ⌊¯2.7|¯15
¯2
      *3 4.7 ¯1.5
20.08553692 109.9471725 0.2231301601
      ⌈¯1.8 0 ¯21 5.6
¯1 0 ¯21 6
      ?3 4 5
1 4 3
      ÷3.5 ¯10 ¯.287
0.2857142857 ¯0.05 ¯3.484320557
      ○1÷180
0.01745329252
      |3.1 0 ¯5.6 ¯8
3.1 0 5.6 8
      !3 5 7 4
6 120 5040 24
      ⌊5.5 6.8 ¯9.1 ¯.12
5 6 ¯10 ¯1
      ?¯1.2 ¯6.7 .52 19.5
DOMAIN ERROR
      ? ¯1.2 ¯6.7 0.52 19.5
      ^
      4×⌈5.8×¯31.046
¯720
      4○1 2 3
1.414213562 2.236067977 3.16227766
      ?10 10 10 10
6 3 1 7   (your random numbers may be different from those shown)
      ⍟14.1 86 .108
2.646174797 4.454347296 ¯2.225624052
      ×¯5.6 0 42
¯1 0 1
      ~0 1 1 0
1 0 0 1
      1○○1 2
1.743934249E¯16 ¯3.487868498E¯16
See comparison tolerance, page 295, for why these are not exactly zero.
      ¯1 ¯2○1 10.5
0.5 1.070796327
```

2.   Floor: $X-1|X$
     Ceiling: $X+1|¯X$ (these expressions work for all real X)

3.
```
      A1←(¯1+A*3)÷2
      *2+A1
3269017.372
      ~(2≤A)∧∨/3=B
0
      C←((A*2)+(A+1)*2)*.5
      C≠⌊C
0
```

4. $0=(⌊N÷10)|N$ or $0=1|N÷⌊N÷10$

5.
```
      A←Y-1969
      LY←⌊.25×A
      B←1+7|3+A+LY   or, on one line:
      B←1+7|3+A+⌊.25×A←Y-1969
```

6.   A $10>|V$ or $0=⌊10⍟|V$
     B $10≤|V$ or $~0=⌊10⍟|V$

7.
```
      M←84.6129999993
      M
84.613
      1E5×M
8461300
      ⌊1E5×M
8461299
```

8. $(\lfloor X \times 10*-(\lfloor 1+10\circledast X)-N)=\lfloor Y \times 10*-(\lfloor 1+10\circledast Y)-N$
9. A $D \div B$
    B $\lceil D \div B$
10. A $(10*-D) \times \lfloor .5+N \times 10*D$
    B $(10*D) \times \lfloor .5+N \times 10*-D$
11. $(\lfloor X+.5)-0=2 | X-.5$ or $(\lceil X-.5)+\sim \times 2 | X+.5$
12. $(\sim A) \vee \sim B$
    1 1 1 0
        $A \vee C \wedge B$
    1 1 0 1
        $(A \wedge \sim B) \wedge A \vee C$
    0 1 0 0
        $(\sim B) \vee A \vee \sim C$
    0 1 1 1
13. $(2 \circ 2 \times \iota 5)=((2 \circ \iota 5)*2)-(1 \circ \iota 5)*2$
    1 1 1 1 1
    For X a scalar, try this:
        $0=-/(2 \ 2 \ 1 \circ 2 \ 1 \ 1 \times X)*1 \ 2 \ 2$
    Can you explain why it doesn't work consistently for all X?
14. $1=+/(1 \ 2 \circ X)*2$
    This version works only for scalar X. For X a vector we can use the outer product as follows:
        $\wedge/1=+/(1 \ 2 \circ . \circ X)*2$
15. $?4 \ 4\rho 100$ or $4 \ 4\rho ?16\rho 100$
16.   The hard way: $(((|N)*.5) \times N>0)+(N*2) \times N<0$
    Much better: $N*.5*\times N$
17. A $S \wedge \sim T$
    B $T \vee \sim J$
    C $(T \wedge S) \vee J$ or $T \wedge S \vee J$
    This ambiguous problem points out that it is more difficult to be precise in English than in APL.
18. $\sim(V1 \wedge V2)$
    1 0 1 0 1 0
        $(\sim V1) \vee (\sim V2)$
    1 0 1 0 1 0
        $\sim(V1 \vee V2)$
    0 0 0 0 1 0
        $(\sim V1) \wedge (\sim V2)$
    0 0 0 0 1 0
    These two equivalences are known in logic as De Morgan's rules.
19. $BETTERGRADES \leftarrow NEWGRADES \lceil 100 \lfloor \lfloor 1.2 \times GRADES$
20. $DED \leftarrow 100 \ 250 \ 500$
        $POL \leftarrow 608 \ 1277 \ 942$
        $PAY \leftarrow .02 \ .035 \ .05$
        $OWNPAY \leftarrow +/DED \times \lfloor POL \times PAY$
21. $DIV \leftarrow .25 \times SHARES$
        $SHAREDIV \leftarrow \lfloor DIV$
        $CASH \leftarrow .01 \times \lfloor .5+100 \times 16.50 \times 1 | DIV$
22. $\lfloor (DATES+1000000 \times 10000 | DATES) \div 10000$
23. $\lfloor 10 | (| NUMBERS) \times 10*-POSITION$
24. $20+\lceil (11 \times 3412+175) \div 144$
25. $(\times X) \times \lfloor .5+ | X$
    Note that the alternate algorithm $\lceil X-.5$, which rounds down numbers ending in $.5$, works in all cases.

Answers for Chapter 8

We haven't explained how to correct typographical errors in defined functions (Chapter 10), so for now you'll have to be very careful entering these exercises. If you do make mistakes, $)CLEAR$ and reenter. Most of the exercises don't depend on any other, so you can usually $)CLEAR$ before each exercise. On some systems you can't even $)CLEAR$ while in function definition, so you may have to enter a ∇ (to close function definition) before you can $)CLEAR$.

1.
```
        ∇Z←EQ X
[1]     Z←0=×/X-2 3 ∇
```
or
```
        ∇Z←EQ1 X
[1]     Z←××/X-2 3 ∇
```

2.
```
        ∇R←H BB AB
[1]     R←H÷AB ∇
```

3.
```
        ∇T←HERO L
[1]     S←.5×+/L
[2]     T←(S××/S-L)*.5 ∇
```

4.
```
        ∇RESULT←REFUND BUCKS
[1]     R1←BUCKS⌊200
[2]     R2←.5×BUCKS-200
[3]     R3←0⌈R2
[4]     R4←R1+R3
[5]     RESULT←R4⌊350 ∇
```
Note the four extra intermediate variables used here. They clutter up the workspace. In Chapter 9 we'll see how to keep this kind of clutter down. Now for a more elegant solution:
```
        ∇RESULT←REFUND1 E
[1]     RESULT←+/.5×E⌊500 200 ∇
```

5.
```
        ∇RT←PR M
[1]     RT←÷+/÷M ∇
```

6.
```
        ∇R←SD X
[1]     R←AVG X
[2]     R←R-X
[3]     R←R*2
[4]     R←(AVG R)*.5 ∇
```
or
```
        ∇R←SD1 X
[1]     R←(AVG(X-AVG X)*2)*.5 ∇
```

7.
```
        ∇M←MR REL V
[1]     M←MR÷(1-(V*2)÷9E16)*.5 ∇
```

8.
```
        ∇Z←X PLUS Y
[1]     Z←X+Y ∇
        ∇Z←X MINUS Y
[1]     Z←X-Y ∇
        ∇Z←X TIMES Y
[1]     Z←X×Y ∇
        ∇Z←X DIVIDEDBY Y
[1]     Z←X÷Y ∇
```

9.
```
        ∇R←A HYPOT B
[1]     R←A×4○B÷A ∇
```

10.
```
        ∇Z←NUM DIVZ DEN
[1]     Z←DEN≠0
[2]     Z←Z×NUM÷DEN+~Z ∇
```

11.
```
        ∇Y←RULEOF72 INT
[1]     Y←⌈72÷INT ∇
```

12. A
```
        ∇Z←EXPENSE UNITS
[1]     Z←50000+(UNITS×20)+5×0⌈UNITS-5000 ∇
```
B
```
        ∇R←SALES PROFIT PRICES
[1]     R←(SALES×PRICES)-EXPENSE SALES ∇
```

Answers for Chapter 9

1.
```
        ∇FICA←P TAX IN
[1]     FICA←.01×P×MAX⌊IN ∇
```
This problem illustrates how a simple APL expression can replace a lot of fuzzy language in the tax code.

2.
```
        ∇A SQDIF B
[1]     T←(A-B)*2 ∇
```

3.
```
        ∇R←FERMAT N
[1]     R←1+2*2*N ∇
```

4.
          $\nabla COMP$
  [1] $(0=A|B)\vee 0=B|A$ ∇
  or
          $\nabla COMP1$
  [1] $0=(A|B)\times B|A$ ∇

5. **A** $\nabla CHANGEA$ V
     [1] $NV\leftarrow NV+\rho V$ ∇
  B $\nabla CHANGEB$ V
     [1] $SV\leftarrow SV++/V$ ∇
  C $\nabla CHANGEC$ V
     [1] $SVSQ\leftarrow SVSQ++/V\star 2$ ∇

6.
          $\nabla Z\leftarrow SD$
  [1] $Z\leftarrow((SVSQ-(SV\star 2)\div NV)\div {}^{-}1+NV)\star.5$ ∇

7. A SQA B lacks the opening ∇
  ∇ $Z\leftarrow B$ HYP monadic arguments must be on the right.
  ∇ A $1FIB$ B illegal function name.
  ∇ A HYP B C most APL systems can't handle more than two arguments.
  ∇ A HYP $B;B;C$ same argument appears twice in the header.

8.
          $(3$ HYP $4)$ HYP 3 HYP 1
  5.916079783
          $4+3$ HYP $4-3$
  7.16227766
          $(4+3)HYP$ $4-3$
  7.071067812

9.
          $)LOAD$ 1 $CLASS$
  $SAVED$ 15.02.39 02/15/83
          $\nabla R\leftarrow ARG1$ D $ARG2$
  $DEFN$ $ERROR$
          ∇ $R\leftarrow ARG1$ D $ARG2$
                              $\wedge$
  D is a variable in 1 $CLASS$. (Execute $)VARS$ D to check.) The system will not let you have two objects with the same name in the same place at the same time.

10.
          $\nabla R\leftarrow PLACE$ $ROUND$ N
  [1] $N\leftarrow N\div PLACE$
  [2] $R\leftarrow\lfloor.5+N$
  [3] $R\leftarrow PLACE\times R$ ∇

11.
          $)LOAD$ 1 $CLASS$
  $SAVED$ 15.02.39 02/15/83
          $CLR\leftarrow 52$ 78 90
  $SYNTAX$ $ERROR$
          $CLR\leftarrow 52$ 78 90
          $\wedge$
  There is already a defined function by the name CLR in this workspace, as can be seen by executing $)FNS$ C.

12.
          $A\leftarrow 1+B\leftarrow 3$
          $T\leftarrow F+7$
  $VALUE$ $ERROR$
          $T\leftarrow F+7$
             $\wedge$
          $T\leftarrow Z+7$
          T
  12
  F is a function name and has no value. When executed, Z receives a value as a global variable.

13.
          $PERIM1$
          R
  14
          B
  2
          C
  5
          M
  7
          S
  1

```
        S←M PERIM2 R
        R
3
        B
2
        C
5
        M
7
        S
20
        S←PERIM3 R
        R
3
        B
2
        C
5
        M
7
        S
10
```

This exercise is designed to give you practice in distinguishing among local, dummy and global variables. To reset the values after each execution, define a function like the following:

```
        ∇SETUP
[1]     S←1 ◇ B←2 ◇ C←5 ◇ M←7 ◇ R←3 ∇
```

14.
```
        ∇M←MARGIN P;S;C
[1]     S←40000-5000×P
[2]     C←35000+2×S
[3]     M←(P×S)-C ∇
```

15.
```
        ∇Z←NTAX COST TAX
[1]     Z←(+/NTAX)+1.05×+/TAX ∇
```

The taxable part of the line could also be written as $+/TAX+TAX\times.05$ or $+/1.05\times TAX$. These are less efficient than the answer given. Why?

Answers for Chapter 10

```
        )LOAD 1 CLASS
SAVED   14.45.33 02/20/83
        ∇STD N
[1]     R←AVG N
[2]     R←R-N
[3]     R←AVG R*2
[4]     ANS←R*.5 ∇
1.      ∇STD[□]
     ∇  STD N
[1]     R←AVG N
[2]     R←R-N
[3]     R←AVG R*2
[4]     ANS←R*0.5
     ∇
[5]     [4□7]
2.   [4]    ANS←R*0.5
        ///1
[4]     R←R*0.5
3.   [5]    [0□5]
[0]     STD N
        5
[0]     R←    STD N
4.   [1]    [Δ2]
```

5.   [5]   [☐]
            ∇ *R←STD N*
    [1]   *R←AVG N*
    [3]   *R←AVG R*2*
    [4]   *R←R*0.5*
            ∇

6.   [5]   [3]
    [3]   *R←AVG (R−N)*2*

7.   [4]   [☐3]
    [3]   *R←AVG(R−N)*2*
    [4]   *R←R*0.5*
            ∇

8.   [5]   ∇

9.   ∇*STD*[1.5]*R←R−N*

10. [1.6] [3☐10]
    [3]   *R←R*0.5*
            /5
    [3]   *ANS ←R*0.5*
    [4]   [.6]

11. [0.6] ρ*N*
  [0.7] ∇

12.   )*ERASE STD*

13.   ∇*STD*[☐] ∇
  DEFN ERROR
         ∇*STD*
             ∧

Answers for Chapter 11

1.   ∇*FN1 S*
    [1]   *S*10* ∇
        ∇*X FN2 V*
    [1]   *2⊛V≤X* ∇
        VAR1←÷1 2 3 4 5 6
        VAR2←⌈/VAR1
)*SAVE WORK1*
   17.54.51 03/12/83
)*CLEAR*
 CLEAR WS
        ∇*FN3 T*
    [1]   ×*T* ∇
        *VAR3←*1 2 3 4 5*
)*SAVE WORK2*
   17.56.04 03/12/83
)*CLEAR*
 CLEAR WS
        ∇*A FN4 B*
    [1]   *A−B*2* ∇
        VAR4←4 6 8 9
)*SAVE WORK3*
   17.56.42 03/12/83
        VAR5←−3 7 10 78
)*SAVE WORK4*
 NOT SAVED, WS QUOTA USED UP
)*LIB*
 WORK1
 WORK2
 WORK3
)*DROP WORK1*
   17.57.32 03/12/83
)*LIB*
 WORK2
 WORK3

```
        )LOAD WORK3
SAVED   17.56.42 03/12/83
        )FNS
FN4
        )VARS
VAR4
        ∇C FN5 D
[1]     (÷C≤?D)×4 ∇
        VAR6←1 0 7 ¯6 ¯8
        )SAVE WORK2
NOT SAVED, THIS WS IS WORK3
        )WSID WORK2
WAS WORK3
        )SAVE
   17.58.19 03/12/83 WORK2
        )CLEAR
CLEAR WS
        )LOAD WORK2
SAVED   17.58.19 03/12/83
        )FNS
FN4     FN5
        )VARS
VAR4    VAR6
        )ERASE FN4 VAR4
        )SAVE
   17.58.42 03/12/83 WORK2
        )LIB
WORK2
WORK3
        )FNS
FN5
        )VARS
VAR6
```

Note that when you load one of your own workspaces and then try to save it with a different name, the system won't let you if a workspace with that name already exists, or if your workspace quota is used up. However, if you execute)$WSID$ $SOMENAME$ prior to saving, any existing version of $SOMENAME$ is overridden. Also, when)$SAVE$ is executed the material will be saved under whatever name the active workspace had prior to saving. The save doesn't take place, however, if the active workspace was not given a name previously.

```
        )LIB 1
ADVANCEDEX
AIDRILL
CLASS
DPDEMO
FILEAID
FORMAT
NEWS
SHAPE
TYPEDRILL
        )LOAD 1 ADVANCEDEX
SAVED    9.40.34 02/10/71
        )FNS
AH       ASSOC     BIN      COMB
DESCRIBE           DTH      ENTER
F        FC        GC       GCD
GCV      HILB      HTD      IN
INV      INVP      IN1      LFC
LOOKUP   PALL      PER      PERM
PO       POL       POLY     POLYB
RESET    TIME      TRUTH    ZERO
```

```
        )VARS
DAH        DASSOC    DBIN     DCOMB
DDTH       DENTER    DESC     DF
DFC        DGC       DGCD     DGCV
DHILB      DHTD      DIN      DINV
DINVP      DIN1      DLFC     DLOOKUP
DPALL      DPER      DPERM    DPO
DPOL       DPOLY     DPOLYB   DTIME
DTRUTH     DZERO     J        M
N          NEW       R        TIMER
X          Z
        DESCRIBE
```

EACH OF THE VARIABLES OF THIS WORKSPACE WHICH BEGINS WITH THE
LETTER D IS THE DESCRIPTION OF THE FUNCTION WHOSE NAME IS
OBTAINED BY REMOVING THE D.

```
        )WSID
IS  1  ADVANCEDEX
        ∇L RECT W
[1]     L×W ∇
        )COPY 1 CLASS RECT
SAVED   14.45.33 02/20/83
        ∇RECT[☐] ∇
    ∇  L RECT H
[1]     2×L+H
[2]     L HYP H
[3]     L×H
    ∇
```

The original *RECT* is replaced by the version in 1 *CLASS*.

```
        )ERASE RECT
        ∇L RECT W
[1]     L×W ∇
        )PCOPY 1 CLASS RECT
SAVED   14.45.33 02/20/83
NOT COPIED: RECT
```

This command copies a global object in the same way as *COPY* only if one doesn't exist with the
  same name in the active workspace.

```
        ∇RECT[☐] ∇
    ∇  L RECT W
[1]     L×W
    ∇
        )SAVE JONES
  12.23.04 03/13/83
        )WSID SMITH
WAS JONES
        )DROP WORK2
  12.23.10 03/13/83
        )SAVE
  12.23.13 03/13/83 SMITH
        )CLEAR
CLEAR WS
        )LOAD 1 ADVANCEDEX
SAVED    9.40.34 02/10/71
        )SAVE 1 ADVANCEDEX
IMPROPER LIBRARY REFERENCE
```

The ordinary user can't save into a common library unless he put it in there originally.

```
        )CONTINUE HOLD
```

(after signing on again)

```
CONTINUE SAVED  12.24.46 03/13/83
        )LIB
CONTINUE
WORK3
JONES
SMITH
```

```
        )FNS
AH          ASSOC     BIN       COMB
DESCRIBE              DTH       ENTER
F           FC        GC        GCD
GCV         HILB      HTD       IN
INV         INVP      IN1       LFC
LOOKUP      PALL      PER       PERM
PO          POL       POLY      POLYB
RESET       TIME      TRUTH     ZERO
        )VARS
DAH         DASSOC    DBIN      DCOMB
DDTH        DENTER    DESC      DF
DFC         DGC       DGCD      DGCV
DHILB       DHTD      DIN       DINV
DINVP       DIN1      DLFC      DLOOKUP
DPALL       DPER      DPERM     DPO
DPOL        DPOLY     DPOLYB    DTIME
DTRUTH      DZERO     J         M
N           NEW       R         TIMER
X           Z
```

The command $CONTINUE\ HOLD$ saves the active workspace in $CONTINUE$ and briefly holds open the phone line. The workspace is available to the user when he signs on again.

3.
```
        )SAVE CONTINUE
        )LOAD GOOD
        )COPY CONTINUE OK
        )SAVE
```
4.
```
        )LOAD 1 CLASS
SAVED   14.45.33 02/20/83
        )GROUP A TAB0 TAB1 TAB2 TAB3
        )GROUP B AVG1 AVG2 AVG3 AVG4 AVG5
        )GROUP A A PI
        )GRPS
A           B
        )GRP A
TAB0        TAB1      TAB2      TAB3      PI
        )GROUP A
        )GRPS
B
```

Answers for Chapter 12

1.
```
        A←0 8 ¯3 4 6 10
        M←2 4ρι8
        V←3 3ρι9
        ρA
6
        ρρA
1
        ρρρA
1
        A⌈0.8×ι6
0.8 8 2.4 4 6 10
        ρM
2 4
        (¯2) 1 2
SYNTAX ERROR
        (¯2) 1 2
              ∧
        ι10
1 2 3 4 5 6 7 8 9 10
        (ι5)+3
4 5 6 7 8
        ¯7×ι1
¯7
```

```
      ι⌈/A
1 2 3 4 5 6 7 8 9 10
      ¯2,1 2
¯2 1 2
      +/ι15
120
      ÷ι5
1 0.5 0.3333333333 0.25 0.2
      ι28÷3+1
1 2 3 4 5 6 7
      ρρV
2
      V,M
LENGTH ERROR
      V,M
      ∧
```

Why the error message?

2.
```
      A←0 8 ¯3 4 6 10
      ρA=6
6
      6=ρA
1
```
The first expression tells us how many elements A has, and the second tells us whether A has 6 elements.

3.
```
      )LOAD 1 CLASS
SAVED  14.45.33 02/20/83
      ×/ρTAB0
1
      ×/ρTAB1
4
      ×/ρTAB2
12
      ×/ρTAB3
24
```
The instructions tell us how many elements are in each of the arrays.

4.
```
      A←0 8 ¯3 4 6 10
      ιρA
1 2 3 4 5 6
      ριρA
6
```
The first expression gives us a vector of indices for the elements in A, while the second is equivalent to $ρA$. Compare $ριρA$ with $⌈/ιρA$. How do they differ? (Don't be too hasty in your answer.)

5. **A**
```
      ∇R←A1 N
[1]   R←+/(ιN)*.5 ∇
```
   B
```
      ∇R←B2 N
[1]   R←(+/ιN)*.5 ∇
```
   C
```
      ∇R←C3 N
[1]   R←(×/ιN)*÷N ∇
```

6.
```
      ¯1+2×ι8
1 3 5 7 9 11 13 15   .
      ¯12+5×ι5
¯7 ¯2 3 8 13
      ¯.3+.3×ι6
0 0.3 0.6 0.9 1.2 1.5
      ¯350+100×ι6
¯250 ¯150 ¯50 50 150 250
      6-ι5
5 4 3 2 1
      2|ι6
1 0 1 0 1 0
```

7.
                ι3*ι3
    RANK ERROR
                ι3*ι3
                ∧

The order of execution is such that ι3 will be generated first and used as powers for 3, resulting in a vector for the right argument of ι on the left. Since interval requires a single element as its argument, the error message appears.

8.
                51≠ι50
                50ρ1
                (ι50)=ι50

9.
                ¯1+2×-/ι5
    5
                +/¯1+ι5
    10
                +/5=1+ι5
    1
                +/0=6=ι5
    5
    or
                +/~6=ι5
    5

10. A
                ∇R←SERIES1 N
    [1]   R←-/÷ιN ∇
    B
                ∇R←X SERIES2 N;T
    [1]   T←¯1+ιN
    [2]   R←+/(X*T)÷!T ∇

11.   0=ρρA
12.   A←3 4 5
                B←ι8
                ρA,ρB
    4
                (ρA),ρB
    3 8

The first expression is equivalent to 1+ρA, while the second is the vector consisting of the lengths of A and B.

13. If E were a dyadic function, we would have to write 6 *E* 8 to execute it. Spaces or other delimiters (e.g., parentheses) are required around a function name.

14.   S←S,ι0 or S←(ι0),S or S←1ρS

15.   11 1ρ1000,.05×ι10
    0
    0.156434465
    0.3090169944
    0.4539904997
    0.5877852523
    0.7071067812
    0.8090169944
    0.8910065242
    0.9510565163
    0.9876883406
    1

This expression generates the values required by the problem, but without identification as to the magnitude (in radians) of the associated angles. With the transpose (Chapter 15) such information can be included: ⍉2 1 1ρ(○A),100A←(¯1+ι11)÷20. The table can also be generated with the outer product. Do you see how?

16.   +/(ιN)×0=2|ιN or +/2×ι⌊N÷2

Looking ahead a bit, once compression is introduced in Chapter 14, a more elegant solution will be +/(Nρ0 1)/ιN.

17.   0 5ρι0

18.   A←(321400÷27.8*.5)-17÷6.5E¯4
                B←5⍟÷(6.8E¯6)*.25
                C←32200*2÷9
                A
    34803.13833
                B
    1.848252091
                C
    10.04027826

```
           L/A,B,C
 1.848252091
```
19.
```
           -/÷1,2×ι29
```
20.
```
           ((ιN)∘.=ιN)×(N,N)ρV
```
21.
```
           (ι4)∘.++4ρ0
```
22.   The sum scan shows that the following series converges fairly rapidly. Try it with some large value of N, say 20:
```
           N+20
           10000×+\÷2*0,ιN
 10000 15000 17500 18750 19375 19687.5
       19843.75 19921.875 19960.9375
       19980.46875 19990.23438 19995.11719
       19997.55859 19998.7793 19999.38965
       19999.69482 19999.84741 19999.92371
       19999.96185 19999.98093 19999.99046
```
23.   A
```
           R≥ιL
```
      B
```
           (L-R)<ιL
```
When the function ↑ is introduced in Chapter 14, these expressions can also be written as $L \uparrow R\rho 1$ and $(-L)\uparrow R\rho 1$.

Answers for Chapter 13

1.
```
           X+'MISSISSIPPI'
           Y+'RIVER'
           'ABCDE'='BBXDO'
 0 1 0 1 0
           ρV+'3172'
 4
           (ρV)ρV
 3172
           3172=V
 0 0 0 0
           X,Y
 MISSISSIPPIRIVER
           1 2<'MP'
 DOMAIN ERROR
           1 2 <'MP'
              ∧
           Y∈X
 0 1 0 0 0
           +/X='S'
 4
           +/X≠'S'
 7
           X,' ',Y
 MISSISSIPPI RIVER
           ρρAL+3 3ρ'ABCDEFGHI'
 2
           X='S'
 0 0 1 1 0 1 1 0 0 0 0
           +/'P'=X
 2
           +/(X,' ',Y)≠'S'
 13
           ∨/X='R'
 0
```
2. D is a character vector consisting of 15 blanks.
3.
```
           ∇F A
 [1]       'THE SHAPE OF A IS ',⍕ρA
 [2]       'THE RANK IS ',⍕ρρA
 [3]       'THE NUMBER OF ELEMENTS IS ',⍕×/ρA ∇
```
4.
```
           (10>I)ρ' ',⍕I
```
This is a formatting problem. Further details in Chapter 17.

5.
```
      )COPY 1 CLASS GEO3 HYP
SAVED  14.45.33 02/20/83
      ∇GEO3[.5]
[0.5] ⍝ THE LITERAL MESSAGES IN THIS FUNCTION
[0.6] ⍝ ARE KEYED TO THE ARGUMENTS USED
[0.7] ∇
      ∇GEO3[⎕] ∇
   ∇ L GEO3 H;X;FLAG
[1]  ⍝ THE LITERAL MESSAGES IN THIS FUNCTION
[2]  ⍝ ARE KEYED TO THE ARGUMENTS USED
[3]  FLAG←((ρ,L)>1)∨(ρ,H)>1
[4]  X←((4×~FLAG)ρ' IS:'),(6×FLAG)ρ'S ARE:'
[5]  'PERIMETER',X
[6]  2×L+H
[7]  'AREA',X
[8]  L×H
[9]  'DIAGONAL',X
[10] L HYP H
   ∇

      3 4 GEO3 5 6
PERIMETERS ARE:
16 20
AREAS ARE:
15 24
DIAGONALS ARE:
5.830951895 7.211102551
```
Comments introduced in this manner don't affect execution of the function, although they do take up space in storage. Note also that in entering the comment the closing del was placed on the next line rather than at the end of the comment. Do you see why?

6.
```
      ∇GPA;GR;CR;M
[1]  M←5 25ρ(25ρ4),(25ρ3),(25ρ2),(25ρ1),(25ρ0)
[2]  GR←M×CR←(3×GR3)+(2×GR2)+GR1
[3]  'STUDENT GRADE POINT AVERAGES ARE ',⍕(+⌿GR)÷+⌿CR
[4]  'THE CLASS AVERAGE IS ',⍕(+/+⌿GR)÷+/+⌿CR ∇
```

7.
```
+/∧⌿'AEIOU'∘.≠CHAR or
(ρCHAR)-+/,'AEIOU'∘.=CHAR  or
+/~CHAR∈'AEIOU'
```

Answers for Chapter 14

1.
```
      A←0 ‾5 ‾8 6.2 15 ‾2 25
      B←1 0 0 1 0 1 1
      C←'ABCDEFGHIJKLMNOPQRSTUVWXYZ ?'
      M←3 4ρι12
      (2<ι5)/ι5
3 4 5
      B/A
0 6.2 ‾2 25
      A[ρA],B[‾2+ρB]
25 0
      A[3 6]←2E5 4E‾4
      A
0 ‾5 200000 6.2 15 0.0004 25
```
Note that A is respecified in this fourth drill problem. This will affect the remaining problems.
```
      'ABD'∈C
1 1 1
      4↑A
0 ‾5 200000 6.2
      2 3ρM
1 2 3
4 5 6
```

```
      M[2;3 1]
7 5
      1 1 0 1\'TWO'
TW O
      A[8]
INDEX ERROR
      A[8]
      ∧
      Aι⌈/A
3
      2 10 15∈M
1 1 0
      ¯3↓C
ABCDEFGHIJKLMNOPQRSTUVWXY
      3 3 ρ1,3ρ0
 1 0 0
 0 1 0
 0 0 1
      1 0 1↑M
 1  2  3  4
 9 10 11 12
      A[1]+A[2 3 4]×A[7]
¯125 5000000 155
      1 0 0 1 1 1\M
 1 0 0 2  3  4
 5 0 0 6  7  8
 9 0 0 10 11 12
      B\2 3 4 5
2 0 0 3 0 4 5
      0 2↓M
  3  4
  7  8
 11 12
      1 3↑M
 1 2 3
      10ρ100
100 100 100 100 100 100 100 100 100 100
```

2. A
```
      D←¯2.1 4 1.9 0 ¯1 ¯4 ¯1.4 .7 2.5 2
      (D<.5)/D
¯2.1 0 ¯1 ¯4 ¯1.4
```
B
```
      (D>0)/D
4 1.9 0.7 2.5 2
```
C
```
      (4=|D)/D
4 ¯4
```
D
```
      ((D<0)∧D>¯1)/D
```
E
```
      (D=2)/D
2
```
F
```
      ((D<1)∧D≥¯2)/D
0 ¯1 ¯1.4 0.7
```

3.
```
      ∇Z←INSERT1 V
[1]   Z←((2×ρV)ρ1 0)\V
[2]   Z[2×ι¯1+ρV]←'o' ∇
```
When laminate is introduced in Chapter 19, this can be done more easily by
```
      ∇Z←CHAR INSERT2 V
[1]   Z←¯1↓,V,[1.2]CHAR ∇
```

4.
```
      ∇Z←INCR V
[1]   Z←1↓V-0,¯1↓V ∇
```

5.
```
      ∇Z←F X
[1]   Z←3×X*2 ∇
      ∇Z←I AREA X
[1]   Z←+/I×F X[1]+I×ι⌊|(-/X)÷I ∇
```

6.
```
      ∇Z←W WITHIN R
[1]   Z←(R≥|W-+/W÷ρW)/W ∇
```

7.
```
(R=⌊R)/R
```

8.
```
      ∇R←A IN INT
[1]    R←(+/INT[2]≥|A-INT[1])×100÷ρA ∇
```
INT is defined here as the vector *B*, *C*.

9.
```
      (⌈/V)>(+/V)-⌈/V or (⌈/V)>+/(V≠⌈/V)/V
```
10.
```
      Y[2×ι⌊(ρY)÷2]   or   (2|1+ιρY)/Y   or   (~2|ιρY)/Y
```
11.
```
      ∇R←S INS X
[1]    R←((S≥X)/X),S,(S<X)/X ∇
```
12.
```
      ∇Z←DELE V
[1]    Z←((ιρV)=VιV)/V ∇
```
13.
```
      ∇R←X SELECT Y
[1]    R←X[Yι⌈/Y] ∇
```
14. The indices as given start with 0, which will result in an index error.

15.
```
      (W=⌈/W)/ιρW or Wι⌈/W
```
16. A
```
      (V<0)/V
```
   B
```
      +/(V<0)/V
```
   C
```
      (V>0)/ιρV
```
   D
```
      (V=⌈/V)/ιρV
```
   E
```
      +/V[2 3 ρ 1 5 6 2 4 8]
```
17.
```
      +/Q[ι8⌊ρQ] or +/Q×8≥ιρQ
```
18.
```
      ¯1 ¯1+1 1+M
```
19. A
```
      ((¯1+ρV,V)ρ1 0)\V
```
   B
```
      ((⌊1.5×ρV)ρ1 0 1)\V
```
   C Same as **B** provided we don't want a zero on the right end when ρ*V* is odd.

20.
```
      ∇R←FACTORS N
[1]    R←(0=(ιN)|N)/ιN ∇
```
   or
```
      ∇R←FACTORS1 N
[1]    R←(~×1|N÷ιN)/ιN ∇
```

21.
```
      ∇R←LONGEST X;J;M;N;P
[1]    J←(X=' ')/ιρX
[2]    P←J,1+ρX ◇ N←¯1+P-0,J ◇ M←⌈/N
[3]    R←X[(P[NιM]+ιM)-1+ριM] ∇
```
   In this solution *J* locates the blanks in *X*. *N* is a vector of word lengths, with *M* the largest. Line 3 generates the indices needed to pick it out of *X*.

22.
```
      ∇R←A COMFACT B
[1]    R←(0=(ιA)|A)/ιA
[2]    R←(0=R|B)/R ∇
```
23.
```
      (~(ιρV)∈I)/V
```
24. The second is a 1 1 matrix, while the first is a scalar. Try ρ of each to check.

25.
```
      W←(W≠'A')/W
```
26. A
```
      ((0=2|X)⌈(0=3|X))/X (∨ may be substituted for ⌈)
```
   B
```
      ((0=2|X)⍱(0=3|X))/X
```
27.
```
      ∇Z←CLOSEST A;M
[1]    M←(1000×(ιρA)∘.=ιρA)+|A∘.-A
[2]    M←,M=⌊/,M
[3]    Z←A[⌈(M/ιρM)÷ρA] ∇
```
   After looking at the matrix *A*∘.-*A*, you should be able to figure out for yourself why the rest of line 1 was necessary. Also compare with the solution given in problem 4.

28. A
```
      M[ι3;]
```
   B
```
      M[1 2;1 2]
```
   C
```
      M[;4 5]
```
   D
```
      M[1 5;1 5]
```
   With the take function, these can be expressed as

   A
```
      3 5↑M
```
   B
```
      2 2↑M
```
   C
```
      5 ¯2↑M
```
   D
```
      1 1↑M    ¯1 1↑M    ¯1 ¯1↑M    ¯1 1↑M
```

29.   A $GALLONS \leftarrow +/INFO[;3\ 5]$ and $TGAL \leftarrow +/GALLONS$
       B $TAX \leftarrow .04 \times INFO[;2]$ and $TTAX \leftarrow +/TAX$
       C $AVMIL \leftarrow INFO[;4] \div 1980 - INFO[;1]$
       D $MPG \leftarrow INFO[;4] \div GALLONS$
       E $GASYR \leftarrow INFO[;3] \div 1980 - INFO[;1]$
       F $GASPM \leftarrow \div /INFO[;3\ 4]$ and $TGASPM \leftarrow \div /+\backslash +/INFO[;3\ 4]$
       G $+/INFO[;3]$
       H $+/INFO[;4]$
       I $\div /(+/INFO[;4]), +/1980 - INFO[;1]$

30. $N \leftarrow \iota 50$
       $COST \leftarrow (.08 \times N) + 10.24 \div N * .5$ (cost)
       $(COST = \lfloor /COST)/N$ (number of items sampled)

31. $\nabla Z \leftarrow T\ CENTER$
  [1] $Z \leftarrow (-1 \uparrow \rho R) - \rho T$
  [2] $Z \leftarrow ((\lceil .5 \times R) \rho '\ '), T\ \nabla$

32. $(^{-}1 \downarrow (\iota \times 1 \uparrow \rho M) \rho 1\ 0) \not\uparrow M$

33. $\nabla Z \leftarrow W\ FWIDTH\ V; L$
  [1] $L \leftarrow ((W=V)/\iota \rho V), 1 + \rho V$
  [2] $Z \leftarrow ^{-}1 + L - 0, ^{-}1 \downarrow L\ \nabla$

34. $100 \times (+/ANS) \div 1 \uparrow \rho ANS$

35. $\nabla HI; A$
  [1] $A \leftarrow (4\ 2 \rho 0\ 8\ 8\ 11\ 19\ 17\ 36\ 17)\ [?4;]$
  [2] $A[2] \uparrow A[1] \downarrow V\ \nabla$

36.   A $?(?8\ 8)\rho 150$
       B $?(?8\ 8)\rho ?299$

37. $(((|V) \epsilon 0, \iota 9)/V$

38. $\wedge /(S1 \epsilon S2), S2 \epsilon S1$ or $\sim 0 \epsilon (S1 \epsilon S2), S2 \epsilon S1$

39. $+/S \epsilon 'ABCDEFGHIJKL'$

40. $C[('X'=C)/\iota \rho C] \leftarrow 'Y'$

41. $(5 < \iota 8)/X$ and $^{-}3 \uparrow X$

42. $(,M)[N? \rho ,M]$

43. $M \leftarrow M + (\rho M) \rho (1 \downarrow \rho M) \rho 0, N$

44. ∇AR
  [1] $M \leftarrow 5\ 15 \rho V1, V2, V3, V4, V5$
  [2] $'TOTALS\ BY\ CATEGORY\ ARE\ ', \overline{\Phi} +/M$
  [3] $'TOTALS\ BY\ CUSTOMER\ ARE\ ', \overline{\Phi} +/M$
  [4] $'THE\ TOTAL\ OF\ ALL\ ACCOUNTS\ RECEIVABLE\ IS\ ', \overline{\Phi} +/+/M$
  [5] $'CUSTOMERS\ WITH\ OVERDUE\ INVOICES:\ ', \overline{\Phi} (\vee /0 \neq ^{-}3\ 15 \uparrow M)/\iota 15\ \nabla$

45. $^{-}3 \uparrow 5 \uparrow V$ and $2 \downarrow ^{-}6 \downarrow V$

46. $P \leftarrow 6.99 + .01 \times \iota 51$
       $Q \leftarrow 600 - 3.7 \times P * 2$
       $TR \leftarrow P \times Q$
     Price: $P[TR \iota \lceil /TR]$
     Production: $Q[TR \iota \lceil /TR]$

47. $A \leftarrow 50?100$
       $B \leftarrow 50?100 \diamond B \epsilon A$

48.   A $(V1 \epsilon V2)/V1$
     If there are duplicate elements in either $V1$ or $V2$, this expression is *not* symmetric with respect to $V1$ and $V2$, i.e., the above would not then be the same as $(V2 \epsilon V1)/V2$.
       B $V1, (\sim V2 \epsilon V1)/V2$
       C $(\sim V1 \epsilon V2)/V1$
     You may recognize these expressions as corresponding to the intersection, union and difference of two vectors.

49. $M1 \leftarrow (((R-1), 1 \downarrow \rho M) \uparrow M), [1](R, 0) \downarrow M$ or $M1 \leftarrow (R \neq \iota 1 \uparrow \rho M) \not\uparrow M$

50. $((,V) \iota S) \downarrow, V$

51. $MAT[I;]$ is a 1 by n matrix, not a vector or scalar. Try instead $(,MAT[I;]) \iota VECTOR$.

52. $ORDERSN \leftarrow ORDERS$
       $ORDERSN[;2] \leftarrow 1.15 \times ORDERSN[;2]$
       $PRICESN \leftarrow PRICES$
       $PRICESN[;2] \leftarrow .9 \times PRICES[;2]$
       $(+/, ORDERSN \times PRICESN) \div +/, ORDERS \times PRICES$

53. $LOWSALES \leftarrow ORDERS < 10000$
       $HIPRICES \leftarrow PRICES > 20$
       A $LOWSALES \wedge HIPRICES$
       B $+/, LOWSALES \wedge HIPRICES$
       C $+/, PRICES \times ORDERS \times LOWSALES \wedge HIPRICES$

Answers for Chapter 15

1.
```
        A←3  2  0  ¯1  5  ¯8
        M←3  4ρι12
        N←4  3ρ9  7  1  2  3  5  6  9  15  22  1
        3φA
 ¯1  5  ¯8  3  2  0
        2φA[ι4]
 0  ¯1  3  2
        ⍋⍒A
 2  3  4  5  1  6
        2↑¯3φA
 ¯1  5
        ¯2  1  3φM
   3   4   1   2
   6   7   8   5
  12   9  10  11
        φ0,ι3
 3  2  1  0
        2φφι7
 5  4  3  2  1  7  6
        φ⊖N
   9   1  22
  15   9   6
   5   3   2
   1   7   9
        A[⍋⍒A]
 5  ¯1  0  2  ¯8  3
        M[⍋M[;1];]
  1   2   3   4
  5   6   7   8
  9  10  11  12
        A[⍒0  1  0  1  0  1]
 2  ¯1  ¯8  3  0  5
        2φ1⊖M
   7   8   5   6
  11  12   9  10
   3   4   1   2
        (φι6)ιM
  6  5  4  3
  2  1  7  7
  7  7  7  7
        (ι6)=⍋A[⍋A]
 1  1  1  1  1  1
        ⍉N
   9   2   6  22
   7   3   9   1
   1   5  15   9
```

2.
```
        ALF←'ABCDEFGHIJKLMNOPQRSTUVWXYZ '
        S←'THE QUICK BROWN FOX JUMPS OVER THE LAZY DOG'
        S[⍋ALFιS]
ABCDEEEFGHHIJKLMNOOOOPQRRSTTUUVWXYZ
```

3.
```
        φ4  3ρ0  1  2  3
```

4.
```
        (V,V1)[⍋V,V1]
```

5.
```
        ∧/V[⍋V]=ιN  or  ∧/(V∈ιN),(ιN)∈V
```

6.
```
        ∇R←MED X
[1]     R←.5×+/X[(⍋X)[⌈⌽¯.5 .5×1+ρX]] ∇
```

7.
```
        ∇R←ELIM V
[1]     R←V=S
[2]     R←((1↑R)↓R≉1φR)/V ∇
```

8. A
```
        ×/LENGTHS
```
   B
```
        +/2×LENGTHS×1φLENGTHS
```

9.
```
        ∇Z←STRAIGHTLINE X
[1]     Z←φX[3]+X[3]×(-/X[1 3])÷X[2]×ιX[2] ∇
```

10. $V[\blacktriangledown V>10]$

11. $\nabla Z\leftarrow MS\ N;Q$
[1] $Z\leftarrow(N,N)\rho\iota N*2$
[2] $Q\leftarrow(-\lceil.5\times N+\iota N$
[3] $Z\leftarrow Q\ominus Q\phi Z\ \ \nabla$

12. A $HAND[;\blacktriangledown'CDHS'\iota HAND[2;]]$
    B $HAND[;DEN\leftarrow\blacktriangledown'23456789TJQKA'\iota HAND[1;]]$
    C $HAND[;DEN[\blacktriangledown'CDHS'\iota HAND[2;DEN]]]$

13. $\nabla Z\leftarrow SORTR\ M;A$
[1] $Z\leftarrow\rho M$
[2] $M\leftarrow,M$
[3] $A\leftarrow\blacktriangle M$
[4] $Z\leftarrow Z\rho M[A[\blacktriangle\lceil A\div 1\downarrow Z]]\ \ \nabla$

If this solution seems a bit weird, it is. It is one which is uniquely APL. Perhaps a more natural approach is to sort one row at a time. This requires that we know how to loop or iterate (Chapter 16). Below is a more conventional branching solution a la Fortran or PL/1, which for arrays with many rows is much slower than $SORTR$:

    $\nabla Z\leftarrow SORTR1\ M;I$
[1] $I\leftarrow 1\uparrow\rho M$
[2] $Z\leftarrow M$
[3] $L:Z[I;]\leftarrow M[I;\blacktriangle M[I;]]$
[4] $\rightarrow L\times\iota I\leftarrow I-1\ \ \nabla$

14. $\nabla R\leftarrow V\ LOC\ W$
[1] $R\leftarrow(\wedge\neq(^-1+\iota\rho W)\phi W\circ.=V)/\iota\rho V\ \ \nabla$

15. $^-2\uparrow G[\blacktriangle G]$ or $2\uparrow G[\blacktriangledown G]$

16. A $(+/\wedge\backslash'\ '=M)\phi M$
    B $(-+/\wedge\backslash'\ '=\phi M)\phi M$

17. $\nabla Z\leftarrow CENT\ MAT;A$
[1] $Z\leftarrow'\ '=MAT$
[2] $A\leftarrow+/\wedge\backslash Z$
[3] $Z\leftarrow(\lceil.5\times A-+/\wedge\backslash\phi Z)\phi MAT\ \ \nabla$

18. $1++(.5\times+/S)>+\backslash S[\blacktriangledown S]$

19. $(+/V[4\downarrow\blacktriangle V])\div ^-4+\rho V$

20. $|/\blacktriangle V$

This expression is dependent on the index origin (see page 294). The authors concede that this is a dirty problem.

21. $+/\vee\backslash\phi 0\neq V$

22. $\nabla Z\leftarrow SCORES\ PRINT\ NAMES;ORDER$
[1] $ORDER\leftarrow\blacktriangledown SCORES$
[2] $'TOURNAMENT\ RANKING:'$
[3] $'\ '$
[4] $Z\leftarrow NAMES[ORDER;],\Phi((\rho SCORES),1)\rho SCORES[ORDER]\ \ \nabla$

23. $(1+\rho V2)-(\phi V2)\iota V1$ or $+/\vee\backslash V1\circ.=\phi V2$

24. A $((V\neq S)\iota 1)\downarrow V$ or $(\vee\backslash V\neq S)/V$
    B $((S\neq\phi V)\iota 1)\downarrow V$ or $(\phi V\backslash S\neq\phi V)/V$

25. $\nabla TRIANGLE\ N;SIDE$
[1] $SIDE\leftarrow(N,N)\rho'\circ',N\rho'\ '$
[2] $SIDE\leftarrow(\ominus SIDE),SIDE$
[3] $(2\times N)\rho'\circ'\ \ \nabla$

26. $\nabla C\leftarrow SUBST\ M;ALF;P$
[1] $ALF\leftarrow'ABCDEFGHIJKLMNOPQRSTUVWXYZ'$
[2] $P\leftarrow 26?26$
[3] ALF
[4] $ALF[P]$
[5] $'\ '$
[6] M
[7] $C\leftarrow ALF[P[ALF\iota M]]\ \ \nabla$

Grade up can be used to improve on the letter substitution by transposing the letters:

    $\nabla C\leftarrow SUBST1\ M;ALF;P$
[1] $ALF\leftarrow'ABCDEFGHIJKLMNOPQRSTUVWXYZ'$
[2] $P\leftarrow\blacktriangle(\rho M)\rho 26?26$
[3] M
[4] $C\leftarrow M[P]\ \ \nabla$

27.
```
      ∇Z← K VIG M;C;D
[1]   ALF←'ABCDEFGHIJKLMNOPQRSTUVWXYZ'
[2]   C←ALFιM
[3]   M
[4]   D←1+26|C+(ρC)ρK
[5]   ALF[(ρC)ρK]
[6]   (ρM)ρ'-'
[7]   Z←ALF[D] ∇
```
Try $K←1$ 2 3 for a test encoding of some message.

28.
```
      ∇R←DECODE C
[1]   R←ALF[PιALFιC] ∇
```
It is assumed that ALF and P are known to the decoder.

29. The result shows that $A×B$ is a maximum when $A=B$, a conclusion well known to calculus students who have worked since time immemorial on problems like the following: show that a square is the rectangle with the greatest area for a given perimeter.

Answers for Chapter 16

1. **A** If $5<W$, go to step 3; if $5>W$, go to 2; if $5=W$, go to the next step. W is assumed to be a scalar or vector of length 1.

   B Go to step 3 if $A=8$, otherwise drop through to the next step.

   C Go to END if $Y>1$, otherwise branch out of the program. At the same time R is reshaped as a 1 1 matrix containing a 1.

   D Go to step 7 if any element of B is a member of C, otherwise drop through to the next step.

   E If $A≤C$ go to 5, otherwise branch out of the program.

   F Go to step 3.

   G Go to step 8 if $0≠J$, otherwise go to the next step. At the same time J is decreased by 1.

   H If the absolute value of X is greater than or equal to I, go to step 4, otherwise leave the program. I is also incremented by 1.

   I Go to $AGAIN$ if $N=10$, otherwise execute the next line. R is reshaped as a 2 4 matrix.

2.
```
      ∇V←REMT;I
[1]   I←1
[2]   L:→(I≥ρT)/0
[3]   V←(T[I]≠V)/V
[4]   I←I+1
[5]   →L ∇
```
This function, which involves branching, solves the problem by brute force. You'll appreciate the power of APL from the following:
```
      ∇V←REM1 T
[1]   V←(~V∈T)/V ∇
```

3.
```
      ∇A←CMPX B
[1]   →BIGGER IF A>B
[2]   →SMALLER IF A<B
[3]   'EQUAL'
[4]   →0
[5]   BIGGER:'GREATER'
[6]   →0
[7]   SMALLER:'LESS' ∇
```

4.
```
      ∇R←MED N
[1]   N←N[♠N]
[2]   →(R=⌊R←.5×ρN)/ST
[3]   R←N[⌈R]
[4]   →0
[5]   ST:R←.5×N[R]+N[R+1] ∇
```
or
```
      ∇R←MED1 N
[1]   N←N[♠N]
[2]   R←N[⌈.5×ρN]
[3]   →L×~2|ρN
[4]   L:R←.5×R+N[1+.5×ρN] ∇
```

5.
```
      ∇R←N DUPL V
[1]   →0×ιρR←(N=V)/ιρV
[2]   'SCALAR NOT PRESENT' ∇
```

6.
```
      ∇Z←ROOT S
[1]   →(0≠ρρS)/0
[2]   Z←S*.5 ∇
```

7.
```
      ∇R←SORT TEXT
[1]   ALF←'ABCDEFGHIJKLMNOPQRSTUVWXYZ'
[2]   R←''
[3]   L:→0×ι0=ρTEXT
[4]   R←R,(TEXT=1↑ALF)/TEXT
[5]   TEXT←(TEXT≠1↑ALF)/TEXT
[6]   ALF←1↓ALF
[7]   →L ∇
```
or, without branching
```
      ∇R←SORT1 TEXT
[1]   TEXT←((ALFιTEXT)≤ρALF)/TEXT
[2]   R←ALF[R[♠R←ALFιTEXT]] ∇
```

8.
```
      ∇R←MODE N;V
[1]   V←R←ι0
[2]   AT:V←V,+/N[1]=N
[3]   R←R,N[1]
[4]   →(0≠ρN←(N[1]≠N)/N)/AT
[5]   R←R[(V=⌈/V)/ιρV] ∇
```

9.
```
      ∇R←FIB N
[1]   R←1 1
[2]   END:→(N>ρR←R,+/¯2↑R)/END ∇
```

10.
```
      ∇HISTOG A;I
[1]   I←⌈/A
[2]   L:I≤A
[3]   →L××I←I-1 ∇
```
To 'clean up' the histogram, change line 2 to $L: ' *'[1+I≤A]$. This function produces a vertical histogram. For a horizontal histogram try the following:
```
      ∇HISTOG1 A
[1]   A[1]ρ'*'
[2]   →×ρA←1↓A ∇
```
The outer product further simplifies the construction of histograms:
```
      ∇HISTOG2 A
[1]   '.□'[1+A∘.≥ι⌈/A] ∇
```

11.
```
      ∇R INT P;IN;I
[1]   'YR PRIN INT'
[2]   ''
[3]   I←1
[4]   L:IN←.01×⌊.5+100×P×R[1]
[5]   I,P,IN
[6]   P←P+IN
[7]   →((I←I+1)≤R[2])/L ∇
```
Here $R[1]$ is the yearly interest rate in decimal form and $R[2]$ the number of years to be evaluated. As in problem 10, the outer product will greatly simplify the job of generating the table. Your table probably will not be formatted properly. If this bothers you, use the formatting operator to be introduced in Chapter 17.

12.
```
      ∇R←ODDS N;A;I
[1]   I←1+R←0
[2]   L:A←5?52
[3]   R←R+3≤+/A≤13
[4]   I←I+1
[5]   →(N≥I)/L
[6]   R←4×R÷N ∇
```
Note that the odds are figured for only one suit (random numbers 1 to 13) on line 3, and the result is multiplied by 4 on line 6, assuming each suit to be equally probable.

13.
```
        (ι4)□TRACE 'ACK'
           2 ACK 1
ACK[1]  →2
ACK[1]  →3
ACK[1]  →2
ACK[1]  →3
ACK[1]  →4
ACK[4]  2
ACK[3]  →0
ACK[1]  →4
ACK[4]  3
ACK[2]  →0
ACK[3]  →0
ACK[1]  →2
ACK[1]  →2
ACK[1]  →2
ACK[1]  →3
ACK[1]  →4
ACK[4]  2
ACK[3]  →0
ACK[1]  →4
ACK[4]  3
ACK[2]  →0
ACK[1]  →4
ACK[4]  4
ACK[2]  →0
ACK[1]  →4
ACK[4]  5
ACK[2]  →0
ACK[2]  →0
         5
```

14.
```
        ∇R←A EQUAL B
[1]     R←(ρρA)=ρρB
[2]     →S×R
[3]     S:R←∧/(ρA)=ρB
[4]     →E×R
[5]     E:R←~0∊A=B  ∇
```
This function tests for equality of rank (line 1), shape (line 3) and elements (line 5). It will distinguish between characters and numerics, e.g., '1' is not equal to 1, and simulates the match function found in APL2.

15.
```
        ∇COND PRINT MESSAGE
[1]     →(~COND)/0
[2]     MESSAGE  ∇
```

16.
```
        ∇R←M DELE NAME;A;D;J
[1]     J←0
[2]     L:→(J≥D←1↑ρM)/END
[3]     J←J+1
[4]     →(~∧/((1↓ρM)↑NAME)=M[J;])/L
[5]     R←(J≠ιD)⌿M
[6]     'DONE'
[7]     →0
[8]     END:'NAME NOT FOUND'  ∇
```
When the inner product is introduced in Chapter 20, the function can be rewritten as
```
        ∇R←M DELE1 NAME;T
[1]     T←M∧.=(1↓ρM)↑NAME
[2]     →(∨/T)/END
[3]     R←(~T)⌿M
[4]     'DONE'
[5]     →0
[6]     END:'NAME NOT FOUND'  ∇
```
DELE1 is more general since it will handle multiple occurrences of NAME in M.

17.
```
        ∇R←GRADE2 M;A
[1]     R←ι1↑ρM
[2]     A←¯1↑ρM
[3]     L:R←R[⍋M[R;A]]
[4]     →L××A←A-1 ∇
```
18.
```
        ∇R←X FINDROW STRING;HOLD;I
[1]     R←ιI←0
[2]     STRING←(¯1↑ρX)↑STRING
[3]     LOOP:I←I+1
[4]     →(I>1↑ρX)/OUT
[5]     HOLD←X[I;]
[6]     →(~∧/HOLD=STRING)/LOOP
[7]     R←R,I
[8]     →LOOP
[9]     OUT:→(0≠ρR)/0
[10]    'NAME NOT FOUND' ∇
```
Or, replace lines 4 6 and 9 as follows:
```
[4]     →OUT⌈ιI>1↑ρX
[6]     →LOOP⌈ι~∧HOLD=STRING
[9]     →0⌈ι0≠ρR
```
The combinations ⌈ι and ×ι, which can be read as 'if,' are less general than compression. Their right arguments *must* be a nonnegative scalar or vector of length one.

19.
```
        ∇Z←CARDSORT MAT;D;ALF
[1]     D←¯1↑ρMAT
[2]     ALF←' ABCDEFGHIJKLMNOPQRSTUVWXYZ0123456789'
[3]     MAT←MAT[⍋ALFιMAT[;,D];]
[4]     L1:→(0=D)/L2
[5]     D←D-1
[6]     →L1
[7]     L2:Z←MAT ∇
```
20.
```
        ∇R←N FIB1 A
[1]     R←A
[2]     →(N=2)/0
[3]     R←(N-1) FIB1 R
[4]     R←R,¯1↑R+(¯1⌽R) ∇
```

Answers for Chapter 17

1. A
```
        10 4⍕TABLE
```
   B
```
        10 ¯3⍕TABLE
```
   C
```
        0 3⍕TABLE
```
   D
```
        (8 3 10 5 6 3,(2ρ10 5))⍕TABLE
```
2.
```
        (⍕Q)[;2×ι(ρQ)[2]] or 1 0⍕Q
```
3.
```
        ∇INC SAL RANGE;A;B;W
[1]     A←1+(|-/RANGE)÷INC
[2]     W←(A,1)ρRANGE[1]+INC×¯1+ιA
[3]     B←52×W
[4]     '        WEEK      MONTH     ANNUAL'
[5]     ''
[6]     10 2⍕W,(B÷12),B ∇
```

4.
```
      ∇NAMES REPORT ACTIVITY;ACT;NO;OD;BAL100;HIBAL;LOBAL
[1]   OD←(0>ACT←+/ACTIVITY)/NO←ι1↑ρNAMES
[2]   BAL100←(100<ACT)/NO
[3]   LOWBAL←⌊/+\ACTIVITY
[4]   HIBAL←⌈/+\ACTIVITY
[5]   ''
[6]   '    CURRENT ACTIVITY REPORT'
[7]   ''
[8]   'THE FOLLOWING ARE OVERDRAWN:'
[9]   ''
[10]  ' NAME       BALANCE'
[11]  NAMES[OD;],20 2⍕ACT[,OD;]
[12]  ''
[13]  'THE FOLLOWING HAVE BALANCES OVER 100 DOLLARS:'
[14]  ''
[15]  ' NAME       BALANCE'
[16]  NAMES[BAL100;],20 2⍕ACT[,BAL100;]
[17]  ''
[18]  'FOLLOWING ARE THE LOW/HIGH BALANCES FOR THE MONTH:'
[19]  ''
[20]  ' NAME        LOW       HIGH'
[21]  NAMES,20 2⍕LOWBAL,(NO,1)ρHIGHBAL ∇
```
5.
```
      ∇R←LITCHK X;Y
[1]   R←2=ρ⍕Y←ιρ1↑,X ∇
```
6.
```
      ∇REPORT DAT;FLAG;REORD;NO
[1]   REORD←DAT[;5]>+/DAT[;2 3])/NO←ι1↑ρDAT
[2]   FLAG←(NO,6)ρ' '
[3]   FLAG[REORD;2+ι4]←'*'
[4]   ' PART NO   IN STOCK   ON ORDER  UNIT COST   REORDER   FLAG'
[5]   ''
[6]   (8 0 11 0 10 0 11 2 9 0⍕DAT),FLAG ∇
```
7.
```
      ∇INSUR BILL;INS
[1]   'BILL IS ',(⍕BILL),' DOLLARS'
[2]   'INSURANCE PAYS ',(⍕INS←(15<BILL)×.6×BILL-15),' DOLLARS'
[3]   'YOUR COST IS ',(⍕BILL-INS),' DOLLARS' ∇
```
8.
```
      DATE←¯1↓,(3 2ρ⍕DATE),'/'
```
Chapter 18 contains features that will simplify formatting expressions like this.
9.
```
      ∇Z←W FORM M;U;R
[1]   R←ρM
[2]   Z←(U←M≠0)/M←,M
[3]   Z←W⍕((ρM),1)ρZ
[4]   Z←(R×1,W[1])ρZ←U\Z ∇
```
10.
```
      ∇R←SPEC COLHEAD HDGS
[1]   R←(SPEC[1]ρ' '),,((ρHDGS)[1],-SPEC[2])↑HDGS ∇
```

Answers for Chapter 19

1.
```
      U←2 3 4ρι24
      C←2 4 3ρ'ABCDEFGHI'
      ⌈/⌈/⌈/U
24
      ⌈/,U
24
      ×⌿U
  13   28   45   64
  85  108  133  160
 189  220  253  288
      +/[2]U
 15  18  21  24
 51  54  57  60
      +⌿U[;2;3]
26
```

```
        ‾1 1 2↓C
F
I
C
        (2 4ρι3)⌽C
BCA
FDE
GHI
BCA

FDE
GHI
BCA
FDE
        +/U[;1;3]
18
        ⍉C
AD
DG
GA
AD

BE
EH
HB
BE

CF
FI
IC
CF
        1 0 1 0/[2]C
ABC
GHI

DEF
ABC
        0 2 2 ↓U
 11 12

 23 24
        ⊖C
DEF
GHI
ABC
DEF

ABC
DEF
GHI
ABC
```

```
        3 1 2⍉C
AD
BE
CF

DG
EH
FI

GA
HB
IC

AD
BE
CF
        1 2 2⍉U
  1   6  11
 13  18  23
```

2.   `U[1;1;]←U[2;3;]`

3.   `R←M[;M]`   Reminder: the indices themselves may have rank >1.

4.   `∇Z←LIST N`
    `[1]`   `Z←⍉(3,N)ρ(⍳N),(!⍳N),÷⍳N ∇`

5. **A**   `+/+/[2]BUDG[;;4 10]`

    B   `BUDG[;3;6]` (per month) or

         `+/BUDG[;3;6]` (per year)

    C   `+/+/[2]BUDG`

    D   `10|Z1←(,Z)⍳⌊/,Z←BUDG[;2;]`(identifies account)

         `⌈/Z1÷12` (identifies month)

    E   `BUDG[;4 5;1 3]`

    F   `∇FORMAT;M`
    `[1]`   `'ACC',6 0 ⍕⍳10`
    `[2]`   `(3ρ'‾'),(54ρ'      ‾'),'      --'`
    `[3]`   `M←12 3ρ'JANFEBMARAPRMAYJUNJULAUGSEPOCTNOVDEC'`
    `[4]`   `M,6 0 ⍕+/[2] BUDG ∇`

    G   `C←BUDG[6+⍳6;;]`
         `D←BUDG[⍳6;;]`
         `BUDG←D,[1](+/D),[1]C,[1]+/C`

6.   `,V,[1.5]';'`

7.   `∇WINNER;A;B;B1`
    `[1]`   `A←⌈/B←+/MAGSALES`
    `[2]`   `B1←B=A∘.+25ρ0`
    `[3]`   `CAL,MAGNAMES[⌈/B1×(12ρ0)∘.+⍳25;] ∇`

8.   `∇Z←UNDER V`
    `[1]`   `Z←V,[.5](V≠' ')\'‾' ∇`
         `UNDER 'TEST  CASE'`
    `TEST` `CASE`
    `‾‾‾‾` `‾‾‾‾`

         `ρUNDER 'TEST  CASE'`
    `2 10`

9. **A**   `+/,SALES[2;;]`

    B   `+/[2]SALES[3 4;;]`

    C   `+/-/SALES[5 3;;]`

    D   `SP[1 2;1 3;2]×SALES[1 2;1 3;2]`

    E   `+/,SP[5;;]×SALES[5;;]`

    F   `SP←SP,[1]1.2×SP[5;;]`

10. **A**   `TEMP←+/SALES[3;;2 4]`
         `100×(-/TEMP)÷TEMP[2]`

    B   `A←+/SALES[4 5;;]`
         `A×50000<A` (0 for those models selling less than 50,000)

11.
```
        ∇REPORT HWR;RH;RPT;CH
[1]     RH←'NAILS' ON 'TACKS' ON 'SCREWS' ON 'TOTAL'
[2]     HWR←(HWR,[1]+/HWR),+/HWR
[3]     RPT←RH,(4 9ρ' '),⍕HWR
[4]     'HARDWARE PURCHASES' CENTER RPT
[5]     ''
[6]     UNDER '  1Q   2Q   3Q   4Q    TOTALS'
[7]     RPT ∇
```
(UNDER is the utility developed in problem 8).

12.
```
        ∇Z←NUMBER LIST;S
[1]     S←1↑ρLIST
[2]     Z←(⍕(S,1)ριS),((S,3)ρ'.  '),LIST ∇
```

13.
```
        ∇R←TABLE M;A
[1]     A←2×∨/(,M)≠⌊,M
[2]     R←A⍕((×/ρM),1)ρM
[3]     R←R,'|'
[4]     R←((1↑ρM),(×/ρR)÷1↑ρM)ρR
[5]     R←'|',R
[6]     R←'_',[1]R,[1]'‾' ∇
```

14.
```
        ∇A←SIDE WITH MATRIX
[1]     A←(' ';[1]' ',[1]SIDE),MATRIX ∇
        ∇R←TOP ABOVE DATA
[1]     R←(,((1↑ρTOP),‾15)↑TOP),[1]' ',[1]15 2⍕DATA ∇
```
ABOVE may have to be adjusted for very wide column headings.

15.
```
        ∇Z←MAT1 BESIDE MAT2;M
[1]     M←(1↑ρMAT1)⌈1↑ρMAT2
[2]     Z←((M,1↓ρMAT1)↑MAT1),(M,1↓ρMAT2)↑MAT2 ∇
```

16.
```
        A,(A,[1]M,[1]A),A
```

17.
```
        ROWHEAD←(5 5ρ'STORE'),⍕ι5
        COLHEAD←9+ι5
        SALES1←(' ',[1]ROWHEAD),(1⌽10 0⍕COLHEAD),[1]10 1⍕SALES
```

18.
```
        1 1 2⍉V∘.+M
```
This procedure is overkill, since the result of the outer product can be a very large array, only a portion of which is really needed. Better is M←(ρM)ρV which is more direct and economical.

19.
```
        1 1 ⍉⌽M or 1 1 ⍉2 0 1 ⌽M
```


Answers for Chapter 21

1.
```
        A←ι4 ◇ B←2 3ρ'ABCDEF'
        C←'ABD' ◇ D←3 1ρι3
        E←3 4 5 ◇ F←4 3ρι10
        G←3 4ρ⌽ι7
        C∘.=B
   1 0 0
   0 0 0

   0 1 0
   0 0 0

   0 0 0
   1 0 0
        D∘.×A
   1  2  3  4

   2  4  6  8

   3  6  9 12
```

```
        1  3  9∘.>D
  0
  0
  0

  1
  1
  0

  1
  1
  1
        E+.=E
3
        F×.-G
  ¯18    0    4    0
    0   ¯6   ¯8    0
    0   24   70   18
   24   12    0   36
        F∨.<G
  1  1  1  1
  1  1  1  1
  0  0  0  0
  1  1  1  1
        A∘.+3×D
   4
   7
  10

   5
   8
  11

   6
   9
  12

   7
  10
  13
        D∘.÷A
  1    0.5    0.3333333333    0.25
  2    1      0.6666666667    0.5
  3    1.5    1               0.75
        B∘.≠C
  0  1  1
  1  0  1
  1  1  1

  1  1  0
  1  1  1
  1  1  1
        E∧.>G
0 0 0 0
        E∨.≠F
LENGTH ERROR
        E∨.≠F
        ∧
        3+.×F
66  48  60
```

```
        ~(A∘.=A)∘.∧1  0  0  1
    0  1  1  0
    1  1  1  1
    1  1  1  1
    1  1  1  1

    1  1  1  1
    0  1  1  0
    1  1  1  1
    1  1  1  1

    1  1  1  1
    1  1  1  1
    0  1  1  0
    1  1  1  1

    1  1  1  1
    1  1  1  1
    1  1  1  1
    0  1  1  0
        ⌽D∘.*A
    1    2    3

    1    4    9

    1    8   27

    1  16   81
        A∘.⌈¯1  3  2  4
    1  3  2  4
    2  3  2  4
    3  3  3  4
    4  4  4  4
        F×.=E
    0  0  0  0
        G|.-F
    0  0  2
    1  0 ¯3
    0  2  0
        (⌽G)⌈.+E
   11  10  9  11
```

2. 4 2 2 or 2 2 4
3.
```
        ∇R←DIST L
[1]     R←⌊.5+(((L[;1]∘.-L[;1])*2)+(L[;2]∘.-L[;2])*2)*.5 ∇
```
or
```
        ∇R←DIST1 L
[1]     R←⌊.5+(+/1 3 2 3⌽(L∘.-L)*2)*.5 ∇
```
4. +/'ABCDEFG'∘.='CABBAGE'
5.
```
        SUM←B|C+D
        CARRY←B≤C+D
        ∇ADDTAB B;T
[1]     INT←¯1+⍳B
[2]     T←INT∘.+INT
[3]     (B|T)+10×B≤T ∇
```
6.
```
        ∇Z←C1 MULT C2
[1]     Z←+⌿(1-⍳⍴C1)⌽C1∘.×C2,0×1↓C1 ∇
```

7. A
```
           X←¯5+⍳9
           F←(⌽X)∘.=|X
           GRAPH

     o           +           o
        o        +        o
           o     +     o
              o  +  o
     + + + + + o + + + +
              +
              +
              +
              +
```

    B
```
           F←(⌽X)∘.=¯5+X*2
           GRAPH

     o           +           o
                 +
                 +
                 +
     + + + + + + + + +
        o        +        o
                 +
                 +
     o           +           o
```

    C
```
           F←(⌽X)∘.≤X+1
           GRAPH

              +        o  o
              +     o  o  o
              +  o  o  o  o
              o  o  o  o  o
     + + + o  o  o  o  o  o
        o  o  o  o  o  o  o
     o  o  o  o  o  o  o  o
     o  o  o  o  o  o  o  o
     o  o  o  o  o  o  o  o
```

    D
```
           F←(⌽X)∘.≤3|X
           GRAPH

              +
              +
     o        o  +        o
     o     o  o  +  o  o        o
     o  o  o  o  o  o  o  o  o
     o  o  o  o  o  o  o  o  o
     o  o  o  o  o  o  o  o  o
     o  o  o  o  o  o  o  o  o
     o  o  o  o  o  o  o  o  o
```

    E
```
           F←((⌽X)∘.≤X+1)∧(⌽X)∘.≥3-|X
           GRAPH

              +        o  o
              +     o  o  o
              +  o  o  o  o
              +     o  o  o
     + + + + + + + o  o
              +           o
              +
              +
              +
```

8.

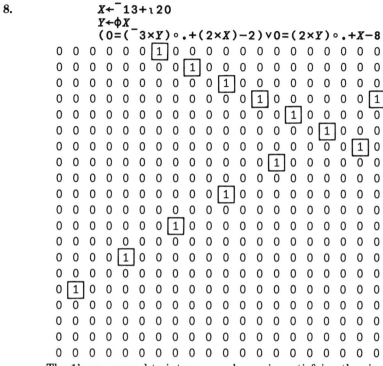

$$X \leftarrow {}^{-}13 + \iota 20$$
$$Y \leftarrow \phi X$$
$$(0 = ({}^{-}3 \times Y) \circ . + (2 \times X) - 2) \vee 0 = (2 \times Y) \circ . + X - 8$$

```
0 0 0 0 0 0 1 0 0 0 0 0 0 0 0 0 0 0 0 0
0 0 0 0 0 0 0 0 1 0 0 0 0 0 0 0 0 0 0 0
0 0 0 0 0 0 0 0 0 0 1 0 0 0 0 0 0 0 0 0
0 0 0 0 0 0 0 0 0 0 0 0 1 0 0 0 0 0 0 1
0 0 0 0 0 0 0 0 0 0 0 0 0 0 1 0 0 0 0 0
0 0 0 0 0 0 0 0 0 0 0 0 0 0 0 0 1 0 0 0
0 0 0 0 0 0 0 0 0 0 0 0 0 0 0 0 0 0 1 0
0 0 0 0 0 0 0 0 0 0 0 0 1 0 0 0 0 0 0 0
0 0 0 0 0 0 0 0 0 0 0 0 0 0 0 0 0 0 0 0
0 0 0 0 0 0 0 0 0 0 1 0 0 0 0 0 0 0 0 0
0 0 0 0 0 0 0 0 0 0 0 0 0 0 0 0 0 0 0 0
0 0 0 0 0 0 0 1 0 0 0 0 0 0 0 0 0 0 0 0
0 0 0 0 0 0 0 0 0 0 0 0 0 0 0 0 0 0 0 0
0 0 0 0 1 0 0 0 0 0 0 0 0 0 0 0 0 0 0 0
0 0 0 0 0 0 0 0 0 0 0 0 0 0 0 0 0 0 0 0
0 1 0 0 0 0 0 0 0 0 0 0 0 0 0 0 0 0 0 0
0 0 0 0 0 0 0 0 0 0 0 0 0 0 0 0 0 0 0 0
0 0 0 0 0 0 0 0 0 0 0 0 0 0 0 0 0 0 0 0
0 0 0 0 0 0 0 0 0 0 0 0 0 0 0 0 0 0 0 0
0 0 0 0 0 0 0 0 0 0 0 0 0 0 0 0 0 0 0 0
```

The 1's correspond to integer number pairs satisfying the simultaneous linear equations 3Y=2X-2 and 2Y=8-X (conventional notation). The point of intersection (4,2) is the common solution of both equations.

9.   Change X to $X \leftarrow \lfloor .5 \times X \div S$

10. $RET \leftarrow PRIN \circ . \times (1 + RATE) \circ . * TIME$

11.   **A** $X \leftarrow \iota 20$
               $Y \leftarrow X \neq 2$
               $Z \leftarrow 2 \times X * 2$
               $20 \ 60 \ PLOT \ X \ VS \ Y$

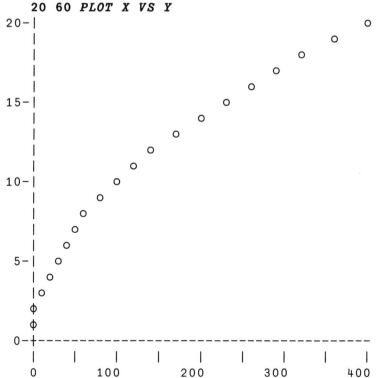

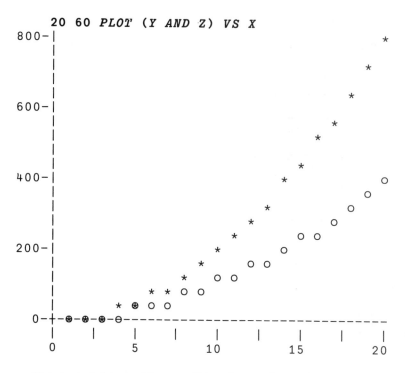

This last plot looks like something the cat dragged in. If we use only one symbol for each 'curve', we are constrained in the fineness of the plot by the 'size' of the print position (1/6 inch vertical by 1/10 inch horizontal). Many APL systems have other plotting routines that take advantage of features of particular terminals, such as the ability to place dots very close together. Your *DESCRIBE* or *HOWPLOT* may contain information on how this may be done. Here is the previous example, using the Tektronix 4015 display terminal:

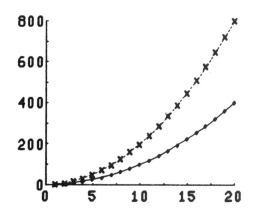

B

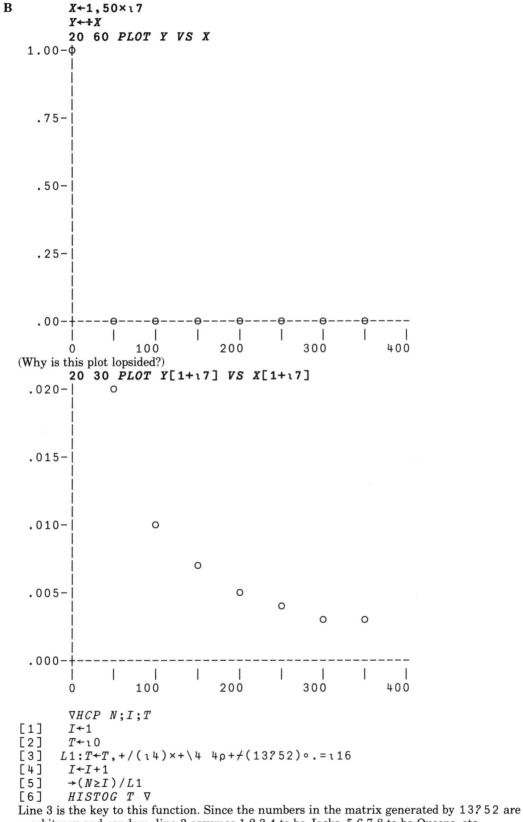

```
        X←1,50×ι7
        Y←÷X
        20 60 PLOT Y VS X
```

(Why is this plot lopsided?)

```
        20 30 PLOT Y[1+ι7] VS X[1+ι7]
```

12.

```
        ∇HCP N;I;T
[1]     I←1
[2]     T←ι0
[3]     L1:T←T,+/(ι4)×+\4 4ρ+≠(13?52)∘.=ι16
[4]     I←I+1
[5]     →(N≥I)/L1
[6]     HISTOG T ∇
```
Line 3 is the key to this function. Since the numbers in the matrix generated by 13?52 are
arbitrary and random, line 3 assumes 1 2 3 4 to be Jacks, 5 6 7 8 to be Queens, etc.

13.
```
          ∇W FIND1 T;A
[1]       A←∧≠(¯1+ιρW)⌽W∘.=T
[2]       T
[3]       A\'↑'  ∇
```

14. **A** $A\wedge.=B$ results in a 1 if A and B are identical, 0 otherwise.

$M\wedge.=B$ yields a logical vector with a 1 for each row of M which is identical to B.

$A+.\neq B$ gives the number of pairs of corresponding dissimilar elements in A and B.

$(M=0)\wedge.\geq U$ produces a logical matrix which reproduces the initial 1's in each row of $M=0$ and fills the rest of the row with 0's, e.g.,

```
            M
  0  0  0  3  2  0  0  0
  0  0  1  7  9  2  8  0
  6  4  0  0  0  1  6  0
          M=0
  1  1  1  0  0  1  1  1
  1  1  0  0  0  0  0  1
  0  0  1  1  1  0  0  1
          (M=0)∧.≥(ι8)∘.≤ι8
  1  1  1  0  0  0  0  0
  1  1  0  0  0  0  0  0
  0  0  0  0  0  0  0  0
```

It may be considered a simulation of the 'and-scan' $\wedge\backslash M=0$.

$A\times.\ast B$ is equivalent to the times reduction of A raised to the B power. One possible use could be in getting a number from its prime decomposition. Here is an example of this latter use:

```
          2 3 5 7×.*2 1 0 1
84
```

Still another use may be seen in the expression $B\times.\ast B<100$. This is the product of all $B<100$.

B $R[I;J]$ is 1 if and only if the Ith row and the Jth column of N have at least one 1 in the same location. It is used to represent two-stage connections, as in pecking orders or circuitry. (See the defined function RUN in this chapter.)

C For $R←C+.=D$, $R[I;J]$ is the number of matching pairs of elements of $C[I;]$ and $D[;J]$. For $R←C\lceil.\lfloor D$, $R[I;J]$ is the largest of the smaller of $C[I;]$ and $D[;J]$ taken pairwise.

15.
```
          ∇R←X POLY C
[1]       R←C+.×X∘.*¯1+ιρ,C  ∇
```

16.
```
          ∇Z←EXP A
[1]       Z←.21 .15 .10+.×(100⌊A),(50⌊0⌈A-100),0⌈A-150  ∇
```
or
```
          ∇Z←EXP1 A
[1]       Z←.01×6 5 10+.×(100 50,⌊/ι0)∘.⌊A  ∇
```
which will handle both vector and scalar arguments. $⌊/ι0$ is the so-called *identity element* for the dyadic operation $⌊$. It yields $7.237005577E75$, the largest number generated by the APL system. The reason it is called an identity element is that when paired with any other number N with $⌊$, it yields N. (Try $+/ι0$, $-/ι0$, $\times/ι0$, $\ast/ι0$, $\lceil/ι0$, etc.)

17. **A**
```
          R←0≠.=4 100 400 4000∘.|Y
```
B
```
          ∇REFUND1 E
[1]       .5×20 500+.⌊1 1∘.×E  ∇
```
This version can handle plural arguments, which the old version could not.

C
```
          ∇R←N DUPL1 V
[1]       R←'SCALAR NOT PRESENT'
[2]       →0×ι0=Nv.=V
[3]       R←(N=V)/ιρV  ∇
```

18.
```
          ORDERS←300 500 200 1000
          PARTS←4 5ρ1 2 0 5 2 0 3 0 1 5 1 1 4 2 2 1 2 4 5 5
          PRICES←32 9.75 3.2 .78 7.2
          PARTORDERS←ORDERS+.×PARTS
          PARTORDERS
1500 4300 4800 7400 8500
          COSTOFALLPARTS←ORDERS+.×PARTS+.×PRICES
          COSTOFALLPARTS
172257
          COSTFOREACHMODEL←PARTS+.×PRICES
          COSTFOREACHMODEL
69.8 66.03 70.51 104.2
```

19.   *WDL.+DS*
20.   *A←3 1 8 9*
              A<.≥1ϕA
       0
              A←1 3 8 9
              A<.≥1ϕA
       1

This expression indicates whether *A* is in strictly ascending order. It is equivalent to
$(\rho A)\leq1++/(1\downarrow A)>(^{-}1\downarrow A)$.

21. **A**   *UCOST+.×QUANT*
       B   *+/QUANT*
       C   *+/QUANT*
       D   *UCOST×+/QUANT*
       E   *UCOST+.×+/QUANT* or *+/UCOST+.×QUANT*
       F   *UCOST⌈.×QUANT*
       G   *(UCOST+.×+/QUANT)÷+/+/QUANT*
       H   *ROW←(FRUIT∧.=(^{-}1↑FRUIT)↑'GRAPES')/ι1↑ρFRUIT*

              UCOST[ROW]+.×QUANT[ROW;]

22.   It compares each row of *M* with every other row of *M* and returns 1 for each row which is smaller than the one being compared, 0 otherwise. The trailing zero is necessary to handle properly the case where a row has leading zeroes. Note that if the columns of the result are summed and graded, the resulting indices applied to *M* will sort the matrix. It is, however, very slow if there are a large number of rows.

23.   ∇*R←VECTOR SEARCH TABLE*
       [1]   *R←(TABLE∧.=VECTOR)ι1* ∇

24.   In general execute ⊞(*N*,*N*)ρ1,*N*ρ0. A specific example might be
              ⊞3 3ρ1 0 0 0
       1 0 0
       0 1 0
       0 0 1

from which it should be evident that the identity matrix is its own inverse.

25.   10 13 3⊞3 3ρ2 13 4 3 ^{-}1 2 1 ^{-}4
       3.5 2.220446049E^{-}16 1

26.   ∇*LIN W;G*
       [1]   *G←(W[1]×W[5])-W[4]×W[2]*
       [2]   *→(0=G)/L1*
       [3]   *'X IS ',⍕((W[5]×W[3])-W[2]×W[6])÷G*
       [4]   *'Y IS ',⍕((W[1]×W[6])-W[4]×W[3])÷G*
       [5]   *→0*
       [6]   *L1:'NO UNIQUE SOLUTION'* ∇

              ∇*ABC SOLVE DEF*
       [1]   ⍝ *ABC IS A 3-ELEMENT VECTOR A,B,C*
       [2]   ⍝ *DEF IS A 3-ELEMENT VECTOR D,E,F*
       [3]   *→(0≠-/×/(ABC,DEF)[2 2ρ1 5 2 4])/OK*
       [4]   *'NO UNIQUE SOLUTION'*
       [5]   *→0*
       [6]   *OK:(ABC,DEF)[3 6]⊞(ABC,DEF)[2 2ρ1 2 4 5]* ∇
27.   ∇*R←F X*
       [1]   *R←X×300+^{-}2×X* ∇
              1E^{-}6 SLOPE 0 100 200
       299.999998 ^{-}100.000002 ^{-}500.0000001
              1E^{-}6 SLOPE 0 20 40 60 80
       299.999998 219.9999972 139.9999974 59.99999757 ^{-}20.00000222
              1E^{-}6 SLOPE 60 65 70 75
       59.99999757 39.99999717 19.99999768 ^{-}2.728484105E^{-}6

The sides of the rectangle are each about 75 feet long.

28.
```
        YR←84+ι7
        SALES←38 52 64 82 98 128 156
        SALES⌹YR∘.*0 1
‾1608.857143 19.28571429
```
The linear equation best fitting the data is $SALES←‾1608.86+19.28×YR$.

29. To solve for R:

R+UR=I

IR+UR=I

(I+U)R=I

(I+U)⁻¹(I+U)R=(I+U)⁻¹I where (I+U)⁻¹ is the inverse of I+U

IR=(I+U)⁻¹I

R=(I+U)⁻¹

Therefore the APL solution is
```
        ⌹((ι1↑ρU)∘.=ι1↑ρU)−U
 1  0  0  0  0  0  0  0  0
 0  1  0  0  0  0  0  0  0
 0  0  1  0  0  0  0  0  0
 1  2  0  1  0  0  0  0  0
 0  1  1  0  1  0  0  0  0
 1  3  3  1  1  1  0  0  0
 3 10  8  3  4  2  1  0  0
 6 12  8  3  4  2  1  1  0
10 33 27 10 13  7  3  0  1
```

30.
```
        W←2000 2200 2500 2750 3000 3500 4000 4500 5000 5500
        C←4.14 4.67 5.35 5.61 6.77 7.39 9.29 10.45 10.95 12.16
        C⌹W∘.*0 1
1.929687474 0.001734030928
```
The equation is $C←1.93+.001734×W$. In these days of energy conservation, what can you deduce from these results?

Answers for Chapter 22

1.
```
        (3ρ40)⊥8 7 2
13082
        1 ‾4.1 .8⊥1 2 3
1.32
        3 3⊤5217
2 0
        (5ρ3)⊤5217
1 1 0 2 0
        (4ρ8)⊥‾14
‾8190
        2⊥5 1 9 6
68
        7 8 9⊥7 8 9
585
        3 3 3⊤5217
0 2 0
        1 4 6⊤345
0 1 3
        1 4 7⊥3 5ρι15
81 117 153 189 225
        3⊤5217
0
        (5ρ3)⊤5217
1 1 0 2 0
        2 4 5⊤78
1 3 3
```

2. **A**   0 4 2⊥2 8 1
    B   0 2000 16⊥3 568 13
3. **A**   8⊥2 1 7 7
    B   2⊥1 0 1 1 0 1
    C   (10⍴3)⊤8933
    D   (10⍴5)⊤4791
4. $X⊤X⊥Y$ and $X⊥X⊤Y$
    More generally, $X⊥X⊤Y$ is the same as $(×/X)|Y$
5.   ∇P←CONV D
    [1]   P←10⊥¯1+'0123456789'⍳(D≠',')/D ∇
6.   N=+/(10 10 10⊤N)*3
7. **A** converts M into a vector of digits.
    B converts M into the corresponding scalar.
    C same as **B**. The *execute* function (Chapter 24) will duplicate the effect of **B** or **C** more succinctly:
            5+⍎M
        1234588
8.   0=11|-/((1+10⍟N)⍴10)⊤N
9.   ∇TRICK N;D1
    [1]   D1←|N-10⊥⌽(3⍴10)⊤N
    [2]   D1+10⊥⌽(3⍴10)⊤D1 ∇
10. **A** same as $+/V$
    B same as $¯1↑V$
    C same as $-/V$
    D separates integer and decimal parts of N.
11.   ∇Z←C EVAL X
    [1]   Z←X⊥C ∇
    (put 0's in for missing powers of X.)
12.   ∇Z←REP ENCODE N
    [1]   Z←((1+⌈REP⍟N)⍴REP)⊤N ∇
    The key here is the use of the characteristic of the log ($⌈REP⍟N$) to determine the positions needed.
13. feet: (0 3 12,÷12)⊥3 0 1 0
    yards: (0 3 12,÷36)⊥3 0 1 0
    or ((÷12 3),1)⊥⌽3 0 1
    and for completeness:
    inches: (0 3 12,÷1)⊥3 0 1 0
    which is the same as 0 3 12⊥3 0 1
14. **A**   ((V≠S)⍳1)↓V or
           (∨\V≠S)/V or
           (((S=⌽V)⊥1)-1)↓V
    B   ((S≠⌽V)⍳1)↓V or
           (⌽V\S≠⌽V)/V or
           (1-(V=S)⊥1)↓V
15.   0 20 12⊤0 20 12⊥1+⌿C
    Jefferson was correct.
16.   ∇R←DIAG M
    [1]   R←10⊥1 1⍉M ∇
17.   (+/V)÷⍴V   +/V÷⍴V   +/V÷+/V=V
        (0⊥+\V)÷⍴V   V+.÷⍴V   1+.×V÷V+.*0
        V⌹((⍴V),1)⍴1   V⌹V÷V   1⊥V÷1⊥V÷V
18. The result is 3521. This suggests that in general decode can be simulated by $W+.×V$, where W is the weighting vector and V is the vector to be decoded, since the weighting vector 1000 100 10 1 is obtained by raising the radix vector 10 10 10 10 to the powers 3 2 1 0.

Answers for Chapter 23

1.
```
        ∇MULT1 N;X
[1]     START:X←?N,N
[2]     (⍕1↑X),'×',⍕1↓X
[3]     L1:→(⎕=STOP,×/X)/0,CORRECT
[4]     'TRY AGAIN'
[5]     →L1
[6]     CORRECT:'CORRECT'
[7]     →START ∇
```

2.
```
        ∇MULT2 N;X
[1]     START:X←?N,N×I←1
[2]     (⍕1↑X),'×',⍕1↓X
[3]     L1:→(⎕=STOP,×/X)/0,CORRECT
[4]     I←I+1
[5]     →(4=I)/ANS
[6]     'TRY AGAIN'
[7]     →L1
[8]     ANS:'ANSWER IS ',⍕×/X
[9]     →START
[10]    CORRECT:'CORRECT'
[11]    →START ∇
```

3.
```
        ∇MULT3 N;X;I
[1]     START:X←?N,N×I←1
[2]     (⍕1↑X),'×',⍕1↓X
[3]     L1:→(⎕=HELP,STOP,×/X)/AID,0,CORRECT
[4]     I←I+1
[5]     →(4=I)/ANS
[6]     RETRY:'TRY AGAIN'
[7]     →L1
[8]     ANS:'ANSWER IS ',⍕×/X
[9]     →START
[10]    CORRECT:'CORRECT'
[11]    →START
[12]    AID:'COUNT THE STARS FOR THE ANSWER:'
[13]    Xρ'*'
[14]    →RETRY ∇
```

4.
```
        ∇MULT4 N;X;I;J;K;A
[1]     K←J←0
[2]     START:X←?N,N×I←1
[3]     J←J+1
[4]     (⍕1↑X),'×',⍕1↓X
[5]     L1:→(⎕=STOP,×/X)/END,CORRECT
[6]     I←I+1
[7]     →(4=I)/ANS
[8]     'TRY AGAIN'
[9]     →L1
[10]    CORRECT:'CORRECT'
[11]     K←K+1
[12]    →L2
[13]    ANS:'ANSWER IS ',⍕×/X
[14]    L2:→START
[15]    END:'YOUR SCORE IS ',(⍕⌈100×K÷J-1),' PERCENT RIGHT' ∇
```

5.
```
        ∇Z←LITPROMPT
[1]     Z←⍈←'          ',0/⎕←'⍈:'
[2]     Z←7↓⍈ ∇
```

6.
```
        ∇SPELL[6] 'THE CORRECT SPELLING IS ',SPL[N+1;] ∇
```

7.
```
        ∇R←ENTER;A
[1]     R←''
[2]     L1:A←,⎕
[3]     →(0=ρA)/DONE
[4]     R←R,20↑A
[5]     →L1
[6]     DONE:R←(1+,0 20⊤¯1+ρR)ρR ∇
```
*ENTER*1 is more general. It pads out the list each time to the width of the widest entry:
```
        ∇R←ENTER1;Z;MAX
[1]     R←0 0ρ''
[2]     NEXT:Z←,⎕
[3]     →(0=ρZ)/0
[4]     MAX←⌈/(ρZ),1↓ρR
[5]     R←((1↑ρR),MAX)↑R
[6]     Z←MAX↑Z
[7]     R←R,Z
[8]     →NEXT ∇
```

8.
```
        ∇R←N LIST L;I
[1]     R←ρI←1
[2]     L1:R←R,L↑⎕
[3]     I←I+1
[4]     →(N≥I)/L1
[5]     R←(N,L)ρR ∇
```

9.
```
        ∇LOOKUP L;M;NAME
[1]     'ENTER NAME'
[2]     NAME←⎕
[3]     NAME←(¯1↑ρL)↑NAME
[4]     M←(L∧.=NAME)/ι1↑ρL
[5]     →(0=ρM)/NOGO
[6]     'NAME IS ON ROW(S) ',(⍕M),' IN THE LIST'
[7]     →0
[8]     NOGO:'NAME NOT FOUND' ∇
```

10.
```
        ∇BALANCE;OPB;TRANS;R
[1]     ⎕←R←'OPENING BALANCE: '
[2]     OPB←(ρR)↓⎕
[3]     ⎕←'TRANSACTIONS: '
[4]     TRANS←⍎⎕
[5]     ''
[6]     R,OPB
[7]     'TOTAL DEPOSITS: ',⍕+/(TRANS>0)/TRANS
[8]     'TOTAL WITHDRAWALS: ',⍕|+/(TRANS<0)/TRANS
[9]     'CLOSING BALANCE: ',⍕(+/TRANS)+⍎OPB ∇
```

11.
```
        ∇Z←MAT INS N;LINE;L
[1]     ⎕←L←'ENTER LINE TO BE INSERTED: '
[2]     LINE←(1↓ρMAT)↑(ρL)↓⎕
[3]     Z←(N≠¯1+ι1+1↑ρMAT)⌿MAT
[4]     Z[N+1;]←LINE ∇
```
INS solves the problem by brute force, actually expanding *MAT* to make room for the new line.
*INS*1 below avoids expansion and uses a sneaky sort on line numbers to rearrange the rows:
```
        ∇Z←MAT INS1 N;LINE;L
[1]     ⎕←L←'ENTER LINE TO BE INSERTED: '
[2]     LINE←(1↓ρMAT)↑(ρL)↓⎕
[3]     Z←(MAT,[1]LINE)[⍋(ι1↑ρMAT),N+.1;] ∇
```

12.
```
        ∇R←MONTHLYINPUT;A
[1]     'ENTER INPUT'
[2]     L1:R←¯1↓A←⎕
[3]     →(12=ρR)/L2
[4]     'WRONG NUMBER OF ENTRIES'
[5]     →L1
[6]     L2:→((+/R)=¯1↑A)/0
[7]     'CONTROL TOTAL DOESN''T CHECK OUT.  REENTER NUMBERS'
[8]     →L1 ∇
```

Answers for Chapter 24

1.
```
         ∇ARITH DATA;A
[1]      A←1↑DATA
[2]      ⍎(A=15)/'ADD DATA'
[3]      ⍎(A=25)/'SUB DATA'
[4]      ⍎(A=35)/'BAL DATA'
[5]      ⍎(~A∊15 25 35)/'ERR DATA' ∇
```
better:
```
         ∇ARITH1 DATA
[1]      ⍎(4 3ρ'ADDSUBBALERR')[''ρ15 25 35⍳1↑DATA;],' DATA' ∇
```
''ρ is needed to make the expression in brackets a scalar rather than a 1-element vector. Why?

2. **A**   ⍎'X','←DAT' or ⍎'X←DAT'
    B   ⍎'NAM',(⍕I),'←D' where $I = 1,2,...$

3.
```
         ∇DECOM FN;M
[1]      ⍝FN IS A CHARACTER VECTOR HOLDING NAME OF FUNCTION
[2]      M←⎕CR FN
[3]      M←(M[;1]='⍝')⌿M
[4]      ⎕FX M ∇
```
This program works only where the comment symbol ⍝ is at the beginning of the line. Where a comment is imbedded elsewhere, more of a challenge is presented. Try to generalize *DECOM*.

4.
```
         ∇Z←FACTEX N
[1]      ⍎3 ¯14[1+N≠0]↑'Z←1 Z←N×FACTEX N-1' ∇
```

5.   ⍎'M[',((¯1+ρρM)ρ';'),'I]'
which is equivalent to $M[;I]$ or $M[;;I]$

6.   ⍎L←'SOMEINSTRUCTION ◊ I←I+1 ◊ ⍎(N≥I)/L'
which is equivalent to the line
       L:SOMEINSTRUCTION ◊ I←I+1 ◊ →(N≥I)/L

7.
```
         ∇ERASEALLBUT M;ERASEALLBUT;A
[1]      A←(11+0 1+.×ρM)↑'M←⎕EX ⎕NL 3'
[2]      ⍎⎕FX('ERASEALLBUT',,';',M),[.5]A ∇
```
This function works equally well for other arguments of ⎕NL. It is an ingenious use of a local variable to shield globals. On line 1 the +.× calculates the number of spaces needed in the header for the names in *M*, including the semicolons, and adds 11 for the width of '*ERASEALLBUT*' to pad out the second line of the canonical representation. When ⎕EX is executed, those names listed in the header will not show in the result of ⎕NL 3 and therefore will not be erased.

8.   Catenates contents of ⍞ to *A* or passes if only RETURN is entered.

9.
```
         ∇Z←REPRES MATRIX;A
[1]      A←',⍝',⍕MATRIX
[2]      Z←⎕FX 'TEMP' ON A ∇
```

```
         ∇Z←RESTORE TEMP;A
[1]      Z←1 1↓⎕CR TEMP
[2]      A←⎕EX TEMP ∇
```
REPRES assigns a temporary name *TEMP* to the matrix in function form (why the ⍝ symbols?). *TEMP* may be edited as a function and recreated as a (character) matrix with *RESTORE*.

10.
```
         ∇REPORT;NAME;PROMPT
[1]      'HERE IS THE REPORT MENU:'
[2]      RPTS
[3]      ⍞←PROMPT←'ENTER THE REPORT DESIRED: '
[4]      NAME←(ρPROMPT)↓⍞
[5]      ⍎NAME ∇
```

11.
```
         ∇OMIT;A;B;NAM;OMT
[1]      A←ρ⍞←'ARRAY NAME? '
[2]      B←⍎NAM←A↓⍞
[3]      L:A←ρ⍞←'OMIT WHICH ROWS? '
[4]      OMT←⍎A↓⍞
[5]      →(∨/OMT>1↑ρB)/ERR
[6]      B←(~(⍳1↑ρB)∊OMT)⌿B
[7]      ⍎NAM,'←B'
[8]      →0
[9]      ERR:'INVALID ROW NUMBER'
[10]     →L ∇
```

12.
```
        )LOAD 1 CLASS
SAVED 14.45.33 02/20/83
        ∇DRILL
[1]     'ENTER YOUR CHOICE OF DRILL EXERCISES'
[2]     'SUB, ADD OR SPELL'
[3]     ⍎⍞ ∇
```

13.
```
        FALSE←'FALSE'
        TRUE←'TRUE'
        ∇A CHECK B
[1]     ⍎5 ¯4[1+A>B]↑'FALSE  TRUE' ∇
        3 CHECK 4
FALSE
        6 CHECK 3
TRUE
```

This illustrates the use of ⍎ to execute only that expression determined by the stated condition. Although in this example the expressions selected are literal, had they instead been instructions requiring considerable computation, some savings could result from avoiding unncessary calculations. Note that ⍎ isn't really necessary in this function; it is used only to make a point.

14.
```
        ∇A CMP B
[1]     ((A>B)/'GREATER'),((A=B)/'EQUAL'),(A<B)/'LESS' ∇

        R←⎕CR 'CMP'
        R
A CMP B
((A>B)/'GREATER'),((A=B)/'EQUAL'),(A<B)/'LESS'
        R[2;8+⍳7]←'MORE   '
        ⎕FX R
CMP
        ∇CMP[⎕] ∇
    ∇ A CMP B
[1]     ((A>B)/'MORE   '),((A=B)/'EQUAL'),(A<B)/'LESS'
    ∇
```

15.
```
        )CLEAR
CLEAR WS
        )COPY 1 CLASS HYP RECT
SAVED  14.45.33 02/20/83
        D←⎕CR 'HYP'
        ⎕EX 'HYP'
        ∇RECT[0⎕0]
[0]     L RECT H;HYP
[1]     [2]
[2]     ⍎'L ',(⎕FX D),' H' ∇
        ∇RECT[⎕] ∇
    ∇ L RECT H;HYP
[1]     2×L+H
[2]     ⍎'L ',(⎕FX D),' H'
[3]     L×H
    ∇
        )FNS
RECT
        3 RECT 4
14
5
12
```

16.
```
        ∇DISP;R;L;M
[1]     'WHAT LETTER(S)?'
[2]     L←⍞
[3]     'LABELS (1), VARIABLES (2), OR FUNCTIONS (3)?'
[4]     R←⎕
[5]     ⎕←M←L ⎕NL R
[6]     I←1
[7]     LP:⎕CR M[I;]
[8]     I←I+1
[9]     →(I≤1↑⍴M)/LP ∇
```

17.
```
[1]    →(7<ρ⎕LC)/EXIT
[2]    ⍝ NORMAL ROUTE HERE
[3]    EXIT:→
```
Don't forget that the first element of ⎕LC in a function is the current line being executed.

18.
```
      ∇LIST;A;B;I;⎕IO
[1]    ⎕IO←1
[2]    A←⎕NL 3
[3]    I←1↑ρA
[4]    →(0∧.=ρA)/0
[5]    ⎕←B←10ρ' '
[6]    L1:⎕CR,A[I;]
[7]    B
[8]    I←I-1
[9]    →(0≠I)/L1 ∇
```

20.
```
      ∇Z←F OPROD A
[1]    Z←⍎'(⍳1↑A)∘.',F,'⍳1↓A' ∇
```
Note that the left argument must be enclosed in quotes when executed.

Answers for Chapter 25

1.
```
3  4  5 simple
(,3) (,4) (,5) nested
(3) (4) (5) simple
3  4  'A' simple
3  (4 'A') nested
((3) (4) (5)) simple
(,3),(,4),(,5) nested
3  4  'AB' nested
'ABC' 'XYZ' nested
'ABC','XYZ' simple
'A' 'B' 'C' simple
'A' ('B' 'C') nested
```

2.

	depth	rank	shape
⊃A 1	0	0	⍳0
⊂A 1 2 3 4 5 6	2	0	⍳0
⊂⊂A 1 2 3 4 5 6	3	0	⍳0
⊂⊃A 1	0	0	⍳0
(⊂A),(⊂B),(⊂C) 1 2 3 99 APL 4 5 6	2	1	3
⊃⊃A 1	0	0	⍳0
⊃A B 1 2 3 4 5 6	1	2	2 3
3 4ρA B C	2	2	3 4

```
3 4ρA B C
1 2 3        99      APL      1 2 3
4 5 6                         4 5 6

   99      APL   1 2 3        99
                 4 5 6

 APL     1 2 3        99      APL
         4 5 6
```

2 3ρC	1	2	2 3

```
APL
APL
```

```
        2 3ρ⊂C                        2       2       2 3
 APL  APL  APL
 APL  APL  APL
        B  B  B                       1       1        3
99 99 99
        ⊂A B C                        3       0       ι0
   1 2 3    99 APL
   4 5 6
```

3.

	depth	shape
`D`	2	3

```
   1 2 3    99 APL
   4 5 6
        D[1]                          2       ι0
   1 2 3
   4 5 6
        ⊃D[1]                         1       2 3
 1 2 3
 4 5 6
        ⊃⊃D[1]                        0       ι0
1
        D[2]                          0       ι0
99
        ⊃D[2]                         0       ι0
99
        D[1],D[2]                     2       2
   1 2 3    99
   4 5 6
        D[1 2]                        2       2
   1 2 3    99
   4 5 6
        (⊃D[1]),D[2]                  1       2 4
 1 2 3 99
 4 5 6 99
        B                            0       ι0
99
        ⊂B                           0       ι0
99
        ⊂⊂B                          0       ι0
99
        ⊃B                           0       ι0
99
        ⊃⊃B                          0       ι0
99
        C,¨B                          2       3
 A 99    P 99    L 99
        A,¨B                          2       2 3
   1 99    2 99    3 99
   4 99    5 99    6 99
        ⊃¨D                           1       3
1 99 A
        ,¨D                           2       3
   1 2 3 4 5 6    99    APL
        ρ¨D                           2       3
   2 3      3
        ρ¨ρ¨D                         2       3
   2 0   1
        ⊃¨ρ¨ρ¨D                       1       3
   2 0 1
        +/¯1↓D                        2       ι0
100 101 102
103 104 105
        (⊂A),¨C                       2       3
   1 2 3 A    1 2 3 P    1 2 3 L
   4 5 6 A    4 5 6 P    4 5 6 L
```

```
        A,¨⊂C                                    2        2 3
    1 APL    2 APL    3 APL
    4 APL    5 APL    6 APL
```

4. $1≥=A$ tests if A is a simple array, and $\Box CR\ ¨\ ⊂[2]\Box NL$ 3 gives a vector of the $\Box CR$'s of all defined functions.

5.
```
        1↓∪' ',¨VECTOR
```
6.
```
        ((' '=VECTOR)/VECTOR)←⊂''' '''
        ⍎'''',(∪VECTOR),'''' HO
```
7.
```
        ⍎(1≥=A)/'A←⊂A'
```
8.
```
        (⍳⊃ρM),M
```
9.
```
        (' ',ROWS),COLS,[1]DATA
```
10.
```
        ∇Z←SHAPES A
[1]     ⍝ SHAPES OF ALL SIMPLE ARRAYS CONTAINED IN ARGUMENT
[2]     Z←⊂ρA
[3]     →(0∈ρA)/0
[4]     →(1≥=A)/0
[5]     Z←(SHAPES ⊃A),SHAPES 1↓,A ∇
```
11. A is reformatted to be of rank $≥2$. After enclosure it becomes a nested scalar, which, when formatted, is always a matrix regardless of its original rank.

12.
```
        X Y Z
```
(This identity is known in some quarters as the 'chipmunk' idiom.)

13.
```
        ⍎(1+X>Y)⊃L2 L1
```
14.
```
        A  B  (A+.×B)
    1  2   3   4    10 20    500   600
    5  6   7   8    30 40   1140  1400
    9 10  11  12    50 60   1780  2200
                    70 80
```
15. First define a function TP to make $TEXT$ into a vector of words (see problem 6):
```
        ∇R←TP STRING
[1]     R←(1+''''=STRING)/STRING ⍝REPLACE ' WITH ''
[2]     ((' '=R)/R)←⊂''' ''' ⍝ REPLACE BLANKS WITH ' '
[3]     R←⍎'''',(∪R),'''' ⍝EXECUTE WITH QUOTES AT BEGINNING AND END
[4]     ⍝R IS NOW A VECTOR OF WORDS
[5]     ∇
```
A Sort $TEXT$ and count the unique items:
```
        TEXT1←TP TEXT
        SORTTEXT←(⍋TEXT1)/TEXT1
        COUNT←+/SORTTEXT∘.(=¨)TEXT1
```
B
```
        ∨/∧/0 1⊖TEXT1∘.(=¨)'AN' 'EXAMPLE'
```
C
```
        (TEXT1~REFERENCE)
```
16. **A**
```
        +/¨ACCOUNTS
```
B
```
        -/¨+/¨ACCOUNTS
```

Answers for Chapter 28

1. **A**
```
        →CONTINUE×(1↑⎕AI)∈NUMBERS
```
B
```
        T←⎕AI[3]
              .
              .
              .
        →(100≤⎕AI[3]-T)/QUIT
```
2.
```
        'S',⎕TC[2],'/'
```
3.
```
        ∇R←DUE BILLS;BILLS1;CHECK
[1]     BILLS1←BILLS
[2]     BILLS1[;2]←12|BILLS1[;2]
[3]     BILLS1←10⊥⍉BILLS[;4 2 3]
[4]     CHECK←(10⊥⎕TS[⍳3])≥BILLS1
[5]     R←CHECK/BILLS[;1] ∇
```
4.
```
        V∘.≥⍳⌈/V
```
This converts integers (4 bytes) to bit representation (1/8 byte), saving considerable space.

5.
```
      ∇Z←DEC DISTRD VALUES;B;C;□CT;□IO
[1]   □CT←□IO←0
[2]   VALUES←VALUES÷DEC
[3]   B←(⌊.5++/VALUES)-+/⌊VALUES
[4]   C←⍋⍒1|VALUES
[5]   Z←DEC×(⌊VALUES)+B>C ∇
```
The expression $1 | VALUES$ contains the error if each element were represented by its floor. B is the total number of additional 1's needed in the vector. C ranks the elements according to the accuracy of their representation, with the least accurate element having C equal to 0.

6.
```
      ∇SMASH;BLANKS
[1]   BLANKS←(□WA-32)ρ' ' ∇
```

7.
```
      ∇Z←RLACC M;□RL;□IO;R
[1]   □IO←0
[2]   □RL←□AI[0]
[3]   R←ρM
[4]   →(0=ρR)/0
[5]   Z←×/R
[6]   Z←Rρ(,M)[Z?Z] ∇
```

8.
```
      ∇Z←DRLACC M;□RL;□IO;R
[1]   □IO←0
[2]   □RL←□AI[0]
[3]   R←ρM
[4]   →(0=ρR)/0
[5]   Z←×/R
[6]   Z←Rρ(,M)[⍋Z?Z] ∇
```

9.
```
      ∇R←TIME;T;W
[1]   W←3↑3↓□TS
[2]   T←(12|1↑W),1↓W
[3]   T←((0=1↑T)/12),((0≠1↑T)/1↑T),1↓T
[4]   R←⍕T
[5]   R[(R=' ')/ιρR]←':'
[6]   R←R,' ',('AP')[1+12≤1↑W],'M EASTERN' ∇
```

10.
```
      ∇DATE;S
[1]   S←3↑□TS
[2]   S[ι3]←S[2 3 1]
[3]   S←⍕S
[4]   S[(S=' ')/ιρS]←'/'
[5]   S ∇
```

11.
```
      ∇FORYOUONLY
[1]   →(1421≠□AI[1])/0
[2]   'THIS IS THE MESSAGE' ∇
```

12.
```
      A←9.222222222222222
      B←9.222222222222227
      A=B
1
      A∈B
1
      A-B
¯4.884981308E¯15
      □CT←0
      A=B
0
      A∈B
0
      A-B
¯4.884981308E¯15
```

13. Because both bracket indexing and interval are affected in the same way by the change of origin.

14.
```
      □IO←0
      ι0

      ι1
0
      ρι0
0
```

```
                ρι1
          1
15.             ∇TIMEOFDAY;T
      [1]       T←4 9ρ(18ρ'MORNING  '),'AFTERNOONEVENING
      [2]       'GOOD ',T[1+⌊⎕TS[4]÷6;] ∇
16.             ∇N CRAPS D;I
      [1]       I←0
      [2]       L1:DICE
      [3]       ⎕DL D
      [4]       I←I+1
      [5]       →(N>I)/L1 ∇
17.             ∇MULTTIME N;X;I;A
      [1]       START:X←?N,N×I←1
      [2]       (⍕1↑X),'×',⍕1↓X
      [3]       A←⎕AI[3]
      [4]       L1:→(⎕=STOP,×/X)/0,CORRECT
      [5]       I←I+1
      [6]       →(4=I)/ANS
      [7]       'TRY AGAIN'
      [8]       →L1
      [9]       CORRECT:'CORRECT'
      [10]      →L2
      [11]      ANS:'ANSWER IS ',⍕×/X
      [12]      L2:A←2↑ 60 60 1000 ⊤⎕AI[3]-A
      [13]      'YOU HAVE USED ',(⍕1↑A),' MINUTES AND ',(⍕1↓A),' SECONDS'
      [14]      →START ∇
18.             ⎕LX←'M[1+(1↑⎕AI)∊1500 1600;]'
19.             ∇USAGE EXPR;A;Z
      [1]       A←((ρEXPR)↑'Z̲'),[.5]EXPR
      [2]       A←⎕FX A
      [3]       A←(1↑1↓⎕AI),⎕WA
      [4]       Z̲
      [5]       TS←(⍕¯6+(1↑1↓⎕AI)-1↑A),' MILLISECONDS, AND '
      [6]       TS,(⍕(¯1↑A)-144+⎕WA),' BYTES' ∇
```

The 'fudge' factors ¯6 and 144 are needed to compensate for extra time and space required as a result of imbedding the expression in a defined function. They will vary with the system and should be adjusted to give zero time and space with a null expression.

Symbol index

Top row

Second row

Third row

α in direct definition, 298

⌈ *monadic* ceiling, 49; *dyadic* maximum, 22; ⌈ /, 36

⌊ *monadic* floor, 49; *dyadic* minimum, 22; ⌊ /, 36

_ underlined letters, 12 13

∇ function definition, 56

Δ *T*Δ trace designator, 150; *S*Δ stop designator, 151; character for names, 12

○ outer product, 203

' character strings, 113 115; empty vector ' ', 120

⎕ evaluated input, 234; system functions and variables, 100 280 292

(in APL expressions, 41; in operating system commands, 289; in strand notation, 262

) in APL expressions, 41; system commands, 13 87 100

A ⎕*FMT* character format, 171

S ⎕*FMT* character substitution, 175

F ⎕*FMT* fixed point format, 169

G ⎕*FMT* picture format, 171

J complex number notation, 302

K ⎕*FMT* scale factor, 172

L ⎕*FMT* left justify qualifier, 172

[ ] indexing or subscripting, 121 178; axis operator, 178 211; scatter indexing or choose, 264

◇ statement separator, 44

⍕ *monadic* execute, 254

⍕ *monadic* format, 161; *dyadic* format, 162 166

Bottom row

⊂ *monadic* enclose, 258 260

⊃ *monadic* pick, 262; *dyadic* first or disclose, 260 261

∩ *monadic* unique, 130

∪ *monadic* unite, 263

⊥ *dyadic* base or decode, 217

⊤ *dyadic* represent or encode, 221

| *monadic* residue, 27; *dyadic* magnitude or absolute value, 48

; in function headers, 73; in indexing, 122; in ⎕*FMT* lists, 170

: for labels, 150; for passwords, 4 95

\ *monadic* scan, 38 209; *dyadic* expand, 126

Z ⎕*FMT* zero fill qualifier, 171

X ⎕*FMT* skip specification, 174

C ⎕*FMT* comma qualifier, 172

B ⎕*FMT* blank qualifier, 172

N ⎕*FMT* right negative decoration, 173

M ⎕*FMT* left negative decoration, 173

, *monadic* ravel, 108; *dyadic* catenate, 108 113 180; *dyadic* laminate, 183; in ⎕*FC*, 166; in ⎕*FMT* left argument, 169

. decimal point, 5; inner product, 191; outer product, 203; in ⎕*FC*, 166

/ *monadic* reduce, 33 34 178; *dyadic* compress and replicate, 123 125

Δ character for names, 12

⍝ comment, 10 44

⍀ *monadic* scan, 38 209; *dyadic* expand, 126

⌿ *monadic* reduce, 33 34 178; *dyadic* compress and replicate, 123 125

≡ *monadic* depth, 258; *dyadic* match, 144

ϵ *dyadic* find, 129

ι *dyadic* find index, 130

⎕ *dyadic* indexing with axis, 264

358

Index

Postscript

All of the functions displayed in the text have been collected together for your convenience into a single workspace, *CLASS*, which may be purchased at a nominal cost on a diskette suitable for most personal computers, or on magnetic tape for VSAPL or APL2. Besides *CLASS*, other workspaces available are:

   AIDRILL, which contains *TEACH* and *EASYDRILL*
   EASYPLOT, which produced most of the plots in Chapter 20
   TYPEDRILL, a typing drill practice
   EASYSCREEN, simple full screen management for the IBM PC
   TABULATE, a simple but effective utility for casual report preparation.

To order any of these workspaces, please send a check or money order to Allen Rose Associates, Box 58, Captain Cook, Hawaii 96704. For disk orders, the first workspace is $35, others are $25 each (in the same order). For tape, the first workspace is $75, others are $40 each. Postage and handling charges are included. To avoid delays, be sure to include information about which hardware and APL software you are using.

Additional materials, including the text-processing programs used in the production of this book, are also available. Please write for further details, or just to exchange ideas.

Pathways to Math Literacy

Second Edition

Dave Sobecki
Miami University Hamilton

Brian Mercer
Parkland College

Mc
Graw
Hill
Education

PATHWAYS TO MATH LITERACY, SECOND EDITION

Published by McGraw-Hill Education, 2 Penn Plaza, New York, NY 10121. Copyright © 2019 by McGraw-Hill Education. All rights reserved. Printed in the United States of America. Previous editions © 2015. No part of this publication may be reproduced or distributed in any form or by any means, or stored in a database or retrieval system, without the prior written consent of McGraw-Hill Education, including, but not limited to, in any network or other electronic storage or transmission, or broadcast for distance learning.

Some ancillaries, including electronic and print components, may not be available to customers outside the United States.

This book is printed on acid-free paper.

7 8 9 LMN 21 20

ISBN: 978-1-260-40493-7   (Bound Edition)
MHID: 1-260-40493-5

ISBN: 978-1-259-98560-7   (Loose Leaf Edition)
MHID: 1-259-98560-1

ISBN: 978-1-260-18930-8   (Annotated Instructor's Edition)
MHID: 1-260-18930-9

Product Developer: *Luke Whalen*
Marketing Manager: *Noah Evans*
Content Project Manager: *Peggy Selle*
Buyer: *Sandy Ludovissy*
Design: *Tara McDermott*
Content Licensing Specialist: *Shannon Manderscheid*
Cover Image: ©*Alfred Pasieka/Science Photo Library/Getty Images RF.*
Compositor: *SPi Global*

All credits appearing on page or at the end of the book are considered to be an extension of the copyright page.

Library of Congress Cataloging-in-Publication Data

Names: Sobecki, Dave, author. | Mercer, Brian A., author.
Title: Pathways to math literacy / Dave Sobecki, Associate Professor of
  Mathematics, Miami University Hamilton, Brian Mercer, Professor of
  Mathematics, Parkland College.
Description: Second edition. | New York, NY : McGraw-Hill Education, [2019] |
  Includes index.
Identifiers: LCCN 2017034142| ISBN 9781259985607 (alk. paper) | ISBN
  9781260189308 (annotated instructor's edition)
Subjects: LCSH: Mathematics—Textbooks.
Classification: LCC QA39.3 .S63 2019 | DDC 510—dc23
LC record available at https://lccn.loc.gov/2017034142

The Internet addresses listed in the text were accurate at the time of publication. The inclusion of a website does not indicate an endorsement by the authors or McGraw-Hill Education, and McGraw-Hill Education does not guarantee the accuracy of the information presented at these sites.

A Letter from the Authors

When we set out to write the first edition of this book, Math Literacy wasn't a particularly well-defined subject. During the planning stages, we did our best to combine our own classroom experiences with information gathered from instructors across the country who were interested in this new non-STEM pathways movement. We're very proud of the result, but over the last four years we've learned a whole lot more about a field that is far more developed than it was in the early days. The result is the second edition of *Pathways to Math Literacy*.

For those who are new to math literacy, let's first address what this whole thing is about. In our view, we as college math faculty have spent too many years teaching developmental courses as if the students were all headed to calculus. We know that most of them aren't, so our approach is based on answering this question: **what is it really useful for non-STEM students to learn?** And what if we agreed to move past the "this is important because it's important" mentality, and thought about the topics and activities that will best serve a group of students that are, for the most part, poorly served by traditional developmental algebra?

Our project is the result of attempting to do just that. Most importantly, it's not about watering down the curriculum in an attempt to pass more students. It's about providing non-STEM students with an alternate but challenging pathway that will get them into the college-credit math courses they need without getting trapped behind the roadblocks that have emerged within the traditional developmental math track. But more importantly, **it's about focusing on context and critical thinking, and showing these students why the math they've struggled with for so many years is relevant in their lives.**

A big part of our approach was developed after studying the results of research that's been done on what exactly employers are looking for in college graduates. Working productively in teams, being able to solve problems without hand-holding, and being able to use technology efficiently are consistently at the top of the list, so we made these the cornerstones of *Pathways to Math Literacy*. Surely we want our students to become better educated, but we also want them to become gainfully employed.

What we've discovered along the way is how much richer the experience can be for non-STEM students when they stop trying to memorize and mimic, and start to really think and learn. By using a workbook format, focusing on active learning, incorporating technology, and approaching every single topic from an applied standpoint, we've been able to build a course (and a book) that elicits our favorite response from students: **"This doesn't feel like a math course. We're kind of using math. . . ."** YES. Yes we are.

This is where we started, and it won't ever change. Based on feedback from far too many gracious instructors to count, we had three main goals for this second edition. The first was to redesign the order of the lessons so that the mathematics flows more logically, and to include additional topics that the market was asking for. Second, we aimed to place more emphasis on the fact that algebra doesn't have to be an abstract, frightening topic, and that having to struggle productively isn't just okay; it's GREAT! The third goal was to add new features and exercises that make the book and its online supplements more flexible and comprehensive so that instructors can adapt our basic ideas to their own needs and philosophies easily. We surely don't expect that everyone, or maybe even anyone, will cover every single lesson in the book. We think we know a lot about math literacy, but you're still the most important expert on what is best for your students. Think of the book as a suggested curriculum that's fully intended to be customized for your needs. No matter which lessons you choose to cover, you'll be fully supported by our entire program. The specifics of these revisions can be found on page v of the book.

If you look very carefully, you'll find many of the topics that typically make up the core of the developmental algebra curriculum. We like to think of it as giving your children medicine they don't want by mixing it into a bowl of ice cream. By making everything contextual, and liberally mixing in important study skills and a variety of topics that are usually in the province of liberal arts math, we're making the process of learning useful problem-solving skills through algebra more palatable for students, which at the end of the day is a significant part of the battle. When your students open their minds to the possibility of really understanding a math course, and really seeing how math can be useful, they blossom into the learner that we try to bring out in all of our students.

Many thanks for looking at our materials, and ALWAYS feel free to reach out to us with questions, comments, suggestions, or support.

Dave and Brian
davesobecki@gmail.com
bmercer@parkland.edu

What's New in the Second Edition?

For those that are familiar with the first edition of *Pathways*, you may have noticed that we seem to have put on some weight. (The book, not Dave and Brian.) We thought it would be a good idea to discuss the variety of reasons for the increase in size.

First, we improved the layout of the book in a couple of subtle but important ways. Many instructors contacted us to say that there wasn't enough space for students to write the kind of thoughtful responses that we hope for, so we spaced out the questions quite a bit more where appropriate. We also found the layout of the **Portfolio** to be very awkward for our students: when they turned in their **Applications,** the Portfolio came along with it and they no longer had access to the **Technology, Reflections,** or **Looking Ahead** questions. That's been rectified by expanding the Portfolio to a second page.

Speaking of expansion, we've added a few new features based on four years' worth of feedback from our wonderful users. Probably the most common request we got was for extra problems that students could practice on, so the **Did You Get It?** feature was born. Whenever a key concept has been covered, we insert an extra question or two to help students reinforce that concept. Answers are included at the end of each lesson, and solutions videos can be found in the online resources. These aren't intended to be in-class activities: they're reinforcement for students who feel that some extra practice would be helpful.

The next new feature is **Prep Skills** for each lesson. In the first edition, the online skills problems were divided into "Prep" and "Practice" categories, but in this edition we took prep to a whole new level. Each lesson begins with a list of specific skills that are needed for that lesson, along with some exposition, solved sample questions, and a list of problems for students to work on. Again, the answers are provided at the end of each lesson, and solutions videos can be found online. (The problems can be worked online as well, of course.) We've found that students with many different academic backgrounds and levels of preparation are taking Math Literacy courses, so a mechanism for letting both students and instructors know exactly what's needed for success in each lesson should help to level the playing field.

The third new feature is end of unit materials. In order to wrap up units and help students prepare for unit exams, we've written extensive summary materials. This starts with an interactive review of all key terms and formulas: rather than just asking students to read yet another list of definitions, we're asking them to test their knowledge of key terms with accessible fill-in-the-blank questions. Next comes a summary of all the learning objectives from the lesson, along with pages of review problems that are similar to those covered within the unit. For units in which new technology skills were particularly important, a tech review is included as well.

Finally, the most obvious way to expand the size of a book is to add new content. This is probably least responsible for our expansion, but we did add some new topics that were requested over the last few years. These topics include gathering and organizing data, expected value and weighted averages, and margin of error in polling. On the algebraic side, there are new expanded sections covering inequalities, systems of equations, and finding linear equations using the point-slope form.

We also did a pretty substantial reorganization of the original topics, again based on feedback from too many generous users to count. While we still believe that a solid foundation in numeracy should come first, we made an effort to incorporate more algebraic skills a bit earlier. This allows much more flexibility in the types of problems students can solve, and also helps to build their algebra skills gradually over the course of the semester.

If you have a moment, please drop us a line and let us know how you feel about the new edition of *Pathways*. Improvement is a never-ending process, and your feedback will allow us to continue on that pathway. Pun intended.

Pathways to Math Literacy Worktext Features

- **NEW Prep Skills:** Appearing directly before nearly every lesson in this book, this new feature provides every unique learner with the knowledge and skills he or she will need to successfully complete the next lesson in the course.
- **NEW Did You Get It?:** Allowing students the opportunity to perform frequent self-checks for understanding and mastery, this new feature is sprinkled throughout lessons to cover the most critical mathematical concepts in the book.
- **Portfolio:** This 2-page section, found near the end of every lesson in the book and printed strategically so that it can be removed by students as needed without affecting other book content, gives students an excellent record of their knowledge and achievements within each lesson. It's also a useful item for instructors to collect as desired, and can be a wonderful study tool at the end of the term.
- **Technology:** The use of technology does not have to be crutch for math students and act as a barrier to success; it should instead *enhance* their mastery of mathematical content, provide opportunity for enrichment and further exploration, and help prepare them for success beyond the classroom. The Technology boxes, videos, and assignments littered throughout *Pathways* lessons aim to achieve all of these objectives.
- **Online Practice:** An enormous bank of adaptive, algorithmic exercises on McGraw-Hill Education's powerful digital learning platforms gives students almost endless opportunities for skills practice as they work on problems that are carefully programmed to mesh seamlessly with the writing and instructional style of the authors.
- **Applications:** In a context-based course, application problems are paramount among homework problems. The problems in the Applications portion of each lesson can be completed on paper and handed in, or can be done online. In either case, the focus is on why the mathematical skills students have studied are useful in their lives.
- **Reflections:** Successful math students—and indeed, successful people—get in the habit of constantly engaging in self-reflection. These critical open-ended questions, located in the Portfolio section of each lesson, help students review mathematical content from the lesson, articulate the purpose of learning that content, and determine what concepts they might still need to continue reviewing and working on to master moving forward.
- **Looking Ahead:** This feature, which appears at the end of the Portfolio section within each lesson, helps ensure continuity and alignment for students as they transition from one lesson to the next throughout the program.

Pathways to Math Literacy Additional Resources for Instructors

- **NEW Quick Start Guide:** This concise tool gives instructors everything they need to successfully implement *Pathways to Math Literacy* with outstanding results starting immediately Day 1, even with minimal prep time available.
- **Annotated Instructor Edition (Includes teaching tips and exercise answers)**
- **Instructor Notes for each lesson:** Created by Brian Mercer, these notes walk an instructor through each lesson sharing an overview, best practices, and common student challenges.
- **Solutions videos:** Solutions videos for every problem in the book are available for the instructor to distribute as needed. (Solutions PowerPoints are also available as needed.)
- **"Math Literacy in action!":** Since not everyone is able to make the trip to Parkland College, Brian Mercer has recorded several of his classes to help instructors get an idea for what a typical class looks like.
- **First Day of Class Presentation:** This resource assists instructors in helping to set up expectations and goals of the course.
- **Unit Exams/TestGen test bank software**
- **Other valuable resources:** These include group projects, evaluations forms, and sample rubrics.

Pathways to Math Literacy Additional Resources for Students

- **NEW SmartBook with Learning Resources:** This powerful digital resource provides students with an assignable, adaptive eBook and study tool that directs them to the content they don't know and helps them study more efficiently.
- **NEW Over 500 new algorithmic skills practice and homework exercises available through ConnectMath Hosted by ALEKS**
- **NEW Dozens of new online videos—in addition to the over 300 such videos that already exist—in a comprehensive online video series, all of which are tied directly to problems from *Pathways to Math Literacy***

- **Expanded ALEKS Math Literacy Pie:** In support of the expanded content in the book, we've expanded content in the math literacy pie as well, which now includes up to 788 topics that students can learn. ALEKS is able to identify what students know and don't know upon entering the course and puts them on a personalized path to success that is aligned with the material you include in the course.
- **Excel Support:** The consistent integration of technology activities is supported by student resources. Author-created video tutorials walk students through all new Excel skills learned in the course, and Excel templates help students get started on Technology assignments.
- **Unit Exam reviews**
- **eBook (rich in media features)**

Digital homework and practice, along with all resources, are available through ConnectMath Hosted by ALEKS and ALEKS

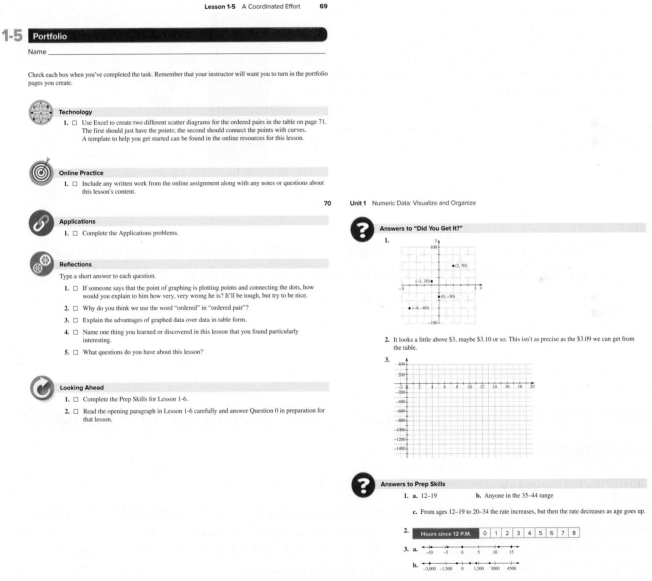

The improved 2-page portfolio in each lesson helps reinforce student learning.

Looking to motivate and engage students? Problem solved!

ALEKS® uses artificial intelligence to precisely map what each student knows, doesn't know, and is most ready to learn in a given course area. The system interacts with each student like a skilled human tutor, delivering a cycle of highly individualized learning and assessment that ensures mastery. Students are shown an optimal path to success, and instructors have the analytics they need to deliver a data-informed, impactful learning experience.

> "ALEKS has helped to create the best classroom experience I've had in 36 years. I can reach each student with ALEKS."
> – *Tommy Thompson, Cedar Valley College, TX*

How can ALEKS help solve your students' challenges?

I did all my homework, so why am I failing my exams?

The purpose of homework is to ensure mastery and prepare students for exams. ALEKS is the only adaptive learning system that ensures mastery through periodic assessments and delivers just-in-time remediation to efficiently prepare students. Because of how ALEKS presents lessons and practice, students learn by understanding the core principle of a concept rather than just memorizing a process.

I'm too far behind to catch up. - OR - I've already done this, I'm bored.

No two students are alike. So why start everyone on the same page? ALEKS diagnoses what each student knows and doesn't know, and prescribes an optimized learning path through your curriculum. Students only work on topics they are ready to learn, and they have a proven learning success rate of 93% or higher. As students watch their progress in the ALEKS Pie grow, their confidence grows with it.

How can ALEKS help solve your classroom challenges?

I need something that solves the problem of cost, time to completion, and student preparedness.

ALEKS is the perfect solution to these common problems. It provides an efficient path to mastery through its individualized cycle of learning and assessment. Students move through the course content more efficiently and are better prepared for subsequent courses. This saves both the institution and the student money. Increased student success means more students graduate.

My administration and department measure success differently. How can we compare notes?

ALEKS offers the most comprehensive and detailed data analytics on the market. From helping the student in the back row to monitoring pass rates across the department and institution, ALEKS delivers the data needed at all levels.

The customizable and intuitive reporting features allow you and your colleagues to easily gather, interpret, and share the data you need, when you need it.

The ALEKS Instructor Module offers a modern, intuitive interface to manage courses and track student progress.

Trusted Service and Support

A unique solution requires unique support. A dedicated team of specialists and faculty consultants ensure that your ALEKS implementation is seamless and painless . . . from start to finish.

ALEKS Service and Support Offers:
- LMS integration that provides single sign-on capability and gradebook synchronization
- Industry-leading technical support and 99.97% uptime
- Flexible courses that can align with any textbook and/or resources, for any classroom model
- Resources for implementation, first day of class orientation, how-to videos and more
- Onsite seminars/worshops and webinars with McGraw-Hill and faculty consultants

McGraw-Hill Education
connect® MATH
HOSTED BY ALEKS

Looking for a consistent voice between text and digital? Problem solved!

McGraw-Hill Connect® Math Hosted by ALEKS® offers everything students and instructors need in one intuitive platform. ConnectMath is an online homework engine where the problems and solutions are consistent with the textbook authors' approach. It also offers integration with SmartBook, an assignable, adaptive eBook and study tool that directs students to the content they don't know and helps them study more efficiently. With ConnectMath, you get the tools you need to be the teacher you want to be.

©Steve Debenport/Getty Images

> "I like that ConnectMath reaches students with different learning styles . . . our students are engaged, attend class, and ask excellent questions."
> – *Kelly Davis, South Texas College*

Trusted Service and Support

A dedicated team of specialists and faculty consultants ensure that your ConnectMath implementation is seamless and painless . . . from start to finish.

ConnectMath Service and Support Offers:
- LMS integration that provides single sign-on capability and gradebook synchronization
- Industry-leading technical support and 99.97% uptime
- Resources for implementation, first day of class orientation, how-to videos and more
- Onsite seminars/worshops and webinars with McGraw-Hill and faculty consultants

How can ConnectMath help solve your students' challenges?

I like to learn by _____.

Whether it's reading, watching, discovering, or doing, ConnectMath has something for everyone. Instructors can create assignments that accommodate different learning styles, and students aren't stuck with boring multiple-choice problems. Instead they have a myriad of motivational learning and media resources at their fingertips. SmartBook delivers an interactive reading and learning experience that provides personalized guidance and just-in-time remediation. This helps students to focus on what they need, right when they need it.

I still don't get it. Can you do that problem again?

Because the content in ConnectMath is author-developed and goes through a rigorous quality control process, students hear one voice, one style, and don't get lost moving from text to digital. The high-quality, author-developed videos provide students ample opportunities to master concepts and practice skills that they need extra help with . . . all of which are integrated in the ConnectMath platform and the eBook.

How can ConnectMath help solve your classroom challenges?

I need meaningful data to measure student success!

From helping the student in the back row to tracking learning trends for your entire course, ConnectMath delivers the data you need to make an impactful, meaningful learning experience for students. With easy-to-interpret, downloadable reports, you can analyze learning rates for each assignment, monitor time on task, and learn where students' strengths and weaknesses are in each course area.

We're going with the _____ (flipped classroom, corequisite model, etc.) implementation.

ConnectMath can be used in any course setup. Each course in ConnectMath comes complete with its own set of text-specific assignments, author-developed videos and learning resources, and an integrated eBook that cater to the needs of your specific course. The easy-to-navigate home page keeps the learning curve at a minimum, but we still offer an abundance of tutorials and videos to help get you and your colleagues started.

About the Authors

Dave Sobecki

I was born and raised in Cleveland, and started college at Bowling Green State University majoring in creative writing. Eleven years later, I walked across the graduation stage to receive a PhD in math, a strange journey indeed. After two years at Franklin and Marshall College in Pennsylvania, I came home to Ohio, accepting a tenure-track job at the Hamilton campus of Miami University. I've won a number of teaching awards in my career, and while maintaining an active teaching schedule, I now spend an inordinate amount of time writing textbooks and course materials. I've written or co-authored either nine or sixteen textbooks, depending on how you count them, as well as a wide variety of solutions manuals and interactive CD-ROMS. I've also worked on an awful lot of the digital content that accompanies my texts, including Connect, LearnSmart, and Instructional videos.

©McGraw-Hill Education

I'm in a very happy place right now: my love of teaching meshes perfectly with my childhood dream of writing. (Don't tell my publisher this—they think I spend 20 hours a day working on textbooks—but I'm working on my first novel in the limited spare time that I have.) I'm also a former coordinator of Ohio Project NExT, as I believe very strongly in helping young college instructors focus on high-quality teaching as a primary career goal. I live in Fairfield, Ohio, with my lovely wife Cat and fuzzy dogs Macleod and Tessa. I'm a recovering sports fan, still rooting for Ohio State and the Cleveland teams in a saner manner. Other passions include heavy metal music, travel, golf, collecting fine art, and visiting local breweries.

Brian Mercer

I can say without a doubt that I was made to be in a classroom. I followed the footsteps of my father, a 35-year middle school math teaching veteran, into this challenging yet rewarding career. My college experience began as a community college student at Lakeland College in Mattoon, Illinois. From there, I received a Bachelor of Science in Mathematics from Eastern Illinois University and a Master of Science in Mathematics from Southern Illinois University. I accepted a tenure-track faculty position at Parkland College, where I have taught developmental and college-level courses for 20 years. I had the opportunity to begin writing textbooks shortly after I started teaching at Parkland. My then department chair and mentor, James W. Hall, and I co-authored several textbooks in Beginning and Intermediate Algebra.

©McGraw-Hill Education

In the fall of 2011, our department began discussing the idea of creating two tracks through our developmental math sequence. The idea stemmed from two issues. First, most of our beginning and intermediate algebra students were headed to either our Liberal Arts Math or our Introduction to Statistics course. Second, we wanted to enhance intermediate algebra to better prepare those students who were headed to college algebra. Obviously, these were two competing ideas! Increasing the algebraic rigor of these courses seemed to "punish" students who were not heading to college algebra. With the two track system, we implemented a solution that best serves both groups of students.

I have to admit that I was initially concerned that offering an alternate path through developmental math for students not planning to take college algebra would lead to a lowering of standards. However, my participation in our committee investigating this idea led me to believe it was possible to offer a rigorous course that was exceedingly more appropriate for this group of students. Since there were no materials for the course, I began creating my own and was paired by McGraw-Hill with Dave Sobecki. The successful partnership that resulted has led to two editions of this book, along with follow-up projects in Quantitative Reasoning and Quantitative Literacy. My thoughts on all three of these projects are summed up by a comment from a trusted colleague who said, "This is just a long overdue idea."

Outside of the classroom and away from the computer, I am kept educated, entertained and ever-busy by my wonderful wife Nikki, and our two children, Charlotte, 10 and Jake, 9. I am an avid St. Louis Cardinals fan and enjoy playing recreational softball and golf in the summertime with colleagues and friends.

Acknowledgments

First, we'd like to thank the following individuals who reviewed or class tested *Pathways to Math Literacy*. Some of you helped make the original version great, others among you contributed to making the second edition even better, and many of you have been helping to enhance *Pathways* along every step of the journey from the very beginning.

Maria Andersen, CEO, Coursetune, Inc.

Amber Anderson, Danville Area Community College

Rachel Anschicks, College of DuPage

Abbey Auxter, Community College of Philadelphia

Jack Bennett, Ventura College

Gale Brewer, Amarillo College

Andrea Buettner, Hennepin Technical College

Cindy Burns, McLennan Community College

Elizabeth Cannis, Pasadena City College

Edie Carter, Amarillo College

Dorothy Marie Carver, Portland Community College

Lori Chapman, Macomb Community College

Mark Chapman, Lansing Community College

Carl Clark, Indian River State College

Brandi Cline, Lone Star College—Tomball

James Condor, State College of Florida

Trey Cox, Chandler-Gilbert Community College

Awilda Delgado, Broward College

Nicole Duvernay, Spokane Community College

Hope Essien, Malcolm X College

Asha Hill, Georgia Highlands College

Jennifer Hill, College of DuPage

Linda Hintzman, Pasadena City College

Brandon Huff, Lewis and Clark Community College

Laura Iossi, Broward College

Gretta Johnson, Amarillo College

Gizem Karaali, Pomona College

Michelle Kershner, Elgin Community College

Taylor Kilman, Indian River State College

Tamela Kostos, McHenry County College

Gayle Krzemien, Pikes Peak Community College

Brian Leonard, Southwestern Michigan College

Christine Mac, Front Range Community College

Caren McClure, Santa Ana College

David Miller, Black Hawk College

Faith Miller, Macomb Community College

Melissa Morgan, Waubonsee Community College

Catherine Moushon, Elgin Community College

Nicole Munden, Lewis and Clark Community College

Bette Nelson, Alvin College

Peter Nodzenski, Black Hawk College

Dawn Peterson, Illinois Central College

Karey Pharris, Pikes Peak Community College

Pat Rhodes, Treasure Valley Community College

Lisa Rombes, Washtenaw Community College

Martin Romero, Santa Ana College

Doug Roth, Pikes Peak Community College

Jack Rotman, Lansing Community College

Cynthia Schultz, Illinois Valley Community College

Jo Lynn Marie Sedgwick, Waubonsee Community College

Mary Sheppard, Malcolm X College

Nigie Shi, Bakersfield College

Craig Slocum, Moraine Valley Community College

Lindsey Small, Pikes Peak Community College

Robin Stutzman, Southwestern Michigan College

Kelly Thannum, Illinois Central College

Ria Thomas, Southwestern Michigan College

Cassonda Thompson, York Technical College

Diane Veneziale, Rowan College at Burlington County

Carol Weideman, St. Petersburg College

Karen White, Amarillo College

Erin Wilding-Martin, Parkland College

Much of the information we needed to bring this vision to life was provided through a variety of focus groups. So next, we thank our focus group participants, whose valuable insights helped focus our efforts. Guess that's why they call them focus groups.

Patricia Anderson, Arapahoe Community College

Beth Barnett, Columbus State Community College

Ratan Barua, Miami Dade College

Jonathan Brucks, University of Texas at San Antonio

Robert Cantin, MassBay Community College

Billye Cheek, Grayson College

Diana Coatney, Clark College

Mahshid Hassani, Hillsbourough Community College

Jessica Lickeri, Columbus State Community College
Rita Lindsay, Indian River State College
Faun Maddux, West Valley College
Tanya Madrigal, San Jacinto College
Teri Miller, Clark College
Jeff Morford, Henry Ford Community College
Arumugam Muhundan, State College of Florida
Bill Parker, Greenville Technical College
Betty Peterson, Mercer Community College
Paul Stephen Prueitt, Atlanta Metro State College
Leslie Sterrett, Indian River State College
Pat Rhodes, Treasure Valley Community College
Wendy Pogoda, Hillsborough CC, South Shore
Saisnath Rickhi, Miami Dade College

Cynthia Roemer, Union County College
Arlene Rogoff, Union County College
Mark Roland, Dutchess Community College
Jorge Sarmiento, County College of Morris
Cathy Schnakenburg, Arapahoe Community College
Pat Suess, St. Louis Community College
Mel Taylor, Ridgewater Community College
Robyn Toman, Anne Arundel Community College
LuAnn Walton, San Juan College
Keith White, Utah Valley University
Valerie Whitmore, Central Wyoming College
Latrica Williams, St. Petersburg College
Mina Yavari, Allan Hancock College

We'd also like to take a moment to thank some of the people at McGraw-Hill Education who helped to make this new edition of *Pathways* a reality and get out the good word about it.

Kathleen McMahon—Managing Director, Math & Physical Sciences
Caroline Celano—Director of Mathematics
Kim Moreno—Director, ALEKS Implementation
Tami Hodge—Director of Marketing
Noah Evans—Marketing Manager, Developmental Mathematics & Non-STEM Pathways
Annie Clarke—Marketing Coordinator
Mary Ellen Rahn—Market Development Manager, Mathematics & Statistics
Robin Reed—Lead Product Developer
Luke Whalen—Product Developer, Developmental Mathematics
Marisa Dobbeleare—Product Development Coordinator
Megan Platt—Product Development Coordinator
Cynthia Northrup—Director of Digital Content, Mathematics
Adam Fischer—Digital Product Analyst
Ruth Czarnecki-Lichstein—Digital Product Analyst
Lora Neyens—Program Manager
Peggy Selle—Content Project Manager (Core)
Rachael Hillebrand—Content Project Manager (Assessment)
Tara McDermott—Designer
Shannon Manderscheid—Content Licensing Specialist

And finally, a few additional people merit above and beyond thanks:

Erin Wilding-Martin, who contributed to this product in so many ways that I'm not even sure she can count all of them.

Jack Rotman, a national leader in the Pathways movement, whose thoughtful and in-depth reviews went about eight miles above and beyond.

Jim Hall, who's almost solely responsible for getting Brian into the wild and crazy world of textbook writing.

The students of Parkland College, who contributed an incredible amount of insight by providing feedback on the earliest incarnations of this book.

Cat Sobecki and Nikki Mercer, our wives. We still can't figure out how two math nerds managed to snag these two beauties.

Detailed Table of Contents

Unit 2: MAKING SENSE OF IT ALL — 149

Unit 1
Numeric Data: Visualize and Organize

©IPGGutenbergUKLtd/Getty Images RF

Outline

Lesson 1-1 Where Does the Time Go?

LEARNING OBJECTIVES

☐ 1. Analyze personal time management for a week of activities.

☐ 2. Solve problems involving percentages.

☐ 3. Create and interpret pie charts.

☐ 4. Create and interpret bar graphs.

©Corbis/agefotostock RF

Time is what we want most, but what we use worst.
    —William Penn

One of the most important aspects of success in college is very underrated: learning how to manage time. This is a skill that you're unlikely to acquire by chance: In order to understand how to use your time most effectively, you have to first become aware of how you're using your time. Then you'll have to develop a plan that will help you best take advantage of your valuable time. This can help you to do better in your classes, and can also help you to have more time to do the things you enjoy.

0. Do you think you do a good job of budgeting your time? Explain.

1-1   Class

Here's a sample time chart put together by a student who was interested in identifying the amount of time she spent for one week. Each hour is marked with C (time in class), H (time spent on homework), S (sleep), W (work), or O (other time commitments). In the Portfolio portion of this lesson, you'll be asked to fill out a similar time chart of your own. For now, we'll analyze this chart.

	Sunday	Monday	Tuesday	Wednesday	Thursday	Friday	Saturday
12am–1:00	O	S	S	S	S	S	O
1:00–2:00	O	S	S	S	S	S	O
2:00–3:00	S	S	S	S	S	S	S
3:00–4:00	S	S	S	S	S	S	S
4:00–5:00	S	S	S	S	S	S	S
5:00–6:00	S	S	S	S	S	S	S
6:00–7:00	S	S	O	S	O	S	S
7:00–8:00	S	S	W	S	W	S	S
8:00–9:00	S	O	W	O	W	O	S
9:00–10:00	O	C	W	C	W	C	S
10:00–11:00	O	C	W	C	W	C	S
11:00–Noon	H	H	H	H	H	H	H
Noon–1:00	H	O	C	O	C	O	H
1:00–2:00	W	C	C	C	C	C	O
2:00–3:00	W	H	C	H	C	H	O
3:00–4:00	W	O	H	O	H	O	O
4:00–5:00	W	O	H	O	H	O	H
5:00–6:00	W	O	O	O	O	O	H
6:00–7:00	W	O	O	O	O	O	H
7:00–8:00	W	H	H	H	H	O	O
8:00–9:00	H	H	H	H	H	O	O
9:00–10:00	H	O	H	O	H	O	O
10:00–11:00	H	O	O	O	O	O	O
11:00–12am	O	S	O	S	O	O	O

1. Count the number of spaces containing each letter in the time chart (C, H, S, W, O). Use the results to fill in the following chart, writing the total number of hours devoted to each activity during one week.

	Hours
Class	
Homework	
Sleep	
Work	
Other	

2. Without adding the hours in the table, how can you decide what the total number of hours should be? Do your values from the table add to the right number of hours?

3. Most college advisors will tell you that a good rule of thumb is to allow 2 hours of study time outside of class for each hour spent in class. Is the student that filled out the table in Question 1 following that advice?

One really good way to analyze the amount of time spent on each activity is to compute percentages. The word "percent" literally means "per hundred." So if you found that you spent 42% of your time playing a trendy new game on your phone, that would mean (1) you should consider psychological help, and (2) for every 100 hours of time, you spend 42 of them playing the game.

4. Write a fraction with the number of hours spent by our hypothetical student in class in the numerator, and the total number of hours in the denominator. You'll find those numbers in your answers to Questions 1 and 2.

5. To convert your fraction from Question 4 to a percent, first use a calculator to perform the division. This gives you a percentage in decimal form. To convert to percent form, move the decimal point two places to the right. The result is the percentage of time that particular student spent in class in one week.

6. Use the steps described in Questions 4 and 5 to fill in the next chart with the percentage of hours in a week devoted to each activity. (Round to the nearest percent.)

	Percentage
Class	
Homework	
Sleep	
Work	
Other	

> ### Math Note
> If you need more practice on working with percentages, have a look at the review box on page 7, and the online prep resources for this lesson.

7. Studies have shown that college students get about 6½ hours of sleep per night on average, but that academic achievement improves when students average 8 hours of sleep. What percentage of the hours in a week would be devoted to sleep if you get 6½ hours of sleep per night? What if you get 8 hours? How do you feel our friend from Question 1 is doing when it comes to sleep? Explain your answer.

Did You Get It

Try this problem to see if you understand the concepts we just studied. The answers can be found at the end of the Portfolio section.

1. Of 118 new enrollees in a college nursing program, 68 are planning on pursuing a four-year degree, 32 a two-year degree, and the rest are undecided. Find the percentage of enrollees that fall into each category.

8. A circle can be divided into 360 equal units of measure, which we call **degrees**. In other words, an entire circle is made up of 360° (the ° symbol represents degrees). Multiply the decimal form of each percentage in Question 6 by 360°, and put the results into the next chart. Round to the nearest whole degree.

	Degrees
Class	
Homework	
Sleep	
Work	
Other	

How Often Do You Wash Your Hands After Using a Public Restroom?

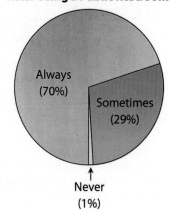

A **pie chart** is a diagram used to compare the relative sizes of different parts of a whole. For example, the pie chart to the right, adapted from a *USA Today* survey, describes people's hand-washing tendencies when using a public restroom. In this case, the whole is the number of people surveyed, and each of the parts is the percentage of folks that gave a certain response. Since 70% of respondents said "Always," the "Always" category fills 70% of the circle. This represents $0.7 \times 360° = 252°$. (See page 7 for a quick review of percents.) The "Sometimes" category fills 29%, which corresponds to $0.29 \times 360° \approx 104°$, and the "Never" category just 1%, corresponding to $0.01 \times 360° \approx 4°$.

Now let's see if we can build a pie chart that illustrates the amount of time spent on various activities for the student survey that began this lesson.

9. Build a pie chart for the information in Question 8 by marking off angles on the circle to the right, starting at the 0° mark, that correspond to the numbers of degrees in Question 8. In this case, the "whole" refers to the total number of hours in a week, and each part is the portion of that time spent on one of the activities. Each of the light gray lines on the graph represents 10°.

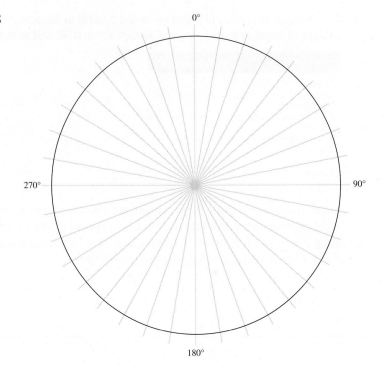

10. Does the pie chart make it easy to analyze the amount of time this student spends on each activity? Explain.

Did You Get It

2. Make a pie chart using the data provided in Did You Get It 1.

Drawing a Pie Chart

1. Find the percentages that fall into each category among the data your chart will describe.

2. Multiply those percentages by 360° to find the number of degrees that needs to be covered by each portion of the chart.

3. Draw an initial boundary line from the center of the chart to the 0° mark. Then, starting at the 0° mark, measure the number of degrees corresponding to your first portion, then draw a boundary. Label this first portion of your chart.

4. Starting at this new boundary, measure the number of degrees corresponding to your second portion, draw in a new boundary, and label that portion.

5. Continue until all categories have been accounted for.

To set up the Group portion of this lesson, we're going to conduct a short class poll to help you learn a little bit about your classmates. Polling is a common and useful way to gather some **data**, which are measurements or observations that are gathered for an event under study.

If we wanted to learn about characteristics of all the students at your college, the ideal approach would be to poll every single one of them. But in most cases, that's not particularly realistic. So instead, we'd likely choose a **sample** of students from the larger **population** of all students at your school. In this case, the sample will be the students in your class. As we learn about statistical studies in this course, we'll need to think about whether or not a chosen sample of subjects provides a good representation of the overall population we're wondering about.

To gather some data, everyone in your class should respond to the two poll questions below. You'll compile and analyze the results in the Group portion of the lesson.

11. Do you think the sample for this poll (students in your class) would or would not provide a good representation of the population in question (all the students at your school)? Explain your reasoning.

How do you feel about math in general?	
I love it	☐
I like it	☐
I can take it or leave it	☐
I don't like it	☐
I hate it	☐

Check all of the boxes that apply to you.	
I live with a parent.	☐
I work and go to school.	☐
I have children.	☐
I'm taking more than 10 credit hours.	☐
I started college right after high school.	☐
At least one of my parents attended college.	☐
I drive to class.	☐
I was born in a year that begins with 1.	☐
I know what my major is.	☐

Math Note

The word "data" is plural, so we say "data are" not "data is." The singular version is "datum."

Review of Percents

1. The word "percent" literally means "per hundred." When we read that 70 percent of respondents to a survey always wash their hands in a public restroom, it means that 70 people per hundred do so.

2. Translating a percent as "per hundred" makes it easy to convert percents to fraction form for using them in calculations: 70% means 70 per hundred, or $\frac{70}{100}$. And there's your fractional form for 70%!

3. This also shows us how to convert percents to decimal form: Dividing any number by 100 moves the decimal two places to the left. That makes 70% equal to 0.70, 5% equal to 0.05, and 23.5% equal to 0.235.

4. If you forget to convert a percent into fractional or decimal form when doing a calculation, you can usually catch your mistake with a bit of thought. In the pie chart on page 5, if we used $70 \times 360°$ instead of $0.7 \times 360°$, we'd have found an angle of 25,200°, which is pretty silly given that a full circle is 360°.

1-1   Group

Numerous studies have shown that one of the best ways to do better in college classes is to study in pairs or groups. To help you get started, if you feel comfortable sharing contact information, exchange the information in the table below. The group you're in now will be your small group for the first unit of this course. When you get used to meeting in class, you'll likely find that meeting outside of class to study and work on homework is a good idea as well, so include some study times that would be convenient for you to meet.

Name	Phone number	Email	Available times

1. Use data from the first class poll on page 7 about what students think about math to complete the table. Then use your results to draw a pie chart comparing the responses.

Feelings toward math	Number	Percent	Degrees
Love it			
Like it			
Take or leave			
Don't like			
Hate it			

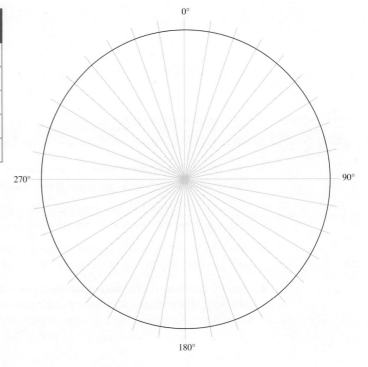

2. Describe how the pie chart allows you to analyze the result of the poll differently than looking at the raw numbers in the chart does.

Using Technology: Creating a Pie Chart

To create a pie chart in Excel:

1. Type the category names in one column (or row).
2. Type the category values in the next column (or row).
3. Use the mouse to drag and select all the data in those two columns (or rows).
4. With the appropriate cells selected, click the **Insert** tab, then choose **Chart** and Pie chart. There are a few different styles you can experiment with, but starting with the simplest is a good idea.

You can add titles, change colors and other formatting elements by right-clicking on certain elements, or using the options on the **Charts** menu. Try some options and see what you can learn!

See the Lesson 1-1-1 Using Tech video in class resources for further instruction.

Pie charts are ideal for representing information where a whole amount is divided into distinct categories. Notice that was the case for the poll on attitudes toward math; every individual could choose only one of the responses. This is reflected in the fact that the percentages for each response add up to 100%. But the second poll is different: It's likely that many respondents will choose more than one response.

3. Use the next table to tabulate the results of that second poll question. Round to the nearest percent again.

Response	Number	Percent
Live with parent		
Work and school		
Have children		
More than 10 hours		
Straight to college		
A parent went to college		
Drive to class		
Born before 2000		
Know major		

As we expected, the percentages add up to far more than 100%, so a pie chart would be a really bad choice for illustrating these data. Instead, we'll use a different way to visualize the data. A **bar graph** is a visual way to compare the sizes of different values. Pie charts are great for comparing parts to a whole; bar graphs are effective for comparing parts to other parts. In a bar graph, the length of each bar gives an indication of how the size of a quantity compares to other related quantities.

Let's look at an example first, then get back to our class polling data. In a telephone poll conducted in October 2016, likely voters were asked two questions about the four candidates for U.S. president: Who are you planning to vote for? and Which of the candidates do you think are qualified to be president? The results are summarized in the following two graphs.

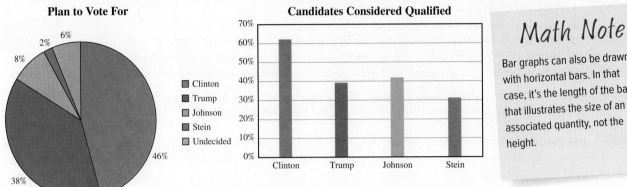

4. Why did we choose a pie chart for the first question and a bar graph for the second?

5. Use the information in the graphs to fill in the table here.

Candidate	Plan to vote for	Qualified
Clinton		
Trump		
Johnson		
Stein		
Undecided		

6. Illustrate the results of the second class poll question with a bar graph. Don't forget to label the responses along the bottom, and label appropriate heights along the left side.

Drawing a Bar Graph

1. Label the name of each category in your data, equally spaced along the bottom of your graph (or along the left if you want to draw horizontal bars).

2. Label an appropriate scale along the left of your graph (or along the bottom for horizontal bars). Make sure your scale starts at zero, and extends out a little bit further than the largest number in your data set.

3. Draw in rectangular bars whose heights or lengths correspond to the number representing each category in your data set.

Using Technology: Creating a Bar Graph

To create a bar graph in Excel:

1. Type the category names in one column (or row).
2. Type the category values in the next column (or row).
3. Use the mouse to drag and select all the data in those two columns (or rows).
4. With the appropriate cells selected, click the **Insert** tab, then choose **Chart** and Column or Bar graph. ("Column" gives you vertical bars, "Bar" gives you horizontal.) Again, there are a few different styles you can experiment with, but starting with the simplest is a good idea.

You can add titles, change colors and other formatting elements by right-clicking on certain elements, or using the options on the **Charts** menu. Try some options and see what you can learn!

See the Lesson 1-1-2 Using Tech video in class resources for further information.

7. Write at least three observations you can make from your bar graph. What do you find interesting or notable about what it tells you?

Did You Get It

3. Of the 118 nursing enrollees from Did You Get It 1, 96 are taking a biology class this semester, 59 a math class, 85 an English class, 16 a psychology class, and 38 a phys ed class. Draw a bar graph illustrating this data.

1-1 Portfolio

Name _____

Check each box when you've completed the task. Remember that your instructor will want you to turn in the portfolio pages you create.

Technology

1. ☐ Fill in a time chart like the one at the beginning of this lesson based on your schedule. Then compile the results and use Excel to create a pie chart and a bar graph showing where your time is spent. For the pie chart, use percentages of time spent on each activity. For the bar graph, use the number of hours spent. There's a sample template in the online resources for this lesson to help you get started. Copy and paste your charts into a Word document, and write a couple of sentences below the charts describing any thoughts you have about what you learned.

Online Practice

1. ☐ Include any written work from the online assignment along with any notes or questions about this lesson's content.

Applications

1. ☐ Complete the Applications problems.

Reflections

Type a short answer to each question.

1. ☐ Do you spend your time efficiently? Explain.

2. ☐ Why are you in college? If you've never thought about a good answer to this question, you certainly should have!

3. ☐ What changes do you plan to make in how you budget your time?

4. ☐ List some benefits of working/studying in groups rather than alone.

5. ☐ Give an example of a survey question that would best be represented by a pie chart, and another that would best be represented by a bar graph. No using any questions from this lesson! Explain your reasoning.

6. ☐ Name one thing you learned or discovered in this lesson that you found particularly interesting.

7. ☐ What questions do you have about this lesson?

Looking Ahead

1. ☐   Complete the Prep Skills for Lesson 1-2.

2. ☐   Read the opening paragraph in Lesson 1-2 carefully and answer Question 0 in preparation for that lesson.

Answers to "Did You Get It?"

1. Four year: 57.6%; two year: 27.1%; undecided: 15.3%

2. **Number of Enrollees**

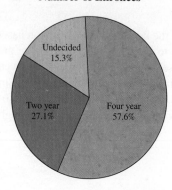

3. **Classes Being Taken by Nursing Majors**

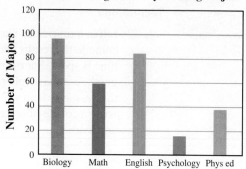

1-1 Applications

Name _____

According to the 2015–2016 National Pet Owners Survey conducted by the American Pet Products Association, 65% of households in the United States have at least one pet. The first table below shows the percentage of households that have each of the most popular pets.

The second table shows the results of a poll done by Public Policy Polling in 2013, in which respondents were asked, "Which of the following exotic animals would you most like to have as a pet: an alligator, a dinosaur, an elephant, a giraffe, a polar bear, or a tiger?"

Percentage of households having various types of pets

Bird	6.1
Cat	42.9
Dog	54.4
Horse	2.5
Fish	13.6
Reptile	4.9

Which exotic animal would you most like to have as a pet?

Alligator	6%
Dinosaur	18%
Elephant	16%
Giraffe	20%
Polar bear	14%
Tiger	26%

1. Which data set is best illustrated with a pie chart? Explain why you feel that way, then draw a pie chart representing the data.

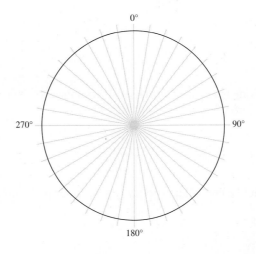

2. Which data set is best illustrated with a bar graph? Explain why you feel that way, then draw a bar graph representing the data.

1-1   **Applications**

Name _____

In May 2015, the Panetta Institute for Public Policy released the results of an extensive survey of college students. One of the questions was, "Do you think the following issues are or are not serious problems facing our country?" Results were divided by political party. Data for those self-reporting as either Democrat or Republican are illustrated by the following bar graph.

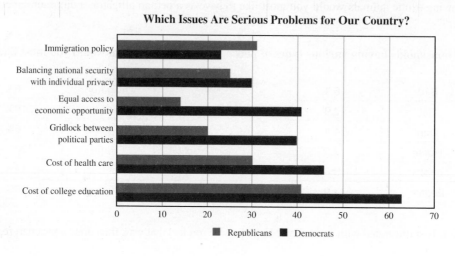

Which Issues Are Serious Problems for Our Country?

3. What issue was seen as serious by most respondents overall?

4. What issue showed the greatest divide between Democrats and Republicans? Explain how you decided.

5. What percentage of Democrats felt like immigration policy was a serious problem? What about Republicans?

6. Of the two political parties, which would you say had the most positive outlook on the current state of the country? Explain.

1-1 Applications

Name _____

On the show *How I Met Your Mother,* Marshall demonstrated the true versatility of pie charts and bar graphs in the most brilliant way possible: by making a pie chart describing his favorite bars, and a bar graph describing his favorite pies. The charts are reproduced below.

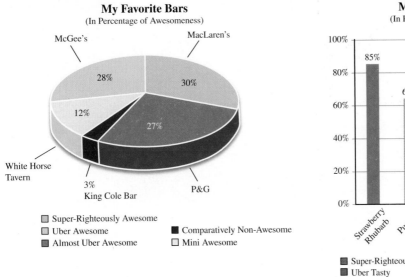

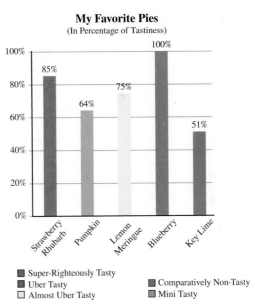

7. Comment on how well you think Marshall did in terms of appropriately using each type of graph based on the data illustrated.

8. What's different about this bar graph that makes it easier to read the data?

9. Look at Marshall's pie chart and try to ignore the percentages for a moment. Which slice appears to be the biggest? Which actually should be?

10. What does your answer to Question 9 tell you about pie charts drawn in a three-dimensional format? Explain.

Lesson 1-2 Prep Skills

SKILL 1: PERFORM ARITHMETIC OPERATIONS ON INTEGERS

- $12 + (-3) = 12 - 3 = 9$ Adding a negative is the same as subtracting.

- $15 - (-8) = 15 + 8 = 23$ Subtracting a negative results in addition.

- $12 \times (-5) = -60$ Multiplying or dividing opposite signs results in a negative.

- $-84 \div (-7) = 12$ Multiplying or dividing same signs results in a positive.

SKILL 2: ADD OR SUBTRACT FRACTIONS

- $\dfrac{3}{7} + \dfrac{2}{7} = \dfrac{5}{7}$ If denominators are the same, rewrite the common denominator and add/subtract the numerators.

- $\dfrac{8}{3} - \dfrac{2}{3} = \dfrac{6}{3} = 2$

- $\dfrac{2}{3} \cdot \dfrac{4}{4} = \dfrac{8}{12}$ To rewrite a fraction with a new denominator, multiply numerator and denominator by the same number.

- $\dfrac{3}{4} - \dfrac{5}{6}$ Find least common denominator: 12 is the smallest number that's a multiple of both 4 and 6.
  $= \dfrac{9}{12} - \dfrac{10}{12}$ Rewrite each fraction with the least common denominator.

  $= -\dfrac{1}{12}$ Rewrite common denominator and subtract numerators.

SKILL 3: ADD DECIMALS

- $2.3 + 0.5$
  $= 2.8$ Add digits in the tenths place to get 8; add digits in the ones place to get 2.

- $3.5 + 5.9$
  $= 9.4$ Add digits in the tenths place to get 14; carry the 1 over to the ones place; add that 1 to $3 + 5$ in the ones place to get 9.

PREP SKILLS QUESTIONS

Perform each operation.

1. a. $12 + 4$ b. $8 + (-10)$ c. $-5 - (-7)$

2. a. 4×6 b. -8×4 c. $(-12) \times (-5)$

3. a. $\dfrac{8}{5} + \dfrac{3}{5}$ b. $\dfrac{2}{9} - \dfrac{23}{36}$ c. $\dfrac{1}{3} + \dfrac{4}{5}$

4. a. $4.8 + 3.1$ b. $0.3 + 1.9$ c. $0.36 + 0.77$

Lesson 1-2   **Do You Have Anything to Add?**

LEARNING OBJECTIVES

☐ 1. Identify circumstances where addition or subtraction is possible.

☐ 2. Add or subtract quantities.

We are what we repeatedly do. Excellence, therefore, is not an act, but a habit.
                    —Aristotle

We've all heard statistics describing the collective weight problem that we as Americans have. So it's not at all surprising that counting calories has become something of a national pastime. Nutritional information labels are now mandated by law on food packaging, and more and more restaurants are including calorie and fat information on their menus. In order to keep track of what you're putting in your body, you need to be able to add up amounts of calories, fat, carbohydrates, protein, and others. This requires identifying and adding the amounts that correspond to like ingredients. This is a skill that will come in handy throughout this course (and beyond).

0. What mathematical topic do you think we'll cover in this lesson, and what does it have to do with nutrition?

©Comstock RF

1-2 Class

My coauthor's daughter Charlotte is in fourth grade, and her favorite lunch consists of a turkey sandwich, carrot slices, yogurt, and juice. The nutrition facts for the food in her lunch are given here. Use these facts to answer questions that follow. A sandwich is made from two servings of bread, one and a half servings of turkey, and one serving of cheese. Charlotte also gets a half-serving of carrots and one serving of yogurt along with one juice box.

Wheat Bread

Nutrition Facts

Serving Size 25g

Amount Per Serving	
Calories 66	Calories from Fat 8
	% Daily Value*
Total Fat 1g	1%
Saturated Fat 0g	1%
Trans Fat 0g	
Cholesterol 0mg	0%
Sodium 130mg	5%
Total Carbohydrate 12g	4%
Dietary Fiber 1g	4%
Sugars 1g	
Protein 3g	

Vitamin A	0%	• Vitamin C	0%
Calcium	4%	• Iron	5%

*Percent Daily values are based on a 2,000 calorie diet.
Your daily values may be higher or lower depending on
your calorie needs.

Sliced Turkey

Nutrition Facts

Serving Size 33g

Amount Per Serving	
Calories 34	Calories from Fat 5
	% Daily Value*
Total Fat 1g	1%
Saturated Fat 0g	1%
Trans Fat 0g	
Cholesterol 14mg	5%
Sodium 335mg	14%
Total Carbohydrate 1g	0%
Dietary Fiber 0g	1%
Sugars 1g	
Protein 6g	

Vitamin A	0%	• Vitamin C	3%
Calcium	0%	• Iron	3%

*Percent Daily values are based on a 2,000 calorie diet.
Your daily values may be higher or lower depending on
your calorie needs.

American Cheese

Nutrition Facts

Serving Size: 1 slice (19g)

Amount Per Serving	
Calories 60	Calories from Fat 40
	% Daily Value*
Total Fat 4g	6%
Saturated Fat 2.5g	12%
Trans Fat 0g	
Cholesterol 15mg	5%
Sodium 200mg	8%
Total Carbohydrate 2g	1%
Dietary Fiber 0g	0%
Sugars 1g	
Protein 3g	

Vitamin A	2%	• Vitamin C	0%
Calcium	20%	• Iron	0%

*Percent Daily values are based on a 2,000 calorie diet.
Your daily values may be higher or lower depending on
 your calorie needs.

Carrots

Nutrition Facts

Serving Size 61g

Amount Per Serving

Calories 25	Calories from Fat 1

	% Daily Value*
Total Fat 0g	0%
Saturated Fat 0g	0%
Trans Fat 0g	
Cholesterol 0mg	0%
Sodium 42mg	2%
Total Carbohydrate 6g	2%
Dietary Fiber 2g	7%
Sugars 3g	
Protein 1g	

Vitamin A 204%	•	Vitamin C	6%
Calcium 2%	•	Iron	1%

*Percent Daily values are based on a 2,000 calorie diet.
Your daily values may be higher or lower depending on
your calorie needs.

Yogurt

Nutrition Facts

Serving Size 125g

Amount Per Serving

Calories 119	Calories from Fat 2

	% Daily Value*
Total Fat 0g	0%
Saturated Fat 0g	1%
Trans Fat 0g	
Cholesterol 2mg	1%
Sodium 72mg	3%
Total Carbohydrate 24g	8%
Dietary Fiber 0g	0%
Sugars 24g	
Protein 6g	

Vitamin A 0%	•	Vitamin C	1%
Calcium 19%	•	Iron	0%

*Percent Daily values are based on a 2,000 calorie diet.
Your daily values may be higher or lower depending on
your calorie needs.

Juice Box

Nutrition Facts

Serving Size 1 Juice Box

Amount Per Serving

Calories 60	Calories from Fat 0

	% Daily Value*
Total Fat 0g	0%
Saturated Fat 0g	0%
Trans Fat 0g	
Cholesterol 0mg	0%
Sodium 10mg	1%
Total Carbohydrate 15g	5%
Dietary Fiber 0g	0%
Sugars 14g	
Protein 0g	

Vitamin A 10%	•	Vitamin C	100%
Calcium 10%	•	Iron	0%

*Percent Daily values are based on a 2,000 calorie diet.
Your daily values may be higher or lower depending on
your calorie needs.

For Questions 1-4, find the total amount of each in Charlotte's lunch.

1. Total calories

2. Total calories from fat

3. Total milligrams (mg) of sodium

4. Total grams (g) of carbohydrates

5. The Food and Drug Administration recommends limiting sodium to 2,300 mg per day for a person with a 2,000-calorie diet. What percentage of the recommended amount of sodium is Charlotte getting in her lunch? What percentage of a 2,000-calorie diet is contained in her lunch? What can you conclude?

Did You Get It

Try this problem to see if you understand the concepts we just studied. The answers can be found at the end of the Portfolio section.

1. How much dietary fiber is Charlotte getting in her lunch? What percentage of the recommended daily allowance of Vitamin C is she getting?

6. If we use the letter P to stand for the phrase "grams of protein," what is the result of the calculation below, and what is the significance of the answer?

$$6P + 9P + 3P + \frac{1}{2}P + 6P + 0P$$

7. Write the number of grams of sugar in Charlotte's yogurt, and the number of milligrams of cholesterol. What happens if you put a plus sign between those two quantities? Can you add them?

8. Suppose that in addition to the amount of carbohydrates in Charlotte's lunch, she also ate some of her friend's mini-pretzels, which added another 3,000 mg of carbs to her intake. At that point, she would have eaten 69.5 g + 3,000 mg of carbs. Can you perform that addition? Why or why not?

9. There are 1,000 milligrams in one gram. Change 3,000 mg into grams. Now can you add up the total number of carbs? If so, do it.

When Can You Add Two Quantities?

Two quantities can only be added when they are **like quantities**: that is, they represent a certain number of the same thing. For example, 3 g of protein and 8 g of protein can be added because each is a number of grams of protein, but 69.5 g of carbs and 3,000 mg of carbs can't be added because grams and milligrams are different things. In some cases, you can convert one quantity to a different unit in order to make the quantities like: 69.5 g + 3,000 mg can be written as 69.5 g + 3 g. In other cases, you simply can't add.

1-2 Group

Here are some addition problems for you to work out. Some can be done very quickly; for some you'll need to do some rewriting; others can't be done at all. Perform the additions that you can. For those that can't be done, explain why.

1. 12 g cholesterol + 5 g cholesterol

2. $\dfrac{3}{11} + \dfrac{7}{11}$

3. 8 yd + 2 ft

4. 10 g sodium + 17 g carbs

5. $5 + 75¢

6. $8x + 5x$

7. $\dfrac{2}{5} + \dfrac{7}{20}$

8. 5 days + 5 hours

Math Note

You probably recognize addition problems like Questions 6 and 9 from the study of **algebra**, where we use symbols (often letters) called **variables** to represent quantities that can VARY.

9. $3y + 7y^2$

10. $0.5 + 0.4$

Did You Get It   ?

2. Perform each addition, if possible.

a. $\dfrac{2}{3} + \dfrac{5}{3}$

b. 125 ft + 230 ft

c. 6 ft + 18 in.

d. 12 days + 19 mi

A bank statement gives you a detailed look at the activity in your account over a period of time. All you need to know to understand a bank statement is a few words of vocabulary, and how to add and subtract positive and negative numbers. Use the sample statement below to answer each question. (Amounts in parentheses are negative.)

Bank Statement

Statement date				
5/17/17		Previous balance		$2,358.25
		11 debits		($1,121.17)
		4 credits		$1,215.20
		Ending balance		$2,452.28

Date	Description	Debits	Credits	Balance
4/17/17	Rent	($400.00)		$1,958.25
4/19/17	Utilities	($120.39)		$1,837.86
4/20/17	Paycheck		$620.34	$2,458.20
4/23/17	Groceries	($79.24)		$2,378.96
4/24/17	New clothes	($93.18)		$2,285.78
4/26/17	Return shirt		$22.01	$2,307.79
5/2/17	Cell phone bill	($78.44)		$2,229.35
5/4/17	Pizza	($11.02)		$2,218.33
5/4/17	Paycheck		$572.29	$2,790.62
5/8/17	Withdraw cash	($200.00)		$2,590.62
5/12/17	Check #278	($40.00)		$2,550.62
5/13/17	Groceries	($48.23)		$2,502.39
5/15/17	Gas	($38.68)		$2,463.71
5/16/17	Netflix streaming fee	($11.99)		$2,451.72
5/17/17	Interest		$0.56	$2,452.28

11. What does a <u>credit</u> refer to?

12. What does a <u>debit</u> refer to?

13. What is meant by a <u>balance</u>?

14. How did this account holder do this month if her goal was to spend less than she made?

15. What would the ending balance be with an additional debit of $50?

16. What would the ending balance have been if the account holder hadn't returned the shirt on 4/26?

17. What would the ending balance be if we remove the $200 cash withdrawal from 5/8?

Did You Get It

3. For each transaction, find what the ending balance would have been had that single transaction taken place. Think of these as three separate questions.

    a. The account holder deposited a birthday check from her mom in the amount of $50.
    b. The account holder withdrew $40 from an ATM.
    c. Check #278 (May 12) was never cashed by the recipient.

At some point in elementary school, you were taught to remember rules for adding and subtracting positive and negative numbers. But did you ever try to understand why those rules make sense? In previous classes, you might have been so focused on *remembering* rules that you never really *thought* about them. Our goal is to *understand* why rules make sense. Let's see if our study of bank statements can shed some light on this important subject.

18. We know that credits add to the balance in an account, while debits subtract from it. If you add two credits to your account, what does that do to the balance?

19. Based on Question 18, fill in the blank: Adding two positive numbers results in a _____ positive number.

20. If you add two debits to your account, what does that do to the balance?

21. Based on Question 20, fill in the blank: Adding two negative numbers results in a larger (further from zero) _____ number.

22. If you add a credit, then follow that with a debit, what happens to your balance?

23. Based on Question 22, fill in the blank: Adding a negative to a positive is the same thing as _____ from the positive.

24. If you remove a debit from your account, what happens to your balance?

25. Based on Question 24, fill in the blank: Subtracting a negative is the same thing as _____ the positive of that number.

Rules for Adding and Subtracting Signed Numbers

1. Adding two positive numbers results in a larger positive number.

2. Adding two negative numbers results in a larger negative number.

3. Adding a negative to a positive is the same thing as subtracting from the positive.

4. Subtracting a negative number is the same thing as adding the positive of that number.

26. Suppose you have a balance of $1,200 in checking, and you make a deposit of $210. What's the new balance?

27. What if you have a balance of $210, and make a deposit of $1,200?

28. Based on Questions 26 and 27, when adding two numbers the order _____ matter. Choose either "does" or "does not."

29. Suppose you have a balance of $1,200 in checking, and you make a withdrawal of $300. What's the new balance?

30. What if you have a balance of $300, and make a withdrawal of $1,200?

31. Based on Questions 29 and 30, when subtracting a number from another, the order _____ matter. Choose either "does" or "does not."

The Significance of Order When Adding or Subtracting

Addition is **commutative**: The order in which you add doesn't matter.

Subtraction is not commutative: The order does matter.

In each phrase in Questions 32–34, pick out the word that's telling you to do a certain arithmetic operation, write the operation it's describing, then perform the calculation.

32. The sum of $4 and $2.50

33. My GPA was 3.1, but it increased by 0.4.

34. The difference between $3.50 per gallon and $2.05 per gallon

35. The colored box summarizes some words that are commonly used to describe either addition or subtraction. Complete each list by writing in the appropriate word from Questions 32–34.

Words and Phrases That Represent Addition or Subtraction

Addition

Plus, is added to, in addition, _____, _____

Subtraction

Minus, is decreased by, is taken away from, _____

Using Excel to Add and Subtract

To add the values in cells A2 and B2, we can use the addition symbol.

In cell C2, we type "=A2+B2". Note that the value in C2 is what you get if you add the values in A2 and B2. The equal sign is a signal to Excel that the stuff you're entering after it is a formula, rather than text, so always begin a formula calculation in Excel with =.

To subtract the values in cells A5 and B5, we can use the subtraction symbol.

In cell C5, we type "=A5−B5".

To add several values listed in multiple cells, we use the SUM command. In the screen below, cell F7 is selected and it reveals the formula =SUM(F2:F6), which has been typed in cell F7 to compute the sum of the values in cells F2, F3, F4, F5, and F6. The colon (:) is used to indicate that we want to include all of the cells between the first one, F2, and the last one, F6. You can type in F2:F6, or you can drag across those cells and Excel will put it in for you.

F7		fx	=SUM(F2:F6)			
	A	B	C	D	E	F
1			Sum			Calories
2	$4	$3	$7			120
3						50
4			Difference			95
5	$3.50	$2.05	$1.45			200
6						35
7					Total	500

1-2 Portfolio

Name _____

Check each box when you've completed the task. Remember that your instructor will want you to turn in the portfolio pages you create.

Technology

1. ☐ Design a spreadsheet to find the ending balance for the bank statement on page 24. If you enter the beginning balance and credits as positive numbers and debits as negative numbers, you can use the SUM command in one column. If you want to try something fancier, you can put the credits in one column, the debits in another, then sum each column and decide how to use each to calculate the ending balance. A template to help you get started can be found in the online resources for this lesson.

Online Practice

1. ☐ Include any written work from the online assignment along with any notes or questions about this lesson's content.

Applications

1. ☐ Complete the Applications problems.

Reflections

Type a short answer to each question.

1. ☐ In your own words, describe the importance of like terms in addition.

2. ☐ Analyze a recent bank statement for your own account, or one for a family member. Describe the significance of the credits and debits.

3. ☐ How do debits to a bank account help us to understand why subtracting a negative results in addition?

4. ☐ Name one thing you learned or discovered in this lesson that you found particularly interesting.

5. ☐ What questions do you have about this lesson?

Looking Ahead

1. ☐ Complete the Prep Skills for Lesson 1-3.

2. ☐ Read the opening paragraph in Lesson 1-3 carefully and answer Question 0 in preparation for that lesson.

Answers to "Did You Get It?"

1. 3 g; 108.5%   2. **a.** $\dfrac{7}{3}$ **b.** 355 ft   **c.** 7½ ft, or 90 in.   **d.** Can't be added

3. **a.** $2,502.28   **b.** $2,412.28   **c.** $2,492.28

Answers to "Prep Skills"

1. **a.** 16   **b.** −2   **c.** 2

2. **a.** 24   **b.** −32   **c.** 60

3. **a.** $\dfrac{11}{5}$ **b.** $-\dfrac{5}{12}$ **c.** $\dfrac{17}{15}$

4. **a.** 7.9   **b.** 2.2   **c.** 1.13

1-2 Applications

Name _____

1. Dwayne and his buddy Sea Bass are over-the-road truckers, and at their weekly chess match on Sundays, they compare the number of miles they drove during the week. The data for last week are illustrated by the bar graph. How far did Dwayne drive last week?

2. Who drove the most overall during the week? By how much?

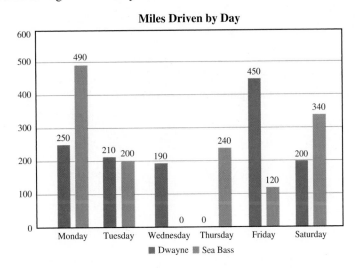

The next bar graph shows the annual net profit or loss for the Ford Motor Company for 2007 to 2015. Use it for Questions 3–5.

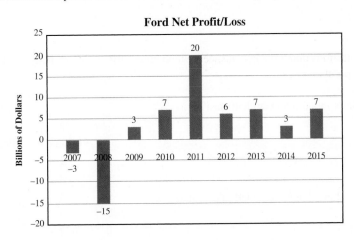

3. What was the difference between net income in 2008 and 2009? Does that represent an increase or a decrease?

4. What was the company's total net income for the years 2007 to 2010?

5. What was the total net income for all years shown in the graph?

1-2 Applications

Name _____

The **perimeter** of a figure is found by taking the sum of the lengths of each side of that figure. Find the perimeter of each figure in Questions 6 and 7.

6.

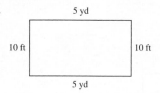

5 yd

10 ft   10 ft

5 yd

7.

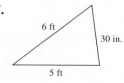

6 ft   30 in.

5 ft

8. Find the length of the unlabeled side of the figure if the perimeter is 86 in.

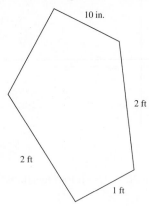

10 in.

2 ft

2 ft

1 ft

Answer the following questions about the spreadsheet, which shows the points earned by a student on a 10-question quiz worth a total of 50 points.

9. What percent of possible points did this student earn?

10. Write down all of the numbers that were added to calculate the value in cell C12.

11. A formula was entered in cell B12, not the number 50. Write the formula that was entered.

C12 fx =SUM(C2:C11)

	A	B	C
1	Problem #	Possible	Points
2	1	4	4
3	2	4	4
4	3	6	5
5	4	8	7
6	5	4	2
7	6	5	5
8	7	4	4
9	8	3	3
10	9	5	0
11	10	7	7
12		50	41

Lesson 1-3   Prep Skills

SKILL 1: RECOGNIZE MULTIPLICATION AS REPEATED ADDITION

- $7 + 7 + 7 + 7 + 7$ is the same thing as 5×7 and is equal to 35.
- $(-4) + (-4) + (-4) + (-4)$ is the same thing as $4 \times (-4)$, and is equal to -16.

SKILL 2: COMPUTE PERCENTAGE OF A WHOLE

To compute a percentage of a whole, compute the given percentage to decimal form by moving the decimal two places to the left. Then multiply that decimal by the whole amount.

- 40% of 100 is $0.4 \times 100 = 40$.   40% in decimal form is 0.40, or just 0.4.

- 5% of 30 is $0.05 \times 30 = 1.5$.   5% in decimal form is 0.05.

PREP SKILLS QUESTIONS

1. Write each repeated addition as multiplication and find the result.

   a. $10 + 10 + 10 + 10 + 10 + 10$

   b. $(-3) + (-3) + (-3) + (-3) + (-3)$

2. Find each requested value.

   a. 50% of 84   b. 35% of 200   c. 4% of 1,000   d. 11.3% of 550

Lesson 1-3   It's About Accumulation

LEARNING OBJECTIVES

☐ **1.** Interpret multiplication as repeated addition.

☐ **2.** Multiply or divide quantities.

A journey of a thousand miles begins with a single step.
　　　　　　　—Lao-Tzu

The best time to plant a tree is twenty years ago. The second best time is now.
　　　　　　　—Chinese proverb

In my experience as both a student and a professor, maybe the single biggest obstacle to succeeding in college is procrastination. As the work you have to do mounts, it's easy to feel overwhelmed at times. We're all familiar with being faced with so much to do that we just don't know where to start. Unfortunately, too many people take the default path, which is to do nothing constructive and put the important stuff off. Sometimes, though, you just have to force yourself to take that first step on the thousand-mile journey. The cumulative effect of doing small bits of work can accomplish a lot!

©Design Pics/Craig Tuttle RF

0. We studied the effects of addition in the last lesson. What do you think we'll study in this one? Justify your response.

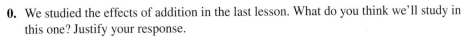

1-3   Group

1. Write about a time you put off something that you had to do, and then regretted it later.

2. Write down an activity that you're good at, like a sport, playing an instrument, a video game, or something else. How good were you when you started, compared to now? How much time went into building your skill at that activity?

3. Write about a task you've performed that required many different small steps to accomplish something bigger.

4. What do you do when you're overwhelmed with work and need to develop a plan?

Some of the problems in the remainder of this activity require calculations. Feel free to use a calculator or computer, but make sure you write down enough work to explain your results.

5. I don't do coffee, but according to an online Starbucks menu, a "Venti" cup of regular coffee costs $2.45. (Evidently, "Venti" is Italian for "really expensive coffee.") Suppose that a regular patron buys two of those every day. How much would she spend in one full year?

6. There are two ways to calculate the amount spent on coffee in Question 5. First, you can add $4.90 + $4.90 + $4.90 + $4.90 + . . . until you've written $4.90 _____ times. Second, you can multiply _____ by ____.

7. Use Question 6 to describe the relationship between multiplication and addition.

8. Going back to our coffee-buying friend in Question 5, complete the table below, based on buying two $2.45 cups of coffee every day. Don't just write an answer: Write the entire calculation.

   How much will she spend . . .

. . . after 1 day?	
. . . after 3 days?	
. . . after 10 days?	
. . . after 180 days?	

9. How much money would she save over the course of the year if she buys coffee at her friendly neighborhood convenience store, where it costs $1.49 per cup?

Did You Get It   ?

Try these problems to see if you understand the concepts we just studied. The answers can be found at the end of the Portfolio section.

1. I also don't drink soda—hello, empty calories!—but I noticed that the soda machine down the hall from my office offers 16-ounce bottles of Coke for $1.50. If a student attends class four days a week during two 16-week semesters and has two bottles of Coke each day, how much money is he spending on Coke per year?

2. You can also get a bottle of water for $1.00. The bottle of Coke contains 185 calories, while the water has none. How much money would he save by going with the water, and how many calories?

10. Tommy (who used to work on the docks) and Gina (who works the diner all day) wisely plan to start saving for retirement. They deposit $1,000 into an account to start out. The plan is to deposit $100 into the account each month for the next 20 years. How much money will they have deposited into the account at the end of 20 years?

11. When you're trying to save money, it can help motivate you to calculate how much money accumulates little by little. Help Tommy and Gina with some of these calculations by filling in the table below, assuming that they stick with their plan of depositing $100 each month after starting with the initial deposit of $1,000. Again, include all calculations, not just the answer.

How much will they have saved . . .

. . . after 1 month?	
. . . after 1 year?	
. . . after 5 years?	
. . . after 10 years? (They're halfway there.)	

12. How much more can Tommy and Gina save in 20 years if they deposit $125 each month rather than $100?

Using Technology: Using the Fill Handle to Auto-Fill Cells

Spreadsheets have the ability to complete cells automatically with either a formula or a value from a selected cell. This is done using the fill handle, which is the bottom-right corner of a selected cell.

	A	B
1	Months	Value
2	0	$1,000.00
3	1	$1,100.00
4		

To auto-fill the cells below B3, click on the little square (fill handle) in the bottom right corner. Then drag to auto-fill cells with either the value or the formula that is contained in cell B3.

See the Lesson 1-3 Using Technology Video in class resources for further instruction.

1-3   Class

Questions 1–5 use the pie charts below. The first illustrates the percentage of energy consumption in the United States by energy source for 2014. The second illustrates the specific breakdown of different renewable energy sources.

U.S. Energy Consumption by Source

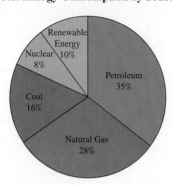

Breakdown of Renewable Energy Sources

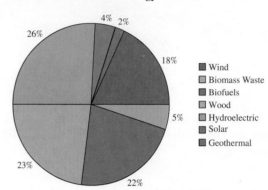

1. The first chart shows that 35% of our energy came from petroleum. The total energy usage for the United States in 2014 was 98.3 quadrillion BTU (British thermal units). What does the result of the calculation 0.35×98.3 tell us about energy usage? Include the result of that calculation in your answer.

2. Does the calculation 98.3×0.35 have the same result? What does this tell you about multiplication?

3. How many quadrillion BTU were generated using renewable energy sources?

4. How much of that energy was generated using wind power? Solar power?

> **Math Note**
>
> In case you're wondering, a quadrillion is almost unimaginably big: It's a million times bigger than a billion. For some perspective, it would take almost 700,000 years to count to 1 quadrillion by ones.

5. Back to the first pie chart: Looking at the natural gas slice, what is the significance of the calculation $100.8 \div 360$? Perform the calculation and describe what it tells us.

6. Does the calculation 360 ÷ 100.8 have the same result? What does this tell you about division?

Did You Get It

3. How many quadrillion BTU were generated by coal in 2014?

4. What is the significance of the calculation 0.26×360 in the renewable energy pie chart?

The Significance of Order When Multiplying or Dividing

Multiplication is **commutative**: The order in which you multiply doesn't matter.

Division is not commutative: The order does matter.

In each phrase in Questions 7–9, pick out the word that's telling you to do a certain arithmetic operation, write the operation it's describing, then perform the calculation.

7. The product of 20 and $2.50

8. Last year I made $2,000 working part time, but this year I made three times as much.

9. The quotient of $24 and 12 gallons

10. The accompanying box summarizes some words that are commonly used to describe either multiplication or division. Complete each list by writing in the appropriate word from Questions 7–9.

Words and Phrases That Represent Multiplication or Division

Multiplication

Multiplied by, _____, _____

Division

Over, divided by, _____

1-3   Portfolio

Name _____

Check each box when you've completed the task. Remember that your instructor will want you to turn in the portfolio pages you create.

Technology

1. ☐ Create a spreadsheet that keeps track of the amount of money accumulated by Tommy and Gina (page 37). In column A, do it the long way: Enter every monthly deposit over a 10-year period, as well as the $1,000 initial deposit. You don't have to enter each amount separately: Use the auto-fill feature. See a template to help you get started in the online resources for this lesson. At the top of columns C and E, create cells in which a user can enter the monthly deposit and the number of years. At the top of column F, enter a formula to calculate the total amount deposited (including the initial $1,000).

Online Practice

1. ☐ Include any written work from the online assignment along with any notes or questions about this lesson's content.

Applications

1. ☐ Complete the Applications problems.

Reflections

Type a short answer to each question.

1. ☐ Describe a situation outside of school where multiplying was useful.

2. ☐ Describe a plan you could follow to keep from getting too far behind in class work.

3. ☐ How can thinking about the cumulative effects of small things help you either in or outside of the classroom?

4. ☐ Name one thing you learned or discovered in this lesson that you found particularly interesting.

5. ☐ What questions do you have about this lesson?

Looking Ahead

1. ☐ Complete the Prep Skills for Lesson 1-4.

2. ☐ Read the opening paragraph in Lesson 1-4 carefully and answer Question 0 in preparation for that lesson.

Answers to "Did You Get It?"

1. $384

2. $128 and 47,360 calories

3. 15.728 quadrillion BTU

4. It provides the number of degrees in the hydroelectric slice of the pie chart.

Answers to "Prep Skills"

1. **a.** $6 \times 10 = 60$ **b.** $5 \times (-3) = -15$

2. **a.** 42   **b.** 70   **c.** 40   **d.** 62.15

1-3 Applications

Name _____

1. If you spend 30 minutes a day goofing off on the Internet during time you've set aside for studying, how much study time (in minutes, and in hours) will you waste over the course of a 16-week semester? What if you waste 45 minutes a day?

Gaining or losing weight comes down to calories burned vs. calories consumed. Burn more calories than you take in, and you'll lose weight. Burn less than you take in, and you'll gain weight. Simple. Let's study some aspects of weight change.

2. George weighed 160 lb when he started college. If he gains just 0.25 lb each month for 4 years of college, how much will he weigh? Suppose he doesn't change his habits after graduation, and continues that modest-sounding weight gain for the next 10 years after college. How much will he weigh for his 10th college reunion?

3. A rule of thumb used by nutritionists is that to lose 1 lb of body fat, you need to burn 3,500 calories above what you take in. If you burn 450 more calories than you take in each day, how long will it take to lose 1 lb? What about 10 lb?

4. An average-sized person will burn about 350 calories in an hour of walking at a fairly brisk pace. How many calories would you burn if you walk an hour a day for 6 months? How many pounds of body fat would that correspond to?

1-3   Applications

Name _____

5. The figure below is made up of some number of smaller squares, like this one: ☐

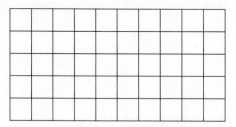

Calculate the number of small squares using first addition, then multiplication.

6. Why do you think the size of a two-dimensional object like this rectangle is measured in square units, like square inches?

7. Now let's add an extra dimension—literally! The next figure is made up of some number of little cubes, like this one:

Calculate the number of small cubes using first addition, then multiplication.

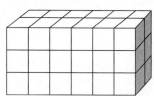

8. If each of the cubes is an inch long on every side, what units do you think would be used to measure the volume of the entire figure? Why?

Lesson 1-4 Prep Skills

SKILL 1: WORK WITH EXPONENTS

An **exponent** is a way to represent repeated multiplication. For example, 4^3 means $4 \times 4 \times 4$.

- $2^5 = 2 \cdot 2 \cdot 2 \cdot 2 \cdot 2 = 32$

- $(-4)^4 = (-4)(-4)(-4)(-4) = 256$ The parentheses show that the negative is included in the number raised to the exponent.

- $-4^4 = -(4 \cdot 4 \cdot 4 \cdot 4) = -256$ Only the 4 is affected by the exponent.

- $\left(\dfrac{1}{5}\right)^2 = \dfrac{1}{5} \cdot \dfrac{1}{5} = \dfrac{1}{25}$

SKILL 2: USE ORDER OF OPERATIONS

Order of operations is a group of agreed-upon rules that allow us to write calculations involving more than one operation without always having to use parentheses to indicate which operation to do first. The order is as follows, with operations higher on the list being performed before those lower on the list.

(1) Parentheses   Perform operations in parentheses first. If there are multiple parentheses, work from innermost outward.
(2) Exponents
(3) Multiplication or division   For operations that live at the same level, work from left to right.
(4) Addition or Subtraction

- $12 + 3 \cdot 4 = 12 + 12 = 24$ Multiplication before addition

- $4(3)^2 = 4(9) = 36$ Exponent before multiplication

- $81 \div (12 - 3) = 81 \div 9 = 9$ Perform the subtraction first because it's in parentheses.

- $52 - 8 \div 4 \cdot 6 = 52 - 2 \cdot 6$ Division before multiplication because it's to the left
  $\quad = 52 - 12$
  $\quad = 40$

- $(-2(3 + 1))^2 - 4 = (-2 \cdot 4)^2 - 4$ Addition in innermost parentheses first, then multiplication inside outer parentheses
  $\quad = (-8)^2 - 4$
  $\quad = 64 - 4$ Exponent before subtraction
  $\quad = 60$

- $\dfrac{7 - 9}{3 + 5} = \dfrac{-2}{8} = -\dfrac{1}{4}$ In a fraction, the fraction bar acts like grouping symbols: interpret the fraction as $(7 - 9) \div (3 + 5)$.

SKILL 3: USE THE DISTRIBUTIVE PROPERTY

The **distributive property** is a method for multiplying some factor by a sum or difference without performing the addition or subtraction first. The factor is multiplied by each of the terms inside the parentheses. In symbols:

$$a(b + c) = ab + ac \qquad a(b - c) = ab - ac$$

- $8(3 - 5) = 24 - 40 = -16$ Matches what you get if you use order of operations
- $4(y + 6) = 4y + 24$ In this case, you CAN'T perform the sum first.
- $-4(2x - 8) = -8x + 32$ Notice that the distributed factor is negative and BOTH signs inside the parentheses changed.

PREP SKILLS QUESTIONS

Perform each operation.

1. a. 3^5 b. $(-2)^6$ c. $\left(\dfrac{1}{2}\right)^4$ d. -5^2

2. a. $8 - 10 \times 2$ b. $4 \cdot (-3) + 12$ c. $19 + -12 \div 3$

3. a. $4 + 3(9 - 1)^2$ b. $-5^2 \cdot 4 - 2$ c. $3 + 4 \cdot 10 \div 2$

4. a. $((8 + 1) \div 3)^4$ b. $6(2 - 5(3 - 4)^2)$ c. $(8 - 3 \cdot 2) - (6 \div 2)^2$ d. $\dfrac{2(3 + 4)}{11 - 9}$

5. Use the distributive property to perform each multiplication.

    a. $10(8 - 3)$ b. $-6(2 + 4)$ c. $x(14 - x)$ d. $-12(2y - 9)$

Lesson 1-4   **Avoiding Empty Pockets**

LEARNING OBJECTIVES

☐ 1. Distinguish between simple interest and compound interest.

☐ 2. Distinguish between linear and exponential growth.

☐ 3. Interpret exponents as repeated multiplication.

☐ 4. Simplify numeric expressions involving exponents and the order of operations.

The most powerful force in the universe is compound interest.
                    —Albert Einstein

Einstein was a smart guy who knew a little something about powerful forces, so that quote is a bit of an eye-opener. In this lesson, we'll study interest, a subject that everyone in our society needs to know something about (unless they want to end up like our friend to the right). If you have a trust fund that will afford you the opportunity to pay cash for a home, a car, a yacht . . . good for you. Feel free to send us a generous donation, care of the publisher. If not, you'll need to borrow money many times during your lifetime, and the amount of interest you pay will be an important part of budgeting your money.

©Stockbyte/Punchstock RF

Then there's saving money, another important part of a financial plan. Putting money in your sock drawer is *not* a sound investment strategy: You'll want to invest in a variety of accounts that will add interest and grow your money. In either case, understanding the power of compound interest will set you on a path to financial success.

0. Explain why you think what you learn in this lesson is likely to be useful in your life.

1-4   Group

1. Discuss any experiences you've had with some of these important financial situations: being responsible for a credit card or checking account, borrowing money to buy a car or home, starting a savings or retirement account, or others.

2. Each of the situations listed in Question 1 is distinct, but all have some common traits. List any you can think of.

Interest is a fee paid for the use of someone else's money. If you borrow money to buy a car, you pay the lending institution for using their money at the time of purchase. If you put money into a savings account, the bank pays you for having access to your money, which they in turn can use to lend to other people.

Simple interest is calculated as a percentage of the original amount of money. For example, if you deposit $100 in an account that pays 4% interest per year, at the end of 1 year, you would have 4% of $100 extra in the account. Since 4% of $100 is $0.04 \times \$100 = \$4$, you would have earned $4 in simple interest, and the account would now be worth $104. In the second year, you'd earn another $4 in simple interest, making the account worth $108.

Compound interest, on the other hand (the force that Einstein was so enamored with), is interest that is paid not just on the original amount deposited, but on interest previously earned as well. To help you to understand the difference between simple and compound interest, let's look at two different accounts:

Account 1: You deposit $1,000 into an account that pays 5% simple interest on that $1,000 each year.

Account 2: You deposit $1,000 into an account that pays 5% of the account balance at the beginning of the current year in interest each year.

3. Answer the following questions about Account 1. Getting an answer is nice, but make sure that you think carefully about how the amount is growing and look for patterns.

How much interest will you earn in the . . .		How much will be in the account at the end of the . . .	
. . . first year?		. . . first year?	
. . . second year?		. . . second year?	
. . . third year?		. . . third year?	

4. Repeat Question 3 for Account 2.

How much interest will you earn in the . . .		How much will be in the account at the end of the . . .	
. . . first year?		. . . first year?	
. . . second year?		. . . second year?	
. . . third year?		. . . third year?	

Computing Simple and Compound Interest

To find the simple interest on an amount of money, you multiply the original amount by the interest rate (written as a decimal) and the amount of time. The units for the time (often years) should match the units on interest rate (often percent per year).

To find the compound interest on an amount of money, first calculate the simple interest for the first year and add it to the original amount to get the new balance after 1 year. For subsequent years, compute the interest as a percentage of the new balance, rather than the original amount.

Did You Get It

Try this problem to see if you understand the concepts we just studied. The answer can be found at the end of the Portfolio section.

1. A small business invests $30,000 in a fund that pays 7% interest per year. Find the amount of interest that would be earned in 2 years if the interest is (a) simple and (b) compound.

5. Fill in the next table by finding the amount in the account at the end of each number of years. You've already found four of the amounts in the table. Hopefully.

	Account 1	Account 2
Start	$1,000.00	$1,000.00
After 1 year	$1,050.00	$1,050.00
After 2 years		
After 3 years		
After 4 years		
After 5 years		

6. Suppose you wanted to find the value of each account after 20 years. Why would that be a much harder calculation for Account 2 than Account 1?

7. This is the calculation used to find the amount after the first year in either account:

Amount = $1,000 + 0.05($1,000)

        Previous plus   5% of
        amount   previous
                     amount

    Can you think of a way to simplify the calculation so that all you have to do is one multiplication?

8. Why does the value of the compound interest account grow faster?

9. Here's a way to describe the difference in growth of the two accounts: Account 1 increases in value by _____ every year, while Account 2 has its value multiplied by _____ every year. So the value of Account 1 at any time looks like $1,000 + _____ × (the number of years passed), and the value of Account 2 at any time looks like $1,000(_____)(_____) . . . , where the multiplication occurs the same number of times as the number of years that have passed.

10. In each of the accounts, the value is growing, but in different ways. Fill in the blank lines in the following box.

The Difference Between Linear and Exponential Growth

In Account 1 (the simple interest account), the values grow by _____ the same constant number.

This type of growth is called **linear growth**.

In Account 2 (the compound interest account), the values grow by _____ by the same constant number.

This type of growth is called **exponential growth**.

Did You Get It

2. Suppose that one savings account is opened with a $500 balance and earns 4% simple interest. To find how the value grows each year, what would you add to the previous year's amount?

3. Suppose that another savings account is opened with a $700 balance and earns 4% compound interest. To find how the value grows each year, what would you multiply the previous year's balance by?

1-4 Class

1. Here's a key observation about the repeated multiplication that occurs when finding the value of Account 2 in the group activity: Repeated multiplication can be expressed more concisely using an _____.

Let's continue working with the two accounts from the Group portion of this lesson. With an initial investment of $1,000 and 5% compound interest, the value of that account after 7 years would be given by

$$1,000(1.05)^7$$

2. Without using a calculator, write that expression without any exponents. Don't perform the calculation: Just write out what it would look like.

3. What is the value of the account after 7 years?

4. In Account 1, where the interest is simple, the account value goes up by 0.05($1,000) = $50 each year. Write a calculation that would find the value after 7 years, then find the value.

Let's take a stab at summarizing what we've learned about linear and exponential growth. Use the calculations for simple and compound interest on this page as models.

5. With linear growth, the value after a certain time is calculated using:

   Starting value _____ a constant _____ a certain number of time periods.

6. With exponential growth, the value after a certain time is calculated using:

   Starting value _____ a growth factor _____.

7. Without trying to give away the answer to Question 6 too much, part of it involves a power. What is the significance of the exponent?

Calculating Values for Linear and Exponential Growth

When a quantity increases based on linear growth, the value after a certain number of time periods can be calculated using this pattern:

New value = Original value + amount of growth per time period × number of time periods

When a quantity increases based on exponential growth, the value after a certain number of time periods can be calculated using this pattern:

New value = Original value × (1 + the growth rate as a percentage)$^{\text{number of time periods}}$

8. Use what you've learned about linear and exponential growth to calculate the value after 20 years in each of the accounts we've been studying. Make sure you write out the calculation that you did.

Did You Get It

4. An investment of $20,000 earns 7.5% interest. Find the value of the investment after 15 years if the interest is (a) simple and (b) compound.

9. If you borrow $500 at 3% simple interest, the amount you'd owe after 4 years is given
    by _____ + 500(_____)(4).

10. To correctly evaluate that expression, you'll need to remember the order of operations, which says that
    _____ comes before _____.

> ### Math Note
>
> If you need some review on order of operations, make sure you check out the prep skills resources for this lesson.

11. Evaluate the expression to find how much you'd owe.

12. Perform the calculation below, then compare your result to Question 11. Describe what you did in terms of order of
    operations. $500(1 + 0.03 \cdot 4)$

13. The reason you got the same answer for Questions 11 and 12 is the _____ property of multiplication
    over addition. (You DID get the same answer, right?)

14. Describe the property you referred to in Question 13 in words, then make up an example of a calculation that uses that
    property.

1-4 Portfolio

Name _____

Check each box when you've completed the task. Remember that your instructor will want you to turn in the portfolio pages you create.

Technology

1. ☐ Create a spreadsheet that uses formulas to recreate the table describing the two bank accounts on page 49. Then extend the table to show the value of each account for the next 30 years. A template to help you get started can be found in the online resources for this lesson.

2. ☐ Do a Web search for different ways to remember the order of operations and find one you like. Warning: You may come across some that are not exactly family friendly.

Online Practice

1. ☐ Include any written work from the online assignment along with any notes or questions about this lesson's content.

Applications

1. ☐ Complete the Applications problems.

Reflections

Type a short answer to each question.

1. ☐ Describe your understanding of the difference between simple and compound interest. How does each relate to the terms "linear growth" and "exponential growth"?

2. ☐ Why do you think Einstein felt so strongly about compound interest?

3. ☐ What's the point of having an order of operations in math?

4. ☐ Name one thing you learned or discovered in this lesson that you found particularly interesting.

5. ☐ What questions do you have about this lesson?

Looking Ahead

1. ☐ Complete the Prep Skills for Lesson 1-5.

2. ☐ Read the opening paragraph in Lesson 1-5 carefully and answer Question 0 in preparation for that lesson.

Answers to "Did You Get It?"

1. **a.** $4,200 **b.** $4,347 **2.** $20 **3.** 1.04 **4. a.** $42,500 **b.** $59,177.55

Answers to "Prep Skills"

1. **a.** 243 **b.** 64 **c.** $\dfrac{1}{16}$ **d.** -25

2. **a.** -12 **b.** 0 **c.** 15

3. **a.** 196 **b.** -102 **c.** 23

4. **a.** 81 **b.** -18 **c.** -7 **d.** 7

5. **a.** $10 \cdot 8 - 10 \cdot 3 = 80 - 30 = 50$

   b. $-6 \cdot 2 + (-6) \cdot 4 = -12 + (-24) = -36$

   c. $14x - x^2$

   d. $-24y + 108$

1-4   Applications

Name _____

Due to a variety of factors including fuel prices and adverse weather patterns, the cost of many groceries is expected to increase by as much as 5% per year. Let's illustrate the effects on consumers using the example of a frozen pizza that currently costs $5.60.

1. If the price of the pizza does go up by 5% next year, find the amount of increase and the new cost.

2. Complete the table below by calculating the new price of several other items for the same 5% increase. Notice the formula in cell C4 which reminds you of the most efficient way to do this calculation.

C4	▲▼	✕ ✓	*fx*	=1.05*B4	

	A	B	C
1	Item	Old price	New price
2	Small potato chips	$0.75	$0.79
3	Half-gallon of milk	$1.79	
4	Frozen pizza	$5.60	$5.88
5	Pound of ground chuck	$3.49	
6	Cooking sherry	$9.49	
7	Bag of chicken breast	$12.29	

3. If the pizza goes up by 5% again the following year, fill in each blank to complete the calculation you'd use to find the price after two 5% increases.

   5.60(1.☐☐)^☐

4. How much would the pizza cost after two 5% increases?

5. Fill in the table below, which shows the cost of the $5.60 pizza after each number of 5% increases. Thinking about your answer to Question 3 should help make the calculations go quicker.

# of increases	New price
1	
2	
3	
4	
10	

6. How does the price of the pizza after 10 years of 5% increases compare to what the price would be if it went up by just 5% of the original cost each year?

1-4 Applications

Name _____

Identify each scenario as illustrating either linear growth, exponential growth, or neither. Show enough work to justify your answer, and if you can, find the next value on the list. A review of the colored box on page 51 will be a BIG help.

7.

	A	B
1		**Taxi Fare**
2	Start	$3.30
3	After 1 mile	$5.70
4	After 2 miles	$8.10
5	After 3 miles	$10.50
6	After 4 miles	$12.90
7	After 5 miles	$15.30

8.

	A	B
1		**Account value**
2	Start	$12,000.00
3	After 1 year	$13,200.00
4	After 2 years	$14,520.00
5	After 3 years	$15,972.00
6	After 4 years	$17,569.20
7	After 5 years	$19,326.12

9.

	A	B
1		**Population**
2	Start	10,000
3	After 1 year	10,200
4	After 2 years	10,404
5	After 3 years	10,612
6	After 4 years	10,824
7	After 5 years	11,041

10.

	A	B
1		**Salary**
2	Start	$40,000
3	After 1 year	$41,500
4	After 2 years	$43,000
5	After 3 years	$44,500
6	After 4 years	$46,000
7	After 5 years	$47,500

11.

	A	B
1		**Stock price**
2	Start	$40.00
3	After 1 month	$42.00
4	After 2 months	$44.50
5	After 3 months	$48.00
6	After 4 months	$52.00
7	After 5 months	$60.00

Lesson 1-5 Prep Skills

SKILL 1: READ INFORMATION FROM A TABLE

The key to finding information accurately from a table is to carefully read the row and column headings so that you know exactly what information is being provided.

Smoking Rates in Canada, 2014

Age group	Males	Females	Total
12–19	8.3%	7.1%	7.7%
20–34	29.6%	19.4%	24.6%
35–44	25.9%	15.5%	20.6%
45–64	22.9%	17.5%	20.2%
65 and older	10.7%	8.4%	9.4%

- Smoking is most prevalent among males in the 20–34 age group (29.6%).
- In every age group, men are more likely to smoke than women.
- The lowest rate is among females 12–19.
- The overall smoking rate is highest for the 20–34 age group.

SKILL 2: SET A TIME SCALE

When data are provided over some time period, like the smoking rate in the United States for selected years from 1965 to 2013, we typically don't use the year, day, clock time, etc. when representing that data graphically. Instead we decide on a certain time as time zero, then use years, days, hours, etc. after that starting time.

Year	1965	1970	1980	1990	2000	2002	2003	2004	2007	2010	2013
% smokers	42.4	37.4	33.2	25.5	23.3	22.5	21.6	20.9	20.8	19.3	17.8

- If we call 1965 time 0, then 1970 would be time 5 (5 years after 1965), 1980 would be time 15, and so on:

Years after 1965	0	5	15	25	35	37	38	39	42	45	48
% smokers	42.4	37.4	33.2	25.5	23.3	22.5	21.6	20.9	20.8	19.3	17.8

SKILL 3: CHOOSE AN APPROPRIATE SCALE FOR A NUMBER LINE

It's a bad idea to always mark off a number line by ones: If we're interested in large numbers, we'd need to keep marking for a long while. Instead, we choose a consistent scale and label it on the number line.

- If we want to graph a variety of numbers between 0 and 20, starting at 0 and counting each tick mark as five numbers would be a good idea:

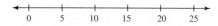

- If we want to graph numbers between −50 and 50, a different scale would be necessary:

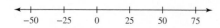

PREP SKILLS QUESTIONS

1. For the table summarizing smoking rates in Canada:
   a.   What group had the lowest overall rate?
   b.   Who is more likely to smoke? A female in the 20–34 range, or anyone in the 35–44 range?
   c.   What happens to the total smoking rates as age goes up?

2. The first table describes the temperature on a certain day between noon and 8 P.M. In the second table, fill in a time scale with noon corresponding to time zero. Also, fill in a descriptive header at the beginning of the top row.

Time	Noon	1:00 PM	2:00	3:00	4:00	5:00	6:00	7:00	8:00
Temperature	42	45	47	48	48	49	46	40	37

Temperature	42	45	47	48	48	49	46	40	37

3. Label an appropriate scale on the number line below, then plot and label each of the numbers on the given list.
   a.   −4, 0, 12, 15, −9

   b.   650, −3,000, 2,500, −500, 1,200

Lesson 1-5   A Coordinated Effort

LEARNING OBJECTIVES

☐ 1. Use a rectangular coordinate system.

☐ 2. Connect data to graphs.

☐ 3. Interpret graphs.

Believe you can and you're halfway there.
               —Theodore Roosevelt

We've already used the word "graph" in this book, when referring to bar graphs. The bar graphs we looked at weren't just pretty pictures, or bars drawn at random heights for no particular reason: They were used to illustrate and understand real data. But the types of graphs we'll study in this unit might be the most misunderstood feature of math: People tend to think of them as just "plotting points and connecting the dots." Nothing could be further from the truth! Just like bar graphs, the graphs that illustrate connections between two variables are all about a visual representation of useful information. So before we talk about the mechanics and terminology involved, we'll use unemployment numbers to vividly illustrate what it's really all about.

©Janis Christie/Getty Images RF

0. How do you think the graphs we study in this lesson will be different from the bar graphs we studied earlier?

1-5 ▌ Class

Most people know that the economy in the United States went through a very rough patch starting in late 2007. How much we've recovered depends on who you ask, as there are conflicting numbers and viewpoints. One common way to measure the strength of the economy is through unemployment numbers.

These tables display the average annual unemployment rate for the years 1992 to 2015. This is an example of **time-series data**, which are quantitative data that have been collected at different points in time.

A **time-series graph** displays values on the *y* axis compared to equally spaced time intervals on the *x* axis.

Year	'92	'93	'94	'95	'96	'97	'98	'99	'00	'01	'02	'03
Rate (%)	7.5	6.9	6.1	5.6	5.4	4.9	4.5	4.2	4.0	4.7	5.8	6.0

Year	'04	'05	'06	'07	'08	'09	'10	'11	'12	'13	'14	'15
Rate (%)	5.5	5.1	4.6	4.6	5.8	9.3	9.6	8.9	8.1	7.4	6.2	5.3

1. Use the table to write a verbal description of trends in the unemployment rate over that 24-year period.

With enough effort, you were probably able to write a reasonable description. But because there's so much data in the table, spotting the trends isn't exactly a simple thing to do. Next, let's look at the same data displayed in graphical form.

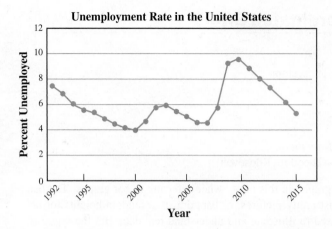

When I look at this graph, two things occur to me: It's a lot easier to see the trends than it was from looking at the table, and the graph looks kind of like a sea monster with a really big nose, which is totally irrelevant but still pretty cool.

2. Use the graph to write a verbal description of trends in the unemployment rate, then explain why the graph makes it easier than the table did.

Without the numbers running along the bottom side of the graph and down the left side, we wouldn't be able to understand any of the information the graph provides. Those numbers provide the **scale** for the graph, and they're ALWAYS crucial in drawing a graph. Each of the number lines that we write the scale on is called an **axis** (the plural of this word is **axes**).

Based on figures from January to October of 2016, the average unemployment rate for that year was expected to be about 4.9%. We can add that piece of information to the graph by finding 2016 on the horizontal axis and 4.9 on the vertical axis, then drawing imaginary lines up from 2016 and right from 4.9 until the lines meet: That's where we put the point corresponding to 2016 and 4.9%.

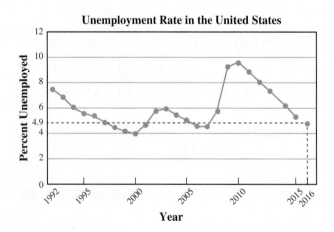

Notice that when we found the location to indicate that the unemployment rate was 4.9% in 2016, the imaginary lines we drew formed a rectangle with the two axes. That's why we call this system of graphing a **rectangular coordinate system**. Each of the numbers we used to locate that point are called **coordinates**. The horizontal axis is usually called the *x* **axis** and the vertical axis is usually called the *y* **axis**. The point where the two axes meet is called the **origin**.

Since we didn't need to worry about negative years or negative unemployment rates, the graph we drew earlier only showed positive values along each axis. But there are plenty of examples of data where negative values make perfect sense, so a rectangular coordinate system is often set up like this:

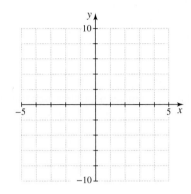

The process of locating information on a rectangular coordinate system, like the 4.9% unemployment rate in 2016, is called **plotting points**. We identify locations by writing the two coordinates together inside parentheses, like this: (2016, 4.9).

3. What are the coordinates of the origin in the rectangular coordinate system above?

4. Look carefully at the numbers on each axis. What distance does each box on the grid represent along the *x* axis? What about the *y* axis?

5. Plot each of the following points on the rectangular coordinate system above. Label the coordinates of each point.
    a. (4, 0)
    b. (0, −8)
    c. (−3, −4)
    d. (2, 7)

Math Note

To be more specific about the term "scale," the distances you found in Question 4 are usually referred to as the scale for each axis.

Did You Get It   ?

Try this problem to see if you understand the concepts we just studied. The answer can be found at the end of the Portfolio section.

1. Draw a rectangular coordinate system, then plot and label the following points on it: (0, −30), (2, 50), (−4, −60), (−1, 10). Make sure you choose an appropriate scale for each axis, and clearly label the scale on your graph.

1-5 Group

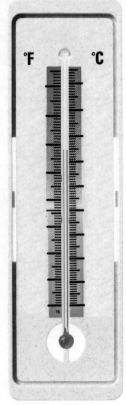

©McGraw-Hill Education/
Ken Cavanagh,
photographer

1. What temperature is this thermometer displaying?

2. Explain why the thermometer is pretty much useless.

3. What are the coordinates of the point drawn on the graph?

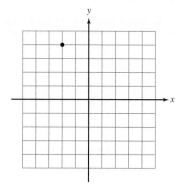

4. Explain why the graph is pretty much useless.

 Important Features of a Good Graph

1. EVERY graph has to have a clearly labeled scale on each axis. A graph with no scale labeled is every bit as useless as a thermometer with no numbers on it.

2. There's no reason the scale has to be the same on both axes. If a graph contains points like (10, 4,000) and (20, 3,000), using the same scale on the x and y axes would lead to a graph that's very difficult to read (try it!).

3. If there are certain points on a graph that are important for some reason, you should label the coordinates of those points directly on the graph.

Being able to understand the connection between a graph and the information that it illustrates is by far the most important skill in graphing. If you can't interpret the meaning of a graph, it's just really bad art!

Almost everyone is interested in gas prices: They can have a very real effect on a household budget. The time-series data in the table below show the average price of a gallon of regular unleaded gas in the United States in January of each year from 2006 to 2016.

5. Write ordered pairs of the form (Years after 2006, Price per gallon) for each pair of values, then plot the points on the graph.

Year	Years after 2006	Jan. price per gallon ($)	Ordered pair (x, y)
2006	0	2.32	
2007	1	2.27	
2008	2	3.05	
2009	3	1.79	
2010	4	2.73	
2011	5	3.09	
2012	6	3.40	
2013	7	3.35	
2014	8	3.32	
2015	9	2.11	
2016	10	1.97	

6. Connect the points you plotted to draw a graph, and describe what that graph illustrates. Then add a verbal label to each axis that describes the information it represents.

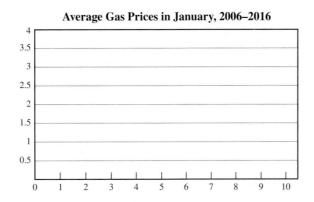

Average Gas Prices in January, 2006–2016

For Questions 7–13, explain how you got your answer using BOTH the table and the graph.

7. What was the highest price of January gas between 2006 and 2016? Is the answer based on the graph different? Why?

8. When was gas most expensive? (Again, you may have two slightly different answers.)

9. When did gas prices stay relatively level from one year to the next?

10. Over what time spans were gas prices rising?

11. Over what time spans was gas getting cheaper?

12. What was the largest single price change in 1 year?

13. Explain why we didn't bother to include negative values along either axis when drawing the rectangular coordinate system for the gas price graph.

Did You Get It

2. Estimate the price of gas in January 2011 using the graph, and write a description of how you got your answer. Then write a description of how your answer compares to the price you can find in the table.

14. If I offered you one of the two accounts detailed below, which would you choose, and why?

	Account 1	Account 2
Start	$1,000.00	$1,000.00
After 1 year	$1,060.00	$1,050.00
After 2 years	$1,120.00	$1,102.50
After 3 years	$1,180.00	$1,157.63
After 4 years	$1,240.00	$1,215.51

15. When we plot points on a coordinate system that correspond to pairs of data, we call the result a **scatter diagram** or **scatter plot**. For the bank accounts in the two tables below, create a scatter diagram for each. First, you'll need to complete the table using skills we practiced earlier in the course. After writing ordered pairs, decide on an appropriate scale for each axis, then plot each point. It would probably be a good idea to use different colors or different markers for each account. (Note: We do NOT connect the points on a scatter plot!)

Time (yrs)	Account 1	Ordered pair
Start	$1,000.00	
After 1 year	$1,060.00	
After 2 years	$1,120.00	
After 3 years	$1,180.00	
After 4 years	$1,240.00	
After 5 years		
After 10 years		
After 15 years		
After 20 years		
After 25 years		

Time (yrs)	Account 2	Ordered pair
Start	$1,000.00	
After 1 year	$1,050.00	
After 2 years	$1,102.50	
After 3 years	$1,157.63	
After 4 years	$1,215.51	
After 5 years		
After 10 years		
After 15 years		
After 20 years		
After 25 years		

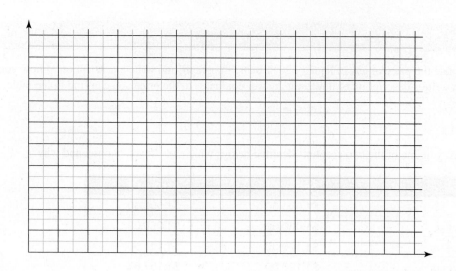

16. Explain why you chose the scale that you did for each axis.

17. Use the two scatter plots to write a verbal description of the differences between the growth of the two accounts. More detail is better!

18. In some cases, if the pattern of points in a scatter plot is relatively clear, we can connect the points to complete a graph. Do that now, drawing two graphs that represent the growth of the two accounts in Question 15. How would you describe the two graphs verbally?

> **Math Note**
>
> In Unit 3, we'll delve deeper into when it's appropriate to connect the points on a scatter plot, and how to find a graph that best fits a given plot.

Did You Get It

3. Draw a scatter plot for the data in the table, which represents the U.S. national surplus/deficit for even-numbered years for the period from 1998 to 2016. Positive numbers indicate the government taking in more money than it spent; negative numbers indicate the government spending more than it took in. All numbers are in billions of dollars. (Seriously. Billions.) Use years after 1998 on the horizontal axis, not the actual year.

Year	Surplus/Deficit
1998	70
2000	236
2002	−158
2004	−413
2006	−248
2008	−459
2010	−1,294
2012	−1,100
2014	−492
2016	−550

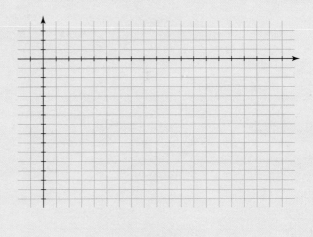

Using Technology: Creating a Scatter Plot

To create a scatter plot in Excel:

1. Type the values that will go on the *x* axis in one column. (This would correspond to the number of years in Question 15.)
2. Type the values that will go on the *y* axis in one column. (This would correspond to the value of the account in Question 15.)
3. Use the mouse to drag and select all the data in those two columns.
4. With the appropriate cells selected, click the **Insert** tab, then **Charts**, and click on Scatter. Then choose the type of scatter diagram you want. Options include plotting only the points, connecting the points with curves, and connecting the points with line segments.

You can add titles and change colors and other formatting elements by right-clicking on certain elements, or using the options on the **Charts** menu. Try some options and see what you can learn!

See the Lesson 1-5 Using Tech video in class resources for further information.

1-5 Portfolio

Name _____

Check each box when you've completed the task. Remember that your instructor will want you to turn in the portfolio pages you create.

Technology

1. ☐ Use Excel to create two different scatter diagrams for the ordered pairs in the table on page 71. The first should just have the points; the second should connect the points with curves. A template to help you get started can be found in the online resources for this lesson.

Online Practice

1. ☐ Include any written work from the online assignment along with any notes or questions about this lesson's content.

Applications

1. ☐ Complete the Applications problems.

Reflections

Type a short answer to each question.

1. ☐ If someone says that the point of graphing is plotting points and connecting the dots, how would you explain to him how very, very wrong he is? It'll be tough, but try to be nice.

2. ☐ Why do you think we use the word "ordered" in "ordered pair"?

3. ☐ Explain the advantages of graphed data over data in table form.

4. ☐ Name one thing you learned or discovered in this lesson that you found particularly interesting.

5. ☐ What questions do you have about this lesson?

Looking Ahead

1. ☐ Complete the Prep Skills for Lesson 1-6.

2. ☐ Read the opening paragraph in Lesson 1-6 carefully and answer Question 0 in preparation for that lesson.

?   **Answers to "Did You Get It?"**

1.

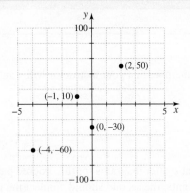

2. It looks a little above $3, maybe $3.10 or so. This isn't as precise as the $3.09 we can get from the table.

3.

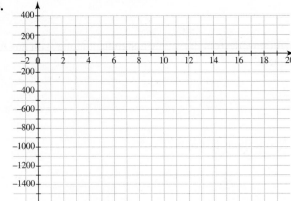

?   **Answers to "Prep Skills"**

1. **a.** 12–19   **b.** Anyone in the 35–44 range

   c. From ages 12–19 to 20–34 the rate increases, but then the rate decreases as age goes up.

2.

Hours since 12 P.M.	0	1	2	3	4	5	6	7	8

3. **a.**

   b.

1-5 Applications

Name _____

The hourly temperatures for Champaign, Illinois, on October 29, 2016, are given in the table. Use hours after midnight (NOT the actual time) as first coordinates, and the temperature as second coordinates.

Time	Temperature	Ordered Pair
12:00 AM	61°	
1:00 AM	63°	
2:00 AM	62°	
3:00 AM	62°	
4:00 AM	62°	
5:00 AM	64°	
6:00 AM	65°	
7:00 AM	63°	
8:00 AM	63°	
9:00 AM	68°	
10:00 AM	71°	
11:00 AM	74°	
12:00 PM	79°	
1:00 PM	81°	
2:00 PM	81°	
3:00 PM	81°	
4:00 PM	79°	
5:00 PM	77°	
6:00 PM	73°	
7:00 PM	70°	
8:00 PM	69°	
9:00 PM	67°	
10:00 PM	66°	
11:00 PM	66°	
12:00 AM	63°	

1. Write an ordered pair for each time and temperature pairing. Remember, the first coordinate is hours after midnight.

2. Decide on an appropriate scale for each axis and create a scatter plot for this data. Then connect the points with a smooth curve. Make sure that the lowest height on the graph corresponds to zero degrees.

Temperatures in Champaign, IL on October 29, 2016

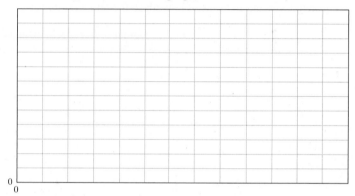

3. What do you need to find in the table to find when the temperature was highest during the day?

4. What do you need to look for on the graph to find when the high temperature was reached?

1-5 Applications

Name _____

5. Use your graph to estimate time spans when the temperature was increasing.

6. Use your graph to estimate time spans when the temperature was decreasing.

7. Draw a second graph for the data: This time make the lowest height on the graph correspond to 50°. Why is this second graph deceiving in terms of how much the temperature varies?

Temperatures in Champaign, IL on October 29, 2016

8. Draw scatter plots for the data in Questions 7 and 8 of Lesson 1-4 Applications, then connect the points with a smooth curve. Describe the shape of each graph, and describe conclusions you can draw for linear and exponential growth graphs.

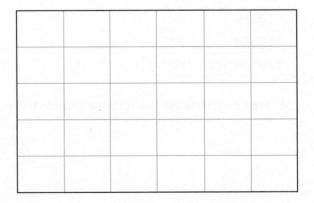

Lesson 1-6   Prep Skills

SKILL 1: REDUCE FRACTIONS

A fraction is in **lowest terms** or is **reduced** if there are no factors (other than 1) common to the numerator and denominator.

- $\frac{4}{6}$ is not in lowest terms because 2 is a factor of both 4 and 6.

- $\frac{6}{25}$ is in lowest terms because the factors of 6 are 1, 2, 3, and 6, while the factors of 25 are 1, 5, and 25.

The process of writing fractions in lowest terms is called **reducing fractions.** It's useful to do because it's easier to work with and interpret fractions when they're in lowest terms. For example, it's a lot easier to see that $\frac{5}{2}$ is two and a half than it is to see that $\frac{180}{72}$ is two and a half. To reduce a fraction, divide BOTH the numerator and denominator by any common factors.

- $\frac{4}{6} = \frac{4 \div 2}{6 \div 2} = \frac{2}{3}$ The greatest factor common to 4 and 6 is 2.

- $\frac{30}{12} = \frac{30 \div 6}{12 \div 6} = \frac{5}{2}$ The greatest factor common to 30 and 12 is 6.

SKILL 2: CONVERT BETWEEN FRACTIONS, DECIMALS, AND PERCENTS

To write a fraction in decimal form, you just need to perform the division, either by hand or with a calculator.

- $\frac{3}{5} = 0.6$

If the decimal doesn't terminate, it's usually appropriate to round. If a certain number of decimal places isn't required, use your judgment based on the context: How accurate would you want your answer to be in a given situation? Note that since you're rounding, the decimal is just an approximation of the exact fractional value.

- $\frac{3}{7} \approx 0.43$

To write a decimal in percent form, move the decimal two places to the right.

- $0.435 = 43.5\%$

To write a percent in decimal form, move the decimal two places to the left.

- $8.2\% = 0.082$

To write a percent in fraction form, write the fraction as $\frac{\text{Percent}}{100}$ and reduce. This makes sense because "percent" literally means "per hundred."

- $70\% = \frac{70}{100} = \frac{7}{10}$

PREP SKILLS QUESTIONS

1. Write each fraction in lowest terms.

   a. $\dfrac{12}{16}$ b. $\dfrac{65}{80}$

2. Write each percent in decimal form.

   a. 60%   b. 12.5%

3. Write each fraction in decimal and percent forms.

   a. $\dfrac{3}{5}$ b. $\dfrac{12}{16}$

4. Write each decimal in percent form.

   a. 0.13   b. 0.058

5. Write each percent in fractional form and reduce.

   a. 75%   b. 15%

Lesson 1-6   What Are the Chances?

LEARNING OBJECTIVES

☐ 1. Compute and interpret basic probabilities.

☐ 2. Translate a probability to a percent chance.

☐ 3. Recognize the difference between theoretical and empirical probability.

The 50–50–90 rule: Anytime you have a 50–50 chance of getting something right, there's a 90% probability you'll get it wrong.

——Andy Rooney

I'm planning on playing golf tomorrow, and my trusty Weather Puppy app tells me that there's a 10% chance of rain. So what exactly does that mean? Will it rain for 10% of the day tomorrow? Actually, a forecast like that is really just an educated guess: The forecaster is saying that there's about a 1 in 10 chance that it will rain at some point tomorrow, which means I'll probably stay dry on the golf course. For our purposes, "probably" is the key word in the last sentence. That word indicates a certain likelihood that something will occur. In this lesson, we'll study *probability,* which is a way to assign a number or percentage to the likelihood of something occurring, like rain in Fairfield, Ohio, tomorrow.

Courtesy of Weather Puppy. Background photo: ©federico stevanin/Shutterstock RF

  0. Write about a time you've heard the word "probability" used outside of school.

1-6   Class

The **probability** of an event occurring is a description of how likely it is that the event will actually happen. Probability can be described using a number ranging from 0 to 1, a percentage between 0% and 100%, or using words like *impossible, unlikely, even chance, likely,* or *certain.*

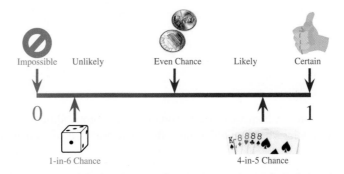

Impossible   Unlikely   Even Chance   Likely   Certain

0   1

1-in-6 Chance   4-in-5 Chance

1. The probability of rolling a 4 with one standard six-sided die is $\frac{1}{6}$ because there is one side with 4 dots, and six sides total that could be showing when the die stops. Write this probability in equivalent forms as a decimal (rounded to three places) and as a percentage (rounded to one decimal place).

2. Write a sentence describing the percent chance of rolling a 4 with one standard die.

3. If you rolled a die 300 times, how many times would you expect it to land on 4?

4. How sure are you that you'd get the number of 4s you'd expect in 300 rolls? Explain.

When we're thinking about a situation in which we'd like to compute some probabilities, we use the word **outcome** to refer to different possible results. For example, when you roll a single die, there are six distinct outcomes: the whole numbers from 1 through 6.

5. When a standard coin is flipped, how many different outcomes are possible in terms of which side lands face up?

6. Based on your answer to Question 5, what is the percent chance that a single coin lands on heads when flipped?

7. Write the probability from your answer to Question 6 as a fraction between zero and one, and describe the likelihood verbally.

Computing a Probability

The probability that a certain outcome occurs is the number of ways that outcome can occur divided by the total number of outcomes. To represent the probability of an outcome, we use a capital P, and briefly describe the outcome in parentheses following the P. So a formula for probability is

$$P(\text{outcome}) = \frac{\text{Number of ways that outcome can occur}}{\text{Total number of outcomes}}$$

For example, the probability of rolling a 4 with one die is

$$P(\text{rolling 4}) = \frac{1}{6} \text{ or just } P(4) = \frac{1}{6}$$

This would be read as "P of 4 is one sixth."

Did You Get It

Try this problem to see if you understand the concepts we just studied. The answer can be found at the end of the Portfolio section.

1. Suppose that you decide to take 1 day off per week from your phone, and just turn it off and leave it at home all day. If you choose the day of the week randomly, what is the probability that you'll go without your phone on Wednesday? What about on a day that ends with the letter y? Use probability notation to write your answers.

8. If you flipped a penny 80 times, about how many times would you expect it to land heads up?

9. Would you definitely get the number of heads you found in Question 8? Discuss.

10. The probability diagram on page 75 contains a picture of a good hand in poker: four 8s. If you were to randomly pick a card from that hand, what's the probability that it would be an 8? Write as a fraction between zero and one and as a percent. Use probability notation.

11. Write a sentence describing the percent chance of drawing the king from that hand of cards.

Each of the probabilities that we've calculated so far can be found without doing any actual experiments: We know for sure that when we roll a die, there are six possible results, and only one of them is a 4. This type of probability is known as **theoretical probability**. Our calculations are based on observing how many outcomes are possible, how many fit a certain criteria, and assuming that each of the outcomes is as likely as any other to occur. If the die were weighted strangely to make 4 more likely to come up than other numbers, our probability calculation wouldn't be accurate anymore.

In that case, we might turn our attention to **empirical probability**. We could roll the die a bunch of times—let's say 100—and record how many times 4 comes up. If we then divide the number of times we got 4 by the total number of rolls, that would give us an approximate percent chance of rolling 4.

1-6   Group

Empirical Probability Lab

Supplies needed: A standard playing card, a dime, and scotch tape.

The point: If you flip a standard playing card and let it fall to the floor, the theoretical probability of it landing face up is 1/2. We can change the probability by making one side heavier; then it would make sense to compute an empirical probability.

The procedure: Tape the dime to the back side of the playing card. Then flip the card from eye level or higher, letting it fall to the floor without hitting anything. Note whether or not the front of the card lands face up. Repeat as many times as you think you need to in order to get a reasonable probability; any less than 20 would be a pretty bad idea. Record your results in the table using tally marks (l):

Number of flips	Times landing face up

1. Based on the results from your table, what is the percent chance that the card will land face up?

2. Write the percent chance as a probability between zero and one, then write a sentence describing how likely you think it is that the card will land face up.

3. Did you find the results of this experiment surprising based on how the card was altered? Explain.

4. Why was empirical probability a better idea than theoretical probability for this experiment?

Math Note

Experts have estimated that the probability of being struck by lightning is three times greater than the probability of winning $1 million or more in a lottery.

Did You Get It

2. The 2016 Cleveland Indians won 94 games and lost 67 during the regular season. What was their percent chance of winning any given game? What was the probability?

5. What's wrong with the logic displayed by Rachel in the following conversation? Explain in depth.

Rachel: I have a 50-50 chance of passing this exam.
Ross: Why do you say that? That doesn't sound very optimistic.
Rachel: Well, it's just like flipping a coin—there are two possibilities. I'll either pass or I won't. So I have a 50% chance of passing.

6. Make a list of some things you can do to change the probability of passing an exam.

7. There are 45 applicants for two really great jobs, and you're one of them. If every applicant has an equal chance, what's the probability that you'll get the job? Write your answer using probability notation.

8. Explain why theoretical probability is probably not a very realistic way of deciding your chances of landing the job in Question 7.

9. The promotional materials for a certain program at a community college boast that out of their 480 most recent graduates, 450 are currently working in the field. If you graduate in this program, describe what you think your chances are of getting a job. Include as many aspects as you can think of.

In many cases, you can use the results of existing surveys to compute empirical probabilities, eliminating the need to do an entire experiment on your own.

In 2016, *USA Today* reported on the results of a study where 1,005 adults were asked how long it took them to know if they could stay in a new job long term. The number of people giving each response is shown in the table.

Response	Number of people
Less than a week	231
Within a month	402
Half a year	241
Within a year	60
Over a year	71

10. What's the probability that a randomly selected worker knew within a week if she could stay in her job long term?

11. What's the percent chance that a randomly chosen worker took more than a month to decide if she could stay in her job long term?

12. Write a sentence or two explaining how likely you think it is that your professor decided if he or she could stay in a job long term in a half year or less.

Did You Get It

3. What's the probability that a random worker feels like it took him just about a month to decide if he could stay in his job long term?

4. What's the percent chance that a random worker took a month or less to decide if he could stay in his job long term?

13. As we pointed out, 1,005 people were surveyed. The survey was done online. How accurate do you think the probabilities computed using this survey are when used to describe the feelings of all American workers? Discuss.

1-6 Portfolio

Name _____

Check each box when you've completed the task. Remember that your instructor will want you to turn in the portfolio pages you create.

Online Practice

1. ☐ Include any written work from the online assignment along with any notes or questions about this lesson's content.

Applications

1. ☐ Complete the Applications problems.

Reflections

Type a short answer to each question.

1. ☐ If someone asked you "What is probability, and why is it called that?", how would you answer?

2. ☐ Describe the relationship between probability and percent chance.

3. ☐ Describe the difference between theoretical and empirical probability. Which do you think is more reliable?

4. ☐ Name one thing you learned or discovered in this lesson that you found particularly interesting.

5. ☐ What questions do you have about this lesson?

Looking Ahead

1. ☐ Complete the Prep Skills for Lesson 1-7.

2. ☐ Read the opening paragraph in Lesson 1-7 carefully and answer Question 0 in preparation for that lesson.

Answers to "Did You Get It?"

1. $P(\text{Wednesday}) = \dfrac{1}{7}$; $P(\text{Ends in y}) = 1$

2. 58.4%; $P(\text{Winning}) = 0.584$

3. $P(\text{Within a month}) = 0.4$

4. About 63%

Answers to "Prep Skills"

1. **a.** $\dfrac{3}{4}$ **b.** $\dfrac{13}{16}$

2. **a.** 0.6   **b.** 0.125

3. **a.** 0.6; 60%   **b.** 0.75; 75%

4. **a.** 13%   **b.** 5.8%

5. **a.** $\dfrac{3}{4}$ **b.** $\dfrac{3}{20}$

1-6 Applications

Name _____

1. According to the United States Census Bureau, just about 51.5% of the adults in America are women. What would you say is the probability that the next adult you run into is female? What's the probability of that person being male?

2. There are 535 members of the United States Congress. Based on Question 1, how many would you expect to be female?

3. In reality, there are 104 women in Congress. What do you think that statistic says about politics in this country?

4. On one game show, contestants get to roll one die one time, and if they roll a number greater than 4, they win an all-expenses paid trip to Bora Bora (which, as it turns out, is an actual place. I used to think it was made up.) What is the probability of winning? Describe how good you'd feel about your chances if you got to play that game.

©Tero Hakala/123RF

5. In one math class, there are 30 students, 12 of whom are "nontraditional" in terms of age. If you randomly pick one person from that class, what's the probability that he or she will be of nontraditional age?

6. An online simulator helps students to understand their chances of passing a course based on study habits, attitude, attendance, work hours, sleep hours, and amount of homework completed. One student runs the simulation 10 times, with results shown in the table. Based on these results, discuss how likely you think it is that the student will pass. More detail is better.

Simulation	Result
1	Fail
2	Pass
3	Pass
4	Pass
5	Pass
6	Fail
7	Pass
8	Pass
9	Fail
10	Pass

7. What do you think is the probability that YOU will pass the math course you're in? Is this a set value, or can it change? If so, how?

Lesson 1-7   Prep Skills

SKILL 1: EVALUATE POWERS OF TEN

When 10 is raised to a positive power, the result is always 1 followed by a number of zeros. That number of zeros matches the exponent.

- $10^7 = 10,000,000$ Exponent is seven: seven zeros

When 10 is raised to a negative power, the result is always a number less than one. The decimal form begins with a number of zeros and ends with 1. The number of zeros is one less than the size of the exponent.

- $10^{-4} = 0.0001$ Exponent is negative four: three zeros

SKILL 2: WRITE REPEATED MULTIPLICATION AS AN EXPONENT

Positive integer exponents are used to represent repeated multiplication. If a number, like 5, is multiplied by itself three times, we write it as 5^3.

- $12 \cdot 12 \cdot 12 \cdot 12 \cdot 12 = 12^5$

Negative integer exponents also represent repeated multiplication, but the negative power indicates that the base should be put into the denominator of a fraction.

- $\dfrac{1}{3 \cdot 3 \cdot 3 \cdot 3} = 3^{-4}$

SKILL 3: MULTIPLY EXPONENTIAL EXPRESSIONS

To multiply two expressions involving exponents that have the same base, you simply keep the base as is, and add the exponents.

- $12^3 \cdot 12^6 = 12^9$ Bases are the same: add the exponents

SKILL 4: DIVIDE EXPONENTIAL EXPRESSIONS

To divide two expressions involving exponents that have the same base, you simply keep the base as is, and subtract the exponents.

- $\dfrac{7^8}{7^2} = 7^6$ Bases are the same: subtract the exponents

PREP SKILLS QUESTIONS

1. Evaluate 10^5

2. Evaluate 10^{-3}

3. Write the expression in exponent form: $8 \cdot 8 \cdot 8 \cdot 8 \cdot 8 \cdot 8 \cdot 8$

4. Write the expression in exponent form, with no fraction:

$$\frac{1}{10 \cdot 10 \cdot 10 \cdot 10 \cdot 10}$$

5. Perform each multiplication, writing your answer with a single exponent:

$10^5 \cdot 10^{12}$ $\qquad$ $8^{-3} \cdot 8^2$

6. Perform each division, writing your answer with a single exponent:

$\dfrac{5^7}{5^3}$ $\qquad$ $\dfrac{10^4}{10^{11}}$

Lesson 1-7   Debt: Bad. Chocolate: Good

LEARNING OBJECTIVES

☐ 1. Convert numbers between decimal and scientific notation.

☐ 2. Describe the significance of writing numbers in scientific notation.

Worrying is like paying on a debt that may never come due.
                    —Will Rogers

©iStockphoto/Getty Images RF

According to an article posted to the *Motley Fool* website in May 2016, the average household in the United States has a little over $93,000 in debt. This is the amount of money that they need to pay back at some point. That's not a good thing, and sounds like an awful lot. Until you realize that as I write this, the federal government's total debt is—get this—$19,804,594,378,489. If I were a betting man, which I'm not on account of being too cheap to risk losing money, I'd be willing to bet that over three quarters of the population can't even pronounce that number, let alone comprehend how ridiculously large it is. (For the record, it's 19 trillion, 804 billion, 594 million, 378 thousand, 489 dollars.) If you decided to pitch in and help out, sending $10 to the government to help defray some of the debt, your contribution would amount to 0.0000000000505% of the debt. Thanks for the effort, big spender!

In certain fields, like governmental finance and the sciences, it's common to work with incredibly large or incredibly small numbers. Using regular decimal notation, this can be pretty cumbersome: do 0.0000004 and 0.000000004 look very different to you? One is a *hundred times as big* as the other! In this lesson, we'll use federal debt and melted chocolate to study a special way of writing very small or very large numbers in a more readable, convenient way.

0. What do you think are some of the reasons we'll be interested in an efficient way to work with really large and really small numbers in this lesson?

1-7   Class

If you track the national debt over the last 90 years or so, it can be modeled fairly accurately by the type of exponential growth we studied in Lesson 1-4. On average, the debt has grown by about 7.9% per year. If that trend continues, by 2050, it would be $276,205,000,000,000, and by 2100 it would be $12,300,000,000,000,000.

If you're like most people (including me, so don't feel bad) you have NO idea what those numbers actually mean. They're just too big to get any perspective on them other than "wow, those are really big." To make it easier to understand and work with numbers of ludicrous size, we'll use a clever method for writing them using exponents.

Consider the number 300, which can also be written as 3×10^2, which is of course 3×100. If you're thinking "that's silly," hang in there . . . there is a point. Take a look at the first handful of powers of 10:

$$10^1 = 10 \qquad 10^2 = 100 \qquad 10^3 = 1,000 \qquad 10^4 = 10,000 \qquad 10^5 = 100,000$$

Do you see the pattern? Each extra power of 10 puts another zero on the decimal equivalent. In fact, the power indicates exactly the number of zeros included. Here's why this is helpful: Five billion is a tremendously large number: 5,000,000,000. Notice that there are nine zeros, so we can write five billion as 5×10^9, which is more concise and easier to read. If that makes sense to you, then you understand the idea behind *scientific notation*.

Now let's take a look at some debt numbers. In 1930, the national debt was about $16 billion. By 1985, it had grown to about $1.823 trillion. Whatever, right? Both are huge numbers. But let's look at them in scientific notation:

$$1930 : \$1.6 \times 10^{10} \qquad 1985 : \$1.823 \times 10^{12}$$

Because the first part of a number in proper scientific notation is ALWAYS a number between 0 and 10, you can easily compare the sizes of numbers by looking at the size of the exponent. The second exponent (12) is 2 bigger than the first (10). That tells us that the second debt has two more digits to the left of the decimal point in its decimal expansion, which makes it 100 times as big. Simple!

1. Earth is about 2.57×10^7 miles from Venus, and about 4.67×10^9 miles from Pluto. About how many times further away is Pluto? (Careful . . . there's more to think about than the size of the exponent.)

Writing Large Numbers in Scientific Notation

1. Write a decimal point at the end of the number, then move it left so that there is just one digit before it.

2. Multiply the result by 10 to some power. The power will be the number of places you moved the decimal.

Example: 3,968,000

3,968,000. (decimal moved six places)

3.968 (the extra zeros are unnecessary)

3.968×10^6

For Questions 2 and 3, write each number in scientific notation.

2. The number of people in the United States in November 2015: 322,146,000

3. The distance in miles from Earth to the Moon: 238,900

We can also use scientific notation to write very small numbers, using negative powers of 10:

$$10^{-1} = \frac{1}{10} = 0.1 \qquad 10^{-2} = \frac{1}{10^2} = 0.01 \qquad 10^{-3} = \frac{1}{10^3} = 0.001 \qquad 10^{-4} = \frac{1}{10^4} = 0.0001$$

This time, the pattern is that when the negative exponent gets larger by one (meaning more negative), the decimal point slides one spot to the left. So, for example, 0.03 is the same as 3×10^{-2}.

Writing Small Numbers in Scientific Notation

1. Move the decimal point right so that there is just one nonzero digit before it. Drop all zeros that come before that digit.

2. Multiply the result by 10 to some power. The power will be the negative of the number of places you moved the decimal.

Example: 0.000437

0.000437 (decimal moved four places)

4.37

4.37×10^{-4}

In Questions 4 and 5, write each number in scientific notation.

4. A typical flu virus measures between 0.000 000 08 and 0.000 000 12 meters in length.

5. *E. coli* is a common bacterium that can cause intestinal issues. A typical specimen is about 0.000 007 meters long.

6. Based on the size of the exponent in scientific notation, which is bigger: a small flu virus, or a typical *E. coli* sample? How many times bigger?

Did You Get It

Try this problem to see if you understand the concepts we just studied. The answer can be found at the end of the Portfolio section.

1. Convert each number to scientific notation.
   a. 0.0098   b. 1,478   c. 54,302,000   d. 0.000 0058

Now that we're good at converting from decimal to scientific notation, it would seem appropriate, if not expected, to work on the reverse: converting back from scientific to decimal notation. So that's just what we'll do.

Converting from Scientific to Decimal Notation

1. If the power of 10 is positive, move the decimal point to the right the same number of places as the exponent. You might need to put in zeros as placeholders when you run out of digits. Putting in commas will make it easier to read a large number.

Example: 4.01×10^8

4.01   (decimal moved eight places)

401,000,000   (fill in extra zeros)

Example: 3.2×10^{-5}

2. If the power of 10 is negative, move the decimal point to the left the same number of places as the exponent, again putting in zeros as needed.

3.2   (decimal moved five places)

0.000032

---

7. Write each number in decimal notation.

   a. The number of red blood cells per microliter of blood in an average healthy man: 5.4×10^6

   b. The mass of an average human ovum: 3.6×10^{-9} kg

Did You Get It

   2. Convert each number to decimal notation.

     a. 6.3×10^7 b. 2.973×10^{-3} c. 4.999×10^5 d. 9.103×10^{-6}

Now let's see if you really understand scientific notation.

8. When a number written in scientific notation has a positive exponent on 10, what can we say for sure about the number?

9. If a number between 0 and 1 is written in scientific notation, what can we say about the exponent on 10?

10. Fill in the blanks: If a number in scientific notation has a negative exponent on 10, to convert to decimal form, move the decimal place _____ because the number is _____.

Using Technology: Scientific Notation in Calculators and Excel

Spreadsheets and graphing calculators are both programmed to provide answers in scientific notation only if the size of the result is especially large or small.

TI-84 Plus Calculator

```
99*125
                  12375
990000*125000
            1.2375E11
(1.5E12)(3.2E-8)
                  48000
```

Source: Texas Instruments

Notice that whether the numbers are entered in decimal or scientific notation, the result is in scientific notation only if it's very large. The calculator displays 1.2375×10^{11} as 1.2375E11.

To input 1.5×10^{12} in scientific notation:

Press 1.5 [2nd] [,] 12. This is listed as "EE" on the calculator.

If you want to force the results of calculations to be in scientific notation, put the calculator in scientific mode:

Press [MODE] [▷] [ENTER] to set the calculator to scientific mode. The result:

```
NORMAL SCI ENG
FL 99*125
RA           1.2375E4
FU
CO
SE
RE
FU
SE
```

Excel

C1 ▼		f_x =A1*B1	
	A	B	C
1	99	125	12375
2	990000	125000	1.24E+11
3	1.50E+12	3.20E-08	48000
4			
5	99	125	1.24E+04

Notice that in rows 1–3, Excel decides whether or not to put the result in scientific notation depending on its size.

To input 1.5×10^{12} in scientific notation, as in cell A3, type 1.5E12. Excel will interpret this as scientific notation.

If you compare rows 1 and 5, you can see that the product is the same in each case: 99 * 125. The difference in the format of the output is based on the formatting option chosen for the cell. In cell C1, the **General** format was chosen from the **Number** menu, in which case Excel decides on the format as mentioned. In cell C5, **Scientific** was chosen from the **Number** menu, so the result is shown in scientific notation regardless of its size.

See the Lesson 1-7 Using Tech video in class resources for further instruction.

11. Write the result of the calculation on the calculator screen in scientific and decimal notation.

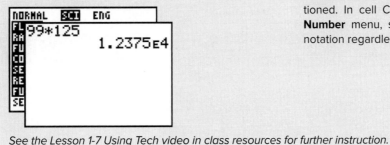

```
(2.4E-8)*(3.1E11
)
             7.44E3
```

In the opening paragraphs for this lesson, we pointed out that when a large number is written in decimal form, it can be pretty difficult to even know how to pronounce the number. In scientific notation, however, it's easier, provided that you know the powers of ten that correspond to various numbers. Some common examples are provided in the following box.

Number	Corresponding power of 10
Hundred	10^2
Thousand	10^3
Million	10^6
Billion	10^9
Trillion	10^{12}

12. The size of the national debt in dollars for selected years from 1930 to 2015 is shown in the table and the graph. In the third column of the table, write how the debt would be read aloud.

Year	Debt in dollars	Pronunciation
1930	1.60E + 10	$16 billion
1940	5.10E + 10	
1950	2.57E + 11	
1960	2.86E + 11	
1970	3.71E + 11	
1980	9.08E + 11	$908 billion
1990	3.233E + 12	
2000	5.674E + 12	
2010	1.3562E + 13	
2015	1.8151E + 13	

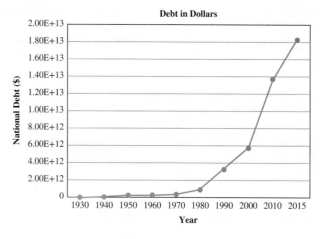

13. The population of the United States was roughly 1.23×10^8 in 1930, and 3.2×10^8 in 2015. If the national debt were to be paid off by dividing the total amount evenly among all citizens, how much would each have owed in 1930? What about in 2015?

Did You Get It

3. The United States government spent about $\$3.7 \times 10^{12}$ in 2015. How much did they spend on average for each person in the country?

1-7   Group

A fun fact: You can use a microwave oven and a bar of chocolate to measure the speed of light. Really! Microwaves are electromagnetic waves, just like visible light. The difference is the wavelength of these waves: For visible light, the wavelengths are in the neighborhood of 10^{-6} m, while microwaves are close to 10^{-2} m. Basically, microwaves emitted in an oven make molecules in food vibrate, which causes heat. The first places to heat up are separated by half of a wavelength, so by using something that starts to melt visibly in certain spots, we can calculate the wavelength. We can then use that to calculate the speed of light, which I think we can all agree is pretty darn cool.

If your teacher is unusually adventurous, he or she might bring in a microwave and chocolate bars, in which case you can perform the experiment on your own. Start with around 20 seconds, and make sure you take out the carousel: The chocolate has to stay stationary. (And now you know why a lot of microwaves have a carousel: Food heats more thoroughly at the spots corresponding to half of the wavelength.)

In case no microwave and chocolate are available, I did the experiment at home and took a picture for you, which is reproduced below. It's a life-size scale, so you can measure the distance between the melted spots with a ruler.

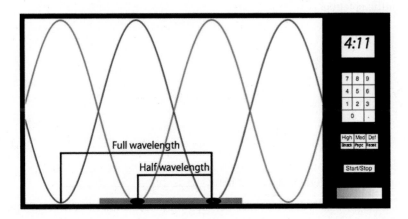

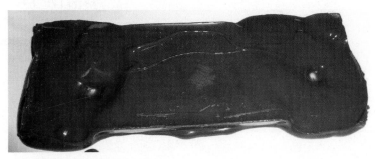

Courtesy of Dave Sobecki

1. Measure the distance between melted spots on your chocolate, trying to measure from center to center. Record your distance below, remembering that this is half the wavelength of the microwaves.

   Distance: _____ cm

2. Convert the half-wavelength to meters. (Think about what the prefix "centi" means!)

   Distance: _____ m

3. Write the full wavelength: _____ m

4. If you have any, eat the chocolate.

5. For electromagnetic waves, the speed of light is the product of the wavelength and the frequency, which is the number of cycles per second (Hz). The frequency of most microwaves is 2.45 GHz: one GHz represents 10^9 cycles per second. Write the microwave frequency in scientific notation.

6. Use your answers to Questions 3 and 5 to calculate the speed of light in meters per second.

7. Use your phone or computer to look up the speed of light and write it here: _____

8. Find the error in your speed of light calculation. This is the difference between your calculation and the actual speed of light. What percent is this difference of the actual speed of light? (This is known as the percent error.) If your answer is WAY off, you might want to check the microwave to see if the frequency is different from 2.45 GHz.

Math Note

There's a link to a really cool video about how microwave ovens work in the online resources for this lesson.

9. This one requires some thought, but it will help you in the homework if you're successful. When a number is written in scientific notation with a negative exponent, it's almost always going to begin with a decimal point and a string of zeros in decimal notation. Looking over the conversion process, develop a rule for the number of zeros to start with.

10. Describe a couple of quantities that your group finds interesting that would be efficiently written in scientific notation. Describe why you think scientific notation would be reasonable for the quantities.

1-7 Portfolio

Name _____

Check each box when you've completed the task. Remember that your instructor will want you to turn in the portfolio pages you create.

Technology

1. ☐ Watch the video on scale linked in the online resources for Lesson 1-7. Then tell everyone you know how cool it is. Even people you don't like.

Online Practice

1. ☐ Include any written work from the online assignment along with any notes or questions about this lesson's content.

Applications

1. ☐ Complete the Applications problems.

Reflections

Type a short answer to each question.

1. ☐ What is the point of scientific notation?

2. ☐ When a number is in scientific notation, how can you tell if it's really large or really small? Explain.

3. ☐ Name one thing you learned or discovered in this lesson that you found particularly interesting.

4. ☐ What questions do you have about this lesson?

Looking Ahead

1. ☐ Complete the Prep Skills for Lesson 1-8.

2. ☐ Read the opening paragraph in Lesson 1-8 carefully and answer Question 0 in preparation for that lesson.

Answers to "Did You Get It?"

1. **a.** 9.8×10^{-3} **b.** 1.478×10^{3} **c.** 5.4302×10^{7} **d.** 5.8×10^{-6}
2. **a.** 63,000,000   **b.** 0.002973   **c.** 499,900   **d.** 0.000009103
3. $11,562.50

Answers to "Prep Skills"

1. 100,000
2. 0.001
3. 8^{7}
4. 10^{-5}
5. 10^{17}; 8^{-1}
6. 5^{4}; 10^{-7}

1-7   Applications

Name _____

1. According to the *Motley Fool,* in 2014 there were 148.6 million personal federal tax returns filed, and the average amount of tax paid per filer was $9,118. Write each of these numbers in scientific notation.

2. How much money total did the government take in from these taxpayers? Perform the calculation in scientific notation, and write how your answer would be pronounced.

©danielfela/Shutterstock RF

3. An American dollar bill is 4.3×10^{-3} inches thick. If all of the tax revenue from Question 2 was paid in dollar bills, how many inches high would it be if they were all put in one stack? Write your answer in decimal notation.

4. To convert a number of inches into a number of miles, you divide by $12 \times 5,280$, which is the number of inches in a mile. How many miles high is our stack of tax proceeds?

5. The earth is 9.3×10^{7} miles from the sun. What percentage of the way to the sun would that big old stack of dollar bills reach? Write in both scientific and decimal notation.

1-7   **Applications**

Name _____

6. Okay, enough silliness: back to more realistic calculations. The total amount of money taken in by the federal government in 2014 was about 3.02 trillion dollars. What percentage of this revenue came from personal income taxes? (Refer back to Question 2.)

7. Among those earning 10 million dollars or more, the average amount of taxes paid was 7.88×10^6. That's an awful lot of money. But what percentage is that of the government's revenue? Write in both decimal and scientific notation.

8. How did the amount of money taken in by the government in 2014 compare to the amount spent, which was 3.51×10^{12}? What can you conclude? (A good answer will say something about the national debt.)

Lesson 1-8   Prep Skills

SKILL 1: READ NUMBERS FROM A DIAGRAM

In Lesson 1-8 it will be really useful to identify information found in different parts of a diagram. The key skill is to clearly identify which part of a diagram is relevant in a given setting.

- The diagram below shows the number of students in the third-floor classrooms of a campus building during the 11:30–12:25 time block on my campus.

- There were 24 students in room 302.

- There were 4 more students in room 305 than there were in room 304.

- If there were 40 students combined in rooms 324 and 327, there must have been 40 − 33 = 7 students in room 327.

PREP SKILLS QUESTIONS

1. How many students were in room 309?

2. How did the number of students in room 305 compare to the combined number in rooms 301 and 302?

3. If there were 235 students total on that floor, how many were in room 327?

Lesson 1-8   What's Your Type?

LEARNING OBJECTIVES

☐ 1. Analyze how your personality type affects how you interact with others.

☐ 2. Create and interpret Venn diagrams.

☐ 3. Describe sets using appropriate terminology.

©Stockbyte/Punchstock RF

The meeting of two personalities is like the contact of two chemical substances; if there is any reaction, both are transformed.
> —Carl Gustav Jung

In almost every walk of life, from social, to academic, to professional, working with and interacting with other people is important. But how many people actually take the time to think and learn about what may be the single most important aspect of their lives? In my view, one of the best things about higher education is being exposed to people with different backgrounds and ideas. When you learn to embrace the value of diversity, a new world of learning and social opportunities opens before you. In this lesson, we'll learn about different personality types and think about how your type affects the way you interact with others in a learning environment.

   In preparation for this class, you should have taken an online personality assessment. The result is a four-letter code that describes your specific personality type. The code is made up of a combination of 8 letters in four pairs, so we'll begin by learning what each letter represents.

First pair: E (Extrovert) or I (Introvert)

Extroverts draw energy from action, preferring to act, then reflect, then adjust actions based on that reflection. Introverts expend energy from action, and prefer to think first, then act upon the thoughtful planning that they've done.

Second pair: S (Sensing) or N (Intuition)

Those with a preference for sensing prefer to base their thoughts and actions on concrete things that they can observe with their five senses; they distrust hunches and "gut feelings." The intuition people tend to trust information that is more abstract or theoretical, and information gathered from previous thoughts and experiences shared by others.

Third pair: T (Thinking) or F (Feeling)

Thinking and feeling are known as the decision-making functions; both are used to make conscious, rational decisions based on the data received from either sensing or intuition. Those with a thinking preference tend to make decisions based on what seems most logical and reasonable with a bit less regard for emotional impact. The feeling preference indicates a tendency toward decision making from a more emotional and empathetic viewpoint, trying to achieve balance and consensus among all people affected by a decision.

Fourth pair: J (Judging) or P (Perceiving)

These types are about the style you prefer when interacting with the outside world. A person with the judging preference is most likely to approach actions with a plan in place, preferring organization, preparation, and staying on schedule. The perceiving style folks are perfectly fine with "playing it by ear," making up the plan as they go. They're flexible and adaptive, and like new opportunities and challenges to pop up.

0. If you took the online personality inventory, write your four-letter code here. If you're unable to take the online inventory, choose one letter from each pairing that you feel best fits your personality, then write the code here.

1-8   Class

Now that we know a little bit about personality characteristics, we'll use a new type of graph known as a **Venn diagram** to see how your personality type compares to others, and later you'll reflect on how this might affect working with others in groups. Venn diagrams are used to represent sets of objects (in this case the letters from the Myers Briggs personality test) and visualize what they have in common, and how they differ.

1. Pair up with someone else in the class, and write your partner's code here: _____
   (It would be a good idea to pick someone who doesn't have the exact same type as you.)

2. Label the two circles in the Venn diagram with one of your names on each line.

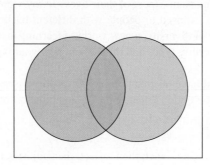

3. Write the letters your personality type has in common with your partner's in the overlapping portion of the two circles.

4. Write any letters in your personality type but NOT your partner's inside the circle labeled with your name, but outside the overlapping portion.

5. Write any letters in your partner's personality type but NOT yours inside the circle labeled with your partner's name, but outside the overlapping portion.

6. Write the remaining letters that don't appear in either code outside the circles, but inside the rectangle.

7. This Venn diagram shows which personality traits you have in common with your partner, and which you each have separately. Write a description of what the diagram says to you.

Venn diagrams are used all the time in studying *sets*. A **set** is any collection of objects, like the letters that make up your personality type. We'll prefer to work with sets that are **well-defined**: A set is well-defined if you can objectively determine (based on facts, not opinion) whether an object does or does not belong in a set.

8. Which of the following sets is well-defined? Why?
   a. The set of all good shows available to binge watch on Netflix
   b. The set of shows with all seasons available on Netflix

Each object in a set is called an **element** or a **member** of a set. One method of describing a set is called the **roster method**, in which elements are listed between braces, with commas between the elements. The order in which we list elements isn't important: $\{2, 5, 7\}$ and $\{5, 2, 7\}$ are the same set.

Often, we will name sets by using a capital letter. We might name the set of objects in the left circle in the diagram in Question 2 using the letter A.

9. Use the roster method to list the elements of the left circle: $A = \{$_____, _____, _____, _____$\}$

The **universal set** is the set of all objects under consideration in a given situation (not all the objects in the universe, which would be silly).

10. In the case of the letters from the personality test, the universal set could be written as: $U = $ _____

The **complement** of a set is the set of all objects from the universal set that are not in that set. The complement of a set A is denoted A'.

11. For the set A that you wrote above, what is A'?

Notice that there are four distinct regions in a Venn diagram illustrating two sets A and B. We'll want to number the regions for reference; we use Roman numerals so that we don't confuse the number of the region with elements in the set.

12. Write the appropriate description next to each region. Pick your answer from the following list:

the elements in set B that are not in set A.
the elements in both sets A and B.
the elements in the universal set that are in neither set A nor set B.
the elements in set A that are not in set B.

Region I represents

Region II represents

Region III represents

Region IV represents

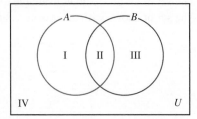

13. The set of elements that are in both sets A and B is called the **intersection of A and B**, and is symbolized $A \cap B$. Write the region or regions in the Venn diagram that correspond to $A \cap B$.

14. The set of elements that are in at least one of sets A and B is called the **union of A and B**, and is symbolized $A \cup B$. Write the region or regions in the Venn diagram that correspond to $A \cup B$.

Did You Get It

Try these problems to see if you understand the concepts we just studied. The answers can be found at the end of the Portfolio section.

1. If the universal set is the days of the week, write the set D of days beginning with the letter T or S using the roster method. Then do the same for the complement of set D.
2. Which region(s) in the Venn diagram correspond(s) to the set A'?

1-8 Group

We can also draw Venn diagrams with three circles to study interactions between three different sets. In this activity, you'll compare characteristics with two other people in your group.

1. Complete the following Venn diagram by placing the letter next to each statement in the appropriate location. For example, if the two people corresponding to the top two circles like to study late at night and the third doesn't, you should put A in the portion marked with the arrow.

A. Like to study late at night
B. Like to study early in the morning
C. Like to get work done early
D. Like to put work off to the last minute
E. Will miss very few classes
F. Usually miss a lot of classes
G. Working a job for 20 or more hours per week

H. Working a job for less than 20 hours per week
I. Taking 15 hours or more of classes
J. Taking less than 15 hours of classes
K. Have children
L. Do not have children
M. Feel confident in most math courses
N. Do not feel confident in most math courses

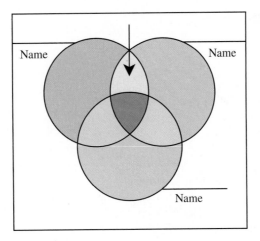

2. Write any observations you find interesting from the completed diagram.

We've seen Venn diagrams where the stuff written inside the circles represents actual elements of the set represented by that circle. Often, when using Venn diagrams to organize information, we'll instead label portions of the diagram with the number of elements that live in that particular set.

The next Venn diagram illustrates the result of a study done on 400 entrees at 75 campus cafeterias. Use the results summarized in the Venn diagram to answer Questions 3–6.

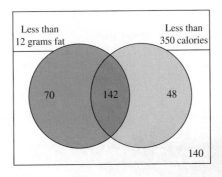

3. How many meals had less than 12 grams of fat and less than 350 calories?

4. How many meals had less than 350 calories?

5. How many had less than 12 grams of fat?

6. How many had over 350 calories and over 12 grams of fat?

Arranging the results of surveys is a really common application of Venn diagrams. The way that questions are asked in a survey can have a big effect on the results. Here are two different ways that students could be surveyed on usage of credit and debit cards:

What type of card do you carry? Choose one	
Credit	☐
Debit	☐
Neither	☐

What type of card do you carry? Choose one	
Credit	☐
Debit	☐
Both	☐
Neither	☐

7. According to Sallie Mae's 2013 "How America Pays for College" report, 800 undergraduate students were asked about their credit and debit card habits: 616 reported carrying a debit card and 240 a credit card. Which of the two questions above was asked? How can you tell?

8. Why does the first question kind of stink as a survey question?

9. The survey reported that 216 of the students reported having both types of cards. Which region in the Venn diagram should be labeled with 216? Label it!

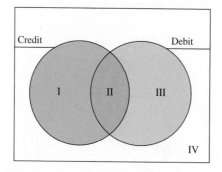

10. Does the fact that the report said that 616 students reported carrying a debit card mean that all 616 carried ONLY a debit card? Explain.

In Questions 11–13, label appropriate sections of the Venn diagram as you find the requested information.

11. How many students carried only a debit card? Think carefully about Questions 9 and 10.

12. How many carried only a credit card?

13. How many carried neither card?

Did You Get It

3. In a 2013 survey reported by Public Policy Polling, 500 Americans were asked about their soft drink preferences. There were 240 who reported drinking regular soda, 185 who drink diet soda, and 15 who drink both. Use a Venn diagram to answer each question.

   a. How many drink only diet soda?
   b. How many drink neither?

According to a survey conducted by the National Pizza Foundation that I just now made up, out of 113 customers surveyed, 47 prefer pizza with pepperoni, 56 prefer sausage, and 30 prefer onion. These results are displayed in the next Venn diagram.

14. According to the information given in the previous paragraph, 47 customers prefer pizza with pepperoni. But notice that 47 doesn't appear in the diagram anywhere. Why not?

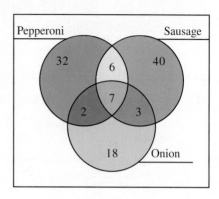

15. How many customers prefer pizza with only sausage (and none of the other two ingredients)?

16. How many customers prefer pizza with all three ingredients?

17. How many prefer pizza with sausage and onion?

18. I hate to call anyone boring, but . . . how many go the boring route (none of these items)?

1-8 Portfolio

Name _____

Check each box when you've completed the task. Remember that your instructor will want you to turn in the portfolio pages you create.

Technology

1. ☐ Find a Venn diagram online based on a topic that interests you. Copy and paste the image into your portfolio, then explain why you found it interesting, and what you learned from it.

Online Practice

1. ☐ Include any written work from the online assignment along with any notes or questions about this lesson's content.

Applications

1. ☐ Complete the Applications problems.

Reflections

Type a short answer to each question.

1. ☐ Think about what you learned about yourself from studying your personality type. How can you use this information in your academic and social lives?

2. ☐ Now consider your personality type as well as the Venn diagram at the top of page 109. How can you use what you learned to help you in this class, and other classes where group work is important?

3. ☐ Name one thing that you learned or discovered in this lesson that you found particularly interesting.

4. ☐ What questions do you have about this lesson?

Looking Ahead

1. ☐ Complete the Prep Skills for Lesson 1-9.

2. ☐ Read the opening paragraphs in Lesson 1-9 carefully and answer Question 0 in preparation for that lesson.

Answers to "Did You Get It?"

1. $D = \{$Tuesday, Thursday, Saturday, Sunday$)$; $D' = \{$Monday, Wednesday, Friday$\}$

2. Regions III and IV

3.

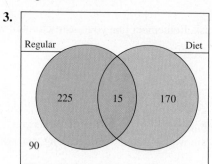

   a. Diet only: 170;   **b.** neither: 90

Answers to "Prep Skills"

1. 19 students

2. There are 12 fewer students in room 305 than in rooms 301 and 302 combined.

3. 24 students

1-8   Applications

Name _____

According to this diagram from Boston Children's Hospital, there are a lot of similarities between the symptoms you experience when you have a cold and symptoms caused by allergies.

1. List the set of cold symptoms using the roster method.

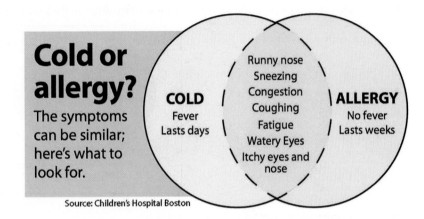

2. If C is the set of cold symptoms and A is the set of allergy symptoms, write the set $C \cap A$

3. Describe the symptoms that help you distinguish between a cold and allergies.

4. If C is the set of cold symptoms and A is the set of allergy symptoms, how would we represent the set below?

   {Fever, lasts days, runny nose, sneezing, congestion, coughing, fatigue, watery eyes, itchy eyes and nose, no fever, lasts for weeks}

In a survey of 130 college students, 108 use Instagram, 37 use Facebook, and 21 use both. Use this information to fill in the Venn diagram to the right, then use it to answer the questions.

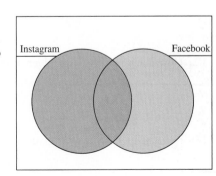

5. How many use Instagram only?

6. How many use Facebook only?

7. How many use neither?

1-8 Applications

Name _____

As the different types of bacteria that cause illness evolve into drug-resistant strains, it's becoming more common for doctors to treat infections with multiple antibiotics. Tuberculosis is one of the diseases where multiple medications are often used. A group of 200 patients with active TB infections enrolled in a clinical trial to test the effects of various antibiotics. The Venn diagram shows the number of patients who were given one or more of the three drugs in the trial. Use the diagram to answer Questions 8–13.

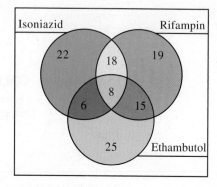

8. How many patients were given all three drugs?

9. How many patients were given just one drug?

10. How many patients were given Rifampin and Ethambutol but not Isoniazid?

11. How many patients were given exactly two of the three drugs?

12. How many patients were given at least Isoniazid and Ethambutol?

13. How many patients were given a placebo containing none of those three drugs?

Lesson 1-9   Prep Skills

SKILL 1: READ DATA FROM A LIST

Unorganized data can be difficult to read, especially if there are a lot of values, or many identical or similar values. In that case, rewriting the list in order is helpful.

The scores for 20 students on a 30-point quiz are listed here.

| 18 | 30 | 27 | 26 | 18 | 29 | 29 | 30 | 30 | 24 |
| 27 | 30 | 12 | 15 | 22 | 28 | 27 | 27 | 24 | 25 |

If we order the list, we get this:

| 12 | 15 | 18 | 18 | 22 | 24 | 24 | 25 | 26 | 27 |
| 27 | 27 | 27 | 28 | 29 | 29 | 30 | 30 | 30 | 30 |

- The most common scores are 27 and 30.
- The lowest score was 12 and the highest was 30.

SKILL 2: DRAW A BAR GRAPH

A bar graph is used to compare the sizes of different data values when those values come from distinct categories. On the list of quiz scores above, we see that there were 2 scores less than 18, 2 from 18–20, 1 from 21–23, 4 from 24–26, and 11 from 27–30. We could represent these numbers with a bar graph:

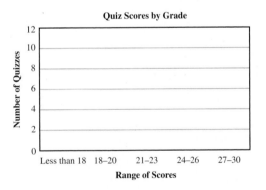

PREP SKILLS QUESTIONS

The data below are the number of classes missed in one semester by all students in a five-day-a-week math class.

| 2 | 4 | 0 | 1 | 1 | 10 | 6 | 2 | 3 | 8 | 0 | 1 |
| 3 | 0 | 18 | 2 | 0 | 3 | 3 | 0 | 1 | 5 | 4 | 2 |

1. Arrange the list in order from smallest to largest.

2. What number of days missed was most common?

3. What were the least and most days missed by anyone in the class?

4. Draw a bar graph that illustrates how many students missed 0 or 1 day, 2–4 days, 5–8 days, and more than 8 days.

Lesson 1-9   News in the Data Age

LEARNING OBJECTIVES

☐ 1. Explain the difference between a population and a sample.

☐ 2. Organize data with frequency distributions and histograms.

☐ 3. Analyze data with stem and leaf plots.

©scanrail/Getty Images RF

Errors using inadequate data are much less than those using no data at all.

—Charles Babbage

With the rise of online news sites and social media, many people have declared the death of traditional news sources in our country. But are newspapers really dead? Are they even sick? Statements like "Everyone just gets news online now" or "Who even reads a newspaper anymore?" aren't evidence—they're opinions. In order to decide if there really has been a significant decline in traditional news sources, we need to do better than listen to anecdotes or read opinions in 140 characters or less.

Instead, we would want to gather some **data**, which are measurements or observations that are gathered for an event under study. The term "data age" is coming into vogue to describe this era because of the vast amount of data that is available to anyone with Internet access and a web browser. But the expense of having access to so much data is that knowing how to gather data appropriately, and how to organize it into a useful form, is more important than it's ever been. So that's what we'll study in this lesson.

0. What types of data do you think it would be useful to look for in studying whether traditional newspapers are dying?

1-9   Class

There are a number of different approaches we could take in trying to evaluate the condition of traditional newspapers, but all of them would begin with gathering relevant data. We could study things like circulation numbers, advertising revenue, how many people read print newspapers compared to online news, and many others.

The table below shows the average daily circulation for newspapers in America for certain years from 2001 to 2015.

Year	2001	2003	2005	2007	2009	2011	2013	2015
Avg. circulation (thousands)	55.6	55.2	53.3	50.7	45.7	43.4	40.7	37.7

Source: Pew Research Center

1. What preliminary conclusions can you draw from the data in the table?

2. Draw a scatter plot of the data. Does this reinforce the conclusions you drew in Question 1, or would you adjust your conclusions now?

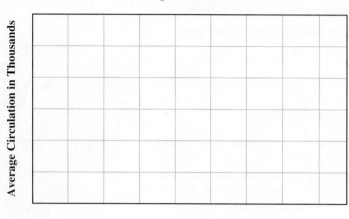

Average Circulation

Average Circulation in Thousands

Year

The data that we've seen so far seem to indicate a clear negative trend for newspaper circulation. But where did that data come from? If this takes into account ALL print newspapers in the country, that would certainly be more compelling than if the numbers came from just a handful. This brings up our first key idea in gathering data.

A **population** consists of all subjects under study. A **sample** is a representative subgroup or subset of a population.

3. In the case of the newspaper circulation numbers, the population would be _____.

4. A sample would be _____.

If we're going to use a sample to draw conclusions on a population, it's important that the sample is **representative**. A sample is considered representative if many different types of members of a population are included.

For Questions 5–8, which of the following do you think would be a representative sample when studying newspaper circulation?

5. Daily newspapers in the 10 biggest cities in the United States

6. One newspaper randomly chosen from each of the 50 states

7. All newspapers affiliated with a national media conglomerate

8. All newspapers in the country are listed alphabetically, and every 10th one is chosen.

Math Note

The word "data" is plural, so we say "data are" not "data is." The singular version is "datum." You don't hear that word very often because it's awfully hard to draw a meaningful conclusion from one tiny piece of information.

The circulation numbers that we've seen so far (as near as I can tell) are population data: While it's not 100% clear from the source, it appears that these numbers are an average of all print newspapers in America. The next data we study are not.

The next table shows the results of a 2015 survey in which adults who read newspapers were asked, "In what format do you read newspapers?"

Format	Percentage
Print only	51%
Print/Desktop computer	11%
Print/Desktop/Mobile device	14%
Desktop only	5%
Desktop/mobile	7%
Print/mobile	7%
Mobile only	5%

9. Which would be most effective in illustrating this data: scatter plot, pie chart, or bar graph? Why?

10. How can you tell that this data came from a sample, rather than a population?

11. It's a relatively common belief that print newspapers are becoming a thing of the past. Do you think the data above supports that idea? Explain.

Did You Get It

Try this problem to see if you understand the concepts we just studied. The answers can be found at the end of the Portfolio section.

1. Suppose that we're interested in the sources that students at your campus use to get news. Classify each of the groups below as population, representative sample, or not representative sample.

   a. A researcher stands next to a box where students can pick up a daily newspaper and asks where they typically get news.
   b. Every student on campus is required to answer a survey on news sources.
   c. Students are divided by class rank, and each student in each class with a student ID number that ends in 4 is surveyed.

1-9   Group

Frequency Distributions

The data collected for a statistical study are called **raw data**. Raw data can be really difficult to interpret; in order to describe situations and draw conclusions, we need to organize the data in a meaningful way. Two methods that we will use are *frequency distributions* and *stem and leaf plots*. First up, we'll study **categorical frequency distributions**, which are a way to organize data that are divided into distinct categories, like gender, your class standing in school, or conferences for college football teams.

A categorical frequency distribution is a table in which you list different categories, then count up how many individuals in a sample or population fall into each category and list those frequencies. In Questions 1 and 2, you'll create a categorical frequency distribution.

1. Twenty-eight college students were surveyed about what source they are most likely to get news from. Their responses are listed below. What should the categories be for this data? Why?

Social media	Print media	TV	Social media
Internet	Internet	Print media	Radio
TV	Radio	Internet	Internet
Print media	Internet	Internet	TV
Radio	Social Media	Internet	Radio
TV	TV	Social media	Radio
Internet	Internet	TV	Print media

2. Build a categorical frequency distribution by writing in your categories, then putting tally marks in the second column as you count the number of individuals in each category.

Categories	Tally marks	Frequency

3. Use your distribution to write some conclusions on the sources typical college students use to keep up on recent news. Do you think that there's enough data for your conclusions to be reliable?

As we saw in Lesson 1-1, we can use a bar graph to illustrate categorical data.

4. Below are two sets of axes that can be used to draw a bar graph illustrating the data in your frequency distribution. Draw a bar graph on each set of axes.

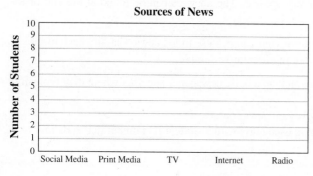

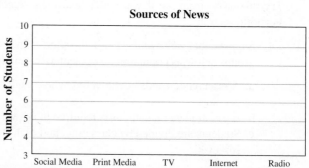

5. Which bar graph would you use if you wanted to exaggerate the difference between the number of students who indicated print media compared to radio? Explain why that graph would be misleading.

Did You Get It

2. A health-food store recorded the type of vitamin pills 35 customers purchased during a 1-day sale. Construct a categorical frequency distribution for the data.

C   C   C   A   D   E   C   E   E   A   B   D   C   E   C   E   C   C

C   D   A   B   B   C   C   A   A   E   E   E   E   A   B   C   B

3. Draw a bar graph based on the results of your frequency distribution.

Another type of frequency distribution that can be constructed uses numerical data and is called a **grouped frequency distribution**. In a grouped frequency distribution, the numerical data are divided into **classes**. For example, if you gathered data on the weights of people in your class, there's a decent chance that no two people have the exact same weight. In that case, everyone would be in a separate category, and each category would have one weight in it. This, of course, would make the frequency distribution no more useful than the original list of raw data!

So it would be reasonable to group people into weight ranges, like 100–119 pounds, 120–139 pounds, and so forth. In the 100–119 pound class, we call 100 the **lower limit** and 119 the **upper limit**.

We'll illustrate by organizing the following data. While the data we've seen indicate that print newspapers have been declining in circulation for many years, most news sources now have a significant online presence. The table lists the number of unique visitors (in thousands) to a number of different online news sources for the month of January 2015.

Site	Unique visitors (in thousands)	Site	Unique visitors (in thousands)
AZCentral.com	6.6	NYDailyNews.com	25.9
BostonGlobe.com	9.8	NYPost.com	22.9
ChicagoTribune.com	12.0	NYTimes.com	54.0
Chron.com	14.4	OregonLive.com	6.3
Cleveland.com	6.5	OrlandoSentinel.com	5.6
DailyMail.co.uk	51.1	SeattleTimes.com	6.1
DallasNews.com	7.0	SFGate.com	19.0
Freep.com	10.6	Telegraph.co.uk	16.8
Independent.co.uk	11.5	TheGuardian.com	28.2
LATimes.com	25.2	USAToday.com	54.5
Mirror.co.uk	12.0	WashingtonPost.com	47.8
Newsday.com	6.0	WashingtonTimes.com	7.0
Nola.com	6.0		

6. Why would a categorical frequency distribution be a bad idea for this data? (Hint: What would the categories be?)

Rather than using each individual data value as a separate category, we'll divide the entire range of data values into evenly spaced portions.

7. Note the classes we chose for dividing the data, and complete a frequency distribution by tallying up the number of sites that fall into each class.

Math Note

In a statistics class, you'll learn a lot about how to make good choices of classes when organizing data with a grouped frequency distribution.

Class	Tally marks	Frequency
5–14.9		
15–24.9		
25–34.9		
35–44.9		
45–54.9		

When data are organized in a grouped frequency distribution, we draw a special kind of bar graph to illustrate. This type of graph is called a **histogram**, and it differs from a bar graph in two main ways. First, the horizontal axis isn't labeled with category names, like Radio or 5–14.9. Because the data values are numerical, we'll label the horizontal axis in number line form, like the scatter plots and time-series graphs we've studied.

As a consequence of that labeling, we get a second difference: The bars won't be physically separated by blank space; instead, they'll be touching each other.

8. Using the axes shown, draw a histogram based on your frequency distribution.

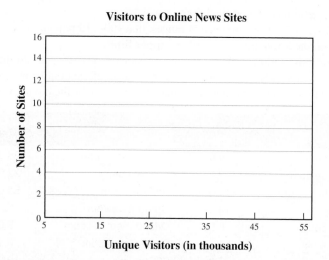

Visitors to Online News Sites

Comparison of Bar Graphs and Histograms

	Bar graph	Histogram
Use	Illustrating categorical data	Illustrating numerical data
Title	Included at top of graph	Included at top of graph
Bars	Include spaces between bars	Edges of bars touch: no spaces
Labels	Vertical scale is frequency or % Horizontal labels are categories	Vertical scale is frequency or % Horizontal labeled with a numeric scale

9. Write down at least three observations you can make based on your frequency distribution and histogram.

10. Look back at the raw data on visitors to news websites. Do any of the data values live exactly on one of the borders of the bars in your histogram?

11. Suppose that a different news site, let's just call it Wuzzup.com, had exactly 25.0 thousand visitors in January 2015. Looking *strictly at your histogram,* which bar would that data point raise the height of? In other words, which group of values does it go into, the ones from 15–25, or the ones from 25–35?

12. Now look at your *frequency distribution.* Which class would Wuzzup.com go into?

Did You Get It

4. The online homework system I use in my calculus classes allows me to track how much time students spend working on homework. In my two Calc 2 sections last semester, here are the average number of hours spent per week for each student. Construct a grouped frequency distribution and histogram for the data. Your classes should be 1–3, 4–6, 7–9, 10–12, 13–15, and 16–18.

1	2	6	7	12	13	2	6	9	5
18	7	3	15	15	4	17	1	14	5
4	16	4	5	8	6	5	18	5	2
9	11	12	1	9	2	10	11	4	10
9	18	8	8	4	14	7	3	2	6

Stem and Leaf Plots

Another way to organize data is to use a stem and leaf plot (sometimes called a stem plot). Each data value or number is separated into two parts. For a two-digit number such as 53, the tens digit, 5, is called the **stem,** and the ones digit, 3, is called its **leaf.** For the number 72, the stem is 7, and the leaf is 2. For a three-digit number, say 138, the first two digits, 13, are used as the stem, and the third digit, 8, is used as the leaf. For values rounded to the tenths place, like 8.4, you can use the value to the left of the decimal place as stem and the tenths place as leaf. In any case, the very last digit is used as the leaf, and what comes before is the stem. Note that we'll include a key with our plot that clarifies what the stems and leaves represent.

Market penetration has been a traditional print newspaper metric. It measures the number of newspapers sold in each market as a percentage of households and includes online readers as well. The top 25 papers in America in terms of market penetration are listed below, along with the percentage of households in their metropolitan area that they reach.

Paper	Market penetration	Paper	Market penetration
Arizona Daily Star	56	Memphis Commerical Appeal	52
Arkansas Democrat-Gazette	62	Milwaukee Journal-Sentinel	59
Austin American-Statesman	51	Minneapolis Star Tribune	52
Buffalo News	64	New Orleans Times-Picayune	64
Chattanooga Times Free Press	53	Oklahoman	49
Cincinnati/Kentucky Enquirer	54	Portland Oregonian	51
Columbus Dispatch	53	Richmond Times-Dispatch	58
Des Moines Register	68	Rochester Democrat and Chronicle	75
El Paso Times	52	San Antonio Express-News	53
Gannett Wisconsin	68	San Diego Union-Tribune	51
Honolulu Star-Advertiser	59	Syracuse Post-Standard	63
Kansas City Star	56	Washington Post	57
Louisville Courier-Journal	58		

13. If you were to build a grouped frequency distribution, what classes would you choose?

14. What will you choose to be the stems for this data? What about the leaves?

15. Do you think the data in this table come from a representative sample of all American newspapers in terms of market penetration? Why or why not?

16. List all of the first digits that appear in percentages in the table. (You don't need to repeat them if they appear more than once.)

17. Write your answers from Question 16 in order under "Stems" in the table below. Write the lowest value first, then larger values as you work your way downward.

18. Go through the data values in the table, and one by one write the second digit in each value under "Leaves," next to the corresponding stem. For example, since the first data value is 56, you'd write a 6 in the leaves column next to 5 in the stems column. Separate leaves that correspond to the same stem with some space, but not with commas. Put in ALL second digits, including repeats.

Stems	Leaves

Key: 5|6 means 56%

19. When drawing a stem and leaf plot, it's traditional to write the leaves in order from least to greatest. This makes it a lot easier to see what the spread of values looks like within one stem. Finish your stem and leaf plot by ordering the leaves.

Stems	Leaves

Key: 5|6 means 56%

Constructing a Stem and Leaf Plot

Step 1: Identify stems and leaves. The leaves will typically be the last digit in numeric data; the stems will be the digits that come before.

Step 2: Write "Stems" and "Leaves" with a horizontal line beneath them, and a vertical line separating them, extending downward.

Step 3: Write the stems you chose in order under "Stems," in order from least to greatest.

Step 4: Working through the data values one at a time, write each leaf to the right of the vertical line next to the corresponding stem. Leave spaces between leaves that are in the same row.

Step 5: Redraw your plot, putting all leaves within a given row in order from least to greatest.

Step 6: Write a key under your plot that describes what the data values mean. For example, if one of the stems is 51 and a corresponding leaf is 6, and this represents a data value of 51.6, write "51|6 means 51.6."

20. Write at least three observations you can make about the market penetration data from looking at your stem and leaf plot.

Did You Get It

5. It's no secret that gas prices have fluctuated wildly in the last few years, but from 1980–1999, they were surprisingly stable. According to the Energy Information Administration, the following data represent the average price (in cents) per gallon of regular unleaded gas for those years. Draw a stem and leaf plot of the data.

119	131	122	113	112	86	90	90	100	115
114	113	111	111	115	123	123	123	106	117

21. Compare grouped frequency distributions, histograms, and stem and leaf plots. How are they similar? Which do you think makes it easier to analyze a set of data?

Using Technology: Using the Sort Feature on a Calculator and a Spreadsheet

To sort data in Excel:

1. Enter the data.
2. Select the cells containing the data.
3. Click on the **Data** tab.
4. Click on **Sort**.
5. Select options and click OK.

To sort data on a TI-84 Calculator:

1. Enter the data in list **L1**. (Access L1 by first pressing **STAT** and **ENTER**.)

2. Press **2nd**, **STAT**, **▶**, **ENTER** to access the **SortA(** feature.

3. Press **2nd**, **STAT**, **ENTER** to input L1 after **SortA(**.

4. Press the **)** key and then press **ENTER**.

5. Go back to L1 and the data you entered should be sorted.

See the Lesson 1-9 Using Technology Video in class resources for further instruction.

1-9 Portfolio

Name _____

Check each box when you've completed the task. Remember that your instructor will want you to turn in the portfolio pages you create.

Technology

1. ☐ Excel can be used to do two tasks from this lesson that are both useful and tedious to do by hand: sorting data and building a grouped frequency distribution. In the online resources for this lesson, there's a spreadsheet that has two of the data sets from this lesson entered: student responses to the media survey, and usage numbers for 25 selected online media outlets. Your first job is to sort the data based on the instructions that appear on the spreadsheet. Note that there's a different worksheet for each data set, and you can change from one to another using the tabs along the bottom. After sorting, there will be further instructions on the template for building the frequency distribution.

Online Practice

1. ☐ Include any written work from the online assignment along with any notes or questions about this lesson's content.

Applications

1. ☐ Complete the Applications problems.

Reflections

Type a short answer to each question.

1. ☐ What is the point of sampling in statistics? What's the difference between a sample and a population?

2. ☐ How do frequency distributions, histograms, and stem and leaf plots help to organize data?

3. ☐ Why is it bad to have too few or too many categories in a grouped frequency distribution?

4. ☐ Name one thing you learned or discovered in this lesson that you found particularly interesting or useful.

5. ☐ What questions do you have about this lesson?

Looking Ahead

1. ☐ Complete the Prep Skills for Lesson 2-1.

2. ☐ Read the opening paragraph in Lesson 2-1 carefully and answer Question 0 in preparation for that lesson.

Answers to "Did You Get It?"

1. a. Not representative sample   **b.** Population   **c.** Representative sample

2.

Type	Tally marks	Frequency
A	⊤⊤⊤⊤ I	6
B	⊤⊤⊤⊤	5
C	⊤⊤⊤⊤ ⊤⊤⊤⊤ II	12
D	III	3
E	⊤⊤⊤⊤ IIII	9

3.

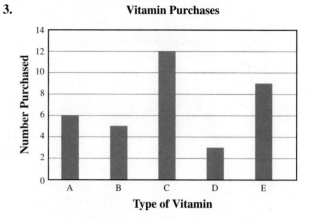

Vitamin Purchases

4.

Class	Tally marks	Frequency
1–3	⊤⊤⊤⊤ ⊤⊤⊤⊤	10
4–6	⊤⊤⊤⊤ ⊤⊤⊤⊤ IIII	14
7–9	⊤⊤⊤⊤ ⊤⊤⊤⊤	10
10–12	⊤⊤⊤⊤ I	6
13–15	⊤⊤⊤⊤	5
16–18	⊤⊤⊤⊤	5

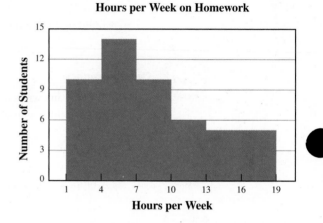

Hours per Week on Homework

5.

Stems	Leaves
8	6
9	0 0
10	0 6
11	1 1 2 3 3 4 5 5 7 9
12	2 3 3 3
13	1

Key: 13|1 means 131

Answers to "Prep Skills"

1. 0   0   0   0   0   1   1   1   1   2   2   2
        2   3   3   3   3   4   4   5   6   8   10   18

2. 0 days   **3.** 0 days; 18 days

4.

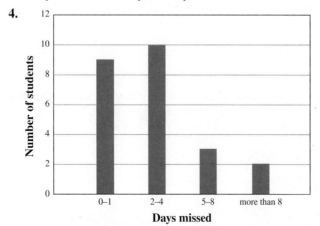

1-9 Applications

Name _____

Thirty random people at a subway station in New York City were asked what their most common source of news is: *The New York Times* (T), the *Post* (P), the *Daily News* (D), or some other source (O).

1. Do you think this would be a representative sample for all New Yorkers? Why or why not?

2. Responses are summarized below. Construct a frequency distribution for the data.

T	O	O	D	P	P	O	P	T	D
T	P	D	D	O	O	O	D	P	O
D	D	O	O	T	P	P	P	O	O

3. What single source do you think was the most common source of news? Can you be certain?

It can be difficult to compare monetary amounts over a large time span because of inflation and changes in the cost of living. For example, the median new home price in the United States in 1980 was about $65,000; in 2015 that number was about $296,000. In short, $65,000 in 1980 doesn't compare to $65,000 in 2015 because it's worth a LOT less.

To combat this, dollar comparisons are often done in inflation-adjusted dollars, which allows more accurate comparison. So if something had actually cost $100 in 1980, the inflation-adjusted cost might be more like $350 in 2015 dollars. The next data set we'll study lists amounts of money in inflation-adjusted 2015 dollars.

1-9   Applications

Name _____

This table shows overall advertising revenue for the American newspaper industry (in billions of inflation-adjusted 2015 dollars) for the years 1980 to 2015.

Year	Ad revenue	Year	Ad revenue	Year	Ad revenue	Year	Ad revenue
1980	42.9	1989	61.8	1998	62.4	2007	51.7
1981	42.8	1990	58.1	1999	64.9	2008	41.6
1982	42.3	1991	52	2000	66.3	2009	30
1983	48.3	1992	51	2001	58.1	2010	27.6
1984	52.5	1993	51.6	2002	56.5	2011	25
1985	55.1	1994	53.8	2003	58.4	2012	22.3
1986	56.9	1995	55.5	2004	60	2013	20.7
1987	61	1996	57	2005	59.8	2014	19.4
1988	62.1	1997	59.9	2006	57.3	2015	17.9

Source: Columbia Journalism Review

4. Build a grouped frequency distribution for the data. Your first class should be 10–19.9, and all others should be the same size.

5. Which class contains the most number of values? Write a sentence explaining what this means using units on any numbers used.

6. Draw a histogram for the ad revenue data on the axes at right. Don't forget to fill in a scale on both axes! You should also include labels on the vertical and horizontal axis describing what those scales represent.

Newspaper Ad Revenues

1-9 Applications

Name _____

The stem and leaf plot below represents the number of daily newspapers in each of the 50 states plus the District of Columbia as of November 2016. Use it to answer Questions 7–10.

Stems	Leaves
0	3 5 7 7 8 8 9 9
1	0 0 0 3 5 5 5 6 9 9
2	0 1 3 5 5 5 7 8 9 9
3	0 2 7 8 8
4	5 9
5	0 0 6 8 9
6	5 6
7	6 6 9
8	9
9	0
11	8
20	0
22	0
23	0

Key: 4|5 means 45 newspapers

7. How many states had 656 newspapers?

8. How many states had 25 newspapers?

9. How many states had less than 30 newspapers? More than 100?

10. What's the largest number of newspapers in any state? Smallest?

1-9 **Applications**

Name _____

The data below are the average weekday individually paid print circulations (in thousands) of select newspapers in the United States as of September 2015. For example, the first row shows that the *Arizona Republic* sells 164,000 copies of their print edition on an average weekday.

Paper	Daily circulation	Paper	Daily circulation
Arizona Republic	164	Minneapolis Star-Tribune	184
Atlanta Journal-Constitution	92	New York Daily News	228
Boston Globe	140	New York Post	245
Chicago Sun-Times	118	New York Times	528
Chicago Tribune	266	Newark Star-Ledger	114
Cleveland Plain Dealer	153	Newsday	217
Dallas Morning News	140	Orange County Register	110
Denver Post	156	Philadelphia Inquirer	138
Honolulu Star-Advertiser	94	San Diego Union-Tribune	117
Houston Chronicle	169	Tampa Bay Times	141
Las Vegas Review-Journal	90	USA Today	299
Los Angeles Times	328	Washington Post	330

11. Build a stem and leaf plot to organize the data.

Stems	Leaves

Key: 13 | 8 means 138,000 copies sold

1-9 Applications

Name _____

12. How useful do you think the stem and leaf plot is in this case? Explain your answer.

13. Based on EVERYTHING you've seen in this lesson, how would you assess the claim that the American newspaper industry is dying?

14. Of the three methods we used to represent data in this lesson (frequency distribution, histogram, stem and leaf plot), which in your opinion is easiest to interpret? Why do you feel that way?

Unit 1   Language and Symbolism Review

Carefully read through the list of terminology we've used in this Unit. Consider circling the terms you aren't familiar with and looking them up. Then test your understanding by using the list to fill in the appropriate blank in each sentence. Hint: One word is used twice.

$A \cap B$	interest	scatter diagram or scatter plot
$A \cup B$	intersection	scientific notation
axis	like quantities	set
bar graph	linear growth	simple interest
categorical frequency distribution	lower limit	stem and leaf plot
classes	origin	theoretical probability
commutative	perimeter	time-series data
complement	pie chart	time-series graph
compound interest	plotting points	union
coordinates	population	universal set
data	probability	upper limit
degrees	raw data	Venn diagram
element	rectangular coordinate system	well-defined
empirical probability	representative sample	x axis
exponential growth	roster method	y axis
grouped frequency distribution	sample	
histogram	scale	

1. A _____ is a diagram used to compare the relative sizes of different parts of a whole.

2. A circle can be divided into 360 equal units of measure, which we call _____.

3. A _____ is a visual way to compare the sizes of different values.

4. Polling is a really common and useful way to gather some _____, which are measurements or observations that are gathered for an event under study.

5. If we wanted to learn about characteristics of all the students at your college, the ideal approach would be to poll every single one of them. But in most cases, that's not particularly realistic. So instead, we'd likely choose a _____ of students from the larger _____ of all students at your school.

6. Two quantities can only be added when they are _____.

7. Addition is _____: The order in which you add doesn't matter.

8. The _____ of a figure is found by taking the sum of the lengths of each side of that figure.

9. Multiplication is _____: The order in which you multiply doesn't matter.

10. _____ is a fee paid for the use of someone else's money.

11. Interest that is calculated as a percentage of the original amount of money is called _____.

12. _____ is interest that is paid not just on the original amount deposited, but on interest previously earned as well.

13. With _____ the values grow by adding the same constant number.

14. With _____ the values grow by multiplying by the same constant number.

15. _____ are quantitative data that have been collected at different points in time. A _____ displays values on the y axis compared to equally spaced time intervals on the x axis.

16. The _____ for a graph is used to describe the distance between the marks on an _____ for a graph.

17. The numbers we use to locate a point on a graph are called _____.

18. The system we use for plotting points on a graph is called the _____.

19. The horizontal axis is usually called the _____ and the vertical axis is usually called the _____.

20. The point where the two axes meet is called the _____.

21. The process of locating information on a rectangular coordinate system is called _____.

22. When we plot points on a coordinate system that correspond to pairs of data, we call the result a _____.

23. The _____ of an event occurring is a description of how likely it is that the event will actually happen.

24. If we assume that both sides of a coin are equally likely to land up, we are using _____.

25. If we performed an experiment and observed 1,000 flips of a coin to determine whether one side was more likely than the other to land up, we would be using _____.

26. _____ is often used to express really large or really small numbers using powers of 10.

27. _____ are used to represent sets of objects and visualize what they have in common, and how they differ.

28. A _____ is any collection of objects.

29. A set is _____ if you can objectively determine (based on facts, not opinion) whether an object does or does not belong in a set.

30. Each object in a set is called an _____ or a member of a set.

31. One method of describing a set is called the _____, in which elements are listed between braces, with commas between the elements.

32. The _____ is the set of all objects under consideration in a given situation.

33. The _____ of a set is the set of all objects from the universal set that are not in that set.

34. The set of elements that are in both sets *A* and *B* is called the _____ of *A* and *B*, and is symbolized _____.

35. The set of elements that are in at least one of sets *A* and *B* is called the _____ of *A* and *B*, and is symbolized _____.

36. A _____ is a subset of a statistical population that accurately reflects the members of the entire population.

37. The data collected for a statistical study are called _____.

38. A _____ is a way to organize data that are divided into distinct categories, like gender, your class standing in school, or conferences for college football teams.

39. A type of frequency distribution that can be constructed using numerical data is called a _____.

40. In a grouped frequency distribution, the numerical data are divided into _____.

41. If one of the classes in a grouped frequency distribution was 100–119 pounds, we would call 100 the _____ and 119 the _____.

42. When data are organized in a grouped frequency distribution, we draw a special kind of bar graph to illustrate. This type of graph is called a _____.

43. A way of organizing data, where each data value or number is separated into two parts, is called a _____.

Unit 1   Technology Review

This is a short review of the technology skills we've used in this unit. In each case, rate your confidence level by checking one of the boxes, If you feel like you're struggling with these skills, consult the online resources for extra practice.

1. Make a pie chart with Excel. (Lesson 1-1)

2. Make a bar graph with Excel. (Lesson 1-1)

3. Use Excel to perform addition. (Lesson 1-2)

4. Use the auto-fill feature in Excel. (Lesson 1-3)

5. Create a scatter plot with Excel. (Lesson 1-5)

6. Use scientific notation. (Lesson 1-7)

7. Sorting a data set. (Lesson 1-9)

Answer each question based on the technology skills from this unit.

1. Make a pie chart from the data in the table.

	A	B
	Grades on an Exam	Number of Students
1		
2	A	4
3	B	7
4	C	5
5	D	1
6	F	3

2. Make a bar graph from the data in the table.

	A	B
	Day of the Week	Total Number of Absences by Day of the Week
1		
2	Monday	12
3	Tuesday	4
4	Wednesday	6
5	Thursday	8
6	Friday	16

3. Write a formula to add all of the values in column B and display the result in cell B19.

⊿	A	B
1	Date	Charge
2	2-Dec	$24.51
3	4-Dec	$45.21
4	4-Dec	$11.89
5	5-Dec	$19.29
6	8-Dec	$16.00
7	9-Dec	$188.22
8	11-Dec	$36.78
9	12-Dec	$44.31
10	15-Dec	$31.97
11	16-Dec	$228.75
12	20-Dec	$22.01
13	21-Dec	$3.75
14	22-Dec	$19.56
15	23-Dec	$9.85
16	24-Dec	$55.08
17	24-Dec	$103.47
18		
19	Total	

4. Use the fill-down feature to complete a spreadsheet like this one, down to row 52.

⊿	A
1	Value
2	$1,000
3	$1,020
4	$1,040
5	$1,060
6	$1,080
7	
8	

5. Use the data in the table to create a scatter plot.

⊿	A	B
1	Age (years)	Height (inches)
2	0	17
3	1	23
4	2	30
5	3	32
6	4	39
7		

6. The values given came from either a calculator or a spreadsheet. Write each value in scientific notation:

a. 3.45E+7

b. 1.72E-04

Use a calculator or a spreadsheet to calculate each value and write the result in scientific notation.

c. $(1.2 \times 10^{12})(8 \times 10^3)$

d. $\dfrac{1}{(389)^{10}}$

7. Sort the list of quiz scores in ascending order.

⊿	A
1	Scores
2	18
3	15
4	17
5	12
6	13
7	19
8	20
9	15
10	16
11	14
12	13
13	18
14	20
15	10
16	18
17	17
18	

Unit 1 Learning Objective Review

This is a short review of the learning objectives we've covered in Unit 1. In each case, rate your confidence level by checking one of the boxes, and then answer the question. If you feel like you're struggling with these skills, consult the lesson referenced next to the objective and see the online resources for extra practice.

I KNOW IT   THINK SO   UNSURE   NO IDEA

1. Analyze personal time management for a week of activities. (Lesson 1-1)

2. Solve problems involving percentages. (Lesson 1-1)

3. Create and interpret pie charts. (Lesson 1-1)

4. Create and interpret bar graphs. (Lesson 1-1)

5. Identify circumstances where addition or subtraction is possible. (Lesson 1-2)

6. Add or subtract quantities. (Lesson 1-2)

7. Interpret multiplication as repeated addition. (Lesson 1-3)

8. Multiply or divide quantities. (Lesson 1-3)

9. Distinguish between simple interest and compound interest. (Lesson 1-4)

10. Distinguish between linear and exponential growth. (Lesson 1-4)

11. Interpret exponents as repeated multiplication. (Lesson 1-4)

12. Simplify numeric expressions involving exponents and the order of operations. (Lesson 1-4)

13. Use a rectangular coordinate system. (Lesson 1-5)

14. Connect data to graphs. (Lesson 1-5)

15. Interpret graphs. (Lesson 1-5)

16. Compute and interpret basic probabilities. (Lesson 1-6)

17. Translate a probability to a percent chance. (Lesson 1-6)

18. Recognize the difference between theoretical and empirical probability. (Lesson 1-6)

19. Convert numbers between decimal and scientific notation. (Lesson 1-7)

20. Describe the significance of writing numbers in scientific notation. (Lesson 1-7)

21. Analyze how your personality type affects how you interact with others. (Lesson 1-8)

22. Create and interpret Venn diagrams. (Lesson 1-8)

23. Describe sets using appropriate terminology. (Lesson 1-8)

24. Explain the difference between a population and a sample. (Lesson 1-9)

25. Organize data with frequency distributions and histograms. (Lesson 1-9)

26. Analyze data with stem and leaf plots. (Lesson 1-9)

1. Use the information about where I spend my 168 hours in a week to complete the table and to create a pie chart. Round to the nearest tenth of a percent and then to the nearest whole degree.

Activity	Number	Percent	Degrees
Teaching Class	15		
Grading & Office Hours	20		
Preparing for Class	10		
Sleep	56		
Other	67		

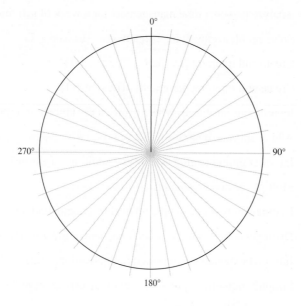

Starting in 2011, the tax rate in Illinois changed to 5% of personal income. Previously, the tax rate was 3% of personal income. These tax rates are represented on the bar graphs provided. The data is the same, but the two graphs use different scales.

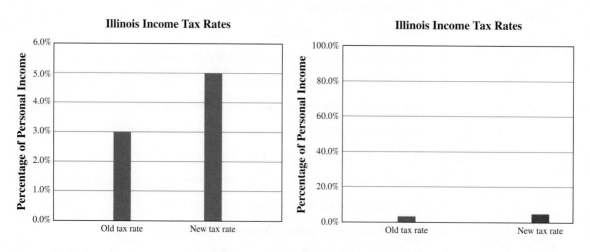

2. Using the old tax rate, how much income tax would an individual pay who makes $32,000 in personal income?

3. Using the new tax rate, how much income tax would an individual pay who makes $32,000 in personal income?

4. Which graph do you think would be used by someone wanting to argue that the tax increase was a huge increase, and which would be used by someone wanting to show that the increase wasn't a big deal? Explain.

Perform each addition or subtraction, if possible. If not, be sure to explain why.

5. $\dfrac{3}{8} + \dfrac{1}{6}$

6. $12x - 5x$

7. 20 miles + 30 hours

Perform each multiplication or division.

8. $\dfrac{3}{5} \times \dfrac{7}{12}$

9. $-12 \div \dfrac{4}{3}$

10. $-2(7)(5)$

Simplify each expression.

11. $10 + 5 \times 3$

12. $(10 + 5)3$

13. $\dfrac{-3^2 + 12}{6(2)}$

14. Rewrite the following expression so that it no longer contains addition. Do not calculate the value!

$50 + 50 + 50 + 50 + 50 + 50 + 50 + 50 + 50 + 50$

15. Rewrite the following expression so that it no longer contains an exponent. Do not calculate the value!

$(1.05)^6$

16. A small aircraft has taken off from an airport. The elevation of the plane has been recorded at various times throughout the flight, shown in the table here. Record each pair of values as an ordered pair and then plot the points on the graph and connect them with lines.

Flight time x (min)	Altitude y (ft)	Ordered Pair (x, y)
0	0	
10	4,000	
20	3,000	
30	2,000	
40	2,000	
50	1,000	
60	0	

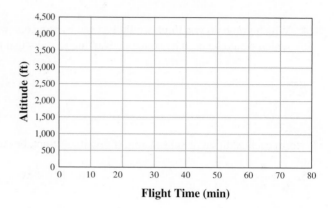

As you answer each question, consider both the table and the graph when you explain your answer.

17. What was the highest altitude reached by the plane?

18. How long after the flight began did the plane reach this highest altitude?

19. When was the plane flying level?

20. How long was the flight?

21. When was the altitude of the plane increasing?

22. When was the altitude of the plane decreasing?

23. The holiday mint M&M's contain 3 colors: red, white, and green. If you reached your hand in the bag and grabbed one M&M, it might be reasonable to calculate the probability of selecting a red one to be 1/3 or about 0.33. Would making this assumption be using empirical or theoretical probability? Explain.

©Ekaterina Minaeva/
Stockimo/Alamy

Suppose you dumped out all of the M&M's from the bag and counted all of them (without eating any) and found that there were 78 red, 96 green, and 82 white. Now if you randomly selected one M&M, determine each probability as a fraction and as a decimal rounded to two decimal places.

24. P(red) =

25. P(green) =

26. P(white) =

27. Are each of the three probabilities you just calculated examples of empirical or theoretical probabilities? Explain.

28. Write a sentence describing the percent chance of drawing a red M&M from the bag based on your answer to question 25.

Write each number in standard decimal notation.

29. 5.62×10^{-4}

30. 3.902×10^{7}

Write each number in scientific notation.

31. 43,450,000,000,000

32. 0.000000728

33. A number often thrown out is that 400 million M&M's per day are produced in the United States. Assuming that number is produced every day of the year, how many M&M's would be produced in a year in the United States? Write the answer in scientific notation.

Consider the two accounts shown.

◢	A	B	C	D	E
1		**Account #1**			**Account #2**
2	Start	$10,000.00		Start	$10,000.00
3	After 1 year	$10,600.00		After 1 year	$10,600.00
4	After 2 years	$11,200.00		After 2 years	$11,236.00
5	After 3 years	$11,800.00		After 3 years	$11,910.16
6	After 4 years	$12,400.00		After 4 years	$12,624.77
7	After 5 years			After 5 years	

34. Account _____ is an example of linear growth because we add _____ to each value to obtain the next value.

35. Account _____ is an example of exponential growth because we multiply each value by _____ to obtain the next value.

36. Which account illustrates simple interest? Explain why.

37. Which account illustrates compound interest? Explain why.

38. What could be typed in B7 to calculate the value in Account #1 after 5 years?

39. What could be typed in E7 to calculate the value in Account #2 after 5 years?

40. Find the value that should appear in cell B7 (it should be the amount in Account #1 after 5 years).

41. Find the value that should appear in cell E7 (it should be the amount in Account #2 after 5 years).

42. Assuming the trend continues for each account, write a numerical calculation that will provide the amount in Account #1 after 60 years.

43. Assuming the trend continues for each account, write a numerical calculation that will provide the amount in Account #2 after 60 years.

44. Find the amount in Account #1 after 60 years.

45. Find the amount in Account #2 after 60 years.

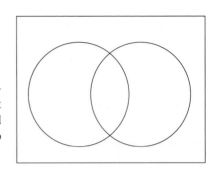

In order to report on which presidential candidate the students at an Illinois community college were supporting, a writer for the school paper surveyed 60 students at that school. They were asked which presidential candidate they thought would do a good job. Of those surveyed, 19 thought Clinton would do a good job, 15 thought Trump would do a good job, and 3 thought both would do a good job.

46. Describe the sample and the population in the previous scenario.

47. Which is more likely to be a representative sample of the student population of a particular school? Explain why.

    a. Asking all students who attend a political rally for one of the candidates.

    b. Asking all students who went through the cafeteria over a two-hour period.

48. Complete the Venn diagram with the appropriate values.

49. How many students thought Clinton would do a good job?

50. How many students thought only Clinton would do a good job?

51. How many students thought Trump would do a good job?

52. How many students thought only Trump would do a good job?

53. How many students thought neither would do a good job?

54. How many students thought both would do a good job?

Consider the data from the table showing the heights of 15 people at a family gathering.

55. Create a stem and leaf plot using the first digit as the stem and the second digit as the leaf for each number.

Stems	Leaves

Name	Height (inches)
Bob	72
Bill	65
Lisa	60
Manuel	42
Hannah	38
Braxton	55
Ava	51
Jake	64
Charlotte	62
Nate	68
Emmett	57
John	54
Mario	60
Ben	61
Luigi	47

56. How many people had a height under 5 feet?

57. If we let A represent the set of names of all people at this gathering whose height is under 5 feet, write that set using the roster method.

58. Give a verbal description of what would be meant by A' in this situation.

59. Write the set A' using the roster method.

60. Complete the frequency distribution, and then use the frequency distribution to make a histogram for the height data.

Class	Tally Marks	Frequency
30–39		
40–49		
50–59		
60–69		
70–79		

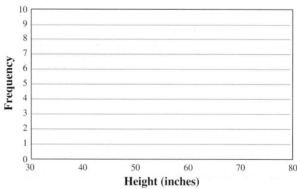

61. Which class contains the largest number of people?

Unit 2
Making Sense of It All

©Colin Anderson/Blend Images RF

Outline

Lesson 2-1 Prep Skills

SKILL 1: CALCULATE A PERCENTAGE

To compute what percentage of a whole a certain amount is, you perform two steps.

Step 1: Divide the portion by the whole. This gives you the percentage in decimal form.

Step 2: Convert that decimal to percent form by moving the decimal two places to the right. This corresponds to multiplying the decimal form by 100.

- $20/50 = 0.4$, which is 40%. So 20 is 40% of 50.

- $110/150 \approx 0.733$, which is 73.3%. So 110 is about 73.3% of 150.

- $8/120 \approx 0.067$, which is 6.7%, so 8 is about 6.7% of 120.

- $200/150 \approx 1.33$, which is 133%, so 200 is about 133% of 150.

SKILL 2: PERFORM CALCULATIONS INVOLVING ORDER OF OPERATIONS IN FRACTIONS

When we have additions or subtractions above or below a fraction bar, order of operations would usually tell us to do division first. But to avoid having to always put parentheses around the entire numerator and denominator, we instead treat the fraction bar as if it implies grouping symbols around the numerator, and around the denominator. That means we perform any calculations in the numerator first, then the denominator, then finally we divide or write the fraction in reduced form, depending on the context.

- $$\frac{8 + 12 + 22 + 15 + 9}{5} = \frac{66}{5} = 13.2$$

- $$\frac{12}{7 + 3 - 1 - 5} = \frac{12}{4} = 3$$

- $$\frac{100 + 250 - 50 + 300}{10 - 5 + 20 + 15} = \frac{600}{40} = 15$$

SKILL 3: ORDER A LIST OF NUMBERS

Here's an efficient method for putting a list of numbers in order:

Step 1: Find the lowest number on the list and write it down, then cross it off the original list.

Step 2: Repeat until there are no more numbers on the original list.

Step 3: Count to make sure you have the same number of entries on your ordered list as there were on the original list.

PREP SKILLS QUESTIONS

1. Fill in each blank.

   a. 120 is _____% of 500.

   b. 11 is _____% of 20.

   c. 7,000 is _____% of 12,500.

   d. $8.32 is _____% of $41.20.

2. Perform each calculation. Convert fractions to decimals rounded to the nearest tenth.

   a. $\dfrac{9 + 12 + 27 + 11 + 16 + 4}{6}$

   b. $\dfrac{100}{12 - 3 - 14 - 5}$

   c. $\dfrac{-8 + 4 + 3 + 16}{10 - 5 - 2 + 8}$

3. Put this list in order from least to greatest.

   20.3   19.1   15.0   15.7   9.2   12.3   19.3   16.8   12.3   10.6   17.7   15.6   15.2

Lesson 2-1   Did You Pass the Test?

LEARNING OBJECTIVES

☐ 1. Consider strategies for preparing for and taking math tests.

☐ 2. Understand the impact of a single question, or a single exam.

☐ 3. Calculate, interpret, and compare measures of average.

©Blend Images - Hill Street Studios/Getty Images RF

Tell me and I'll forget; show me and I may remember; involve me and I'll understand.

—Chinese proverb

When's the last time you were tested? If you think of that only in an academic sense, you may be consulting a calendar. If you're more of a metaphorical person, you may be thinking "I get tested every day." Life tests us in many different ways, and how we deal with tests goes a long way to determining our character. In fact, that's one of the reasons that an education is so important. The tests that you take in college classes are a metaphor for some of the most important events in life: With the pressure on, can you perform your best? What have you learned, and can you apply that knowledge when you need to?

0. Discuss some ways an instructor might decide how well or how poorly a class did on a test.

2-1   Class

In this lesson, we're going to look at exams in a math course. How do you prepare? How is your grade for the exam determined? What impact does this score have on your grade in the course? How does an instructor determine how well the class as a whole understood the material?

Answer each question in your groups and then prepare to share your answers with the class.

1. What are some strategies you use to prepare for an exam?

2. What are some habits you have or have seen that are not helpful when preparing for an exam?

3. What are some strategies you use during an exam?

4. When a test has been graded and returned, students (and instructors) are usually interested in knowing what the "class average" was. Explain the meaning of the word "average" in your own words. Don't think in terms of formulas, but what it tells you.

	A	B	C
1	Student	Exam 1 (%)	Exam 2 (%)
2	Michael	80	89
3	Andy	77	93
4	Pam	68	84
5	Jim	81	88
6	Dwight	96	91
7	Stanley	54	75
8	Phyllis	75	54
9	Kevin	81	86
10	Creed	71	0
11	Darryl	89	83
12	Gabe	56	64
13	Toby	81	65
14	Holly	92	73

In math and stats, the term "average" is sort of a generic term, with several interpretations. Loosely defined, the average of a list of numbers is the most typical value. But what exactly does that mean? The one that appears most often? The one right in the middle? Or some mathematical combination?

There are three different measures that we'll study in this lesson, and all of them fall under the umbrella of "average." And in some cases, they can take on completely different values. This means that interpretation becomes far more important than being able to do calculations.

> The **mean** of a set of numbers is what you probably think of as the "average." You find it by adding all of the numbers, then dividing by how many numbers there are on the list.

5. Find the mean test score on Exam 1.

> The **median** of a list of numbers is the value that lives right in the middle of the set if it's arranged in order. To find the median:
> **Step 1:** List the numbers in order from either largest to smallest or smallest to largest (you can pick).
> **Step 2:** If there is an odd number of values, the median is the value that has the same number of values above and below it on the list.
> **Step 3:** If there is an even number of values, the median is the mean of the two values right in the middle of the list.

6. Find the median test score on Exam 1.

> The **mode** of a list of numbers is the value that appears most often. If all values appear only once, there is no mode.

7. Find the mode of the Exam 1 scores.

Math Note

A data set can have more than one mode if there are multiple values that appear the same number of times.

Did You Get It

Try this problem to see if you understand the concepts we just studied. The answers can be found at the end of the Portfolio section.

1. Here are the number of points that Creed earned on each question on Exam 1. Find all three measures of average for these scores.

Question	1	2	3	4	5	6	7	8
Points	5	12	10	10	6	12	9	7

Computing Measures of Average Using Excel

To compute the three measures of average in Excel, use these commands:

- Mean: =AVERAGE(cell range)
- Median: =MEDIAN(cell range)
- Mode: =MODE(cell range)

	80
	77
	68
	81
	96
Mean	80.4
Median	80
Mode	#N/A

80
77
68
81
96
=AVERAGE(B1:B5)
=MEDIAN(B1:B5)
=MODE(B1:B5)

The samples shown here calculate measures of average for the first five scores from Test A earlier. The first spreadsheet shows the results of the calculations. The second displays the formulas that were used to get those measures of average. The "#N/A" indicates that there is no mode for the data.

See the Lesson 2-1 Using Tech video in class resources for further instruction.

2-1 Group

If it doesn't make you uncomfortable, exchange the following information with the classmates in your Unit 2 group. This will be your small group for the second unit. It would be a good idea to schedule a time for the group to meet to go over homework, ask/answer questions, or prepare for exams. You can use this table to help schedule a mutually agreeable time.

Name	Phone Number	Email	Available times

The spreadsheet summarizes the results for one student on a 15-question math test with partial credit awarded.

1. Complete the totals at the bottom of each column using addition.

2. What percent of the total possible points did this student earn? (Round all percentages in this lesson to one decimal place.)

3. What letter grade did this student get? (The grading scale is 90% = A, 80% = B, 70% = C, 60% = D.)

	A	B	C
	Problem	Points	Points
1	Number	Possible	Earned
2	1	2	2
3	2	2	2
4	3	2	0
5	4	5	4
6	5	5	2
7	6	8	4
8	7	8	3
9	8	9	9
10	9	4	4
11	10	5	5
12	11	5	5
13	12	6	6
14	13	6	6
15	14	10	6
16	15	10	10
17	Totals		
18			
19			

4. Problem 15 on the test was an application (what some folks call "story" or "word" problems). What letter grade would this student have earned if she'd wimped out and skipped that question?

5. What's the highest grade you could get on this test if you skip problem 15 because it's a scary word problem?

6. Does Question 5 sound familiar to you? Have you ever been in that position? Explain.

7. What do these questions make you think about in terms of taking tests, and the importance of trying every question?

Did You Get It

Suppose that the instructor who wrote the test in Questions 1–5 had added two more questions, one worth 8 points and another worth 5.

2. What percentage would this student have earned if she didn't even notice those questions were part of the test?

3. How much would her percentage have improved if she got both of those questions completely correct?

So here's the big question: Why three measures of average? Let's look into it. The first list below shows the percentage of points earned by 25 students on a quiz. The mean score is 69.4%. The second shows the number of hours spent by the students preparing for the quiz in their online homework system. The mean number of hours is 3.5.

Scores

100 100 100 100 100 100 100 100 100 100 100 100 88 85 82 78

71 70 60 0 0 0 0 0 0

Study Time

28 6 5.3 4.3 4 3.7 3.5 3.5 3.4 3.3 3.2 2.2 2.2 2.1 1.9 1.8 1.7 1.7 1.7

1.7 1.4 1.1 0 0 0

8. After returning the quiz, the professor scolds the class mercilessly, making four students cry and sending six others to RateMyProfessor.com to say really mean things. His justification: The average grade was a D! Ugh. Do you think this is an accurate measure of how the class performed on the quiz? Explain.

9. Compute the other two measures of average, then decide which of the three measures of average provide the most accurate description of how the class did.

10. The professor is really puzzled by that D average because students spent an average of 3.5 hours studying, which isn't bad for a quiz (but would probably be a little low for a test). Assess his confusion. Is the mean a good measure of average for the time spent studying? Why or why not?

11. Find the other two measures of average, and discuss which of the three you think provides the most accurate representation of the time spent by students.

12. Do you think the scores came from a math class? Why or why not?

At the beginning of the course, you should have been provided some information on how exactly you're going to be graded. Most instructors have their own standards, so you should make an effort to understand how your grade will be calculated. Most likely it was on a syllabus provided by your instructor.

13. How well do you feel you understand the grading standards for your course? If you don't know them, consult the syllabus or ask your instructor.

Let's look at a fairly basic points system for grading. We'll say that your course grade comes from 4 exams worth 100 points each, a homework score worth 200 points, and a final exam worth 200 points.

14. How many total points can be earned in the course?

15. What percentage of the total score is accounted for by the first exam?

16. If you don't show up for the first exam and take a 0%, then average 82% for everything else the rest of the course, what would your final percentage be?

	A	Exam 1	Exam 2	Exam 3	Exam 4	Homework	Final Exam	Total Points	Overall %
1		Exam 1	Exam 2	Exam 3	Exam 4	Homework	Final Exam	Total Points	Overall %
2	**Points possible**	100	100	100	100	200	200		
3	**Your scores**								

17. What would your final percentage be if you score 100% on Exam 1, then average 82% for the rest of the course?

▲	A	B	C	D	E	F	G	H	I
1		Exam 1	Exam 2	Exam 3	Exam 4	Homework	Final Exam	Total Points	Overall %
2	Points possible	100	100	100	100	200	200		
3	Your scores								

18. What does the difference between your answers to Questions 16 and 17 tell you?

2-1 Portfolio

Name _____

Check each box when you've completed the task. Remember that your instructor will want you to turn in the portfolio pages you create.

Technology

1. ☐ Create a spreadsheet that calculates final grades for the grading system described on page 158. You can use the samples there as a template. Your sheet should use formulas to add up the number of points possible, your total score when you enter individual scores for exams and homework, and your final percentage. Experiment with your spreadsheet to find the effects of one unusually bad test score. A template to help you get started can be found in the online resources for this lesson.

2. ☐ The four scores below show where one student stands going into a 200-point final. Enter the current scores, then experiment with values on the final to see the range of grades this student could get. Follow further instructions on the template.
   Exam 1: 73　Exam 2: 78　Exam 3: 84　Exam 4: 82　Homework: 164

Online Practice

1. ☐ Include any written work from the online assignment along with any notes or questions about this lesson's content.

Applications

1. ☐ Complete the Applications problems.

Reflections

Type a short answer to each question.

1. ☐ Write down a list of things that you think are most likely to affect how well you do on tests in this course. Then describe what you can do to make that information work for you.

2. ☐ There are many websites with test-prep and test-taking hints. Find one that you think is helpful, and describe some tips that you can use.

3. ☐ Describe the three measures of average we studied.

4. ☐ When a data set has one or two values that are much higher than all of the others, which measure of average is most likely to be deceiving? Why?

5. ☐ Name one thing you learned or discovered in this lesson that you found especially interesting.

6. ☐ What questions do you have about this lesson?

Looking Ahead

1. ☐ Complete the Prep Skills for Lesson 2-2.

2. ☐ Read the opening paragraph in Lesson 2-2 carefully then answer Question 0 in preparation for that lesson.

? **Answers to "Did You Get It?"**

1. Mean: 8.9; median: 9.5; mode: 10 and 12

2. 68%

3. She could have improved by about 2.8%.

? **Answers to "Prep Skills"**

1. **a.** 24   **b.** 55   **c.** 56   **d.** about 20.2

2. **a.** $\dfrac{79}{6} \approx 13.2$ **b.** -10 **c.** $\dfrac{15}{11} \approx 1.4$

3. 9.2   10.6   12.3   12.3   15.0   15.2   15.6   15.7   16.8   17.7   19.1
   19.3   20.3

2-1 Applications

Name _____

Here's another look at a group of exam scores:

1. Find the mean for all Exam 2 scores.

◢	A	B	C
1	**Student**	**Exam 1 (%)**	**Exam 2 (%)**
2	Michael	80	89
3	Andy	77	93
4	Pam	68	84
5	Jim	81	88
6	Dwight	96	91
7	Stanley	54	75
8	Phyllis	75	54
9	Kevin	81	86
10	Creed	71	0
11	Darryl	89	83
12	Gabe	56	64
13	Toby	81	64
14	Holly	92	74

2. Find the median for all Exam 2 scores.

3. Find the mode for all Exam 2 scores.

4. Find the mean, median, and mode for the scores on Exam 2 if you throw out Creed's zero (dude didn't even show up . . . Come on, man!).

5. You've found six measures of average for the Exam 2 scores so far on this page: mean, median, and mode for all the scores, then for the scores without the zero. Of the six, which single one do you think is the best representation of how students performed on the test? Needless to say, you should explain why you chose that one.

6. After the Exam 2 scores were listed on the class online site (without names, of course, which would violate several federal laws), one of the students said, "Wow, we did great on this test," while the instructor said, "I disagree. The average was a low C!" Who's right? Justify your answer, including information about measures of average.

Lesson 2-2   Prep Skills

SKILL 1: USE ORDER OF OPERATIONS

Order of operations is a group of agreed-upon rules that allow us to write calculations involving more than one operation without always having to use parentheses or other grouping symbols to indicate which operation to do first. The order is as follows, with operations higher on the list being performed before those lower on the list. If there are two operations tied (like two multiplications), they are performed left to right. Grouping symbols can indicate a different order.

Parentheses

Exponents

Multiplication or division

Addition or subtraction

- $12 + 3 \cdot 4 = 12 + 12 = 24$ Multiply $(3 \cdot 4)$ first.

- $4(3)^2 = 4(9) = 36$ Exponent first

- $81 \div (12 - 3) = 81 \div 9 = 9$ Calculation in parentheses $(12 - 3)$ first

- $52 - 8 \div 4 \cdot 6 = 52 - 2 \cdot 6$ Divide $(8 \div 4)$ first, then multiply $(2 \cdot 6)$.
  $= 52 - 12$ For two operations at the same level,
  $= 40$ perform the leftmost one first.

- $\dfrac{7 - 9}{3 + 5} = \dfrac{-2}{8} = \dfrac{-1}{4}$ Fraction bar acts like parentheses around the numerator $(7 - 9)$ and denominator $(3 + 5)$.

When a calculation contains multiple parentheses, the innermost parentheses are done first:

- $(-2 (3 + 1))^2 - 4 = (-2 \cdot 4)^2 - 4$ Inner parentheses $(3 + 1)$ first, then outer $(-2 \cdot 4)$
  $= (-8)^2 - 4$ Exponent before subtraction
  $= 64 - 4$
  $= 60$

PREP SKILLS QUESTIONS

Perform each operation.

1. a. 3^5 b. $(-2)^6$ c. $\left(\dfrac{1}{2}\right)^4$ d. -5^2

2. a. $12 + 20 \div 2$ b. $(-4)(-6) - 7$ c. $7 \times 4 - (-60) \div 12$

3. a. $20 + 2(9 - 4)^2$ b. $-3^3 \cdot 2 - 42$ c. $12 + 2 \cdot 30 \div 5$

4. a. $((8 - 1) \times 3)^2$ b. $2{,}000(1 + 0.05)^{12}$ c. $10{,}000(1.045)^2 - (10{,}000 + 10{,}000(0.045) \cdot 2)$

   d. $(7 - (3 + 4)^2)^2$

Lesson 2-2   Ins and Outs

LEARNING OBJECTIVES

☐ 1. Distinguish between inputs (independent variables) and outputs (dependent variables).

☐ 2. Evaluate expressions and formulas.

☐ 3. Write and interpret expressions.

©Gyro Photography/
amanaimagesRF/Getty Images RF

Experience is a hard teacher because she gives the test first, the lesson afterward.
                                                           —Vernon Law

The holy grail of energy research: a process that outputs far more energy than you put in. Develop a safe, clean process that does that, and you'll be rich beyond your wildest dreams. There's a worthwhile metaphor here: In many instances, the output (result you get) is determined by what you input. Don't practice and stay out all night before a big game, your output will probably stink. Put in a ton of work and effort, and you're likely to do your best. In this lesson, we'll study input and output from a mathematical sense, and hopefully give you a MUCH better idea of just what in the world a "variable" really is.

0. Provide a couple more examples of where an input leads to an output.

2-2   Class

First, let's talk about variables. Answer this question honestly and to the best of your ability without any outside help:

1. What is a variable?

If you're like most people, your answer was probably something like this: "A variable is a letter instead of a number." I am very sorry to inform you that, and I say this in the most caring possible way, your answer stinks. Think about what the word "variable" should mean in plain English: able to vary. And THAT is the key to understanding variables:

> A **variable** is a quantity that is able to change, or vary.

Contrast this with a **constant**, which can't vary. The number 12 is a constant, because no matter what, it still has the same value. The number of hours you spend studying, on the other hand IS a variable, because it can vary according to how much effort you choose to expend.

But what about the whole "letter" thing? Isn't x a variable? Technically, the answer is no. We use letters to REPRESENT variables, since that distinguishes them from numbers, which never change. But a variable is NOT a letter: It's a *quantity* that can vary, which is usually represented by a letter. To save time, we often refer to the letter itself as a variable, but try to keep in mind it's actually the quantity represented by that letter that is really a variable.

2. Which sentence makes more sense? Explain your reasoning.
   a. The amount of time you spend studying depends on the grade you earn in a course.
   b. The grade you earn in a course depends on the amount of time you spend studying.

3. List other factors that are likely to impact your grade in this course.

Because these factors can cause a change in your course grade, and not the other way around, the course grade (which can vary) is referred to as a **dependent variable** in this situation. Other factors, like the amount of time you spend studying, are called **independent variables**. Independent variables cause changes in dependent variables. Think of it as "Your grade *depends* on the factors you identified."

4. Consider the following relationships, where one quantity or event causes another to change. Identify the independent and dependent variable in each case, and don't forget to think about WHY it makes sense that these things are variables.

   a. The age of a tree and the height of a tree

   b. The number of practice sessions and the quality of a musical performance

   c. Your score on a placement test and the math courses you've taken previously

   d. Your blood pressure and the amount of time you spend exercising each week

   e. The value of a share of Apple stock and what year it is

   f. The number of songs a band sells on iTunes and the amount of money spent on marketing

   g. The cost of a cab ride and the number of miles you're driven

h. The number of customers that want to buy a certain product and the price of that product

---

Did You Get It

Try this problem to see if you understand the concepts we just studied. The answers can be found at the end of the Portfolio section.

1. For each situation, describe which is the best choice for the independent and dependent variable, and justify your answer.
   a. The amount of money spent by a candidate for the presidency, and the percentage of the population that votes for that candidate.
   b. The taste test rating of a certain soft drink, and the number of teaspoons of sugar in each 12 ounces of that drink.

2-2 Group

1. A few key terms used in this section are listed below. Discuss each term with your group and note how the definitions are similar, and how they're different.

Expression – A combination of variables and constants using mathematical operations and grouping symbols

Examples: $4x + 2y$, $\dfrac{11}{t-2}$, $\sqrt{x^2 - 20}$, $(4n - 6)(2 + n)$

Equation – A statement that two quantities are equal that is built using expressions and an equal sign (=)

Examples: $3x + 2 = 7$, $y = z^2 - z - 6$, $100e^{0.02t} = 500$

Formula – An equation with multiple variables that is used to calculate some quantity that we're interested in

Examples: $A = \pi r^2$, $P = 2l + 2w$, $A = P + Prt$

In many cases, relationships like the ones we thought about in the Class portion of this lesson can be described mathematically using a formula. For example, it might cost $2 for a cab ride plus $2.50 for each mile; in that case we could write the formula

$C = 2 + 2.50m$

where C represents the variable cost of the cab ride, and m represents the variable number of miles. It's the number of miles that affects the cost, so m is the independent variable and C is the dependent variable. We might say that the number of miles is the **input**, while the cost is the **output**. Think of it like a machine: You input a number of miles, and the machine gives you back the cost.

2. If we wanted to know the cost of a 7-mile cab ride, we could replace the variable m, which represents miles, with the number 7; the result would be $C = 2 + 2.50(7)$. Finding the value of the calculation to the right of the equal sign will tell us the cost. We call this **evaluating** the expression (or formula) for cost. Find the cost of the 7-mile cab ride.

> **Math Note**
>
> There's no reason you HAVE to use a letter to represent a variable quantity: You could use a smiley face, a zodiac sign, a picture of your mom, whatever. But we'll use letters because we don't know what your mom looks like.

3. Evaluate the cost formula for $m = 4$, then attach units to your answer and write a sentence describing what it tells us. Include information about each variable.

Did You Get It

2. If a streaming service charges a monthly fee of $3, then adds $0.75 for each movie or TV show watched, then the formula $C = 3 + 0.75n$ describes the monthly cost C in terms of variable n, which represents the number of movies or shows watched. Use this formula to find the cost of watching 13 movies or shows.

In Lesson 1-4, we studied simple and compound interest. One of the things we discovered is that to compute the value in an account that earns simple interest, we can use this procedure:

New value = Original value + interest earned

which is

Original value + Original value × interest rate × number of time periods

Whether you realized it or not at the time, you were doing algebra! Each of the quantities in that verbal description can change, so they are variables that can be represented by symbols. Instead of writing the long verbal description above, it's a whole lot quicker and more concise to write it as a formula using letters to represent the variable quantities:

Computing Future Value Using Simple Interest

The new value of an account A (known as the **future value**) is given by

$$A = P + Prt$$

where P represents the original amount (or **principal**), r represents the interest rate in decimal form, and t represents the number of time periods.

If it makes perfect sense to you that we've written the expression describing future value twice, and the second one is simpler, then congratulations: You get algebra.

4. When using the formula $A = P + Prt$ in a given situation, you'll usually know the principal amount and the interest rate, so P and r will be constants. That leaves A and t as the only variables. Which of those variables would you say is the input? Which would you say is the output? Why?

5. Now forget about formulas for a second, and pretend we're back in Lesson 1-4, computing interest using what we know about percents. If you start with $2,000 in an account and earn 3% simple interest each year, how much interest would you earn each year? Make sure you show your calculation.

6. Now substitute the values provided in Question 5 into the formula $A = P + Prt$ and simplify just a bit. Does your answer to Question 5 make sense based on the resulting formula?

7. Complete the table of values for your shiny new formula.

t	A = 2,000 + 60t
0	2,000
1	
2	
3	
4	
5	
6	

8. What's the value of the account after 2 years?

9. How long does it take for the account to reach a value of $2,240?

Did You Get It

3. If $42,000 is invested at 4.5% simple interest, write a formula that calculates the value of the account after t years. Then use your formula to find the value of the account 12 years after it was opened.

When working with formulas, especially complicated ones, calculators and spreadsheets really come in handy for doing repeated calculations. So let's have a look at some cool features that will save you a lot of work in this class—and any other class that uses formulas.

Evaluating a Formula with a Calculator or Spreadsheet

To make a table of values for an expression on a TI-84 Plus:

1. Press ⬭ Y= to get to the equation editor screen.

2. Enter the right side of the formula you are finding values for; use ⬭ X,T,θ,n for the independent variable.

3. Press ⬭ 2nd ⬭ WINDOW to get to the table setup screen. Enter the first input value you want an output for next to TblStart, and the distance between input values next to ΔTbl. (In Question 1 of the group activity, these would be 0 and 50, respectively.) The **Indpnt** and **Depend** settings should be **Auto** so the calculator does all of the values automatically.

4. Press ⬭ 2nd ⬭ GRAPH to display the table of values.

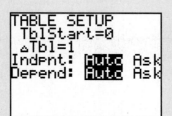

See the Lesson 2-2-1 video in class resources for further information.

To make a table of values for an expression in Excel:

1. Enter the inputs you want in one column. If they're evenly spaced, you can enter the first, then use a formula to add a certain amount to the first input, and copy that formula down or use the fill-down feature. See samples.

2. Enter the formula for the expression in the output column next to the first input. Use the cell that the first input value lives in to replace the variable in the expression.

3. Copy the formula down, or use the fill-down feature to complete the table.

	A	B		A	B
1	Input	2000+60t	1	Input	2000+60t
2		0	2000	2	0	=2000+60*A2
3		1	2060	3	=A2+1	=2000+60*A3
4		2	2120	4	=A3+1	=2000+60*A4
5		3	2180	5	=A4+1	=2000+60*A5
6		4	2240	6	=A5+1	=2000+60*A6
7		5	2300	7	=A6+1	=2000+60*A7
8		6	2360	8	=A7+1	=2000+60*A8

See the Lesson 2-2-2 Using Tech video in online resources for further information.

We also studied compound interest in Lesson 1-4, and found that when a quantity increases based on exponential growth, the value after a certain number of time periods can be calculated using this pattern:

New value = Original value × (1 + the growth rate in decimal form)$^{\text{number of time periods}}$

Once again, we can write an algebraic formula for this pattern that makes it more concise. In most cases, the time period is years, so we'll be using that in our algebraic formula.

Computing Future Value Using Compound Interest

$$A = P(1 + r)^t$$

where *A* is the new value, *P* is the principal, *r* is the interest rate in decimal form, and *t* is the number of years.

10. Evaluate this formula for $P = 10{,}000$, $t = 40$, and $r = 0.06$. Then write a sentence or two explaining what the resulting calculation tells us.

11. Write a formula that describes the value of an account that starts with $5,000 and earns 4% compound interest.

12. Use a calculator or spreadsheet to complete this table. Round to the nearest cent.

t	A
0	
10	
20	
30	
40	
50	
60	

13. What's the value of this account after 20 years?

14. To the nearest year, how long does it take the account to reach a value of $24,000? Did it reach $24,000 before or after this time? Explain.

2-2 | Portfolio

Name _____

Check each box when you've completed the task. Remember that your instructor will want you to turn in the portfolio pages you create.

Technology

1. ☐ One of the big advantages to using Excel when doing calculations involving formulas is that Excel can easily handle formulas with multiple variables. The table feature on a graphing calculator restricts you to one. A classic problem in both algebra and calculus involves the connection between area and perimeter for rectangles. Does a certain perimeter give you a fixed area? Or do the lengths of the sides change the area even if they add up to the same perimeter? In the online template for this assignment, you'll find a table that allows you to input various lengths and widths for rectangles. Your job is to use formulas to calculate the perimeter and area, then experiment with different values and write any conclusions. The geometry formulas you need are $A = lw$ and $P = 2l + 2w$.

Online Practice

1. ☐ Include any written work from the online assignment along with any notes or questions about this lesson's content.

Applications

1. ☐ Complete the Applications problems.

Reflections

Type a short answer to each question.

1. ☐ What is a variable? Why is it wrong to answer "a letter"?

2. ☐ When two variables are related, what does it mean to say that one is the independent variable and the other is the dependent variable?

3. ☐ Describe the difference between an equation and an expression.

4. ☐ How do the terms input and output apply to the relationships we discussed in this lesson?

5. ☐ Describe something you learned or discovered in this lesson that you found particularly interesting.

6. ☐ What questions do you have about this lesson?

Looking Ahead

1. ☐ Complete the Prep Skills for Lesson 2-3.

2. ☐ Read the opening paragraph in Lesson 2-3 carefully then answer Question 0 in preparation for that lesson.

Answers to "Did You Get It?"

1. **a.** Amount of money is independent. How much you spend definitely affects the number of votes you get, but not the other way around.
   b. Amount of sugar is independent. That will affect how the drink tastes.

2. $12.75

3. $A = 42{,}000 + 42{,}000(0.045)t$; $64,680

 Answers to "Prep Skills"

1. **a.** 243   **b.** 64   **c.** $\dfrac{1}{16}$ **d.** −25

2. **a.** 22   **b.** 17   **c.** 33

3. **a.** 70   **b.** −96   **c.** 24

4. **a.** 441   **b.** 3,591.71   **c.** 20.25   **d.** 1,764

2-2 Applications

Name _____

1. If we were to find a formula that relates the distance it takes an average car to stop when the brakes are applied and the speed at which the car is traveling, which would be the input and which would be the output? Why?

2. The formula $D = R + 0.05R^2$ describes the total stopping distance in feet for an average car under ideal driving conditions, where R is the speed of the car in miles per hour. This distance includes the time needed for the driver to react and the time for the car to come to a full stop. Use the formula to fill in this table. I'd suggest using a spreadsheet or the table feature on a calculator, but you can do whatever you want. You're an adult.

Speed (mph)	Stopping Distance (ft)
5	
10	
15	
20	
25	
30	
35	
40	
45	
50	

Math Note

This formula was developed based on experimental data from drivingtesttips.biz. Later in this course we'll see how to develop formulas from experimental data.

3. If you're driving at 25 miles per hour through a school zone and a child runs out in front of you, how much distance will your car cover before stopping?

4. How slow would you have to go in order to decrease that stopping distance by 30 feet?

5. At the scene of an accident, a traffic investigator determines that the stopping distance for one of the cars involved was 103 feet. The speed limit in that area was 30 mph, and conditions were ideal. Was the driver speeding? Explain.

6. According to the U.S. Department of Transportation, in 2014 alone, 3,179 people were killed and 431,000 injured in motor vehicle crashes involving distracted drivers. If you're sending a text while driving on the freeway at 67 mph, how much stopping distance would you need to avoid an accident? (Legal disclaimer: NEVER EVER EVER EVER EVER do this.)

7. What are some factors that would affect stopping distance? Remember, stopping distance factors in both the reaction time of the driver and the time needed to come to a complete stop after braking.

Lesson 2-3   Prep Skills

SKILL 1: RECOGNIZE QUANTITIES THAT CAN BE ADDED

Quantities can only be added if they're **like quantities.** For example, you can easily add $10 and $8, but you can't add $10 and 8 bran muffins. The easiest way to decide if quantities are like is to cover up the number part: If what's left over is identical, the quantities are like. If there are any differences, then the quantities are NOT LIKE and CANNOT be added.

- 202 lb + 15 lb = 217 lb   Without the numbers, both quantities are pounds.

- 202 lb + 15 oz   Not like quantities (lb and oz) so can't be added.

- $12y + 22y = 34y$ Without the numbers, both quantities are y.

- $12y + 22y^2$ Not like quantities (y and y^2) so can't be added.

In some cases, quantities that aren't like can be changed into like quantities by changing units.

- 4 lb + 3 oz = 64 oz + 3 oz = 67 oz   4 lb is 4 × 16 = 64 oz; now they're like quantities.

- $3 + 50¢ = $3 + $0.50 = $3.50   Usually you can convert to whichever of the
                                                        units you prefer.
    = 300¢ + 50¢ = 350¢

SKILL 2: MULTIPLY POWERS OF A VARIABLE QUANTITY

We know that integer exponents represent repeated multiplication. For example, $5^4 = 5 \times 5 \times 5 \times 5$. The same applies to variable quantities, which can be represented by letters, like x, or units of measurement, like feet, meters, or others.

- $x \cdot x = x^2$

- $4y^2 \cdot 2y = 8y^3$ Numbers and variables get multiplied separately.

- $4 \text{ in.} \times 2 \text{ in.} = 8 \text{ in.}^2$ Numbers and units get multiplied separately.

- $6 \text{ m}^2 \times 10 \text{ m} = 60 \text{ m}^3$

SKILL 3: WRITE A PROCEDURE AS A FORMULA

One of the most common and important uses of variables in math is writing formulas to represent mathematical procedures. For example, in order to find your average speed over a trip, you would divide the distance you went by the amount of time you traveled. (This is exactly why a common measure of speed is "miles per hour": It's a distance divided by a time.) Instead of writing that procedure out in words, we could more concisely write

$$s = \frac{d}{t}$$

where s represents the average speed, d represents the distance, and t represents the time.

PREP SKILLS QUESTIONS

1. Add the quantities if possible, or describe why they can't be added.

   a. $132 \text{ yd} + 40 \text{ yd}$

   b. $-12t^3 + 4t$

   c. $18y^2 + 10y^2$

2. If possible, rewrite the quantities so they can be added.

   a. $4 \text{ ft} + 8 \text{ in.}$

   b. $12 \text{ yd} + 16 \text{ sec}$

   c. $10 \text{ decades} + 5 \text{ years}$

3. Perform each multiplication.

   a. $4y \cdot 6y$

   b. $(4 \text{ km})(6 \text{ km})$

   c. $x^2(-3x)$

   d. $8 \text{ yd}^2 \times 12 \text{ yd}$

4. To find the amount of simple interest earned, multiply the original amount, the interest rate, and the number of years. Write this procedure as a formula, and describe what each symbol in your formula represents.

5. The temperature in degrees Fahrenheit can be calculated by multiplying the temperature in Celsius by $\frac{9}{5}$ and adding 32. Write this procedure as a formula, and describe what each symbol in your formula represents.

Lesson 2-3   **From Another Dimension**

LEARNING OBJECTIVES

☐ 1. Determine units for area and volume calculations.

☐ 2. Use formulas to calculate areas and volumes.

☐ 3. Discuss important skills for college students to have.

☐ 4. Simplify expressions.

Even if you're on the right track, you'll get run over if you just sit there.

—Will Rogers

Courtesy Dave Sobecki

In a couple of lessons in Unit 1, we worked with lengths and distances. When you measure distance along a line, you're measuring in just one dimension. But unless you reside in South Park, you live in a three-dimensional world, and many measurements are used for two- and three-dimensional objects. How much carpet do you need for a certain room? That's an area—two dimensions. What's the cargo capacity of an SUV you're considering buying? Volume—three dimensions. How much paint do you need to buy when repainting a couple of rooms? Area. How large of a hot water tank do you need if you have five people in your house? Volume. Measurements like this play a very real role in everyday life, and understanding how to do calculations for measurement in multiple dimensions gives you a real perspective on size in our world.

0. Think of some units of measurement that are applied to areas, and to volumes.

2-3 Group

This activity is a bit less guided than most: The idea here is to promote some qualities that we'll study in the Class portion of this lesson, like problem solving, agility, adaptability, initiative, imagination, and (of course) collaboration, which is always one of the key goals in group work.

We'll begin by working with area and volume. **Area** is the measure of size for two-dimensional objects, like floors, walls, posters, fields, etc. **Volume** is the measure of size for three-dimensional objects, like beer mugs, swimming pools, buildings, and so on.

1. Notice that each of the small boxes in the figure here is a square that's one inch on each side. You could find the area of the large rectangle by adding up the number of boxes, but there's a quicker way. What is it? Use it to find the area.

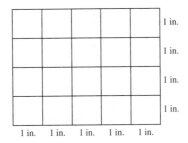

1 in.   1 in.   1 in.   1 in.   1 in.

2. When length is measured in inches, the correct units for area are _____ _____.

3. Use your answer from Question 1 to write a formula for the area of a rectangle based on the length and the width.

4. This time, we have a three-dimensional figure made up of a bunch of little cubes. You could find the volume by counting all the little cubes, but you're more clever than that! Describe a quicker method, then use it to find the volume.

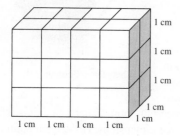

5. When length is measured in centimeters, the correct units for volume are _____ _____.

6. Use your answer from Question 4 to write a formula for the volume of a rectangular solid based on the length, width, and height.

Did You Get It

Try this problem to see if you understand the concepts we just studied. The answers can be found at the end of the Portfolio section.

1. Find the area of one figure and the volume of the other figure, whichever is more appropriate.

a.

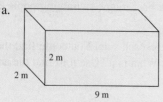

b.

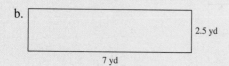

7. My friend David Najar is an acclaimed artist. The value of a painting is to some extent determined by the area of the canvas. A Najar piece I recently acquired has dimensions as shown, and you can find the area using the formula $A = lw$, where l is the length and w is the width. What is the area?

Area = _____ × _____. (Include units on each number.)

Area =

The area units for the canvas are _____ _____ because there are _____ factors multiplied together, each of which has _____ as units.

24 in.

32 in.

Painting courtesy of David Najar, Photo courtesy of Dave Sobecki

8. The volume of a cylindrical oil storage tank can be found using the formula $V = \pi r^2 h$, where r is the radius of the top and bottom, and h is the height. Use the second diagram (not one of my best, but to be fair I'm a mathematician, not a graphic artist) to find the volume of the tank.

Volume = _____ × _____ × _____ × _____
(Write four separate factors, and again include units on all measurements.)

Volume =
(Round to the nearest tenth.)

The volume units for the oil tank are _____ _____ because there are ____ factors that have _____ as units.

9 m

5 m

In Questions 9–13, perform each calculation. Then describe whether the result is an area or a volume, and make an educated guess as to what type of figure you think the result measures. (If necessary, round results to one decimal place.)

9. (6 m)(4 m)

10. (3 ft)(5 ft)(10 ft)

11. $\dfrac{4\pi(4 \text{ in.})^3}{3}$

12. $\dfrac{4\pi}{3}(1.5 \text{ cm})^3 + \pi(1.5 \text{ cm})^2(3 \text{ cm})$

> **Math Note**
>
> It would be a good idea to locate the π button on your calculator, and use it anytime a calculation involves pi. You'll get better results than if you use a decimal approximation like 3.14, and it's less work! Bonus.

13. $\frac{1}{2}\pi(2\ \text{ft})^2 + (8\ \text{ft})(4\ \text{ft})$

Did You Get It

2. For each calculation, describe if it's an area or a volume, then calculate the result, including units.

   a. $\frac{1}{2}(4\ \text{mi} + 5\ \text{mi})(3\ \text{mi})$

   b. $13(14\ \text{ft}^2)9\ \text{ft}$

   c. $\frac{4}{3}\pi(7\ \text{mm})(5\ \text{mm})(11\ \text{mm})$

2-3 Class

In his 2010 book *The Global Achievement Gap,* educational consultant Tony Wagner outlines seven survival skills that students have to master to reach their academic potential. Define what each of these skills means to you.

1. Critical thinking and problem solving

2. Collaboration across networks and leading by influence

3. Agility and adaptability

4. Initiative and entrepreneurialism

5. Accessing and analyzing information

6. Effective written and oral communication

7. Curiosity and imagination

Here's a key quote from Wagner's book: *"Today knowledge is ubiquitous, constantly changing, growing exponentially. . . . Today knowledge is free. It's like air, it's like water. It's become a commodity. . . . There's no competitive advantage today in knowing more than the person next to you. The world doesn't care what you know. What the world cares about is what you can do with what you know."*

8. What does this quote mean to you? Do you agree with it? Why or why not?

At this point, you should be pretty comfortable multiplying units of length to find the correct units for area and volume calculations. Multiplying two terms with variables is very similar to multiplying dimensions with units.

9. Perform each multiplication. For parts a and b, include units.

   a. 2 ft × 3 ft = _____

   b. 6 ft^2 × 5 ft = _____

   c. $(2x)(3x)$ = _____

   d. $(6x^2)(5x)$ = _____

When reviewing addition of similar quantities in Lesson 1-2, we saw that we can add the expressions $8x$ and $5x$ to get $13x$. Since $8x + 5x$ and $13x$ would give you the same output no matter what input you choose, we say that those expressions are **equivalent**.

When working with expressions, equations, and formulas it's often useful to simplify expressions. This involves replacing an expression with a simpler but equivalent one. As we saw in the previous paragraph, adding or subtracting like terms is one way to simplify an expression.

10. Use the formula $P = a + b + c$ to find the perimeter of this triangle. The length of each side is measured in inches. First write the formula, then substitute the expressions for each side of the triangle into the formula, then simplify the result. Make sure each step is a complete formula (has both a left side and a right side), and include units.

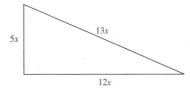

11. Repeat Question 10, but this time use the formula $A = \dfrac{1}{2}bh$ to find the area of the triangle. In this case, b represents the length of the triangle's base and h is the height.

12. Use your answers to Questions 10 and 11 to find the perimeter and area of the triangle if x is 4.

Did You Get It

3. Simplify each expression, and state whether each could be a volume, an area, or neither.
   a. $\pi(4x)^2 x$
   b. $lw + lw + wh + wh + lh + lh$
   c. $8y^2(10y^2)$

2-3 | Portfolio

Name _____

Check each box when you've completed the task. Remember that your instructor will want you to turn in the portfolio pages you create.

Online Practice

1. ☐ Include any written work from the online assignment along with any notes or questions about this lesson's content.

Applications

1. ☐ Complete the Applications problems.

Reflections

Type a short answer to each question.

1. ☐ Pick two of the seven survival skills from the Class portion of the lesson that you think are most important to you. Discuss why you chose them, and how strong you think you are in these skills.

2. ☐ Why are units so important in measurement? Giving some examples of measurements with no units should help.

3. ☐ What does it mean to say that two expressions are equivalent?

4. ☐ Name one thing you learned or discovered in this lesson that you found particularly interesting.

5. ☐ What questions do you have about this lesson?

Looking Ahead

1. ☐ Complete the Prep Skills for Lesson 2-4.

2. ☐ Read the opening paragraph in Lesson 2-4 carefully and answer Question 0 in preparation for that lesson.

Answers to "Did You Get It?"

    1. a. 36 m^3
                b. 17.5 yd^2

    2. a. Area: 13.5 mi^2
        b. Volume: $1{,}638 \text{ ft}^3$
        c. Volume: $1{,}612.7 \text{ mm}^3$

    3. a. $16\,\pi x^3$, volume
        b. $2lw + 2wh + 2lh$; area
        c. $80y^4$; neither

Answers to "Prep Skills"

    1. a. 172 yd
        b. cannot be added; t^3 and t are not like
        c. $28y^2$

    2. a. $4\frac{2}{3}$ ft or 56 in.
      b. cannot be added
      c. 10.5 decades or 105 years

    3. a. $24y^2$
        b. 24 km^2
        c. $-3x^3$
        d. 96 yd^3

    4. $I = Prt$, where I represents the amount of interest earned, P is the original amount, r is the interest rate, and t is time in years.

    5. $F = \dfrac{9}{5}C + 32$, where F is the temperature in degrees Fahrenheit and C is the temperature in degrees Celsius.

2-3 Applications

Name _____

Tennis balls are packaged in a cylindrical can, and since they're round, that leaves a lot of empty space in the can. How much space? The radius of a tennis ball is 3.3 cm; the can has the same radius for a nice tight fit, and the height of the can is six times that radius, which is 19.8 cm.

1. The calculation below is intended to find the volume of the empty space in the can, but there's something wrong with it. Explain how you can tell, without doing any calculations or looking up any formulas, that the answer will be wrong. (Hint: The terms "units" and "like terms" might come into play.)

$$\text{Volume} = \underbrace{\pi(3.3\text{ cm})^2(19.8\text{ cm})}_{\text{Volume of can}} - 3\underbrace{\left(\frac{4}{3}\pi(3.3\text{ cm})^2\right)}_{\substack{\text{Volume of}\\\text{each ball}}}$$

©McGraw-Hill Education/
Ken Karp, photographer

2. Find the fix needed to correct the mistake in the calculation. If you need help, do a Web search for "volume of a sphere." Then find the volume of empty space in the can. Round to the nearest hundredth.

3. Use your corrected formula to find the volume of the can, and the volume of all three balls in the can combined. Round each to the nearest hundredth.

4. What percentage of the volume of the can is filled by the tennis balls? When you set up your calculation, make sure to include units on all volumes. Round to the nearest hundredth.

5. After performing the division in Question 4, what units remain? Do you think this will always happen when finding percentages?

2-3 Applications

Name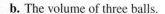

6. Racquetballs have a radius of about 2.8 cm. If three balls are packaged in a can like we described for tennis balls earlier, find each volume. Round to the nearest hundredth.
   a. The volume of one ball.

   b. The volume of three balls.

   ©Comstock Images/Alamy RF

   c. The volume of the can. (Remember, the height is six times the radius.)

   d. The volume of empty space in the can.

   e. The percentage of the can filled by the racquetballs. How does it compare to the tennis ball percentage? Does this surprise you?

7. Golf balls also come in packages of three, but they are usually packaged in a rectangular box with a square bottom. The radius of each ball is about 2.2 cm. The length and width of the box's square base are twice the radius, and the height is six times the radius.

   a. Would you guess that there would be more or less empty space by percentage than there is in a tennis ball can? Why?

   b. Use your procedure from Question 4 to find the percentage of the golf ball box that is filled. Round volumes to the nearest hundredth.

   ©Arina Zaiachin/123RF
   .com

Lesson 2-4   Prep Skills

SKILL 1: REDUCE FRACTIONS

The process of writing fractions in lowest terms is called **reducing fractions**. It's useful to do because it's easier to work with and interpret fractions when they're in lowest terms. For example, it's a lot easier to see that $\frac{5}{2}$ is two and a half than to see that $\frac{180}{72}$ is equal to two and a half. To reduce a fraction, divide BOTH the numerator and denominator by any common factors.

- $\dfrac{4}{6} = \dfrac{4 \div 2}{6 \div 2} = \dfrac{2}{3}$ The greatest factor common of 4 and 6 is 2.

- $\dfrac{30}{12} = \dfrac{30 \div 6}{12 \div 6} = \dfrac{5}{2}$ The greatest factor common of 30 and 12 is 6.

SKILL 2: BUILD UP FRACTIONS

Sometimes it's useful to do the opposite of reducing fractions: rewriting fractions so that they have a bigger numerator and denominator. This is called **building up** a fraction. Since it's the opposite of reducing fractions, we do exactly the opposite: Instead of dividing the numerator and denominator by the same number, we multiply the numerator and denominator by the SAME number.

- $\dfrac{3}{5}$ can be written as a fraction with denominator 20: $\dfrac{3 \cdot 4}{5 \cdot 4} = \dfrac{12}{20}$

- $-\dfrac{2}{3}$ can be written as a fraction with denominator 60: $-\dfrac{2 \cdot 20}{3 \cdot 20} = -\dfrac{40}{60}$

SKILL 3: MULTIPLY FRACTIONS

To multiply two fractions, you just multiply numerators and multiply denominators to find the fraction for the product.

- $\dfrac{2}{3} \cdot \dfrac{7}{11} = \dfrac{14}{33}$

- $\dfrac{5}{2} \cdot \dfrac{12}{7} = \dfrac{60}{14} = \dfrac{30}{7}$ Often, the result can be reduced.

If one of the factors isn't a fraction, you can make it a fraction by just giving it a denominator of 1.

- $100 \cdot \dfrac{3}{5} = \dfrac{100}{1} \cdot \dfrac{3}{5} = \dfrac{300}{5} = 60$

The same process can be used to multiply three or more fractions.

- $\dfrac{6}{1} \cdot \dfrac{1}{3} \cdot \dfrac{2}{1} \cdot \dfrac{4}{1} = \dfrac{48}{3} = 16$

SKILL 4: REDUCE FRACTIONS WITH VARIABLES

Variables in fractions can sometimes be a common factor. For example, in the expression $\frac{7a}{2a}$, we can divide the numerator and denominator by a to get $\frac{7}{2}$.

- $\dfrac{y(3 - y)}{y} = 3 - y$ Numerator and denominator divided by y

- $\dfrac{12t}{t^2} = \dfrac{12}{t}$ Numerator and denominator divided by t

SKILL 5: RECOGNIZE UNIT EQUIVALENCES

You almost certainly know that 12 inches and 1 foot represent the same length. This is an example of a **unit equivalence**, which is a statement that two measurements in different units represent the same size. The following tables are a list of unit equivalences. The goal is certainly not to memorize these equivalences (although it wouldn't be a bad idea to learn some of them by heart). Just familiarize yourself with them so that you know where to refer back to when needing an equivalence throughout the remainder of the course.

English Measures and Equivalents

Length	Weight
12 inches (in.) = 1 foot (ft) 3 feet = 1 yard (yd) 5,280 feet = 1 mile (mi)	16 ounces (oz) = 1 pound (lb) 2,000 pounds = 1 ton (T)
Liquid Volume	**Time**
3 teaspoons (tsp) = 1 tablespoon (tbs) 8 fluid ounces (oz) = 1 cup (c) 2 cups = 1 pint (pt) 2 pints = 1 quart (qt) 4 quarts = 1 gallon (gal)	60 seconds (sec) = 1 minute (min) 60 minutes = 1 hour (hr) 24 hours = 1 day 7 days = 1 week 52 weeks = 1 year 365 days = 1 year

Metric System

Kilo	Hecto	Deka	Base Unit	Deci	Centi	Milli
km	hm	dam	**Length** Meter (m)	dm	cm	mm
kg	hg	dag	**Weight** Gram (g)	dg	cg	mg
kL	hL	daL	**Volume** Liter (L)	dL	cL	mL

Move decimal right ⟶

⟵ Move decimal left

Conversions between Systems

Length	Weight	Volume	Temperature
2.54 cm = 1 in. 1 m ≈ 3.28 ft 1.61 km ≈ 1 mi	28.3 g ≈ 1 oz 2.2 lb ≈ 1 kg	1.06 qt ≈ 1 L 3.79 L ≈ 1 gal	$F = \dfrac{9}{5}C + 32$ $C = \dfrac{5}{9}(F - 32)$ $C = K - 273.15$ $K = C + 273.15$

PREP SKILLS QUESTIONS

1. Write each fraction in lowest terms.

   a. $\dfrac{12}{18}$ b. $-\dfrac{5}{35}$ c. $\dfrac{20}{45}$

2. Write each fraction with the given denominator.

   a. $\dfrac{1}{3}$; 21   b. $\dfrac{7}{3}$; 18   c. $-\dfrac{3}{8}$; 80

3. Perform each operation, and reduce your answer if necessary.

   a. $\dfrac{2}{5} \cdot \dfrac{9}{2}$ b. $12 \cdot \dfrac{9}{8}$ c. $\dfrac{12}{1} \cdot \dfrac{1}{3} \cdot \dfrac{600}{1}$ d. $5 \cdot \dfrac{11}{5} \cdot \dfrac{12}{11} \cdot \dfrac{7}{12}$

4. Simplify each fractional expression by dividing out common factors.

   a. $\dfrac{8b}{3b}$ b. $\dfrac{5x(x + 4)}{x}$ c. $\dfrac{4y^2}{8y}$

5. Use the table on the previous page to find an equivalent measure for each amount.

   a. 1 gal = _____ qts   b. 1 in. = _____ cm   c. 1 gal = _____ L

   d. 1 T = _____ lbs   e. 1 kg = _____ lbs

Lesson 2-4   It Works Like Magic

LEARNING OBJECTIVES

☐ 1. Convert units using dimensional analysis.

☐ 2. Convert units within the metric system.

☐ 3. Convert rates of change.

☐ 4. Convert temperatures.

©David A. Tietz/Editorial Image, LLC RF

If you don't like change, you are going to like irrelevance even less.
　　　　　　　　　　—Eric Shinseki

Have you ever thought about the number of different ways we have to measure objects? Inches, feet, yards, miles, centimeters, meters, kilometers . . . and these cover only length; there are many more ways to measure length, as well as different units of measure for temperature, time, area, volume, mass, and other quantities. Why so many different measurements? The short answer is efficiency. Things come in so many different sizes that being stuck with just one unit of measurement would be very inconvenient. For example, it's about 5,892,480 inches from Chicago to Milwaukee. Clearly, measuring the distance in miles (93) is far more efficient.

　　On the other hand, this mysterious beaker is only about 0.00016 miles tall. Do you have even the first clue of how tall that is compared to, say, a house cat? Me neither. So measuring its height in inches (10) makes a whole lot more sense. In this lesson, we'll learn an incredibly valuable skill called **dimensional analysis** in the process of converting units. It sounds fancy, but don't worry: You'll be able to handle it just fine, and it'll help you out with a lot of day-to-day calculations that might have seemed puzzling before.

0. Think of a situation you've encountered where converting the units of some quantity did, or would have, come in handy.

2-4　Class

According to the unit equivalence table in the Prep Skills (which we'll use a TON in this lesson), 1 kg is equivalent to about 2.2 lb. Quick, without thinking about it too deeply, if you wanted to convert your weight from pounds to kilograms, would you multiply or divide by 2.2? Not so easy, is it? (Don't feel bad, it's confusing for me too, and I have all sorts of degrees and stuff.) Our first goal in this lesson is to develop a systematic procedure that takes thinking and guessing out of the business of converting units. It's based on an idea that's so brilliantly simple you should probably send us a sizeable cash donation: If measurements in two different units represent the same actual weight, like 1 kg and 2.2 lb, then a fraction formed from dividing those units is just a fancy way to say 1. In other words, 1 kg and 2.2 lb are different ways to express the exact same amount, so

$$\frac{1 \text{ kg}}{2.2 \text{ lb}} \text{ and } \frac{2.2 \text{ lb}}{1 \text{ kg}} \text{ are both equal to } 1.$$

We call a fraction of this type a **conversion factor**, and *multiplying any measurement by a conversion factor won't change the size of the measurement* because we're just multiplying by one; it will just change the units used to measure.

　　So here's our genius idea for converting units for a measurement: We'll multiply the measurement by a conversion factor in a way that makes the units we don't want divide out, leaving behind the units we do want. To see how this works, we'll return our attention to the beaker at the beginning of the lesson. It turns out that this particular beaker contains a revolutionary product, Dr. Phail's Magic Love Potion: guaranteed to lure the affection of that special someone, or your money back (minus a processing fee of just $29.95). The 450 mL of potion in the beaker can be converted to liters if we multiply by a convenient conversion factor.

1. Write two different conversion factors based on the fact that 1 liter is equivalent to 1,000 mL.

2. There are two ways we could multiply our measurement of 450 mL by a conversion factor:

   $$450 \text{ mL} \cdot \frac{1 \text{ L}}{1,000 \text{ mL}} \quad \text{or} \quad 450 \text{ mL} \cdot \frac{1,000 \text{ mL}}{1 \text{ L}}$$

   Which of these two calculations correctly eliminates milliliters and leaves behind liters? Why?

   > **Math Note**
   >
   > If multiplying a number by a fraction, as in Question 2, bothers you at all, feel free to write the number as a fraction by giving it a denominator of 1.

3. What are the units for the other calculation? Do they have any meaning?

4. So how many liters of magic potion are in the beaker?

5. According to our handy-dandy conversion chart, 1 gallon is approximately equivalent to 3.79 L. Write two different conversion factors based on this fun fact.

6. Use one of the two conversion factors to convert your answer from Question 4 into gallons.

Did You Get It

Try this problem to see if you understand the concepts we just studied. The answers can be found at the end of the Portfolio section.

1. There are four quarts in a gallon. How many quarts are in the beaker at the beginning of the lesson? (You'll need your answer to Question 6.)

7. Now here's one of the great things about dimensional analysis: Notice that it took us two steps to get from 450 mL to gallons. First we converted to liters using one conversion factor, then from liters to gallons using another. If you're really clever, you can get there directly in one calculation by using BOTH of the conversion factors you used in Questions 4 and 6. Do it!

8. My house is just about 15 miles from the Gulf of Mexico on the Florida coast. How far is this in inches? Use two conversion factors in one calculation, like you did in Question 7.

Did You Get It

2. There are 2 cups in a pint, and 8 pints in a gallon. If a large recipe calls for 7 cups of sweet cream, how many gallons is that?

Converting Units within the Metric System

When we converted 450 mL to L we used dimensional analysis, but it turns out that we could have just moved the decimal point. If you look at the conversion chart for metric units in the Prep Skills for this lesson, going from mL to L requires a move of 3 columns to the left. This corresponds to moving the decimal point 3 places to the left:

450. mL = 0.450 L

If, on the other hand, a unit you're converting to lives to the right on the chart, count the number of columns and move the decimal point that many places to the right.

9. Convert 0.44 L of love potion into dL and kL by shifting the decimal. Which is the more reasonable measurement in this case?

Did You Get It

3. Use the metric conversion table to convert 275 grams into cg and dag.

10. Dr. Phail's potion also comes in a 0.75-gallon container. Convert this to cubic centimeters (cc) using equivalances in the Prep Skills table and dimensional analysis. (Hint: You will also need to know that 1 cubic centimeter (cc) = 1 mL.)

Now here's a key idea: Another way to write cubic centimeters is cm^3, or $cm \cdot cm \cdot cm$. We can use this idea to convert units of volume.

11. According to the table of equivalences, 1 in. = 2.54 cm. What is the result of the following calculation? Pay close attention to the units.

$$1{,}000 \text{ cm}^3 \cdot \frac{1 \text{ in.}}{2.54 \text{ cm}} \cdot \frac{1 \text{ in.}}{2.54 \text{ cm}} \cdot \frac{1 \text{ in.}}{2.54 \text{ cm}}$$

12. Use the idea from Question 11 to convert your answer from Question 10 into cubic inches.

13. Based on what you just did, fill in the blank to create a shortcut to convert between cubic centimeters and cubic inches.

    1 in.^{3} = _____ cm^3

Converting Area and Volume Units

You can use known conversion factors involving length to convert units in two dimensions (area) and in three dimensions (volume). You'll just need to use them enough times to be sure the area or volume units you started with have been completely divided away.

For example, my bedroom has an area of 196 ft². This area can be converted to square inches by using the fact that 1 ft = 12 in.

$$\frac{196 \text{ ft}^2}{1} \cdot \frac{12 \text{ in.}}{1 \text{ ft}} \cdot \frac{12 \text{ in.}}{1 \text{ ft}} = 28{,}224 \text{ in}^2$$

Did You Get It

4. Use the procedure for converting units of area or volume to convert 4 square miles into square feet.

2-4 Group

Rates of Change

A **rate** is a ratio that compares two quantities. Examples of rates include $\frac{75 \text{ mi}}{1 \text{ hr}}$, $\frac{10 \text{ mg}}{1 \text{ mL}}$, and $\frac{\$15.00}{2 \text{ tickets}}$. The first two are also called **unit rates** because they have a 1 in the denominator.

1. Explain what is meant when we say a car is traveling $\frac{75 \text{ mi}}{1 \text{ hr}}$ (more commonly written as 75 mph).

2. The entire 450 mL of Dr. Phail's Love Potion (from the beginning of the lesson) is supposed to be slowly dripped into a mixture over a 5-hour period. (Kind of a pain, but hey—love doesn't come easy.) Express this quantity as a rate.

> ### Math Note
>
> You know how sometimes we write fractions using a slanted line, like 5/2? DON'T do that when using dimensional analysis. The whole process relies on clearly recognizing which units are in the numerator, and which are in the denominator.

3. Simplify the rate you wrote in Question 2 so that it's a unit rate.

4. It might seem like it would be really complicated to convert this rate into liters per minute, but dimensional analysis will save the day. If we're going to end up with liters per minute, we'll need to get rid of mL in the numerator and replace it with L, and we'll need to get rid of hr in the denominator and replace it with min. This can be accomplished in one calculation if we multiply by two different conversion factors that eliminate the unwanted units, just like we did in the class portion. Do that now. Focus on putting the units you want to eliminate on the OPPOSITE side of the fraction when writing your conversion factors. Write your answer in decimal and scientific notation.

Did You Get It

5. By several recent estimates, global sea levels are rising by at least 0.32 cm per year. Convert this rate to inches per century. (A century is 100 years.)

Converting Temperatures

Unlike other unit conversions, temperature conversions are done using a formula. (We'll get a quick look at why in the Applications.) There are two common temperature units for everyday use: degrees Fahrenheit in the English system, and degrees Celsius in the metric system. There's a third unit often used in science, particularly chemistry, known as degrees Kelvin.

5. While in production, the love potion needs to be kept below 400 K at all times. The thermometer on the most recent batch currently reads 200°F. One of the formulas provided will convert that temperature to degrees Celsius. Which formula would you use? Why?

$$F = \frac{9}{5}C + 32 \qquad C = \frac{5}{9}(F - 32)$$

> ## Math Note
>
> In the Celsius and Fahrenheit scales, we use the degree symbol (as in 32°F or 21°C), but in the Kelvin scale, we just use a K (as in 200 K).

6. Use the appropriate formula to convert 200°F to Celsius.

7. Use one of the two formulas provided to convert that temperature to Kelvin. Explain why you chose that formula. Will the batch of love potion be ruined?

$$C = K - 273.15 \qquad K = C + 273.15$$

8. Use a calculator or spreadsheet along with an appropriate formula to complete the table, which compares Fahrenheit and Celsius temperatures.

Degrees Celsius	Degrees Fahrenheit
0	
10	
20	
30	
40	
50	
60	
70	
80	
90	
100	

Did You Get It

6. The hottest temperature ever reliably recorded was 129.2°F in Death Valley, California, in June 2013. The lowest was −89.2°C at Vostok Station, a Soviet research installation on Antarctica, in July 1983. Convert the high temperature to Celsius and the low temperature to Fahrenheit.

We'll close this lesson with a bit more practice on dimensional analysis problems, coming to us from the world of nursing, where I promise you it comes in handy. We'll look at some related examples in the Applications.

9. According to the online dosage guide for one brand of insulin, the recommended delivery is 0.2 units of insulin per kilogram of weight each day. How many daily units would be indicated for a 178-pound patient?

10. A dosage of 1,700 mg of cefadroxil is to be delivered to a patient in an IV drip over 75 minutes. It's supplied in a solution that contains 1 gram of the drug in 20 cm^3 of solution. The pump used to deliver the drug uses units of cc's per hour. At what rate should it be set?

2-4 Portfolio

Name _____

Check each box when you've completed the task. Remember that your instructor will want you to turn in the portfolio pages you create.

 Technology

The method of dimensional analysis is all about multiplying by an appropriate factor, and spreadsheets are really good at doing multiplication, right? So it should be possible to build a spreadsheet that does unit conversions. Starting with the template in the online resources for this lesson, build a spreadsheet that converts lengths in meters to each of feet, inches, yards, and miles. To figure out how to write the formulas, it'll be helpful to first do a couple of sample conversions by hand, then apply that knowledge to the spreadsheet. See the template for further instructions.

 Online Practice

1. ☐ Include any written work from the online assignment along with any notes or questions about this lesson's content.

 Applications

1. ☐ Complete the Applications problems.

 Reflections

Type a short answer to each question.

1. ☐ Describe the process we developed for converting units; focus on the fact that we're multiplying by one.

2. ☐ What's a conversion factor? Where do they come from? What are they used for?

3. ☐ What's a rate? What about a unit rate?

4. ☐ How can we use length conversion factors to convert areas or volumes?

5. ☐ Name one thing you learned or discovered in this lesson that you found particularly interesting.

6. ☐ What questions do you have about this lesson?

 Looking Ahead

1. ☐ Complete the Prep Skills for Lesson 2-5.

2. ☐ Read the opening paragraph in Lesson 2-5 carefully and answer Question 0 in preparation for that lesson.

Answers to "Did You Get It?"

1. 0.48 qt

2. 0.4375 gal

3. 275 g = 27,500 cg = 27.5 dag

4. 111,513,600 ft^2

5. About 12.6 $\dfrac{\text{in.}}{\text{century}}$

6. High: 54°C; Low: −128.56°F

Answers to "Prep Skills"

1. **a.** $\dfrac{2}{3}$ **b.** $-\dfrac{1}{7}$ **c.** $\dfrac{4}{9}$

2. **a.** $\dfrac{7}{21}$ **b.** $\dfrac{42}{18}$ **c.** $-\dfrac{30}{80}$

3. **a.** $\dfrac{9}{5}$ **b.** $\dfrac{27}{2}$ **c.** 2,400   **d.** 7

4. **a.** $\dfrac{8}{3}$ **b.** $5(x + 4)$ **c.** $\dfrac{y}{2}$

5. **a.** 4 qts   **b.** 2.54 cm   **c.** 3.79 L   **d.** 2,000 lbs   **e.** 2.2 lbs

2-4 Applications

Name _____

For Questions 1–5, use dimensional analysis with conversion factors to convert each measurement to the given units. You'll need unit equivalences from this section and from page 192 to build your conversion factors. Round to two decimal places if necessary.

1. How many miles is a 10-kilometer race?

2. How many feet is a 10-kilometer race?

3. The average offensive lineman in the National Football League weighs 141.3 kilograms. How many pounds is that?

4. A surgical patient needs to have her liquid intake carefully monitored. How many mL of fluid did she consume if she drank $\frac{1}{2}$ L of water, a pint of milk, and 8 oz of juice?

5. The earth moves at about 98,000 feet per second as it revolves around the sun. How fast is that in miles per hour? (Recall that 1 mile is 5,280 feet.)

©Getty Images/Digital Vision RF

Glaciers are large masses of ice that flow like rivers across the ground. Really, really slow rivers—did I mention that they're ice? Most move less than a foot per day. At one point, the San Rafael glacier in Chile was moving 203 millimeters per day.

6. How fast was it moving in inches per hour? (1 inch is 25.4 mm.)

Source: Photograph by Bruce F. Molnia, U.S. Geological Survey

7. Find the speed in miles per hour, then explain why that's a silly unit of speed in this case. Write your answer in scientific notation.

8. How long would it take the glacier to move the length of a football field (100 yards)? Write your answer in decimal notation rounded to the nearest tenth of an hour, then in scientific notation.

9. A patient needs 175 mg of a low-dose pain reliever. The pharmacy sends pills marked 0.35 g. How many should be administered?

Lesson 2-5 Prep Skills

SKILL 1: LOCATE NUMBERS ON A NUMBER LINE

When numbers live exactly at one of the labels on a number line, it's pretty easy to decide where to put them, as in this example:

- Locate −15 on the number line

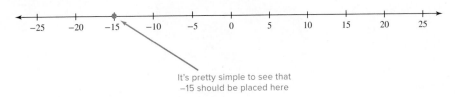

It's a more interesting question, and typically involves some estimation, when locating numbers that live in between labels.

- Locate 3, 8.2, 13.4, and 19.9 on the number line

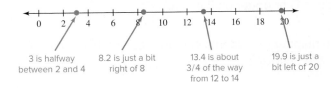

SKILL 2: READ BAR GRAPHS, PIE CHARTS, AND SCATTER PLOTS

These skills have been previously covered in this book. Cool! Bar graphs and pie charts are in Lesson 1-1, and scatter plots were introduced in Lesson 1-5.

PREP SKILLS QUESTIONS

1. Locate −40, 15, −15, 27, and −2 on the number line.

2. The pie chart shows the distribution of grades on a final exam I just finished grading for a Calc 2 class with 31 students. Use it to answer each question.

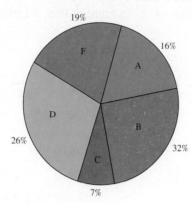

Grades on Calc 2 Final

a. What percentage of students got a B on the final?

b. How many students got a C on the final?

c. How many students got a D or better on the final?

3. The bar graph shows the number of students that got each of the first five questions on the final completely correct. Use it to answer each question.

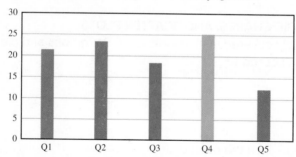

Students Getting Full Credit by Question

a. Which question was answered correctly by the most students?

b. How many people answered Question 2 correctly?

c. What percentage of the 31 students taking the test got Question 5 completely right?

4. The scatter plot shows the final grades for all 31 students. On the horizontal axis is the student's position alphabetically on the class roster. The vertical axis shows their score out of 160 on the final.

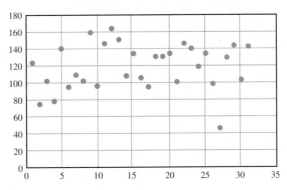

Student Scores on Calc 2 Final

a. How many students scored less than 80 points?

b. How many students scored 140 or more points?

c. About what was the lowest score on the test?

Lesson 2-5   Take a Guess!

LEARNING OBJECTIVES

☐ 1. Identify the steps in a systematic problem-solving procedure.

☐ 2. Make educated guesses.

☐ 3. Compare numbers using inequality symbols.

©Rich Legg/Getty Images RF

Don't be afraid to fail. Be afraid not to try.
            —Michael Jordan

Consider this scenario: You're a contestant on a game show, and you're given a trivia question worth $50,000. Pressure! The question is "Which state was first to secede from the union in 1860?" Do you know the answer? If so, terrific—drinks are on you. But if you don't know the answer, you'd have to guess. Would your list of guesses include the Pacific Ocean, Justin Bieber, Twinkies, and a goat? Of course not. Those would be completely ridiculous, and you're not a goof.

The point is that "guessing" doesn't usually mean just throwing out some random answer and praying for a miracle. Instead, we use information we know to be true and some reasoning ability to make an **educated guess**. In this section, we'll try to gain some confidence with educated guessing, which sometimes goes by a different name in math: **estimation**.

From an instructor's point of view, it seems like in math classes, a lot of students are afraid to make educated guesses. But sometimes that's a completely reasonable step in problem solving. Nobody likes to be wrong, but if you're not willing to at least answer a question, you have no chance at ever being right. Not being afraid of failure is one of the characteristics shared by almost everyone that's very successful in their chosen field.

Think Michael Jordan never failed? Do a Google search sometime for "Michael Jordan high school team." If one of the greatest athletes of all time can overcome the occasional fail, then surely we can, too. So let's get over the fear of being wrong and gain the confidence to make educated guesses.

0. Describe a situation, either in the classroom or out, where having the confidence to make an educated guess would be helpful.

2-5 Class

1. Write a brief description of two or three problems that you've had to solve outside of school.

2. What are some methods that you use to solve problems in your life? Do you think that they apply to solving problems in college classes?

We're now well into the second unit of this course. So what is it really about? Math would be the easy answer, but we're sure hoping that you've recognized by now that this isn't a typical math course. A better answer to that question would be "problem solving." Hopefully you've noticed that we haven't done any abstract math: Every topic we've covered has been in an attempt to solve some problem. So by now, we've gotten some pretty good experience in solving problems. And without even thinking about it, we've carved out some general guidelines for attacking problems.

A Hungarian mathematician named George Pólya published a book on problem solving in 1945. In it, he described a problem-solving procedure that he felt was common to most of history's greatest thinkers. His book has been translated into at least 17 languages and is still a big seller on Amazon, so obviously he must have been on to something! Pólya's procedure isn't exactly earth shattering: Its brilliance really lies in its simplicity. Pólya's basic steps are listed in the colored box, followed by our spin on each step.

Polya's Four-Step Procedure for Solving Problems

Step 1: Understand the problem. The best way to start any problem is to write down relevant information as you read it. Especially with longer word problems, if you read the whole problem at once and don't DO anything, it's easy to get panicked. Instead, read the problem slowly and carefully, writing down information as it's provided. That way, you'll always at least have a start on the problem. Another essential step: Carefully identify AND WRITE DOWN what it is they're asking you to find; this almost always helps you to devise a strategy.

Step 2: Devise a plan to solve the problem. Good planning is the key to any successful operation! This is where problem solving is at least as much art as science—there are many, many ways to solve problems. A short list of common strategics includes making a list of possible outcomes; drawing a diagram; trial and error; finding a similar problem that you already know how to solve; and using arithmetic, algebra, geometry, or good old-fashioned common sense.

Step 3: Carry out your plan to solve the problem. There's no point in making a plan if you don't carefully execute it. If your original plan doesn't work, don't settle for failure and give up—try a different strategy! There are many different ways to attack problems. Be persistent!

Step 4: Check your answer. In ANY problem-solving situation, you should think about whether or not your answer is reasonable. In many cases you'll be able to use math to check your answer and see if it's exactly correct. Even if you can check an answer, before you start solving a problem (or after you finish it) the ability to make an estimate to decide whether your answer is reasonable is a valuable skill.

Estimation is a valuable skill when it comes to reading information from charts and graphs. In fact, we used that skill (without even realizing it!) several different places in Unit 1. For example, when reading a bar graph, if the length of a bar falls between two lines, we have to estimate its height. We can practice this useful skill by looking at number lines.

This number line is a timeline of important advances in medical science. Use it to answer Questions 3–10.

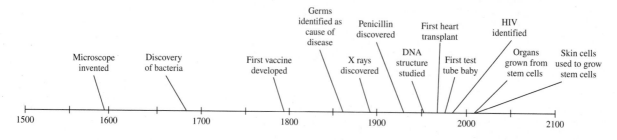

3. Estimate the year that the microscope was invented, and describe how you got your answer.

4. Estimate the year that germs were identified as the cause of disease, and describe how you got your answer.

5. Which happened first: the first test tube baby, or the first heart transplant? Estimate the year for each.

6. Which happened first: organs grown from stem cells, or the identification of HIV? Estimate the year for each.

There are several places in this course where comparing the sizes of numbers plays a key role. So it's worth a bit of our time to review some of the symbols and terminology that go along with these comparisons. In some cases our example comparisons will involve just numbers; in others, we'll be using letters to represent variable quantities.

Comparing Numbers

Verbal Description	In Symbols	Relationship on a Number Line
10 and $\frac{20}{2}$ are equal.	$10 = \frac{20}{2}$	10 and $\frac{20}{2}$ are the same point.
x is approximately equal to 10.	$x \approx 10$	The quantity x is close to 10, but they aren't necessarily the same point.
10 is not equal to 15.	$10 \neq 15$	10 and 15 are different points.
10 is less than 12.	$10 < 12$	10 is to the left of 12.
y is less than or equal to 10.	$y \leq 10$	The quantity y is either to the left of or on 10
10 is greater than 6.	$10 > 6$	10 is to the right of 6.
n is greater than or equal to 10.	$n \geq 10$	The quantity n is either to the right of or on 10

7. Use your answer from Question 5 to write an inequality involving < that compares the dates for the advances mentioned in that question.

8. Use your answer from Question 6 to write an inequality involving > that compares the dates for the advances mentioned in that question.

9. The two most recent events on the timeline are organs grown from stem cells, and skin cells grown into stem cells. How do the dates compare?

Your first instinct might be that growing stem cells from skin cells came later because the words are set farther right, but their position on the graph indicates that they might also have occurred in the same year. When comparing two quantities that may be equal, we can use the symbol ≤ , which is read "less than or equal to," or ≥ , which is read "greater than or equal to."

10. Use one of the symbols introduced in the previous paragraph to describe the relationship between the dates for organs being grown from stem cells, and stem cells being grown from skin cells. Do so using verbal descriptions of those quantities first, then assign a letter to represent each quantity and write a second inequality with your variables.

Did You Get It

Try this problem to see if you understand the concepts we just studied. The answers can be found at the end of the Portfolio section.

1. Use the timeline to make an estimate of the year in which the first vaccine was developed. Then write an inequality that compares that date to the date when penicillin was discovered.

Now we'll practice estimation using a bar graph. The next graph shows the average monthly cost of homeowners insurance in five states that are common destinations for people hoping to move to a warmer climate. Use it for Questions 11–15.

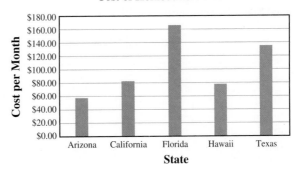

Cost of Homeowners Insurance

11. Estimate the monthly cost of homeowners insurance in California.

12. Do you think your estimate may be too high, or too low? Why?

13. Using your answers to Questions 11 and 12, write an inequality using either $\geq$ or $\leq$ that describes the cost of home-owners insurance in California. Use letter C to represent the cost.

14. Suppose that you were planning a move to Arizona and wanted to budget a monthly amount for homeowners insurance. Would you prefer an overestimate or an underestimate? Explain.

15. What estimate would you use for the monthly cost of homeowners insurance in Arizona?

Did You Get It

2. Use the bar graph on insurance to fill in the blanks: The cost of homeowners insurance in Florida $\geq$ _____ per month, which means my estimate was an _____ (overestimate or underestimate).

Another type of graph that we often have to estimate values from is the scatter plot, like the one here. This graph illustrates the federal minimum wage in the United States by year starting in 1978. Use the graph for Questions 16–18.

Minimum Wage

16. Estimate the minimum wage in 2009.

17. Do you think your estimate may be too high, or too low? Explain.

18. Suppose that a high school graduate in 2009 was trying to figure out how to budget for college while working a minimum wage job. Would she have preferred an underestimate of the minimum wage, or an overestimate? Why?

The following box describes some words in English that are used to describe the inequality symbols we've been working with.

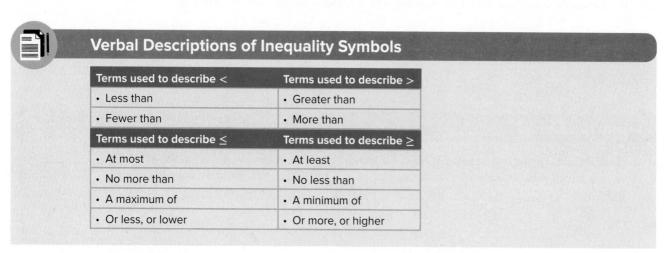

Verbal Descriptions of Inequality Symbols

Terms used to describe $<$	Terms used to describe $>$
• Less than	• Greater than
• Fewer than	• More than
Terms used to describe $\leq$	**Terms used to describe $\geq$**
• At most	• At least
• No more than	• No less than
• A maximum of	• A minimum of
• Or less, or lower	• Or more, or higher

In Questions 19–22, write the statement as an inequality, then give an example of an actual value that would match each description. For example, if I say, "Man, I need to get at least a 2.2 GPA this semester or I'll be on double-secret probation," then 2.5 would be a value matching the description. Assign a variable to each quantity.

19. We can fit at most 12 people on the Slow Ride pedal bus.

20. It's estimated that there are at least 50 ways to leave your lover.

21. I get a text alert from my bank if the balance in my checking account drops below 100 bucks.

22. Any amendment to the U.S. Constitution will only be enacted if more than 37 states vote to accept it.

Did You Get It

3. Write each statement as an inequality. Assign a variable to each quantity.
   a. If I don't get 80% or higher in this class, my parents are going to sell me to a traveling circus.
   b. I took a volcano tour in Hawaii Volcanoes National Park that allowed no more than 10 people near the crater at any one time.

2-5 Group

An **isotherm** is a curve on a map that connects locations where the temperature is the same. By looking at a large map with isotherms, you can get a rough idea of what the temperature is like in many different locations. Using the map, estimate the temperature in each city.

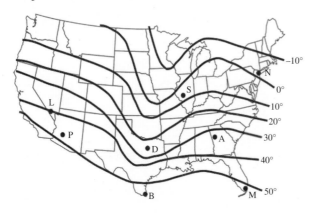

1. Las Vegas, NV (L) _____

2. Phoenix, AZ (P) _____

3. Dallas, TX (D) _____

4. Springfield, IL (S) _____

5. Atlanta, GA (A) _____

6. Miami, FL (M) _____

7. New York, NY (N) _____

4. The southernmost city in Texas is Brownsville, located at point B on the map. Estimate the temperature there. Why is this one harder than the cities in Questions 1–7?

At this point, we've talked about estimation, and learned a little bit about Pólya's problem-solving method. This is a theme that we'll carry on as we work through the course: Being able to estimate an answer to a problem is *always* a valuable skill, but better still if you can then solve to find an exact answer. For now, we'll focus on doing some estimates, and we'll revisit many of these questions later on.

Spend some time thinking about Questions 8–12. After talking with your group, make your best guess and explain your reasoning. Remember, these are supposed to be EDUCATED guesses, not shots in the dark, so think about using some basic calculations to help you. No using phones or computers to look anything up yet!

8. Estimate the monthly payment if we borrow $10,000 at 7% interest for 3 years to buy a car. If we were planning a budget, would we want an overestimate or an underestimate? Why?

9. An average cup of plain old coffee (not one of those designer blends in a monster cup that you could bathe a small dog in) has about 80 mg of caffeine. How long would it take for that caffeine to leave your system? Based on your guess, how many mg do you think will be in your system in half that time? What are you assuming when you make that estimate?

10. About how much would you spend in a year if you bought two $2.80 cups of coffee each weekday (Monday through Friday)? Does this amount surprise you? Does it sound worth the expense?

11. If you put $1,000 into an Individual Retirement Account (IRA) right now, how much would it be worth when you retire? What are some of the things you need to factor in to make a reasonable estimate here?

12. How much money are you completely wasting every time you skip a college class? What information would you need to calculate this exactly?

2-5 **Portfolio**

Name _____

Check each box when you've completed the task. Remember that your instructor will want you to turn in the portfolio pages you create.

Online Practice

1. ☐ Include any written work from the online assignment along with any notes or questions about this lesson's content.

Applications

1. ☐ Complete the Applications problems.

Reflections

Type a short answer to each question.

1. ☐ What kinds of things would you think about when making an educated guess in a math problem?

2. ☐ Describe at least one situation where estimating is good enough, and one where it isn't.

3. ☐ Describe the four steps in Pólya's problem-solving method. Then write about a time in this course that you've used each step.

4. ☐ Name one thing you learned or discovered in this lesson that you found particularly interesting.

5. ☐ What questions do you have about this lesson?

Looking Ahead

1. ☐ Complete the Prep Skills for Lesson 2-6.

2. ☐ Read the opening paragraph in Lesson 2-6 carefully and answer Question 0 in preparation for that lesson.

Answers to "Did You Get It?"

1. The first vaccine was developed around 1795; the year when the first vaccine was discovered < the year when penicillin was discovered.

2. $160, underestimate

3. **a.** $G \geq 80\%$ where G is the grade needed
   b. $P \leq 10$ where P is the number of people allowed near the crater

4. It's definitely more than 50°, but we can't gauge how much more because there's no 60° isotherm on the map.

Answers to "Prep Skills"

1.

   ```
   ←—+——●——+——+—●—+—●—+——+—●—+—●—+——+——+——→
    −50 −40 −30 −20 −10   0   10  20  30  40  50
   ```

2. **a.** 32   **b.** 2 students   **c.** 25 students

3. **a.** Question 4   **b.** about 23   **c.** about 39%

4. **a.** 3   **b.** 9   **c.** about 47 out of 160

2-5 Applications

Name _____

1. According to a survey reported by the Nielsen Corp., in the fourth quarter of 2014, the average American adult spent just about 11 hours a day using electronic media of some sort. The pie chart displays the percentage of time spent using various types of media. Use the chart to make an educated guess on the amount of time spent using the media types in the table, and briefly explain how you made your estimates.

Time Spent Using Electronic Media

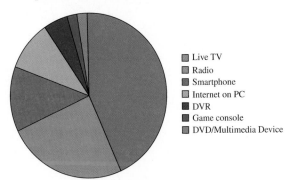

■ Live TV
■ Radio
■ Smartphone
□ Internet on PC
■ DVR
■ Game console
■ DVD/Multimedia Device

Media	Time
Live TV	
Radio	
Smartphone	
DVD/Multimedia	

2. Write the set of described numbers using the roster method.
   a. The number of people in a boat that can hold at most 7 people.

   b. The number of days you'll work out next week if you plan to work out at least twice.

Shopping provides a really good example of the value of estimation. Most people have a rough idea of how much they have to spend in a given shopping trip. While you could pull out the old cell phone calculator and add up all of your purchases to the cent, who has time for that? Instead, it's helpful to round prices to easy-to-use numbers and keep rough track of the total. Use this idea to estimate the total cost of each group of items in Questions 3–5. Round each price to the nearest dollar, then try to estimate the overall cost in your head.

3. Four boxes of mac and cheese (89 cents per box)

   A gallon of orange juice ($3.79)

   A loaf of bread ($1.79)

   Two pounds of ground turkey ($2.97 per pound)

4. Two pairs of jeans ($24.95 and $32.95)

   A three-pack of socks ($7.99)

   Three workout shirts ($11.99 each)

5. Two Xbox games (regular price $29.50 each, on sale for 50% off)

   iPhone case ($18.95)

   Headphones ($22.49)

6. Estimation is useful for tipping when you're dining out, too. If the service is good, 20% of the overall bill is a nice tip to leave. Here's a clever way to find that: Move the decimal of the total amount one place to the left: that gives you 10%. Round this value to the nearest dollar and double the amount, and voila! Twenty percent. Use this to find a reasonable tip for good service on each bill.
   a. $31.45

   b. $129.80

This graph shows the violent crime rate in 2014 for five different American cities, measured in violent crimes per 100,000 citizens. Use it for Questions 7–10.

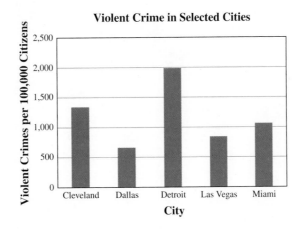

Violent Crime in Selected Cities

7. Estimate the number of violent crimes per 100,000 citizens in Detroit.

8. Do you think your estimate may be too high, or too low? Why?

9. Write an inequality that uses your estimate from Question 7 and your answer to Question 8. Assign a variable to the quantity you're illustrating.

10. Describe the number of violent crimes per 100,000 citizens in Miami using either the words "at least" or "at most."

Lesson 2-6 Prep Skills

SKILL 1: CONVERT FRACTIONS INTO PERCENT FORM

To find the percentage that corresponds to a given fraction, we can do these two steps: (1) Divide the numerator by the denominator, and (2) convert the resulting decimal into percent form by moving the decimal point two places to the right (multiply by 100).

- $\dfrac{38}{50} = 0.76$; moving the decimal two places to the right, we get 76%.

- $\dfrac{8 - 12}{12} \approx -0.333$; moving the decimal two places to the right, we get −33.3%.

SKILL 2: FIND THE AREA OF A RECTANGLE

We covered area of rectangles in Lesson 2-3: Recall that the area is the length times the width. It's very important that the two measurements are in the same units!

- The area of a rectangle with length 15 in. and width 3 ft can be calculated in one of two ways. We could convert 15 in. to 1.25 ft, and get area (1.25 ft)(3 ft) = 3.75 sq. ft. Or we could convert 3 ft into 36 inches and get area (15 in.)(36 in.) = 540 sq. in. We could then do a unit conversion to show that these two areas are the same.

SKILL 3: CONVERT UNITS OF AREA AND VOLUME

This skill was covered in Lesson 2-4. We use dimensional analysis, keeping in mind that we'll have to multiply by the same conversion factor either twice or three times when the units we're trying to eliminate are squared or cubed.

- $27 \text{ in.}^2 \cdot \dfrac{1 \text{ ft}}{12 \text{ in.}} \cdot \dfrac{1 \text{ ft}}{12 \text{ in.}} = 0.1875 \text{ ft}^2$

- $4 \text{ cm}^3 \cdot \dfrac{1 \text{ in.}}{2.54 \text{ cm}} \cdot \dfrac{1 \text{ in.}}{2.54 \text{ cm}} \cdot \dfrac{1 \text{ in.}}{2.54 \text{ cm}} \approx 0.244 \text{ in.}^3$

PREP SKILLS QUESTIONS

1. Convert each fraction into percent form.

   a. $\dfrac{12}{40}$ b. $-\dfrac{0.3}{1.6}$ c. $\dfrac{58.3 - 60}{60}$

2. Find the area of a building made up of three rectangular rooms that are 12 ft by 18 ft, and a hallway that's 22 ft long and 4 ft wide.

3. Using only the fact that 1 yd = 3 ft, convert 10 cubic yds into cubic feet.

4. Using only the fact that 12 in. = 1 ft, convert 5,000 sq. inches into sq. feet.

Lesson 2-6   It's All Relative

LEARNING OBJECTIVES

☐ 1. Compare change to relative change.

☐ 2. Apply percent error.

When you sit with a nice girl for two hours you think it's only a minute, but when you sit on a hot stove for a minute you think it's two hours. That's relativity.
       —Albert Einstein

Source: Library of Congress, Prints and Photographs Division [LC-USZ62-60242]

In a nutshell, Einstein's theory of relativity says that even the passage of time is not an absolute, but rather is relative to your frame of reference. In this lesson, we'll study appropriate ways to compare numbers, focusing on the importance of relativity. Consider these two scenarios: 1) I owe you $20, and I give you $10 instead. Will that work for you? 2) You win $5 million in a lottery, but you only get paid $4,999,990. Would that ruin your day? You're out ten bucks either way, but clearly that's a much bigger deal when the amount owed is $20. If that makes sense to you, then you have an instinctive understanding of the concept of relative change.

0. How does Einstein's quote about relativity connect to the examples of being shorted by $10? And how cool is Einstein's hair?

2-6 Class

When asked to compare the sizes of two numbers, most people think of subtraction, but the example above shows that this isn't necessarily the best choice. The **change** between two quantities is found by simply subtracting the new value from the old. This is sometimes referred to as **actual change**.

The Change in a Quantity

$$\text{Change} = \text{New value} - \text{Original value}$$

If we use x_n to represent the new value and x_o to represent the original value, we get

$$\text{Change} = x_n - x_o$$

    In both scenarios in the opening paragraph, the change in what was owed and what was paid is $10, which leads us to conclude the significance of that $10 is the same in each case. But doesn't it seem clear that the $10 shortfall is more significant when the total amount owed is $20? That's where relative change comes in. The **relative change** between two quantities measures the change as a fraction of the original value.

The Relative Change in a Quantity

$$\text{Relative change} = \frac{\text{Change}}{\text{Original value}} = \frac{\text{New value} - \text{Original value}}{\text{Original value}}$$

Using the same variables as in our definition of change,

$$\text{Relative change} = \frac{x_n - x_o}{x_o}$$

From our first scenario:

$$\text{Relative change} = \frac{\$10 - \$20}{\$20} = -\frac{1}{2} \text{ or } -50\%. \text{ (The negative indicates that you got shorted. Bummer.)}$$

This shows that the change between the amount owed and the amount received is half of the amount owed. That's a big deal!

1. Find the relative change if you win $5,000,000 and get paid $4,999,990. Write as a fraction, not a decimal.

> ## Math Note
>
> Relative changes are often written as percentages, but they don't have to be. Fraction or decimal form is fine, too.

Did You Get It

Try this problem to see if you understand the concepts we just studied. The answers can be found at the end of the Portfolio section.

1. A stock that was worth $65 per share yesterday is now trading at $38 per share after the CEO was arrested for fraud. Find the actual change and the relative change in the value of the stock.

2. Compare the relative change for the two scenarios in the opening paragraph from this lesson. Does this match your intuition about the scenarios?

3. Your instructor tells you that you're going to get an additional 2 points on a recent test or quiz. Describe when this would be great news, and when it wouldn't help very much.

For Questions 4 and 5, write a sentence that describes in your own words what exactly the given statement means. For example, when we found that the relative change from $20 owed to $10 paid was $-1/2$, this means the amount paid was too low by an amount half of what it was supposed to be.

4. The relative change in my budget was 7% compared to last year.

5. The relative change in enrollment this year compared to last year at my college was −3.5%.

For Questions 6 and 7, write a statement using the term "relative change" or "percent change" to describe the information provided. This is pretty much the opposite of what you did in Questions 4 and 5.

6. Apple's profit in 2016 was 14.4% lower than it was in 2015.

7. The value of my retirement fund was 5.5% more at the end of this year than it was at the end of last year.

Did You Get It

2. I'm at the Cincinnati airport (CVG) right now, and I just learned that the number of passengers flying in or out of CVG was about 7% higher in 2016 than it was in 2015. Write a sentence using the phrase "relative change" that describes this statistic. Make sure your answer has a − or + in it.

If you want some interesting reading, look up "baseline budgeting." Currently, the federal budget has an automatic annual increase of 7% to many programs.

8. Suppose that $435 million is spent for improvements to interstate highways for 2017. If the automatic increase of 7% applies to this budget, how much is expected for that program in 2018? (Round to the nearest million.)

9. Suppose that only $440 million is budgeted for that program, not the expected amount that you found in Question 8. Find the actual change and the relative change in the amount spent from 2017 to this budgeted amount of $440 million for 2018. Is it positive or negative? What does this change mean?

10. A news article reports that this program has been cut by 5.4%. Does this match what you found in Question 9? What values have been used to come up with that calculation? (Hint: It is still relative change.)

11. Write a sentence or two describing the 5.4% cut and what is misleading about it.

2-6 Group

Next up is a really useful topic that's related to relative change. We've already talked quite a bit about estimation in this course. In most cases, when some quantity is estimated there's going to be some error in that estimate. When comparing an estimate to an exact value, the **error** or **actual error** in the estimate can be expressed by subtracting the actual value from the estimated value. That is,

$$\text{Error} = \text{Estimated value} - \text{actual value}$$

The percent error is calculated just like the relative change. The idea is to measure how far off the estimate is as a percentage of the actual value.

The Percent Error in an Estimate

When an estimate is made of some quantity, the percent error in the estimate is given by

$$\text{Percent error} = \frac{\text{Estimated value} - \text{actual value}}{\text{Actual value}}$$

If we use x_e to represent the estimated value and x_a to represent the actual value,

$$\text{Percent error} = \frac{x_e - x_a}{x_a}$$

This calculation gives you percent error in decimal form; we'll usually want to rewrite that as a percentage.

Some sources use an absolute value in the numerator of this formula so that the percent error is always positive. But since we're all about interpretation in this course, we'll want to preserve the sign so that we can tell if the estimate is too high (positive percent error) or too low (negative percent error).

If you're ever in the market for some new carpet, you might consider searching the Web for the Carpet Buyer's Handbook. The site has many useful resources on buying and installing carpet. It turns out that figuring out how much you're going to spend is more complicated then you might think. Carpet is sold by the square foot, and you can measure the square footage of a room. But you can't buy exactly a certain number of square feet because carpet comes on rolls of a certain width (usually

12 feet). If you need a 2 ft × 3 ft piece for a closet, you can't buy just 6 square feet: You'd have to buy 2 feet off of the roll, which would be 24 square feet.

In addition, there are certain guidelines that installers will adhere to in order to get the best result. These govern how the pieces off the roll can be situated, leading to more potential waste. The bottom line is that when a professional installer measures a room to estimate the amount of carpet needed, the result will usually be quite a bit different from the actual square footage that will be covered.

1. When you're buying carpet, do you want an overestimate or an underestimate? Explain.

A carpet installer estimated that $24\frac{2}{3}$ square yards of carpet would be needed for the bedroom and closet shown in the diagram.

2. Find the area of the bedroom only in square inches. (Recall that the area of a rectangle is length times width.)

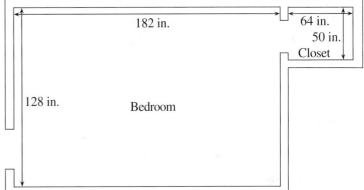

3. Find the area of the closet in square inches.

4. Each of the doorways shown is 30 inches wide, and the walls are 4 inches thick. Carpet is needed for the entire doorway between the bedroom and closet, and in half of the doorway into the bedroom. How many square inches does this add to the total carpeted area? What is the total carpeted area?

5. Convert the total carpeted area to square yards. Round to one decimal place. (You may find it useful to look back at the colored box on converting area and volume measurements on page 198.)

6. Write a sentence or two describing how the professional estimate compares to the actual carpeted area.

7. Find the percent error in the estimate. Round to one decimal place. Write a sentence explaining what this tells us about how the estimate compares to the actual carpeted area.

Did You Get It

3. One of the guest rooms in my house has two walls that are 15′6″ by 8 ft, and two others that are 12′3″ by 8 ft. When buying paint for the walls, I estimated the wall area to be about 450 sq. ft. Find my percent error.

8. Not everyone realizes this, but when you buy carpet, you pay for the estimated amount, not the actual amount covering your floors. If the family that owns the house in the diagram picked carpet that costs $28 per square yard installed, how much would they have paid?

9. Use the actual error in the estimate to find the dollar value of wasted carpet.

10. According to the Internet (which knows everything), a good rule of thumb is to plan for 5–10% waste when buying carpet. How did the estimator do?

11. One suggestion for estimating carpet is to measure each room in inches and round up to the nearest half foot (and ignore the doorways). Using the measurements for the closet and the bedroom, make an estimate for the square feet needed. How does this estimate compare to the actual area?

12. List some situations where relative change is a much more useful number than actual change.

2-6 Portfolio

Name _____

Check each box when you've completed the task. Remember that your instructor will want you to turn in the portfolio pages you create.

Technology

1. ☐ The first few rows of a spreadsheet designed to compute change and relative change are shown here. Your job is to download the template in online resources, then fill in formulas in row 3 for computing the change and relative change from one row to the next for each account. Then copy those formulas down to fill in the rest of the sheet. Finally, write any observations you have based on the result.

	A	B	C	D	E	F	G
1	**Account #1**	**Change**	**Relative Change**		**Account #2**	**Change**	**Relative Change**
2	$ 10,000.00				$ 10,000.00		
3	$ 10,700.00				$ 10,500.00		
4	$ 11,400.00				$ 11,025.00		

Online Practice

1. ☐ Include any written work from the online assignment along with any notes or questions about this lesson's content.

Applications

1. ☐ Complete the Applications problems.

Reflections

Type a short answer to each question.

1. ☐ How would you explain to someone you know that relative change is often much more meaningful than actual change?

2. ☐ Both Shawna and John found out that they're getting a $1,000 annual raise this year. John went out to celebrate, while Shawna yawned and said "Yeah, whatever." Use the topic of this section to describe what you think might be likely to account for this discrepancy in their reactions to the news.

3. ☐ Name one thing you learned or discovered in this lesson that you found particularly interesting.

4. ☐ What questions do you have about this lesson?

Looking Ahead

1. ☐ Complete the Prep Skills for Lesson 2-7.

2. ☐ Read the opening paragraph in Lesson 2-7 carefully and answer Question 0 in preparation for that lesson.

Answers to "Did You Get It?"

1. Actual: −$27; Relative: about −41.5%

2. The relative change in the number of passengers from 2015 to 2016 was +7%.

3. About 1.4% error

Answers to "Prep Skills"

1. **a.** 30%   **b.** −18.75%   **c.** about −2.8%

2. 736 ft^2

3. 270 ft^3

4. about 34.7 ft^2

2-6 Applications

Name _____

After moving into a new house, a couple wants to have a concrete patio poured to support a hot tub, because . . . well, because it's a hot tub. The plans call for a 14 ft by 16 ft slab of concrete 4 inches thick. Round any calculations to two decimal places if you need to.

1. How many cubic feet of concrete will be needed?

2. Convert the volume of concrete to cubic yards.

3. The coolest thing about ordering ready-mix concrete is that a concrete mixer will show up at your house. Most companies require orders by the cubic yard. Our couple's patio was estimated at 3 cubic yards. How much extra concrete was ordered?

©Photographer's Choice/Getty Images RF

4. Find the percent error in the estimate compared to the actual amount of concrete needed. Write a sentence explaining exactly what the percent error means.

5. In 2016, an average cost for concrete was $140 per cubic yard. How much would be spent on concrete for the patio at that price?

6. Find the dollar value of the wasted concrete.

7. Suppose that you've budgeted $250 per month for a new car, but the salesperson goes into sales mode and talks you into one with a few extra snazzy features. Next thing you know, you have a car payment of $265 per month. Find the actual change and the relative change needed for our car payment budget to accommodate our impulsive decision to go with the fancy car.

8. If the total of all payments for the original budgeted amount is $12,000, how much extra would you end up paying for the snazzy features? Do you think that would be worth it? Discuss.

9. A certain pain medication has a recommended dosage of 0.3 mg per pound of body weight, and is reported to only be effective if the dosage administered is within 5% of the recommendation. Would a dosage of 50 mg be effective for a 175-pound patient?

Lesson 2-7   Prep Skills

SKILL 1: FIND A MEAN

Mean, or what is commonly called "average," is one of the main topics of Lesson 2-1. In short, the mean of a list of numbers is computed by adding all of the numbers and dividing by how many numbers there were on the list. But you already knew that, didn't you?

SKILL 2: INTERPRET INFORMATION FROM A DIAGRAM

Identifying information from a diagram plays an important role in this lesson. The skill you'll need is pretty similar to reading info from a pie chart, like this example:

- The chart represents the final grades for 51 students in two sections of a math class. Students that earned a C or better were eligible to move on to the next class. If we add the percentages for the A, B, and C categories, we find that 74% of students qualified to move on. This represents (0.74)(51), or 38 students.

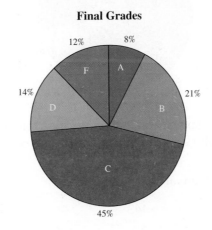

Final Grades

SKILL 3: FIND PROBABILITY FROM A PERCENT CHANCE

Recall that probability is really the same thing as the percent chance that some event will occur. The only difference is that probability is typically written in fraction or decimal form.

- If there's a 41% chance that some event will occur, we find the probability of it occurring by converting 41% to decimal form. Move the decimal point 2 places to the left to get a probability of 0.41.

SKILL 4: WRITE INTERVALS IN INEQUALITY NOTATION

The inequality symbols $<$ and $>$ can be used to describe an interval of numbers. For example, if we want to write an inequality that represents all of the real numbers that are less than 12, we could write $x < 12$. The letter that we choose to represent the variable quantity is immaterial: we could have used any letter.

- The set of all real numbers that are more than -8 is written $x > -8$.
- The set of all real numbers that are no more than 5 is written $x \le 5$.
- The set of all real numbers that are no less than 100 is written $x \ge 100$.

PREP SKILLS QUESTIONS

1. Find the mean of the numbers listed.

   23   34   45   56   67   78   89   11   22   33

2. The pie chart represents the breakdown of customers by day for a breakfast restaurant in a downtown area. There were 2,431 customers for the week.

   a. What percentage of customers visited on the weekend?

   b. How many customers visited on a weekday?

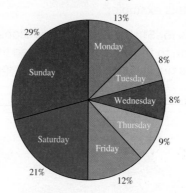

Customers by Day

3. In an average year, there is at least some measurable precipitation on about 42% of days in Seattle, WA. If you choose a random day during the year, what's the probability of precipitation?

4. Write a verbal description of each interval described.

   a. $x \geq -11$ b. $x < 9$ c. $x > 143$

5. Write an inequality that describes each interval.

   a. The set of all real numbers that are less than 40.

   b. The set of all real numbers that are more than 3.2.

   c. The set of all real numbers that are at least 5.

Lesson 2-7   Is That Normal?

LEARNING OBJECTIVES

☐ 1. Identify the steps in computing standard deviation, and describe why they lead to a measure of variation.

☐ 2. Compute and interpret standard deviation.

☐ 3. Use a normal distribution to find probabilities.

The only normal people are the ones you don't know very well.
                    —Alfred Adler

©Dserov/Shutterstock RF

When I was in college, I had a button on my favorite jacket that said "Why be normal?" Some people tend to want to be different, while others would prefer to blend in. But what exactly does "normal" mean? Is it what's most common? Most accepted? If you have "just a normal day," is that a good thing or a bad thing? I suppose that a normal day would be a day where things happen like they usually do, and that's not a bad description of how we'll be using the word "normal" in this lesson. We've already learned a lot about measures of average, but it turns out that a data set often has more of a story to tell than simply what the average is (whatever that means). We'll begin this lesson by thinking about whether a lot of the values in a data set are "normal" (meaning similar to the others), or if there are a lot of values that do their best to stand out from the crowd.

0. After reading the opening paragraph, how do you think we're going to apply the word "normal" to studying sets of data?

2-7 ▐ Group

Two golfers were competing in a televised competition for a scholarship to play on a college golf team. The scores for each golfer over all six rounds of the competition are shown in the table. If you're not familiar with the sport, in golf a lower score is better.

Player	Rd. 1	Rd. 2	Rd. 3	Rd. 4	Rd. 5	Rd. 6
Brittany	75	80	72	81	75	77
Ji-Min	69	77	71	75	80	83

1. Compute the mean score for each player. Round to one decimal place.

2. Find the range of scores for each golfer. (The **range** of a data set is calculated by subtracting the highest value minus the lowest value.)

3. Which golfer do you think was the better player in this competition? Which do you think was more consistent? Explain your reasoning.

4. Can you make up four exam scores that have a mean of 80, and a highest score of 100? Are the scores close together, or spread out?

5. Can you make up four exam scores that have a mean of 80 and a highest score of 84? Are the scores close together or spread out?

6. What do the previous two questions tell you about how there's more to the story told by a data set than just the measures of average?

Did You Get It

Try these problems to see if you understand the concepts we just studied. The answers can be found at the end of the Portfolio section.

1. If nine of the ten houses on one street are all worth about $210,000 and the one at the end of the street is valued at $1,200,000, how does the mean price on the street compare to a similar neighborhood that only has the nine houses worth $210,000?
2. Is the range a meaningful measure of how spread out the home values are in the first neighborhood?

2-7 Class

As we saw in the Group portion of this lesson, while the mean is a very useful tool in analyzing data, there's more to the story than just the mean because it can't factor in how spread out a group of values is. The range is one way to analyze spread, but it totally ignores all but the highest and lowest values. So if there's just one value that's really low or high compared to the others, the range will make it seem like the data are more spread out than they actually are.

For this reason, we'll study a more detailed measure of spread known as the **standard deviation**. In short, standard deviation, which is often represented by a lowercase Greek sigma (σ), is a measure of how far on average the values are from the mean. A large standard deviation means there are a lot of values far away from the mean. A small standard deviation means that most of the values are close to the mean. Here are the steps for computing standard deviation, using Brittany's golf scores from the Group portion as an example: 75, 80, 72, 81, 75, 77.

Step 1: Find the mean. Standard deviation is all about measuring distance from the mean, so we better start by finding the mean. We already found the mean in group Question 1: It's 76.7.

Step 2: Subtract the mean from each data value in the data set. This is where we're really measuring the spread.

  1. Fill in the second column of the table below.

Step 3: Square the differences from Step 2. This is a simple way to eliminate the signs: We're trying to measure how far away from the mean the values are, not whether they're bigger or smaller.

Score	Score − Mean	(Score − Mean)^2
75		
80		
72		
81		
75		
77		

  2. Fill in the third column of the table by squaring each value in the second column.

Step 4: Find the mean of the squares. This is almost finding the average of the distances of each data value from the mean: The only problem is that we're really averaging the squares. We'll fix that soon.

  3. Find the mean of the values in the third column of the table.

Step 5: Find the square root of the mean from Step 4. In essence, this is "undoing" the squares used to eliminate the signs.

  4. Find the standard deviation by computing the square root of your answer from Question 3.

Using Technology: Computing Standard Deviation

TI-84 Plus Calculator

1. Enter the data in list **L1**; press **STAT** then **ENTER**.

2. Enter the list of values under **L1**.

3. We want choice 1 under the **STAT-CALC** menu, which you get to by pressing **STAT** ► **ENTER**.

4. Choose **1: 1-VarStats.** Among the information displayed will be the mean, which is denoted $\bar{x}$, and the standard deviation (σ_x).

5. If appropriate, select Calculate and press **ENTER**.

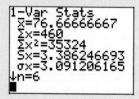

```
1-Var Stats
x̄=76.66666667
Σx=460
Σx²=35324
Sx=3.386246693
σx=3.091206165
↓n=6
```

Excel Spreadsheet

B8	f_x =STDEV.P(B2:B7)	

◢	A	B	C
1		Score	
2		75	
3		80	
4		72	
5		81	
6		75	
7		77	
8	Standard Deviation	3.1	
9			

1. Enter the values in a row or column.
2. Enter = STDEV.P(B2: B7); note that this is the range of cells containing the data values.
3. Format the cell where you entered the formula to display the number of decimal places you want.

See Lessons 2-7-1 and 2-7-2 Using Tech videos in class resources for further instruction.

The Normal Distribution

How many people do you know that are taller than 6′5″, or shorter than 5′1″? For most people, the answer to that question is "not very many." The heights of humans tend to exhibit a phenomenon shared by many characteristics of living things: There are a lot of values close to the mean, and less and less as you get farther from the mean. The picture to the right is an example of 100 maple seed pods that I collected from my back yard, arranged by length; note the pattern that appears.

5. Describe the pattern made by the seed pods, and explain what it says about their lengths.

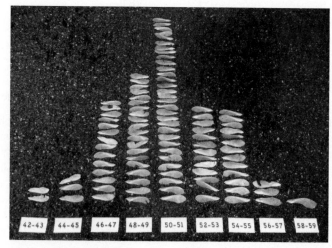

Courtesy of Dave Sobecki

This phenomenon is so common, in fact, that data sets that follow a similar pattern are said to be **normally distributed**. Things like sizes of individuals, IQ scores, weights of packaged products, and lifespans of batteries or lightbulbs are often normally distributed.

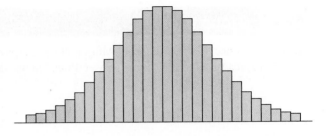

I only collected 100 pods, out of thousands (maybe millions) on the tree. If I had collected a lot more of them, the picture would most likely have started to look a lot like the nice, symmetric diagram to the right. When a group of data is normally distributed, and we know the mean and standard deviation, there's a rule that allows us to estimate how many data values fall within certain ranges. This is known as the **empirical rule,** and it's illustrated by the following diagram.

The empirical rule says that when a data set is normally distributed, about 68% of all values will fall within 1 standard deviation of the mean; about 95% will fall within 2 standard deviations of the mean; and about 99.7% will fall within 3 standard deviations of the mean.

An Illustration of the Empirical Rule

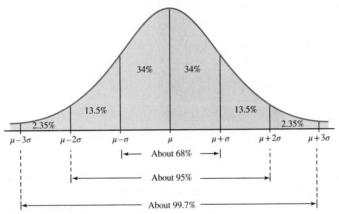

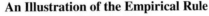

> **Math Note**
>
> The mean for data that are normally distributed is often represented by the lowercase Greek letter mu (μ).

For example, the heights of American men are normally distributed with mean 5 feet 9.3 inches and standard deviation 2.8 inches. That is, μ is 5 feet 9.3 inches, and σ is 2.8 inches.

6. Use the information just given about μ and σ to fill in the blanks on the next empirical rule diagram with heights, using the formulas below the blanks for guidance.

7. Based on your diagram, about what percentage of American men fall into the height range from 5 feet 6.5 inches to 6 feet 0.1 inch?

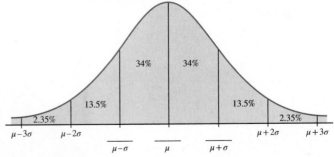

Did You Get It

3. About what percentage of American men are between 5 feet 9.3 inches and 6 feet 0.1 inch tall?

2-7   Group (Again)

1. Find the standard deviation for Ji-Min's golf scores (provided on page 243). Compute first by hand, then using a calculator or spreadsheet to check your answer. Round to one decimal place.

2. Discuss how comparing the two standard deviations can help you to decide which of the two golfers is a more consistent player.

A standard package of Oreos is supposed to contain 510 grams of chocolatey goodness. But there's variation in just about anything, including production and packaging, so some packages will contain more and some will contain less. In fact, this is exactly the sort of quantity that tends to be normally distributed. The folks that run Nabisco aren't stupid, and they know that customers won't be very happy if they weigh a package of cookies and find that it contains less than the labeled amount. The typical approach to keep that from happening is to design the packaging process so that the mean is something more than 510 grams, with a standard deviation that guarantees that the vast majority of packages contain 510 grams or more.

3. Let's say that the mean is 518 grams and the standard deviation is 4 grams.

   a. Fill in all of the blanks on the empirical rule diagram with weights in grams. Use the formulas below the blanks for reference.

   b. What percent of all Oreo packages would contain between 514 and 522 grams?

©McGraw-Hill Education/John Flournoy, photographer

34%   34%

13.5%   13.5%

2.35%   2.35%

$\overline{\mu-3\sigma}$ $\overline{\mu-2\sigma}$ $\overline{\mu-\sigma}$ $\overline{\mu}$ $\overline{\mu+\sigma}$ $\overline{\mu+2\sigma}$ $\overline{\mu+3\sigma}$

4. Using what we know about the connection between probability and percent chance, what's the probability that a randomly chosen package contains between 514 and 522 grams?

The probability of a package of Oreos containing between 514 and 522 grams can be written as $P(514 < x < 522)$, where x represents the weight. This uses a *compound inequality*, which is a combination of two inequalities. In this case, $514 < x < 522$ means that x is both greater than 514 (that's the $514 < x$ part) AND less than 522 (which is the $x < 522$ part). *In other words, x is between 514 and 522.*

Writing Compound Inequalities

There are many occasions where we'd like to represent an interval between two specific numbers. To do this concisely, we use a **compound inequality**. An inequality of the form

$$a < x < b$$

describes the set of all numbers that are between a and b. When writing an interval in this form, we only use the *less than* symbol. The first number is the lower boundary of the interval we're describing, and the last number is the upper boundary.

5. Write a compound inequality with variable x that describes the set of all weights between 510 and 526 grams.

6. Write an expression using your answer to Question 5 that describes the probability of a randomly selected Oreo package containing between 510 and 526 grams of joy (cookies, actually).

7. Use the empirical rule to find the probability in Question 6.

Did You Get It

4. Write an expression using a compound inequality that represents the probability of a randomly selected Oreo package weighing between 514 and 530 grams, then use the empirical rule to find that probability.

8. Write a description of the probability represented by the expression $P(x < 510)$, where x represents the weight of a randomly selected package of Oreos. Shoot for a description that one of your classmates could easily understand.

9. Find the probability described in Question 8. (This will require some interpretation of the diagram illustrating the empirical rule.)

10. Based on your answer to Question 9, if 1,000 Oreo packages are sampled, how many will have less than 510 grams of cookies?

Did You Get It

5. Use the empirical rule to find the probability that a randomly selected Oreo package weighs more than 514 grams.

11. Is it unusual for a package to weigh more than 530 grams? Explain.

2-7 Portfolio

Name _____

Check each box when you've completed the task. Remember that your instructor will want you to turn in the portfolio pages you create.

Technology

1. ☐ Using the Internet as a resource, find a data set that you find interesting, then use a spreadsheet to compute the mean, median, and standard deviation. Then write a brief report about what these measures of average and spread tell you about the data. Make sure that you list the source of your data.

Online Practice

1. ☐ Include any written work from the online assignment along with any notes or questions about this lesson's content.

Applications

1. ☐ Complete the Applications problems.

Reflections

Type a short answer to each question.

1. ☐ Describe exactly what the standard deviation of a data set tells us. More detail, as usual, is better.

2. ☐ What can we learn from analyzing the standard deviation for a data set that we couldn't learn from just looking at measures of average?

3. ☐ Look back at your answer to Question 0 at the beginning of the lesson. How did you do? Would you change your answer now?

4. ☐ Name one thing you learned or discovered in this lesson that you found particularly interesting.

5. ☐ What questions do you have about this lesson?

Looking Ahead

1. ☐ Complete the Prep Skills for Lesson 2-8.

2. ☐ Read the opening paragraph in Lesson 2-8 carefully and answer Question 0 in preparation for that lesson.

Answers to "Did You Get It?"

1. The mean for the second neighborhood is obviously $210,000. For the first it's $309,000.

2. The range is huge—almost $1,000,000—which makes it seem like the values are very spread out. But they're not since all but one are identical.

3. About 34%.

4. $P(514 < x < 530) = 0.8385$

5. 0.84

Answers to "Prep Skills"

1. 45.8

2. **a.** 50%   **b.** 1,215 or 1,216

3. 0.42

4. **a.** The set of all real numbers that are no less than −11
   b. The set of all real numbers that are less than 9
   c. The set of all real numbers that are more than 143

5. **a.** $x < 40$ **b.** $x > 3.2$ **c.** $x \geq 5$

2-7 Applications

Name _____

1. In Lesson 2-1, you found the mean of the exam scores shown in the table. Find the standard deviation for these scores, using whatever method you prefer. Then describe what the mean and standard deviation tell you about the data.

	A	B	C
1	Student	Exam 1 (%)	Exam 2 (%)
2	Michael	80	89
3	Andy	77	93
4	Pam	68	84
5	Jim	81	88
6	Dwight	96	91
7	Stanley	54	75
8	Phyllis	75	54
9	Kevin	81	86
10	Creed	71	0
11	Darryl	89	83
12	Gabe	56	64
13	Toby	81	64
14	Holly	92	74

2. According to numerous online resources, the mean height for American women is 5 feet 5 inches, with a standard deviation of 3.5 inches. Use the empirical rule to find the probability that a randomly chosen American woman is between 5 feet 1.5 inches and 5 feet 8.5 inches.

3. Write an expression of the form P(inequality) that represents the probability you found in Question 2. Use h to represent the height of a randomly chosen woman, and write heights in inches.

4. In a group of 500 women, how many would you expect to be taller than 6 feet? (You'll need to interpret the diagram that illustrates the empirical rule.)

2-7   Applications

Name _____

5. On one campus, about 95% of students work between 6 and 12 hours per week, and the number of hours worked is normally distributed. What is the mean number of hours worked likely to be? What is the standard deviation? (This one requires a little bit of ingenuity.)

For each of the quantities in Questions 6–9, decide whether you think each is likely to be normally distributed, and explain why or why not.

6. The SAT scores for all high school juniors in Texas.

7. The amount of tax revenue taken in by the United States government over the last 60 years.

8. The length of daylight hours over the course of a year.

9. The amount of time it takes all students in a class to finish a given homework assignment without a time limit.

Lesson 2-8   Prep Skills

SKILL 1: COMPUTE A BASIC PROBABILITY

The simplest way to compute a probability is to divide the number of outcomes in a certain event by the total number of outcomes possible. For example, when flipping a coin, you can either get heads or tails: There are two outcomes. Exactly one of those satisfies getting tails, so the probability of getting tails is ½.

- A board game spinner has 8 spaces, numbered from 1 to 8. For each spin, there are 8 possible outcomes. Three of those 8 are more than 5, so the probability of getting a number more than 5 is

$$\frac{\text{Number of ways to get more than 5}}{\text{Total possible outcomes}} = \frac{3}{8}$$

SKILL 2: CONVERT FROM PERCENT FORM TO DECIMAL FORM

When we're given a percentage, to convert it into decimal form, we execute two steps: (1) Move the decimal point two places to the left (divide by 100); (2) drop the percent symbol.

- $90\% = 0.90$

- $12.5\% = 0.125$

- $4\% = 0.04$

PREP SKILLS QUESTIONS

1. There are 52 cards in a standard deck, equally divided among hearts, clubs, diamonds, and spades. Find the probability of drawing a club with one randomly selected card, and the probability of not drawing a spade.

2. When you roll one six-sided die, what's the probability of getting a number less than 3?

3. Convert each percentage to decimal form:
   a. 87%   b. 33.5%   c. 9%   d. 1.3%

Lesson 2-8 Meeting Expectations

LEARNING OBJECTIVES

☐ 1. Estimate expected value experimentally.

☐ 2. Compute expected value.

☐ 3. Compute weighted grades and GPA.

©McGraw-Hill Education/Mark Steinmetz, photographer

Don't lower your expectations to meet your performance. Raise your level of performance to meet your expectations.
    —Ralph Marston

If you bought 10 $1 scratch-off lottery tickets that have prizes ranging from "you get nothing and like it" to $10,000, how much money would you expect to end up winning or losing? If that question makes sense to you, great—it means you have an understanding of what the topic of expected value is about. When some game or experiment involving probability has numeric outcomes, like the amount of money won or lost when buying 10 lottery tickets, expected value is used to describe what would be expected to happen, on average, if you repeated that experiment a boatload of times. It's a tremendously useful calculation in many different settings: It's not hard to think of many situations where you'd like to have some idea of whether or not the end result is likely to be favorable. Games of chance are obvious applications, but there are tons of others: Buying insurance, investing, job decisions, and what items a store should put on sale are four that come to mind. By the way, if you guessed that you'd lose somewhere between $6 and $7, for most instant lottery games, you'd be right. Now let's jump in and learn about expected value. I expect that you'll do fine.

0. Describe what you think it means to say that the expected value of buying 10 $1 lottery tickets is $7.

2-8 Class

Expected Value Lab

Supplies needed: At least one 6-sided die for each group. (A phone app will work just fine.)

The point: The expected value of an event is the value that can be expected, on average, to occur. In this case, you'd probably guess that the expected value is one of the numbers from 1 to 6. But does it have to work out that way? We shall see!

The procedure: One really good way to gain some perspective on what expected value is all about is to play a game and see how the results compare to what we might expect. It's a pretty simple game: Roll one die, and you win the dollar amount of the number facing up—$1 for a 1, $2 for a 2, $3 for a 3, etc. So each group should roll their die 100 times, and record the result of each roll. You can either split the rolls among the group, or have a roller and a recorder.

Record results in the following table. If you have access to a computer, you might want to record the results in a spreadsheet instead, which will help make the calculations we need to do easier.

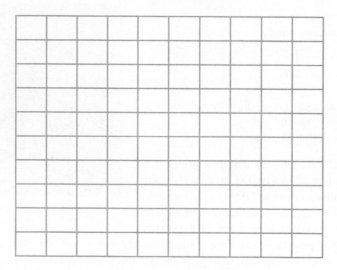

1. Add the numbers across each of the 10 rows, and write the sum to the right. Then add up all of those sums. How much money would you have won on those 100 rolls?

2. On average, how much did you win per roll?

3. Add the answers from Question 2 for every group in your class. It's a good idea to have each group write their answer on the board. Then divide by the number of groups to find the average amount won for the entire class.

4. Congratulations: You've just found the expected value for one roll in this game, which is the average amount you'd expect to win per roll if you played this game a LOT. Is it possible to win this amount on one roll? Explain.

5. What is the probability of getting a 1 when rolling one die?

6. What is the probability of getting any individual number from 1 to 6 when rolling one die?

7. Complete the second column of this table by writing in the probability of each outcome. Then complete the third row by multiplying each outcome by its probability.

Outcome (X)	Probability P(X)	Product X · P(X)
$1		
$2		
$3		
$4		
$5		
$6		

Math Note

Do all of your probabilities add up to one? If not, you must have made a mistake.

8. Find the sum of the values in the third column. How does it compare to the expected value for your class?

9. Obviously, playing this game for free would ROCK: You'd always win something for nothing. How likely is that to happen in real life, though? (Hint: Not at all.) Instead, you'd typically pay to play. What do you think would be a fair price to charge to play this game? Explain your choice.

10. Let's say you were setting up this game somewhere on your campus. Would you expect to make money if you were charging students $2 to play? What about $5?

Finding Expected Value

To compute the expected value of a probability experiment:

Step 1: List out all possible numeric outcomes.

Step 2: Write the probability of each outcome.

Step 3: Multiply each numeric outcome by its probability.

Step 4: Add the results. The sum is the expected value.

11. If you were charging $2 to play, the outcomes for each roll would be different. For example, instead of winning $1 for a roll of 1, you'd lose $1 because you paid $2 to play, and the outcome would be –$1. This in turn changes the expected value. We've revised the table you filled in earlier to reflect this change in the outcome for each roll. Use the new table to find the expected value for the player. Does your answer agree with your prediction in Question 10?

Roll	Outcome (X)	Probability P(X)	Product X · P(X)
1	–$1	$\frac{1}{6}$	$-\$\frac{1}{6}$
2	$0	$\frac{1}{6}$	$0
3	$1	$\frac{1}{6}$	$\$\frac{1}{6}$
4	$2	$\frac{1}{6}$	$\$\frac{2}{6}$
5	$3	$\frac{1}{6}$	$\$\frac{3}{6}$
6	$4	$\frac{1}{6}$	$\$\frac{4}{6}$

Did You Get It

Try these problems to see if you understand the concepts we just studied. The answers can be found at the end of the Portfolio section.

1. Suppose that you buy travel insurance after booking a trip, at a cost of $49. If you take the trip as scheduled, you've lost that $49, which would be an outcome of –$49. If something happens that forces you to miss the trip, you get back the $1,400 you originally paid, which would be an outcome of +$1,351. Let's say there's a 0.98 probability that you'll be able to go on the trip and a 0.02 probability that you won't. Find the expected value.
2. Will the company offering the insurance make or lose money in the long run? Why?

2-8 Group

Just about every college syllabus contains information about a grading policy and a grading scale. Are you aware of the policies for this course? Do you understand the policies? If not, make sure that you talk to your instructor.

Here's a potential grading scale that could be used in this course. A scale like this is called a **weighted scale**, because some assignments count for a bigger portion of the overall grade than others. We'll refer to the percentage of the overall grade corresponding to a given category as the **weight** for that category.

Grading:	Grading Scale:
20% Homework	A 90%
• Technology	B 80%
• Skills	C 70%
• Applications	D 60%
• Reflections	F Below 60%
20% Group work and class participation	
• Group projects and presentations	
• Exam reviews	
• Attendance and participation	
• Binder check	
• Final portfolio assignment	
40% Unit exams	
20% Final exam	

Let's try to figure out the final grade for a fictional student named Christine. She earned 220/320 points on homework assignments (boo!!), 365/410 points on group work and class participation, 77/100 on exam 1, 82/100 on exam 2, 71/100 on exam 3, 85/100 on exam 4, and 162/200 on the final. This table can be used to organize all of her scores.

Category	Student's Average (as a percent)	Weight (in decimal form)	Points for category (out of 100)
Homework			
Group work and class participation			
Unit exams			
Final exam			
		Grade =	

1. Using the scores provided, find the percentage of points earned in each category and put them in the Student's Average column.

2. Use information on the grading scale to fill in the weights for each category. Remember, the weight is the percentage of overall points corresponding to a category. Make sure you're writing the weights in decimal form, not percent form.

3. The points out of 100 earned for each category is the student's average multiplied by the weight: Use this to fill in the last column.

4. The overall grade, out of 100, is the sum of all the points earned. Write this total in the bottom right-hand corner.

5. What letter grade did Christine earn?

6. Which category would you say had the most negative effect on Christine's grade? Discuss why you feel that way. Provide evidence, not gut feelings.

7. As a check on the grading system, what should all of the weights add up to? Is that the case here? What would it mean if they didn't add up to that total?

Did You Get It

3. Find the final course grade for this history student.

Category	Student's Average (as a percent)	Weight (in decimal form)	Score (as a percent)
Quizzes	70	0.2	
Exams	75	0.3	
Final paper	87	0.5	
		Grade =	

Now that we know how to compute weighted grades, let's do something more useful. It's certainly a good idea to figure out your grade and make sure your instructor got it right. But it's even a better idea to figure out where you stand at some point in a course, and use that information to decide on how well you need to do the rest of the way to get a grade you're shooting for.

So let's say that you have the following scores in the week before your final exam.

Category	Student's Average (as a percent)	Weight (in decimal form)	Score (as a percent)
Homework	95.0	0.1	
Quizzes	88.0	0.15	
Unit exams	89.0	0.5	
Final exam		0.25	
		Grade =	

8. Complete the score column as much as you can.

9. If you don't even show up for the final, what would be your final grade?

10. How many points on a 200-point final would you need in order to get an A in the course? Feel free to use trial and error, trying out some different percentages at the bottom of the first column. You can assume that the professor would round your average to the nearest whole number using standard rounding rules.

Hopefully you noticed that the calculations we did for computing a weighted grade average are the same as the calculations we did to find an expected value. In each case, a value is multiplied by a percentage in decimal or fraction form (the weight, or the probability of an outcome), and the results are added. Cool. We'll close the Group portion with another expected value calculation to make sure you've got it down.

In a classic carnival game, you have to plunk down $2 to spin the lucky wheel, shown below. If the pointer lands on red, you're the proud owner of $3 (which means the net result is a gain of $1). If it lands on yellow, you get to spin again for free (net gain $0). If it lands on purple, you my friend are out two American dollars (net loss of $2), and if it lands on blue, you get paid $5. Rock on!

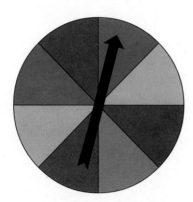

11. What's the net gain if you land on blue? Write your answer at the bottom of the Gain column next to Blue.

Color	Gain (X)	Probability P(X)	Product X · P(X)
Red	$1.00		
Yellow	$0.00		
Purple	−$2.00		
Blue			
		Expected value =	

12. Compute and record the probability for each gain (X). You'll need the picture of the spinner.

13. Calculate and record the product for each X*P(X).

14. What's the expected value? Record in the table, then describe exactly what the result means.

15. A game of chance is called a **fair game** if the expected value is 0. Why do you think that is?

16. A game favors the player if the player's expected value is positive, and favors the house (a nickname for those running the game) if the expected value is negative. Is the spinner game fair? Does it favor one side? Explain.

17. If you played this game 100 times, how much would you expect to win or lose?

Did You Get It

4. Let's make a minor change to the spinner game: If landing on blue pays out $6 instead of $5, what's the new expected value? Is the game fair, or does it favor one side?

2-8 Portfolio

Name _____

Technology

1. ☐ Can a spreadsheet roll a die? Physically, no. Numerically, yes. The command "=RANDBETWEEN(1,6)" generates a random number from the set 1, 2, 3, 4, 5, 6, which is exactly the same thing as rolling a die. That means you can repeat the experiment that started this lesson many, many times by just copying and pasting—if you're clever. The technology template for this lesson will get you started. The goal is to repeat the experiment enough times that the average expected value gets really close to the theoretical expected value that you calculated in Question 8 of the Class portion.

Online Practice

1. ☐ Include any written work from the online assignment along with any notes or questions about this lesson's content.

Applications

1. ☐ Complete the Applications problems.

Reflections

1. ☐ For all but one bet in standard American roulette, the expected value on a $1 bet is −$0.053. Explain what that means.

2. ☐ Betting on 0, 00, 1, 2, and 3 in roulette has an expected value of −$0.079. Is that a smarter bet, or a dumber one? Explain.

3. ☐ What makes a grading system weighted?

4. ☐ Name one thing you learned or discovered in this lesson that you found particularly interesting.

5. ☐ What questions do you have about this lesson?

Looking Ahead

1. ☐ Complete the Prep Skills for Lesson 3-1.

2. ☐ Read the opening paragraph in Lesson 3-1 carefully and answer Question 0 in preparation for that lesson.

Answers to "Did You Get It?"

1. The expected value is −$21.

2. The company will make money because in the long run, customers will lose $21 each time they buy.

3. 80%

4. The expected value is now $0, and the game is fair.

Answers to "Prep Skills"

1. $\frac{1}{4}; \frac{3}{4}$

2. $\frac{1}{3}$

3. **a.** 0.87　　**b.** 0.335　　**c.** 0.09　　**d.** 0.013

2-8   Applications

Name _____

The goal of the first few questions will be to compute a grade point average, which is a good example of weighted grading: Courses with more credit hours contribute more to the GPA than those with less.

   Below are the grades that our friend Christine earned last semester. You'll be filling in the rest of the table as you work through Questions 1–4.

Course	Grade	Grade Value	Credit Hours	Grade Points
English	A		3.0	
Math	C		4.0	
History	B		3.0	
Science	D		5.0	
		Totals:		

1. In most GPA systems, an A is worth 4 points, a B is worth 3 points, a C 2 points, and a D 1 point. Fill in the appropriate values in the Grade Value column.

2. In a GPA system, the number of credit hours act like the weights in a weighted grading system: The number of grade points for each course is the product of the grade value and the credit hours. Fill in the Grade Points column.

3. The GPA is calculated by dividing the number of grade points by the total number of credit hours. Fill in the Totals row, then use the results to find Christine's GPA. GPAs are almost always rounded to two decimal places.

4. What would her GPA have been if all courses were weighted the same? How did you decide?

Next, we'll study a traditional carnival game that we just now made up. The player rolls a single die. If the roll is 1, you win $1. You lose $2 if you roll a 2, 3, or 4. You win $3 if you roll a 5 or 6.

5. Without doing any calculations, does this game sound fair? Would you be willing to play it? Explain.

6. Find the expected value of this game. The table, which we're generously providing at no added cost, should help.

Result	Outcome (X)	Probability P(X)	Product X · P(X)
1			
2, 3, 4			
5, 6			

7. Would you prefer to be the player in this game, or the person running the game? Why?

8. What should the player expect to happen if he overstays his welcome and plays the game 500 times?

9. The grading structure for my Calc 2 class last semester is described here, and one student who shall remain nameless (because otherwise he or she could sue me back to the Stone Age and probably get me fired as well) had the scores shown. What was this student's overall average?

4 Tests: 40% total	Test scores: 78/100, 85/100, 68/100, 92/100
6 Quizzes: 20% total	Quiz score (overall): 140/150
Final: 20%	Final score: 175/200
Homework: 10%	HW score: 88/94
Projects: 10%	Project scores: 38/50, 50/50

Unit 2   Language and Symbolism Review

Carefully read through the list of terminology we've used in Unit 2. Consider circling the terms you aren't familiar with and looking them up. Then test your understanding by using the list to fill in the appropriate blank in each sentence.

$A = P(1 + r)^t$	expected value	mode
$A = P + Prt$	expression	normally distributed
area	fair game	output
change	formula	percent error
compound inequality	future value	principal
constant	greater than	range
conversion factor	greater than or equal to	rate
dependent variable	independent variable	relative change
dimensional analysis	inequality	standard deviation
empirical rule	input	time
equation	interest rate	unit rate
equivalent	less than	variable
error	less than or equal to	volume
estimation	mean	weighted scale
evaluate	median	

1. The _____ of a set of numbers is found by adding all of the numbers, then dividing by how many numbers there are in the list.

2. The _____ of a list of numbers is the value that lives right in the middle of the set if it's arranged in order.

3. The _____ of a list of numbers is the value that appears most often.

4. A _____ is a quantity that is able to change, or vary.

5. A _____ is a quantity that can't vary.

6. Course grade is an example of a _____ because other factors cause your course grade to vary.

7. The amount of time you spend studying is an example of an _____ because the amount of time spent studying can cause changes in your course grade.

8. An _____ is a combination of variables and constants using mathematical operations and grouping symbols.

9. An _____ is a statement that two quantities are equal, built using expressions and an equal sign (=).

10. A _____ is an equation with multiple variables that is used to calculate some quantity that we're interested in.

11. The independent variable is sometimes called the _____ and the dependent variable is sometimes call the _____.

12. To _____ an expression (or a formula), replace all occurrences of the variable or variables with specific numbers. This allows us to find a numeric value.

13. The future value of an account using simple interest is given by _____.

14. The future value of an account using compound interest is given by _____.

15. In Questions 13 and 14, the new value of an account A is known as the _____, P represents the original amount or _____, r represents the _____ in decimal form, and t represents the number of _____ periods.

16. Two expressions that would give you the same output no matter what input you choose would be considered _____ expressions.

17. _____ is the measure of size for two-dimensional objects, like floors, walls, posters, fields, etc.

18. _____ is the measure of size for three-dimensional objects, like beer mugs, swimming pools, buildings, and so on.

19. _____ is the incredibly valuable skill we use in the process for converting units.

20. Multiplying any measurement by a _____ won't change the size of the measurement because we're just multiplying by one; it will change the units used to measure.

21. A _____ is a ratio that compares two quantities.

22. A _____ is a rate that has a 1 in the denominator.

23. _____ is another name for making an educated guess.

24. A statement that involves one of the symbols $>$, $\geq$, $<$, or $\leq$ is called an _____.

25. A phrase used to describe $<$ is _____.

26. A phrase used to describe $>$ is _____.

27. A phrase used to describe $\leq$ is _____.

28. A phrase used to describe $\geq$ is _____.

29. The _____ between two quantities is found by simply subtracting the new value from the old, $(x_n - x_o)$.

30. The _____ between two quantities measures the change as a fraction of the original value, $\dfrac{x_n - x_o}{x_o}$.

31. When comparing an estimate to an exact value, the _____ in the estimate can be expressed by subtracting the actual value from the estimated value.

32. The _____ is calculated just like relative change. The idea is to measure how far off the estimate is as a percentage of the actual value.

33. The _____ of a data set is calculated by subtracting the highest value minus the lowest value.

34. _____, which is often represented by a lowercase Greek sigma (σ) is a measure of how far on average the values are from the mean.

35. Things like sizes of individuals, IQs, weights of packaged products, and lifespans of batteries or lightbulbs are often _____.

36. When a group of data is normally distributed, and we know the mean and standard deviation, the rule that allows us to estimate how many data values fall within certain ranges is known as the _____.

37. A combination of two inequalities is known as a _____.

38. The _____ of an event is the value that can be expected, on average, to occur.

39. A grading scale where some assignments count for a bigger portion of the overall grade than others is called a _____.

40. A game of chance is called a _____ if the expected value is 0.

Unit 2   Technology Review

This is a short review of the technology skills we've used in this unit. In each case, rate your confidence level by checking one of the boxes, and then answer the question. If you feel like you're struggling with these skills, consult the online resources for extra practice.

				1. Computing measures of average using Excel (Lesson 2-1)
				2. Evaluating a formula with a calculator or spreadsheet (Lesson 2-2)
				3. Computing standard deviation (Lesson 2-7)

1. Compute the mean, median, and mode for the lengths of my 10 favorite Arnold Schwarzenegger action movies in the list.

	A	B
1	**Movie**	**Length (min)**
2	Collateral Damage	108
3	Commando	90
4	Conan The Barbarian	129
5	Predator	107
6	Teminator 2	137
7	Terminator	107
8	Terminator 3	109
9	Terminator Genisys	126
10	The Running Man	101
11	True Lies	141
12		
13		
14	Mean	
15	Median	
16	Mode	

2. A prepaid calling card starts with a value of $40. It costs $0.06 per minute to use the card. The formula $V = 40 - 0.06x$ gives the value remaining on the card after x minutes of talking time. Use a calculator or a spreadsheet to complete this table.

x (min)	V (value remaining)
0	
60	
120	
180	
240	
300	

3. Compute the standard deviation for the lengths of my 10 favorite Arnold Schwarzenegger action movies in the list.

	A	B
1	**Movie**	**Length (min)**
2	Collateral Damage	108
3	Commando	90
4	Conan The Barbarian	129
5	Predator	107
6	Teminator 2	137
7	Terminator	107
8	Terminator 3	109
9	Terminator Genisys	126
10	The Running Man	101
11	True Lies	141
12		
13		
14	Standard Deviation	

Unit 2   Learning Objective Review

This is a short review of the learning objectives we've covered in this unit. In each case, rate your confidence level by checking one of the boxes, and then answer the question. If you feel like you're struggling with these skills, consult the lesson referenced next to the objective and see the online resources for extra practice.

1. Consider strategies for preparing for and taking math tests. (Lesson 2-1)

2. Understand the impact of a single question, or a single exam. (Lesson 2-1)

3. Calculate, interpret, and compare measures of average. (Lesson 2-1)

4. Distinguish between inputs (independent variables) and outputs (dependent variables). (Lesson 2-2)

5. Evaluate expressions and formulas. (Lesson 2-2)

6. Write and interpret expressions. (Lesson 2-2)

7. Determine units for area and volume calculations. (Lesson 2-3)

8. Use formulas to calculate areas and volumes. (Lesson 2-3)

9. Discuss important skills for college students to have. (Lesson 2-3)

10. Simplify expressions. (Lesson 2-3)

11. Convert units using dimensional analysis. (Lesson 2-4)

12. Convert units within the metric system. (Lesson 2-4)

13. Convert rates of change. (Lesson 2-4)

14. Convert temperatures. (Lesson 2-4)

15. Identify the steps in a systematic problem-solving procedure. (Lesson 2-5)

16. Make educated guesses. (Lesson 2-5)

17. Compare numbers using inequality symbols. (Lesson 2-5)

18. Compare change to relative change. (Lesson 2-6)

19. Apply percent error. (Lesson 2-6)

20. Identify the steps in computing standard deviation, and describe why they lead to a measure of variation. (Lesson 2-7)

21. Compute and interpret standard deviation. (Lesson 2-7)

22. Use a normal distribution to find probabilities. (Lesson 2-7)

23. Estimate expected value experimentally. (Lesson 2-8)

24. Compute expected value. (Lesson 2-8)

25. Compute weighted grades and GPA. (Lesson 2-8)

After you've evaluated your confidence level with each objective and gone back to review the objectives you weren't sure about, use the problem set as an additional review.

1. How did things go for the first exam? What do you plan to do the same for the second exam? What do you plan to change?

Question #	Points Possible
1	3
2	2
3	6
4	5
5	4
6	6
7	8
8	6
Total	40

2. The table shows the number of points possible on an 8 question quiz. What is the highest percentage a student could earn if he skipped the question worth the lowest number of points? What if he skipped the question worth the highest number of points instead?

Consider the table showing points earned on exam 1 for a group of students as you answer Questions 3–6.

	Exam 1
Beavis	28
Butthead	28
Hank	78
Bart	84
Lisa	100
Homer	71
Marge	92

3. Determine the mean of these scores.

4. Determine the median of these scores.

5. Determine the mode of these scores.

6. Which measure of average would you use if you wanted to brag about how well these students did on the exam?

7. According to http://www.boeing.com/, the Boeing 747 consumes about 5 gallons of fuel per mile. If a plane starts with 63,500 gallons of fuel and consumes fuel at that same rate, which expression would best represent the number of gallons of fuel **remaining** in the tanks of a plane after *x* miles had been flown? Circle the correct choice, and then explain why you believe it is correct.

©imageshop–zefa visual media uk ltd/
Alamy RF

   A. 63,500   **B.** $63,500 - x$

   C. $63,500 - 5x$ **D.** $12,700x$

   Explain:

8. Use your calculator or a spreadsheet to complete the table where the miles flown is *x* and the gallons remaining is given by the correct expression from question 7.

Miles flown	Gallons remaining
0	
250	
500	
750	
1000	
1250	
1500	
1750	
2000	

9. How many gallons would be remaining after 1,000 miles were flown?

10. How many miles were flown if there were 56,000 gallons of fuel remaining?

11. Write a sentence or two using the terms **input, output, independent,** and **dependent** to describe the relationship between the miles flown and the gallons remaining.

12. Which is most likely the correct way to compute the volume of a cone? Circle the correct choice and clearly explain your reasoning using the units (not by looking up a formula).

   A.   **Volume** $= \dfrac{1}{3}\pi(1.2 \text{ in.})^2(3 \text{ in.})$

   B.   **Volume** $= \dfrac{1}{3}\pi(1.2 \text{ in.})(3 \text{ in.})$

13. The formula $A = \pi r^2$ can be used to find the area of a circle with radius *r*. Find the area of the circle in the figure. Round to the nearest tenth.

3 cm

14. The formula $V = \pi r^2 h$ can be used to find the volume of a cylinder with radius r and height h. Find the volume of the cylinder in the figure. Round to the nearest tenth.

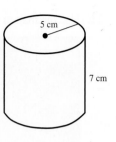

In Questions 15 and 16, simplify each expression.

15. $2(3x)(4x)$

16. $5x + 6y + 2x + 3y$

17. Determine the number of cups that are in a 2-liter bottle of Dr Pepper.

18. Determine the speed in inches per second of a space-shuttle crawler that travels at 2 miles per hour.

19. A 5-k race is 5 kilometers long. How long is that in millimeters?

20. Convert 68° Fahrenheit to Celsius.

21. Write a brief summary of Polya's 4-step problem-solving procedure.

22. Use the map to estimate the distance from St. Louis to New York, and explain your reasoning.

Distance:

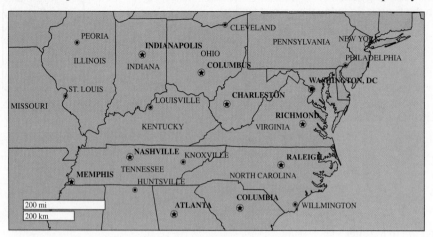

Reasoning:

23. If in a typical month your cell-phone bill is around $54, you might want to budget at least $60 for cell-phone expenses. Write an inequality to state that the amount budgeted c for cell-phone expenses was at least $60.

24. A seven-passenger van can transport at most seven people safely. Write an inequality stating that the number of passengers n is at most seven.

25. On March 1, 2017, the Dow Jones Industrial Average closed at $21,115.55. The next day it closed at $21,002.97. What was the actual change in value of the Dow from March 1 to March 2, 2017? What was the relative change?

26. If a jet was fueled with 68,000 lbs of fuel and was supposed to be given 72,000 lbs of fuel, what's the percent error? Then write a sentence using your answer to describe the impact this mistake would have on the amount of time the plane could remain flying.

Runners often keep a training log to keep track of the distance they run over a period of time. Nikki's running log is displayed here showing total miles run by month for 2015 and 2016.

	Miles in 2015	Miles in 2016
Jan	40	29
Feb	43	48
March	38	22
April	49	21
May	47	44
June	55	80
July	41	75
Aug	35	10
Sept	42	49
Oct	48	45
Nov	29	43
Dec	35	38

27. In which year did Nikki run more miles?

28. Compute the standard deviation for the miles run for each year. Feel free to use your favorite form of technology to assist with the calculations.

29. Write a sentence or two describing the meaning of the standard deviations you just computed.

30. It has been reported that credit card debt for college seniors is normally distributed with a mean of $3,262 and a standard deviation of $1,100. Fill in the missing values under the normal curve.

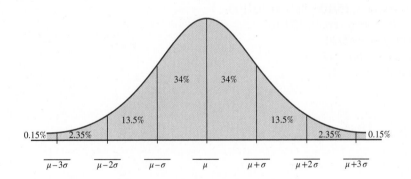

31. Write an expression that describes the probability of a randomly selected college senior having credit card debt over $4,362, and use the empirical rule to find this probability.

32. Use the empirical rule to find $P(2,162 < x < 5,462)$ and write a sentence explaining what it means.

Suppose you decide to set up a simple dice-rolling game at a carnival and you plan to pay $1 for a 1 or 2, $2 for a 3 or 4, and $3 for a 5 or 6. If each player pays you $2 for each roll, YOU would make $1 if the player rolled a 1 or 2, $0 if the player rolled a 3 or 4, and lose $1 if the player rolled a 5 or 6. Those outcomes have been completed in the table.

Outcome (X)	Probability P(X)	Product X · P(X)
$1		
$0		
−$1		

33. Complete the associated probabilities for each outcome and then complete the third column and use it to find the expected value of this game.

34. Is this a fair game? Would it make sense for you to offer this game? Explain.

35. The grading structure for a Stats course is described here, and one student had the scores shown. What was the student's overall average? If necessary, round the student's scores to the nearest full percent.

3 Tests: 30% total   Test scores: 65/100, 88/100, 93/100
8 Quizzes: 20% total   Quiz score (overall): 139/160
Homework: 5%   HW score: 65/70
Project: 15%   Project scores: 48/50
Final: 30%   Final score: 191/200

Unit 3
Thinking Linearly

©Brand X Pictures/PunchStock RF

Outline

Lesson 1: 88 Miles Per Hour!
Lesson 2: A Snow Job
Lesson 3: All Things Being Equal
Lesson 4: All Quantities Are Not Created Equal
Lesson 5: What's Your Problem?
Lesson 6: Big Mac Exchange Rates
Lesson 7: The Effects of Alcohol
Lesson 8: Party Planning
Lesson 9: The Great Tech Battle
Lesson 10: All Systems Go
End of Unit Review

Lesson 3-1   Prep Skills

SKILL 1: USE DIMENSIONAL ANALYSIS

Dimensional analysis was the main skill we learned in Lesson 2-4: It's the process we used to convert measurements from one unit to another. If you don't remember the process very well, it would be an excellent idea to review that lesson before starting Lesson 3-1. Try the Prep Skills Questions first to see how you do, then refer back to Lesson 2-4 if necessary.

SKILL 2: BUILDING UP FRACTIONS

Sometimes it's useful to do the opposite of reducing fractions: rewriting fractions so that they have a bigger numerator and denominator. This is called **building up** a fraction. Since it's the opposite of reducing fractions, we do exactly the opposite: Instead of dividing the numerator and denominator by the same number, we multiply the numerator and denominator by the SAME number.

- $\frac{3}{5}$ can be written as a fraction with denominator 20: $\frac{3}{5} \cdot \frac{4}{4} = \frac{12}{20}$
- $-\frac{2}{3}$ can be written as a fraction with denominator 60: $-\frac{2}{3} \cdot \frac{20}{20} = -\frac{40}{60}$

SKILL 3: DRAWING A SCATTER PLOT

This important skill was introduced in Lesson 1-5. The key things to remember are (1) write the given information as ordered pairs; (2) put the information corresponding to the first coordinates on the horizontal axis and the information corresponding to the second coordinates on the vertical axis; and (3) put an appropriate scale on those axes so that all of the points on your plot fit in the space you have, and don't leave a ton of empty space with no points. In almost every case, you'll want the scale on the vertical axis to begin at zero so that the heights of points don't give a misleading view of differences in the data.

SKILL 4: INTERPRETING INFORMATION FROM GRAPHS

Interpreting graphs is the most important skill we covered in Lesson 1-5. As we pointed out at the time, if you can't use a graph to get information, then it's just really bad art. In essence, this is the exact opposite of drawing a scatter plot. When you draw a plot, you're taking two corresponding pieces of information and drawing a point that represents them. When you interpret a graph, you're looking at a point and recognizing what those two pieces of information are. In both cases, the key is the same: carefully identifying exactly WHAT INFORMATION is represented by the scale on each axis.

PREP SKILLS QUESTIONS

1. Use dimensional analysis to perform each conversion. The unit equivalence reference tables can be found on page 192.

   a. 1,100 yards to feet

   b. 93 km to meters

   c. 2 miles to yards

   d. 32 hours to seconds

2. Rewrite each fraction with the given denominator.

   a. $\frac{5}{3}$; 21

   b. $-\frac{2}{5}$; 60

   c. $\frac{14}{4}$; 10

3. Draw a scatter plot of the data provided, which are the global sales (in millions) for each of Metallica's first 9 albums, as of January 1, 2016.

Album number	1	2	3	4	5	6	7	8	9
Sales (millions)	5.5	7.1	7.8	9	23	8.5	7	4.3	2.3

4. The graph shows the number of hours of daylight over the course of a year in Portland, Oregon. Use it to answer the questions.

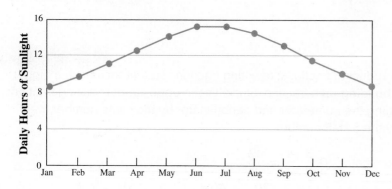

a. About how many hours of daylight could I expect on my birthday, July 8?

b. About when does the daylight time get longer than 12 hours in the spring?

c. What are the highest and lowest amounts of daylight during the year?

Lesson 3-1 **88 Miles Per Hour!**

LEARNING OBJECTIVES

☐ 1. Interpret a rate of change.

☐ 2. Predict a future value from a rate of change.

☐ 3. Calculate a rate of change.

☐ 4. Find the intercepts of a line.

☐ 5. Interpret the meaning of the intercepts of a line.

*The future is something which everyone reaches at the rate of
60 minutes an hour, whatever he does, whoever he is.*
　　　　　　　　—C.S. Lewis

©Universal Pictures Photographer: Ralph
Nelson, Jr./Photofest

Anyone familiar with the classic movie *Back to the Future* instantly recognizes the significance of 88 miles per hour: It's the speed the DeLorean time machine needed to reach in order to travel through time. Speeds (like 88 miles per hour) are familiar examples of the topic of this lesson, **rates of change**. Our world is a dynamic, ever-changing place, so studying the rate at which things change is an excellent way to study the world around us. The amount your grade changes as you spend more time studying? That's a rate. Your hourly wage if you work a part-time job? Rate. A waiter's decrease in tips as less customers eat at a restaurant? Rate. They're everywhere! Fortunately, studying rates will tie together some of the skills we've already practiced in this course, meaning we're in a good position to make the most of this useful topic.

  0. Think of an example of a rate of change different from the ones listed in the opening paragraph.

3-1 Class

A rate is a ratio that compares two quantities. By rate of change, we mean a rate that compares the change in one quantity to the change in another. A speed like 88 miles per hour qualifies, because we can write it this way:

$$\frac{88 \text{ mi}}{1 \text{ hr}}$$

This quite literally compares a change in distance (88 miles) to a change in time (1 hour). That's exactly why we measure speeds in miles per hour.

  The word **equivalent** is an important word in math, and one that we'll use often in this course. Make sure you clearly understand what that word means. For our purposes, we'll say that two quantities are equivalent if they have the same value or are interchangeable even if they look different.

  1. If you make $100 a day for doing a certain job, how much money would you make in a 5-day work week?

  2. Are $\dfrac{\$100}{\text{day}}$ and $\dfrac{\$500}{5 \text{ days}}$ equivalent rates? What does that mean?

Question 2 demonstrates a useful fact about rates of change: They can be scaled up or scaled down to fit a given situation. Scaling up a fraction is done by writing an equivalent fraction (that is, one that has the same value) using larger numbers. Scaling down is writing an equivalent fraction with smaller numbers. These processes are done by either multiplying BOTH the numerator and denominator by the same number, or dividing BOTH the numerator and denominator by the same number.

3. Write a fraction equivalent to $\dfrac{60 \text{ mi}}{4 \text{ hr}}$ that has 2 in the denominator.

4. Write a fraction equivalent to $\dfrac{60 \text{ mi}}{4 \text{ hr}}$ that has 1 in the denominator. This is known as a **unit rate**.

5. Write a fraction equivalent to $\dfrac{\$320}{4 \text{ days}}$ that has 10 in the denominator. (Hint: First scale down, then up.)

6. If one bicyclist is pedaling at a rate of 40 miles in 3 hours, and another at a rate of 50 miles in 4 hours, which is faster? (Scaling either up or down can be used!)

Did You Get It   ?

Try this problem to see if you understand the concepts we just studied. The answer can be found at the end of the Portfolio section.

1. If I leave my home and drive for 2 hours, covering 128 miles, what was my rate?

Most experienced runners get to a point where they can comfortably jog long distances at a consistent pace. This "pace," of course, is another way to say "rate of change," because speed is the rate at which distance changes compared to time. One particular runner jogs one lap around a 400-meter track in 2 minutes. In Questions 7–16, you can assume that the runner can maintain this pace for a long time.

7. For every _____ minutes, the runner jogs _____ meters.

8. Complete the table, continuing the pattern for times and finding the associated distances for this runner.

Time (Min)	Distance (m)
2	400
4	

9. Notice that the rate at which the runner's distance changes is constant. When the rate of change is constant, a quantity illustrates what type of growth (that we encountered in Unit 1)?

10. Write the runner's rate as a fraction using meters in the numerator.

> **Math Note**
>
> Using rates of change to calculate sizes of quantities is one of the most important applications of dimensional analysis.

11. Write this rate as a unit rate in meters per minute.

12. Convert your rate from Question 11 to meters per second using dimensional analysis. (Round to two decimal places.)

13. What distance will the runner cover in 40 minutes?

14. What distance will he cover in 40 seconds?

15. Based on the previous two questions, can you write a formula for finding the distance traveled by an object when you know the speed and amount of time traveling at that speed?

Did You Get It?

2. Based on the rate you found in Did You Get It 1, what distance could I cover in 3.5 hours driving at that rate?

16. What would this runner's total time be for a 10k race? (Ten kilometers, that is. Recall that 1 km = 1,000 m. Your answer to Question 11 will help.)

3-1   Group

At this point, we know that a rate of change measures how some quantity is changing. Now ponder this question: Do rates of change change? That might look like a typo, but it's not. The rate at which some quantity changes either stays constant, or changes. For example, if you make $9 per hour at a job, the rate at which your pay changes as you work more hours is always the same: Your pay grows at the rate of $9 per hour. But if you're driving in traffic, the rate of change of your position (what we commonly call speed) probably changes quite a bit. Our next order of business is to study situations where the rate of change of a quantity stays constant: In that case, modeling that situation with an equation or a graph is very manageable.

1. According to taxifarefinder.com, a cab ride from the airport in Las Vegas will cost you an initial charge of $5.10, plus $2.60 per mile. Use this information to fill in the rest of the table describing the total cost for various distances. Then create a scatter diagram, using the distance as x coordinate and the cost as y coordinate.

©Stockbyte/Punchstock RF

Distance	Cost ($)
0	$5.10
1	$7.70
2	$10.30
3	
4	
5	

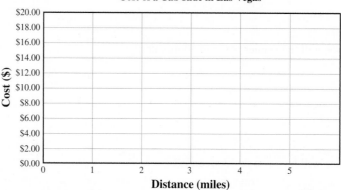

2. What do you notice about the pattern that the points on your scatter diagram are making? Use that observation about a pattern to connect the points, drawing a graph that represents the cost of a cab ride based on distance.

3. The point where any graph crosses the y axis is called the **y intercept** for the graph and a point where the graph crosses the x axis is called an **x intercept**. Write the coordinates of the y intercept for the graph that you drew. More importantly, what information does the y intercept represent? Does the graph have an x intercept? Why or why not?

4. How much more will you pay for a 3-mile ride than for a 2-mile ride?

©Glow Images RF

5. How much more will you pay for a 5-mile ride than a 2-mile ride? Explain why that makes sense based on your answer to Question 4.

6. Pick any two points on the graph that you drew, and subtract the second coordinates. Then divide the result by the difference of the first coordinates. Each person in your group should pick a different pair of points. What does the result represent about the cab ride?

In dividing the difference of the two costs by the difference of the two distances in Question 6, you found the rate of change of the cost as distance changes. When applied to the graph of a line, we call this number, which describes how steep the line is, the **slope** of the line.

The Slope of a Line

The slope of a line is a number that describes how steep a line is. This is accomplished by comparing the change in height over some span to the change in horizontal position.

As a formula, if the two points are (x_1, y_1) and (x_2, y_2), the slope (usually represented by the letter m) is

$$m = \frac{y_2 - y_1}{x_2 - x_1} = \frac{\text{Difference of second coordinates}}{\text{Difference of first coordinates}}$$

The key to interpreting slope is to recognize that each of the numerator and denominator is a change in some quantity. So slope compares the change in two quantities, which makes it a rate of change. Specifically, slope is the rate at which the second coordinate changes compared to the first coordinate.

Did You Get It

3. Find the slope of a line that connects the points (3, 10) and (8, 30).

7. If you were to connect the points (1, 7.70) and (5, 18.10) on the graph in Question 1 with a triangle, it would look something like this. Label the coordinates of the two given points on this triangle.

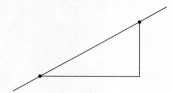

8. How much more distance was added to the ride going from (1, 7.70) to (5, 18.10)? Label this value on the triangle.

9. How much cost was added to the ride going from (1, 7.70) to (5, 18.10)? Label this value on the triangle.

10. Find the slope of the line using your answers to Questions 8 and 9. What do you notice?

11. How much would 4 miles add to the cost of a taxi ride? Would it matter if the change was from 1 mile to 5 miles or if it was 20 miles to 24 miles?

12. The thing that makes a line a line is the fact that the slope never changes. We now know that the slope of a line describes the rate at which the *y* coordinate changes compared to the *x* coordinate. Based on this, how can you decide if the relationship between two quantities might be modeled well by a straight line?

13. Estimate the distance of a $16 cab ride. You can use either the table or the graph, but make sure you explain how you got your answer.

Everyone knows that after you buy a car, in most cases its value decreases as it gets older. Suppose you bought a used car for $15,000 a few years ago, and its value has been decreasing at the rate of $2,000 per year since then. **Make sure you answer each of the remaining questions with a full sentence,** with punctuation and everything!

©Vladimiroquai/iStock/Getty Images RF

Time (yrs)	Value ($)
0	$15,000
1	$13,000
2	$11,000
3	$9,000
4	$7,000
5	$5,000

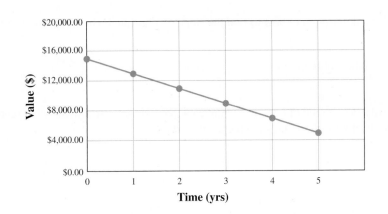

14. Find the *y* intercept of the graph and explain what it means. (Remember, the *y* intercept is a point, not a number.)

15. Find the slope of the line and explain what it means. In particular, what's the significance of the sign?

16. Estimate the value of the car after 42 months. (Careful about time units!)

17. Estimate the number of years it took for the car to reach a value of $6,000.

Math Note

The process of an object losing value as time passes is called **depreciation**. This concept is used by businesses in calculating net assets for tax purposes.

Did You Get It

4. Estimate the value of the car 18 months after it was purchased.
5. About how long after it was purchased was the car worth $10,000?

18. Give a description of how to find the slope of a line, and why it represents a rate of change. Be specific!

19. Give a description of how to find the y intercept of a graph, and the x intercept as well. Include a definition in your own words of what the y and x intercepts of a graph are.

3-1 Portfolio

Name _____

Check each box when you've completed the task. Remember that your instructor will want you to turn in the portfolio pages you create.

Technology

1. ☐ When you know the rate at which a quantity changes, you can build a spreadsheet to calculate the size of that quantity. Build a spreadsheet that calculates pay given hours worked and hourly rate, like the one shown here. You should be able to enter any rate you like in dollars per hour, and have a formula calculate the pay corresponding to any time you enter. Also enter a formula to calculate total pay for all employees. A template to help you get started can be found in the online resources for this lesson.

	A	B	C	D
	Employee	Time (hrs)	Rate ($/hr)	Pay ($)
2	Napoleon	10	$8.75	$87.50
3	Deb	20		
4	Rico	32		
5	Me	40		
6			Total Pay	
7				

Online Practice

1. ☐ Include any written work from the online assignment along with any notes or questions about this lesson's content.

Applications

1. ☐ Complete the Applications problems.

Reflections

Type a short answer to each question.

1. ☐ In this section, we learned that the speed of an object is a rate of change; specifically, the rate at which distance traveled changes as time changes. Think of at least three other rates of change, and describe specifically what they measure. If you want to impress your instructor, try to come up with one that doesn't have a unit of time in it.

2. ☐ Explain in your own words what the slope of a line is. You should discuss both what it means graphically and what the practical significance is.

3. ☐ What are the intercepts of a graph?

4. ☐ Name one thing you learned or discovered in this lesson that you found particularly interesting.

5. ☐ What questions do you have about this lesson?

Looking Ahead

1. ☐ Complete the Prep Skills for Lesson 3-2.

2. ☐ Read the opening paragraph in Lesson 3-2 carefully and answer Question 0 in preparation for that lesson.

Answers to "Did You Get It?"

1. 64 mi/hr   2. 224 miles   3. 4   4. About $12,000   5. About 30 months

Answers to "Prep Skills"

1. a. 3,300 ft   b. 93,000 m   c. 3,520 yd   d. 115,200 sec

2. a. $\dfrac{35}{21}$ b. $-\dfrac{24}{60}$ c. $\dfrac{35}{10}$

3.

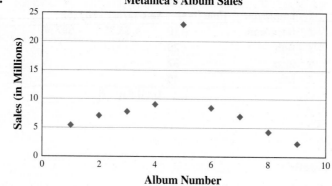

4. a. about 15 hours   b. around March 28   c. about 15 hours; about 8.5 hours

3-1 Applications

Name _____

When advertising special financing deals, car makers often use rates to describe what your monthly payment will look like. (This is because the amount you need to borrow varies widely based on the car you choose and the down payment you make.) In January 2013, Hyundai offered 2.9% financing on the Genesis coupe which would result in monthly payments of $22.09 per $1,000 borrowed for 48 months.

1. For every _____ borrowed, the monthly payment will be _____.

Courtesy of Dave Sobecki

2. Complete the table of loan payments using your answer to Question 1.

3. Write the rate Hyundai advertised as a fraction.

Amount Borrowed	Loan Payment
$1,000	$22.09
$2,000	
$3,000	
$4,000	
$5,000	
$6,000	
$7,000	
$8,000	
$9,000	
$10,000	

Use your answer to Question 3 and dimensional analysis for Questions 4 and 5.

4. What would your monthly payment be if you borrowed $18,000?

5. If your monthly payment is $331.35, how much did you borrow?

6. If you agree on a price of $23,900 (including taxes and fees) for a Genesis and the dealership offers you $7,500 in trade for your old car, how much would your monthly payment be?

3-1 Applications

Name _____

A manufacturing company buys a new stamping machine for $28,000. The maker of the machine informs the company's CEO that on average, it depreciates in value according to the schedule shown in the table.

7. If the depreciation continues at the same rate, how long will it take until the machine has no value?

Months	Value
0	$28,000
6	$24,500
12	$21,000
18	$17,500

8. Based on the pattern you see in the table, how do you know that the graph will be a straight line?

9. Pick an appropriate scale for each axis, and graph the value of the machine until it reaches zero. Use the number of months as first coordinate.

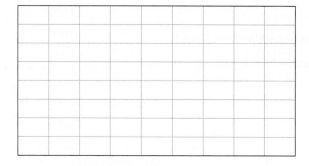

10. Find the slope of the graph and explain what it means.

11. Find the intercepts of the graph, and describe what each means.

Lesson 3-2   Prep Skills

SKILL 1: ADD OR SUBTRACT LIKE TERMS

In Lesson 1-2, we saw that quantities can only be added if they're like quantities, which means they're identical except possibly for the numeric part. For example, $8n$ and $12n$ are like quantities because they're both just n without the 8 and the 12, while $8n$ and $12n^2$ are not like quantities because n and n^2 aren't identical.

The individual pieces of an expression containing addition and subtraction are called **terms**. In this case, we use the phrase *like terms* rather than like quantities. Deciding which terms can be added or subtracted is an important part of simplifying algebraic expressions.

- $10k + 8 - 3k + 4$ $10k$ and $-3k$ are like terms; 8 and 4 are like terms
  $= 7k + 12$

- $4n - 7n^2 + 11n + 7 - 4n^2$ $4n$ and $11n$ are like terms; $-7n^2$ and $-4n^2$ are like terms
  $= 15n - 11n^2 + 7$

SKILL 2: FIND SLOPE AND Y INTERCEPT

Slope was one of the key concepts we learned about in Lesson 3-1. It's discussed in the Group portion of that lesson, with a reminder on how to compute slope in the colored box on page 287. Finding and interpreting the y intercept of a graph is also in that Group portion. In short, the y intercept is the point where a graph crosses the y axis. It always tells you the value of the output for an equation when the input is zero.

SKILL 3: EVALUATE EXPRESSIONS

This was one of the most important skills we studied in Lesson 2-2. When we use an algebraic expression to model some quantity, it's very common to calculate the value of that quantity by replacing an input variable with some number. This is what we called evaluating an expression. The only thing you need to think about is replacing every single occurrence of the variable or variables with the given number(s).

- For the future value formula $A = P(1 + rt)$, if we want to know the future value of a $5,000 initial investment at 6% interest for 5 years, we're given values of $P = 5,000$, $r = 0.06$, and $t = 5$. So we replace each letter in the formula with the associated value:

  $A = \$5,000(1 + 0.06(5)) = \$6,500$

SKILL 4: DRAW A SCATTER PLOT

This important skill was introduced in Lesson 1-5 and reviewed in the Prep Skills for Lesson 3-1.

PREP SKILLS QUESTIONS

1. Perform each addition or subtraction.

   a. $3x + 8x - 12$ b. $14y + 6 - 2y - 10$ c. $11a + 12b - 13 + 7a - 20b$

2. The graph on the next page shows the value of an antique painting based on the number of years since it was found in someone's attic. Find the slope of the line and write a description of what it tells us about the painting.

3. What is the *y* intercept of the graph? What does it tell us?

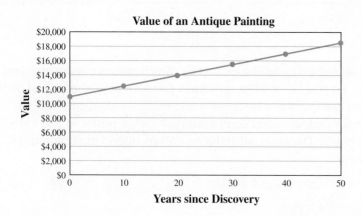

4. Evaluate each expression for the given value of the variable(s).

a. $K = C + 273.15$; $C = 35$

b. $A = lw$; $l = 10$, $w = 35$

c. $C = 4,200 + 1.35x$; $x = 675$

Lesson 3-2   A Snow Job

LEARNING OBJECTIVES

☐ 1. Write expressions based on given information.

☐ 2. Interpret algebraic expressions in context.

☐ 3. Evaluate and simplify expressions.

©Richard Ellis/Alamy

"Between calculated risk and reckless decision-making lies the dividing line between profit and loss."
                                        —Charles Duhigg

Most folks that start a business do so with the goal of making money. And running a business isn't easy—there are tons of things you need to keep track of. Where is your money being spent? Is your investment of time and money worthwhile? How many customers do you have, and how much money are you bringing in? If you plan to just start a business without a plan for carefully monitoring every aspect of the company, you have about the same chance of success as an entrepreneur planning to sell snow cones at the South Pole. Before this course, you may have thought that algebra was just an abstract thing that pointy-headed intellectuals do to amuse themselves, but we've already seen a ton of ways that algebra is used to make sense of things in our lives. In this lesson we're going to show how some of the skills we've been working on are useful in monitoring a business. And that's no snow job.

   0. In your own words, what is algebra?

3-2   Class

If you were running a business, like one that sells snow cones, you'd probably have a lot of data related to your costs and the amount of money you can make. And if you had also completed the first two units of this course, you'd know a lot about organizing and working with data, so let's put some of the stuff we've learned to work by studying the operation of a snow cone stand. First, we'll need to know some terminology from business and economics.

The amount of money that a business needs to spend for their operation is known as their **costs**. The amount of money that customers pay them for their goods or services is called the **revenue**. The difference between these two numbers is the amount of money that the company makes or loses, which is called the **profit**.

   1. When a company is making money—which is the goal—the profit will be positive. What is the relationship between revenue and costs when this happens?

The spreadsheet describes the costs associated with a snow cone business, as well as the revenue and profit.

	A	B	C	D	E	F	G	H	I	J	K	L
	Snow cones sold	Cups	Cost of cups	Syrup (oz)	Cost of syrup	Ice (oz)	Cost of ice	Combined supply costs	Fixed costs	Total costs	Revenue	Net profit
1												
2	0	0	$0.00	0	$0.00	0	$0.00	$0.00	$245.00	$245.00	$0.00	-$245.00
3	100	100	$1.00	200	$4.00	500	$7.00	$12.00	$245.00	$257.00	$75.00	-$182.00
4	200	200	$2.00	400	$8.00	1000	$14.00	$24.00	$245.00	$269.00	$150.00	-$119.00
5	300	300	$3.00	600	$12.00	1500	$21.00	$36.00	$245.00	$281.00	$225.00	-$56.00
6	400	400	$4.00	800	$16.00	2000	$28.00	$48.00	$245.00	$293.00	$300.00	$7.00
7	500	500	$5.00	1000	$20.00	2500	$35.00	$60.00	$245.00	$305.00	$375.00	$70.00

2. If 300 snow cones are sold, how many ounces of syrup are needed? What about if 500 snow cones are sold?

3. A formula was typed into cell D5 to obtain the result you used to answer Question 2. What formula would give the correct result? (The formula should use cell A5.)

4. Write a verbal description of the relationship between the number of snow cones sold and the number of ounces of syrup that will be needed.

5. Complete the following sentence. If x represents the number of snow cones sold, then _____ represents the number of ounces of syrup used.

When writing an expression that represents some quantity, we'll often turn that expression into an equation (or formula, if you like) by using a letter to represent the value of the expression.

6. Using the letter S to represent the amount of syrup used, write a formula that describes the ounces of syrup needed in terms of the number of snow cones sold.

Courtesy of Greg Stiff

How do we know so much about the snow cone business? Because one of us used to own one!

Did You Get It

Try these problems to see if you understand the concepts we just studied. The answers can be found at the end of the Portfolio section.

1. A hot dog vendor makes \$0.60 on each hot dog sold. Write an expression to describe how much she makes, in dollars, from selling x hot dogs.
2. Using the letter D for the amount she makes, write a formula that describes the amount she makes in terms of number of hot dogs sold.

---

7. Does the number of snow cones sold depend on the amount of syrup used, or does the amount of syrup used depend on the number of snow cones sold?

8. In your formula from Question 6, which is the independent variable (input), and which is the dependent variable (output)?

9. Is the relationship between the amount of syrup used and the number of show cones sold linear, exponential, or neither? Explain.

10. If x represents the number of snow cones sold, what quantity described in the spreadsheet would be represented by $5x$?

11. If 70 snow cones are sold, the value of 5x is _____. Write a sentence or two explaining exactly what that result tells us about the snow cone business.

12. If you were to graph the data in columns A and J from the spreadsheet, with number of snow cones on the horizontal axis and total costs on the vertical axis, would the graph be a line? How can you tell?

13. Now plot points corresponding to columns A and J. Do they form a straight line? What is the y intercept?

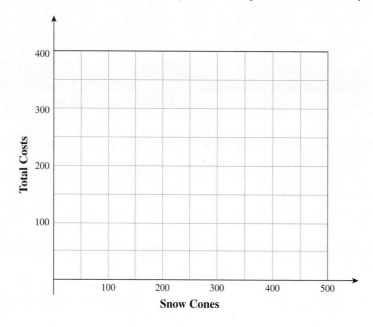

14. Write a unit rate that describes the combined costs of all supplies needed per snow cone sold.

15. Pick two points from the graph (remember, the points are coming from the table) and find the slope of the line connecting them. What do you notice?

16. If each cup costs $0.01, write an expression for the total cost in dollars of the cups based on *x*, the number of snow cones sold.

17. If $0.04 is spent on syrup for each snow cone sold, write an expression for the total cost in dollars of the syrup based on *x*, the number of snow cones sold.

18. If $0.07 is spent on ice for each snow cone sold, write an expression for the total cost in dollars of the ice based on *x*, the number of snow cones sold.

19. The total combined supply costs for making one snow cone looks like this:

cost of cups + cost of syrup + cost of ice

Write an algebraic expression for this, and then simplify your expression. Your previous three answers will surely help.

20. The total cost of selling snow cones is the sum of the variable cost for supplies (which you just found) and the **fixed costs**: These are costs that aren't affected by the number of snow cones sold, like rent, insurance, licensing, etc. Look back at the table to find the fixed costs for this business, then use that to write an equation of the form $C =$ _____ that represents the total cost based on *x*, the number of snow cones sold.

Did You Get It

3. A company that makes paper plates has fixed costs of $750 and it costs them $0.43 to make each package of plates. Write an equation of the form $C =$ _____ that represents the total cost based on *x*, the number of packages of plates they make.

3-2 Group

Next, we'll study the profit made by the business, beginning with a graph. The graph was drawn using information from the data table at the beginning of the lesson.

Answer each question with a full sentence or face consequences too dire to mention in polite company.

©RoongsaK/Shitterstpcl RF

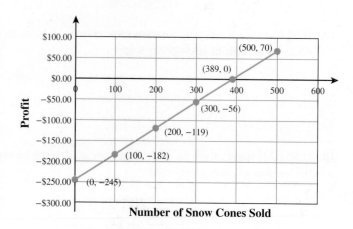

1. Find the *y* intercept of the graph and explain what it means.

2. Find the *x* intercept of this graph and explain what it means.

3. Find the slope of the line and explain what it means.

4. Estimate the net profit if 150 snow cones are sold. What's the significance of the sign?

5. Estimate the number of snow cones that need to be sold to make a profit of $50.

6. Fill in the blanks: The profit starts at _____ when no snow cones are sold, and goes up by _____ for each sale.

7. Use your answers to the previous question to write an equation of the form $P =$ _____ that gives the profit made from selling x snow cones.

Now that we're representing data with equations, we can use a calculator to draw graphs. This can be useful in checking an equation that you've written: If its graph matches the data that you started with, then you know you have the right equation.

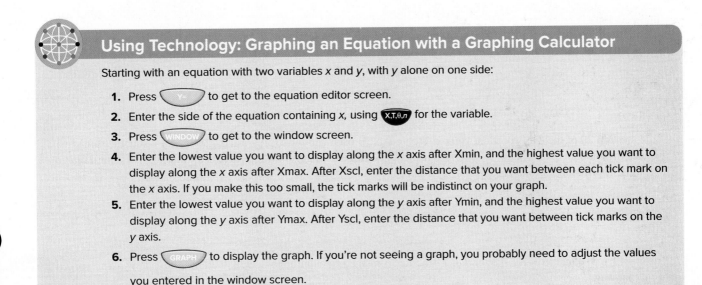

Using Technology: Graphing an Equation with a Graphing Calculator

Starting with an equation with two variables x and y, with y alone on one side:

1. Press ⬭Y= to get to the equation editor screen.
2. Enter the side of the equation containing x, using ⬭X,T,θ,n for the variable.
3. Press ⬭WINDOW to get to the window screen.
4. Enter the lowest value you want to display along the x axis after Xmin, and the highest value you want to display along the x axis after Xmax. After Xscl, enter the distance that you want between each tick mark on the x axis. If you make this too small, the tick marks will be indistinct on your graph.
5. Enter the lowest value you want to display along the y axis after Ymin, and the highest value you want to display along the y axis after Ymax. After Yscl, enter the distance that you want between tick marks on the y axis.
6. Press ⬭GRAPH to display the graph. If you're not seeing a graph, you probably need to adjust the values you entered in the window screen.

See the Lesson 3-2 Using Tech video in class resources for further information.

8. Use a graphing calculator to graph the equation you wrote in Question 7. Does it match the graph provided earlier? Draw a quick sketch of what your calculator screen looks like.

Use the spreadsheet at the beginning of the lesson to answer the following questions.

9. Find the total cost from selling 400 snow cones.

10. Find the revenue from selling 400 snow cones.

11. A formula that uses cells J7 and K7 was typed in cell L7. What is that formula? (Focus on the dollar amounts in cells J7 and K7.)

12. Write a verbal explanation of the relationship between the profit made from selling a certain number of snow cones and the revenue and total costs from selling that number of snow cones.

13. If we use P to represent profit, C to represent total costs, and R to represent revenue, write a formula that describes the profit in terms of C and R.

14. In Question 20 of the Class portion, you represented total costs with the expression $0.12x + 245$. Using the same line of reasoning, find an expression that describes the revenue from selling x snow cones. (Recall that we used a unit rate to find the expression for total costs.)

15. Is $5 - (7 - 3)$ equal to $5 - 7 - 3$, or $5 - 7 + 3$? Perform each calculation to decide, then try to explain why it worked out that way.

16. Subtract the expression $0.12x + 245$ from the one you wrote in Question 14. Use what you discovered in Question 15 to perform the subtraction. Then write a description of what exactly this new expression represents.

17. Use your expression to find the profit made if the company sells 8,000 snow cones at a festival.

Did You Get It

4. If the company from Did You Get It 3 that makes paper plates sells their plates for $2.49 per package, write and simplify an expression that describes the company's profit in terms of the number of packages sold.

5. Would the company make or lose money if it sells 250 packages? How much money?

3-2 Portfolio

Name _____

Check each box when you've completed the task. Remember that your instructor will want you to turn in the portfolio pages you create.

Technology

1. ☐ The spreadsheet on page 298 is in the online resources for this lesson. Make a copy of the spreadsheet, then use the fill-down feature to extend the existing pattern to show up to 2,100 snow cones sold. This should be in row 23 if all goes well.

2. ☐ Now create a scroll bar that changes the values in cell A23. (We learned how to make scroll bars in the online resources for Lesson 2-1.) The settings should be Current = 2,000, minimum = 0, maximum = 2,000. Adjust the scroll bar to the point where the profit is as close to zero dollars as possible. Record the value on the scroll bar, and describe what that tells you about the business.

Online Practice

1. ☐ Include any written work from the online assignment along with any notes or questions about this lesson's content.

Applications

1. ☐ Complete the Applications problems.

Reflections

Type a short answer to each question.

1. ☐ Describe how we used algebra in this lesson to study the operation of a snow cone business.

2. ☐ Describe what each of costs, revenue, and profit mean in terms of operating a business.

3. ☐ If a company's costs start out at $3,000 when no items are produced, and it costs $1.25 to produce each item, describe how you can write an expression that provides the cost of making x items. Don't just write the expression: Describe how you got it.

4. ☐ Name one thing you learned or discovered in this lesson that you found particularly interesting.

5. ☐ What questions do you have about this lesson?

Looking Ahead

1. ☐ Complete the Prep Skills for Lesson 3-3.

2. ☐ Read the opening paragraph in Lesson 3-3 carefully and answer Question 0 in preparation for that lesson.

Answers to "Did You Get It?"

1. $0.6x$ 2. $D = 0.6x$ 3. $C = 750 + 0.43x$

4. $2.06x - 750$ 5. They'd lose $235.

Answers to "Prep Skills"

1. **a.** $11x - 12$ **b.** $12y - 4$ **c.** $18a - 8b - 13$

2. The slope is about 150; this means the value of the antique painting increases $150 every year after being found in the attic.

3. The y intercept is about (0, 11,000). This means the painting was worth $11,000 when it was discovered.

4. **a.** $K = 308.15$ **b.** $A = 350$ **c.** $C = 5,111.25$

3-2 Applications

Name _____

Unfortunately for the snow cone business we studied within the lesson, they're not the only game in town when it comes to frosty treats. They compete fiercely with Frosty the Cone Man, a nearby ice cream stand. The table describes the profit that Frosty can make based on the number of cones he sells. We'll be using this information throughout the Applications.

Cones sold	Profit
0	–$375
200	–$181
400	$13
600	$207
800	$401
1,000	$595

1. Use the grid to graph the points from our table. Put cones sold on the horizontal axis and profit on the vertical axis.

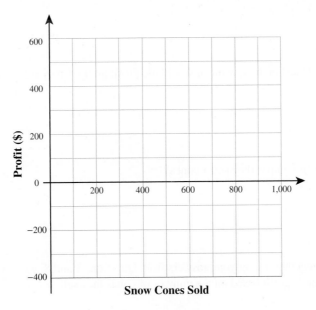

Snow Cones Sold

2. Based on the plotted points, does the graph appear to be a line? If so, draw it in.

3. Find the *y* intercept of your graph, and describe what it tells us about Frosty's business.

3-2   Applications

Name _____

4. Estimate the x intercept based on your graph, and describe what it tells us about the business.

5. Find the slope of the line using two of the points from the table.

6. Notice that in calculating the slope, you subtracted two profits in the numerator, and two numbers of cones sold in the denominator. Based on this, what are the units for your slope? What does it tell us about the business?

7. Based on your answer to Question 6, how much would the profit go up if they sell 10 cones? Twenty cones?

8. How much would the profit go up if they sell x cones?

9. Now let's put the pieces together. Using your answers from Questions 3 and 8, write a formula in the form $P =$ _____ that describes the company's profit based on the number of cones they sell.

10. Remember that festival where the snow cone business sold 8,000 units? How much profit would Frosty the Cone Man make if he sells 10,500 cones at that festival?

Lesson 3-3 Prep Skills

SKILL 1: ADD OR SUBTRACT LIKE TERMS

Just in case you missed this in the last lesson. . . . In Lesson 1-2, we saw that quantities can only be added if they're like quantities, which means they're identical except possibly for the numeric part. For example, $8n$ and $12n$ are like quantities because they're both just n without the 8 and the 12, while $8n$ and $12n^2$ are not like quantities because n and n^2 aren't identical.

The individual pieces of an expression containing addition and subtractions are called **terms**. In this case, we use the phrase *like terms* rather than like quantities. Deciding which terms can be added or subtracted is an important part of simplifying algebraic expressions.

- $10k + 8 - 3k + 4$ $10k$ and $-3k$ are like terms; 8 and 4 are like terms
  $= 7k + 12$

- $4n - 7n^2 + 11n + 7 - 4n^2$ $4n$ and $11n$ are like terms; $-7n^2$ and $-4n^2$ are like terms
  $= 15n - 11n^2 + 7$

SKILL 2: EVALUATE EXPRESSIONS

Hey, here's another one we just covered in the last lesson. Good deal. When we use an algebraic expression to model some quantity, it's very common to calculate the value of that quantity by replacing an input variable with some number. This is what we called *evaluating an expression*. The only thing you need to think about is replacing every single occurrence of the variable(s) with the given number(s).

- For the future value formula $A = P(1 + rt)$, if we want to know the future value of a $5,000 initial investment at 6% interest for 5 years, we're given values of $P = 5{,}000$, $r = 0.06$, and $t = 5$. So we replace each letter in the formula with the associated value:

  $A = \$5{,}000(1 + 0.06(5)) = \$6{,}500$

SKILL 3: WRITE A LINEAR EQUATION GIVEN A BEGINNING VALUE AND RATE OF CHANGE

This was one of the most important skills we practiced in Lesson 3-2. If some quantity begins at some value when the input is zero and has a *constant* rate of change, then we can write a linear equation that models that quantity. In every case, the equation will be of the form

Output = initial value + rate of change(input variable)

- If you start a job making $11 per hour and get a raise of $1.25 per hour every year, a formula for your hourly wage (W) in terms of years after you started is

  $W = 11 + 1.25t$

  Beginning   Rate of   Input
    value   change   variable

PREP SKILLS QUESTIONS

1. Simplify each expression by combining like terms.

   a. $8t + 7 - 3t - 4$

   b. $14x + 12 - (7 - x)$

   c. $5(10 - 4x) - 5(2x + 2)$

2. Evaluate each expression for the given value of the variable(s).

   a. $V = 21{,}000 - 1{,}700t;\ t = 4$

   b. $C = 4.25 + 0.9x;\ x = 12$

   c. $P = 2l + 2w;\ l = 35,\ w = 50$

3. Marlene rented a new apartment for $1,400 a month, and was told that the rent increases by $20 per year if she decides to stay. Write an equation that describes the rent (R) in terms of years after she moves in (y).

4. A stock that has been tanking lately was at $42 per share a while ago, and has been losing value at the rate of $1.75 per week since then. Write an equation in the form $V =$ _____ that describes the value of the stock in terms of w, the number of weeks since it was at $42.

Lesson 3-3   **All Things Being Equal**

LEARNING OBJECTIVES

☐ 1. Explain what it means to solve an equation.

☐ 2. Demonstrate the procedures for solving a basic linear equation.

☐ 3. Solve a literal equation for a designated variable.

3. Find x.

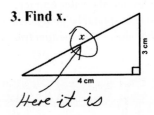

Here it is

Thinking is like loving and dying. Each of us must do it for himself.
—Josiah Royce, American philosopher

What is an equation? If your answer is "a thing you solve to find *x*," you're (a) not alone, and (b) not correct. Of all the things that contribute to students struggling in algebra, probably the biggest is a simple lack of understanding of what the important words and procedures actually mean. As the famous graphic reproduced here illustrates, not understanding what the words mean can lead to some embarrassing answers. (By the way, if you don't think that's funny, you REALLY need this lesson.) In it, we'll review basic equation-solving techniques that you probably feel like you know. In fact, you might even feel like you're expert at them. Try not to focus so much on the *how* — this lesson is about understanding the *what* and *why* of solving equations.

0. What is your current view of what it means to solve an equation?

3-3   Class

Consider the following four statements:

- New York City is the capital of Guatemala.
- Over a million distinct species of animals have been cataloged and named.
- $8 = 5$
- $13 - 10 = 3$

The first and third statements are false, while the second and fourth are true. As you probably noticed, the connection between the last two statements is that each states that two things are equal. This simple exercise illustrates the two key ideas behind understanding equations.

Key Equation Ideas

1. An **equation** is simply a statement that two quantities are equal.

2. Like verbal statements, equations can be either true or false.

1. The statement below contains a variable quantity. Is it always true or always false? Explain.

The number of hours you'll spend on homework this week is 14.

An equation written to represent a statement like this is called a **conditional equation**, and is the type we use most commonly in areas of math (and other fields of study) that use algebra.

If we use the letter h to represent the number of hours you spend on homework, we can write our equation as $h = 14$. In this case, it should be pretty clear that if the value of h is 14, the equation is true, and otherwise it's false. So *14 is the only number that makes the equation true,* which brings us to some important definitions.

Key Equation Definitions

1. A number that makes an equation a true statement when substituted in for the variable is called a **solution** of an equation.

2. The set of ALL numbers that make an equation true is called **THE solution** of an equation.

When an equation looks like $h = 14$, the solution is pretty obvious. That's good. But when an equation looks like $-12y + 17 = 2y - 11 \ldots$ not so much. Our goal in solving equations is to develop a systematic approach to turning an equation whose solution isn't obvious into one with an obvious solution. But that only helps if we keep this next key idea in mind, which in some sense is the most important thing in this lesson:

The Process of Solving Equations

When changing the form of an equation in an attempt to find the solution, anything you do to the equation should not affect what makes the equation true or false.

2. The equation $5 = 5$ is obviously true, while the equation $5 = 10$ is false. Multiply BOTH SIDES of each equation by 2. What can you conclude?

Here's what you should have learned from Question 2: multiplying both sides of the equation by the same number (2 in this case) doesn't change when the equation is true and false, which means we can do that to a conditional equation *without changing the solution.* And ultimately, THAT is what this lesson is about.

3. We know the equation 1 ft = 12 in. is a true statement. So it's also true that 3 ft = 36 in. Explain why.

4. The equation 1 mi = 5,280 ft is true, while the equation 1 yd = 1 m is false. Multiply both sides of each equation by zero. Explain why multiplying both sides of a conditional equation by zero is a bad idea when trying to find the solution.

> ### Math Note
>
> When two equations have the same solution, we call them **equivalent equations**. So our goal in solving equations is to transform the original equation into an equivalent equation with an obvious solution.

5. Fill in the blank to complete a description of our first useful tool for solving equations, then use it to solve the equation, and check your answer.

> ### Equation Solving Tool #1: Multiplication
>
> We can _____ both sides of an equation by the same number or expression as long as that number or expression isn't equal to zero.
>
> Example: Use your answer above to solve the equation $\dfrac{d}{360} = 0.35$.
>
> Now check your answer by seeing if it makes the original equation a true statement.

6. Is the solution you found in the colored box the only solution to the equation? How can you tell?

> ### Did You Get It
>
> Try this problem to see if you understand the concepts we just studied. The answer can be found at the end of the Portfolio section.
>
> 1. Solve the equation $\dfrac{y}{8} = -12$.

7. We know that the equation 1 min = 60 sec is true. So is it also true that 1/2 min = 30 sec? What did we do to both sides to produce an equivalent equation?

8. Use the result of Question 7 to fill in the blank, completing a description of our next tool for solving equations. Then use it to solve the equation, and check your answer.

> ### Equation Solving Tool #2: Division
>
> We can _____ both sides of an equation by the same number or expression as long as that number or expression isn't equal to zero.
>
> Example: Use your answer above to solve the equation $5x = 60$.
>
> Now check your solution by seeing if it makes the original equation true.

An equation stating that two ratios are equal is called a **proportion**. The equation we solved in Question 5 can be written as a proportion if we write the percentage (35%) in fraction rather than decimal form:

$$\frac{d}{360} = \frac{35}{100}$$

A procedure called "cross multiplying" is often used to solve proportions: In this case, you'd multiply down one diagonal, giving you $100 \cdot d$, and multiply up the other diagonal, giving you $360 \cdot 35$. (This is shown in the diagram.) Setting those two results equal to each other, the resulting equation is $100d = 360 \cdot 35$, which you can solve using Tool #2. But why does this work?

$$\frac{d}{360} \diagdown \frac{35}{100}$$

9. Use Tool #1 to multiply both sides of the original proportion by the number $100 \cdot 360$, and do any obvious reducing of fractions. What do you notice about the result?

10. Use cross-multiplying to solve the proportion $\dfrac{x}{12} = \dfrac{15}{36}$.

Did You Get It

2. Solve the equation $\dfrac{10}{y} = \dfrac{35}{81}$.

Now let's work on building our next equation-solving tool.

11. We know that 1 min = 60 sec. Is it okay to add the number 3 to both sides of the equation, resulting in 4 min = 63 sec? Why or why not?

12. Is it okay to add 3 seconds to both sides of the equation, resulting in 1 min 3 sec = 63 sec? Why or why not?

13. Use the result of Question 12 to fill in the blank, completing a description of our next tool for solving equations. Then use it to solve the equation, and check your answer.

Equation Solving Tool #3: Addition

We can _____ the same quantity or expression to both sides of an equation.

Example: Use your answer above to solve the equation $x - 142 = 70$.

Now check your solution by seeing if it makes the original equation true.

Did You Get It

3. Solve the equation $230 = 63 - x$.

14. Given the fact that 36 in. = 3 ft, subtract 5 in. from each side of the equation. Is the resulting equation still true?

15. Use the result of Question 14 to fill in the blank, completing a description of our last tool for solving equations. Then use it to solve the equation, and check your answer.

Equation Solving Tool #4: Subtraction

We can _____ the same quantity or expression from both sides of an equation.

Example: Use your answer above to solve the equation $n + 1,361 = 2,094$.

Now check your solution by seeing if it makes the original equation true.

The types of equations that we've been solving in this lesson are called **linear equations,** because we've seen that the graph of an equation with the input appearing only to the first power is a line. Here's a review of the steps we've discovered, along with some bonus material.

Summary of the Steps for Solving Linear Equations

Step 1: Simplify both sides of the equation, if necessary, by multiplying out any parentheses and combining any like terms.

Step 2: Use Tools #3 and/or #4 to rearrange the equation so that the term containing the variable is isolated on one side.

Step 3: Use Tool #1 or #2 to change the coefficient of the variable to 1.

Note: If the equation you're trying to solve contains any fractions, like the one in Question 9, the FIRST thing you should do is multiply both sides by a common denominator. This will eliminate any fractions.

Did You Get It

4. Solve the equation $4(x - 3) = 10 + x$.

3-3   Group

In Lesson 3-2, we were provided with a graph describing the profit made by a snow cone business in terms of the number of snow cones sold, which is reproduced here. We used the graph to estimate the net profit if 150 snow cones were sold, and also to estimate the number that we'd need to sell to make a profit of $50.

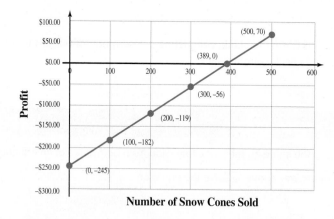

Number of Snow Cones Sold

And using the graph was just fine, except for that pesky "estimate" thing. What if we want exact answers instead? In that case, we'd need to have an equation representing the profit, so it's a darn good thing that we found one in that lesson: $P = -245 + 0.63x$, where P is the profit, and x is the number of snow cones sold.

1. Given the fact that x represents the number of snow cones sold, what should we do to find the profit made from selling 150 snow cones? Describe what you'd do, then find that profit.

2. How does this compare to the estimate you found in the previous lesson?

3. Given that P represents the profit, what should we do to find the number of snow cones needed to make a profit of $50? What happens when you do this? Why is this question in this lesson?

4. Now you should be able to solve an equation to find the number of snow cones needed to make a profit of $50. If your solution requires rounding, think about what it represents before deciding on a final answer.

5. Check your answer by plugging it back into the equation you wrote. Does it make the equation exactly true? What can you conclude about the company making $50?

6. Use the equation to find the profit if 700 snow cones are sold.

7. Use the equation to find the number of snow cones they'd need to sell to make a profit of $400.

8. Look very carefully at the steps you did to solve the equations in Questions 4 and 7. Write those steps in words here.

9. Start with $P = -245 + 0.63x$. Perform the exact same steps you described in Question 8 on this equation to solve for x. Be prepared for the fact that you won't get a number this time as your solution: You'll get an expression involving P.

What you just did is solve a **literal equation.** This is an equation with more than one variable, so that when you solve for one of the variables, the result is an expression rather than a number. In this case, we were given an equation that told us P for a given value of x. We turned it into an equation that tells us x for a given value of P. Why would we do that? Let's see.

10. Suppose we were interested in using this spreadsheet to calculate the number of snow cone sales that would be necessary to make certain levels of profit. What formula could you type into cell B2 to calculate the number of snow cones needed to break even (that is, make a profit of $0)? Your answer to Question 9 should be quite helpful.

	A	B
1	P	X
2	$0	
3	$250	
4	$500	
5	$1,000	

11. Use a calculator or spreadsheet to complete the table, then describe why solving the equation for x was helpful.

Earlier in the course, we worked with two equations for converting temperatures between Fahrenheit and Celsius:

$$F = \frac{9}{5}C + 32 \quad \text{and} \quad C = \frac{5}{9}(F - 32)$$

Let's start with the formula that calculates F in terms of C, and see if we can solve for C.

12. First, subtract _____ from both sides. Fill in the blank, then perform that step on the equation.

13. Now multiply both sides by _____, which is the reciprocal of the fraction in the equation.

14. What do you notice?

Solving a Literal Equation

1. Pretend that all variables other than the one you're solving for are just numbers, not letters.

2. Use normal equation-solving procedures to solve for the desired variable.

Did You Get It

5. Solve the equation $A = P + Prt$ for t.

3-3 Portfolio

Name _____

Check each box when you've completed the task. Remember that your instructor will want you to turn in the portfolio pages you create.

Technology

1. ☐ You'll need to complete the first few questions in the Applications before attacking this Tech assignment. One of the real advantages of being able to solve literal equations is that you can rearrange a formula to find the variable you're interested in calculating, rather than whatever variable happens to be isolated in the original formula. In the Applications, we'll revisit the cab problem from Lesson 3-1, and work with a formula that provides the number of miles that can be driven for a certain cost. Your job is to make a spreadsheet that calculates the trip length for every dollar amount from $5 up to $100, then draw a graph of your result using the connected scatter plot command. There's a template in the online resources for this lesson to help you get started.

Online Practice

1. ☐ Include any written work from the online assignment along with any notes or questions about this lesson's content.

Applications

1. ☐ Complete the Applications problems.

Reflections

Type a short answer to each question.

1. ☐ Explain in your own words what it means to solve an equation. If your answer doesn't use the word "true," it probably stinks.

2. ☐ Describe the four equation-solving tools we covered in this section, and what they all have in common.

3. ☐ What is a literal equation? What's the point of solving them?

4. ☐ Name one thing you learned or discovered in this lesson that you found particularly interesting.

5. ☐ What questions do you have about this lesson?

Looking Ahead

1. ☐ Complete the Prep Skills for Lesson 3-4.

2. ☐ Read the opening paragraph in Lesson 3-4 carefully and answer Question 0 in preparation for that lesson.

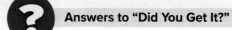

Answers to "Did You Get It?"

1. $y = -96$ 2. $y = \dfrac{162}{7}$ 3. $x = -167$ 4. $x = \dfrac{22}{3}$ 5. $t = \dfrac{A - P}{Pr}$

Answers to "Prep Skills"

1. **a.** $5t + 3$ **b.** $15x + 5$ **c.** $-30x + 40$

2. **a.** $V = 14{,}200$ **b.** $C = 15.05$ **c.** $P = 170$

3. $R = 1{,}400 + 20y$

4. $V = 42 - 1.75w$

3-3 Applications

Name _____

In Lesson 3-1, we studied a cab ride by looking at the price for certain distances in table and graph form. We found that the initial cost of starting the trip was $5.10, which means that you'd pay $5.10 for zero miles traveled. We also found that the slope of the line was $2.60, which means that you'd pay $2.60 per mile. Using what we learned in Lesson 3-2, we can write a formula that describes the cost of a trip (C) in terms of miles traveled (m): $C = 5.1 + 2.6m$.

1. How much would it cost for a 17-mile trip to the airport?

2. If you have budgeted $18 for a cab ride to tour the downtown area, how far can you go? Set up and solve an equation.

3. Here's a smaller version of the graph describing cab rides from Lesson 3-1. Does your answer to Question 2 match the information on the graph? Draw an arrow to the location on the graph that you used to decide.

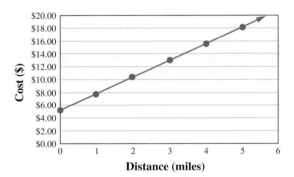

4. Solve the equation for m. What is the significance of the result?

3-3   Applications

Name _____

5. Use your answer to Question 4 and a calculator or spreadsheet to fill in the table. Round to the nearest tenth of a mile.

Cost of trip	Miles travelled
$8	
$10	
$15	
$25	

In Lesson 3-1, we also studied how the value of a car depreciates after it's purchased. The original value of the car (zero years after purchased) was $15,000, and we found that the value decreased by $2,000 each year.

6. Write a formula in the form $V =$ _____ that describes the value of the car in terms of the number of years after it was purchased (t).

7. How much was the car worth 6 years after it was purchased?

8. When was the car worth half of what it was purchased for? Provide your answer in years and months.

9. Here's a smaller version of the graph describing the value of the car from Lesson 3-1. Does your answer to Question 8 match the information on the graph? Draw an arrow to the location on the graph that you used to decide.

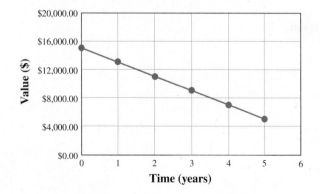

3-3 Applications

Name _____

10. How long does it take the car to have no value?

11. Find an equation that provides the number of years since the car was purchased in terms of its value.

12. The formula $P = 2l + 2w$ calculates the perimeter of a rectangle (P) when you know the length (l) and width (w). Solve this literal equation for the width.

13. Let's examine the relationship between the perimeter of a rectangle and its area. If the perimeter is 200, fill in this table using your answer to Question 12 and a calculator or spreadsheet.

Perimeter	Length	Width	Area
200	10		
200	30		
200	40		
200	50		
200	80		

14. What conclusions can you draw about the relationship between perimeter and area for a rectangle?

Lesson 3-4   Prep Skills

SKILL 1: WORK WITH INEQUALITY NOTATION

Inequality notation in algebra is typically used to represent an interval of numbers. For example, the set of numbers that are more than 10 is an interval: We could represent that in inequality notation by $x > 10$. (Of course, the choice of specific letter is immaterial: $y > 10$ describes the same interval.) There are basically two skills you need to be comfortable with: interpreting the meaning of an expression in inequality notation, and the opposite, writing an expression in inequality notation when an interval is described.

- The set of all numbers less than or equal to -5 can be written as $x \leq -5$.

- The set of numbers that are between 6 and 12 can be written as $6 < x < 12$. This is called a **compound inequality**, and is always used to describe an interval between two specific numbers. You should NEVER write a compound inequality with both a $<$ and a $>$ symbol. To be on the safe side, always write the smallest number first, then $<$, then your choice of variable, then another $<$, then the largest number in the interval.

- The expression $t \geq 8$ represents the set of all real numbers that are 8 or greater.

- The expression $y < 4$ represents the set of all real numbers that are less than 4.

- The expression $-3 \leq x < 2$ represents the set of all real numbers between -3 and 2 including -3.

SKILL 2: RECOGNIZE TERMS THAT INDICATE AN INEQUALITY

The following are some of the terms commonly used to describe inequalities.

- Used to represent:

    $>$: greater than, more than

    $<$: less than, not as much as

    $\geq$: greater than or equal to, at least, no less than, a minimum of

    $\leq$: less than or equal to, at most, no more than, a maximum of

SKILL 3: SIMPLIFY ALGEBRAIC EXPRESSIONS

We've already reviewed adding and subtracting like terms in the Prep Skills for both Lessons 3-2 and 3-3. Sometimes we'll also need to use the distributive property (which was reviewed in the Prep Skills for Lesson 1-4). Combining the two, and using order of operations, we can develop a general strategy for simplifying algebraic expressions.

1. Use the distributive property to multiply out any parentheses.

2. Combine any like terms using addition or subtraction.

    - $2(x + 4) - 5x$ Distribute 2 through $(x + 4)$

      $= 2x + 8 - 5x$ Subtract $2x - 5x$

      $= -3x + 8$

    - $4y + 10 - (3y + 5)$ Distribute -1 through $(3y + 5)$

      $= 4y + 10 - 3y - 5$ Subtract $4y - 3y$; subtract $10 - 5$

      $= y + 5$

SKILL 4: SOLVE BASIC LINEAR EQUATIONS USING EQUATION-SOLVING TOOLS

You just completed an entire lesson based on solving linear equations, so consider the Prep Skills Questions here to be an opportunity to get a little more practice.

PREP SKILLS QUESTIONS

1. Write an inequality to represent each set of numbers described.

   a. All real numbers that are at least 17

   b. The numbers between −5 and 5, along with 5

   c. A group of test scores that are no more than 90

   d. The positive numbers that are a maximum of 32

   e. The variable quantity represented by y is at most $\dfrac{3}{2}$.

2. Write a verbal description of the interval described by each inequality.

   a. $t \leq 3$ b. $x > -10$ c. $300 < P < 500$ d. $0 \leq k < 9$

3. Simplify each expression as much as possible.

   a. $4(2t - 11) + 3t$

   b. $8y + 4 - 4(7 - 3y)$

   c. $5(2x + 1) - (5x + 3) + 2x + 10$

4. Find all solutions to each equation.

   a. $x + 2 = 5$

   b. $y - 3 = -10$

   c. $5x = 35$

   d. $\dfrac{P}{365} = 10{,}000$

Lesson 3-4   **All Quantities Are Not Created Equal**

LEARNING OBJECTIVES

☐ 1. Demonstrate the procedures for solving a linear inequality.

☐ 2. Solve application problems that involve linear inequalities.

©Stockbyte/Getty Images RF

We hold these truths to be self-evident: that all men are created equal . . ."
—The Declaration of Independence

The lesson quote above is one of the fundamental bedrocks that our nation was built upon. Society isn't perfect, and we can all work harder to live up to that ideal. But at the end of the day, we as a society believe that all people are equal in the eyes of the law. Notice that the Declaration of Independence didn't say anything about quantities, though. Equality certainly plays a key role in algebra, but what about inequality?

We've seen that solving linear equations is a very useful tool in solving problems from a wide variety of areas. But think about the following situation: You've finished school and are looking for a real job. As you nervously wait for your big interview, you decide not to be too demanding, but that the minimum compensation you're willing to accept in salary is $40,000 per year. So "Acceptable salary = $40,000" seems like an adequate description of your standards. But nobody has ever gone into an interview and said, "I want 40k and I won't accept a penny more!" Of course, you would be perfectly happy with any amount over $40,000 as well. This is when using a statement like "Acceptable salary ≥ $40,000" is much more reasonable. And this is just one of many modeling situations where inequality is a *good* thing.

0. Think of some of the scenarios we've modeled in this unit so far. Describe at least one where an inequality would be a more realistic model than an equation.

3-4   Class

Remember the snow cone business from Lesson 3-2? Of course you do. That was like two days ago. In one of the questions in Lesson 3-3, we found the number of snow cones they'd need to sell in order to make a profit of exactly $400. But wouldn't it make more sense to find the number they'd need to sell to make AT LEAST $400?

A statement that one quantity is more or less than another is called an **inequality**. The inequality $2 < 5$ is the true statement that two is less than five. The inequality $x > 3$ is a statement that the variable quantity represented by x is more than 3. Just like with equations, **the solution to an inequality is the set of all numbers that make the inequality a true statement when substituted in for the variable**.

1. Name a number that makes $x > 3$ true.

2. Name a number that makes $x > 3$ false.

In many ways, solving inequalities is similar to solving equations. For example, the first step we identified in solving equations was to use the distributive property and combine like terms to simplify each side of the equation as much as possible. The same is true for inequalities: Surely most folks would prefer to work with a simpler inequality rather than a more complicated one.

After doing that, we'll use tools similar to the ones we learned for equations to rearrange inequalities, with the goal of isolating the variable we're solving for.

First, here's a summary of the tools we can use to solve equations:

#1. Multiply the same nonzero number or expression on both sides.
#2. Divide both sides by the same nonzero number or expression.
#3. Add the same number or expression to both sides.
#4. Subtract the same number or expression from both sides.

Do these tools work for solving inequalities too? Let's see. (Remember, by "work," we mean that we can do these procedures to an inequality without changing whether it's true or false.) We'll use less than (<) to explore new rules, but the rules will also apply to greater than (>), less than or equal to (≤), and greater than or equal to (≥). In Questions 1–4, fill in the comparison symbol that makes the inequality true after performing the operation.

1. Add 8 to both sides.

Left side	Comparison symbol	Right side
10	<	20

2. Add −8 to both sides.

Left side	Comparison symbol	Right side
10	<	20

3. Subtract 6 from both sides.

Left side	Comparison symbol	Right side
10	<	20

4. Subtract −6 from both sides. (Be careful!)

Left side	Comparison symbol	Right side
10	<	20

5. Fill in either "does" or "does not" to complete our first tool for solving inequalities. Then follow the remaining instructions in the box.

Inequality Solving Tool #1

Adding or subtracting the same number on both sides of an inequality _____ change the direction of the comparison symbol.

   Use inequality Tool #1 to solve each inequality. Then graph the solution set on the number line. Finally, choose any number in the solution set and plug it back into the inequality to check that it makes the inequality true. (Note: When graphing a set of numbers on a number line, include a filled-in circle at an endpoint that IS included in the set, and an empty circle if the point is NOT included.)

$x - 5 > 9$ $t + 11 \leq 5$

   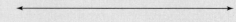

Check: Check:

6. Write a verbal description of what the solution sets to the two inequalities in the colored box really tell us. The first has been done as an example.

Any value of x greater than 14 will cause $x - 5$ to be greater than 9.

Math Note

The inequality $3 > x$ says exactly the same thing as $x < 3$. In each case, the quantity that's less is on the closed end of the comparison symbol. But we'll almost always write $x < 3$, with the variable on the left.

Did You Get It

Try this problem to see if you understand the concepts we just studied. The answer can be found at the end of the Portfolio section.

1. Solve each inequality.
   a. $x - 32 < 11$
   b. $y + 6 \geq -2$

---

7. Multiply both sides by 2.

Left side	Comparison symbol	Right side
10	<	20

8. Multiply both sides by −2.

Left side	Comparison symbol	Right side
10	<	20

9. Divide both sides by 5.

Left side	Comparison symbol	Right side
10	<	20

10. Divide both sides by −5.

Left side	Comparison symbol	Right side
10	<	20

11. Write "stays the same" or "changes" in each blank to complete our second tool for solving inequalities. Then follow the remaining instructions in the box.

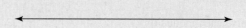

Inequality Solving Tool #2

If you multiply or divide both sides of an inequality by a positive number, the direction of the comparison symbol _____. If you multiply or divide both sides by a negative number, the direction of the comparison symbol _____.

    Use inequality Tool #2 to solve each inequality. Then graph the solution set and choose one number from the solution set and check to see that it makes the inequality true.

$2x < 10$ $-3z \geq 12$

Check: Check:

$\frac{1}{4}t > -3$ $-\frac{1}{3}b \leq 2$

                                                    Check:

Check:

Did You Get It

2. Solve each inequality.

   a. $\frac{2}{3}x < -12$ b. $-4a \geq 20$

The types of inequalities that we've been solving in this lesson are called linear inequalities, because we've seen that the graph of an equation with the input appearing only to the first power is a line. Here's a review of the steps we've discovered, along with some bonus material.

Summary of the Steps for Solving Linear Inequalities

Step 1: Simplify both sides of the inequality, if necessary, by multiplying out any parentheses and combining any like terms.

Step 2: Use Tool #1 to rearrange the inequality so that the term containing the variable is isolated on one side.

Step 3: Use Tool #2 to change the coefficient of the variable to 1. Make sure that you change the direction of the inequality if you multiply or divide by a negative number.

Note: If the inequality you're trying to solve contains any fractions, the FIRST thing you should do is multiply both sides by a common denominator. This will eliminate any fractions.

Did You Get It

3. Solve the inequality $-2(x - 5) \geq x - 8 - 5x$.

3-4 Group

Now let's get back to our good friends in the snow cone business. We were able to model the company's profit using the equation $P = -245 + 0.63x$, where x is the number of snow cones sold. Let's say that the goal is to make a profit of at least \$100 in a day.

1. Write an inequality that states in symbols that the profit for this business will be at least \$100.

2. Solve this inequality.

3. Graph the solution on the number line.

4. Show that one value from the solution set checks.

5. What does the solution to the inequality tell us about the company?

6. Write a verbal description of what this inequality represents in the context of the snow cone business: $-245 + 0.63x < 0$.

7. Solve this inequality.

8. Graph the solution on the number line.

9. Show that one value from the solution set checks.

10. What exactly does the solution to the inequality tell us about the business?

4. Find the number of snow cones the company will need to sell in order to make more than $600 in profit.

The temperature inside a room housing computer servers is important to proper function. A Google search for "server room temperature" yields the following (among other results): According to OpenXtra, server room temperatures should not dip below 50 degrees Fahrenheit, and should not exceed 82 degrees Fahrenheit. The optimal temperature range is between 68 and 71 degrees Fahrenheit.

11. Write an inequality to express the statement "server room temperatures should not dip below 50 degrees Fahrenheit" mathematically using the letter F to represent the temperature.

12. In Lesson 2-4, we learned that Fahrenheit and Celsius temperatures are related by the equation $F = \frac{9}{5}C + 32$. Use this to turn your inequality from Question 11 into an inequality with variable C.

13. Solve this inequality, and describe what the solution tells us.

14. Write an inequality to express the statement "and should not exceed 82 degrees Fahrenheit" mathematically using F.

15. Use the Celsius conversion formula to turn your inequality into one involving variable C.

16. Solve this inequality, and describe what the solution tells us.

17. Putting your answers to Questions 13 and 16 together, write a single compound inequality to describe the allowable server room temperatures.

18. Write a single compound inequality to describe the optimal server room temperatures in degrees Fahrenheit.

19. Use the conversion formula to rewrite your compound inequality from Question 18 with variable C. Then solve this inequality to determine the optimal server room temperatures in degrees Celsius. Does this match your answer to Question 17? (Note: To solve a compound inequality, use the same steps you've been using: Just do the same thing to all three sides.)

3-4 Portfolio

Name _____

Check each box when you've completed the task. Remember that your instructor will want you to turn in the portfolio pages you create.

Online Practice

1. ☐ Include any written work from the online assignment along with any notes or questions about this lesson's content.

Applications

1. ☐ Complete the Applications problems.

Reflections

Type a short answer to each question.

1. ☐ Explain why inequalities are often a more realistic way to model situations than equations.

2. ☐ How does our procedure for solving linear inequalities differ from our procedure for solving linear equations?

3. ☐ What do the solution sets for inequalities look like? How do they compare to the solution sets for equations?

4. ☐ Name one thing you learned or discovered in this lesson that you found particularly interesting.

5. ☐ What questions do you have about this lesson?

Looking Ahead

1. ☐ Complete the Prep Skills for Lesson 3-5.

2. ☐ Read the opening paragraph in Lesson 3-5 carefully and answer Question 0 in preparation for that lesson.

Answers to "Did You Get It?"

1. **a.** $x < 43$ **b.** $y \geq -8$

2. **a.** $x < -9$ **b.** $a \leq -5$

3. $x \geq -18$

4. More than 1,341

 Answers to "Prep Skills"

1. **a.** $x \geq 17$ **b.** $-5 < x \leq 5$ **c.** $0 \leq t \leq 90$ **d.** $0 < x \leq 32$ **e.** $y \leq \dfrac{3}{2}$

2. **a.** All real numbers that are at most 3

   b. All real numbers that are greater than -10

   c. All real numbers between 300 and 500

   d. All real numbers between 0 and 9, along with 0

3. **a.** $11t - 44$ **b.** $20y - 24$ **c.** $7x + 12$

4. **a.** $x = 3$ **b.** $y = -7$ **c.** $x = 7$ **d.** $P = 3{,}650{,}000$

3-4 Applications

Name _____

Much of this assignment follows up on the work we did in the Applications for Lesson 3-3. In that lesson, we were solving equations to learn more about situations we had previously modeled. In this lesson, we'll use inequalities to learn a bit more about those situations.

In Lesson 3-1, we used the equation $C = 5.1 + 2.6m$ to model the cost of a cab ride (C) in terms of miles traveled (m).

1. What does the inequality $5.1 + 2.6m \leq 20$ represent in this scenario?

2. Solve the inequality and graph the solution on a number line.

3. Write a sentence describing what your solution tells us.

4. Explain why an inequality is a more natural choice than an equation for this situation.

5. Suppose that you're running some errands for your boss, and she says, "I imagine you'll need to spend at least 30 bucks on cab fare. Don't spend more than 50, though." Write an inequality that matches these conditions. (Think about whether to use $<$ or $\leq$.)

6. Solve the inequality you wrote in Question 5.

7. Describe what information is provided by your solution.

3-4   Applications

Name _____

8. Suppose that you have a maximum of $50 to spend on cab fare, and you need to make a round trip, both to and from a certain location. Which of the following inequalities best describes this situation?

   a. $5.1 + 2.6x \leq 2 \cdot 50$

   b. $10.2 + 2.6x \leq 50$

   c. $2(5.1 + 2.6x) \leq 50$

   d. $\dfrac{5.1 + 2.6x}{2} \leq 50$

9. Solve the inequality you chose and write an interpretation of the solution.

10. In Lesson 3-1, we also studied the depreciation in the value of a car, which was modeled by the equation $V = 15,000 - 2,000t$. The owner of the vehicle decides he'll hang onto it at least until it's worth less than $2,000. Write and solve an inequality that describes how long he'll keep the vehicle, and write a sentence that describes your solution.

Lesson 3-5 Prep Skills

SKILL 1: TRANSLATE STATEMENTS INTO SYMBOLS

In the last few lessons, we've seen that when using algebra to model data or solve problems, it's important to recognize what can change (or vary) in a situation, and represent those quantities (called variables) with letters. Once you've done that, the key skill becomes writing verbal statements regarding those variable quantities in symbols.

- If you work a part-time job making $9 per hour, the number of hours you work per week might vary. If you represent the hours using h, then $9h$ describes your pay for working h hours.

- If a rectangular parking lot is being designed to be 120 feet long, but the width hasn't been decided, then the area is unknown. We could use w for the width and A for the area, then the equation $A = 120w$ describes the area.

- If you plan to study a certain number of hours this week, then 3 hours more than that next week because you have a test coming up, you can use N for the number of hours this week, and $N + 3$ for the number of hours next week.

SKILL 2: SOLVE LINEAR EQUATIONS

This has been the main skill we've been working on for the past two lessons, so you know where to go for reference on this skill. Above all else, remember the basics:

- Simplify both sides of an equation separately before trying to solve.

- When using the equation-solving tools to isolate the variable, make sure you do the same thing to BOTH SIDES of the equation.

SKILL 3: SOLVE FORMULAS FOR ONE OF THE VARIABLES

This was the third objective in Lesson 3-3, where we called it solving literal equations. This just means solving an equation with more than one variable for one of those variables. The procedure is exactly the same as the one used for solving equations with one variable: You just have to pretend that every letter *other than the one you're solving for* is just a number.

- $A = lw$ To solve this formula for l, divide both sides by w.

  $l = \dfrac{A}{w}$

Why would anyone want to do this? Convenience. In its original form, the formula above tells you area when you know length and width. After solving for l, it's a formula that tells you the length if you know the area and the width. That's how we'll use this skill in the forthcoming lesson.

- $A = P(1 + rt)$ To solve this formula for t, first simplify the right side.

  $A = P + Prt$ Subtract P from both sides.

  $A - P = Prt$ Divide both sides by Pr.

  $t = \dfrac{A - P}{Pr}$

SKILL 4: USE DIMENSIONAL ANALYSIS

We initially learned dimensional analysis as a means for converting units of measure, but it can actually be used for many types of calculations.

- How long would it take you to drive 130 miles if you average 48 miles per hour?

$$130 \text{ mi} \times \frac{1 \text{ hr}}{48 \text{ mi}} \approx 2.7 \text{ hr}$$

As always, the key is the units: We started with a number of miles and wanted a time, so we used a fraction that had miles in the denominator and hours in the numerator.

PREP SKILLS QUESTIONS

1. An account starts out with an initial deposit of $400, and has $30 added to it each week. Write an expression using variable w to describe the total deposits after w weeks.

2. The length of a rectangular climbing wall is 8 feet more than the height. Write two expressions, one describing the length and one the height. Make sure you describe what any letters you use represent.

3. Lindor truffles (my personal weakness) are on sale for $12 per pound. Write an equation that describes the cost of buying truffles if you plan to spend $20.

4. Solve each equation.

   a. $3x + 5 = 20$　　　　b. $\dfrac{y - 5}{3} = 8$　　　　c. $4 = -2(5 - 2t)$

5. Solve each equation for the requested variable.

   a. $3x + y = k$ for y　　　　b. $\dfrac{y - n}{3} = W$ for n　　　　c. $z = -2(y - 2t)$ for t

6. Use dimensional analysis to solve each problem.

   a. Marlene makes $14 per hour. How many hours would she have to work to make $100?

   b. A groundskeeping crew can mow 12,000 square yards in an hour. How long would it take them to mow a 125,000-square-foot field?

Lesson 3-5   What's Your Problem?

LEARNING OBJECTIVES

☐ 1. Solve application problems using numerical calculations.

☐ 2. Solve application problems using linear equations.

©Brand X Pictures/PunchStock RF

Avoid problems, and you'll never be the one who overcame them.
                        —Richard Bach

It just occurred to me that snakes and word problems in math have a lot in common. Most people are afraid of them, and that fear is usually irrational. In each case, education is the key to overcoming your fear. While you may be able to avoid snakes, you can't avoid problems—they're an inevitable part of life. And there's a good reason that math problems are called "problems"! The skills and thought processes you practice when working your way through word problems will come in handy when dealing with other types of problems outside of the hallowed halls of academia. So in this lesson, we'll focus on problem-solving techniques.

0. What's the first thing you think of when you hear the phrase "word problem" in math class? Be honest.

3-5 Class

We were first exposed to Polya's procedure for solving problems in Lesson 2-5. This lesson is all about solving problems using the algebra that we've been practicing, so it seems like a good time to review the steps. If you want to review them in more detail, refer to the colored box at the beginning of Lesson 2-5.

A Review of Polya's Four-Step Procedure for Solving Problems

Step 1: Understand the problem.

Step 2: Devise a plan to solve the problem.

Step 3: Carry out your plan to solve the problem.

Step 4: Check your answer.

Now let's practice using Polya's procedure.

Here's the first problem we'll tackle: Jack and Diane are going to start saving for retirement. They deposit $1,000 in an account to start out. Then they plan to deposit $50 each month. How long will it take until they've deposited $4,500?

Step 1: Understand the problem.

1. What information is provided in the statement that you're likely to need? Write it all down.

2. What is it that the problem is asking you to find?

Step 2: Devise a plan

3. First let's plan to do this using arithmetic. How much is added each month? How much needs to be added total to get to $4,500?

Step 3: Execute the plan

4. Perform an arithmetic operation based on your answers to Question 3 to solve the problem.

Step 4: Check your answer

5. What would the total deposits be after 70 months? Perform a calculation to check.

Now let's redo steps 2 and 3, this time using algebra.

Step 2: Devise a plan

6. Use letter m to represent the quantity in this problem that can change, and describe what that quantity is. (With a variable, we can write an equation to describe the given information.)

Step 3: Execute the plan

7. If $50 is being deposited each month, how much will be deposited after m months? Use this to write an equation that describes the problem. Then solve the equation and write a solution to the problem.

When you develop a strategy to solve a specific problem, then adapt that strategy to a variety of related problems, that's called **generalizing** your approach. In this case, the essence of the problem is that we had a starting value of some quantity ($1,000 in this case) and were adding $50 to it at regular intervals.

8. Generalize this problem to develop a framework that would allow someone to input any starting amount and any monthly amount, and be able to quickly determine how long it would take to reach a specific savings goal. (Hint: Look very carefully at the equation you wrote in Question 7, and identify EXACTLY what every number or letter in your equation represents.)

Did You Get It

Try this problem to see if you understand the concepts we just studied. The answer can be found at the end of the Portfolio section.

1. A manufacturer of custom drinking mugs has a fixed setup cost of $1,000 per order plus a variable cost of $1.50 per mug. How many mugs were produced when the total cost was $2,800?

A useful reminder before moving on: The two most important elements of understanding the problem are the two things you should ALWAYS do when attacking a word problem:

 ### Key First Steps in Attacking Word Problems

1. Write down any relevant information AS YOU COME TO IT, rather than reading the whole problem all at once. If you're not sure if something is relevant or not, write it down and decide later.

2. Identify AND WRITE DOWN exactly what it is the problem is asking you to find. After you've done that, carefully read the problem again to make sure you understand the context.

3-5   Group

In this activity, you'll be working on four problems of different types. We'll help you to follow Polya's general guidelines on the first. After that, you're on your own. I know you won't let me down.

1. Suppose that you have four people in your family, and you want to hang a picture of each family member. Aww, that's sweet. Anyhow, the wall you choose is 60 inches wide, and each of the picture frames is 8 inches wide. To make everything look just right, you want to make the wall space between the edges of each frame identical, and put that same amount of space between the ends of the wall and the edge of the nearest frame. Each frame has a single hook in the center of its back. Where should you put the four nails needed to hang the pictures?

Step 1: Understand the problem.

   a. Write down the relevant information provided by the problem.

   b. What exactly are you being asked to find?

Step 2: Devise a plan.

When a problem describes something physical that can be drawn, a diagram is usually a good idea.

   c. Draw a diagram based on the description of the problem including the relevant information you wrote down.

Based on your diagram, you should be able to note how much space will be covered by frames, and how many blank spaces there will be. Once you know that, you can find the total blank space and divide by the number of spaces to find how far from the edges of the wall the edge of each frame will be.

Step 3: Carry out the plan.

   d. How much of the 60 inches will be covered by picture frames? How many empty spaces are there? What is it we're trying to find? Give that quantity a variable name.

   e. Note that the total 60 inches of the wall can be described by space covered by frames plus space in between frames. Use this idea to write and solve an equation that finds the space between frames. Then use that to describe the locations of all four nails.

Step 4: Check your answer.

   f. Use your diagram to decide if the spots you found for the nails will work according to the statement of the problem.

2. Now let's think about generalizing our approach. Here's a verbal description of the equation you should have written in part e:

   (# of pictures)(Width of each picture) + (# of pictures + 1)(x) = Total width

   where x is the space between pictures. Choose variable names for all quantities in this problem and write a general equation as described above.

> ## Math Note
>
> What you're doing in Question 3 is a GREAT way to test out a general solution: See if it works on a specific problem that you already know the answer to.

3. Use the numbers from the problem we already solved to verify that your formula provides the same solution we already found.

4. Hey, great news! Your family now has five members since you decided to adopt a puppy. Puppies are awesome! Now you have five pictures to evenly space on that wall. Use your answer to Question 3 to find where to put the nails, and describe why this is better than just starting over from scratch.

Courtesy of Dave Sobecki

Did You Get It

2. In the interest of thwarting the efforts of nosy neighbors, a homeowner plans to plant three 10-foot-wide bushes along a 48-foot fence. If she wants consistent spacing between the bushes, and between the bushes and the end of the fence, where should she dig the holes?

Now you're on your own. Remember that the point of this activity is to think about a problem-solving procedure that can be used on any problem, so focus on our systematic procedure rather than just trying to figure out an answer.

5. The riding mower in the classic movie *Forrest Gump* was a 1962 Snapper HiVac with a 28″ cut that averaged about 4 miles per hour in regular use. A standard football field is 120 yards long and 160 feet wide. How long would it take Forrest to mow a football field with this fine machine?

©AF archive/Alamy

6. Can you generalize what you did to solve Problem 5? How long would it take Forrest to mow two football fields if he upgraded to a 54-inch John Deere ZTrak that can mow at 9 miles per hour? (Okay, so the timing doesn't work, but indulge us. Anything can happen in the movies!)

7. What are we not accounting for in our calculations in Problem 6? How can you make your answer more accurate?

Did You Get It

3. A field cultivator is the tool that is pulled behind a tractor to work ground in a field. How long would it take to work a 320–acre field (1 mi long and 0.5 mi wide) with a field cultivator that is 60 ft wide if the tractor pulling it goes 7.5 mi/hr? (Don't worry about turnaround time.)

8. Last problem: A crop-dusting service is hired to spray a chemical pesticide over a field of broccoli, which I personally think tastes like feet, but some people seem to like. The plane has a 350-gallon tank that at the moment contains 80 gallons of a 0.5% solution, which means that 0.5% of the liquid in the tank is actually pesticide: The rest is water. The goal is to find how many gallons of a pre-mixed 1% solution would need to be added to increase the concentration in the tank to 0.8%.

   a. How many gallons of pesticide are currently in the tank?

   b. If we add x gallons of the 1% solution, how many gallons total will be in the tank?

   c. If we're adding x gallons of a 1% solution, how many gallons of pesticide are we adding? How many gallons of pesticide will we have total?

d. Now set up an equation that has two different expressions to describe the new amount of pesticide in the tank. One expression uses your answer to Question 8b, along with the fact that the new solution is 0.8% pesticide. The other expression is your answer to Question 8c. Then solve to find the number of gallons that would be needed to make the mixture 0.8% pesticide.

e. How many gallons of the 1% mix would we need to raise the concentration of the tank to 0.9%? Don't start over from scratch! Just adapt your work from part c.

3-5 Portfolio

Name _____

Check each box when you've completed the task. Remember that your instructor will want you to turn in the portfolio pages you create.

Technology

1. ☐ **a.** Trial-and-error isn't the greatest strategy for solving every problem, but it does come in handy from time to time. And technology can help shoulder the burden of repeated calculations. Suppose that Jack and Diane from Class Questions 1–7 start with $2,000 and invest $175 every month. Set up a spreadsheet with number of months in column A and the value of the account in column B. Use a formula that you can fill down each column after putting in the original values. Then find how long it will take for the retirement account to reach $10,000. A template to help you get started can be found in the online resources for this lesson.

   b. On a second tab of your spreadsheet, use the generalized formula developed in Class Question 8 to build a calculator that will tell you the time required to reach an investment goal, and use it to solve the problem in part a without trial-and-error.

Online Practice

1. ☐ Include any written work from the online assignment along with any notes or questions about this lesson's content.

Applications

1. ☐ Complete the Applications problems.

Reflections

Type a short answer to each question.

1. ☐ Write an honest assessment of your experience with word problems in math: the good, the bad, and the ugly. What do you think is most responsible for these experiences, either good or bad?

2. ☐ What are some advantages to using algebra instead of arithmetic to solve problems?

3. ☐ What does it mean to generalize a solution to a specific problem?

4. ☐ Name one thing you learned or discovered in this lesson that you found particularly interesting.

5. ☐ Do you have any questions about this lesson?

Looking Ahead

1. ☐ Do an Internet search for "exchange rates" and find the value of one U.S. dollar in Russian rubles today. You'll need this number at the beginning of Lesson 3-6.

2. ☐ Complete the Prep Skills for Lesson 3-6.

3. ☐ Read the opening paragraph in Lesson 3-6 carefully and answer Question 0 in preparation for that lesson.

Answers to "Did You Get It?"

1. 1,200 mugs

2. The first goes 9.5 ft from the end of the fence, the next goes 14.5 ft away, then the last is another 14.5 ft past the second.

3. About 5.87 hours, or 5 hours 52 minutes.

Answers to "Prep Skills"

1. $400 + 30w$

2. The length is $h + 8$, where h is the height of the wall; the height is $l - 8$, where l is the length of the wall.

3. $20 = 12p$, where p is the number of pounds purchased.

4. **a.** $x = 5$ **b.** $y = 29$ **c.** $t = \dfrac{7}{2}$

5. **a.** $y = k - 3x$ **b.** $n = y - 3W$ **c.** $t = \dfrac{z + 2y}{4}$

6. **a.** About 7.1 hours   **b.** About 1.16 hours or 1 hour and 9.6 minutes

3-5   Applications

Name _____

For the first question, we'll provide some suggestions on how to proceed. Of course, if you can think of a different way that works for you, that's not just okay, it's GREAT.

On the way to the airport a few years ago, my wife's car hit a huge hole in a construction area, damaging the front right wheel. Huge. I think there may have been alligators living in it. The temporary tire forced us to decrease our average speed by 15 miles per hour. If the 39-mile drive usually takes us 45 minutes, how much time should we have budgeted for the drive home from the airport?

1. Write down all the information that seems relevant to a solution. (Hint: The alligator thing isn't relevant.)

2. What is the usual speed described by the problem?

3. Now you should have enough to get you started. Good luck. We're all counting on you.

4. Want to read about something wild? Of course you do. Do a search for "Barkley Marathons." This is a race so grueling that often nobody actually finishes. The race consists of five loops of 20 miles through the mountains of Tennessee. For those who make it to the last lap, the racers go in alternate directions around the course, which of course means they'll meet in the middle somewhere. Let's say that only two racers make it to the last lap, and it's close: In fact, both start the last loop around the course at the same time. If one averages 2 miles per hour and the other 1.92 miles per hour, how many hours would it be until they meet? (Hint: Use a letter to represent the time until they meet. Then write expressions for the distance traveled by each racer. What do their distances have to add up to?)

3-5   **Applications**

Name _____

5. A landscape architect is planning a new nature area in the middle of an urban campus. She wants the length to be twice the width, and wants to put a 3-foot-high retaining wall around the perimeter. There will be 309 total feet of wall installed. How wide will this area be?

6. Adapt the procedure you did in Question 5 to solve the problem if the length is three times the width instead of two times.

7. A pool is being built in a new student rec center at Falcon Community College. The pool is designed to be a 60 ft by 26 ft rectangle, and the deck around the pool is going to be lined with slate tiles that are 1-ft squares. How many tiles are needed? (This is not quite as easy as it seems at first . . .)

3-5 Applications

Name _____

8. Generalize your result from Question 7 to solve any problem like this where 1-foot square tiles are bordering a rectangular area with length *l* feet and width *w* feet.

A landscaping company sells two types of grass seed mixes that are popular in its area: a premium mix that sells for $1.25 per pound and a standard mix that sells for $ 0.95 per pound.

9. If the store manager dumps a 20-lb bag of each mix into a large barrel, what is the total value of the grass seed in the barrel?

10. At what price per pound should the company sell this new mix to produce the same income as selling the two mixes separately?

11. If the store manager started with 20 lb of the premium mix in a large barrel, how many pounds of the standard mix should be added to create a mix that could be sold for $1.00 per pound?

3-5 Applications

Name _____

12. How many pounds of grass seed must the barrel hold in order to contain all the mixture created in Question 11?

13. How many pounds of the standard mix should be put in a barrel with 20 lb of the premium mix to create a mix worth $1.10 per pound?

● **Lesson 3-6 Prep Skills**

SKILL 1: WORK WITH PROPORTIONS

We were introduced to proportions in Lesson 3-3. A proportion is simply a statement that two ratios (fractions) are equal. Like any equation, proportions can be true or false. Here's a true proportion:

$$\frac{4}{12} = \frac{1}{3}$$

Proportions often arise in practical situations. For example, if you make $12.50 for 1 hour of work, you'd make $25 for 2 hours: This can be described by a proportion:

$$\frac{\$12.50}{1 \text{ hr}} = \frac{\$25}{2 \text{ hr}}$$

When a proportion contains a variable, then solving it (like any equation) means finding all values for the variable that make it a true statement. The main tool we have for solving proportions is cross-multiplying. When you multiply the numerators from each fraction by the denominators from the other, the two products that result are also equal.

- Solve the proportion: $\dfrac{25.00}{2} = \dfrac{x}{7.5}$ Cross-multiply

    $2x = 187.50$ Divide both sides by 2

    $x = 93.75$

Did you notice the connection to the previous proportion? The left side of this equation is the ratio of dollars earned ($25) to time worked (2 hours). So that must be what the ratio on the right side of the equation represents as well. It's comparing $x to 7.5 hours, so our solution tells us how much you'd make for working 7.5 hours. This is exactly how we'll use proportions in the upcoming lesson.

SKILL 2: SOLVE LINEAR AND LITERAL EQUATIONS

Yep, here it is again. Are you starting to get the impression that solving equations is an important skill?

SKILL 3: WRITE CONVERSION FACTORS FROM AN EQUIVALENCE

When using dimensional analysis to convert units, you need conversion factors to multiply by. The thing that makes conversion factors work is that they're really just different ways to say 1: As such, the numerator and denominator have to be equal to each other. When we're told that two quantities are equal even if they're measured differently, we can turn that into two different conversion factors.

- The amount of snowfall that corresponds to 1 inch of rain depends on temperature and some other factors, but a general rule of thumb used by meteorologists is that 10 inches of snow corresponds to 1 inch of rain. We can write two conversion factors from this equivalence:

$$\frac{10 \text{ in. snow}}{1 \text{ in. rain}} \quad \text{and} \quad \frac{1 \text{ in. rain}}{10 \text{ in. snow}}$$

Each of these is equal to 1 so we could multiply by either in a calculation without changing the actual size of the quantity.

SKILL 4: USE DIMENSIONAL ANALYSIS

Another important skill that keeps coming up, this was reviewed in the Prep Skills for Lessons 3-1 and 3-5.

PREP SKILLS QUESTIONS

1. Write a proportion that describes this situation: 8 of 10 people surveyed liked a certain new soft drink, so if 200 people are surveyed we'd expect about 160 to like it.

2. Solve each proportion.

   a. $\dfrac{y}{84} = \dfrac{5}{7}$ b. $\dfrac{4}{9} = \dfrac{x+2}{20}$

3. Solve each equation.

   a. $34 = k \cdot 5$ b. If $y = 220$ and $x = 40$, find k in the equation $y = kx$.

4. Solve for n: $B = nw$.

5. On February 21, 2017, one ounce of gold was worth $1,283.50. Write two conversion factors based on this information.

6. Use one of the conversion factors you wrote to find the value of 10.5 ounces of gold, and use the other to find how much gold could be purchased for $30,000.

Lesson 3-6   Big Mac Exchange Rates

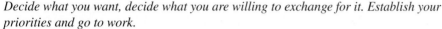

LEARNING OBJECTIVES

☐ 1. Identify situations where direct variation occurs.

☐ 2. Write an appropriate direct variation equation for a situation.

☐ 3. Solve an application problem that involves direct variation.

Decide what you want, decide what you are willing to exchange for it. Establish your priorities and go to work.
                    —H.L. Hunt

©Ingram Publishing/SuperStock RF

One of the most confusing things about traveling abroad is different currency. Since you're so familiar with dollars, you instantly have an idea of how cheap or expensive something is when the price is in dollars. What if I told you that a Big Mac costs about 75 rubles in Russia and 43 kroner in Norway? Those certainly sound like awful prices, but unless we know what a ruble or a kroner is worth, we have no idea how much or how little that actually is. In this lesson, we'll use exchange rates between currencies to study the topic of variation, which can be used to model the connection between many useful quantities.

   0. Have you ever heard the phrase "is directly proportional to"? What do you think it means?

3-6 Class

An **exchange rate** is a number that describes how much of one currency you can trade for another currency. For example, if the U.S. exchange rate for Canadian currency is 1.2, it means that you could trade one U.S. dollar for $1.20 Canadian. When travelers talk about how expensive or cheap a certain country is, it's often a reflection of the exchange rate. The Big Mac costs mentioned earlier? The average cost in the U.S. in July 2016 was $5.06. In Russia it was just $2.15, and in Norway the cost was almost $6.

   1. Using the exchange rate you found online in the Looking Ahead portion of Lesson 3-5, write the exchange rate as an equation: $1 US = _____ rubles.

   2. Write the rate above as a conversion factor with U.S. dollars in the denominator.

   3. Complete the table that shows the relationship between the number of U.S. dollars and Russian rubles that can be exchanged for those dollars.

U.S. Dollars	Russian Rubles
0	
10	
20	
30	
40	
50	

   4. Draw a graph based on your table. Make sure to mark a scale on each axis, and include a verbal label that shows the quantity represented on each axis.

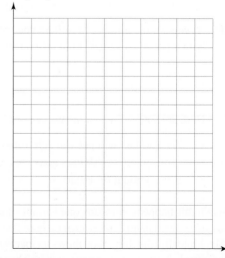

5. Find the slope of the line you graphed. What does it represent?

6. Write an equation using x and y that calculates the number of rubles (y) that you can trade x American dollars for. Which variable is the input and which is the output?

7. Use your equation to find the current cost of a Big Mac in Russia, using $2.15 as the equivalent in American dollars.

8. Use your graphing calculator to verify the table and graph from Questions 3 and 4.

9. How many rubles do you think you'd get if you exchanged zero U.S. dollars?

10. If you doubled the number of dollars you are exchanging, what do you think that would do to the number of rubles you'd get in exchange? Find an example in the table to confirm your answer.

11. If you tripled the number of dollars you are exchanging, what do you think that would do to the number of rubles you'd get in exchange? Find an example in the table to confirm your answer.

12. If you cut the number of dollars you are exchanging in half, what do you think that would do to the number of rubles you'd get in exchange? Find an example in the table to confirm your answer.

Here are some conclusions we can draw about exchange rates:

- Zero dollars will get you zero rubles.
- If the amount of dollars goes up, the number of rubles goes up by the same factor.
- If the amount of dollars goes down, the number of rubles goes down by the same factor.

When this happens, it means one variable quantity is found simply by multiplying a second variable quantity by a constant. We say these two quantities **vary directly** or that they are **directly proportional**. We call this type of relationship **direct variation**. Algebraically, the thing that shows us that two quantities x and y vary directly is an equation of the form $y = kx$, where k is some real number. (So if your equation from Question 6 doesn't look like that, you might think about changing it.)

Did You Get It

Try this problem to see if you understand the concepts we just studied. The answer can be found at the end of the Portfolio section.

1. As of February 2017, 1 U.S. dollar equals 0.81 British pounds. Write an equation to give the number of British pounds (y) you would receive in exchange for x U.S. dollars. Then use the equation to find the number of British pounds you would receive if you exchanged $50.

 ## Direct Variation

The following are various ways of illustrating what it means to say that two variable quantities vary directly.

Verbally	Algebraically	Numerically		Graphically
The quantity y varies directly as the quantity x, and the constant of variation is k.	$y = kx$ Example: $y = 3x$	x | $y = 3x$ 1 | 3 2 | 6 3 | 9 4 | 12 5 | 15		

3-6 Group

1. Earlier in this unit, we put a lot of energy into modeling the cost of taking a cab in Vegas. There was an initial charge of $5.10, plus $2.60 per mile. Is this an example of direct variation? Explain.

Now let's talk about a painful experience that we almost all go through at some point: buying gasoline.

2. Do you think the amount spent at a gas pump and the number of gallons of gasoline purchased are quantities that vary directly? Explain.

3. Let's say you stop in at the local gas station just to buy an energy drink, and don't pump any gas. How much would you pay for zero gallons of gas?

If 5 gallons of gas costs $11.10:

4. How much would you expect to pay if you double the amount purchased to 10 gallons?

5. How much if you cut the amount in half to 2.5 gallons?

Now the more interesting question: How much would you expect to pay for 15.2 gallons of gasoline? That's not quite as straightforward. First we'll attack this problem using proportions. Then we'll see if maybe it's more efficient to use variation.

6. In Lesson 3-3, we learned that an equation stating that two ratios are equal is called a proportion. Solve this problem by setting up a proportion. On one side, the ratio should compare the 5 gallons purchased to the cost of that purchase. On the other side, the ratio should compare 15.2 gallons of gas to the cost (which is what you're trying to find).

Did You Get It

2. On my campus last year, I was involved in a survey of first-year students. We got 140 responses, and 105 students indicated that they had declared a major at that point. At the time, there were about 1,600 first-year students on campus. How many would you guess had declared a major?

7. Now let's see how we can solve the gasoline problem using direct variation, then see why that might be a good idea. First, write a direct variation equation describing the cost C of buying G gallons of gas.

8. We know that 5 gallons costs $11.10, so plug those values into your variation equation. Then solve the resulting equation for the constant of variation.

9. Now you can rewrite your variation equation so that the only unknowns in it are *C* and *G*. Do it!

10. What does the constant of variation you found describe about buying gas at this station?

11. How much would you expect to pay for 15.2 gallons?

12. Which method of finding the cost of 15.2 gallons makes it easier to complete this table? Pick one method, explain why, and fill in the table.

Gallons	Cost
0	
3	
6	
9	
12	
15	

13. What would it cost you to put 11.55 gallons in your car from this pump?

14. If you spent $40 on gasoline at this pump, how many gallons did you get?

Solving Problems with Direct Variation

1. Identify the two quantities that vary directly.

2. Note which is the input and which is the output, and write an initial equation of the form $y = kx$.

3. Use a given input and output to find the constant of variation k.

4. Rewrite the equation in the form $y = kx$ where you've replaced k with a number. (It might help to write units on y, k, and x and to think about dimensional analysis.)

5. Use your equation to solve the problem.

15. If you get paid hourly at your job, the total amount of money you earn varies directly with the number of hours you work. Let's say you worked 14 hours last week and made $163.80. Write a variation equation describing your total pay P in terms of hours worked h. Then use it to find how much you'd make for working 20 and 25 hours.

Did You Get It

3. When taking a multiple choice test, the number of points that you get varies directly with the number of questions you get right. If you got 12 questions right and scored 75 points, write a variation equation to describe the test, then use your equation to find the score for someone who got 14 questions right.

---

16. **a.** Solve the general direct variation equation $y = kx$ for k.

16. **b.** What does this tell you about the ratio (fraction) involving x and y? (Hint: Does k vary in a direct variation equation?)

Some advantages of using a direct variation equation rather than a proportion:

1. Proportions answer questions one at a time, but you can use a direct variation equation to answer multiple questions very quickly.

2. With the table feature on a graphing calculator, or a spreadsheet, you can speed up the process even more when you have a direct variation equation.

3. With proportions, you never actually see the conversion factor (constant of variation). Look at the gasoline problem: The variation equation shows us easily that gas was $2.22 per gallon.

The best gift I got for my birthday last year was my very own Mini Me. Not a living one, which would have been the best gift that *anyone* ever got for their birthday, but a bobblehead made to look like me. (Don't laugh at the shorts. Custom clothes would have cost extra.) When scale models of real objects are made, the scale is often given as a ratio. In this case, the ratio of my Mini Me's size to the real thing (me) is 1/13.

17. My Mini Me is 5.82 inches tall, that handsome little devil. How tall am I in feet and inches? Either set up and solve a proportion, or use an equation of variation.

Courtesy of Dave Sobecki

18. The actual Mini Me from the *Austin Powers* movies is 32 inches tall. If he had a bobblehead made at the same scale as mine, how tall would it be?

19. The sales commission earned by a saleswoman varies directly with her gross sales. In one quarter, her commission was $7,200 on $180,000. What was her sales commission rate?

20. Use the sales commission rate to write an equation relating the commission earned to the amount of gross sales for that quarter. Make sure you describe what any letters you use represent.

21. Use your equation to complete the table of values.

	A	B
1	Gross Sales ($)	Commission ($)
2	$40,000	
3	$80,000	
4	$120,000	
5	$160,000	
6	$200,000	
7	$240,000	
8	$280,000	
9	$320,000	
10	$360,000	

22. Earlier, we observed that as the number of rubles goes up, so does the number of dollars. And we also saw that as the amount of gas you buy goes up, so does the cost. Is that always the case? If the constant of variation is negative, what is the effect on y if x increases? Explain. Studying the generic equation that describes direct variation will help.

In Questions 23–25, decide if the graph illustrates a situation where *y* varies directly as *x*, and explain your reasoning.

23.

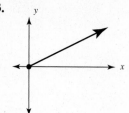

24.

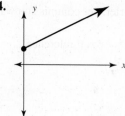

25.

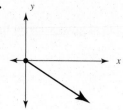

3-6 Portfolio

Name _____

Check each box when you've completed the task. Remember that your instructor will want you to turn in the portfolio pages you create.

Technology

1. ☐ As you know, when you copy and paste a formula in Excel, it changes the cell reference accordingly: If the original formula is =A1/B1 in cell C1, copying and pasting in C2 changes the formula to =A2/B2. But sometimes we want to have all copied calculations use the same cell in a formula. In that case putting a dollar sign in front of the row and column will "lock" the cell reference and keep it from changing when we paste. This is useful in building an Excel table to convert currency.

    Look up the exchange rate for converting U.S. dollars to the currency for a country you would like to visit. Type that rate in cell E1. Then create a table and graph similar to the ones in the Class portion of this lesson. Make sure you include the name of the country and the website where you got your exchange rate. A template to help you get started can be found in the online resources for this lesson.

Online Practice

1. ☐ Include any written work from the online assignment along with any notes or questions about this lesson's content.

Applications

1. ☐ Complete the Applications problems.

Reflections

Type short answer to each question.

1. ☐ How would you decide whether or not two quantities vary directly?

2. ☐ What are some advantages to writing a direct variation equation rather than solving a problem using a proportion?

3. ☐ Name one thing you learned or discovered in this lesson that you found particularly interesting.

4. ☐ What questions do you have about this lesson?

Looking Ahead

1. ☐ Complete the Prep Skills for Lesson 3-7.

2. ☐ Read the opening paragraph in Lesson 3-7 carefully and answer Question 0 in preparation for that lesson.

Answers to "Did You Get It?"

1. $y = 0.81x$; 40.5 pounds   2. 1,200 students   3. $y = 6.25x$; 87.5 points

Answers to "Prep Skills"

1. $\dfrac{8 \text{ like it}}{10 \text{ people}} = \dfrac{160 \text{ like it}}{200 \text{ people}}$

2. **a.** $y = 60$

   b. $x = \dfrac{62}{9}$

3. **a.** $k = \dfrac{34}{5}$

   b. $k = 5.5$

4. $n = \dfrac{B}{w}$

5. $\dfrac{1 \text{ oz gold}}{\$1,283.50}$; $\dfrac{\$1,283.50}{1 \text{ oz gold}}$

6. 10.5 ounces of gold is worth \$13,476.75; \$30,000 will purchase about 23.4 ounces of gold.

3-6   Applications

Name _____

1. Use the Internet to find and write the current exchange rate for converting the U.S. dollar to the Chinese yuan.

2. Complete the table using the current exchange rate.

U.S. Dollar	Chinese Yuan
0	0
20	
40	
60	
80	
100	

3. Write an equation that will convert U.S. dollars to Chinese yuan.

4. Which is the independent variable in your equation? Which is the dependent variable? Describe each using the terms input and output.

5. The average cost in China of an imported Volkswagen is the equivalent of $24,000. How much is that in yuan?

At various times over the past ten years, economists in Western countries have felt that China was manipulating the value of its currency, keeping it artificially low in order to give the country an export advantage. The point is that if the yuan is valued at less than it's actually worth, imported goods will cost more in yuan than they should, and that will make imports less attractive to Chinese buyers, leading to an export advantage.

Some economists feel that the yuan is valued at 20% less than it should be compared to the U.S. dollar.

6. If that's accurate, one dollar should be worth less yuan than the actual exchange rate. If the yuan is undervalued by 20%, then one dollar should be worth 20% less yuan. Find what the exchange rate should be.

7. How much would that affect the price of a Volkswagen in China?

8. Forensic scientists often examine scaled-up crime scene photos to search for evidence that might be hard to identify at regular size. Studying bite marks on a photo of a victim's leg at 500% magnification, a technician measures the distance between two punctures from the bite to be 165 mm. What is the actual distance between the punctures?

$\left(\text{Hint: The ratio of the photo size to actual size is } \dfrac{5}{1}\right).$

©Mikael Karlsson/Alamy

Here's a look at a map of the east side of Dubuque, Iowa. It shows a driving path from a casino on the river to a golf course on the other side. According to the maps app on my phone, the driving distance is 3.0 miles. We're most interested in the graphic at the bottom left, which indicates that 1 inch on the map (measure if you don't believe me) corresponds to 2,000 feet in real life.

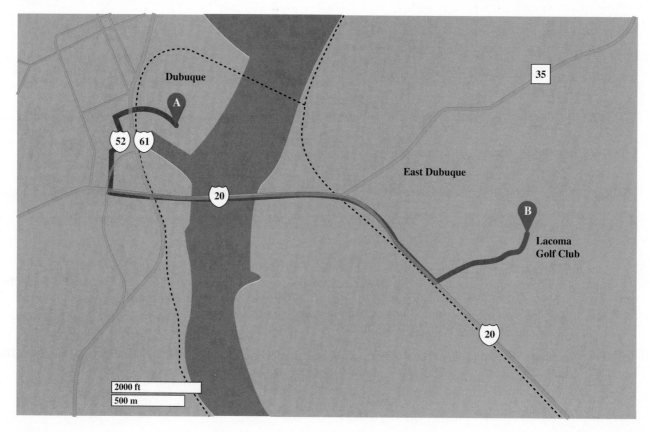

9. Write a ratio that compares size on the map to size in real life.

10. Points A and B on the map are 4.06 inches apart. How far apart are the casino and golf course in miles? Use a proportion to decide.

11. Write an equation of variation that relates the distance on the map m to the distance in real life R. Then use information you know to solve for the constant of variation and update your equation.

12. If we looked at a satellite photo at the same scale as this map, do you think we could see any boats on the river? Answer yes or no and explain your reasoning.

13. Let's say that a 50-foot boat was out on the river. That's a pretty good-sized boat: The typical recreational motorboat is in the 18- to 24-foot range. Use your variation equation to find how big that boat would be on the satellite photo. Do you think we'd be able to see it?

Lesson 3-7   Prep Skills

SKILL 1: TRANSLATE STATEMENTS INTO SYMBOLS

This is a skill that we've been using throughout Unit 3, and you're probably getting better at it than you ever thought you would. More practice certainly doesn't hurt though.

- One conservative estimate for the global rise in sea levels over the next 100 years is 0.22 inches per year. If that happens, sea levels will rise 0.22y inches in y years.

- If a new TV show got a lot of hype but turns out to stink, and it loses 700,000 viewers each week after the premiere, then $-700{,}000w$ represents the total change in viewership after w weeks.

- If 12.5 million people watched the first episode, then the number of viewers after w weeks looks like $12{,}500{,}000 - 700{,}000w$.

SKILL 2: DRAW A GRAPH FROM A TABLE OF VALUES

We've practiced scatter plots several times—this is when we match up inputs and outputs from a table as points, then plot those points on a grid with a choice of scale that displays all the points distinctly in the space provided. You can also connect those points with lines or curves to illustrate trends in data.

- This table displays the number of viewers for the TV show described in Skill 1 over the first five weeks of its (presumably short) life. The data are illustrated in graphic form next to the table.

Weeks after premiere	Viewers
0	12,500,000
2	11,100,000
4	9,700,000
6	8,300,000
8	6,900,000
10	5,500,00

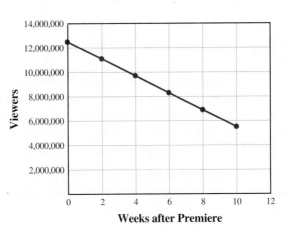

SKILL 3: SOLVE LINEAR INEQUALITIES

This was the key topic in Lesson 3-4. The key thing to know is that solving a linear inequality uses the same steps as solving a linear equation with one important exception: If at any point you multiply or divide both sides by a negative number, you have to reverse the direction of the inequality sign. That is, < becomes > and vice versa.

- $y + 13 \leq 5$ Subtract 13 from both sides
  $y \leq -8$

- $-6t > 54$ Divide both sides by −6; change > to <
  $t < \dfrac{54}{-6}$
  $t < -9$

- $12 + 3x \geq 80$ Subtract 12 from both sides
  $$3x \geq 68$$ Divide both sides by 3; inequality sign stays the same
  $$x \geq \frac{68}{3}$$

SKILL 4: COMPUTE SLOPE

In this unit, we've been working with slope in terms of a known constant rate at which some quantity changes, which is great. But remember that we can also compute slope when we have two points on a graph. Rather than think of it as a formula, like you may have learned it in an algebra class, just think of it as the change in y value divided by the change in x value.

- The TV show we've been working with had 12,500,000 viewers for its premiere, and 9,700,000 four weeks after its premiere. The slope of the graph connecting the two points corresponding to this information is

$$m = \frac{\text{Change in viewers}}{\text{Change in weeks}} = \frac{9,700,000 - 12,500,000}{4 - 0} = \frac{-2,800,000}{4} = -700,000$$

SKILL 5: INTERPRET SLOPE AND y INTERCEPT

Speaking of slope, when we find the slope of a line, as we just saw, we're finding a comparison between the change in output and the change in input. This measures the rate at which the quantity described by the output is changing.

- In this case, the $-700,000$ indicates the number of viewers is decreasing at the rate of 700,000 viewers per week.

  Notice the units: Since the output describes number of viewers and the input describes number of weeks, when we divide change in output by change in input, we get units of viewers per week. This is often the easiest way to interpret what slope is telling us in a given situation.

  The y intercept of a graph is the point that has first coordinate zero. The first coordinate of any point represents an input, so the y intercept always tells us the value of the output when the input is zero.

- In the TV show example, since the first point we have is (0, 12,500,000), this means that there were 12,500,000 viewers for the premiere. (In this case, we're calling the premiere time zero, because it's zero weeks after the premiere.)

PREP SKILLS QUESTIONS

1. Translate each statement into symbols.
   a. According to a report on CNNMoney in 2015, 869,000 new pieces of computer malware were released per day in that year. Write an expression for the number released in x days.
   b. If you owe your parents $600 and pay them $50 per month, write an expression describing how much you owe after m months.

2. The table describes the amount of money earned by a cotton candy vendor at a ballpark based on how many bags she sells. Draw a graph of the data.

Bags	0	20	40	60	80
Money earned	0	$8	$16	$24	$32

3. Find the slope of your graph, and describe what it means.

4. What is the y intercept of your graph? What does it mean?

Lesson 3-7   The Effects of Alcohol

LEARNING OBJECTIVES

☐ 1. Write an equation of a line given a description of the relationship.

☐ 2. Write an equation of a line that models data from a table.

☐ 3. Write an equation of a line from a graph of the line.

☐ 4. Graph a line by plotting points.

©Doug Menuez/Photodisc
Green/Getty Images RF

As long as algebra is taught in school, there will be prayer in school.
                    — Cokie Roberts

It's no secret that alcohol consumption by college students is common, and that overindulgence can have many negative effects, in both the short and long term. And if anything, the problem is getting more serious. At my school alone, 21 students were hospitalized for alcohol poisoning during ONE recent weekend. When someone makes the choice to drink, they're affected as long as the alcohol remains in their blood stream. There are many theories on how to hasten the sobering up process: black coffee, ice cold showers, greasy food, drinking lots of water. . . . The truth is that none of these have any effect whatsoever on blood alcohol concentration (BAC). You can try every mythical treatment known to man, but at the end of the day the only thing that will bring down BAC is time. So far, we've studied a wide variety of quantities that can be modeled using linear equations. In this lesson, we'll use the time required to sober up, and other quantities, to study writing linear equations that model situations in greater depth. But first, let's talk about something much more positive: pizza!

0. When a person drinks, how do you think alcohol leaves the body over time? At a steady rate, or some other way?

3-7 Class

A student org you're involved in is planning a year-ending pizza party to celebrate another successful year on campus. As chair of the planning committee, you've wisely worked a deal with a local pizza place to provide large pizzas at $9 each. The budget will allow at most $175 to cover the food, and of course you'd like to know how many pizzas you can get and stay under budget. We'll attack the problem in several different ways.

1. Use a numerical calculation. Include all details, and don't forget to write the number of pizzas you can buy.

2. Write an equation that represents the total cost C of ordering p pizzas. What does this tell you about how the cost varies when you change the number of pizzas ordered?

3. Complete the table, then use it to estimate the number of pizzas you can buy.

Pizzas Bought	Total Cost
0	
5	
10	
15	
20	
25	
30	

4. Use the information from the table to draw a graph with the number of pizzas on the horizontal axis and the total cost on the vertical axis. Make sure you label the scale on each axis. Use your graph to estimate the number of pizzas that can be bought for $175. Try to ignore the answer you found in Question 1, and use only the graph.

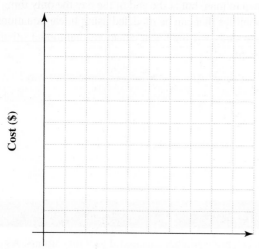

Number of Pizzas

5. Since we want to spend AT MOST $175, this is a good place to use an inequality. Write an inequality that can be used to find the number of pizzas you can buy for at most $175. Then solve that inequality and use the result to decide on the number of pizzas you can buy.

Did You Get It

Try these problems to see if you understand the concepts we just studied. The answers can be found at the end of the Portfolio section.

1. If hot dogs cost $1.50 at Ball Park Frank night at the ballpark, write an equation that describes the cost C of buying h hot dogs.
2. Write and solve an inequality that will tell you how many hot dogs you can buy for your family if you want to spend less than $20.

6. What's the slope of the line you drew in Question 4? What does it represent?

7. What's the *y* intercept of the line? What does it represent?

Nice job so far, but did we forget to mention the $10 delivery charge? Sorry. You'll have to rework the problem, keeping in mind that we want to know how many pizzas we can get for at most $175 at $9 each, plus a flat fee of $10 for delivery.

8. Write an equation that describes the cost *C* of buying *p* pizzas with the delivery charge included.

9. Complete the table, then use it to estimate the number of pizzas you can buy.

Pizzas Bought	Total Cost
0	
5	
10	
15	
20	
25	
30	

10. Use the information from the table to draw a graph with the number of pizzas on the *x* axis and the total cost on the *y* axis. Don't forget to label a scale on each axis. Use your graph to estimate the solution to the problem.

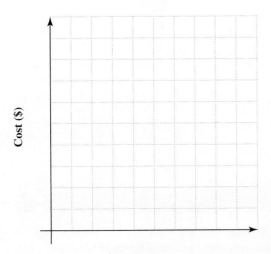

Cost ($)

Number of Pizzas

11. Write and solve an inequality that can be used to find the number of pizzas you can buy with the delivery charge added. **Write the solution to the problem in a full sentence.**

12. In this situation, would you say that the cost of ordering pizza varies directly with the number of pizzas? Explain.

13. What is the slope of the line you drew? What does it represent?

14. What is the y intercept of the line you drew? What does it represent?

Did You Get It

3. Refer to Did You Get It 2. You can't have the family choke down 13 hot dogs with nothing to drink. What is wrong with you? If you need to spend $18 on drinks, write a new equation that describes the cost of buying h hot dogs.
4. What are the slope and y intercept of your equation? What do they tell us about the situation?

15. Now here's the key idea: Look back at your answers to Questions 8, 13, and 14. The slope was _____,
the *y* intercept was _____, and the equation was _____.

This fits the form of many of the linear models we've studied previously, where the equation was of this form:

$$y = \text{starting value of the quantity} + \text{constant rate of change} \cdot x$$

(Remember, "starting value" means the output associated with input zero.) In algebra, we call this the **slope-intercept form** of a line, because the two constants in the equation are the slope (rate of change) and the *y* intercept (starting value). The slope-intercept form is usually written as $y = mx + b$ but can also be written as $y = b + mx$ to match the order we've been using.

Writing the Equation of a Line

When a line has slope *m* and the second coordinate of its *y* intercept is the number *b*, then the equation of that line is $y = mx + b$.

16. A small business had just 12 employees when they opened their doors, but have been adding employees at the rate of 4 per month since then. Write a linear equation that describes the number of employees in terms of the number of months after the company was founded.

17. What are the slope and *y* intercept of this line? What do they tell us about the company?

18. Use this information to draw a graph of your equation. Be sure to label a scale and the axes.

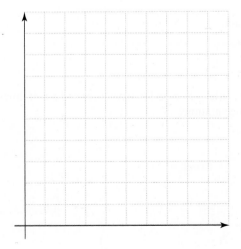

Graphing an Equation in Slope-Intercept Form

Step 1: Plot the *y* intercept; its first coordinate is always zero, and its height is the constant term in the equation.

Step 2: Find at least one other point on the graph. You can either plug an input into the equation, or use the slope. For example, if the slope is 2/3, that indicates a vertical change of 2 units for every 3 units of horizontal change. So you can find another point by moving two units above and three units to the right of the *y* intercept. Remember, the slope is the coefficient of the variable in the equation.

Step 3: Draw a line through the points you plotted. If they don't all line up, then you must have plotted one or more of them wrong.

Did You Get It

5. Use the procedure in the colored box to graph the line

$$y = \frac{7}{3}x - 5.$$

3-7 | Group

Now we turn our attention to studying the effects of alcohol. Blood alcohol concentration is a percentage of alcohol in the blood stream. The legal limit for operating a motor vehicle in most states is 0.08: This means that 0.08% of a person's blood is alcohol. The table here is borrowed from WebMD. It shows the ways that alcohol can affect a person at different BAC levels.

The Effects of Drinking Alcohol	
Estimated blood alcohol concentration (BAC) %	**Observable effects**
0.02	Relaxation, slight body warmth
0.05	Sedation, slowed reaction time
0.10	Slurred speech, poor coordination, slowed thinking
0.20	Trouble walking, double vision, nausea, vomiting
0.30	May pass out, tremors, memory loss, cool body temperature
0.40	Trouble breathing, coma, possible death
0.50 and greater	Death

1. After being arrested for driving under the influence, a well-known starlet was found to have three and a half times the legal limit of alcohol in her blood. What was her blood alcohol concentration?

2. Explain exactly what your answer to Question 1 means.

3. Describe some of the effects the arresting officers may have been able to observe at the time of the arrest.

John Q. Bonehead decides it would be a good idea to drive when he shouldn't. Fortunately, he gets pulled over before anything tragic happens, and a BAC test finds a level of 0.16 at 2 A.M. Unlike most other drugs, studies have shown that alcohol leaves the blood stream at a constant rate. The table shows his BAC every hour after the arrest.

Hours after 2 A.M.	BAC
0	0.16
1	0.145
2	0.13
3	0.115
4	0.1

4. What is the slope of the line describing John's BAC? What does it tell us?

5. What is the y intercept of the line describing John's BAC? What does it tell us?

6. Write the equation describing John's BAC, with x representing hours after 2 A.M., and y representing BAC.

7. When using an equation to model a situation, it's important to recall what specific information the equation provides. Restate your answer to Question 6 in the form of a statement like this: "If x represents _____, then $y =$ _____ represents _____." (Don't physically fill in the blanks: write a full sentence below.)

8. We've learned about several features of graphing calculators that allow us to study the information provided by an equation: substituting in values for variables, making a table, and making a graph come to mind. Using these features, discuss whether or not the equation you wrote tells the story that it's supposed to. More detail is always better!

9. What would Mr. Bonehead's blood alcohol concentration be at 3:30 A.M.? (Remember, eating greasy food won't change it!)

10. How many hours would it take for his BAC to drop below the legal driving limit of 0.08? (He can take a cold shower if he likes, but it won't help.) Set up and solve an inequality to answer this question, please.

Did You Get It

6. Set up and solve an inequality that will tell you what times John's BAC is more than half of the legal limit.

11. What information would you need in order to draw the graph of your equation? Be specific.

12. Graph the line on the coordinate system provided. Make sure that you choose and label an appropriate scale on each axis.

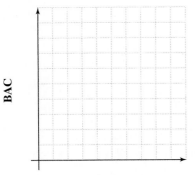

Hours after 2 A.M.

13. What is the *x* intercept? What does it mean?

 The Connection Between Slope and Direction

- When the slope of a line is positive, it means that the quantity modeled by the line is increasing. This in turn means that the graph will slant upward from left to right.

- When the slope of a line is negative, it means that the quantity modeled by the line is decreasing. This in turn means that the graph will slant downward from left to right.

14. Sketch an example of a line with a positive slope. Label this line on the graph below.

15. Sketch an example of a line with a negative slope. Label this line on the graph below.

16. Can you describe what a line with a slope of 0 would look like? Sketch an example and label this line on the graph below.

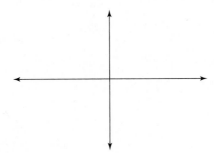

3-7 Portfolio

Name _____

Check each box when you've completed the task. Remember that your instructor will want you to turn in the portfolio pages you create.

Technology

1. ☐ Use Excel to create a table and graph for both of the pizza party problems in the Group portion of this lesson. Make sure that you use a formula for calculating the costs. For each formula, explain how that formula relates to the equation that describes the cost of the pizzas. Type your explanation in the text box which is included in the template that you can find in the online resources for this lesson.

Online Practice

1. ☐ Include any written work from the online assignment along with any notes or questions about this lesson's content.

Applications

1. ☐ Complete the Applications problems.

Reflections

Type a short answer to each question.

1. ☐ Describe the connection between the graph of a line and how we use the line's equation to solve problems like the pizza party problem. How would you find the solution on a graph?

2. ☐ Explain how to find the equation of a line when you know the slope and the y intercept.

3. ☐ Describe what you learned about the time required to sober up from the Group portion of this lesson.

4. ☐ Explain how you would graph a line if you had the equation in $y = mx + b$ form.

5. ☐ Name one thing you learned or discovered in this lesson that you found particularly interesting.

6. ☐ What questions do you have about this lesson?

Looking Ahead

1. ☐ Complete the Prep Skills for Lesson 3-8.

2. ☐ Read the opening paragraph in Lesson 3-8 carefully and answer Question 0 in preparation for that lesson.

Answers to "Did You Get It?"

1. $C = 1.50h$ **2.** $1.5h < 20$; you can buy at most 13 hot dogs.   **3.** $C = 18 + 1.5h$

4. The slope is 1.5: This is the cost per hot dog. The y intercept is (0, 18); that's the cost if you buy no hot dogs, which is the drinks alone.

5.

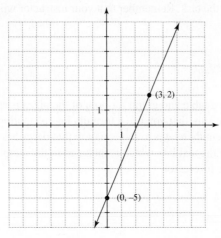

6. $0.16 - 0.015x > 0.04$; when less than 8 hours have passed, his BAC is still more than half the legal limit.

 Answers to "Prep Skills"

1. a. $869,000x$ **b.** $600 - 50m$

2.

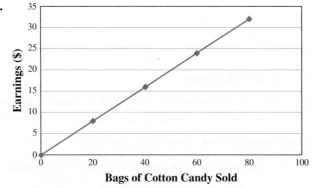

3. 0.4; The vendor earns $0.40 for every bag of cotton candy she sells.

4. (0, 0); If she doesn't sell any cotton candy, she earns no money.

3-7 Applications

Name _____

If you're interested in weight loss, there certainly isn't a shortage of information, diet plans, supplements, and flat-out gimmicks available to you. But the simple truth is this: Gaining or losing weight ultimately comes down to one thing. If you consume more calories than you burn, you'll gain weight, and if you consume less calories than you burn, you'll lose weight. In this activity we'll study some aspects of weight change.

©Stockbyte/Getty Images RF

1. Bubba weighed 170 pounds when he started college, and never really thought about his weight much. Then a funny thing happened: He got super-busy, moderately poor, and started eating a lot of cheap fast food. He also started sleeping less and not drinking enough water. The result? He started gaining weight at the rate of 0.4 pounds per month. No biggie right? We shall see. Write a linear equation describing Bubba's weight (y) in terms of months after he started college (x).

2. Restate your answer to Question 1 in the form of a statement like this: "If x represents _____, then $y =$ _____ represents _____." (Don't physically fill in the blanks: write a full sentence below.)

3. If Bubba continues this modest-sounding weight gain, how much will he weigh after three years of college?

4. How long will it take our buddy Bubba to pass the big two-zero-zero at this rate? Use an inequality, please.

3-7 Applications

Name _____

5. Draw the graph of your equation, including (as usual) an appropriately chosen scale on each axis.

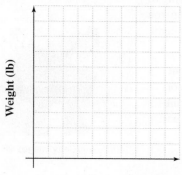

Months after Starting College

6. Find the slope of the line and explain what it means.

7. Find the *y* intercept and explain what it means.

Now let's study what it takes to lose weight. In Lesson 2-5, we saw that an average person can lose one pound if he burns 3,500 calories more than he consumes. Let's say that after reaching the 200-pound plateau, Bubba has had enough and decides to work on losing some weight. The table shows his weight if a certain number of calories are burned.

8. Find the slope of a line based on the data in the table. Use weight for *y* coordinates and thousands of calories burned as *x* coordinates. Recall that slope is change in output divided by change in input.

Calories burned (thousands)	Weight
0	200
14	196
28	192
42	188
56	184

9. Write a linear equation that describes Bubba's weight (*y*) in terms of thousands of calories burned (*x*). Your answer to Question 8 will help.

3-7   Applications

Name _____

10. Restate your answer to Question 9 in the form of a statement like this: "If x represents _____, then $y = $ _____ represents _____."

11. Use your equation to find Bubba's weight if he burns 50,000 calories above what he consumes.

12. Use your equation to find how many extra calories Bubba would have to burn to get back to the weight at which he started college.

13. According to the Mayo Clinic website, a man of Bubba's size would burn about 755 calories when running for an hour. How many hours of running will Bubba need to put in to get back to his original weight?

Math Note

Interested in overcoming the famous "freshman fifteen"? A Google search for that phrase yields some very informative and useful results.

3-7 Applications

Name _____

14. Based on this entire activity, what would have been Bubba's best approach when starting college?

A movie download service has a $14 monthly fee for membership; it then costs $3 to rent each movie.

15. If we model the cost (y) of renting a certain number of movies in a month (x), what is the slope of the line? What does it mean?

16. What is the y intercept of the line? What does it mean?

17. Use slope-intercept form to write an equation that models the cost in terms of movies rented.

Lesson 3-8   Prep Skills

SKILL 1: FIND AND INTERPRET SLOPE

We've worked with slope quite a lot in Unit 3. In some sense, knowing how to compute AND interpret the slope of a line are very closely related skills. If you think of slope as some abstract formula, it's hard to interpret what it means. But if you think of slope as change in output divided by change in input it's a lot easier to recognize that the slope measures the rate at which the output changes compared to a one-unit change in the the input.

   This is especially simple to recognize when you consider the units attached to both the numerator and denominator of a slope calculation.

- A podcast has 423,000 downloads of its first episode, and 510,000 for its fifth. If we connect two points on a graph representing that data, the slope is

$$\frac{(510{,}000 - 423{,}000) \text{ downloads}}{(5 - 1) \text{ episodes}} = \frac{87{,}000 \text{ downloads}}{4 \text{ episodes}} = 21{,}750 \frac{\text{downloads}}{\text{episode}}$$

The units (downloads per episode) are really helpful in interpreting what this means: The number of downloads went up by 21,750 downloads per episode.

SKILL 2: GRAPH A LINE

The nice thing about drawing the graph of a line is that it doesn't change direction. This means all we really need is two points on the graph, since you can then draw a straight line that connects them. On the other hand, unless you never, ever make mistakes, it's a pretty good idea to find at least three points when drawing a line: If the three points you found don't line up, then you know at least one of them must be wrong.

   Of course, this relies on knowing in advance that the graph is a line. And how do we do that? There are two main ways. First, if the situation described involves a quantity changing at a constant rate, then the graph is going to be a line. Why? See Skill 1 above! Constant rate of change means constant slope, and constant slope means that the graph never changes direction — that's a line. Second, if you're graphing an equation with two variables, and both variables appear only in the numerator and only to the first power, then the graph will be a line.

- To graph $y = 15x - 12$, we first recognize from the form of the equation that the graph is a line. Then we find three points by substituting three values in for x:

x	y
0	−12
−5	−87
5	63

Now we set up a coordinate system, labeling the axes so that all of the points will fit on the graph. Then we plot the points, connect with a line, and include arrows on each end because there's nothing that says the line should have a beginning or an end.

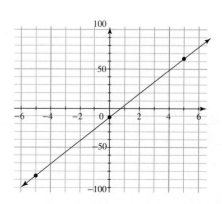

SKILL 3: SOLVE LINEAR EQUATIONS AND INEQUALITIES

There's not much we can say here that hasn't already been said like nine times, but a couple extra practice problems certainly won't hurt you any. Heck, it might even help.

PREP SKILLS QUESTIONS

1. After spending only 10 minutes on his first homework assignment, Ben slowly begins to realize that he needs to take his math class a little more seriously, and starts to increase his study time. By the sixth assignment, he's spending 45 minutes on homework. Find the slope of a line that describes the amount of time Ben is spending on homework, and describe what it means.

2. Draw the graph of the equation $y = -20x + 45$.

3. Find all solutions to each equation or inequality.

   a. $5x + 12 = 100$ b. $3(2 - y) = y - 10$ c. $50 + 12.5x \geq 99$

Lesson 3-8   Party Planning

LEARNING OBJECTIVES

☐ 1. Find the *y* intercept and equation of a line given two points.

☐ 2. Find the equation of a line using point-slope form.

☐ 3. Convert between forms of a linear equation.

©Ingram Publishing RF

Spring is nature's way of saying "Let's Party!"
            – Robin Williams

Everyone loves a good party, with the possible exception of the person in charge of planning it. A backyard barbecue with a handful of friends is not a big deal, I suppose, although they can be surprisingly expensive depending on who you invite. But the big shindigs—weddings, New Year's Eve, charity balls—those take a TON of planning. And a lot of money. Anybody can throw a great bash with an unlimited budget, but for most folks the most important aspect of planning is keeping track of spending based on a target amount that's been budgeted. And that takes math skills! In this lesson we'll take our modeling to the next level: the party level.

0. What aspects of a big party would require math skills? Write down some ideas.

3-8   Class

Congratulations! Your boss thinks highly enough of your organizational skills to put you in charge of a gala to benefit a local no-kill shelter. (Whatever you do, don't screw it up.) You find an appropriate banquet hall and are told that hosting 150 people will cost $6,500. If you up the number of guests to 200, the bill jumps to $8,500.

1. If you make the reasonable assumption that the relationship between the number of people and cost is linear, do we have enough information to find a model for the cost? (By model, we mean an equation that provides the cost for a certain number of people.) Discuss.

2. Which quantity should be the independent variable, and which should be the dependent variable? Explain.

3. Using your answer to Question 2, write two points based on the cost information provided. Then use those points to find the slope of a line.

4. What does your slope tell us about the cost?

Now the big question: Can we find the equation of the line? If we knew the y intercept, we'd be golden, but we don't. So we'll need to be clever.

5. Using x for your independent variable and y for your dependent variable, write a generic equation for cost using the slope-intercept form. Then substitute in the slope you found and information from one of the points. This will give you an equation that you can solve to find the y intercept of the line.

6. What does your y intercept mean? Explain.

7. Write the linear model in the form $y = mx + b$.

Finding the Equation of a Line Through Two Points Using Slope-Intercept Form

1. Find the slope in the usual way: Divide the difference of the y coordinates by the difference of the x coordinates.

2. Substitute the slope in for m, and the x and y coordinates of one of the points in for x and y in the equation $y = mx + b$. This results in an equation you can solve to find b.

3. Now that you know both m and b, you can use $y = mx + b$ to write the equation of the line.

8. Graph the line you found, and then the two points you were originally given. If the line doesn't go through the points, what does that mean?

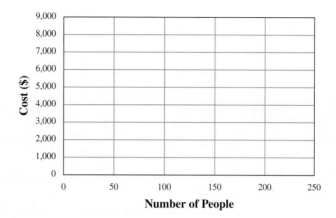

Now we're going to use our new favorite word: generalize.

9. We know that the slope of the line connecting ANY two points on the line is _____.

10. Call one point on the graph (x, y). Find the slope of the line between that generic point and the point $(150, 6{,}500)$.

11. Multiply both sides of the equation you wrote by the denominator to clear fractions.

What you have now is called the **point-slope** form of a line. Since that equation has to be true for every point on the line, it acts as a formula for finding the equation when you know the slope and one point on the line. How is this different from slope-intercept form? Glad you asked. Slope-intercept form requires that you know a *specific point* on the line, namely the y intercept. Point-slope works with ANY point on the line, making it more flexible.

Point-Slope Form

$$y - y_0 = m(x - x_0)$$

x and y are the variables; m is the slope; (x_0, y_0) is any point on the graph.

Example: A line through $(2, 7)$ with a slope of -3 has equation $y - 7 = -3(x - 2)$.

12. Solve the equation from Question 11 for *y*. What do you notice?

Did You Get It

Try these problems to see if you understand the concepts we just studied. The answers can be found at the end of the Portfolio section.

1. Write the point-slope form of the equation describing the cost of the party using the point (200, 8,500). Then show that you get the same result by solving for *y*.
2. Find the equation of a line through $(-3, 8)$ with slope 5. Write your answer in slope-intercept form.

3-8 Group

A small business has been selling 200 digital locking cookie jars per week, which has led to them losing $150 each week (a net profit of -150). According to their business plan, their net profit will increase by $12 for each unit sold.

©Getty Images/Blend Images RF

1. What evidence do you see that would lead you to conclude that this is a linear relationship between net profit and units sold?

2. Identify the independent and dependent variables.

3. What's the slope? How do you know that?

4. Write the equation in slope-intercept form. (If you use point-slope form, convert it to slope-intercept form.)

5. What is the *y* intercept? What does it mean?

6. How many cookie jars do they need to sell in order to break even? What is the significance of this point on the graph? Think about what the profit would be if the business breaks even.

7. Fill in the table of values, then use it to draw a graph of your equation. Label the scale and axes as appropriate.

x	y
0	
200	
400	
600	

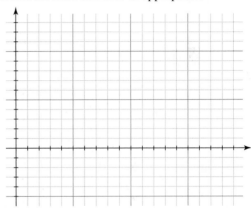

8. Find the number of units needed to make a profit of at least $500 per week.

A custom shirt shop charges a setup fee plus an additional fixed amount per shirt. An order for 20 shirts costs $188, and an order for 25 shirts costs $228.

©Mawardibahar/Getty Images RF

9. What evidence do you see that would lead you to conclude that this is a linear relationship between the number of shirts ordered and the total cost of the order?

10. Identify the independent and dependent variables.

11. What is the slope? What does it mean?

12. Find an equation that will allow you to calculate the cost of ordering any number of shirts.

13. What is the *y* intercept? What does it mean?

14. Graph your equation. Label the scale and axes as appropriate.

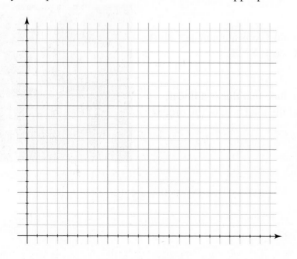

15. How much would 35 shirts cost?

16. How many shirts could you order if you wanted to spend at most $500?

Did You Get It

3. Find the slope-intercept equation of the line that goes through the points (8, 150) and (18, 400).

3-8 Portfolio

Name _____

Technology

1. ☐ We now know how to find the equation of a line through two points. But what if you have data that are kind of linear, but not exactly? The world isn't always as orderly as we'd like, so many quantities that can be modeled effectively by a linear equation aren't exactly linear. In that case, we'd like to find the line that comes closest to matching the data. This is actually the topic of the next lesson, but in this tech assignment we'd like you to start kicking the tires, so to speak. Follow the instructions on the tech template, located in online resources for the course, and see if you can find the line that comes closest to modeling some sort-of-linear data.

Online Practice

1. ☐ Include any written work from the online assignment along with notes or questions about this lession's content.

Applications

1. ☐ Complete the Applications problems.

Reflections

1. ☐ When finding the equation of a line, do you prefer using point-slope or slope-intercept form? Why? Does it depend on the situation?

2. ☐ Once you have the equation for a linear model, what's the advantage of writing it in slope-intercept form?

3. ☐ Describe the process you prefer for finding the equation of a line when you know two points on that line.

4. ☐ Name one thing you learned or discovered in this lesson that you found particularly interesting.

5. ☐ What questions do you have about this lesson?

Looking Ahead

1. ☐ Make sure you complete the Technology assignment! It's a really important part of preparing for the next lesson.

2. ☐ Complete the Prep Skills for Lesson 3-9.

3. ☐ Read the opening paragraph in Lesson 3-9 carefully and answer Question 0 in preparation for that lesson.

Answers to "Did You Get It?"

1. $y - 8{,}500 = 40(x - 200)$; this also simplifies to $y = 40x + 500$

2. $y = 5x + 23$

3. $y = 25x - 50$

Answers to "Prep Skills"

1. 7; The amount of time Ben spends on homework increases by 7 minutes per assignment.

2.

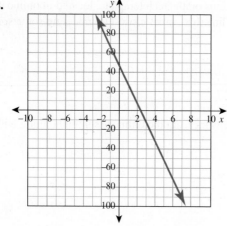

3. **a.** $x = \dfrac{88}{5}$ **b.** $y = 4$ **c.** $x \geq 3.92$

3-8 Applications

Name _____

Tires have tread on them to channel away water and improve grip on both wet and dry surfaces. The height of the treads on a tire is referred to as tread thickness. The table shows the tread thickness of a particular set of truck tires based on the number of miles on those tires.

Miles (thousands)	Tread thickness (mm)
15	7.2
35	4.8

1. As you might expect, this table shows that the more miles you put on a set of tires, the less tread there is left on those tires. That's why tires don't last forever. Do you think it's reasonable to predict that the relationship between tread thickness and miles driven is linear? Why or why not?

2. Let's continue on the assumption that tread thickness and miles driven are linearly related. Find the rate at which the thickness is changing compared to thousand miles driven by comparing change in thickness to number of miles driven in thousands. What does this number describe about a line that can be used to model tread thickness?

3. Why was it smart to write miles in thousands, rather than the actual number of miles?

4. Use either one of the ordered pairs in the table to write the point-slope form of the equation that describes the relationship between the tread thickness and the number of thousands of miles the tire has been used.

3-8 Applications

Name _____

5. Write the slope-intercept form of the equation that describes the relationship between the tread thickness and the number of thousands of miles the tire has been used. You can either use the previous question or create a new equation from the data in the table.

6. Graph the equation and the two points from the table. If they don't live on the line, that would be bad, right? Label the scale and axes as appropriate.

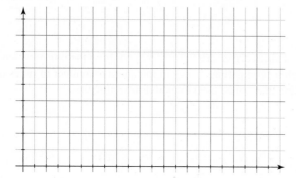

7. Use your equation to predict the tread thickness when the tires have been used for 50,000 miles.

3-8 Applications

Name _____

8. According to the U.S. Department of Transportation, the minimum safe tread thickness is $\frac{1}{16}$ in. Convert this thickness to millimeters, then decide how many more miles the owner of these tires can drive before he risks life and limb driving on unsafe tires. (1 in. is about 25.4 mm. Assume that the current number of miles is the later data in the table.)

9. That particular model of tire has tread thickness of 9.2 mm when brand new. Does that match what your model predicts? What can you conclude?

Lesson 3-9   Prep Skills

SKILL 1: DRAW A SCATTER PLOT

This skill was introduced in Lesson 1-5 and reviewed in the Prep Skills for Lesson 3-1. Remember that the first coordinates go along the horizontal axis and the second coordinates go along the vertical axis. Always focus on the scale you choose for the axes: Identify the biggest value on each axis and use that as a guide to help you choose. The horizontal axis should extend a little bit beyond the largest first coordinate, and the vertical axis should extend a little bit beyond the largest second coordinate.

SKILL 2: FIND THE EQUATION OF A LINE THROUGH TWO POINTS

Of course, we just studied this skill in the last lesson, so hopefully a quick refresher will suffice. In order to find the equation of any line, you need to know the slope, so that's the first step. If you have two points on the line, you can just use

$$\frac{\text{Difference of } y \text{ coordinates}}{\text{Difference of } x \text{ coordinates}}$$

to find the slope, and you're off and running.

The next thing you need is a point on the line. In this situation, you'll have two to choose from. Either is fine, but be smart about it: If one point has a zero coordinate, always choose that one. In general, choose the point that has the simplest coordinates. Avoid fractions and negative numbers if you can, as those make you more likely to make an arithmetic mistake.

Once you have the slope, a known x coordinate, and a known y coordinate, you can plug directly into the formula

$$y - \text{known } y \text{ coordinate} = \text{Slope}(x - \text{known } x \text{ coordinate})$$

and there's your equation. We'll usually get a simpler equation by multiplying out parentheses on the right, then solving for y.

- Find the equation of the line through (2, 6) and (−1, 20).

$$m = \frac{20 - 6}{-1 - 2} = \frac{14}{-3} = -\frac{14}{3}$$

I would pick (2, 6) since both coordinates are positive.

$$y - 6 = -\frac{14}{3}(x - 2)$$

$$y - 6 = -\frac{14}{3}x + \frac{28}{3}$$

$$y = -\frac{14}{3}x + \frac{28}{3} + 6$$

$$y = -\frac{14}{3}x + \frac{28}{3} + \frac{18}{3}$$

$$y = -\frac{14}{3}x + \frac{46}{3}$$

PREP SKILLS QUESTIONS

1. Draw a scatter plot for the data here, which relate the test scores of 15 math students to their homework average.

HW average (x)	40	95	77	100	22	85	88	81	93	100	95	0	50	78	90
Test score (y)	51	88	62	91	15	83	94	77	89	97	98	32	67	72	67

2. Find the equation of the line through each pair of points.

   a. $(0, 9)$ and $(12, 57)$

   b. $(-3, -4)$ and $(-4, 8)$

   c. $(2, 5)$ and $(-3, 8)$

Lesson 3-9   The Great Tech Battle

LEARNING OBJECTIVES

☐ 1. Determine whether two variables have a linear relationship.

☐ 2. Calculate the line of best fit for a set of data using a spreadsheet.

☐ 3. Calculate the line of best fit for a set of data using a calculator.

☐ 4. Interpret the correlation coefficient for a data set.

One machine can do the work of fifty ordinary men. No machine can do the work of one extraordinary man.
        — Elbert Hubbard

That quote says an awful lot about the dangers of too much reliance on technology, a peril with the potential to affect every modern student. The most interesting thing about it, though, is that it was written in 1903! When used correctly in math, technology allows us to focus more on understanding and interpretation, and less on computation. That's great. But when you try to use any technology as a substitute for thinking, nothing good is likely to happen. In this lesson, we'll learn how technology can help us to decide when a given data set is likely to be modeled well with a linear equation. Better still, calculators and spreadsheets will be able to find the best linear model for such situations, freeing us to focus on interpreting the model and using it to further study the data.

0. Without using technology, what are some ways you could tell if a data set might be modeled well with a linear equation?

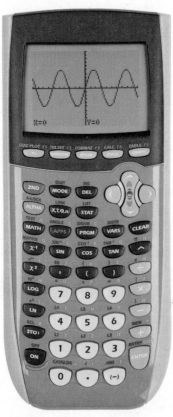

©DonNichols/Getty Images RF

3-9 Class

In Lesson 3-7, we examined the relationship between calories burned and weight loss. While we needed to study data to model the exact nature of the relationship, you were probably able to figure out that the two quantities are related in some way. There are many quantities that *seem* like they might be related, but it's not clear that they really are, or if so, how. So it would be nice to have a way to study relationships (if they even exist) between data sets. Fortunately, the lovely folks who program spreadsheets and graphing calculators have done most of the heavy lifting for us. Still, in our continuing quest to not rely on technology more than our brains, it's a good idea to think about when quantities are likely to be related in some way.

1. Decide if you think the two quantities are likely to be related numerically, and explain your answer.

a. Dollars spent by a political candidate and the number of votes he gets

b. An adult test subject's height and IQ

c. A person's height and shoe size

d. The age of a car and its resale value

2. Is there a relationship between the total fat in a fast-food burger and the total calories? The table here lists calorie and fat information for a standard hamburger at a variety of fast-food restaurants. Begin your study of this question by drawing a scatter plot based on the table.

Fast Food Restaurant	Total Fat (g)	Calories
McDonald's	9	250
Burger King	12	290
Wendy's	8	230
Hardee's	12	310
Carl's Jr	17	470
Sonic	15	310
White Castle	7	140
Dairy Queen	14	350
Jack in the Box	14	310
In-N-Out Burger	19	390

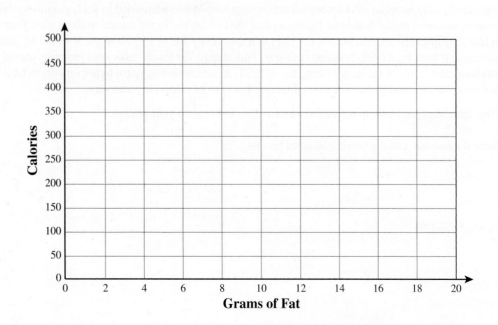

3. The points on your scatter plot don't form a straight line, but there should be a linear trend you can observe. Use a straightedge to draw a line that you think looks like the best fit for your scatter plot. Note that it's possible that the line that fits the data best doesn't go through any of the points.

4. Identify two points on the line of best fit that you drew on your scatter plot, and use them to find an equation for the line.

Using Technology: Finding the Line of Best Fit with a Graphing Calculator

To find a line of best fit for two data sets that appear to have an approximate linear relationship:

1. Press **STAT** **ENTER** to get to the list editor.

2. Enter the data set you want to use as inputs (*x* values) under **Ll**.

3. Use the right arrow key (▶) to access **L2**. Then enter the data set you want to use as outputs (*y* values). When entering data from a table, make sure you enter the second list in the same order as the first.

4. Turn on **Plot1** by pressing **2nd** **Y=** **1**. Set up the screen as shown below.

5. Press **Y=** and if the **Y =** screen isn't blank, move the cursor over any entered equations and press **CLEAR**.

6. Press **ZOOM** **9** which is the **Zoom Stat** option; this automatically sets a graphing window that displays all of the plotted points.

7. Press **STAT** followed by the right arrow key to access the **STAT CALC** menu, and choose the **LinReg** (for linear regression) option, which is choice 4. Then press **ENTER** to calculate the line of best fit. Depending on which version you have, it might be necessary to use the arrows to move down to select **Calculate** before pressing enter.

8. Press **Y=** and enter the equation of the line of best fit, then press **GRAPH** to display the scatter plot along with the line of best fit.

See the Lesson 3-9-1 video in class resources for further instruction.

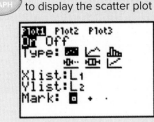

5. Use the procedure in the Using Technology box to find the equation of the line of best fit using a graphing calculator. Round to one decimal place.

6. Use your answer to Question 5 to predict the number of calories in a Whataburger, which has 25 grams of fat. How does the answer compare to the number of calories predicted by your own line of best fit in Question 4? The Whataburger actually has 590 calories. Which line gave a more accurate prediction?

Did You Get It

Try this problem to see if you understand the concepts we just studied. The answer can be found at the end of the Portfolio section.

1. The table shows the gold-medal lengths for the men's Olympic long jump for selected years from 1900 to 2000. Using years after 1900 as input and length as output, find the line of best fit for this data. Round to three decimal places. Then use it to predict the length of the winning jump in 1984.

Year	X	Length (meters)
1900	0	7.18
1912	12	7.60
1920	20	7.15
1932	32	7.64
1948	48	7.82
1960	60	8.12
1972	72	8.24
1980	80	8.54
1996	96	8.50
2000	100	8.55

7. A classic roast beef sandwich from Arby's has 360 calories and 14 grams of fat. What does your line of best fit predict for calories? Is this expected? Explain.

When finding the line of best fit using a graphing calculator, the last line in the display should be a value for a quantity labeled r, which is known as the **correlation coefficient**. If your calculator is not displaying r, press 2nd 0, then use the down arrow to scroll down and choose "DiagnosticOn" and try the calculation again. This number measures how well the line seems to fit the data. The closer r is to 1 (positive slope) or -1 (negative slope), the more accurately the data you entered can be modeled using a linear equation. Here are some examples, based on data from two of my classes last semester:

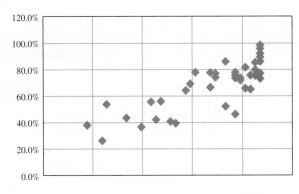 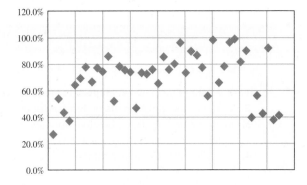

8. One of these scatter plots has a correlation coefficient of 0.19; the other has a correlation coefficient of 0.82. Discuss which you think is which, and why.

9. One of the scatter plots has each student's homework score for the semester on the x axis and the corresponding overall percentage in the course (from 0 to 100) on the y axis. The other again has overall percentage on the y axis, but along the x axis is the student's position alphabetically in the class. (The student whose name comes first alphabetically is 1, the next alphabetically is 2, and so on.) Which plot is which? Again, discuss your reasons.

10. What is the value of the correlation coefficient r for the fast-food sandwich plot? Round to two decimal places.

Did You Get It

2. Find the correlation coefficient for the line of best fit you found in Did You Get It 1. Does this indicate a strong linear relationship?

Using Technology: Finding the Line of Best Fit with a Spreadsheet

To find a line of best fit and correlation coefficient on a spreadsheet:

1. Enter the data in two columns and create a scatter plot.
2. Click on one of the points on the scatter plot, then choose "Add Trendline" from the **Chart** menu.
3. In the formatting dialog box that appears, click "Options," then click the checkboxes for "Display equation on chart" and "Display r^2 value on chart."
4. Calculate the square root of the r^2 value that appears on the chart. This is the correlation coefficient.

See the Lesson 3-9-2 video in class resources for further instruction.

11. Based on all of the work done in this activity, how strong do you think the relationship is between the number of grams of fat in a fast-food hamburger and the number of calories in it? Make sure you justify your answer.

An Important Note on Lines of Best Fit

Hopefully, you noticed right from the beginning of our study of burgers that you can't draw a straight line that goes exactly through all of the points. That in turn means the predictions made by our equation for any sandwich are unlikely to be perfectly accurate. This will almost always be the case when finding a line of best fit for a data set with more than two values. There's a good reason we call it "the line of best fit," not "the line of perfect fit"! The equations we're finding are models for data that allow us to make approximations and predictions; they're not exact representations of data.

12. Look back at the original table of fat and calories near the beginning of this lesson. Use the calculator-generated line of best fit to predict the number of calories in the Hardee's burger. Then find the difference between the actual number of calories and your predicted value.

When using a line of best fit to model data, we use the term *residual* to refer to the difference between predicted values obtained from a model and actual values. You just computed the residual for the Hardee's burger. Remember: the output we get from the equation of the line of best fit is the predicted value.

The Residual of a Data Point

When a data set is modeled by a line of best fit, the difference between the actual value from that data set and the value predicted by the equation is called the **residual** for that value.

Residual = Actual value − predicted value

The sign of the residual tells you if the actual value was higher (positive residual) or lower (negative residual) than the predicted value.

13. Find the residual for the White Castle burger.

Did You Get It

3. Continuing our study of Olympic men's long jump champions from Did You Get It 1, find the residuals for the winning long jumps in 1920 and 1980.

3-9 Group

Correlation Lab: How Much Candy Can You Grab?

Supplies needed:

- A large bowl filled with Hershey's miniatures candy (or some other relatively small, WRAPPED candies). One bowl per group is nice, but somewhat costly.
- A ruler for each group

(Thanks to our friends from Cincinnati State Technical and Community College for inspiring this activity.)

1. What factors would be likely to go into how many candy bars you can grab out of a bowl? List some.

In this activity we're going to see how closely hand size correlates to the number of candy bars you can grab. First you'll need to decide on some parameters to make sure that everyone's data are comparable.

2. Decide which hand everyone will use. Right? Left? Dominant? Nondominant? Describe why you made the choice you did.

3. How should you measure hand size? And what units will you use? Describe your choice.

At this point, you should have a short class discussion to decide on choice of hand and how to measure for the entire class so that results are consistent. Write the choices made here for reference.

4. Now it's time to begin the activity. For each person in your group, measure the size of his or her hand, then have each person reach into the bowl and grab as many candy bars as possible IN ONE TRY. Count the number, put the candies back in the bowl, then record the data in the table. Finally, share your data with your instructor or other groups so that data for the entire class are included. (Note: In this question, you're only using the first two columns of the table. The other columns will be filled in later.)

Hand size (x)	# Candy bars (y)	Predicted #	Residual

5. Draw a scatter plot of the data on the grid supplied.

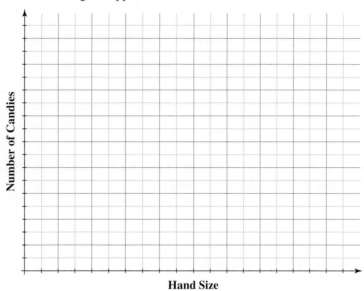

Hand Size

6. Use a calculator or spreadsheet to draw a scatter plot for the data, then find and write the equation of the line of best fit.

7. Add the line to your hand graph.

8. Find the correlation coefficient for the data. How closely are the two quantities related?

9. Use the line of best fit to predict the number of candy bars that your instructor should be able to grab. Then have your instructor grab some candy. How accurate was the prediction?

10. Use your equation and either the table feature on a graphing calculator or a spreadsheet to calculate the predicted number of candy bars for everyone in your chart based on hand size. Fill that data into the table in the Predicted # column.

11. Compute the residual for everyone in the class, and add that to the table as well.

12. Find the sum of all residuals. What can you conclude?

13. Write any conclusions you can draw about the connection between hand size and the number of candy bars you can grab, then start eating those candies (like you haven't already).

3-9 Portfolio

Name _____

Check each box when you've completed the task. Remember that your instructor will want you to turn in the portfolio pages you create.

Technology

1. ☐ Enter the Olympic men's long jump data from Did You Get It 1 in the first two columns of a spreadsheet, then create a scatter plot and find the line of best fit. In the third column, use the equation of best fit to calculate the predicted winning jump for each year in the table, then in the fourth column compute the residual for each winning jump. Finally, use the SUM command to add all residuals.

2. ☐ One of the years conspicuously absent from the long jump data was 1968. American Bob Beamon jumped 8.90 meters (over 29 feet) that year to beat the previous world record by almost 2 feet—in a sport where new records usually pass the old by an inch or two. Many people consider this the single most remarkable athletic feat in human history—Beamon himself literally fell over from shock when he realized how far he'd jumped. Rework Question 1, but this time include that 1968 jump in the data set. How much does it affect the line of best fit? Discuss.

Online Practice

1. ☐ Include any written work from the online assignment along with any notes or questions about this lesson's content.

Applications

1. ☐ Complete the Applications problems.

Reflections

Type a short answer to each question.

1. ☐ What is a line of best fit for two sets of data?

2. ☐ Does the line of best fit provide useful information about every pair of data sets? Why or why not? Your answer should probably mention the correlation coefficient.

3. ☐ Does a line of best fit have to go through a lot of the data points? Explain.

4. ☐ Name one thing you learned or discovered in this lesson that you found particularly interesting.

5. ☐ What questions do you have about this lesson?

Looking Ahead

1. ☐ Complete the Prep Skills for Lesson 3-10.

2. ☐ Read the opening paragraph in Lesson 3-10 carefully then answer Question 0 in preparation for that lesson.

Answers to "Did You Get It?"

1. $y = 0.015x + 7.179$; 8.44 m

2. 0.96; this does indicate a strong linear relationship.

3. 1920: –0.329; 1980: 0.161

Answers to "Prep Skills"

1.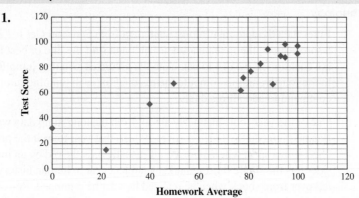

2. **a.** $y = 4x + 9$ **b.** $y = -12x - 40$ **c.** $y = -\dfrac{3}{5}x + \dfrac{31}{5}$

3-9 Applications

Name _____

This table shows the average annual cost for tuition, room, and board at all colleges in the United States between the 2000 and 2014 school years.

1. Draw a scatter plot on the axes provided. The *x* values are given in the table; use values from the Cost column as *y* values. Do you think a linear equation will model the data accurately?

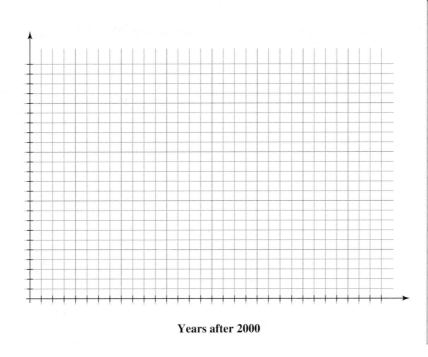

Years after 2000

School Year	x	Cost ($)
2000–01	0	$10,820
2001–02	1	$11,380
2002–03	2	$12,014
2003–04	3	$12,953
2004–05	4	$13,793
2005–06	5	$14,634
2006–07	6	$15,483
2007–08	7	$16,231
2008–09	8	$17,092
2009–10	9	$17,650
2010–11	10	$18,475
2011–12	11	$19,401
2012–13	12	$20,233
2013–14	13	$20,995
2014–15	14	$21,728

2. Use a graphing calculator or spreadsheet to create a scatter plot and find the line of best fit for the data, then add the line to your scatter plot.

3. What is the slope of the line? What does it mean?

3-9   Applications

Name _____

4. Use your equation to predict total tuition, room, and board costs for the 2019–2020 school year.

5. Use your equation to predict total tuition, room, and board for the 1990–1991 school year. (Hint: What x value would correspond to 10 years BEFORE 2000?)

6. Use your equation to predict the school year in which total tuition, room, and board will reach $30,000.

7. What is the correlation coefficient for the data? Are you surprised based on your answer to Question 1? Explain.

8. Find the residuals for the 2002–2003 and 2008–2009 school years. What do your results mean?

Lesson 3-10   Prep Skills

SKILL 1: COMPUTE A UNIT PRICE

Unit pricing is used very commonly in grocery stores as a way for shoppers to compare prices. If one box of coffee k-cups has 12 cups for $8.99 and another has 16 cups for $12.89, it's not at all obvious which is the better deal. So the tag in the store (if you look closely enough) probably tells you the unit price, which is the cost of one unit of a given item.

- In this case, for the first box: $\dfrac{\$8.99}{12 \text{ cups}} \approx \$0.749$ per cup

  For the second: $\dfrac{\$12.89}{16 \text{ cups}} \approx \$0.806$ per cup

Now we can see that the first box is the better price: Each cup is about 75 cents, compared to about 81 cents for the bigger box.

SKILL 2: SUBSTITUTE AN EXPRESSION INTO AN EXPRESSION

By now you should be very comfortable evaluating expressions, which typically involves replacing the variable with a number. For example, to evaluate the expression $120 + 9x$ for $x = 4$, we'd get $120 + 9(4) = 156$. Sometimes it's useful to evaluate expressions not just for numbers, but for other expressions as well.

- Substitute $15 - 2y$ for x into the expression $120 + 9x$:

  $120 + 9(15 - 2y) = 120 + 135 - 18y = 255 - 18y$

- If $y = 100 - x$, rewrite the equation $4x - 2y = 425$ with only variable x.

  Since we're told that $100 - x$ is the same as y, we can consider $100 - x$ to simply be a new name for y. In that case, we can replace y in that equation with $100 - x$, to get $4x - 2(100 - x) = 425$. The left side could then be simplified by multiplying out parentheses and combining like terms, to get $6x - 200 = 425$.

SKILL 3: WRITE A LINEAR EQUATION FROM A DESCRIPTION

This specific skill was reviewed in Lesson 3-3 Prep Skills, but we've practiced writing algebraic expressions based on given information throughout this entire unit. When it comes to writing equations, one of the key ideas is that an equation comes from two different ways to express the same quantity.

- Let's say you make $12.75 per hour at a part-time job and you're interested in setting up an equation to calculate how many hours you'd need to work to make $200. You could use letter h to represent the number of hours worked, in which case $12.75h$ is the amount you'd make for h hours. The situation states that we want that amount to be $200, so in essence both $12.75h$ and 200 are ways to describe the amount of money earned. So it makes perfect sense to write the equation $12.75h = 200$.

This can also be done with situations that have more than one variable quantity. If you had a second part-time job that pays $10 per hour, and you represented the number of hours worked at that job with variable k, then the total amount you earn is now $12.75h + 10k$, so if you're still interested in earning $200, the equation would be $12.75h + 10k = 200$.

PREP SKILLS QUESTIONS

1. Which has the cheaper unit price: a bag of 40 Reese's cups for $6.99, or a package of 16 for $3.79?

2. Which has the cheaper unit price: 4 pounds of ground chuck for $8.19, or 24 ounces of ground chuck for $3.49?

3. Substitute $18 + 3y$ for x into the expression $15 - x$.

4. Substitute $3x - 1$ for y into the expression $2y - 25$.

5. If $y = 14 - x$, rewrite the equation $5x - 10y = 85$ with x as its only variable.

6. For the unit price of Reese's cups in the bag of 40, write an equation that describes how many of those Reese's cups you could buy for $25.

7. A semi-private golf course has an initiation fee of $800 which allows players to play golf as much as they like. But they do have to pay a $12 cart fee each time they play. Write an equation that describes how many times a member could play for $1,100.

8. Players can choose to walk the course, in which case they only have to pay a $2 fee that goes toward course maintenance each time they play. Write a new equation describing the number of times a player could play in a riding cart or walking for $1,100.

Lesson 3-10   All Systems Go

LEARNING OBJECTIVES

☐ 1. Solve an application problem involving a system of equations.

☐ 2. Illustrate the solution to a system of equations using a table.

☐ 3. Illustrate the solution to a system of equations using a graph.

In the long run, we shape our lives, and we shape ourselves. The process never ends until we die. And the choices we make are ultimately our own responsibility.
— Eleanor Roosevelt

If a problem comes knocking at your door, you can hide behind the sofa and hope it goes away, or you can answer the door and see an opportunity. Many successful people will tell you that this mindset is what separates the winners from the pretenders in life. It's about taking personal responsibility for your own success, and seeing every obstacle as one more chance to achieve success. Throughout this unit, we've learned skills and strategies that can be used to write equations describing situations, and use those equations to solve problems.

©REB Images/Blend Images LLC RF

But the world is a complicated place, and there are many very real situations where more than one quantity varies, which means we'll need more than one variable. In that case, we'll also need more than one equation that models the situation. Fortunately, we'll have a system in place for dealing with these situations: a system of equations, in fact.

0. Think of all of the equations we've solved in Unit 3. Can you think of any situations where we solved equations that had more than one variable in them?

3-10 | Class

1. Summarize Polya's problem-solving strategy from Lesson 2-5.

We do have some experience in solving equations that have multiple variables in them: We called that solving literal equations. The idea was to solve a formula for one of the variables to turn it into a more convenient form. But we never got a number as a solution when we did that: The result was always another formula with variables in it. This isn't ideal when solving specific problems: If I ask you how big the area of your campus is and you say *"l* times *w,"* I'm probably going to look at you funny and slowly back away.

When we're studying a situation with two variable quantities, we may be able to set up a **system of equations**. This is two or more related equations that share common variables. Let's start off with a situation that might lead to a system of equations.

The shipping manager at a small business sent out a shipment of three coffee mugs and six promotional packets on Monday, and the total shipping weight was 42 ounces. On Wednesday, she sent six more mugs and three more packets, and this time the total weight was 48 ounces. Now the boss wants to know the shipping weight for each packet, and for each mug. Our goal is to help the shipping manager out.

2. In this problem, there are two variable quantities that we don't know: the shipping weight of a packet and the shipping weight of a mug. If we use x to represent the weight of one mug and y to represent the weight of one packet, write an expression that describes the combined weights of three mugs and six packets.

3. Use your answer from Question 2 to write an equation that describes the weight of the first shipment.

If we repeat what you did in Question 3 for the second shipment, we get our first look at a system of equations:

$$3x + 6y = 42$$
$$6x + 3y = 48$$

4. Solve each equation for y.

5. Make a table of values for each equation.

x	1st Equation: $y =$	2nd Equation: $y =$
2		
4		
6		
8		
10		

6. Graph both equations on the same grid. Make sure you label which is which.

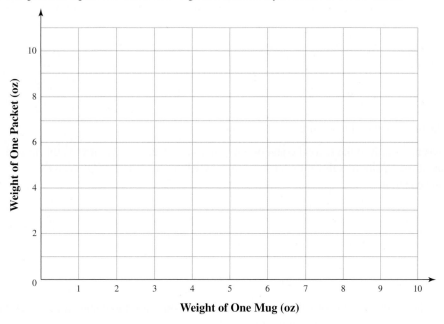

7. Where does it look like the two lines intersect?

8. Plug the coordinates of that point back into each of the ORIGINAL equations. What do you notice?

Congratulations! You just solved a system of equations! The point (6, 4) provides a value for each variable ($x = 6$ and $y = 4$) that makes both equations true, and that's what a solution is.

A **solution to a system** of two equations is a pair of numbers, one for each variable, that make both equations true when substituted in. **Solving a system** means finding all pairs of numbers that are a solution.

9. What does the solution we found tell us about the shipping weights?

10. How could you have found the solution to the system from the table you made without graphing?

Our next goal will be to develop an algebraic method for solving a system of equations.

11. Write the result you got earlier when you solved the second equation for *y*. If you look at it the right way, this provides another name for *y*: the right side of the equation. Substitute that for *y* in the ORIGINAL FIRST EQUATION. How many variables are in the resulting equation?

12. Solve the resulting equation for *x*, then find the value of *y* that corresponds to it. (You'll need to decide for yourself how to do that.) Did you end up with the same solution you got from graphing?

The method that we used to solve this system is called substitution, because what makes it work is substituting a new name for one of the variables that leaves an equation with only one variable.

Solving a System of Equations Using Substitution

Step 1: Solve one of the equations for one of the variables. You can choose either equation and either variable, but it's almost always worth thinking about a choice that makes it less likely you'll end up with fractions.

Step 2: Substitute the result of Step 1 for the variable you solved for in the OTHER equation. This results in an equation with only one variable.

Step 3: Solve that equation, and you'll have a value for one of the variables.

Step 4: Substitute the value from Step 3 back into the result of Step 1. This will give you a value for the other variable.

Step 5: Write the solution of the system. You can write it either as a point, like (6, 4), or as two equations, like $x = 6, y = 4$.

Did You Get It

Try this problem to see if you understand the concepts we just studied. The answer can be found at the end of the Portfolio section.

1. Solve the system of equations.

$$4x + 3y = -2$$
$$y - 4x = -6$$

Interestingly, this technique can also be used to solve problems that could be solved by writing a single equation, like the next one.

While traveling on business, Eldrick bought a $50 prepaid international cell phone to call his girlfriend Lindsey. Calls cost $0.07 per minute. How many minutes has he used if the display shows $32.15 remaining?

To answer this question we could think about two different equations. One states that the value of the card V is $32.15.

13. Write that equation here:

Next we can write another equation that states that the value V started at $50 and decreased by $0.07 for each minute used x.

14. Write that equation here:

15. Complete the table.

x	1st equation: $V =$	2nd equation: $V =$
0		
100		
200		
300		
400		
500		

16. Graph both equations on the grid.

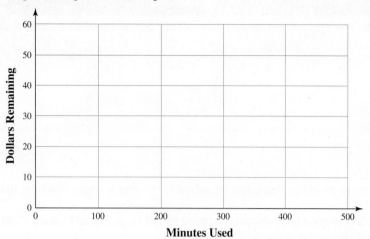

17. Use your graph to estimate the solution to the system of equations. How confident are you of your answer? Why?

18. Now solve the system using the substitution method. Did you get the same solution? Use this result to solve the original problem.

19. How would you determine the second coordinate of the solution?

Did You Get It

2. A taxi company charges a fixed initial charge of $4 plus an additional $1.80 per mile. How long was the taxi ride if the total cost was $14.62? Write an equation showing the constant total cost. Write a second equation showing the total cost based on the fixed initial cost and the cost per mile. Solve this system of equations and answer the question.

3-10   Group

1. The members of an intramural softball team decide to get custom t-shirts made. There are two screening shops in town that they can choose from. Wave Graphics charges a setup fee of $22, and then each shirt is $7. The Shirt Shack doesn't charge a setup fee, but each shirt is $9. If for some bizarre reason the team decided to only order three shirts, which shop would be the cheaper choice?

2. The goal is to find the number of shirts for which the two shops would charge the same.

   a. Write an equation that describes the cost C of buying x shirts from the Shirt Shack.

   b. Write an equation that describes the cost C of buying x shirts from Wave Graphics.

   c. Now you have a system of equations! Good job. Let's examine the costs associated with each shop by making a table of values.

Number of shirts (x)	Cost at Shirt Shack (C)	Cost at Wave Graphics (C)
3		
6		
9		
12		
15		

   d. Based on the table, estimate the number of shirts that would make the total cost the same at each shop.

e. Graph the lines corresponding to each of the equations you wrote in parts a and b on the same coordinate system. Make sure you choose a scale so that the point where the two lines cross is visible.

f. What quantity does the height of every point on each line represent?

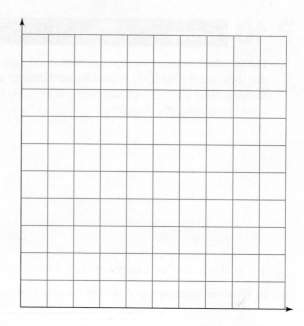

g. The point where the graphs cross is where the two heights are the same. What does this represent in the problem?

h. Based on your graph, estimate the number of shirts that will lead to the same cost at each shop.

i. Solve the system of equations algebraically to find the exact solution.

j. What will the total cost be for the number of shirts found in part i?

Now that we've practiced the process of setting up and solving a system of equations to solve a problem, we'll close the lesson by giving you a problem to solve, and providing just a couple of suggestions to get you started.

3. The Shirt Shack operates on a daily fixed cost plus a variable cost that depends on the number of shirts screened in one day. The total cost for screening 260 shirts on Friday was $1,015. The total cost for screening 380 shirts on Saturday was $1,345. What is the fixed daily cost? What is the cost to screen each shirt?

   a. We're asked to find two things in this problem. Assign a variable to each.

   b. Now use your variables to write and solve a system of equations, then write your solution to the problem in the form of a sentence or two.

Did You Get It

   3. The Sugar Buzz has two popular kinds of candy. The owner is trying to make a mixture of 100 pounds of these candies to sell at $3 per pound. If the gummy crickets are priced at $2.50 per pound and the sour cubes are $3.75 per pound, how many pounds of each should be mixed in order to produce the mixture he's shooting for?

3-10 Portfolio

Name _____

Check each box when you've completed the task. Remember that your instructor will want you to turn in the portfolio pages you create.

Technology

1. ☐ This refers to the problem in Questions 1–7 of the Applications section of this lesson. Use your equations for the cost of buying diapers with the Amazon Family membership and the cost without the membership to complete the table shown in an Excel spreadsheet. Then graph the system of equations. Explain how the graph shows when it is worth joining Amazon Family.

	A	B	C
	Boxes of diapers bought	Cost with membership	Cost without membership
1			
2	0		
3	2		
4	4		
5	6		
6	8		
7	10		
8	12		

Online Practice

1. ☐ Include any written work from the online assignment along with any notes or questions about this lesson's content.

Applications

1. ☐ Complete the Applications problems.

Reflections

Type a short answer to each question.

1. ☐ What is a system of equations? What kinds of situations are likely to be modeled by a system of equations?

2. ☐ How can you solve a system of equations using graphing?

3. ☐ If it's possible to solve a system of equations by graphing, why is it often better to solve algebraically?

4. ☐ Name one thing you learned or discovered in this lesson that you found particularly interesting.

5. ☐ What questions do you have about this lesson?

Looking Ahead

1. ☐ Complete the Prep Skills for Lesson 4-1.

2. ☐ Read the opening paragraph in Lesson 4-1 carefully and answer Question 0 in preparation for that lesson.

Answers to "Did You Get It?"

1. $x = 1, y = -2$

2. $C = 14.62, C = 4 + 1.80x$; the ride was 5.9 miles long.

3. 60 pounds of gummy crickets, 40 pounds of sour cubes

Answers to "Prep Skills"

1. A bag of 40 Reese's cups for $6.99 is the better deal at $0.17 per cup compared to $0.24 per cup.

2. Four pounds at $8.19 is the better deal at $2.05 per pound compared to $2.33 per pound.

3. $-3 - 3y$ 4. $6x - 27$ 5. $15x - 140 = 85$

6. $0.17c = 25$, where c represents the number of Reese's cups purchased.

7. $800 + 12c = 1,100$, where c represents the number of rounds of golf played with a cart.

8. $800 + 12c + 2w = 1,100$, where c represents the number of rounds of golf played with a cart and w represents the number of rounds played walking.

3-10 Applications

Name _____

Parents with young babies buy a lot of diapers (to say the very least), so getting the best deal is pretty important. Comparing prices can be harder than you would think, though — retailers don't all sell diapers in the same size boxes. A recent check of prices on Pampers Swaddlers in Size 1 revealed the following:

> Amazon.com: 234 diapers for $46.99
> Meijer: 160 diapers for $34.99

1. Find the unit price for each box of diapers and use it to decide which is the best deal. (There's free shipping, so don't worry about shipping or tax.)

Amazon offers an interesting deal: If you pay $99 per year to join their Amazon Family club, you get 20% off all diaper purchases.

2. What would the $46.99 box of diapers cost with that discount?

3. Write an equation that provides the total cost C of buying x boxes of diapers in one year with the Amazon Family membership.

4. Write another equation that provides the total cost C of buying x boxes of diapers in one year from Amazon without being a member of Amazon Family.

3-10 Applications

Name _____

5. Complete the table of values for each equation.

x	1st equation: C =	2nd Equation: C =
0		
3		
6		
9		
12		
15		

6. The equations you wrote in Questions 3 and 4 form a system of equations. Solve that system using substitution and use your result to find how many boxes of diapers you'd need to buy in a year for the two costs to be the same. What would the cost be?

7. Under what circumstances would you want to join Amazon Family to buy diapers? (Well, obviously having a baby would be one of those circumstances. What other ones?)

8. After her first two exams in psychology, a student has a mean score of 90 and a range of 12. What were her scores on the two exams?
   a. Define two variables corresponding to two unknowns in the problem.

3-10 Applications

Name _____

b. Write an equation stating that the mean of the two exam scores was 90, and one stating that the range was 12.

c. Solve the system of equations you wrote using your favorite method, then write a sentence answering the question about exam scores.

9. A hospital needs 80 liters of a 12% solution of disinfectant. This solution is to be prepared from a 33% solution and a 5% solution. How many liters of each should be mixed to obtain this 12% solution? There are different ways to solve this problem, but using a system of equations is the simplest way.

Unit 3 Language and Symbolism Review

Carefully read through the list of terminology we've used in Unit 3. Consider circling the terms you aren't familiar with and looking them up. Then test your understanding by using the list to fill in the appropriate blank in each sentence.

building up
conditional equation
correlation coefficient
direct variation
equation
equivalent
equivalent equations
exchange rate
generalizing
inequality

line of best fit
linear equation
literal equation

$$m = \frac{y_2 - y_1}{x_2 - x_1}$$

proportion
rate of change
slope
solution

solution to a system
solving a system
system of equations
terms
x intercept
$y = mx + b$
y intercept
$y = kx$
$y - y_0 = m(x - x_0)$

1. Rewriting fractions so that they have a bigger numerator and denominator is called _____ a fraction.

2. A _____ is a rate that compares the change in one quantity to the change in another.

3. Two quantities are _____ if they have the same value.

4. The point where any graph crosses the y axis is called the _____ for the graph.

5. When applied to the graph of a line, the _____ of the line describes how steep the line is.

6. The formula for the slope of a line is _____.

7. The individual pieces of an expression containing addition and subtraction are called _____.

8. A point where a graph crosses the x axis is called an _____ of the graph.

9. An _____ is simply a statement that two quantities are equal.

10. A _____ can be either true or false, depending on what value we choose for the variable quantity.

11. A number that makes an equation a true statement when substituted in for the variable is called a _____ of an equation.

12. When two equations have the same solution, we call them _____.

13. An equation stating that two ratios are equal is called a _____.

14. An equation with the input appearing only to the first power has a graph that is a line and is called a _____.

15. A _____ is an equation with more than one variable, so that when you solve for one of the variables, the result is an expression rather than a number.

16. A statement that one quantity is more or less than another is called an _____.

17. When you develop a strategy to solve a specific problem, then adapt that strategy to a variety of related problems, that's called _____ your approach.

18. An _____ is a number that describes how much of one currency you can trade for another currency.

19. It's called a _____ relationship when one variable quantity is found simply by multiplying a second variable quantity by a constant.

20. The algebraic equation that describes the relationship when two quantities vary directly looks like _____.

21. The slope-intercept form of the equation of a line is _____.

22. The point-slope form of the equation of a line is _____.

23. When two data sets appear to have an approximately linear relationship, _____ is the line that best represents the data on a scatter plot.

24. The _____ is a number that measures how well the line of best fit seems to fit the data.

25. A _____ is two or more related equations that share common variables.

26. A _____ of two equations is a pair of numbers, one for each variable, that make both equations true when substituted in.

27. _____ of two equations means finding all pairs of numbers that are a solution.

Unit 3   Technology Review

This is a short review of the technology skills we've used in Unit 3. In each case, rate your confidence level by checking one of the boxes, If you feel like you're struggling with these skills, consult the online resources for extra practice.

			1. Graphing an equation with a graphing calculator (Lesson 3-2)
			2. Finding the line of best fit with a graphing calculator (Lesson 3-9)
			3. Finding the line of best fit with a spreadsheet (Lesson 3-9)

1. Use a graphing calculator to graph the equation $P = 0.25x - 50$. Use a scale that displays the x values from 0 to 500 with a distance of 50 units between each tick mark and displays the y values from -100 to 100 with a distance of 10 units between each tick mark.

2. Use a graphing calculator to create a scatter plot and determine the equation of the line of best fit for the data in the table. Also include the correlation coefficient.

x	y
2	4
5	7
7	8
9	11
12	15
14	19

3. Use a spreadsheet to create a scatter plot and determine the equation of the line of best fit for the data in the table. Also include the correlation coefficient.

x	y
10	18
15	16
19	12
26	9
29	6
34	2

Unit 3 Learning Objective Review

This is a short review of the learning objectives we've covered in Unit 3. In each case, rate your confidence level by checking one of the boxes. If you feel like you're struggling with these skills, consult the lesson referenced next to the objective and see the online resources for extra practice.

1. Interpret a rate of change. (Lesson 3-1)

2. Predict a future value from a rate of change. (Lesson 3-1)

3. Calculate a rate of change. (Lesson 3-1)

4. Find the intercepts of a line. (Lesson 3-1)

5. Interpret the meaning of the intercepts of a line. (Lesson 3-1)

6. Write expressions based on given information. (Lesson 3-2)

7. Interpret algebraic expressions in context. (Lesson 3-2)

8. Evaluate and simplify expressions. (Lesson 3-2)

9. Explain what it means to solve an equation. (Lesson 3-3)

10. Demonstrate the procedures for solving a basic linear equation. (Lesson 3-3)

11. Solve a literal equation for a designated variable. (Lesson 3-3)

12. Demonstrate the procedures for solving a linear inequality. (Lesson 3-4)

13. Solve application problems that involve linear inequalities. (Lesson 3-4)

14. Solve application problems using numerical calculations. (Lesson 3-5)

15. Solve application problems using linear equations. (Lesson 3-5)

16. Identify situations where direct variation occurs. (Lesson 3-6)

17. Write an appropriate direct variation equation for a situation. (Lesson 3-6)

18. Solve an application problem that involves direct variation. (Lesson 3-6)

19. Write an equation of a line given a description of the relationship. (Lesson 3-7)

20. Write an equation of a line that models data from a table. (Lesson 3-7)

21. Write an equation of a line from a graph of the line. (Lesson 3-7)

22. Graph a line by plotting points. (Lesson 3-7)

23. Find the y intercept and equation of a line given two points. (Lesson 3-8)

24. Find the equation of a line using point-slope form. (Lesson 3-8)

25. Convert between forms of a linear equation. (Lesson 3-8)

26. Determine whether two variables have a linear relationship. (Lesson 3-9)

27. Calculate the line of best fit for a set of data using a spreadsheet. (Lesson 3-9)

28. Calculate the line of best fit for a set of data using a calculator. (Lesson 3-9)

29. Interpret the correlation coefficient for a data set. (Lesson 3-9)

30. Solve an application problem involving a system of equations. (Lesson 3-10)

31. Illustrate the solution to a system of equations using a table. (Lesson 3-10)

32. Illustrate the solution to a system of equations using a graph. (Lesson 3-10)

After you've evaluated your confidence level with each objective and gone back to review the objectives you weren't sure about, use the problem set as an additional review.

1. The following two graphs show the distance traveled in miles based on time in hours for two different cars.

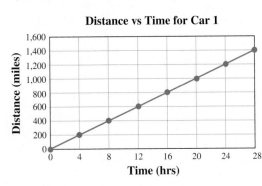

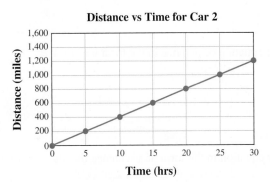

Which statement is more accurate? Circle your choice and show good mathematical evidence to support your choice.

Choose:

A. Car 1 is moving at a faster speed than car 2.
B. Car 2 is moving at a faster speed than car 1.
C. Both cars are moving at the same speed.
D. It cannot be determined from these graphs.

Explain:

In this graph the input *x* is the number of units produced by a machine in a factory. The output *y* is the profit made by the sale of these units when they are produced.

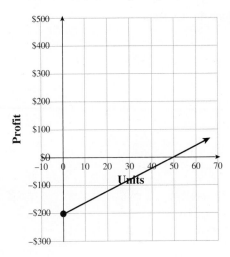

2. Determine the *x* intercept and interpret its meaning.

3. Determine the *y* intercept and interpret its meaning.

4. Determine the slope of this line and explain what it means.

5. Determine the equation of this line in the form $y = mx + b$.

6. Describe your equation in the form of a sentence like this: "If x represents _____ , then $y =$ _____ represents _____"

7. Use your equation to determine the profit if 60 units are produced and sold.

8. Use your equation to determine the number of units that must be produced and sold in order to generate a profit of $100.

9. The following equation has been solved. Provide an explanation of what was done in each step.

$$-2.5x + 70 = 65$$
$$-2.5x = -15$$
$$x = 6$$

Solve each equation in Questions 10–13.

10. $3x = 12$

11. $t + 4 = 28$

12. $b - 250 = 200$

13. $\dfrac{y}{2} = 11$

In Questions 14 and 15, solve each equation for *a*.

14. $P = a + b + 2c$

15. $y = 2ab - c$

16. The following inequality has been solved. Provide an explanation of what was done in each step, and insert the correct inequality symbol between the left side and the right side of the inequality in each step.

$$-2x - 13 < 9$$

$$-2x \quad 22$$

$$x \quad -11$$

17. Is -15 a solution to the inequality in Question 16? Is 0? Is 15?

18. Graph the solution to Question 16 on a number line.

Solve each inequality in Questions 19–22.

19. $\dfrac{a}{4} \le 20$

20. $z - 4 > 10$

21. $-3b \le 60$

22. $x + 5 < 11$

For Questions 23–25, refer to the following: A marketing firm has been hired to make custom foam fingers. They charge a setup fee of $40 and then charge an additional $5 per foam finger.

23. Write an equation that describes the total cost for an order of x foam fingers.

24. Write the algebraic inequality needed to indicate that the cost for an order of foam fingers would be at most $150. Solve this inequality.

25. Explain the significance of the answer you found for Question 24.

26. In a 200-gallon tank, a farmer has 120 gallons of an insecticide and water solution that is 4% insecticide and 96% water. If he adds 30 gallons of pure water to this tank, what is the percentage of the new solution that is insecticide? What is the percentage of the new solution that is water?

27. Turns out the farmer in Question 26 wanted to get the concentration lower. If he started with the 120 gallons of 4% insecticide mixture in the 200-gallon tank, how many gallons of water would he need to add to get a mixture that is 3% insecticide? Set up and solve an equation to answer this question. Be sure to clearly define any variable used.

For Questions 28–32, assume $20 U.S. can be exchanged for 18.16 Euro.

28. How many Euros do you think you would receive in exchange for $0 U.S.?

29. Would you say that $y = mx + b$ or $y = kx$ would be an appropriate form for an equation that gives the number of Euros based on the number of U.S. dollars? Explain your reasoning.

30. Determine the equation that gives the number of Euros based on the number of U.S. dollars.

31. Use your equation and a calculator or spreadsheet to complete the table.

U.S. dollars	Euros
20	18.16
40	
60	
80	
100	

32. Use your equation to determine the number of Euros that you would receive in exchange for $500 U.S.

33. An appliance repair shop charges $50 for a house call. They charge an additional $30 per hour for labor. Write the equation of a line in slope-intercept form to model this situation. Explain the meaning of your independent and dependent variables.

34. Graph the equation you wrote in Question 33.

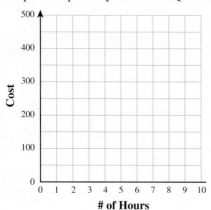

35. An airplane starts at an altitude of 36,000 ft and begins descending at a constant rate. Write the equation of a line in slope-intercept to model this situation. Explain the meaning of your independent and dependent variables.

Minutes	Altitude
0	36,000
5	28,500
10	21,000
15	13,500

36. Determine an equation of the line in slope-intercept form that passes through $(-4, 9)$ with a slope of -2.

37. Determine an equation of the line in point-slope form that passes through $(-2, 4)$ and $(-1, -3)$. Then write your equation in slope-intercept form.

Consider the following as you work Questions 38–43. A math teacher asked his students to keep track of the number of hours they spent doing homework for a particular unit of a math course. After the unit exam, the grade obtained by each student was recorded next to the amount of time that student spent doing homework. The results are displayed in the table.

Study Time	Exam Score
22	94
18	85
13	77
14	88
17	89
12	91
15	61
8	73
16	84
16	90
5	55
20	99

38. Determine the equation of the line of best fit for this data. Round all coefficients to 4 decimal places.

39. Determine the meaning of the slope of this equation.

40. Determine the meaning of the y intercept of this line.

41. Determine the value of the correlation coefficient r. What does this tell you about how closely the quantities are related?

42. Based on this equation, predict the exam score (rounded to the nearest whole number) if a student spends 18 hours doing homework for this unit.

43. Compute the residual for the point where the study time was 18 hours, and explain what it means.

44. A jet has a fuel tank containing 40,000 gallons of jet fuel when it takes off on an international flight at midnight. If the plane consumes 3,000 gallons of fuel per hour, determine the number of hours into the flight when the jet's fuel tank contains 4,000 gallons of jet fuel. Set up and solve an equation to answer this question.

45. Use part of the equation you wrote in Question 44 to create a graph and a table. Use the graph and the table to illustrate the solution to Question 44. Indicate where you would find the solution on the graph and in the table.

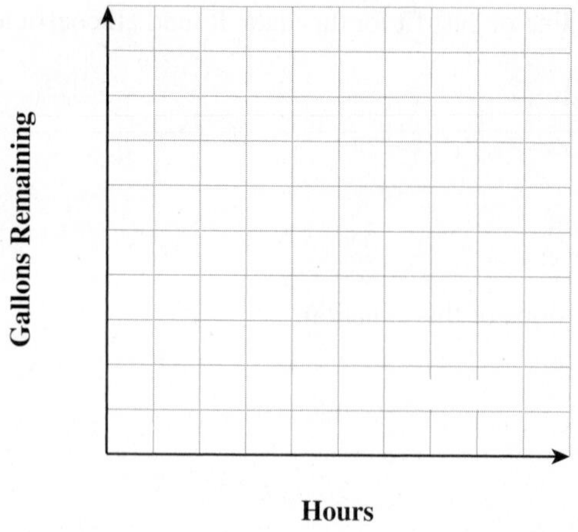

Hours	Gallons Remaining

Graph with y-axis labeled "Gallons Remaining" and x-axis labeled "Hours"

Paul works for an organization that prints a color newsletter. The organization is trying to decide whether to send the newsletter out for printing, or buy a color copier of its own. The local copy shop will print the newsletters for $0.35 per page. If the organization buys its own printer for $2,200, then it can print the newsletters itself for $0.13 per page.

46. Write equations for the cost C of each option.

47. Solve the system of equations you wrote in Question 46. Explain the significance of the solution for this system.

Unit 4
Living in a Nonlinear World

©Design Pics/Bilderbuch RF

Outline

Lesson 4-1   Prep Skills

SKILL 1: ADD OR SUBTRACT LIKE TERMS

In Lesson 1-2, we saw that quantities can only be added if they're like quantities, which means they're identical except possibly for the numeric part, which we call the **coefficient**. For example, $8n$ and $12n$ are like quantities because they're both just n without the 8 and the 12, while $8n$ and $12n^2$ are not like quantities because n and n^2 aren't identical.

When an expression has several pieces that are added or subtracted, the individual pieces are called **terms.** In this case, we use the phrase *like terms* rather than like quantities. Deciding which terms can be added or subtracted is an important part of simplifying algebraic expressions.

- $10k + 8 - 3k + 4$ $10k$ and $-3k$ are like terms; 8 and 4 are like terms
  $= 7k + 12$

- $4n - 7n^2 + 11n + 7 - 4n^2$ $4n$ and $11n$ are like terms; $-7n^2$ and $-4n^2$ are like terms
  $= 15n - 11n^2 + 7$

SKILL 2: DIVIDE TWO TERMS BY ONE TERM

When performing a division like $\frac{4 + 12}{2}$, begin by combining like terms in the numerator, then divide. But when the numerator has terms that can't be combined, as in $\frac{4n + 12}{2}$, that won't work.

Instead, to simplify the expression, we'll essentially do the OPPOSITE of adding fractions. Look at the fraction as the *answer* to an "adding fractions" problem: There are two terms added in the numerator, with a single denominator. As an addition problem, this would look like $\frac{4n}{2} + \frac{12}{2} = \frac{4n + 12}{2}$. To perform the division, we'll just do that process in reverse, breaking the original fraction into two separate fractions, each with the common denominator.

- $\dfrac{4n + 12}{2} = \dfrac{4n}{2} + \dfrac{12}{2}$ Now perform the two easier divisions
  $= 2n + 6$

PREP SKILLS QUESTIONS

1. Simplify each expression by combining like terms.

   a. $12x + 7 - 13 - 4x$ b. $4m^2 - 3m + 5 + 7m - 10m^2$ c. $4y + 7y^3 + 9$

2. Perform each division.

   a. $\dfrac{20x + 16}{4}$ b. $\dfrac{-12n - 96}{6}$

Lesson 4-1 Oh Yeah? Prove It!

LEARNING OBJECTIVES

☐ 1. Apply inductive reasoning to make a conjecture.

☐ 2. Disprove a conjecture by finding a counterexample.

☐ 3. Apply deductive reasoning to solve a problem.

©Pixtal/age Fotostock RF

When you have eliminated the impossible, whatever remains, however improbable, must be the truth.
– Sherlock Holmes

Here's a hypothetical situation: You're in an English literature course, and the prof reads a passage from a Shakespearean sonnet, then says "Clearly, Shakespeare was referring to the forthcoming rise of reality television when he wrote that passage." Would you (a) mumble "Wow, no kidding" and write his claim down in your notebook, or (b) respectfully disagree and challenge him to back up his claim? If you understand what getting an education is all about, you'll choose option b. Most students would. But for some reason, those same students will dutifully scribble down every formula and example a math professor puts on the board without ever questioning where it all comes from or why it makes sense. Today, we fight back! In this lesson we'll study two different types of reasoning used in math. Ultimately, what it's about is being able to think in a logical, orderly way. And what skill could possibly be more useful than that?

0. What do you think the word "reasoning" means?

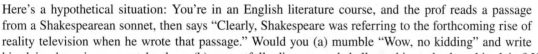

4-1 **Group**

©MCT/Getty Images

Each day that the United States Supreme Court is in session, the nine justices perform the traditional "conference handshake" that began during the late 19th century under Chief Justice Melville W. Fuller. Each justice shakes hands with all of the others to indicate that their differences of opinion won't prevent them from focusing on justice and a fair judicial process.

Here's a question to ponder: Just how many total handshakes are necessary? Will there be any time left over for things like doing their actual job? It's not such an easy question. So let's see if we can look at some simpler cases to give us some guidance.

1. How many handshakes would there be if there were just two justices?

We can illustrate the situation by drawing two dots, one for each justice, and connecting them with a line, ●———● which represents them shaking hands with each other.

You might think that drawing the diagram for two justices was silly, but it gives us an idea of how to figure out the number of handshakes for larger groups.

2. Connect each pair of dots with a line to indicate a handshake that will take place. Then count the number of lines (handshakes) for each group size.

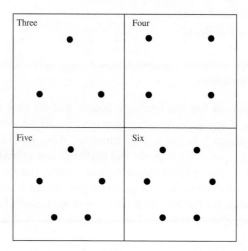

Inductive reasoning is the process of reaching a conclusion based on specific examples. After finding the number of handshakes for two through six justices, can we use those examples to draw a conclusion about how many are needed for all nine?

3. Fill in the table with the results you've already discovered, then see if you can use inductive reasoning to find a pattern and finish the rest of the table.

Number of Justices	Number of Handshakes
2	
3	
4	
5	
6	
7	
8	
9	

Did You Get It

Try this problem to see if you understand the concepts we just studied. The answer can be found at the end of the Portfolio section.

1. A polygon is a closed geometric figure with three or more sides, like a triangle, rectangle, pentagon, etc. Each point where two sides meet is called a vertex. A diagonal of a polygon is a line segment from one vertex to another that isn't one of the sides of the polygon. If you look at your drawings from Question 2, you'll see that a polygon with 3 sides has no diagonals, one with 4 sides has 2 diagonals, one with 5 sides has 5 diagonals, and one with 6 sides has 9 diagonals. Use inductive reasoning to make a prediction for the number of diagonals in polygons with 7, 8, 9, and 10 sides.

In Question 3, you made an educated guess about the number of handshakes necessary for nine justices using inductive reasoning. **Conjecture** is another name for an educated guess based on available evidence. Proving that a conjecture is true almost always involves more than inductive reasoning. For example, after watching a couple of races on TV, you might conjecture that all NASCAR drivers are men. In order to prove that conjecture, you would need to confirm the sex of every single driver in NASCAR; just watching a bunch of races won't prove anything conclusively.

Proving that a conjecture is false is much easier — all you need is a single example that violates the conjecture. If Danica Patrick drives in the next race you watch, she provides a **counterexample** that proves your conjecture was false.

In Questions 4–6, find a counterexample to prove that each conjecture is false.

4. Every time it rains, my softball game gets cancelled. Our game was cancelled last night.

   Conjecture: It must have rained last night.

   Counterexample:

5. Look at the equation $y = (x + 3)(x - 7)(2x - 1)$.

   a. Substitute -3 in for x and find the corresponding value for y.

   b. Repeat part a for $x = 7$.

   Conjecture: Any number substituted in for x will make $y = 0$.

   Counterexample:

6. These three right triangles are all isosceles.

   Conjecture: Every right triangle is an isosceles triangle.

   Counterexample:

> **Math Note**
>
> A triangle is **isosceles** when exactly two sides have the same length.

Did You Get It

2. Prove that each conjecture is false by finding a counterexample.

   a.   Every month of the year has at least four letters in its name.

   b.   No U.S. city is farther north than Toronto, Canada.

7. The numbers illustrated here are called **triangular numbers**. Use inductive reasoning to find the fifth and sixth triangular numbers. You can either draw diagrams or notice a pattern.

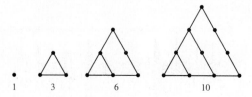

8. This pattern should look familiar. . . . If it doesn't, go back to page 458. Looking at the diagrams, can you think of a reason that the triangular numbers match the number of handshakes needed, starting with two people? Or do you think it's a coincidence?

9. The next triangle is called **Pascal's triangle** in honor of the 17th-century French mathematician Blaise Pascal. Even though it's relatively simple, it turns out to have a wide variety of applications in math. Use inductive reasoning to complete the 6th and 7th rows of the triangle.

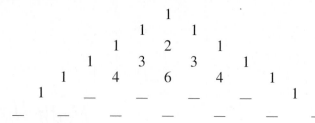

10. Here's a clever number trick. Pick any number you like, and multiply it by 8. Add 40, then divide by 4. Subtract 10 from the result, then subtract your original number. What do you get? Try some specific examples, and use inductive reasoning to make a conjecture as to what the result will always be.

4-1 Class

Now it's time to take a closer look at deductive reasoning. **Deductive reasoning** is the process of reasoning that arrives at a conclusion based on known rules or principles. Inductive reasoning is great for seeing patterns and making educated guesses about general results. For example, after completing Question 10 in the Group section, you're probably pretty darn sure that the result of the number trick is always the original number. But no matter how many different numbers you choose, you can't be 100% certain that it ALWAYS works that way unless you try every number in the world. Of course, that's impossible.

This is where deductive reasoning comes into play. Instead of looking at specific examples, we'll start with an **arbitrary number** and represent it with the letter n. By arbitrary, we mean a symbol that is able to represent ALL possible numbers. That's what makes using a variable so great: Since we want n to represent ANY number, we need it to be a number that can change. In other words, a variable!

1. Starting with a number n, multiply that number by 8.

2. Now add 40 to the result of Question 1.

3. Next, divide the result of Question 2 by 4. Be careful! Make sure you divide BOTH TERMS by 4.

4. Subtract 10 from the result of Question 3.

5. Now subtract the original number n. What is the result?

6. Describe why this is different from the specific calculations we did in the group activity, and why it PROVES that the result will ALWAYS be the original number.

Did You Get It

3. Try the procedure with a handful of numbers then make a conjecture as to what the result will always be. Then use deductive reasoning to prove your conjecture.

Take a number.
Double it.
Add 12.
Subtract 4.
Divide by 2.
Subtract your original number.

This is an example of deductive reasoning because we used a general calculation to draw a conclusion, not a handful of specific calculations. Let's see if we can use a similar approach to find a general formula that solves the handshake problem once and for all.

7. Pretend that you're one of the nine justices: How many people's hands do you need to shake?

8. Choose one other justice. How many hands does he or she need to shake?

9. If we number the justices from 1 through 9, this table shows how many hands each needs to shake.

Justice	1	2	3	4	5	6	7	8	9
Number of handshakes	8	8	8	8	8	8	8	8	8

This results in how many handshakes total? (Write as a multiplication.)

10. This result doesn't match the answer we got using inductive reasoning. Explain why this answer is twice as big as it should be. (Think about handshakes, not math!)

11. Conclusion: The number of handshakes needed for nine justices is $\frac{9 \times 8}{2}$. Write a general formula with variable n that would describe the number of handshakes needed for a group of n people. Then verify that your formula gives the values you found for the table on page 458.

Did You Get It

   4. Look back at the Did You Get It 1, where we studied the number of diagonals in a polygon. Write a formula with variable n (the number of sides) that describes the number of diagonals. (Hint: The formula we developed for the number of handshakes is a good starting point.) How does the number of diagonals differ from the total number of lines drawn in Question 2?

To wrap up our study of inductive and deductive reasoning, decide if the type of reasoning used in each example is inductive or deductive.

12. After failing the first two tests in math class, John decided that he better start doing the homework regularly.

13. Marlene was having a hard time keeping up with minimum payments on her credit card, so she started to make a budget to make sure she wouldn't spend more money than she was making.

14. In spite of his friends' pleas, Mark tried to drive home after drinking too much. None of them were surprised when he got busted for DUI.

15. My favorite professional team started off the new season 12–0, so I'm sure they're going to make the playoffs.

4-1 Portfolio

Name _____

Check each box when you've completed the task. Remember that your instructor will want you to turn in the portfolio pages you create.

Technology

1. ☐ Complete the following spreadsheet down to the row for 30 people. In the Group section, you noticed a pattern using inductive reasoning: Use that pattern to write formulas in column B. In the Class section, we developed a formula for the number of handshakes required. Use that formula in column E. A template to help you get started can be found in the online resources for this lesson.

	A	B	C	D	E
1	**Inductive Reasoning**			**Deductive Reasoning**	
2	Number of people (n)	Number of handshakes (H)		Number of people (n)	Number of handshakes (H)
3	2	1		2	
4	3	3		3	
5	4	6		4	
6	5			5	

Online Practice

1. ☐ Include any written work from the online assignment along with any notes or questions about this lesson's content.

Applications

1. ☐ Complete the applications problems.

Reflections

Type a short answer to each question.

1. ☐ Describe the difference between inductive and deductive reasoning.

2. ☐ Describe a time in your life that you used inductive reasoning, and one when you used deductive reasoning.

3. ☐ What's the point of a counterexample?

4. ☐ Name one thing you learned or discovered in this lesson that you found particularly interesting.

5. ☐ Do you have any questions about this lesson?

Looking Ahead

1. ☐ Complete the Prep Skills for Lesson 4-2.

2. ☐ Read the opening paragraph in Lesson 4-2 carefully and answer Question 0 in preparation for that lesson.

Answers to "Did You Get It?"

1. 7 sides has 14 diagonals, 8 sides has 20, 9 sides has 27, 10 sides has 35.

2. **a.** May has only 3 letters.

   b. The entire state of Alaska is well north of Toronto, as are many cities in the northern portion of the mainland U.S.

3. The answer is always 4. $\dfrac{2x + 12 - 4}{2} - x = \dfrac{2x + 8}{2} - x = \dfrac{2x}{2} + \dfrac{8}{2} - x = x + 4 - x = 4$

4. Subtract the number of sides from the total number of handshakes and you're left with the number of diagonals, so $\dfrac{n(n-1)}{2} - n$ will work.

Answers to "Prep Skills"

1. **a.** $8x - 6$ **b.** $-6m^2 + 4m + 5$ **c.** $7y^3 + 4y + 9$

2. **a.** $5x + 4$ **b.** $-2n - 16$

4-1 Applications

Name _____

In the Group section, we looked at triangular numbers. We can also define square numbers and pentagonal numbers.

1. Use inductive reasoning to find the fifth square number.

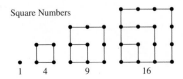

Square Numbers

2. Use inductive reasoning to find the fifth pentagonal number.

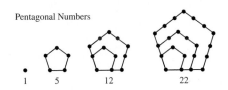

Pentagonal Numbers

3. A formula for the nth triangular number is $\frac{n}{2}(1n - (-1))$; this simplifies to $\frac{n(n+1)}{2}$.

 A formula for the nth square number is $\frac{n}{2}(2n - (0))$; this simplifies to n^2.

 A formula for the nth pentagonal number is $\frac{n}{2}(3n - (1))$; this doesn't simplify. Sigh.

 Using inductive reasoning, a formula for the nth hexagonal number is $\frac{n}{2}(\_n - (\_))$.

 (Hint: Look at the pattern in the missing numbers for the previous three formulas.)

4. Use the formulas from Question 3 to complete this table. Feel free to use a calculator, or (better still) a spreadsheet.

	Triangular Numbers	Square Numbers	Pentagonal Numbers	Hexagonal numbers
1st				
2nd				
3rd				
4th				
5th				
6th				
7th				

4-1   Applications

Name _____

In Questions 5 and 6, find a counterexample that shows the conjecture is false.

5. Conjecture: Every eight-legged creature is a spider.

6. Conjecture: No number with last digit zero can be divided evenly by 3.

In Questions 7–10, decide if inductive or deductive reasoning was used.

7. Charles Manson has been denied parole 12 times. Applying again would be a big waste of time.

8. In this state, to be a nurse you need at least a two-year degree. So when I was in the emergency room after an accident, I asked the super-cute nurse where she went to college.

9. We got four inches of spring snow last night, so instead of the softball game I had scheduled, I'll make other plans.

10. Last night while playing blackjack, the dealer's first card was an ace four times in a row. So I really couldn't believe it when it happened again on the next hand.

Lesson 4-2   Prep Skills

SKILL 1: COMPUTE OR APPROXIMATE SQUARE ROOTS

A square root of a positive number a is a number you have to square to get a back. For example, since 7^2 is 49, 7 is a square root of 49. Here's another way to think of it: If you're my square, I'm your square root. Notice that $(-7)^2$ is also 49, so -7 is a square root of 49, too. In fact, every positive number has two square roots, one positive and one negative. The symbol $\sqrt{}$ is used to represent the *positive* square root of the number enclosed by the symbol. So we would write $\sqrt{49} = 7$.

- $\sqrt{25} = 5$ because $5^2 = 25$
- $\sqrt{144} = 12$ because $12^2 = 144$

Each of 49, 25, and 144 are called **perfect squares** because each is the square of a whole number. When numbers get larger, it can be really hard to tell if a number is a perfect square, and really hard to compute square roots mentally. In that case, a calculator becomes an essential tool. Scientific calculators (nongraphing) have a $\sqrt{}$ key: You enter the number you want the square root of, then hit the square root key. On many graphing calculators, you'll press 2nd then x^2 to get the root symbol, then key in the number and press ENTER.

- $\sqrt{841} = 29$

If the number we're finding the square root of isn't a perfect square, the decimal equivalent of the square root will always have infinitely many digits. Since you can't write all the digits, you'll have to round at some point, turning the decimal equivalent into a decimal approximation. This is another situation where a calculator (or spreadsheet, using the "= SQRT( )" command) is pretty much essential.

- $\sqrt{8} \approx 2.83$

- $\sqrt{1{,}243} \approx 35.3$

SKILL 2: FIND DISTANCE ON A GRAPH

When two points on a graph have the same y coordinate, it means they live at the same height. In this case you can find the distance between them by just finding the difference of their x coordinates.

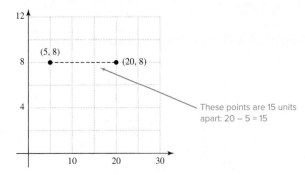

These points are 15 units apart: $20 - 5 = 15$

When two points on a graph have the same *x* coordinate, it means they live on the same vertical line. In this case you can find the distance between them by just finding the difference of their *y* coordinates.

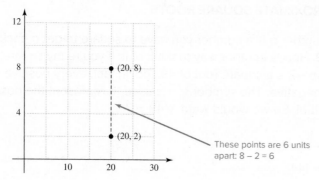

These points are 6 units apart: 8 − 2 = 6

SKILL 3: SET UP AND SOLVE A PROPORTION

In the applications for this lesson you'll set up a proportion to find the size of something that we have a scale model for. We did this in Lesson 3-6 (the famous Dave Sobecki bobblehead problem). The procedure is based on writing a ratio that compares the size of the model to the size of the actual object on both sides of an equation.

- On a map, 1 inch corresponds to 1,000 feet. How far apart are two buildings that are $4\frac{1}{4}$ in. apart on the map?

$$\frac{\text{Map distance}}{\text{Real distance}}: \quad \frac{1 \text{ in.}}{1{,}000 \text{ ft}} = \frac{4\frac{1}{4}\text{in.}}{x \text{ ft}} \quad \Rightarrow \quad x = 1{,}000 \times 4\frac{1}{4} = 4{,}250 \text{ ft}$$

PREP SKILLS QUESTIONS

1. Compute the square root exactly without using a calculator or spreadsheet.

   a. 16   b. 36   c. 100

2. Compute the square root exactly using a calculator or spreadsheet.

   a. $\sqrt{289}$ b. $\sqrt{961}$ c. $\sqrt{12{,}769}$

3. Approximate the square root to two decimal places using a calculator or spreadsheet.

   a. $\sqrt{14}$ b. $\sqrt{140}$ c. $\sqrt{1{,}107}$

4. Find the distance between points *A* and *B*, and between points *B* and *C*.

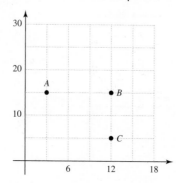

5. While on vacation last year, my wife and I bought a scale model of the space needle in Seattle. The model is 5 in. tall, and the actual building is 605 ft tall. How tall would a model of the Statue of Liberty (305 ft) be at this scale? Round to the nearest hundredth.

Lesson 4-2   **A Road Map to Success**

LEARNING OBJECTIVES

☐ 1. Solve application problems using the Pythagorean Theorem.

☐ 2. Solve application problems involving the distance formula.

©Ilene MacDonald/Alamy RF

Map out your future, but do it in pencil. The road ahead is as long as you make it.
        —Jon Bon Jovi

While a road map to success is a useful metaphor, in this lesson we'll study a particular type of map that will help us to introduce some key ideas in geometry. When you're looking at a road map, it's very much like looking straight down from a plane, and the roads all look two-dimensional. But of course, we live in a three-dimensional world, and what you're missing is the change in height. Because of this, the actual distance you'd drive on a road isn't always the distance you'd measure on a map. We'll use the change in height for roads to learn about two important results used to study our physical world: the Pythagorean theorem and the distance formula.

0. What do you think the sign in the picture means?

4-2   Class

The road sign above describes a mountain road with a grade of 8%. This is a warning that the road is steep enough to require some extra caution, but what exactly does it mean? The slope of a road is very much like the slope of a line: It's a comparison between how far the road goes up or down for a certain horizontal distance. A grade of 8% means that for any horizontal distance, the change in height is 8% of that distance.

1. What's the change in elevation over a 1-mile horizontal stretch for a road with a 8% grade? Fill in that change in height on the diagram. Why did we write 1 mile as 5,280 feet on the diagram?

5,280 ft

Did You Get It?

Try this problem to see if you understand the concepts we just studied. The answer can be found at the end of the Portfolio section.

1. The steepest road in America is Canton Avenue in Pittsburgh, with a 37% grade. To be fair, it's only that steep for about 25 feet, but whatever. If the road was that steep for a full mile, what would be the elevation change in feet?

The diagram now illustrates the situation we described in the lesson opener: The horizontal distance (5,280 feet) would appear on a map of the road, but the slanted line at the top of the triangle represents the road. So the actual distance you drive is the length of that slanted side, which we don't know based on the horizontal distance and the change in height.

Fortunately, there's a very old and very famous result from geometry that will allow us to find the actual driving distance: the Pythagorean theorem. This provides a mathematical relationship between the lengths of sides in a triangle when two of the sides are perpendicular. In the following diagram, we'll call the lengths of the three sides *a, b,* and *c*. The little square at one of the angles indicates that those two sides are perpendicular: We call that angle a **right angle**, and the triangle a **right triangle**.

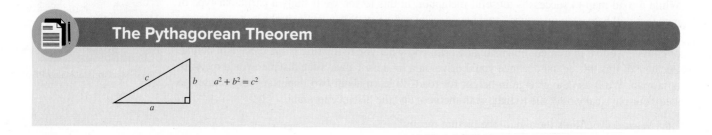

The Pythagorean Theorem

$$a^2 + b^2 = c^2$$

In words, the Pythagorean theorem says that if you square the lengths of the two shorter sides in a right triangle and add the results, you'll get the square of the length of the longest side. The longest side is called the **hypotenuse**, and it's always across from the right angle.

In using the Pythagorean theorem, we're going to work with square roots quite a lot. It turns out that approximation plays a really important role when dealing with roots. For example, we know that $\sqrt{49} = 7$ because $7^2 = 49$. But what is $\sqrt{47}$? Since 47 is a little bit less than 49, it seems reasonable to estimate that $\sqrt{47}$ is a bit less than 7. But how much?

To get more accurate (but still approximate) values for square roots, we can use a calculator or a spreadsheet.

Using Technology: Approximating Square Roots

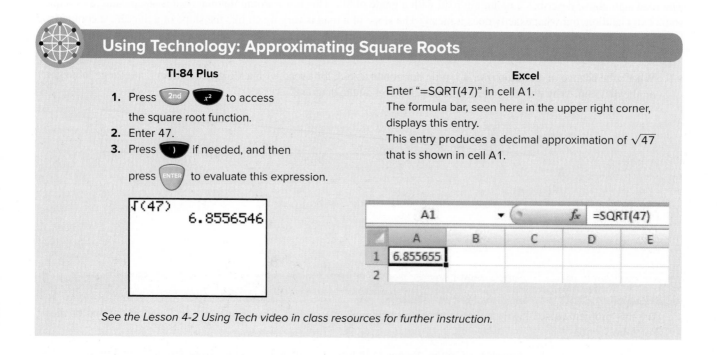

TI-84 Plus

1. Press [2nd] [x^2] to access the square root function.
2. Enter 47.
3. Press [ )] if needed, and then press [ENTER] to evaluate this expression.

√(47)
     6.8556546

Excel

Enter "=SQRT(47)" in cell A1.
The formula bar, seen here in the upper right corner, displays this entry.
This entry produces a decimal approximation of $\sqrt{47}$ that is shown in cell A1.

A1		f_x	=SQRT(47)

	A	B	C	D	E
1	6.855655				
2					

See the Lesson 4-2 Using Tech video in class resources for further instruction.

2. Complete the following table of common square roots.

Fill in the correct value to make each equation true. No calculators!		Estimate each square root to the nearest whole number and fill in the relationship between the square root and your estimate with either < or >.	Use a calculator or a spreadsheet to approximate the following square roots to the nearest hundredth.
$\sqrt{1} = 1$	$\sqrt{64} = 8$	$\sqrt{11}$	$\sqrt{11} \approx$
$\sqrt{4} = 2$	$\sqrt{81} =$		
$\sqrt{} = 3$	$\sqrt{100} = 10$	$\sqrt{78}$	$\sqrt{78} \approx$
$\sqrt{16} = 4$	$\sqrt{121} =$		
$\sqrt{25} = 5$	$\sqrt{} = 12$	$\sqrt{99}$	$\sqrt{99} \approx$
$\sqrt{} = 6$	$\sqrt{169} =$		
$\sqrt{49} =$	$\sqrt{196} =$	$\sqrt{124}$	$\sqrt{124} \approx$
	$\sqrt{} = 15$		

Let's look at how we can use the Pythagorean theorem to study grade.

3. Notice that the diagram on page 471 is a right triangle. Use the Pythagorean theorem to write an equation involving the length of the missing side of the triangle. Then simplify the side with only numbers on it.

Math Note

There are actually two numbers that make the equation $c^2 = 28{,}056{,}821.76$ true: 5,296.9 and −5,296.9. But in this setting, c is a physical distance, so we ignore the negative solution in Question 4.

4. In order to solve your equation to find the missing length, you'll need to "undo" the square: This is exactly what square roots are designed to do. So apply a square root to both sides to find the missing length.

5. How much farther would you drive on that road than the 1 mile that would appear on a map?

Did You Get It?

2. Waipio Road in Hawaii is actually steeper than the road described in Did You Get It 1 (at least in some stretches), but access is restricted to four-wheel-drive vehicles and people on foot, so most don't count it as a legitimate road. According to Fixr.com, this road goes up 800 feet in a horizontal span of 3,170 feet. How far does a hiker cover in walking that span?

4-2 Group

1. Suppose that we know that the distance between points A and B is exactly five miles. If the contour of the road followed the solid path in each of the three figures below, would the distance traveled by the car be more than, less than, or equal to five miles?

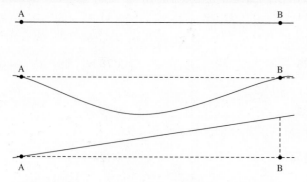

Contour maps might remind you of the isotherm maps we learned about back in Lesson 2-5. But instead of the lines representing locations that have the same temperature, the lines represent locations that have the same altitude. This is a way to overcome the two-dimensional nature of maps, allowing us to see both straight-line distance from above, and changes in height as well. The top part of the next diagram is the contour map; under the map is an illustration of a side view that shows what the elevations look like based on the map.

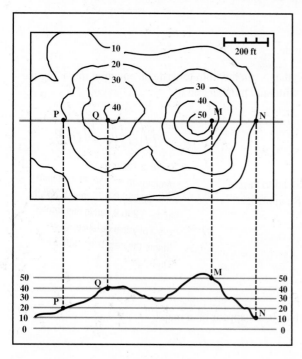

2. How does the distance between points P and Q compare to the distance between points M and N on the map? Use the scale on the map.

3. The lower illustration also shows points P, Q, M, and N, but this time the elevations are shown as well. How does the actual hiking distance from P to Q compare to the hiking distance from M to N? What can you conclude about apparent distance on a contour map?

4. Based on the scale provided on the two-dimensional contour map, the distances from P to Q and from M to N are both about 200 feet. Use the lower illustration to estimate the actual trail length between points P and Q, making sure to describe how you got that estimate. Then repeat for the trail between points M and N.

5. Illustrate the grade of each trail by drawing a right triangle.

6. Use the Pythagorean theorem to estimate the true length of each trail.

7. The road sign at the beginning of this lesson is from a road with an 8% grade for a horizontal span of 8 miles. By how much does the elevation change over that 8-mile span?

8. How far would you actually drive in covering that 8-mile span?

Before selling his house, Brian needs to remove a dead mouse that got trapped under the bathtub. (Clearly, "includes a deceased animal" is not a feature buyers are looking for.) Using the corner of the room as the origin, and using a patented, high-tech rodent corpse location device, he was able to determine that the mouse was located at coordinates $(4, -2)$. An access panel under the sink is located at coordinates $(1, -5)$. Assuming that the units are feet, the goal is to find the distance from the access panel to the mouse.

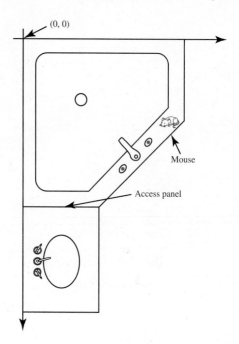

9. Estimate the distance by plotting the two given points on the graph below. If you're creative, you can use a group member's page with the same grid as a ruler to make a good estimate.

10. Using your plot from Question 9, use the Pythagorean theorem to find the exact distance, first in exact form (which will have a square root in it), then in decimal form rounded to the nearest tenth of a foot.

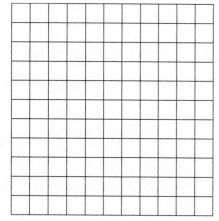

4-2 Class (Again)

The process used to find the distance from the access panel to the mouse in Group Questions 9–10 can be mimicked to develop a generic formula for finding the distance between any two points on a graph. Let's start with two arbitrary points, labeled (x_1, y_1) and (x_2, y_2). Since we're not labeling specific number coordinates, but using symbols, these points can represent ANY pair of points.

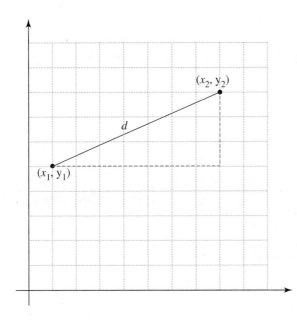

1. What are the coordinates of the point where the two dotted lines meet to form a right angle? (Hint: That point is at the same height as (x_1, y_1) and lives directly below (x_2, y_2).)

2. Use your answer to Question 1 to find the length of the two dotted sides of the right triangle, then label those lengths on the diagram. Taking another look at the mouse problem calculation might help.

3. Use the Pythagorean theorem to set up an equation containing the distance d that we're looking for. (Hint: Putting parentheses around the expression you wrote for the lengths in Question 2 is a good idea.)

4. Solve the equation to find a formula for the distance between any two points.

Math Note

Even though the diagram we're using is in the first quadrant, the fact that we used arbitrary points means that our formula will work for any two points. It also doesn't matter which point you call (x_1, y_1) and which you call (x_2, y_2).

The Distance Formula

The distance between any two points (x_1, y_1) and (x_2, y_2) can be found using the formula:

$$d = \sqrt{(x_2 - x_1)^2 + (y_2 - y_1)^2}$$

5. A map of a national park has a grid on it to help reference locations. The camping office is located at the point $(-5, 10)$ on the grid, and the lodge is at $(2,4)$. Each square on the grid represents a distance of two miles. Use your formula from Question 4 to find the distance from the camping office to the lodge.

Did You Get It?

3. Grids are often used at crime scenes to help in locating evidence, and to document exactly where any evidence was located. At one crime scene, two shell casings were found: one at coordinates $(3, 12)$ and another at coordinates $(-5, 6)$. Each square on the grid represents 3 feet. How far apart were the two shell casings?

4-2 | Portfolio

Name _____

Check each box when you've completed the task. Remember that your instructor will want you to turn in the portfolio pages you create.

Online Practice

1. ☐ Include any written work from the online assignment along with any notes or questions about this lesson's content.

Applications

1. ☐ Complete the applications problems.

Reflections

Type a short answer to each question.

1. ☐ What does the Pythagorean theorem say? When can you use it?

2. ☐ Why can't you just find the distance between two points by plotting them on a grid, then counting the number of boxes between them?

3. ☐ Name one thing you learned or discovered in this lesson that you found particularly interesting.

4. ☐ What questions do you have about this lesson?

Looking Ahead

1. ☐ Complete the Prep Skills for Lesson 4-3.

2. ☐ Read the opening paragraph in Lesson 4-3 carefully and answer Question 0 in preparation for that lesson.

Answers to "Did You Get It?"

1. 1,953.6 ft   2. 3,269.4 ft   3. 30 ft

Answers to "Prep Skills"

1. **a.** 4   **b.** 6   **c.** 10

2. **a.** 17   **b.** 31   **c.** 113

3. **a.** 3.74   **b.** 11.83   **c.** 33.27

4. Distance between A and B: 9

    Distance between B and C: 10

5. About 2.52 inches tall

4-2   Applications

Name _____

Questions 1–3 are based on the contour map provided, which is of Mount St. Helens in Washington. All elevations on the contour lines are given in meters.

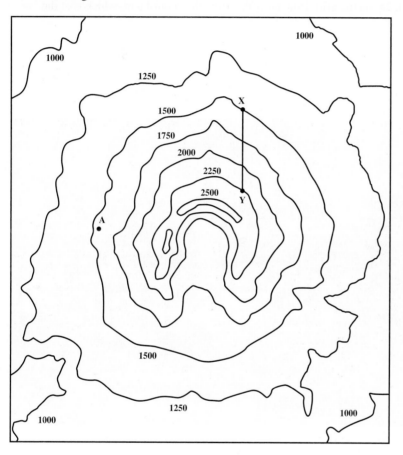

Source: John Pallister/USGS

1. Estimate the elevation of point A.

2. If points X and Y are 5,100 m apart looking straight down at the map, find the grade of a trail that connects those two points. (Hint: Find the change in elevation first.)

3. How far would you walk along the trail from point X to point Y? Assume that the elevation changes in a straight line. Round to the nearest tenth of a meter, then convert the distance to feet and miles.

4-2   Applications

Name _____

4. An archaeological dig is marked with a rectangular grid where each square is 5 feet on a side. An important artifact is discovered at the point corresponding to (−50, 25) on the grid. How far is this from the control tent, which is at the point (20, 30)?

Courtesy of Dave Sobecki

I took this photo from the deck of a cruise ship in the harbor just west of downtown Seattle. The road jumped out at me because it looks just like the diagrams we often draw to illustrate slope and grade, and I figured I'd be able to use it for a problem at some point. Well, here's that point.

5. Using proprietary software hacked from the NSA, I was able to tremendously enlarge a second photo that shows more of the bridge without losing any clarity. This allowed me to identify the make and model of every vehicle on the bridge to identify their lengths. (Okay, that's not true — I used Adobe Fireworks to measure the cars in pixels, and looked up the length of an average passenger car. It just sounded cooler the other way.)

In any case, the average car is 14 feet long, and the average length of the cars I could measure on the bridge was 34.4 pixels. The length of the bridge is 2,709 pixels. How long is that span in feet? (Hint: Set up a proportion that compares photo length in pixels to actual length in feet for cars on one side of the equation, and the bridge on the other.)

4-2 Applications

Name _____

6. I was also able to use my software (allegedly) to find that the change in vertical height when driving the length of the bridge is 89.6 feet. What horizontal distance do you cover when driving the bridge?

7. If the highway department put up a sign on each side of the bridge warning that the grade is 8%, how accurate would that be? Compute and discuss.

Lesson 4-3   **Prep Skills**

SKILL 1: FIND THE ANGLES FOR A SECTOR IN A PIE CHART

We studied pie charts a million years ago, way back in Lesson 1-1. The information needed to build a pie chart is percentages: the percentage of the full circle corresponding to each sector. A full circle measures 360°, so to find the angle we need we multiply the given percentage (in decimal form) by 360°.

- In a July 29 Gallup poll, 38% approved of the president's handling of the office, 57% disapproved, and 5% had no opinion. To build a pie chart for this survey you would need:

  $0.38 \times 360° = 136.8°$

  $0.57 \times 360° = 205.2°$

  $0.05 \times 360° = 18°$

SKILL 2: APPROXIMATE QUANTITIES INVOLVING SQUARE ROOTS

When a number is a perfect square, like 25, its square root is a whole number (5 in this case). But if a number isn't a perfect square, it turns out that it's impossible to write an exact decimal form because there will be infinitely many digits. In that case, the best you can do is an approximation, and for that we'll almost always use a calculator or spreadsheet. If you're using a graphing calculator, you'll push 2nd, then x^2 to get the square root feature, then key in the number you're finding the square root of and hit Enter. When using a spreadsheet, pick any cell and enter **=SQRT**(number you're computing the square root of)

- $\sqrt{39} \approx 6.24$

- $\sqrt{1,104} \approx 33.23$

- $\sqrt{-18}$ is not a real number because there's no real number whose square is negative.

SKILL 3: SQUARE A RADICAL EXPRESSION

In some sense, the whole point of square roots is that they're the opposite of squares. So if you take any non-negative number, apply a square root, and then square the result, you get right back where you started.

- $(\sqrt{3})^2 = 3$

- $(\sqrt{n+5})^2 = n + 5$ as long as we know that $n + 5$ isn't negative

In short, it doesn't make any difference what the stuff inside the square root is (as long as it isn't negative): If you compute the square of a square root expression, that simply eliminates the square root and you're left with the expression that was inside the radical.

SKILL 4: SOLVE AN EQUATION WITH THE VARIABLE IN THE DENOMINATOR

Students have a tendency to kind of freak out and do some strange things when they need to solve equations that contain fractions. But the truth is that you never actually have to solve equations with fractions, because with one simple step you can always eliminate the fractions and turn an equation with fractions into an easier one without fractions.

And what is this brilliant step? Multiplying both sides by a common denominator for all fractions involved. I promise that this will get rid of all fractions.

- $\dfrac{12}{x} = 8$ Common denominator is x: Multiply both sides by x

  $x \cdot \dfrac{12}{x} = 8 \cdot x$ Simplify left side: $x/x = 1$

  $12 = 8x$ Divide both sides by 8

  $x = \dfrac{12}{8} = \dfrac{3}{2}$

PREP SKILLS QUESTIONS

1. In a pie chart, one sector represents a data value that's 47% of a whole. Find the angle that sector covers in the pie chart.

2. Use a calculator to find an approximate value for $\sqrt{18.4}$. Round to two decimal places.

3. Use a calculator to find an approximate value for $\sqrt{\dfrac{0.4(1 - 0.4)}{800}}$. Round to two decimal places.

4. Find the square of $\sqrt{\dfrac{12}{n}}$. You can assume that n represents a positive number.

5. Solve the equation: $\dfrac{36}{n} = 4$

6. Solve the equation: $\dfrac{0.027}{n} = 3.5$

Lesson 4-3   The Error of Your Ways

LEARNING OBJECTIVES

☐ 1. Determine the margin of error in a given poll.

☐ 2. Explain the meaning of the margin of error in a given poll.

☐ 3. Calculate the number of poll respondents needed for a given margin of error.

Courtesy of Dave Sobecki

Better to trust the man who is frequently in error than the one who is never in doubt.

　　　　　　　　　　—Eric Sevareid

Do you know what percentage of Americans think that Bigfoot exists? Me neither. But I bet you can find that information online somewhere. In our information society, it seems like there's a poll for everything, from approval of the president to favorite type of underwear. And since so much information is provided to citizens and consumers in the form of polls, an understanding of how polls operate has become a pretty important survival skill. In this lesson, we'll study a key aspect of interpreting the results of a poll, the margin of error. And we'll find out that understanding error in polls can prevent errors in judgment.

0. When a poll says that a certain percentage of college students feels a certain way on a subject, how do you think they determine that?

4-3 ▐ Group

Polling has become big business, and two of the biggest names in that business are Gallup and Pollster. One of the more widely quoted polls they run is used to determine the president's current approval rating among citizens. But of course, they can't ask everyone in the country every week whether they approve or disapprove of the president's performance, so instead they ask a sample of citizens and use sampling and statistical techniques to try to decide if the results are truly indicative of the general population.

1. Go to the website www.pollster.com, then find the link for the presidential approval survey and click on it. What is the president's most current approval rating? Write a couple of sentences explaining what that means.

2. How do you think the approval rating was calculated? Be specific. Make sure your answer contains both of these key words: "population" and "sample."

3. Draw a pie chart describing the most current approval rating. Your chart should have three sectors.

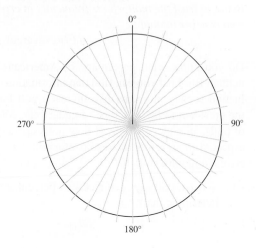

4. How would you describe the trend in approval rating over the last six months?

5. Scroll down a bit and find the first link to the Gallup survey and click on it. You'll see an approval rating and a brief description of how the poll was conducted, including a line that says "Margin of error," followed by something like "±3 percentage points." What do you think the term "margin of error" means in this context?

6. Can you think of another situation in life, school, or work where you've heard either "margin of error" or "margin for error"? Describe.

7. What do you think is better to have, a small margin of error or a big one? Why? Does it depend on the situation?

Did You Get It

Try this problem to see if you understand the concepts we just studied. The answer can be found at the end of the Portfolio section.

1. Back at the Pollster website, find and click on a link for "Congress Job Approval."
   a. What is the approval rating for Congress?
   b. What's the margin of error?
   c. Compare the approval rating to the one for the president and discuss what you think that says.

4-3 **Class**

Because it's not possible to poll every individual all the time to ask their opinions, sampling plays a really important role in polling. As you know, sampling is the process of choosing a portion of a population in such a way that the individuals chosen are in some way representative of an entire population. The downside of sampling is that it introduces uncertainty in the results of a poll, since to some extent the pollster is making an educated guess.

> The **margin of error** for a poll is a statistical measure that provides a range of values that the true outcome of the poll is likely to be inside. A margin of error of 5% means that the true value of the statistic reported by the poll is likely to be within 5% of the reported value.

Let's look at an example. If someone reports that 84% of Americans like pizza (which sounds awfully low to me, by the way), and the margin of error is ±3%, this means they're confident that the actual percentage of Americans that like pizza is some-where between 81% and 87% (since those are the percentages that are within 3% of 84.)

Here's the catch: How confident is confident? For margins of error, confidence is measured as a percentage. One way of computing margin of error is with a 95% confidence level. In our example above, a 95% confidence level would mean that the polling institution is 95% sure that the accurate percentage of Americans that like pizza is between 81% and 87%.

1. Take another look at the Gallup presidential approval rating, and find the margin of error. Then describe exactly what the poll result means, referring to both the approval rating and the margin of error.

2. An Associated Press poll indicated that 63% of teachers below college level feel like the amount of homework students get is not excessive. The poll had a margin of error of ±3.5% with a 95% confidence level. Write a sentence or two explaining what that result means.

A formula for computing margin of error is provided in the colored box. Sadly, it means absolutely nothing until you know what all of the symbols stand for, which is why you should read everything in the colored box.

Computing Margin of Error

When n people are polled, and $\hat{p}$ give a particular response, the margin of error with a 95% confidence level is given by the formula

$$\text{Margin of Error} = 2\sqrt{\frac{\hat{p}(1 - \hat{p})}{n}}$$

Note that both the margin of error and $\hat{p}$ (which is often called the **sample proportion**) are percentages written in decimal form. The symbol $\hat{p}$ is usually read "p hat."

The margin of error means that if this poll were conducted many times, we would expect that at least 95% of the time the actual percentage of the entire population that would give a particular response is somewhere between $\hat{p}$ − the margin of error and $\hat{p}$ + the margin of error.

3. On December 18, 2015, an organization called Public Policy Polling released the results of a poll with 532 responses. Of those respondents, 181 supported one particular candidate for the presidency in 2016. Among those folks, 41% were in favor of bombing Agrabah, which as it turns out is the fictional country from the Disney movie *Aladdin*. Use the formula in the colored box to find the margin of error for this reported percentage.

©Marka/Alamy

4. Write a sentence describing exactly what your answer to Question 3 tells us about all American voters who supported that candidate. More detail is always better.

5. Among all respondents to the survey, 30% supported bombing a cartoon country, and Public Policy Polling reported a margin of error of 4.3%. Does that number match what you get from the formula above?

Did You Get It

2. A *Wall Street Journal* poll conducted in December 2014 asked 1,000 adult Americans if they or a family member had ever been notified by a credit card company of a possible data breach involving their personal information. Forty-five percent reported that they had been notified. Use the formula in the colored box to find the margin of error for this result, then describe what the poll tells us.

6. For this question, don't look at the margin of error formula. Seriously, no peeking or I'll know. Based on what margin of error measures, do you think the margin of error for a poll should go up or down as the number of people surveyed gets larger? Justify your answer.

7. Now look at the margin of error formula. Based strictly on that formula, what should happen to the size of the margin of error if the number of people surveyed gets larger? Does this match your answer to Question 6? Explain.

8. What if the folks from Public Policy Polling who conducted the Agrabah poll got a little bit lazy, and decided to only survey 100 people, then go bowling. Recalculate the margin of error for the overall poll. Did it get bigger or smaller?

While it's absolutely fine and dandy to calculate the margin of error after conducting a poll, in many cases it's more useful to think about what the margin of error might be like BEFORE you're done sampling. This would allow you to decide how many people need to be surveyed in order to make your result reliable.

Suppose that you begin surveying students on your campus about their attitudes on race relations in the United States. After 70 surveys are returned, you find that 32% of respondents think that race relations are a serious problem facing our society.

9. What is the margin of error at that point in the survey?

10. If you decide that you'll only consider your survey a success if the margin of error is at most 4%, it would be perfectly reasonable to want to know how many more people you'd have to survey. Assuming that the result holds at 32%, set up the margin of error formula with a 4% margin of error, a 32% sample proportion, and variable n representing the number of people surveyed. (Remember, percentages need to be written in decimal form.)

In order to find the sample size needed to get that 4% margin of error, we'd need to be able to solve the equation you wrote in Question 10 for n. There are two issues to address: First, the quantity we want to solve for is inside a square root, and second, it's in the denominator of a fraction.

Let's begin by eliminating the radical. To accomplish this, we can square both sides of the equation, because we know that squaring a square root eliminates the radical. But first, it's helpful to rearrange so that the square root is the only thing on one side of the equation.

11. Starting with the equation $0.04 = 2\sqrt{\dfrac{(0.32)(0.68)}{n}}$ (Aw man, I just gave away the answer to the last question . . .), divide both sides by 2 to isolate the radical.

12. Now square both sides of the equation.

13. Keeping in mind that the goal is to solve for *n*, what can we do to BOTH SIDES of the equation in order to get *n* out of the denominator? Explain what we can do, then, you know, do it.

14. Now you should be able to solve for *n*, so write how many MORE PEOPLE you'd need to survey to get that 4% margin of error we were shooting for.

> ## Math Note
> Remember, *n* represents the MINIMUM number of people that would be needed to get a particular margin of error. So if *n* doesn't work out to be a whole number, you'll need to round UP to the next whole number.

15. Do you find that number surprising? Discuss.

Did You Get It

3. Preliminary results of a survey show that 11% of Americans lack health insurance. How many people need to be surveyed in order to have a margin of error of 2%?

16. Now let's go back to the presidential poll we started this lesson with. Use the approval rating you discovered, along with the margin of error, to find the number of people that were polled. Now look again at the description of the poll. How does your result compare to the number of people that were actually surveyed? What do you think accounts for any discrepancy?

17. Suppose that the result of a public opinion poll shows that just 9% of people would be willing to give up their cell phone for one week in exchange for $100. How many people would need to be surveyed in order to have a margin of error of ±2%?

©Hero/Corbis/Glow Images RF

18. Repeat Question 17, but this time for a poll where 50% of respondents say they'd be willing to give up their phone for a week. How does this affect the number of responses needed to get the 2% margin of error?

Math Note

Remember, the formula we're using provides 95% confidence in our margin of error. For other confidence levels, the coefficient in front of the root changes.

19. Bonus Question: Look carefully at the margin of error formula. What about it, mathematically, makes your conclusion from Question 18 make perfect sense? Detailed explanation if you want bonus points!

20. Now design your own problem. Find a survey online that interests you, and using the result and the reported margin of error, calculate the number of respondents.

4-3 Portfolio

Name _____

Check each box when you've completed the task. Remember that your instructor will want you to turn in the portfolio pages you create.

Technology

1. ☐ Find an article on either Gallup.com or Pollster.com that has the term "margin of error" in it, and briefly explain what that means in the context of that particular poll.
2. ☐ As we saw in this lesson, being able to find the number of people that are needed to get an acceptable margin of error is really useful. Build a spreadsheet like the one here that uses a formula to compute the value of n needed to achieve a certain margin of error given a value of $\hat{p}$. (Hint: You'll need to solve the equation that computes margin of error for n. Questions 10–14 in the Class portion will be a big help.)

	A	B	C
1	p	Margin of error	n
2	0.32	0.01	8704
3	0.32	0.02	2176
4	0.32	0.03	967
5	0.32	0.04	544

Online Practice

1. ☐ Include any written work from the online assignment along with any notes or questions about this lesson's content.

Applications

1. ☐ Complete the Applications problems.

Reflections

Type a short answer to each question.

1. ☐ What is the margin of error for a poll? When is it used, and why?
2. ☐ Describe how being familiar with margin of error might help you in the future.
3. ☐ Name one thing you learned or discovered in this lesson that you found particularly interesting.
4. ☐ What questions do you have about this lesson?

Looking Ahead

1. ☐ Complete the Prep Skills for Lesson 4-4.

2. ☐ Read the opening paragraph in Lesson 4-4 carefully and answer Question 0 in preparation for that lesson.

Answers to "Did You Get It?"

1. Answers vary depending on recent poll numbers.   2. 3.1%; Descriptions vary.
3. 979 people

Answers to "Prep Skills"

1. 169.2°   2. 4.29   3. 0.02   4. $\dfrac{12}{n}$ 5. $n = 9$ 6. $n \approx 0.008$

4-3 | Applications

Name _____

A stats class was interested in determining the percentage of students on their campus who are opposed to a new policy eliminating all paper books from the campus bookstore in favor of eBooks. After surveying 90 students, the class finds that 33% are opposed to the policy.

1. Calculate the margin of error for this survey. Round the percentage to one decimal place.

©Fancy/Veer/Corbis/Glow Images RF

2. Write a sentence or two describing exactly what your answer to Question 1 tells you about the percentage of the overall student body that is opposed to the policy.

3. The class conducting the poll was unhappy with the margin of error (as well they should be), so they decide to survey another 90 students. With the additional data, the percentage of students opposed to the policy goes up to 35%. What's the margin of error now?

4. If surveying more students keeps the percentage at 35%, how many more would need to be surveyed in order to be 95% confident that the correct percentage for the entire student body is between 32% and 38%? Don't forget to consider the number of students that had already been surveyed. (Hint: What would the margin of error be in this case?)

4-3 Applications

Name _____

You may have noticed that the margin of error formula only factors in the *sample* size, not the *population* size. If you think about it, this sounds kind of fishy: If you survey 30 members of a club out of a population of 40, you'd expect your results to be much more reliable than if you survey 30 people out of the entire U.S. population of 325 million. But the margin of error formula would treat both polls the same.

It turns out that the margin of error formula we've been using works consistently well as long as the sample surveyed is less than 5% of the overall population. In cases where the sample is larger than 5% of the population, we would want to adjust the margin of error to reflect the fact that we're actually polling a large sample relative to the population. For that purpose, statisticians developed a statistic called **finite population correction** (FPC) to account for the smaller margin of error that should result.

5. Suppose that the campus in Questions 1–4 is a small satellite campus, with only 400 students. After surveying 180 students (Question 3), almost half of everyone on campus would have been surveyed. The formula for finite population correction is below. Find the value, and in the next question we'll learn what to do with that number.

$$FPC = \sqrt{\frac{N-n}{N-1}} \quad \text{where } N \text{ is the population size, and } n \text{ is the sample size.}$$

6. The FPC acts as a multiplier: To get the adjusted margin of error, multiply the value of the FPC by the margin of error that came from the usual formula. Find the new margin of error for the situation where 180 students have been polled out of a campus population of 400. (Use the margin of error you found in Question 3.)

7. Without referring to any formulas, describe what should happen to the margin of error as the size of the sample gets really close to the size of the population. Then use the FPC formula to argue that your conclusion matches what would happen mathematically.

Lesson 4-4 Prep Skills

SKILL 1: USE DIRECT VARIATION EQUATIONS

We learned all about direct variation in Lesson 3-6. Here are some of the important ideas:

The most notable characteristic of quantities that vary directly is that if one doubles, the other does as well, and if one is cut in half, the other is too. There's more to it than that—the quantities go up or down proportionally—but this is a nice basic way to think about what direct variation means.

More specifically, if two quantities x and y vary directly, the relationship between them can be described by an equation of the form $y = kx$, where k is some constant. This number is known as the constant of variation.

- When you fill your gas tank, the cost C varies directly with the number of gallons g. So we know that these quantities can be modeled by the equation $C = kg$.

In order to find the constant k in a variation situation, you need values for each quantity. This results in an equation where k is the only unknown, so you can solve for it.

- Continuing the gas example, if it costs \$30.69 to pump 14.2 gallons:

$$30.69 = k \cdot 14.2$$
$$k = \frac{30.69}{14.2} \approx 2.16$$

Now we know that the equation relating cost and number of gallons is $C = 2.16g$.

SKILL 2: MAKING A TABLE OF VALUES FOR AN EQUATION

This is another skill that we've practiced multiple times in this course. It was originally introduced in Lesson 2-2. More recently, we practiced this a lot in Lesson 3-7. Focus on questions where you're given an equation with two variables, and you build a table of inputs and the associated outputs. If you're not sure how to do the one in the Prep Skills Questions, look back at Lessons 2-2 and 3-7.

SKILL 3: MAKING A SCATTER PLOT

This important skill was introduced in Lesson 1-5, and of course we've used it several times since then. There are additional practice questions in the Prep Skills for Lessons 3-1, 3-2, and 3-9. Are you starting to get the idea that we think being able to draw scatter plots is a pretty big deal?

PREP SKILLS QUESTIONS

1. The force required to move an object varies directly as the resulting acceleration of that object. Write a direct variation equation that describes the force in terms of acceleration.

2. More fun with physics: The direct variation equation $F = kx$ describes a relationship between the distance in meters that a spring stretches or compresses (x) when a force of F newtons is applied. If one particular spring stretches 0.3 meters when a force of 60 newtons is applied, find the specific direct variation equation for this spring.

3. For the equation $y = \frac{200}{x}$, fill in the table of values.

x	1	5	10	20	40	150
y						

4. Make a scatter plot using your table from Question 3.

Lesson 4-4   Where's My Jetpack?

LEARNING OBJECTIVES

☐ 1. Identify situations where inverse variation occurs.

☐ 2. Solve problems involving direct and inverse variation.

Nothing is too small to know, and nothing is too big to attempt.
        — William Cornelius Van Home

Courtesy Everett Collection

If you talk about modes of travel with most Americans who grew up before the 1990s, you'll likely find that they feel kind of cheated. Based on movies, TV shows, and books from the 1950s through the 1980s, we all pretty much figured we'd have flying cars and jetpacks by the time 2017 rolled around, just like James Bond. What a letdown! For the most part, we're still stuck with modes of transportation that have been around for over 100 years. Sigh. Jetpacks exist of course, but they're not exactly widely available. In this lesson, we'll use modes of transportation, including the long-promised jetpack, to study the relationship between speed and time for a given trip. Clearly those quantities are related, but it turns out that exactly how they're related will lead us to study a new type of variation.

  0. Think about the direct variation that we studied in Lesson 3-6. Do you think speed and time for a trip will vary directly? Why or why not?

4-4   Group

In studying direct variation in Lesson 3-6, we found that when two quantities vary directly, if one goes up the other does as well by the same factor. But think about speed and time when traveling: The faster you go, the sooner you get there. So as speed goes up, time goes down. The goal of this activity is to study that relationship in depth. Let's say you need to travel 40 miles, and you have several different choices of how to get there.

  1. For each mode of travel, find how long it will take to make the 40-mile trip.

Mode	Speed (mi/hr)	Time (hr)
Mosey	1	
Walk	3	
Jog	5	
Bike	10	
Bus	20	
Car	40	
Jetpack	80	

2. The speed doubles when going from jogging (5 mi/hr) to biking (10 mi/hr). What happens to the time?

3. The speed doubles when going from bus (20 mi/hr) to car (40 mi/hr). What happens to the time?

4. The speed is cut in half when going from bus (20 mi/hr) to bike (10 mi/hr). What happens to the time?

5. The speed is divided by four when going from jetpack (a zippy 80 mi/hr) to bus (20 mi/hr). What happens to the time?

6. Does time depend on speed in this problem, or does speed depend on time? Explain your answer.

Did You Get It

Try this problem to see if you understand the concepts we just studied. The answer can be found at the end of the Portfolio section.

1. The amount of time it takes to boil a pan of water varies inversely with the wattage of the stove it's sitting on.

   a. If a stove is turned up so that the wattage is doubled, what happens to the time required to boil water?

   b. If it took 4 minutes for a pan of water to boil, then the wattage was reduced to one-third of the previous wattage, how long would it take another pan with the same amount of water to boil?

7. Graph the values in your table and connect them with a curve. Put the independent variable (as decided in your answer to Question 6) on the *x* axis and the dependent variable on the *y* axis. Include labels on each axis.

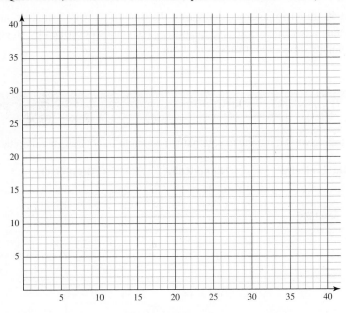

8. Use your graph to estimate the time it would take to travel 40 miles at 7 mi/hr.

9. Use your graph to estimate the speed needed to make the 40-mile trip in two and a half hours.

Did You Get It

2. According to the graph, about how long would it take to travel 40 miles at 32 miles per hour? What speed would be needed to make the trip in 6 hours?

---

10. (This one will impress your instructor.) Find an equation that relates speed to time for a 40-mile trip.

11. Use your equation to find how long it would take to make the trip at 65 miles per hour.

4-4   Class

In the Group portion of this lesson, we saw that for a 40-mile trip, as speed increases, the time of the trip decreases, and vice versa. This is typical of **inverse variation,** a relationship between two variable quantities that can be described by an equation of the form $y = \frac{k}{x}$, where k is some constant. Let's compare direct and inverse variation.

Comparison of Direct and Inverse Variation

The following are various ways of illustrating what it means to say that two variable quantities vary directly.

Verbally	Algebraically	Numerically	Graphically
The quantity y varies directly as the quantity x, and the constant of variation is k.	$y = kx$ Example: $y = 3x$	see table below	see graph below

x	$y = 3x$
1	3
2	6
3	9
4	12
5	15

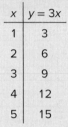

And these are various ways of illustrating what it means to say that two variable quantities vary inversely.

Verbally	Algebraically	Numerically	Graphically
The quantity y varies inversely as the quantity x, and the constant of variation is k.	$y = \frac{k}{x}$ for $x \neq 0$ Example: $y = \frac{12}{x}$	see table below	see graph below

x	$y = \frac{12}{x}$
1	12
2	6
3	4
4	3
5	2.4

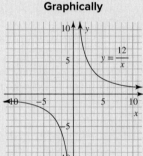

1. When you exchange currency, the value of currency you trade in varies directly with the amount you get back. So as the amount you trade in increases, the amount you get back _____.

2. When you drive a certain distance, the time it takes varies inversely with your speed. So if your speed increases, the amount of time for the trip _____.

In Questions 3–5, write an equation of variation for the situation, using k as the constant of variation.

3. The price P at which a manufacturer is willing to sell a certain product varies inversely as the number of items that consumers are willing to buy u.

4. When a store has discounted gallons of milk by a certain amount, the total savings T varies directly as the number of gallons bought g.

5. Isaac Newton discovered that the gravitational force between two bodies F varies inversely as the square of the distance between them d.

Did You Get It

3. Write a variation equation using constant k for the situation described in Did You Get It 1.

6. The gross pay P for working a certain hourly job varies directly as the number of hours worked h. Use that fact to fill in the table.

h	P
5	$56
10	
15	
20	
25	

7. The number of days d it takes for a construction crew to repave a certain road varies inversely as the number of workers w that work on the project. Use this to fill in the table.

w	d
6	30
12	
18	
24	
30	

The weight of an object on Mars varies directly as its weight on Earth. Suppose that a 170-lb astronaut becomes the first human to set foot on Mars. (Note: Matt Damon didn't actually go there. That was a movie.) He or she would weigh 64.6 lb on Mars.

8. Find the constant of variation.

9. Write an equation relating the weight of an object on Mars to its weight on Earth.

10. Use your equation from Question 9 to fill in the table of values.

Weight on Earth (lbs)	Weight on Mars (lbs)
120	
135	
150	
165	
180	
195	

11. Suppose that a second excursion to Mars happens, and the landing craft holds an extra astronaut and more equipment, which makes it twice as heavy on launch as the first manned trip. How much heavier would this craft be when it lands on Mars?

12. On the next trip advances in lightweight materials lead to the landing craft weighing 1/3 as much as the previous trip. How do the weights compare on Mars?

When a wheel rolls along, the number of times it completes a full revolution to cover a certain distance varies inversely as the circumference of the wheel.

13. Explain why this makes perfect sense.

14. The wheels on my Explorer have a circumference of just about 240 cm. If they make 150 revolutions in traveling a certain distance:

   a. Find the constant of variation.

   b. Write an equation relating the number of revolutions made by a wheel to its circumference in centimeters for this particular distance.

Did You Get It

   4. Refer back to Did You Get It 3. With a stove set on high, it provides 1,400 watts of power, and boils a quart of water in 320 seconds. Write a variation equation that models the relationship between wattage and time to boil a quart of water.

15. Use your equation from Question 14 to complete the table of values.

Circumference (cm)	Number of revolutions
100	
150	
200	
250	
300	

16. What happens to the number of revolutions if the circumference is tripled?

17. What happens to the number of revolutions if the circumference is cut in half?

Did You Get It

5. Use the equation you wrote in Did You Get It 4 to find how many watts would be needed to boil a quart of water in 2 minutes.

4-4 Portfolio

Name _____

Check each box when you've completed the task. Remember that your instructor will want you to turn in the portfolio pages you create.

Technology

1. ☐ Use Excel to create a table and graph illustrating the rate-time problem at the beginning of this lesson. You should use a formula to calculate the times corresponding to a variety of speeds. Begin by using a total distance of 40 miles. Then create a second worksheet using a parameter that allows you to change the distance to anything you like in a single cell and have that automatically change the table and graph. There's a template to get you started in the online resources for this lesson.

Online Practice

1. ☐ Include any written work from the online assignment along with any notes or questions about this lesson's content.

Applications

1. ☐ Complete the Applications problems.

Reflections

Type a short answer to each question.

1. ☐ Describe the differences between direct and inverse variation from as many different aspects as you can think of.

2. ☐ Explain why the topic of inverse variation is in this unit. (Hint: Look at the unit title.)

3. ☐ Body mass index (BMI) is essentially a comparison between a person's weight and height. A BMI between 18.5 and 24.9 is considered healthy; over 25 is considered overweight, and over 30 is considered obese. How do you think a person's height varies with BMI? What about weight with BMI? Explain.

4. ☐ Name one thing you learned or discovered in this lesson that you found particularly interesting.

5. ☐ What questions do you have about this lesson?

Looking Ahead

1. ☐ Complete the Prep Skills for Lesson 4-5.

2. ☐ Read the opening paragraph in Lesson 4-5 carefully and answer Question 0 in preparation for that lesson.

Answers to "Did You Get It?"

1. **a.** The time is cut in half. **b.** It would take 12 minutes.

2. A little over an hour; a little over 7 mph

3. $t = \dfrac{k}{w}$, where t is time to boil and w is wattage.

4. $t = \dfrac{448{,}000}{w}$

5. About 3,733 watts

Answers to "Prep Skills"

1. $F = ka$, where F is the force and a is the acceleration

2. $F = 200x$

3.

x	1	5	10	20	40	150
y	200	40	20	10	5	1.33

4.

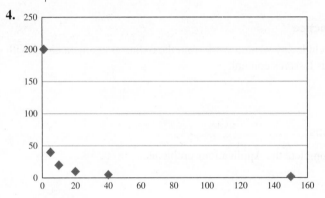

4-4 Applications

Name _____

For each problem, the game plan is to use the information to write an equation of variation. The information provided will allow you to find the constant of variation. Then use your equation to solve the problem.

1. The UV (ultraviolet light) index is a measure of how intense the sun's rays are at a given location and time. The UV index would be low on a cloudy day and much higher on a sunny day. Fill in the blank with either *directly* or *inversely:*

   The time it takes to get a sunburn varies _____ as the UV index.

2. Write a general variation equation relating the time it takes to get a sunburn and the UV index. Make sure you define what any variables stand for.

3. According to *CBS News* online Consumer Tips, at a UV rating of 6, an average person can get a sunburn in as little as 15 minutes. Use this fact to find the constant of variation and rewrite your variation equation using that value of k.

4. How long would it take to get a sunburn when the UV rating is 8.5?

5. Fill in the blank with either *directly* or *inversely:*

   The amount of newsprint used by a newspaper varies _____ as the number of people in the area served by that paper.

4-4   Applications

Name _____

6. According to the North American Newsprint Producers Association, the newsprint used to supply the annual needs of 1,000 people is 34,800 kg. How many kilograms would be needed to supply Tampa, Florida, which has a population of about 353,000? Write a variation equation and use it to solve this problem. How much is that in pounds?

7. Fill in the blank with either *directly* or *inversely:* The length of skid marks left when a driver slams on the brakes varies _____ as the square of the speed of the car v.

8. A child was struck by a car in a crosswalk. The driver of the car had slammed on his brakes and left visible skid marks that were 31 feet long on the pavement. He told the police he had been driving at 25 miles per hour. The police know that, under the conditions at that time, skid marks would be 62 feet long for a car traveling at 40 miles per hour. If the man is telling the truth, how long should the skid marks be? Write a variation equation and use it to solve this problem.

9. The illumination provided by a car's headlight (L) varies inversely as the square of the distance from the headlight (d). A headlight produces 19 foot-candles (fc) at a distance of 26 ft. What will the illumination be at 60 ft?

Lesson 4-5   Prep Skills

SKILL 1: CONVERTING BETWEEN PERCENTS AND DECIMALS

To write a decimal in percent form, move the decimal point two places to the right and include the percent symbol.

- $0.435 = 43.5\%$

To write a percent in decimal form, move the decimal point two places to the left and remove the percent symbol.

- $8.2\% = 0.082$

SKILL 2: RECOGNIZING LINEAR OR EXPONENTIAL GROWTH OR DECAY

When a quantity grows according to linear growth, the same number is repeatedly ADDED to the total.

- 8, 11, 14, 17, 20, 23, . . . is a sequence of numbers growing linearly because every new value is obtained from adding 3 to the previous value.
- 100, 95, 90, 85, 80, 75, . . . is a sequence of numbers decaying linearly because every new value is obtained from subtracting 5 from the previous. We can think of this as adding −5.

When a quantity grows according to exponential growth, the total is repeatedly MULTIPLIED by the same number. We call this multiplier the **growth factor**, or **multiplication factor**.

- 1, 3, 9, 27, 81, 243, . . . is growing exponentially because every new value is obtained from multiplying the previous value by 3.
- 10, 8, 6.4, 5.12, 4.096, . . . is decaying exponentially because every new value is obtained from multiplying the previous value by 0.8.

SKILL 3: FINDING RELATIVE CHANGE

This skill was the main topic of Lesson 2-6. Recall that when a quantity changes, the actual change is simply the new value minus the original value. The relative change is the actual change divided by the original value. Written as a formula (kind of):

$$\text{Relative change} = \frac{\text{New value} - \text{Original value}}{\text{Original value}}$$

SKILL 4: INTERPRETING INFORMATION FROM A GRAPH

The key to interpreting information from ANY graph is recognizing what quantity is represented by the values on each axis. Finding the coordinates of a point does you no good unless you know what each coordinate represents. Once you've done that, it's simply a matter of reading the scale on each axis, and locating points corresponding to values along each axis.

- The following graph represents the value of an investment account in dollars (vertical axis) in terms of years (horizontal axis) since the account was opened.

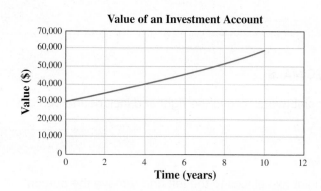

Value of an Investment Account

- The value of the account was $30,000 at the time it was opened because the point (0, 30,000) is on the graph. We can see from the labels that the first coordinate represents years after the account was opened, and the second represents the value in dollars.

- It took the account just about 4 years to pass $40,000 in value because the point where the graph goes above height 40,000 is just a bit to the right of 4 on the horizontal axis.

PREP SKILLS QUESTIONS

1. Convert each percent to decimal form.

   a. 4%   b. 81%   c. 11.4%

2. Convert each decimal to a percent.

   a. 0.37   b. 0.914   c. 0.019

3. Does this sequence represent linear growth, exponential growth, or neither?

   7, 16, 25, 34, 43, 52

4. Does this sequence represent linear growth, exponential growth, or neither?

   2, 3, 4.5, 6.75, 10.125, 15.1875

5. Write the growth factor for any sequence in Questions 3 and 4 that is exponential.

6. In one year, Chad's salary was raised from $31,500 to $35,250. Find the relative change.

7. The graph here shows the concentration of a certain drug in a patient's bloodstream in milligrams per liter in terms of the number of hours since the drug was administered. Use the graph to answer the questions.

   a. What was the original concentration at the time the drug was administered?

   b. How long did it take for the concentration to drop below 4 mg/L?

   c. This particular patient needs a concentration of at least 2 mg/L for the drug to be effective. About how long was this dose effective?

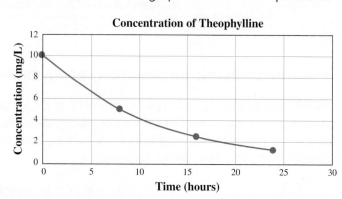

Concentration of Theophylline

Lesson 4-5 Sit Back and Watch Your Money Grow

LEARNING OBJECTIVES

☐ 1. Define function and use function notation.

☐ 2. Identify the significance of a and b in an equation of the form $y = ab^x$.

☐ 3. Find exponential models.

☐ 4. Compare exponential models using graphs, tables, and formulas.

©Picturenet/Getty Images RF

If I take 30 steps linearly, I get to 30. If I take 30 steps exponentially, I get to a billion.
— Ray Kurzweil

Raise your hand if you hope to be rich someday. There's a pretty good chance that your hand is up right now: Financial independence is a goal for a lot of people. We've already studied the differences between quantities that grow linearly and those that grow exponentially. Now that our skills at interpreting graphs have grown, well, exponentially, it's a good time to revisit exponential growth to learn a little bit more about its magic. We already know that the long-term growth of money is an ideal way to study exponential growth, so we'll start there, and on the way start you on the path to riches!

0. If a person invested $15,000 today in a reasonably successful fund, how much do you think it could be worth in 40 years?

4-5 Class

1. Describe the differences between linear and exponential growth based on what we know from earlier in the course.

If most people won $15,000 on a game show, they'd go on a spending spree. But not you! You're too smart for that. Instead you'd decide to invest that money to make it grow. I'm not sure how patient you are, but what if you were super-patient? Like patient enough to let that money grow for 40 years in a fixed-rate investment? Let's take a look. Make sure that you answer every question with a complete sentence.

Time (years)	Value ($)
0	$15,000.00
1	$16,050.00
2	$17,173.50
3	$18,375.65
4	$19,661.94
5	$21,038.28
6	$22,510.96
7	$24,086.72

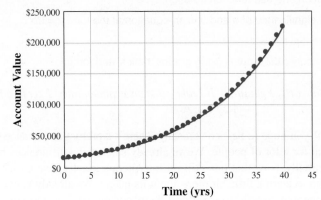

2. For each value in the table after the initial investment, divide the amount by the value of the account the previous year. What do you notice?

3. What does your result in Question 2 say about the type of growth this account exhibits?

4. Find the relative change in value for each year in the table compared to the previous year. What can you conclude?

5. Find the value of the account after 10 years. Don't multiply by 1.07 ten times … that's what exponents are for!

6. Use your answer to Question 3 to write an equation in the form "y = expression," where the expression describes the amount of money in the account after x years. (Hint: Starting with $15,000, how many times have you multiplied by your answer to Question 3 after x years?)

7. Verify that the equation you wrote generates the account values in the table. Ideally, you would use either the table feature on a graphing calculator or spreadsheet, but in any case, make sure you describe how you got your values.

Did You Get It

Try this problem to see if you understand the concepts we just studied. The answer can be found at the end of the Portfolio section.

1. Elaine keeps an investment whose value x years after opening the account can be described by the equation $y = 12,500(1.05)^x$. What was her initial investment? By what percentage does it grow each year?

We'll continue studying your genius plan to grow your winnings in a bit. For now, we'd like to point out that we've been working with a really important idea in math for quite a while now without giving it a name. Look at the spreadsheet, which shows tournament scores for five members of the Findlay College golf team at the 2016 NCAA championships. If you wanted to find the total team score in cell B7, what formula would you use?

If you said "=SUM(B2:B6)," you win. The key elements of that command are SUM, which is the name of the formula that you're asking Excel to use, and B2:B6, which tells Excel what numbers to apply that formula to. This may remind you of the terminology we used back in Lesson 2-2: inputs and outputs. The input here is the range of cells, and the output is the sum.

This process of matching up inputs and outputs in math is given a special name: function.

	A	B
1	Player	Score
2	Kasey Petty	69
3	Shelby Warner	73
4	Makenzie Torres	75
5	Samantha Hatter	80
6	Kelsey Koesters	81
7		

A **function** is a relationship between two quantities where each input produces a unique output.

Our Excel sum qualifies as a function, because when you specify the input (cells B2 through B6) there is a unique output (the sum). The equation we wrote describing the value of the $15,000 investment is also a function: The input is the number of years, and for each number of years there is a unique output (the value of the account after that many years). It's not like the bank would let you choose between two different amounts: There's a single value, and that's that.

In order to distinguish that a formula defines a function, we use **function notation.**

Function Notation

The output of a function named f is described by the symbol $f(x)$, which is read "f OF x." Warning: NEVER read $f(x)$ as "f TIMES x." It's NOT a multiplication.

So we would write the investment equation as $f(x) = 15{,}000(1.07)^x$ and read this as "f of x equals 15,000 times 1.07 to the x power." It's not a coincidence that this looks JUST like the syntax for Excel formulas. In fact, if you look up Excel documentation, it refers to things like =SUM, =AVERAGE, and =MEDIAN as functions. Everything ties together and life is good.

8. For the spreadsheet displayed earlier, find the output for the function =SUM(B3:B4).

9. For the function describing the value of our $15,000 investment, find $f(12)$, and describe what it means.

Did You Get It

  2. a. For the spreadsheet on the previous page showing golf scores, find the output for the function =SUM(B2:B5).
     b. For the function describing the value of our $15,000 investment, find $f(23)$ and describe what it means.

---

10. Look back at the graph that illustrates the value of the account. Trace along the graph slowly from left to right, and describe what the changing steepness of the graph tells you about how the value is growing.

11. How much interest will you earn from zero to five years into the investment? This will be the difference in the value after five years and the initial investment. You could use the formula for the function, but the table of values printed earlier is a better choice.

12. How much interest will you earn between years 35 and 40? This time the formula is your only option.

13. Describe what you can learn from comparing the answers to Questions 11 and 12. Also describe how that fits in with your answer to Question 10.

Did You Get It

3. Elaine from Did You Get It 1 never touches the money in that account, and it gets passed down through three generations. After 94 years in the bank, how much would the account be worth?

4-5 Group

We've now studied exponential growth a couple of different times in this course. But there's a flip side to exponential growth, known as **exponential decay**. The thing that distinguishes exponential growth is that the growth starts off relatively slowly, then speeds up dramatically as time passes. Let's see how exponential decay compares.

Coffee is a popular morning drink because the caffeine it contains acts as a temporary stimulant. Once the caffeine gets into your system, the amount dissipates exponentially (assuming that you don't add more, of course). Answer every question (except for 2 and 6) with a full sentence.

©Ingram Publishing/Alamy RF

Time (hours)	Caffeine (mg)
0	180.0
1	144.0
2	115.2
3	92.2
4	73.7
5	59.0
6	47.2
7	37.7

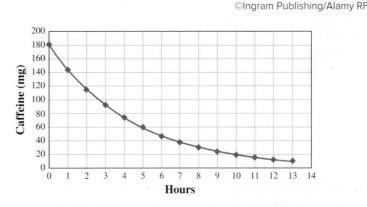

1. If you're the coffee drinker represented by the table and graph, how much caffeine was initially in your system?

2. Find the relative change in caffeine for each one-hour period listed in the following table. Round to the nearest full percent.

Hours	Relative change
0–1	
1–2	
2–3	
3–4	
4–5	
5–6	
6–7	

3. Complete this important statement about exponential change: A quantity either grows or decays exponentially when the

   _____ _____ in that quantity is _____.

4. Looking at the graph of the caffeine remaining in your system, describe what exponential decay looks like compared to exponential growth.

5. What's the multiplication factor that you'd need to multiply by a previous hour's amount to get the next hour's amount? (Hint: If 10% of something goes away each hour, 90% remains.)

6. Use your answer to Question 5 to write a function of the form "$f(x) =$ expression" where the expression describes the amount of caffeine left in your system after x hours. Your answer to Question 6 in the Class portion is a good place to look if you need help.

Did You Get It

4. The radioactive elements used in medical imaging are good examples of substances that decay exponentially. Iodine-123 is a radioactive substance used in diagnosing thyroid conditions. This particular isotope decays in such a way that 95% of the initial sample remains after each one-hour period. If an initial sample is 200 mg, write a function that describes the amount remaining after x hours.

7. Use a graphing calculator to verify that the equation you wrote in Question 6 gives you the values in the table, and the given graph. Describe your results.

8. Use the function you wrote to find the amount of caffeine left in your system after 150 minutes.

9. Use the graph to estimate the amount of time needed for the amount of caffeine to drop to 40 mg. Describe how you found your answer.

10. Use either TABLE or TRACE commands on your calculator to try and come up with a more accurate estimate of the time needed for the caffeine level to reach 40 mg.

Did You Get It

5. Use the equation you wrote in Did You Get It 4, along with a graphing calculator, to answer each question.

   a. How much of the initial 200-mg sample of Iodine-123 remains after 8 hours? One week?

   b. About how long does it take until half of the original sample remains?

11. Make up a situation that could be modeled by each of the following exponential graphs. As always, extra points for creativity!

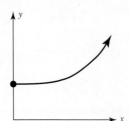

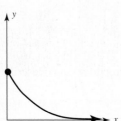

4-5 Portfolio

Name _____

Check each box when you've completed the task. Remember that your instructor will want you to turn in the portfolio pages you create.

Technology

1. ☐ Use a spreadsheet to extend both the table and the graph for the caffeine problem (p. 521) out to the point where there's less than 1 mg left in your system. How long does this take? A template to help you get started can be found in the online resources for this lesson.

Online Practice

1. ☐ Include any written work from the online assignment along with any notes or questions about this lesson's content.

Applications

1. ☐ Complete the Applications problems.

Reflections

Type a short answer to each question.

1. ☐ Compare exponential growth and exponential decay. What do they have in common? How are they different? A really good answer will say something about relative change.

2. ☐ What did you learn in this lesson about the value of leaving money invested for long periods of time? How can you apply this to retirement?

3. ☐ Name one thing you learned or discovered in this lesson that you found particularly interesting.

4. ☐ What questions do you have about this lesson?

Looking Ahead

1. ☐ Complete the Prep Skills for Lesson 4-6.

2. ☐ Read the opening paragraph in Lesson 4-6 carefully and answer Question 0 in preparation for that lesson.

Answers to "Did You Get It?"

1. $12,500, 5%   2. a. 297   b. $71,107.95: This is the value of the account after 23 years.

3. $1,226,603.29   4. $y = 200(0.95)^x$

5. a. 8 hours: 132.7 mg, 1 week: 0.036 mg   b. 13.5 hours

Answers to "Prep Skills"

1. a. 0.04   b. 0.81   c. 0.114

2. a. 37%   b. 91.4%   c. 1.9%

3. linear growth   4. exponential growth

5. Growth factor for Question 4 is 1.5   6. 11.9%

7. a. 10 mg/L   b. about 11 hours   c. about 18 hours

4-5   Applications

Name _____

We'll begin this assignment by looking at the savings plan for Joe, a 30-year-old with a steady job making $30,000 a year, with an annual raise of 4%. Looking ahead to the future, Joe commits to saving 12% of his earnings every year. He chooses a fixed fund investment that returns 9% annually. The following graph shows Joe's earnings, the amount of money he spends, and the amount of money that is generated in interest on his investment each year. The purple curve isn't the amount he's saved; it's the amount of interest earned each year. The values on the *x* axis represent Joe's age in years.

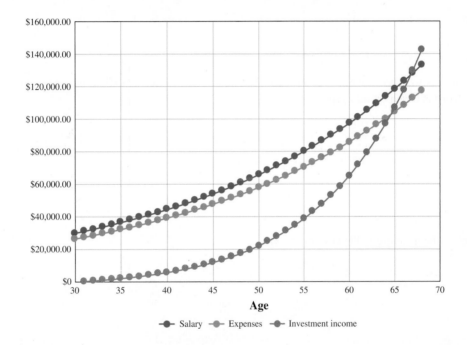

The investment income graph displays the true magic of exponential growth: The income is limited when Joe's a young guy, but as he gets closer to thinking about retirement, the income really takes off. Notice that at age 65, something awesome happens: The income that Joe's making from his investments is more than his living expenses. At that point, he can retire and live as well as ever without, you know, working for a living. Sweet! This age is known in financial circles as the **crossover point**.

Use the information provided to answer Questions 1–5.

1. How much money is Joe earning when he's 30?

2. How much money is he allowing himself to spend when he's 30? Show a calculation, then describe whether or not your answer seems correct based on the graph.

4-5   Applications

Name _____

3. How much is Joe earning when he's 35? Show a calculation based on the annual relative growth rate of 4%. Then describe whether or not your answer seems correct based on the graph.

4. How much money is Joe allowing himself to spend when he's 35? Show a calculation, then describe whether or not your answer seems correct based on the graph.

5. Carefully explain the meaning of the crossover point.

Now turn your attention to the graph to answer Questions 6–8.

6. How much is Joe earning in salary when he's 60?

7. How much is Joe allowing himself to spend when he's 60?

4-5 Applications

Name _____

8. How much is Joe earning from his investments at 60?

9. Write a function of the form "$f(x)$ = expression" where the expression describes the amount Joe earns x years after age 30. If you need guidance, look at the answers to Applications Question 3 and Class Question 6.

10. Use your answer to Question 9 to find how much Joe earns at age 60. How does it compare to the estimate you got from the graph?

11. Write a function of the form "$f(x)$ = expression" where the expression describes the amount Joe spends x years after age 30.

12. Use your answer to Question 11 to find how much Joe spends at age 60. How does it compare to the estimate you got from the graph?

4-5 Applications

Name _____

Now let's look at a coworker of Joe's named Fran. She has the same job as Joe, makes the same amount of money, and in an amazing coincidence happens to be the same age. Sounds like she and Joe should get together and go bowling or something. Anyhow, Fran is much more frugal than Joe: She commits to spending only 70% of her salary and saving the rest in the same retirement plan that Joe is invested in. Let's see what Fran's graph looks like. Again, the horizontal axis is her age.

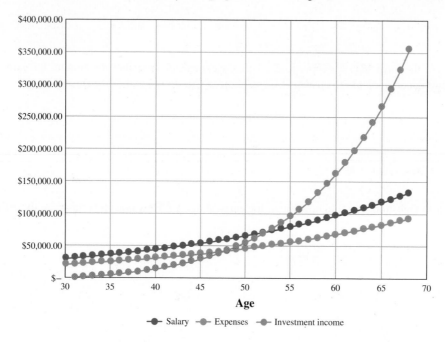

13. How much less money does Fran spend at age 30 than Joe?

14. How much earlier does Fran reach her crossover point?

15. Describe what impact this article might have on your saving vs. spending plan in the future.

Lesson 4-6   Prep Skills

SKILL 1: RECOGNIZE LINEAR OR EXPONENTIAL GROWTH/DECAY

This skill was covered earlier in the course, and was reviewed in the Prep Skills for Lesson 4-5.

SKILL 2: FIND A LINE OF BEST FIT

This skill was the topic of Lesson 3-9, where we learned how to use both calculators and spreadsheets to find regression lines. Refer to the Tech boxes in that lesson along with the accompanying videos in online resources if you need a refresher. In Lesson 4-6, we'll be using very similar procedures to find different types of equations.

SKILL 3: INTERPRET PARAMETERS IN AN EXPONENTIAL EQUATION

We learned how to do this in Lesson 4-5. Here's a quick refresher. For an exponential equation of the form $y = a(b)^x$ that describes the size of some quantity in terms of time, the coefficient a tells us the initial size of the quantity being represented by the equation. This is pretty easy to see: If you input time zero, b^x is just 1, so the output is a. The base b of the exponent describes the percentage by which the quantity is changing each time period. For exponential growth, the base is of the form $1 + r$, where r is the growth rate as a percentage in decimal form. For exponential decay, the base is of the form $1 - r$, where r is the decay rate as a percentage in decimal form.

- The population of a town is described by the formula $P = 12{,}400(1.04)^t$, where t is the number of years after 2000. The 12,400 tells us that the population was 12,400 in 2000. The 1.04, which can be written as $1 + 0.04$, tells us that the growth rate is 0.04 in decimal form, making it 4%.

- The amount of a drug in milligrams in a patient's system is described by the formula $A = 110(0.72)^x$, where x is the number of hours after the drug has entered her system. The 110 tells us that there were initially 110 mg of the drug in her bloodstream. If we write 0.72 as $1 - 0.28$, we can see that the amount of the drug was decreasing at the rate of 28% per hour.

SKILL 4: FIND RELATIVE CHANGE

This skill was covered in Lesson 2-6, and reviewed in the Prep Skills for Lesson 4-5.

SKILL 5: USE FUNCTION NOTATION

Function notation was just introduced in the last lesson, but in case you didn't catch it, here are the essentials. We've used the terms *input* and *output* fairly often to describe quantities in modeling. The input is often represented by x and the output by y. Not always, mind you—we sometimes use letters that are indicative of the quantity they represent, like C for cost, or t for time. But if we're using x for the input, we can also use the symbol $f(x)$ for the output. This is read as "f of x" and indicates that we're defining a function named f whose input is the variable x. Basically, instead of writing an equation like $y = 2.4 + 0.8x$, we'd write it as $f(x) = 2.4 + 0.8x$. To indicate the output that goes along with input 5, for example, we'd use $f(5)$, and find that $f(5) = 2.4 + 0.8(5) = 6.4$

PREP SKILLS QUESTIONS

1. Does this sequence represent growth that is close to linear, exponential, or neither?

   12, 33, 53, 75, 98

2. Does this sequence represent decay that is close to linear, exponential, or neither?

   400, 320, 254, 200, 162, 130

3. Use a calculator or spreadsheet to find the line of best fit for the data in the table.

x	12	24	36	48	60	72
y	$312	$600	$1,040	$1,279	$1,703	$2,041

4. A quantity is described by the equation $y = 26(1.2)^x$. What was the initial size of the quantity? By what percentage is it increasing each time period?

5. The first time a new course is offered at a college, 73 people signed up for it. The following semester, only 60 signed up. Find the relative change.

6. For the function $f(x) = 3 \cdot 5^x$, find $f(0)$, $f(2)$, and $f(-1.2)$.

Lesson 4-6   Follow the Bouncing Golf Ball

LEARNING OBJECTIVES

☐ 1. Gather and organize data from an experiment.

☐ 2. Find an exponential curve of best fit for an experimental data set.

☐ 3. Study the decay rate for exponential decay.

Courtesy of David Sobecki

It's just a glorious day. The only way to ruin a day like this
would be to play golf on it.
                        —David Feherty

Avid golfers have a classic love-hate relationship with the game. They enjoy it enough
to spend a lot of time and money pursuing it, but they also know how downright mad-
dening it can be. Golf is a whole lot harder than it looks, and sometimes it seems like the ball just moves and bounces with a
mind of its own—an evil mind intent on ruining the golfer's day.

Even so, like everything else in our world, golf balls are bound by the laws of physics and their motion actually is
predictable—at least in a lab setting, if not on the golf course. In this lesson, we'll follow a bouncing golf ball to help us further
our study of exponential growth and decay, relying on technology to find exponential equations that best fit a data set.

0. Suppose that you drop a golf ball from a height of 10 feet onto a hard surface, and the ball bounces back up to a height
of 8 feet. Could you make a prediction on how high it would bounce if dropped from 5 feet? Why or why not?

4-6 Group

Here's the list of supplies needed for our golf ball experiment:

1. A golf ball; without this, it's not a golf ball experiment, is it?

2. A meter stick or tape measure with metric units

3. A chair or short stepladder

4. Masking tape and a marking pen

5. A hard, smooth floor area next to a wall

6. A graphing calculator or spreadsheet program with a regression feature

Part 1: The Bounce Lab

Location is everything here: You'll need a relatively high ceiling, and a smooth concrete or other hard floor. Tile with grout
lines won't work: The grout lines will affect the bounces of the ball. The key is to get consistent bounces straight up with no
deflection. Have the tallest member of your group stand on a chair or short stepladder, and run a strip of masking tape vertically
along the wall from the floor to the highest point they can reach. (Ideally, the starting point will be at least 250 cm above the
floor.) Using your meter stick/tape measure and the marking pen, label heights on the masking tape every 10 cm starting with
0 cm at floor level.

Now you're ready to bounce. Hold the golf ball a few inches from the wall with the bottom of the ball at the highest height
marked on the tape. Drop the ball and have someone in the group note the approximate height the ball reaches at the top of its
first bounce. This will give you a rough idea of where to look.

Now repeat the drop, and have the person who watched the height of the first bounce put their finger on the tape at the height the ball reaches on the first bounce (the bottom of the ball, that is). Then mark that height with the pen. Repeat twice more FROM THE SAME HEIGHT, then calculate and record the *average* of the three bounce heights. (Use the table to record your results. Once you add the bounce heights in the Total bounce height column, you just need to divide by 3 to get the average bounce height.)

Next, we'd like to calculate the height of the second bounce. But rather than having the ball bounce twice, use the height of the first bounce that you calculated as the new release point. Clever, right? Repeat three times, recording the bounce heights in the table and calculating the average. Then use that average height as release point to calculate the height of the third bounce, and so on. Continue until you have heights for the first 8–10 bounces.

1. Record the data from your experiment in the table.

x Bounce #	Trial 1 bounce height (cm)	Trial 2 bounce height (cm)	Trial 3 bounce height (cm)	Total bounce height (cm)	y Average bounce height (cm)
0					
1					
2					
3					
4					
5					
6					
7					
8					
9					
10					

2. Use these data to create a scatter plot. Use the average bounce height as your y coordinates.

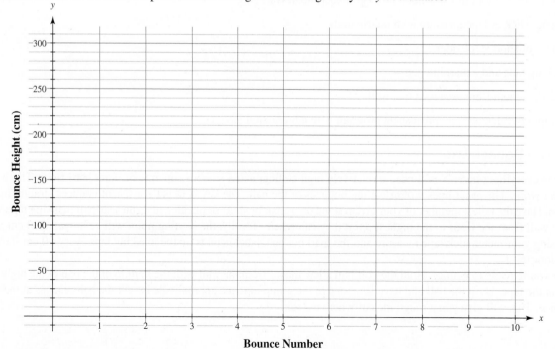

Part 2: Modeling Your Data

Hopefully, you can see that a linear model would be a bad choice for our bounce height data. The scatter plot should remind you of the exponential decay models we saw in Lesson 4-5. In order to find a model, we'll use exponential regression commands on either a graphing calculator or spreadsheet.

Finding an Exponential Equation of Best Fit

Whether using a graphing calculator or spreadsheet, the setup is the same as when finding the line of best fit: Enter the data as before. Then:

Graphing Calculator

Press **STAT** followed by the right arrow key to access the **STAT CALC** menu, and choose **ExpReg,** which is choice 0 on that menu. Then press **ENTER** to calculate the exponential equation of best fit.

Spreadsheet

Create a scatter plot, then point the cursor at one of the data points. Right click (Windows) or option click (Mac) and choose "Add Trendline" from the contextual menu, and choose Exponential. To display the equation, you'll need to locate the Format Trendline menu. For some spreadsheets, you can find it by right or option clicking on one of the data points again. On others, the menu will automatically appear to the right after you choose Add Trendline. In any case, you'll find check boxes for Display Equation on Chart and Display R-squared value on chart.

Here's where things get funky: Spreadsheets provide exponential equations in the form $y = ae^{kx}$, rather than the $y = ab^x$ provided by a graphing calculator. The number e is known as the *natural base:* It's a bit more than 2.7. To convert the spreadsheet formula into the form we want, compute 2.7^k, where k is the coefficient of x in the equation provided by the spreadsheet. The result is the base you need (b) in the formula $y = ab^x$.

See the Lesson 4-6 Using Tech video in online resources for further information.

3. Use either a calculator or spreadsheet to find the exponential function of best fit for your bounce data. Write your answer in the form $f(x) = ab^x$.

4. Use your function to approximate the height of the 7th bounce. How does the result compare to the value in your table? Does this surprise you?

5. Find $f(0)$. What does your answer mean?

Did You Get It

Try this problem to see if you understand the concepts we just studied. The answer can be found at the end of the Portfolio section.

1. When trying this experiment at my campus, I got the model $f(x) = 263(0.84)^x$.
   a. What was the approximate height I dropped the ball from originally?
   b. About how high was the seventh bounce?

Now let's analyze the significance of every symbol in our equation.

6. What does the variable x represent?

7. In the function $f(x) = ab^x$ that models your data, what is the value of a? What does it tell us about the experiment? Your answers to Questions 5 and 6 should help. Does it match the results in your table? Why do you think that is?

8. In the function $f(x) = ab^x$ that models your data, what is the value of b? What does it tell us about the experiment?

Did You Get It

2. Look back at the bounce height function I got in Did You Get It 1. What is the significance of the 0.84 in that function? What does it tell you about the difference between my golf ball experiment and yours?

Part 3: The Connection Between Exponential Decay and the Rate of Decay

We've put a considerable amount of energy into studying exponential growth or decay. The independent variables we've worked with have typically been whole numbers: years after an account was opened, hours since caffeine was introduced to the bloodstream, number of bounces for a golf ball, etc. In each case, the distinguishing feature is that each new output comes from multiplying the previous by the same fixed number. In the bounce lab, we see that same pattern: Each bounce is a certain percentage of the height the ball was dropped from. The result is a function where the input is an exponent, and that's why we call this type of function an **exponential function**.

Now let's study the rate of decay.

9. Using data from your original table, fill in this new table. The drop height corresponds to the height of the previous bounce; start with the original height the ball was dropped from. Use the average bounce heights from the original table. Note: The difference between this table and the previous one is that the input is no longer the bounce number: It's the *height of the previous bounce.*

x Drop height (cm)	y Bounce height (cm)

x Drop height (cm)	y Bounce height (cm)
	—

10. Use these data to create a second scatter plot.

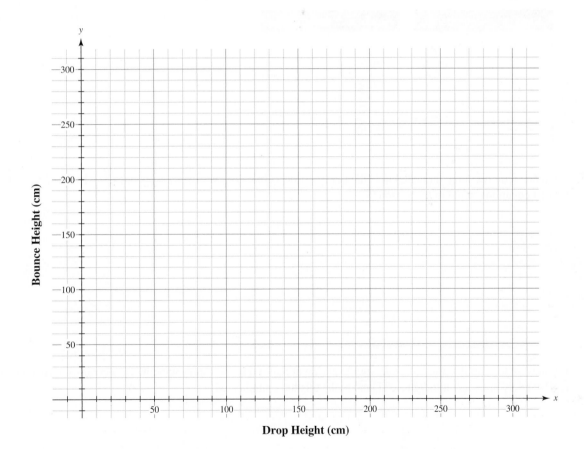

11. Based on the scatter plot, what kind of equation seems to be a good choice for modeling this data?

12. Use your graphing calculator to find the equation of best fit. Round to two decimal places.

$y = $ _____

13. Your equation has a variable in it, but also has **parameters**: These are constants in an equation of a certain form that are determined by the data for a particular model. For example, when you found a function of the form $f(x) = ab^x$ earlier, x was the variable, while the values you found for a and b were parameters. Identify the variables and parameters in your answer to Question 12, then describe what each means in this setting.

14. Find the relative change in height from one bounce to the next. If you need a reminder, we studied relative change in Lesson 2-6. Then find the average relative change for all bounces.

Bounce	Rel. Change
0–1	
1–2	
2–3	
3–4	
4–5	

Bounce	Rel. Change
5–6	
6–7	
7–8	
8–9	
9–10	

15. (This one requires some thought, but is the key question.) How does your answer to Question 14 relate to EACH of the best-fit equations found in this lesson?

16. If you were to drop the golf ball from your experiment out of a second story window 20 feet above a concrete patio, how high would you expect it to bounce? Don't make this too complicated!

Did You Get It

3. Recall that the function giving the height of the bounces in terms of bounce number (from Did You Get It 1) was $f(x) = 263(0.84)^x$.

a. What should the relative change in bounce heights work out to be? In other words, if I'd made a table comparing the drop height to the bounce height, like in Question 9, what should I have gotten for the average relative change (Question 14)?

b. If my experiment had worked out ideally, with perfectly consistent bounces and completely accurate measurements, what would I have gotten for the equation of the line of best fit for the data comparing drop heights to bounce heights? Your answers from Questions 13 and 15 will save the day here.

17. List as many factors as you can think of that contribute to the data from this experiment not working out to be a perfect exponential equation.

According to the International Federation of Tennis, a regulation tennis ball should bounce about 55 inches when dropped from a height of 100 inches.

18. What's the bounce height as a percentage of the drop height for a regulation tennis ball?

19. Write an expression that calculates the bounce height for a regulation tennis ball dropped from 200 inches.

20. Write an equation that describes the bounce height (y) of a regulation tennis ball when it's dropped from x inches.

21. Using your answer to Question 18, it's possible to write an equation that describes the height of the xth bounce when a regulation tennis ball is dropped from a height of 100 inches. Do it! The things we learned in the golf ball experiment will definitely come in handy.

22. If you were to toss a tennis ball a bit forward from 10 feet above the ground, draw a graph of what you think the path of the ball would look like. The horizontal axis should measure lateral distance from where it was tossed, and the vertical axis should measure height. In essence, your graph should be a side view of watching the ball bounce forward.

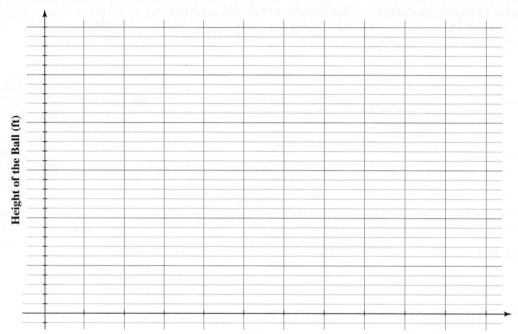

Horizontal Distance Covered (ft)

4-6 | Portfolio

Name _____

Check each box when you've completed the task. Remember that your instructor will want you to turn in the portfolio pages you create.

Technology

1. ☐ Questions 1, 2, and 3 in the Group section are great examples of the three ways we've modeled data: numerically, graphically, and algebraically. Build an Excel spreadsheet that illustrates each of those models, using a table, connected scatter plot, and a formula. A template to help you get started is available in the online resources for this lesson. Remember that Excel will give you a formula in the form $y = ae^{kx}$. You can leave the equation in that form, or convert it to the form $y = ab^x$, as described in the Using Technology box on page 535.

Online Practice

1. ☐ Include any written work from the online assignment along with any notes or questions about this lesson's content.

Applications

1. ☐ Complete the Applications problems.

Reflections

Type a short answer to each question.

1. ☐ We've studied linear and exponential equations of best fit in this course. If you're looking at a set of data, how can you decide which of those would be most appropriate for the data?

2. ☐ How could you tell if neither of those types of equations is a good fit for a data set?

3. ☐ Name one thing you learned or discovered in this lesson that you found particularly interesting.

4. ☐ What questions do you have about this lesson?

Looking Ahead

1. ☐ Complete the Prep Skills for Lesson 4-7.

2. ☐ Read the opening paragraph in Lesson 4-7 carefully and answer Question 0 in preparation for that lesson.

? **Answers to "Did You Get It?"**

1. a. 263 cm   **b.** 77.6 cm   **2.** It's an average of what percent of the previous height each bounce reaches. By comparing to your result, you can tell if my golf ball bounces more or less than yours.   **3. a.** −0.16   **b.** $y = 0.84x$

? **Answers to "Prep Skills"**

1. linear growth   **2.** exponential decay   **3.** $y = 29.03x - 56.8$ **4.** 26; 20%

5. −17.8%   **6.** $f(0) = 3; f(2) = 75; f(-1.2) \approx 0.43$

4-6 Applications

Name _____

1. The function $f(x) = 81.15(1.013)^x$ can be used to model the population of the United States in millions of people based on the number of years since 1900. Identify the variables and the parameters in this equation, and describe what the significance of each is in terms of population.

2. Use the function in Question 1 to complete the table, then use the table to draw a graph of the function. Don't forget to label an appropriate scale on each axis.

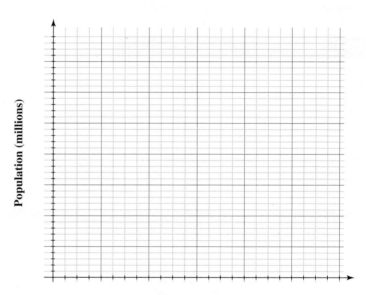

Years after 1900	Population (Millions)
0	
20	
40	
60	
80	
100	

Population (millions)

Years after 1900

3. The function $f(x) = 81.15(1.013)^x$ illustrates _____ growth. The population was growing by _____% each year.

4. The model used in Questions 1–3 was obtained using official data for every census from 1900 to 2010. (The census is conducted every 10 years.) Use your model to predict the population in 2015. Then find the population of the United States in 2015 online and compare to your result. How accurate is it?

4-6 **Applications**

Name _____

5. What do you think the result of your answers to Question 4 say about population growth in the 21st century?

6. What if we use only more recent data? Since the census is conducted only every 10 years, we'll have to use a different source. I used estimates from a site called Worldometers, which are based on multiple data sources that are likely to make them more accurate than the census. In fact, the census is historically not the best measure of the true population for a wide variety of reasons. The table has data for years from 1990 to 2010. Use the data to find the exponential function of best fit. Include FIVE digits in all parameters. *Note that x now represents years after 1990.*

Year	Yrs. after 1990	Population (Millions)
1990	0	254.51
1995	5	268.04
2000	10	284.59
2005	15	298.16
2010	20	312.25

7. Based just on the base of the exponential in your function, do you think this equation is likely to give a better estimate for the 2015 population than our first model? Why or why not?

8. Use your function from Question 6 to estimate the population in 2015 and 2050. Compare the 2015 estimate to the population you already found on the Internet. Then search for a site that does population projections and see how your prediction compares. What does the comparison say about that site's population growth forecast?

Lesson 4-7   Prep Skills

SKILL 1: USE PERIMETER AND AREA FORMULAS FOR A RECTANGLE

A rectangle has two dimensions: length and width. If we use l to represent length and w to represent width, then the perimeter of the rectangle is $P = 2l + 2w$. This is really just adding up the lengths of each individual side. The area of the rectangle is the product of the length and the width: $A = lw$.

- This rectangle has perimeter $P = 2(8) + 2(12) = 40$ cm. It has area $A = 8(12) = 96$ cm^2.

12 cm

8 cm

- If a rectangle has perimeter 240 inches and the length is 50 inches, we can find the width by subtraction. Since the length is 50 in., there are 2 sides of that length, which accounts for 100 in. That leaves 140 in. left over for the other two sides, so each is 70 in.

SKILL 2: USE THE DISTRIBUTIVE PROPERTY

This skill was reviewed in the Prep Skills for Lesson 1-4. In this lesson, we'll be distributing a variable into an expression, so you also need to be familiar with rules for exponents, as in this example. We'll first apply the distributive property, multiplying the y by both terms in the parentheses.

- $y(40 - 5y) = y \cdot 40 - y \cdot 5y$ When multiplying y by itself, add the original exponents (both 1) to get y^2

   $= 40y - 5y^2$

SKILL 3: SUBSTITUTE AN EXPRESSION INTO AN EXPRESSION

This skill was covered in the Prep Skills for Lesson 3–10. We're all very comfortable with substituting NUMBERS into an expression by now. Just do the same thing when substituting in an expression! Replace every occurrence of the variable with that expression, making sure to keep the expression in parentheses, then simplify if possible.

SKILL 4: FIND AND INTERPRET INTERCEPTS

Intercepts were introduced in Lesson 3-1. Here's a quickie review: The intercepts of a graph are the points where the graph crosses one of the axes. The y intercept is the point where the y axis is crossed. This happens exactly when the x (or first) coordinate is zero. So this intercept tells us the output of the equation when the input value is zero. The x intercept is the point where the x axis is crossed. This happens exactly when the y (or second) coordinate is zero. So this intercept tells us what values of the input will result in an output of zero.

   In order to effectively interpret the story told by intercepts, you have to be completely aware of what quantity each of the input and output represents. Then just think of each intercept as what happens when one of those quantities is zero.

- This graph represents the total amount owed on a student loan, where *x* is the number of years since the borrower graduated from college.

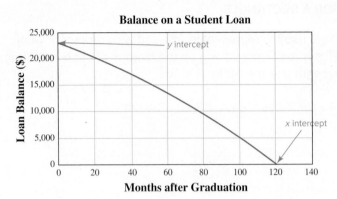

Balance on a Student Loan

The graph crosses the *y* axis at about 23,000, so the *y* intercept is (0, 23,000), and the initial amount owed at the time of graduation was $23,000. The graph crosses the *x* axis at 120, so the *x* intercept is (120, 0), and the balance of the loan falls to $0 after 120 months.

PREP SKILLS QUESTIONS

1. Find the perimeter and area of a rectangle that is 13 ft wide and 4.5 ft long.

2. A rectangle with perimeter 148 m is 42 m long. How wide is it?

3. Multiply out the parentheses:

   a. $3w(w + 5)$

   b. $10x(8 - x + 2x^2)$

4. Substitute $90 - 2w$ for *l* in the expression $P = 2l + 2w$, then simplify the result.

5. This graph describes the height of a drone in terms of number of seconds since it took off. Find all intercepts, and describe what each tells us.

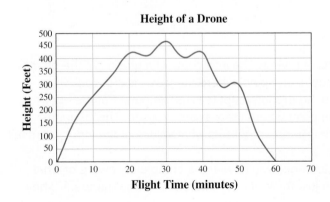

Height of a Drone

Lesson 4-7 Irate Ducks

LEARNING OBJECTIVES

☐ 1. Identify a parabolic graph.

☐ 2. Solve problems using the graph of a quadratic equation.

I can't change the direction of the wind, but I can adjust my sails to always reach my destination.

— Jimmy Dean

We've studied two distinct types of graphs in depth: linear and exponential. While these two types clearly have some key differences, they have one thing in common: They don't change direction. If every quantity in the world that started to increase kept doing so we'd be covered, but of course that's not the case. So to continue our study of modeling, we'll want to branch out to graphs that are allowed to change direction. We'll begin our study of one such type of graph by looking at the motion of some very, very angry winged creatures. But we'll soon see that this new type of function can be applied to many different real quantities.

0. Write down at least three real quantities you can think of that are likely to change direction when graphed.

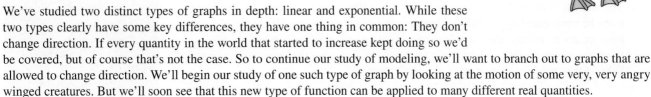

1. Ducks seem awful mild-mannered, always floating placidly on a pond, or waddling in a little line across the street. But like anyone else, push them too far and it turns out that they can be downright irate! (Especially when you couldn't get legal permission to use a different group of angry birds.) A group of beavers has started to build a dam that will flood our ducks' nests, and it's time to strike back! Draw four flight paths: one from the duck cannon on the left to each of the beavers on the right. Keep in mind that gravity exists! It's not possible to fly in a straight-line path. And birds can't fly through wooden posts. Use your imagination to change the launch angle of the cannon as necessary.

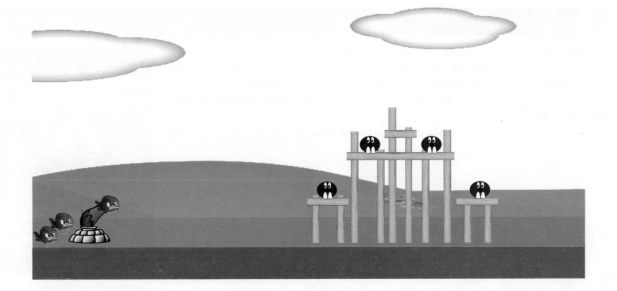

This lesson was inspired by Jake Mercer, who commandeered his dad's phone to play a certain video game involving birds. Afterwards, Dad (Brian) noticed that the smudges left on the screen resembled a well-known shape to math folks. (Young boys are not exactly known for clean hands.)

2. Describe the shape of each path in your own words. How are they similar? How are they different?

The shape of the path that an object moving through the air under the influence of gravity follows is called a **parabola**. This is illustrated in the time-lapse photo of a bouncing ball. Parabolas have several distinguishing features, but the two most obvious are the change of direction when reaching a high (or in some cases low) point, and the fact that the two halves on either side of the direction change are mirror images. This is known as **symmetry**.

3. The amount of profit that a company makes when they produce *x* units of a product can often be represented by a parabola similar to the one in the photo. Of course, if a company makes no product they'll lose money. Explain why a parabola is a good choice to model the profit. (Hint: How much profit will they make if they produce no items? What if they produce so many they can't sell them all?)

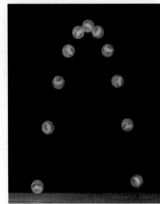

©Custom Life Science Images/ Alamy

Did You Get It

Try this problem to see if you understand the concepts we just studied. The answer can be found at the end of the Portfolio section.

1. Suppose you were modeling the temperature on a certain location from midnight until noon the following day. Do you think a parabola might make a reasonable model? Why or why not?

4-7   Group

A homeowner is planning to fence in a play area for his dog Moose, and he decides that he'd like to spend no more than the cost of 160 feet of fence. But since he wants Moose to have plenty of room for chasing squirrels, he decides to use the full 160 feet. He also wants the play area to be rectangular, as shown in the diagram. **Answer each question (except 3 and 8) with a full sentence.**

1. If he decides to make the play area 5 feet wide, how long would it be? Don't forget to consider all four sides.

Courtesy of Dave Sobecki

2. What would the length be if the play area is 50 feet wide?

3. Complete the table, then plot the points; your ordered pairs should look like (width, area), or (w, A). Recall that the area of a rectangle is the length times the width.

Width	Length	Area	Ordered Pair (w, A)
5			
10			
20			
30			
40			
50			
60			
70			
80			

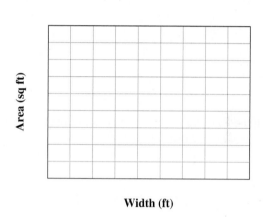

Area (sq ft)

Width (ft)

4. Based on the graph, what width makes the area as large as possible?

5. What's the area of the largest possible pen he can make out of 160 feet of fence?

6. Describe the shape that the play area should be to make the area as big as possible.

7. Write an explanation of the process used to calculate the length needed for each width.

8. Write an expression with w representing the width to describe the length when the width is w feet. Your answer to Question 7 should be a big help.

9. Write the formula for the area of a rectangle with length l and width w.

10. Substitute your expression for the length from Question 8 into the area formula for l, then simplify the result. What's the largest power of w that appears?

Did You Get It

2. Suppose that the homeowner in Questions 1–9 doesn't love Moose nearly enough, and decides to only use 100 feet of fence for the play area.

   a. What would the area be if the width is 20 feet? What about 35 feet?

   b. Write an expression for the length of the play area when the width is w feet.

   c. Use part b to write an expression for the area of the play area when the width is w feet.

The profit made by a company that manufactures wind turbines is illustrated by the following graph. The first coordinates represent the monthly number of kilowatt hours of electricity generated by their turbines in millions. We'll use the letter x to represent this variable quantity. The second coordinates of points are the company's profit in dollars. Answer every question with a complete sentence.

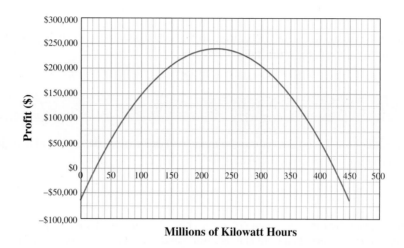

Millions of Kilowatt Hours

11. What's the y intercept of the graph? What does it tell us?

12. What are the x intercepts of the graph? What do they tell us?

13. How much electricity would need to be generated in order to make a profit of $100,000?

14. What's the maximum profit the business can earn? How much electricity needs to be generated to reach that profit?

15. The function that describes the profit made by the company is $f(x) = -6x^2 + 2,700x - 63,750$, where x represents the amount of electricity generated in millions of kilowatt hours, and $f(x)$ is the associated profit. Use a graphing calculator or computer program to recreate the graph from this problem, and use a trace and/or a table feature to verify your answers to Question 14.

A function in which the variable appears to the second power, and no other power except perhaps first, is called a **quadratic function**. Here's the general form for a quadratic function:

Definition of a Quadratic Function

A function is quadratic if it can be written in the form $f(x) = ax^2 + bx + c$, where all of a, b, and c are numbers. Note that a can't be zero, but b and c can be.

Notice that in our definition of quadratic function, a can't be zero. This is because to qualify as quadratic, a function has to have a term with the variable squared. If a is zero, that term is gone. But b and c can be zero, which tells us that the other two terms may or may not be there. Notice also that the definition says "can be written in the form." Sometimes you may have to do a bit of simplifying to recognize a quadratic function.

16. Which of the following functions is quadratic?

a. $f(x) = 4x^2 + 16x - 3$

b. $f(x) = 8x - x^2$

c. $f(x) = x^2 + 2x^3$

d. $f(x) = 2x(x - 4)$

e. $f(x) = 2x^2 + 3\sqrt{x}$

> ### Math Note
> Other than the algebraic form of the function, every quadratic function has one main thing in common: The graph is a parabola.

Did You Get It

3. a. Adapt your answer from Did You Get It 2c into a function describing the area when the width is w feet. Did you get a quadratic function?

   b. Use a calculator or computer to graph your function and use the graph to find the width that will provide the greatest play area if the cheapskate homeowner buys 100 feet of fence.

4-7 Portfolio

Name _____

Check each box when you've completed the task. Remember that your instructor will want you to turn in the portfolio pages you create.

Technology

1. ☐ Use Excel to create a graph describing the width and area of the rectangular play area in the Group portion of this lesson. Use the table on page 549 as a model for your spreadsheet. A smooth marked scatter plot should get the job done nicely. Print your graph and add labels on the key points that were discussed in Questions 1, 2, 4, and 5.

Online Practice

1. ☐ Include any written work from the online assignment along with any notes or questions about this lesson's content.

Applications

1. ☐ Complete the Applications problems.

Reflections

Type a short answer to each question.

1. ☐ If you're looking at a graph, what are some key things that will tell you that it might be a parabola?

2. ☐ How can you tell if a function is quadratic?

3. ☐ Think of some quantities that could be modeled with quadratic graphs. Did you do better than you did in Question 0 at the beginning of this lesson?

4. ☐ Name one thing you learned or discovered in this lesson that you found particularly interesting.

5. ☐ What questions do you have about this lesson?

Looking Ahead

1. ☐ Complete the Prep Skills for Lesson 4-8.

2. ☐ Read the opening paragraph in Lesson 4-8 carefully and answer Question 0 in preparation for that lesson.

Answers to "Did You Get It?"

1. It depends on the particular day, but on average this would probably be reasonable. You'd expect the temperature to decrease overnight, reaching a low early in the morning, then increase after the sun rises.

2. a. $w = 20$, $A = 600$ sq ft; $w = 35$, $A = 525$ sq ft   **b.** $50 - w$ **c.** $w(50 - w)$

3. a. $f(w) = 50w - w^2$; this is a quadratic function   **b.** 25 ft

Answers to "Prep Skills"

1. perimeter: 35 ft; area: 58.5 sq ft   **2.** 32 m   **3. a.** $3w^2 + 15w$ **b.** $80x - 10x^2 + 20x^3$

4. $P = 180 - 2w$

5. $(0, 0)$; this tells us that the drone was on the ground before it took off (flight time 0 minutes).

$(60, 0)$; this tells us that the drone landed back on the ground after being in flight for 60 minutes.

4-7   Applications

Name _____

After a football is kicked by a punter, it's subjected to gravity, and follows a parabolic path. The height of one particular punt is shown in the graph. The first coordinates represent the horizontal distance from the punter, and the second coordinates represent the height of the ball above the ground. Both measurements are in feet. **Answer each question with a full sentence.**

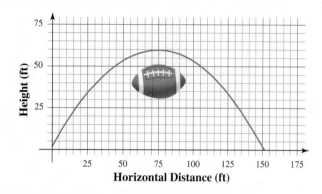

Height (ft)

Horizontal Distance (ft)

1. About how high above the ground was the ball when it was kicked?

2. How far away from where it was kicked did the ball land?

3. How high did the punt go?

4. Use the graph and some ingenuity to estimate the actual distance the punt traveled. (This is different from how far away it landed! Think of the parabola as a road, and estimate how far you'd travel on that road.) There's no right answer here: A big part of the question is describing how you got your estimate.

4-7 Applications

Name _____

The next graph also shows the height of the ball on the *y* axis, but this time the *x* coordinates are the number of seconds since the ball was kicked.

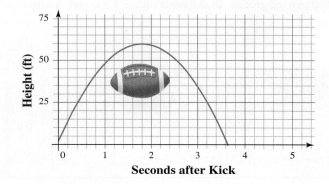

Seconds after Kick

5. The hang time of a punt is how long it's in the air before returning to the ground. What was the hang time for this punt?

6. After how many seconds was the ball 45 feet above the ground?

7. The equation of the parabola representing the ball's height is $f(x) = -18(x - 1.8)^2 + 60$, where $f(x)$ is the height in feet and *x* is the number of seconds after it was kicked. Find the exact height after the number of seconds you found in Question 6. How accurate were your answers to Question 6?

4-7 Applications

Name _____

8. If you find the value $f(4)$ in that function, why does the result not apply to the punt?

9. Explain why the shape of the graph on the previous page does NOT tell you what the flight path of the ball looked like from a side view.

Lesson 4-8 Prep Skills

SKILL 1: FIND THE EQUATION OF A LINE GIVEN TWO POINTS

We've previously studied two ways to find the equation of a line. If you know the slope of the line and the y intercept, you can use the formula $y = mx + b$, where m is the slope and b is the second coordinate of the y intercept. This allows you to just write the equation directly. That formula is called slope-intercept form.

- The equation of the line with slope $\frac{2}{3}$ and y intercept $(0, -8)$ is $y = \frac{2}{3}x - 8$.

If you know the slope and one point on the line, you can use the formula $y - y_0 = m(x - x_0)$, where m is the slope, and x_0 and y_0 are the x and y coordinates of the point that you know. This is called point-slope form.

- The equation of the line with slope -2 that goes through the point $(1, 5)$ is $y - 5 = -2(x - 1)$. You can then simplify to write in the standard form $y = mx + b$.

If you know two points on the line, you have two choices. First, you definitely need to find the slope using the slope formula $m = \frac{\text{difference of } y \text{ coordinates}}{\text{difference of } x \text{ coordinates}}$. Then you can either choose one of the two points you know and use the point-slope form, or you can use the procedure outlined below to find the equation using the slope-intercept form.

- Find the equation of line through the points $(2, 5)$ and $(-3, 15)$.

  The slope is $m = \frac{15 - 5}{-3 - 2} = \frac{10}{-5} = -2$. If we want to use the point-slope formula, we can choose either point. I'll go with $(2, 5)$.

  $$y - 5 = -2(x - 2) \quad \Rightarrow \quad y - 5 = -2x + 4 \quad \Rightarrow \quad y = -2x + 9$$

  If we want to use the slope-intercept formula, we know the equation looks like $y = -2x + b$, but we don't know what b is. Pick one of the points and substitute in for x and y. This allows us to solve for b. If we again choose the point $(2, 5)$, we substitute 5 for y and 2 for x into our equation. $5 = -2(2) + b \Rightarrow$ $5 = -4 + b \quad \Rightarrow \quad b = 9$

  Again, we get $y = -2x + 9$.

SKILL 2: COMBINE LIKE TERMS

Way back early in Unit 1, we talked about how you can only add or subtract quantities when they're like. For example, everyone knows that 12 grams of protein + 8 more grams of protein is 20 grams of protein, and that if you went toys-in-the-attic crazy and bought 42 pineapples, if someone not quite as loco as you stole 30 of them, you'd have 12 left. But 12 grams of protein + 8 grams of fat is just 12 grams of protein + 8 grams of fat: The quantities can't be added.

This idea also applies to expressions involving variable quantities. For example, $12x + 8x$ is $20x$ for the same reason that 12 grams of protein + 8 grams of protein is 20 grams of protein. We call $12x$ and $8x$ **like terms** because they each represent a certain number of the same thing: the variable quantity x. We could also subtract $42y - 30y$ to get $12y$. But $12x$ and $8y$ aren't like terms, so they can't be added or subtracted.

- $5x + 12 - 2x - 17 = 3x - 5$ $\qquad$ 5x and 2x are like terms and can be subtracted; so are 12 and 17.
- $13x - 4y + 8x - 7y + 10 = 21x - 11y + 10$

SKILL 3: MULTIPLY FACTORS

When multiplying two factors of the form ax^n, where a and n are numbers and x is a variable, you multiply the numeric coefficients together, then multiply the variable factors by adding the exponents.

- $(9y)(3y) = 27y^2$
- $(-10x^2)(7x^4) = -70x^6$

SKILL 4: USE THE DISTRIBUTIVE PROPERTY

This skill was reviewed in the Prep Skills for Lesson 1-4. In this lesson, we'll be distributing a variable into an expression, so you also need to be familiar with rules for exponents, as in this example. We'll first apply the distributive property, multiplying the y by both terms in the parentheses.

- $y(40 - 5y) = 40 \cdot y - y \cdot 5y$
$$= 40y - 5y^2$$

PREP SKILLS QUESTIONS

1. Find the equation of the line that has slope -5 and goes through the point (10, 2). Write your answer in the form $y = mx + b$.

2. Find the equation of the line that goes through the points (7, -10) and (4, 32).

3. Simplify each expression by combining like terms.
   a. $9x + 12 + 3x - 9$ b. $2a - 3b - 4a - 5 + 6b$

4. Perform each multiplication.
   a. $(12t)(5t)$ b. $\left(-\frac{5}{2}x^2\right)(4x^3)$

5. Perform each multiplication.
   a. $x(x + 5)$ b. $-4y(12 - y)$

Lesson 4-8   Minding Your Business

LEARNING OBJECTIVES

☐ 1. Combine algebraic expressions using addition or subtraction.

☐ 2. Demonstrate the relationships between revenue, cost, and profit functions.

☐ 3. Combine algebraic expressions using multiplication.

☐ 4. Write a revenue function from a demand function by multiplying algebraic expressions.

An economist is an expert who will know tomorrow why the things he predicted yesterday didn't happen today.
— Laurence J. Peter

At its core, business is simple: come up with a product or service that people want, and sell it to them. It gets complicated by competition, though. If you're the only person selling a product that people want or need, you're golden. But how often does that happen? Pretty much never. One of the most important aspects of business is studying financial figures and using them to predict future conditions. And since those figures are numbers, it should come as no surprise that we can use algebraic equations to model them. In this lesson, we'll use some common economic concepts to study some ways that we can combine expressions involving variables in order to model more complicated things in our world.

©Erik Isakson/Blend Images RF

0. How do you think studying financial figures might impact how much a company decides to charge for a certain product or service?

4-8   Group

After studying two years' worth of sales records, the owner of a popular boutique has found that she can sell 400 jars per month of a brand of bath beads that was featured on *Shark Tank* when she prices them at $12. When she temporarily lowered the price to $10, she sold 480 per month.

1. If the relationship between price and sales is linear, write an equation that relates the price p to the number of jars of bath beads sold x. Your equation should be in the form $p = mx + b$. Hint: Start by writing ordered pairs of the form (jars sold, price), then find the slope.

In economics, the word **revenue** refers to the amount of money that a business takes in as a result of selling a product or service. Revenue is pretty easy to calculate, especially if you know the amount of sales and the price: Revenue is simply the selling price times the number of units sold. Using the symbols from Question 1, revenue R is number of units sold x times price p.

2. Write an equation that represents the revenue made on bath beads for our boutique owner by using the equation $R = xp$. Then simplify your expression by multiplying out the parentheses using the distributive property. Your answer to Question 1 will be helpful.

The **costs** of doing business for a company come in two flavors: fixed and variable. Fixed costs are things like rent, utilities, insurance, and wages, which stay the same whether the company makes and sells anything or not. Variable costs refer to what it costs to produce the items being sold, which varies depending on the number of items produced.

3. The portion of the boutique's fixed monthly costs attributed to bath beads is $325; the cost of each jar of bath beads from the supplier is $3.50. Write an equation that represents the total cost C to the boutique of acquiring x jars of bath beads. Your equation should be in the form $C = mx + b$.

4. Since revenue is the amount of money a business takes in, and cost is the amount the business pays out, the difference between revenue and cost is the **profit** made by the business. That is, profit P is revenue R minus costs C. Write an equation that represents the profit made on bath beads by the boutique. (Hint: Substitute your answers to Questions 2 and 3 into the formula $P = R - C$.) Don't simplify your expression yet.

5. The costs consist of two distinct terms, and when we subtract we need to make sure to subtract ALL of the costs, not just some of them. To make sure this happens, we put parentheses around the entire cost expression; if you didn't already do this, add parentheses to your answer from Question 4. Then perform the subtraction, keeping in mind that the parentheses are there to remind you to subtract EVERY term in the expression for cost. The result is an equation describing profit in terms of jars of bath beads sold that's relatively easy to work with.

> ## Math Note
>
> In algebra, **terms** are individual parts of an expression that are added or subtracted. For example, in $250x + 30$, the terms are $250x$ and 30.

Did You Get It

Try this problem to see if you understand the concepts we just studied. The answers can be found at the end of the Portfolio section.

1. A company that makes portable Bluetooth speakers can sell x units if they price them at $p = 32 - 0.04x$ dollars. Find an equation that describes their revenue R in terms of the number of units they sell.
2. The cost function for the company in Did You Get It 1 is $C = 11.2x + 785$. Find the profit equation in the form $P = $ expression.

6. Find the profit the boutique makes if it sells 200 jars of bath beads per month.

7. Find the profit made from selling 600 jars per month.

8. How in the world can the boutique make LESS money for selling MORE bath beads? Explain.

9. What's the profit if the boutique sells no bath beads in a month? What does the result mean?

10. Use a calculator or computer to graph the profit equation you wrote and then use your graph to estimate the number of jars that must be sold to make the biggest possible profit.

11. What's the largest monthly profit that can be made on bath beads? (Use your answer to Question 10.)

12. What selling price results in the largest possible profit?

Suppose that our boutique owner decides to donate the proceeds from five sales of bath beads to a local women's shelter each month. In that case, the revenue isn't $x(-0.025x + 22)$ anymore: It's $(x - 5)(-0.025x + 22)$ because the number of items that we need to multiply by the price is five less (the proceeds from five sales donated). Could we still use the distributive property to multiply out the parentheses? We surely can. Let's have a look.

The expression that results is the product of two **binomials**, which is a fancy math term for an expression with two terms. To understand how we would perform this multiplication, let's first pretend that the $(x - 5)$ is just a number, say 10. Then the multiplication would look like

$$10(-0.025x + 22)$$

and the distributive property tells us that we can expand this as

$$10 \cdot (-0.025x) + 10 \cdot 22 = -0.25x + 22$$

No big deal, right? Now let's put the $(x - 5)$ back where it belongs, and do exactly the same thing.

$$(x - 5)(-0.025x + 22) = (x - 5) \cdot (-0.025x) + (x - 5) \cdot 22$$

Multiply $(x - 5)$ Multiply $(x - 5)$
by first term   by second term

13. Now you can use the distributive property twice because you have two terms that each have something multiplied by a difference. Multiply out both sets of parentheses. Don't combine any like terms yet. (Don't let it bother you that the term being distributed is on the right side of the parentheses! You can move it to the left if it makes you feel better.)

Using multiple applications of the distributive property is a routine you can always use to multiply two expressions that each have two or more terms. And that's fine. But if you look a little deeper, you can see a shortcut pattern. Notice that there are four terms in our answer, and those terms come from multiplying every term in the first expression by every term in the second. That's a nice general rule for this type of multiplication.

14. Combine like terms to simplify your answer to Question 13.

Multiplying Multiple-Term Expressions

To multiply two expressions that each have two or more terms, you have two choices.

1. Treat the first expression as if it were just a number, and distribute it to each term in the second expression. Then you can use the distributive property to multiply out any remaining parentheses, and finally combine any like terms.

2. Multiply every single term in the first set of parentheses by every term in the second set, then combine like terms.

15. In designing the boutique's parking lot with a 4-foot landscaping strip on three sides, an architect found that the total area could be expressed as $(w + 4)(2w + 8)$, where w is the width of the paved portion. Multiply out the parentheses in this expression and simplify.

Math Note

If you're familiar with the FOIL procedure for multiplying two binomials, feel free to use it. But remember it only works if you have two binomials!

Did you get it

3. Multiply out the parentheses: $(x + 3)(x - 5)$

The form $(w + 4)(2w + 8)$ is called the **factored form** of an expression. Notice that it's written as a product: $(w + 4)$ TIMES $(2w + 8)$. Each of $(w + 4)$ and $(2w + 8)$ is called a **factor** of the expression. Factors are things that are multiplied together; terms are things that are added or subtracted. Your answer to Question 15 is called the **expanded form** of an expression, and it's written as a sum or difference. These are two different forms of the same expression: If you input ANY value for the variable quantity x, you should get the same result from either expression. (We say that the expressions are **equivalent**.)

4-8 | Class

An algebraic expression consisting of one or more terms that look like either a real number, or a real number times a variable raised to a whole number power is called a **polynomial**. In this lesson, we've studied operations on polynomials: combining polynomials using addition, subtraction, and multiplication. Let's summarize what we've learned.

In Questions 1–4, simplify each expression. Aside from what we covered in the Group portion of this lesson, here are some things you should keep in mind:

- Order of operations: Multiplication always comes before addition or subtraction.

- The distributive property is needed when multiplying a number or variable by a sum or difference.

- When subtracting, don't forget to subtract EVERY term in an expression. That's what the parentheses are there for!

1. $(3x^2 + 3x + 5) + (2x^2 - 3x - 10)$

2. $(5x^2 + 3x + 2) - (x^2 - 2x + 7)$

3. $3(x^2 + 3x + 5) + 2(x^2 - 3x - 10)$

4. $2(3x^2 + 4x - 5) - 3(4x^2 - 5x + 1)$

Did You Get It

4. Simplify the expression as much as possible: $3(4y^2 + 7y - 3) - (8 - 4y + 6y^2)$.

You probably already noticed that multiplying expressions is more challenging than adding and subtracting them. For that reason we're going to get some more practice on multiplying and also develop a method to check and see if your result is correct when you multiply expressions. (It also works for adding and subtracting, by the way.)

5. Perform each multiplication, keeping in mind that our procedure involves multiplying every term in the first factor by every term in the second factor.

    a. $(y - 5)(y + 7)$ **b.** $(2x + 6)(3x - 8)$

6. Use the distributive property to multiply: $2x(3x + 4)$. Does this match the description in Question 5? Explain.

Now about checking our answers. Earlier we pointed out that the goal when simplifying is to get another expression that provides the exact same output as the original no matter what input you choose.

7. If two expressions satisfy that condition, what should the relationship between their graphs be? Think about what the graph of an equation really is.

8. Use a calculator or computer program to graph both $(2x + 6)(3x - 8)$ and your answer to Question 5b. Do you think your answer is correct? Explain.

9. Our next goal is to multiply $(x - 5)$ by $(x^2 + 3x + 4)$.

   a. First, multiply x by each term of $x^2 + 3x + 4$, and list the three products.

   b. Now multiply -5 by each term of $x^2 + 3x + 4$, and again list the three products. (Careful with the negative sign!)

   c. Add all six products from parts a and b, combining any like terms. This is (we hope!) the product of $(x - 5)$ and $x^2 + 3x + 4$.

10. Use a graph to decide if your answer to Question 9c is right. Explain.

Did You Get It

   5. Perform the multiplication and check your answer with a graph: $(2x + 1)(x^2 - 3x + 2)$.

4-8 Portfolio

Name _____

Check each box when you've completed the task. Remember that your instructor will want you to turn in the portfolio pages you create.

Technology

1. ☐ Create an Excel spreadsheet to explore whether or not your answer to Question 9c in the Class portion of this lesson is correct. Make sure to input a wide variety of *x* values: positive, negative, fractions, decimals, even irrational numbers if you want to impress your teacher. Can you be sure that the two expressions are equivalent by inputting a variety of values? Explain. (Bonus points for doing some online research about when two polynomials are equivalent. . . .) There's a template to help you get started in the online resources for this lesson.

	A	B	C
1	Input (x)	(x–5)(x^2+3x+4)	Answer to 9c
2			
3			
4			

Online Practice

1. ☐ Include any written work from the online assignment along with any notes or questions about this lesson's content.

Applications

1. ☐ Complete the Applications problems.

Reflections

Type a short answer to each question.

1. ☐ What is a polynomial? What is meant by the phrase "operations on polynomials"?

2. ☐ Describe the significance of each of these words in the context of this lesson: revenue, costs, profit.

3. ☐ Describe the process we developed for multiplying two expressions that each have two or more terms.

4. ☐ Name one thing you learned or discovered in this lesson that you found particularly interesting.

5. ☐ What questions do you have about this lesson?

Looking Ahead

1. ☐ Complete the Prep Skills for Lesson 4-9.

2. ☐ Read the opening paragraph in Lesson 4-9 carefully and answer Question 0 in preparation for that lesson.

Answers to "Did You Get It?"

1. $R = 32x - 0.04x^2$

2. $P = -0.04x^2 + 20.8x - 785$

3. $x^2 - 2x - 15$

4. $6y^2 + 25y - 17$

5. $2x^3 - 5x^2 + x + 2$

Answers to "Prep Skills"

1. $y = -5x + 52$ 2. $y = -14x + 88$ 3. a. $12x + 3$ b. $-2a + 3b - 5$

4. a. $60t^2$ b. $-10x^5$ 5. a. $x^2 + 5x$ b. $-48y + 4y^2$

4-8 Applications

Name _____

Based on the results of an extensive market research study that I totally made up, an economist hired by a company that makes a popular line of indoor grills predicts that consumers in one market will buy x units per week if the price is $p = -0.27x + 61$ dollars.

1. Recall that revenue is price times number of units sold, and write an equation that represents the revenue the company will make from selling x units of the grill in that market. Simplify your answer.

2. It costs the manufacturer $C = -0.12x^2 + 14x + 570$ dollars to make x units of this particular grill. Write an equation describing the profit made from selling x units of the grill in this market. The simpler your answer is, the easier it will be to work with in the next couple of questions.

3. Find the profit made if 10 grills are sold per week. What does this mean?

4. Find the profit made for sales of 100 and 250 grills. How do they compare?

5. Use a calculator or computer program to graph the profit equation you wrote in Question 2 and use it to estimate the number of grills they'd need to sell to make the largest possible profit.

4-8 Applications

Name _____

6. What's the largest profit the company can make from indoor grills in that market, and what should they set the price at to make that happen?

7. Suppose that one month the company runs a promotion where they send a rebate of the full purchase price to four randomly selected customers. To find the revenue in Question 1, you multiplied x (the number of units) by the price formula. What would you need to multiply the price by in this case?

8. Write and multiply out the revenue equation in this case.

9. Find the new profit equation using your revenue equation and the original cost equation.

10. Graph this new profit equation and see what effect this promotion has on the largest profit the company can make.

Lesson 4-9 Prep Skills

SKILL 1: IDENTIFY WHEN A LINEAR EXPRESSION IS ZERO

This is a skill that too many people try to commit to memory, rather than learning a simple procedure so that you don't have to memorize anything. To decide when an expression like $x - 7$ is zero, the most reliable method is to set up an equation with that expression on one side and zero on the other, then solve that equation.

- $x - 7$ is zero for any x that makes the equation $x - 7 = 0$ true.

  $x - 7 = 0$ Add 7 to both sides

  $x = 7$

- $y + 12$ is zero for any y that makes the equation $y + 12 = 0$ true.

  $y + 12 = 0$ Subtract 12 from both sides

  $y = -12$

Of course, if you're able to just look at $x - 7$ and figure out that it will be zero when x is replaced by 7, that's fine. But if you have ANY doubt whatsoever, set up and solve the equation.

SKILL 2: EVALUATE ALGEBRAIC EXPRESSIONS

This is a skill that we've used repeatedly throughout this book. All you really need to keep in mind is that when you're substituting in a number for a variable, you need to replace every occurrence of that symbol with the given number, then use order of operations to complete the calculation.

- Evaluate $12x^2 - 6x + 1$ for $x = 3$

  $12(3)^2 - 6(3) + 1 = 12(9) - 18 + 1 = 108 - 18 + 1 = 91$

Notice the use of parentheses around the 3. It's usually a good idea to put parentheses around the number you're substituting in, but it's especially important to do so when negatives are involved.

- Evaluate $12x^2 - 6x + 1$ for $x = -3$

  $12(-3)^2 - 6(-3) + 1 = 12(9) + 18 + 1 = 108 + 18 + 1 = 127$

Without the parentheses, some common mistakes often result:

$12 \cdot -3^2 - 6 \cdot -3 + 1$

First, -3^2 doesn't mean the same thing as $(-3)^2$: Order of operations says that -3^2 means -9, not 9. Second, it's easy to mistake the $-6 \cdot -3$ for subtraction rather than multiplication.

SKILL 3: MULTIPLY BINOMIALS

We saw in Lesson 4-8 that to multiply two algebraic expressions with more than one term, you need to multiply every term in the first expression by every term in the second, then combine like terms.

- $(x - 5)(x + 2) = x \cdot x + x \cdot 2 - 5 \cdot x - 5 \cdot 2 = x^2 + 2x - 5x - 10 = x^2 - 3x - 10$

    x from first expression
    multiplied by both terms
    in second expression

    -5 from first expression
    multiplied by both terms
    in second expression

PREP SKILLS QUESTIONS

1. Identify all x values that make the output of each expression equal to zero.

   a. $x - 4$ b. $y + 3$ c. $2x + 5$

2. Evaluate each expression for the given values of the variable.

   a. $4x - 12$; $x = 0, 4, -3$ b. $2x^2 + 3x - 1$; $x = 0, 2, -3$ c. $-3(y + 4)(y - 6)$; $y = -4, 0, 1, 6$

3. Perform each multiplication.

   a. $(x + 3)(x + 6)$ b. $(t - 4)(t + 4)$ c. $(2y - 3)(3y + 7)$

Lesson 4-9   The F Word

LEARNING OBJECTIVES

☐ 1. Explain why factoring is useful in algebra

☐ 2. Explain the connection between zeros and *x*-intercepts.

☐ 3. Factor a trinomial.

©BDS/123RF

Confidence is the most important single factor in this game, and no matter how great your natural talent, there is only one way to obtain and sustain it: work.
— Jack Nicklaus

Relax— the F word we're talking about is perfectly acceptable by FCC standards. It's only in math classes that some people feel it's a dirty word: factoring. Depending on who you ask, factoring can be thought of as anything from an essential part of every college student's curriculum, without which they would surely perish, to an archaic procedure with very limited and artificial applications in the modern world. The truth is that you can type any polynomial into Wolfram Alpha and get its factored form. The trick is in understanding what the point is, and being able to efficiently use the factored form of a polynomial to solve problems. So that will be our first order of business. We'll look at the actual process of factoring later in the lesson, just in case your school is in the "you really, really, really, really need to be able to do this" camp.

0. Without looking ahead at all, provide a description of what you think factoring is.

4-9 Group

1. Perform the multiplication: $5 \times 7 =$ _____

2. Turn your answer from Question 1 around backwards to write 35 as a product: $35 =$ _____ × _____

Congratulations—you have just factored. Isn't it bizarre that a topic that has such a bad reputation is based on such a simple idea?

Factoring is simply the process of writing a number or expression as a product. In that regard, it's essentially the opposite of performing multiplication.

Here's an example from our study of economics. In Lesson 4-8, we multiplied a variable quantity (number of units sold, represented by *x*) by the expression $-0.025x + 22$, which represented price, to get an equation describing revenue: $R = -0.025x^2 + 22x$. If we "undo" that multiplication to recover the price:

$$-0.025\,x^2 + 22x = x(-0.025x + 22)$$

we have factored, because we've written $-0.025x^2 + 22x$ as a product. Simple!

As you probably know, computers have a master volume setting that controls the volume of everything it sends through the speakers. But many applications have volume control as well, like web browsers when playing videos from YouTube. If the master volume is set to 100% and the volume in the YouTube window is set to 60%, the sound in the video will play at 60% of its max. Easy. Now let's look at some other combinations.

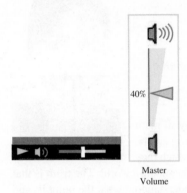

Master
Volume

3. If the volume in the YouTube window is set at half and the master volume for the computer is at 40%, what percent of the max volume do you think you'll hear from your speakers? Explain your answer.

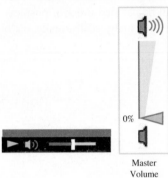

Master
Volume

4. If the volume in the YouTube window is set at half and the master volume for the computer is at 0, what percent of the max volume do you think you'll hear from your speakers? Explain your answer.

Master
Volume

5. If the volume in the YouTube window is set all the way to the left and the master volume for the computer is at 80%, what percent of the max volume do you think you'll hear from your speakers? Explain your answer.

Conclusions:

6. To get the overall volume, we _____ the percentages in decimal form from the master volume and the YouTube volume.

7. You can only get zero as the overall volume if _____.

So what does this have to do with factoring?

8. For what value of the variable quantity x does the expression $x - 4$ have output zero? What about the expression $x + 5$? (Don't over-think these. They're really easy.)

9. Now look at the product $(x - 4)(x + 5)$, which is a polynomial in factored form. Find the value of the product when . . .

a. $x = 2$ **b.** $x = 4$ **c.** $x = 0$ **d.** $x = -1$ **e.** $x = -5$

Conclusion:

10. The only way a product of algebraic expressions can have value zero is if _____ .

Did You Get It

Try this problem to see if you understand the concepts we just studied. The answer can be found at the end of the Portfolio section.

1. Find all values of y for which the output of the expression $(y - 8)(y + 5)$ is zero.

And THAT'S why factoring is a big deal in algebra. It provides an important technique for solving equations that have zero on one side.

11. Write the number 37 as a product.

12. Write the polynomial expression $3x + 5$ as a product.

In Questions 11 and 12, there's only one way to write the given number or expression as a product (unless you're willing to use fractions, which we are not at the moment): one times the number or expression itself. In the case of 37, we call it a **prime number**. For the polynomial $3x + 5$, we say that it is a **prime polynomial**.

The point: Not every expression can be factored if we restrict our attention to integer coefficients.

4-9 Class

Other than what it means to factor, the main point of the Group portion of this lesson is why factoring is a **big deal**: It makes it simple to see when an expression has output equal to zero, which has important applications in solving equations.

If $x = c$ is an input value for which the output of a function $f(c)$ is zero, we call the input c a **zero** of the function. There's a useful relationship between the factors of a polynomial, the zeros of the related function, and the x intercepts of the graph.

The Connection Between Factors, Zeros, and Intercepts

For a given polynomial $P(x)$ and a real number c, each of these statements say the same thing:

The point $(c, 0)$ is an x intercept of the graph of $P(x)$. **(Graphical)**	The input c is a zero of $P(x)$, which means that $P(c) = 0$. **(Numerical)**	The expression $(x - c)$ is one of the factors of $P(x)$. **(Algebraic)**

1. For the polynomial $P(x) = (x - 1)(x + 5)$, find each output. Use P in this factored form.

   a. $P(-5)$ **b.** $P(-3)$

   c. $P(-1)$ **d.** $P(1)$

2. Use the table and graph provided for $P(x) = (x - 1)(x + 5)$ to answer each question.

x	$P(x)$
−5	0
−4	−5
−3	−8
−2	−9
−1	−8
0	−5
1	0

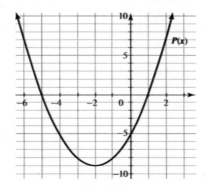

   a. List the factors of $P(x)$.

b. List the zeros of $P(x)$.

c. List the x intercepts of the graph.

3. Now let's look at the function $f(x) = x^2 + 2x - 3$.

x	f(x)
−4	5
−3	0
−2	−3
−1	−4
0	−3
1	0
2	5

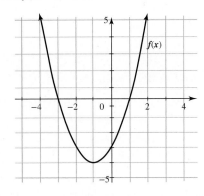

a. List the zeros of $f(x)$.

b. List the x intercepts of the graph.

c. Use parts a and b to write the factored form of $f(x) = x^2 + 2x - 3$. If you're not sure how to do this, look back at the colored box that comes before Question 1.

Use the factored form of each polynomial to list the zeros and x intercepts of the polynomial's graph.

4. $P(x) = 2(x - 3)(x - 4)$

Zeros:

x intercepts:

5. $y(x) = (x + 5)(x + 4)(x - 2)$

Zeros:

x intercepts:

Did You Get It

2. The x intercepts of the parabola $f(x) = x^2 + 2x - 35$ are $(5, 0)$ and $(-7, 0)$. Write a factored form of the function.
3. List the zeros and x intercepts for the function: $P(x) = -3(x + 2)(x - 10)$.

At this point you should have a pretty solid grasp on what factoring means, and some of the information you can get from the factored form of a polynomial. That leaves the $100,000 question: *How do you get that factored form?* Factoring is a topic that you could spend a couple of weeks studying in depth, but we just want to give you a quick look at one particular type of factoring that pops up a lot in the study of quadratic equations and functions.

There are many different theories and techniques on how to do this type of factoring, and in many ways we're going to leave it up to your instructor to decide how (or even if) to cover factoring. We'll just make some general suggestions, which are based on a key skill we learned in the last lesson: multiplying two binomials.

6. Perform the multiplication: $(x + 2)(x + 12)$. DO NOT combine like terms.

7. When you multiply two binomials, you'll always get four terms at first. If both of those binomials have a first power term and a constant, two of the four terms will be like terms, so you can combine them to get a final answer with three terms. Do that now.

8. What you did in Question 6 was quite literally the *opposite* of factoring. Why?

The final result of the multiplication you did is a quadratic expression with three terms: one with the variable squared, one with the variable to the first power, and one constant term. An expression of this type is called a **trinomial** because it has three terms, and the key to factoring expressions of this form is recognizing that they're the ANSWER to a "multiply binomials" problem.

Now let's look carefully at the multiplication:

$$(x + 2)(x + 12) = x^2 + 14x + 24$$

The first term of the resulting trinomial (x^2) came from multiplying the first terms of the binomials ($x \cdot x$). The last term of the trinomial (24) came from multiplying the second terms of the binomials ($2 \cdot 12$). And the middle term ($14x$) came from a combination of the outside terms ($12 \cdot x$) and the inside terms ($2 \cdot x$). We can take advantage of these observations to turn this process around backwards.

The expression $x^2 + 5x + 6$ can be factored into the product of two binomials (not obvious, but trust us for a moment). In that case, we can set up an equation as follows:

$$x^2 + 5x + 6 = (\_\_ + \_\_)(\_\_ + \_\_)$$

Our job is to fill in the blanks.

9. What product would give us x^2? Write your answers in the first blank in each factor.

$$x^2 + 5x + 6 = (\_\_ + \_\_)(\_\_ + \_\_)$$

10. One pair of numbers that could give us a constant term of 6 is $1 \cdot 6$. Write those in the second blanks, then multiply out the parentheses and see if you get $x^2 + 5x + 6$.

11. Think of another pair of numbers with product 6, write them on the blank lines and multiply out the parentheses again to see if you get the right product this time.

$$(x + \_\_)(x + \_\_)$$

This is a reliable process for factoring trinomials. I like to think of it as a game of hangman: Set up the parentheses with four blanks to fill in, then figure out what needs to go in each blank to get the right product. When you practice the process a bit, you'll be able to figure out what to put in the blanks much more efficiently. (If your instructor thinks it's important for you to do so, that is.)

Let's try another example: Factor $y^2 - 3y - 10$.

12. How can you get y^2 as a product? Set up parentheses like we did in Question 9, and use your results to fill in the first blank in each set of parentheses.

13. List all pairs of numbers whose product is the constant term, -10. Don't forget to think about the sign!

14. Find a pair of numbers from your list that you can put into the second blanks in each set of parentheses to get a product of $y^2 - 3y - 10$, then write the factored form of that polynomial.

15. Now try one more factoring problem. Don't let the coefficient of x^2 bother you: The same process works just fine, but you'll have to be careful when placing the pairs of numbers with product -20 in the second blanks: Try them in both orders.

$$2x^2 - 3x - 20$$

Did You Get It

4. Factor each trinomial.

   a. $x^2 + 6x + 8$ b. $y^2 - y - 30$ c. $2x^2 - 17x - 9$

Dude, what's the point?

I'm glad you asked. We have seen that when you know the factored form of a polynomial, it's super easy to find the x intercepts of its graph. And this can be used to solve many problems, like this one.

   If you make your living from growing produce, say apples, the more apples you grow, the more you can sell. Duh. So why not just plant a million apple trees? Space and resources. If the trees are too densely planted, they compete with each other for resources, and each tree produces less. So too many trees could mean less apples. And it's pretty obvious that not enough trees means less apples. Hey—maybe it's useful to find the ideal number of apple trees to plant.

In one orchard, there are 50 trees, each of which produces 800 apples. For every additional tree planted, the average output per tree drops by 10 apples. Bummer. How many additional trees should be planted to get the largest total number of apples?

16. If x more trees are planted, how many trees will there be total?

17. If the current yield per tree is 800, and will go down by 10 for each new tree planted, what will the yield per tree be if 5 more trees are planted?

18. If the current yield per tree is 800, and will go down by 10 for each new tree planted, what will the yield per tree be if x more trees are planted?

19. The total number of apples produced will be the total number of trees times the yield per tree. Write a function $T(x)$ describing the total number of apples, using your answers to Questions 16 and 18.

20. Find the x intercepts of the function you wrote in Question 19.

21. The graph of this function is a parabola that opens down, and parabolas are symmetric. That means the high point we're looking for has to be halfway between the x intercepts. How many new trees should they plant, and how many apples will be produced?

4-9 Portfolio

Name _____

Check each box when you've completed the task. Remember that your instructor will want you to turn in the portfolio pages you create.

Technology

1. ☐ As we mentioned in the opening paragraph of this lesson, the website Wolfram Alpha (the URL, shockingly, is wolframalpha.com) can factor pretty much anything that is factorable. So go to the site and ask Wolfram Alpha to factor the polynomials from Questions 14 and 15 in the Class portion of this lesson. In exchange for your effort, you'll get back a factored form of the polynomials, and a whole lot more. Put a printout of the result in your portfolio, then type a brief report on some of the other things you can learn about the polynomials this way.

Online Practice

1. ☐ Include any written work from the online assignment along with any notes or questions about this lesson's content.

Applications

1. ☐ Complete the Applications problems.

Reflections

Type a short answer to each question.

1. ☐ What is the value of having the factored form of a polynomial? Think of as many different aspects as you can.

2. ☐ Describe the relationship between factoring and multiplication.

3. ☐ Name one thing you learned or discovered in this lesson that you found particularly interesting.

4. ☐ What questions do you have about this lesson?

Looking Ahead

1. ☐ Complete the Prep Skills for Lesson 4-10.

2. ☐ Read the opening paragraph in Lesson 4-10 carefully and answer Question 0 in preparation for that lesson.

Answers to "Did You Get It?"

1. $y = 8$ and $y = -5$ **2.** $(x - 5)(x + 7)$

3. Zeros: $x = -2, 10$; x intercepts: $(-2, 0)$ and $(10, 0)$

4. a. $(x + 4)(x + 2)$ **b.** $(y - 6)(y + 5)$ **c.** $(2x + 1)(x - 9)$

Answers to "Prep Skills"

1. a. $x = 4$ **b.** $y = -3$ **c.** $x = -2.5$

2. a. $-12, 4, -24$ **b.** $-1, 13, 8$ **c.** $0, 72, 75, 0$

3. a. $x^2 + 9x + 18$ **b.** $t^2 - 16$ **c.** $6y^2 + 5y - 21$

4-9 Applications

Name _____

A trendy nightclub has a $10 cover charge, and gets 540 patrons on an average night. After surveying customers, they're able to estimate that for each additional $1 they add to the cover charge, they'll lose an average of 20 patrons per night.

1. If they add x one-dollar increments to the cover charge, write an expression describing the new charge.

2. If they add x one-dollar increments, how many patrons will they lose on average? What will be the new average number of customers?

3. Write a function $R(x)$ that describes the average nightly revenue if they raise the current price by $$x$. (Hint: You'll need your answers to Questions 1 and 2.)

4. Find $R(0)$ and describe what it means.

5. Find the x intercepts of your function and describe what each tells us about the nightclub's cover charge and revenue.

6. If all has gone well, the graph of your revenue function should be a parabola that opens down. Since parabolas are symmetric, the highest point on the graph is halfway between the x intercepts. Use that fact to find the highest point on the graph, and describe in detail what it tells you about the nightclub's cover charge and revenue.

4-9   Applications

Name _____

As part of a stunt for a late-night TV show, an intern throws a golf ball upward from a Manhattan balcony at a speed of 32 feet per second. Any halfway competent physicist would tell you that in that case, the height of the ball t seconds after it's released can be modeled by the function $h(t) = -16(t^2 - 2t - 3)$. For what it's worth, this is only true if you're willing to ignore friction and wind resistance (which I do as often as I can—I hate those guys), but for a golf ball those are reasonably negligible.

7. From what height is the ball thrown? (Hint: How many seconds after it was released is the time when it was released?)

8. Factor the polynomial $t^2 - 2t - 3$.

9. Using your answer to Question 8, find the zeros of the height function, and describe what each of them tells us about the golf ball.

Lesson 4-10   Prep Skills

SKILL 1: EVALUATE FUNCTIONS

Evaluating an algebraic expression for a certain input is probably one of the two or three skills that we've used most in this entire course, so I have to think you're pretty comfortable with that by now. The only thing that's a little bit different now is the notation, since we've introduced functions. Before, we may have given you an expression like $3x^2 - 10$ and asked you to evaluate it for an input like $x = 2$. So you'd replace x with 2, do some arithmetic, and life is good. Now, we'll give you a function $f(x) = 3x^2 - 10$ and ask you to find $f(2)$. *This means exactly the same thing!* When you see the symbol $f(2)$, you just think of it as finding the value of the function f when the input variable is replaced by 2.

SKILL 2: PLUG NUMBERS INTO A COMPLICATED FORMULA

Wait, we just got done talking about evaluating a function for a given input. Isn't this the same skill? It is, but most of the formulas that we've plugged numbers into have been relatively simple. But in this lesson, you'll need to evaluate a formula that has a lot going on, so a little practice at that would be a nice preparation for the lesson.

- For $f(x) = \dfrac{\sqrt{x^2 - 2x} + x}{2x}$, find $f(5)$ and $f(-4)$.

  As always, the goal is to first replace the variable (x in this case) with the given input. Then we'll have to be extra careful with the arithmetic.

  $$f(5) = \frac{\sqrt{5^2 - 2(5)} + 5}{2(5)} = \frac{\sqrt{25 - 10} + 5}{10} = \frac{\sqrt{15} + 5}{10} \approx \frac{3.87 + 5}{10} = \frac{8.87}{10} = 0.887$$

  $$f(-4) = \frac{\sqrt{(-4)^2 - 2(-4)} + (-4)}{2(-4)} = \frac{\sqrt{16 - (-8)} + (-4)}{-8} = \frac{\sqrt{24} - 4}{-8} \approx \frac{4.90 - 4}{-8} = \frac{0.9}{-8} \approx -0.11$$

SKILL 3: REVIEW ECONOMIC TERMS

In Lesson 4-8, we used the economics of operating a business to study quadratic functions. This is just a quick review of the econ concepts.

   The **price** p that a company charges for a certain item is often described as a function of the number of items that sell. An example is something like $p = -0.02x + 18$, where p is price in dollars, and x is units sold.

   The **revenue** is the total amount of money brought in by the company for selling x items. To find revenue, multiply the number of items sold x by the price function p. In this case, the revenue is $R = x(-0.02x + 18) = -0.02x^2 + 18x$.

   The **cost** function describes the cost to the company of making and/or selling x items. It's also a function with variable x.

   The **profit** function describes the amount of money left over from the revenue after costs are subtracted. So a formula for profit is $P = R - C$, where R is the revenue and C is cost.

- If the cost function for the product above is $C = 850 + 3.5x$, the profit is

  $$P = R - C = -0.02x^2 + 18x - (850 + 3.5x)$$
  $$= -0.02x^2 + 18x - 850 - 3.5x$$
  $$= -0.02x^2 + 14.5x - 850$$

SKILL 4: FIND AND INTERPRET INTERCEPTS FOR A GRAPH

This skill was reviewed in the Prep Skills for Lesson 4-7 if you need a refresher.

PREP SKILLS QUESTIONS

1. For $f(x) = 1.3x^2 + 5x - 10$, find $f(0)$, $f(60)$, and $f(330)$.

2. Evaluate the formula for $a = -6.2$ and $b = 12.1$:
$$\frac{7a - \sqrt{b^2 - 4(3a)}}{5b}$$

3. When selling x units of a certain product, a company can charge $p = 8.5 - 0.035x$ dollars per item. The cost of producing and shipping the items is $C = 1{,}462 + 1.8x$. Find functions that describe the revenue and the profit for this product.

4. For the price function in Question 3, find the intercepts and describe what each means in the situation.

Lesson 4-10   Going. . . Going. . . GONE!

LEARNING OBJECTIVES

☐ 1. Solve a quadratic equation using the quadratic formula.

☐ 2. Find the vertex of a parabola using $x = \dfrac{-b}{2a}$.

☐ 3. Solve application problems using the quadratic formula.

Every strike brings me closer to the next home run.
                    — George Herman "Babe" Ruth

Baseball purists will tell you that a well-pitched game is the pinnacle of the sport, but the average fan goes to the park hoping to see some home runs—and the longer, the better. There's just something cool about seeing a ball hit back back back, and gone. And in the information age, fans don't just want to speculate on how far a home run was hit: They want a measurement, and want it RIGHT NOW. So most ballparks and TV broadcasts now supply a distance after a home run is hit. But how do they calculate the distances? If you guessed "math," you're pretty smart. We've already seen that objects flying through the air tend to follow a parabolic path. In this lesson, we'll learn more about studying parabolas from an algebraic standpoint. This allows us to get more information about things like—you guessed it—how far a home run travels.

©Akihiro Sugimoto/agefotostock RF

0. What information do you think we would need about the flight of an object in order to find an equation that models its path?

4-10 | Class

As of this writing, it's been over 8 years since a major league baseball player hit a home run longer than 500 feet. There have been a few close calls, the longest of which was hit on August 6, 2016, by Giancarlo Stanton of the Miami Marlins. Based on information provided by a cool website called "Home Run Tracker," we can approximate the flight of that ball with this function: $f(x) = -0.00146x^2 + 0.718x + 2.5$. The input x represents the number of horizontal feet from where the ball was hit, while the output $f(x)$ is the height above the ground after the ball had traveled x feet horizontally. In order to find the total distance the ball was hit, we'd need to find the horizontal distance (x) that corresponds to a height of zero feet (when the ball would have returned to ground level if it hadn't been stopped by the stands).

So we'd need to solve this equation:

$$-0.00146x^2 + 0.718x + 2.5 = 0$$

In Lesson 4-9, we learned how to solve a quadratic equation if the side with the variable is factored. But that's not the case here, and we don't know how to factor something with decimals. So we need a method to solve a quadratic equation that isn't in factored form.

Math Note

If you want to learn more about the math behind estimating home run distance, do a Google search for "how hit tracker works."

Fortunately, there's a formula that provides solutions to any quadratic equation, as long as it's written in the **standard form** $ax^2 + bx + c = 0$, where a is not zero.

The Quadratic Formula

The solutions to a quadratic equation in the form $ax^2 + bx + c = 0$ are

$$x = \frac{-b + \sqrt{b^2 - 4ac}}{2a} \text{ and } x = \frac{-b - \sqrt{b^2 - 4ac}}{2a}$$

This is sometimes written more concisely as

$$x = \frac{-b \pm \sqrt{b^2 - 4ac}}{2a}$$

where the symbol "$\pm$" is read "plus or minus" and means one solution comes from adding and the other from subtracting.

Important Note
a is the coefficient of the term with the variable squared, b is the coefficient of the variable to the first power, and c is the constant term.

1. For the equation describing Giancarlo Stanton's home run on the previous page, what numbers correspond to a, b, and c in the quadratic formula?

2. Use the quadratic formula to find the two solutions to that equation. Round to one decimal place if necessary.

3. One of the solutions provides the length of the home run. What was it?

4. What is the significance of the other solution in the physical situation?

Did You Get It

Try this problem to see if you understand the concepts we just studied. The answer can be found at the end of the Portfolio section.

1. In Did You Get It 1 and 2 in Lesson 4-8, we found that the revenue for a company that makes speakers was $R = 32x - 0.04x^2$ and the profit was $P = -0.04x^2 + 20.8x - 785$, where x in each case is number of speakers sold. Find the number of units that will make each of the revenue and profit equal to zero.

If we rewrite the two solutions provided by the quadratic formula just a bit, something interesting happens:

$$x = -\frac{b}{2a} + \frac{\sqrt{b^2 - 4ac}}{2a} \text{ and } x = -\frac{b}{2a} - \frac{\sqrt{b^2 - 4ac}}{2a}$$

Let's visualize that a bit differently:

$$x = -\frac{b}{2a} + some\ number \text{ and } x = -\frac{b}{2a} - that\ same\ number$$

This allows us to see that the x value $-\dfrac{b}{2a}$ is exactly halfway between the two solutions.

5. What's the connection between the solutions of the equation $ax^2 + bx + c = 0$ and the x intercepts of the graph of $f(x) = ax^2 + bx + c$?

6. The point where a parabola changes direction is called the **vertex** of the parabola. How do we know that the vertex has to be halfway between the x intercepts?

Combining Question 6 with the observation at the top of the page, we get a simple way to find the vertex of a parabola when we know the equation:

The Vertex Formula

For a quadratic function $f(x) = ax^2 + bx + c$, the x coordinate of the vertex can be found using the formula

$$x = -\frac{b}{2a}$$

Once you know the x coordinate, you can find the y coordinate by substituting the x coordinate in for x in the function and simplifying.

7. Use the vertex formula to find the first coordinate of the vertex for the function describing Stanton's home run:
$f(x) = -0.00146x^2 + 0.718x + 2.5$.

8. What does your answer describe about the home run?

9. Now evaluate $f(x)$ for the input you found in Question 7. What does that tell you about the home run?

Did You Get It

2. Find the vertex of the parabola $f(x) = 4x^2 - 12x + 65$. Remember that the vertex is a POINT, not a number.
3. Find $f(0)$. Based on your results, is the vertex the highest or lowest point on the graph? How can you tell?

4-10 | Group

In Lesson 4-8, we learned a lot about the economics of a boutique that sold a popular brand of bath beads. This was because we had enough information to model their revenue and profit with quadratic functions. But when it came down to analyzing those functions to find things like the maximum profit and the number of items they'd need to sell to break even, we were limited by having to estimate values from the graph.

There's nothing *wrong* with doing that—one of the central themes of this course is the value of visualizing data graphically. But now that we know the quadratic and vertex formulas, we can find exact answers to questions that we had to estimate before.

1. The price function for bath beads was $p = -0.025x + 22$, the revenue function was $R = -0.025x^2 + 22x$, and the profit function was $P = -0.025x^2 + 18.5x - 325$. Do you think the same number of items would make BOTH the revenue and profit have output zero? Don't use the formulas: Think about what revenue and profit mean, and explain your answer.

2. Use the quadratic formula to find the zeros of the revenue and profit functions and discuss whether what you find matches your thoughts in Question 1.

3. Do you think the number of units that provides the most revenue is the same as the number of units that provides the most profit? Again, this isn't based on the formulas. Think about the situation.

4. Find the number of units that provides the maximum revenue and the maximum profit and discuss whether what you found matches your thoughts in Question 3.

5. Find the exact maximum profit that the boutique can make from these bath beads.

6. What should they charge for each jar to make the most profit?

7. What price provides the largest revenue? What would the profit be at that price?

8. Superficially, you might think that charging more for a product will lead to making more money; that selling more items will lead to making more money; and that taking in the most revenue would lead to making the most money. Discuss what you've learned in studying the boutique business about all of those statements. More detail means you learned more!

Did You Get It

4. For the company in Did You Get It 1, the price function was $p = 32 - 0.04x$. Find the number of items and the price that would lead to the largest possible profit. How much would the company make in that case?

4-10 Portfolio

Name _____

Check each box when you've completed the task. Remember that your instructor will want you to turn in the portfolio pages you create.

Technology

1. ☐ Build a spreadsheet that finds the solutions of any quadratic equation of the form $ax^2 + bx + c = 0$ when values for a, b, and c are entered. Then use your spreadsheet to confirm the distances you found for the home run described on the first page of this lesson. Do the results agree with your answers to Question 2 in the Class portion of this lesson? A template to help you get started can be found in the online resources for this lesson.

	A	B	C	D	E
1	a	b	c	Solution 1	Solution 2
2					

Online Practice

1. ☐ Include any written work from the online assignment along with any notes or questions about this lesson's content.

Applications

1. ☐ Complete the Applications problems.

Reflections

Type a short answer to each question.

1. ☐ What is the quadratic formula used for? Why is that so useful? Discuss.

2. ☐ What types of applied problems can be solved using the vertex formula?

3. ☐ Name one thing you learned or discovered in this lesson that you found particularly interesting.

4. ☐ What questions do you have about this lesson?

Looking Ahead

1. ☐ Complete the Prep Skills for Lesson 4-11.

2. ☐ Read the opening paragraph in Lesson 4-11 carefully and answer Question 0 in preparation for that lesson.

Answers to "Did You Get It?"

1. Revenue: 0 and 800 units; Profit: About 41 and 479 units

2. (1.5, 56)

3. $f(0) = 65$; since there's a point higher than 56, the vertex must be the lowest point.

4. 260 items at $21.60 profit is $1,919

Answers to "Prep Skills"

1. $f(0) = -10; f(60) = 4,970; f(330) = 143,210$

2. -0.96

3. $R = 8.5x - 0.035x^2$
   $P = -0.035x^2 + 6.7x - 1,462$

4. p intercept: (0, 8.5); This means if the company sells no product, they can charge $8.50 per item (this doesn't really make sense in real life).

   x intercept: (243, 0); This means if the company gives the items away (price is $0), they would give away about 243 items.

4-10   Applications

Name _____

The height of a golf ball in meters can be described by the equation $h = -4.9t^2 + 23.5t$, where t is the number of seconds after it was hit. (Note: This is different from our home run equations, where the input x represented the number of horizontal feet traveled.)

1. Use a calculator or spreadsheet to make a table of inputs and outputs for this function. The variable t should start out at zero and increment by 0.2. Then use the result to draw a detailed graph of the function.

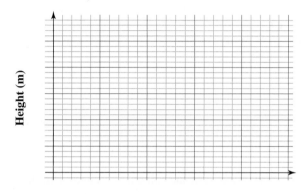

Time (sec)

2. Find the vertex of the parabola using the formula we developed in this lesson, rounding each coordinate to the nearest tenth.

3. Explain what each coordinate of the vertex means.

4. Find the intercepts for the function.

4-10 Applications

Name _____

5. Explain what each intercept means.

6. Describe when the ball is headed upward, and when it's coming back down.

7. The function $d(t) = 49.2t$ describes the horizontal distance (in meters) traveled by the ball after t seconds. How far did it go?

8. The distance for golf shots is traditionally measured in yards. Given that there are 3 feet in a yard and that 1 meter is 3.28 feet, how far in yards did the shot go?

On November 2, 2016, Rajai Davis of the Cleveland Indians hit a 2-run home run that tied game 7 of the World Series in the bottom of the eighth inning. Using Home Run Tracker data, I was able to find a function that models the flight of the ball:

$$f(x) = -0.00175x^2 + 0.6315x + 1.9$$

where x is the horizontal distance in feet from where the ball was hit and $f(x)$ is the height in feet.

4-10 Applications

Name _____

9. How high was the ball at the time it was hit?

10. Find the solutions to the equation $-0.00175x^2 + 0.6315x + 1.9 = 0$ and describe what each tells us about the home run.

11. The home run fence is 19 feet high at the point where the ball went over it, which is about 325 feet from where the ball was hit. By how much did the ball clear the fence?

Lesson 4-11 Prep Skills

SKILL 1: INPUT DATA AND FIND A REGRESSION EQUATION

This skill was the topic of Lesson 3-9, where we learned how to use both calculators and spreadsheets for finding regression equations. Refer to the Tech boxes in that lesson along with the accompanying videos in online resources if you need a refresher. We also practiced this skill in Lesson 4-6, where we found exponential equations of best fit. You should probably review the Tech box in that lesson as well.

SKILL 2: FIND THE CORRELATION COEFFICIENT AND RESIDUALS

Each of the correlation coefficient and residuals are means for deciding how accurately a given regression equation matches the data that it came from. In the case of correlation coefficient, this is provided by the technology used to find the equation. But you need to know that in some cases the technology provides r^2, which is the square of the correlation coefficient r. In that case, you'll need to find the square root.

The residual of a data point is defined to be the difference between the actual value and the value predicted by the regression equation. So the way you find a residual is

1. Evaluate the regression equation for the input of a known data point. This is the value predicted by the equation.

2. Compute Actual value − Predicted value.

SKILL 3: USE THE QUADRATIC FORMULA

This was the main skill that we studied in Lesson 4-10. The quadratic formula is good for exactly one thing: solving quadratic equations in the form $ax^2 + bx + c = 0$. The order is really important here: a always stands for the coefficient of the x^2 term, b is always the coefficient of the x term, and c is always the constant term. Once you have an equation in that form, you should identify and WRITE DOWN a, b, and c. Then substitute those values into the quadratic formula

$$x = \frac{-b \pm \sqrt{b^2 - 4ac}}{2a}$$

and do the arithmetic to find the solutions. Remember that there are TWO solutions. The symbol "$\pm$" is read as "plus or minus" and it means BOTH add and subtract. So another way to look at the quadratic formula is that it supplies two solutions:

$$x = \frac{-b + \sqrt{b^2 - 4ac}}{2a} \text{ and } x = \frac{-b - \sqrt{b^2 - 4ac}}{2a}$$

- The solutions of $4x^2 - 8x - 9 = 0$ are

$$x = \frac{-b \pm \sqrt{b^2 - 4ac}}{2a} = \frac{-(-8) \pm \sqrt{(-8)^2 - 4(4)(-9)}}{2(4)} \qquad a = 4, b = -8, c = -9$$

$$= \frac{8 \pm \sqrt{64 - (-144)}}{8} = \frac{8 \pm \sqrt{208}}{8} \approx \frac{8 \pm 14.4}{8}$$

This provides two solutions: $\dfrac{8 + 14.4}{8} = 2.8$ and $\dfrac{8 - 14.4}{8} = -0.8$.

SKILL 4: FIND THE VERTEX OF A PARABOLA

The vertex of a parabola is the key point on the graph: It's where a parabola changes direction, making it either the highest or lowest point on the graph. There's a simple procedure for finding the vertex, and it uses the same symbols as the quadratic formula. The first coordinate of the vertex is given by the formula

$$x = -\frac{b}{2a}$$

where b is again the coefficient of the x term and a is the coefficient of the x^2 term. Once you have the first coordinate from this formula, you find the second coordinate the same way you would find the second coordinate for any input: by plugging back into the equation.

- The graph of the function $f(x) = -3x^2 + 12x - 4$ is a parabola. The first coordinate of the vertex is $x = -\frac{b}{2a} = -\frac{12}{2(-3)} = -\frac{12}{-6} = 2$. The second coordinate is $f(2) = -3(2)^2 + 12(2) - 4 = -12 + 24 - 4 = 8$. So the vertex is the point (2, 8).

PREP SKILLS QUESTIONS

1. Find an exponential function of best fit for the data in the table.

x	0	5	10	15	20	25
y	12,406	9,430	6,023	4,803	3,411	1,000

2. Find the correlation coefficient for the exponential model in Question 1, then find the residuals for each data point.

3. Find all solutions to each equation.

   a. $x^2 + 15x - 3 = 0$ b. $4y^2 - 3y - 10 = 0$ c. $-0.03x^2 + 0.276x + 12.6 = 0$

4. Find the vertex of the parabola for each quadratic function that makes up the left side of the equations in Question 3.

Lesson 4-11   Down the Drain

LEARNING OBJECTIVES

☐ 1. Calculate the equation of best fit for a set of quadratic data using technology.

☐ 2. Solve application problems that involve a quadratic set of data.

A great accomplishment shouldn't be the end of the road, just the starting point for the next leap forward.

> —Harvey Mackay

©Shutterstock/Pavel Ilyukhin RF

So this is it, friends: the end of our journey. But as the quote indicates, we're hoping that you won't see this as the end of math literacy, but the beginning of the rest of your life, a life that you can proudly live as someone who understands the value of using math in our world. We've modeled so many different things using math that it seems appropriate to finish up with one more lesson on modeling. You may have wondered where exactly the functions we used to model home runs in the last lesson came from. Does the Home Run Tracker website give formulas? The answer is no. But it does give more than enough information for us to use the regression techniques that we've learned to find a parabola of best fit. In this lesson, we'll get you up out of your seats for one more shot at active learning, and develop some data that might be modeled well by a quadratic function.

0. Do you think that data can be modeled by a quadratic function even if it doesn't change direction? That is, if it always increases or decreases?

4-11   Group

Experiment: The Time Needed to Drain a Bottle

Supplies needed:

- A clear 2-liter plastic bottle (or larger) with a hole drilled near the bottom of the straight-walled portion. The heights in the table on the next page should be marked on the bottle either with a permanent marker, or by attaching a paper strip with height markings. Height zero should be marked at the height of the hole. Experiment with the hole size so that it takes roughly 3 minutes for the bottle to drain. About 1/4 inch is a good place to start. You might also consider different size holes for different groups.

- Water and a bucket to drain water into.

- A watch that displays seconds. The stop watch feature on a smartphone works well.

1. Cover the drain hole, then fill the bottle up to the 20-cm mark. Set the time to zero seconds. Then uncover the drain hole and take the cap off the bottle. As the water drains out, record the time for each height in the table.

x Time (sec)	y Height (cm)
0	20
	18
	16
	14
	12
	10

x Time (sec)	y Height (cm)
	8
	6
	4
	2
	0

2. Use your data to create a scatter plot on the grid provided.

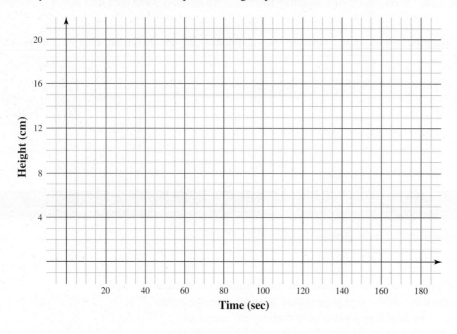

3. Do you think a linear or quadratic model is best suited to fit the data from this experiment?

4. What information in the table or graph supports your choice in Question 3? Explain why you think your choice makes sense.

5. Now try your best to ignore the scatter plot and data. Was there anything about what physically happened during the experiment that you think supports your choice in Question 3? Explain.

6. Find either the line or parabola of best fit, depending on which you chose in Question 3. You might encounter coefficients in scientific notation, so watch out for that. Round to four decimal places. Find the correlation coefficient if you choose a linear model, and the value of r^2 if you choose a quadratic model. (Calculators and spreadsheets will most likely show only r^2 if the model isn't linear: the correlation coefficient r is designed to measure how close to linear a model is.) The closer r^2 is to one, the closer a quadratic model fits the actual data.

7. Use your model to predict the time when the water in the bottle reaches 2 cm above the drain hole. How does this compare to your experimental data?

8. What's the value of y when x is 50? Explain the meaning of these values.

9. Find the value of x when y is 11. Explain what these values mean, and compare to what you would predict based strictly on the table.

Did You Get It

Try this problem to see if you understand the concepts we just studied. The answer can be found at the end of the Portfolio section.

1. Find the quadratic equation of best fit for the data shown, which represent the profit made by one company when they produce and sell x items. Find the value of r^2 as well.

x (Items)	0	100	200	300	400	500
y (Profit in $)	−1,243	−12	1,161	2,503	3,211	3,617

2. How much does the model predict the company would make if they sell 700 items?

---

10. In case you're not wet enough already, we're going to repeat the experiment. This time, instead of noting the time every 2 centimeters, we're going to note the height every 10 seconds. Fill in the table with your group's results. If the bottle isn't empty by the time you get to the end of the table, that's okay. You should still have plenty of data.

x Time (sec)	y Height (cm)
0	
10	
20	
30	

x Time (sec)	y Height (cm)
40	
50	
60	
70	

x Time (sec)	y Height (cm)
80	
90	
100	
110	

11. Find a best fit model for the new data, and write the correlation coefficient or r^2, whichever is appropriate.

12. Compare your two models, both algebraically and graphically. Discuss similarities and differences. Which is the better fit for the data you found? How do you know?

13. Why do you think the bottle didn't drain at a constant rate? Think about what's happening physically.

14. In the table, use your equation of best fit to find the residual for each data point. Are there any points that jump out as being very unusual? Why do you think that is?

x Time (sec)	y Height (cm)	Predicted height from equation	Residual
10			
20			
30			
40			
50			
60			
70			
80			
90			
100			
110			

Did You Get It

3. Find the residuals for your quadratic model in Did You Get It 1. Are you surprised by the results, based on the value of r^2?

4-11 Portfolio

Name _____

Check each box when you've completed the task. Remember that your instructor will want you to turn in the portfolio pages you create.

Online Practice

1. ☐ Include any written work from the online assignment along with any notes or questions about this lesson's content.

Applications

1. ☐ Complete the Applications problems.

Reflections

Type a short answer to each question.

1. Would you change your answer to Question 0 at the beginning of the lesson now? Explain.

2. Why is it useful to first draw a scatter plot for data before deciding on what type of model to use?

3. Name one thing you learned or discovered in this lesson that you found particularly interesting.

4. What questions do you have about this lesson?

Looking Ahead

1. Start preparing for your final!

2. Consider sending us some feedback on the book. We love to hear from students! Our email addresses can be found in the front of the book.

Answers to "Did You Get It?"

1. $y = -0.0107x^2 + 15.433x - 1{,}339$ $r^2 = 0.99497$

2. $4{,}221.10

3.

x (Items)	y (Profit in $)	Predicted Profit	Residual
0	-1243	-1339	96
100	-12	97.3	-109.3
200	1161	1319.6	-158.6
300	2503	2327.9	175.1
400	3211	3122.2	88.8
500	3617	3702.5	-85.5

Answers to "Prep Skills"

1. $y = 14{,}767.183(0.913)^x$

2. $r = -0.9500$; residuals: $-2{,}361.18$, 61.89, 80.00, $1{,}032.84$, $1{,}019.26$, -517.29

3. **a.** $x = 0.20, -15.20$ **b.** $y = 2, -1.25$ **c.** $x = 25.60, -16.40$

4. **a.** $(-7.5, -59.25)$ **b.** $(0.375, -10.5625)$ **c.** $(4.6, 13.2348)$

4-11   Applications

Name _____

1. The table shows data describing a batted ball in a baseball game. Find a quadratic function of best fit for the data.

Feet from home plate	Feet in the air
0	4
100	75
200	95
300	46

2. How far away from home plate did the ball land?

3. How high did it go?

4-11 Applications

Name _____

4. Did the ball reach its highest point exactly halfway in between where it was hit and where it landed? Should it have? Discuss, and keep in mind that the model is a parabola!

5. The Home Run Tracker data actually describes where the ball WOULD land if nothing stopped it from reaching the ground, like a fielder, the stands, or home run fence. In the direction this particular ball was hit, the fence is 344 feet from home plate, and is 8 feet high. Did the ball clear the fence?

6. Find the value of r^2 and the residuals for your model, then use both to discuss how well you think the model fits the data.

Unit 4   Language and Symbolism Review

Carefully read through the list of terminology we've used in Unit 4. Consider circling the terms you aren't familiar with and looking them up. Then test your understanding by using the list to fill in the appropriate blank in each sentence.

$$d = \sqrt{(x_2 - x_1)^2 + (y_2 - y_1)^2}$$

$$x = \frac{-b \pm \sqrt{b^2 - 4ac}}{2a}$$

$$x = -\frac{b}{2a}$$

	exponential decay	parameters
	exponential function	perfect squares
	exponential growth	polynomial
	$f(x)$	prime polynomial
	factored form	profit
arbitrary	factoring	quadratic function
binomial	factors	revenue
coefficient	function	right triangle
conjecture	growth factor	standard form
counterexample	hypotenuse	symmetry
deductive reasoning	inductive reasoning	terms
equivalent	inverse variation	trinomial
expanded form	isosceles	vertex
	margin of error	zero
	parabola	

1. When an expression has several pieces that are added or subtracted, the individual pieces are called _____.

2. For a term that has a number multiplied by some power of a variable, the number part is called the _____.

3. _____ is the process of reaching a conclusion based on specific examples.

4. _____ is another name for an educated guess based on available evidence.

5. A _____ is an example that proves your conjecture was false.

6. _____ is the process of reasoning that arrives at a conclusion based on previously accepted general statements.

7. An _____ number is a number that is able to represent ALL possible numbers.

8. Each of 49, 25, and 144 are called _____ because each is the square of a whole number.

9. A triangle with two sides that are perpendicular is called a _____.

10. The longest side of a right triangle is called the _____.

11. The distance between two points (x_1, y_1) and (x_2, y_2) is given by _____.

12. The _____ for a poll is a statistical measure that provides a range of values that the true outcome of the poll is likely to be inside.

13. An _____ relationship exists between two variable quantities when that relationship can be described by the equation $y = \frac{k}{x}$, where k is a constant.

14. When a quantity grows according to exponential growth, the total is repeatedly MULTIPLIED by the same number. We call this multiplier the _____.

15. A _____ is a relationship between two quantities where each input produces a unique output.

16. The function notation used to indicate the output of a function named f for an input x is _____.

17. In an _____ equation like $y = a \cdot b^x$, a will be positive and the value of b will be greater than 1.

18. In an _____ equation like $y = a \cdot b^x$, a will be positive and the value of b will be between 0 and 1.

19. A function where the input is an exponent is called an _____.

20. _____ are constants in an equation of a certain form that are determined by the data for a particular model.

21. The shape of the path that an object moving through the air under the influence of gravity follows is called a _____ .

22. When a graph can be cut in half so that one half is the mirror image of the other, this is known as _____ .

23. A _____ can be written in the form $f(x) = ax^2 + bx + c$.

24. In economics, the word _____ refers to the amount of money that a business takes in as a result of selling a product or service.

25. The difference between revenue and cost is the _____ made by the business.

26. _____ is a fancy math term for an expression with two terms.

27. The _____ of an expression is written as a product.

28. Multiplying factors in an expression will give what is called the _____ .

29. If you have two _____ forms of the same expression you should be able to input ANY value for the variable quantity x and get the same result from either expression.

30. An algebraic expression consisting of one or more terms that look like either a real number or a real number times a variable raised to a whole number power is called a _____ .

31. _____ is simply the process of writing a number or expression as a product.

32. When the only way to write a polynomial as a product is one times the polynomial, the polynomial is called a _____ .

33. If $(c, 0)$ is an x intercept of the graph of $P(x)$, then c is a _____ of $P(x)$.

34. If $(c, 0)$ is an x intercept of the graph of $P(x)$, then $x - c$ is one of the _____ of $P(x)$.

35. A polynomial expression with three terms is called a _____ .

36. _____ of a quadratic equation is $ax^2 + bx + c = 0$, where a is not zero.

37. The quadratic formula is _____ .

38. The point where a parabola changes direction is called the _____ of the parabola.

39. The x coordinate of the vertex of a parabola defined by the function $f(x) = ax^2 + bx + c$ can be found using _____ .

Unit 4   Learning Objective Review

This is a short review of the learning objectives we've covered in Unit 4. In each case, rate your confidence level by checking one of the boxes. If you feel like you're struggling with these skills, consult the lesson referenced next to the objective and see the online resources for extra practice.

1. Apply inductive reasoning to make a conjecture. (Lesson 4-1)

2. Disprove a conjecture by finding a counterexample. (Lesson 4-1)

3. Apply deductive reasoning to solve a problem. (Lesson 4-1)

4. Solve application problems using the Pythagorean Theorem. (Lesson 4-2)

5. Solve application problems involving the distance formula. (Lesson 4-2)

6. Determine the margin of error in a given poll. (Lesson 4-3)

7. Explain the meaning of the margin of error in a given poll. (Lesson 4-3)

8. Calculate the number of poll respondents needed for a given margin of error. (Lesson 4-3)

9. Identify situations where inverse variation occurs. (Lesson 4-4)

10. Solve problems involving direct and inverse variation. (Lesson 4-4)

11. Define function and use function notation. (Lesson 4-5)

12. Identify the significance of a and b in an equation of the form $y = ab^x$. (Lesson 4-5)

13. Find exponential models. (Lesson 4-5)

14. Compare exponential models using graphs, tables, and formulas. (Lesson 4-5)

15. Gather and organize data from an experiment. (Lesson 4-6)

16. Find an exponential curve of best fit for an experimental data set. (Lesson 4-6)

17. Study the decay rate for exponential decay. (Lesson 4-6)

18. Identify a parabolic graph. (Lesson 4-7)

19. Solve problems using the graph of a quadratic equation. (Lesson 4-7)

20. Combine algebraic expressions using addition or subtraction. (Lesson 4-8)

21. Demonstrate the relationships between revenue, cost, and profit functions. (Lesson 4-8)

22. Combine algebraic expressions using multiplication. (Lesson 4-8)

23. Write a revenue function from a demand function by multiplying algebraic expressions. (Lesson 4-8)

24. Explain why factoring is useful in algebra. (Lesson 4-9)

25. Explain the connection between zeros and x-intercepts. (Lesson 4-9)

26. Factor a trinomial. (Lesson 4-9)

27. Solve a quadratic equation using the quadratic formula. (Lesson 4-10)

28. Find the vertex of a parabola using $x = -b/2a$. (Lesson 4-10)

29. Solve application problems using the quadratic formula. (Lesson 4-10)

30. Calculate the equation of best fit for a set of quadratic data using technology. (Lesson 4-11)

31. Solve application problems that involve a quadratic set of data. (Lesson 4-11)

After you've evaluated your confidence level with each objective and gone back to review the objectives you weren't sure about, use the problem set as an additional review.

In Questions 1 and 2, determine whether the type of reasoning used is inductive or deductive. Explain how you decided.

1. Eric knew Jamal was late the last three times they met for lunch, so he decided to lie and tell Jamal to meet 15 minutes before he really planned to show up.

2. Beth was worried that if she didn't do enough homework, she might fail her class.

3. Find a counterexample to the conjecture: This unit review only has three questions.

4. A roller coaster is being built to include a section that is set at 40% grade. How much vertical distance will this roller coaster rise along this section that covers a horizontal distance of 160 ft? Draw a picture to help illustrate your work.

5. What would the length of the actual track be in this section? Round to the nearest tenth of a foot if needed.

6. With the origin at Champaign, the coordinates for Springfield and Bloomington on the map shown are $(-74, -21)$ and $(-29, 27)$, respectively. Assuming the coordinates are given in miles, find the distance between the two cities. Round to the nearest tenth of a mile. Show your work!

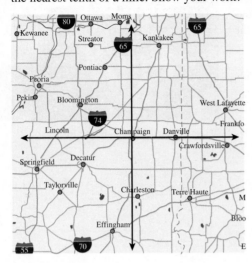

7. A recent news article reported that according to a poll, only 29% of Americans support a proposed infrastructure plan. At the bottom of the article was the following sentence: "The Post-ABC poll was conducted by telephone Jan. 12–15, 2017, including landline and cellphone respondents. Overall results have a margin of sampling error of plus or minus 3.5 percentage points." The confidence level was not given. Supposing the confidence level was 95%, write a sentence or two explaining the results of the poll.

For Questions 8 and 9: In conducting a survey of 200 students, a researcher found that 22% had significant (more than $1,000) credit card debt.

8. Calculate the margin of error with a 95% confidence level for this survey.

9. If the researcher wanted to get a margin of error of 4%, how many total students would she need to survey? Assume the number of students with significant credit card debt stays at 22%.

For Questions 10–13: While running for city council, Erika plans to hand out fliers to every house or apartment in the largest neighborhood in her district. The time it takes to hand out fliers to the entire neighborhood varies inversely with the number of people who help hand out the fliers. From her previous election, she knows it takes 25 hours for 2 people to hand out fliers to the neighborhood.

©Sata Production/Shutterstock RF

10. Write an equation that relates the time required to the number of people.

11. Use the equation to complete the table. Round to the nearest tenth of an hour if needed.

People	Time
1	
2	
3	
4	
5	
6	
7	
8	
9	
10	

12. How long does it take for 10 people to hand out these fliers?

13. Does this result make sense with what you know about inverse variation? Explain.

14. Thinking in terms of exponential growth, what factor would you want to multiply by in order for a quantity to grow by 15% (that is, <u>gain</u> 15% of its value)?

15. Write an exponential growth function that describes an investment that starts at $500 and grows exponentially by 15% of its value each year x.

16. For the function in Question 15, find $f(4)$ and describe what it means.

17. Thinking in terms of exponential decay, what factor would you want to multiply by in order for a quantity to decay by 15% (that is, <u>lose</u> 15% of its value)?

18. Write an exponential decay function that describes a quantity of bacteria that have been treated with an experimental antibiotic that starts at 800,000 and decays exponentially by 15% of its value each day x.

19. For the function in Question 18, find $f(4)$ and describe what it means.

20. The graph shows the number of bacteria over a 20-day period based on your equation in Question 18. Use the graph to estimate how many days it takes for the number of bacteria to drop below 100,000.

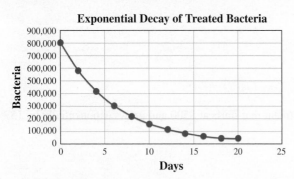

Exponential Decay of Treated Bacteria

The amount of money in an investment account has been recorded in the table. Use the table to answer Questions 21–23.

Years	Value
0	$10,000
1	$12,320
2	$15,120
3	$18,610
4	$22,880

21. Use a spreadsheet or your calculator to find the exponential equation of best fit for this data. Write your equation in the form $y = a(b)^x$.

22. Based on your equation, describe the rate at which this investment has been growing over this 4-year period.

23. A common legalish statement in advertisements for investment opportunities is, "Past performance is not indicative of future results." If we assume this trend will continue, what would this investment be worth after 6 years?

The graph shows the daily profit y in dollars of an auto parts maker where x parts are produced in a day. Use the graph to answer questions 24–27. Answer each question with a complete sentence.

24. Estimate the y-intercept of this graph. Explain what it means.

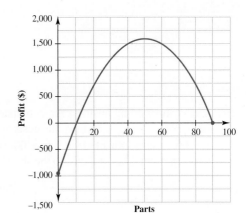

25. Estimate the x-intercepts of this graph. Explain what they mean.

26. Estimate the number of parts that will need to be produced in order to make a $1,500 profit.

27. Estimate the maximum profit the business can generate. How many parts need to be produced to reach that profit?

For Questions 28–37, refer to the following: From years of experience, a bagel shop has determined that at a price of $p = \$2.50$, they will sell $x = 450$ bagels each week. If they lower the price to $p = \$2.00$, they will sell $x = 550$ bagels each week.

28. Assuming this relationship is linear, write an equation that relates the price, p, to the number of bagels, x, that will be sold. Your equation should look like $p = mx + b$.

29. The revenue generated by selling these bagels is the product of the price p times the number of bagels sold, x. Write an equation that represents revenue by substituting your result from above into the equation $R = xp$.

30. The costs of doing business for a company can be found by adding fixed costs, such as rent, insurance, and wages, and variable costs, which are the costs to purchase the product you are selling. The portion of the bagel shop's fixed weekly costs allotted to bagels is $200, and the supplies to actually produce each bagel cost $0.75. Write an equation that represents the total cost to the shop of producing x bagels. Your equation should look like $C = mx + b$.

31. The profit made by the sale of these bagels is found by subtracting the costs from the revenue: $P = R - C$. Find an equation that represents profit by substituting your expressions for R and C into the profit formula. Simplify your answer.

32. What is the profit made by selling 300 bagels each week?

33. What is the profit made by selling 450 bagels each week?

34. What is the profit made by selling 0 bagels each week?

35. Find the number of bagels sold per week that will generate the highest profit.

36. What is the maximum profit that can be generated by this business?

37. At what price would you sell the bagels to realize this profit?

According to the baseball tracking system installed at a ball park, a home run was at the following horizontal and vertical positions along its path. Assume x represents the horizontal distance in feet from home plate and y represents the height in feet.

Horizontal distance	Height
0	3
100	128
200	161
300	75

©imac/Alamy RF

38. Use a calculator or spreadsheet to find the quadratic equation of best fit for this data. (Do not round your results.)

39. How far did the home run travel?

40. What is the highest point reached by the ball?

In Questions 41–48, simplify each expression by performing the indicated operations.

41. $(x + 8) + (3x - 5)$

42. $2(x + 3) - 3(x - 4)$

43. $(x^2 - 7x - 9) + 2(5x^2 - 11)$

44. $-(3x^2 + 4x - 5) - 2x(2x + 5)$

45. $-5x(3x - 6)$

46. $(x + 4)(x - 7)$

47. $(x - 3)(x - 8)$

48. $(2x - 5)(3x + 7)$

In Questions 49–52, factor each trinomial.

49. $x^2 - 7x + 10$

50. $x^2 + 11x + 18$

51. $2x^2 + x - 6$

52. $3x^2 - 4x - 15$

53. Solve the equation $x^2 - 7x + 10 = 0$ using the quadratic formula. Compare your answers to those for Question 49. What do you notice?

Index